7/98

Lighting Design Handbook

Other McGraw-Hill Books of Interest

*For more information about other McGraw-Hill materials,
call 1-800-2-MCGRAW in the United States. In other
countries, call your nearest McGraw-Hill office.*

Lighting Design Handbook

Lee Watson

McGraw-Hill, Inc.
New York   St. Louis   San Francisco   Auckland   Bogotá
Caracas   Hamburg   Lisbon   London   Madrid
Mexico   Milan   Montreal   New Delhi   Paris
San Juan   São Paulo   Singapore
Sydney   Tokyo   Toronto

Library of Congress Cataloging-in-Publication Data

Watson, Lee.
  Lighting design handbook / Lee Watson.
    p. cm.
  Includes bibliographical references.
  ISBN 0-07-068481-2
  1. Electric lighting. 2. Stage lighting. I. Title.
TK4169.W38 1990   89-39104
621.32 — dc20   CIP

Four copyrighted articles by Robert Benson are reprinted in their entirety in Appendix B with the permission of Rodale Press. These articles are from the October 1977, November/December 1977, March/April 1978, and September 1978 issues of *Theatre Crafts*.

Credits for Plates 67, 68, and 69: Cinematographer: Vilmos Zsigmond, ASC. Gaffer: Rick Martens. (*From* American Cinematographer, Oct. 1978).

1234567890   RAEHQR   9876543210

ISBN 0-07-068481-2

The sponsoring editor for this book was Joel E. Stein, the editing supervisor was Susan Thomas, the designer was Naomi Auerbach, and the production supervisor was Dianne L. Walber. It was set in Optima by Progressive Typographers.

Printed by Rae Printing; bound by Horowitz & Sons.

For information about our audio products, write us at:
Newbridge Book Clubs, 3000 Cindel Drive, Delran, NJ 08370

Dedication

Funding from the estate of Furba (Walker) Dooley Cable (the author's maternal grandmother) and from Hazel Dooley Watson (the author's mother) provided for the necessarily extensive research and graphics costs of this *Handbook*. This volume is dedicated to Furba in fond remembrance by her daughter and her grandson. Brief sketches and photos of Furba and Hazel follow:

Furba Elizabeth Walker
Born November 25, 1890
Edmonton, Kentucky

"Mother grew up in a family of 13 children. She married my father, Frank Dooley, at an early age. She had a special talent for making dolls' clothes which she used to advantage in making clothes for her daughter (me). She could design or copy from a picture in a magazine, producing beautiful garments. Her love for music was another lifetime pleasure. She passed away August 27, 1978. Were she here today, she would be a very proud and happy grandmother — having a part in her only grandchild's publication of this book."

Hazel Watson

Hazel Emma Dooley
(Mrs. Dallas V. Watson)
Born May 20, 1906
Curtis, Kentucky

"My mother's early artistic talents were evident in her music, her work in high school drama, and her encouragement of my own intense interest in theatre. Hazel's full life as a mother still leaves her time to continue her involvement in politics, through which she has achieved national recognition. Prominent socially in her community — my boyhood home — her continued support in my own lifelong study of lighting and design has been vital to me. The words *courageous, determined,* and *considerate* best describe this remarkable woman."

Leland (Lee) H. Watson

About the Author

The late Lee Watson worked extensively in nearly all fields of lighting design. He designed lighting for 42 Broadway productions, including the world premieres of *Diary of Anne Frank* and Arthur Miller's *A View From the Bridge*. For 12 years, he lighted numerous Off-Broadway productions and worked in New York City with CBS network TV and other television groups. His lighting credits include over 60 operas, the Seattle World's Fair, the Cincinnati Ballet, regional theatres, industrial shows, and many architectural projects. A professor at Purdue University, he was coauthor with Joel Rubin of an earlier book, *Theatrical Lighting Practice*. He served on the Board of Directors of the International Association of Lighting Designers and of United Scenic Artists local #829 in New York City. He was formerly president of the U.S. Institute for Theatre Technology and was a USITT Fellow, as well as holder of a USITT Founders' Award.

Contents

Part 1   Some Basics

Part 2   The Specialty Areas: Design and Practice

Foreword

John Gleason

Lee Watson worked for many years compiling the myriad of sources, techniques, and ideas cited in this update to the earlier Rubin and Watson *Theatrical Lighting Practice* (many years out of print). Indeed, this volume far surpasses the earlier book in its scope and content. Whether in his travels to New York to see the latest shows, going around the country designing productions, or attending meetings and trade shows, Lee was searching out information. Many of us can recall early morning phone calls, with Lee asking about new techniques he had seen us use or an article just published. The reading, research, scholarship, and insight that Lee brought to this veritable encyclopedia of lighting borders on the heroic.

Lee had a passion. A passion to communicate his knowledge and an excitement about the almost unending fields of lighting design being taught and practiced during his lifetime. This volume will enable both the student and the practitioner to sample what others are doing in their own as well as in other related fields of lighting. And if, as Lee intended, a spark is kindled and an interest in a different discipline is aroused, his listing of additional sources will provide enough food to satisfy anyone's hunger to learn.

This book is a wonderful tribute to a life filled with a ceaseless study and appreciation of an art that he helped to create.

JOHN GLEASON
New York
January 22, 1990

Foreword

Richard Pilbrow

In 1955 I was an assistant stage manager at Her Majesty's Theatre in London. I had lived and breathed theatre since childhood and had achieved the pinnacle of my ambition so far: stage management in a long-running West End show.

My disillusionment was swift. Far from being the Craigian ideal of the "Master of the Art and Science of the Stage," I seemed an automaton, calling cues as routinely as the dreariest bureaucratic wage slave. Then I read *Theatrical Lighting Practice* by Joel E. Rubin and Leland H. Watson. It was a revelation! There was a *profession of lighting design* (then unknown in Britain). You could earn a living doing it!

It was enough. I told a sceptical London theatre world that I was a "lighting designer." It was hard for a while, but the times were fortunate.

The profession of the stage lighting designer has seen exponential growth since 1954, when Lee and Joel wrote their first book about its infancy. With this new volume, Lee Watson has done the profession another mighty service in bringing together an encyclopedia survey of the craft and business of lighting design.

Today thousands of people earn their living designing lighting. From its beginnings as an element in theatrical production, it has grown to be an important design factor in every branch of entertainment, as well as in the world outside — in architecture, for example. This book celebrates that diversity and surveys it in extraordinary depth. It is a unique and vital handbook to the professional and to the many who seek to pursue a career in this exacting but rewarding career.

The word *rewarding* must be qualified. Few lighting designers get rich (although today more than a handful can be very successful), but lighting can provide a well-compensated career in many diverse fields. Each field is extraordinarily interesting. The ability to control, manipulate, and create with LIGHT is a special skill. It demands technical ability, professional competence, and most importantly TALENT. If you, the reader, possess that talent—if you have guts, dedication, and much determination—stage lighting design would be a noble and creative way of life for you.

Lee has performed a great service with this monumental work. A lifetime of love and dedication has gone into it. Those who knew Lee will always miss him. But many in the future will also be grateful to him again and again for the rich resources in this book.

It is a most fitting tribute to, and memorial of, a . . . *lighting designer.*

RICHARD PILBROW
January 22, 1990

Preface

This *Lighting Design Handbook* evolved rather curiously. As long ago as 1969, the late Robert MacGregor, a publisher, asked Dr. Joel E. Rubin and myself to revise and update our earlier work, *Theatrical Lighting Practice*. Neither of us was very enthusiastic about a revision, both lacking time and being aware of the shortcomings of that brief, early work. Discussions between Dr. Rubin and me ultimately resulted in the decision that I would undertake a book entirely on my own, a volume to be somewhat based upon the earlier work, yet different in nature. This handbook is the result.

The first 10 chapters of *The Lighting Design Handbook* were written to address several basic needs in the industry, which translate into the reasons for this book's existence (and character) listed below:

1. All too often any one group of lighting design specialists is unaware of what others in lighting are doing or how they do it. To spread knowledge of the many different areas of lighting design is one aim of this book.

2. There exists no unified source for bibliographical information (annotated) concerning the mass of printed material produced in the last hundred years to help guide the serious practitioner or student to further information and research sources.

3. A photographic record of outstanding design work exists for the costume and scenic designer, but because this kind of history is more difficult to document in the field of lighting design, there is little available that tries to record and perpetuate outstanding work or provides a broad view of levels of design work. To answer the need, this *Hand-book* includes extensive illustrations. While the selection of the illustrations was mine, designers from all parts of the industry graciously submitted photographs. It is hoped that a documented and representative view of our field is presented herein and that these photographs will ''open the eyes'' of people in all segments of the industry to the truly remarkable amount of quality lighting design being created today. (These photographs are very useful, although it must be recognized that photographs do not necessarily present the ''radiant energy'' light/shade/color picture seen with the human eye by those people present at an actual production. Photography can never exactly duplicate firsthand vision.)

4. Scattered examples of light plots, switchboard hookups, and focus charts have been available in magazines, but few examples have appeared in textbooks. This handbook presents many full-page light plots by leading designers from all segments of the industry. Comparison of different styles leads to a better understanding of accepted methods of communication — both their forms and their existing standards and practices.

5. With the possible exception of Richard Pilbrow's *Stage Lighting*, all standard lighting texts deal extensively with technology, that is, with lighting equipment and technical practices. No single volume exists which successfully deals only with the intangible art of designing lighting. This *Handbook* sets out to focus primarily on *designing* (although other areas of concern to the designer, such as lighting equipment selection, color use, scenic projection, lasers, holograms, and energy conservation, are presented where necessary).

Part 3 of this handbook, entitled "The Business of Lighting Design," was written out of a recognition of several basic needs in the industry:

1. Little has been written about the business of lighting design: the number of people involved, unions, agents, and professional organizations. There is a need for wider dissemination of accurate information about the United Scenic Artists Lighting Entrance Examination and the union itself.

2. I undertook an extensive Industry Survey because it seems that the industry needs to know more about how many people are working in various specialties; what the income ranges are; how long working designers have practiced lighting design; and what the influence of sex, union membership, and education is on employability. Students particularly are entitled to have at hand "hard facts" about their proposed lifetime career area.

This handbook is for the advanced student; it presumes familiarity with the contents of basic texts. Besides being a handbook, it is also a nonalphabetized *reference encyclopedia*. In that sense, it does not attempt to be exhaustive and definitive in any one area. Whole books, for example, have been written about television lighting alone, but this volume devotes only a few pages to that specialty. This book is intended to (1) survey the broad outlines of many areas of specialization and make that information available to practitioners in other, allied, specialties, and (2) extensively supplement and summarize existing knowledge by providing a wide range of new light plots, photographs, and extensive bibliographical references to lead to further study. Each section's footnotes are somewhat self-contained, with the expectation that the reader may not have consulted other portions of this volume.

It is hoped that the serious student who intends to make lighting design his or her life's work will find this *Handbook* useful throughout his or her career. It is intended that working professionals will find in it a quick, basic survey about their own specific areas of endeavor *plus* much new knowledge about the work of other practitioners in related fields.

This book is for the *designer* of lighting. It is not a technical manual or a how-to guide. It is intended to put a lifetime's accumulation of design-related information *in one place*.

Two notes of caution must be added here. The first is that abbreviations are used liberally throughout. For example, United Scenic Artists is consistently shortened to USA, and United States Institute for Theatre Technology becomes simply USITT. A list of some abbreviations and their spelled-out forms is provided at the end of the front matter, for easy reference.

Secondly, portions of the *Handbook* inevitably are biased. The selection of graphics must of necessity reflect my choices and criteria. The text is inevitably prejudiced by my own lengthy career as a working lighting designer, author, and teacher. In many cases I have attempted to indicate in the text that a certain offering is my opinion and is not necessarily correct or infallible. The reader is asked to read the book accordingly. This handbook is *one person's* view of the lighting design industry. It is for the reader to judge my accuracy and to make a critical evaluation when my acknowledged bias may have "crept in."

Acknowledgments

Assembling a study of this magnitude involved the assistance and active cooperation of virtually the entire industry. Such cooperation was most willingly offered. Thousands of photos passed through the author's office and the staff's hands.

Special thanks goes to William Roggenkamp for supervising all early graphics selection. Gail Reid (Mrs. Robert Reid) was the original typist, as well as a critic. In New York City my longtime friend and former assistant, Bruce Martin, spent endless hours on the telephone and in person acquiring and copying light plots and hookups and some photographs. A Broadway designer does not readily part, even briefly, with the one original drawing of his current hit show. Bruce handled this delicate situation with skill, diplomacy, and dedication. Invaluable in assisting him were Henry Robson and Raymond Costanza, photographers at Merit Studios/National Blueprint in New York City. We received useful technical advice and graphics work from Ron Smith, owner of Twin Cities Typesetting in Lafayette, and from his brother, Tom Smith, who opaqued negatives and did camera-ready pasteups of switchboard hookups, charts, etc. The personnel of the U.S. Post Office in West Lafayette offered patience and guidance through the arrival and departure of priceless original photos and graphics shipped via Priority Mail, registered mail, and certified mail. My father, Dallas Watson, supervised the typing.

A number of students worked as paid research assistants, clerical help, or in whatever capacity was needed. Those that deserve special mention include David Lyons, Frank Butler, Susan Senita, Jon Lear, the late Eddie Elias, Kirk Bookman, Evan Lenhardt, Tom Fleming, Don Stikeleather, Dan Madura, and B. J. Moffatt. Thanks also is due to Purdue University for making available office space, photocopy service, audiovisual production services, and facilities of the various Purdue libraries — particularly interlibrary loan and the Engineering Library. Credit should be given to Jeff Struckman (then of Webster College) and Lee Pilcher (USA #829) for help with the humor in Chap. 16. Also, special thanks goes to Austin McCormick, computer genius and patient critic.

Thanks also to the USA #829 (New York City), particularly Elmon Webb, and USA #350 (Chicago). Essentially the entire lighting design industry freely and willingly answered questionnaires and contributed information or graphics which are credited in the text, in the footnotes, or in the photo credits. Where otherwise unattributed, graphics were supplied by the listed designer.

A select few stand out as offering assistance way beyond "the call of duty." Nananne Porcher and Marion Kinsella were invaluable. Nan supplied numerous photos of her own design work which appear throughout the handbook. Imero Fiorentino made available, mostly through his staff assistant, Rosemary Kalikow, both light plots and his entire file of production photographs of the work of the many prominent lighting designers of his staff. Jules Fisher likewise opened his files, as did John Watson. James Moody, President of Sundance Corporation, not only sent some 40 light plots and 25 color photographs of his and his firm's work, but also phoned frequently to offer any needed additional assistance. Robert Lobi of Digital Controls, Inc., and

Bill McManus of McManus Enterprises were equally interested and helpful.

Two theatre magazines and a major film organization extended much assistance: *Lighting Dimensions* magazine made available photographs requested from the entire file of back issues; Patricia MacKay (then editor and now owner-publisher of *Theatre Crafts*) generously obtained the necessary permission to reprint the copyrighted articles by Robert Benson from *Theatre Crafts* magazine's "Buyer's Guide" series. I found a new friend in the person of Three Tyler, former public relations director of the American Society of Cinematographers. Ms. Tyler not only supplied illustrations from the files of *The American Cinematographer* (of which she was for a while assistant editor), but she also read and made editorial suggestions about the accuracy of Chap. 7, concerning cinematography. In addition she delicately steered through the officers of that organization basic approval (but not official endorsement) of the simplified treatment of this subject herein—certainly an area where I needed help.

Professor Van Phillips of Purdue University offered useful material about theatre consulting, as well as endless patience as I devoted much time to the preparation of this handbook.

I am especially indebted to two more mature friends (the term "older" is now avoided by this aging author): Dr. Harold I. Hanson of Brigham Young University, who supplied the Hill Cumorah photographs, and Charles Elson, who assembled and supplied the drawings and production photos of his lighting design for *Compulsion* on Broadway.

A large number of members of the architectural lighting specialty spent time, offered advice, and supplied photographs and graphics. These include William M. C. Lam, Howard Brandston, Leslie Wheel, Donald Gerstzoff, Edison Price, the late James Nuckolls, and Jules Horton. Abe Feder works in many areas and was most helpful, as was his office manager, Mrs. Wenslova.

Very special thanks to United Scenic Artists Lighting Union #829 members Curtis Osterman, Candice Dunn, and Patricia Stern. Each generously supplied their USA #829 Lighting Entrance Examination.

Additional thanks to the many who took the time to answer my Industry Survey. Your names and financial information will remain undisclosed forever.

Not to be overlooked are two other major figures in the field of lighting design: Richard Pilbrow and John Gleason. Each contributed a Foreword.

My gratitude to my parents and my grandmother for both encouragement and financial assistance in making this work possible has been expressed in the dedication of this handbook.

In short, a great many people helped to bring this study to you. Ours is a generous industry, freely sharing insights and knowledge, and filled with warm, dedicated artists of first rank. *They* brought you this book. Faults, omissions, and errors are my responsibility. I sincerely hope that this study proves to be of value to all of us in our rather young design industry and that it can be ultimately revised and updated as needed.

LEE WATSON
West Lafayette, Indiana

Special thanks are due to Van Phillips of Purdue University and to Fred Weller of Weller & Associates, who generously volunteered to review the proofs after the author passed on.

Some Abbreviations Used in This Book

AATE   American Alliance for Theatre and Education

AATSE   American Association of Theatre in Secondary Education

AATY   American Association of Theatre for Youth

ABT   American Ballet Theatre

ABTT   Association of British Theatre Technicians

ACT   American Conservatory Theatre

ADC   Associated Designers of Canada

ADIA   American Discotheque Industry Association, Inc.

AEICP   Association of Entertainment Industry Computer Professionals

AFTRA   American Federation of Television and Radio Artists

AGMA   American Guild of Musical Artists

AHLI   American Home Lighting Institute

ALA   American Lighting Association

ALD   Association of Lighting Designers (British)

AMI   Association for Multi-Image, International, Inc.

APIAD   Associazione Produttori Italiani Attrezzure per Discotheque e Teatri

ASC   American Society of Cinematographers

ASLD   American Society of Lighting Directors, Inc.

ASTC   American Society of Theatre Consultants

ATA   American Theatre Association

ATHE   Association for Theatre in Higher Education

AWC   additional weekly compensation

BKSTS   British Kinematography, Sound, and Television Society

BRH   Bureau of Radiological Health

BSTD   British Society of Theatre Designers

BSTLD   British Society of Television Lighting Directors

CIE   Commission Internationale de L'Eclairage

DLF   Designers Lighting Forum

FOH   front-of-house

HID   high-intensity discharge

HMI   hydrargyrum-medium iodides

IALD   International Association of Lighting Designers

IATSE   International Association of Theatre and Stage Employees

IES, IESNA   Illuminating Engineering Society of North America

ILDA   International Laser Display Association

IOSTT   International Organization of Scenographers and Theatre Technicians

LED   light-emitting diode

LORT   League of Regional Theatres

MALE   Mexican Association of Lighting Engineers

MIC   modulation-induced color

mm   millimeter

mW   milliwatt

NAB   National Association of Broadcasters

NABET   National Association of Broadcast Engineers and Technicians

NFA	National Feature Artists	TLA	Theatre Library Association
PLASA	Professional Lighting and Sound Association (British)	TOLD	Training of Lighting Designers
PMPEA	Professional Motion Picture Equipment Association	TTFL	Theatre, Television, and Film Lighting Committee
SMPTE	Society of Motion Picture and Television Engineers	TUTS	Theatre Under the Stars
SRES	Specular Reflector Engineering Society	TV	television
STLD	Society of Television Lighting Directors	USA	United Scenic Artists
TAP	Technical Assistance Project	USITT	United States Institute for Theatre Technology
TCG	Theatre Communications Group, Inc.	W	watt
TDA	Theatrical Dealers Association	WCTU	Women's Christian Temperance Union

Introduction The Nature, Extent and Diversity of the Lighting Design Field

> The artist is the creator of lighting effects, the scientific method can only analyze the finished product.
>
> P. R. BOYCE, *Human Factors in Lighting.*[1]
>
> Lighting is a creative process not a technical one. Most bad lighting comes from the fact that people don't understand that. Lighting is all about reading plays and talking to directors and understanding what's in the directors' and designer's and actors' and writers' heads. Not about lamps and wire and computers. The boring and bad lighting is because people get it the wrong way around.
>
> RICHARD PILBROW in *Theatre Crafts,* 1984.[2]

[1] *P. R. Boyce*, Human Factors in Lighting. *N.Y.; Macmillan; 1981.*

[2] *Patricia MacKay, "Technology Is Supremely Unimportant: Richard Pilbrow Talks about his Career as Head of Theatre Projects and as a Lighting Designer,"* Theatre Crafts, *vol. 18, no. 4 (April 1984), p. 53.*

From the beginning of time, Man has been influenced — emotionally and artistically — by the light around him. He has been terrified by lightning and angry storms, calmed by a peaceful sky filled with white fleecy clouds, made depressed and moody by a gloomy overcast sky, and entranced by the sheer beauty of sunrises and sunsets. Light has always influenced Man's moods and activities.

Beyond that, vision — which is dependent upon and influenced by available light — is probably the most prized of the five senses. Man's early discovery and utilization of fire not only enabled him to keep warm and to prepare and preserve food, but also enabled him to extend his vision by "pushing back the darkness." In this way, fire encouraged Man to be active and productive *beyond* the normal daylight hours, because with fire he could see in the dark. Since that time, Man has been striving for constant improvement in his ability to *control* and extend natural light. The hand-carried torch, the candle, the kerosene lamp, the gaslight, the electric arc, the limelight, and, finally, the miraculous range of today's electric light sources have all been part of Man's drive first to create illumination after dark and then to control that light for productive and artistic needs.

For a long time, improvements in lighting only increased the *illumination* that was available after dark or in a dim place. But then, with the advent of electric incandescent light sources just over 100 years ago, Man had the technology to start *creating* and *designing* with lighting, rather than just illuminate with it. Because of the relative newness of the necessary technology, the history of the lighting design industry is indeed a short one, spanning approximately the last 100 years. But the industry has taken great strides in this short time, and it now extends into almost all phases of modern life. Lighting has become a new art form. The planned use of light can shape and control our lives, and it can release and reveal the beautiful and the magnificent in people, architecture, musical performance, human and dramatic relationships, dance, and countless other activities. The creative use of light has become an art that celebrates life!

Along the way, the industry—the art—has survived those developmental artists and technicians who would use light only to glorify themselves or their splashy inventiveness. It has survived those who would use light to imitate the terrifying destructive splendor of a volcanic eruption.

The lighting design industry is just beginning to reach for the sky. In the past, much of our teaching and many of our textbooks have been concerned only with narrow, specialized technology. We teachers have often trained practitioners in the skills of a craft when we should have been helping newcomers to develop and expand their artistic insight and vision. Technology is an important *tool,* and design is the creative use of that tool, but the progress of the artistic mastery of light as a design element has sometimes been almost lost in the welter of developing technology and craft skills.

Also, our industry has too often divided itself and its artistic development into useless little compartments—theatre lighting, television lighting, cinematic lighting, architectural lighting—*when really they are all one and the same.* Each specialty is based upon (1) what light is, (2) how it is perceived, (3) how it is produced and shaped, and (4) how it can be used (designed) to meet the larger needs of Man. Specific *technology* and *craft* practices may vary from field to field, but the same *art* underlies them all. Lighting designers are all in the same business—the designed use of light to reveal and enhance—and lighting design has now "come of age."

As of 1988, the international market for lamps was $7 billion, with another $20 billion expended for luminaires and/or fixtures. The largest market was in the United States and Canada: $10.8 billion total, with $2.7 billion expended for lamps and $8.1 billion for fixtures/luminaires. Worldwide the lamp market involved 41% for incandescent light sources (49% in the United States), 36% for fluorescents, 13% for HID (high intensity discharge), and 4.4% miscellaneous (TV, etc.). These figures were reported at the 1989 Lighting World International conference in New York City. As the worldwide total lighting/illumination market increases, so does the need for lighting designers in all areas of design specialization.

See also: Ben Bova, THE BEAUTY OF LIGHT. N.Y.; John Wiley & Sons, Inc., Wiley Science Editions; 1988. In this thought-provoking volume of 350 pages by a leading science fiction and futuristic novels author of more than 70 books, award-winning Bova says in his Foreword: "This book began with the title The Beauty of Light *and the idea that I wanted to write about how light affects us and how we use light in art, science, industry, and our everyday lives. The more I studied and wrote on the subject, the more I found to study and write about. Light affects us in so many ways. We use light every moment of our waking lives. . . . As a result, this book touches on hundreds of topics—lightly." It is well worth any* lighting *designer's time to ramble through this volume.*

Part 1

Some Basics

Chapter 1

On Being a Creative Artist: Designing[3]

[3] *The reader should be familiar with several of the following basic texts:*

Bernard R. Boylan, The Lighting Primer. *Ames, Iowa; Iowa State University Press; 1987. 150 pp., illus., 2 color plates. Excellent basic text covering technology and design fundamentals.*

Willard F. Bellman, Lighting the Stage: Art and Practice. *N.Y.; Harper & Row, 2d ed.; 1974. Detailed basic text. 480 pp., illus., color.*

W. Oren Parker, Harvey K. Smith, and R. Craig Wolf, Scene Design and Stage Lighting. *N.Y.; Holt, Rinehart and Winston, 7th ed.; 1989. A good basic text; well illustrated. 596 pp., illus., color.*

Hunton D. Sellman, Essentials of Stage Lighting, *2d ed. Englewood Cliffs, N.J.; Prentice-Hall; 1982. Excellent, highly readable text for the beginner; good plots and illustrations. 214 pp., illus., color.*

Richard Pilbrow, Stage Lighting. *London; Studio Vista; revised ed., 1979. 175 pp., illus., color. The most readable semi-text about the actual working of the business; good illustrations. British practice.*

Neil Fraser, Lighting and Sound. *Oxford, England; Phaidon Theatre Manual, 1988. 132 pp., well illustrated, color; brief, readable paperback covering all aspects of beginning lighting design and sound.*

Harvey Sweet, Handbook of Scenery, Properties, and Lighting. Volume II: Lighting. *Boston, London, Sydney, Toronto; Allyn and Bacon,*

Most lighting design training starts from the wrong end. If a teacher's objective is to develop lighting design artists, the teacher should begin by helping to

- Develop the designers' "how to see" skills and deepen the skills involved in visual analysis and retention.
- Develop the designers' "problem analysis" skills.
- Broaden the designers' understanding and abilities in "design concept" development.
- Develop the lighting designers' understanding of light (radiant energy), the way it can be used (optics), and the way its use can affect human response (optics and human behavior).
- Develop the designers' ability to communicate via light plots, "light and shade" sketches, storyboard presentations, switchboard layouts, focus charts, and shop orders.
- Develop, expand, and deepen those personality traits of designers which seem to distinguish most creative artists and which can be observed to be universally present in today's leading lighting designers.

These are the training foundations upon which must rest any worthwhile career as a creative artist of lighting design. Yet most lighting design training starts at the other end with practical experience working backstage, hanging and repairing lighting equipment, operating switchboards, etc. Consequently, such training produces expert "techies"— a few of whom even blunder on through to become creative artists of light. Let's see what others say about the above-listed aspects of training creative lighting artists.

Design the space first, then go back and do the backup engineering to find out what is needed to implement that design. Today, so much of it is done the other way. They do the engineering and then the design will be miraculously produced from that. It's all backwards. . . . Lighting design should be taught before lighting application. . . . [There is a] big difference between teaching lighting application and teaching lighting design. Until the lighting community understands this difference, there will continue to be a lot of poor lighting throughout the U.S. Visual perception should be taught before anything else. Students must be taught to understand how people see and how the mind modifies those visual perceptions, which are more important than people realize. We must consider the effectiveness of the design of the luminous environment and not just the lighting system. *William Dombroski, Ohio University*[4]

At school I learned part of the *science* of illumination and at work I am discovering the *art* of illumination. *Thomas Thompson, designer, Howard Brandston Lighting Design, Inc., New York City*

Theory has allowed me to *think* with an open mind, where the interaction with practicing professionals has taught me to *see*— that is, to observe and evaluate projects critically, and to *communicate* in a professional manner. *Mark L. Roush, Manager of Light and Vision Conferencing Center, architectural products designer, Holophane Co.*

I feel that my background from school in architectural lighting, lighting calculations, and the psychological aspects of architectural lighting is very strong. I feel that I would have benefited, however, by exploring lighting through course work outside of the architectural realm. Some exposure to theatrical lighting or light as an art form would provide another angle on lighting that would be useful to me as a designer. *Helen K. Diemer, head of Lighting Department, Flack & Kurtz Consulting Engineers, New York City*[5]

To see; to sense, perceive and understand; to feel; and to respond; these are the elements of the visual experience. Light is the catalyst between the objects and events, and the viewer for whom the design is made. . . . Design begins with people, is done by people, for people. *Louis Erhardt, Lighting Design & Application, vol. 13*[6]

The man who knows *how* (to light) will have no trouble finding a job — a job working for the man who knows *why*. Understand the reasons for each bit of illumination; where to apply it, its amount, color, direction. Learn to see, to feel, and to create. *Louis Erhardt, Lighting Design & Application, Contributing Editor*[7]

Visual Skills: Learning to See[8]

Training and sharpening one's observation powers is very similar to learning to drive a car, play a piano, type, or speed-read. No one is born with any of these various skills; they must be developed through training. "Learning to see" also involves training: analyzing sunsets, sunrises, foggy days, the pattern of light in a city at night at various hours, and the effect of flat illumination on a brick wall versus sharp shafts of sunlight. If a student is to grow as a lighting design artist, he or she must develop this trained visual skill, whether the aim is theatre, architectural lighting, film, or TV. It is wise for the student to become familiar with the five factors in seeing: contrast, luminance, size, time, and color.

The development of visual observation skills is not readily taught. William M. C. Lam calls this part of the visual process "the experience filter."[8] Every light and shade pattern which the eye transmits to the brain is "referenced" against previous visual experiences for interpretation. V. Liekovsky, consultant in biophysics of vision with Biomedical Injury Analysis, Inc., set this concept forth most clearly in the May 1984 issue of *Lighting Design & Application:*

The philosopher Kemeny out of Dartmouth noted that when we see a "table," in reality all we see is a perspectively distorted rectangle, brown on the top, and there is nothing in our visual impression which would contraindicate our approaching it and

attempting to push our fist through the top — as we could easily do so with a tubful of water, or the thick coat of sheep. It is our past experiences — he says — our learned memory, which warns us that a brown-topped, four legged trapezoid appearing object, about 31 inches in height, is *solid*. Solidity is in our experience, not in our visual perception. He also observes that we hardly ever see a table as a rectangle; from almost any perspective, it appears as a trapezoid. Still, we never state its true appearance in those precise terms.

Kemeny uses the example to point out the necessity of separating facts from assumptions. We should not be inclined to say that we see a solid table until we touch it; it could be a hologram.[9]

While Liekovsky's example may seem to be somewhat outlandish, it does forcefully point to the need for lighting designers to enlarge their store of visual images on "file." Most people, including many of us in lighting design, "look without seeing." The theatre designer needs an extensive "visual card file" of analyzed information about the nature of sunsets, rainy days, cities at night, and so on. Both the theatrical designer and the architectural specialist need mental visual images of how a brick wall looks in bright sunlight from different angles, on a grey day, at night, by lightning. All of us too often take for granted the composition and nature of the multitude of visual images we see around us constantly. Deepening this "card file" can only be done by the individual. The references cited in footnote 8 will give a better understanding of the visual process and suggest useful exercises to increase our ability to "learn to see." But the actual expansion rests primarily with the individual. It is important to work constantly at seeing — throughout a lifetime. The sources listed in footnote 8 contain knowledge that is as essential for the designer as is anything to be found in this Handbook.

Problem Analysis[10]

The theatrical lighting designer begins by reading the script (score, choreography) of the film, television show, play, opera, or dance under consideration. From this reading the designer will learn both specifics (time, place, weather, light changes, etc.) and, much more importantly, what the material is trying to accomplish. Is the audience to be moved emotionally? Stimulated intellectually? Informed? Amused? Agitated to action? Further, what clues of a specific nature has the author (choreographer, composer) supplied for the

Inc.; 1989. 116 pages, spiral-bound, well illustrated. Covers all of the beginner's fundamentals of lighting from the American viewpoint.

Paul Carter, Backstage Handbook. *N.Y.; Broadway Press; 1988. Section #4. "Electrics" is well illustrated and presents basic terms, formulas and codes the electrician/lighting designer might use. Not a basic lighting design text.*

Useful supplemental references are:

Jean Rosenthal and Lael Wertenbaker, The Magic of Light. *Boston; Little, Brown and Co. and Theatre Arts Books; 1972. Excellent volume with Ms. Rosenthal's career and design philosophy plus numerous plots and illustrations. 256 pp., illus.*

Stanley McCandless, A Method of Lighting the Stage. *N.Y.; Theatre Arts Books, Inc.; 1947. An early, basic study by the father of lighting instruction in the United States. Now out-of-date. 144 pp.; illus.*

J. Michael Gillette, Designing with Light: An Introduction to Stage Lighting. *Palo Alto, Calif.; Mayfield Publishing Co.; 2nd ed., 1989. In-print book with the best coverage of educational theatre practices. 244 pp., illus.*

Theodore Fuchs, Stage Lighting. *Boston; Little, Brown and Co.; 1929. Available in reprint. The first stage lighting text; much information still of value. 500 pp., illus.*

Joel E. Rubin and Leland H. Watson, Theatrical Lighting Practice. *N.Y.; Theatre Arts Books; 1954. Out-of-print but still useful. 142 pp., illus.*

Francis Reid, The Stage Lighting Handbook. *N.Y.; Theatre Arts Books; 3rd ed., 1987. A basic book of British practice; 130 pp., illus.*

Also: Theatre Arts Books/Methuen.

Also available in Spanish: Manuel de Illuminacion Escenica, *published by the Foundacion Diputacion de Sevilla. Translation was by Hector Morales, a student of Francis Reid's. A Swedish edition, Teaterljus, with translation by Hans-Ake Sjoquist, was published by Entre of Stockholm in 1982.*

Roger W. Maas, Lighting for Historic Buildings: A guide to Selecting Reproductions. *Washington, D.C.; Preservation Press; 1988. Around $13. Traces the beginnings of lighting through the candle to gas and electricity.*

Frederick Bentham, The Art of Stage Lighting. *N.Y.; Theatre Arts Books; 2d ed., revised & expanded, 1976. Very good British text. 361 pp., illus., color.*

Richard H. Palmer, The Lighting Art: The Aesthetics of Stage Lighting Design. *Englewood Cliffs, N.J.; Prentice-Hall; 1985. Illus., color, 237 pp. A basic text on stage lighting design with application primarily to educational theatre practices rather than to professional practices. Limited useful material.*

[4] *Wm. Dombroski (Ohio University, Interior Design) in "Lighting Education: An Overview,"* Lighting Design + Application, *vol. 15, no. 2 (Feb. 1985), pp. 41–42.*

[5] *These three quotes come from the following sources which students in architectural lighting will find useful: "Four Young Lighting Designers Speak Out — What Did You Learn in School? What Do You Wish You Had Learned?,"* Lighting Design + Application, *vol. 16, no. 3 (Mar. 1986), pp. 10–12, and "Letters," vol. 16, no. 5 (May 1986), p. 2. An astute commentary by Sidney Feltman.*

[6] *Louis Erhardt, "Views on the Visual Environment,"* Lighting Design + Application, *vol. 13, no. 9 (Sept. 1983), p. 4.*

[7] *Louis Erhardt, "Views on the Visual Environment,"* Lighting Design + Application, *vol. 14, no. 1 (Jan. 1984), p. 8.*

[8] *For further study, see also:*

George Nelson, How to See: Visual Adventures in a World God Never Made. *Boston; Little, Brown and Co.; 1977. 234 pp. Written by a critic, editor, designer, and architect, this is an excellent guide to expanding visual perception skills. Illus.*

William M. C. Lam, Perception and Lighting as Formgivers for Architecture. *N.Y.; McGraw-Hill; 1977. 310 pp. Lavishly illustrated. Excellent text touching upon "how we see."*

Frederick Bentham, The Art of Stage Lighting. *N.Y.; Theatre Arts Books, 2d revised ed.; 1976. See Chapter 11: "Painting With Light," pp. 226–231. Brief treatment.*

Johan Jansen and Otto Lührs, Art In Light, Lighting Effects in Painting and Sculpture, Art and Technology. *Deventer, Netherlands; Kluwer; 1985. 124 pp. Color throughout. Most useful study in "Learning To See."*

George C. Izenour, Theatre Technology. *N.Y.; McGraw-Hill; 1988. 553 pp. Glossy paper, excellent illustrations, oversized (11 3/4" × 12 1/4") volume which frequently touches upon the history of lighting and lighting design but is heavily shaped by Prof. Izenour's concepts as a theatre consultant worldwide. For a "pro and con" review of this controversial volume, see: Theatre crafts, vol. 22, no. 8 (Oct. 1988), p. 92 (Dr. Joel E. Rubin, pro) and p. 93 (H. X. Pert, con).*

Ann Daly, "Ways of seeing: Grenald Associates, Ltd., Deals in LIght, Perception, and Behavior," Lighting Dimensions, *vol. 13, no. 4 (May/June 1989), pp. 62–65, 77, 79–80. Illus., color. A major article of value particularly to those engaged in architectural lighting — but useful for all lighting designers.*

Robert H. McKim, Thinking Visually: A Strategy Manual for Problem Solving. *Belmont, California; Wadsworth, Inc.; 1980. 310 pp., illus. Chapters entitled "Seeing," "Imagining" and "Idea-Sketching" are particularly useful to lighting designers.*

Dennis J. Sporre, "Visual Adaptation and Stage Lighting," Theatre Design and Technology, *no. 17 (May 1969), pp. 7–8.*

James J. Gibson, The Perception of the Visual World. *Boston; Houghton Mifflin Co. (Riverside Press, Cambridge); 1950. Illus., 238 pp. Excellent basic study of seeing.*

Louis Erhardt, "Seeing," Lighting Design + Application, *vol. 16, no. 7 (July 1986), pp. 6, 56. Good basic article on how we see. Also: "Seeing Brightness," vol. 16, no. 8 (Aug. 1986), p. 48.*

R. L. Gregory, The Eye and Brain. *London; World University Library; 1966. Basic text on vision.*

H. C. Weston, Sight, Light and Work. *London; Her Majesty's Stationery Office (available through York House); 1963. One of the best studies of basics of design and vision by an illumination engineer with a designer's perspective. Well-illustrated. Valuable. 360 pp.*

Robert L. Smith and Brian R. Winkleman, "Education: The Third Dimension of Lighting: Reflections, Refractions, Filterings, and Radiations," Lighting Design & Application, *vol. 15, no. 2 (Feb. 1985); pp. 27–30. Illus., color. Basic information concerning light, well presented and illustrated, from Professor Smith's beginning course in architectural lighting at the University of Illinois.*

Hayden N. McKay, "Energy Optimization and Quality Lighting Design," Lighting Design + Application, *vol. 16, no. 3 (Mar. 1986), pp. 26–33. Illus., color. Essential reading about the basics of architectural lighting design by an architect/lighting designer on the staff of Howard Brandston Lighting Design, Inc., New York City. Lavishly illustrated.*

"Seeing the Light: The Wonders of the Exploratorium Now in San Francisco and New York," Lighting Design + Application, *vol. 16, no. 7 (July 1986), pp. 36–37. Illus., color.*

Malcome W. Browne, "City Again Boasts a Science Museum," The N.Y. Times, *Sept. 5, 1986. More about the "Seeing the Light" permanent exhibit.*

John P. Frisby, Seeing, Illusion, Brain and Mind. *N.Y.; Oxford University Press; 1979. 160 pp., illus., color. A readable presentation of the visual process, with excellent graphics.*

Leo M. Hurvich and Dorothea Jameson, The Perception of Brightness and Darkness. *Boston; Allyn and Bacon; 1966. 141 pp. Charts and graphs. A standard basic study of the psychology of seeing. For the advanced student.*

P. R. Boyce, Human Factors in Lighting. N.Y.; MacMillan Publishing Company, and Toronto, Collier MacMillan Canada, Ltd.; 1981. 421 pp., illus. Excellent recent summary of the basics of optics and vision.

Louis Erhardt, "Views on the Visual Environment," Lighting Design + Application, vol. 14, no. 4 (Apr. 1984), p. 4. Erhardt writes:

"Perhaps we should regard vision as an information-processing procedure. . . . Light is visible radiation. Without vision there is no light, without light, no vision. There interdependence demands that they be considered together. For many years illumination has been "engineered." There is a growing appreciation that lighting must first be designed, then implemented using the vast body of information developed by the engineers. Why must lighting be "designed"? A designer is an artist whose imagination and creativity are directed toward lighting usefully and beautifully. An artist is a self-taught appreciator of light and vision. He has learned to see [italics by Watson]. With a canvas before him, nearly uniform in its illumination, he chooses and mixes his selective reflectors — his paint colors. He depicts forms, textures, and relationships by allocating and applying color values. He captures sunlight, morning dewdrops and may even suggest the fragrance of a flower. . . . The lighting designer is not blessed with such total freedom. He is given a scene, often fixed in its reflective properties. He can emphasize, subdue, or modify, but only within the limits given.
  Deane Judd appreciated the artist's ability: "Artists having no formal acquaintance with visual science have created some very impressive scenes, and have sold them at some very astronomical prices. . . . I have only admiration for this ability of the artist because I am only now commencing to understand how it is achieved. . . . The rule is that artists lead, and scientists follow."

Tom O'Mahony, "Light as Emotion; as Aesthetic — The World Is Really People and Emotion, and Light Is the Revealment of It — Abe Feder," Lighting Design + Application, vol. 15, no. 9 (Sept. 1985), p. 25.

Jeffrey L. Brown and Gary R. Steffy, "A Philosophy on the Solving of Lighting Design Problems," Lighting Design + Application, vol. 17, no. 2 (Feb. 1987), pp. 13–15. Illus., color. Excellent analysis of lighting problem solving.

Louis Erhardt, "Views on the Visual Environment," Lighting Design + Application. There are many highly readable, essential articles in this series. Consult:
"Twenty Answers to Questions of Brightness," vol. 16, no. 10 (Oct. 1986), p. 2.
"Seeing Brightness," vol. 16, no. 8 (Aug. 1986), p. 48.

"Constancy," vol. 17, no. 4 (Apr. 1987), p. 61
"Measure Brightness?" vol. 16, no. 9 (Sept. 1986), p. 45.
"Twenty Answers to Questions of Color," vol. 17, no. 1 (Jan. 1987), p. 55.
"Specifying Color," vol. 16, no. 12 (Dec. 1986), p. 51.
"Seeing Color," vol. 16, no. 11 (Nov. 1986), p. 2.
"Colorimetry," vol. 17, no. 2 (Feb. 1987), p. 61.

Gary Gordon, "The Design Department," Architectural Lighting. There are highly readable, essential articles in this series with basic information not readily available elsewhere. Consult:
"Color," vol. 1, no. 5 (May 1987), pp. 85–86. Illus., color.
"Three-Dimensional Form is Seen as a Relationship between Highlights and Shadows," vol. 1, no. 4 (Apr. 1987), pp. 38–39. Illus., color.
"Brightness Contrast," vol. 1, no. 3 (Mar. 1987), p. 47.
"Designing Shadows," vol. 1, no. 1 (Jan. 1987), pp. 53–54. Illus., color. Essential reading. From p. 54: "Only in the shadows . . . can much of light be appreciated. A good listener appreciates conversations by its pauses. Let us also appreciate light by its shadows."

Robert G. Davis, "Closing the Gap: Research, Design and the Psychological Aspects of Lighting," Lighting Design + Application, vol. 17, no. 5 (May 1987), pp. 14–15. Illus. Important information for the designer concerning the influence of light on impressions and behavior and how to design these effects.

James Nuckolls, "IES Papers Report," Lighting Dimensions, vol. 11, no. 1 (Jan./Feb. 1987), pp. 24, 82–83. Nuckolls reports on an IES paper which raises the questions, Does good lighting lead to poor thinking? and the place of wall lighting in the office for the worker.

Liv Arvesen, "Painting with Light: Experimenting with Coloured Light at Trondheim University, Norway," International Lighting Review, 40th year, 2nd quarter, 1989. Pp. 65–67, illus., color. An important study of monotony, room size and light used to direct movement — all related to color studies with excellent color graphics.

Joost van Santen, "Catching the Light: Light Art in the Ordiance Survey Building, Emmen, The Netherlands," International Lighting Review, 40th year, 2nd quarter, 1989. Pp. 70–73, illus., color. A useful study concerning the use of daylight as an architectural lighting design factor.

[9] V. Liesovasky, "Letters," Lighting Design + Application, vol. 14, no. 5 (May 1984), pp. 4, 6.

[10] For further study see: Robert L. Beneditti, "The Designer–Director Relationship: Form and Process," Theatre Crafts, vol. 13, no. 1 (Jan./Feb. 1979), pp. 36, 58–65. Overly discursive; useful.

Robert L. Benedetti, "The Designer/Director Relationship: The Integration of Action and Environment," Theatre Crafts, vol. 13, no. 5 (Oct. 1979), p. 30.

Jean Rosenthal and Lael Wertenbaker, The Magic of Light. Boston; Little, Brown and Co. and Theatre Arts Books; 1972. See Chapter 5, pp. 59–72. Excellent analysis; very readable.

J. Michael Gillette, Designing with Light: An Introduction to Stage Lighting. Palo Alto, Calif.; Mayfield Publishing Co.; 1978. See Chapter 9, "Analyzing the Script," pp. 107–113. Good basics.

Willard F. Bellman, Lighting the Stage: Art and Practice, 2d ed. N.Y., Harper & Row; 1974. See Chapter 18: "Design Procedures," pp. 371–375. Very basic; sketchy. Also see "Return to the Script," p. 416.

Gerald Zekowski, "How to Grab a Footcandle," Lighting Design + Application, vol. 16, no. 6 (June 1986), pp. 60–61. Illus. A wise and witty article about light and vision by the National Director of Education and Labs, Lightolier. Essential reading.

Ernest Wotton, "Lighting is for People," Lighting Design + Application, vol. 12, no. 6 (June 1982), pp. 24–26.

For an excellent but lengthier discussion of the ramifications and importance of script analysis, see: Jo Mielziner, Designing for the Theatre. N.Y.; Bramball House; 1965, p. 7–9.

Those in architectural lighting should refer to: Louis Erhardt, "Views on the Visual Environment: Design Process Part 1 — Project Analysis," Lighting Design & Application, vol. 13, no. 10 (Oct. 1983), pp. 8–9.

Glenn Loney, "Designers on Design: Tom Skelton," Theatre Crafts, vol. 23, no. 4 (April 1989), pp. 45–51, 67–71, 74. Illus., color. Designer Skelton is noted for extensive and careful preplanning and early analysis of anything he is to design for. This interview/article contains his own words, extensively, on this process.

lighting designer's guidance? Beyond this, prior to any meeting with the director and the other creative artists (designers of scenery, costumes, cinematography, etc.), the lighting designer should gather as much insight as is possible about the production's budget, time allocation, performance place (or places), and, if available, specific scenic environment (setting), costumes, and even selected performers. Only then can designers meet with fellow artists and contribute their speciality: a knowledge of how light and shade and color can add to the production's total effectiveness. The designer possesses specialized knowledge concerning the way other humans *respond* to light.

Implied in this process of problem analysis is a deep familiarity with the field of lighting design. The designer should arrive at a first conference with as complete an understanding of the script and its objectives (and the structure used to achieve those objectives with an audience) as the director brings to the conference. The director's task involves coordinating many different arts and skills. The task of the lighting designer is to expand audience response by knowing what is to be accomplished and how creative use of light can help. If the designer arrives with less than a thorough understanding of the script and its central "problem," he or she will only provide the barest necessities called for by the author, or else merely "flesh out" the demands of the director. That is not designing! Script analysis (the initial part of problem analysis) does not come from seeing a few films, a lot of television, and a few live shows. It does not come from reading half a dozen plays/operas/ballets. Instead, it is the end product of extensive research and training combined with an obsessive interest in all that can be learned from the past. It stems in part from a study of the contemporary works of others and an ability to understand and appreciate experimental work. The theatrical lighting artist needs to "flesh out" a basic knowledge of theatre/film/TV, history, literature, architecture, music, dance, philosophy, economics, psychology, and so on. Without a broad range of interests and an even broader range of knowledge, the lighting designer will arrive at the initial conference with only a minuscule amount of knowledge about a very little thing: lighting. Anyone who wishes to be a lighting designer must grow to the status of artist via a broad understanding of life, people, *and* the selected art

through which the individual wishes to express this understanding creatively.

The process is much the same for the architectural lighting designer. Prior to the first conference, the designer needs to study the architect's plans and ask many questions. What is the budget? Why is the space being built or rebuilt? Who will use it? For what purpose? Is it exterior or interior? Public or private? For work or amusement? What can be discovered about the tasks to be performed there? Are they complex? Simple? And who is to be the user of the space? Why? What is the focus of the space? The total project? Lighting designers also must ask themselves if they know enough about architecture, interior design, landscaping, engineering, and heat-ventilation-construction requirements to make their lighting creativity a useful (or vital) part of the total project. Like the theatrical lighting specialist, the architectural lighting designer needs a perspective much broader than just a command of lighting if he or she is to have anything worthwhile to contribute to a project. Even a disco designer needs to know to which age or interest group a client intends to appeal. So does the designer for a theme/amusement park. Whether they call it script analysis or problem analysis, *all* lighting designers must develop this skill and insight. Most theatre/dance/music schools offer training in this fundamental. So do architectural/engineering programs. Further guidance is suggested in the sources cited in footnote 10.

On the topic of problem analysis a few other matters need to be stressed. Lighting designers, be they theatrical or architectural, can only benefit from entering the problem analysis process *at the earliest possible moment* in the overall planning, regardless of whether the project is a theatrical production, a building, or a parking mall. A constant complaint of *all* working lighting designers is that they are brought into project processes at a point where their creative options are very limited. If the play has already been cast, the set has been designed and built, the costumes have been approved and constructed, and the production has been fully conceived by the director, then the creative contribution of the lighting designer really suffers. He or she can no longer suggest solutions with the scenic designer for feasible modifications in the set to allow space for hanging lights, or warn the costume designer about colors which will be modified or deteriorated by lights, or help the director use lights as a transition device in a multiscene/place/time production such as much of Shakespeare. The options, as well as the potential for contribution, are now limited, creatively and technically. For these reasons, the lighting designer must begin problem analysis with the production team as early as possible.

Late timing can be even worse for the architectural/interior/landscape lighting designer. If all plans are nearly complete ("now, let's just add the necessary lighting"), the task remaining is merely technical. No longer can the designer find usable space for "wall washers" in a huge marble lobby, nor can selected features of the space or building be accented or played down. That they are brought into projects late in the planning stage is a constant complaint of all architectural lighting personnel. The lighting designer's function is a *creative* one, and, ideally, he or she must get in on the planning at the earliest possible moment — or find vastly limited what he or she can contribute. It is too late for a designer to begin designing when a completed set of building plans has been handed over!

The theatrical specialist should take a similar approach. It was indicated earlier that problem analysis in the theatre consists of much more than just reading the script. Professional theatre, however, has made extensive use of a communications device uniquely its own: the "concept." Since the designer is expected to arrive at the first production meeting with a fully formed concept, the concept as a communication device (which it is) merits attention here, rather than later in this chapter.

Concepts

Much too much fuss has been made over formalizing a very simple process: the generation and presentation of concepts. The use of "concepts" in theatre came about through lighting educators working closely with the annual United Scenic Artists (USA) #829 Lighting Entrance Examination in New York City. Educators liked the ideas of a design concept and rapidly adopted its use. Working Broadway lighting designers soon adopted it, too, for it gave them a usable communication tool for that all-important

first meeting with the director. However, many of the educators who train lighting designers remain confused about what a concept in this context is. USA #350 in Chicago defines it in a way that is different from the definition used by USA #829 in New York City. In New York the nature of the concept has shifted in the Union exam from year to year. In 1984, USA #829 identified a concept as a "description of the lighting."

Various authorities have written about concepts,[11] which are really quite simple to define and use. First, let's look at what they are *not:*

- A concept is not a literary analysis of the script or of the script's characters, plot, structure, or message. These elements are but pieces of necessary prerequisite information that help the designer to form a concept.
- A concept is not a description of how a designer intends to use light for a specific production (although this information may be required *after* the designer has arrived at a concept).

A concept *is:*

1. *An image.* It may be visual: the designer may see a play as clashes or swirls or jagged lines, or as texture — smooth and satiny or rough. The image may be a painting (used frequently) or a photograph which captures the designer's reaction to the script, TV show, opera, or dance. It may even be a cartoon. It may be an auditory symbol: a selection from classical or contemporary music which captures for the designer the necessary meanings of the material. A concept is a *real* image — not a philosophical one. Eliminated forever are such abstract images as *truth, justice,* and *beauty.* One cannot pick up, display, measure, or feel/taste/smell justice. The qualities of justice can only be described in other terms or by use of examples.

2. *A communications device.* Producers and directors think in visual terms about visual matters (lighting). The concept a designer presents *describes in graphic terms a personal design approach.* It is a means of establishing communication between the lighting designer and the director. If the designer says, "This play describes the discovery and elimination of a worm from a luscious red apple," the director will understand. If the designer says, "This play is about good and evil," he or she has failed to communicate any

[11] *Robert Brand, "Contrast: More about USA #829 Lighting Design Exam,"* Lighting Dimensions, *vol. 1, no. 6 (Dec. 1977), p. 54. Mr. Brand writes about "concepts" as they apply to the USA #829 Exam in New York City.*

Donna Hart, "Concepts in Lighting," Lighting Dimensions, *vol. 2, no. 4 (Apr. 1978), p. 54.*

J. Michael Gillette, Designing with Light: An Introduction to Stage Lighting; *Palo Alto, Calif.; Mayfield Publishing Co.; 1978. See Chapter 12, "Design Examples," pp. 143–164; concept analysis of* The Glass Menagerie *by Tennessee Williams.*

Ann Daly, "Dancing in the Dark: Dana Reitz Choreographs with Light, As Well As Movement," Lighting Dimensions, *vol. 13, no. 4 (May/June 1989). Pp. 84, 86, 89. Illus. An interesting and useful article explaining how a noted choreographer works with designed light by Jennifer Tipton, Beverly Emmons, and others.*

[12] E. I. Mostepanenko, "Opportunities for the Artistic Use of Light to Convey a Play's Images" ABTT News, Nov. 1984, p. 4. Mr. Mostepanenko is a Russian critic. This article first appeared in Stage Technologies and Technology, No. 1, 1978, and appeared in ABTT News in translation.

[13] See also footnote 8, and the following:

Jane E. Brody, "Surprising Health Impact Discovered for Light," The New York Times, "Science Times," pp. 19–20, Tuesday, Nov. 13, 1984. The subtitle — "Studies Reveal Light Has Surprisingly Wide Impact on Health"— indicates the subject covered. Illus.

Jane E. Brody, "Ways to Offset Lack of Light In the Shorter Days of Winter," The New York Times, "Living" section, Wed., Nov. 14, 1985, pp. 17–18. More on the same subject. (Both of these articles by Ms. Brody were reprinted in the IALD Newsletter, Jan. 1985, pp. 3–4)

Louis Erhardt, "Views on the Visual Environment: Light — What Is It?", Lighting Design + Application, vol. 16, no. 4 (Apr. 1986), p. 52.

Sarah Shankman, "Light in the Laboratory: A Biomedical Scientist Explores the Effects of Light on Mammals," Lighting Design + Application, vol. 16, no. 5 (May 1986), pp. 11–15. Illus., color. Useful summary of current research.

Judith H. Heerwagen and Dean R. Heerwagen, "Lighting and Psychological Comfort," Lighting Design + Application, vol. 16, no. 4 (Apr. 1986), pp. 47–51. Charts. Two architects write about the effect of light on comfort.

Los Angeles Times Syndicate, "Full-Spectrum Lights May Improve Health." Lafayette Journal & Courier, July 13, 1988, p. B4. Lab studies by a psychiatrist of 5- to 9-year-olds indicate that they stay healthier under full-spectrum fluorescent lighting.

"Health: Danger: Lights at Work," Lighting, vol. 2, no. 6 (Dec. 1988), pp. 25–26. Reprint of a report by the Medical Research Council of England, reprinted from the May 1988 Design magazine.

understanding to the director. Concepts often exist solely as a means of getting another artist to understand what an artist visualizes about the meaning and content of a project. Playwrights don't need them: they use words. Scene and costume designers can communicate through sketches. Lighting, being intangibly visual, requires something else; hence, the concept.

3. *An organizational device.* The designer develops a conceptual approach to a design task. Once it has been developed, all that the designer conceives thereafter can be measured against it. This is the primary purpose of the concept in union exams. Does this light color, angle, or intensity further the expression of the conceptual approach that has been adopted? For illustration, let's assume that a designer's concept of Shakespeare's play *Hamlet* is that young Hamlet is psychotic. Hamlet *imagines* the ramifications of the mother/uncle relationship. He is "mad as a hatter." If this is the lighting concept, then Hamlet should always be lighted in colors and angles and intensities of light which are unreal and bizarre, suggesting disorientation and madness. Those around him, in sharp contrast, must appear in perfectly normal lighting. Hamlet must appear "out of kilter" through the use of lighting design, which springs from the concept. Hamlet is insane; the other characters aren't. Thus, the designer utilizes a concept (which also could be called a *design approach*) as a unifying element and brings shape, form, consistency, intention, and meaning to his design.

There are plenty of working professional lighting designers (yes, even on Broadway) who have no other "concept" than to "light the show" — but they probably won't admit it. The concept has become a popular design tool, but one that continues to be modified as each year passes.

> Like music, light has a spontaneous influence over the feelings and moods of the audience. That is why in the revelation of the more deeply implied layers of a play light is frequently more powerful even than the word, which can be analyzed and discarded while the emotional reactions of the spectator cannot.[12]

Understanding Light[13]

The technician *assembles* light, by means of wires and bulbs; the designer *uses* light as an expressive tool. There is

a great difference between solving the illumination problem and designing with light. To be a successfully practicing lighting designer, a person needs to know just about everything there is to know about light and vision. What is light? How is it produced, modified, controlled? What is the human visual process? How does it work? Are there any flaws or distortions in the human visual process? How does the cinematic camera's or the television camera's response to luminous energy differ from the response of the human eye? Can this light/shade/color image be altered, distorted, or improved in the studio or the laboratory? What, then, is the effect upon the "seeing" of the ultimate human viewer? Are there by-product effects of radiant energy (ultraviolet light, for example) which damage or affect the human seeing mechanism? Can eyes and productivity be affected by long hours spent in the office in front of a badly lighted computer screen? And, most important of all, just *how do* humans respond — emotionally and intellectually — to varying patterns of radiant energy? That knowledge is the ultimate key to lighting design — in any speciality.

It is not the specific purpose of this handbook to deal at length with the vast body of knowledge involved in optics, vision, radiant energy, and human responses to light, although these subjects will be touched upon throughout. To treat this body of information herein would lengthen this book tenfold. Nonetheless, light is the ultimate (perhaps the only) tool of designers, and their whole career is devoted to evoking human responses from the use of it. Students are urged to delve as deeply into this body of information as possible if they choose to practice the art of lighting design.[14] Josef Svoboda, in a talk entitled "The Theatre Today — The Theatre Tomorrow" said: "Light, which is the most beautiful medium used by the theatre and its space, since it is weightless, is capable of reacting to every change in situation, is able to transform one space into another in an instant and to create an entirely different atmosphere."[15]

The Planning Stage

The initial conferences are over. Now comes the period of translating all of the useful information gleaned during the problem analysis into a workable, artistic solution. Since

Perhaps one of the most useful activities for a new student of lighting design is to arrange a visit to one of the now-numerous "lighting labs" or training programs, some of which are listed below:

Philips Lighting Center at Somerset, New Jersey. At an initial cost of over $2 million and with annual upkeep of $750,000, Philips has opened a unique lighting training center. Under the direction of Mark L. Roush, the Center deals with not only fundamentals of light production, control, and designed utilization, but in over 20,000 square feet it exhibits application use of light for industrial, office, retail, and residential uses as well as roadway and headlight design problems. International Lighting Review, *39th year, 3rd quarter of 1988, pp. 98–103 contains text by Mark Rousch ("Lighting Center, Somerset, USA") and extensive color illustrations of the new Lighting Center. "London Gallery,"* Lighting Dimensions, *vol. 13, no. 2 (March 1989), p. 29. Details Marlin's Light Gallery at 14 Warren Street, off Trittenham Court Road in London. It opened October 1988 and features seminars as well as a lighting lab.*

"Light Lab Opens," Lighting, *vol. 1, no. 1 (June 1987), p. 10. Canada's Canlyte, Inc., opened Canada's first light lab, called The Lighting Concept Center, in the Toronto Design Centre.*

"Lighting Lab Opens in Los Angeles," Lighting Dimensions, *vol. 12, no. 3 (April 1988), p. 17. The Lighting Group, a division of Westwood Wholesale Electric Co., opened a lab at 11900 Santa Monica Boulevard in West Los Angeles.*

*"Concept Centre, Educating the Lighting Design Team. "*Lighting, *vol. 2, no. 1 (Feb. 1988), pp. 16, 18. Illus. A more lengthy illustrated article concerning the Canlyte lighting lab listed above in Toronto.*

"Philips Lighting Centre Lets Designers See How Systems Work at First Hand," Lighting, *vol. 2, no. 2 (April 1988). p. 25. Illus. Details concerning the Philips lighting lab in Toronto on Milner Avenue, titled the Philips Centre.*

"Lighting Concepts Center Launched," Lighting Dimensions, *vol. 11, no. 6 (Nov. 1987), p. 26. Details concerning the Massachusetts Gas & Electric new Lighting Concept Center at 222 Canal Street, Boston.*

"Philips Lighting Center Opens," Lighting Dimensions, *vol. 12, no. 6, (Sept./Oct. 1988), p. 28. Illus. Further description and photos of the excellent Philips Lighting Center in Somerset, New Jersey.*

"Lighting GE's Lighting Institute," Lighting Dimensions, *vol. 12, no. 6 (Sept./Oct. 1988), p. 22. Employed by General Electric to redesign and update their Nela Park light lab were: Lesley Wheel of Wheel-Gersztoff, Howard Brandston, David Mintz, Ray Grenald, and Gary Steffy—all top architectural lighting designers, each with their own large firm.*

Architectural Lighting Showcase, *vol. 2, no. 12 (Dec. 1988), pp. 28, 30. Illus., color. Details and photos about the lighting laboratory at the General Electric (GE) Energy Resource Center in Tualatin, Oregon.*

General Electric (GE) Training Seminars at Nela Park, Cleveland, Ohio. Two- and three-day instruction in lavish facilities (partly subsidized by GE) and with a top-rated staff. Covers variously: architectural lighting and interior design, theatrical lighting, film lighting, TV lighting, and so on. Reopened updated on June 21, 1987.

Lightolier. This firm has excellent showrooms and instructional staffs in New York City, Kentucky, and on the West Coast. Contact: Lightolier, 1071 Avenue of the Americas (at 41st Street), New York, N.Y., 10018. (212) 719-1616.

Halo/ELA Tech Center, 6 W. 20th St., New York, N.Y. 10011. (212) 645-4580.

Fashion Institute Lighting Lab. A lavish lighting laboratory partly underwritten by the New York State Department of Education as a part of the Interior Design Department, Fashion Institute of Technology, 227 West 27th St., New York, N.Y. 10001.

Luminatae, Inc., 8515 Keystone Crossing Ave., Indianapolis, Ind. 46204. (317) 251-1100.

Moto-Light, 3119A South Scenic, Springfield, Mo. 65805. (417) 883-4549.

York Lighting Corp., St. Laurent (Montreal), Quebec, Canada, has opened a large showroom at its head office.

University of Kansas, Lawrence, Kan., % Dr. Ronald N. Helms, Lum-I-Neering 3316 Westridge Court, Lawrence, Kansas 66044 (913) 864-3434.

See: "Showrooms," Interior Design, *Apr. 1987. Illus., color.*

Also, visits to the Exploratorium *in San Francisco and the* Museum of Holography *in New York City and in Chicago (see Chapter 3) can provide valuable training. See: "Seeing the Light,"* Lighting Design + Application, *vol. 16, no. 7 (July 1986), pp. 36–37.*

There are many other light labs and showrooms, with new ones being added weekly around the country; this list is only a starting point.

[14] *A most useful tool for the beginning theatrical lighting designer is:*

Delbert Unruh, Composition in Light. *Published privately by Professor Unruh, University of Kansas, Lawrence, Kan. 66045.*

For further guidance, see also:

Sophus Frandsen, "NEW CONCEPTS: The Scale of Light," International Lighting Review, *38th year, 3rd quarter 1987, pp. 108–112. Illus., color. Excellent test about the importance of scale in understanding light.*

Delbert Unruh, "Composition in Light—Aesthetic and Functional Considerations," Theatre Design and Technology, *no. 38 (Oct. 1974), pp. 17–22. Illus.*

Bob Davis, "Stage—Frontlight Positions—An Informal Plea for Diversity," Lighting Design + Application, *vol. 5, no. 6 (June 1975), pp. 62–68. Illus.*

Arthur E. Alvis, Jr., Programmed Lighting Design. *Ph.D. dissertation, University of Missouri (Columbia), 1982.*

Lee Watson, "Splash, Sensitivity, or Structure—Styles of Lighting Design," Lighting Dimensions, *vol. 2, no. 1 (Jan. 1978), pp. 17–18. The author discusses his design criteria.*

[15] *Josef Svoboda, "The Theatre Today — The Theatre Tomorrow," ABTT News, Feb. 1985, pp. 2–3.*

[16] *William B. Warfel,* Handbook of Stage Lighting Graphics. *N.Y.; Drama Book Specialists/Publishers; 2d ed. 1974. 41 pp., illus. Standard "bible" of light plot communication.*

Harvey Sweet, Graphic for the Performing Arts. *Boston; Allyn and Bacon; 1985. Illus., 281 pp. Guide to basic drafting and sketching skills. Little on lighting design.*

USITT Graphics Standards Board, "A Standard Graphic Language for Lighting Design," Theatre Design & Technology, *vol. 20, no. 4 (Winter 1985), pp. 14–15. Illus. Codified standard symbols and style recommended by a United States Institute for Theatre Technology (USITT) committee following years of study and inquiry. Not yet universally adopted.*

designers usually do not hang or install the luminaires (lights) themselves, their solution must be organized for the inspection and use of others. This involves communication. Any artist must master the existing vocabulary of an art form, whether it consists of words and images of poetry/prose or of musical notation. Here is a list of the established means of communication which a student needs to master for the planning stage:

1. The Light Plot. A *light plot* is a work order. It is a method for communicating the shape, form, and details of the "lighting machine" which the artist needs to have at hand for the creation and execution of a concept. Examples of various designers' plots abound throughout this *Handbook*, and the student should study them. Architectural lighting designers use similar drawings to communicate to both the architect and the electrical engineer or contractor. For the theatre, the standard reference work is Professor William Warfel's *Handbook of Stage Lighting Graphics*.[16] There is no need to repeat that information here, but the student is advised to master this form of understandable communication.

In the theatre there are two types of light plots. One type is the simplified professional and Broadway work order containing only the theatre's permanent structural shape, a title block, a symbol key, unit (luminaire) location and identification number, and dimension and location lines. It does *not* contain information concerning dimmer, color, and focus. These bits of information are in the switchboard hookup sheets, which will be discussed next. The second type of light plot is the study, or classroom, light plot, which is used by most educators in the teaching of lighting design and for the USA Entrance Examination. In addition to the elements listed for the professional light plot, this plot indicates dimmer control number, color media, major focus, sometimes circuit connection number, and any other pertinent technical details about lighting equipment. All theatrical designers need to know how to do both types. A show *can* be hung from either type of plot. The professional light plot is much cleaner and less cluttered with information; also, it preserves many of the lighting details from the prying eyes of ill-informed setup electricians and "stage managers who light," since only the production's master electrician

has a copy of the switchboard hookup sheets. The classroom light plot is a much better communication device, rather than just existing as a work order. It allows other lighting designers and educators to understand easily the student's intention in creating his "lighting machine" without their having to cross-reference the switchboard hookup sheets. Examples of both types of light plot occur throughout this volume. Warfel also deals with both.

Since the exact form of the theatrical light plot is in constant evolution, this volume presents many variations from Warfel's suggested practice. Each working designer finds minor modifications which best communicate that designer's work-order demands. Students should study the plots in this book and decide which works best for them — within the general guidelines suggested by Warfel.

It should be noted that a light plot can be accompanied by a section drawing, although not all working designers do section drawings (there are relatively few in this volume). Much of the information contained in the section drawing (for example, trim heights for masking and beam spreads for adequate area coverage) can be worked out by the designer in "roughs," and then that information can be transferred onto the light plot. Nonetheless, since the Union exam and many types of classroom instruction *require* a section drawing, the student will need to know how to do one and have examples in his portfolio.

2. Sketches. Increasingly, lighting designers (in both the theatrical and the architectural fields) are learning how to present their ideas in "light and shade" sketches. These sketches are often a cross between an advertising agency's storyboard and the more finished "presentation" sketches of a scenic designer. The one purpose of these sketches is to convey to others the lighting design intention. These sketches are not finished "works of art," as are most sketches prepared by scenic and costume designers, or by architects and interior designers. Both USA #829 and USA #350 now require study sketches as a part of their entrance examinations. Most leading lighting design educators now encourage their students to become proficient in sketching and rendering.

Prior to beginning any such sketches of a lighting concept, the designer should study most carefully the scenic

Figure 1.1 Rendering of desired lighting for Richard Strauss's *Electra*, Teatre "La Fenice," Venice. Scene design: Andreas Nomikos; director: Rudolph Hartman.

designs prepared for the production. Most scenic designers give strong clues in their sketches as to the desired light distribution. If the scenic design indicates sunlight pouring through the bay window of a set, that's what the scenic designer expects to see when the set gets on stage! Figure 1.1, a sketch by Andreas Nomikos for a production of Richard Strauss' opera *Elektra*, contains innumerable clues for the lighting designer and deserves careful study.

Once designers have gleaned all of the information they can from the scenic designer's sketches, they should be prepared to do some roughs of their own — to communicate to both the director and the scenic designer the "high points" of their use of light. Figure 1.2 presents one such set of storyboards by Professor Delbert Unruh (see footnote 14). Figures 1.3 through 1.6 present another such set of storyboards done by one of my students.

If design students discover that they cannot sketch (a problem faced by many of the older professional lighting designers), they should consider an alternative: building a model of the set or using the scenic designer's model, lighting it with miniature lights, and then photographing it. USA #350 will accept such photographs in lieu of sketches.

Architectural lighting specialists have long known the value of submitting "light and shade" sketches to both the client and the architect. Theatrical lighting designers are rapidly learning that they not only *can* sketch, but *must*.

3. Switchboard Hookups. Switchboard hookups are the vital part of the light plot for the master electrician. In tabular form by control circuit number (dimmer), the hookup tells the color media, type of lighting instrument, wattage, location in the theatre, and necessary specialized details (funnels or hi-hats, gobos or patterns, etc.). The conventional form for hookups again varies slightly from designer to designer. The student can be guided by Warfel's suggestions or by the examples presented throughout this *Handbook*. The switchboard hookup has replaced the older "instrument schedule," which listed lighting units by mounting position ("balcony front," "first electric pipe," etc.). The switchboard hookup and the instrument schedule contain the same information, but it is arranged differently.

On rare occasions the student may be asked to prepare "hanging cardboards." Popularized as an instructional tool by Professor Gilbert Hemsley, Jr., at the University of Wisconsin, these are simply the older instrument schedule, neatly drafted. They have been prepared by master electricians (usually on the back of laundry shirt cardboards) for as long as I can remember. They are rarely needed if the lighting project has a competent master electrician.[16a]

4. Focus Charts. During the setup, an accurate record of the precise focus of each lighting unit must be kept by the lighting designer, the assistant lighting designer, or the stage manager. The exact focus chart form used varies widely from designer to designer (examples appear throughout this *Handbook*). The focus chart is a vital record, because, for example, the original production may move through several different theatres, there may be national road companies performing the show (or bus-and-truck tours), or there may be foreign reproductions of the show. Even within a given theatre, lighting units may inadvertently be knocked out of focus. The focus chart is a vital record.

5. Magic Sheets. Some working designers assemble on one sheet of paper a condensed summary of their equipment design setup. Warfel calls these "color keys." If the de-

[16a] *For more detailed information and an example of hanging cardboards, the student should consult the Yale University School of Drama Technical Brief No. 1110, by Eugene Leitermann, October 1981.*

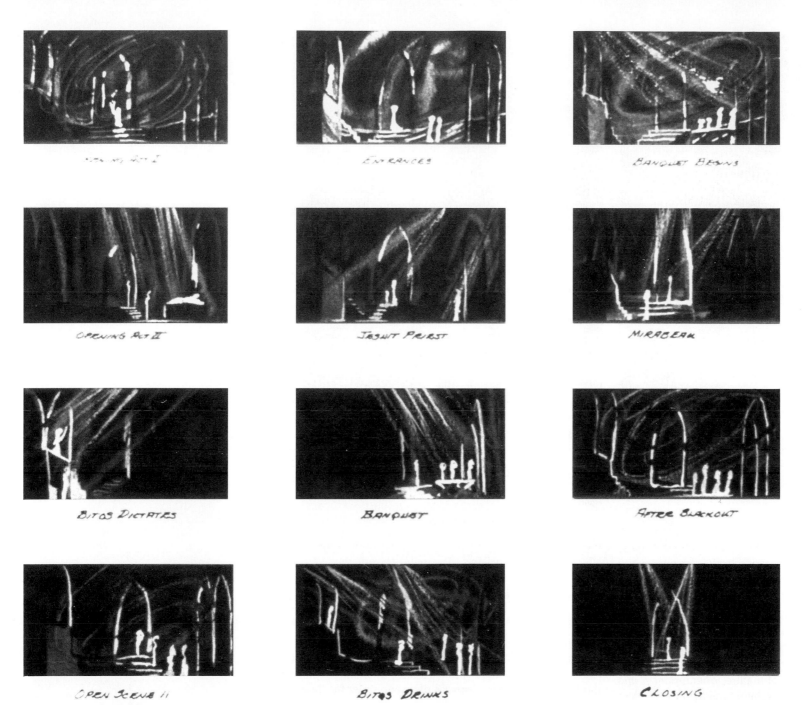

Figure 1.2 Thumbnail sketches or storyboard samples by Professor Delbert Unruh for *The Dream Weaver*, Nebraska University, 1968.

Figure 1.3 Light study sketch by Richard Lloyd, Purdue University graduate student, for *Electra:* Chrysothemis's first entrance.

Figure 1.4 *Electra:* Electra giving Aegisthus light.

Figure 1.5 *Electra:* Electra confronting Clytemnestra.

Figure 1.6 *Electra:* Finale.

signer chooses to take the time to prepare such a summary, it can be of considerable assistance to the designer when setting lighting cues (changes) and intensity levels and bringing about a lighting concept in the theatre.

6. Shop Orders. Schools own their own lighting equipment, as do most regional theatres, many Off- and Off-Off-Broadway groups, and TV studios. On the other hand, much movie lighting equipment is rented, as is nearly everything used for professional theatre, opera, dance, and industrial and trade shows. Architectural lighting involves the purchase of permanent equipment. Outdoor theatres almost always own lights. The need to rent thus varies. Schools normally teach nothing or very little about shop orders and the rental process, yet the practicing professional needs this knowledge. Sooner or later the designer has a show which does *not* have a master electrician on the payroll to order rented lighting equipment. A fuller explanation of shop orders can be found in Appendix A of this *Handbook.* An example appears in this volume concerning the USA examination. Portions of a shop order by Gilbert

[17] Lee Watson, "About Shop Orders," Lighting Dimensions, vol. 1, no. 6 (Dec. 1977), pp. 15–16, 20.

[18] "The Dream Team on Collaboration," Theatre Crafts, vol. 16, no. 7 (Aug./Sept. 1982), pp. 12–15, 40, 42–43. Illus. Useful interview with producer-choreographer-director Michael Bennett, Robin Wagner (scene design), Tharon Musser (lighting design), Theoni V. Aldredge (costume design), and Bob Avian (sound) on their communication process.

Beeb Salzer, "To Robert L. Benedetti," Lighting Dimensions, vol. 3, no. 7 (July 1979), pp. 53, 58. Thoughts on director–designer communication.

"Lighting Team Pros—Problems and Goals," Lighting Design + Application, vol. 14, no. 4 (Apr. 1984), pp. 17–37. Most of this issue of Lighting Design + Application is devoted to communication with others as a vital element in architectural lighting design. Includes: "Lighting Design — Who's in Charge?" (a panel discussion of experts from several lighting disciplines), and the lighting designer as a source of technical information, as a client psychologist, as a team worker with the client, the engineer, and the interior designer. Lewis Sternberg writes: "Lighting specialists aren't born, they're trained and developed." The combined articles by prominent professionals portray the necessity of team communication.

August Everding, "A German View on Lighting the Stage Today," Cue, no. 49 (Sept./Oct. 1987), pp. 4–5. An excellent article, written from the viewpoint of the German regisseur (producer/director) by a leading German concerning the design relationship/communication process.

Ann Daly, "Show and Tell: Designers Share Techniques for Presenting Lighting Concepts to Their Clients," and: Bonnie Schwartz, "Airbrush: Renderings That Make the Difference," and "Film: Backlit Images Pack a Punch," and Michael S. Eddy, "Computer Graphics: Lighting in the Third Dimension," and Bonnie Schwartz, "Models: Dramatic Presentations in Small Packages," and Mark Loeffler, "Mock-ups: Simulation as the Clearest Form of Presentation," Lighting Dimensions, vol. 13, no. 4 (May/June 1989). pp. 47–53.

Hemsley, Jr., are found in Scene Design and Stage Lighting.[3] The most lengthy treatment of shop orders in print can be found in my article titled "About Shop Orders."[17]

These six written forms are the ones in common use in the planning stage. The point is that somewhere, on paper, the lighting designer must think through the design problems and create a "lighting machine" to solve them; he or she must then prepare the necessary work orders which communicate that which is needed to hang the show or build the building and how to use that "machine" wisely and rapidly. Whether the show calls for one simple light plot and a hookup, or an instrument schedule, with or without a section, matters not. The objective is a well-designed final production. The forms are merely the means. Outlined above are today's commonly accepted vocabulary and presentation style. Mastering each will help the designer to communicate with others more readily.

I have largely bypassed the large body of technical knowledge which the designer must possess. Other volumes have covered extensively the necessary knowledge about light and vision, light sources, light control, color theory and use, lighting equipment (luminaires or units or instruments), drafting skills, and so forth. These sources are cited in earlier footnotes. This Handbook presumes a fundamental knowledge of lighting technology, stressing the design arts which grow from the use of technology.

Communication

One of the largest problems the lighting designer faces is that no one else, with the exception of other lighting designers, understands and can make use of a light plot, hookup, etc. The director doesn't. If it is architectural work, the client doesn't. Yet always the lighting designer is working as part of a design team. The poet, the novelist, the painter, and the composer can each create alone. Not the lighting designer! This chapter has already touched upon several vital devices which can help to improve the lighting designer's communication with collaborating artists, including the concept and sketches, to name but two. Yet, if the designer cannot find an acceptable way to communicate lighting ideas following the planning stage, it is unlikely that he or she will work often. What should the lighting designer do when finding that the director has absolutely no visual sense — that is, the director is totally word- and idea-oriented? When the director, who has seen a model, sketches, and a floor plan, says to the scenic designer, "Oh, is this door over here and does it open offstage rather than onstage?" The lighting designer punts — and finds a way! Past those systems suggested here, there is no easy way to teach communication. Each lighting designer must constantly work at it. The student for whom communication is a very real problem should consult the articles listed in footnote 18.

Creativity

Where, then, in this welter of problem analysis, writing a concept, drafting and sketching plans, and communicating with fellow artists/technicians/engineers, does any creativity come into play? Is lighting design merely an uninspired skill? Certainly not! Each individual lighting designer can express creative powers to an unlimited degree in the following ways:

- The designer selects the best lighting unit to solve the design objectives. The designer has artistic control of wattage, type of luminaire (instrument, unit), and the use to which it is put.
- The designer controls media selection and color usage.
- The designer controls luminaire focus and placement. Through this control the designer directs (or obscures) audience/client attention, causing the observer/user to look at a certain person or space. In theatre/film/TV, this is the most powerful creative tool in assisting the director to create an ever-changing pattern of attention focus, resulting in a progression of endlessly changing mobile stage pictures. Mobility of focus is also a factor in architectural lighting design.
- The designer controls timing. The rate, pace, and propriety of light changes and light cues will always remain an artistic decision matter.[19]
- The designer controls special effects. Particularly in the fields of spectacle (discos, theme parks, circuses, musicals, ice shows, etc.), the creation and selection of stunning effects can be the basis of a highly successful lighting design career.

■ The designer controls interpretation of the meaning of the script (building, dance, opera) and desired audience reactions, as far as they are dependent upon the use of light. As a member of the creative production/design team, the lighting designer has at hand endless subtle variations of angle, color, intensity, and flow (form and movement) with which to expand, clarify, accent, and reinforce what the other creative artists are doing. However, the designer must avoid ''taking over the show'' and ''showing off'' personal abilities in order to get attention.

This brings us to a brief treatment of a vital element: the objectives of lighting design, what lighting is all about. Each objective is considered in detail below.

1. Selective Visibility. A careful analysis of the script/building and of the director's/architect's production presents a pattern of what the audience/client should be looking at (focus) at any given moment. ''Visibility'' implies some comfortable level between the extremes of excessively flat overlighting (*glare,* which can be most painful) and underlighting (*gloom,* which can be equally painful). Too little light and too much light are equal sins. So is unimaginative dullness. ''Selective'' implies mobility — light pattern changes. In theatre, the performers move, and the attention constantly shifts to differing parts of the performance space. Light is the principal tool available to assist the director in the ever-changing focus pattern. The theatre/film/TV lighting artist paints a series of light/shade/color portraits for the audience which clarify, focus, and expand the production. In architecture/display lighting, the artist of light assists in featuring those elements which are primary (be it a work area or a decorative planting space) and subordinating those of less consequence (hallways, storage areas, etc.). Mobility and change of lighting/focus is equally possible in architectural lighting. A restaurant's lighting should be vastly different for the noon meal and for ''after work'' leisure-time evening dining. The designer should not be afraid of shadow and darkness. Contrast is one of the lighting designer's best tools. The hero in a shaft of intense white light in a surrounding pool of darkness is one of the designer's most effective theatrical tools. Flat, even ''visibility'' illumination belongs in the football stadium — and very few

other places. There is a very real difference between *lighting design* and *illumination.*

2. Mood. So much has been written and researched about the power of light to influence audience/client mood response that little need be added here. It frequently is the mood-evoking ability of the lighting designer which separates the great disco design from the ordinary design. For the architectural lighting designer it is mood evocation and control which separates the monumental building from the factory-office box with seemingly endless evenly spaced fluorescent troffers.

3. Composition. Nothing exists or is seen until light is present. In both theatrical and architectural lighting, the designer begins with a ''clean slate.'' The designer composes, paints, and reveals (or subordinates) what the viewer sees with light. Ever-changing ''painting with light'' applies equally to *all* lighting fields.

4. Dealing with Nature. William M. C. Lam, in his book *Perception and Lighting as Formgivers for Architecture,* (see footnote 8), writes about human biological needs, one of which is the need of humans to know where they are and to be oriented sufficiently to feel safe and secure. The architectural specialist must deal with the presence or absence of daylight. The theatrical designer must immediately clarify for the audience as the curtain rises the ''representation of nature'' information: Where are we? In the tropics? At the North Pole? Is it day or night? Is it raining, lightning, snowing? The designer satisfies the *biological information needs* of the audience by imitating with light the known lighting patterns of nature. *Then* the audience can sit back and become familiar with the characters and the story line offered. But the first question is always, Where (when, in what situation) are we? That first question is usually answered in part by lighting.

Creativity in lighting? There is lots of room for it. Rarely, however, are design considerations ideal. Time and the budget or unsuccessful communication can intrude. Rarely does lighting artistry reach the perfectionist level the designer had in mind during the planning stage. When it does

Illus., color. A priceless group of articles dealing with various methods of presenting lighting design concepts (most frequently in architectural lighting) to the client.

See also:
Albert F. C. Wehlburg, Theatre Lighting: An Illustrated Glossary. *New York; Drama Book Specialists; 1975. 62 pp., illus.*

''A Glossary of Commonly Used Terms in Theatre, Television and Film Lighting,'' Lighting Design & Application, *vol. 13, no. 11 (Nov. 1983), pp. 43–46, 48. An extensive glossary, prepared over several years, by 36 members of the Illuminating Engineering Society. A useful and up-to-date communication reference.*

N. Peter Cutchey, ''Technically Speaking, Glossary of Technical Terms Commonly Found in the Lighting Business,'' Discotech, *vol. 3, no. 1 (Jan. 1987), pp. 14–15. Useful glossary, particularly for the disco design specialty.*

[19] *See Francis Reid, ''Calling the Show,''* Cue, *no. 36 (July/Aug. 1985), pp. 12–13. Excellent article on cueing.*

come close, the achievement offers the designer one of life's great satisfactions.

What is good lighting? Perhaps my own lighting standards as a critic quoted here from my articles in *Lighting Dimensions* and *Lighting Design + Application* will help answer that question.

What is good lighting? Such a simple question. Yet it has resulted in thousands of hours of panel discussions and near endless coverage in books, magazines and journals.

As a relative newcomer to the pages of *Lighting Design + Application* it seems appropriate to explain my criteria in answering this all-important question about lighting design in the performing arts. As the only (foolhardy) critic of lighting design in the Western Hemisphere, here are the things I look for:

(1) *Cues.* Does the material call for a light change or is the designer merely showing off his/her cleverness? Do the cues fit the action, movement and rhythmic pattern and flow of the show, whether it be drama, opera, dance, television, film, disco, concert lighting, theme park or a world's fair and exposition? Is the cue "count" (execution) too abrupt or too drawn out? Are there too many lighting changes or too few?

(2) *Visibility.* Is there enough light for comfortable vision or too much, on the edge of glare? Some productions have scenes which are unnecessarily "artsy" in dimness; others are just "illuminated" with such an intense, flat level of lighting that all design is eliminated.

(3) *Realism.* Many productions call for a plausible representation of reality. Does the sunlight pour through windows on opposite sides of the stage (yes, I've seen that at the New York City Opera)? Does a supposedly oil lantern dim out on cue with no performer going near it (to be found in one recent Broadway production of a Greek tragedy)? Can the audience grasp time-of-day, weather and geographic locale from lighting "signals" when the curtain goes up or the production begins?

(4) *Composition.* Has the designer provided carefully composed light/shadow/color pictures? Involved here is the whole element of composition: what is revealed, obscured, accentuated or subordinated by the use of all revealing light in the overall visual environment.

(5) *Focus.* A primary function of light in theatrical performance is to direct the audience's attention as needed in the visual field, assisting the director/playwright/performers in centering on that which is (at each moment) most important. Did the designer plan both area control and specials to assist in this vital process? Were there enough areas or was it necessary to light half the stage when only a sofa was important for a short scene? Or was the performance space "chopped up" into so many small areas that constant light changes distracted from the flow of the production?

(6) *Depth* and *Plasticity.* Are crosslight, backlight and modeling (or key) light used effectively to accent the performers and cause them to "stand out" from the visual surround? Does light help us to understand the solidity, weight, depth and texture of the elements in the scene presented? Or is everything flat, evenly lighted with no sense of depth? This element becomes paramount in films and television when the light and shade image viewed is presented on a flat surface (movie screen or TV tube).

(7) *Mood.* What, if anything, did the lighting designer do — good or bad — to reinforce the mood desired by the playwright/choreographer/composer? Influencing and evoking mood response is both one of the more difficult and most important things which an artist of light brings to a production.

(8) *Effects.* What was done in the use of projections, lasers, holograms, gobo patterns, special effects, fire, smoke, pyrotechnics, etc., to add or detract from the production's overall effectiveness? I call this "glitz and glitter" or "splash." It is highly important in musicals, some opera and almost all industrial shows plus all fairs, expositions and circuses. Were "practicals" (lamps, chandeliers, wall sconces, torches, candles) believable and well handled?

(9) *Spectacle.* Closely allied to #8 is spectacle. This is an essential component in ice shows, huge outdoor productions (The *Liberty* weekend for example). Is the designer up-to-date (or even ahead) in the latest spectacular effects available?

(10) *Followspots.* As long as the designer's name is on the program, the designer remains responsible for smooth, frequently unobtrusive use of followspots. The designer planned the cues and colors. Are the followspots "soft-edged" in a realistic production? Check the Metropolitan Opera lighting: only an observant expert can detect the presence of follows. Were the spots operated with correct "pickups"? Were they obtrusive or helpful?

(11) *Color.* How wisely was colored light used? Did it add or detract? Was the designer's color palette too saturated, too intense or too emotional for the nature of the material? Or were the color selections too pale, pastel, bland and unobtrusive to fit the blood and guts (dramatic strength) of the material presented? Color and selection is highly personal with each designer and frequently the most difficult artistic decision to deal with.

(12) *Maintenance and upkeep.* If the production has been running for some time, were light cues and followspot work still smoothly operated? Or was the production allowed to deteriorate, becoming slovenly? The designer's lighting credit remains on the program — whenever and wherever it performs. The designer remains ultimately responsible for the visual effectiveness of all you see, even if the designer was not "running the show." Furthermore the excuse: "that's what the director insisted upon" does not hold water. Your credit is still there. The designer should have: (a) somehow changed the director's mind, or (b) withdrawn from the production (or had the credit removed) if

the end product the audience sees as a cash customer is just plain bad lighting design.

(13) *Design.* Most important of all: Did the lighting expand, deepen, improve or change the art of using light as a design element? Or are we just viewing another example of technical cleverness? Are we seeing a production which will be immediately popular, rapidly forgotten and have absolutely no effect whatsoever upon the forward thrust of lighting design? Example: Ms. Tharon Musser's introduction of a memory electronic switchboard for the Broadway production *Chorus Line* was a tremendous step forward in expanding the tools available to an imaginative "user of light." Finally, does the lighting of the production being critiqued further the art and expand the artistry?

You can add others. These are the basics I use. If we were setting forth "What is good lighting?" for architectural, landscape and interior design, many others would need to be added (energy efficiency; task adequacy; reinforcement or architectural ambience; cost, both initial and upkeep maintenance). Others on my list would be dropped.[20]

The Production Process

In spite of near-perfect analysis and planning, the production process is a time during which frantic pandemonium prevails for *all* lighting designers. For those working architecturally, it could be that some of the specified luminaires haven't arrived yet. Or the wall washers don't do what was expected at all. The client, the architect, *and* the contractor may all be yelling at the lighting designer at the same time, while he is checking, altering or modifying, and adjusting. Usually the designer wishes they would leave him alone until he is *finished,* and then critique, if they must.

The production process is equally nerve-racking for the theatrical designer. For example, he may find that the equipment is all in place, but that one ellipsoidal spotlight just will *not* shine through a new scenic drop that is immediately upstage of the light. Or that the costumes aren't at all the shade he thought they would be when he examined the sketches. Or that many lighting approaches which looked brilliant on his planning papers just don't work out at all as he sets intensity levels and cues. Perhaps the director has even reblocked three whole scenes, affecting the critical focus of ten "specials," and no one ever told the poor lighting designer.

These are the realities of lighting design. In the face of these unexpected circumstances it becomes apparent how well the lighting designer has

- Used available time and resources (conferences, analysis, crew/installation personnel, rehearsal, etc.) to the maximum.
- Used available funding (be it equipment cost/rental, crew size, setup/installation costs, etc.).
- Learned how to "cover his ass" by working through the unexpected problems calmly, rapidly, and knowledgeably with the others on the production team to obtain maximum creative results for the audience/client.

The pressure is nearly unbearable. A designer's "workability" in the production process is *the* element which most often determines whether or not he will ever work again. My personal definition of a *great* lighting designer is the designer who, with a given amount of time and personnel and equipment, achieves *more* in lighting artistry, from which the audience/client benefits, than could any other lighting designer faced with the same constraints. It is a difficult goal to achieve!

Beeb Salzer, in *Lighting Dimensions,* described the production process much better than I can ever hope to in "A Letter to a Young Designer." Here are some excerpts:

> Dear Friend, I watched you at work in the auditorium, your drawings spread over the wide desk and the shaded lamp lighting the changes in your expression. The intercom was in your hand while your other hand searched over lists of numbers and symbols on your plot. People were sitting all around you talking. Other voices came over your intercom; voices came from the stage, all of them urging, begging, commanding, flattering, damning. You were a lightning rod for all the psychological electricity unloosed on the final day before opening.
>
> We had talked about what might happen to you on this, your first professional job. But nothing could truly prepare you. . . . You did survive, even triumphed. Your lighting was close to what you wanted it to be and the experience made you a veteran, slightly battle-scarred, but confident in your ability, stamina, and purpose.
>
> Those last few days of rehearsal are completely different for the lighting designer than for anyone else. He is the sprinter on the team. He must summon up one fast concerted burst of energy to do his job. Or maybe he is like the last runner on a relay team. The pressure is on him, regardless of how slow the others have been.

[20] Lee Watson, "*The Mind and Methods of a Lighting Critic,*" Lighting Dimensions, *vol. 8, no. 7 (Nov./Dec. 1984), pp. 11–12. Professor Watson writes about the critical standards used to judge good (effective) lighting design versus poor design. Also covered in "Watson on The Performing Arts,* Lighting Design + Application, *vol. 16, no. 10 (Oct. 1986), pp. 46–47.*

[21] *Beeb Salzer, "A Letter to a Young Designer,"* Lighting Dimensions, *vol. 7, no. 3 (June 1983), p. 11.*

See also:

"My First Broadway Show," Lighting Dimensions, *vol. 9, no. 2 (Mar./Apr. 1985), pp. 42–50. Illus., color. Lighting designer Peter Maradudin talks about his first professional production, the Broadway production of* Ma Rainey's Black Bottom.

James L. Moody, "How to Cope with Failure," Lighting Dimensions, *vol. 9, no. 4 (July/Aug. 1985), pp. 39, 41–42. Veteran concert, theatre, and TV lighting designer writes about knowing how to make the best of a bad situation.*

[22] *Clive Barnes, "Critic's Notebook: Comments, Not Complaints, About Broadway, Mr. Papp and the Irish,"* The New York Times, *Dec. 8, 1976.*

. . . Sure, you had a bit of time to focus and set a few levels, but after what seemed like minutes, the army of Genghis Khan descended with demands for space and time to practice their barbaric rites. They sang and danced, moved sets around, and shouted through the once dark and calm theatre.

Until then you were working with equipment, steel and glass, cables and lamps. When the hordes arrived you also had to deal with egos, personalities, prejudices, and insecurities.

. . . It was also at this time that the others looked to you to be a god. A lighting designer does appear to have supernatural powers. His control over arcane technical equipment, combined with the visible magic he performs, gives him an aura of influence and at the same time creates expectations that are hard to satisfy.

"I'd like that girl levitated about three feet. Can't you do it with light?"

At other times you were expected to be a janitor, a kind of artistic garbage man, carting away the mess that others have made.

"That red sofa should disappear in this scene. Can't you light it out?"

Frustration! It is the motor that drives every sort of aberrant behavior in the final days of rehearsal. It is the Eumenides, never invited but always present to needle, push, and betray one's best instincts and moral resolves. The interesting thing is not your own frustration; that can be defined in terms of your goals and how far you are from them. Nor is it the collective frustration, one that joins the whole company in a shared concern for a flawed production. The fascinating thing to watch is the way the individual frustrations grate against each other causing friction, heat, and pain.

Young designers, like you, are often unaware that everyone else, or should I say the real artists working on a production, have fallen short of what they envisioned their work to be. It is never as good or as beautiful as what their mind's eye saw in those quiet moments of preparation. . . .

Directors are especially prone to fits of frustration. Theirs is the central vision, yet they have no direct control over anything. They have no concrete tools but must rely on intelligence, persuasion, strength of character. In those last rehearsals, the one thing a director might actually control is the lighting. There it is being worked on in front of him. It seems that all one must do to effect changes is to say a few words into a headset. There you are, the lighting designer, prey to the frustrations of the director. . . . At this point doing anything is better than doing nothing.

There are, of course, variations of the frustrated director syndrome. The show is so far gone that the director has given up and does not bother you. The director is not an artist so he is not frustrated. The leading man can't remember his lines so the director spends his time working with him. The director is technically ignorant and visually blind and is afraid to mess with the production. In some ways it is therefore better to have a director badgering, screaming, and cursing because it is a sign that the show is close enough to fight for and there are no larger problems.

I know that you would like to have advice on ways to handle each situation. My frustration is that I cannot tell you how. You will deal with things in one way while others cope in their own ways. Each one finds a combination of wheedling, cajoling, lying, tricking, and a good dose of being so efficient, talented, and right that one is beyond criticism.. . . .

You are on your way. Godspeed.[21]

Summary

The creative artist called a lighting designer is born, not made. Yet each person is given a certain amount of creativity, and if designers are not willing to use their inherent gifts to the fullest, they should not design. Proper guidance and training (self-teaching or guidance from others) allows designers to expand and utilize their creative gifts. Add the old bromide "Genius is 90 percent perspiration and 10 percent inspiration" to the equation for success, and the equation approximates the truth.

It is fitting to close this chapter with an excerpt from a critical piece by New York City drama critic Clive Barnes, which was printed in the December 8, 1976 edition of *The New York Times:*

Why cannot Broadway musicals be as imaginatively staged and designed as the Met Opera's new *Esclarmonde?* Beni Montresor . . . designed with such wit and feeling, such a sense for the stage, for light and for theatrical magic. Montresor uses lighting and gauzes, scrims and drapes in a modern way.

Theatrical design trends can be seen just as easily in the N.Y. City Opera or in dance. . . . Operas such as *The Makropoulos Affair, Mefistofele, A Village Romeo and Juliet* and *Die Tote Stadt* were all fantasticated ventures that broadened the concept of the lyric theatre.

All these productions have used light projections and, quite often, film in a manner apparently unknown to Broadway producers. . . . Consider, in dance, the bold, out-of-the-ordinary visual work on Alwin Nikolais.

. . . Certainly we have never seen on Broadway the sort of total visual theatrical concept that can occasionally be seen in opera and dance. Wake up, Broadway! There are images out there to be captured. They are not using gaslight any more.[22]

Chapter 2

Keys to Mastery

Through all the years of teaching, I discovered that teaching design—being a part of theatre process—is really teaching a way of living. Design is dealing with life and everything that it entails. The best kind of design is that.[23]

I remember a demonstration by Gordie Pearlman—assisted by a modem and long distance—of three-dimensional scenic elevations generated by ground plans somehow placed in a large mainframe computer some 2000 miles distant. Then there was Tharon Musser's lighting for *A Chorus Line* with the first computer board on Broadway. . . . These were but a few examples of what the new technology could do in the theatre; hundreds and thousands of other applications were to come along to make our work easier and faster.

Better? George Balanchine is quoted as having said, "Less is better." To my way of thinking, it all depends on the way you use the technology. Just because we have a machine that can memorize 500 light cues with varying rates of change or rigging systems operated by one flyman who needs only to push the correct controller on cue doesn't necessarily mean that we have a more perfect production or better art. It is very probable that the play, opera, or musical doesn't need an infinite number of changes in the lighting or 30 differest settings all driven by very expensive electronic machinery controlled by computers. . . . Which brings me back to the last sentence in my first paragraph above—Someone has to pay the bill for all of this electronic wizardry and one thing we know very well: most of it is custom built and it doesn't come cheap.

Our new—and potentially liberating—technology is very expensive and must be handled with great care. Call me old fashioned but I don't buy the argument that was advanced to rationalize the enormous complexity of (the musical) *Legs*. Robert Allan Ackerman, the director, was quoted as saying that: "Modern audiences don't have the patience to sit through crossover material while stagehands are changing the scenery manually. . . . Sophisticated audiences come into the theatre expecting to be bombarded by constantly changing visual effects."[23A] I think any audience—modern or otherwise—will accept what it sees on the stage *if the production is well done!* A good script,

a good score, good performers, and good direction ought to insure a good production. The visual support—scenery, lighting, costumes, props, and whatever else is *needed*—ought to be dictated by good sense and good taste. Just because our technology can provide 30 moving settings and/or 500 light cues doesn't mean they have to be there. Put on stage only what the audience needs to believe in the actors as the characters they are portraying.

Let us not be ruled by technology. It's a very expensive dead end! Remember the old definition of *theatre?* "All you need is four boards and a passion." I've left out the horses—too much technology![23B]

---

[23] *Ming Cho Lee, Adjunct Professor of Design at Yale University, from the* Yale Drama Annual Report, 1982–83.

[23a] *Marilyn Stasio, "Legs: Long March to Opening Night,"* New York Times, *Dec. 18, 1988, Arts & Leisure section, p. 6.*

[23b] *Tom Watson, "There's No Business . . ."* Theatre Design & Technology, *vol. 25, no. 1, (spring 1989), pp. 5, 62–63. Tom Watson taught lighting at the University of Delaware until retirement. He was also the USITT's editor of* Theatre Design & Technology *from 1972 to 1977.*

All potential lighting designers seek both to discover *how* those at the top (their personal heroes) achieved success and to recreate such a path in their own development. This *Handbook* is as much concerned with presenting ways to become a continuously working lighting designer as it is with exploring the basically unteachable, but developable, design concept. In this field, process is often more marketable than is artistry.

This chapter attempts "walking above water." My 45 working years in the lighting design industry may not have made me wise—but they *have* made me experienced.

Throughout those years in professional theatre, in television, in teaching, and in writing I have tried to isolate those personality traits and attitudes which seem to be common to nearly all who are at the top in lighting. It is my belief that if these traits and attitudes were clearly listed, someone with a beginner's interest in lighting design could quickly and accurately determine whether he or she had the basic qualities needed to succeed in this line of endeavor. Jean Eckart, a professional designer and teacher, quotes a standard saying of George Gebhart, who was for many years an outstanding Broadway production electrician: "Young electricians should work with experienced designers. Young designers should work with experienced electricians."[23C]

Perhaps that is why the master–apprentice system persists today as a means of completing the training of promising newcomers. In that same spirit, here is a list of seven traits ("the keys to mastery") which seem to be the necessary attributes of a top lighting designer. In most cases, a top lighting designer is:

An Organized Individual. Organization in lighting design is paramount. Lighting designers are obsessively planned and tidy. They keep endless lists. They put things down on paper. Given tasks worth doing, they are much like dogs with bones: a good designer will *not* let go of a job until it can be crossed off the list. Sometimes a designer's operation may not *seem* to have organization; for example, things may be heaped everywhere. But, believe me, in reality, everything in heaps is meticulously organized according to the designer's own unique system. Lighting designers, as a consequence of basic habits and traits, can cope marvelously with schedules, crew-work allocations, and any disasters which may arise. I have always admired Tharon Musser's remarkable organization, which is far superior to my own. I have yet to meet a beginner whose room was a disaster area of scattered socks, sports equipment, papers and letters — or books and records not arranged along some logical pattern — who in later years turned up anywhere near the top in lighting. There is a place for the disorganized person, but not in lighting.

A Disciplined Individual. Lighting designers are really remarkable about forcing themselves to do unpleasant tasks. A top lighting designer is never a "flower child," or a successful procrastinator, or someone who does not show up for meetings (or, worse yet, crew calls) or does not return phone calls. The whole "I'll do it when I have my head together and am in the mood" attitude does not go far in lighting. This does *not* mean that lighting designers always *enjoy* the many impossible tasks forced upon them, but they do tackle whatever needs to be done. Anyone who is aware of Peggy Clark or Robert Brand or Tony Quintavalla faithfully forging through grading USA #829 Entrance Exams for 60+ hours (not a real "turn on") can understand and appreciate this trait.

A Responsible Individual. Most lighting designers can be counted on. If lighting designers say they will do something, they will do it — and as nearly on time as they can manage. I once phoned Ed Kook (then owner of Century Lighting) and requested nearly $100,000 in additional electronic dimmers on a rush order for the 1962 Seattle World's Fair. Ed asked only, "Lee, do *you* stand behind payment for this order?" I replied yes, and the entire order arrived and was installed in the Seattle Opera House (on schedule) before the paperwork for payment had even begun. Being regarded as responsible and dependable by the industry is a lot like a good credit rating — it takes years to build up, and it can be destroyed in a minute. All top lighting designers are noted for dependability.

A Team Player. Theatre, unlike sculpture or composing or writing, is a team art. Athletics (football), musical performances (a symphony orchestra), dance, and theatre can only be created by individual artists who have mastered the ability to perform *together*. Buildings are only built by a team.

The lighting designer is almost always the "lowest person on the totem pole," so learning give-and-take is essential. The producer, the director, and usually the scenic designer or scenographer are ahead in the "pecking order." Only the electrician and crew (if the designer is lucky) are under the lighting designer. A designer who can't learn to play on the team will not go far in this business. Those who must have everything "their own way" — or else they pick up their marbles and go home — just don't belong in this game.

A Leader. Being a leader may seem to be the opposite of being a team player, but it really isn't. Leadership in a designer means initiative; strong, purposeful drive; ambition; and, when necessary, aggressiveness. A designer who exhibits such "leadership" is a "workaholic," one who loves lighting and lives and breathes it 25 hours each day, 8 days a week. If designers are less dedicated than that, most of the time someone who *is* that dedicated will get the shows *they* want. Maybe that's why lighting designers frequently make poor husbands/wives/lovers. The meek are a long time inheriting the world in this industry! Howard Bay wrote: "Exhibitionism must rear its smiling head if your career rests

[23c] *From a telephone conversation between Jean Eckart and the Leland Watson, June 1979.*

[23d] *Howard Bay,* Stage Design. *N.U.: Drama Book Specialists; 1974. See Chapter 5: Lighting, p. 144.*
[23e] *Based upon Mary Alice Kellogg's "Fast Track," TWA Ambassador, vol. 11, no. 12 (Dec. 1978), p. 27–28, 46, 48, 50, 53.*
[23f] *Ibid.*
[23g] *John E. Gibson, "People Quiz/Does Your Personality Affect Your Creativity?", Family Weekly, Sept. 16, 1979, p. 21.*

solely on whether or not those rays are noticed or whether that gauze transformation is admired by the daily press."[23d]

An Egotist. If an individual lighting designer doesn't believe that he or she is good (or talented or creative), no one else will. Theatre — show business — is a veritable cesspool of uncontained ego and ambition, which is why it produces all of the fights, scenes, and lawsuits that fill the daily papers, scandal sheets, and movie magazines. Lighting designers (with few exceptions) are flamboyant, theatrical, and often impossible; but they are able to create magic with light.

A Scholar. This characteristic may not seem to go with the others, but almost any successful lighting designer's office will verify that it does. Good lighting designers are "up" on the articles in trade journals, the profound scholarly books and texts, the dull lectures and papers of every trade convention. A favorite game played by top lighting designers at social get-togethers is to discover who knows the most obscure facts about the history of lighting and lighting design. Any front-rank designer is remarkably well-informed about the mysteries of color, color theory, color psychology, optics, and vision. This kind of scholasticism may not be a prerequisite for designing lights, but it is difficult to locate good designers who are not deeply aware of the accumulated knowledge about lighting. Someone like John Gleason reads far more lighting textbooks and journals *each year* than students still in school do in all of their courses.

There they are — some basic character traits. If a beginning designer has been "shortchanged" in any appreciable number of them, he or she should try to develop and strengthen latent potential in the other areas.

Just to say it twice (a common practice with educators): May Alice Kellogg, in her book *Fast Track,* also listed seven basic qualities of superachievers (in *all* areas, not just lighting design). Here is a summary of *her* list of general superachiever characteristics:

1. Superachievers are loners — they were rarely the most popular people in high school.
2. Superachievers had strong ties to the adults around them as children. The achievers felt most comfortable with and were more strongly influenced by adults than by their peer group.

3. Superachievers made constructive use of youth. As young people, the achievers frequently selected mentors to emulate and were often restless, with short attention spans.
4. Superachievers have an excess of energy — a scattering of resources in early years with a multiplicity of interests at any one time. They have a restlessness leading to frequent changes of job; They are interested in many different fields and may be employed initially in several widely different career areas.
5. Superachievers have a constant willingness to work, i.e., they are usually "workaholics."
6. Superachievers usually have early seasoning, such as exposure to tragedy (death of a parent or sibling)
7. Superachievers display a willingness to take risks that stems from developed self-awareness and self-knowledge.[23e]

Kellogg says, "Each [Achiever] was able to see opportunity and each was not afraid to grab it, or, he or she was afraid, but grabbed it anyway. The Achievers took tremendous risks, offering a chance for growth and success."[23f]

So, there you have it: two lists. No one can achieve anything close to perfection in *all* of the seven traits listed, but perhaps having the list available to aid with self-inspection can give an individual a clearer view of the potential for growth and development.

Just for fun, here's a "quiz" about the creative process, which contains many kernels of wisdom. It is from John E. Gibson's "People Quiz: Does Your Personality Affect Your Creativity?"[23g]

(1) The capacity to think original, creative thoughts is associated with certain personality traits. TRUE or FALSE?
(2) There is one characteristic that is almost invariably found in highly creative people. TRUE or FALSE?
(3) The most creative people rely chiefly on their intuition. TRUE or FALSE?

His answers are most revealing:

(1) TRUE. Studies at Middle Tennessee State University (showed that): Subjects scoring high in original thinking were characterized as possessing "self-confidence in matching talents against others, willingness to take risks, dislike for doing things in a prescribed way and the ability to translate their thoughts into action, reducing them to practice."

(2) TRUE. Creativity Studies at Pasadena City College (California), showed that "creative people tend to be more sensitive than the less creative. They are more aware of more problems, of more facets of a given problem, of relevant evidence, of their own conscious impulses. . . . It is the capacity to be born anew every day."

(3) FALSE. They rely on a combination of intuition and logical thinking. Evaluations of studies in neurophysiology and observations of creativity in renowned scientists have concluded that "major acts of creative genius require activity in both the intuitive right hemisphere of the brain and the rational (or logical) left hemisphere."

While this quiz and its answers are not specifically applicable to lighting design, they do make the point that geniuses cannot be created. However, the quality of original creativity in lighting design, as in other areas, can be expanded and developed further than *that which the artist initially possesses*. Should a person interested in lighting turn out to be completely devoid of even the slightest traces of originality and creativeness, he or she is more likely to find a meaningful place for any abilities as either a technician or as an engineer, both of which are sorely needed and most creative in their own ways. (I do not imply that technicians or engineers never exhibit originality or genius; it is just that their genius is not the exact *sort* needed by the designer.)

Chapter 3

On Being a Master Technician: The Building Blocks

The use of light as a design tool has largely been controlled by the technology available, usually borrowed from inventions and developments intended for other industries. Lighting in TV, film, theatre, discos, and concerts and in the architectural field cannot be any more imaginative than the means available for achieving any desired lighting design.

Consequently, switchboard and control network development frequently determined what the designer was able to do. Evolving from older gas tables, early switchboards offered increasingly complex control over basically only one of the three controllable properties of light: intensity or on/off switching. Designer control of the other two properties, color and distribution (distribution concerns form and movement), was largely dependent upon modification of the light's intensity. Thus when the designer desired a color change, he used additional luminaires with a different color medium but the same focus area. For distribution control, the lighting artist hung additional sets of luminaires to cover a different area or hired a follow spotlight operator if the artist wished to make use of movement of light as a design tool. Quite primitive!

Because on/off functions and intensity variations readily lend themselves to control via modern technology, control networks have become quite flexible. Computer memory is available and has become invaluable to the designer who has anything to say with lights. Computer-generated light plots, switchboard hookups, and instrument schedules are now in common use. Yet this technological control over only *one* of the variables of lighting still limits the creativeness of lighting designers and leaves much space for future design growth.

No designer should overlook the important contribution of the engineer and the technologist. A brief excerpt from a letter to me from Dr. Richard Iacobucci, founder and head of Roctronics Entertainment Lighting, emphasizes this point:

> It's just that we think it's high time that the creative efforts on the manufacturing side of the curtain should be recognized as just as significant to the advance of technology for the benefit of the industry, as are the spectacular musical and dramatic achievements on stage.
>
> Since you are doing a section on careers and employment in the lighting industry, let me point out our own disappointing experience. We have many students, graduates of so-called drama schools, come to us for employment. We find them totally unprepared to assume the responsibilities of technical theatre. They don't know the difference between a watt and a pipe clamp. It is our opinion that so-called technical theatre schools

are totally inadequate in preparing the students to face the technologically complex demands of today's sophisticated lighting control and manipulation equipment.[24]

This chapter offers a brief treatment of the *technology* of lighting. The designer, to be effective, must understand and have mastered the use of his tools. He must be aware of the knowledge possessed by the engineer, the scientist, and the laboring technician. This *Handbook* is about design. The technology covered in this chapter is intended as a supplement to extant technical texts cited earlier in the footnotes.[24a]

Power Production and Distribution

Lighting design has already been affected by an awareness of potential energy shortages. Present means of utilizing energy for illumination are inefficient and are becoming more and more costly. With worldwide recognition of this problem at hand, in the near future we will witness the development of alternative sources of energy. Meanwhile, more efficient energy distribution methods are needed. Many lighting designs already guard against charges of frivolous and wasteful use of a vital basic commodity: oil. Yet it is the lighting engineers, with the wise assistance of the designers, who hold the ultimate key to elimination of inefficiency. Energy conservation is discussed in Chap. 10.

Sources, Luminaires, and Lighting Equipment

The tungsten filament incandescent electric light is among the most inefficient methods of producing visible energy (light). Present necessity has directed research toward more powerful sources which last longer, are more compact, cost less, and produce more output.

Alternate sources are being developed. Improvements in fluorescent control, miniature sources, metallogen (hydrargyrum-medium iodides, HMI), and other short-arc luminous flux sources, as well as developments in laser technology and fiber optics, are all technological advances which demand the designer's attention. Until the 1970s, no light-

ing designer could expect to produce more than barely adequate wide-angle scenic projections. Then came the HMI light source and everything changed.[25] We designers still await the development of a compact, low-heat, high-output light source which permits us to mount 60 luminaires in the space of a 30-foot light pipe. Further progress in light as a design tool is dependent upon further progress in sources and fixtures equal to the great strides that have been taken in applying computer technology to control networks. Neon is now dimmable down to 3 percent of total voltage. Solid-state electronic high-frequency ballasts can now be controlled by adjustable photosensor controls for low-noise, high-efficiency operation. The energy crunch may have been a blessing in disguise. The electrical industry rarely develops any step forward for the infinitely small and specialized lighting design market. Thomas L. Pincu places the size of the lighting, distribution, and control equipment market in the theatre and television industries as "something in excess of $300 million every year."[26] This is a minuscule market when compared to most industries. Yet, as Pincu points out, the equipment purchased by that market must be good, because it is expected to serve satisfactorily throughout an anticipated 25 to 50 years of projected use.

Lighting designers are often the ones consulted for either the selection of new equipment or the upgrading of existing facilities. They need guidelines for making the best possible equipment selection from the multitude of available competing products. Much of this appropriate guidance has been assembled and presented by Robert Benson in a series of "Buying Guides" published in *Theatre Crafts* magazine. Some sample "Buying Guides" are shown in Appendix B of this volume.[27]

Intensity

The architect selects wattages and luminaires which produce the desired intensity. For the most part, the architect relies upon on/off switching for control by adding timers, dimmers, and even more complex intensity-control devices. Film and TV designers use more sophistication because of the known absolutes in film response to luminos-

[24] *Letter to the author from Dr. Iacobucci, dated November 14, 1979.*

[24a] *Steven R. Terry, "Contrasts," Lighting Dimensions, vol. 6, no. 4 (May/June 1982), pp. 17, 25. The most sensible presentation in print regarding repairing and servicing complex computer switchboards. Clarifies the separation between the lighting engineer-technician and the lighting artist-designer—they are not one and the same.*

See also:

Michael Callahan, "Bright New World?", Lighting Dimensions, vol. 7, no. 1 (Mar. 1983), pp. 62–64, 66, 72–73, illus.; vol. 7, no. 2 (Apr./May 1983), pp. 27–32, 35, 38–39, illus.; vol. 7, no. 3 (June 1983), pp. 35–42, illus. Brilliant analysis of the potentialities and problems of improved control of intensity, color, form, and movement in light sources from the perspective of a concert lighting designer/engineer.

"Memory Lighting Controls, Including Guide to Technical Comparison," Lighting + Sound International, vol. 1, no. 7 (May/June 1986), pp. 37–47. Illus., comparison chart of features on pp. 38–39. Excellent analysis of most switchboard types from the primary manufacturers, particularly British and European manufacturers.

"More Memory Lighting Controls," Lighting + Sound International, vol. 1, no. 10 (Sept./Oct. 1986), p. 44. Additional information about three control systems by Dynamic Technology, Ltd., which were left out of the article cited above.

Steve Pollock, Larry Opitz, Douglass Sisk, and Ron Olson, "Lighting Control R+D: High End Products," Theatre Crafts, vol. 20, no. 4 (Apr. 1986), pp. 26–31, 43–44, 46–48, 49, 51–56. Illus. A valuable analysis of available control boards; covers units from AVAB, Colortran, Electro Controls, Kliegl and Strand. Contains a performance feature comparison chart.

"Lighting Controllers Follow-up," Theatre Crafts, vol. 21, no. 4 (Apr. 1987), pp. 4, 6. Comments concerning the article listed above by John F. West ((West Star Corp.), Douglass F. Sisk, Damian Delaney (Kliegl), Debra Garcia (Colortran).

Mark Loeffler, "From Toybox to Toolbox, A Look at Lighting System Peripherals," Theatre Crafts, vol. 23, no. 3 (March 1989), pp. 19–21, 24. An

illustrated series of articles, appearing in nearly each issue, with illustrations which summarize new technology developments.

Robert C. Heller, "New Products," Theatre Design + Technology, vol. 14, no. 2 (Summer 1988), pp. 37–38. Illus. Similar coverage of new products appearing in most issues.

Susan Dandridge, "PALS: Precision Automated Lighting Systems," Strandlight, No. 8 (Spring 1989), p. 1. Illus. Explains developmental progress of control systems: 1967—Memory Control Boards, 1972—Tungsten Halogen, 1989—Remote Memory Controlled Lighting of Focus and Color.

James Twynam, "States or Moves?" Cue, no. 51 (January/February 1988), p. 3. A philosophical discussion of the differing orientation of computer-controlled switchboards guided by either British or American design philosophy.

Rod Litherland, "BriteBeam, BriteArc, Brighton," Society of Television Lighting Directors, no. 35 (Winter 1987–88), pp. 14–15. Illus. Covers the manufacture of HMI lamps.

Bree Burns, "News: The Future of Lighting Is Automatic," Theatre Crafts, vol. 22, no. 3 (March 1988), p. 22. Illus., color. Useful details concerning Vari*Lite utilization in lighting opera for the Los Angeles Center Opera with lighting designed by Wally Russell.

Bob Anderson, "Sweet 16, Zero 88 Celebrates Its 16th Birthday Far Away from the Attic Days of Its Youth," Cue International, no. 59 (May/June 1989), pp 38–41. Illus. Covers switchboard development and improvement by several firms in Europe.

Bert Morris, Getting the Most From Your Followspot. Washington, D.C.; Theatrical Technicians, Inc.; 1988. Approximately $2. Useful 20 pp. guide to followspot operation.

Mark Loeffler, "In Charge of the Light Brigade: Production Electrician Robert Febribach on Broadway," Lighting Dimensions, vol. 13, no. 2 (March 1989), pp. 32, 34–35. An interview with a leading Broadway production electrician (Phantom of the Opera, Les Misérables, Big River), which gives a good insight into the work and attitudes of a master technician.

[25] Keiichiro Ryu, HMI sources are now dimmable. See: SMPTE Journal, vol. 93, no. 1 (Part II, Jan. 1984), p. 117.

Michael Cahana, "A Growing, Glowing Source: Electroluminescent Light Is Coming of Age," Lighting Dimensions, vol. 10, no. 4 (July/Aug. 1986), pp. 16, 58–59. Illus., color.

Michael Cahana, "Electrodeless Discharge Lighting, Finding a Home in Industry—What's Next?", Lighting Dimensions, vol. 10, no. 3 (May/June 1986), pp. 48, 50–51. Illus.

S. Newton Hockey, "New Concepts: Piping Light," International Lighting Review, 2d quarter, 36th year (1985), pp. 69–71. Illus., color. Light "pipes," similar to fiber optics, are being used to channel light and are becoming important in architectural lighting.

Bentley Miller, "Light Sources: Softlights and Fluorescent Light," Broadcast + Technology, vol. 13, no. 2 (Oct. 1987), pp. 48, 50–51. A useful summary concerning light sources integrated into luminaires used in television and cinematography lighting.

John Gleason, "Sources Wish List: The T-3," Lighting Dimensions, vol. 10, no. 3 (May/June 1986), pp. 70, 72. Illus. Gleason's plea for new lamp development to better meet the theatre's needs.

Bentley Miller, "Light Sources: A History of the Development of Light Sources," Broadcast + Technology; Part One appears in vol. 12, no. 2 (Nov./Dec. 1986), pp. 62, 64–66; Part Two appears in vol. 12, no. 3 (Jan. 1987), pp. 32, 34. Very useful survey summary.

Keiichiro Ryu, "Dimmable HMI Lighting System for a TV Studio," SMPTE Journal, vol. 93, no. 7 (July 1984), pp. 667–671. Illus. Complete information about a Japanese TV news studio which dims HMI lamps 50 percent, including technical details on how this is achieved and the effect on lamp life, color, intensity, and output.

Karl Ruling, "How To: Build an Ellipsoidal Reflector Xenon Flash Unit," Theatre Crafts, vol. 20, no. 4 (Apr. 1986), pp. 106–115. Illus. Details of a useful lighting unit.

Designers should also give new consideration to neon as a design source. See:

Michael Webb, "The Magic and Art of Neon," Lighting Dimensions, vol. 8, no. 1 (Jan./Feb. 1984), pp. 28–29, 31–35. Illus., color. Excerpted from Michael Webb's book, The Magic of Neon, this article offers both a history of and design uses and technology of neon as a light source.

Eric Zimmerman, Michael Heyden, "Neon In Art, Architecture, and Consumer Lighting." A videotape of this conference presentation at Lighting World IV, May 1986, is available from Conference Copy, Inc., 204 Avenue M, Brooklyn, N.Y. 11230.

Ronald Naversen and Keith Cornelius, "How To: Simulate Neon," Theatre Crafts, vol. 20, no. 2 (Feb. 1986), pp. 102–103. Illus.

"Neon—A Revival," International Lighting Review, 38th year, 1st quarter of 1987, pp. 2–17, illus., color. Several key articles about worldwide use of neon as a design element by various authors, including A. L. C. Vreven, G. A. C. Trommar, K. Seshadri, Peter Wang, Randy Burkett, and others uncredited. Excellent and numerous color plates.

Michael Webb, The Magic of Neon. Salt Lake City; Gibbs M. Smith Books; 1984. Illus., color, 87 pp. Presents history, technique, bibliography, and sources for neon. Lavishly color illustrated.

"Neon Goes High-Tech—From Boardroom to Corporate Image," Architectural Lighting, vol. 1, no. 2 (Feb. 1987), p. 9. Illus., color.

Garreth Fenley, "Neon—A Hands-on Craft with Its Own Vocabulary," Architectural Lighting, vol. 1, no. 2 (Feb. 1987), pp. 36–41. Illus., color. Useful article that lists neon training schools.

Michael Webb, "New Life for Neon," Lighting Dimensions, vol. 6, no. 4 (May/June 1982), pp. 26–27, 29–31. Illus., color.

"Words on the Streetscape," Lighting Design & Application, vol. 9, no. 11 (Nov. 1979), pp. 16–17. Illus., color. Designed used of neon.

ity; however, they make little use of dimmers because of the resultant change in color temperature (Kelvin rating) from dimming. Even though TV designers have more flexibility than do film designers, they still use intensity variations only hesitantly because of critical color–temperature response requirements. It is in the theatre and the wider range of performance arts that we find the most extensive use of intensity control networks.[28]

Distribution

Distribution is the least controllable of the designer's tools. Distribution consists of two factors: light form (pattern) and movement. The architect controls distribution by luminaire selection and has little control beyond that initial selection. The performance arts have only primitive means of control of distribution: Rosco Lab's line of distribution-altering diffusers, the strobe light, an additional luminaire hung to cover another area, a few primitive ellipsoidal reflector units, and follow spotlights with limited potential variation of beam spread. Designers hang a new unit to alter area coverage, or they change the lens or insert shutters and gobos by hand.

If the design artist had available a more flexible way to alter beam shape, distribution, and form, remotely and economically, design ability would be greatly enhanced. To this end, two European firms (Ludwig Pani in Vienna, Austria, and Adrian de Backer in Zavantum, Belgium) have pioneered workable, economical, remote memory control of focus.[29] Century Lighting, under the earlier guidance of Edward Kook, produced a few remote-focus control units for the circus movie *The Greatest Show on Earth,* but they were not durably engineered. Pani and de Backer have for several years been mass-producing luminaires with remote control of direction and focus. These, aided by their memory computer systems, are used extensively in TV stations and theatres in such places as Austria, Central Europe, and even at the Bolshoi Opera House in Moscow. Other firms which have entered this market include: Cameleon/Telescan of France; Vari-Lite/Showco of Dallas in 1980; SynchroLights of Dallas; Panaspot/Panabeam from Mor-

pheus Lighting of San Jose, California; and Avab (the Swedish Emil Niethammer group). The remote-control units were expensive at first. I received a bid of approximately $5,000 per luminaire from de Backer in 1975 for remote control of ellipsoidals (i.e., motor control of insertion and angle-of-tilt of four shutters, barrel focus, pan and tilt of the entire luminaire, and a five-color changer).

Two distinct advantages make such remote-control systems a future necessity:

1. **Economy.** Fewer luminaires are needed since each one is capable of more flexible use. Personnel requirements are reduced, and over a period of time in locations constantly in production, such as theme parks, TV and film studios, opera houses, etc., the personnel savings outweigh the high initial cost. Energy conservation may ultimately dictate moves toward many fewer luminaires in each performance place —with each liminaire given maximum use.

2. **Added Design Potential.** Any lighting designer who has worked on a musical, an ice show, a disco, a concert, an opera, or a dance knows how indispensable the mobility of a follow spotlight is.[30] While the rapid, broad movement of the unpredictable performer *may* always necessitate a light with an operator, there are limitless times when the designer would *like* to be able to redirect a luminaire without hanging a second unit.

Films and television have created a generation accustomed to mobility of place, time, and focus. Psychedelic lighting and the disco craze were the direct product of a generation on wheels and in the air, comfortable with multiple stimuli of increasing complexity and variability. To keep up with this generation, the lighting industry needs improved technology to make control of light distribution a basic design tool.

Color (Production and Design Use)

The human eye can recognize *5 million* colors. Colored light production, color theory, and color perception must be understood by the designer. These subjects are well covered in basic texts,[31] but here are a few related thoughts.

Rudi Stern, Let There Be Neon. *N.Y.; Harry N. Abrams; 1979. 160 pp., illus., color. The definitive volume on neon covering history, design uses, the technological craft, a glossary, chronology, and bibliography.*

Sarah Pattee, "Night Lights, Neon is Back, and It's Glowing Brighter Than Ever,"U.S. Air, vol. 10, no. 12 (December 1988), pp. 42–46, 48. Illus., color. Informative summary.

"Everything You Wanted to Know about Neon. . . ."Disco Tech, vol. 3l, no. 3 (July 1987), pp. 22–27. Illus. Excellent source material about all aspects of neon.

"NEON," Pro Light & Sound, vol. 2, no. 5 (February/March 1988), pp. 41–43. Illus. Excellent basic summary of neon light production and utilization.

[26] *Thomas L. Pincu, "Lighting and Control Equipment for the Theatre: Where are the Standards?"Theatre Crafts, vol. 12, no. 1 (Jan./Feb. 1978), pp. 73–75.*

Fred Bentham, "Book Review: A Narrow View of a Wide Subject,"Sightline, vol. 23, no. 2 (April 1989), p. 34. Bentham, in a review of George Izenour's Theatre Technology, points out: "What is certain is that the Izenour launch at Yale in 1947 was of 44 channels with 10 presets. In contrast my own first Strand Light Console (Strand, England, where Bentham was then president) had in 1935 70 channels and 24 instant-memory presets." Bentham takes several strong swipes at both Izenour's work and Izenour's second major book.

[27] *See also: Steve Pollock (editor), "Special Report: Are They All the Same?", Theatre Crafts, vol. 19, no. 8 (Oct. 1985), pp. 30–37, 64, 66, 68–70, 72, 77–78, 80–84, 86–87 for an analysis of luminaires (fixtures or instruments) for theatre from Altman, Colortran, GTE Sylvania, Electro Controls, Kliegl, General Electric, Lighting and Electronics, and Strand, with comments by Tharon Musser, Jules Fisher, Ken Billinton, Beverly Emmons, and Richard Nelson.*

[28] *Robert Davis, "There's No Voltage Like Low Voltage,"Theatre Crafts, vol. 19, no. 7 (Aug./Sept. 1985), pp. 44–45, 92, 94, 96–97. Illus., color. "Part II: Engineering and Design*

Applications for Theatre Production" presents photos and drawings concerning the increasing use of low-voltage lamps in U.S. productions.

M. J. Dyer, "Low Voltage Luminaires," ABTT News (Aug. 1985), pp. 13–14. Reprinted from Lighting Equipment News, Aug. 1985. Good overview article.

Steve Pollock, "PARS for the Course, Low Voltage Part Three: A Guide to Sealed Beam Lamps," Theatre Crafts, vol. 20, no. 1 (Jan. 1986), pp. 31, 48–51. Illus.

Steve Pollock, "Accents Onstage, Low Voltage Part Four: A Buyer's Guide to Architectural Lighting Fixtures," Theatre Crafts, vol. 20, no. 2 (Feb. 1986), pp. 37–38, 40, 42–43. Illus.

[29] *Some remote-control spotlight settings are also produced in England, by Spectrum Audio, Ltd. in Conventry. The product is called "Tipspot." From: ABTT News (Jan./Feb. 1979), p. 22.*

Richard Glickman, "Automated Lighting Systems at Nipp on Hoso Kyokai—Part I," Lighting Dimensions, vol. 3, no. 4 (Apr. 1979), pp. 26–29, 31. Illus., color.

The first U.S. patent of a remote control of pan, tilt, beam size adjustment was received by C. Andreino in 1930. Joseph Levy and Edward B. Kook patented a remote color changer in 1940. From: Michael Callahan, "Bright New World?" Lighting Dimensions, vol. 7, no. 1 (Mar. 1983), pp. 62–63.

See also:

Rudiger Kreckel, "A Revolution in Studio Lighting Techniques," TABS, vol. 41, no. 1 (Mar. 1984), pp. 14–15. Illus., color. Article on remotely focused lighting equipment in a German TV facility.

Fred Humphrey and Steve Futers, "'Cordial Accommodation,'" TABS, vol. 41, no. 1 (Mar. 1984), pp. 16–17. Illus., color. Description of a British TV studio with remote control.

*"Remote Control of Luminaires," ABTT News (Nov./Dec. 1984), pp. 15–17. Detailed information about the remote-controlled Vari*Lite and the French Telescan MKII.*

*Francis Reid, "Vari*Lite, A Quantum Leap for Stage Luminaires," Cue, no. 33 (Jan./Feb.*

*1985), p. 23. Excellent summary by Reid of Vari*Lite remote control of focus and color.*

*Steve Pollock, "Remote-controlled Luminaires," Theatre Crafts, vol. 20, no. 8 (Oct. 1986), pp. 30–31, 67–70, 72–74. Illus., color. Useful analysis and details concerning Dyna-Might, Morpheus, Strand ShowChanger, Vari*Lite units.*

*Mike Williams, "An Industry Milestone: Vari*Lite Unveils the Long-Awaited Models 2 and 3," Lighting Dimensions, vol. 10, no. 6 (Nov. 1986), pp. 53–65. Illus., color.*

*Bob Anderson, "Vari*Lite Encore," Cue, no. 47 (May/June 1987), pp. 18–20. Illus., color.*

"A Worthy Test for Panaspot," Lighting Dimensions, vol. 10, no. 4 (July/Aug. 1986), p. 47. An interesting commentary about the use of Morpheus Lights's Panaspot in concert lighting.

*"Vari*Lite, Take a Closer Look," Society of Television Lighting Directors, Summer 1987, no. 34, pp. 17–19. Illus. Summary of British demonstration of Vari*Lite for television.*

"Abstract's New Lantern Lights The Way," L. S. & V. Magazine, premiere issue November/December 1988, p. 13. Illus. Description of the Swedish Abstract Electronics new Eagle Lantern—a remote controlled unit.

"Moto-Light," Theatre Design & Technology, vol. 23, no. 2 (Summer 1987), inside cover. Illus., color. Information about remote-controlled Moto-Yoke, Moto-Cannon, Moto-Zoom and Moto-64.

"Lighting," SMPTE Journal, vol. 97, no. 4 (Part I/April 1988), pp. 270–272. Information concerning the Japanese remote-controlled spotlight manufactured by RDS Corporation.

*Steve Terry, "A Technical Commentary," Lighting Dimensions, vol. 12, no. 2 (March 1988), pp. 32, 38–43. A careful analysis of current (1988) Vari*Lite units (including noise problems, when used for opera), beam control, and quality and color management. The VL2 model can provide 125 colors and utilizes a 250 watt HTI arc lamp source; the VL-3 model provides 300 colors and utilizes a 53-volt, 475-watt tungsten light source.*

"Small Yet Powerful," Cue International, no. 58 (March/April 1989), p. 43. Illus. Description of the first remote-controlled moving light with an MR-16 light source produced by Abstract Electronics AB in Stockholm, Sweden, named the Colibri.

Mark Loeffler, "Designer-Friendly: A Modular, Integrated System of Moving Lights Called Pan-Command," Lighting Dimensions, vol. 12, no. 4 (May/June 1988), pp. 44–47. Illus., color. Also: Mike Williams, "Blinded By the Light," pp. 46–47. Illus. Two articles concerning the use of Morpheus Lights, Inc., "Pan-Command" moving light by William Klages for the 1988 Grammy Awards Show and for John Cougar Mellencamp's 1987–88 concert tour, as well as the 1988 Bruce Springsteen Tunnel of Love concert tour.

[30] *Other useful information concerning follow-spots can be found in:*

Steve Pollock, "Equipment Buyers Guide: Followspots, Who's Hot and Who's Hotter," Theatre Crafts, vol. 20, no. 9 (Nov. 1986), pp. 37–42. Contains a useful several-page chart comparing the luminaires (instruments) of Altman, Colortran, Lighting and Electronics, Lycian, Packaged Lighting Systems, Phoebus, Strong International, and Times Square.

"Letters: Followspots Continued," Theatre Crafts, vol. 20, no. 10 (Dec. 1986), p. 3. Reader comments concerning an article cited above.

[31] *In addition to basic chapters on color in the standard theatre texts cited earlier, see also:* Frans Gerritsen, Theory and Practice of Color: A Color Theory Based on Laws of Perception. *N.Y.; Van Nostrand Reinhold Co.; 1975. 180 pp., illus., color. Fundamentals, particularly of color perception, lavishly treated in a basic volume.*

Life Library of Photography, Color. *New York; Time-Life Books; 1970. 240 pp., illus., color. While dealing mainly with film, this volume is so well-illustrated and readable that it is of value to all lighting designers.*

Tom Douglas Jones, The Art of Light and Color. *New York; Van Nostrand Reinhold Co.; 1972. 120 pp., illus., color. This book presents not only the basics, but also covers color music and organs, psychedelic lighting, light and color sculpture, psychotherapy, and color as an art form. Of primary interest to the disco and concert lighting fields. Beautifully illustrated presentation of Jones's work in color.*

Faber Birren, Light, Color and Environment. *New York; Van Nostrand Reinhold Co.; 1969. 132 pp., illus., color. A study of the functional aspects of color; the biological, physiological, visual, and psychological elements of color and its effect on humans. Lavishly illustrated. Of value to all lighting designers. Chapters for the architect on offices, industrial plants, schools, hospitals, motels and hotels, shops and stores, food service, apartments, and homes. Basic information on color responses.*

William B. Warfel and Walter R. Klappert, Color Science for Lighting the Stage. *New Haven, Conn.; Yale Press; 1981. 158 pp., illus., color, spiral bound with color chart included. The most definitive study available on analysis of and use of the 530 gel colors in use today.*

Josef Albers, Interaction of Color. *New Haven, Conn; Yale Press; revised edition in paperback, 1975. 82 pp., illus., color. No designer of lighting should be practicing without having studied Professor Albers's brief version of his original lengthier book. The best study on the effects of color upon other colors and perception. Widely available; used as a text in many art departments.*

Ralph M. Evans, An Introduction to Color. *New York; John Wiley & Sons (or London; Chapman & Hall); 1948. 340 pp., illus., color. A standard college text but quite readable; well illustrated; good bibliography.*

Clarence Rainwater, Light and Color, A Golden Science Guide. *New York; Golden Press (or Racine, Wis.; Western Publishing Co.); 1971. 160 pp., illus., color. This source recently went out of print. Color on every page on high-quality paper. Pocket-size and inexpensive. Covers light sources, illumination, physics, vision, perception, color systems, color use. The ideal volume for beginning lighting students.*

Rollo Gillespie Williams, Lighting for Color and Form. *N.Y.; Pitman; 1954. 340 pp., illus., color. Now out-of-print. Written by a lifelong theatre practitioner. Good basics for all lighting specialties. Well illustrated. Still quite useful.*

Egbert Johnson, Basic Color. *Chicago; Paul Theobald; 1948. 208 pp., illus., color. An interpretation of the Ostwald color theory and system. High-quality paper; excellent illustrations. Still quite useful when a copy can be located.*

A. H. Munsell, A Color Notation. *Baltimore; Munsell Color Co.; 1947. 74 pp., illus., color. A handy little volume about the Munsell system. In print through many editions for several years.*

Matthew Luckiesh, The Language of Color. *New York; Dodd, Mead & Co.; 1918. 282 pp., illus., color. Hard-to-find. The original work on color responses and reaction.*

Matthew Luckiesh, Color and Its Applications. *New York; D. Van Nostrand Co.; 1927. 420 pp., illus., color. A more extensive basic text. Much early work on color use, as well as theory. Also hard-to-find.*

"Colour Filter Developments," ABTT News, *June '85, pp. 14–15. About dichroic color filters and sources. In this issue, see also "Correspondence," p. 4, for comments by Ned Bowman of Rosco Labs.*

Deborah T. Sharpe, The Psychology of Color and Design. *Totowa, New Jersey; Littlefield, Adams & Co.; 1979. 170 pp., illus., color. Available in both paperback and hardcover. A much lighter weight volume dealing only with color uses and applications (little theory or basics).*

See also:

"A Light-and-Color relationship," Light *magazine, vol. 38, no. 3 (1969), p. 6. Excellent color illustrations of the effect of daylight, fluorescent, standard cool white, deluxe cool white, 5000° K and 7000° K on the same painting. Excellent presentation of the effect of color source output upon color values of an apparent object.*

William B. Warfel, "Working With White Light," Lighting Dimensions, *vol. 6, no. 6 (Sept./Oct. 1982), pp. 26–29, 31–32. Illus., color.*

"The Color of Light" is a 20-minute ½-inch VHS videocassette with an accompanying workbook for beginners. Available from Rosco Labs, Inc., 36 Bush Ave., Port Chester, N.Y. 10573, for approximately $40 (U.S.). Very amateurish.

Belinda L. Collins, "Color and Lighting: Color Occurs When Three Pieces of Information Are Processed," Lighting Design + Application, *vol. 17, no. 4 (Apr. 1987), pp. 4–6, 54. Illus., color. Basics of color vision, primarily for architectural lighting specialists. Rather amateurish writing but useful graphics.*

John Gleason, "What Color Is White Light? . . . Or, The Telltale Temperature," Lighting Dimensions, *vol. 10, no. 4 (July/Aug. 1986), pp. 76–77. A chatty, fundamental piece on color temperature for theatrical designers.*

Bentley Miller, "Light Source: A Lens Primer for Lighting Directors," Broadcast + Technology. *"Part I" appears in vol. 12, no. 8 (May/June 1987) and "Part II" in vol. 12, no. 9 (July/Aug. 1987), pp. 107–108. Illus. Color basics for television directors.*

John Gleason, "Understanding Color: A Black and White Look at This Phenomenon of Light," Lighting Dimension, *vol. 11, no. 5 (September/October 1987), pp. 32, 34, 36–37, Part II. Also: John Gleason, "The Higher the Temperature, the Bluer the Light — How the Color of Light Reacts on Pigment," Part I, vol. 10, no. 5 (September/October 1986), pp. 76–77, 79. A beginner's series of articles about color by a master teacher.*

Sam Mills, "Lighting Graphics," Architectural Lighting, *vol. 1, no. 9 (October 1987), pp. 37–39. Illus. First of three articles about color basics. Well written and well illustrated. Also: vol. 2, no. 1 (January 1988), pp. 39–40.*

"Designers Speak Out On Color," RoscoNews, *Spring 1987, p. 3. Comments by Ken Billington, Howard Bay, Nananne Porcher, and John Gleason on color usage in theatre.*

David R. Batcheller, "A Colorimetric Study of Stage Lighting Filters," Theatre Design and Technology, *no. 30 (Oct. 1972), pp. 14–22. And, in the same issue:*

William D. Little, "A Uniform Numerical Color Media Coding System," pp. 23–25. Two early basic studies of color identification and nomenclature in the theatre.

Rosco Labs, "Designers on Color" and "Color Media Guide." Two useful booklets (1981) distributed free by: Rosco Labs, 36 Bush Avenue, Port Chester, N.Y. 10573. Telephone: 914/937-1300.

Norah McNutty, "Chromoid," TABS, vol. 38, no. 2 (Oct. 1981), p. 22. Illus. In-depth description of the manufacturing process and development of Rank-Strand's heat-resistant color media.

William H. Stocks, "Burnout Rate of Color Media," Theatre News, vol. 12, no. 11 (Nov. 1980), p. 15. Report of testing of media burnout.

R. Craig Wolf, "History of Colored Light on the Stage," thesis at University of California at Los Angeles, 1967.

Lee Watson, "Color Concepts in Lighting Design," Educational Theatre Journal, vol. 10, no. 3 (Oct. 1958), p. 254.

Morgan Christensen, "Paint Colors for HPS Lighting and a Practical Technique for Determining Reflectance under Various Lighting Systems," Lighting Design & Application, vol. 13, no. 1 (Jan. 1983), pp. 20–27. Illus., color.

Videotape:
Rosco, How To Use the COLOR OF LIGHT. A 20-minute videotape available from Rosco, 36 Bush Avenue, Port Chester, NY 10573. Quite sophomoric text by lighting designer Mark Stanley. Of some (but relatively minimum) value.

"Crystal Color Comes Alive," L S & V Magazine, premier issue November/December 1988, p. 16. Artifex Corp. of Costa Mesa, California introduced the first liquid crystal cell color system in the U.S.

Michael S. Eddy, "Color in Light, From Gelatin to Plastics and Beyond," Theatre Crafts, vol. 23, no. 4 (April 1989) pp. 40, 100, 103, 105–106. An excellent article explaining the origins and dates thereof for theatrical color media. The second part of this film series appears in the next issue. Most useful.

Fred Bentham, "A Chromatic Diversion in C or D," Cue, no. 52 (March/April 1988), pp. 10–14. Illus. Bentham outlines the history of his own color control switchboards (for Strand, England) and the work of Rollo Gillespie Williams in this field.

Mark Loeffler, "Pick a Color, Any Color—A Look At Drop-In Color Changers," Theatre Crafts, vol. 22, no. 2 (Feb. 1988), pp. 38–39, 59–62. Illus. Illustrates and surveys presently available color wheels, dichroics, scrollers, and boomerangs. Most useful.

In terms of color control, lighting design in the United States has lagged technologically. Only when the German source of imported gelatin color media was cut off by World War I did we begin to develop our own media. This development was largely due to the efforts of R. Monroe Peaver in Boston. Following World War II, England was producing and marketing worldwide the product Cinemoid before American equivalents came along. Until fairly recent times the wide range of glass color media was mostly imported from France for distribution in the United States. There was a brief flurry of installation of remote-controlled color changers following World War I, but their use did not catch on in the United States.

Today such firms as Rosco Labs and Lee Filters have widened the available range of color media and increased the heat-resistant qualities. However, little is being done today toward providing *infinite* color control flexibility.

There are several fundamental factors that tend to hinder a designer's development of the ability to use color as a design element:

■ Color nomenclature has never been standardized. No descriptive language of agreed-upon color names exists on a popular level. Color *can* be described and analyzed most accurately, but only through the use of extensive scientific terminology which is frequently beyond both the ability and interest level of the working artist/designer.

■ Little accurate knowledge (usable on a practical level) is at hand in the whole area of human response (psychologic and symbolic/associational) to color. We know that warm colors excite and stimulate and that cool colors calm or depress. We commonly accept purple as being associated with royalty. However, behavioral scientists have discovered little that is useful for the lighting designer. Color usage is still largely dependant upon the experience, the educated "guesses" and the intuitions of the artist. Human reaction to color is subjective and individually variable, and for that reason color use is often considered to be *the* most challenging design area.

■ Tools and technology available for infinitely flexible use of color are quite primitive. For the most part designers must drop bits of colored paper into a luminaire or turn a color wheel or mix the desired color palette primitively by directing several differently colored luminaries at the same spot and then producing color additively with numerous dimmers at varying intensity settings.

Because of these current realities of color and lighting, a confident and comfortable use of color is usually the last design ability an artist develops. A few basic words of advice to beginning lighting designers concerning color *use* may be helpful here:

■ Do not lean too heavily upon highly saturated colors or pure primaries unless the dramatic material (or building or movie) obviously calls for it. The novice designer who either "wants to be different (original, creative)" or comes equipped with an inordinately outrageous color preference sense is usually the one who revels in an excess of gaudy color.

■ On the other hand, do not depend exclusively upon the timid tints and pastels, i.e., the standard acting area colors such as No Color Pink, Daylight Blue, Straw, Bastard Amber, and Lavender or Violet. While these "safe" tints are the ideal colors to complement human skin tone, they belong in the designer's palette for light comedies. They hardly will suffice for Lady Macbeth following the murder of the king.

■ Also, do not be afraid of theatrical use of color, when appropriate, but be careful not to be overindulgent with it. Let the color choice fit the need. Use color as a design element; take chances; experiment; watch audience reaction; become a master of both color theory and color application. It all takes time, experimentation, mistakes, and the gradual development of color taste.

Two developments, one realized and the other technologically possible, should be mentioned in connection with color:

1. Color Wheels. Some theatrical lighting firms now manufacture and market "Indexing Color Wheels." Tharon Musser used wheels produced by the Lycian Stage Lighting Co. for *Ballroom* on Broadway in December 1978, and other designers have used them since. Jules Fisher used

British units in the London production of *Joseph and the Technicolor Dreamcoat*, as did David Hersey for *Nicholas Nickleby*. While still a relatively primitive solution, these units do make it possible to have a choice of previously selected colors available, at will, from a single luminaire.

2. Modulation-Induced Color. The other potential solution is more fundamental. It offers the possibility of completely changing the nature and use of color. Michael Wolfe and John Schwiller wrote an illustrated article entitled "Instant Color" in *TABS* magazine in 1977.[32] Manufacturers and working lighting designers should read this two-page article. The authors experimented with liquid crystals as a color-control element (at the University of Nottingham, England), and in this article they explain and diagram the technology of what they have named MIC. (modulation-induced color). In simplest form, MIC involves remote memory electrochemical control of thin liquid-crystal–impregnated molecules treated with dyes. Thus *any* color of light (including a blackout, most useful for new nondimmable short-arc light sources) can be reproduced—instantaneously or at leisure—from a single luminaire at will, and this system can replace either an iris or shutters. By use of a matrix structure it is possible to produce an infinitely variable series of gobos. What is lacking is the necessary research to overcome basic problems of light loss and heat factors, as are the funds necessary for production and marketing costs.[33]

Picture the possibilities open to the designer of dance, ballet, or opera if any and all luminaires could change to any color at will. Picture the possibilities in architectural illumination of buildings, monuments, churches, and museums. Consider the added design possibilities for ice shows, musicals, revues, discos, theme parks, expositions, industrial shows—everywhere light is used to design. Consider, just for a moment, the complete change in lighting applications and design choices that would occur if such control were in designers' hands.

Projections

Among the highly sophisticated techniques available, few hold such fascination for the young and such challenge for

the experienced as projections. Edward Kook said in 1975 at a United States Institute for Theatre Technology (USITT) Opera Projections Symposium in Newark, New Jersey:

I believe that projections are more workable [than built scenery], in a practical way, to do multiscene plays. It's flexible. It frees the spatial limitations of the stage. It enables great speed in changes, increases fluidity of action. It's a timesaving tool. It is *not* a substitute for scenery; it augments it. For touring, it minimizes bulk. It reduces substantially, therefore, the cost of packing, transportation, and loading; and it is economical.

But many disclaim that money savings are their reasons for utilizing projections. They contend that the high cost of the machines, the preparation of slides, and long periods of adjustment, equals and often exceeds those of painted scenery. I believe that unfamiliarity with the medium, the fear of failure, and long hours demanded for adjustment are basic reasons why today there are still no extensive uses of projections.

We cannot deny that projections have the artistic advantage of vividness and are possessed with a luminous quality of brilliance, of color, and immeasurably enhance environment and poetic illusions. . . . Scenery, painted in the studios, [is] all imitation of the scenic artist's hand. *Nothing* is more impossible than to attempt to create [three-dimensional] structure [on stage] via light images. (Three-dimensional scenery is also needed). Yet we can extend architecture and landscape if it supports the illusion of the continuation of the structure.

I think what hits the crux of the resistance to the use of projections is the undue darkness of a scene that is forced upon us which diminishes the brightness of the acting area to ensure an effective projection, lest it be washed out by ambient light. Our agony is heightened when the director, with his impatience during rehearsal hours, orders us to kill the projections.

I believe the future of the art of projections depends as much on education as it does upon a bold attitude and improved instruments. It challenges the imagination of the playwright and his director, the creative talents of the scenic and lighting designer, the expertise of the specialists in projection, the skill of the craftsman [and] progressive makers of lamps, to uncover new and more efficient and dimmable lamp sources with pinpoint filaments.

I believe that projections, integrated with live performances, will raise the quality of theatrical performances and will, at the same time, simplify the operation and control of projections. Above all else, projections will serve creatively, the art underlining the ideas of the playwright. But if [use of] projections remain[s] a beauty unto itself, it is, in the words of Francis Bacon,

[32] TABS, *Summer 1977, vol. 35, no. 2, pp. 18–19. Illus., color.*

[33] *See also:*

Arthur Miller, "*Electrically controlled Variable-Color Optical Filters,*" Lighting Dimensions, *vol. 1, no. 5 (Nov. 1977), p. 17. Another variation using polarized filters. Illus.*

[34] "Opera Scenery Projections Symposium," Symphony Hall, Newark, N.J. May 11, 1975. Tape recording of proceedings in possession of author.

[35] Graham Walne, "Projecting the Right Image," Lighting + Sound International, vol. 1, no. 11 (Nov. 1986), pp. 11–12, 14–16. Illus., color. Excellent summary of British and continental projection practices with many photos and a listing of British manufacturing sources.

[36] Willard Bellman, p. 419, op. cit. (see footnote 3).

[37] "Opera Scenery Projections Symposium," Symphony Hall, Newark, N.J., May 11, 1975.

"petty wonderment." For, if we are asked in the end, Where is the play?, it will wind up as an empty art.[34]

In this brief statement Mr. Kook touched upon most of the factors of concern about projections, which are as follows: (1) the philosophy of use of projections, (2) types of projection, (3) projector light sources, (4) light collectors, (5) slide material, (6) objective lens systems, (7) projections surfaces (screen) and projector location, (8) ambient light and performer visibility, and (9) design considerations.[35] Each of these topics will be touched upon as the chapter progresses. The reader should keep in mind two things: (1) projections can be infinitely complex or diabolically simple, so the beginner need not be excluded, and (2) if a designer thoroughly understands the basics of projections, the new developments of sophisticated equipment will not be confusing or difficult to grasp. A look at the basic mechanics of projection is useful for putting its components in perspective:

> Projection depends upon the partial or complete interception of a light beam by a gaseous, fluid or solid material (the *slide*). This material serves as the object to be projected. The receiving surface upon which the projected image is registered (the *screen*) may partially or completely intercept what we may now term the *projection*. Our ability to perceive the projection is conditioned by (1) the intensity of the original light beam, (2) the intensity of other light which may also be incident upon the projection surface (*ambient light*) and (3) its reflectivity or transmission abilities and the density of the intercepting object (*slide*).[36]

Philosophy (When to Use Projections)

The history of projected images goes far back into history. Early magic lantern shows and stunning sunrises and sunset effects were recorded long before the advent of today's powerful electric light sources. Projections were used with the kerosene lantern, the limelight, and the carbon arc. Recorded history does not go far enough back in time to chronicle the origins of the Balinese shadow-and-puppet plays, but there are records dating back to the second century, B.C. During the mid-1800s, projections (and overall lighting intensity levels) were quite dim. The stage was filled with painted wings and borders, the scenery was in forced perspective, and the available gas light was barely strong enough to illuminate the performer adequately. The performer was most frequently found far away from the scenic background — downstage, nearest the brightest source available, the footlights.

Powerful electric light sources changed all that. It also changed the nature of scenic investments placed before the audience: in 1895 Adolphe Appia demanded and in 1905 Edward Gordon Craig delivered three-dimensional scenery — steps, columns, levels, and solid walls. Audiences began demanding realism and naturalism. Spectacle, for a brief time, became less important than realism. Illusion, however, never lost its importance. The first full projected theatre setting used in North American theatre was created by designer Lee Simonson for *Back to Methuselah* in 1922.

As technology advanced, designers began to understand the *difference* between light (or projections) and painted scenery. One was not necessarily a substitute for the other. Each had its place. Each offered possibilities unattainable with the other media. Thus the question arose: When should projections be used? Jo Mielziner, at the New Jersey Projections Symposium, said: "The thing that makes projections beautiful is it's non-realistic element. I'm very much opposed to projection of a photograph. Theatre is a symbol, a suggestion, non-realism. When we get very realistic, we loose our strength."[37] There are many who would disagree with Mielziner. Basic to any attempt to define the rightness or wrongness of projections is the acceptance of one fundamental. In the words of Mielziner, "Projections must spring from the original concept — not be an additive." This concept is important. The decision that the qualities projected images offer are right for a particular contemplated production must be made at the very beginning of the creative process by the playwright, director, producer, scenographers, and lighting designer. Given this imperative, there can be no hard-and-fast "lists" of when to use or not to use projections. However, here is a list of production situations in which projections are *apt* to be of value:

1. The script or production calls for multiple rapid scenic changes or mobility of place and time. Example: Ibsen's *Peer Gynt.*

[38] *Willard Bellman, op. cit. (see footnote 3).*

2. The production uses surrealism, abstraction, constructivism, expressionism, or impressionism as a style of production. Example: Elmer Rice's *Adding Machine.*

3. The production is a fantasy or a children's drama. Example: *Jack and the Beanstalk.*

4. The production is a political commentary drama or a historical survey drama. Willard Bellman titles this use of projections as *didactic* use of projections.[38] The audience is intentionally aware of the use of projections and of multiple screens to convey messages to the audience. Examples: Weill-Brecht *Three Penny Opera* or *The Makropoulous Secret* or the Broadway *Beatlemania*. A variation is found in the entire field of multi-image production used for entertainment or to convey a sales message or for instruction/indoctrination.

5. The production calls for realism or naturalism. Uses of projections in these cases are more restricted. In many realistic productions a night sky or a city skyline or a cloudy sky can be projected and add more realism than a flat, evenly lighted sheet of blue canvas cyclorama. Bellman refers to *integrated scenic element* projections which allow the audience to be unaware of the use of projections as such. In these cases the projected background is often a most effective substitute for a painted backcloth.

A list of situations in which projections are *not* suitable would be just as long as that given above. Determination of insuitability rests on the following two tenets (and sub-issues):

1. Projections are *not* quick, easy, and economical substitutes for built or painted scenery. Full-scale projections should never be considered unless:

   a. There is sufficient *funding* (or possibilities for borrowing) to cover the costs of obtaining suitable specialized projection equipment and paying for the slide/image development, processing, and replacement; and an adequate projection surface is available.

   b. Sufficient *time* is allowed for planning, preparation, experimentation, and adjustment in the production process. Projections should *never* be added at the last moment as an afterthought. If the designer is new to projections or is breaking new ground, experimentation time is vital. Designers must also allow for delays and mistakes in areas they do not completely control: for example, an outside artist/photographer/research facility delivering slide/image material on schedule; photographer/artist delays in processing slides; or delays in obtaining rented projectors, specialized lamps, or rare parts. Additionally, time must *always* be allowed for the added complexities of lighting the performer and adjusting the cast, director, other designers, show crew, and technicians to this new, different, technically and artistically sophisticated element of projections.

2. Projections must not be used at the expense of *consistency. Do* the projected images meld with the particular production's other visual elements? With the scenery, costume, sound, acting, and directing styles? Do *all* production elements contribute *together* toward a unified objective? If for any of these questions the answer is no, projections should not be used. They should never be used as a novelty unless such spectacle is consistent with the total thrust of the rest of the production. Have other members of the production team adjusted to some basic technical necessities (as follows):

   a. Does the scenic designer agree that a dark or black, nonreflective and highly light-absorbent floor covering may be used; that the projections reinforce, complement, and expand the built visual element; that middle-ground "transition" built pieces can be present for a smooth transition from one media (the real, three-dimensional performer) to the projected media (the two-dimensional illusion)?

   b. Does the director understand that performers must be kept an agreed-upon distance away from projection surfaces to avoid giveaway shadows; that the lighting will be rather highly theatrical and dramatic (crosslighting and backlighting, rather than the more common flat frontlights) in style; and that some slight concession from farce or comedy visibility is likely?

   c. Does the business manager/producer realize that additional costs, both for equipment and supplies and

[39] *See also:*

Jules Fisher, "Shadows in the Light," Theatre Crafts, *Jan./Feb. 1974, pp. 18–22, 24–26, 28–31. An excellent illustrated article by one of America's leading designers. Treats all aspects of pattern production and use including distortion correction and use of polarization for an appearance of motion.*

J. M. Chapman, "Gobos for Performance Lighting," Theatre Design & Technology, *vol. 19, no. 3 (Fall 1983), pp. 24–25. Excellent short treatment of the technology of gobos by a design educator at Trent Polytechnic in Nottingham, England.*

"Stage Lighting and Patterns: An Underused Device," RoscoNews, *Spring 1985, pp. 3–4. Illus. A survey of the gobo template use.*

Joe and Andrea Tawil, "The Painted Slide," Society of Television Lighting Directors, *no. 31 (Spring 1986), pp. 29–33. Illus. Excellent presentation by the Tawils on gobos and the Great American Scene Machine. Also reprinted in ABTT News, May/June 1986, pp. 2–5.*

"Light Source: Designer Patterns Offer Creative Lighting at Low Cost," Broadcast + Technology, *vol. 12, no. 4 (Feb. 1987), pp. 42–44. Illus. An article about gobos or patterns supplied by Rosco for television lighting directors.*

"DHA," ALD # Magazine, No. 7 (July 1988). p. 9. *Describes the most advanced gobos (patterns, kukoloris, or cukoloris) available from David Hersey Associates in London and New York City, as well as other slides, fiber optics effects, and silk screen printing. The present (1989) new address for DHA is: 3 Jonathan Street, London SE11 5NH; tel. 01-582-3600.*

"Soft-17, Inc.," Theatre Crafts, *vol. 22, no. 5 (May 1988), p. 53. An advertisement by Soft-17, Inc. [3345-3 Sunrise Blvd., Rancho Cordova, California 95742; tel. (916) 635-7118] concerning a new process for adding color images to gobos. The ad also lists eight distributors from coast to coast in the U.S.A.*

"Previews," International Photographer, Film & Video Techniques Magazine, *vol. 61, no. 4 (April 1989), p. 4. Illus. "New Micro Patterns From the Great American Market," is the subtitle.*

for added technical crew time and theatre use, may be involved?

d. Does everyone understand that patience will undoubtedly be called for as the lighting designer ventures off into the world of one of the most sophisticated, yet challenging, design tools available?

Many other specialized areas of lighting design besides the theatre make constant use of projections in a more sophisticated (yet very different) manner. Projections are used in

- Film and cinematography
- Television, with sophisticated and complex matte and "insert" techniques
- Industrial shows, conventions, and trade shows using multi-image technology
- Exhibitions, world's fairs, and theme parks

Types of Projection

Everything from a pool of sunlight splashing through the trees, to snow falling outside a window, to a full-stage scenic environment *may* be the result of judicious use of projected images. It is necessary to create some classification of types of projection. These categories are based upon the nature of the projection equipment utilized. There are five basic groups: (1) projections of patterns (gobos) and other special effects (fire, rain, etc.), which Fred Bentham calls "profile projection" or "low-definition optical projection"; (2) lensless wide-angle projection (from a Linnebach projector or variations thereof), which Willard Bellman labels "square law or shadow projection"; (3) lens wide-angle projections (usually referred to as "projected scenery"), which Bentham names as "high-definition optical projection"; (4) multi-image projection (also called *multimedia*), involving the synthesis of related multiple images by the viewers; and (5) film (loop or motion picture) projection. Each of these categories is discussed in some detail here, and then there is a discussion of basic elements common to most projection equipment: the light source, the light collector lens train, the slide, the objective lenses, the screen

or projection surface, projector location, and performer illumination.

Effects and Patterns. Patterns[39] (also called *gobos*, or "kukaloris" or "kookies") were originally borrowed by the theatre from the cinematography world. Film makers had long used objects of all types of material in nearly every conceivable shape, placed in a beam of light to either create shadows or to modify (disperse) beam form. Theatre folk extended this by inserting a relatively heat-resistant "pattern" at the gate (shutter) focal plane of ellipsoidal reflector spotlights. Color use was not possible because of the high heat levels at the gate (over 1000°F). But aluminum foil, pie plates, stainless steel, copper, quartz, and mica were found to withstand the heat, and soon anything that could be drawn in a black-and-white India ink pattern could be primitively, but inexpensively, projected. Frequent use was made in the beginning of extruded radiator grillwork patterns. Television used them to break up the flat wall monotony behind news commentators and commercial announcers. Theatre created a whole new world of patterns based upon sunlight through every architectural type of window and door: the ever-popular venetian blind pattern, sunlight and moonlight through foliage, lightning, clouds, stars, etc. Next came abstract patterns, such as spirals, swirls, jagged lines, and even distorted "essences of tree branches." The early process was primitive. Cut by hand with a matte knife or razor blade or with power tools, the desired pattern was created in lightweight metals such as copper and aluminum (however, these did not stand up well under intense heat). Soon more intricate designs were being demanded, challenging even the skills of a New York City jeweler everyone had used to hand-file new designs. Design demands produce technological solutions. Mica glass and quartz were used briefly, but ultimately it became simpler and less expensive to use photochemical methods to acid-etch patterns in stainless steel. These stainless steel patterns withstood the heat from prolonged use. Today hundreds of different commercially fabricated stainless steel gobos patterns are readily available from most supply houses and manufacturers. If a designer produces his or her own gobos patterns, they can cost as little as $1 each (produced in quantity). Methods for doing this are cited in footnote 40. The range of patterns which can be created is limited only by the designer's imagination and effort.

Gobos or kukaloris or projected patterns (by any name) remain one of the designer's most valuable tools for expressing individual creativity. While the ability to break up and modify a shaft of light can be overused and create only busy confusion, when they are applied with taste and restraint—properly motivated by both the visual and textual material onstage—gobos patterns remain one of the designer's greatest assets.

Standard theatre "effects heads" (also called "sciopticons") are another projection device. Consisting of a slide and objective lens train, the whole unit slips readily into the color frame holders of most standard plano-convex (not Fresnel or ellipsoidal reflector) spotlights. Variable-speed, reversible motor-driven rotating discs (either hand painted on mica or photographically reproduced on glass discs) are readily available to provide a theatrical version of moving fireworks, stars, fire, flames, rain, snow, and clouds. Over 90 different such moving effects can be found by searching the catalogs of the major rental firms. Some, such as moving clouds, are used so frequently that many producing groups own them. Rental prices are reasonable. The customer must supply the rental firm with only three pieces of information: the effect desired, the distance between the projector mounting position and the surface to be projected upon, and the size of the projected image desired. They are an old theatrical effect, but they work!

There are two other standard effects, shadowgraphs and water-ripple effects. Shadowgraphs spring from the centuries-old Balinese dance/drama and are made up of a light source shining on an object or performer, resulting in a shadow being cast on a bed sheet or screen. Nowadays shadowgraphs are used mostly in puppetry. The other standard effect, water-ripple projection, can be created by directing a spotlight onto bits of broken glass mirror at the bottom of a shallow container of water. The water is agitated, and the reflections are diffracted for a perfect simulation of water ripples. The effect is usually very weak and is useful only for short throws. A second way of creating a water-ripple effect is by using a standard "water ripple effect head," which consists of a spotlight with three or more metal (or glass) screens rotating in clockwise and counterclockwise directions by motor drive, thus breaking up the light beam in the process. Usually the light output is quite weak. Other unique projection "effects" methods exist wherever there is an inventive mind with some mechanical aptitude.

Both patterns and effects are almost always intended to cover a small physical space onstage: a fire from a fireplace or stove; rain outside a window; a splotchy sylvan glade. This type of projection and projection equipment is rarely used as the entire scenic environment.

Lensless Wide-Angle Projection[41]. Many people are familiar with the Linnebach or shadow projector. Attributed to German architect-technician Adolphe Linnebach, the projector simply consists of a concentrated light source in a black box (which controls maximum angle spread and coverage of the resultant image)—and a place to insert slide material. The more concentrated the light source, the sharper the projected image. The more powerful the light source, the brighter the projection. Figure 3.1 shows graphically the interrelationship between source size, slide detail, position, and image clarity. Figure 3.2 shows front and side views of a commercially built Linnebach and slide. Slides are easy to produce. They can be cardboard or lightweight metal cutouts for a black-and-white pattern (similar to those used for a gobo). Color can be added by using as slide material either sheets of glass (high heat is not a significant factor) or, more commonly, clear plastic color media painted with heat-resistant inks and dyes. Many local art stores carry a complete line of plastic-base, heat-resistant inks and dyes, as does Rosco Labs. Plastic, dyes, a brush, and some imagination can put the lighting designer in business. Remember that linear detail in any shadow projection will not ever be as sharp as projection using lenses. Linnebach projections are commonly used for

- Low-budget productions: Funds are not available for more sophisticated equipment.
- Talent and experience limitations: Those providing the projections have not had the necessary training to deal with

[40] Stephen B. Pollock, "Making Your Own Gobos By Photofabraction," Theatre Crafts, vol. 10, no. 4 (Sept. 1976), pp. 30–31, 62, 64–66, 68, 70–71. A "home" process presented in detail with cost factors, supplies, processes; illustrated.

Paul J. Spika, "Lighting Templates from Offset Printing Plates, Etched Method," Theatre Crafts, vol. 12, no. 5 (Sept. 1978), pp. 47, 83. Illus.

Keith W. Clark, "A Method of Etching Gobos," Theatre Design & Technology, vol. 12, no. 1 (Spring 1976), pp. 29–30, 38. Illus.

J. Michael Gillette, "Lighting Templates: Handcut Method," Theatre Crafts, vol. 12, no. 5 (Sept. 1978), pp. 46, 82. Illus.

Susan Dandridge, while a graduate student at Purdue University, developed yet another process in conjunction with Purdue's Chemistry Department. We were able to produce custom-designed gobos in quantity for her thesis production of Shakespeare's The Tempest at a cost of around 70¢ per gobo. Here is our process:

Materials: Silk or organza for silkscreening; .15-gauge aluminum flashing from local hardware store; copy camera from the Art Department; Kodolith film from Eastman; polyblue, a photo-sensitive plastic film; asphaltium from the local bookstore (a tarlike acid-resistant substance); a solution of half hydrochloric acid and half water; a solution of half 3% hydrogen peroxide from the local drugstore and half water.

Process: Enlarge original design to twice desired size of finished gobo. Photograph this with copy camera containing Kodolith film. This produces a high-contrast negative finished the size of the desired gobo. Lay this onto the sheet of polyblue. Place a sheet of glass over this seal to it. Expose for approximately half an hour to strong light; R-40s, Fresnels, etc. The polyblue will appear not to have changed. Place in a tray of equal parts 3% hydrogen peroxide and water. Soak 3 to 5 minutes. The plastic will harden. Lay this in a pan and run warm water gently over it (minus frame). Let it dry approximately 1 hour. Peel away the acetate of the polyblue and the stencil is left on the screen material. From here on, it is a simple silkscreening process. Cut the aluminum into 4-inch squares. Paint asphaltium on one side. On the other side place the stencil. Then simply use the asphaltium as ink in the silkscreen process. When dry, place in acid solution. Time in solution will vary with the strength of the solution. Use 5 minutes at first; expand to 10 minutes as the acid solution weakens. Rinse well with water. Asphaltium will dissolve with turpentine.

For many years the author has had acid-etched copper gobos created by a multitude of photoengraving and etching commercial firms around the country at a reasonable cost. Such firms can be located in any larger city's telephone Yellow Pages.

[41] Holger Steve, "Constructing a Variable Effects Projector," Theatre Crafts, May/June 1974, p. 19.

L. I. Renolds, "The Use of the Linnebach Projector for Scenic Projection," thesis, Stanford University, 1950.

John A. Conway, "Build Your Own Direct Beam," Players Magazine, Jan. 1953.

W. Joseph Stell, "Moving Pictures from a Linnebach," Theatre Crafts, Jan. 1969.

1. VARIATIONS IN THE SIZE OF THE SOURCE

OPTIMUM PROJECTION CONDITIONS COULD ONLY BE ACHIEVED WITH A POINT SOURCE. FOR LARGER SOURCES THE SIZES OF THE DETAILS OF THE PROJECTION MUST BE AT LEAST AS LARGE AS THE SOURCE.

 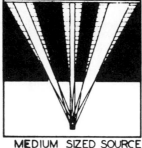 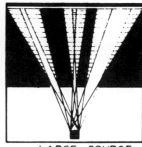

POINT SOURCE   MEDIUM SIZED SOURCE   LARGE SOURCE

2. VARIATIONS IN DISTANCE BETWEEN TEMPLATE & SCREEN

SINCE A POINT SOURCE IS NOT AVAILABLE, THE DISTANCE BETWEEN TEMPLATE & SCREEN ASSUMES IMPORTANCE. A MAXIMUM OF EFFECTIVENESS IS ACHIEVED BY A MINIMUM OF DISTANCE BETWEEN TEMPLATE & SCREEN.

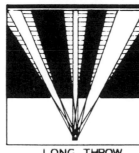 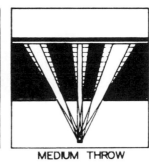 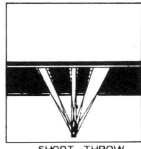

LONG THROW   MEDIUM THROW   SHORT THROW

3. VARIATIONS IN DISTANCE BETWEEN TEMPLATE & SOURCE

THE LACK OF CLARITY IN PROJECTION DUE TO THE PENUMBRA EFFECT IS AMELIORATED BY INCREASING THE DISTANCE BETWEEN TEMPLATE & SOURCE

 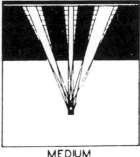 

CLOSE   MEDIUM   LONG

Figure 3.1 Basic considerations in shadow projections. (*Courtesy of Wm. H. Allison.*)

LINNEBACH LANTERN

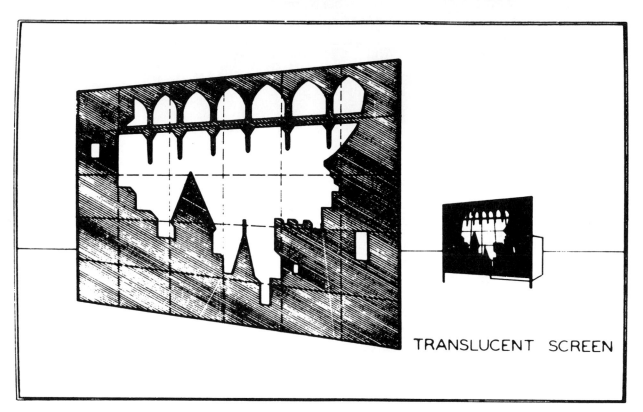

TRANSLUCENT SCREEN

Original Drawing

1.

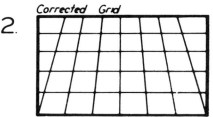

2. *Corrected Grid*

3. *Corrected Slide*

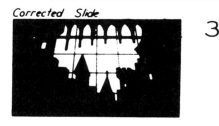

THE LINNEBACH LANTERN

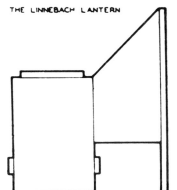

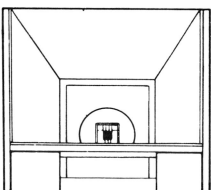

Figure 3.2 Linnebach lantern. (*Courtesy of Wm. H. Allison.*)

I. <u>ORIGINAL DRAWING</u> WITH A SUPERIMPOSED REFERENCE GRID.

2. <u>CORRECTED GRID</u> TEMPLATE LINES ADJUSTED TO FORM PARALLEL LINES ON THE SCREEN

3. <u>CORRECTED SLIDE</u> DRAWING (1) ADJUSTED TO CORRECTED GRID (2), MAINTAINING SAME RELATIONSHIPS BETWEEN DESIGN FORMS & GRID

more complicated projection (for example, many elementary school productions use Linnebach projections).

- Children's drama and fantasy: The child's world of imagination may make the broad, colorful imprecision of Linnebach projections the *preferred* media.
- Scenic backgrounds that lend themselves readily to lack of detail: city skylines, sunsets, sunrises, mountain landscapes, forests, etc.
- Abstract expressionistic/impressionistic productions: for example, Linnebach projections were used for the mathematical abstract figures in a production of Elmer Rice's play *The Adding Machine*.

Other equally valid situations occur to the reader where exact reproduction of excessive detail is not needed.

Several readily available light sources best suit the needs of Linnebach work. The filament dimension of most stage lamps is too large. A whole family of low-voltage light sources with highly concentrated filaments is available. Willard Bellman discusses this in detail in both of his books (see footnote 56). Also, lamps manufactured primarily for use in the smaller home projection equipment have highly concentrated filaments. While these lamps entail a relatively high cost, they are often ideal because they can be operated at overvoltage, which shortens their already short life but vastly increases their light output. Several usable tungsten-halogen (quartz) sources are better than most standard tungsten lamps. *All* of the projected pattern from a Linnebach *must* come from one light source. If a large area is to be covered, you need both maximum output and minimum filament size—a difficult compromise to achieve.

Distortions can be dealt with in any of three ways. Linnebachs are usually bulky. The University of Michigan at Ann Arbor has two huge Linnebachs that are nearly the size of a small dormitory room each. (If equipped with running water, they could be rented out as living quarters!) Since Linnebachs are bulky, they are often either placed on the stage floor in front of a drop or cyclorama or hung from overhead electronic pipes at the top of the cyc. Figure 3.2 shows one method of slide distortion correction.

An ordinary stage Fresnel spotlight with the lens removed can serve as a Linnebach. For the Broadway production of Eugene O'Neill's *Moon for the Misbegotten* (Bijou Theatre, May 1957), I used several such units on the upstage side of the set, directed toward the cyc. By painting streaks of color on the sheets of clear Cinemoid and then crossfading between Fresnels mounted above the stage floor level to lower Fresnels nearer the floor line, and combining this with realistic full-cyc sky projections from two 5-kilowatt wide-angle projectors, I was able to create a stunning, yet plausible, sunrise that prompted *The New York Times* drama critic Brooks Atkinson to devote a whole paragraph of his review to "the most beautiful, realistic, theatrically effective" sunrise he had ever seen in a theatre. Happily, both performers were required to point to the sunrise and call the audience's attention to its beauty in dialogue provided by playwright O'Neill. Linnebach projections need not be restricted to amateur theatre; the Linnebach can be a powerful design tool in the lighting artist's arsenal.

Two innovative approaches to slide treatment deserve mention. Professor Hunton D. Sellman, while at the State University of Iowa, developed the first of a series of home-built Linnebachs in which the slide holder was a curved slot which exactly followed the curvature of the full cyc. By painting on plastic color media (rather than glass), he could consistently produce a distortion-free image (vertically and horizontally) on the cyc. He further mounted the lamp socket in sliding grooves (forward-and-back, side-to-side), allowing accurate compensation for hanging more than one Linnebach off of the center line of the cyc.

Thomas Wilfred evolved the Direct Beam projector. As can be seen in Figure 3.3, this consisted of a multiplane sequence of slide materials and a color-change device. Since the color modifier was nearest to the light source, no sharp definition appeared. The whole projection could be faded from night through sunrise into daylight. The fact that the slide material was on three separated planes affected image sharpness, giving softness of detail for the "far distance" portion of the projection, increased sharpness of detail for "middle distance," and extreme precision (at the expense of a rather large piece of slide material) for all "foreground detail." This is just as it is seen in nature or from an aerial perspective. Further refinements along these

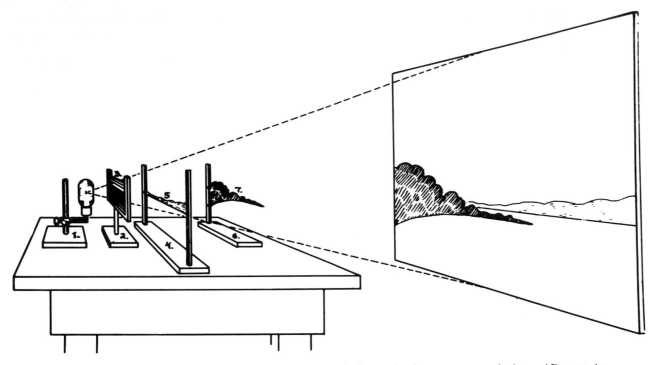

1. Lamp
2. Frame for diffused background coloring by means of I
3. Laminated glass filters (sky, water, and so forth)
4. Middle-distance plane with
5. Coastline cut-out of colored plastic
6. Foreground plane with
7. Promontory cut-out of colored plastic

Figure 3.3 Thomas Wilfred's Direct Beam scenic projector, with background, middle-distance, and foreground planes for interposition of form and color elements. *(Courtesy of Art Institute of Light, West Nyack, N.Y.)*

In the actual projector, two or more background filters may be moved in and out of the beam by remote control, thus permitting a gradual transition from day through sunset to night and vice versa, with any suitable setting. An additional attachment for moving clouds consists of a drum rotating around the lamphouse and holding a plastic cylinder with painted clouds which pass through the beam of light between planes 2 and 4.

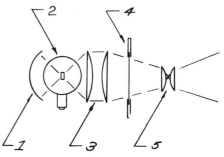

1. Spherical reflector
2. Concentrated filament lamp
3. Condensing lens system
4. Slide and slide holder
5. Objective lens system

Figure 3.4 Simple lens projector components.

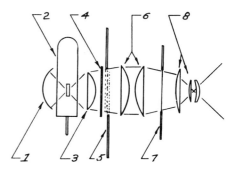

1. Spherical reflector
2. Concentrated filament lamp
3. First condenser element or "collector" condenser
4. Heat-reflecting filter
5. Color blender
6. Condenser lens elements
7. Slide and slide holder
8. Objective lens elements

Figure 3.5 Complex lens projector components.

same lines make it possible to introduce movement into the final image.

Linnebach projections, with the many possible variations and modifications, are not at this time in vogue. Lighting, like fashion, evolves in cycles. The astute designer will not overlook the many possibilities Linnebach projections offer and the opportunity to use a design tool which may seem startlingly new to most audiences today.

Wide-Angle Projection, with Lens. For any projection requiring great brightness and an absolute minimum of distortion plus maximum accurate reproduction of linearity, lens projectors are a must. Figure 3.4 shows the components of a simple lens projector. Figure 3.5 is a more sophisticated projector. Each component will be treated in detail in the material which follows. The designer should keep in mind a few fundamentals:

[42] *Michael F. Kenny and Raymond F. Schmitt, Images, Images, Images: The Book of Programmed Multi-Image Production. Rochester, New York; Eastman Kodak Co.; 1979. 240 pp., illus., color. The entire volume deals with projection equipment, design, use, and technology for the multi-image field. Focuses on Carousel-type slide projectors and film, with very little application to wide-angle scenic background projection. Invaluable in its field. Beautifully printed and illustrated in color on top-quality paper. Highly readable text.*

See also:

Mary Luder, "Multi-Image Programming Hardware and Software," Theatre Crafts, vol. 13, no. 5 (Oct. 1979), pp. 40–41, 66–68, 70. Illus. Good basic information.

Roberta Lord, "Wow Voyager: Light Sculpture as Sets," Theatre Crafts, vol. 19, no. 3 (Mar. 1985), p. 19. Illus., color. A detailed explanation of use of multimedia projections as scenic background for a Kansas City Ballet production. Artist Dale Eldred explains his design approach and technical execution.

"Kodak on Broadway," Theatre Crafts, vol. 18, no. 2 (Feb. 1984), p. 10. Illus. Describes Kodak's new Duratrans process for producing large photographic transparencies used by Michael Hotopp and Paul de Pass in the 1983 Broadway musical, Tap Dance Kid.

Louis M. Brill, "The Theatre of Performing Lights," Lighting Dimensions, vol. 3, no. 9 (Sept. 1979), pp. 16–17, 19. Illus., color. A description of a multimedia theatre with lasers and holography.

Lowell Fowler, "Multi-Image As a Lighting Tool," Lighting Dimensions, vol. 4, no. 3 (Mar. 1980), pp. 30–31, 33, 37. Illus., color.

1. No present-day lens projector is very efficient. The best projectors deliver only approximately 5 percent of the initial-source visible light output onto the projection surface. Further loss occurs when one adds such factors as the inverse square law (light loss due to projection distance) and the amount of radiant energy reflected back from the projection surface (reflectivity of screen) as viewed by the audience.

2. With very few exceptions (apart from opaque and overhead projectors; see Bellman's *Scenography*, p. 559, footnote 56), no existing high-precision lens projector available today will deliver much more than a 1:1 image size. This means that the projected image is 1 foot wide for every foot between the projector and the screen. A few sophisticated units can deliver 1:1.6 (18-inch-wide image with 1 foot of distance between the projector and the screen), but that is always with some distortion present.

3. Theatre projection is also complicated by the necessity to illuminate the live performer in proximity to the projection surface. The advantages of the darkened movie house (with its near-total absence of ambient light) are removed. Nor can the theatre lighting designer approximate the potential control of ambient light that TV makes possible.

Multi-Image Projection. Multi-image projection consists of (1) an assemblage of smaller projection areas in a given playing space which is synthesized by the viewer's mental response into one total image, composed of definable parts; (2) many different images in a given space, each of which is interrelated and each of which makes its own individual comment on the total production being presented; or (3) multiple images used to stimulate, to attract interest and attention, or to serve as a novel means of presentation. This use is most evident in industrial/trade shows, conventions, theme parks, and discos, wherein distraction away from the live performer is not a problem.

Multi-image production is the easiest place for the beginner to start. Today's youth, highly conditioned by rock shows, TV, movies, and disco, respond readily to multi-stimulation. Further, multi-image projection can be done with readily available, reasonably inexpensive, technological equipment: Carousel projectors, 8-mm film, etc. However, on its most sophisticated level, multi-image can be more complex, more demanding creatively, and more costly than any other form of projection except moving film.

Multi-image projection appears in all areas of lighting design:

- Multi-image projection is used in *serious theatre production.* The multi-image work of Czech scenographer Josef Svoboda in *Magica Laterna* is world renowned. Multi-image is used in all forms of dance (ballet, modern dance, ethnic) and opera. It is to be found in musicals and sometimes in lighter comedy.

- Multi-image is at the heart of much that is created for use in *industrial shows, conventions, display and merchandising,* and *trade shows* — wherever a product or process is to be explained or sold.

- Early *discos, light shows, psychedelic lighting,* and *concert tours* made heavy use of multi-image techniques.

- *Cinema* is, by its very nature, multi-image. So is *television.* Rapid intercuts of multiple images is the most common simple use.

- Early *discos* used batteries of Carousel projectors and thousands of slides. In this environment, multi-image projection has recently been largely replaced by motion in more abstract forms.

- *Theme parks, world's fairs, expositions,* and a whole range of productions *advertising* the activities and merits of a city or tourist attraction or specific product make extensive use of multi-image productions — frequently without the use of any live performers.

Since this field is a complex one still in the midst of day-to-day development and expansion, it is not covered at length here. For more information, refer to *Images, Images, Images: The Book of Programmed Multi-Image Production,*[42] which covers the specialized area of multi-image production in great depth.

Film Projection. The same diversity of use presented in the list offered in the "Multi-Image" section applies to projected moving film. Without further discussion of film projection in other areas, I'll make a few brief comments about uses of film in live theatre. The United States is ahead of European counterparts in this area of projections. While

European technology and inventiveness is superior in "still" wide-angled projected images and in the insertion of moving objects at the focal plane of wide-angle projectors (particularly at Bayreuth's annual Wagner *Ring Cycle*), designers in the United States remain ahead in use of film sequence as a part of opera, ballet, modern dance, and dramatic production.[43]

The history of scenic projection of moving film images in theatrical productions began around 1920. Svoboda used film as a design element in *Laterna Magica* in Prague, Czechoslovakia, in the mid-1950s and, later, for his Czech Pavilion at the Montreal World's Fair. During the mid-1960s Gardner Compton and Emile Ardolino designed the film usage in the Joffrey Ballet's production of *Astarte*. They also collaborated with opera director Frank Corsaro on the film and still projections used in the New York City Opera production of Janacek's *The Makropoulos Affair* in November 1970. About the same time Ronald Chase began experimenting with film projection as a part of the scenic environment for director Richard Pearlman's Washington Opera production of Benjamin Britten's *The Turn of the Screw* in 1969. Corsaro and Chase joined forces for the Washington Opera's production of Delius' *Koanga* at the Kisner Auditorium in December 1970. At about the same time, Chase again worked with Pearlman on a production of the rock opera *Tommy* for the Seattle Opera. The first collaboration of Chase and Corsaro on *Koanga* led to their joint efforts for Delius' *Village Romeo and Juliet* at the Kennedy Center Opera in April 1972 and Korngold's *Die Tote Stadt* in April 1975. Many of the Chase and Corsaro operas utilizing film first played at the Washington Opera, then playing the New York City Opera's State Theatre in Lincoln Center.

Winston Tong and Bruce Geduldig won an Off-Broadway "Obie" Award for their use of film in *Bound Feet* at the La Mama Theatre in New York City. *Illuminations* on a European tour used film by this same team. *Frankie and Johnny* was produced using film inserts at San Francisco's Magic Theatre.

Beatrix Cenci, the commissioned opera which opened the Kennedy Center in Washington, D.C., involved film and projections by Chase in 1971. Chase was involved in the Los Angeles Opera's *Anna Karenina* on March 16, 1983, and the Eastman School of Music's production of *The Turn of the Screw,* also integrating film projections into these productions. Several Corsaro–Chase operatic collaborations using film projection have been presented in the 1980s at the summer St. Louis Opera Theatre: *Fennimore and Gerda* (1981), Delius' *Margot la Rouge* (1983), and Poulenc's *Les Mamelles de Tirésias* (1983). The opera, *Doktor Faust,* was presented using film projections at Washington, D.C.'s Wolf Trap Theatre. There was an operatic production of *Lulu* in Houston.

Fenimore and Gerda was also offered at the King's Theatre during the Edinburgh, Scotland, Summer Festival in 1983. A new production of Richard Strauss' *Die Frau Ohne Schatten* was offered for the 1984 season of the Chicago Lyric Opera with Frank Corsaro directing and design by Ronald Chase.[44]

Mr. Chase began as a sculptor and became a cinematographer. Creative mastery of film technology applied to opera production is his forte. Mr. Carsaro is a noted director, much of whose reputation rests upon opera productions. He has a high level of inventiveness and is very open to experimentation. Sometimes in tandem, often separately, these two men have been responsible for several opera productions combining multi-image still projection with extensive use of film. Mr. Chase's representatives at the New Jersey Opera Projection Symposium described the technique he has helped to evolve as a "sandwich" approach to projections use: projections from both front-of-house and backstage are projected upon a scrim at the curtain line, front and rear projections are produced on an upstage screen, and live actors perform in the middle. (This is, of course, a highly simplified version of the process involved.) The only other production in which I have seen this technique applied was a production of Karl Orff's opera, *A Play for the End of Time,* performed at the Salzburg (Austria) summer festival in 1975. This production was technically most successful, but the opera itself was weak.

Many of the Corsaro–Chase opera productions have been heavily subsidized by individuals and foundations. As an example, it has been reported that 3,000 feet of film (around 15 minutes) plus over 500 stills were involved in *Die Tote Stadt.* Much of the footage was filmed on location in Bruges, Belgium, at a reputed cost of over $200,000.

[43] See:

Stephen Ford, "An Experiment in the Extension of the Opera Stage: Integration of Live Theatre and Film Techniques," Theatre Design + Technology, no. 7 (Dec. 1966), pp. 17–19. Illus. Early work of Wallace Russell using film projections in opera.

Paul Planer, "Projected Opera Settings," Opera News, vol. 18 (Feb. 15, 1954), pp. 4–5.

X. Ted Barber, "Scenic Effects Using the Motion Picture," The Passing Show, Newsletter of the Shubert Archive, vol. 8, no. 2 (Summer 1984), pp. 2–3. Illus. A fascinating account of motion picture backgrounds in 1914 by scenic designer Frank D. Thomas for the Shubert Revue.

[44] Ronald Chase, "Cinematic Approaches to Theatre," Theatre Crafts, vol. 17, no. 7 (Aug./Sept. 1983), pp. 32–35, 70–72, 74, 76. Illus. Excellent article by the foremost U.S. practitioner of film integration into scenic design. Good brief history of film use in live theatrical production. Analysis of when to use and when to avoid adding film and projected images to a production. Analyzes possible future uses of film as yet unrealized.

Harold C. Schonberg, "City Opera 'Tote Stadt' Exploits Film Technique," The New York Times, Apr. 3, 1975.

Allen Hughes, "'Village Romeo and Juliet' Sparkles at City Opera," The New York Times, Oct. 8, 1973.

Gilda Guttman, "Multi-Media Projected Scenery at the New York City Opera," Ph.D. thesis, 1980, New York University.

Harold C. Schonberg, "Films—A New Dimension For Opera," The New York Times, Sunday, Apr. 20, 1975. Illus.

Mr. Chase also received program credit for "additional material, staging, lighting, projection design" for Jump Street Rag at the Chi Chi Theatre in San Francisco on February 2, 1983.

Thomas Lask, "Frank Corsaro Is Projecting a Novel Image for Opera," The New York Times, May 1, 1975.

"Fennimore and Gerda" by Delius. Review of Opera Theatre of St. Louis production with Ronald Chase. Opera News, vol. 46, no. 4 (Oct. 1981), p. 31.

Alan Rich, *"The Lively Arts: Dead Weight,"* New York *magazine, Apr. 21, 1975, pp. 84–88.*

"Anna Karenina" by Iain Hamilton. Review as produced by the Los Angeles Opera Theatre. Opera News, *vol. 47, no. 17 (June 1983), p. 42.*

"Fennimore and Gerda" by Delius. A review in Opera News, *vol. 48, no. 8 (Jan. 7, 1984), p. 36.*

"Margot la Rouge" by Delius and Poulenc's Les "Mamelles de Tiresias." Reviewed by Opera News, *vol. 48, no. 4 (Oct. 1983), p. 92.*

David Fingleton, "Stage Design," Cue, *no. 48 (July/August 1987), p. 6. Illus. Chase's lighting, with director Frank Corsaro, of* L'enfant et les Sortilèges *by Ravel at England's summer Glyndebourne Festival.*

Mark Loeffler, "From Manon To Madonna, The State of the Art in Scenic Projections," Theatre Crafts, *vol. 22, no. 1 (Jan. 1988), pp. 34–37, 50–54, 56. Illus., color. Excellent coverage of available projection equipment, from the simple Carousel to the complex Pani HMI, with photos of recent productions utilizing extensive projections.*

Audio Visual Promotion Aids, Inc., "Projection Clarification," Theatre Crafts, *vol. 22, no. 3 (March 1988), p. 14. Some technical corrections on Mark Loeffler's January article (above).*

[45] The New York Times, *April 3, 1975, op. cit. (see footnote 44).*

[46] *Alan Rich,* New York *magazine, p. 84, op. cit. (see footnote 44).*

Critical reactions were mixed. Of *Die Tote Stadt,* music critic Harold C. Schonberg wrote in *The New York Times:* "This is a dream opera, a hallucinatory one, and the Corsaro–Chase team has aimed the films at interpretation as well as background. The object is to mirror what goes on in the mind of the central character, and to do so in a manner that conventional stage techniques cannot begin to do. . . . But the techniques (Chase–Corsaro's) nevertheless are trailblazers, and it is not impossible that in years to come they will usurp conventional procedures." [45]

On the negative side, critic Alan Rich wrote in the April 21, 1975 issue of *New York* magazine:

> Try as I might, I can come up with no rational explanation for the City Opera's decision to revive Erich Korngold's *Die Tote Stadt.* I can only come up with one irrational explanation, for that matter: the notion of providing Frank Corsaro with the perfect vehicle for his directional extravagances, and opera that he couldn't possibly make worse than it is. If that be the case, the company sold Mr. Corsaro short.
>
> But the basic flaw in Corsaro's work in *Die Tote Stadt,* it seems to me, is the assumption that the technique works *per se,* and can somehow redeem any opera of any quality. That is fallacious; *Village Romeo* worked only because the mixed medium was conceived as a visual extension of the music, as stage settings in any form must be. Here, where it has apparently been designed as an exact duplication of the music, we are simply buried in twofold banalities. [46]

There are often opposing views on a production. The point of this example is that some of the most progressive work in use of film as a scenic and lighting design element is taking place in the United States today.

Having looked at the factors affecting use of, or abstinence from, projected images and having analyzed the various types at hand, we now turn to an examination of the basic elements and problems connected with high-definition lens projectors.

The Light Source

The perfect light source for projection would be

- A point source in dimension. Since a "point" is an abstract idealization and does not really exist, we lose right at the beginning. Obviously the smaller in dimension the light source actually is, the better it serves the demands of an optical projection train.

- Of infinite brightness; dimmable. Again, we lose. Sources each year become more powerful in luminous output, but they are never likely to come anywhere near having the power of the sun in a point-source dimension (which would theoretically be ideal). Being "dimmable" is a moot feature. Several light sources which are far superior to the readily dimmable tungsten filament electric lamp are in use and are preferred because of their high output or their smaller dimension in comparison to the standard electric light filament. Many cannot be *electrically* dimmed (a whole family of high-intensity short arcs, for example), yet their advantages are such that mechanically controlled shutters become acceptable.

- Of low- (or no-) heat output. The infrared (heat) portion of the energy spectrum contributes nothing usable in visible radiant energy. Its presence cracks lenses and warps and burns slides. A "cold" light source is highly desirable.

- Of the correct (maximum usable) color balance (temperature) output. Few artificial light sources meet this requirement. Anyone in an industry in which color matching is important (for example, printing or textiles) knows the difficulties involved. A properly balanced color output is a problem in projection light sources, too.

So right from the start there is no way to design the ideal projector, because nearly every requirement cannot be met by today's technology. Like the ideal automobile (inexpensive, fast, durable, comfortable, attractive, fuel-efficient), the ideal projector will probably never exist. Designers must seek out and accept the best compromises available.

Here are some rough guidelines concerning presently available sources, suitable or unsuitable, for projection work:

Neon, Fluorescent, Mercury Vapor, Sodium Vapor lamps. These sources are not usable at all. Neon and fluorescent sources are "line" rather than "point" sources. Their dimension is wrong. Mercury and sodium are of limited spectral output.

Tungsten Filament at Line Voltage. These sources are rapidly becoming obsolete because of high heat production, excessive filament size, and poor color balance. In spite of its cheapness and ready intensity control, the tungsten filament projection lamp at line voltage lingers on mostly in small slide/film projectors for home, office, and amateur use and in older 5-kilowatt and 10-kilowatt wide-angle scenic projectors. Even in home projectors, HMI and other sources are rapidly replacing this "old faithful."

Tungsten Filament at Regulated Low Voltage. This source is also just "hanging on." Reducing the voltage allows for big reductions in filament size without a corresponding loss of brightness (output). Specialized lamps of this type are still useful, but they do not appear in newer projection units.

Carbon Arc. The carbon arc is almost entirely obsolete. While the electric carbon arc is the brightest source available (as well as being of small dimension and of an acceptable color balance, particularly in the blues), safety regulations require a human operator and a fireproof booth enclosure. These two cost factors negate the value of its brightness. In addition, it is not readily dimmable electrically.

Xenon Arc Lamps[47]. Xenon arc lamps are not used much because of necessary safety precautions. The xenon arc is a very compact source, and it has a high brightness and a good color balance. But since it operates at an internal pressure of several atmospheres and is subject to a series of events which can prompt a dangerous explosion, regulations in the United States now require such extensive safety precautions and bulky safety equipment that the xenon arc's usefulness in theatrical projectors is limited. If an operator is unprotected from exposure to the raw light output of the xenon lamp, very serious (and permanent) injury can result to skin and eyes.

Tungsten Halogen (Quartz) Lamps. The quartz lamp is better than the standard tungsten incandescent, first of all because the color balance output is better (stronger in the blues). Also, the quartz lamp is more compact in size, and it does not blacken during its usable life, which is usually long. Available since 1976 in 10,000-watt (T-24 bulb) size with

nearly twice the life expectancy of its tungsten incandescent counterpart, the quartz lamp has largely replaced the older tungsten in projection equipment.

The HMI Lamp[48]. The most promising light source to appear, rapidly replacing all others in sophisticated projection equipment, is the hydrargyrum (mercury) medium iodides (HMI) lamp. The HMI lamp is of the mercury arc family, specifically the high-intensity metal-halide type. First developed by the company Osram GmbH, of Munich, West Germany, in 1969 for German television, it has become the most usable tool available for many fields, particularly as a light source for powerful projectors. First shown by Osram at the 1970 *Photokina Exhibition* in Cologne, Germany, it was used by light designer/electrician Kurt Winter to replace xenon at the Wagner *Ring Cycle* in Bayreuth, Germany, in the summer of 1973. Later that year Winter leased the development rights to his supplier, Ludwig Pani of Vienna, Austria. Pani, who had long produced the "Rolls Royce" of the projector line, rapidly developed a new series of projectors based upon the HMI source.

By the summer of 1975, when I returned to Europe, over 50 HMI wide-angle scenic projectors were in use throughout Europe. I talked with opera house owners (of the Paris Opera, Berlin Staatsoper, etc.) about the use and operation of these new units. Later that year Pani supplied the first four such projectors to be used in the western hemisphere for my production of *Carmen* by the New Jersey State Opera in Trenton and Newark, New Jersey. I designed the scenery, lighting, and projections for this production. (At that time the USITT Opera Projection Symposium referred to at the beginning of this chapter was held in Newark for 225 theatre designers, technicians, and manufacturers.) Pani units are now in common use by the Met Opera, Toronto Opera, San Francisco Opera, and others.

The HMI lamp (a tungsten short-arc) is filled with mercury and argon under high vapor pressure (see Figure 3.6). The additional introduction of other rare-earth metal iodides—dysprosium, holmium, and thulium, plus bromides to prevent blackening—produces the excellent "full daylight spectrum" of nearly continuous radiation throughout the visible spectrum, a color output [5600°K (Kelvin)] which

[47] W. A. Ward, "Xenon Arc Light Source for the Theatre," thesis, University of Southern California at Los Angeles, 1967.

"Xenon," Lighting Dimensions, vol. 2, no. 9 (Nov. 1978), pp. 29–30.

Richard Glickman, "CID: The Latest Compact Source AC ARC Lamp for Film and Television," Lighting Dimensions, vol. 4, no. 5 (May 1980), pp. 10–12. Illus.

[48] Richard Glickman, "HMI Update, Parts I & II," Lighting Dimensions, vol. 3, no. 1 (Jan. 1979), pp. 28–29, 31, 33–35, and vol. 3, no. 2 (Feb. 1979), pp. 24–27. This two-part series not only analyzes the basics of HMI lamps but also gives a wide range of ballast and filter solutions to most problems which have arisen with the use of HMI in film and TV applications.

Thomas M. Lemons, "TTFL: HMI Lamps," Lighting Design & Application, vol. 8, no. 8 (Aug. 1978), pp. 32–37. Detailed illustrated technical information about both basics and ballast problems. Very understandable how-to information for users of HMI lamps.

Osram, "Osram Halogen-Metalldamflampen HMI Metallogen." A full-color 12-page brochure issued by Osram (Gesellschaft mit beschränkter Haftung, Berlin-München) in three languages (English, German, French) by Osram. Excellent color photos of HMI use in opera, film, TV, and dance. Good technical information. Obtained by author in Germany from Osram.

William Bamberg, "Ruggedized 'Double Seal' for Use in a 6000-watt Lamp," SMPTE Journal, vol. 91, no. 12 (Dec. 1982), pp. 1175–77. Illus.

"Lighting," SMPTE Journal, vol. 92, no. 4 (April 1983), pp. 380–81. Describes in great technical detail the new 6000-watt HMI lamp and its use in motion picture lighting.

Ryle Gibbs, "The Use of Metal Halide Lamps on Exteriors," SMPTE Journal, vol. 84 (Aug. 1975), pp. 610–13. Contains an illustrated short history of the evolution of the HMI, its application to various types of luminaires, color rendition, flicker problems with film. Primarily a report of French experiences with HMI. Corrected information for this Handbook's text was supplied to the author by Keith Gillum, HMI Marketing, Macbeth Sales Corp. in a letter dated 3/18/80 and is incorporated herein.

Robert E. Levin, "Performance Characteristics of HMI-Type Lamps," SMPTE Journal, vol. 94, no. 6 (June 1985), pp. 660–666. Illus. Complete analysis of HMI, Brite Arc, and Brite Beam lamps.

Production Arts Lighting, 636 Eleventh Avenue, N.Y., N.Y. 10036, telephone: (212) 489-0312, is, as of late 1985, the authorized dealer and factory service center for Ludwig Pani equipment in the United States.

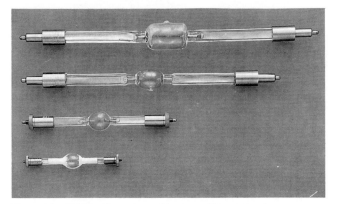

Figure 3.6 HMI Metallogen lamp. (*Courtesy of Osram Corp.*)

HMI lamp is converted into UV (ultraviolet) energy, a non-visible portion of the energy spectrum; 45 percent is converted into visible light; and 42 percent of the output is in the infrared region of the energy spectrum (i.e., it is registered as heat, not as visible light). This compares most favorably with incandescent lamps, in which 85 percent of the electrical energy consumed is converted to heat (infrared) and only 15 percent of the output is visible light. Further, and of importance in projection, this low heat factor becomes of great value in protecting slides and lenses from heat/burnup damage. While UV output is quite high for HMI lamps, most of this UV energy is removed by having the radiant energy pass through heat-resistant glass. *Extreme caution should be exercised by operators of HMI lamps never to expose either their eyes or skin to unmodified HMI lamp output, since rapid and severe sunburn and eye damage can result.*

Available Sizes, Costs, and Life Expectancy. HMI lamps are available in the following wattages:

Wattage	Approximate cost (1988)	Burning time (life expectancy) in hours
200	$ 290	300
575	410	750
1200	580	750
2500	1005	500
4000	1275	500
6000	2100	350
12,000	3950	250

While the initial cost per lamp is quite high, it should be remembered that little else approaches the HMI lamp's color balance, efficiency of usable visible light for energy consumed, or compactness of source. In addition, the operating cost (output versus energy consumption) during operation is sufficiently low to help outweigh the initial cost for TV, film, or projection use.

Operation. The HMI is an enclosed arc. An ignition circuit is required to fire it (for approximately 1 second). A ballast is needed. A warm-up time lasting from 30 seconds to 3 minutes is required for the arc to reach full output and full color stabilization. It cannot be easily dimmed (dimming

makes the HMI so valuable. The center of the arc (once fired with the use of ignition circuits and associated ballasts) operates at about 5600°K in a highly-heat-resistant T-shaped quartz bulb with a "bubble" surrounding the arc. Several characteristics of the HMI lamp merit discussion here.

Efficiency. HMI consumes very little electrical energy for its high visible-lumen output. Per watt of electrical energy consumed, HMI produces 85 to 110 lumens. The standard carbon arc produces a mere 32 lumens per watt. Incandescent lamps produce 27 to 34 lumens of light per watt (9 lumens or less if filtered to produce a daylight color balance output). Low-pressure sodium vapor lamps can produce nearly 200 lumens, but the restricted color output eliminates them from serious consideration. Thus, the HMI is at least six times as efficient, per watt of electricity consumed, as common incandescent sources.

Color Output. Since the color output is 5600° to 6000°K, the HMI produces an evenly balanced color range closely approximating daylight. Few other sources do. If anything, HMI is slightly "strong" in the blue end of the spectrum (the opposite of incandescent), which makes it highly useful for projecting blue skies. The Kelvin temperature output of the HMI does, however, gradually decrease 300°K from its initial 5600°K during lamp life. This decrease can be an important factor in film and color TV use. Approximately 11 percent of the electrical energy consumed by an

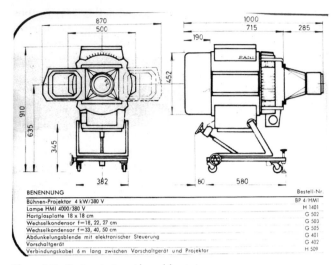

BENENNUNG	Bestell-Nr.
Bühnen-Projektor 4 kW/380 V	BP 4/HMI
Lampe HMI 4000/380 V	H 1401
Hartglasplatte 18 x 18 cm	G 502
Wechselkondensor f=18, 22, 27 cm	G 503
Wechselkondensor f=33, 40, 50 cm	G 505
Abdunkelungsblende mit elektronischer Steuerung	G 401
Vorschaltgerät	G 402
Verbindungskabel 6 m lang zwischen Vorschaltgerät und Projektor	H 509

Figure 3.7 Pani projector, side and front view.

Figure 3.8 Pani projector.

less than 50 percent of full brightness produces wide fluctuation in color temperature output). The HMI is very sensitive to voltage variations, although recent developments have allowed for dimming up to 40 percent of full brightness. A remote-controlled mechanical dimmer has been developed for intensity control and dousing of projectors. The HMI arc will re-fire, once extinguished, quite rapidly. It must be operated on an alternating current of 207 volts. Equipment is available so that many HMI lamps can be operated on standard American electric voltage service. Lamps with technology and output similar to the HMI are Sylvania's Brite Arc and Brite Beam in 200-watt, 575-watt, 1200-watt, 2500-watt, and 4000-watt sizes.[49]

Figures 3.7 and 3.8 show the Pani 4000-watt HMI scenic projector and side-plus-front-view line drawings. In summary, for the first time in the history of scenic projection, a light source is available which begins to meet the ideal requirements of a projection light source: the HMI is extremely bright, highly efficient, relatively "cool", and compact, and it has an excellent balanced color output. On the negative side, HMI is expensive, it cannot be readily dimmed electrically past a certain level, and it has a relatively limited lamp life.

Most projectors are equipped with aklo-glass heat filters (similar to the yellowish-green tinted glass used in some auto windshields to reduce sunlight glare). These filters remove much of the infrared heat, yet allow most of the visible light to pass through freely. The filters are strips of tinted glass mounted in a metal frame to allow for contraction and expansion of the glass. If the filters are damaged or removed, slide material will normally burn up in a few seconds.

Light Collectors (Reflectors and Condensers)

Light sources normally emit radiant energy in all directions. The usable portion of this output (in either a spotlight or a projector) is commonly termed the *angle of acceptance.* More specifically, if a straight line is drawn from the lamp filament to top and bottom outer edges of a lens, the result-

[49] *Donald A. Richardson and Warren C. Gungle, "The Care and Handling of Sylvania Brite Arc® and Brite Beam® Lamps,"* SMPTE Journal, *vol. 93, no. 6 (June 1984), pp. 588–91. Illus.*

ing angle is the angle of acceptance. Obviously, moving the light source closer to the lens (possible in a Fresnel lens of short focal length) greatly increases the angle of acceptance. However, lenses of short focal length are more difficult to cast or grind flaw-free. Thus, as the lamp is brought closer to the lens (in design), two things happen: the lens becomes more costly, and the heat from the lamp–lens proximity may crack the lens (also, a thick lens heats up more rapidly by retaining more light internally).

To make maximum use of all the light flux output of a projector, a reflector is added behind the source to redirect light rays optically back through the filament toward the lens (thus increasing the usable angle of acceptance and, at the same time, intensifying the heat on the filament coil, causing it to burn more brightly and produce more output). The reflector should be (1) as large as luminaire design makes possible; (2) of maximum reflectivity; (3) slightly adjustable in positioning to retain perfect optical alignment, or else so rigidly mounted that its relationship to the light source cannot be misaligned; (4) of an optically usable shape for its own luminaire — spherical (the most common) or ellipsoidal or some other designed form. A second way to make maximum use of the light flux output of a projector is to position the largest possible diameter lens (or lenses) as near to the source as is operationally safe. This combination — large size and closeness to source — allows maximum use of lamp output. Obviously there are practical limits to lens diameter: it cannot be 3 feet in diameter and fit into any plausible projector housing. Past a certain diameter, the increase in angle acceptance produces little additional "light gathering." Both the largest possible reflector surface and the condenser lens train markedly increase total projector light output. The collector lenses (or condenser lenses) themselves will absorb up to 10 percent of the light energy directed through them. This absorption can be decreased by using optically coated lenses, but the cost is usually prohibitive. These condenser lenses have a major function: they "bend" the light output, that is, change the direction of travel of the light and compress the light rays together into a smaller bundle. This beam needs to be converged into the approximate size of the slide/image material. These lenses need not be of high optical quality, nor

excessively expensive. See Figures 3.4 and 3.5 for further clarification of this relationship.

The Slide/Image Material

Nearly anything can be placed at the slide aperture of a projection system — a standard slide (hand-painted or photographically produced), metal shapes, ripple glass, color media, etc. — if it will withstand the heat. While lighting designers in the United States tend to think only of standard "still" slides as projection material, their European counterparts, in productions such as those given at the Wagner Festival at Bayreuth, Germany, make extensive use of a variety of objects, often moving or rotating them.

The positioning of the slide aperture should be slightly movable on the projection train for maximum flexibility. Sharp focus, however it is obtained, is the ultimate objective.

Slide Size. Aperture physical dimensions are fairly standard throughout the world. Most common is the 35-mm transparency used in Carousel projectors, 35-mm film projectors, etc. In film work, 8-mm, 16-mm, and 70-mm filmstrips are not uncommon. There are other sizes in general use in "still" slide work. One is the 3¼- by 4-inch slide, found in older classroom projectors. Most larger scenic projection slides used in the United States are 5 by 7 inches in size. European practice dictates 7 by 7 inches and 9½ by 9½ inches for the newest 6-kilowatt HMI Pani projector. Obviously, the larger the slide, the easier it is to force powerful quantities of radiant energy through the slide without heat/ ventilation problems. As with an excessively large diameter condenser lens, however, the practicality of projector luminaire size is an operating limitation.

Heat Problems and Ventilation. The prevention of heat destruction of slide material is always a major problem. Powerful luminous energy, reinforced by a reflector and compressed into a smaller space by condenser lenses, reaches the slide. An aklo-glass filter (mentioned earlier) can remove a portion of the destructive infrared heat energy. Yet there remains UV energy and visible energy to deal with. Early projectors used slides enclosed in transparent glass water jackets with associated pumps and hoses circulating cooled water on both sides of the slide (much like the radiator in an automobile). These projectors are not used today because of the bulk and added complexity of the water circulation equipment.

The ventilation problem is currently dealt with in two ways: (1) by using air circulation fans to keep a constantly moving column of free air flowing across the slide material to cool it and (2) by selecting and mounting slide material with the highest possible resistance to heat damage. Cooling fans can cause noise problems. To be effective, fans need to have the largest possible blades (a fan with large blades can operate at a much slower rotation speed, as compared to a fan with smaller blades, yet move the same amount of air). The fan must be securely mounted to minimize vibration noise. Part of the noise is caused by the blades agitating moving air and part by motor movement. I have used celotex (or any other acceptable sound-baffling material) surrounding a noisy fan to absorb and muffle unwanted noise. Specially designed fans and careful mounting are a design necessity. Some of the heat problem is eliminated if the slide itself is in motion (as with motion picture film strips passing through a projector, rotating glass cylinders, etc.). In any case, slide destruction by heat must be addressed by the lighting designer.

Slide Materials. Slides are often painted on glass. Pyrex heat-resistant glass is well worth its slightly higher cost, because it effectively eliminates cracks caused by heat. It is fairly inexpensive and easy to obtain. Two basic "corrections" must be made when using slides: *distortion correction* and *color correction*. If the slides are hand painted, distortion correction is accomplished easily (see Fig. 3.2). Several standard texts, listed in the footnotes, provide formulas for determining grid correction and also provide illustrated examples. The inks needed for glass slides should be heat-resistant. Painted slides usually withstand heat better than do photographically reproduced slides. Hand-painted slides are quite common in Europe. In the United States there are few artisans who paint tiny slide detail (miniature work) with ease; thus, photography correction is the easier method. Inks and dyes for slide preparation are readily available in 16 colors from Rosco Labs; Craft-Tint in Cleveland, Ohio (represented in most art stores); Deka-Lasur Co.

in Germany (the materials are imported by Kliegl Bros., New York City); Reprolon (the trade name of a product produced by Haussman Co. in Germany); or Venus Corp. (Flow Master Inks) in the United States. Inks are readily subject to creative scratching, rubbing, blotting, and washes in slide design preparation. Several specifics about distortion correction information for photographic slide material are listed below:

1. The designer should *always* use original photographic material that is at least as large as the final slide size. Enlargement of a 35-mm transparency to 7- by 7-inch slide size will not work because the amount of detail present in the original material is insufficient. Graininess will be the result. A dot or hair's width on the projection slide may be enlarged by projection so that it occupies a 6- or 7-foot space on the projection surface. Most of the work I have used for full background scenic projections was shot on 8- by 10-inch negatives under ideal conditions.

2. The camera used to photograph slide material must be in exact duplicate scaled position so that its lens is located where the full-sized projector objective lens will be in relation to the sketch or other slide material. It must be shaped, sized, and located where the projection surface will be. All distortion is thereby corrected.

3. It is most helpful to overlight the slide sketch material to be photographed. This allows the camera to be "stopped down" (placed on the lowest possible f stop) and also greatly increases the "depth of field" in focus. This is very important if the projection surface is curved or if it is not perpendicular to the axis of the projection. For *Carmen* I stopped the camera to f 64.

4. The designer (or photographer) should shoot several related "exposure times." After the pictures have been developed, the designer can pick the one most suited to the show's needs. A "thin" negative (pastels and tints) will allow more projected light through to the projection surface than a "thick" one (in terms of density of color pigmentation on the negative).

5. An attempt should be made to control color correction in both the photographing and developing processes. Color can even be helped by control exercised in the prep-

aration of the original artwork. For example, sky can be painted a paler blue than normal so that the blue area on the film will transmit more light. It is also possible to compensate slightly for depth of focus problems in the art preparation. A sketch that is being photographed is composed of paints and pigments, and its reflectivity is important, just as is the light source color output used for photographing. The designer must also carefully study the color output of the light source of the designated projector (HMI versus tungsten, for example) and the color reflectivity of the projection surface if the final projected image, *as viewed by the audience,* is to appear the same as the original artwork. It is important to remember that the process goes through several media which operate differently from one another. The image goes from paint-and-pigment-sketch, to photographic-negative illuminated by projector source, to reflected image from a projection surface. Once a designer has explained his or her objectives to almost any good photographic lab, in most cases the lab will willingly supply several photographic copies of the material to be developed. Each print will have slightly differing development balances. I have yet to find *any* competent color lab which is exorbitant in price once it discovers that its work will appear nightly before an audience of hundreds or thousands in 40- by 70-foot size and that the lab will receive proper program credit. It just isn't a "run of the mill" lab job! The designer should be extremely wary of having slide photography and preparation done by friends and acquaintances who "do" photography or by other amateurs. For any large-scale production work, it is wise to use experts who develop color film themselves rather than sending it away. Costs, per 8- by 10-inch print or negative (exclusive of original photography), will usually run from $30 to $50 *per slide.* Budget accordingly, and *do not turn to the unqualified* in an attempt to save money.

6. It is often helpful to build a model of the stage set to exact scale and make miniature duplicates of all "built" scenery which will appear in front of the projection area. The designer can make the miniatures out of black velour (or paint them black) and then move this black "scenery" into position in front of the art material to be photographed/projected, scene by scene. This will give a black

area on the negative where built scenery is to appear. There will be no "spill" or "leakage" of projected image where it should not be. This procedure was used for all slides for my production of *Carmen* (see Color Figs. 1, 2, and 3). At no time did any projection image appear on built scenery, yet extreme distortion projection angles were used throughout. This model method works!

Slide Preparation. Because heat deterioration is a problem, the mounting of photographic slides requires careful treatment. If the negative is to be mounted between two pieces of glass (a "sandwich"), some free space should be allowed between the two pieces of glass for the film stock to expand or contract. Normally such slides are bound with photographic slide tape only at the four corners, rather than all the way around the four sides. Two other solutions are possible; both are superior to the sandwich. Having slides prepared by Background Engineering, Inc. [729 North Seward Avenue, Hollywood, California 90038; telephone: (213) 465-4161] is one solution. This firm, in existence for many years, is the only one in the world (to my knowledge) which uses a secret process to dissolve the acetate film base chemically, floating the color pigmentation off onto heat-resistant Pyrex-glass. At a cost of around $50 to $75 per slide, the end result is a single piece of glass with the negative's color (but no film stock) deposited on it and chemically treated to be highly heat-resistant. The process, which takes several days, involves the chemical dissolving of the film stock in an absolutely vibration-free underground room, allowing the color pigment to "settle" on the glass. Background Engineering has long been a leading supplier of such slides to the cinematography world. With this type of slide, the column of air passing over the color pigmentation provides proper cooling. The prevention of deterioration is almost guaranteed. A second good solution, used only in Europe, hinges on the use of double-faced Scotch brand clear transparent tape in 7-inch wide rolls. The tape is applied to a *single* glass slide, the photographic negative is then pressed onto the adhesive surface of the tape, and bubbles are pressed out with a towel. Thus, only a single piece of slide glass is used, and the negative is exposed to free air movement on one side. Unfortunately, I have not been able to find a source of supply for this tape in the

7-inch width in the United States. (Note that none of these problems exists if you are using a moving film strip, a loop, or other traveling slide material.[50])

Slide Changers. The simplest slide changer is the standard two-slide carriage holder, operated by hand. However, with this system the operator can easily jar the projector, resulting in a huge, jiggling projection image. Carousel-type slide projectors come with straight and circular slide trays, usually holding 80 or more 35-mm transparencies per loading, and are remote-controlled. For larger slide sizes (also with remote control possible), two standard solutions are used. One solution is to have slides racked up in trays on one side of the projector that are automatically pushed into position and accumulated, after use, in an identical tray on the opposite side. A second solution is for slides to be mounted around the perimeter of a revolving disc and for the disc to move ahead one slide each time. This system limits the number of slides according to the overall size of the wheel. In any case, remote control is advisable, both because of the possibility of jarring the projector and the usual inaccessibility of the projector's location.

Dissolves, Wipes, Blackouts. Most projectors provide some remote means of controlling focus, slide change, and (frequently) dissolves between two or more projectors. In the case of powerful light sources (such as HMI lamps) which cannot be easily electrically dimmed, mechanical dimming is provided. The more sophisticated projectors also allow for precise positioning (by knobs) of the slide (rotation, etc.) in the aperture. These items and slide changers are discussed extensively in the great number of technically oriented texts and catalogs which are readily available (many such sources are cited in footnotes 41, 42, and 56).

Objective Lenses[51]

The final item in a projector lens train — the objective lens system — is both the most expensive and the most critical. *All* lenses create some distortion (keystoning, barrel-and-pincushion distortion, color aberration, etc.). A good objective lens system usually consists of several lenses affixed to each other, forming one composite lens. The combination of different types of lenses in the composite allows each lens design to contribute to overcoming distortion factors inherent in the other lens elements. Designing and delivering quality lenses for relatively narrow-angle projection work (for example, standard movie projectors and slide projectors) is relatively easy. The wide-angle spread which is demanded of a lens used in theatre is more difficult to design and fabricate. As a generally accepted rule of thumb, the best objective lenses will deliver *at most* a 1:1.6 ratio (18-inch-wide image at 1-foot throw distance), but some distortion is always inherent. Obviously, short-focal-length lenses are desired. Additionally, the lowest possible *f* rating (focal length divided by the lenses' diameter) is sought — preferably *f* 4.5 or less. See Bellman's two texts (*Scenography* and *Lighting the Stage,* footnote 56), for a fuller treatment. Most projectors used in television and cinematography projection work have a maximum spread of 1:.75 (9-inch spread at 1-foot throw distance). The lenses in these short-spread projectors are much easier to fabricate and less expensive. Short projection distances are much less common in film and TV studios. Some use has been made (by Ludwig Pani's firm in Austria, for example) of the *zoom* lens assembly on scenic projectors; however, overall, high light loss has discouraged experimentation with zooms for theatre projection use.

Figure 3.9 is a reproduction of the first page of the patent filed in the United States on February 19, 1950, by Paul Planer. Planer was the *P* of the famous early German projection firm, G.K.P. (Geyling, Kann, and Planer). For reasons unknown to me, the decision was made in Germany in the late 1940s to send Planer and several projectors to the United States. Dr. Joel E. Rubin and I became well-acquainted with Mr. Planer. We received much valuable projection information in the early 1950s prior to Mr. Planer's untimely death while undergoing surgery. Examples of his firm's work in Germany and his own projections in this country appear later in this chapter. Most quality wide-angle projection objective lenses obtainable in the United States, England, Germany, Austria, and Japan are based upon or are improvements of the G.K.P. objective lens train shown in Patent #2,586,436 (Fig. 3.9).[52]

Objective lenses can be either purchased or rented from

[50] *Andrea Tawil, "Designing Slides for Theatre and Concert Projection,"* Theatre Crafts, *vol. 16, no. 3 (Mar. 1982), pp. 23, 28–34. Illus.*

Merrill Lessley, "Photographic Techniques for Creating Projected Effects," Lighting Dimensions, *vol. 2, no. 10 (Oct. 1978), pp. 26–32. Illus. in color and with diagrams.*

Joseph N. Tawil, "Projections for Theatre and Television," Lighting Design & Application, *vol. 9, no. 3 (Mar. 1979), pp. 17–21. Highly useful, well-illustrated article on slide design and production.*

Kodak, "Cementing KODACHROME and EKTACHROME Transparencies to Glass." Publication E-34. Available from Eastman Kodak, Motion Picture and Education Markets Division, Rochester, N.Y. 14650.

Paul S. Hoffman, "Sharper Projected Images in T.V.," Lighting Dimensions, *vol. 2, no. 10 (Oct. 1978), pp. 19–21. Illus., color. Hoffman describes in detail his use of Color-Key, a photosensitive graphic arts product from 3-M, as slide material. Color-Key is available in 48 different transparent colors.*

Edward Kyvig, "Technique for the Elimination of Distortion from Projected Images in Stage Lighting," thesis, State University of Iowa, 1937.

Charles Lown, "Technical Method of Removing Distortion from Lens Projections," M.A. thesis, State University of Iowa, 1945.

Ronald Fedoruk, "The Caligula Slides, Predictable Distortion and Corrected Projections," Theatre Design & Technology, *vol. 24, no. 2 (Summer 1988), p. 23–25. Illus. Fedoruk is now a Canadian designer who early trained with Josef Svoboda. This article presents excellent material about distortion correction.*

M. Barrett Cleveland and Mark W. Shanda, "Low-Cost Transparencies For Large-Format Projectors," Theatre Design & Technology, *vol. 24, no. 4 (Winter 1988), pp. 39–40.*

[51] *Walter R. Klappert and Ira Domser, "Projected Scenery Using a Large Plastic, Fresnel Lens,"* Theatre Crafts, *vol. 12, no. 5 (Sept. 1978), pp. 52–53. Illus., Brief text description of how to achieve a wide-angle image most economically using readily available materials.*

[52] See also:

Fred Bentham, "Projecting Back Over Fifty Years," Cue, no. 32 (Nov./Dec. 1984), pp. 11–13. Illus. Reminiscences (with photos) by Bentham about early projected scenery, including reproduction of an Oct. 3, 1931 article in The London Illustrated News about G.K.P. projection.

photographic or theatrical supply houses. Normally rental firms need only know (1) the projection distance involved and (2) the desired image spread (size). As mentioned earlier, the expensive objective lens system is the most critical element in any projector.

Projection Surface or Screen

Designers ordinarily think of theatrical projected images as images that are directed toward a screen, projection sheet, or cyclorama, but such need not be the case. Alwin Nikolais is world renown as a choreographer partly as a result of his imaginative projection of patterns upon costumed dancers' bodies. Josef Svoboda long ago moved past the static, rectangular screen to mobile projection surfaces in a multiplicity of shapes hung at a whole range of angles. Perhaps more than any other scenographer, Svoboda has used projections as an essential basic design element. He exercises effective control over not only the slide material but also the surfaces upon which it is to appear. The rapid expansion of both the technology and the artistry of cinematography, television, and the newer fields of multimedia and multi-image production has freed projections from the bonds of a picture on a sheet behind the performers. Such Broadway designers as the late Ralph Alswang developed other innovations. The Living Screen was largely the work of Alswang. Rather than hanging a solid projection sheet, Alswang hung 6-inch- to 1-foot-wide vertical strips of projection material that pivoted at the top and bottom (much like a vertical venetian blind). These pivoting strips allowed the performers to move through the projection surface. The technique was particularly useful for ice shows. Film depicting skaters would be shown, then suddenly the live skater depicted in the film would burst through the film image. Strictly an effect, but highly theatrical. Theatre has moved past the day when the stage contained only a single projection surface. Svoboda often projects on tightly spaced rope structures, on balloons, and on built pieces of scenery — and each unconventional "screen" contributes to reinterpretation and redesign of the resultant projection image. The Makropoulos Affair was projected on many layers of free-form scrim hung freely in space.

Given this diversity of surfaces, several factors still need

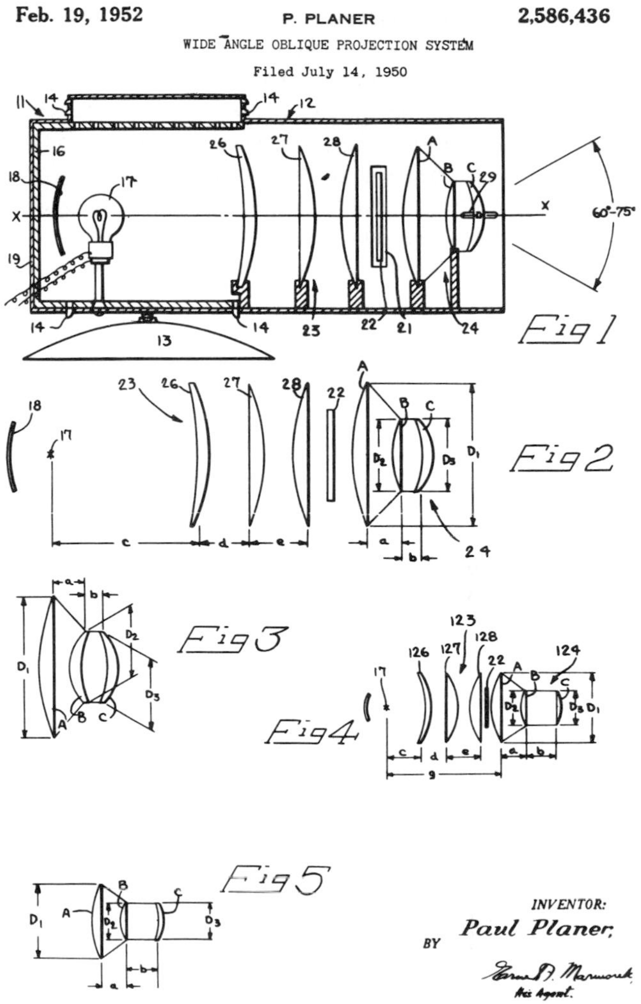

Figure 3.9 Planer patent.

to be considered: (1) the advantages and disadvantages of front projections versus rear projection, (2) the nature of and reflectivity (or transmission) of the screen surfaces available, and (3) projector location in relation to the projection surface and the performer.

Front versus Rear Projection. The experts divide almost evenly on this one, because each position has almost equal advantages and disadvantages. Table 3.1 lists some advantages and disadvantages of front projection.

Front projection is the *only* possible answer in most U.S. and British theatres because of limited backstage space. A front-projection surface has two basic requirements: (1) it should be as reflective as possible (preferably white), and (2) it should be a "firm" surface, free from wrinkles, bulges, tears, and other aberrations. A solid curved plaster sky dome is nearly ideal; however, very few exist in the United States. Front projection can be done from a theatre balcony front, a ceiling cove, the footlights, the first electric pipe ends, or the backstage side towers.

The advantages and disadvantages of rear-screen projection are shown in Table 3.2.

Rear projection offers many advantages. It is often ruled out because of lack of adequate backstage space or cost of rear-projection screens. I prefer rear projection but have had few opportunities to use it.[53]

Table 3.1 Advantages versus Disadvantages of Front Projection

Advantages	Disadvantages
Less backstage space is needed, so it is the only possible solution when stage depth is limited.	The scenic projector is more likely to be located in a less accessible place, making remote control necessary and making repairs, adjustments, slide changes, and servicing more difficult.
It does not require expensive, hard-to-obtain, specialized rear-projection surfaces.	The high reflectivity of the screen surface necessary creates many additional problems with ambient bounce light from the performers and other scenic elements.
	Distortion of the projected image (due to projector location) is more likely and may require more complex correction.
	The fact that a highly reflective projection surface is vital limits the scenographer's design choices: a bright "white sheet" *must* be worked into the design (while a darker, less obtrusive surface is possible in rear projection).
	Performers must be kept a good distance away from the projection surface to avoid unwanted shadows.

Table 3.2 Advantages versus Disadvantages of Rear-Screen Projection

Advantages	Disadvantages
The projection equipment is readily accessible.	Extensive backstage space is necessary.
Rear-screen projection is more efficient (needing less projector output or "power").	Specialized rear-screen projection surfaces are necessary; in-house substitutes are complicated to fabricate.
Performers can work much closer to the projection surface (as close as 18 inches away under ideal conditions).	
Distortion correction problems are minimized.	
Noise interference problems are reduced because the projectors are upstage, away from both the performers and the audience.	
Ambient light problems are reduced, both because the luminous projected image exists "in depth" in the thickness of the screen (and so is harder to "wipe out") and because lower front-surface-reflectivity screens can be used.	

[53] *Peter Edwards and Richard B. Glickman,* "Cyc Screen—A New Approach to Cyclorama for Television Stages," SMPTE Journal, *vol. 91, no. 1 (Jan. 1982), p. 61. Description of a new plastic film surface for cycs which can be used for either front or rear projection.*

Michael J. Hall, "Rear Projection, or Something to Look Forward To," Cue, *no. 6 (July/Aug. 1980), pp. 26–29. Illus., color. Excellent British article on rear-screen TV projection.*

Gerald Janesick, "Low-cost Rear Projection Screen: A Technical Production Casebook in Developing Three Surfaces on Visqueen," Theatre Crafts, *vol. 12, no. 3 (Mar/Apr. 1978), pp. 30–31, 50, 52–53. Illus. Excellent low-cost solution providing workable screen at the nonprofessional level.*

Stephen P. Hines, "Front-Projection Screens: Properties and Applications," SMPTE Journal, *vol. 95, no. 9 (Sept. 1986), pp. 903–11. Illus. Of primary use to those in film lighting.*

Richard Huggins, "Giant Rear Projection Screens, Big Screen for Small Bucks," Lighting Dimensions, *vol. 2, no. 4 (Apr. 1978), pp. 36–37. Illus. Description of how to use large sizes of transparent polyethylene film (readily available plastic) to create a low-cost rear-screen projection surface.*

John F. Dreyer, "Operational Characteristics of Rear Projection," SMPTE Journal, *vol. 68, no. 8 (Aug. 1959), pp. 521–24. Highly technical discussion of rear-screen projection.*

Armin J. Hill, "Analysis of Background Process Screens," SMPTE Journal, *vol. 66, no. 7 (July 1957), pp. 393–400. Illus. Excellent, highly technical analysis of projection screens for cinematography process work.*

"Something To Look Forward To: New Screen Materials," RoscoNews, *Spring 1985, p. 3. Illus.*

PROJECTION SCREEN SOURCES

Bodde Screen & Projector Co., 8829 Venice Blvd., Los Angeles, Calif.

D.O. Industries, East Rochester, N.Y. Manufacturers of Navilux screen.

Polacoat, Inc., 9750 Conklin Road, Cincinnati, Ohio 45242, (513) 791-1300. Manufacturers of Lenscreen. Screens made of both glass and acrylic materials.

OTHER PROJECTION MATERIALS SOURCES

Eastman Kodak, Rochester, N.Y. 14650.

Buhl Optical Co., 1009 Beech Avenue, Pittsburgh, Penn. 15233, (412) 321-0076.

[54] *Rosco Labs, 36 Bush Avenue, Port Chester, N.Y. 10573, (914) 937-1300. Manufacturers of Roscoscreen, sold by the yard for front or rear projection at low cost in black, white, clear, and grey. Maximum size: 100 feet by 120 feet.*

Trans-Lux Corp., 625 Madison Avenue, N.Y., N.Y. (212) 751-3110.

Gerriets International, R.R. 1, 950 Hutchinson Road, Allentown, N.J. 08501, (609) 758-9121. Inexpensive, custom-made German rear-projection screens.

[55] *Robert Segrin, "Scenic Projection on a Budget," Theatre Crafts, vol. 10, no. 3 (May/June 1976), pp. 12–13, 49–50. Illus. Solutions to the problem of finding and working with low-budget projection equipment.*

Andrea Tawil, "Projection — The New Popularity," Lighting Dimensions, vol. 2, no. 10 (Oct. 1978), pp. 24–25. Vivid color illustrations and good text about the use of projections in concert lighting.

George Lefteris, "Front Screen Projection — Good News," Lighting Dimensions, vol. 2, no. 10 (Oct. 1978), pp. 48–49, 51–54. Good text and excellent color illustrations concerning projected backgrounds in TV.

Davi Napoleon, "The Chelsea Theatre Center: Bringing Film, Video, and Projections to the Stage," Theatre Crafts, vol. 11, no. 5 (Oct. 1977), pp. 12–17, 47–48, 50–52, 54. Useful, well-illustrated article about the Chelsea Theatre production of Saul Levitt's play, Lincoln, with actor Fritz Weaver in 1976–1977. Lighting by William Mintzer.

Glenn Loney, "New Visions in Opera Design, Rudolph Heinrich in Retrospect," Theatre Crafts, vol. 10, no. 6 (Nov./Dec. 1976), pp. 12–17, 36–38, 40. Many illustrations and much useful information concerning Heinrich's use of projections in opera design.

Glenn Loney, "Romantic Realism and the Cosmic Gunther Schneider-Siemssen: Designs the Literal and the Symbolic," Theatre Crafts, vol. 12, no. 6 (Oct. 1978), pp. 28–33, 40–44, 46. Detailed description with many fine photos

There are other considerations. Commercially manufactured screens are fabricated from a wide range of plastics and in a multitude of sizes. They must be designed thin enough to allow a maximum amount of light to pass through from the rear projector, but dense enough to eliminate a "hot spot" in the center (the projector lens seen through the screen). It is difficult to create your own rear-projection screen. Nearly anything (a bed sheet, cyc, wallboard, etc.) can be used as a projection surface for front projection; such is not the case for rear screens.

There are many sources for rear screens.[54] Important in the selection of any rear screen is its *transmission factor.* Rear screens vary from transmitting 30 percent of the light projected on the rear side to a maximum of around 80 percent. Transmission factors are determined by (1) the substance of which the screen is composed, (2) the density of the screen, and (3) the color of the screen material. Rear-screen projectors are normally mounted in the center of the screen. If they are mounted at the base of the screen or on a pipe at the top, distortion correction becomes necessary.[55]

Ambient Light and Performer Visibility

A major problem in theatre use of projections will always be how to light the live performers without ambient light destroying a clear, bright, sharp projected image. Stages filled with live actors tend to be quite bright. Here are some solutions:

- The lighting designer should insist that the floor covering be quite dark. Absorbent black is ideal, but not always possible. The same applies to built scenery (particularly up to performer head height), which should be as dark as can be accepted by the scenographer. If the scenographer must have a white marble floor (or else his whole design "just won't work"), *the projections should be eliminated.*

- The lighting designer should make sure that the director understands the necessity of keeping performers an agreed-upon distance in front of the projection surface for front projection. This point may seem trivial, but I have known directors to insist — in the hectic throes of final rehearsal — upon bringing actors closer. The image is suddenly filled with human shadows and all theatrical illusion

and plausibility goes out the window! A lighting designer who is using rear projection should check with the scenographer about the possibility of hanging a black scrim in front of projection surfaces. This will markedly decrease ambient light spill on the front screen surface and add a tremendous sense of depth and spaciousness.

- The lighting designer should get the director and all other artists to accept the fact that the lighting will consist heavily of crosslighting, backlighting, and downlighting. Flat front "fill" (balcony rail or normal ceiling port coverage of areas) should be minimized or avoided completely. If the director seems inclined to insist upon a farce or comedy full-up, the designer should *eliminate the projections.* Sharply sculptural lighting must, of course, be suited to the production values being sought. Don't try to use projections for the wrong show: a full-up "pink and bastard amber" comedy!

- To avoid direct spill on the projection surface, all luminaires should be equipped with louvers, barn doors, funnels, or shutters in ellipsoidals. Lighting for projected images is much like designing lighting for an arena production. In arena, all ambient light should be prevented from spilling into the audience area surrounding the playing space. Arena lighting involves high-angle instrument mounting positions, as does lighting for projections. Careful preplanning must be given to instrument placement and focus coverage from the inception of planning through the light plot and in final execution.

- The lighting designer ought to strive for maximum *contrast* (black-and-white values as well as color contrasts) in the slide artwork. This contrast will be of help in dealing with ambient light. A slide with powerful, stark contrasts can project through even when too much undesired light begins to soften and grey it out.

Design Considerations

The range of available wide-angle projectors is very large. Detailed information concerning most available projection equipment can readily be located in Mark Lipschutz's two booklets.[56]

Some design examples from specific productions that are

of projections. Includes Schneider-Siemssen's work in opera.

Stephen Ford, "An Experiment in the Extension of the Opera Stage: Integration of Live Theatre and Film Techniques," Theatre Design & Technology, no. 7 (Dec. 1966), pp. 17–19. Illustrated article about Canadian use of projections for opera.

Mark Lipschutz, "Motion Interfusion, The Dynamic Structuring of Computer-Generated Images to Create Animated Scenery Projected in Space." A pamphlet published by Pennsylvania State University, University Park, Penn. 8 pages. No date. Mimeographed and illus. Discusses use of computer-generated multicell animation (abstract) for a production of Wagner's Ride of the Valkeries film. Cost and technical details included.

[56] *Mark Lipschutz, Selected 'Still' Projection Apparatus for Scenic and Effects Projection. N.Y.; USITT; 1973. 230 pages. An invaluable reference handbook: a slim volume with technical data, drawings, and photos of all projection equipment adaptable to theatre scenic projection in use in 1973.*

Mark Lipschutz, Supplement to Selected 'Still' Projection Apparatus. N.Y.; USITT; no date. A brief updating of Mark Lipschutz's earlier Penn State University study, published and distributed by USITT.

Mark Loeffler, "Product Report," Theatre Crafts, vol. 22, no. 7 (August/September 1988), pp. 86–87. Illus. A brief report about the newest Great American Scene Machine projector.

See also:

W. Joseph Stell, "Increasing the Density and Breadth of Theatrical Communication Through Projections," Theatre Design & Technology, vol. 19, no. 3 (Fall 1983), pp. 14–18. Illus. A useful article by Professor Stell which summarizes the history of theatrical uses of projections as a scenic device. Useful illustrations.

Ronald Chase, "Cinematic Approaches to Theatre," Theatre Crafts, vol. 17, no. 7 (Aug./Sept. 1983), pp. 32–35, 70–72, 74, 76. Illus. Excellent article by the foremost U.S. practitioner of film integration into scenic design. Good brief history of film use in theatre. Brilliant!

Thomas Wilfred, Projected Scenery, A Technical Manual. N.Y.; Drama Book Specialists; 1965. 60 pages. Spiral-bound handbook by one of the early masters. Wilfred devoted his life to projection, color music, and projection equipment. Contains also a glossary, a bibliography, and biographical notes about Wilfred.

Erwin M. Feher, The Art of Light in the Theatre. N.Y.; privately printed; 1970. The best history of projection. Mimeographed; 310 pages; 150 illus. Appended technical summary material on optics, distortion, lasers, and projection theory. Valuable.

Erwin M. Feher, Towards a Theatre of Light. Toronto; privately printed; no date. Another version by Feher of some of the same material but with much more technical information and drawings.

Erwin M. Feher, The History, Theory and Practice of Projections. A different title for Feher's The Art of Light. Also available from Feher are mimeographed lectures: Elements of Scenography; Projections; Light and Form. Illus.

Glenn Loney, "Caravaggio in College: Jo Mielziner Creates a Projection Spectacular," Theatre Design & Technology, no. 32, (Fall 1973), p. 25.

Josef Jelinek, Promitaci Technike Ve Scenograffi. Prague, Czechoslovakia; Scenograficky Ustav; 1968. Excellent illustrations, charts, and photos. Command of the Czech language is necessary for effective use of this fine study.

Edward F. Kook, Images in Light for the Living Theatre. N.Y.; Ford Foundation; 1963. 248 pages. Illus. Covers the basics plus a questionnaire submitted to leading working lighting designers about their use of projections. Followed by useful technical data summary and bibliography.

Eric Strange, "The Inverse Square Law," Sightline, vol. 14, no. 1 (Spring 1980), pp. 15–20. Illus. Excellent presentation of British practices.

Freddie Grimwood, "Projection a la Chinoise," Cue, no. 6 (July/Aug. 1980), pp. 4, 6–7. Illus. Color. Excellent, informative report on the Chinese projection of full backdrops from a short throw distance.

Bob Anderson, "CCT at 21," Cue, no. 43 (Sept./Oct. 1986), pp. 11–13. Illus. Details and photos about a range of British projection equipment.

INFORMATION ON PROJECTION DESIGN AND USE

Jarka Burian, The Scenography of Josef Svoboda. Middletown, Conn.; Wesleyan University Press; 1971. 200 pages. An excellent, invaluable study with top photographs and text of the work of the modern scenography master. Includes much of his use of projections in productions. Inspiring.

Jarka M. Burian, "A Scenographer's Work: Josef Svoboda's Designs, 1971–1975," Theatre Design & Technology, vol. 12, no. 2 (Summer 1976), pp. 11–34. A continuation and updating, with photos and drawings, of Burian's book.

Frederick Bentham, "Super Projection in the Garden at the Gate," TABS, vol. 29, no. 1 (Mar. 1971), pp. 16–21. Multiple color illustrations and text description of projections used for The Knot Garden at the Royal Opera House Covent Garden.

Frederick Bentham, "A Multi-Projector Complexity," TABS, vol. 31, no. 2 (June 1973), pp. 57–62. Description and photos in color of projections used for I and Albert at the Piccadilly Theatre in London.

B. Bear, "Project Seagul Chichester," TABS, vol. 31, no. 2 (Sept. 1973), pp. 115–18. Illus. Projections applied to a serious play production.

Joseph N. Tawil, "Staging with Light Patterns and Scenic Projectors," Lighting Design + Application, vol. 8, no. 1 (Jan. 1978), pp. 26–33. Color illus. Excellent basic summary of gobo and pattern information and use.

Gene E. Diskey and Mary B. Moore, "Image Amplification." A paper presented to the Illuminating Engineering Society Theatre, Television, and Film Lighting (IES TTFL) convention at Nashville, Tennessee, on Nov. 30, 1978. Reprints available from G. Emerson Diskey & Associates, Dallas, Texas. Excellent technical description of the use of electronic amplification (television) as used in commercial conventions, training sessions, and demonstrations.

Gerald Millerson, TV Lighting Methods. *N.Y.; Hasting House (Communications Arts Books, Media Manuals, Focal Press book); 1975, pp. 114–17. Brief but helpful in this field.*

PROJECTIONS CHAPTERS IN STANDARD WORKS

Richard Pilbrow, Stage Lighting. *London; Studio Vista (in United States: Drama Book Specialists, New York); revised edition 1979, pp. 170–171. Brief.*

W. Oren Parker and Harvey K. Smith, Scene Design and Stage Lighting. *N.Y.; Holt, Rinehart and Winston; 4th edition 1979. Chapter 18, pp. 468–493. Lengthy treatment, most useful for excellent illustrations of projection use in productions and of recent projection equipment.*

Willard F. Bellman, Scenography and Stage Technology, An Introduction. *N.Y.; Thomas Y. Crowell; 1977. Chapter 29, pp. 541–65. One of the best recent treatments of the whole range of projection information. Brief. Good text; excellent illustrations, drawings, and production photos.*

Willard F. Bellman, Lighting the Stage, Art and Practice. *N.Y.; Chandler; 2d edition, 1974. Appendix I, pp. 418–64. An earlier and more extended treatment by Professor Bellman with different text and photographs.*

Hunton D. Sellman, Essentials of Stage Lighting. *N.Y.; Appleton-Century-Crofts; 1972. Chapter 5, pp. 77–95. Brief, early treatment; illus.*

Frederick Bentham, The Art of Stage Lighting. *N.Y.; Theatre Arts Books; 2d edition, 1976. Chapter 12, pp. 275–309. Extensive, well-illustrated treatment of the entire range of projection and effects.*

Howard Bay, Stage Design. *N.Y.; Drama Book Specialists; 1974; pp. 141–42, op. cit. (see footnote 23d). Chatty, but well stated.*

Jill Dolan, *"Love of Light, Leni Schwendinger's Painterly Projections," Theatre Crafts, vol. 20, no. 2 (Feb. 1986), pp. 22–25, 52, 54–55. Illus., color. Schwendinger is a leading artist of slide design for dance. Very useful, colorfully illustrated article.*

THESES ON PROJECTION

Robert B. Payne, *"Projected Scenery: Its Design, Preparation and Technique," M.A. thesis, San Jose College, 1958.*

Curtis Jay Senie, *"Scenic Projection: Current Equipment and Practice in the U.S.," M.F.A. thesis, Yale, 1966.*

D. E. Butler, *"Projected Scenery," thesis, University of Washington, 1955.*

R. E. Kremptz, *"An Investigation of Current Trends in Light Projection," thesis, San Jose State University, 1967.*

Sidney Zanville Litwack, *"Study of Projection Scenery — History, Technology, Design," thesis, North Carolina University, 1954.*

John J. Moore, *"Projected Scenery — Static and Dynamic — Its Uses and Limitations," thesis, Syracuse University, 1952.*

[57] Willard Bellman, Lighting the Stage *p. 423, op. cit. (see footnote 56).*

[58] George R. Snell, *successor to Genarco. Manufacturers of advanced projection equipment: 155 Route 22, East, Springfield, N.J. 07081, (201) 467-2666.*

heavily dependent upon projections will be helpful at this point to tie together the information presented thus far. Jules Irving has said, "Projections are the closest thing you can put on stage to how you think." Willard Bellman, in *Stage Lighting*, writes: "As a space-changing device [projections] can define, divide, integrate, texture, and even expand or contract the virtual space of a production."[57]

Figure 3.10 shows early background projections for a production of *The Magic Flute* at the Royal Opera House, Stockholm, in 1947. Undoubtedly G.K.P. projection equipment with an arc source was used. Figure 3.11 is a rarity. This is a reproduction of a German hand-painted slide (with distortion correction) for the opera *Vasantasena*, first produced at the Burd Theatre in Vienna in the 1940s. At that time over 70 mid-European opera houses, mostly German, were equipped with identical G.K.P. projectors. Slides for scenic backgrounds were shipped from opera house to opera house just as today imported opera scenery is rented. Figure 3.12 shows the resultant projected image.

Contrast these early projection efforts against the projections in Figs. 3.13 and 3.14, which are from *Beatrix Cenci*, an opera commissioned for the opening of the John F. Kennedy Opera House in Washington, D.C., September 1971. Cinematography was supervised by Ronald Chase with Nananne Porcher serving as lighting designer. The problems of lighting the performer and the use of large-scale abstract images are apparent here.

Stage and film designer/director/producer Harry Horner engaged me to design lighting for the North American premiere of Benjamin Britten's opera, *Midsummer Night's Dream*, at the Queen Elizabeth Playhouse in Vancouver, Canada (August 1961). Horner directed and designed the revolving turntable sets and costumes and projection sketches. Color Figs. 4 and 5 are copies of two slides used. It is easy to visualize these two projections with scenery, costumes, and actors in front of them and under fluid stage lighting. These were but 2 of over 30 sets of slides used throughout the production.

In 1975 I designed lighting for the Philadelphia Opera's production of *Tosca*. George R. Snell[58] had just developed the North American version of a projector using the 1200-watt HMI lamp with a 3¼ by 4-inch slide. We decided to

Figure 3.10 *The Magic Flute* at the Royal Opera House, Stockholm, 1947. This is an early example of wide-angle background projection.

Figure 3.12 *Vasatasena,* an opera ultimately produced in over 70 European opera houses utilizing standard GKP wide-angle projectors with projected backgrounds from hand-painted slides.

Figure 3.11 Photograph of a 3½-inch by 4½-inch hand-painted glass slide with distortion correction in the slide, for *Vasantasena.* This slide was used with the standardized GKP projectors in 10 opera houses throughout Europe in the 1930s and 1940s. First performed at the Burd Theater, Vienna. (*Courtesy of Paul Planer.*)

Figure 3.13 *Beatrix Cenci* at the premiere of the John F. Kennedy Opera House, Washington, D.C. This commissioned opera was premiered in September of 1971. Cinematography: Ronald Chase; costumes: Theoni Aldredge; director: Gerald Freedman; lighting design: Nananne Porcher.

[59] *Jo Mielziner*, Designing for the Theatre. *N.Y.; Bramball House; 1965, p. 51.*

[59a] *Complete details on this Laser Vision Systems development (Broadway Chambers, 14–26 Hammersmith Broadway, London W6 7AF; telephone: 01-741-1921) is contained in the* ABTT News *issue from Mar./Apr. 1985 (p. 17).*

Figure 3.14 Another production photo of *Beatrix Cenci.*

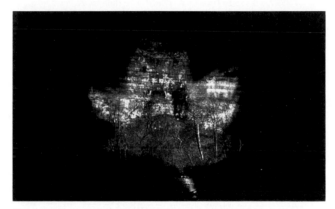

Figure 3.15 Projection of the Canadian national symbol (the maple leaf) on the gorge wall of the American Falls at Niagara during testing by lighting designer Nananne Porcher and engineer Clyde Nordheimer, 1979. (*Photo: Clyde Nordheimer.*)

enhance the rented sets from Tony Stivanello in New York City for *Tosca* by adding three "show curtain" projections on a scrim at the curtain line. To have had these show curtains dye-painted on scrim at a union shop would, at that time, have cost approximately $6,000 per drop for materials and painting — a total cost of $18,000. Using sketches prepared by Van Phillips and HMI projectors rented from Snell, I was able to project three powerful, full-proscenium pictures at a cost of $1,000 (a savings of $17,000). See Color

Fig. 6. The projectors were located in the motion picture projection booth at the rear of the Philadephia Academy of Music Theatre. The resulting images were so bright that there was no problem in achieving a standard "bleed" through the scrim (with lighting on the stage set and the cast brought up as the projectors were faded out). There are times when projections will save large sums in the scenic budget.

Figure 3.15 presents a most unusual example of projections used in commercial, rather than theatrical design. Nananne Porcher and Clyde Nordheimer of Jean Rosenthal Associates redesigned the lighting of Niagara Falls from 1978 to 1980. Part of their redesign involved the installation of a powerful scenic projector so that images could be projected upon the Gorge Wall of the American Falls, using the falling sheet of water as a screen. The illustration shown is a projection of the Canadian national symbol, the maple leaf, which was projected on the falls *on the American side* during the projection testing. Porcher and Nordheimer's American employers as well as local American newspapers did not find this choice of test projection amusing.

Projections can save production money, but they should be used only if they fit the show; if everyone connected with the production is willing to cooperate with the demands projections impose; and if the designer and technicians have absorbed the necessary know-how about projections, projectors, and their use. Jo Mielziner wrote in *Designing for the Theatre:*

> So much of the initial designing of these projected images [for *Death of a Salesman*] is guesswork. It is virtually impossible to determine by the design alone if enough chiaroscuro has been used, with extreme light values contrasted with extreme dark values, or if there is too much definition and detail. Trial and error is the only method when projections are used. But when they turn out well they are always worth the experimentation and trouble."[59]

The newest wrinkle in projections is the use in England of 5-watt laser light sources in a video projector. This newest technological development offers potential promise for even more successful use of light projections as a design element.[59a]

Lasers

The word *laser* derives from the longer term *light amplification by stimulated emission of radiation*. The term *laser* actually defines a very special type of light beam with its own unique properties. The beam is composed of coherent light, which means that it is of one color and wavelength, absolutely pure. Neon gas is used to produce a red laser beam; argon or krypton gas for blue and green. The radiant energy (light waves) of a laser are all of the same wavelength and in phase (synchronized) with each other. Helium gas is often mixed with the other gases in the plasma tube (the major expensive item, with a life expectancy of around two years) which is surrounded by a power supply (magnetic coil) that creates a magnetic field. High voltage passing through the gas-filled tube causes ionization and radiation of light. The influences of the powerful magnetic field causes this radiation to oscillate laterally from one end of the tube to the other. At each end of the tube are surface reflecting mirrors perfectly aligned with each other. One mirror is nearly 100 percent efficient in reflectivity; the other is a special mirror which allows radiation to pass through it at a certain threshold velocity. Internal oscillation continues to build the energy level of the radiation (both by bouncing it between mirrors and by the influence of the magnetic field) until the beam "breaks through" the front mirror at the desired threshold energy level.[60]

The laser light beam is unique. Unlike incoherent light (incandescent particles, which scatter and disperse), the laser beam is polarized (in phase and with particles lined up in planes). Consequently, a laser beam diverges (spreads) infinitesimally, remaining a highly concentrated beam of radiant energy of high amplitude and great power. The beam appears to be "grainy" (uneven). The observer does not see "light" in space from a laser unless smoke or dust or a surface from which it can reflect is present. So an observer never sees a laser beam — only reflected laser light. Since the "dot" of light (or beam) is ordinarily moved faster than the eye can assimilate the movement, an appearance of a continuous image (just as that seen on a TV screen) is the result. The grainy pattern moves as the beam moves, but it is actually filled with what Robert Bloom calls "black holes."[61]

[60] *"Lasers,"* Lighting Dimensions, *vol. 2, no. 2 (Feb. 1978), pp. 23–39, 52. Entire issue covers lasers and holography. Contains: "Laser Introduction," by Jason Sapan (p. 24); ". . . Laser," by Robert Bloom (p. 24); "Theatrical Use of Lasers," by Dick Sandhaus (p. 26); "The Practical Application of the Laser to Performance Lighting," by Alvin E. Alvis and Richard Hansen (p. 28); "Laser Safety in Entertainment," by Bruce Rogers and Gary Levenberg (p. 33); "Laserium," (p. 36); "The Beginners Guide to Laser Lighting," by Frank Lodge (p. 38); "Technical," (p. 40); and "Index to Laser Companies," (p. 52). Hard-to-locate issue, but invaluable. Illus. in color.*

Allen A. Boraiko (text) and Charles O'Rear (photos), *"The Laser: 'A Splendid Light' ",* National Geographic, *vol. 165, no. 3 (Mar. 1984), pp. 335–63. Illus., color. The best short summary that has appeared on the entire field of lasers and laser use. Well-written and lavishly illustrated.*

T. Kallard, Laser Art and Optical Transforms. *N.Y.; Optosonic Press (P.O. Box 883, Ansonia Station, N.Y. 10023); 1979. In readable, nontechnical English, this work covers: history, lasers, safety, modualtors, laser in theatre, optical transforms, and holography, and includes a bibliography. 170 pages, 242 photos, 143 drawings.*

T. Kallard, Exploring Laser Light. *Same publisher as work cited above. Earlier work.*

Bruce Rogers and Gary Levenberg, *"XY Scanning in Laser Entertainment,"* Lighting Dimensions, *vol. 2, no. 4 (Apr. 1978), pp. 21–22. Technical scanner and controller details. Illus., color.*

Laser. *The Laser Arts Society for Education and Research holds bimonthly meetings in San Francisco and publishes a quarterly newsletter. Contact: LASER, P.O. Box 42083, San Francisco, CA 94101, (415) 431-9581.*

Barnaby J. Fede, *"Market Challenges for Lasers,"* The New York Times, *April 28, 1982; p. 39, Finance section, Chicago edition.*

Richard F. Shepard, *"Laser Light Show in Park,"* The New York Times, *May 16, 1980, p. C19.*

Arthur Hill, *" 'Nonpractical' Laser Still Zooming,"* Houston Chronicle, *Dec. 6, 1967. Good early history of laser information.*

Richard Stevenson, *"Lasers in Lighting: Technical Demands vs. Creative Potential,"* Lighting Dimensions, *vol. 4, no. 3 (Mar. 1980), pp. 38–41. Illus.*

Annabel Hecht, *"FDA Trying to Shed Light on Dazzling Laser Shows,"* Chicago Tribune, *Dec. 30, 1978. Section 1, pp. 9–10.*

John Wolff, *"The Future Looks Bright for Lasers,"* ABTT News, *Mar. 1979, p. 10. From Stage and Television Today, Feb. 15, 1979.*

J. M. Peterson, *"Laser Art,"* Lighting Design & Application, *vol. 2, no. 3 (Mar. 1977), pp. 22, 25. A detailed description with photos of eight experiments the beginning laser artist can use to develop and expand knowledge of laser potential as an art medium.*

Rod Litherland, *"A Demonstration of Lasers,"* Society of Television Lighting Directors, *Spring 1986 (#31), pp. 21–22. Illus.*

"Monterrey's Rivers of Light," Lighting Dimensions, *vol. 10, no. 1 (Jan./Feb. 1986), pp. 22–25, 27. Illus., color. A lavishly illustrated article about Monterrey, Mexico's new Lighthouse of Commerce which nightly beams lasers to featured buildings in the city.*

Paul Goldberger, *"The Relationship of Light to Architecture — Lasers,"* Lighting Design + Application, *vol. 15, no. 9 (Sept. 1985), pp. 18–19. Illus., color. Illustrated examples of recent laser shows and theatrical usage.*

"Laser Performance for the Senzasai at Shiga Sacred Garden," Lighting Design + Application, *vol. 15, no. 10 (Oct. 1985), pp. 22–23. Illus., color. A laser show in a religious event in the orient — winner of an IES Edwin F. Guth Memorial Award of Excellence.*

"The Splitting Image: John Offord Explores the Multi-Direction of Laserpoint," Lighting + Sound International, *vol. 1, no. 6 (Apr. 1986), pp. 25–28. Illus., color. Excellent article covering the history of laser use and current involvement by England's oldest and best established laser firm. See also p. 44 for use of laser in the play* Time.

Andrew Kagen, *"La Serium: New Light on an Ancient Vision,"* Arts Magazine, *vol. 52, no. 2 (Mar, 1978), pp. 126–131. Illus. Excellent summary and illustrations.*

Bart Johnson, Laser Displays, Inc. Catalog. *Available from: Laser Displays, Inc., 755 Boylston Street, Boston, MA 02166, (617) 354-0567. 20 pages. $5.00. A catalog combined* with basic equipment and technique information. An evaluation of various manufacturer's equipment plus safety and legal aspects.

John Hillkirk, "The Laser," Lafayette Journal and Courier, *Living section D*, p. 1, Jan. 30, 1983. *Illus.*

Dr. Brian B. O'Brien, "Laser Theatre Technology," Lighting Dimensions, *vol. 4, no. 5 (May 1980), pp. 28–29, 31–32. Illus. Color.*

"'Lasers on the Dunes' Runs Through Labor Day," Lafayette Journal and Courier, *June 30, 1989, p. C1. Description of an outdoor live laser show in Michigan City, Indiana.* "Designers Forum," Disco Tech, *vol. 3, no. 3 (July 1987), pp. 6–7. Illus. A forum of lighting designers with extensive contribution by Dick Sandbaus, president of Science Faction Corp., a key laser firm.*

Mark Sutton-Vane, "Music and Light at the London Laserium," Society of Television Directors, *no. 36 (Summer 1988), pp. 35–38. Illus., color. Covers a British laser show and gives useful information concerning British laser safety regulations.*

Gavin Birkett, "Lasers For Television," Society of Television Lighting Directors, *no. 36 (Summer 1988), pp. 38–39. The only article this author is aware of concerning British laser safety regulations.*

"Laser Media Lighting the Future," L S & V Magazine *(Light, Sound & Video for the Nightclub and Entertainment Industries), vol. 1, no. 3 (March/April 1989), p. 16. Presents a profile of Ron Goldstein and his firm, Laser Media.*

Peter Cutchey, "Everything You Need to Know About Laser," Pro Light & Sound, *no. 3 (Summer 1987), pp. 35, 39–40. Illus. Includes* "Where to Find Low Cost Lasers." *Also: Dick Sandbaus,* "Lasers—Laying Down the Guidelines," *p. 44.*

Walter Gundy, "Introducing the World's Largest Laser Show: A Gold Medal Performance at Seoul '88," L S & V Magazine, *vol. 1, no. 2 (January/February 1989), pp. 45, 54.*

Stephan Harper, "The Class IIIa Entertainment Laser: Safety and Design Aspects of Low-Power Laser Projectors," L S & V Magazine, *vol. 1, no. 2 (January/February 1989), pp. 29, 46–47, 54, 60. Excellent basic article about lasers by the president of Summa Technologies, Inc., in California.*

Beth Howard, "Laser Days: Richard Sandbaus Collaborates With Juggler and High-Wire Artist in Grand Central Dances," Lighting Dimensions, *vol. 11, no. 7 (January/February 1988), pp. 38, 40–42. Illus., color. Laser expert Sandbaus devises a laser accompaniment for a modern dance.*

Ron Goldstein, "Laser Media: Lighting the Future," L S & V Magazine, *vol. 1, no. 3 (March/April 1989), p. 16. Illus. A description of the Laser Media Company by its chief executive officer. Laser Media was founded in 1974, now located in both Los Angeles and New York City. Includes a description of many of their larger designs for nightclubs, advertising, concerts, olympics, television, etc.*

"Lasers Over the Grand Coulee," Lighting Dimensions, *vol. 13, no. 4 (April 1989), p. 36. Grand Coulee Dam in Washington state is now the site of a nightly laser show.*

THE LASERIST, *a magazine published twice yearly by the International Laser Display Association. Contact: Barbara Inatsugu, 1126 Ashland Ave., Santa Monica, CA 90405. Tel:(213) 826-3838.*

"Short circuits," Lighting Dimensions, *vol. 13, no. 4 (May/June 1989), p. 28. Information about the permanent laser show as art at Miami's Bayfront Park, designed by Richard Sandbaus of Science Faction.*

INFORMATION ABOUT SPECIFIC PERFORMANCE USES

Mike Williams, "Filling the Space with Lasers—Laservision's Ron Alpert Transforms a Washington, D.C. Nightclub with Custom Special Effects," Lighting Dimensions, *vol. 10, no. 5 (Sept./Oct. 1986), pp. 34–35, 58, 60–61. Illus., color.*

Dick Sandbaus, "The Xenon File, The Design Challenge," Lighting Dimensions, *vol. 3, no. 2 (Feb. 1979), pp. 40–41, 43, 45. Illus., color. Detailed description of the design problems and solutions involved with a large-scale laser installation in the Xenon disco in New York City. Useful information about federal safety requirements, solutions to these problems, and costs.*

Dick Sandbaus, "For a Laser, All the World's a Stage," Lighting Dimensions, *vol. 5, no. 1 (Jan./Feb. 1981), pp. 36–37, 40–41. Illus. Color.*

Bruce Rogers, "The Star Wars Craze That Swept the Nation," Lighting Dimensions, *vol. 2, no. 7 (Sept. 1978), pp. 26–28. Detailed description with color photos of a laser/light show used in conjunction with several symphony orchestra performances.*

Arthur E. Alvis, Jr., "Laser Projections for Performance Lighting," Theatre Crafts, *vol. 12, no. 7 (Nov./Dec. 1978), pp. 44–47, 51–52, 54–57. Illus. (photos and drawings). Useful information about various inexpensive scanner/control systems used in actual productions.*

Dick Sandbaus, "Creating Light Sculpture: Lasers in Three Dimensions," Lighting Dimensions, *vol. 3, no. 9, (Sept. 1979), pp. 20–21. Illus. Color.*

Terry Helbing, "The Use of Lasers in The Damnation of Faust," Theatre Design & Technology, *vol. 14, no. 3 (Fall 1978), pp. 15–16. A detailed description of uses of lasers in Sarah Caldwell's Boston Opera production of* Faust *in March 1978 and problems encountered by David Infante (the laser designer and founder-president of Laser-Physics, Ltd., New York, New York).*

Jennifer Morris, "Laser Graphics," Lighting Dimensions, *vol. 3, no. 10 (Oct. 1979), pp. 24–26. Illus., color.*

"Interview: Motoko Ishii," International Lighting Review, *1985/1; front cover and p. 18. Illus., color. Use of lasers at Japan's Tsukuba Expo '85.*

LASER SAFETY INFORMATION SOURCES

Director, Division of Compliance, Bureau of Radiological Health (BRH), 12720 Twinbrook Parkway, Rockville, MD 20852. Telephone: *(301) 443-4874. Prime federal government agency enforcing laser safety standards and regulations. Information available. Ask for* "Laser Light Show Safety Criteria," *by L. Dale Smith and Jerome E. Dennis;* "Philosophy and Overview of the Federal Laser Products Performance Standard," *by Joanne B. Long; and* "Enforcement Policy for Certain Laser Light Shows, Displays, and/or Devices," *by John C. Villforth.*

"Seeing the Light with Music," Lighting Design + Application, *vol. 10, no. 5 (May 1980), pp. 24–28. Illus., color. Lengthy treatment of Laserium.*

Laser intensity is maintained over long distances. This highly concentrated beam is of such high energy and velocity that, in sufficient power, it can be used to burn through steel plate, be used for delicate eye surgery, be beamed to the moon and reflected back to earth, or be used as a vehicle for communications. Such a tremendous quantity of organized, coherent light energy is concentrated into one narrow beam that exposure to any but the weakest laser beams can instantly cause blindness or permanent eye damage, light a cigarette, start a fire, or burn human skin. More powerful lasers exceed in destructive power the blinding output of the sun. Laser safety precautions are discussed at length later in this chapter. Both the federal government and many states have passed laws and established policing agencies to help avoid lethal danger to laser operators or audiences when lasers are used where the uninformed or careless might be present. At this moment the U.S. government has the legal right to impose fines of up to $300,000 and to issue court cease and desist orders when lasers are improperly used.

The Bureau of Radiological Health (BRH) classifies lasers as follows:

- *Class I:* Low-power lasers that are harmless and produce no biological damage. These are the type that can be used in the limited number of "home" laser units.
- *Class II:* Lasers of up to 1-milliwatt (one one-thousandth of a watt) in power. These are the lasers used in the entertainment field. Careful controls are advisable. This class of lasers can produce eye damage after prolonged exposure.
- *Class III:* Lasers of up to ½ of a watt in power. These lasers are dangerous and constitute the upper power limit usually permissible in the entertainment field. They can damage human tissue from a direct, short exposure.
- *Class IV:* Lasers of more than ½ of a watt in power. Lasers in this class are extremely hazardous and can cause tissue damage by diffuse reflection, as well as by direct exposure. These lasers are not permitted in any entertainment usage. *A 1-watt laser exceeds the brightness of the sun.* Normally Class IV lasers are used only in scientific and industrial applications, under very strict controls.

So far we have been discussing only the raw laser beam of light as it emerges from the plasma tube. However, this beam can be modified in an almost limitless manner. Under certain conditions it can be expanded or dispersed with lenses. The beam of light can be shaped, formed, moved, and agitated by the use of controlled mirrors and prisms. (While a laser beam – generating unit is itself costly, it is the additional equipment to modify and control the *use* of a laser beam which complicates and quickly raises the expense of the process.) Three elements of a laser beam can be modified: (1) the *wavelength,* or *color* (all colors visible to the human eye can be produced by control modifiers);[62] (2) the *mode* (that is, the shape of the beam and its light distribution are modifiable); and (3) the *modulation,* or variation in intensity. Using these three modifiable variables — color, shape, and intensity — the designer creates with lasers.

History[63]

The origin of lasers is still in dispute. Much like Sir Joseph Swan and Thomas Edison in the field of electricity, more than one genius was pursuing the workable technology of lasers (as of then unnamed) at the same time. Patent suits and court battles are still in progress.

In 1951, Dr. Charles H. Townes, then a staff research physicist at Columbia University in New York City, developed a concept about something he called "masers." By 1957, R. Gordon Gould, another physicist, was also doing research on solid-state lasers, at the Columbia University Radiation Laboratory while working toward a Ph.D. Meanwhile, Dr. Townes had been joined in his research at home by his brother-in-law, physicist Dr. Arthur L. Schawlow, then with the Bell Telephone Labs, Inc. (Dr. Schawlow now teaches at the Stanford University Physics Department.) During 1957 both groups were at work. On November 13, 1957, Gould recorded in a notebook — which he promptly had notarized — his calculations. These involved the first known use of the word *laser* and the first written description. At about the same time Dr. Townes and Dr. Schawlow filed for patent rights on "masers." The ensuing court disputes, minus quite involved technical interpretations of the law, will be highlighted here as the subsequent history is related.

"Laser and Holographic Directory," Lighting Dimensions, *vol. 3, no. 9 (Sept. 1979), pp. 23, 25, 28. Invaluable list of laser and holograph firms with addresses and description of firm's products.*

State of New York, Department of Labor, Division of Safety and Health, Radiological Health Unit, 69th Floor, Two World Trade Center, New York City, 10047. Similar agency for New York state. New York has its own laws and regulations.

Laser Institute of America, P.O. Box 1744, Waco, Texas 76703. Telephone: (817) 772-9782. Laser safety courses.

LASER SAFETY ARTICLES

Laser Institute of America, Laser Safety Guide. *Available from Laser Institute of America (see above).* $2.50.

ANSI, American National Standard for Safe Use of Lasers. *Available from: American National Standards Institute, 1430 Broadway, N.Y., N.Y. 10018.* $10.00.

Robert M. Weiner, "Laser Safety Update," a publication of Weiner Assoc., 544 23rd St., Manhattan Beach, CA 90266. Telephone: (213) 545-1190. A copyrighted publication by one of the larger laser safety consultation firms. 1979. Also summarized in Lighting Dimensions, *vol. 3, no. 9 (Sept. 1979), pp. 43–44.*

R. James Rockwell, Jr., Radiant Resources Newsletter, *published quarterly (since Fall 1979) by Rockwell Association, Inc., P.O. Box 43018, Cincinnati, Ohio 45242. Telephone: (513) 217-1568. Another key laser safety consultation firm.*

Dick Sandhaus, "Laser Regulations: This Time It's For Real," Lighting Dimensions, *vol. 2 no. 3 (Mar. 1978), pp. 21, 44. Useful summary and layman's explanation of safety situation.*

Arnie Ehrlich, "Laser Zap Bum Rap," Lighting Dimensions, *vol. 2, no. 6 (July/Aug. 1978), p. 13. Brief review of laser safety by a spokesman for IALHAS (International Association of Laser and Holographic Arts & Sciences).*

ACGHI, ACGHI's Guide for Control of Laser Hazards. *Published by the American Conference of Government Industrial Hygienists, P.O. Box 1937, Cincinnati, Ohio 45201.* $3.25. *The basic reference source upon which most existing legislation is based.*

DIRECTORIES OF MANUFACTURERS, MODELS, SPECIFICATIONS, AND PRICES

Optical Industry and Systems Directory, *published each September by the Optical Publishing Co., P.O. Box 1146, Pittsfield, MA 01201.*

The Laser Focus Buyer's Guide, *published each January by Advanced Technology Publishers, 385 Elliott St., Newton, MA 02164.*

MAGAZINES

New Renaissance, *published monthly at 5267 Eleventh Avenue, Seattle, WA 98105. $25 per year.*

NEW DISCOVERIES

Charles Ih, "Laser Process May Keep Color Film Fadeproof," Lighting Dimensions, vol. 2, no. 6 (July/Aug. 1978), p. 13. Description of a new process by Dr. Ih (University of Delaware) which translates color motion picture film into preservable black-and-white laser-hologram images for accurate reconstitution.

[61] *Robert Bloom, "Lasers!", p. 24, op. cit. (see footnote 60).*

[62] *Laser Displays, Inc., produces laser beams in an advertised 256 colors.*

[63] *The author drew much factual information from "Laser Patent Upsets the Industry," Lighting Dimensions, vol. 2, no. 2 (Feb. 1978), pp. 40–41.*

[64] *William J. Broad, "New Laser Offers Great Power and Flexibility," The New York Times, Aug. 19, 1986, Chicago edition, p. 21. Illus.*

The year 1960 brought the first public display of lasers. In 1964 Dr. Townes received the Nobel Prize in physics for his early laser work. By the early 1970s lasers were being used by such rock groups as *Led Zeppelin, The Who,* and *The Electric Light Orchestra* (see the reference for John Wolff's article cited in footnote 60). John Wolff, England's foremost authority on lasers used in the entertainment field, first used lasers for *The Who.* Laser displays were appearing in museum displays. Movies, many the work of laser specialist Chris Outwater, used lasers: *Logan's Run, Lipstick,* and *Demon Seed,* for example (*Star Wars* was to come later). During 1971 the first of a series of court patent disputes between Townes and Gould was settled in Townes's favor. In 1973 there was a nationally publicized laser art exhibit by Rockne Krebs at the Walker Art Center in Minneapolis. Bart Johnson designed the laser equipment employed. The year 1973 also brought a second court decision, this time giving Gould patent rights to the basic laser amplifier.

In November 1973, Ivan Dryer, film expert, opened the first *Laserium* show at the Griffith Observatory in Los Angeles. This was followed by duplicate *Laserium* (and later *Laserock*) shows in many cities in the United States, Canada, Britain, and Japan. By the mid-1970s lasers had begun to appear in discos. Also in 1973, the Federal Drug Administration (FDA) conducted its first survey of laser activity in the entertainment industry. This led to the initial FDA laser safety standards of August 1976.

Arthur E. Alvis, Jr., while a graduate student at the University of Missouri, Columbia, purchased and began experimenting with inexpensive lasers in 1977. That year lasers were used for the show *Hell Fire* (just lasers, sound and light) and also for a production of *Biedermann and the Firebug* and for *Hell Fire II* (lasers, mime, sound, and light). Descriptions of this early theatrical use of lasers appear in some detail in an article by Alvis. By 1978 Sarah Caldwell was using laser expert David Infante for a production of the opera *Faust* in Boston. Discos were turning increasingly to lasers, and concert shows continued their growth. (Refer to footnote 60 for more information about these projects and designers.)

"Free electron" lasers, which are much more efficient than other lasers and offer new use possibilities, are cur-

rently being developed, promising great strides forward.[64]

In 1982, the laser industry had a $120 million market. By 1990, the industry is expected to generate $970 million annually (see *Fede* reference in footnote 60).

Uses

Lasers have been used in an amazing range of applications. They are used to "read" coded product labels at supermarket checkouts; for metal cutting, welding, drilling, and machining; for pollution detection; as the vehicle for transmitting words and pictures in the communication industry; in tailoring, to cut fabric in quantity from patterns; in a wide range of surgical operations and as a delicate cutting tool; for fingerprint identification; in a whole group of measuring surveying situations; to measure the distance to the moon or for minute cell measurement; and in the production of holograms (three-dimensional projections in space). The world of entertainment has seen lasers used in *Laserium,* lasers used as displays for advertising and in amusement parks, lasers used in film creation, lasers used in mime and trade shows and multimedia shows, laser shows in discos and for rock group concerts, and lasers as part of sound-and-light shows and in plays and operas. The potential seems to be nearly limitless. In May of 1980 the New York City Parks Department presented a laser light show in Central Park.

Laser designs as pure "art" have also come into their own. In October 1984 the Italian firm Krypton presented *Eneide* (at the La Mama Theatre), a laser/computer interpretation of Virgil's *Aeneid.* Color Fig. 7 shows lasers designed and installed by Science Faction Corp. in use in discos. Color Fig. 8 is an abstract laser composition designed and produced by Richard V. Werth of Spectrolaze, Inc., Los Angeles. Recent citywide celebrations utilizing lasers include celebrations in Calgary, Canada (during the 1987 Winter Olympics); Stone Mountain, Georgia; and Houston, Texas. Lasers were also used in the ground-breaking ceremony for the Tower City Center in Cleveland.

Safety

Lasers can be highly dangerous, not only to an uninformed

or careless operator but also to any audience member exposed to uncontrolled laser beams over 1 milliwatt in power. State governments have passed laws to protect citizens from burns, death, or permanent loss of vision, and in August 1976 the Division of Compliance, Bureau of Radiological Health of the Food and Drug Administration, Public Health and Service, U.S. Department of Health and Welfare was charged with formulation and enforcement of federal regulations. These regulations are quite complex.[65] They are subject to modification as the technology and understanding of lasers advances. The only safe approach is this: *No one should use lasers above 1 milliwatt in power anywhere before having mastered current safety literature.* An extensive list of this literature is offered in footnote 60. As a specific guide to laser use in the entertainment industry, Rogers and Levenberg offer the laser user/designer these imperatives:[66]

1. Keep direct laser light out of the audience.
2. Ensure that a trained operator is always present.
3. Remove or cover specular surfaces in the performance area.
4. Completely enclose the laser system.
5. Do all alignment without an audience.
6. Alert show security and other personnel to laser hazards.
7. Don't use more power than is required.

Lasers are *not* a theatrical toy. At their worst lasers can approach the fabled "death ray" in permanent destructiveness.

Cost

Lasers are expensive. The simplest low-power unit for home experimentation from Spectra-Physics costs $500 to $1000 (1980). A 2-watt laser costs around $10,000 with an additional $2,000 needed for supplemental mirrors, prisms, and controls. A 3.5 millihertz (mHz) laser is listed by Metrologic for around $500. The range of prices currently quoted by Laser Displays Inc. is provided below:

Purchase:
    $1,600 to $72,000 for projector *only*
    $8,500 to $18,000 for an image synthesizer
    $14,000 to $17,000 each for image programmers
    $16,500 for computer animation

Rental:
    $150 per hour for studio programming
    $500 per day rental for a 10 milliwatt neon laser
    $1,100 per day for a 250 milliwatt argon laser

Science-Faction Corp. quotes a base price of $7,000 and up for a small laser and accessories suitable for home use. Clearly the expenses involved eliminate most interested amateurs. Also, laser equipment is quite fragile.

None of this information is meant to discourage the use of lasers by lighting designers. Laser applications increase daily. However, before lighting designers apply lasers in their own work, they must *know what they are doing with lasers and know the cost, effort, and danger involved.*

Fiber Optics[67]

The lighting designer is not yet equipped technologically to snake a garden-hose-like bundle of fiber optics around corners to wherever they are needed in the set and spray a desired area with a directed wash of light; however, that day may not be far off. What is possible with fiber optics, one of newest miracles of modern science, has but limited application to lighting design at this moment. (Much the same could have been said of lasers, holograms, the computer, and the transistor but a short time ago.)

A century ago Alexander Graham Bell invented what he called a "photophone," which used sunlight to transmit messages. He wrote: "I have heard a ray of sun laugh and cough and sing." The photophone did not catch on because it was bulky and unreliable. Many years later, however, in 1966, Charles Kao, vice president and chief scientist for International Telephone and Telegraph, proposed research to transmit message-bearing beams of light in glass fibers. The 1960 advent of the laser had made this feasible. By 1970 Corning Glass had developed a glass fiber of sufficient quality to carry light short distances without amplification. (It is interesting to note that in the late 1950s optical engineers and doctors developed the endoscope, which makes use of fiber optics to peer deep inside human bodies.)

[65] *Similar standards were published in England by the Health and Safety Executive in December 1980 (Guidance Note PM19).*

[66] *Rogers and Levenberg, p. 35, op. cit. (see footnote 60).*

[67] *See: Richard Pilbrow, "Fiber Optics in the Theatre,"* Sightline, *vol. 13, no. 2 (Autumn 1980), pp. 104–107. Illus. Very detailed description. Best information available at this time.*

Charles K. Kao, Optical Fiber Systems: Technology Design, and Applications. *N.Y.; McGraw-Hill; 1982. Illus., 205 pages. The basic book for laymen. Invaluable.*

Allen A. Boraiko, "Fiber Optics, Harnessing Light by a Thread," National Geographic, *vol. 156, no. 4 (Oct. 1979), pp. 516–35. Lengthy, definitive article about fiber optics. Filled with excellent color illustrations and readable, informative text.*

"Stars for Stars," Lighting + Sound International, *vol. 1, no. 10 (Sept./Oct. 1986), p. 10. An informative article about the Upstart Fibre Optic Company (Plymouth, England) and the first use of a fiber optics star cloth in television. Contains both technical information and pertinent history of fiber optics use in theatre, concert lighting, and television.*

Bentley Miller, "A History of the Development of Light Sources — Part II," Broadcast + Technology, *vol. 12, no. 3 (Jan. 1987), p. 34. Technical explanation and history of the use of fiber optics to light the interior of an automobile during a night scene in CBC television.*

Paul Chapple, "Peter Pan and the Fibre Optic Stars," Lighting + Sound International, *vol. 1, no. 4 (Feb. 1986), pp. 17–19, 21. Illus., color. Several useful articles concerning fiber optics production and use in the production of* Peter Pan *by British firms Eurotec Optical Fibres, Ltd., Par Opti, and Litework. The* Peter Pan *production was at the Plymouth Theatre Royal.*

Barry Gregson, "Starlight Magic," Cue, *no. 44 (Nov./Dec. 1986), pp. 9–10. More about the use of fiber optics supplied by Eurotec Optical Fibres of Doncaster.*

Michael Cahana, "Fiber Optics; From Lighting Around the Corners to Communications Around the World," Lighting Dimensions, *vol.*

11, no. 2 (Mar./Apr. 1987), pp. 128, 130–131. Useful summary of current use of fiber optics in nightclubs, Starlight Express *musical, world's fairs, and display and billboards.*

S. Newton Hockey, *"Piping Light into High Atria,"* Lighting Design + Application, *vol. 14, no. 7 (July 1984), pp. 15–16. Illus., color. Describes the newest variation of fiber optics: "light pipes" in the Insurance Corp. of British Columbia, Vancouver.*

Robert Kearns, *"Fiber Optics Is a Bright Light in Technology,"* Chicago Tribune, *May 8, 1982; section 5, p. 11. Illus.*

David Hodges, *"Ahead with Fiber Optics: Applications from Video Transmission to Heart Surgery,"* Video Systems, *vol. 8, no. 6 (June 1982), pp. 24–27. Illus., color. Good basic summary.*

Andrew Pollack, *" 'Lightwave Era' Is Ushered In,"* The New York Times, *Business section, p. 29, Feb. 11, 1983. Illus. Basic progress report.*

Stephen Mallery, *"Catching Some Rays: New Device Delivers Filtered Sunlight Indoors,"* Architectural Lighting, *vol. 1, no. 9 (Oct. 1987), pp. 27–30. Illus., color. Coverage of a Tokyo skyscraper with extensive internal lighting using natural light and fiber optics.*

[68] Boraiko, p. 523, op. cit. (see footnote 60).

[69] *Taped telephone interview by Lee Watson with David Hersey in London for* Lighting Dimensions, *Jan. 30, 1983.*

[70] *LTM Corp. of America, 1160 North Las Palmas Ave., Hollywood, CA 90038, (213) 460-6166; or LTM France, 104 Boulevard Saint-Denis, 92400 Courbevoie, France. Telephone: 788-44-50.*

[71] *In England contact Fiber Optics Designs, Ltd., Torbay Works, Hunslet Rd., Leeds LS10 1AT. Telephone: 0532-436220.*

FOCI, Fiber Optics Concepts International, Inc., 10016 Pioneer Blvd., Suite 103 & 104, Santa Fe Springs, CA 90670, (213) 942-7207 and 942-2624.

Quicer Industries, Fiber Optic Signs, P.O. Box 16361, Long Beach, CA 90806, (213) 427-2842.

The principle of fiber optics is simple: A beam of light confined within a very tiny thread of purest glass travels the length of the thread. Bounced off the walls (because of total internal reflection), the beam emerges at the other end of the thread with little loss of strength. One technical hangup has been the ability to produce flaw-free glass threads smaller in diameter than human hair. This technological feat is now possible. Through the *encoding* of light impulses (using computer-encoded digital language), amazing communications possibilities are opened up.

Fiber optics are used

- To expand medical diagnosis. Tiny bundles of optic fibers can be inserted in accessible parts of the body for diagnostic examination.
- To perform other analyses. The same basic process used in medicine (via the endoscope) is used to look inside nuclear reactors, engines, tanks, etc. Fiber optics strands are used to monitor auto brake and backup lights, as well as headlights.
- To carry light to otherwise unreachable places. This includes inside the body; saving space in autos by piping light from one source to several instrument displays. Fiber optics is excellent for underwater applications — it illuminates without the possibility of electrical "shorts."
- In night-vision goggles for after-dark flights and for fire detection.
- In traffic signs. Fiber optics bundles can be brighter than traditional neon and incandescent sources and use less energy.
- In communications. A pair of fibers which are only 39 millionths of an inch in diameter can carry 10,000 simultaneous conversations.

Another major technological hangup was the lack of tiny light sources (smaller than a period on this page). Then semiconductor lasers and light-emitting diodes (used to light up pocket calculators) were developed. Some of these miniature light sources can be pulsed a billion times each second. Laser authority Allen Boraiko (see footnote 67) writes: "Theoretically, one light beam could accommodate every telephone message, radio broadcast, and television program in North America simultaneously. In a tenth of a second, it could flash every word in a thirty-volume *Encyclopedia Britannica.*" [68]

Optical fibers which carry light rather than electrical signals do not pick up "cross talk" and are unaffected by lighting and short circuits; also, they cannot readily be tapped or jammed. However, both infrared and ultraviolet light causes fiber optics to age and deteriorate.

It is now possible to produce fibers in continuous six-mile lengths, and lengths can be fused to each other. With such amazing potential, fiber optics technology is finding widespread application around the world. With increased application and continuing research, fiber production costs are coming down.

To date, fiber optics bundles have only been used as a decorative novelty in theatrical productions — for twinkling stars, fireworks effects, burning flames, and flowing liquids (lava). The total development and recent rapid increase in technology make this a promising area for adaptation to the lighting designer's needs for increased flexibility in power and light transmission. Fiber optics has been utilized by Richard Pilbrow as a backdrop for the ill-fated musical *Swing* (sets by Robin Wagner), which closed in Washington, D.C. (see Color Fig. 9); by Pilbrow again for a fireworks effect on a backdrop in *Joking Apart;* by Allen Ayckbourn in London at the Globe Theatre during the summer of 1979 with photoflash lamps behind the fiber optics bundles; for Pilbrow's production of *Oklahoma!* at the Palace Theatre in London as a "star cloth"; and on Broadway by Tharon Musser in *Dreamgirls,* by David Hersey in *Cats,*[69] and by Hersey in *Starlight Express.* As early as February 16 to 19, 1964, fiber optics were used in a primitive form for the modern dance, *Fantastic Gardens,* by the Judson Dance Theatre at the Judson Memorial Church in Greenwich Village in New York City.

In 1982, LTM Corporation[70] began public marketing of fiber optics lighting instruments for use in motion pictures, videotapes, and live theatre. Its system consists of a daylight color temperature HTI Osram, 250-watt light source (average life is 250 hours) in a "light box" with ballast (30-second warm-up time), with 2½-foot or 8-foot fiber optics cables; also available are accessories which convert the light output to Fresnel-type light, controllable by barn doors.[71] TIR Systems, Ltd., has come out with its Light Pipe, a variation on fiber optics reflectivity usable in both entertainment and architectural lighting.[72]

I call the interested reader's attention to a definitive 95-page terminal project, "Utilization of Fiber Optics in Theatrical Lighting," by James A. deVeer, completed at Purdue University in May 1984. It covers fiber optics at a length not possible here. Not only does this study summarize existing printed information about fiber optics, but it also reports on extensive experimentation deVeer conducted. Further, deVeer analyzes the advantages and, as yet, unsolved problems in the widespread use of fiber optics as a light conductor in theatrical situations.

Holograms and Holography

"Holography is the most under-used, least understood communications tool to come out of the scientist's laboratory in the past 30 years."[73] Thus did Larry Goldberg, marketing manager of Holex Corp., summarize the mystery involved in this new image projection technique.

What Is Holography?

Some distinctions are in order first: *holograms* are the actual pieces of film upon which has been recorded pertinent information about light waves; from these holograms, *holographic projections,* or images, can be produced. A holographic image *seems to be* a three-dimensional object, frequently existing in free space. It can be viewed from various angles (viewpoints) or walked around. The viewer sees the object in the image from constantly shifting viewpoints, just as if it *were* an actual three-dimensional object. Yet a holographic image exists in free space and is a visual *image,* nothing more. A holographic image is created by a complicated scientific/optical process in such a manner that the human mind visually recreates and accepts the accurately reproduced light-and-shade image as a three-dimensional object.

The technical process by which this grand illusion is achieved is beyond the proper scope of this *Handbook.* Holographic images are not created by amateurs, and up to this time the materials and expertise involved have made holographic image production in any usable size quite expensive. The necessary technical information is, however, readily available (consult sources listed in footnote 74).

There are many readily understood aspects of holography with which the lighting designer should be familiar. These aspects include types of holograms and holographic images, current applications of holograms, basic problems of the medium which hamper more widespread application, costs involved, and future potentials of the technique. Each will be covered in the paragraphs that follow.

Types of Holograms and Holographic Images

Holograms and holographic images can be classified in two different ways: (1) according to the way they are produced or created, and (2) according to the way they are used or viewed. Let's take production first. Larry Goldberg provided a useful breakdown:[75]

1. A *conventional transmission hologram* is a hologram on a film base. It can be illuminated with any source except fluorescent. The image is a single color, and the holographic image appears (a few inches to a few feet) *behind* the film. The largest size created to date has been 18 by 24 inches. Sizes ranging from 1 inch square to 9 inches square (but not *necessarily* square) are standard and are mass-produced and reasonably priced.

2. A *projected image hologram* is a second-generation hologram made from another hologram. The image appears in front of the film. The largest to date has been from a 2- by 3-foot plate with the image approximately 18 inches in front. These holograms are available in 9-inch square plates in production quality but are quite expensive. They are lighted from the rear of the film.

3. A *reflection hologram* is a hologram film lighted from the front of the film with a small filament source. Currently an 8- by 10-inch plate is the largest available. The image appears behind the film.

4. A *spectral hologram* is a hologram illuminated from behind by any source except fluorescent. The image is ex-

[72] See "The Light Pipe" by TIR Systems, Ltd., 2227 Quebec St. Vancouver, B.C., Canada V5T 3A1. Illus., color.

[73] Larry Goldberg, "Technology Update: Holography, A New Dimension for Marketing Programs," Lighting Dimensions, vol. 2, no. 2 (Feb. 1978), pp. 46–47. Diagrams. The best available article explaining holography in simple terms; defines the five basic existing types, outlines uses to date, and offers tips on marketing potentials.

[74] Edward A. Bush, "Holography: An Introduction," Theatre Design & Technology, vol. 14, no. 3 (Fall 1978), pp. 4–8. Illus. Good basics by the director of educational services for the Museum of Holography, New York City.

Dr. H. John Caulfield (text) and Charles O'Rear (photos), "The Wonders of Holography," National Geographic, vol. 165, no. 3 (Mar. 1984), pp. 364–77. Illus., color. The cover of this issue depicts the most widely distributed hologram to date. Excellent text and color photos. Invaluable summary for those interested in further information.

"The Holographic Process," Lighting Dimensions, vol. 2, no. 2 (Feb. 1978), p. 51. Two simple sketches and a simplified text covering the basics of holography.

Strawberry Gatts, "Holography: Something New in Image-Making," Lighting Dimensions, vol. 2, no. 2 (Feb. 1978), pp. 48–50. Easily readable article outlining holography basics, use, costs, and problems.

Edith Sapan, "A Short History of Holography — The Vision of Tomorrow," Lighting Dimensions, vol. 2, no. 2 (Feb. 1978), pp. 42–43. Article reprinted from Laser Focus magazine. Illus., color.

James D. Lyon, Jr., "Scenery Projected in Space," Theatre Design & Technology, 26(October 1971), p. 27.

Chris Outwater, "Application of Laser and Holography in Theatre and Motion Pictures," Theatre Design & Technology, vol. 14, no. 3 (Fall 1978), pp. 8–10. Summary of progress to date.

Robert Howell, "Multiplex and Projected Holograms," Theatre Design & Technology, vol. 14, no. 3 (Fall 1978), pp. 11–13. Illus. Good technical information.

"Soviets Explore Several Systems for Holographic Movies," Holosphere, vol. 6, no. 1 (Nov. 1977). Reprinted in Theatre Design & Technology, vol. 14, no. 3 (Fall 1978), pp. 13–14. Excellent progress report and explanation.

"White-light Holographic Displays," Lighting Dimensions, vol. 2, no. 2 (Feb. 1978), pp. 44–45, 50. Illus. Detailed history, listing of active firms, and report of present technology.

Arthur E. Alvis, Jr., "Holography: Further Thoughts," Theatre Crafts, vol. 12, no. 3 (Mar./Apr. 1978), p. 6. Comments by Alvis concerning both the high cost of and the need for advanced technical knowledge in holography experimentation.

Louis M. Brill, "The Blue Skies of Holography," Lighting Dimensions, vol. 4, no. 7 (July 1980), pp. 22–25, 40. Illus., color. Good basic article.

Additional Information can be obtained from The Laser Arts Society for Education and Research (LASER), P.O. Box 42083, San Francisco, CA 94101, (415) 431-9581. The group meets bimonthly and publishes a newsletter covering both lasers and holograms.

[75] Larry Goldberg, pp. 46–47, op. cit. (see footnote 73).

[76] Louis M. Brill, "A Dimensional Gateway to 3D — The Possibilities for Holography Have Been Blasted Wide Open Through New Technology," Lighting Dimensions, vol. 11, no. 1 (Jan/Feb. 1987), pp. 18, 83–86. Illus., color. Somewhat optimistic report by Brill (of the Wavefronts holographic firm) about recent applications of holograms, including theatrical applications.

Dudley, Holography: A Survey. New York; Museum of Holography; 1973. 129 pages.

Mary Lucier, see footnote 77.

Hildebrand and Brenden, An Introduction to Acoustical Holography. New York; Museum of Holography; 1972. 224 pages.

Susan Schenk, ed., WHO'S WHO IN DISPLAY HOLOGRAPHY. New York; Museum of Holography; 1978. 140 pages.

[77] Mary Lucier, "Holography: State of the Art," Theatre Crafts, vol. 11, no. 4 (Sept. 1977), pp. 8–10, 98, 100. Illus. An excellent description of

tremely bright in color (not necessarily that of the original object) due to prismatic effect and viewing angle. Reasonable in price, these holograms can be mass-produced in sizes up to 9 inches square.

5. A *moving hologram or an internal hologram* involves a motion-picture film process whereby the image seems to have movement when either the subject or the viewing angle is altered. Such holograms are currently available in sizes 9 inches in height by 20 to 60 inches in length, as well as in an 18- by 6-foot size, and are the basis of experimental work in Russia and elsewhere using lasers as the light source. A *multiplex hologram* (not a true hologram) can create motion on 35-mm film.

Each of these five basic types is diagrammed with easy-to-understand drawings and more technical details by Larry Goldberg in the article cited in footnote 73.

Uses

Like lasers, our present primitive holograms have appeared in many places.[76] In the scientific fields, holography is used

- To study sound waves in three-dimensional volumes (acoustic and ultrasonic holography)
- In microscopy
- For earth testing and exploration (seismic holography)
- As a diagnostic tool in medicine (bioholography and ophthalmology)
- In ocean surveillance
- In microwave technology
- In nuclear technology

Holography has been most utilized in the fields of display and advertising and marketing — often as a fascinating novelty and attention-getter. Both the Flamingo Hotel and the Aladdin Hotel in Las Vegas, Nevada, have holographic panels in walls and floors. Fisherman's Wharf in San Francisco and a haunted house on the pier in Ocean City, Maryland, use holographic effects.

Holography has attracted people in the fine arts and has appeared in museums as a featured display. The Museum of Holography in New York City has been host to numerous combined holography–poetry reading exhibitions. Chicago now (as of 1984) has its own Museum of the Fine Arts Research and Holographic Center.[77]

A few expensive, but quite brief (in duration), holographic movies have been created (usually of the multiplex type). Lloyd Cross of San Francisco first used a holographic-type image in the movie *Logan's Run*. Bonnie Kozek created a one-minute holographic movie called *Mystery*. The major work in this area however has been in the Soviet Union.[78]

Holograms have not often been successfully used in the theatre (other than when the theatre auditorium is being used as a place of assemblage).[79] Robert Howell summarized this problem:

> What does all this mean to the theatre profession? For the time being — very little. We keep getting scintillating hints of the fantastic effects that could be done on the stage, but the technology is still very much lacking. Artists, advertisers, cinematographers have all seen the possibilities for expression through holography. It is now up to the theatre professionals to help generate their own enthusiasm for the medium. For the theatre designer a whole new dimension is being offered up for use in filling up and redefining the theatre space. But the energy, ingenuity, and imagination of theatre designers and technicians with a real interest in holography will be needed to make all the dreams a reality.[80]

Problems

There are at least six basic problems which have thus far deterred widespread use of the existing potentials holograms offer:

1. Hologram photography and production of holographic images work best with *laser* light sources; coherent light is vital. Why? First, lasers are of a single wavelength. Since holography basically consists of photographing the reflected light pattern of an object from several (two or more) different viewpoints, then producing an *apparent* image in space by optical *interference* patterns of phased light[81] in space to create a believable (virtual) image which really only exists when seen by human eyes and synthesized and interpreted by a human brain, using *coherent light* (lasers) rather than incoherent light (which scatters in all directions) makes the whole process easier. Yet, as was explained in the earlier part of this chapter, production and control of laser light can be expensive, can require exten-

sive technical know-how, and can be extremely dangerous to the human eyes and body (in powerful quantities, improperly used). Holography, to reach its highest potential, requires laser light power well above the danger point.[82]

2. Experimentation with and production of strong, bright, large-sized holographic images ("still" or movie) is, at this time, very *costly.*

3. Up to this time, we have only been able to produce *true* holographic images which are no larger than the size of the original holographic film.[83] This has been a major deterrent to the use of holography. Film of the high-quality, fine-grain type necessary for good holograms just isn't made in sizes that large (or at least not at a price that present experimenters can afford). The largest film plates available are a 3-by 3-foot size. The largest film is 4 by 150 feet.

4. Viewing angle has been a problem. Only from a limited range of viewing angles (with present technology) is it possible for the viewer's mind to assimilate a three-dimensional holographic image. This, of course, has eliminated the dreamed-of creation of Hamlet's ghost onstage in a holographic form which will appear as a holographic image to a widely scattered audience in a theatre.[84]

5. *Color* is a problem. Holographic images of great brilliance and color can be produced, but not with colors intermixed in a believable, realistic blend. But do we *want to* project an image of a green orange, a red pear, a purple apple? Until there is a breakthrough in the problem of accurate color reproduction in holograms, holography will remain a fascinating novelty.

6. *Technical complexity* is a big problem. Holographic production and experimentation (on any workable level for the entertainment industry) *is not for the amateur.* It requires complex, sophisticated, and costly equipment in the hands of inventive, trained scientists. The world of theatre is not, at this moment, overrun with a wealth of such scientific geniuses.[85]

All of these current facts about holograms provide this picture: holograms fascinate the public, intrigue the artist, and are expensive and complex to produce on a large scale. They are used in museums, in very exciting experimental work, as an advertising gimmick, and as a "curiosity" com-

the evolution of the Museum of Holography and basic information about holograms.

"A Museum Devoted Only to Holography," Lighting Dimensions, vol. 2, no. 2 (Feb. 1978), p. 6. Brief description of the Museum of Holography.

F. N. D'Alessio, "Chicago Museum Devoted Solely to Holograms," Lafayette Journal and Courier, July 5, 1984, p. D3. Describes the Museum of the Fine Arts Research and Holographic Center (executive director Loren Billings, director John Hoffman), an extension of the School of Holography at 1134 West Washington Blvd., Chicago, IL 60607, (312) 226-1007.

Richard F. Shepard, "Holography Takes Root in SoHo in a Museum Devoted to Future," The New York Times, Dec. 26, 1976, section C, p. 16. Details about the Museum of Holography.

Museum of Holography. A 12-page, folding brochure available from the Museum of Holography, 11 Mercer Street, N.Y., N.Y., 10013, (212) 925-0526. This booklet explains the origin, nature, and services of the Museum and membership. The Museum has an information service (925-0581); publishes the annual Who's Who in Display Holography and the monthly Holosphere magazine (925-0577); operates an extensive bookstore which sells holographic movies, portraits, plates, prints, pendants, key chains, and books and reprints on the subject (925-0577); operates an educational service (925-0577); and operates a reference library, exhibition services, and a traveling exhibition service (753-7478). The Museum is a nonprofit organization supported by public funds and tax-deductible contributions. See also: Lee Watson, "Museum of Holography," Lighting Dimensions, vol. 3, no. 9 (Sept. 1979), p. 31.

"Illusive Treasure-Trove at Holography Gallery," The New York Times, Dec. 21, 1986, p. 27. Describes the Museum of Holography— Fifth Avenue at 745 Fifth Avenue near 58th Street.

Museum of Holography's Bookstore Catalog. Published annually, with prices. The latest edition lists 33 available books/articles on the subject, 9 reflection holograms, 25 intergrals, 25 pendants, and assorted specialty items and displays which are for sale.

Holosphere. This magazine is published monthly by the Museum of Holography, 11 Mercer Street, N.Y., N.Y. 10013.

[78] Chris Outwater, see footnote 74.

"Soviets Explore . . .," see footnote 74.

[79] Fran Minarik, "Simone Forti's Holographic ANGEL," Theatre Design & Technology, vol. 14, no. 3 (Fall 1978), pp. 17–18. Illus. An explanation and photograph of one holograph creation and its use in a production at Judson Church in New York City.

Mel Gussow, "Theatre: 'Pretty Boy' and a Beckett Play," The New York Times, June 15, 1985. Chicago edition, p. 16. The Mabou Mines production at the Performing Garage (33 Wooster St., New York City) of Samuel Beckett's Imagination Dead Imagine used holograms. It lasted only 14 minutes in performance time. The production was directed by Ruth Malec-zech, with holographic design by Linda Hartinian, holographic stereograms by Hart Perry, and lighting design by Toby Scott (with Anne Militello and L. B. Dallas). Gussow states in his review:

The current adaptation is the equivalent of hearing poetry read to sculpture. . . . A beam of light falls on a catafalque and the intricate design on the exterior changes color and texture as we watch it—from gold to bright white, from sandstone to marble. Faces and objects seem to appear on the surface. Atop the cata-falque floats a holographic image of a prone "woman-child," played by Clove Galilee. She rotates and swims as if she were a mermaid in a minature fishtank. . . . Light, voice, hologram, and music play against one another in undulating patterns. . . . It is a paradigmatic example of the Mabou Mines mastery of technology in the name of art.

[80] Robert Howell, p. 13, op. cit. (see footnote 74.

[81] Edward A. Bush writes: "Holography's ability to record differences in phase relationships is what makes possible the recording of three-dimensional images." p. 6, op. cit., (see footnote 74.

[82] *Edward A. Bush, p. 7, op. cit. (see footnote 74).*

[83] *Strawberry Gatts writes: "No effective emulsions have yet been invented to use specifically with laser light. The industry is, amazingly, still utilizing the same silver halides and dichromtes used by the film and printing industries." p. 50, op. cit. (see footnote 74).*

[84] *See Chris Outwater, p. 10, op. cit. (see footnote 74).*

[85] *Edward A. Bush writes: "According to Stephen Benton, however, even with suitable equipment, 'holography remains a tedious and painstaking craft, requiring considerable technical competence . . . for first rate results.' The staff would have to be well-grounded in physics and chemistry in order to insure a bright, useful image." p. 7, op. cit. (see footnote 74).*

[86] *Edward A. Bush, p. 8, op. cit. (see footnote 74).*

[87] *See Edith Sapan, op. cit. (see footnote 74).*

[88] *See footnote 77.*

ponent in jewelry, trinkets, and medallions. No one should write off holograms in the future work of lighting designers in *all* specialties, although much more work needs to be done to expand hologram applicability. Edward A. Bush wrote:

"Yet even though the possibility for large-scale, three-dimensional imagery has existed in principle since holography's invention, currently, the practical use of holography in theatre still appears to be as much a dream as holographic images one could hope to create are dreamlike. Engineering problems and financial constraints continue to pose barriers to development for the holographers, worldwide, conducing research into this, and other similar applications." [86]

History

In 1891 French physicist Gabriel Lippman created color photos by interferometry. Light sources and technology were not up to the demands of present-day holography, and his work, which could not be duplicated by others, was largely forgotten.[87]

The origins of present-day holography are generally attributed to the work of Dr. Dennis Gabor, performed in 1947 while he was doing research at the British Laboratories at Rugby. In 1970 Dr. Gabor applied for a patent on a holographic projection system which was not further developed. In 1972 Dr. Gabor received the Nobel Prize for his original pioneering research leading to present-day holography. It is Dr. Gabor who first used the term *holography*.

By 1960 Yu N. Denisyuk was producing three-dimensional visual recordings (holograms) in the Soviet Union. Denisyuk had read Gabriel Lippman's obscure works and applied the newly developed laser light to hologram development.

In 1964 and 1965, Emmett Leith and Jarvis Upatnieks gave holography a major boost forward in the western world. They are generally given credit for applying laser technology to Dr. Gabor's earlier research. Their work at the University of Michigan resulted in the first practical holograms in this country. Nile Hartman also produced similar results in this same period.

By December 1969 the first international conference on holography and computers was held at the Rice Hotel in Houston, Texas. In this same period, Stephen Benton, of Polaroid Corp., developed several technical improvements in holograms and obtained patents on his work.

In 1972 Tung Hon Jeong and Lloyd G. Cross developed the first white light internal holograms which reduced hologram production costs. Cross, of San Francisco, was also the founder of Multiplex Co., which is still a major manufacturer of holographic equipment. Cross also obtained patents. Jeong and Cross produced the first 360° (viewing angle) single-shot transmission holograms. Cross continued development of the multiplex hologram which made possible the first motion picture work in holograms in this country.

A major exhibition — "Holography '75" — took place in 1975 at the International Center for Photography in New York City. By 1976, Rosemary ("Rosy") H. Jackson had established the Museum of Holography on Mercer Street in New York City. She had earlier worked with Jody Burns at a now-defunct school of holography and arranged a major holography exhibition in Sweden. The Museum of Holography was chartered as a tax-free institution by the State of New York on July 1, 1976.[88] This museum currently owns over 450 pieces of holographic work, perhaps the most significant collection anywhere in the world. The Museum of Holography is the main clearinghouse for information in this field.

Also in the mid-seventies the movie *Logan's Run* was produced. Chris Outwater was the consultant for the holographic work used; Multiplex Co. produced the holographic film (six multiplex holograms). In England, Holoco Corp. grew out of the work of Nicholas Phillips, John Wolff, film director Anton Furst, and David Proter at Loughborough University. Phillips and Porter reduced the granularity of holographic film and improved film developing processes. Money from the rock group The Who provided funding for research by Holoco Corp., which produced holograms for one of the group's tours (although the group did not use them on tour for very long). Lloyd Cross produced the now-famous multiplex holographic film *Angel*, using dancer Simone Forti, in 1976. This film was exhibited for three performances in New York City. The first was at

Judson Church in Greenwich Village and was called "Evenings on a Revolving Turntable." The second, in April 1976, also involved artist Peter Van Riper. Jean Dupuis organized these early gatherings. The third performance was called "Some Images" at the Fine Arts Building.

Undoubtedly, with secret research in progress in England and Russia and widely scattered locations in the United States, there are many exhibits, developments, and people involved in holography evolution which I have missed. Nonetheless, an overall picture of slow beginnings and rapidly accelerating activity from 1970 onward is evident.

Costs

A few hard facts about cost are enough to make clear that even if a working lighting designer has the necessary technical/scientific expertise to use holography, cost will deter usage. However, it is likely that the increasing interest in holograms and new developments may rapidly change this picture.

A person having a holographic photograph made can expect to spend from $500 to $1,000 just for the photo. Effective advertising displays in hologram run from $1,000 each (very simple) to $25,000 each. For producing (or purchasing) film holographic images in quantity, prices for plastic film, in quantities of 100,000 or more, can run as follows:

Size, inches	Viewable with any light source	Viewable using sunlight or a point source
2½ × 2½	$1.50–$2 each	15¢ each
2¼ × 5		30¢
4 × 5		60¢

A 2- by 3-foot panel starts at $5,000, a 4- by 4-foot panel at $7,000. In addition, bright, high-quality holographic work can *only* be photographed and viewed with high-quality, rather powerful *phased* laser light sources, and such lasers (at least two are needed) begin at $15,000 each.

Inevitably, as holograms begin to be used in the entertainment arts, the designer will be forced to turn to firms and individuals who specialize in this field. Larry Goldberg offers several valuable suggestions about "how to deal with

holographers," [89] summarized below. According to Goldberg, the designer should

1. Check out the financial and service reliability of the company being dealt with through Dunn & Bradstreet or one of the better business bureaus.

2. Visit the holography company, check its size and dependability, and request a performance bond, if the designer has any doubts about it.

3. Be prepared to make both a deposit and progress payments (25 to 30 percent in advance is reasonable). The designer may be asked to fund research development of new products, with no guarantee of success.

4. Allow maximum time for delivery. Currently firms and facilities are often small and quite busy. Custom holograms take time.

5. Establish good communications once a reliable holographer has been selected. The holographer should feel free to let the designer know about any problems, delays, or cost increases that occur. The designer must communicate objectives and expectations clearly.

Computers

Approximately 10 years ago computer technology burst upon the scene in the "high-tech" countries as both the "in" thing and as a marked advance in technology. First used in the entertainment/theatre world to control "memory" switchboards, computers are now being used to help with the lighting designer's paperwork and, with very recent developments, to generate light plots. Like all advances in the machinery of civilization, computer technology has both advantages and (a few) drawbacks. The computer industry has become a $110 billion industry. Computers offer both existing and potential applications for the lighting designer.

Robert Meden, professor of architecture at Ball State University, Muncie, Indiana, stated his philosophy of computer use in a panel discussion reported in *Lighting Design + Application* magazine: "The computer is a great tool for the designer and can alleviate some of the more tedious aspects of lighting design. At the same time, it's not going to solve everything." [90] In the same panel discussion, Profes-

[89] *Larry Goldberg, p. 47, op. cit. (see footnote 73).*

[90] *Vol. 15, no. 2 (Feb. 1985), p. 34.*

[91] *Ibid., p. 36.*

[92] *Forrest Wilson, "How We Create,"* Lighting Design + Application, *vol. 17, no. 2 (Feb. 1987), pp. 8–11, 45–55. Illus. Priceless comments by several authors.*

[93] Indianapolis Star, *Feb. 18, 1985, p. 16.*

[94] *Sources of basic computer information:*

Srully Blotnick, Computers Made Ridiculously Easy. *N.Y.; BYTE Books/McGraw-Hill; 1984. 198 pp., illus. Good beginning book on computer technology and use. Not specifically for lighting applications.*

David Lord, "The Computer Department," Architectural Lighting, *vol. 1, no. 6 (June 1987), pp. 47–50. Illus. Latest information concerning microcomputer lighting program software.*

Robert G. Davis and Craig A. Bernecker, "An Evaluation of Computer Graphic Images of the Lighted Environment," IES Journal *(1984 IES Annual Conference Papers issue), vol. 14, no. 1 (Oct. 1984), pp. 493–514. A rather academic presentation of the need for and value of computer-generated graphics in architectural lighting along with the discussion which followed this paper's presentation.*

"Special Report — Computers in Lighting," Lighting Design + Application, *vol. 14, no. 6 (June 1984) pp. 17–36. Illus., color, articles by Toni Napoli. An early survey of computer-aided design, drafting, calculations, and technical information storage as it affects the architectural lighting field. Fourteen articles, including a "questions and answers" pro and*

con discussion by experts. A useful summary of currently available facilities and user evaluations of them. Also available from IES as a reprinted 16-page publication for $1.75. Contains a helpful listing of available software programs for architectural lighting.

John Markoff, "Making Computers Compatible," The New York Times, May 11, 1988, p. D8. Illus. New software to smooth the transition to faster machines is detailed.

Leonard Harman, "Computer-Assisted Lighting Design Using AutoCAD," Theatre Design & Technology, vol. 23, no. 1 (Spring 1987), pp. 18, 20, 23. Most useful.

sor James Benya of the California University Department of Architecture and owner of Luminae, Inc., said:

> We don't have to assume that computers are going to take over lighting design. There are two sides to lighting design to be concerned with; one is the technical performances of the lighting system. That can be calculated and I find the computer a useful tool to work out these calculations. But lighting should also be aesthetic, must be functional, and must provide all of the needs of the people in the space. I don't see the computer moving into that area. The two must be balanced."[91]

In *Lighting Design + Application* Forrest Wilson wrote:

> A survey made last year [1986] by the *Wall Street Journal* concluded that much of the $40 billion a year spent on micro-electronic equipment to improve productivity is wasted. The quantity and quality of work is as much a social as a technical issue. An ability to create accident, ambiguities, and malapropisms, which present computers cannot do at all but humans do without effort, may be as or more important to creative thinkers than a host of fiber-optic connected devices.
>
> One question might be — is the computer in its present form the right tool to inspire imaginative decisions? Computers change one set of symbols for another and expect to be commended for their cleverness in doing so. They monitor what is said to them and if they do not like it the answer is a rude noise. They snitch to the boss if a worker goes to the bathroom or relaxes for one second. But humans cannot tell whether a micro chip is producing or sitting on its arse.[92]

Professor David Di Laura of the University of Colorado Department of Civil, Environmental, and Architectural Engineering, writing in the *Indianapolis Star*, made the point that: "Computers are merely the mechanisms that generate . . . information. The issue is information." In their weekly newspaper column, "The Business Computer," Frank Lynn Peterson and Judi K-Turkel made this insightful observation: "Computers do not solve problems, people do. If you cannot eliminate messy inventory, late taxes, or writing errors without a computer, you cannot do it with a computer."[93]

Computers and computer technology are firmly entrenched in almost every aspect of society, and young people seem to be particularly drawn to computerization. There is now even an Association of Entertainment Industry

Computer Professionals (AEICP), headed by Lawrence Saltzman, who is also the president of Entertainment Computer Systems, Inc. In England we have Alan Healy of Playlight Hire, Ltd. Speaking of the possibilities of computer-generated graphics in theatrical projection in the entertainment/theatre field of lighting design, there are several good software programs available (see footnote 94) which markedly help the busy professional lighting designer with assembling, correcting, and updating instrument schedules; color cutting lists; switchboard hookups; and the other paperwork which accompanies lighting a show.[94] If a designer is responsible for designing the lighting for three to five productions per year, the investment of money and time to master computer usage may not justify that designer's involvement. If, on the other hand, a designer is a working professional lighting designer whose full-time career effort is directed toward lighting productions, a computer and some of the current software packages may well be a vital investment. The computer is an invention much like the typewriter: it speeds up the drudgery and offers rapid clean copies, but it does not help anyone to have anything more worthwhile to say (or design) than did the ancient quill pen and parchment paper.

In respect to the use of computers to generate light plots (eliminating potentially many hours of drafting), software technology is really forging ahead. A designer must have a computer with a plotter and learn a whole new group of techniques to utilize existing programs. For some people the initial programming involves so much time and effort, as does learning to use the software, that it is easier just to continue drafting. If, however, a designer's work requires numerous light plots throughout the productive year, computer-generated light plots should by all means be investigated.

The uses and requirements of a computer are somewhat different in the architectural lighting field. Since literally thousands of different luminaires are on the market, a computer software program (see footnote 94) becomes an almost priceless information tool. Further, much architectural lighting design requires extensive and accurate mathematical illumination engineering calculations. A computer (if programmed with accurate information) can

Natalie Langue Leighton, Computers in the Architectural Office. *N.Y.; Van Nostrand Reinhold; 1984. 192 pp. A useful "beginners" volume about the use of computers as a design tool in architectural work.*

Donald J. Jung and Michael J. Bethel, "Selecting a Plotter," Theatre Crafts, *vol. 18, no. 9 (Nov./Dec. 1984), pp. 19, 101–107. Illus. Excellent, understandable information concerning plotter selection to accompany a basic computer.*

J. Mark Kelman, "Spotlight on Computers," Lighting Dimensions, *vol. 8, no. 7 (Nov./Dec. 1984), pp. 56–57, 59–61, 63. Illus., color. A basic primer about computer use in theatre/entertainment lighting design with examples of various available software programs. Invaluable information for the beginner.*

Bob Fisher, "Is This the Time to Buy? Getting into Computers: A Guide for Production Companies and Individuals," On Location, *Feb. 1985, pp. 94–95, 99. Useful basic information about hardware purchases.*

Douglass F. Sisk, "Computer-Assisted Lighting Controllers," Theatre Crafts, *vol. 21, no. 2 (Feb. 1987), pp. 36–41. Offers excellent chart comparing numerous manufacturers' switchboard controllers. Most useful analysis and information.*

Michael Cabana, The Use of Computers by Lighting Aestheticians: Surveys and Suggestions. *M.F.A. thesis; 1987; Parsons School of Design, New York City. Thesis examines existing software usable in lighting design.*

Computer Graphics World publishes the Computer Graphics Directory *annually. It is a useful guide to both hardware and software. PennWell Directories, P.O. Box 21278, Tulsa, OK 74121.*

Bob McClintock, "Computers: Theatrical Hardware, Computer Style," Theatre Crafts, *vol. 19, no. 1 (Jan. 1985), pp. 14–15, 80–84. McClintock, of ArtSoft, discusses usable hardware, prices, and sources for lighting programs. Basic information, well presented.*

John Weygandt, "Software Report, Filevision for Your Lighting Design," Theatre Crafts, *vol. 19, no. 8 (Oct. 1985), pp. 100, 102–104, 106–107. Illus.*

Charles Drucker, "The Lights of Illusion," Computerland, *vol. 1, no. 2 (Jan./Feb. 1986),*

pp. 30–33, 52. Illus., color. Brief, well-written article about adaptation of Apple computers for memory switchboard control.

ALD/Pro (Assistant Lighting Designer) software from John W. McKernon, 148 W. 23rd St., #5-D, N.Y., NY 10011.

Steve Pollock, "Programming Madonna," Theatre Crafts, *vol. 19, no. 9 (Nov. 1985), pp. 38–39, 41, 44. Use of computers for a concert tour. Illus., color.*

Eric Sandberg-Diment, "Computer-Aided Design Dooms Lesser Tools," The New York Times, *Chicago edition, Nov. 12, 1985, p. 17.*

Ken M. MacGregor, "Computer Graphics," Society of Television Lighting Directors, #31 (Spring 1986), pp. 5–11. Illus. British Practice.

Available software lighting programs for theatre/entertainment lighting designers:

"Lights" program from Jacques Design, Inc., 13282-1 S.W. 114 Lane, Miami, FL 33186. Tel: (305) 386-5559.

"Bravo" program from Arts Research Technology Systems, Inc. (A.R.T.S.), 8200 Normandale Blvd., Suite 405, Bloomington, MN 55437.

"ShowPlot" from the Great American Market, 826 N. Cole Ave., Hollywood, CA 90038. Tel: (213) 461-0200.

"StageLights" from Rosco Laboratories, Inc., 36 Bush Ave., Port Chester, NY 10573. Also "ALD" (Assistant Lighting Designer) program.

"C.A.L.D." (Computer Assisted Lighting Design), "CADPad," "TouchCAD," "CADCamera" and "AutoCAD" programs from Artsoft, 60 South Hartford Turnpike, Wallingford, CT 06492; or 135 Fifth Avenue, N.Y., NY 10010; or P.O. Box 1538, Kingston, Ontario, Canada K7L 5C7.

"Quick-Temp" program from Quality Lighting, Inc., 11530 Melrose Ave., P.O. Box 309, Franklin Park, IL 60131-0309. Telephone: (312) 451-6768.

Sources of information about theatre/entertainment software programs:

Merrill Lessley, "Inside Rosco's Stagelights," Lighting Dimensions, *vol. 9, no. 1 (Jan./Feb. 1985), pp. 53–57, 66. Subtitled "Software Review," this is a critical analysis of Rosco's "Stagelights" software program by Dr. Lessley and a response by Rosco.*

Lewis E. Lawrence, Jr., "Lighting Software For a Song," Lighting Dimensions, *vol. 9, no. 2 (Mar./Apr. 1985), pp. 25, 27–28, 30. Illus. Subtitled "Software Review, What They Do and How to Get Them," this article describes the*

"CompuLight," "Instrument" and "Light," "Lighting Design Aid" and "LightPrint" software programs for theatre lighting developed in various universities.

Robert Heller, "Software Report," Theatre Crafts, *vol. 10, no. 1 (Jan. 1985), pp. 16–19, 80. A review of "ALD," a Rosco software program, and the "Lights" program from Jacques Design, Inc.*

David Jacques, "Letters: More Lights," Theatre Crafts, *vol. 19, no. 3 (Mar. 1985), p. 8. A response by the president of Jacques Design, Inc., to the January 1985 critique of the "Lights" software program.*

Louis Racine, "The MacPoint," Theatre Crafts, *vol. 19, no. 2 (Feb. 1985), p. 3. A Canadian designer's comments on use of the Macintosh computer in lighting design work.*

James L. Moody, "Software: A New Program for Lighting Designers," Theatre Crafts, *vol. 19, no. 7 (Aug./Sept. 1985), pp. 28, 86–88. Illus. Excellent detailed summary of the capabilities and practical applications of one of the better software lighting design packages available.*

Craig Miller, "Computers: Using your Apple to Handle Lighting Paperwork," Theatre Crafts, *vol. 19, no. 3 (Mar. 1985), pp. 16, 57–61. Illus. An excellent article by a working Broadway lighting designer about his use of an Apple computer.*

David E. Patrick, "Computers: An Instrument Schedule for the Master Electrician," Theatre Design & Technology, *vol. 20, no. 3 (Fall 1984), p. 18. Illus. A computer-generated software program for creation of lighting paperwork (but not plots) developed at Western Illinois University.*

Michael Klepper, "Computers: The Macintosh: Is It the Answer For Designers?" Theatre Crafts, *vol. 18, no. 7 (Aug./Sept. 1984), pp. 20–21, 76. Illus. Thoughtful information, well-presented and well-illustrated.*

Robert J. Thurston, "TRS-80 Model III Light Plots Using Profile 3 Plus," Theatre Design & Technology, *vol. 20, no. 2 (Summer 1984), pp. 26, 33. Illus. A description by Professor Thurston of the use of the Radio Shack "Profile III Plus" software program to generate lighting paperwork (but not plots).*

Francis Reid, "Shopping at USITT," Cue, #29 (May/June 1984), p. 15. Illus. A description by British lighting designer, educator, and critic Reid of computer displays and sessions at the 1984 United States Institute for Theatre Technology (USITT) Conference in Orlando, Florida.

"Streets with Style," Lighting Dimensions, vol. 8, no. 3 (May/June 1984), pp. 27–34. Illus., color. An interview with cinematographer Andrew Laszlo and lighting designer Marc Brickman about the rock-concert sequences in the feature film Streets of Fire. Includes the first computer-generated light plot used for a feature film. This plot is reproduced in this volume as Figure 22.

Robert Heller, "Software Report: ALD-PRO updates original ALD," Theatre Crafts, vol. 20, no. 3 (Mar. 1986), pp. 20, 70–71.

Available software lighting programs for architectural lighting designers:

"Lumen-Point," "Lumen $" and "Lumen-Micro" from Lighting Technologies, 3060 Walnut Street, Suite 209, Boulder, Colorado 80301. Lighting Technologies also publishes Lumenews, a very useful quarterly newspaper. Lighting Technologies has programs that prepare light distribution sketches of rooms.

"CADLight I: Daylighting" and "CADLight II: Artifical Lighting" from Energyworks, Inc., Watertown, Mass. Available through Wiley & Sons, Inc., P.O. Box 063, Somerset, NJ 08873.

"Micro-Site-Lite," "Micro-Cost-Lite," and "Micro-Eye-Lite" from Murray and Gillespie Computer Solutions, Inc., 90 Nolan Court, Unit 22, Markham, Ontario, Canada L3R 4L9. Telephone: (416) 477-0260.

See also the annual reports of the IES Computer Committee which list available software.

"Available Lighting Computer Programs: A Compendium and a Survey," Lighting Design + Application, vol. 15, no. 6 (June 1985), pp. 54–59. This article lists 24 sources (firms) and also offers a brief review of new books on the subject.

"Available Lighting Computer Programs: A Compendium and a Survey," Lighting Design + Application, vol. 16, no. 6 (June 1986), pp. 42–43. Names, addresses, and a chart comparison of available lighting software in the architectural lighting area.

"Available Lighting Computer Programs: A Compendium and a Survey," Lighting Design + Application, vol. 16, no. 9 (Sept. 1986), pp. 40–41. Prepared by the IES Computer Committee. In chart form; details sources of manufacture.

Sources of information about architectural lighting programs:

"Light & Design: Computer Graphics in Lighting Design," Interior Design, vol. 55, no. 11 (Nov. 1984), pp. 264–65. Illus., color. Eight color graphics and abstracted texts, excerpted from a paper presented at the August 1984 IES meeting by Naomi Johnson Miller (Peerless Electric), Peter Y. Ngai (Peerless), and David D. Miller (independent computer graphics consultant). Copies of the full paper can be obtained from IES, 345 East 47th Street, N.Y., NY 10017. Very useful.

Naomi Johnson Miller, Peter Y. Ngai, and David D. Miller, "Presentation Techniques: Computer Graphics in Lighting Design," International Lighting Review (Amsterdam, Netherlands), 4th quarter 1984, pp. 122–126. Illus., color. Similar article to that listed above, but with outstanding color graphics concerning client presentation sketches computer generated. This same information is also available in the Journal of the IES (1984 IES Annual Conference Papers), vol. 14, no. 1 (Oct. 1984), pp. 6–26, but in this version the illustrations are all black/white.

David L. DiLaura, Denis P. Igoe, and Richard G. Mistrick, "Synthetic Photography," Lighting Design + Application, vol. 15, no. 8 (Aug. 1985), pp. 24–27. Illus. A useful, well-illustrated article about combining architectural lighting calculations with computer graphics.

The General Electric Lighting Institute (Nela Park, Cleveland, OH 44112) began a series of conferences about the use of computers in lighting design and analysis in November 1985. The fee for the two-day, hands-on conference was $125 (covering some meals and transportation). Contact W. S. Fisher, Manager, Lighting Education, GE Lighting Institute.

"Computers in Lighting," Lighting Design + Application. See: "Software available," vol. 15, no. 9 (Sept. 1985), pp. 12, 41–42; vol. 15, no. 10 (Oct. 1985), p. 56; vol. 16, no. 1 (Jan. 1986), p. 58; and vol. 16, no. 6 (June 1986), p. 59.

Sarah Shankman, "Is the Computer Just More Stuff in the Carpetbag of the Snake Oil Salesman Trying to Sell a Lighting System?" Lighting Design + Application, vol. 16, no. 6 (June 1986), pp. 9–16. Six experts discuss the computer — its uses and value in lighting design.

Michael J. Leite, "Computers and the Typical Design Practice, A Step-By-Step Guide to What a Microcomputer Can Do for You," Lighting Design + Application, vol. 16, no. 6 (June 1986), pp. 20–24.

Craig A. Bernecker and Richard G. Mistrick, "Using the Computer to Teach Lighting," Lighting Design + Application, vol. 16, no. 6 (June 1986), pp. 26–28. Illus., color. The Penn State director of illumination studies writes about computer use in teaching architectural lighting design.

Dr. Ian Lewin, "Using Microcomputers in the Lighting Industry," Lighting Design + Application, vol. 16, no. 6 (June 1986), pp. 29–35. Illus., color. The president of Lighting Sciences, Inc. (Scottsdale, AZ), a laboratory of optics, vision, testing, and illumination design, writes about computer use.

Robert G. Davis, "Computer Graphics as a Design Tool," Lighting Design + Application, vol. 16, no. 6 (June 1986), pp. 38–40. Illus., color.

Stuart M. Lewis, "Software Buyers' Guide, Special Report," Electrical Construction Technology, vol. 41, no. 8 (Aug. 1989), pp. 10–12. A two-page chart listing available lighting computer software, the manufacturer/vendor, a description, current prices, type of computer it will run on, and other system requirements. Most useful.

Michael S. Eddy, "Ready or Not: Is CADD Right For You?" Lighting Dimensions, vol. 13, no. 3 (April 1989), pp. 44, 46–48. Illus. Also contains a list of selected resource guides to CADD.

Michael S. Eddy, "Computer Graphics: Lighting in the Third Dimension," vol. 13, no. 4 (May/June 1989), pp. 50–51. Illus., color. An excellent summary of the available software and systems for studying and presenting to clients a three-dimensional 'picture' printout of lighting design solutions, mostly in the architectural lighting field.

David Lord, "The Computer Department," Architectural Lighting. An excellent series of columns covering available software and basic

do this more rapidly and more accurately than a person can. The most advanced software now on the market offers sketchlike renditions of the illumination distribution throughout a space, which can be used for client presentations. As this *Handbook* is being written, color graphics programs for architectural lighting software are being developed.[95]

Because both the available computers (hardware) and the technology available for using them (software programs) change from day-to-day, neither can be a major subject in this text. Two points need to be strongly stressed. The first is that the computer is here to stay. This is the "computer age," and it behooves every lighting designer —student or practicing professional—to keep abreast of the evolving technology. The second point is that a computer is merely a useful tool. It does not now, nor is it ever likely to, design lighting. The process of programming a computer to deal with the infinite variables of client taste, preference, unavoidable schedule reshuffling, selection of where light cues/changes should come and of what duration, remains a human design element.

There is one main drawback to the advent of computers in lighting design. Unfortunately, in some cases computer technology is beginning to replace the established master-teacher–student relationship. Why should a busy designer hire an assistant (at rather high union rates) to do the drudgery of drafting, programming, and scheduling when a computer can do it better and less expensively? As this shift happens the industry begins to lose one of its valuable traditions (assets): the breaking in and training of the newcomer on the job as an apprentice to the established artist. On the other hand, the computer is of great value to established designers, allowing them to spend more time on design—relieved of time-consuming information storage and processing tasks.

Summary

It is clear that this brief treatment of scenic projection, lasers, fiber optics, holograms, and computers does not begin to supply all of the information on these subjects the lighting designer needs to know. These relatively new areas are in rapid evolution and are not adequately covered in any of the existing standard lighting texts. The material offered in this chapter presents basic insights into the potential contribution of these technologies as design elements and, through the extensive footnotes, steers the evolving designer to more extended sources of technical and application information which may be needed.

As the chapter closes, it is fitting to present a few examples of the new technology at work. Figure 3.16 shows one of the earliest computer-generated light plots for the movie *Streets of Fire,* created on an Apple Macintosh computer and Imagewriter in 1984. Figure 3.17 is a computer-generated light plot, and Fig. 3.18 is one page of the switchboard hookup for the 1986 Purdue University production of *G. R. Point* by designer Glen Goodwin. Figures 3.19 and 3.20 are production photos from *G. R. Point.*

computer information for the architectural lighting designer, in the following issues:
Vol. 1, no. 7 (July/Aug. 1987), pp. 38, 40, 42. Illus.
Vol. 1, no. 9 (October 1987), pp. 40–41. Illus., color.
Vol. 1, no. 11 (December 1987), pp. 32–34. Illus., color.
Vol. 2, no. 1 (January 1988), pp. 37–38, 40. Illus., color.
Vol. 2, no. 3 (March 1988), pp. 42–44. Illus., color.
Vol. 2, no. 5 (May 1988), pp. 38, 40. Illus., color.
Vol. 2, no. 6 (June 1988), pp. 37–39. Illus., color.
Vol. 2, no. 8 (August 1988), pp. 48–50. Illus. Energy analysis programs.
Vol. 2, no. 10 (October 1988), pp. 38–39. Illus.
Vol. 2 no. 11 (November 1988), pp. 40–42. Illus. Indoor, outdoor lighting calculation programs.
Vol. 3, no. 4 (April 1989), p. 38. "CD-ROM."
Vol. 3, no. 5 (May 1989), pp. 48, 50. Illus.
Vol. 3, no. 8 (August 1989), pp. 40–41. Illus.

[95] *See* Lumenews, *vol. 2, no. 4 (Aug. 1986).*

D. L. DiLaura, D. P. Igoe, P. G. Samaras, and A. M. Smith, "Verifying the Applicability of Computer Generated Pictures to Lighting Design," Journal of the I.E.S., *vol. 17, no. 1 (Winter 1988), pp. 36–61. Illus. Experts from the Universty of Colorado and Lighting Technologies, Inc. of Boulder present a lengthy engineering appraisal of the use of computer graphic images utilized in architectural lighting design.*

Gregory J. Ward and Francis M. Rubinstein, "A New Technique for Computer Simulation of

Illuminated Spaces," Journal of the I.E.S., *vol. 17, no. 1 (Winter 1988)*, pp. 80–91. Illus. More about architectural lighting calculations graphically illustrated by computer.

"Overseas, OISTAT Amsterdam," ABTT News, Jan. 1988, pp. 3–4. An extensive report on Richard Pilbrow's projected uses of computers and computer technology in theatrical lighting in the near future. Very thought-provoking.

"The Future of Luminaire Design Is At Hand," Lumenews, *vol. 4, no. 1 (April 1988)*, pp. 1–6. Illus. Lumenews *is published regularly by Lighting Technologies, 3060 Walnut Street, Suite 209, Boulder, Colorado 80301 United States of America, tel: (303) 449-5791. Describes and illustrates Lighting Technologies' newest computer software FIELD (Finite Element Luminaire Design) for designing luminaires.*

A. K. Bennett-Hunter, "Luddite Among the Lasers, Not Everyone at the PQ Computer Symposium Was in Favour of the Future," Sightline, *vol. 21, no. 2 (Autumn 1987)*, pp. 23–24. A summary of use of computer technology at the Prague quadrennial meeting in 1987 (a worldwide conference of theatre specialists held every fourth year). The article presents the views of Bran Ferren (U.S.), Helmut Grosser (West Germany), Ken Smalley (Britain), Dr. Kensuka Mori (Japan), Bernard Desfarges (France), Sergei Barchin (USSR), and Josef Svoboda (Czechoslovakia). An excellent summary of present-day and potential future computer usage in lighting design.

Rosco Laboratories [36 Bush Ave., Port Chester, N.Y., tel: (914) 937-1300] now produces the following computer software: Lightwright, Stagelights, Candlepower, and Tickets.

Michael Stauffer, "CADD For the Theatre Designer, A Comparison of Low-Cost Programs," Theatre Crafts, *vol. 23, no. 1 (January 1989)*, pp. 66, 68–71. Chart. A highly useful source for information and addresses of companies with CADD usable software aimed at those lighting designers who use variations of the CADD system for drafting light plots.

Robert Chase, "Lightwright for Lighting Designers, A Review of Rosco's Computerized Assistant," Theatre Crafts, *vol. 23, no. 2 (Feb. 1989)*, pp. 28–29.

"Product Report," Theatre Crafts, *vol. 23, no. 2 (Feb. 1989)*, pp. 74–75. Details about the ETCEDIT software program by the firm Electronic Theatre Controls for use by lighting designers.

Mark Loeffler, "Lighting Director for Lighting Designers, Drafting by Cursor Instead of Pencil," Theatre Crafts, *vol. 22, no. 9 (Nov. 1988)*, pp. 94, 96–97. Illus. An analysis and description of the lighting designer's software program supplied by Specialized Lighting Services in New York City.

"Dramatic Software," Theatre Crafts, *vol. 22, no. 7 (August/September 1988)*, p. 26. An advertisement by Dramatic Software in California about their software called "The Light Plot."

Patrick M. Finelli, "Software and the Stage," Theatre Design & Technology, *vol. 24, no. 3 (Fall 1988)*, pp. 35–37. An excellent summary and history of software use in the theatre.

William D. File and Robert Reinecke, "Computers," Theatre Design & Technology, *vol. 24, no. 1 (Spring 1988)*, pp. 17, 45. Results of an extensive survey of theatre computer users. IBM and compatible computers now dominate (52.75%), but new microcomputer purchases indicate that 61.2% plan to purchase MacIntosh and only 14.3% plan to purchase IBM or compatible units.

Bob Anderson, "Graphpads for Christmas," ALD # Magazine, *no. 9 (May 1989)*, pp. 17–21. Extensive material concerning British computer usage, both in lighting design and as switchboard controllers.

Joseph P. Oshry, "ShowPlot Update," Theatre Crafts, *vol. 22, no. 4 (April 1988)*, pp. 102–103. Illus. Update about the Great American Market line of software for lighting.

Michael Mell, "Upgrading Your Lighting Booth," Theatre Crafts, *vol. 21, no. 10 (Dec. 1989)*, pp. 32, 34–35. Subtitled: "Retrofitting the Sixties," the article by a Brannigan Lorelli Associates member deals with updating control units.

"Anti-Tandy Bias?" Theatre Crafts, *vol. 21, no. 9 (Nov. 1987)* p. 6. A "Letters to the Editor" correcting errors in Douglass F. Sisk's "Computers in Theatre" in the August/September 1987) Theatre Crafts.

Douglass F. Sisk, "Computers in Theatre," Theatre Crafts, *vol. 21, no. 7 (August/September 1987)*, pp. 38, 92–95. Analysis of numerous theatre lighting software packages and sources.

Product News: Lighting by Computer and Calculations Made Easy," Lighting Dimensions, *vol. 12, no. 4 (May/June 1988)*, p. 96. Announcement of new Lighting Technologies software enabling improved color perspective graphics and lighting calculation programs from Illuminating Software, Inc.

William J. Wallace, "Computer Graphics: CAD and the Small College Theatre," Theatre Design & Technology, *vol. 25, no. 2 (Summer 1989)*, pp. 29–31. Illus. Useful article for smaller producing groups. Also: Patrick M. Finelli, "Computer Graphics: Advancing Production Technology," pp. 35–40. Illus. A fall 1986 survey of computer usage in theatre and lighting.

"JCN," Cue International, *no. 57 (January/February 1989)*, p. 42. An advertisement by JCN (Oakland, California) about their Show Master software program for lighting by a firm specializing in "Computer Technology for the Entertainment Industry."

"Computer Aided Lighting Design Program," Lighting *vol. 1, no. 1 (June 1987)*, pp. 10–11. Description of CALA (Computer Aided Lighting Analysis) for the Canadian market from Holophane. Bill Smelser, "Design: Sophisticated Software Packages Aid Lighting Design by Computer," Lighting, *vol. 1, no. 3 (Nov. 1987)*, pp. 22, 24. Illus.

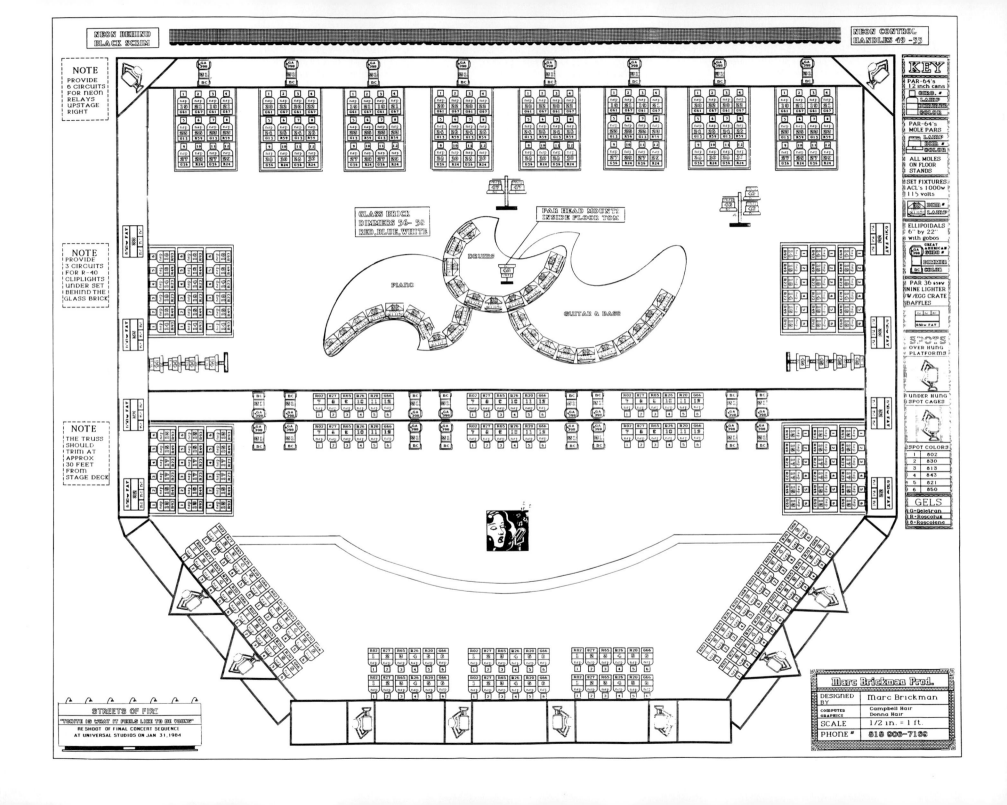

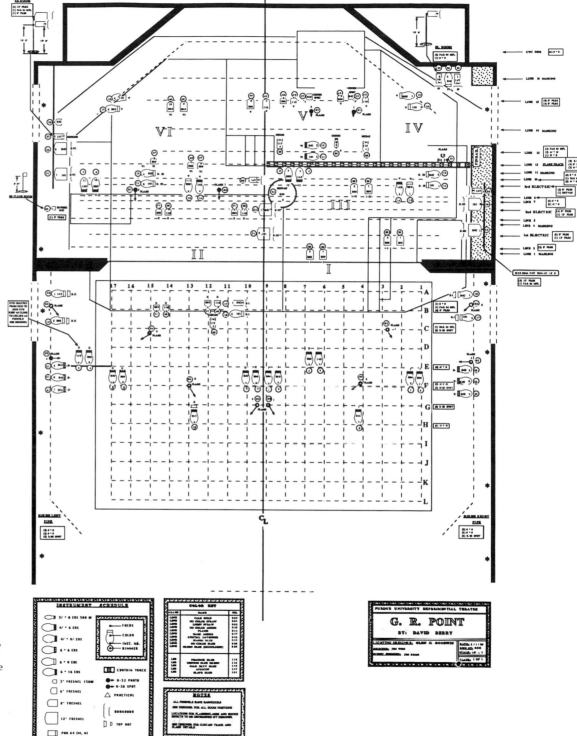

Figure 3.16 An early computer-generated light plot, created by Marc Brickman for the 1984 film *Streets of Fire*. Cinematographer: Andrew Laszlo. Computer graphics by Campbell Hair and Donna Hair. Graphics generated on an Apple Macintosh computer and Imagewriter.

Figure 3.17 Computer-generated light plot by Purdue University graduate student lighting designer Glen C. Goodwin. Created on a Macintosh 512-kilobyte computer for the February 1, 1986 production of *G. R. Point* in Purdue's Experimental Theatre with direction by James Wise and set design by James Ream.

G. R. POINT HOOKUP SCHEDULE

DIMMER	FOCUS	TYPE	COLOR	WATTS	LOCATION	INST #	CIRCUIT
1	AREA I	4/ X 9/	804	750 W	GRID F1	2	
1	AREA I	4/ X 9/	804	750 W	GRID F9	5	
2	AREA I	4/ X 9/	850	750 W	GRID F1	1	
2	AREA I	4/ X 9/	850	750 W	GRID F9	4	
3	AREA I	4/ X 9/	842	750 W	GRID H4	1	
4	AREA II	4/ X 6	803	750 W	GRID E18	3	
4	AREA II	4/ X 6	803	750 W	GRID E7	2	
5	AREA II	4/ X 6	143	750 W	GRID E18	4	
5	AREA II	4/ X 6	143	750 W	GRID E7	1	
6	AREA II	4/ X 6	803	750 W	LINE 10	10	
6	AREA II	4/ X 6	803	750 W	LINE 12	5	
7	AREA II	4/ X 6	143	750 W	LINE 10	11	
7	AREA II	4/ X 6	143	750 W	LINE 12	4	
8	AREA II	4/ X 9/	N/C	750 W	GRID F10	7	
8	AREA II	4/ X 9/	N/C	750 W	GRID F17	10	
9	AREA II	4/ X 9/	850	750 W	GRID F10	6	
9	AREA II	4/ X 9/	850	750 W	GRID F17	9	
10	AREA II	4/ X 9/	842	750 W	GRID H13	2	
11	X-III	6 X 9	161	750 W	LINE 10	1	
11	X-III	6 X 9	161	750 W	LINE 10	3	
11	AREA VI	4/ X 9/	161	750 W	LINE 13	2	
12	X-III	6 X 9	N/C	750 W	LINE 10	2	
12	X-III	6 X 9	N/C	750 W	LINE 10	4	
12	AREA VI	4/ X 9/	N/C	750 W	LINE 13	3	
13	AREA V	6 X 9	N/C	750 W	LINE 8	1	
13	AREA V	6 X 9	143	750 W	LINE 8	5	
14	AREA V	4/ X 6	143	750 W	LINE 8	2	
14	AREA V	4/ X 6	N/C	750 W	LINE 8	4	
15	AREA V	6 X 9	803	750 W	CYC PIPE SL	1	
15	AREA V	6 X 9	803	750 W	CYC PIPE SR	3	
16	AREA V	6 X 9	143	750 W	CYC PIPE SL	2	
16	AREA V	6 X 9	143	750 W	CYC PIPE SR	4	
17	X-I	PAR 64-W	N/C	750 W	GRID B11	1	
17	X-I	6 X 9	161	750 W	HR PIPE	2	
18	X-I	6 X 9	161	750 W	GRID B11	2	
18	X-I	6 X 9	N/C	750 W	HR PIPE	1	
19	X-II	6 X 9	803	750 W	HL PIPE	2	
20	X-II	6 X 9	143	750 W	HL PIPE	1	
21	X-	6 X 6	842	750 W	HL PIPE	5	

Figure 3.18 The switchboard hookup for *G. R. Point*. (*Courtesy of Glen C. Goodwin.*)

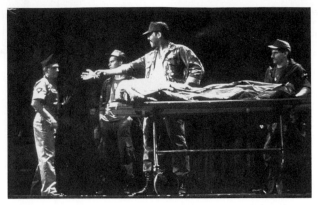

Figure 3.19 Production photo of *G. R. Point*. (*Courtesy of Glenn C. Goodwin.*)

Figure 3.20 Production photo of *G. R. Point*. (*Courtesy of Glenn C. Goodwin.*)

Part 2

The Specialty Areas: Design and Practice

Chapter 4

Nonmusical Performance Theatre

[96] *For useful information concerning the location of performance places nationally and internationally, see:*

Beatrice Handel, Janet Spencer, Nolanda Turner (eds.), The National Directory for the Performing Arts and Civic Centers. *Dallas, Tex.; Handel & Co., Inc. (2800 South, Suite 231, Dallas 75201); 1973. 604 pp. Intended to be an annual publication. State-by-state listing all U.S. performance places with pertinent details.*

Leo B. Pride (ed.), International Theatre Directory. *N.Y.; Simon and Schuster; 1973. 577 pp.; illus. Gives pertinent details on all theatres, listed by country.*

Jennifer Merin and Elizabeth B. Burdick, International Directory of Theatre, Dance and Folklore Festivals. *Westport, Conn.; Greenwood Press; 1979. 481 pp. Descriptive details concerning all national and international performance festivals.*

No area of lighting design has been more written about than the lighting of the nonmusical (serious drama) performance stage. Its paragon, the Broadway theatre (or London's West End), still remains both a touchstone and an objective toward which most practicing lighting designers aspire. Its practices influence all other forms of theatrical lighting.[96]

Design Considerations

In almost all cases, if the aspiring lighting designer has in hand the following three basic pieces of information about a particular show, 90 percent of the lighting design is predetermined and will be nearly identical from production to production, regardless of who "lights the show":

1. *The Play.* Much of the lighting of a show is specifically dictated by the dramatic material. The author of a piece wrote it to be performed, and the script tells the designer much about how the piece is to be presented.

2. *The Place.* When the lighting designer knows which theatre (or performance place — it may be an open field) is to be used, much of the lighting design is decided. Lighting instruments can only be mounted in certain places in a particular physical environment; switchboards have limitations. The realities of a production to a great extent determine the possible design solutions.

3. *The Set.* Someone (the scenographer; a scenic de-signer; the lighting designer, if that person performs all design jobs) has determined a visual environment — a scenic setting or performance milieu. This environment further limits the positions from which the designer can light and also limits the way the lighting can be achieved.

The same basic premise is used for repertory lighting.

Given these three basics — the show, the theatre, and a specific setting — much of the lighting design is decided. However, as a creative artist, the lighting designer can decisively create within the structure of each of these factors:

The Play. Shakespeare can be done (successfully) in many ways. Variations in lighting design approach are almost limitless if the designer is designing lighting for the same *Romeo and Juliet* the rest of the artists are presenting. Certain design approaches are wrong; for example, psychedelic lighting for a realistic *Romeo and Juliet* just won't work. The lighting designer may, if fortunate, have a voice with the production group about which play the group produces. Once this decision has been made, choices narrow.

The Place. The lighting designer has important input here. He or she can ask for false beams to conceal lighting units or ask to create new mounting positions in the theatre. Once the performance place and its modification is determined, so is much of the lighting design.

The Set. Prior to the scenic designer's arriving at finalized visual environment (settings) decisions, the lighting de-

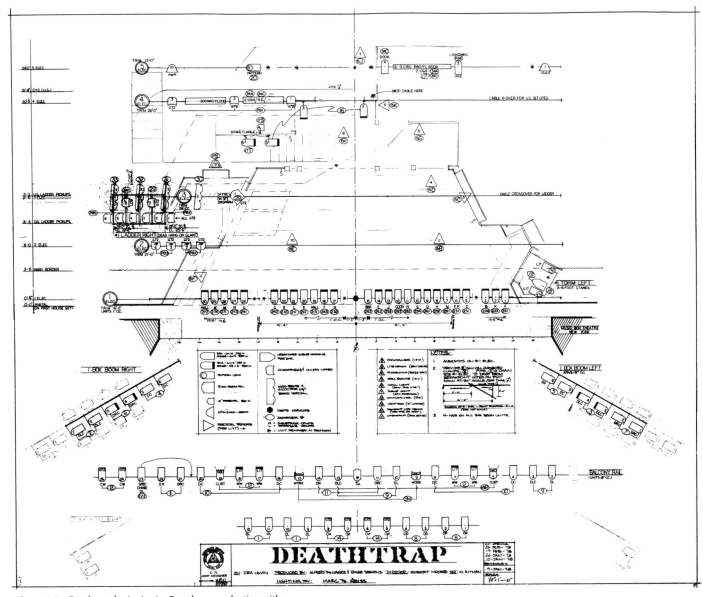

[97] *"Roger Morgan: Tony Aware,"* Lighting Dimensions, *vol. 3, no. 11 (Nov. 1979), pp. 29, 31–34. Illus. Interview. Includes Morgan's light plot on p. 32.*

Figure 4.1 *Deathtrap,* by Ira Levin. Broadway production with lighting design by Marc B. Weiss; scenery by William Ritman. (*Photo:* © *Marc B. Weiss.*)

DEATHTRAP – BOARD HOOKUP
Music Box NYC 26 Feb 1978

1	BOOTH-9-10-11-12		DL
2	BBR-1-2		DLC
3	BBL-3-4		DLC
4	BBR-5-6		DC
5	BBL-5-6		DC
6	BBR-3-4		DRC
7	BBL-1-2		DRC
8	BOOTH-1-2-3-4		DR
9	BR-2-3-10-13		DL
10	BR-4-8-16-20		DC
11	BR-11-14-21-22		DR
12	BR-6-7-17-18		WW
13	BR-24-25		CW
14	BOOTH-5-6-7-8		CW
15	Switchbox - PRACTICALS		
16	SET-2-3-5		HALL B/L
17	Switchbox -		BACKINGS
18	TL-2-3		FIRE
19	TL-1		FLAME
20	5P-9		LIVING RM
21	AUX	211-214	UL
22	AUX	221-224	UL
23	AUX	231-234	DL
24	AUX	241-244	DC
25	AUX	251-254	DC
26	AUX	261-264	DR
27	AUX	271-274	UR
28	AUX	281-284	UR
29	3P-1 + LR-7		MOON
30	3P-2	SUN	SKYLITE-HI
31	LR-9	SUN	SKYLITE-MID
32	LR-10	SUN	SKYLITE-LOW
33	LR-11	SUN	FRENCH DOOR
34A	4P-strip	circ-1	
	+ 5P-strip	cir 1	CW
34C	4P-strip	circ-2	
	+ 5P-strip	circ 2-3	
	+ 5P-4 + LR-8		WW

Dim17:	swS	SET-4+prac-9	Kitchen
	swT	SET-6	Stairs

Lightning – push buttons:

PB1	5P-3
PB2	2P-1-3
PB3	2P-2-4
PB4	LR-4-5-6
PB5	LR-1-2-3
PB6	4P-1-2-3-

211	1P-21	L
212	1P-20	K
213	1P-19	WALL
214	------------	
221	1P-1	F
222	BR.23	CHAIR DL
223	1P-2	K
224	1P-3	B
231	1P-6	FIREPLACE
232	1P-17	A
233	1P-22	B
234	1P-10	G
241	1P-26	C
242	1P-23	G
243	1P-18	F
244	------------	
251	1P-5	C
252	1P-8	H
253	1P-13	J
254	------------	
261	1P-9	D
262	1P-14	E
263	1P-15	BAR
264	------------	
271	1P-28	M
272	1P-30	HALL
273	1P-27	H
274	1P-29	J-N
281	1P-7	M
282	1P-11	N
283	1P-12	DOORS
284	------------	

Dimmer 15

swA	------------
swB	Chandelier
swC	Track UL
swD	Floor lamp
swE	Track over desk
swF	Track over bar
swG	Vestibule sconce
swH	Hall chandelier
swJ	Living room lamp
swK	Outside bug light

Figure 4.2 *Deathtrap* switchboard hookup sheets.

signer can have a meaningful creative input with the design team. Once the set is determined, so is much of the lighting.

Since there is no one correct answer, this chapter places emphasis on current practices as shown in numerous examples. Design theory was treated in Chapter 1. Offered here is an extensive selection of light plots by practicing artists for proscenium theatre, thrust theatre, arena theatre, dinner theatre, and experimental or avante-garde theatre from contemporary examples.

Figures 4.1 and 4.2 are Marc B. Weiss's plot and hookup for *Deathtrap,* which are included here for several reasons: the final lighting design was excellent artistry; few Broadway shows have box set scenic designs with a ceiling over everything these days, and this plot shows how Weiss solved the problem; and the melodrama had a long run in New York City and many readers have seen it. Figure 4.3 shows the lighting. Weiss leaned heavily upon naturalism and realism as motivating light sources in this design.

Figures 4.4, 4.5, and 4.6 depict Roger Morgan's plot, section, and hookup for *Crucifer of Blood* in New York City. Figure 4.7 is a scene from this Tony Award – winning production. Designer Morgan leaned heavily upon both special effects (the storm scene) and mood creation.[97] Figures 4.8 and 4.9 offer Tharon Musser's plot and hookup for the single-setting (but multi-place) serious drama *Whose Life Is It Anyway?* This design departed from then-standard practice in that Musser used an FOH (front-of-house) light pipe suspended over the orchestra area (in sight of the audience) instead of the more common balcony front and box boom instrument-mounting positions. She thereby obtained "arena stage" high-angle front lighting in a proscenium theatre to sharply define each of three hospital rooms with minimum spill into adjacent areas. Notice also the carefully designed "light rig" in the production photo (Fig. 4.10), in sight of the audience and suspended above the acting area. It was *designed.* Light was used to create *selective* visibility where it was needed — yet faces were clearly visible.

Figures 4.11 and 4.12 take us away from the proscenium theatre into arena production, which will be treated at greater length later in this chapter. The production is *Arturo Ui* by designer William Mintzer at Washington D.C.'s 1,800-seat Arena Theatre. Figures 4.13, 4.14, and 4.15 are

Figure 4.3 *Deathtrap* production photo. (*Photo: © Sy Friedman.*)

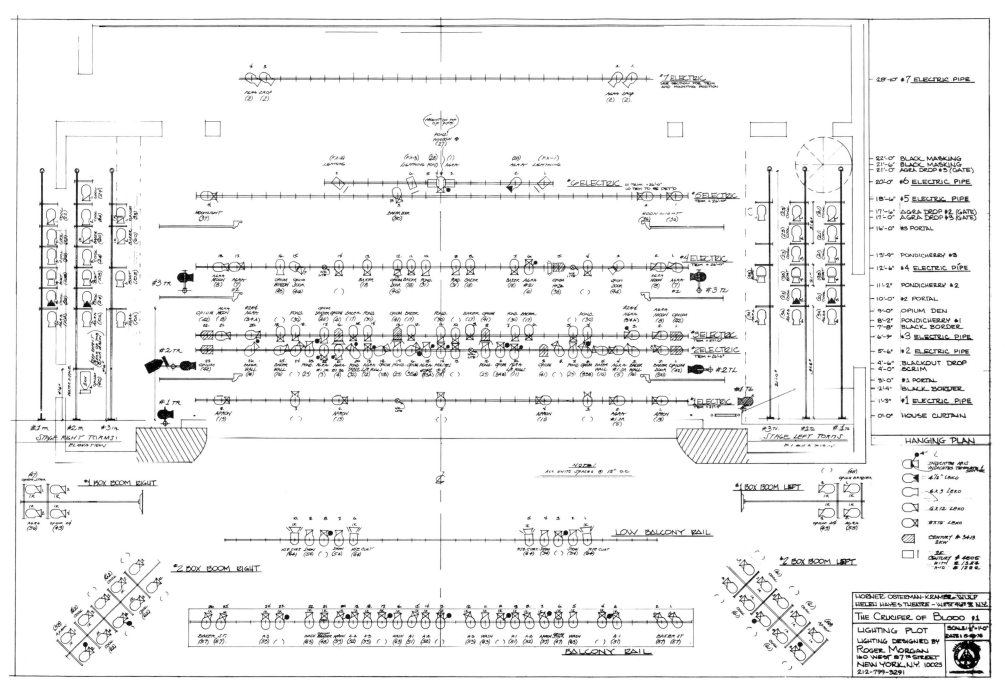

Figure 4.4 Light plot for Broadway production of *The Crucifer of Blood*; lighting design by Roger Morgan.

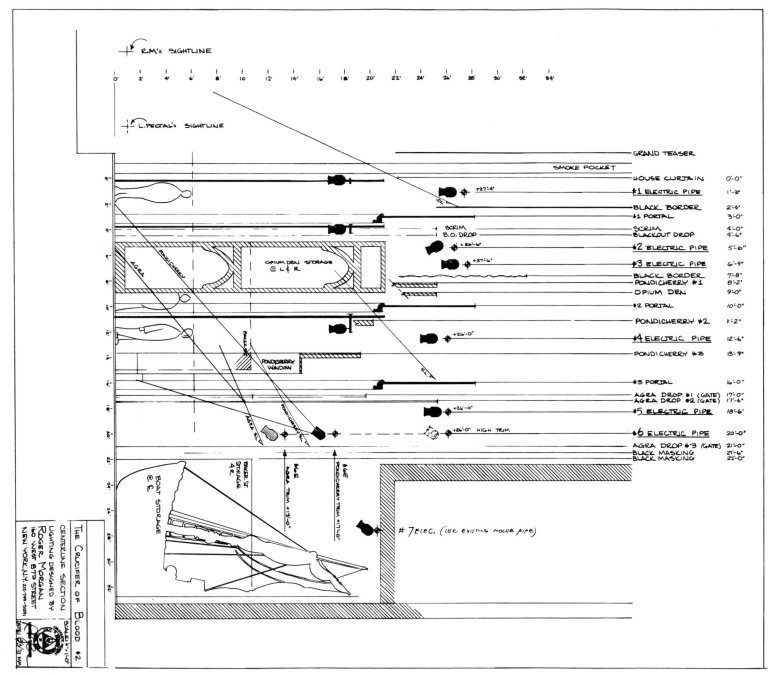

Figure 4.5 Section drawing for *The Crucifer of Blood.*

DIM	USE	QUAN.TYPE	WATTS	TOT.LOAD	LOCATION	COLOR
1	AGRA SUN	1 BIG BROAD	2K	2K	6P3	GOLD G-36
2	AGRA					
3	LANTERN #1 DR. SMALL	1 6x16 IRIS	750	750	2P22	VLL R-53
4	LANTERN #1 DR. BIG	1 6x12 IRIS	750	750	2P21	VLL R-53
5	LANTERN #1 BR. L.SIDE	2 6x16	750	750	1P2 2P4	VLL R-53
6	LANTERN #2 U.L.C. @ ARCH	1 6x16 IRIS	750	750	4P6	VLL R-58
7	LANTERN #2 U.L.C. SIDES	1 6x12 / 1 6x16	750	1500	4P1-17	VLL R-53
8	AGRA MOON	4 6x12	750	3K	3P2-24 4P2-18	AMBER R-16
9A	LOW SUN SL.	3 6x9	750	2250	1TL6 2TL6 3TL3	AMBER R-16
9B	BOAT TORM L.	3 6x9 T+S	750	2250	1TL4 2TL4 3TL2	NC
10A	LOW SUN SR.	3 6x9	750	2250	1TL6 2TL7 3TR4	AMBER R-16
10B	BOAT TORM R.	3 6x9 T+S	750	2250	1TR4 2TR5 3TR3	NC
11A	L. LANTERN POOL @ CHEST	1 6x16 IRIS	750	750	2P10	VLL R-53
12A	R. LANTERN POOL	1 6x16 IRIS	750	750	2P19	VLL R-53
13	BAKER ST. SL. PRACTICAL 3				2 SCONCES + 1 TABLE LAMP	— —
14	BAKER ST. SR. PRACTICAL 1				TABLE LAMP	— —
15	HOLMES SR DR	1 6x16 IRIS	1K	1K	2P14	LT.BL R-62
16	BAKER ST. WALLS	4 6x12	750	3K	2P3-5-25-26	B.A. R-02
17	BAKER ST. BACKLTS D.S.	4 6x16	750	3K	3P6-9-12-15	LT.GR R-87
18	BAKER ST. BACKLTS U.S.	4 6x16	750	3K	4P7-8-11-13	LT.GR R-87
19	APRON SIDE LTS	4 6x16	750	3K	1P1-4-6-8	LT.BL G-70
20	AGRA SUN #2 SL.	1 4½x16	750	750	6P2	AMBER R-16
21	DL. COOL TORM	1 4½x16 / 2 6x12 / 1 6x9	750	3K	1TL1-2-3-5	LT.BL G-70
22	DR. COOL TORM	1 4½x16 / 2 6x12 / 1 6x9	750	3K	1TR1-2-3-5	LT.BL G-70
23	UL. COOL TORM	1 4½x16 / 2 6x12	750	3K	2TL1-2-3-5	LT.BL G-70
24	UR. COOL TORM	1 4½x16 / 2 6x12	750	3K	2TR1-2-4-6	LT.BL G-70
25						
26	COFFIN INTERIOR LIGHTING	TO BE DET'D				NC —
27	ROUND WINDOW	1 6x16 IRIS	750	750	6P4 (OVER MOUNT)	VLL R-53
28	BIG WINDOW	1 BIG BROAD	2K	2K	6P5	VLL R-53
29	DS. BACK LTS	4 6x12	750	3K	2P7-12-17-23	DK.BL R-68
30	MID STG. BACK LTS	5 6x12	750	3750	3P4-7-11-14-18	DK.BL R-68
31	U.S. BACK LTS.	2 6x12	750	1500	4P9	DK.BL R-68
32	TABLE DN. LT.	1 6x12 IRIS	750	750	2P20	VLL R-53
	REPLUGS					
11B	OPIUM STAIR SPECIAL	1 6x12 T+S	750	750	1P18	VLB R-60
12B	BOAT RUNNING LIGHTS				SET- PRACTICALS	— —
33A	LANTERN #2 @ C LARGE	1 6x12 IRIS	750	750	2P15	VLL R-53
34A	LANTERN #2 @ C SIDES	2 6x16 IRIS	750	1500	3P-3-20	VLL R-53
35A						
36B	OPIUM S.L. PRACTICAL				SL OPIUM SET	— —
37B	OPIUM S.R. PRACTICAL				SR OPIUM SET	— —

DIM	USE	QUAN.TYPE	WATTS	TOT.LOAD	LOCATION	COLOR
33B	OPIUM	1 6x16 IRIS	750	750	2P6	MAGENTA R-45
34B	OPIUM	1 6x16 IRIS	750	750	2P11	BL-GR R-93
35B	OPIUM	1 6x16 IRIS	750	750	2P16	MAGENTA R-45
36A	MOONLIGHT SL.	2 6x16	750	1500	5P1	L BG R-63
37A	MOONLIGHT S.R.	1 6x16	750	750	5P4	L BG R-63
38	BACK ROOM HAZE	1 8" FRESNEL (CENTURY #2419)	1K	1K	4P5	V.DK.BL R-80
39	BACK ROOM DOOR GOBO	1 6x12 T+S	1K	1K	3TR1	LT.BL G-70
40	WATER RIPPLE	1 1172 PROJ	2K	2K	2TR8	VLB R-60
41	FRESNEL DN. LTS.	4 8" FRESNEL (CENTURY #2419)	1K	4K	2P9 3P8-13-16	DK.BL R-68
42	FRESNEL SIDE LTS	4 8" FRESNEL (CENTURY #2419)	1K	4K	2P1-27 3P1-22	DK.BL R-68
43	OPIUM S.R. WINDOW	1 6x16	750	750	4P16	LT.BL G-70
44	SLOP HOUSE DOOR	1 6x9	750	750	4P3	RED R-45
45	BRAZIER D.S.R.	1 6x12 IRIS	750	750	5P17	NC —
46	OPIUM DOOR GOBO	2 6x12 T+S	1K	2K	4P12-15	LT.BL G-70
47	STAIR SL. AREA OPIUM	2 6x16 T+S	1K	2K	BR6 #1BBR1	VLB R-60
48	BRAZIER SL. AREA OPIUM	2 6x16 T+S	1K	2K	BR21 #1BBL1	VLB R-60
49	DL. X.LTS.	2 6x16	1K	2K	#1BBL4 #1BBR4	VLB R-60
50	BAKER ST. DOORS	2 6x16	1K	2K	2P2 5P-3	LAV R-51
51	AREA 1 D.S.L.	3 6x16	1K	3K	BR 3-9-15	VLB R-60
52	AREA 2 C	3 6x16	1K	3K	BR 8-14-19	VLB R-60
53	AREA 3 DS.R.	5 6x16	1K	3K	BR12-18-24	VLB R-60
54	SHOW CURTAIN	4 6x12	750	3K	LOW BALC.R. 2-4-7-9	LT.BL G-70
55	DC → SR AGRA	1 6x16	1K	1K	#1BBL2	VLL R-53
56	DC → SR AGRA	1 6x16	1K	1K	#1BBR2	VLL R-53
57	BAKER ST. RAIL	4 6x16	1K	4K	BR1-2-25-26	STRAW R-08
58	APRON BOX	2 6x16	1K	2K	#2BBL1 #2BBR1	VLB R-60
59	WARM C APRON	2 6x16 IRIS	1K	2K	BR7-20	VLL R-53
60	BAKER ST. WINDOW	2 6x12	1K	2K	#2TR3 #3TR2	NC —
61	COOL SIDES L.	4 6x16	1K	4K	#2BBL 3-4-7-8	LT.BL G-70
62	COOL SIDES R.	4 6x16	1K	4K	#2BBR 3-4-7-8	LT.BL G-70
63	DK.BL. WASH	4 6x12	1K	4K	BR 5-11-16-22	DK.BL G-65
64	HOUSE CURTAIN	4 8"FRES	1K	4K	LOW BALC.R 1-5-6-10	PINK R-01

COLORS ARE ROSCOLUX OR GELATRAN

Figure 4.6 Switchboard hookup for *The Crucifer of Blood.*

Figure 4.7 Production photo of *The Crucifer of Blood*. Written and directed by Paul Giovanni. Scene design: John Wulp; lighting design: Roger Morgan; assistant lighting designer: Marcia Madeira; costumes: Ann Roth. (*Photo: © Martha Swope*.)

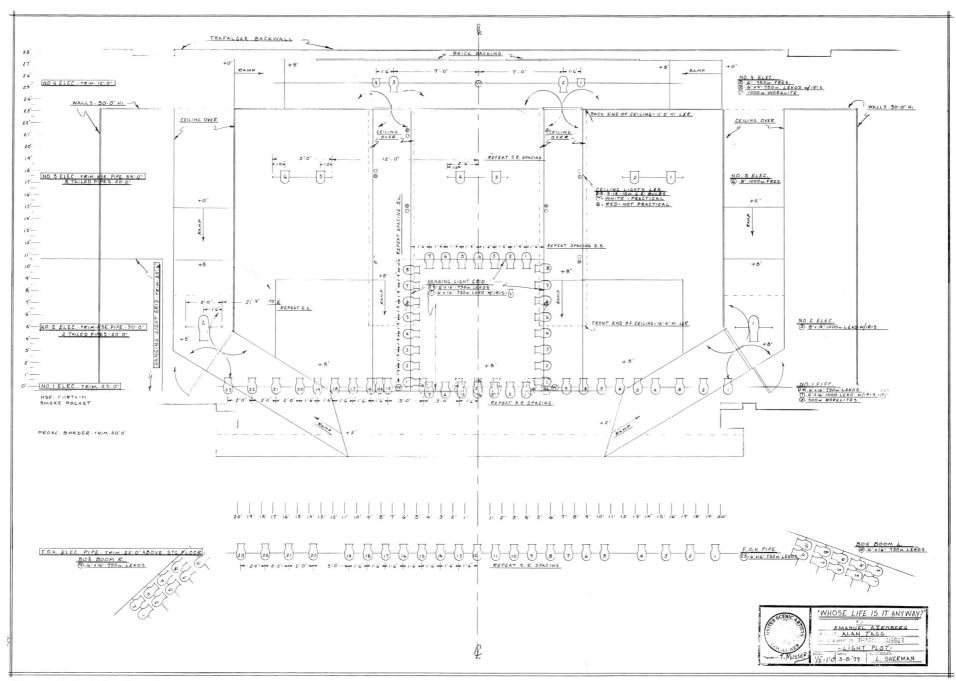

Figure 4.8 Light plot for *Whose Life Is It Anyway?* by Brian Clark.
Scene design: Alan Tagg; lighting design: Tharon Musser; assistant
lighting designer: Jo Mayer; costumes: Pearl Somner.

HOOK-UP KLIEGL PERFORMANCE - 56 CONTROL CH.

CIRCUIT	POSITION & UNIT NO.	TYPE	FOCUS	COLOR
1	BOX BOOM L 3-4 / BOX BOOM R 1-2	6X16 750W LEKOS	DL 3/4 HIGH HATS	L-3 R-13 N.C. / L-4 R-2 R-60
2	BOX BOOM L 1-2 / BOX BOOM R 3-4	6X16 750W LEKOS	DR 3/4 HIGH HATS	L-1 R-3 N.C. / L-2 R-4 R-60
3	BOX BOOM L 7-8	6X16 750W L	WASH L HIGH HATS	R-68
4	BOX BOOM R 7-8	6X16 750W L	WASH R HIGH HATS	R-68
5	F.O.H. PIPE 1-2-3	6X16 750W L	ENDS L HIGH HATS	R-60
6	F.O.H. PIPE 21-22-23	6X16 750W L	ENDS R HIGH HAT	R-68
7	NO. 1 ELEC. 1-2-3	6X16 750W L	ENDS L	N.C.
8	NO. 1 ELEC. 21-22-23	6X16 750W L	ENDS R	R-68
9	F.O.H. PIPE 4-9	6X16 750W L	ROOM L HIGH HATS	4. R-60 / 9. N.C.
10	NO. 1 ELEC. 4-6-8	6X16 750W L	ROOM L	4. 8. N.C. / 6. R-60
11	F.O.H. PIPE 12-15-20	6X16 750W L	ROOM R HIGH HATS	12-15 N.C. / 20. R-60
12	NO. 1 ELEC. 16-18-20	6X16 750W L	ROOM R	16. 20. N.C. / 18. R-60
13	F.O.H. PIPE 8-10- 14-16	6X16 750W L	ROOM L HIGH HATS	8. 16. N.C. / 10. 14. R-60
14	HANGING LT. GRID D.S. 1-7	6X16 750W LEKOS	KEN D.S.	1. N.C. / 7. R-60
15	HANGING LT. GRID D.S. 2-3-5-6	6X16 750W LEKOS	KEN U.S.	N.C.
16	HANGING LT. GRID L 1-3-5-7	6X16 750W LEKOS	KEN L	N.C.
17	HANGING LT. GRID L 2-4-6-8	6X16 750W LEKOS	KEN L	R-60

HOOK-UP KLIEGL PERFORMANCE - 56 CON-P.J.L.CH.

CIRCUIT	POSITION & UNIT NO	TYPE	FOCUS	COLOR
18	HANGING LT. GRID R 1-3-5-7	6X16 750W LEKOS	KEN R	N.C.
19	HANGING LT. GRID R 2-4-6-8	6X16 750W LEKOS	KEN R	R-60
20	HANGING LT. GRID US 1-3-5-7	6X16 750W LEKOS	KEN BK	N.C.
21	HANGING LT. GRID US 2-4-6	6X16 750W LEKOS	KEN BK	R-60
22	HANGING LT. GRID DS 4	6X16 750W IRIS	DSC IRIS KEN'S ROOM	R-60
23	BOX BOOM R 5-6	6X16 750W L	PATH L HIGH HATS	5. N.C. / 6. R-60
24	F.O.H. PIPE 13	6X16 750W L	CORRIDOR RIGHT DS HIGH HAT	N.C.
25	BOX BOOM L 5-6	6X16 750W L	PATH R HIGH HATS	5. N.C. / 6. R-60
26	F.O.H. PIPE 11	6X16 750W L	CORRIDOR LEFT DS HIGH HAT	N.C.
27	F.O.H. PIPE 5-6-7	6X16 750W L	PATH L D.S. HIGH HAT	N.C.
28	F.O.H. PIPE 17-18-19	6X16 750W L	PATH R. D.S. HIGH HAT	N.C.
29	NO. 1 ELEC. 10-11-13-14	6X16 750W L	PATH BK	R-60
30	NO. 1 ELEC. 9-9A	6X16 750W L	CORRIDOR LEFT US	R-60
31	NO. 1 ELEC. 15-15A	6X16 750W L	CORRIDOR RIGHT US	R-60
32	NO. 1 ELEC. 5	6X16 750W L	RAMP SL	R-60
33	NO. 2 ELEC. 1	8X14 1KW LEKO IRIS	DOOR L BK	R-60
34	NO. 1 ELEC. 19	6X16 750W L	RAMP SR	R-60
35	NO. 2 ELEC. 2	8X14 1KW LEKO IRIS	DOOR R BK	R-60

HOOK-UP KLIEGL PERFORMANCE - 56 CONTROL CH.

CIRCUIT	POSITION & UNIT NO.	TYPE	FOCUS	COLOR
36	NO. 3 ELEC. 1	8" 1KW FRESNEL	WALL L	N.C.
37	NO. 3 ELEC. 2	8" 1KW FRESNEL	WALL L	R-60
38	NO. 3 ELEC. 3	8" 1KW FRESNEL	WALL C	N.C.
39	NO. 3 ELEC. 4	8" 1KW FRESNEL	WALL C	R-60
40	NO. 3 ELEC. 5	8" 1KW FRESNEL	WALL R	N.C.
41	NO. 3 ELEC. 6	8" 1KW FRESNEL	WALL R	R-60
42	NO. 4 ELEC. 1-4	6" 750W FRESNELS	US. WALL	N.C.
43	NO. 4 ELEC. 2-3	6X9 750W LEKOS IRIS	U.S. DOORS BKS.	R-60
44	CEILING LIGHTS	(20) S-14 40WATT G.E. BULBS	410 WHITE APE PRAC.	
45	NO. 1 ELEC. 7	6X16 750W LEKO	SISTER DOORWAY	N.C.
46	NO. 1 ELEC. 17	6X16 750W LEKO	KEN DOORWAY	N.C.
47				
48	DESK LAMP - BULLETIN BD.	60 W. STD.	SISTER OFF.	
49	WALL SCONCE	40 W. STD.	KEN'S RM.	—
50	BOX BOOM L 9-10 / BOX BOOM R 9	6"X16" 750W L	RIGHT OFFICE FILL	9. N.C. / 10. R-60 / N.C.

NOTE: 1 HOT PATCH CABLE TO C PLATFORM —

NOTE: U.S. DOORS HAVE R-104 BEHIND GLASS.

Figure 4.9 Switchboard hookup for *Whose Life Is It Anyway?*

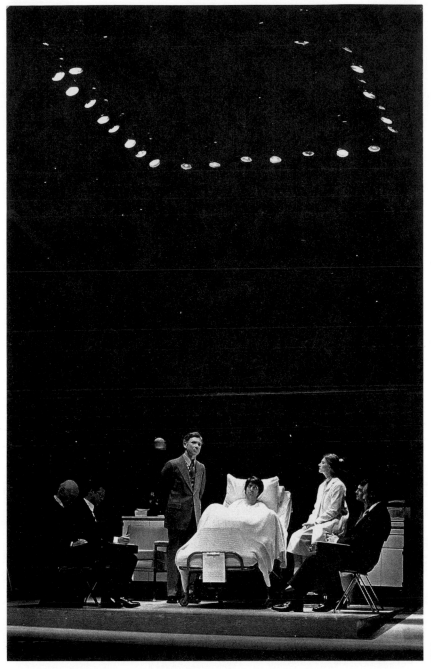

Figure 4.10 Production photo of *Whose Life Is It Anyway?* on Broadway. (*Photo:* © *Martha Swope.*)

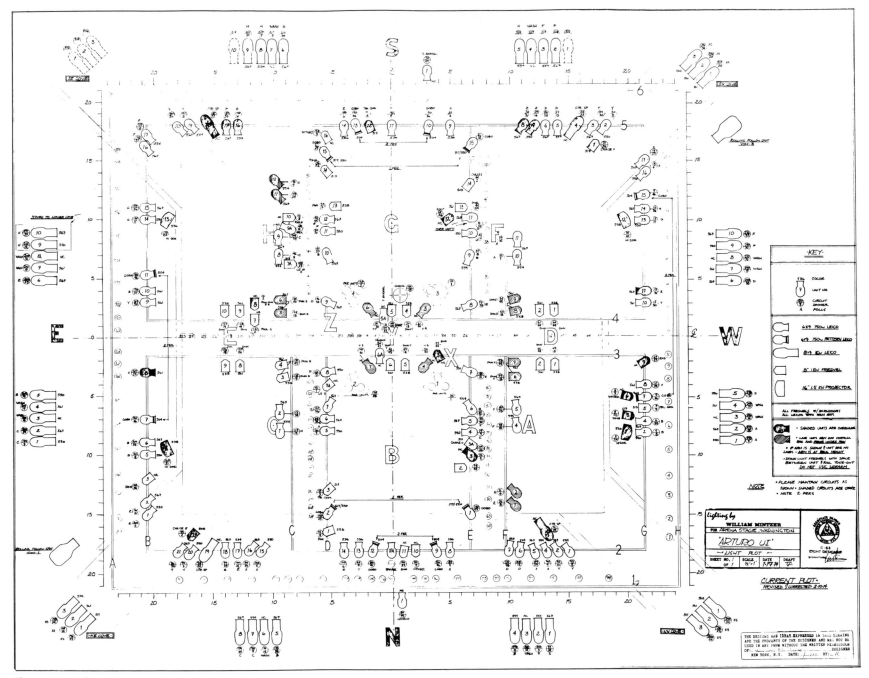

Figure 4.11 Light plot for *Arturo Ui* by Ugo Betti at Washington, D.C.'s Arena Stage in 1974. Director: Carl Weaver; scenic design: Karl Eigsti; lighting design: William Mintzer; costumes: Marjorie Slaiman.

WILLIAM MINTZER — *lighting design*

Production: "ARTURO UI"
Producer: ARENA STAGE, WASHINGTON. DC 1/74

·HOOK-UP·

REVISED 2·10·74

pg 1-

Table 1

CIR	SW	FOCUS	POSITION-NO	TYPE	CLR	NOTES
35·72 / 137	1	PARS 1·3·4	FLY 1·3·4	PAR 56 300W	NC	3
121		UI SP. S.DRUM	D·7A	8" 1KW FRES.	NC	SC·12 · 1
150 / 151 / 151	2	UI SWING·1	4P·7 / G·18	8" 1KW FRES	NC	3
95 / 44		CHAISE ·5	2P·22 / E·14	8" 1KW FRES	503	2 · 6
74		JUDGE ·5	E·3	6×9 750WL	NC	1
111 / 191	3	TBL·SOFA	D·5 / SP·8	8" 1KW FRES	517	2
86 / 158		WITNESS·9	2P·10 / D·16 / D·6	8" 1KW FRES	NC	3 · 6
90 / 155	4	X	2P·4 ¢ C·12	6×9 750WL	554	2
102 / 18		X	2P·15 ¢ G·16		550	2 · 6
87 / 22		X	2P·8 ¢ SP·9		536	2
93 / 181	5	Y	2P·1 ¢ SP·19		554	2
97 / 30		Y	2P·20 ¢ SP·2		550	2 · 6
83 / 192		Y	2P·13 ¢ SP·11		536	2
71 / 177	6	Z	F·2 ¢ B·17		554	2
160 / 25		Z	B·1 ¢ SP·7		550	2 · 6
103 / 189		Z	2P·14 ¢ SP·14		536	2
254·36 / 116·248	7	A	N·COVE·2 ¢ F·10 / D·5 ¢ W·COVE·1	8×9 1KW·6×9 750 / 6×9 750·8×9 1KW	554 / 550	4
253·37 / 43·4	8	B	N·COVE·1 ¢ E·9 / E·COVE·1 ¢ E·4	8×9 1KW·6×9 750 / 6×9 750·6×9 750	554 / 550	4
195·146 / 199·75	9	C	N·COVE·7 ¢ C·8 / E·COVE·1 ¢ E·4	8×9 1KW·6×9 750 / 8×9 1KW·6×9 750	554 / 550	4
78·227 / 150·240	10	F	F·4 ¢ N·COVE·3 / D·11 ¢ W·COVE·9	6×9 750·8×9 1KW / 6×9 750·8×9 1KW	554 / 550	4
81·224 / 174·15	11	G	E·6 ¢ S·COVE·5 / B·14 ¢ G·13	6×9 750·8×9 1KW / 6×9 750·6×9 750	554 / 550	4
177·222 / 212·40	12	H	C·1 ¢ S·COVE·8 / W·COVE·9 ¢ E·10	6×9 750·8×9 1KW / 8×9 1KW·6×9 750	554 / 550	4
68·27 / 122·243	13	D	2P·6 ¢ SP·5 / D·8 ¢ W·COVE·9	6×9 750·6×9 750 / 8×9 1KW·8×9 1KW	554	4
170·184 / 202·82	14	E	2P·17 ¢ SP·16 / E·COVE·5 ¢ E·7	6×9 750·6×9 750 / 8×9 1KW·6×9 750	554	4
252·194	15	WASH N	N·COVE 3 ¢ 6	8×9 1KW LEKO	NC	2
225 / 221		WASH S	S·COVE 4 ¢ 7		NC	2 · 4
200 / 204	16	WASH E	E·COVE 5 ¢ 8		NC	2
246 / 237		WASH W	W·COVE 3 ¢ 8		NC	2 · 4

Table 2

CIR	SW	FOCUS	POSITION-NO	TYPE	CLR	NOTES
201 / 210	17	WASH E	E COVE 4 ¢ 7		561	2
245 / 239		WASH W	4 COVE 4 ¢ 7		561	2 · 4
59 / 33	18	DWN X	F·6 ¢ 8	8" 1KW FRES	538	2
49 / 50		DWN Y	3P·5 ¢ 4P·4		538	2
133 / 154		DWN Z	C·3 ¢ 5		538	2
63·112 / 126	19	DWN A·B·C	3P·1 ¢ D·1 ¢ 3P·9	8" 1KW FRES	538	3
64·153 / 127		DWN F·G·H	4P·1 ¢ D·13 ¢ 4P·10		538	3 · 6
3 / 173	20	HIGH SIDE	G·1 / B·13	16" 1.5 KW 8P	536	2
145 / 14	21	HIGH SIDE	B·4 / G·12		538	2
91 / 182	22	CENTER	2P·3 / SP·18	8×9 1KWL	NC	2
98 / 28			2P·19 / SP·4			2 · 4
251 / 212·232	23	XS CLEAR	NW COVE 2 / NE COVE 2 / SW COVE 2	8×9 1KWL	561	3
249 / 248·50	24	XS AMB	NW COVE 3 / NE COVE 3 / SW COVE 3		502	3
250 / 233	25	XS FLAME	NW COVE 1 / NE COVE 1 / SW COVE 1		811	3
162 / 45	26	DEFENDENT·9	B·3 / E·12	8" 1KW FRES	NC	2
109 / 31		CHAISE ·11	E·3 / SP·1	8" 1KW FRES	550	2 · 6
156 / 5		TOMB ·15	D·14 / G·5	8" 1KW FRES	517	2
104 / 53 / 52	27	END·SP	2P·11 / 3P·3 / SP·13	8" 1KW FRES	NC	3
145		UI·'Z'	C·7A	8" 1KW FRES	517	SC·4 · 1 · 4
138	28	PARS 2	FLY 2	PAR 56 300W	NC	1
89 / 154	29	X	2P·5 / C·11	6×9 750W L	567	2
101 / 19		X	2P·16 / G·17		567	2 · 6
167 / 10		X	B·8 / G·8		561	2
92 / 180	30	Y	2P·2 / SP·20		567	2
96 / 29		Y	2P·21 / SP·3		567	2 · 6
169 / 12		Y	B·9 / G·10		561	2
70 / 176	31	Z	F·1 / B·16		567	2
161 / 24		Z	B·2 / SP·B		567	2 · 6
170 / 13		Z	B·10 / G·11		561	2

Table 3

CIR	SW	FOCUS	POSITION-NO	TYPE	CLR	NOTES
77·30 / 118·247	32	A	N·COVE·1 ¢ F·11 / D·6 ¢ N·COVE·2	8×9 1KW·6×9 750 / 6×9 750·8×9 750	567	4
193·147 / 164·6	33	B	N·COVE·5 ¢ D·10 / B·6 ¢ G·4	8×9 1KW·6×9 750 / 6×9 750·8×9 1KW	567	4
159·149 / 201·73	34	C	N·COVE·8 ¢ G·9 / E·COVE·2 ¢ E·5	8×9 1KW·6×9 750 / 8×9 1KW·6×9 750	567	4
80·226 / 152·236	35	F	F·5 ¢ S·COVE·2 / D·12 ¢ W·COVE·10	6×9 750·8×9 1KW / 6×9 750·8×9 1KW	567	4
120·225 / 175·16	36	G	D·7 ¢ S·COVE·6 / B·15 ¢ G·14	6×9 750·8×9 1KW / 6×9 750·6×9 750	567	4
179·220 / 211·41	37	H	C·2 ¢ S·COVE·9 / E·COVE·10 ¢ F·17	6×9 750·8×9 1KW / 8×9 1KW·6×9 750	567	4
68·26 / 130·235	38	D	2P·5 ¢ SP·6 / D·9 ¢ W·COVE·6	6×9 750·6×9 750 / 8×9 1KW·6×9 750	567	4
99·183 / 206·57	39	E	2P·18 ¢ SP·6 / E·COVE·6 ¢ E·8	6×9 750·6×9 750 / 8×9 1KW·8×9 750	567	4
141·140 / 52·51	40	VOMS 1·2	4P·3 / 3P·7 / 4P·6	6×9 750W	NC	4
96		GHOST DWN	F·3	8" 1KW FRES	561	1 · S
20·32 / 105·108	41	BULBS PAN	PANS ¢ NASE UNIT C 5A	15 W A·15 / 6×9 750	NC	*PROVIDE CIRCUIT — BULBS ¢ 1 LEKO
339 / 340	42	BULBS BAND	BAND PLATFORM	1KW A·S	NC	" " — PLK AS
58 / 54	43	DWN X	F·7 ¢ 9	8" 1KW FRES	561	2
48 / 45		DWN Y	3P·6 ¢ 4P·5		561	2 · 6
132 / 135		DWN Z	C·4 ¢ 6		561	2
62·75 / 129	44	DWN A·B·C	3P·2·E·2 ¢ 3P·B		561	3
61·42 / 128		DWN F·G·H	4P·2·E·13·4P·9		561	3 · 6
84	45	LEGEND	1P·1 ¢ 3P·6A	6×9 750W	NC	2
86 / 190	46	GOBO CTR	2P·9 ¢ 12 / SP·10 ¢ 13	6×9 750 T ¢ S	504	4
166 / 9		GOBO EDGE	B·7 ¢ 11 / G·7 ¢ 15		504	4 · 8
110 / 46	47	GOBO BRANCH	D·2 ¢ E·1 / D·15 ¢ E·15		517 / 550	STRIPS
54 / 139		S·BARREL·SONG CHANDELIER	4P·5A ¢ G·1 / CTR PANS	8" 1KW FRES	NC	SC·4 · 2 · *PROVIDE GRID CIR
335		GHOST WAGON	DECK V·4		521	PROVIDE CIR V·4
331	48	CAR	V·4	6×9 750W L	NC	2
336 / 538		F·S DECK	DECK V·1 / DECK V·3		NC	*PROVIDE CIR V·1 " " V·3 · 2 · 4
	49	DEAD				
	50	DEAD				

Figure 4.12 Switchboard hookup for *Arturo Ui*.

Figure 4.13 Production photo of *Arturo Ui*. (*Photo: ©Anton Miller.*)

Figure 4.14 Production photo of *Arturo Ui*.

Figure 4.15 Production photo of *Arturo Ui*.

production photos from this highly theatricalized presentation.

Figures 4.16 and 4.17 show my plot and hookup for *Pueblo* (an original script which later became a nationally televised ABC Special) for the Washington Arena Stage production. I have intentionally included my unrevised hookup as a sample of the type of rough presentation done by a busy designer under pressure. This plot and hookup were done during one Sunday afternoon in the theatre. The lighting was hung the next day and focused thereafter. All revisions done through opening night are shown in this hookup. Many of the plots and hookups used in this volume were carefully redrafted by the designers for publication use *after* the show was open and running, so it seemed useful to include at least one sample of an unrevised working hookup done in haste. Figure 4.18 shows a production photo from the scene where the American spy ship *Pueblo* is being fired upon by the North Koreans prior to capture. The entire stage floor was trapped and covered with open wire grillwork which became the surfaces below deck level. Actors played scenes under the stage floor in full light. The ship's "bridges" were elevators which came up out of the floor. Steel catwalks and ladders and superstructure allowed the large cast to climb all the way to the overhead light grid, as the performance was blocked by director Gene Frankel. It is useful to contrast the design work on this 1971

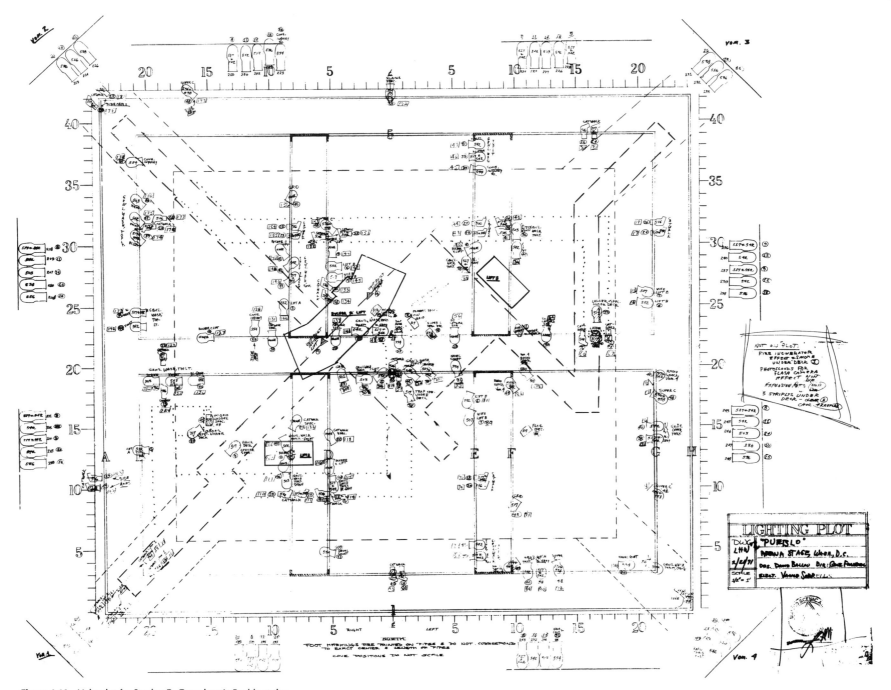

Figure 4.16 Light plot for Stanley R. Greenberg's *Pueblo* at the
Arena Stage in Washington, D.C., March 1971. Director: Gene
Frankel; scene design: David R. Ballou; lighting design: Lee Watson;
costumes: Marjorie Slaiman.

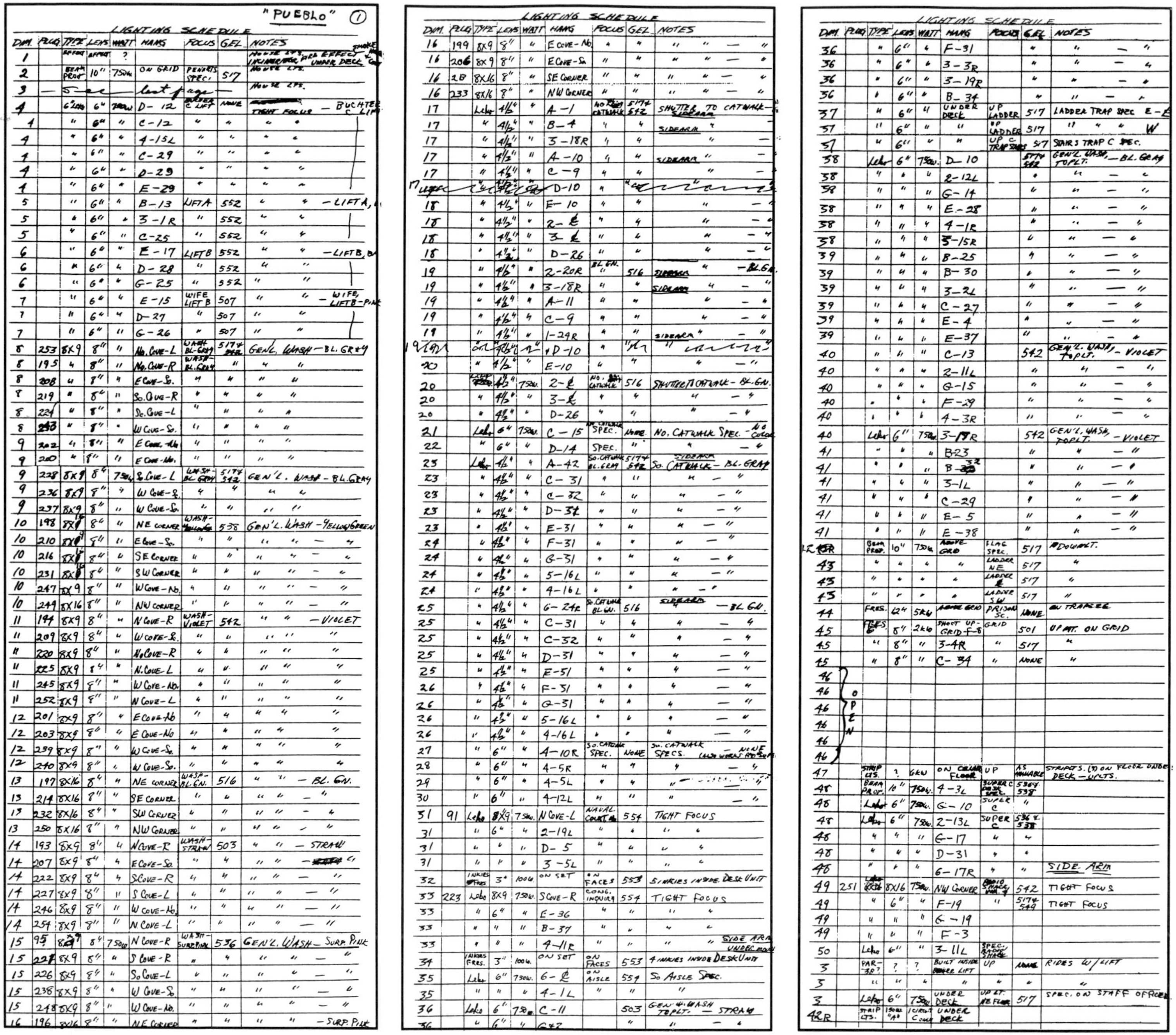

Figure 4.17 Switchboard hookup for *Pueblo.*

Figure 4.18 Production photo of *Pueblo*. (*Photo:* © *George de Vincent.*)

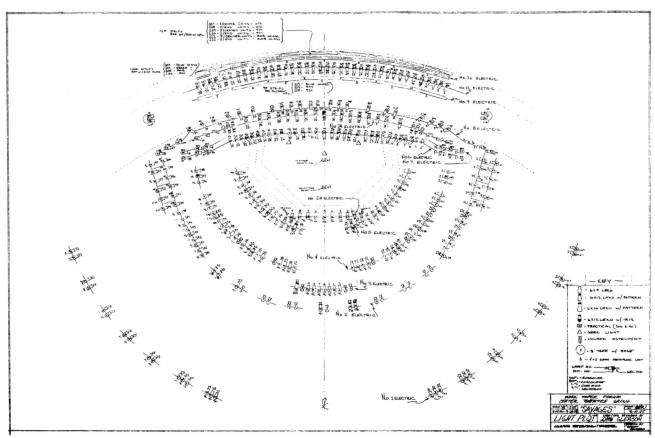

Figure 4.19 Light plot for *Savages* at the Mark Taper Forum, Los Angeles, in June 1974. Set and costume designs: Sally Jacobs; lighting design: John Gleason; director: Gordon Davidson.

production with designer Mintzer's work for a different production in the same theatre in 1974. Each design is valid; however, the designs used the same space very differently and the plays were quite dissimilar.

Figures 4.19 and 4.20 offer yet another contrast. In these figures, *Savages,* designed by John Gleason, is presented in light plot and hookup and photos. Figure 4.21 depicts the show as it was lighted from that plot and that hookup at the Mark Taper Forum in Los Angeles within the framework of a basic seasonal repertory light setup in 1974 (repertory light is discussed in greater detail in Chap. 6). Figures 4.22, 4.23,

and 4.24 present John Gleason's light plot, hookup, and production photo for the same show, *Savages,* when presented at New York City's Hudson Guild Theatre in a proscenium stage in 1977. Same show, same designer, same director; different city and theatre type. (Los Angeles is a thrust theatre; Hudson Guild is a proscenium theatre). These two productions merit careful comparison. They also convey a message: the lighting designer shouldn't throw any light plots away, because the same show may be repeated elsewhere, at a later time.

David Hersey's brilliant lighting design for the 8½ -hour

MARK TAPER FORUM
PERMANENT HOOK-UP
Revised: May, '74

Switches 1 thru 60 = 7000w / 4way
Switches 61 thru 100 = 7000w / 6way
Switches 101 thru 120 = 12000w / 12way
Non-Dims 1 thru 10 = 4way

SAVAGES

Switch	Position	Type	Focus	Color
1	4P-12-37 / 3P-6	3/ 6" Leko	Area 1 DDC	N/C
2	3P-3 / 4P-4-30 / 6P-14	4/ 6" Leko	Area 2 DL	N/C
3	3P-5 / 4P-10-39	3/ 6" Leko	Area 3 DC	N/C
4	3P-8 / 4P-19-45 / 6P-29	4/ 6" Leko	Area 4 DR	N/C
5	4P-6-24 / 5P-19 / 6P-11	4/ 6" Leko	Area 5 L	N/C
6	4P-13-28 / 5P-24	3/ 6" Leko	Area 6 L/C	N/C
7	4P-18-31 / 5P-2-29	3/ 6" Leko	Area 7 E	N/C
8	4P-21-36 / 5P	3/ 6" Leko	Area 8 R/C	N/C
9	5P-12 / 5P-25-43	4/ 6" Leko	Area 9 R	N/C
10	4P-3-23 / 5P	3/ 6" Leko	Area 10 UL	N/C
11	4P-15-34 / 5P-5-26	4/ 6" Leko	Area 11 UC	N/C
12	4P-26-46 / 5P	3/ 6" Leko	Area 12	N/C
13	4P-1 / 5P-15-21	3/ 6" Leko	Area 13 UUL	N/C
14	5P-3-11-20-28	4/ 6" Leko	Area 14 UUC	N/C
15	4P-48 / 5P-10-16	3/ 6" Leko	Area 15 UUR	N/C
16	5AP-4 6P-22 / 8P-14	3/ 6" Leko	Bed Position 1	N/C
17	5AP-6 6P-29 / 8P-15	" "	Pos 2	N/C
18	3P-4 / 6P-21	2/ 6" Leko	Pos 3	N/C
19	6P-7	6" Leko	SP. SL CRAWFORD	N/C
20	6P 4,5 / 34,35	4/ 6" Leko	L MS end Pipe	N/C
21	5P-1-30	2/ 6" Leko	Area 1 DDC BACK	950
22	7AP-8	1/ 6" Leko	Area 2 DL BACK	950
23	7AP-12-18	2/ 6" Leko	Area 3 DC BACK	950
24	7AP-22	1/ 6" Leko	Area 4 DR BACK	950
25	7AP-10	1/ 6" Leko	Area 5 L BACK	950
26	7AP-13	1/ 6" Leko	Area 6 L/C BACK	950
27	7AP-14-16	1/ 6" Leko	Area 7 E BACK	950
28	7AP-17	1/ 6" Leko	Area 8 R/C BACK	950
29	7AP-20	1/ 6" Leko	Area 9 R BACK	950
30	7AP-7-11	2/ 6" Leko	Area 10 UL BACK	950
31	7AP-9-21	2/ 6" Leko	Area 11 UC BACK	950
32	7AP-19-23	2/ 6" Leko	Area 12 UR BACK	950
33	8P-11	1/ 6" Leko	Area 13 UUL BACK	950
34	8P-12-17	2/ 6" Leko	Area 14 UUC BACK	950
35	8P-18	1/ 6" Leko	Area 15 UUR BACK	950
36	5AP-5	"	Bed Pos 1 SP	N/C
37	3P 7	"	L Path	N/C
38	5P-4,6	2-6" Leko	Bed Pos 3 end Area	N/C
39	5P 25,27	"	"	N/C
40	6P-1-2-3	3/ 6" Leko	US Ends L	67
41	7P-1-2-3	3/ 6" Leko	US Ends L	805
42	8P-1-2-3	3/ 6" Leko	US Ends L	38
43	6P-36-37-38	3/ 6" Leko	US Ends R	67
44	7P-4-5-6	3/ 6" Leko	US Ends R	805
45	8P-26-27-28	3/ 6" Leko	US Ends R	38
46	2P-1-4-5-8	4/ 6" Leko	US Sides L	N/C
47	2P-2-3-6-7	4/ 6" Leko	US Sides L	811
48	2P-13-15-17-19	4/ 6" Leko	Sides L	17
49	2P-14-16-18-20	4/ 6" Leko	Sides L	N/C
50	2P-54-55-56-57	4/ 6" Leko	US Sides R	N/C
51	2P-53-56-57-60	4/ 6" Leko	US Sides R	811
52	2P-41-43-45-47	4/ 6" Leko	Sides R	17
53	2P-42-44-46-48	4/ 6" Leko	Sides R	N/C
54	2P-10-12-50-52	4/ 6" Leko	Sides L & R	38
55	3P-9 / 6P-20	2/ 6" Leko	Bed Pos 3 SP	N/C
56	2P-9,11 / 4P-9	3/ 6" Leko	DS Bed	Gelatran 971
57	2P 49,51 / 4P-40	"	"	67
58	5AP	1/ 6" Leko	SP 4	N/C
59	6P 17	"	SP 5	N/C
60	6P 19	"	L Down Lite	N/C
61	5AP-3	"	MSC CRAWFORD	N/C
62	UPSTAGE PRACTICAL	150w	OVERBED	N/C
63	DN STAGE PRACTICAL	"	"	N/C
64	11P 10,14,18 21,25,29	6/ 6" Leko	US WASH BL	N/C
65	11P 11,15,17 22,24,28	"	"	45
66	11P 9,13,16 23,26,30	"	"	Gelatran 3d
67	5AP-2	1/ 6" Leko	X-1	N/C
68	5AP-7	"	X-2	N/C
69	5AP-8	"	X-3	N/C
70	6P 6,33	2/ 6" Leko	DS Bed Green Tone	67
71	4P 11,38	"	"	38
72	11P 6,7,8 31,32,33	6/ 6" Leko	Change Lite	956
73	5P 8,23 / 6P 10	3/ 6" Leko	Office	N/C
74	8P 8,16	2/ 6" Leko	"	67
75	4P 41,42	Template	Sc14 SP Temp for Indians	52
76	4P 16,17 32,33	4-6x12	Templates Reeds	67
77	7AP-5,6 24,25	4-6x12 Template	Template Reeds	8:1
78	3P 11	6x16 Template	Window	849
79	2P 28,29,38,39 21	5-6x12 Template	Barkey Leaf F	38
80	5P 17	6x16 Temp	Shutter Window	67
81	7AP 15	6x12 IRIS	Fire Down Lite	914
82	6P 15,24	2/ 6" Leko	Fire Circle	805
83	5AP 1	1/ 6" Leko	West Opening SP	N/C
84	6P 32	"	COT SR SP	N/C
85	ON SET L+R	2-3"400w	X-Lite Indians	N/C
86	"	"	"	67
87	11P-1-2-3-4 35-36-37-38	4/ 6" Leko	Final Look	67
88	6P 12,13,26,27	4/ 6" Leko	Sc4 Ind DL	940
89	4P 2,47 / 5P 9,22 / 6P 8,31	6/ 6" Leko	Sc5	4P-N/C 5P-940 6P-67
90	8P-4,7 23,25	4/ 6" Leko	Indians US 36	38
91	4P 44,22,27,5 / 6P 9 / 4P 29	6/ 6" Leko	Sc7	4P N/C 6P N/C 7P-38
92	8P 6,10,22	3/ 6" Leko	Indians Sc7	805
93	8P 5,9,13,20,24	5/ 6" Leko	Sc 8 Indians	N/C
94	2P 40,37,35, 31, 27	"	Sc 10 Perimeter	N/C
95	1P 17,18,19,30,31,32	6/ 6" Leko	Sc 10	N/C
96	1P 1,2,3,14,15,16	"	"	67
97	11P 5,12,19,20,27,34	Template	Ind.Temp Inner Below Leafs	N/C
98	8P 21 6P 30 / 5P 14	3/ 6" Leko	USR Inner Below	N/C
99	6P 16,23	2-6x12 Temp	Decoc. Metal Temp	N/C
100	6P 18	1/ 6" Leko	USC Totems Final Flash	N/C
101	1P 4,5,6,7,8,9,10,11,12,13	10/ 6" Leko	Flash	N/C
102	1P 20,21,22,23,24,25 26,27,28,29	"	"	N/C
103	CYC - Foots	500w R-40 Floods	Drop Rear	Glass Blue
104	CYC "	"	"	Amber
105	CYC "	"	"	Green
106	CYC "	"	"	N/C
107	CYC 12P	PAR 64 500w WFL	"	N/C
108	CYC "	"	"	967 977
109	CYC "	"	"	Glass Amber
110	CYC 9P	PAR 56 300w WFL	Drop Front	Blue
111	CYC "	"	"	977
112	CYC "	"	"	914

Non-Dims	Position	Type	Focus	Color
1	BANK of PHOTOFLASH		6-	
2	"			
3	"			
4	"			
5	BANK of PHOTOFLOODS			
6	"			
7	"			
8	"			

Figure 4.20 Switchboard hookup for the Mark Taper Forum production of *Savages*.

Figure 4.21 *Savages* production photo, Mark Taper Forum, Los Angeles. (*Photo: ©Steven Keull.*)

adaptation of *The Life and Adventures of Nicholas Nickleby* as presented by the Royal Shakespearean Company at New York City's Plymouth Theatre in 1981 is offered for study next. Hersey is an American who has long worked and lived in England. He is best known in this country as the designer of *Evita, Cats,* and *Starlight Express.* The American production of *Nickleby* was a nearly identical reproduction of the London version. Figures 4.25 and 4.26 depict the plot and hookup. Production photos in Figs. 4.27 through 4.31 are self-explanatory from the captions. Because there were many noteworthy design elements in Hersey's work on this

show, I have taken the liberty of quoting at length from my *Lighting Dimensions* article "Nicholas Nickleby: A Dickens of a Show," from the March 1982 issue:

There are several elements in David's style which merit careful study and possible emulation. Among these are:

1. *Economy of Units.* Using only 296 lighting units on 154 dimmers, David masterfully lighted 8½ hours of short scenes which took place all over the theatre: on stage, on ramps and scaffoldings built inside auditorium boxes, on overhead rampways in the normal "balcony front" lighting position and on a ramp from the stage extending into the orchestra.

2. *Simplicity of Design Line.* Unlike the more common Ameri-

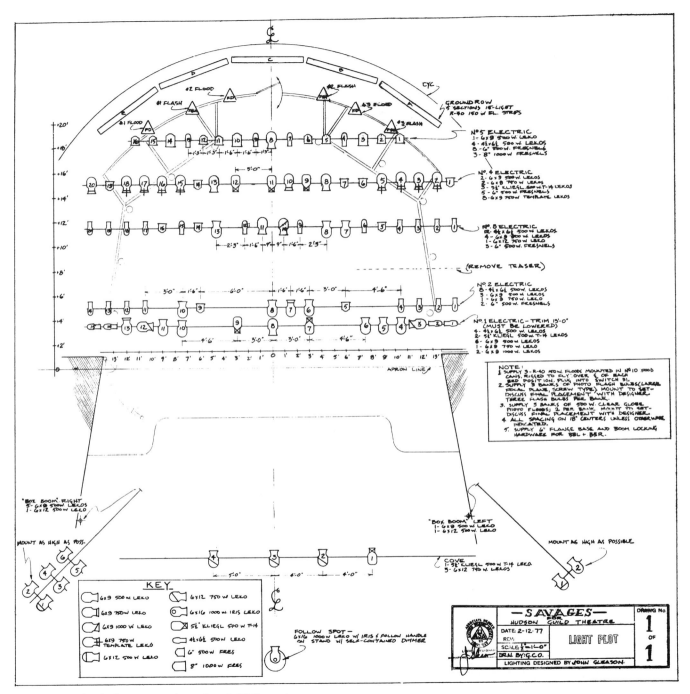

Figure 4.22 Light plot for *Savages* at the Hudson Guild Theatre in New York City, February 1977. Lighting design: John Gleason; sets and costumes: Sally Jacobs; director: Gordon Davidson.

Figure 4.24 Production photo of *Savages* in New York City (Hudson Guild Theatre). (*Photo: © Charles Marinaro.*)

SHOW: SAVAGES N.Y.C.

Board # FOH 2-6 PLATE 2000 W.

Board # FOH 1-6 PLATE 2000W / 1-6 PLATE 1800W

Board # BACKSTAGE 1 6-PLATE 3600W / 1 6-PLATE 1000W

SWITCH	LOCATION & No.	TYPE & WATTAGE	COLOR	FOCUS
1	2E 8 / 3E 8.13 / 4E 8	4-6x9 500W	2E - N/C 567	BED POSITION 1 - US
2	2E 6.10 / 3E 7 / 4E 13	4-6x9 500W	2E - N/C 567	BED POSITION 2 - MS
3 (B.B.s 6x12)	BBL 1 / BBR 1 / 1E 6.10	6x12 500W / 6x12 500W / 2-6x9 500W	N/C N/C 567	BED POSITION 3 - D.S.
4	2E 5.9 / 3E 14 / 4E 6	4-6" 500W FRES.	3E-N/C 805	WEST HOUSE U.S.
5	BBL 2 / BBR 2 / 1E 4	3-6x9 500W	1E-567 N/C	PEREIRA S.L.
6	1E 5.11 / 3E 5.16	2-6x9 500W / 2-6" 500W FRES.	N/C 567	MS & WEST
7 (OVERLOAD?)	1E 13 / 2E 7 / 4E10.20	4-6x9 750W	869 869 N/C	BRIGG SCENE
8	2E 1.3 / 3E 1.3	4-4½x6½ 500W	869	WASH L
9	2E 2.4 / 3E 2.4	4-4½x6½ 500W	849	WASH L
10	2E 12.14 / 3E 18.20	4-4½x6½ 500W	869	WASH R
11	2E 11.13 / 3E 17.19	4-4½x6½ 500W.	811	WASH R
12	1E 1.2.14.15	4-4½x6½ 500W	849/849	ENDS L+R
13	5E 1.5.12.16	4-6" 500W FRES	N/C	INDIANS U.S.
14	5E 2.6.11.15	4-6" 500W FRES	850	INDIANS U.S.
15	4E 1.7.14.19	4-6" 500W FRES	869	INDIANS U.S.
16	BBR 3.4.5.6	4-6x9 500W	N/C	SCENE 10
17	3E 6.9.12.15	4-4½x6½ 500W	850	BACKLITE D.S.

SWITCH	LOCATION & No.	TYPE & WATTAGE	COLOR	FOCUS	NOTES
18	5E 4.7.9 13	4-4½x6½ 500W	850	BACKLITE U.S.	
19	4E 9.12	2-5½" KLEIGL T-14 500W	805	FIRE CIRCLE	
20	4E 11	1-5½" KLEIGL T-14 500W	N/C	TOTEM DL USC	
21	COVE 3	1-6x12 750W		SP.1	BRIGG SC
22	1E 3.12	2-6x9 1000W	N/C	HIDEOUT #3 SIDES	
23	COVE 2	1-6x12 750W		SP.3	BRIGG SC
24	1E 7	1-5½" KLEIGL T-14 500W		SP.2	
25	GROUND ROW	5 SECTIONS 15-LITE R-40 150W FLOODS	N/C	CYC	
26	GROUND ROW	"	871 OR PRIMARY GREEN ROUNDEL	CYC	
27	GROUND ROW	"	R-85 OR PRIMARY BLUE ROUNDEL	CYC	
28	5E 3.10.14	3-8" 1000W FRES	R-80 / R-103	CHANGE LIGHT	
29	4E 2.3.17.18	4-6x9 750W TEMPLATE	N/C	INDIANS INNER AREA	TEMPLATES
30	4E 4.5.15.16	4-6x9 750W TEMPLATE	869	TEMPLATE-STAGE COVERAGE	TEMPLATES
31	HANGING PRACTICALS 1.2.3	3- R-40 150W FLOODS	N/C	HIDEOUT PRACS.	REPLUGS: ONE ONLY ON DIMMER AS CUED.
32	1E 9	1-5½" KLEIGL T-14 500W	N/C	CRAWFORD AREA DR.	
33	COVE 1	1-5½" KLEIGL T-14 500W	N/C	KWARUP SPEC S.L.	
34	1E 8 / 3E 11 / 5E 8	3-6x9 500W	849	HIDEOUT BACKLITES	REPLUG
35	3E 10	1-6x12 750W LEKO	N/C	& D.L.	
36	COVE 4	1-6x12 750W	N/C	OPEN SPEC.	
FOLLOW SPOT		6x16 1000W		IRIS LEKO w/ FOLLOW HANDLE AND DIMMER.	

Figure 4.23 Switchboard hookup for *Savages* in New York City.

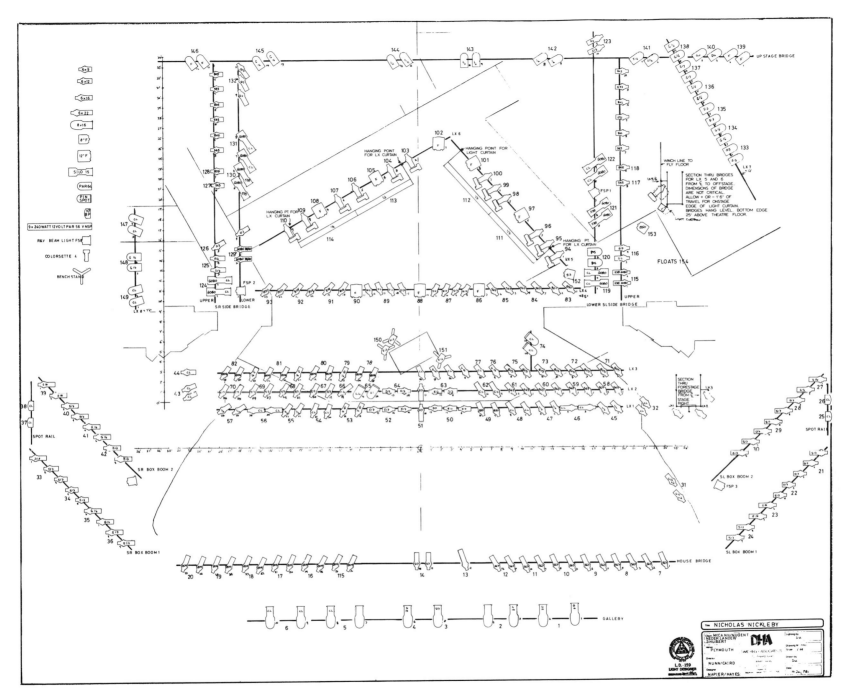

Figure 4.25 David Hersey's light plot for the New York City production of *The Life and Adventures of Nicholas Nickleby* at Broadway's Plymouth Theatre, 1982.

DHA — Plymouth Theatre Hook-Up — Front of House

POSITION	NO	TYPE	SETTING		COLOUR	CIRCUIT
GALLERY	1,2	8x16	SR Warm fill		Gelatran 16	1
	3,4	"	SL "		"	2
	5	"	Special	Cinemoid	517	3
	6	"	Special	GelaTRAN	16	4
	7,8	"	SL clear fill		cl	5
	9,10	"	SR "		"	6
HOUSE BRIDGE	1,2	6x16 1K	DL	Cinemoid	567	7
	3,4	"	SL		"	8
	5,6	"	DC		"	9
	7,8	"	SC		"	10
	9,10	"	DR		"	11
	11,12	"	SR		"	12
	13	6x22 1K	Special		"	13
	14,15	6x16 1K	Ramp	"	517	14
	16,17	"	SL	Rosco	804	15
	18,19	"	DL		"	16
	20,21	"	SC		"	17
	22,23	"	DC		"	18
	24,25	"	SR		"	19
	26,27	"	DR		"	20
BOXBOOMS						
SL 1	1	6x16 750	Walk round	Cinemoid	517	21
	2	6x12 750	"		"	"
	3	6x9 750	"		"	"
	4,5	6x9 750	"		"	22
	6,7	6x16 1K	Warm Truck	Gelatran	16	23
	8,9	"	Cool Truck	Cinemoid	517	24
SL SPOT RAIL	1	10"8.P	Spec		cl.	25
	2	"	"		cl.	26
SL 2	1,2	6x16 1k	Warm X/L	Gelatran	16	27
	3,4	"	Cool X/L	Cinemoid	517	28
	5,6	"	Warm X/L	Gelatran	16	29
	7,8	"	Cool X/L	Cinemoid	517	30
UNDERWALKWAY	1,2	6x12 750	Theatre Spec. Exact position to be agreed		6x16x2	31
	3,4	6x9 750	XL Exact position to be agreed on site.		cl.	32

DHA — Plymouth Theatre Hook-up — Front of House Cont

POSITION	NO	TYPE	SETTING		COLOUR	CIRCUIT
BOXBOOMS	1	6x16 750	Walk Round	Cinemoid	517	33
SR 1	2	6x12 750	"		"	"
	3	6x9 750	"		"	"
	4,5	"	"		"	34
	6,7	6x16 1K	Warm Truck	Gelatran	16	35
	8,9	"	Cool Truck	Cinemoid	517	36
SRSPOT Rail	1	10"8.P	Special		cl	37
	2	"	"		cl.	38
SR 2	1,2	6x16 1K	Warm X/L	Gelatran	16	39
	3,4	"	Cool X/L	Cinemoid	17	40
	5,6	"	Warm XL	Gelatran	16	41
	7,8	"	Cool X/L	Cinemoid	517	42
UNDERWALKWAY	1,2	6x12 750	Low X/L EXACT position to be Agreed		cl.	43
SR	3	"	Smoke XL, EXACT Position to be agreed		cl.	44
FORESTAGE BRIDGE: Note LX 1and 2 are treated as separate pipes on the underside of						
			the bridge. Lx 3 is in the middle of the onstage			
			side as per M.P.J's Dwg no. 6			
LX 1	1,2	6x12 750	Truck	Gelatran	Blue	45
	3,4	6x16 1K	DS X/L		cl.	46
	5,6	6x12 750	Truck	Gelatran	Blue	47
	7,8	"	Fill		cl.	48
	9,10	6x9 750	Cool Pool	Rosco	850	49
	11,12,13	6x9 750	Side Boxes	Cinemoid	517	50
	14,LX2 13	6x16 1K	Ramp		"	51
	15,16,17	6x9 750	Side Boxes		"	52
	18,19	6x12 750	Warm Pool	Gelatran	16	53
	20,21	"	Fill		cl.	54
	22,23	"	Truck	Gelatran	Blue	55
	24,25	6x16 1K	DS X/L		cl.	56
	26,27	6x12 750	Truck	Gelatran	Blue	57
LX 2	1,2	"		Cinemoid	567	58
	3,4	"			"	59
	5,6	"			"	60
			xxxxxxxxxxxxxxxxxxxxxxxxxxxxxxxxxxxxxxxxxxxxxxxxxxx			
	7,8	"			"	61
	9,10	6x16 1K	Hawk Truck		cl.	62
	11,12	6xx9 750	Side Boxes	Cinemoid	517	63

DHA — Plymouth Theatre Hook-up — F.O.H. Cont. and Stage

POSITION	NO	TYPE	SETTING		COLOUR	CIRCUIT
LX 2	14,15	6x9 750	Side Boxes	Cinemoid	517	64
	16,17	PAR 64 120 watt Pin Spot (LSI)			cl	65
	18,	6xx16 1K	Spec		cl.	66
	19,20	6x12 750		Cinemoid	517	67
	21,22	"			"	68
	23,24	"			"	69
	25,26	"			"	70
LX 3	1,2	"		Rosco	305	71
	3,4	"			"	72
	5,6	"			"	73
	6A,6	PAR 64 120 watt Pin Spot (LSI) Sidearmed up stage			cl.	74
	7,8	6x12 750		Rosco	805	75
	9,11,13	"	US Truck	Gelatran	16	76
	10,12,14	"	Arches		cl.	77
	15,16	"		Rosco	804	78
	17,20,23	"	US Truck	Gelatran	16	79
	18,19	"		Rosco	804	80
	21,22	"			"	81
	24,25	"			"	82
LX 4	1,2	6x12 750	Lhera Truck	Rosco	850	83
	3,4	"		Cinemoid	567	84
	5,6	"			cl.	85
	7	12"Fres	2K P/L	Gelatran	Full Blue	86
	7,9,10,11	6x9 500		Cinemoid	517	87
	12	12"Fres	2K P/L	Gelatran	F.Blue	88
	13,14,15,16	6x9 500		Cinemoid	567	89
	17	12"Fres	2K P/L	Gelatran	F.Blue	90
	18,19	6x12 750		Rosco	804	91
	20,21	"			"	92
	22,23	"			"	93
LX 5	1	6x12 1K	COLORCHANGE 1.850 2.Gel16,3.805 4.517			94
	2	"	"			95
	3	"	"			96
	4	12"Fres	2K	Gelatran	F.Blue	97
	5	6x12 1K	COLORCHANGE 1=850,2=Gel16.3=805.4=517			98
	6	"	"			99
	7	"	"			100
	8	12"Fres	2K	Gelatran	F.Blue	101

Figure 4.26   Switchboard hookup for *Nicholas Nickleby*.

POSITION	NO	TYPE	SETTING	COLOUR	CIRCUIT
LX 6	1	12"Fres.	2K B/L Gelatran F.Blue		102
	2	6x12 1K	COLOURCHANGE 1=850,2=Gel16,3=805,4=517		103
	3	"	"		104
	4	12"Fres.	2KB/L Gelatran F.Blue		105
	5	6x12 1K	COLORCHANGE 1=850,2=Gel16,3=805,4=517		106
	6	"	"		107
	7	12"Fres.	2K B/L Gelatran F.Blue		108
	8	6x12 1K	COLORCHANGE 1=850,2=Gel16,3=805,4=517		109
	9	"	"		110
LIGHT CURTAINS SL		9x 240watt 12volt PAR 56 VNSP in series	Gelatran	Blue	111
		"	"	"	112
	36	"	"	"	113
		"	"	"	114
SL SIDE BRIDGE					
Upper Pipe	1,2	6x16 1K	TEMPLATE	Cinemoid 538	115
	3,4	6x12 750	X Above	517	116
	5,7,9,11	6x9 500	Cool Dressing	543	117
	6,8,10,12	"	Warm "	Rosco 805	118
Lower Pipe	1,2	Silo 15	1K Gobo	cl.	119
	3,4	PAR 64 NSP		Rosco 805	120
	5,6	Silo 15	1K Gobo	Cinemoid 538	121
	7	FSP 1	24Volt 500watt R&V Beam Light c/w local Dimmer		
	8,9	Silo 15	1K Gobo	cl.	122
	10,11	6x16 1K	Note: Sidearm US of Bdn if necessary	517	123
SR SIDE BRIDGE					
Upper Pipe	1,2	Silo 15	1K Gobo	cl.	124
	3,4	6X12 750	X Above	Cinemoid 517	125
	5,lower4	6x12 750		"	126
	6,8,10,12	6x9 500	Cool Dressing	543	127
	7,9,11,13	"	Warm "	Rosco 805	128
Lower Pipe	1	FSP 2	24 Volt 500watt R&V Beam light c/w local dimmer		
	2,3	6x16 1K	TEMPLATE opera gobo	Cinemoid 538/540	129
	5,6	Silo 15	1K Gobo	538	130
	7,8	"	"	cl.	131
	9,10,11	6x16 750		Cinemoid 517	132

POSITION	NO	TYPE	SETTING	COLOUR	CIRCUIT
LX 7	1,2	PAR 64 VNSP		cinemoid 517	133
	3,4	"		Gelatran 16	134
	5,6	"		cinemoid 517	135
	7,8	"		gelatran 16	136
	9,10	"		cinemoid 517	137
	11,12	"		gelatran 16	138
6XX8					
UPSTAGE BRIDGE					
	1,2	"		gelatran F.blue	139
	3,4	"		cl.	140
	5,6	"		gelatran 16	141
	7,8	"		Blue	142
	9,10	"		"	143
	11,12	"		"	144
	13,14	"		gelatran 16	145
	15,16	"		F.Blue	146
LX 9	1,2	"		cl.	147
	3,4	PAR 64 FSP		gelatran 16	148
	5,6	PAR 64 VNSP		cl.	149
UNDER STAGE					
	1,2	10"B.P on short stand		cinemoid 517	150
	3	"	"	"	151
SL SET	1	8"Fres.	1K ringed in net to be agreed on site	538 517	152
	2	"	" "	850	153
FLOATS					154

Figure 4.27 John Napier's set for *Nicholas Nickleby* with lighting by David Hersey. (*Photo: © Chris Davies/NETWORK.*)

Figure 4.28 The opening scene of *Nicholas Nickleby*. (*Photo: © Chris Davies/NETWORK.*)

Figure 4.29 A candle-lighted scene from *Nicholas Nickleby*. (*Photo:* © *Chris Davies/ NETWORK*.)

Figure 4.31 Detail of David Hersey's lighting of the performers on an audience catwalk (*Nicholas Nickleby*). (*Photo:* © *Chris Davies/ NETWORK*.)

Figure 4.30 The play-within-a-play: Romeo and Juliet scene from *Nicholas Nickleby*. (*Photo:* © *Chris Davies/NETWORK*.)

can practice of using multiple backlights and front- and side-lights on a given stage space, Mr. Hersey uses a real minimum. The units he uses are often more powerful in wattage than those used here. This results in a "clean" line with distinct highlights and shadows rather than the multiple softened shadows from many units. The result is much closer to the clarity of a single shaft of sunlight — our most common viewing situation. Photographers have long known this technique, particularly when shooting an automobile for magazine ads. Roger Morgan's "Single Source" lighting is an American example. Bev Emmons calls this Hersey trademark: "single shadow backlight."

3. *Lack of Repetition of Lighting "Setups."* Because British practice (particularly in the Royal Shakespeare's Aldwych Theatre where Mr. Hersey most often designs) does not involve a "patch panel" or "hookup" (interconnecting or interplugging), he does not "gang" units on opposite sides of the stage (or auditorium) on a single dimmer. Thus two units on the auditorium left Box Boom are not paired on the same dimmer with two others on the right Box Boom on one dimmer. Consequently David lights the first scene in a given space onstage from *one* side only. The next scene in that same space will be "key" lighted from the opposite side of the auditorium. This introduces a degree of flexibility which results in each scene looking differently lighted — even if played in the same stage space used a couple of scenes earlier. That same technique is applied to backlights and sidelights. Thus the designer has many possible combinations to use in designing the lighting of any given location onstage. To this writer each scene throughout the 8½ hours had its own individualized design "look." The only exceptions were a limited number of "full-stage" scenes. Assistant lighting designer Beverly Emmons comments: "He does not use areas. He's broken that up. He doesn't need to think (in terms of areas). He gets his tone by playing one angle and one color against another."

4. *Simplicity of Cues.* While the production utilized nearly 500 cues, this critic was aware of none within scenes! Unlike the more common American practice of "now it is time for another light change — let's show just how important lighting design can be!" all changes took place going out of one scene and into the next. As a result the focus was where it should be: on the actors and the show! Maybe we are too influenced here by discos, concert lighting and the remanents of psychedelic lighting! Further Hersey used lighting most effectively to control the flow of the production as it moved from scene to scene. Light changes were used to terminate a scene: to tell the audience that now it was time to move on to the next place and episode. Light changes were used to "build" into each subsequent scene. Frequently there were many cues as a new scene was introduced: backlights and crosslights would come up on a wagon in an extreme upstage position; these lights then faded into a second --or even third — set of different units as the wagon slowly "snaked" its way downstage in guided tracks to its ultimate position — marvelously sculpturally lighted throughout its journey. When it arrived at its final destination for the scene to follow, the designated lighting for that scene flowed smoothly into place. But there were few (or no) changes of light *within* a scene. Isn't that what lighting design *should* do?

5. *Use of New Units and Techniques.* The followspots (four in number: two "out-front" high in the Boxes and two backstage) are a lighting designer's dream for a dramatic play. They are German Reische & Vogel units similar to the American "beam projector" with 24-volt, 500-watt lamps (with silvered reflector built into the lamp) and a parabolic reflector. They have no lens; no iris. Color was changed "by hand." The beam could not be "irised" or "shaped." Because these units are extremely "hot" (powerful) in the center of the beam (and then drop off in intensity subtly as one moves away from the beam center), the viewer was rarely aware of "follow spotlighting." Rather it seemed as if a powerful, dimensional pool of light was where it was needed. Principals were never "followed." The spots were used as "mobile sidelights" on scene playing spaces. Those few times when they *did* move location within a scene, it was done slowly and unobtrusively as the action swirled to another place. You were rarely aware of their presence — as it should be in a dramatic piece. The two follow spotlights backstage were used much less than those "out front." Bev says, "The reason why he had this problem was that the man in London on stage left side was not very good."

David also used European low-wattage PAR-56 lamps in two striplights with "flipper shields." They were used to backlight several downstage areas in the "V." (See the Light Plot). Each strip was "rigged" on three conterweighted "fly" lines so that its quite narrow band of light could be directed either upstage, midstage or for downstage coverage as desired by the flyman. Bev: "Three trim marks were established and they had cues." This both eliminated an extra union electrician and yet offered the designer additional flexibility. Of low-voltage PAR lamps, Bev says: "It's the narrowness and blast quality of those strips which is important. Those are his trademark also."

Mr. Hersey used also two other units not unknown in American practice: a dozen low-voltage remotely controlled color changers on two racks of backlights (upstage on each side on the "V"). Ms. Emmons comments: "We debated not using the color changers because they're so unreliable. These came from England. We didn't have any trouble at all. They came ready to go. They are great. They are very light weight. It would have needed 60 Lekos to do what those 12 are doing." Additionally Hersey made extensive use of larger Fresnels which are commonly found only in TV studios here: 10" and 12" units. Bev called these "good big Fresnels." She adds: "I think one of the most interesting things about David's lighting is the different kinds of light sources which he makes available to himself. Because he works in Europe, he gets all their stuff as well as our stuff."

[98] Lee Watson, "Nicholas Nickleby: A Dickens of a Show," Lighting Dimensions, vol. 6, no. 2 (Mar. 1982), pp. 18–25. Illus., color.

See also C. Lee Jenner, "Nicholas Nickleby Comes to Broadway," Theatre Crafts, vol. 15, no. 9 (Nov./Dec. 1981), pp. 12–15, 55–56, 58–61. Illus.

[99] Patricia MacKay, "The Elephant Man," Theatre Crafts, vol. 14, no. 1 (Jan./Feb. 1980), pp. 24–25, 80–84. Illus., includes Bev Emmons light plot, hookup, and focus chart.

Glenn M. Loney, "Recreating Amadeus," Theatre Crafts, vol. 15, no. 3 (Mar. 1981), pp. 10–15, 65–68, 70, 72, 74–75. Illus. See particularly pp. 14–15 and 74–75 for Bev Emmon's light plot, hookup, and text.

Peter Maradudin, "My First Broadway Show," Lighting Dimensions, vol. 9, no. 2 (Mar./Apr. 1985), pp. 42, 47, 49–50. Illus., color. Yale graduate Peter Maradudin describes lighting his first Broadway production, Ma Rainey's Black Bottom.

"Lighting Fugard's The Blood Knot. Yale's William Warfel made his Broadway debut with Athol Fugard's The Blood Knot. Warfel talks about the evolution of his design for this important production," Lighting Dimensions, vol. 10, no. 2 (Mar./Apr. 1986), pp. 28–37. Illus., color light plot.

Mike Williams, "Tom Skelton's Dark Dreams, The Iceman Cometh Returns to the Stage," Lighting Dimensions, vol. 10, no. 3 (May/June 1986), pp. 97–98, 100–102. Illus., color.

"There's Intelligent Life on Broadway," Lighting Dimensions, vol. 10, no. 2 (Mar./Apr. 1986), pp. 80–83, 85–88, 90–92. Illus., color, light plot. A description of Neil Peter Jampolis's lighting of Lily Tomlin's revue, Search For Signs of Intelligent Life in the Universe, a Broadway revue.

"Ming Cho Lee—An Interview," Lighting Dimensions, vol. 10, no. 2 (Mar./Apr. 1986), pp. 39–44. Illus., color. Yale's co-chairman of design and prominent professional scenic designer discusses lighting from the scenic designer's viewpoint.

[100] Rubin and Watson, p. 46, op. cit. (see footnote 3).

His color *palette* for Nicholas was quite limited. Except for a few "specials," he used only seven colors: Geltran #16 (Bastard Amber); clear; Cinemoid #517 (Steel Blue) and #567 (Steel Tint); Roscolene #804 (No Color Straw); and both the Lee Filters 1/2-blue and full blue (#201 and #202). He used pink, lavender or violet. There was one color change on lights backstage, done by the backstage follow spot operators between the 1-hour intermission. The total production was operated by only the 4 follow spot operators and one switchboard operator.[98]

These examples by an assortment of working designers, and from proscenium as well as thrust and arena physical facilities, offer the reader current practice as well as the inference that there is no *single* way to do lighting design for a particular show. Each design must be tailored to the script, the production place, the setting, the production style, and the abilities of the individual designer. The examples also illustrate that there is a common thread of *communication form* which runs through all of them — and yet the individual variations of differing artists are apparent.

Techniques

Since time, advance preparation, organization, and response to disaster make up such an important portion of that which is expected by the employer of a professional theatre lighting designer, it is useful to compare the step-by-step procedures used to "get a show lighted." There are of course infinite variations. However, they tend to fall into one of two major groupings: (1) the system used in training and academic theatre and (2) the system used in commercial or professional theatre. They are, in some points, quite different. I do not imply judgment values. I am aware of the brilliant theatrical productions, both with simplistic and with quite lavish theatre plants and production equipment, that can flourish in academic theatre environments. I define "commercial" or "professional" theatre to be that theatre produced by artists whose main employable profession is theatre, rather than teaching. The salaries or work product or physical plant facilities of these professionals, so defined, may be skimpy or quite grandiose. The resultant production may be relatively inferior or brilliant. *Quality* is not the criterion. Table 4.1 presents a step-by-step comparison of the differences and the similarities of approach in lighting design for professional practice versus academic practice.

Procedures and Practices

Lighting design *style* is greatly influenced by the physical form of the performance place.[99] Outdoor theatres are discussed in Chap. 6, along with other production types. Below is a discussion of the influence upon lighting design of four basic theatre types/forms: arena, thrust, dinner, and avant-garde or experimental.

Arena Theatre

In 1954 (in *Theatrical Lighting Practice*), Dr. Joel Rubin and I wrote:

> To the lighting designer, central staging may provide a sense of emancipation from the physical scenic element. But added to this is a responsibility for a larger portion of the production's visual design. Such responsibility re-stresses the need for close cooperation between actor, director and lighting designer. This becomes even more important when the production is less realistic in concept, tending toward a frankly presentational style of theatre. In this instance, the lighting designer must create an individual light concept which helps interpret each moment of the play and serves essentially as a background for the words and the action.[100]

This applies equally today.

Problems

Arena production presents the lighting designer with specific additional technical design problems:

1. All (or most) lighting equipment must be mounted overhead, and the resulting high-angle lighting, which will *not* blind members of the audience sitting on any of the four sides of the acting area, makes clean, clear *visibility* illumination of the performer's faces difficult.

2. There is little or no scenery (as such) present; basically the arena show is made up (physically) of props, performers and costumes, a playing space, and light. Therefore, delineating place, time, weather — and even mood — becomes more difficult and rests largely with the lighting.

3. There no longer is a proscenium "frame" separating the audience and the performer. Scenes may be played

Table 4.1 Comparison of Professional and Academic Approaches to Lighting Design

Professional	Academic
The lighting designer is contracted by a producer, director, star, general manager, or friends to design the lighting of a show. A meeting takes place where details of the production team, the show, the performance place, and "contracted payment for services to be rendered" (a union contract, a letter of agreement, or payment terms) are discussed and agreed upon. A contract is filed with the Union (most often it is United Scenic Artists).	Usually the lighting designer is selected and assigned by a faculty member, and the only reward is academic credit (grades).
The designer reads the script and possibly checks out the theatre to be used.	The designer reads the script and gets an inventory of available house equipment and physical drawings and details.
A conference is held with the director, other designers, the business manager, etc., to set design objectives and understanding, budget, schedule, crews, etc.	A conference is held with the director, other designers, the business manager (if the student designer has indirect access to school funding); schedule, crews (assigned by faculty), and set design objectives.
A light plot and hookup and shop order are prepared and submitted to management; three bids from rental firms are solicited and given to the business manager.	A light plot and hookup are prepared and submitted to a faculty instructor, lighting class, etc., for critique and revision. Special supplies (lamps, effects, color media) for the specific production may be ordered.
The designer confers as necessary with the business manager to select a production electrician and others on the production team (such as an assistant) who work under the designer.	The designer confers as needed with follow classmates who will hang and prepare the show.
The designer focuses the lighting for the show during "fit-up" or "setup" in the first theatre in which the show is to be performed.	The designer, who focuses the lighting for the show, may also be called upon to serve as electrician and to help hang the show.
The designer sets light cues and levels. This *may* be done with both the director and the stage manager. Under pressure, the designer will do this while other rehearsals are taking place, subject to later discussion with the director/stage manager.	The designer sets light cues and levels, usually with the guidance of a faculty instructor, the director, the stage manager, and other production designers. It is usually a separate call.
A technical rehearsal is held in which all cues are integrated with the cast and the show. This is the *only* "stop and go" rehearsal allowed by the director, producer, and cast, in which major attention and focus is on lighting/technical problems.	A technical rehearsal is held in which all the cues are integrated with the cast and the show. This is a stop-and-go rehearsal, in which the major focus is on lighting/technical problems.
Several dress rehearsals follow with cleanup calls as needed for modification of focus, color, cues, and other design elements; however, the director does not expect to stop for *any* lighting problems. He or she will give the designer notes (frequently through the stage manager) or confer with the designer following each dress rehearsal. The director expects the concerns expressed in notes to be "cleaned up" or discussed with him by the lighting designer without further involvement. The management does not expect — or look kindly upon — mistakes or delays, if they are avoidable. The designer is expected to be an experienced and talented professional, not a student who is learning and experimenting.	Several dress rehearsals follow with cleanup calls as needed for modification and correction of any aspect which requires such. While it is the intention of the director not to stop at any dress rehearsal for lighting problems, this intention is more often violated than respected. The students involved are learning, and they are expected to make mistakes and to grow in the process. Much time is consumed in this way, but much is learned.
The production opens. The designer is finished (subject to contractual agreements to "look in" on the production and be sure that it is being "kept up"). No further changes in the lighting design are possible without a new contract and a new design fee.	The production opens. Depending upon the director and the school's policy, further modifications and changes may be incorporated during the run to enable students to learn and grow and experiment.
The designer may be further involved in (1) national touring company duplicates, (2) foreign productions, and/or (3) movie or TV use of the production or scenes from it. All subsequent uses of the lighting design (which designers own, the right to use their creative concept having been "leased" to the management for specific use situations) are the province of the designer.	The designer may be called upon to be present at various performances. Usually a critique of the designer's work by faculty and/or other students takes place to guide the student designer toward further growth.
The show closes and is struck.	The show closes and is struck.

Basic	
In professional theatre the lighting designer's fellow workers are *paid*. The designer does not (should not) need to motivate stagehands to hang lights. He will mostly deal with other strong, creative, decisive theatre artists who have their own concepts of what a lighting designer's contribution should be. The designer must learn to work with them.	In academic theatre environments, the lighting designer's fellow workers are there to learn or to gain academic credit — in either case, of their own free will. They must be treated with respect and be motivated to do the dirty, time-consuming, dull but necessary tasks if the show is to "get on." They are not paid, and they must understand from the lighting designer why they should choose to do the things asked of them.

[101] *Willard F. Bellman*, Lighting the Stage: Art and Practice. *N.Y.; Harper & Row; 2d ed., 1974. "Lighting the Arena and Thrust-Apron Stage, Appendix IV," pp. 468–73. Good basics; brief.*

W. Oren Parker and Harvey K. Smith, Scenic Design and Stage Lighting. *N.Y.; Holt, Rinehart and Winston; 4th ed., 1979. "Designing the Lighting for Other Forms of Production, Arena," pp. 541–48. Well illustrated; light plot; good basic text.*

Joel E. Rubin and Leland H. Watson, Theatrical Lighting Practice. *N.Y.; Theatre Arts Books; 1954. See Chapter IV, "Arena Production," pp. 46–62. The first text treatment; somewhat dated; illus. (see footnote 3).*

Roger Morgan, "Single Source Lighting," Theatre Crafts, (Mar./Apr. 1970), pp. 13–15, 34–36. Required reading.

Stanley Abbott, "Arena Lighting: An Analysis of Four Methods," Theatre Annual, 1965–1966, pp. 76–87. Analysis of 3-, 4-, and 5-instruments-per-area design approaches.

Joseph Stephan, "Lighting for Theatre in the Round," Tabs, vol. 22, no. 3 (Sept. 1964), pp. 25–31. Good illus., article.

Bruce Griffiths, "Arena Lighting: A Survey," thesis, M.F.A., Yale, 1951.

Donald Mullin, "Lighting the Arena Stage," Tabs, vol. 23, no. 2 (June 1965), pp. 27–35. Excellent basic article.

Kelly Yeaton, "Lighting Arena Corners," Players Magazine, 28:74 (Jan. 1951). Good illus., article.

Kelly Yeaton, "Single Source Arena Light," Players Magazine 28:74 (Dec. 1951). Illus.; early article prior to Roger Morgan's.

Fred Clinton Bock, Scheme for Arena Theatre Lighting Grid Design in Terms of Grid Spacing, Walkway Space, and Masking by Louvres. Ph.D., dissertation, Ohio Stage, 1966.

Bennet Averyt, "An Annotated Bibliography for Lighting the Arena Stage," USITT Committee on Theatrical Presentation. No date, out of print. Mimeographed.

Kenneth N. Kurtz, "Motivational Lighting for Open Stage Realism," Theatre Crafts, (Nov./Dec. 1973), pp. 18–21, 28–30. Excellent illus., plots, text.

(Continued on page 114)

(and must be lighted) in the aisles or sometimes even behind part of the audience.

4. The audience is extremely *close* to the performers and the playing space. Tricks and illusions (fires for example) that work when there is a stage apron and an orchestra pit between the performer and the first row of audience may no longer be acceptable.

5. Not only is the range of vertical angles of light now restricted and the intense color range limited, but the audience is on all four sides surrounding the performers. In many circumstances this completely destructs the designer's normal repertory of lighting tools, e.g., frontlight, backlight, sidelight, key light.

6. The range of usable instrument-mounting positions is severely restricted in an arena production.

The sum of these points means that arena lighting design demands extensive *technical knowledge* and ability from the designer before he or she is ever called upon for an *artistic design* contribution. To me, arena lighting is frequently more difficult—and often less rewarding—than lighting for either thrust or proscenium production. The problems can be solved, however, and sensitive design can result.

Solutions

As part of the solution, the lighting designer should plan on lighting from high angles. The designer should also demand of the director and scenic designer that the floor covering be a useful lighting tool. If the show is a comedy, a light and brightly reflective floor covering will reflect much overhead lighting *upward* to softly fill in the performers' faces for good visibility. Should the show require the opposite effect, a darkened stage with performers in stark and dramatic pools of light can in part be achieved by use of a dark floor covering. The floor can also often be used as a design element via light images or patterns projected upon it. The floor usually is the major scenic background element for the audience, since seats in most arena theatres are steeply raked.

Another part of the lighting designer's solution is *area control* to assist the director in audience focus and *selective visibility*. The basic arena light plot usually provides for a controllable action area in the center of the arena (the strongest position for the performer) and separate surround areas. Whether the lighting designer divides the arena into four additional areas or twelve depends upon the show being presented and the designer's work. It *is* possible to semi-isolate portions of the playing space with light and even to "follow" a performer around the stage. In a few cases, high-angle followspots can even be used.

There is no need here for a lengthy discussion about the basic equipment layout approach. Both the light plots included herein and the sources listed in bibliographical footnotes[101] deal with 3 lights per area (120° separation) and 4 lights per area (90° separation), both of which are standard. Always more important is the ability to light faces clearly. Figures 4.32 to 4.35 clarify various design approaches.

Mood is most frequently achieved through color selection. Overall color "washes" of the arena from either Fresnel spotlights or carefully shielded striplights help solve the problem of separating night and day scenes.

Representation of nature can be partially achieved by using gobos in ellipsoidal spotlights to project a pattern of sunlight or moonlight on the arena floor from imagined windows. Photoflash bulbs can simulate lightning, fireworks, etc.

Plasticity normally is somewhat difficult to achieve. The necessarily high, steep angle of most lighting units will automatically introduce theatricality and considerable three-dimensionality (plasticity or revelation of form). As mentioned earlier, single-source lighting (the performer in a single shaft of light), if used very sparingly, can add moments of plastic, sculpt modeling.

Scenic and dramatic composition is the same in the arena as it is in a proscenium picture except that you are "painting" a series of pictures in free space rather than within a framework.

Most special effects used in proscenium productions can be reproduced in an arena in modified form. For example, I used rings of heater cones and sal ammoniac (ammonium chloride) smoke rising to the domed ceiling of the Casa Manana Theatre in Fort Worth, Texas, for a production of the *Damn Yankees* musical number "Steam Heat." Floor lamps and practicals can be plugged into electrical floor outlets around the arena (during scene-shifting "blackouts"). Patterns and gobos can project on either the stage

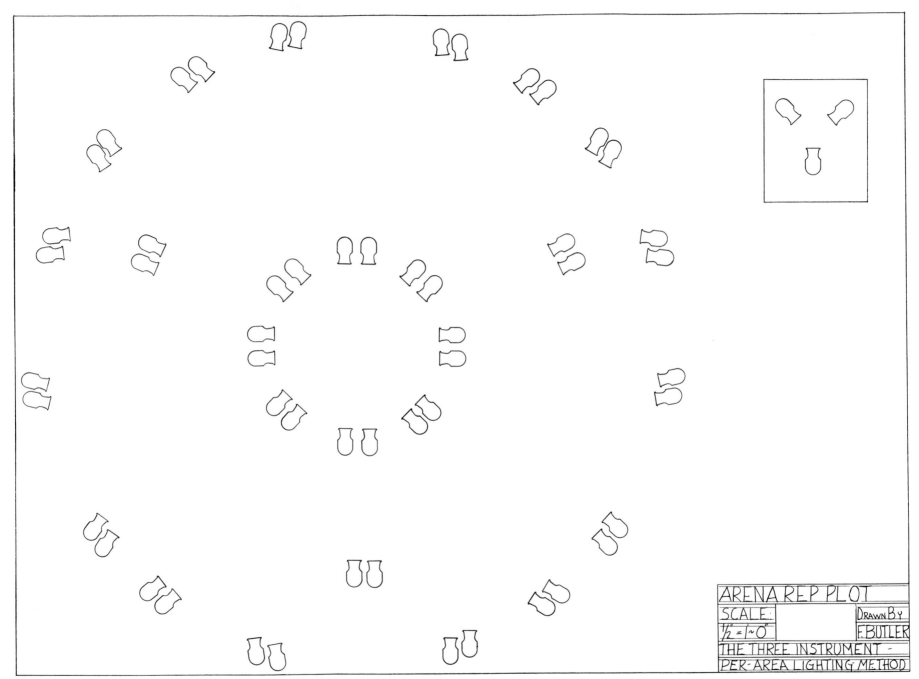

Figure 4.32 Arena rep plot: 3 instruments per area as an arena lighting method.

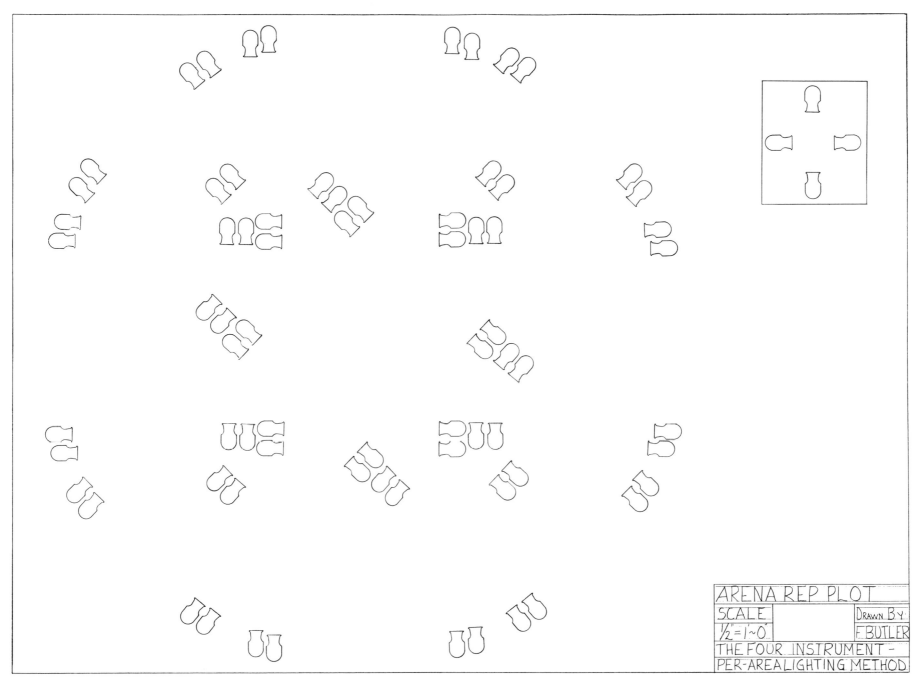

Figure 4.33 Arena rep plot: 4 instruments per area as an arena lighting method.

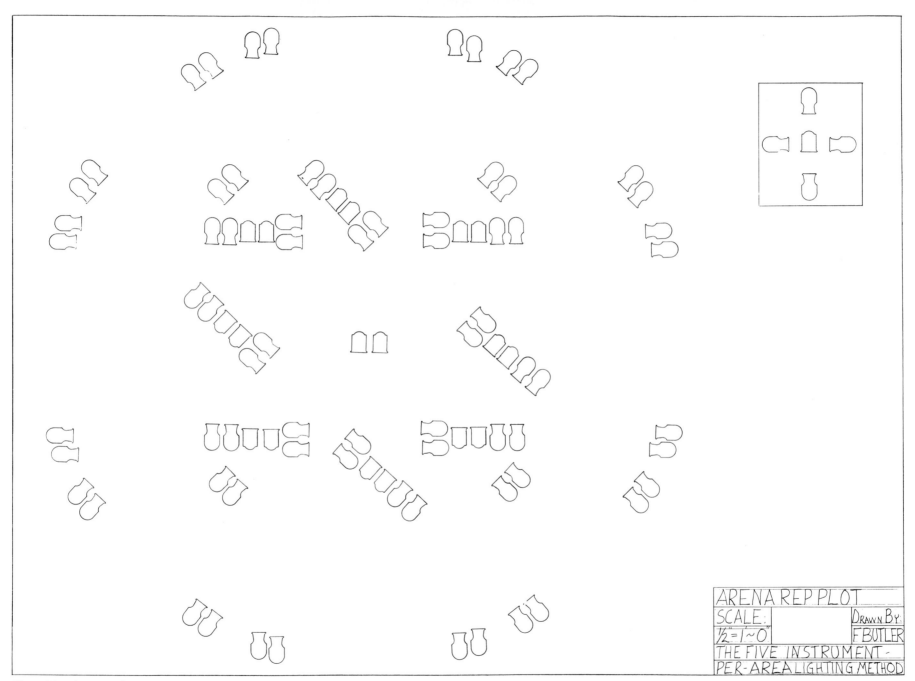

Figure 4.34 Arena rep plot: 5 instruments per area as an arena lighting method.

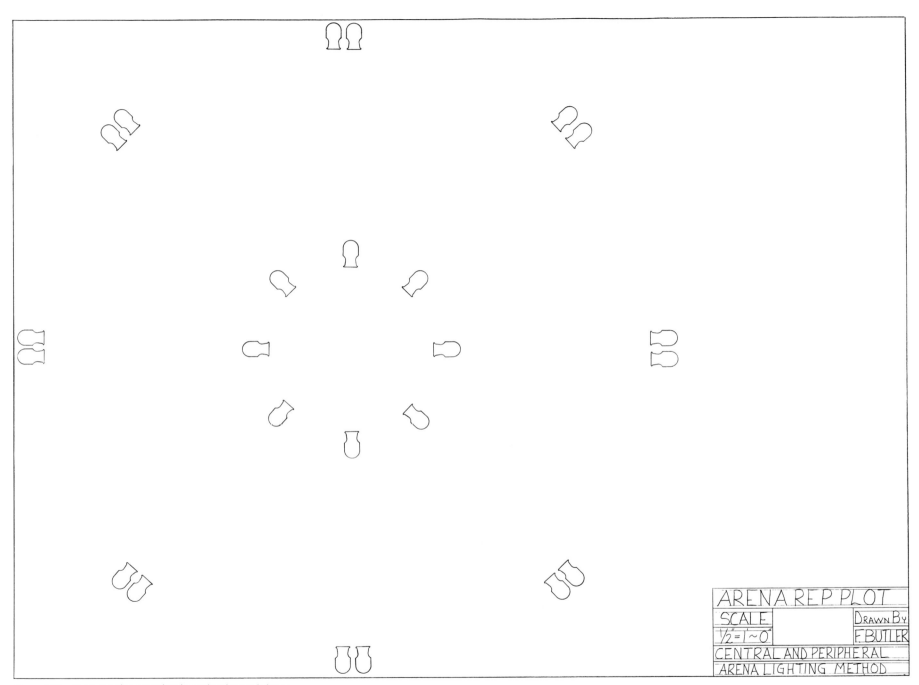

Figure 4.35 Arena rep plot: central and peripheral arena lighting methods.

floor or, in the case of some carefully designed arenas, on the surround wall behind the audience seating area (completely surrounding the audience and putting them "inside" the play). Blacklight (ultraviolet) can be used. The designer must always remember that the audience is much closer than in most other theatre types, so effects frequently must *seem* to be more realistic.

Many arena theatres have overhead rigs (sometimes called "valances") where lighting equipment finds its home (most often in sight of the audience). Clever scenic designers use the outside circular surface to paint, apply, or design a motif show curtain for each production. Chandeliers and garlands of "bee" lights and lanterns can frequently be flown in from these overhead light rigs (or pipes and catwalks that are permanently in place).

The lighting designer must keep in mind that the director will often play entrances, exits, and short scenes in the aisles (or sometimes in the midst of or behind the audience). These areas must always be part of the basic setup. Only sharp-edged beam ellipsoidal reflector units will work readily here. Performers can only be illuminated from the top (audience exit area) and stage ends of the aisles without spilling light into audience seating areas and blinding the cash customer. This setup inevitably leads to theatricality and contrasty lighting.

If an arena is also equipped to present musicals, an orchestra pit will be present somewhere on the outside perimeter of the arena. If the pit is in use, care must be taken to shield orchestra stand lights. The designer must avoid the temptation to design lighting from either the pit location or the side of the arena where the switchboard is located, because cash customers are on *all* sides — 360° around. The designer is obliged to design for all of them.

The "corners" of an arena playing area can be particularly troublesome spots. If performers play right to the edge of the stage, they may be only inches away from front-row customers. Yet the performers' faces must be clearly lighted without blinding the audience. These edge locations frequently call for additional luminaires (beyond those assigned to "area" duty) to crosslight faces strongly.

Lastly, and probably most important of all, light (direct emanation) must be kept *out of the audience area*. It is possi-

ble to fit every overhead luminaire with a hi-hat (or "funnel" or "top hat") or with barn doors. These can be homemade from tin cans and black paint and color frames, and can make all the difference in the finished look and professionalism of an arena production.

Figure 4.36 is a photograph from *Charley's Aunt* by designer Gary W. Gaiser at the Brown County Playhouse, Nashville, Indiana. While this is a thrust rather than an arena production, it shows clearly the interrelationship between playing space, scenery, audience, and overhead light-mounting positions.

Thrust Theatre

Thrust theatre falls somewhere between arena theatre and proscenium theatre. There is a scenic area behind one end of the thrust, but the audience is on three sides of the performance area. Little more need be said. Thrust is either the best of both worlds or the worst of both worlds, depending on a designer's individual viewpoint. The light plots, hookups, and photographs in this chapter for *Savages* (Figs. 4.19 to 4.21) at the Mark Taper Forum theatre in Los Angeles with lighting by John Gleason and for *Black Angel* in Chap. 6 (Mark Taper Forum; by Tharon Musser and including the season's repertory light plot and hookup, Figs. 6.17 to 6.22) are for thrust stage productions.

Figure 4.36 A thrust-stage production of *Charley's Aunt* at the Brown County Playhouse, Nashville, Indiana; summer of 1978. Lighting by Gary W. Gaiser.

"Edinburgh International Festival," Tabs, *vol. 33, no. 1 (Spring 1975), pp. 12–13. Illus., color. British arena productions.*

"A Theatre Inspired—The New Victoria Theatre, Europe's First Purpose-Built Theatre-in-the-Round Opens in North Staffordshire," Lighting & Sound International, *vol. 1, no. 9 (Aug. 1986), pp. 20–23. Illus. Gives extensive details of Europe's first arena theatre including plans and available lighting equipment and resident staff.*

[102] *Francis Reid, "Angles for Thrusts,"* Tabs, *vol. 33, no. 2 (Summer 1975), pp. 20–21. Chatty; well-diagramed basics.*

Charles E. Williams, "Lighting for Isolation on the Thrust Stage," Theatre Design and Technology, *no. 16 (Feb. 1969), pp. 10–11. Illus.*

"Edinburgh International Festival," TABS, *vol. 33, no. 1 (Spring 1975), pp. 12–13. Illus. Color. British thrust productions.*

[103] *Henry David Rosso, "Dinner Theatres May Face Hard Times,"* UPI Story in Indianapolis Star, *Sept. 4, 1984, p. 30.*

[104] *Deborah Dryden, "Chanhassen, The Cadillac of Dinner Theatres,"* Theatre Crafts, *vol. 14, no. 5 (Oct. 1980), pp. 24–27, 78–80, 82. Illus.*

[105] *Denis Bablet,* Revolutions in Stage Design of the XXth Century. *Paris-New York; Leon Amiel (publisher); 1977. 388 pages. Exquisitely illustrated in black-and-white and in color. Brilliant text. Invaluable addition to any research collection. Best, most up-to-date source on avante-garde theatre trends.*

Brooks McNamara, Jerry Rojo, and Richard Schechner, Theatres, Spaces, Environments: Eighteen Projects. *N.Y.; Drama Book Specialists; 1975. 182 pages. Well-illustrated. The basic available text on avant-garde theatre.*

Eldon Elder, Will it Make a Theatre? *N.Y.; Off-Off-Broadway Alliance (distributed by Drama Book Specialists); 1979. 206 pages. The how-to manual for innovative "found space" theatre performance place creation.*

See also "Street Theatre," Theatre Crafts, *vol. 6, no. 2 (Apr. 1972). Entire issue is devoted to this subject. Basic; illus.*

"Street Theatre," Theatre Review, *Jan. 1979, p. 5.*

Kate Davey, "Richard Foreman's Scenography," Theatre Crafts, *vol. 12, no. 4 (May/June 1978), pp. 34–35, 56–58, 60–62. Illus.; good text.*

Timothy L. Kelly, "Mobile Stage for Summer Touring," Theatre Crafts, vol. 12, no. 4 (May/June 1978), *pp. 36–40, 42–43. Illus.*

"The Festive Face," Theatre Crafts, *vol. 11. no. 2 (Mar./Apr. 1977), pp. 8–9, 45–48, 50, 52, 54.*

Figure 4.37 Purdue University's 1979 production of Shakespeare's *Twelfth Night;* scene design: Don McBride; lighting design: Lee Watson; costumes: Stephanie A. Schoelzel (Rutherford); director: Dale Miller.

I have also included here a production photo of Shakespeare's *Twelfth Night* (Fig. 4.37) from my own lighting at Purdue University as a sample of the type of facial modeling and sculpting which the designer seeks in the treatment of performers' faces.[102]

Dinner Theatre

Dinner theatre is in most cases either arena or thrust; it is rarely proscenium. It is included here as a separate category because of the specific lighting practices usually used for it. Rarely with dinner theatre productions is there a lighting designer, per se. The exception is when the production is a "package" playing a chain of dinner theatres. Then there is often a designer for the initial theatre's presentation. Usually the local "lighting designer" is also the stage manager and, often, the entire design/technical staff. Dinner theatres operate with a limited number of pieces of lighting equipment and switchboard capacity.

The performance bill of fare for dinner theatre is often recent Broadway comedies and musicals. Little scenery is used (as in arena shows). Dinner theatres are a good place for a designer to begin a career and to learn, although they have been decreasing in popularity.[103] They are rarely a long-term employment situation for lighting designers. Fig-

ure 4.38 presents the light plot for the dinner theatre production of *Blithe Spirit* at Elmsford, New York, by production designer Michael J. Hotopp. Hotopp is co-owner of Design Associates in New York City, a firm which designs sets, costumes, and lighting for chains of dinner theatres. Their shop also builds and paints the sets. Their staff assembled the entire production for its "first stand." This particular production played thrust. Figure 4.39 shows a production photo of the set, the lighting equipment, and the audience arrangement.[104] Before I leave this subject, a brief historical aside: The first dinner theatre was the Barksdale Tavern in Hanover, Virginia, started in 1953.

Avant-Garde or Experimental Theatre

There are as many other fringe types of performance places as there are imaginative producing groups. The literature on such groups and performances is fascinating and worth reading.[105] Some groups play street theatre, performing at "found" outdoor locations and carrying minimum illumination lighting. Others, such as the well-known Performance Garage in Greenwich Village in New York City, constantly rearrange the entire interior of their building for each production. This group frequently moves the audience around during a performance; the play's action causing the spectators to shift positions on balconies, stairs, catwalks, and the main floor to get out of the way of the performers playing a scene. It works. Any portion of the interior of the building — or even the street outside — may become a lighted playing space. I hope that this type of imaginative use of performance place will continue throughout the future of theatre. Much of Robert Wilson's "Opera" can also be readily classified as avante-garde, as can the Brooklyn Academy of Music's "New Wave" performance series.

Figures 4.40 through 4.47 and Color Figs. 10 through 17 are examples of a wide range of nonmusical productions from commercial, educational, and amateur productions. The common element is excellence of lighting design. They are examples of the fine lighting design to be found in a multitude of places throughout the United States and internationally.

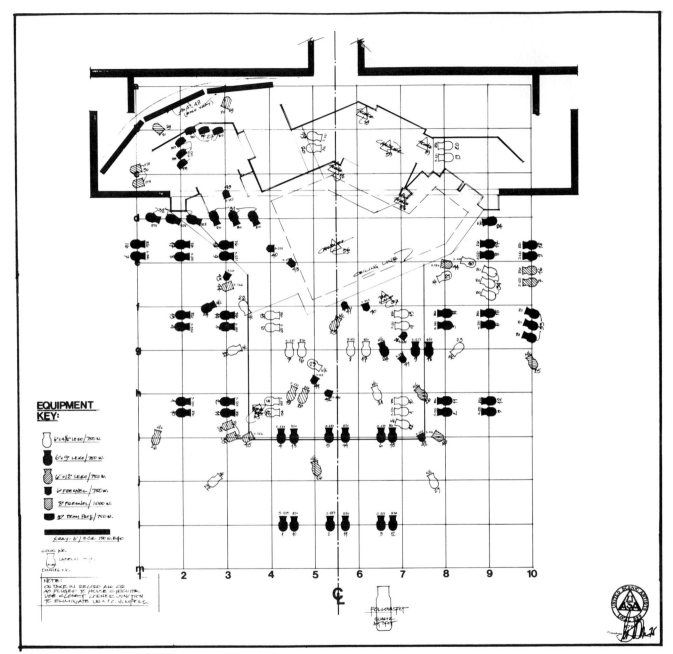

EQUIPMENT KEY:

6" x 4½" LEKO / 750 W.

6" x 9" LEKO / 750 W.

6" x 12" LEKO / 750 W.

6" FRESNEL / 750 W.

8" FRESNEL / 1000 W.

8" BEAM PROJ. / 750 W.

X-RAY - 6' / 3 CIR. 150 W. R40

COLOR MK.

LATERAL TILT.

DIMMER NO.

NOTE:
ON TAKE IN RECORD ALL CIR.
AS PLUGED TO HOUSE CIRCUITS.
USE CLOSEST CONNEC JUNCTION
TO ELIMINATE UN-NEC. JUMPERS.

FOLLOWSPOT

QUARTZ
AM 3 FT

Figure 4.38 Light plot for *Blithe Spirit,* January 1975, at An Evening Dinner Theatre in Elmsford, N.Y. Production designed by Michael J. Hotopp.

Figure 4.39 Production photo of *Blithe Spirit.*

Figure 4.40 *Julius Caesar* at the American Conservatory Theatre (ACT), San Francisco, 1976. Director: Edward Payson Call; scenic design: Richard Seger; costumes: John Conklin; lighting design: Richard Devin.

Figure 4.41 *The Lark* by Jean Anouilh in 1977 at Southwest State University, Marshall, Minnesota. Sets and lighting designed by Charles E. Howard, Jr.

Figure 4.42 *Richard III* in February 1977 at Chicago's Goodman Theatre. Director: Bill Woodman; set design: J. Jenson; costumes: J. Brady; lighting design: F. Mitchell Dana.

Figure 4.43 *Spoon River Anthology* in June 1974 at the SUNY–Albany Summer Theatre, Albany, New York; lighting design by Harry Feiner.

Photographs of Robert Wilson's *Einstein on the Beach production at the Met Opera. Lighting by Beverly Emmons. Photo by Nathaniel Tileston.*

Carroll Britch, "Profile Staging, Designs for Found Theatre spaces," *Theatre Crafts, vol. 9, no. 5 (Oct. 1975), pp. 16–17, 27–30. Illus.; useful text.*

"Tech Theatre Takes to the Streets: Lighting and Sound Equipment for Outdoors," Theatre Crafts, *Mar./Apr. 1972, pp. 14–15, 37–38. Illus.*

"Non-Lighting For the Theatre: Single Source and Work Light Effects Vie with Total Light Environments," Theatre Crafts, *Sept. 1971, pp. 16–21, 42–43. Very important avant-garde theatre article; illus.; covers work of Peter Brook, Richard Schechner, and Alwin Nikolais.*

Mary Lucier, "From Meat Loaf to Pirates," *Theatre Crafts, vol. 15, no. 6 (June/July 1981), pp. 18–19, 63–64. Illus. Light plots and switchboard hooks by Dennis Parichy and Victor En Yu Tan for cost-effective Off-Off-Broadway productions.*

We Are Strong, A Guide to the Work of Popular Theatre Across The Americas, *vol. I. Mankato, Minn.; Institute for Cultural Policy Studies; 1983. 244 pp., illus. The definitive guide to avant-garde theatrical experimentation.*

Mel Gussow, "The Theater's Avant-Garde Branches Out," *The New York Times, Sunday, Mar. 18, 1984. Arts and Leisure, pp. 1, 18. Illus. A "round up" article, well illustrated, of the latest in theatre, music, and dance experimentation. Includes Robert Wilson's work.*

John Rockwell, "Is 'Performance' a New Form of Art?" *The New York Times, Sunday, Aug. 15, 1983. Arts and Leisure, pp. 1, 13. Another "roundup" of avant-garde theatrical activity. Again includes Robert Wilson.*

The foremost avant-gardist is probably Robert Wilson. Of Wilson's work, John Rockwell has written:

A first encounter with (Wilson's) works can be literally overwhelming. The sheer beauty of his theatrical visions, the dreamy rightness of the action, the hypnotic blend of non-linear disjunction and deeper coherence—all of these seize one's attention and compel one into thinking that nothing like this can ever have happened on stage before.

Figure 4.44 *Troilus and Cressida.* Set design: John Wright Stevens; lighting design: Dan Boylen.

Figure 4.45 *Macbeth* at the Utah Shakespearean Festival, Cedar City, Utah, in July 1973. Set design: Michael Meyers; lighting design: Tom Ruzika.

Figure 4.46 Purdue University's production of *Tobacco Road* in 1978 at West Lafayette, Indiana. Set design: Joni Johns; lighting design: Kirk Bookman; costumes: Stephanie A. Schoelzel (Rutherford).

Figure 4.47 Goethe's *Faust* at the University of North Carolina–Greensboro in 1974. Set design: Andreas Nomikos; lighting design: Robert Thurston.

Wilson's many productions in Europe and America have included The Life and Times of Joseph Stalin, The Life and Times of Sigmund Freud, The $ Value of Man, *and (with composer Philip Glass)* Einstein on the Beach. *His latest,* the CIVIL warS: a tree is best measured when it is down, *is multilingual, and it will run 12 hours and cost around $14 million. The* American Theatre *critic writes: "The scenes . . . communicate primarily through sounds, imagery, stage design and movement, rather than narration or plot." (See: "The Whims of 'Wars'",* American Theatre, *May 1984, p. 16.) On the other critical side, British producer Peter Hall in his* Peter Hall's Diaries: The Story of a Dramatic Battle, *writes of Wilson's work, "This is Emperor's new clothes theatre. And it is bullshit: aestheticism run riot," an opinion which would muster an equal number of advocates.*

Philip Auslander, "Staying Alive, The Living Theatre in the '80s,' American Theatre, *vol. 1, no. 4 (July/Aug. 1984), pp. 10–14. Illus. A useful piece about Julian Beck and Judith Malina's* Living Theatre *troupe, another leading experimental theatre group.*

Rob Baker, "Directors on Design: The Mystery Is in the Surface, A Day in the Mind of Robert Wilson," Theatre Crafts, *vol. 19, no. 8 (Oct. 1985), pp. 22–27, 88–99. Illus., color.*

Corinna Boskovsky, "Pictures of Mystery, Erich Wonder's Stage Design Makes German Audiences Draw Their own Conclusions," Theatre Crafts, *vol. 20, no. 8 (Oct. 1986), pp. 32–35, 90–97. Illus., color. Includes a chronology of Wonder's avant-garde designs.*

Stephen Holden, "Avant-Garde Antics For the Adventurous," The New York Times, *Weekend, Sept. 15, 1986, p. 19. Illus.*

Jennifer Dunning, "Avant-Garde Extravaganza on the East Side," The New York Times, *Weekend, Feb. 6, 1987, pp. 13, 15. Illus.*

Stephen Holden, "International Network of Venues Nourishes Avant-Garde Works," The New York Times, *July 28, 1987, p. 18. Illus.*

Chapter 5

Musical Theatre

[106] *The 1985–1986 Central Opera Service annual survey offers the following information: 14.4 million people attended an opera performance during 1985–1986. There were 18,073 performances of opera in 1986. There were 39 major opera companies with budgets over $1 million, and 170 opera companies with budgets over $100,000 in 1986; there were 404 university, college, and conservatory opera departments in 1986. Forty-nine institutions were granting degrees in either opera or music-theatre in 1983. A total of 961 different operas were performed during the 1985–1986 season.*

Maria F. Rich, "U.S. Opera Survey 1985–86, Cause of Concern," Opera News, vol. 51, no. 5 (Nov. 1986), pp. 32, 34, 36–38, 40, 42.

The demands placed upon a lighting designer by musical theatre forms frequently differ markedly from those engendered by nonmusical theatre, as discussed in Chap. 4. This chapter deals with those differences as they affect opera, dance, musicals, revues, and operetta. As in previous chapters, numerous light plots and photographs of productions by noted designers are presented as guides.

Opera

Opera, the most dramatic form of theatrical presentation, has a lengthy and noteworthy history. It dates back to at least *Orfeo* in Mantua, Italy, in 1472. Opera requires a sophisticated, trained audience; people are not born preferring grand opera. Opera appeals more to the ear than to the eye, and it basically reaches its audience through music, rather than through the spoken word or a story line. These characteristics set opera apart as a dramatic form, and they influence the design of lighting for operatic productions. It is interesting to note that opera, both live and on TV, has increased tremendously in popularity in the United States in recent years.[106]

Design Considerations

This section presents some keys to opera design which I have compiled from my own experience designing lighting for over 50 opera productions: for the New York City Opera (seven productions); for the Houston Grand Opera (four years); for the New Jersey State Opera (two seasons); and in Baltimore, Philadelphia, Milwaukee, and Vancouver (Canada).

"Suspension of Disbelief" On The Part of The Opera Audience Is Basic. When confronted with life's moments of intense passion, grief, or tragedy, humans do *not* naturally sing with beautiful clarity, accompanied by a talented orchestra of 70 to 120 musicians and backed up by a chorus of 50 to 100 vocalists. The opera audience knows and accepts this. Because the audience is composed of sophisticated opera goers looking forward to a near-perfect fusion of music, story, vocal achievement, and "grand" scenic/visual decor, lighting design can be planned to match. In many senses opera is the quintessence for the mature adult of the child's game of "let's pretend." Grand opera can free the imagination, bringing about a "suspension of disbelief" unattainable in the other dramatic forms. Accordingly, lighting design springs from a base of *heightened dramatic theatricality*. Grand opera *must* be "grand." Since the members of the audience are eager to assist, by their presence conveying a willingness to believe, use their cooperation wisely.

The Music Is Key. Only in disco or concert lighting (and sometimes in dance) is the lighting artist expected to use lights and knowledge of light's influence upon human emotional response to expand and interpret pure *music* rather than words and story line. Yet, like disco or concerts, opera depends upon use of light to help interpret and to heighten the effect of music. It is the *music* in opera which prompts it to soar to the heavens. To highlight perfectly the all-important music with light, the lighting designer should study the score; listen to existing recordings; and talk with the musical director or conductor, who can provide design approach keys as readily as the staging director does. In opera production the conductor or musical director has more real power to determine interpretation than the stage director. The combination of a conductor and an operatic star agreeing on a bit of staging, or phrasing, or timing of a physical movement on stage will always receive top priority, regardless of what the stage director may ask for. The savvy lighting designer makes friends with the conductor so that the big "cross-dim into sunset" will work for the audience!

The Physical Size of The Opera Stage Is Important. Opera is almost always performed in proscenium theatres, even when done outdoors. It is rarely presented in either thrust or arena performance places. Recently, however, there have been a number of experimental productions moving in the direction of arena presentation of opera. Usually the opera selected either is very contemporary or is from *opera buffa* and will lend itself to this treatment. It is a trend which a designer should keep an eye on.[107]

Opera stages are among the largest in overall physical dimensions for several good reasons: (1) it is necessary to assemble as large an audience as possible before a company can even come near to covering the costs of opera production; (2) composers of traditional grand opera wrote for both large casts and many sets of scenery, so space is needed backstage and in the "fly" space overhead; (3) an orchestra in an orchestra pit takes up much physical space (and can make a lot of noise or beauty, depending upon its skill). A big theatre is called for to achieve the necessary auditory balance between the singers and the orchestra. For these reasons, opera is almost always produced on a large scale in a big performance place (chamber opera is an exception). Consequently, the lighting units used for opera must be more powerful, have longer throw distances, be more numerous, and cover larger performance areas than lights used for other shows. These necessary characteristics inevitably affect the designer's task.

Accumulated Tradition Affects Design. Through the long history of opera, specific customary ways of presenting

opera have accumulated. For the most part these traditions are upheld today, even though the original reason for doing a particular special effect may have changed. For example, a certain traditional blocking may have been developed to show off the strengths of a particular diva who is no longer even with us. Still, change should be introduced only because it is *better*, not just because it is new and different. Opera audiences, directors, and singers are immersed in the traditional way of presenting opera. They will reluctantly — and slowly — accept change, but only if it is a markedly successful improvement over tradition. A lighting designer should research, study, and learn the traditional way of doing things before introducing a new approach.[108]

Contemporary Presentation Trends Can Be Very Important To The Lighting Designer. Not so long ago, opera was in a decline in the United States; it was the sleep-inducing province of the old-line aristocracy and the ultra-rich. Then along came opera performed in English. Productions sung in the audience's native language made opera going easier and the box office sales larger, but at the same time it antagonized the Purists, who often felt that they "owned" opera and its associated snob values. The opera audience base has recently been broadened even more by the introduction of opera productions on national television and in selected film versions (although opera "on the air" goes back to the early days of NBC radio). For operas performed in their original languages, subtitles projected above the proscenium have become popular. Opera companies have discovered that to avoid bankruptcy they must have the income from telecasting in addition to revenues from recording if they are to make a successful transition from private benefactor financing to broad public support and (eventually) to government support. Telecasting operas and presenting them in English improved the product onstage and the size of the audience out front, but many opera companies have still had to move firmly toward simplified but effective physical decor (sets) to economize. The New York City Opera company has been "out front" in this direction, as has Herbert Kurt Adler's San Francisco Opera. These companies have turned to unit set groupings of levels and platforms that can serve for trilogies of related operas; extensive use of projected scenic backgrounds; and any

[107] See "Ring Around the Opera, Glenn Giffen Sits In on the Birth of a New Company in Denver, Opera Colorado," Opera News, vol. 48, no. 1 (July 1983), pp. 14–16. Illus. A description of one opera company working "in the round."

[108] Edward Rothstein, "A New Breed of Directors Changes the Face of Opera," The New York Times, March 11, 1984, section 2, Arts and Leisure, pp. 1, 32. Illus. A balanced, illustrated presentation of the pros and cons of avant-garde operatic changes by such directors as Frank Corsaro, Jonathan Miller, and Andrei Serban.

John Rockwell, "Opera Design Is Going Neo-Baroque," The New York Times, Arts and Leisure section, pp. 19, 22, Jan. 6, 1985. Critic Rockwell believes that the visual arts have assumed a dominant position in opera productions of the present day.

Jan Strasfogel, "A Galaxy of Light: An Expressionistic Staging of a Modern Opera," Theatre Crafts, vol. 22, no. 3 (March 1988), pp. 64–68. Illus., color. An ultramodern Oper Frankfurt production in Germany with direction by Strasfogel and design by Hans Hoffer. The production leaned heavily upon lighting as the major design element.

Martin Hall, "Translations Tactfully Conveyed," Cue, no. 56 (November/December 1988), pp. 17–18. A description of how the British summer Glyndebourne Festival and its touring opera deals with surtitles.

Robert Turnbull, The Opera Gazetteer. London; Trefoil; 1988. A British publication which gives basic information concerning over a hundred opera theatres, including policy, seasons, capacity, and price ranges. Useful for lighting designers.

simplification that can work in the best interests of effective opera presentation. In addition, they have hired the very best (worldwide) scenographers, scenic designers, and lighting designers in an attempt to reduce costs without compromising the grandness of grand opera. Sometimes "grand" can be achieved more by a great soloist in a shaft of brilliant light on a nearly darkened stage than by adding ten more 40- by 80-foot painted backdrops at a cost of $5,000 to $10,000 each.

Opera Always Loses Money. I have never worked for an opera company that was not in debt. It has been estimated that if the Metropolitan Opera ("the Met") were to break even financially each season solely on box office ticket sales, each and every seat in the theatre — all season long — would have to be priced at $250 per performance (which just isn't possible). Opera companies are always somewhat chagrined when they realize that the more public performances they present, the more money they lose. Full houses help — but no performances at all are the only way to avoid a deficit! The reality that opera companies survive on gifts, subsidies, and great community goodwill benefits new lighting designers in a strange way: opera companies are more willing to give a newcomer an opportunity to design than are most other theatre groups. Opera companies don't pay much; consequently, they provide more opportunities for the "new kid on the street." This abundance of opportunity applies more to the 50 or so regional opera companies than it does to the 10 giants, i.e., the Met, the New York City Opera, the San Francisco Opera, and companies in Chicago, Dallas, Miami, and so on.

Repertory Is Costly. This ties in with the topic discussed in the previous paragraph. Any designer who can work within the necessary repertory system of the larger opera companies — yet find a way to cut production costs without sacrificing quality — will have a steady job. Most regional opera companies — because they cannot hope to afford the costs of repertory performances — present *one* opera for two to six performances, usually over a one- to two-week period. Such companies offer two to five attractions per season. However, the larger companies (1) offer continuous repertory, i.e., a *different* opera each evening with two on matinee days; (2) usually tour nationally or regionally between their seasons at their own house; (3) frequently have adjunct programs. One type of adjunct program involves presentation of simplified excerpts on tour to surrounding schools and communities to build an ongoing opera audience. Other adjunct programs include summer productions outdoors (for example, by the St. Louis Municipal Opera; the Met in the Park; the La Scala basic group at Arena di Verona; the Vienna opera at Bregenz, Austria; or the world-famous Glyndebourne Opera with the London Philharmonic in the pit.

Winter repertory affects the lighting designer. On Thursday evening, for example, an opera is presented to the public. A night crew takes over after the performance and strikes it. The crew may put onstage another opera (not yet premiered) for rehearsal the next morning. Once the rehearsal (probably with full lighting) is over, that opera is struck and a third one put in place for the Friday evening performance. *Ad infinitum.* Is it any wonder that repertory opera is costly? Or that opera lighting designers frequently come to believe that they live in the opera house 24 hours per day during the height of the season? Or that they find that they must, as working designers, turn to a basic repertory arrangement of lighting equipment?

Some Hints Can Help With Repertory Lighting Equipment Layout. Dramatic theatre commonly can be "blocked" by dividing the stage into six basic acting areas: DL, DC, DR, UL, UC, UR (where D and U are *down* and *up,* while R, L, and C are *right, left,* and *center).* Opera does not lend itself to this six-part division. In opera, ten areas are more common: DL, DLC, DC, DRC, DR, UL, ULC, UC, URC, UR. The reason is simple: DC is a perfect place for the star singer to do his or her great aria. If two singers are involved in a matchless duet, they almost always can be found singing DLC and DRC. Five areas across the front is not only traditional but also vital to successful design, particularly in repertory. The lighting designer for an opera should plan on the following lighting basics from the outset:

- Ten areas — each controllable in at least warm and cool (for the day or "up" scenes, pink or amber or bastard amber or some close relative; for night scenes, one of the blues). More elaborate setups (at the Met or the New York City

Opera, for example) will have bastard amber, one of the pinks, lavender or violet, a warm blue, a steely-cool blue-green, and a pale-daylight blue constantly available for each of 10 standard acting areas. Opera directors know of this 10-area arrangement and will block the staging of the principal singers so that the singers "come to rest" for vocal numbers smack in the center of a standard area.

- Maximum crosslight wash in a range of standard colors from box booms or side ports FOH (front-of-house) and on bridge or pipe ends or ladders or floor booms backstage (always at hand).
- Simplified backlight setup, controllable by areas or "zones" ("In One" is downstage; "In Two," midstage; "In Three," upstage; "In Four," extreme upstage; etc.).
- Gobo specials and background or special projection equipment (as determined by the season's designer).
- Unassigned specials throughout the layout, usually in places most readily accessible for rapid color change and focus. These specials are used as needed, and are on separate dimmers or power lines.
- Floor units and specials. Light booms or towers or floor stands backstage can be easily recolored and refocused for each individual scene. They "bail out" many a lighting designer by rapidly covering entrances, exits, platforms, doors, windows, etc.
- Follow spotlights. A few opera directors hate followspots, but most couldn't do without them (and neither could the lighting designer). While there are a few scenes in the Metropolitan Opera's repertory which are entirely lighted behind a curtain-line scrim (although there are always three operator-controlled followspots on the light bridge backstage), the lighting for most scenes depends heavily upon three (or more) powerful FOH followspots in the hands of trained, skillful operators following exact pre-planned pickups and moves.

In the opinion of lighting designers who work opera regularly, many singers are born with a God-given gift *always* to go to a different spot onstage for *each* performance of a given scene. Only a followspot can help in such cases. Other singers—widely loved by lighting designers—can be counted on always to go to an exactly designated spot.

Little embarrasses a lighting designer more than a lengthy, elaborately rehearsed light cue which dims stage left and brightens stage right just as the principal (world-famous) suddenly lurches *down left* to sing, thrushlike, in complete gloom, as critics scribble notes about the ineptness of the lighting design!

Follow spotlights *can* be thrown to soft focus (eliminating the "steak knife" hard edge) and be used as mobile balcony rail frontlights. Followspots can be effective when used with taste and restraint. They have saved many an opera lighting designer's career.

The chorus and the edges of the stage should not be overlooked. While traditional operas focus upon two to ten principals, they also include large choruses. The faces of chorus members need not be crisply visible, but their bodies should be. Chorus singers are present for a reason (usually to provide commentary on the main action, reaction to it, and mood values). They can be backlighted or crosslighted, and, as mobile human figures, can be used to "paint a picture." The edges of the stage must also receive light. Few things show amateurishness more than dark corners down left and down right at the curtain-line with chorus members hovering there, not quite certain whether the lighting designer really *wanted* them onstage at all. And in many poorly lighted productions, the principals do not dare venture far away from the "pool" of light down center.

The Lighting Designer Should Be Prepared To Serve As Technical Director. The large opera companies have huge technical staffs. Lighting designers may find counterweights dropping all around them if they attempt to undertake duties assigned to someone else. However, regional opera companies often expect the lighting designer to serve as technical director for rented or borrowed sets. Since the lighting designer has to work out a hanging plot to determine where the lighting equipment will be, it is common also to modify the scenery hanging plot to fit into the theatre being used. Consequently, the lighting designer normally does this drawing and works most closely with the opera's (or theatre's) carpenter and flyman. Any training a lighting designer has had in scenic design and in technical theatre will come in most handy if he or she must assume this position.

[109] *Fred Bentham, "A Light at the Opera,"* Sightline, *vol. 21, no. 1 (Summer 1987), pp. 27–29, 31, 33. Illus. Bentham reminisces about early British opera lighting at Covent Garden with Charles Bristow, Robert Nesbitt, and William Bundy in the early 1950s.*

Lighting Should Be Designed To Light The Singers, Not The Scenery. Opera leans heavily upon lighting design. Sets are expensive, and they often stay in repertory for 40 years or more (the Metropolitan Opera still has opera sets intact and in use which date back to World War I and have been constantly refurbished). Ancient sets can be both handsome and believable.

While an audience comes expecting to see the "grand" in scenic splendor (even though the sets and costumes may have seen better days), primarily they come to hear (first) and see (second) the performers and the opera. Mood and scenic splendor are all very well, but opera is about singing, and the lighting design should acknowledge this. I have not forgotten seeing the world-renowned production of *Parsifal* at Bayreuth, Germany, designed and lighted by Wieland Wagner — Richard Wagner's grandson — in 1973. Everything was so dim and "moody" that much of the evening I was trying to decide which end of the auditorium contained the stage from which all the beautiful sound was issuing. Fortunately, that style of opera lighting is not in vogue at the present time.

Communications Form

As for theatre, for opera the traditional light plot and switchboard hookup serves as the work order. Figure 5.1 shows the current Metropolitan Opera basic light plot. Figure 5.2 is the FOH equipment allocation. Figure 5.3 shows the projection setup. This is the layout for the entire season. Since the Met has a long history and has many operas constantly available in repertory, changes happen only over a period of years. In fact, when the Met moved from its old home on Thirty-ninth Street in New York City to the new house in Lincoln Center, little changed. All the lighting equipment layout had to remain basically the same (except with newer and more powerful luminaires being introduced as replacements). The Met has (finally) added a new memory switchboard — but all the old circuits remain, with new ones now available in addition. To do away with the old circuits would require the complete redesigning of the lighting for over 60 operas in rep (repertory)!

Figure 5.4 shows a production photo of *The Turn of the Screw* in the current repertory of the New York City Opera at the New York State Theatre in Lincoln Center. It carries a lighting design credit for Hans Sondheimer. The original production was designed at the older Fifty-fifth Street Masonic Temple (former home of the New York City Opera) by me. When the company moved to Lincoln Center, all new Union (USA #829) lighting design contracts were filed (with payment) for the entire repertory. Hans Sondheimer then had the freedom to modify and adapt the lighting design of each opera to the conditions of the new house. With all due respect to designer Sondheimer, he kept intact everything from my original production: the colors, cue placement and duration, focus, and concept are all as they were in the original. Only the program credit was changed.

Figure 5.5 shows the designer Gil Wechsler's specific light cues and circuit checklist (the only one available for this volume — only repertory opera would have continued use of such a list) for the specific production of *Tannhauser* within the season's framework. Color Fig. 18 and Figs. 5.6, 5.7, and 5.8 show photographs of this production. In Chap. 6, Figs. 6.8 through 6.12 offer the light plot, hookup, and production photos of *Salome*, lighted by designer Stephen Ross at the outdoor Santa Fe Opera in its rep setup. Color Fig. 19 is also from this production. Color Fig. 48 and Color Fig. 48a in Chap. 6 offer production photos of opera at Arena di Verona (Milan, Italy). Figure 5.9 and Color Figs. 20, 21, and 22 are the design work of Nananne Porcher. Figures 5.10 through 5.14 are other examples by various designers of outstanding opera lighting design.

The history of lighting design at the Metropolitan Opera is of particular interest. When I was a youth and first in New York City, Jacob Buchter [IATSE (International Association of Theatre and Stage Employees) Local Union #1] ruled lighting design there with an iron hand. He controlled the electricians, supervising their work and assigning their duties. In conjunction with the scenic designer, the Met's impressario (then Rudolph Bing), the stage director, and anyone else who could successfully participate, Buchter served as a focal point and clearinghouse for *all* lighting setup, design, and operation in repertory. Much of the same system prevails (except in England and the United States) in opera houses throughout the world today.[109] When Buchter retired (his was the reign at the Thirty-ninth

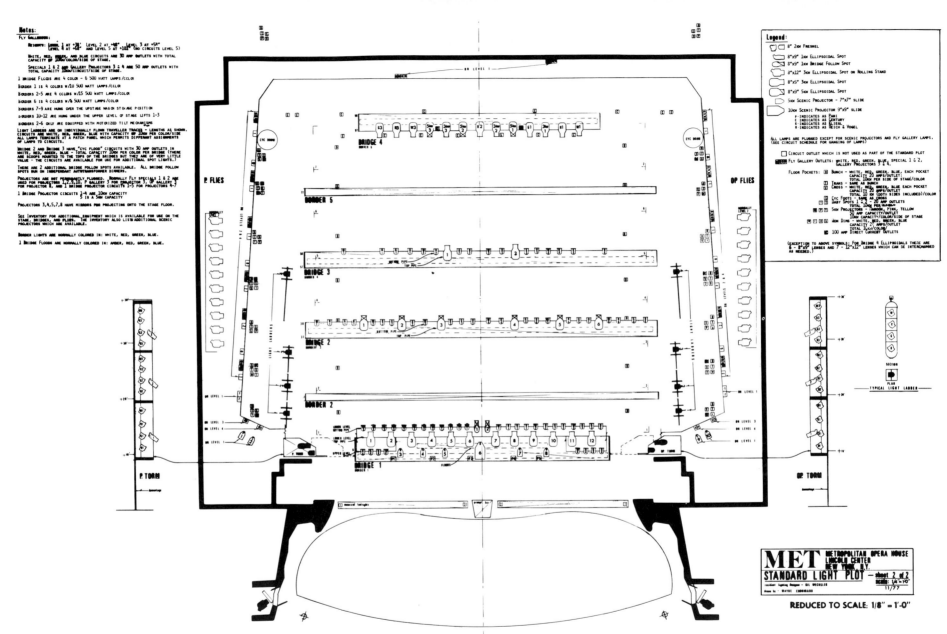

Figure 5.1 Basic Metropolitan Opera season light plot in 1979 by lighting designer Gil Wechsler.

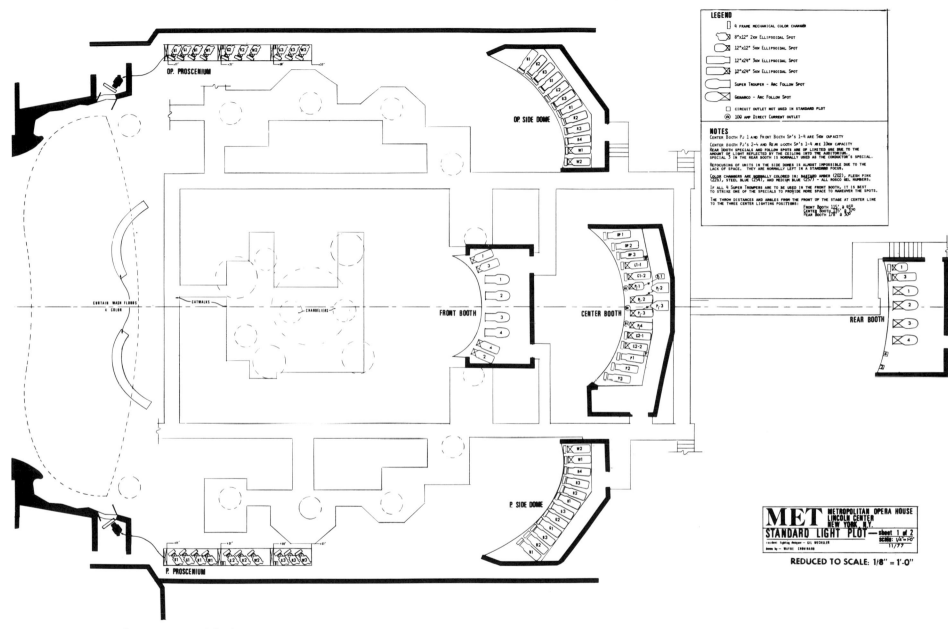

Figure 5.2 Basic Metropolitan Opera season light plot.

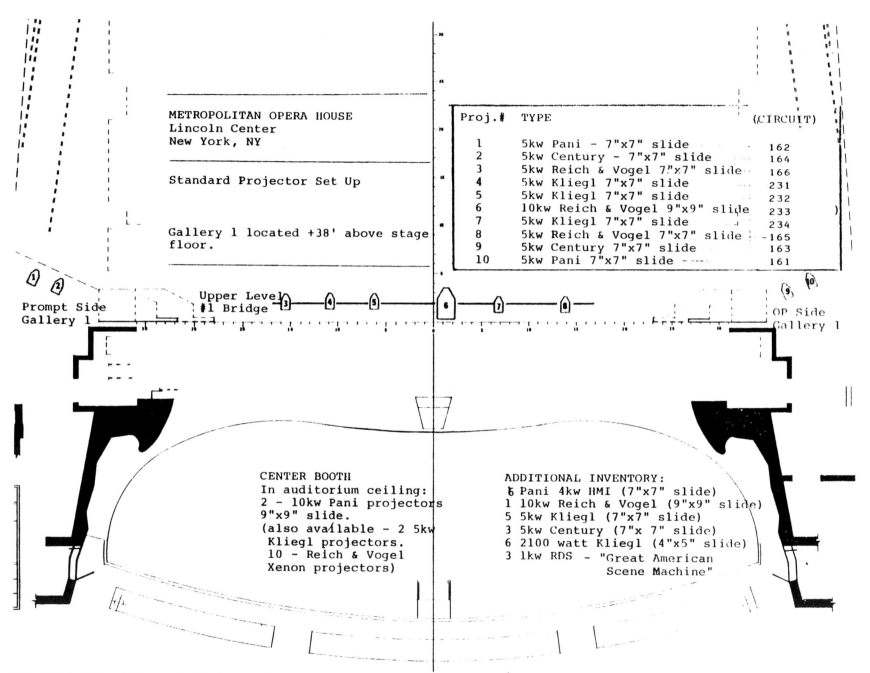

METROPOLITAN OPERA HOUSE
Lincoln Center
New York, NY

Standard Projector Set Up

Gallery 1 located +38' above stage
floor.

Proj.#	TYPE	(CIRCUIT)
1	5kw Pani - 7"x7" slide	162
2	5kw Century - 7"x7" slide	164
3	5kw Reich & Vogel 7"x7" slide	166
4	5kw Kliegl 7"x7" slide	231
5	5kw Kliegl 7"x7" slide	232
6	10kw Reich & Vogel 9"x9" slide	233
7	5kw Kliegl 7"x7" slide	234
8	5kw Reich & Vogel 7"x7" slide	165
9	5kw Century 7"x7" slide	163
10	5kw Pani 7"x7" slide	161

Prompt Side
Gallery 1

Upper Level
#1 Bridge

OP Side
Gallery 1

CENTER BOOTH
In auditorium ceiling:
2 - 10kw Pani projectors
9"x9" slide.
(also available - 2 5kw
Kliegl projectors.
10 - Reich & Vogel
Xenon projectors)

ADDITIONAL INVENTORY:
6 Pani 4kw HMI (7"x7" slide)
1 10kw Reich & Vogel (9"x9" slide)
5 5kw Kliegl (7"x7" slide)
3 5kw Century (7"x 7" slide)
6 2100 watt Kliegl (4"x5" slide)
3 1kw RDS - "Great American
              Scene Machine"

Figure 5.3 Standard projection setup in the basic Metropolitan
Opera 1979 season light plot by Gil Wechsler.

Figure 5.4 New York City Opera production of Benjamin Britten's *The Turn of the Screw*. Scenic design: Jac Venza; lighting design: Hans Sondheimer, based on design by Lee Watson for the original New York City Opera production. (*Photo: ©Fred Fehl.*)

Figure 5.6 Metropolitan Opera's production of Wagner's *Tannhauser*. Set design; Gunter Schneider-Siemssen; lighting design: Gil Wechsler; costumes: Patricia Zipprodt; director: Otto Schenk. (*Photo: James Hefferman.*)

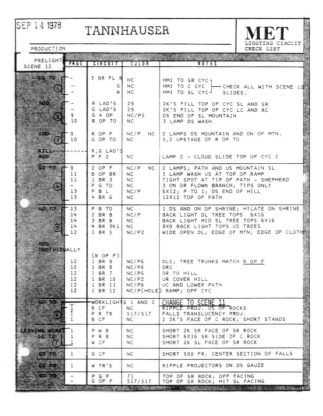

Figure 5.5 Metropolitan Opera's *Tannhauser*. Cues and circuit checklist by lighting designer Gil Wechsler.

Figure 5.7 *Tannhauser* production photo. (*Photo: James Heffenan.*)

Figure 5.8 *Tannhauser* production photo. (*Photo: James Hefferman.*)

Figure 5.9 Dallas Civic Opera production of *Aida* at the State Fair Music Hall in 1960. Set and costume design: Peter Hall; lighting design: Nananne Porcher; director: Elias Rabb.

Figure 5.10 *Galileo Galilei* by Ezro Laderman and Joe Darion in February 1979 for the Tri-Cities Opera Co. in Binghamton, N.Y. Director: Carmen Savoca; set design: John E. Bielenberg; lighting design: John Eloy Vestal.

Figure 5.11 *Marriage of Figaro* by Mozart at the Cincinnati Conservatory's Corbett Auditorium in February 1975. Set design: Paul R. Short; lighting design: Suellen Childs.

Figure 5.12 Wagner's *Flying Dutchman* in August 1978, performed by the Indiana University Opera theatre, Bloomington, Indiana. Set design: Max Röthlisberger; lighting design: Allen R. White; projections: James Mulder.

Street Metropolitan Opera), he was replaced by Rudy Kuntner, another IATSE #1 stagehand who headed all lighting. Kuntner oversaw nearly every detail of the construction of the new Lincoln Center Metropolitan Opera House. Were it not for Kuntner's devoted attention to detail, many aspects of lighting there would not be as good as they are today. When Kuntner suffered a series of heart attacks,

rather than using a stagehand from IATSE #1, the Met finally hired a USA #829 lighting designer: Gil Wechsler. Heading the stagehands electrical crew is Sandy Hacker, a brilliant production electrician with whom I have worked many times on Broadway. The two make an excellent team.

Other lighting designers have established strong careers basically in opera lighting. Robert Brand, once a student of

[110] *Jean Rosenthal and Lael Wertenbaker,* The Magic of Light. *Boston; Little, Brown and Co.; 1972. Chap. 7: "Lighting the Opera," pp. 87–103. A brilliant analysis of the history and nature of opera and its effect upon lighting and lighting designers. Filled with personal memories which communicate Rosenthal's love of both opera and lighting.*

Joel E. Rubin and Leland H. Watson, Theatrical Lighting Practice. *New York; Theatre Arts Books; 1954. Chap. III, "The Opera Stage," pp. 37–45. The first text treatment of opera lighting. Still usable.*

Basic references:

Leslie Orrey, A Concise History of Opera. *London; Thames and Hudson; 1972. Available in paperback. Contains 254 illustrations, 32 in color. Orrey interrelates changing theatrical conditions, architecture, and production style in a readable, well-illustrated history of opera, in the United States and abroad. He also treats briefly operetta and musical comedy.*

Rudolf Hartman (ed.), Opera. *New York; William Morrow & Co., Inc.; 1977. 268 pages. Lavishly printed and illustrated in-depth study of opera production by 64 world-renowned designers, directors, and producers of opera. Of particular interest: "Lighting and Projection" by Gunther Schneider-Siemssen and "Plastic Projection in Stage Design" by Heinrich Wendel. Each of 11 operas is presented as designed by several major artists, discussed by each, and compared:* Don Giovanni, The Magic Flute, The Barber of Seville, Don Pasquale, Don Carlos, Die Meistersinger, Die Gotterdammerung, Fidelio, Tales of Hoffmann, Pelléas et Mélisande, *and* Die Frau Ohne Schatten.

Metropolitan Opera National Council publishes regularly the Central Opera Service Bulletin. *These list (annually) the "Opera Repertory" (operas produced in the United States each year); seasonal information (finances, premieres, subsidies, translations, new books, awards, etc.); and the "Directory of Opera Companies and Workshops in the U.S. and Canada." This last publication gives extensive information about each opera-producing group — its address, executives, policies, etc. — and is an invaluable reference tool that is useful when seeking design employment.*

Figure 5.13 San Francisco Spring Opera production of *St. Matthew's Passion* by J. S. Bach. Set design: Ming Cho Lee; lighting design: John Wright Stevens.

Figure 5.14 Boston University Opera Workshop production of *Summer and Smoke* in 1976. Set design: Michael Anania; lighting design: Pat Collins. (*Photo courtesy of M. Anania.*)

mine, has for years designed up to 25 operas per season in the regional opera circuit and is constantly employed and widely respected by opera managements, directors, and designers. Tom Munn became staff lighting designer for the San Francisco Opera, replacing Bob Brand. He is a rising star as a result of his dedication, artistic talent, and inventive use of projections. Hans Sondheimer was technical director, stage manager, and lighting designer for the New York City Opera from its inception until recently, in addition to his career in teaching and in designing lighting for numerous industrial shows. After Sondheimer retired, Gil Hemsley, Jr. assumed the lighting duties at New York City Opera, until his death in 1983. Stephen Ross (whose Santa Fe Opera work appears in Chap. 6) established a growing reputation with the Greater Opera Co. of St. Louis, the Santa Fe Opera, and the Cincinnati Summer Opera before moving to Canada, where he is quite in demand. Tharon Musser was long the technical director and frequently the lighting designer for the Dallas Opera. Miami Opera utilizes a series of "name" designers: Robert Brand, Tharon Musser, Duane H. Schuler (who followed Gil Wechsler into the Chicago Lyric Opera). Houston Grand Opera, Washington Opera Co., and Santa Fe Opera, along with many others, turn to various well-known designers such as Nananne Porcher

and Neil Peter Jampolis. Jean Rosenthal had a long career in opera lighting,[110] primarily with the New York City Opera Company.

The Challenge

Opera is one of the most exciting design challenges encountered in a lifetime of lighting design. It is huge, theatrical, imaginative, sometimes unbearably beautiful (visually and vocally), and devilishly difficult to do under the necessary technical limitations imposed. Only at the very top does it pay well. Yet lighting designers would not wish to be deprived of its design challenge.

Dance

Almost overnight dance became tremendously popular in the United States. The youth of the nation danced in ever-increasing numbers at discos. People of all ages turned to aerobic dancing to keep fit. Theatres presenting dance programs were packed, whether presenting an ethnic import (the dancers of Senegal with their bare, bouncing breasts) or classical ballet by the Bolshoi Ballet from Russia. The National Association of Regional Ballet reported that in 1968 members of American ballet audiences numbered one mil-

The magazine, Opera News, *is a valuable reference source. It is published approximately 26 times per year on a frequency schedule corresponding to the height of the winter opera season by the Metropolitan Opera guild, Inc., 1865 Broadway, NY 10023.*

See also:

Lee Watson, "Genesis of an Opera," Lighting Dimensions, *vol. 5, no. 4 (May 1981), pp. 17–19, 21–23. Light plot, hookup, color production photos for the author's* One Night In Venice, *with text.*

Ken Billington, "Notes on Lighting for Opera," Lighting Dimensions, *vol. 5, no. 4 (May 1981), pp. 33–35. Illus., color.*

Catherine Wanek, "Santa Fe Opera, Part I Background," Lighting Dimensions, *vol. 2, no. 1 (Jan. 1978), pp. 30–34; also, same issue: "Santa Fe Opera, Part II Stephen Ross," pp. 35–37. Extensive color illustrations and a season repertory light plot for this key (outdoor) opera company. Good text.*

Robert Brand, "Lighting Design in Regional Opera," Lighting Dimensions, *vol. 5, no. 4 (May 1981), pp. 38–40. Illus., color.*

Glenn Loney, "New Visions in Opera Design: Rudolph Heinrich in Retrospect," Theatre Crafts, *vol. 10, no. 6 (Nov./Dec. 1976), pp. 13–17, 36–38, 40. Good text, extensive illustrations of important design work.*

Glenn Loney, "If It Burns, Forget It — British Designer Randolf Koltai on Concepts and Materials," Theatre Crafts, *vol. 11, no. 1 (Jan./Feb. 1977), pp. 10–15, 64–68. Well-illustrated work of another important living designer.*

Glenn Loney, "The Bayreuth Festival, A Centenary Ring Cycle," Theatre Crafts, *vol. 11, no. 2 (Mar./Apr. 1977), pp. 16–17, 36–38, 40. Another illustrated look at a major production group.*

Glenn Loney, "Designing for a new vision — Director–Designer Jean-Pierre Ponnelle's Controversial Settings," Theatre Crafts, *vol. 12, no. 3 (Mar./Apr. 1978), pp. 14–19, 59–60, 62–66, 68–69. Another provocative set of illustrations and text in this series of leading opera design.*

Glenn Loney, "Romantic Realism and the Cosmic — Gunther Schneider-Seimssen Designs

the Literal and Symbolic," Theatre Crafts, *vol. 12, no. 6 (Oct. 1978), pp. 28–33, 40–44, 46. Extensive illustrations, including many of the Met's* Tannhauser, *shown elsewhere in this Handbook.*

"Lighting for Opera and Ballet in Repertory — An Interview with Hans Sondheimer at the New York State Theatre," Theatre Crafts, *Jan./Feb. 1973, pp. 12–15, 34–38. Well-illustrated.*

Lee Watson, "A Salute to Hans," Lighting Dimensions, *vol. 2, no. 10 (Dec. 1978), pp. 12–14 and color cover. More about Sondheimer. Illus., color.*

Richard Pilbrow, Stage Lighting. *New York; Von Nostrand Reinhold Co.; revised edition, 1979. Opera, p. 104. Brief.*

Frantisek Deak, "Satyagraha," and Richard Riddell, "Notes on Lighting Satyagraha," Theatre Design & Technology, *vol. 17, no. 2 (Summer 1981), pp. 10–14. Illus. Light plot. Avant-garde opera by Robert Wilson.*

Glenn M. Loney, "It's All in the Plot: Tom Munn of the San Francisco Opera," Theatre Crafts, *vol. 17, no. 9 (Nov./Dec. 1983), pp. 20–23, 65–69. Illus. Light plot included. Munn discusses opera repertory lighting in San Francisco.*

Charles Osborne, The World Theatre of Wagner. *London; Phaidon Press or Macmillan Publishing Co. in New York; 1982. Illus., color, 224 pp.*

Rudolph Hartman, Richard Strauss, The Staging of His Operas and Productions from the Premieres to the Present. *N.Y.; Rizzoli; 1982. Illus., color, 302 pp.*

Susan Lieberman, "Northern Lights," Theatre Crafts, *vol. 18, no. 7 (Aug./Sept. 1984), pp. 40–45, 95–98. Illus., color. Contains Duane Schuler's season repertory light plot for the Chicago Lyric Opera.*

Leslie Rubinstein, "Spettacolo!" Opera News, *vol. 49, no. 16 (May 1985), pp. 16–17, 19–20. Illus., color. A useful article about Verona (Italy) opera in the outdoor ancient Roman ampitheatre each summer.*

Michael F. Ramsaur, "The Staging of Wagner's Ring," Lighting Dimensions, *vol. 8, no. 7 (Nov./Dec. 1984), pp. 42–50, 52. Illus., color.*

Includes light plot. A description of technical innovation in the annual production of Wagner's Ring Cycle *in West Germany.*

"Speed, Simplicity are Design Elements at NYC Opera," Rosconews, *Spring 1986, pp. 2, 4. Illus. A description of opera rep lighting by New York City Opera resident designer Mark Stanley.*

"Grand Designs at the Met," Lighting Dimensions, *vol. 10, no. 2 (Mar./Apr. 1986), pp. 54–58, 60–61, 63–66, 68, 70–71, 94. Illus., color. Light plot. An extensive, well-illustrated description of Gil Wechsler's lighting design at the New York City Metropolitan Opera.*

Cole Mobley, "Light Show — Behind the Scenes with Gil Wechsler and His Staff, Who Illuminate the Metropolitan Opera Stage," Opera News, *March 14, 1987, pp. 14–16, 18. Illus. Well-written overview of lighting at the Met.*

"Overseas, Oistat Amsterdam," ABTT News, *November/December 1987, pp. 5–6. A summary by British lighting designer Bob Davis of the use of surtitles in opera.*

Michael S. Eddy, "Under the Stars: Craig Miller Heads Into 11th Year At Santa Fe Opera," Lighting Dimensions, *vol. 13, no. 4 (May/June 1989), pp. 56–59, 71–72. Illus., color. Light plot.*

[111] *Robert Jackson, "Viewpoint,"* Opera News, *vol. 24, no. 22 (June 1978, p. 5. A brief summary of the growth and popularity of dance.*

Leslie Bennetts, "New York City in the Performing Arts: Still the Capital, but with a Difference," The New York Times, *Mar. 5, 1983, p. 11.*

Anna Kisselgoff, "Diversity Is the Word for American Dance Today," The New York Times, *Art and Leisure Section, p. 10, Mar. 10, 1985. Good background survey of dance today.*

lion; in 1978 — 10 years later — that audience was estimated at 15 million, and by 1986 the dance audience had grown to 20 million. In 1968 roughly 80 percent of the dance audience was concentrated in New York City; by 1978, 80 percent was outside of New York City.[111] The number of dance companies grew from 35 to 213 in 1986! Dance has evolved from a few straggling imported companies playing the big cities and a few impoverished modern dance troupes traipsing around the collegiate circuit into a major attraction. The current high stature of dance is evidenced by the popularity of the "Dance in America" series on network television (Public Broadcasting Service) and by the intense competition between the big commercial networks to present the outstanding Christmas *Nutcracker* ballet special. Touring companies, both American and foreign, are everywhere. Movies such as *The Turning Point* are based upon ballet and play to overflow crowds. Dance has become popular. But what is "dance"?

Webster's defines *dance* thus: "to perform a rhythmic and patterned succession of bodily movements, usually to music." That definition is hardly sufficient to describe what is happening that is called "dance" in our theatres today. In an attempt to define *dance* more precisely as it relates to theatre, several of my Purdue University graduate scenography seminars discussed this topic at length. First we eliminated all dance in which one actively participates, rather than being a spectator (this removes most disco). We were aware of many modern performances where dance is performed to silence (to a counted beat rather than music) and to other auditory stimuli which could not properly be called music. We were aware that a few dance groups basically improvise before an audience; each performance is different (sometimes changing with altered musical stimuli and lighting, as well as with other variables). Yet such is also the case with *commedia dell'arte*. Both have a basic, organized outline, or structure. We discussed the fringe outer edges of dance: pantomime, the martial arts (judo and karate), formal gymnastics, marching bands at football games, the classical striptease, and jazz and tap dancing. Mime, martial arts, and gymnastics are certainly the "performance of a rhythmic and patterned succession of bodily movements" and are frequently presented before an enthusiastic audience of admirers of skill and technique. Much the same could perhaps be said of such popular sports as swimming and tennis. It seems necessary to understand and address the problem of defining the term *dance*, prior to discussing how dance is to be lighted.

The graduate students and I eventually arrived at this definition of "dance as theatre": *Dance is a form of communication for an audience that is an organized expression employing bodily movement and using rhythm as a base.* While it may not be approved by *Webster's,* this is the definition which will be used throughout this chapter.

Because lighting design is different for various forms of dance, my students and I then selected "types" of dance. We found that types could best be differentiated by understanding that there are four basic dance-related *variables.* Each type of dance differently grouped the primary and secondary emphases of these variables. The variables are as follows:

1. *Dance Objective.* The objective may be to tell a story, to delineate a mood, or to bring about a desired result (rain, please the gods, celebrate a victory, etc.). What is the dance intended to accomplish?

2. *Dance Technique and Vocabulary of Movement.* In ballet there are formal techniques (for example, females dance *on point;* males normally do not).

3. *The Accompaniment.* What music, rhythm, or sound generators are used?

4. *The Production Form. Swan Lake* or *The Cage* are built around specific scenery and utilize it; more abstract dances do not. Alwin Nikolais utilizes his own specific production tools: sound, light, costumes, and scenery. Without them, much of his choreography would be meaningless. Much the same can be said of costume use by either Martha Graham or *Mummenchantz.*

Dance types, for purposes of discussing lighting design, can be divided into the following:

1. *Classical Ballet.* The primary variable is story and technique.

2. *Mood Dance.* This kind of dance is also commonly referred to as modern dance or interpretative dance. This category would include the work of Martha Graham, Ruth

Page, Robert Joffrey, Gerald Arpino, Alvin Ailey, Merce Cunningham, Hanya Holm, Geoffrey Holder, Isadore Duncan, Loie Fuller, Alwin Nikolais, and many others.

3. *Entertainment Dance.* This category includes tap, jazz, TV disco programs, dance marathons, June Taylor Dancers on TV, Busby Berkley, dance "Happenings" (John Cage's work), freeform spontaneous dance, and the classical striptease.

4. *Production Dance.* A production dance is a part of an opera or a musical comedy: for example, the dances in *Oklahoma, Slaughter on Tenth Avenue,* and the musical *Fancy Free;* dance interludes in opera; and dancing in *Billy the Kid* (also a ballet).

5. *Ethnic or Regional Dance.* American Indian dances, the *Ballet Folklorico* of Mexico, the *Bayanihan* of the Philippines, the *Peking Ballet,* Spanish flamenco, Egyptian "belly dancing," Tahitian "hand" dancers, etc., fall into this category.

6. *Pantomime.* Without sound but with a story line and a rhythm, pantomime is a fringe area.

7. *Martial Arts, Gymnastics, and Some Other Sports.* These disciplines make up another fringe area.

While this analysis may seem to the casual reader to be a lengthy digression, it is useful background to the nine design considerations and the six technique specifics which follow.

Design Considerations

The next few pages offer some basic considerations which a lighting designer for dance needs to be aware of before preparing plans and designs.

The Floor. At a United States Institute for Theatre Technology (USITT) national panel in Phoenix in 1978 (involving the collective experience of Nananne Porcher, Chenault Spence, and Martin Aronstein), all dance lighting designers stressed that the floor surface selected was of even more importance to lighting than the purchase of instruments and controls. Their point was most valid. Much of the scenic background for dance is the floor surface. Classical dancing is often about "feet." The floor's reflectivity, color, and/or pattern is not only the decor, but "bounce" light from it also affects the dancers' appearance. Some designers prefer a fairly dark surface, because it bounces little light on the dancers or on a cyclorama (cyc) and yet makes the lighted dancers' feet and bodies stand forth. Others prefer a very light, reflective surface, because bounce light enhances the performers' visibility and sets off their feet. Almost all designers dislike the mirrorlike, highly varnished hardwood floor. Preferences vary, but in any case, the color and reflectivity of the surface upon which dance takes place is a major factor for the lighting designer and is largely unmodifiable once the floor covering has been purchased and is in place.

The Dancers. Dance lighting is often the opposite of opera lighting, because it is the body motions of the living dancers which is paramount, rather than voice and facial interpretation, as in drama. In opera, voice and music are paramount. The emphasis on the body in dance cannot be stressed enough. Here is how this principle affects lighting design for common mounting positions:

1. Lighting designers should use all the *crosslight* they can manage. That is what dance lighting is all about, and that is why it rarely is performed in arena or thrust theatres. Crosslighting (from pipe ends, from booms on the sides of the stage and FOH, or from ladders backstage, as well as from low-angle "shin kickers") does more to dramatize, sculpt, and reveal and enhance the body form, as well as structure and clarify movement, than does light from any other angle. Unlike drama, in which the designer must be concerned about one performer casting a shadow on another's face, dance movement is so free that this is not a concern.

2. *Backlight* is a real godsend. It separates the dancer from the relatively unimportant scenic background (be it a drop or a sky cyc or blacks) and isolates the three-dimensional moving body in what lighting designer Jean Rosenthal called "jewel-like lighting". Dance can be, and is, performed without backlight, but not when there is a choice. Backlight is more necessary in dance lighting design than in any other area of theatrical lighting (with the possible exception of the "two-dimensional media," television and film).

3. *Frontlight* is much less important than backlight. Classical story ballets and mood dance with a story line may call for more light from the front than is normally needed — but

even then it should be a subtle "fill," much like footlights (i.e., used in moderation). Often frontlighting is used in dance to "lay down" an overall mood throughout the dancing space for the particular piece being presented (a "blue ballet" versus a "white," "amber," or "pink" ballet). Almost always in dance, *plasticity* takes precedence over excessive *visibility*.

4. *Followspots* are useful (when available), particularly in classical ballet — not, in the usual sense, to accentuate the star performers, but instead to assist the audience in keeping a properly balanced focus on the lead dancers in a stage filled with the moving bodies of a large *corps de ballet*. It is the one device (other than dancer groupings) available to the choreographer to direct the audience's attention where desired. A designer should not be afraid to use followspots with dance, but they should be thrown to soft focus and used with subtlety.

Dance is based upon groupings, patterns, and movement. The designer can rapidly discover whether the companies' choreographers incline toward diagonal line patterns or static groupings. This knowledge affects how the designer plans equipment layout and how equipment is used.

Repertory Flexibility. Drama and opera present one continuous and complete story in an evening's performance time. Dance presents many. With the exception of the full-length ballet or mood story dance, in most cases many different dances in many different moods go together to make up one evening's program. If a company is performing constantly, there may be 50 or more complete dances in repertory. Lighting design for dance must be tailored to the overall type of presentation of the specific dance company, yet flexible enough to deal with the range of choreographed content within that company's repertory. In most cases the content is amazingly broad.

Dancing Space. Dancing space is important, not decor. This point has been mentioned above. Dancers need a lot of performance space. Lifts may be involved so the designer must light above the usual head height. If built scenery or large props are present, the choreographer will use them — dancers become tactilely involved, or else the pieces are eliminated. Normally lots of open space for movement is

what is needed. The most important design elements (other than dancers, of course) are costumes and lighting and sound. Dance leans as heavily upon the creative power of light as any of the theatre forms.

Areas. Traditional drama can usually be fitted into standard stage areas, as can opera. Dance cannot. Much like the musical (to be discussed next in this chapter), dance is often lighted in *zones*. Downstage ("In One") is where the principals are most apt to be. Midstage ("In Two") is the next choice. Upstage ("In Three" or "In Four") is where the decorative groupings of the *corps* are to be found (with the exception of entrances and exits by the principals, mostly upcenter). There are, however, many story dances which demand pools of light in standard *areas*. The lighting designer may need both control devices in a season setup. Beyond that, there is a constant need for color *washes* (toning and blending light) throughout the entire dance area. Not only does lighting require available zone control, plus area control, plus color washes, but many dances also will demand *specials*. These can be pools of light nearly anywhere onstage, or a *silhouette* opening with dancers' bodies framed against the background. Whether lighting for a specific dance involves areas or zones or washes or specials, the lighting design *must* spring from the needs of the dance and must respond to and reinforce the rhythm of the accompanying sound/music. The design approach springs out of the dance material; the designer cannot force the choreographer, dancers, and company to fit into a preconceived design approach. Because of all these things, dance, properly lighted, can call for a lot of lighting and control equipment.

Budget and Time. Budget and time are important factors. The fact that an evening's program may consist of from one (full-length) to twenty or more individual dances means that the designer must use time and equipment wisely. Add to the regular constraints the constant program changes due to dancer injury or a desire to present maximum variety to the audience, and the lighting problems double. Dance companies are never rich. Trained dancers "live" dance — 24 hours a day — and subject themselves to unbelievable physical training and rigors which would shame many a star athlete. Since they freely give so much of themselves for "their art," they expect the lighting designer to do the same. Miracles are always expected from a minimum of both time and equipment. If the company can't afford elaborate sets, then the lighting designer ought to be able to come up with imaginative projected gobo patterns on the floor and cyc. Inexpensive inventiveness is the name of the game in dance. Lighting designers who are not prepared for this game should do their lighting in other areas of theatre.

Differences Between Dance and Opera. It is useful here to recap the differences between dance and opera. As compared with opera, dance involves:

- More performer mobility
- Scenery that is at best only a background (and rarely is a performer)
- Interpretation that is achieved through body stance and movement, rather than with the voice or facial expression
- Dance numbers that are of shorter duration and more numerous for an evening's program
- An emphasis on "poetic beauty" rather than "grandness" (there are exceptions to this)
- An emphasis in lighting on angle of light, intensity, form and movement, and, lastly, color.

The last point is the most important design point. There is a huge interpretational difference between the human body lighted from a pool of light directly overhead; "shin kickers" from each side; or a special in the footlights casting a large shadow behind the dancer. The "selective" part of selective visibility is not crucial in lighting dance. Few dances (there are a few) call for separate playing areas and figures isolated in a single shaft of light on a darkened stage. Plasticity (or three-dimensionality, or revelation of form) is all-important. Scenic and dramatic composition ("painting a picture") is vital, but it must follow the fluid movement of the dancers and the dance. Mood can be most important in dance lighting, primarily because scenery is kept to a minimum and lighting must replace it in fulfilling this function.

Scrims and Translucent Backdrops. Scrims and translucent backdrops can be vital to dance. If a dance company can possibly afford it (after it has purchased a suitable floor covering), it should buy a translucent backdrop rather than

a cyclorama. This area is the scenic background for much of dance. It is the lighting designer's key mood and scenic composition tool. The company should give him every design opportunity by owning (or having available) a good surface upon which can be worked lighting magic. If the company must use a cyclorama, it should invest in a good black or white scrim to put in front of the cyc. This will help eliminate bounce light from the stage floor graying-out the lower half of the supposed sky. It will help add the all-important illusion of infinite depth in front of which the dancer's bodies perform. It will eliminate the audience's being conscious of telltale seams in the cyc. It is easily the second most important piece of lighting equipment (the floor being number one). Lastly, a dance company should invest — as soon as possible — in a properly designed and constructed, readily transportable, curved ground row. The curved ground row allows the lighting designer to conceal striplights on the stage floor to light evenly the base of the cyc and at the same time helps to eliminate the horrible line which seems to cut right through the dancer's bodies when the lighting designer attempts to achieve a smooth transition between the lighted tone value of the floor surface (horizontal) and the cyclorama (vertical) behind it. The curved ground row is a most valuable investment.

Concept Hints. Finally, this section presents a grab bag of important design considerations.

Any dance company should give first consideration to securing a permanent company lighting designer. (The Phoenix USITT panel all agreed on this and gave it number-one priority.) A company may choose a diverse assortment of guest lighting designers, but ahead of equipment purchases, or even a dance floor surface, there should be the means to make one person *responsible for lighting*. That person (in small companies) may also be the stage manager, or even one of the dancers who has a visual design/technical sense. It should be a paid position if the company can afford it; it may be a volunteer position if necessity dictates. Lighting design should channel from the choreographer's ideas and requests through to the single lighting designer, then on to the workers. Nothing confuses a switchboard operator more than receiving conflicting lighting suggestions from the choreographer, the stage manager, *and* the lighting designer. Lines of communication and channels of authority should be set up to ensure a smooth performance.

Designers should study, analyze, and come to know the dance company by which they are employed. Dance lighting begins with an analysis of what dance is, the variables and the types. Designers should learn their company's repertory, style, command structure (who makes the final decisions), and financial base. Most important of all is the dance company's *purpose,* which the designer should become acquainted with as soon as possible. Why does the company exist? How does it differ from other dance companies?

Designers should also study and analyze each dance carefully, listening to the music (if any) and its rhythm; watching dance rehearsals; and becoming familiar with the movement, the story (if there is one), the mood, and the dance patterns. Designers should make it a point to talk with the choreographer about each dance and its intention (not with the dancers). After all that is done they can begin to think about designing the lighting.

It helps a designer to understand the members of the company's audience. Why did they come? What do they expect to see or to happen? Why did they come to see this company rather than another? The answers to these questions are vital to good lighting design for the company. Dance lighting is much more than mere mechanical formulas.

Designers need to analyze the performance place (or places) in which the company is to perform. What mounting positions are always available for luminaires? Sometimes available? Rarely or never available? They should also check sight lines and acoustics; auditorium decor; and amount of room backstage. The Beverly Emmons "Technical Information Questionnaire" in *Theatre Design and Technology* [see footnote 113 ("Panel: Dance Production")] can be of great assistance here. What is the theatre crew like? How much time is allowed in the theatre for load-in and setup? For rehearsal? Are there other performances or groups using the stage during the setup or rehearsal period? What is the lighting budget? Is there money for contingencies (such as blown fuses, burned-out lamps, need for fresh color media —all frequent "just before the curtain" emergencies)?

Dance Types/Variables. Here is a checklist of the various types of dance along with the variables which are most important for each:

Classical Ballet. Emphasis is on story and dance technique, then scenery and mood. Sculpting the dancer's body with light is very important.

Mood Dance. Sculpting the body and mood are paramount.

Entertainment Dance. Color, spectacle, and adequate visibility are most important. Sculpting the body is frequently less important.

Production Dance. Emphasis is on mood, suitability of lighting, sculpting figure, and contrast (with the rest of the production).

Ethnic or Regional Dance. The story, its objective, and its authenticity of detail (either literally or in essence) take precedence.

Mime. Clear, clean visibility is the main objective.

Martial Arts, Gymnastics, Sports. Since these arts require skill, rhythm, and organized precision in bodily movement, they match our definition of dance. Sharp visibility is important, but the performer must not be blinded. While it may seem unusual to continue to include this category under "Dance Types," it is not really out of line. A student of mine was recently hired (at good pay) to light a regional gymnastic competition.

While these suggestions may not result in a designer's immediately being engaged to design lighting for the greater works of the Bolshoi Ballet, the American Ballet, the New York City Ballet, the Martha Graham Dance Co., the Nikolais Dance Co., or even those wonderful dance creations of Jose Limon, they are at the heart of dance lighting. Many professional lighting designers begin in dance. Tharon Musser did. So did Jennifer Tipton, Jean Rosenthal, and Nananne Porcher. Many designers have spent the majority of their professional time lighting dance. Ron Bates (New York City Ballet; also production stage manager), Chenualt Spence (Alvin Ailey Dance Co.), and Nick Cernovitch are prime examples. Others, such as Thomas Skelton,

Richard Nelson, Gil Hemsley, and Beverly Emmons have established excellent reputations in dance lighting. Alwin Nicholais is a creative genius with lighting who also designs his sets, choreographs dance, and has his own internationally known dance company. Thomas Skelton serves as Associate Artistic Director of the Ohio Ballet as well as lighting designer. I was lighting designer with the Cincinnati Ballet for three seasons.

The greatest of dance lighting is pure poetry. Recently I attended an evening by the Martha Graham Dance Co. with many dances still lighted just as Jean Rosenthal had originally designed them. In my humble opinion, few designers today can equal that work. Tracing the careers of those who design dance lighting is most difficult. Beginning in September 1984, "Bessies" (like Tonys, Oscars, and Emmys) were awarded for annual achievements in dance at New York City's Joyce Theatre.

Techniques

There are a number of specific technical considerations which should be within the designer's working knowledge. These considerations are described in the paragraphs that follow.

One of the basic necessities of dance lighting is that of providing a *sheet of light* of consistent intensity across the width of the stage with crosslights. Dancers near the wings (either exiting or entering) should not pass through unbearable "hot spots" on the upper portion of the torso, while remaining completely unlighted from the waist down. Nor should the edges of the dancing area, nearest the wings, be great puddles of gloom. How can this problem be solved? It's easy — if, in each wing (on booms, ladders, or pipe ends) the designer has provided (1) a 4½-inch ellipsoidal or a 6-inch Fresnel to cover the short throw, nearest the wing; (2) a 6- by 9-inch ellipsoidal or a 6- by 12-inch ellipsoidal (for large stages) to cover the dancer center stage: and (3) a 6- by 12-inch ellipsoidal or a 6- by 16-inch ellipsoidal (for large stages) for the far side of the stage. *Voila!* The problem is solved. Because each unit decreases in beam spread width (concentrating a given amount of illumination in a smaller bundle), and because each unit selected progressively illu-

minates a longer throw distance, this setup produces even crosslighting across the entire stage.

Backlights, if available, need to be powerful. Approximately five times as much wattage is needed for backlighting as for flat-frontal illumination. Much of the light strikes the hair, shoulders, etc., and is reflected up into the flies or to the ceiling of the auditorium. Only that amount which is sufficiently diffused reaches the eyes of the audience. It just takes a lot of backlight to achieve sculpting and to separate the dancer from the background. Further, most designers soon discover that properly used backlight is the finest tool for controlling the mood values of the dancing/performing space. Much of this light bounces up from the floor and serves — much better than traditional footlights — to tone the entire area in whatever color or mood is desired. Yet it does not affect frontal face/body tonality because it comes from upstage of the performer.

"*Shin kickers*" (i.e., luminaires placed in the wings near the floor to crosslight the dancers from a low angle) are wonderful — if they are not overused. They pick up feet and ankles and legs, adding desired highlights. They add plasticity to the entire human figure. Used too often, they may become a bore. Here are some tips from Peggy Clark's "Dance Tour Lighting for Small Companies," which may help the designer to prevent injuries that occur when dancers run into "skin kickers":

1. Mount a special circuit of "guidelights" in little basket guards on the bottoms of booms, dimmed very low for dark ballets, brighter for more strongly lighted dances.

2. Mount a head-high small red light on each boom.

3. Run a strip of fluorescent tape or paint down each boom.

4. During spacing rehearsals on stage, encourage dancers to learn where the booms are located.[112]

Spacing rehearsals are an integral part of dance production. As a company on tour moves from performance place to performance place, the size of the stage will vary. In general, the designer should attempt to adjust the proscenium opening and mask it to the usual space required by the company. If the company normally plays a 40-foot opening, and then moves into a theatre with a 100-foot proscenium,

[112] *Peggy Clark, "Dance Tour Lighting for Small Companies,"* Theatre Design and Technology, *vol. 15, no. 2 (Summer 1979), pp. 17–32. See p. 19. Lengthy USITT report with a wealth of technical suggestions from top dance lighting experts (usually no two agree). Scattered throughout are worthwhile suggestions concerning designing light for dance; numerous charts, drawings, and light plots; and further comments by Jennifer Tipton, Nananne Porcher, James C. Wright, and Beverly Emmons. A dance company "Technical Information Questionnaire" by Bev Emmons is included and is of real value.*

[112A] Lee Watson and Kirk Bookman, *"The Genesis of a Ballet,"* Lighting Dimensions, *vol. 2, no. 5 (May/June 1978), pp. 25–31. Extensively illustrated (including color) narration of the lighting of a new modern ballet for the Cincinnati Ballet. Includes photos of many light cues (full-stage), a light plot, focus charts, switchboard cue sheets and hookup, and a detailed description of step-by-step evolution of the lighting. Continued description (see below) in the next issue.*

Lee Watson and Kirk Bookman, "The Genesis of a Ballet, Part II," Lighting Dimensions, *vol. 2, no. 6 (July/Aug. 1978), pp. 40–41. Contains the balance of the color photos left out of the original article and brief additional text.*

it should be masked in to 40 feet, if possible. When adjustments *must* be made (more the rule than the exception), the choreographer and dancers will need to have a spacing rehearsal ahead of their public performance to adjust entrances, exits, and — frequently — the entire dance pattern to the new dimensions. For designers, this rehearsal provides a wonderful time period during which to check the light levels against the dancers and determine their own success in adapting the light to the playing space in use.

Lighting designers who are involved in *planning company expenditures* should consider the following:

1. Most important is a good floor, both for the designer and for the dancers.

2. Next in importance is the scenic surround area. Use a transluscent backdrop, if at all possible; or, a good cyc and scrim; black velours if you are traveling deluxe (much better than the usual "house" golds, tans, greys, or pinks).

3. If the company has a performance place it uses on a regular basis, thought must be given to equipping it *and* having units to tour with, which may not always require the same equipment. Both setup time and audience expectations are greater in a company's home facility.

4. Fittings and accessories are next in importance. The designer should get booms, bases, cables, color frames, sidearms, and ladders to make maximum use of the older lights the company already owns.

5. Equipment maintenance and upkeep are crucial. Rather than buying all new units, the designer should fix (or send out to a good stage parts and expert repairmen) what the company already owns and should *take good care of it.*

6. The designer must calculate carefully (and be absolutely correct most of the time) such things as setup time (both on road tour and at home), focus, setting light levels and cues, full rehearsal, and strike. Accuracy here (both about time and money expended) will do much to cause the business manager, the choreographer, and the dancers to have confidence in the designer.

Special effects are useful in dance lighting. The lighting designer shouldn't forget about blacklight (ultraviolet), fog (tricky to use with dancers), gobos, and projections. All are potentially troublesome but often worth the time and effort.

Switchboard operation is critical. The designer should try to find enough dimmers to put stage right luminaires and their same-color counterparts on stage left on *separate dimmers.* This setup vastly increases the design/sculpting possibilities. Also, dance is about counts and music. *Timing* of cues (when they begin, how long they take, and when they end) is often a matter of operator response to the music, particularly if the company uses live music. The selection of the switchboard operator is the one area in which designers should exercise whatever authority they might conceivably have. Without a good switchboard operator, concepts and beautiful pictures can go down the drain! Fluidity, flow, and preciseness in cue execution are what dance — and dance lighting — is all about.

Communication Form

Again, the traditional theatre light plot and switchboard hookup are the standard work orders. Figure 5.15 presents Thomas Skelton's light plot and Figure 5.16 the hookup and "magic sheets" (condensed list of dimmers and luminaires controlled by them for the lighting designer's use while setting cues and levels) for the Ohio Ballet. Figures 5.17 and 5.18 show production photos.

Figure 5.19 is Richard Nelson's light plot for the Merce Cunningham Dance Company. Figure 5.20 is the switchboard hookup and Figures 5.21 and 5.22 are production photos indicating Nelson's imaginative use of this layout.

Figure 5.23 is my light plot for *Poulenc's Organ Concerto* by Artistic Director/Choreographer David McLain for the Cincinnati Ballet. Figure 5.24 is the hookup. Figures 5.25 through 5.28 are the focus charts, which are not readily available to accompany most other plots included in this study. Color Figures 23 through 28 present one of the documentation studies available: a full-stage color photograph of selected major light changes or cues. By combining a study of the light plot and hookup and focus charts with these photographs, it is possible to reconstruct mentally the total use of all light plot equipment, cue by cue. Figure 5.29 shows the switchboard "track sheets" used for each cue, with a typical cue presented. Figures 5.30 and 5.31 are photographs taken from upstage, aimed toward the auditorium, which can help some one studying this show to visu-

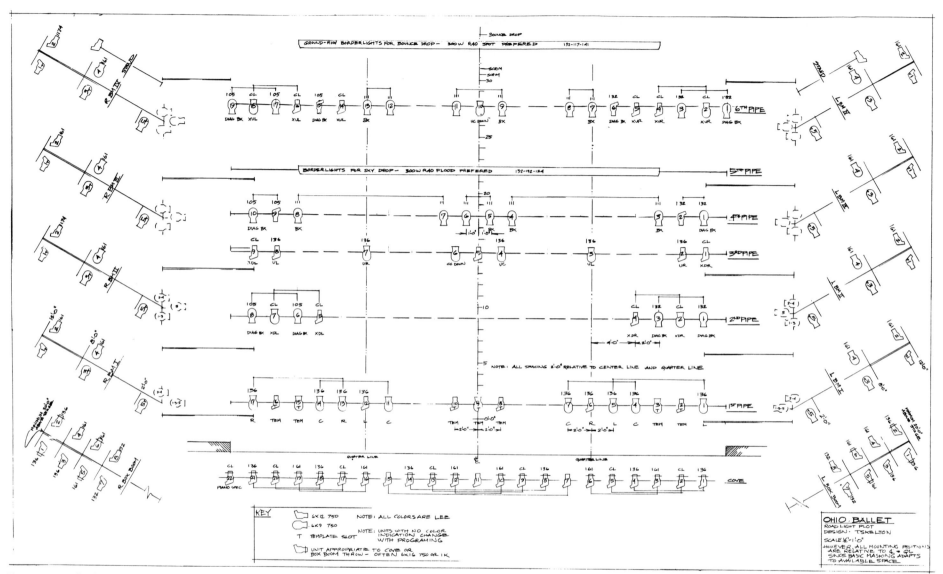

Figure 5.15 Light plot for the Ohio Ballet by Thomas R. Skelton.

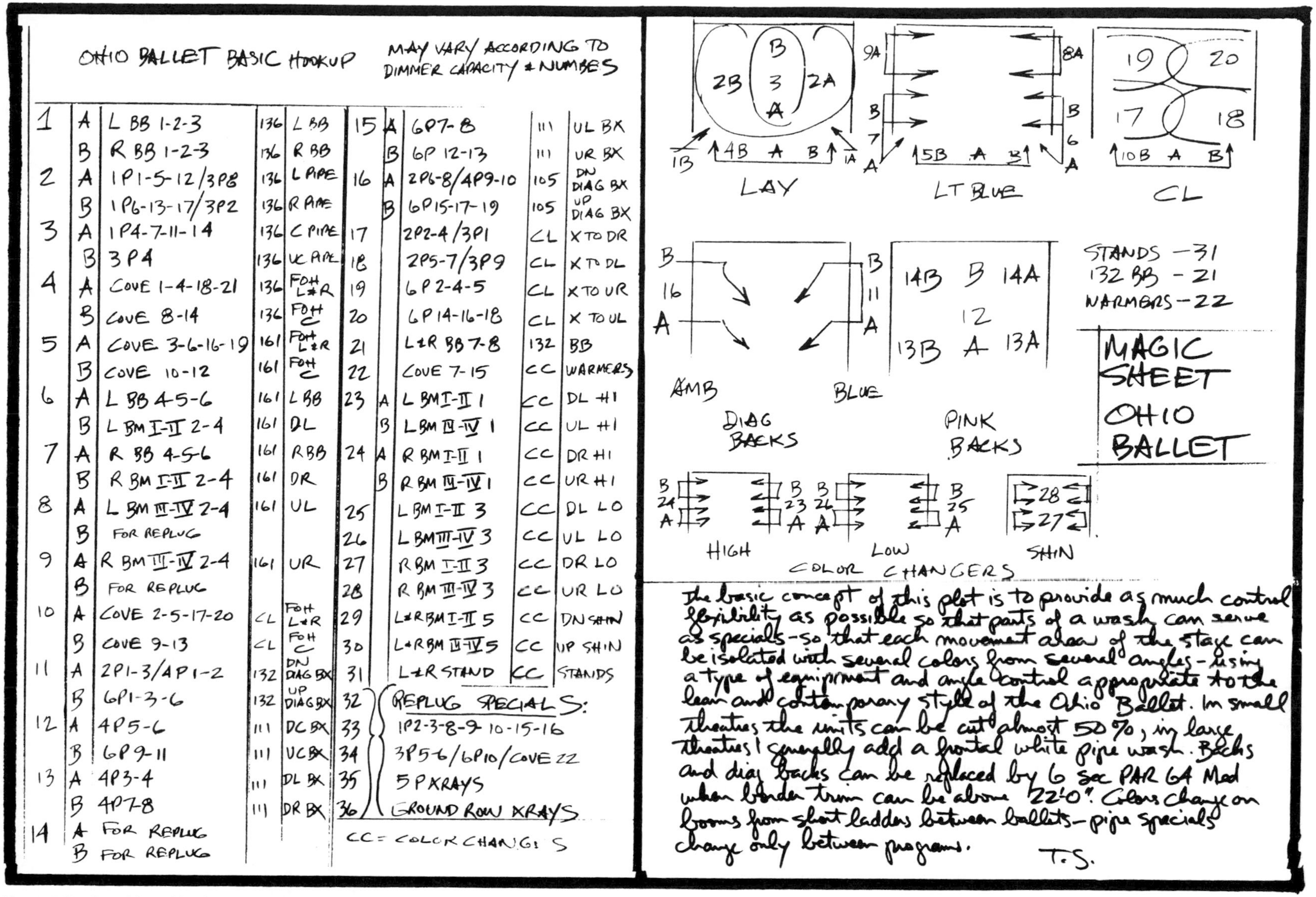

OHIO BALLET BASIC HOOKUP — MAY VARY ACCORDING TO DIMMER CAPACITY & NUMBERS

1	A	L BB 1-2-3	136	L BB	15	A	6P7-8	111	UL BX
	B	R BB 1-2-3	136	R BB		B	6P 12-13	111	UR BX
2	A	1P1-5-12/3P8	136	L PIPE	16	A	2P6-8/4P9-10	105	DN DIAG BX
	B	1P6-13-17/3P2	136	R PIPE		B	6P15-17-19	105	UP DIAG BX
3	A	1P4-7-11-14	136	C PIPE	17		2P2-4/3P1	CL	X TO DR
	B	3P4	136	UC PIPE	18		2P5-7/3P9	CL	X TO DL
4	A	COVE 1-4-18-21	136	FOH L+R	19		6P2-4-5	CL	X TO UR
	B	COVE 8-14	136	FOH C	20		6P14-16-18	CL	X TO UL
5	A	COVE 3-6-16-19	161	FOH L+R	21		L+R BB 7-8	132	BB
	B	COVE 10-12	161	FOH C	22		COVE 7-15	CC	WARMERS
6	A	L BB 4-5-6	161	L BB	23	A	L BM I-II 1	CC	DL HI
	B	L BM I-II 2-4	161	DL		B	L BM III-IV 1	CC	UL HI
7	A	R BB 4-5-6	161	RBB	24	A	R BM I-II 1	CC	DR HI
	B	R BM I-II 2-4	161	DR		B	R BM III-IV 1	CC	UR HI
8	A	L BM III-IV 2-4	161	UL	25		L BM I-II 3	CC	DL LO
	B	FOR REPLUG			26		L BM III-IV 3	CC	UL LO
9	A	R BM III-IV 2-4	161	UR	27		R BM I-II 3	CC	DR LO
	B	FOR REPLUG			28		R BM III-IV 3	CC	UR LO
10	A	COVE 2-5-17-20	CL	FOH L+R	29		L+R BM I-II 5	CC	DN SHIN
	B	COVE 9-13	CL	FOH C	30		L+R BM III-IV 5	CC	UP SHIN
11	A	2P1-3/4P1-2	132	DN DIAG BX	31		L+R STAND	CC	STANDS
	B	6P1-3-6	132	UP DIAG BX	32		REPLUG SPECIALS:		
12	A	4P5-6	111	DC BX	33		1P2-3-8-9-10-15-16		
	B	6P9-11	111	UC BX	34		3P5-6/6P10/COVE 22		
13	A	4P3-4	111	DL BX	35		5P XRAYS		
	B	4P7-8	111	DR BX	36		GROUND ROW XRAYS		
14	A	FOR REPLUG							
	B	FOR REPLUG							

CC = COLOR CHANGES

The basic concept of this plot is to provide as much control flexibility as possible so that parts of a wash can serve as specials—so that each movement area of the stage can be isolated with several colors from several angles—using a type of equipment and angle control appropriate to the lean and contemporary style of the Ohio Ballet. In small theatres the units can be cut almost 50%, in large theatres I generally add a frontal white pipe wash. Backs and diag backs can be replaced by 6 sec PAR 64 Med when border trim can be above 22'0". Colors change on booms from short ladders between ballets—pipe specials change only between programs. T.S.

Figure 5.16 Switchboard hookup and magic sheets for the Ohio Ballet.

alize the placement of all lighting equipment and the performing space. Additionally, a reprint here of some of the two-part article "Genesis of a Ballet," by myself and Kirk Bookman (*Lighting Dimensions,* May/June and July/August 1978) (see footnote 112A), can provide insight into the day-to-day problems encountered by a professional lighting designer on a new ballet:

A day-by-day running description of the *process* of designing lighting for the Cincinnati Ballet's new production of *Poulenc's Organ Concerto* is undoubtedly the best way to explain the accompanying light plot, focus chart, sample cue sheet, and the cue descriptions. In addition, we offer herewith a truthful (if sometimes embarrassing) account of the things that went well (and badly) along the way.

Thursday, July 23: Lighting Designer Lee Watson, potential Scenic Designer Van Phillips and Lighting Graduate Assistant Kirk Bookman drove from Purdue University (West Lafayette, Indiana) to Cincinnati for a first meeting with Artistic Director David McLain and Associate Artistic Director David Blackburn. McLain, also a major choreographer, had indicated that a new set and costumes for his *Organ Concerto* were a major objective of the upcoming season. Phillips had been suggested as designer by Watson. McLain's opening statement to Phillips was that Van's portfolio in no way indicated a competence in the type of decor McLain was seeking. David reached up on the library shelf and leafed through to photos of artist Barbara Hepworth as the style he had in mind. All present had already listened to the Poulenc music, looked at sketches and photos of the previous production's decor, and viewed a rehearsal-quality videotape. It immediately became clear that McLain was seeking a setting which incorporated "movement," the "visual change of a wire sculpture as you walk around it," "geometric without becoming cubistic or solid." It should also be "transparent or translucent" and "linear." This brief, intense meeting ended with an agreement for Phillips to submit rough study sketches in the genre required. It was further agreed that the set was to serve as a mobile structure with very heavy reliance on lighting design and changes to reinforce the mood variations of both the choreography and music.

October–November: Van Phillips and McLain held further brief meetings. Phillips used Naum Gabo's "Linear Construction 1949" as an additional source. The contracts (United Scenic Artists #350, Chicago) were filed for the designers and both a finished sketch of the final set and a working model (½") were provided, discussed and approved. Working drawings were completed and a contract for construction by the shop at the Cincinnati Music Hall under the direction of technical director Roy Hopper and master carpenter Leroy Adams (both members of IATSE Local #5, Cincinnati) was agreed upon. General man-

ager Patricia Losey (of the Cincinnati Ballet) bird-dogged the endless details of obtaining pipe, fittings, and strings for a set that was far from conventional for classical ballet.

December 1–3: Lee Watson was at the Music Hall with McLain for the first season program in Cincinnati and modified lighting design concepts as a direct result of working with the company. The decision to move the entire (linoleum) dance floor area downstage 7 feet (past the curtain line and out onto the apron) was made by McLain and Watson. While this would entail McLain and Blackburn re-staging all three ballets for February 16–18 (with the "In-One" downstage entrance of dancers no longer possible), it would guarantee more separation between the extreme upstage dancing position and the cyclorama. It would also allow flying space for Phillips' setting upstage of the dancing area and eliminate the problem which had developed from strong reflected light bouncing off the new (highly reflective pale gray) stage flooring onto the cyc surface. The new floor certainly enhanced the audiences' ability to see dancers' feet, but markedly increased lighting-bounce problems.

January 27, 1978: Watson completed and mailed to the Music Hall the light plot for the three ballets to be presented in February: *Swan Lake,* Act II; *Le Combat;* and *Organ Concerto.* Watson's basic approach consisted of three pipes of intense backlight in bright pink, moonlight blue green, and violet (the upstage pipe to also light through the string structure set for *Organ*); major concentration of instruments on the permanently in-place ladders on each side of the stage for strong cross-lighting of the dance area in flesh pink, lavender, no color (white), and light blue — these colors also to duplicate in the balcony ends and house coves (sidelighting) position to cross-light the apron forestage dance area; flat front lights from the house balcony rail and under-balcony positions in several color washes: pale violet, moonlight blue green, medium blue, slate blue, dark blue and steel blue. Added to this was a cyc light setup with two house borderlights in red, blue and amber glass roundels, plus 1 circuit of daylight blue; in addition, 10 cyc scoops in medium green with the addition of low-wattage striplights on the stage floor in red, blue and amber glass roundels.

The remainder of the plot calls for 10 dimmers and associated lighting instruments used only for the *Organ Concerto:* a house borderlight in red, amber and blue (glass roundels) and no color (white) to top-light all three string structures of the set (rear strings, wings, and fans); one pipe (4th Electric Pipe on Dimmer #81) of 10 Lekos (6" × 13" with 750w. lamps) in brite pink to downlight in fan and wings; two booms of 11 Lekos (6" × 9" with 750-W lamps) on each boom (stage left and right) to cross-light the entire string structure in no color (white), yellow, pale blue and brite pink. The only additional dimmer on units consisted of two 8" Lekos (200w. each) on Electric Pipe #13 (dimmer #63) in no color to create a stage center pool of backlight for Cue #9. Looking back (with the magnificent hindsight which always

Figure 5.17 Ohio Ballet production of *Galante Taenze* with choreography by Heinz Poll. Set design: Edward Burbridge; lighting design: Thomas R. Skelton; costumes: A. Christina Giannini. (*Photo: Lillian Knight.*)

Figure 5.18 Ohio Ballet's *Adagio for Two Dancers* with choreography by Heinz Poll. Costumes and lighting design: Thomas R. Skelton. (*Photo: Thomas A. Myers.*)

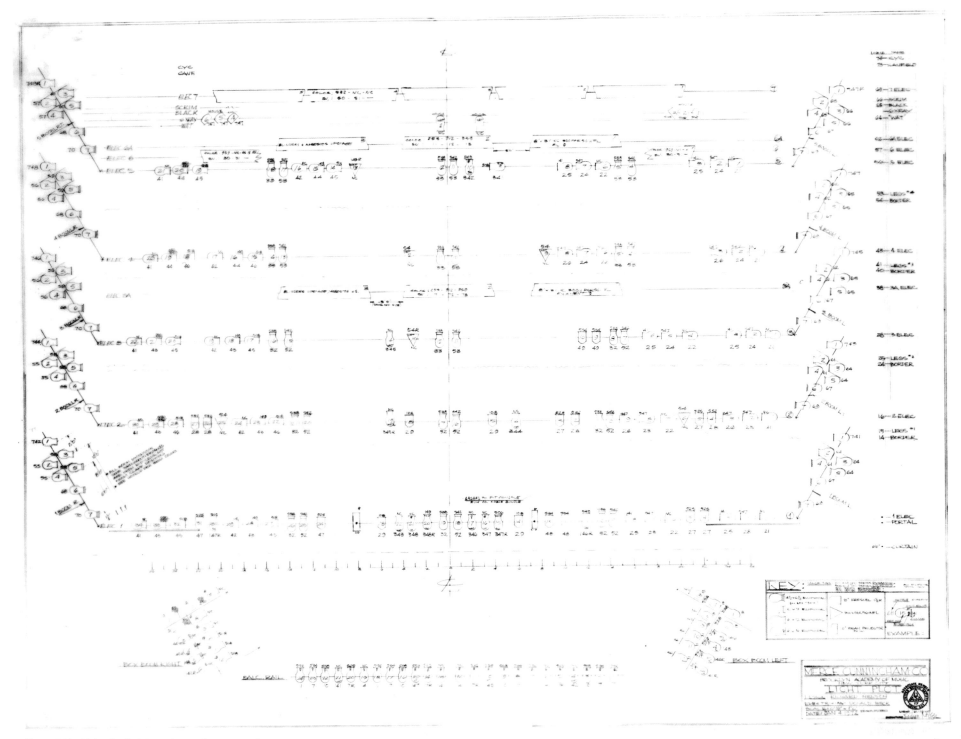

Figure 5.19 Light plot for Merce Cunningham Dance Co. in 1972 at the Brooklyn Academy of Music. Lighting by Richard Nelson.

A FEW NOTES ABOUT THE CUNNINGHAM/ACADEMY OF MUSIC PLOT

THE BOARDS AT THE ACADEMY HAD TO SIT ON THE SL FLY FLOOR IN A SINGLE ROW, NECESSITATING FOUR OPERATORS; THE HOUSE BOARD ON DECK DSL. THEIR CONFIGURATIONS ARE CORRECT. And unusual.

LASERS ON FIRST PIPE, FOR "SIGNALS", WERE FED TO POWER AND MODULATION EQUIPMENT IN ORCH PIT- OPERATED BY DESIGNER.

PLOT USED IN-HOUSE INVENTORY ONLY.

SEVERAL COLORS USED IN THIS INITIAL REPERTORY PLOT ARE NO LONGER MANUFACTURED. THE 100 and 200 SERIES ON THE PLOT AND IN THE HOOKUP WERE DYNAMOID, MFD. BY CENTURY; THE 900 SERIES WAS ROSCOLAR. BELOW IS A CONVERSION CHART COMPARING THESE COLORS TO THE NEAREST MATCHES I'VE COME UP WITH:

PLOT COLOR		EQUIVALENT
Dynamoid	253	Lee 104
"	141	Lee 132
"	247	532 cinemoid
"	108	578 plus 503
"	149	804 plus 805
Roscolar	912	803 plus 811
"	959	Lee 165 (not it but closest)
Cinemoid	747	??????

THE "PECULIAR" NUMBERING OF THE BOARDS WAS A DEVICE TO MAKE THE MEMORIZATION OF THE ENTIRE HOOKUP, AND THE UTILIZATION OF SAME, FAST . if you generate your own 'magic sheet' from the plot and hookup, you'll see how it worked. The operators went along in this case, but I don't advise you do it to anyone used to running road boards.

SWBD HOOKUP BOARD I 14 PL x 3600W
8 PL x 1200W
CUNNINGHAM ACAD. OF MUSIC

SW	UNITS	COLOR	FOR	NOTE
1.	Rail 1-7-18-24	532	wash	all front washes straight-in, leg to leg, cut ds edge to us off drops.
2.	Box L 10-11-12	541	x-wash	
3.	Box R 10-11-12	518	x-wash	
4.	Rail 6-12-13-19	CL	wash	
5.	Box L 8-9-13	CL	x-wash	x-washes are 3 units each. focus long-ctr-short w/ "long" foc to head ht at opp ¼line, then connect others.
6.	Box R 8-9-13	CL	x-wash	
7.	Rail 2-8-17223	534	wash	
7R.	Rail 5-11-14-20	525	wash	
8.	Box L 1-2-7	538	x-wash	DO NOT SUBSTITUTE COLORS FOR 508 pt or 525 if unavailable. See dsr.
9.	Box R 1-2-7	2x550	x-wash	
10.	Rail 3-9-16-22	508	wash	
11.	Elec 6A 1-2-3 circ I	253	us bax	
12.	Elec 6A 1-2-3 circ II	912	us bax	
13.	Elec 6A 1-2-3 circ III	959	us bax	
14.	AUX MASTER 141 to 148 ....4 maximum aux dimmers at once			
141.	Rail 21	CL	"WALKAROUND TIME" set	
141R.	Box L 6	CL	"HOW TO PASS, KICK..."reader 1.	
142.	Rail 4	CL	"WAT" set	
142R.	Box R 6	CL	"how to" reader #1.	
143.	Box L 4	553	"SECOND HAND" spec	
143R.	5E 13	CL	"WAT" us transparent cube back.	
144.	Box R 3	CL	"HOW TO" reader 2.	
144R.	Box L 5	553	"SECOND HAND" dc	
145.	Rail 10	553	"HOW TO" reader 1.	
145R.	Box R 4	CL	"SEC. HAND" dc	
146.	Box L3	CL	"HOW TO" reader 2.	
146R.	1E 11	549	"SEC. HAND" cc spec	
147.	Rail 15	553	"HOW TO" reader 2.	
147R.	1E 30	510	"SEC HAND" cc spec.	
148.	Box R5.	CL	"SEC HAND" dc backup spec	

SWBD. HOOKUP BOARD II 14 PL x 6000W
8 Pl x 1200W
CUNNINGHAM ACAD OF MUSIC

NUMBERING STARTS WITH 21! NO DIMMERS 15 to 20!

SW	UNITS		COLOR	FOR	NOTES
21.	1E1-2E1-3E1-4E1-5E1		CL	x to sr	hot ctr. top&bot to ¼line
22.	1E6-2E7-3E4-4E6-5E6		CL	x to sr	hot r¼ top to legs bot to ctr
23.	1E2-7 2E2-8		547	x to sr (DS)	overlay corresponding units in 21-22
24.	3E2-5 4E2-7 5E2-7		547	x to sr (US)	
25.	1E3-8 3E3-6 5E3-8		141	x to sr	cover full depth!
26.	2E3-9 4E3-8	***	247	x to sr	ds to #4legs
27.	1E4-5 2E5-13		525	wash ctr to sl	
28.	2E 4- 12- 26- 27		532	us wash	
29.	1E 14- 23 2E15-18		108	us wash	
30.	6E 1-2-3-4-5 circ I		959	cyc or wall	
31.	6E 1-2-3-4-5 circ II		CL	cyc, wall or drops	
32.	{1E 10- 19- 26 2E11-17-21 / 3E 8-16}		538	ds & ctr sides downlts	
33.	3E 12 4E5- 11- 14 5E5-12-18		538	su & ctr-ctr downlites	
34.	AUX MASTER 341 to 348				
341.	5E9		508	"SIGNALS" us chairs	
342.	5E 10		549	"SIGNALS" cc backlt	
343.	1E 22		CL	"WAT" set	
344.	2E 14		CL	"WAT" set	
345.	3E 14		CL	"WAT" set	
345R.	2E 19		CL	"WAT" set	
346.	1E 17		CL	"WAT" set	
347.	1E 16	*	CL	"CANFIELD" DROP/see below	
347R.	1E 15	**	506	"SIGNALS" arrow gobo-cyc	
348.	1E 21	*	CL	"CANFIELD" DROP/see below	

* THESE TWO UNITS ARE CENTURY DIECAST 6 x 12 LEKOS WITH DOUBLE-FLATTED REFLECTORS$ AND FRONT LENS REMOVED . Focus image of reflector and lamps onto ctr of cyc.. no cuts.. sharpen until you can read the manufacturer's name printed on lamps.

** The arrow template extends from 6 ft sr of ctr to the left ¼ line, arrowhead pointing sl. shaft about 9 ft above deck.

*** The units in dimmers 21-22, 23-24, and 25-26 all do essentially the same thing, but their ganging at board is different, as are colors

SWBD. HOOKUP BOARD III 14PL x 6k
BOARD IV 6PL x 3600W
BAM! CUNNINGHAM!

NUMBERING STARTS WITH 41! NO DIMMERS 35 to 40!

SW	UNITS	COLOR	FOR	NOTE
41.	1E34-2E30-3E22-4E20-5E21	CL	x to sl	see notes for dim 21 to 26 * reverse dir'n.
42.	1E29-2E24-3E19-4E17-5E16	Cl	x to sl	
43.	1E28-33 2E23-29 3E18-21	long 149 short dbl 550	x to sl (DS)	
44.	4E16-19 5E15-20	ditto	x to sl	
45.	1E27-32 #3E17-20 5E14-19	518	x to sl	
46.	2E22-28 4E15-18	518	x to sl	
47.	1E24-31	525	wash ctr to sr	works w/27
48.	1E 12-13	534	cs wash thru ctr	
49.	3E9-10	534	us wash ctr to sl	
50.	7E 1-2-3-4-5 circ I	532	cyc	
51.	7E 1-2-3-4-5 circ II	CL	wall	
52.	{1E9-18-25 2E10-16-20 / 3E 7-15}	542	downlites	
53.	3E11 4E 4-10-13 5E4-1--17	542	downlites	
54.	2E6-25 4E9-12	CL	"WAT" set bax	
54R.	3E13	CL	"WAT" set backlt	

BD IV

SW	UNITS	NOTES
55.	I & II BM R 2-4	
56.	III & IV BM R 2-4	
57.	V BM R 2-4	DIMS 55 to 60 color-chg units
58.	I & II BM R 3-5	
59.	III & IV BM R 3-5	
60.	V BM R 3-5	

SWBD HOOKUP BOARD V 14 PL x 3600W
8 PL x 1200

SW	UNITS	COLOR	FOR	NOTES
61..	I & II BM SL 2-4			
62.	III & IV BM SL 204			
63.	V BM SL 2-4			
64.	I & II BM L 305			
65.	III & IV BM L 3-5			
66.	V BM L 3-5			DIMS 61 to 70 color change units
67.	I to V BMS 1 6		head-hi x	
68.	I to V BMS R 6		head-hi x	
69.	I to V BMS L 7		kickers	nothing but 4½ units available in theatre inventory.
70.	I to V BMS R 7		kickers	
71.	3A ELEC 1-2-3 circ I	253	ds bax	
72.	3A ELEC 1-2-3 circ II	912	ds bax	
73.	3A ELEC 1-2-3 circ III	959	ds bax	
74.	AUX MASTER 741 to 748................only 4 aux loads at a time!			

741.	1 BM L 1	745.	III BM 1 1
742.	1 BM R 1	746.	III BM R 1
743.	II BM L 1	747.	IV BM L 1
744.	II BM R 1	748.	IV BM R 1

HOUSE SWBD

75.	"6XRAY PIPE" 4-5-6	747	diag bax thru ctr
76.	"6XRAY PIPE" 1=2=3	504	diag bax thru ctr.
77.	"WAT SET PIPE" 1-2	CL	"WAT" flying set dnlts
78.	CANFIELD LIGHT BEAM COLUMN ***NOT ON PLOT***SEE NOTE BELOW		
79.	CANFIELD SLIDE PROJECTOR, BALC RAIL **NOT ON PLOT*** No SLIDE CHANGES		
HOT.	CANFIELD LIGHT COLUMN MOTOR		

***The set for "CANFIELD" is a motorized vertical column 18 inches wide by 6 inches deep by 24 feet high, which travels at 3 feet per minute the full length of proscenium, and automatically reverses direction at the completion of each full-width run. It carries up to 8 G.E. # Q4559 low-voltage aircraft landing lamps which are focused to create an intense vertical beam of light on the CANFIELD cyc, which is coated with a highly reflective beaded paint. The face of the column acts as a 'scanning screen' for the rail SLIDE.

Figure 5.20 Switchboard hookup for Merce Cunningham Dance Co., by Richard Nelson.

Figure 5.21 *Canfield* by the Merce Cunningham Dance Co. at the Brooklyn Academy of Music in New York City. Lighting by Richard Nelson. (*Photo: James Klotsky.*)

Figure 5.22 *Canfield.* (*Photo: James Klotsky.*)

comes *after* the show is open), Watson has decided that for the *next* Cincinnati Ballet (spring) engagement at the Music Hall, he will move at least half of the lighting units off of the house ladders and onto counterweighted pipe ends for stronger cross-lighting from a shorter throw distance. At this point, all designers had completed preplanning, the *Organ* set and costumes were built, with everyone awaiting February 13th load-in to the Music Hall.

February 12: Watson (accompanied by Purdue graduate students Bookman and Robert Reid who was to serve as Watson's assistant) and Phillips departed early from Lafayette.

February 13: Promptly at 8 a.m., the 15-man crew at the Music Hall began unloading trucks and hanging the three ballets and lighting equipment. A word needs to be added here about the delightful efficiency of the IATSE crew from Local #5. Under the benevolent discipline of Roy Hopper, truly one of the top technicians in the business, they hang a show rapidly and seemingly effortlessly. However a snag *did* develop. The rear string structure pipe framing bent and buckled when assembled. The unit could not be flown in and out! Since Phillips' design was most definitely far from traditional lumber-scenery construction, the argument went on for several days as to where the blame could be assigned: (1) a lack of trial setup in the theatre for a new set, (2) substitution of parts due to budget and deadlines for final construction, (3) etc. In any case, it was clear that technician Hopper had warned at the beginning that he had grave doubts about the framing structure.

An estimated 24 labor-hours of crew time was lost at this point from the normal, budgeted hanging and focusing of lights and setup of scenery and stage flooring. Watson left the Music Hall at 6 p.m. Monday evening with the beginning of a very black mood.

The dance company and orchestra rehearsed on stage that evening with work lights. Scenery moves could not yet be rehearsed because the string structure was being rebuilt that same evening. Throughout this period every attempt was being made to conserve electricity with an impending threat of no opening Thursday evening due to a coal strike.

February 14: Crew call at 9 a.m., but the stage crew reduced from 15 to 10 stagehands. Watson's (interior) black mood increased. Having lost 24 labor-hours of normal lighting setup time, it becomes necessary to cut every corner to get back on schedule. Continued hanging of lighting units until 7 p.m., when the dancers and orchestra arrived. Continued hanging around them until 11 p.m. Not only was Watson now well behind schedule but, during the day, it was discovered that both the stage left and stage right light ladders were not in the correct positions indicated on the light plot. Consequently, spotlights for cross-lighting would be pointed toward black legs rather than clearly shooting through the open space between legs "In One, Two, Three and Four." A quick conference with Music Hall Electrician Glenn Parrish resulted in re-hanging and correcting the ladders on stage right. Those on stage left were already up and cabled. The decision was made to "go with it" and correct by breasting the (up-and-down stage) vertical pipe from which the ladders hung down toward the proscenium, partly correcting the problem. Little or no time was wasted by any of the parties involved in trying to assign the blame. It really didn't matter with the shortness of time. Parrish and his crew remain one of the best in Watson's mind, so he assumed responsibility for not watching the setup carefully enough.

By this time, the linoleum floor was in place and taped down;

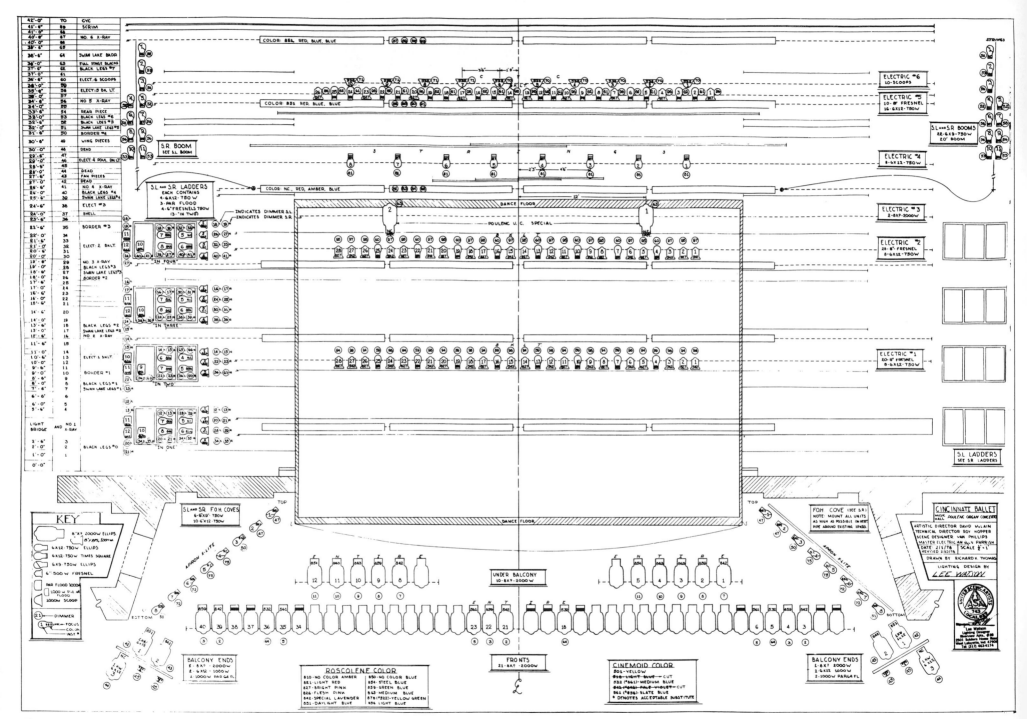

Figure 5.23 Lee Watson's light plot for the Cincinnati Ballet's 1978 production of the *Poulenc Organ Concerto* in the Music Hall.

KEY	KEY IDENT. NO.	INSTRUMENTS	COLOR	FOCUS
	FL-1,2,12	3-3" Lekos	R42	FRONTS: Pale Violet
		3-3" Lekos	R57	FRONTS: Moonlt.,Pl.Green
		3-3" Lekos	R61	FRONTS: Slate Blue
	Under Bal.1,5	3-8" Lekos	R42	FRONTS: Pale Violet
		2-8" Lekos	R59	FRONTS: Moonlt.,Bl.Gn.
		2-8" Lekos	R65	FRONTS: Dk. Blue
	4,9	2-8" Lekos	R65	FRONTS: Dk. Blue
	5,10	2-8" Lekos	R54	FRONTS: Steel Blue
	1st Ladder,L-1,7,11	1-6" Fres.,1-6x12" Leko,1-PAR-	R26	"In One," L--Pink
	1st Ladder,R-1,7,11	same Flood	R26	"In One," R--Pink
	2nd Ladder,L-1,6,10	same	R26	"In Two," L--Pink
	2nd Lad.,R-1,6,10	same	R26	"In Two," R--Pink
	3rd Lad.,L-1,7,11	same	R26	"In Three," L--Pink
	3rd Lad.,R-1,7,11	same	R26	"In Three," R--Pink
	4th Lad.,L-1,7,11	same	R26	"In Four," L--Pink
	4th Lad.,R-1,7,11	same	R26	"In Four," R--Pink
	1st Lad.,L-2,8,12	same	R42	"In One," L--Lav.
	1st Lad.,R-2,8,12	same	R42	"In One," R--Lav.
	2nd Lad.,L-2,8,12	same	R42	"In Two," L--Lav.
	2nd Lad.,R-2,8,12	same	R42	"In Two," R--Lav.
	3rd Lad.,L-2,8,12	same	R42	"In Three," L--Lav.
	3rd Lad.,R-2,8,12	same	R42	"In Three," R--Lav.
	4th Lad.,L-2,8,12	same	R42	"In Four," L--Lav.
	4th Lad.,R-2,8,12	same	R42	"In Four," R--Lav.
	1st Lad.,L-3,5,	1-6" Fres., 1-6x12" Leko	NC	"In One," L--NC
	1st Lad.,R-3,5,	same	NC	"In One," R--NC
	3rd Lad.,L-3,5	same	NC	"In Three," L--NC
	3rd Lad.,R-3,5	same	NC	"In Three," R--NC
	4th Lad.,L-3,5	same	NC	"In Four," L--NC
	4th Lad.,R-3,5	same	NC	"In Four," R--NC
	1st Lad.,L-4,6,10	1-6" Fres.,1-6x12"Leko,1-PAR-	R56	"In One," L--Blue
	1st Lad.,R-4,6,10	same	R56	"In One," R--Blue
	2nd Lad.,L-3,5,9	same	R56	"In Two," L--Blue
	3rd Lad.,L-4,6,10	same	R56	"In Three," L--Blue
	3rd Lad.,R-4,6,10	same	R56	"In Three," R--Blue
	4th Lad.,L-4,6,10	same	R56	"In Four," L--Blue
	4th Lad.,R-4,6,10	same	R56	"In Four," R--Blue
	Bal.Ends,L&R-1	2-6" Lekos, 1000w.	R51	FRONTS: Apron Xlts.,Lt.Fl.
	Bal.Ends,L&R-2	2-6" Lekos, 2000w.	R42	FRONTS: Apron Xlts.,Lav.
	Bal.Ends,L&R-3	2-6" Lekos, 1000w.	NC	FRONTS: Apron Xlts.,NC
	Bal.Ends,L&R-4,5	PAR Fl., 1000w. (4)	R56, R59	FRONTS: Apron Xlts., Blue, Moonlt.,Bl.Gn.
	Apr.Xlts.,L&R-1,2	2-6x9" Lekos, 2-6x12" Lekos	R51	FRONTS: Apr.Xlts.,Lt.Fl.
	Apr.Xlts.,L&R-3	2-6x12" Lekos	R42	FRONTS: Apr.Xlts.,Lav.
	Apr.Xlts.,L&R-4	2-6x12" Lekos	R59	FRONTS: Apr.Xlts.,Moonlt.
	Booms,L&R-1,2,3	6-6x9" Lekos		String Booms-NC
	Booms,L&R-1,2,3	6-6x9" Lekos		String Booms-Yellow
	Booms,L&R-1,2,3	6-6x9" Lekos	R45	String Booms-Turq. Blue
	Booms,L&R-1,2	4-6x9" Lekos		String Booms,Pink

63	3rd Elec.-1,2	2-8" Lekos		Poulenc
64	F5,1&,36	3-8" Leko	R52	
65	2nd Lad.,L-4	1-6x12" Leko		"In Two," L
66	2nd Lad.,R-4	1-6x12" Leko		"In Two," R
69	2nd Lad.,R-3,5,9	1-6" Fres.,1-6x12"Leko,1-PAR Fl	R56	"In Two," R--Blue
70	6th Elec.-1 thru 6	6-Cyc Scoops		Cyc--Green
71	6th Elec.-7 thru 10	4-Cyc Scoops		Cyc--Green
72	Apr.Xlts.,L&R-6,7	2-6x9" Lekos,2-6x12" Lekos		FRONTS: Apr.Xlts.--Bl.
75	Apr.Xlts.,L&R-4,5	same	NC	FRONTS: Apr.Xlts.--NC
78	Cyc Floor Xrays	4 sects. striplights	Red	(Roundels,Glass)
79	Cyc Floor Xrays	same	Blue	same
80	Cyc Floor Xrays	same	Amber	same
81	4th Elect.-1 thru 8	3-6x12" Lekos (Glass Sq.)		String Borders,Pink
82	4th Borderlt.			Trans--NC (Roundels)
83	4th Borderlt.		Red	Trans--Red (Roundels)
84	4th Borderlt.		Blue	Trans--Blue (Roundels)
85	4th Borderlt.		Amber	Trans--Amber (Roundels)
86	5th Borderlt.			Cyc Borders (Roundels)
87	6th Borderlt.		Red	Cyc Borders (Roundels)
88	5th Borderlt.		Blue	Cyc Borders (Roundels)
89	6th Borderlt.		Amber	Cyc Borders (Roundels)
90	5th Borderlt.		Blue	Cyc Borders (Roundels)
91	6th Borderlt.		Blue	Cyc Borders (Roundels)
92	5th Borderlt.			Cyc Borders (Roundels)
93	6th Borderlt.			Cyc Borders (Roundels)
94	1st Elec.-2,5,8,11, 14,17,20,23,26,28	10-8" Fresnels		Warm Wash
95	2nt Elec.-2,5,8,11, 14,17,20,23	10-8" Fresnels		Warm Wash
96	5th Elec.-1,4,7,10,13, 16,19,22,25	10-8" Fresnels		Warm Wash
97	3rd Elec.-1,4,7,10,13, 16,19,22,25	10-8" Fresnels		Warm Wash
98	1st Elec.-1,4,7,10, 13,16,19,22,25	10-8" Fresnels		Cool Wash

Revised: 2/16/72

*Reproduction of actual Focus Charts,
Switchboard Track Sheets and
Switchboard layout for POULENC'S
ORGAN CONCERTO.*

Figure 5.24 Switchboard hookup for the *Poulenc Organ Concerto*.

Focus Chart — Production POULENC ORGAN CONCERTO — CINCINNATI BALLET - MUSIC HALL — Unit Location — Page

Unit #	Unit Type	Dimmer	Focus Location / Hot Spot (ERS) / Flood/Spot (Fres)	Top	Bottom	Left	Right	Notes/Accessories
			BACK LIGHTS PIPE #32					
	8 F	75,77	FULL FLOOD / U DSTAGE WASH					
	6X12	60	HOT SPOT / U DSTAGE WASH	OPEN	OPEN	OPEN	OPEN	
			PIPE #38 (POULENC CONCERTO)					
2	8X?	63	HOT SPOT / UP CENTER	OPEN	OPEN	OPEN	OPEN	
			DOWN LIGHT PIPE 46					
8	6X12	81	HOT SPOT - DOWN LIGHT CYC STRUCTURE	OPEN	OPEN	OPEN	OPEN	
			BACK LIGHT PIPE 58					
	8 F	96	FULL FLOOD / UP STAGE WASH					
	6X12	61	HOT SPOT / UP STAGE WASH	OPEN	OPEN	OPEN	OPEN	
	6X12	62	HOT SPOT / UP STAGE WASH					
			STRING STUCTURE BOOMS- SL & SR					
	6X?		HOT SPOT / CYC STRUCTURE	OPEN	OPEN	OFF OF CYC	OFF OF DANCE FLOOR	

Figure 5.25 Switchboard hookup.

Focus Chart Production POULENC ORGAN CONCERTO

Unit Location _____ CINCINNATI BALLET - MUSIC HALL

Unit #	Unit Type	Dimmer	Focus Location Hot Spot (ERS) Flood/Spot (Fres)	Shutter Cut offs Top	Bottom	Left	Right	Notes Accessories
			SL IN I III IV LADDERS					
1, 3	6" F	12, 20, 28, 34	½ SPOT "IN" LEFT OFF OF LEGS					
2	6×12	"	HOT SPOT "IN" CENTER	OPEN	OPEN	OFF OF LEGS	OFF OF LEGS	
	PAR FLOOD	12, 20, 28	CENTER OF SHAFT "IN" RIGHT					
			SL IN II LADDER					
2	6 F	6, 22, 36	½ SPOT IN TWO LEFT OFF OF LEGS					
5, 7	6×12	14, 22, 28, 36	HOT SPOT "IN II" CENTER	OPEN	OPEN	OFF OF LEGS	OFF OF LEGS	
6	PAR FLOOD	14, 22, 28, 36	CENTER OF SHAFT IN TWO" RIGHT					
			BACK LIGHTS PIPE #13					
4, 5, 6, 8, 9, 7, 2	8 F	94, 98	FULL FLOOD DOWN STAGE WASH					
13, 16, 19, 21	6×12	59	HOT SPOT DOWN STAGE WASH					

Figure 5.26 Switchboard hookup.

Focus Chart Production POULENC ORGAN CONCERTO

Unit Location _____ CINCINNATI BALLET — MUSIC HALL

Unit #	Unit Type	Dimmer	Focus Location Hot Spot (ERS) Flood/Spot (Fres)	Shutter Cut offs Top	Bottom	Left	Right	Notes Accessories
			SL FOH COVE					
1, 4, 6	6×9	47, 75, 72	HOT SPOT DOWN - LEFT	OPEN	BOTTOM EDGE OF DANCE FLOOR	OPEN	OFF OF PROS	
2, 3, 5, 7, 8	6×12	75, 50, 75, 72, 51	HOT SPOT DOWN - RIGHT	"	"	OFF OF PROS.	OPEN	
			SR IN - I, III, IV LADDERS					
1, 2, 3, 4	6" F	13, 21, 29, 35	½ SPOT "IN" RIGHT OFF OF LEGS					
5, 6, 7, 8	6×12	"	HOT SPOT "IN" CENTER	OPEN	OPEN	OFF OF LEGS	OFF OF LEGS	
10, 11, 12	PAR FLOOD	13, 21, 35	CENTER OF SHAFT "IN" LEFT					
			SR IN II LADDER					
1, 2, 3	6 F	9, 23, 69	½ SPOT "IN" RIGHT OFF OF LEGS					
4, 5, 6, 7	6×12	15, 23, 66, 69	HOT SPOT "IN" CENTER	OPEN	OPEN	OFF OF LEGS	OFF OF LEGS	
8, 9	PAR FLOOD	"	CENTER OF SHAFT "IN" LEFT					

Figure 5.27 Switchboard hookup.

Unit #	Unit Type	Dimmer	Focus Location Hot Spot (EHS) Flood/Spot (Fres)	Shutter Cut Offs				Accessories
				Top	Bottom	Left	Right	
			FRONTS					
3,4, 5,6	6x?	2, 3, 6A, 5	HOT SPOT CENTER — SL	BASE OF CYC	BOTTOM EDGE OF DANCE FLOOR	OPEN	OFF OF TEOU	
18, 21, 22, 23	8x?	6A, 21, 22, 23	HOT SPOT CENTER				OPEN	
35, 36, 39, 40	8x?	5, 64, 2, 3	HOT SPOT CENTER—SC			OFF OF PROS.	"	
			UNDER BALCONY					
1, 2, 3,4,5	8x?	7, 8, 9, 10, 11	HOT SPOT CENTER — SL	6 " OF SW CYC	BOTTOM EDGE OF DANCE FLOOR	OPEN	OFF OF PROS.	
6, 9	8x?	"	HOT SPOT CENTER—SC			OFF OF PROS.	OPEN	
			BALCONY ENDS					
1—8	8x? 12 NEW 20, 24	42—49	HOT SPOT DOWN CENTER	OPEN	BOTTOM EDGE OF DANCE FLOOR	OPEN	OPEN	
	SR		FOH COVE					
4	2x?	50, 55	HOT SPOT DOWN — RIGHT	OPEN	BOTTOM EDGE OF DANCE FLOOR	OFF OF PROS.	OPEN	
8	2x?	54, 50, 55, 53	HOT SPOT DOWN — LEFT				OPEN	

Figure 5.28 Switchboard hookup.

SWITCHBOARD TRACK SHEETS   MUSIC HALL—CINCINNATI BALLET   POULENC'S ORGAN CONCERTO 2/16/78

Figure 5.29 Cue sheets.

Figure 5.30 View from the side of the stage of dancers and light ladders used for Lee Watson's lighting of the *Poulenc Organ Concerto*. (*Photo: Robert Reid.*)

Figure 5.31 View through the string structure toward the audience during a rehearsal of the *Poulenc Organ Concerto*. (*Photo: Robert Reid.*)

all scenery, borders, legs and cyc were "in the air." All of the color media problems solved under the guidance of assistant Bob Reid. Watson had made the decision to go with the color media already on hand in the Music Hall plus that which the Cincinnati Ballet normally carries in their Road Box. This meant many substitutions. Since Watson was unwilling to substitute for the Roscolene #827 (brite pink) or #859 (moonlight blue green), these additional sheets of color were purchased locally and cut. Back to the hotel at 11 p.m., with lighting units still to be hung and cabled and not one unit yet focussed.

February 15: Crew call at the Music Hall at 11 a.m. Finally, there was time for Parrish and his crew to tackle the problem of hanging lighting units on the Balcony Ends horizontal pipes and

in the very cramped (vertical) House Coves. A quick hauling up of lighting equipment established that 5 of the 8″ Lekos (2000w.) could *not* be mounted on the [Balcony] Ends pipes. They would neither safely support the weight nor could the units be reached for accurate focus. Watson made a quick decision to keep one 2 kw. on each side in violet; to change two units to 6″ × 12″ Lekos (1000w. each) for the no color (white) and pink circuits; and, to use two PAR-64 Flood quartz units for the two blue circuits. Only 4 lines to the switchboard could be made available rather than the 5 separate circuits called for — so, the blues were combined (the other outlet was in a floor pocket now underneath the huge organ pipes). Stagehand William Shukas (normally the Road IATSE Road, L.U. #IA man with the Cincinnati

Ballet on tour) was a major value in keeping this moving forward. He also did the major portion of the focus of lighting units backstage during the day. During the early part of the day, the string set booms were put up and cabled backstage. These lamps were from the 30 units (6" × 9" Lekos, 750w.) owned for road tours of the Ballet. The Music Hall Inventory includes nothing wider in beam spread than a 6" × 12" Leko.

While this was under way (booms, Coves and Bal. Ends), Watson was focussing the backstage ladder cross-lights. All three electrical pipes of backlights over the stage were "dead focussed" [focussed or painted while not lighted at the floor level rather than at show high trim] by Watson on Tuesday, as were the two *Organ* Center Specials. When taken up to trim, 92 units were already correctly focussed from the deck without using crew time to bring out a ladder. Only the upstage pipe (Electric #5) was brought in to the stage floor once to tip all lights slightly higher.

According to the agreed schedule, McLain was to have arrived at 2 p.m. to look at light cues. This had been pushed back to 3:30 p.m. by agreement on Tuesday. As it worked out, the last of the Front-of-House Cove units were being focussed at 4:30 p.m. at the same time that Watson was on switchboard talkback out in the auditorium setting cues and levels for *Swan Lake* and *Combat* (done between 3–4:30 p.m.). Choreographer Fredrick Franklin remained amazingly understanding as he checked and modified and approved the various setups for these two ballets while individual circuits (3 or more spotlights) were flashing on and being focussed. McLain also assisted in determining final levels.

Finally, at 4:30 p.m., all was ready and work began on the 14 cues for the *Organ Concerto!* With professional understanding, McLain had already surrendered his scheduled one hour "spacing rehearsal" on stage with his dancers—a vital concession. This allowed, at very maximum, *exactly 6 minutes per cue* to call through to the switchboard the dimmer levels to be used, discuss the visual result, set counts with Stage Manager Vicky Zimmerman, and record on the Kliegl memory switchboard. The Music Hall has 100 dimmers and approximately 1000 terminations to connect lights. We were using 305 lighting units (including borderlights) in a first class theatre with a top crew. Still, 6 minutes per cue seemed a very real limitation to Watson. At this point, Watson had cut only 8 front lights (8" lekos, 2000w.) from his planned setup (the "curtain warmer" circuit of 2 units because of the energy shortage and a circuit of pink and of amber frontlights). The total connected load at this point was 366,000 watts.

With the very real assistance that a group of stagehands can and do muster when time is short, the final lighting cue for *Organ Concerto* was completed at 4 minutes before 6 p.m.—the normal dinner break time before dress rehearsal. There were, indeed, many moments when Watson, Hopper, and McLain doubted completion by the deadline. Wednesday evening's dress rehearsal with orchestra and costumes went quite smoothly. The normal amount of adjustment of cue timing and intensity modification ran smoothly concurrently with the rehearsal. All of the 12 scenery moves (by the flymen) for *Organ* were smooth enough and at the proper place to suggest a good opening night.

February 16: Opening night! All parties involved arrived at 6 p.m. for an 8 p.m. curtain. The time was well utilized to run a "light check," replace burnt out lamps, refocus 3 units on the "In One" left ladder which were still spilling on the first black masking leg, etc. The opening went well until Watson was told by David Blackburn after the final curtain to "report to David McLain's dressing room for discussion of some serious flaws in the lighting of *Swan Lake*. With some trepidation, Watson reported, only to find that surprise birthday gifts and a cake awaited him in honor of his 52nd birthday on February 18. Even lighting design has its warm, human moments.

Figure 5.32 is the light plot by Nananne Porcher for the 1978 season road tour of one of America's large ballet companies, the American Ballet Theatre (ABT). ABT does not have a permanent home. Its entire design/technical setup is planned to be completely portable. The company carries its own floor covering, plus drops and legs in black, and lighting is planned for rapid assembly and rapid strike. It is a treat to be in the theatre to watch one of ABT's setups or strikes. They are as beautifully planned and executed as many an onstage ballet seen by the paying audience. Much of this efficiency is the result of years of careful preparation by scenic designer and former co-artistic director Oliver Smith and longtime lighting designer Porcher. Figure 5.33 shows the season's hookup, and Figure 5.34 presents Porcher's focus chart.

Several production photos of lighting design by other designers (without accompanying plots or hookups) are included here. Figure 5.35 is a dramatic view of Ronald Bates's work for *Serenade* by the New York City Ballet Co. This work is a staple in the repertory. Notice the highly effective use of crosslight in a classical ballet.

Figure 5.36 is from the work of Alwin Nikolais—choreographer, set designer, costume designer, and lighting designer for his own company. Nikolais is by popular agreement a one-of-a-kind genius. He relies heavily upon endless experimentation and light patterns and projections in his choreography. His dancers are trained to move to precise locations where they often become a living projection screen (or, rather, their costumes do) for projections

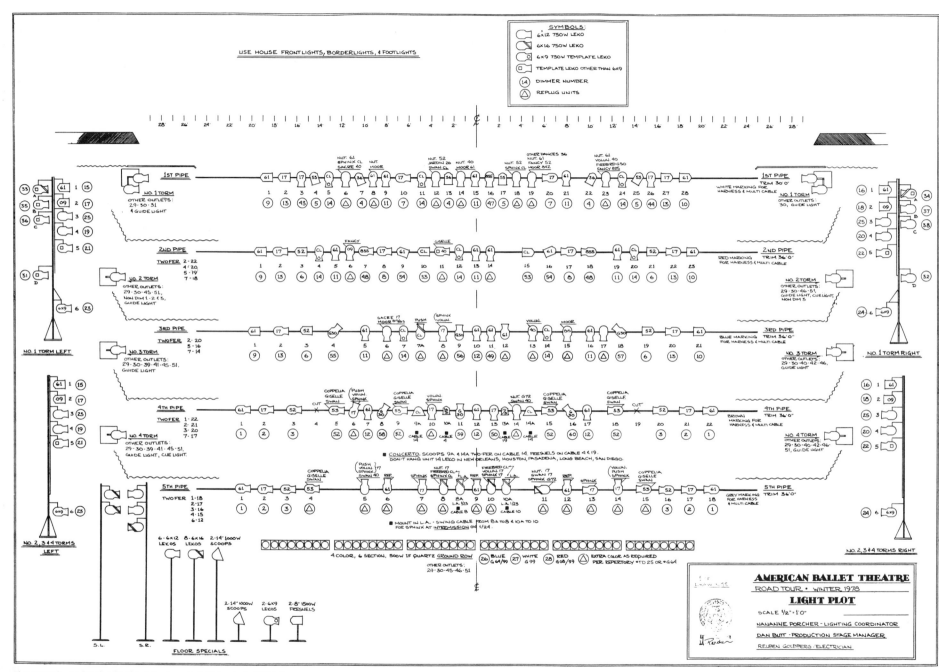

Figure 5.32 Light plot for the American Ballet Theatre's (ABT's) season road tour in 1978, by lighting designer Nananne Porcher.

Left Table — AMERICAN BALLET THEATRE SHOW BOARD HOOKUP 1978

SWITCH	WAT.	POSITION & UNIT NO.	TYPE	FOCUS	COLOR
1	6K	4TH PIPE 1-22 / 5TH PIPE 1-18	6X12 750W LEKO	U.S. L&R BLUE ENDS	61
2	6K	4TH PIPE 2-21 / 5TH PIPE 2-17	6X12 750W LEKO	UP L&R ENDS LIGHT BLUE	17
3	6K	4TH PIPE 3-20 / 5TH PIPE 3-16	6X12 750W LEKO	U.S. L&R WARM ENDS	52
4	6K	1ST PIPE 7-13-22	8" 1500W FRESNEL	LAVENDER MID. WASH	36
5	6K	1ST PIPE 4-17-25	8" 1500W FRESNEL	MID. STAGE PINK WASH	53
6	6K	2ND PIPE 3-21 / 3RD PIPE 3-19	8" 1500W FRESNEL	MID STAGE L&R WARM	52
7	6K	1ST PIPE 10-20	6X12 750W LEKO	D.S. STAR TURN	17
8	6K	2ND PIPE 8-17	6X12 750W LEKO	MID STAGE STAR TURN	17
9	6K	1ST, 2ND & 3RD PIPE UNITS 1	8" 1500W FRESNEL	LEFT BLUE ENDS	61
10	6K	1 PIPE 28, 2 PIPE 23 / 3 PIPE 21	8" 1500W FRESNEL	RIGHT BLUE ENDS	61
11	6K	1ST PIPE 9-15-21 / 2ND PIPE 5-13-19 / 3RD PIPE 5-16	6X12 750W LEKO	DOWNLIGHT I-II & III	61
12	6K	3RD PIPE 10 / 4TH PIPE 7-12-17	6X12 750W LEKO	DOWNLIGHT III & IV	61
13	6K	1ST PIPE 2-27 / 2ND PIPE 2-22 / 3RD PIPE 2-20	8" 1500W FRES / 6X12 750W LEKO	LIGHT BLUE ENDS L&R	17
14	6K	1ST PIPE 5-11-24 / 2ND PIPE 4-12-20 / 3RD PIPE 7-14	6X9 750W PATTERN LEKO	LEAF PATTERN	CL
15	6K	NO. 1-2-3-4 TORMS LEFT 1	8" 1500W FRESNEL	XLIGHT	61
16	6K	NO. 1-2-3-4 TORMS RIGHT 1	8" 1500W FRESNEL	XLIGHT	61
17	6K	NO. 1-2-3-4 TORMS LEFT 2	8" 1500W FRESNEL	XLIGHT	09
18	6K	NO. 1-2-3-4 TORMS RIGHT 2	8" 1500W FRESNEL	XLIGHT	09
19	4K	NO. 1-2-3-4 TORMS LEFT 4	6X12 750W LEKO	XLIGHT	●
20	4K	NO. 1-2-3-4 TORMS RIGHT 4	6X12 750W LEKO	XLIGHT	●
21	4K	NO. 1-2-3-4 TORMS LEFT 5	6X12 750W LEKO	XLIGHT	●
22	4K	NO. 1-2-3-4 TORMS RIGHT 5	6X12 750W LEKO	XLIGHT	●
23	4K	NO. 1-2-3-4 TORMS LEFT 6	6X9 750W LEKO	SHINBUSTER	●
24	4K	NO. 1-2-3-4 TORMS RIGHT 6	6X9 750W LEKO	SHINBUSTER	●
25	6K	NO. 1-2-3-4 TORMS LEFT 3 & RIGHT 3	6X12 750W LEKO	XLIGHT	●
26	6K	GROUND ROW 6 SECTIONS	500W IF QUARTZ	BLUE	G64
27	6K	GROUND ROW 6 SECTIONS	500W IF QUARTZ	WHITE	CL
28	6K	GROUND ROW 6 SECTIONS	500W IF QUARTZ	RED	G08
29	6K	FLOOR CABLE ALL POSITIONS			
30	6K	FLOOR CABLE ALL POSITIONS			

Right Table

SWITCH	WAT.	POSITION & UNIT NO.	TYPE	FOCUS	COLOR
31	2K	NO. 1 TORM LEFT "D"	6X12 750W PATTERN LEKO	■	●
32	2K	NO. 1 TORM RIGHT "D"	6X12 750W LEKO	■	●
33	2K	NO. 1 TORM LEFT "A"	6X16 750W PATTERN LEKO	■	●
34	2K	NO. 1 TORM RIGHT "A"	6X16 750W PATTERN LEKO	■	●
35	2K	NO. 1 TORM LEFT "B"	6X12 750W PATTERN LEKO	■	●
36	2K	NO. 1 TORM LEFT "C"	6X12 750W PATTERN LEKO	■	●
37	2K	NO. 1 TORM RIGHT "B"	6X12 750W LEKO	■	●
38	2K	NO. 1 TORM RIGHT "C"	6X12 750W LEKO	■	●
39	2K	FLOOR CABLE U.L.			
40	2K	FLOOR CABLE U.R.			
41	2K	FLOOR CABLE U.L.			
42	2K	FLOOR CABLE U.R.			
43	2K	1ST PIPE 3	6X12 750W LEKO	DOWN LEFT POOL	17
44	2K	1ST PIPE 26	6X12 750W LEKO	DOWN RIGHT POOL	17
45	2K	FLOOR CABLE S.L.			
46	2K	FLOOR CABLE S.R.			
47	2K	1ST PIPE 16	6X12 750W LEKO	DOWN ₵ POOL	835
48	2K	2ND PIPE 7-18	6X12 750W LEKO	₵ POOL	835
49	4K	3RD PIPE 11	6X12 750W LEKO	MID ₵ POOL	61
50	4K	4TH PIPE 13	6X12 750W LEKO	UP ₵ POOL	17
51	4K	FLOOR CABLE UP LEFT & UP RIGHT			
52	4K	4TH PIPE 5-9-15-18	6X12 750W LEKO	COPPELIA GISELLE SWAN LAKE	53
53	4K	2ND PIPE 10-15	8" 1500W FRESNEL	₵ CLEAR XLIGHT	CL
54	4K	2ND PIPE 9-16	8" 1500W FRESNEL	₵ BLUE XLIGHT	61
55	2K	3RD PIPE 4	6X12 750W LEKO	X TO D.R.	G30
56	2K	3RD PIPE 9	6X12 750W LEKO	BACKLIGHT ₵	G30
57	2K	3RD PIPE 18	6X12 750W LEKO	X TO D.L.	G30
58	2K	4TH PIPE 8	6X12 750W LEKO	X TO MID RIGHT	G30
59	2K	4TH PIPE 11	6X12 750W LEKO	BACKLIGHT MID ₵	G30
60	2K	4TH PIPE 16	6X12 750W LEKO	X TO MID LEFT	G30

SWITCHES 61 THRU 72 ARE FOR SPECIAL REPLUGS AS REQUIRED BY REPERTORY. LIGHT PLOT SYMBOL △ ALL ARE 2K DIMMERS.

■ FOCUS CHANGES FOR INDIVIDUAL BALLETS.

● COLORS CHANGE FOR INDIVIDUAL BALLETS

NOTE: 4TH CIRCUIT OF GROUND ROW IS COLORED & REPLUGED AS REQUIRED BY REPERTORY

Figure 5.33 ABT switchboard hookup for season road tour.

and patterns. Throughout the years Nikolais has remained endlessly creative, always moving on to new experimentation. In *Crossfade,* one of his older dances, the dancers perform a relatively "normal" Nikolais dance. At the final moment all are choreographed into a line downstage. Suddenly, Carousel projectors concealed in the footlights project genitals and breasts (in the exact proper locations, a triumph of careful choreography) on the all-white body-tight costumes of the entire company — just as the curtain falls to a gasp, followed by thunderous applause.

Chapter 7 contains several dance production photos from television productions. Figure 7.11 and Color Figs. 61 through 63 are from the "Dance in America" series of Public Broadcast Service of Martha Graham's world-famous *Clytemnestra,* taped at Opryland studios in Nashville, Tennessee, with the creative lighting of CBS's Ralph Holmes. Color Fig. 66 is from the movie *The Turning Point* — a classic about ballet — with lighting by Nananne Porcher. Included also are the stage lighting plot and hookup used by Porcher while this movie was being filmed. Figure 5.37 and Color Figs. 29 and 30 are additional examples of striking dance lighting (Fig. 30 makes effective use of neon).

A careful study of these plots, hookups, magic sheets, and production photos should give the reader a thorough knowledge of communications forms in the broad range of dance: ballet, large or small and on tour; modern dance; the unique work of Nikolais; and in television.

Procedures and Practices

Because James C. Wright expresses his ideas very well, it is fitting to close the dance lighting portion of this chapter with a brief quote from the "Notes of James C. Wright" from Peggy Clark's USITT study, "Dance Tour Lighting for Small Companies," published in the Summer 1979 issue of *Theatre Design and Technology:*

> Most important is the issue of *style* . . . A standardized light plot may do more harm than good. . . . The idea is not codification but inspiration.
>
> If the lighting has grown organically from the dance, as it should, the designer will be able to limit the plot and cues to those which are necessary only for the specific piece. Thus, where color control is generalized, this should be specific unless great color control is needed. The lighting is part of the dance,

Figure 5.34 Focus chart for ABT road tour.

and suffers greatly when it is tacked on at the end or near the end. The use of films and slides is the same—all must grow from the piece as a single entity. Even when the choreographer has no specific lighting ideas, he/she generally has a textural or concrete feeling about the piece which might be used as a theme; the lighting must reflect the depth, not the surface values of the piece. Any lighting that exists for effect or to display lighting design is extraneous and should be cut. Any experimentation should be the logical outgrowth of the piece. Too many dances are destroyed by overlighting or ineptly handled cues—the designer or person responsible for the lighting should use no more light than he/she can control, even if this means dancing under worklights.

Over 90% of the work of the lighting designer is the setting of the cues. Except where demanded by the dance or the contextual change of the dance, one should not execute a cue. *The goal of lighting the dance is to light the dance—not have the dancers accompany the light.*"[113]

Musicals

Attempting to define what a musical is—and to separate cleanly the musical as a form from a play with music, opera, dance, revue, and operetta—is a nearly impossible task. The modern musical and modern musical comedy (not all musicals are intended to be strictly entertaining and funny) are almost purely of American invention. The musical grew as a form of escapist entertainment before the advent of movies and TV. It borrows freely from burlesque, vaudeville, variety shows, boy-meets-girl plays, melodrama, spectacle, and anything else that is lying around loose. With no hesitation at all, musicals incorporate stolen pieces from opera, operetta, all forms of dance, and—lately—both TV and movies. There are musicals which are almost opera, such as *A Little Night Music* and *Sweeney Todd, The Demon Barber of Fleet Street.* Also in the hard-to-classify category is *Dancin',* an all-dance musical with no connecting plot and only a theme to unify it, as well as *Jesus Christ, Superstar* and *Godspell,* both of which have an underlying serious message. Because it is impossible to draw clear dividing lines, we will turn our attention to what a musical is supposed to do and how the musical does it.

Jean Rosenthal described musicals beautifully: "A musical is bigger and brighter and busier than other forms." She further added:

[113] Clark, pp. 26–27, 32, op. cit. (see footnote 112).

See also:

Jean Rosenthal and Lael Wertenbaker, The Magic of Light, op. cit. (see footnote 110), Chap. Nine: "To Dance in Light," pp. 115–31; "Martha Graham" light plot, section on pp. 202–05. Jean's personal reminiscences about her lengthy, diversified career lighting the key dance companies and how to design for them. Since dance was her first love, her memories, analyses, and suggestions are priceless.

Douglass F. Sisk, "When the Dance Speaks . . . Allen Lee Hughes 'Listens' to the Nuances of Choreography before Creating His Environments of Light," Lighting Dimensions, vol. 11, no. 1 (Jan./Feb. 1987), pp. 28–33, 48–49. Illus., color. Includes Feld Ballet light plot.

Joel E. Rubin and Leland H. Watson, Theatrical Lighting Practice, op. cit. (see footnote 110), "Ballet and Modern Dance," pp. 31–37. Now somewhat out-of-date.

Tom Skelton, "Handbook of Dance Stagecraft," Dance magazine. A series of 27 articles by Thomas Skelton appearing from Oct. 1955 through Oct. 1957. Well-illustrated. Article topics vary from important basic fundamentals to how-to home remedies. Well worth reading. Discussed are the nature of dance lighting, areas and cross lighting, lighting instruments, color media and theory and practical use, projections, switchboards and control, angle and intensity as design tools, modern dance lighting design, jazz and ballet pas de deux lighting, budget problems, improvised and homebuilt lighting equipment, followspots, cue timing and sequence, masking, the dance recital, sets and props, effects, production problems, and staff and touring. In short, a complete beginner's manual.

Adrian Dightam, "Give to Forms and Images a Breath," Cue, no. 1 (Sept./Oct. 1979), pp. 20, 22–23. Illus., color. Excellent British article on designing light for dance.

Rae Ellen Ballard, "Dance Lighting in Alternative Spaces—Edward Effron in Profile," Theatre Crafts, vol. 16, no. 3 (Mar. 1982), pp. 18–19, 45–47. Illus.

Leslie Armstrong, AIA, and Roger Morgan, Space for Dance. N.Y.; Publishing Center for Cultural Resources, 625 Broadway, NY, 10012; 1984. 191 pp, illus. While this volume deals primarily with the design of theatre spaces for dance, lighting designer Roger Morgan includes much of interest to the lighting designer.

David M. Clark, "Ballet, Lighting, Television," Lighting Dimensions, vol. 2, no. 5 (May/June 1978), pp. 34–36, 44. Fine text and color illustrations of dance lighting of the "Little Women Ballet" on TV.

Jennifer Tipton, "Some Thoughts About Dance Lighting," Lighting Dimensions, vol. 2, no. 5 (May/June 1978), pp. 37, 46, 48, 55. Valuable discussion of the differences in lighting design for dance and for drama by a leading dance designer. Includes photographs.

Thomas Skelton, "Tom Skelton, On the Ohio Ballet," Lighting Dimensions, vol. 2, no. 5 (May/June 1978), pp. 39–41. Illus., color. Description by Skelton of touring with the ballet company for which he is both associate director and lighting designer.

Miami Garrard Dance Co., Cortli. New York; Miami Garrard Dance Co., 155 Wooster St., N.Y., NY 10012; 1978. Text on using computer control for dance lighting. 225 pages. Illus.

Thomas Skelton, "Jean Rosenthal's Dance Lighting," Theatre Crafts, vol. 7, no. 4 (Sept. 1973), p. 46. A wonderful tribute to Rosenthal and her work by one of today's leading dance lighting designers; Skelton lists Rosenthal's pioneer contributions to dance lighting.

Ronald L. Bates, "A Viewpoint on Lighting for Dance," Lighting Dimensions, vol. 2, no. 6 (July/Aug. 1978), pp. 42–43. Thoughts on dance lighting by the production manager and lighting designer for the New York City Ballet.

"Panel: Dance Production," Theatre Design & Technology, no. 22 (Oct. 1970), pp. 12–16. A national convention discussion reported. Comments by Marcia Segal (critic), Alwin Nikolais, Jennifer Tipton, Beverly Emmons, and Michael Rabbitt (technical director). Both good philosophical analysis of dance and useful technical information.

"Budget Lighting for the Bucks County Ballet," Theatre Crafts, vol. 7, no. 2 (Mar./Apr. 1973), p. 50. Lighting budget for the 150 smaller regional dance companies.

"Lighting: Capturing desert sun and building palace walls," Theatre Crafts, vol. 7, no. 4 (Sept. 1973), pp. 12–13, 47–48. Well-illustrated article on the "lighting designer for dance, virtually a magician." Photos of the work of Alwin Nikolais, the early Cincinnati Ballet and the Merce Cunningham Co.

Kenneth P. Bowen, "Letters to the Editor," Theatre Design & Technology, vol. 21, no. 3 (Fall 1985), p. 11. Very important statement about dance and dance lighting design.

Basic reference:

Cyril W. Beaumont, Ballet Design, Past and Present. New York; Studio Publications, Inc.; 1946. 216 pages. Still available. An early book filled with photographs, black-and-white and color, of ballet production and design. Most useful.

Mary Clarke and Clemet Crisp, Design for Ballet. New York; Hawthorn Books, Inc.; 1978. 288 pages. The modern counterpart of Beaumont but with much more extensive text. Excellent illustrations, black-and-white and color.

Ballett International magazine, published by Ballett-Buehnen-Verlag, P.O. Box 270443, D-5000 Koeln 1, Germany, since 1982.

Oren Parker and Harvey Smith, "Dance," pp. 553–558, op. cit. (see footnote 3). Brief text; useful for plot and illus.

Richard Pilbrow, Stage Lighting, pp. 114–15, op. cit. (see footnote 3). Brief.

Lee Watson, "A Space For Dance," Lighting Dimensions, vol. 9, no. 4 (July/Aug. 1985), pp. 13, 15–16, 18, 30. A critical comparison of the lighting of the 10 key American ballet companies.

Sharon Jackman, "Lighting the Joffrey Ballet," Lighting Dimensions, vol. 9, no. 2 (Mar./Apr. 1985), pp. 52–53, 54–55, 56–58, 60, 62–63. Illus., color. Light plot and text for the 1985 lighting of Romeo and Juliet by Tom Skelton.

"A Garden of Darkness and Light, Martha Clarke Brings Hieronymus Bosch's Beautifully Terrifying Images to Life in The Garden of Earthly Delights, with the Help of Lighting Designer Paul Gallo," Lighting Dimensions, vol. 9, no. 7 (Nov./Dec. 1985), pp. 78–81, 83–85. Illus., color.

Ken Bowen, "Lighting for the Real World of

Dance," Lighting Dimensions, *vol. 10, no. 2 (Mar./Apr. 1986), pp. 47–53. Illus., color. Suggestions about economy dance lighting on a limited budget by a Chicago designer.*

William James Lawson (editor), Stern's Performing Arts Directory. *N.Y.; Dance magazine, Inc.; 1989. The annual guidebook of dance and music resources, managers, and presenters. Although it contains much advertising in its 500 pages, it remains the only usable guidebook for dance. It lists dance lighting designers, their addresses, and telephone numbers. It sells for around $35.*

"Works in Progress: Dance Theory," The New York Times Magazine, *March 12, 1989, p. 110. Illus., color. The experimental choreography of Trisha Brown where for* Astral Convertible *all lights for the 35-minute dance are triggered by movement (sound waves) and sound — different each performance. Light thus becomes a key part of the choreography.*

Mark Loeffler, "Stan Pressner: A Colorful, Sometimes Strident Style for Modern Dance," Lighting Dimensions, *vol. 12, no. 6 (September/October 1988), pp. 66–69, 84–85. Illus., color. The design work of lighting designer Stan Pressner in modern dance. His work is presented with an interview and graphics.*

Beth Howard, "Carol Mullins," Lighting Dimensions, *vol. 12, no. 7 (November 1988), pp. 46–49, 62, 65. Illus., color.* "What the Consultants Say," Theatre Crafts, *vol. 22, no. 10 (December. 1988), pp. 20, 22–23. Subtitled "Architecture 88, Dance Spaces That Work," the next article is "What the Users Say," pp. 24, 26–27. With opinions by Bev Emmons, Roger Morgan, Ron Jerit, and Robert Davis — as well as others prominent in dance, this is a usable commentary. "Architecture 88" continues the series about dance spaces on pp. 31–37, 53–55. Illus. This issue covers dance in other places, including Jacob's Pillow and the National Ballet School.*

Tom Watson, "LDs and Choreographers Discuss 'Lighting the Dance' at Connecticut Sympo-sium," Lighting Dimensions, *vol. 12, no. 2 (March 1988), p. 17. Illus. A description of an important dance lighting symposium at the University of Connecticut, October 29–31, 1987. Participants in Storrs, Connecticut, included Allen Lee Hughes, Jane Reisman, Chenault Spence, Jennifer Tipton, and Craig Miller.*

Beth Howard, "A Legacy Evolves: Mark Stanley Lights — and Relights — the New York City Ballet," Theatre Crafts, *vol. 22, no. 2 (February 1988), pp. 40–45, 62–63. Illus., color. Includes light plot.*

Ann Daly, "Dancing in the Dark: Dana Reitz Choreographs With Light, As Well As Movement," Lighting Dimensions, *vol. 13, no. 4 (May/June 1989), pp. 84, 86, 89. A description of choreographer Reitz's use of light as a design element in her choreography (much as does choreographer/designer Nikolais), even when working with lighting designers Jennifer Tipton and Beverly Emmons.*

Ken Tabachnick, "On Reconstruction: the LD's Archeological Dig For 'Lost' Lighting," Lighting Dimensions, *vol. 13, no. 4 (May/June 1989), pp. 50, 52, 54–58. Dance/opera lighting designer Tabachnick explains the detailed and time-consuming process he must use with the Martha Graham Dance Company in reconstructing Jean Rosenthal's original lighting following revisions by Gilbert Hemsley (1978–1980) and Beverly Emmons (1982).*

[114] Jean Rosenthal, p. 75, op. cit. (see footnote 110).

[115] Ibid., p. 76.

[116] Ibid.

You treat the script, or book, with the same respect as a dramatic script, whether it deserves it or not. The songs are an integral part of the script; the words are important. You study the movement, the integrated dancing, as you would for a ballet. You soak in the score as you do for an opera. And you seek the emotional key to the whole. After which you are free to admit that the musical is not a drama or an opera or a ballet, but a form of amusement which incorporates the technical demands of all other forms." [114]

The word *amuse(ment)* is key, and Rosenthal repeats it with other choice words in another description of *musical*: "A musical is expected to beguile, amuse, please, surprise and entertain its audience." [115] Musicals could have been included in Chap. 9, which is concerned with spectacle. The elements of spectacle involved in ice shows, circuses, and outdoor theatrical pageantry all find their proper place in the musical form.

Design Considerations

There are at least six basic factors to consider when designing lighting for a musical.

1. Space. Most musicals should be performed in large theatres. There are exceptions: *I Do, I Do* (a two-person musical), *Fantasticks,* and others come to mind. Musicals require an orchestra, room to dance, often a rather large cast, masses of scenery, and frequent change of locale. Rosenthal wrote: "A musical is seldom as heavy scenically as an opera — it is larger than life rather than heroic in scale — but it moves faster." [116] The larger performance space and multiple scenic requirements obviously lead to complex light plots, lots of luminaires, and more than a saltwater dimmer board.

2. Zones. The traditional musical (there are exceptions to everything in lighting design) alternates — scenically — between short scenes "In One," midstage numbers involving "In One" and "In Two," and three or four big, full-stage numbers (the spectacle; the scenes where dancing room is needed; the act and show finale). Authors write that way; scenic designers and scenographers design that way; directors block that way. So, rather than using standard (i.e., dramatic show) acting/lighting areas, the lighting designer lights in zones — and with as much available variation in color and angle as possible. Crosslighting is nearly as important in musicals as in dance.

3. Followspots. Because the designer is not often set up for area control, and because musicals traditionally have two to eight principals, use of one or more followspots has become the key to most musical lighting. In *Sweeney Todd,* Ken Billington was faced with the problem of a huge factory onstage and an overhead glass roof which effectively eliminated most of the more commonly used lighting positions. So what did he do? He effectively used 3 arc follow spotlights from the projection booth at the rear and had 4 more located onstage—in clear view of the audience—high in the air on steel beam structures on the set. In moments of real crisis there are large Fresnel spotlights in sight as a part of the set that can be brought full-up to act as crosslight "shin kickers" when needed.

Followspots need not be "hard-edged" and obtrusive. Jo Mielziner often used them on Broadway in serious plays. He used incandescent 3000-watt and 5000-watt Dynabeams with great unobtrusive effect. In a musical followspots are vital. They pick out the principals, keeping the audience's attention where the director wants it. Most other lighting in a musical illuminates the scenic environment (scenery and drops) and provides a colorful mood wash into which are inserted the powerful followspots which carry the show. To my knowledge, only designer Peggy Clark has ever designed lighting on Broadway for a musical and dispensed entirely with followspots—in *Beggar's Holiday,* in production in 1946 and 1947. During the same season for *Brigadoon,* Clark used followspots only for flooding. There have been no repeats of this approach.

4. Doubling Lights. Since followspots carry the main action, most of the rest of the lighting equipment (tons of it) serves to "paint a picture," set the mood, and sculpt the performers' bodies. Not only are strong colors often used—musicals are supposed to be colorful and visually stimulating—but lighting equipment must "double." With a multiplicity of scenes, combinations of lights must be used over and over throughout the show. Of course there are specials in the plot for effects, dramatic moments, and individual scenes which do not fit conveniently into the overall setup, but almost every luminaire works many times. With lots of scenery, many scenes, and a large cast, space is at a premium. There just isn't much room left over for lights. Each light (or electric pipe) must perform many critical tasks. Jean Rosenthal called the musical "a giant jigsaw puzzle into which it is necessary to fit all the pieces, including lighting equipment, flying, and moving scenery."

5. Complex Cues. Many sets and the necessity to fit light changes into the flow of music and dance lead to a great number of light cues.

6. Close Coordination. Since nearly all creative elements of theatre are blended together in a musical—words, acting, singing, dancing, effects, complex scenery, colorful costumes, and (maybe) bizarre makeup—all must coordinate. The performance/design staff has no choice except to work together. Disaster is the only other alternative. Unlike opera (in which the musical director is usually king) or dance (in which the choreographer controls all) or serious drama (in which the director has supreme control), in a musical nearly everyone is "boss." This general equality leads to many problems until it becomes apparent who is making the important, key decisions. It behooves the lighting designer to detect who is in final control at the earliest possible moment and act accordingly.

Communications Form

Again the standard light plot and hookup are used. However, the designer must carefully consider the multiple sets and/or scenes involved. Several light plots, switchboard hookups, and production photos are included here which exemplify lighting design styles and specific practices.

In Chap. 6 there are some production photos of musicals: Fig. 125, *Gypsy;* Fig. 126, *The Boyfriend.* In Chap. 10, Color Figs. 90, 91, 91a, and 91b are pictures of the *Pontiac '74* show, which was actually a musical.

The next plot and hookup presented in this chapter are from Thomas Skelton's Broadway production of *Peter Pan* (see Figs. 5.38 and 5.39 and Color Fig. 31). Figures 5.40 and 5.41 are the plot and hookup from a hit musical in New York City which radically departs from the usual musical comedy format: *Sweeney Todd, The Demon Barber of Fleet Street* by designer Ken Billington, *Sweeney Todd* is a "serious"

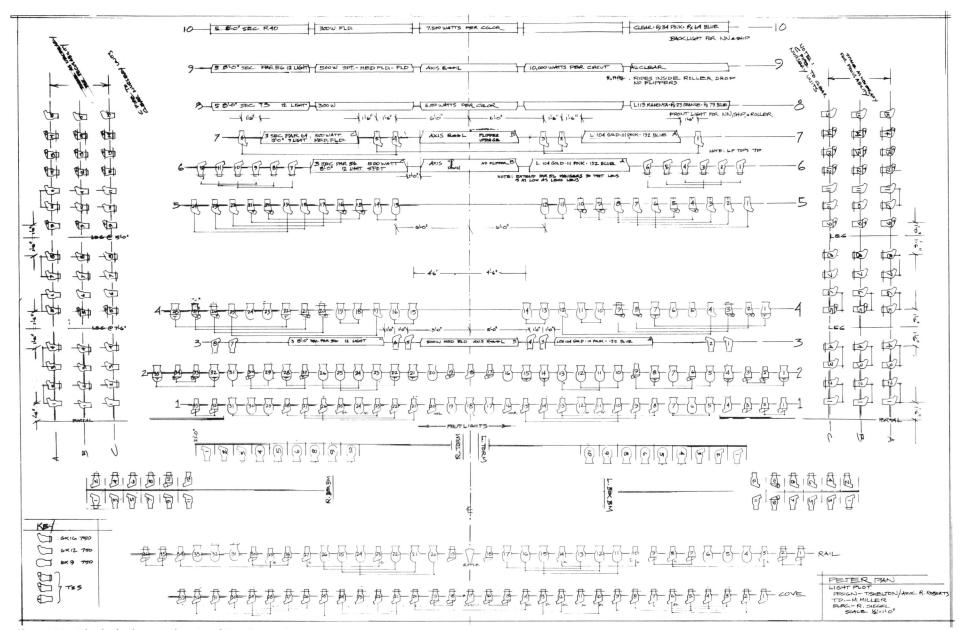

Figure 5.38 Light plot for the musical version of *Peter Pan*, starring Sandy Duncan, at the Lunt-Fontaine Theatre, New York City. Set design: Peter Wolf; costumes: Bill Hargate; lighting design: Thomas R. Skelton; associate lighting designer: Ruth Roberts.

PETER PAN HOOKUP ①

1	COVE 1-11-23-33	CL	C- DC CL
2	" 12-14-20-22	Rx 33	DC pink
3	" 2-6-10-13	Rx 49	From DL pan
4	" 21-24-28-32	Rx 49	From DR pan ⓣ
5	" 15-16-18-19	15-19=869 / 16-18=104	
6	" 17	805	Window
7	" 5-9-25-29	849	Blue wash
8	L+R BB 1-2	CL	BB DC CL
9	L+R BB 3-4	CL	BB DL-DR CL
10	L BB 5-6/COVE 3-7	813	L BB Amb
11	R BB 5-6/COVE 27-31	813	R BB Am
12	L BB 7-8/COVE 4-8	Rx 44	L BB Pink
13	R BB 7-8/COVE 26-30	Rx 44	R BB Pink
14	L+R BB 9-10	CL	BB ⓣ
15	L+R BB 11-12	132 / 869 / 104	BB 32
16	RAIL 1-2-19-35-36	869 / 104	R ⓣ 6x16
17	7-9-18-28-30	849	6x12
18	10-14-23-27	CL	R C CL
19	3-8-29-34	CL	R L+R CL
20	11-15-22-26	132	R Blue Lo
21	4-33	132	Hi
22	12-16-21-25	817	Amb Lo
23	5-32	817	Hi
24	13-17-20-24	Rx49	Purple Lo
25	6-31	Rx49	Hi
26	FOOTS	Rx26	Foots Red
27	FOOTS	Rx82	Blue
28	FOOTS	Rx525	Mauve
29	L+R TORM 1/1P12-24	CL	T DC CL
30	L TORM 5-12	CL	L Tom CL
31	R TORM 5-12	CL	R Ta CL
32	L TORM 2-6/1P 10-15	Rx 64	L T Blue
33	R TORM 2-6/1P 21-26	Rx 64	R T Blue
34	L TORM 3-8/1P 9-14	813	L T Amb
35	R TORM 3-8/1P 22-27	813	R T Amb
36	L TORM 4-10/1P 8-13	Rx26	L T Red
37	R TORM 4-10/1P 23-28	Rx26	R T Red
38	L+R TORM 7-11	Rx73	Shin Green ⓣ
39	9-13	Rx79	Shin Blue ⓣ
40	1P 16	CL	x DR
41	1P 20	CL	x DL
42	1P 4	825	Ship
43	1P 5-7-29-31	Rx 52	1 P Lav
44	1P 11-25	827	1 P DC Pink
45	1P 1-2-3-32-33	874	1P ⓣ Green
46	1P 6/2P 16	825	DL BED
47	1P 18/2P 11-13-23-25	CL	C pract CL
48	1P 17/2P 5-7-29-31	802	C pract BA
49	1P 19	Rx 52	1P Down
50	2P 10-12-24-26	Rx 52	11 LAV
51	28-1-4-32-33	Rx15	2P 6x9 2nd ⓣ

52	2P 8-14-22-28	Rx73	2P LC 6x9 inside ⓣ
53	2P 2-3-33-34	Rx70	2P LC 6x12 2-1 ⓣ
54	2P 6-9-17	Rx22	CAVE ⓣ WALLS
55	2P 19-27-30	Rx51	2P 6x12 inside ⓣ R
56	2P 15-21	Rx70	2P 6x9 NN ⓣ
57	2P 18/4P 6-23	349	CAVE OVER
58	2P 20	825	UR BED
60	3P 1-3-6-8	874	LC 3r GR
61	3P 2-4-5-7	854	LC 3x 854
62	3P PAR 56	104	Soft
63	3P PAR 56	111	Pink
64	3P PAR 56	132	Blue
65	4P 1-7-22-28	828	4P 6x9 ⓣ
66	4P 2-8-21-27	849	6x12 ⓣ
67	4P 3-9-20-26	Rx 51	6x16 ⓣ
68	4P 4-12-17-25	802	CAVE UNDER
69	4P 5-24	802	SHIP 602
70	4P 10-11-18-19	Rx52	4P LAV
71	4P 13-14-15-16	104	m I BX
72	L+R A Pipe 1-2	Rx89	LC
73	B P 1-2	Rx63	LC
74	C P 1-2	Rx52	LC
75	L AP 3-4-7-8	CL	DL CL
76	R AP 3-4-7-8	CL	DR CL
77	L B P 3-4-7-8	827	DL pink
78	R B P 3-4-7-8	827	DR pink
79	L C P 3-4-7-8	813	DL Amb
80	R C P 3-4-7-8	Rx44	DR Maj
81	L A P 5-6-10-11	849	UL Bl
82	R A P 5-6-10-11	849	UL Bl
83	L B P 6-10-11/5P 2-7	Rx49	UL Purp
84	R B P 6-10-11/5P 18-23	811	UR Amb
85	L C P 6-10-11/5P 3-8	813	UL Amb
86	R C P 6-10-11/5P 17-22	Rx44	UR Pink
87	L+R B P 5-12/L AP 12	Rx26	Red T
88	L+R C P 5-12/R AP 12	Rx94	Green T
89	L+R A PIPE+B PIPE 9	849	Iris T
90	5P 1-6-19-24	849	5P 849
91	5P 5-10-15-20	858	5P ⓣ
92	5P 4-9-16-21	827	5P ⓣ
93	5P 11-12-13-14	104	CAVE BX
94	6P 1-4-9-12	139	6P GR
95	6P 2-5-8-11	11	6P MAG
96	6P 3-6-7-10	132	6P BL
97	6P PAR 64 A-C	139	GREEN
98	6P PAR 64 A-C	111	PINK
99	6P PAR 64 A-C	132	BLUE
100	7P 1-3-4-6	CL	Act II stain
101	7P 2-5	861	GR
102	6-7 P PAR 64 B	139	GR
103	7 P PAR 64 A-C	139	GR
104	6+7P B	111	PINK

105	7P Hi AC		111
106	6+7P B		132 BLUE
107	7P A-C		132
108	8P		LEE 113 MAGENTA
109	"		
110	8 P		Rx 23 ORANGE
111	"		
112	8 P		Rx79 Blue
113			
114	10th P	Baby 9th	Rx 64 Blue
115	"	Pipe Act	
116	10th Pipe	I-III	Rx34 pink
117	"		
118	10th Pipe		CL
119	"		
120	L A PIPE 13-14		827	Iris ⓣ
121	R A PIPE 13-14		104	"
122	L B PIPE 13-14		Rx64	"
123	R B PIPE 13-14		Rx64	"
124		PRACT.	
125			
126			
127			
128			

HOMELESS L+R A-B-C PIPE 13-14-15
L+R C PIPE 9
~~RIPPLE EFFECT~~
~~FLOOR SPECIALS~~

Figure 5.39 Switchboard hookup for *Peter Pan*.

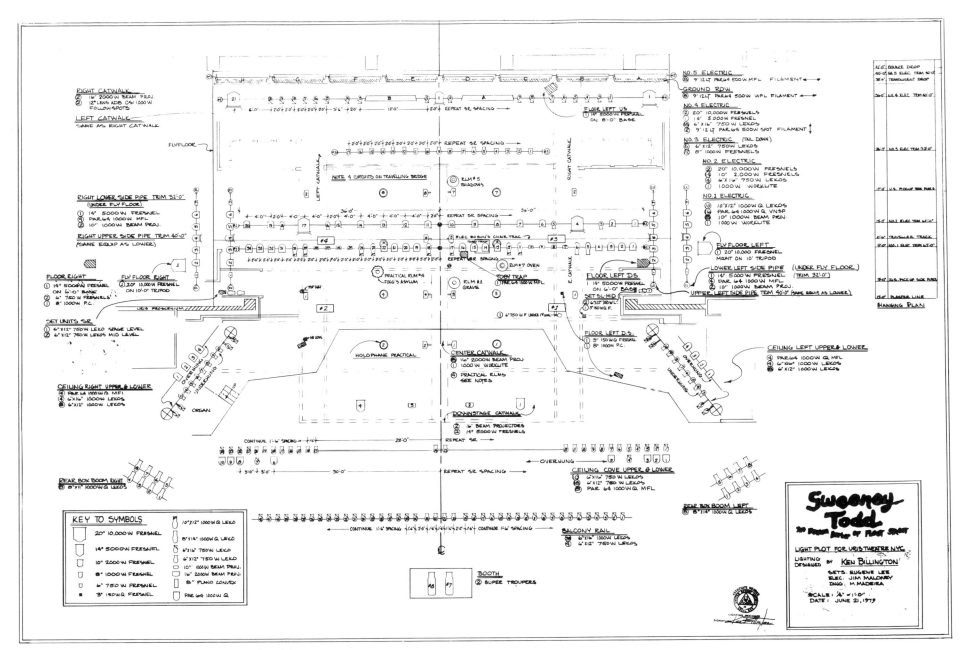

Figure 5.40 Light plot for *Sweeney Todd, the Demon Barber of Fleet Street* at the Uris Theatre in New York City in 1979. Director: Harold Prince; production designers: Eugene and Franne Lee; lighting design: Ken Billington; assistant lighting designer: Marcia Madeira.

SWITCH	POSITION & UNIT NO.	TYPE	FOCUS	COLOR
1	BALC. RAIL 1-2-3	6"x16" 1000w L	L	N.C.
2	BALC. RAIL 30-31-32	6"x16" 1000w L	L	N.C.
3	BALC. RAIL 6-7-8	6"x16" 1000w L	C	N.C.
4	BALC. RAIL 35-36-37	6"x16" 1000w L	C	N.C.
5	BALC. RAIL 11-12-13	6"x16" 1000w L	R	N.C.
6	BALC. RAIL 40-41-42	6"x16" 1000w L	R	N.C.
7	BALC. RAIL 5-17-24	6"x16" 1000w L	ABOVE L	N.C.
8	REAR BOX R 5-6	8"x11" 1000w L	ABOVE L	161
9	BALC. RAIL 4-16-25	6"x16" 1000w L	BELOW L	N.C.
10	REAR BOX R -8	8"x14" 1000w L	BELOW L	161
11	BALC. RAIL 19-26-38	6"x16" 1000w L	ABOVE R	N.C.
12	REAR BOX L 5-6	8"x11" 1000w L	ABOVE R	161
13	BALC. RAIL 18-27-39	6"x16" 1000w L	BELOW R	N.C.
14	REAR BOX L 3-8	8"x14" 1000w L	BELOW R	161
15	BALC. RAIL 10-15-28-33	6"x16" 1000w L	WASH	161
16	FAR BOX L 1-2-4-7	8"x16" 1000w L	WASH L	G-60
17	FAR BOX R 1-2-4-7	8"x15" 1000w L	WASH R	849
18	CATWALK C 1	16" 2000w B.P.	GRAVE	530
19	CATWALK C 2	16" 2000w B.P.	TRIO ABOVE R	530
20	CATWALK C 3	16" 2000w B.P.	LOVE SEAT "KISS ME"	530
21	CATWALK C 4	16" 2000w B.P.	BARBER SHOP	530
22	CATWALK C 5	16" 2000w B.P.	PIRELLI MURDER	530
23	CATWALK C 6	16" 2000w B.P.	BARBER SHOP	530
24	BALC. RAIL 9-14	6"x16" 1000w L	STEAM ENGINE	N.C.
25	STEAM ENGINE INNERS 1 BELOW 2 ABOVE	3150w G.F. NO LENS	STEAM ENGINE	N.C.
26	CEILING FIXTURES 1-2-3-4-5-6-7-8	500w CLEAR	HOLOPHANE	
27	UNDER BRIDGE RLM'S 7 8	75w A-19 CLEAR		
28	BALC. RAIL 34	6"x16" 1000w L	ORGAN	N.C.
29	CEILING LEFT LOWER 3-4-7-8	6"x12" 1000w L	ROOF DS	N.C.
30	CEILING LEFT LOWER 1-2	6"x16" 1000w L	SKYLIGHT DS	N.C.
31	CEILING LEFT LOWER 5-6-9-10	6"x12" 1000w L	ROOF DS	117
32	CEILING COVE 1 CEILING COVE OVER 4	6"x12" 1000w L	SKYLIGHT DS	117
33	CEILING LEFT UPPER 3-4 CEILING COVE OVER 1-2	PAR 64 1000w QMFL	SKYLIGHTS RED	NC
34	CEILING LEFT UPPER 1-2 CEILING COVE OVER 1-2	" "	SKYLIGHTS RED	106
35	CEILING RIGHT LOWER 3-4-7-8	6"x12" 1000w L	ROOF DS	NC
36	CEILING RIGHT LOWER 1-2	6"x16" 1000w L	SKYLIGHT D.S.	NC
37	CEILING RIGHT LOWER 5-6-9-10	6"x12" 1000w L	ROOF DS	117
38	CEILING COVE 26 CEILING COVE OVER 7	6"x16" 1000w L	SKYLIGHT DS	117
39	CEILING RIGHT UPPER 3-4 CEILING COVE OVER 8-10	PAR 64 1000w QMFL	SKYLIGHTS	NC
40	CEILING RIGHT UPPER 1-2 CEILING COVER OVER 6-9	"	RED	106
41	#1 GRAVE 500w CL #5 SHADOW 300wCL #4 FOG'S 25wCL #7 OVEN 150wCL	—	HANGING RLMS	—
42	1ST PIPE 1-2-3-4	6"x16" 1000w L	SKYLIGHT SL	NC
43	1ST PIPE 31-32-33-34	" "	SKYLIGHT SR	NC
44	LEFT PIPE UPPER 2-3 LOWER 2-3	PAR 64 1000w QMFL	RED SKYLIGHTS CUPOLA	106
45	RIGHT PIPE UPPER 2-3 LOWER 2-3	" "	"	106
46 A	LEFT PIPE UPPER 5-6 LOWER 5-6	PAR 64 1000w H.FL.	SKYLIGHT	N.C.
46 B	RIGHT PIPE UPPER 5-6 LOWER 5-6	" "	SKYLIGHT	NC
47 A	BALC. RAIL 20-21-22-23	6"x12" 750w L	SHOW CURTAIN	N.C.
47 B	4TH PIPE 2-3-19-20	6"x16" 750w L	WINDOWS U.S.	NC
48 A	4TH PIPE A-B	10"-1.5KW PAR	BACK U.S.	N.C.
49 A	4TH PIPE A-B	10"-1.5KW PAR	BACK U.S.	G-60
49 B	4TH PIPE A-B	" "	BACK U.S.	R-70
50 A	D.S. CATWALK 2-4-7	16" 2000w BEAM PROJ	TABLE ACT II	N.C.
50 B	FLOOR D.S.C. 1-2	2000w G.T-3	SHADOWS	N.C.
51 A	4TH PIPE 15-16-17-18	6"x16" 750w L	ENDS R	N.C.
51 B	UNDER B' UNIT L	6"x7 750w F	OVEN	R-20
52 A	CATWALK L 1	16" 2000w B.P	R.o/L	N.C.
52 B	CATWALK L 2	16" 2000w B.P	U.S.R.o/L	N.C.
53 A	CATWALK R 1	16" 2000w B.P	L.o/L	N.C.
53 B	CATWALK R 2	16" 2000w B.P	U.L.o/L	N.C.
54	4P 8-9-13-14	6"x12" 750w L	BOAT WATER	516
55	JUDGE DOOR S.R. RLM	500w A-19 CLEAR	DOOR	N.C.
56 A	FLOOR TRAP 1-	PAR 64 1000w Q.H.FL.	TRAP	117
56 B	MP 5-6	10"x12" 1000w	GREEN FINCH	N.C.
57	CATWALK CENTER CATWALK LEFT & RIGHT	25w CLEAR	PRACTICAL A-19's	
58 A	ORCHESTRA PIT	25w A19 CL	PIT	
58 B	BRIDGE PRACTICAL RLMS	3-250w PAR 38	OVER HEAD	N.C.
59 A	CEILING COVE 23	6"x16" 750w L	ORGAN	N.C.
59 B	CENTER CATWALK #8	16" 2000w BEAM TYPE	TABLE ACT II	530
59 B	DOOR LEKOS L 1+2	6"x12" 750w L	X	N.C.
60	DOOR LEKOS R 1+2	6"x12" 750w L	X-ABOVE	N.C.
61	1ST PIPE 21-22	PAR 64 1000w	TABLE & NSP	N.C.
62 A	FLOOR SL 1	6" 1000w P.C.	SHADOWS	N.C.
63	FLOOR S.R. 1-2	6" 750w F	SHADOWS	N.C.
64	RIGHT DOOR 3 (UNDER B' LEVEL)	6"x12" 750w L	X	N.C.
65	WORKING CABLE SL 1 BOAT 2 OVEN	6" 750w B.P. 100w A19 CL	HAND HELD NO LENS 6" 750w F	N.C. R-20 6-10
66	PRACTICALS LEFT	25w CL		N.C.
67 A	PRACTICALS RIGHT	25w CL		
68 A	CEILING COVE 5-7-9-11	6"x12" 750w L	ROOF	R-35
69	CEILING COVE 16-18-20-22	6"x12" 750w L	ROOF	R-35
70	CEILING COVE 6-8-10-12	6"x12" 750w L	ROOF	161
71	CEILING COVE 15-17-19-21	6"x12" 750w L	ROOF	161
72	5TH PIPE A-B-G-H	8"-1.5KW PAR S6 300w HFL	BOUNCE	N.C.
73	5TH PIPE C-D-E-F	10"-1.5KW PAR S6 300w HFL	BOUNCE	N.C.
74	GROUND ROW A-B-G-H	6"-9FT PAR 64 500w NFL	BOUNCE	N.C.
75	GROUND ROW C-D-E-F	6"-9FT PAR 64 500w NFL	BOUNCE	N.C.
76	5TH PIPE A-B-G-H	8"-1.5KW PAR S6 300w HFL	BOUNCE	R-81
77	5TH PIPE C-D-E-F	10"-1.5KW PAR S6 300w HFL	BOUNCE	R-81
78	GROUND ROW A-B-G-H	6"-9FT PAR 64 500w NFL	BOUNCE	R-80
79	GROUND ROW C-D-E-F	6"-9FT PAR 64 500w NFL	BOUNCE	R-80
80	5TH PIPE A-B-G-H	8"-1.5KW PAR S6 300w HFL	BOUNCE	R-20
81	5TH PIPE C-D-E-F	10"-1.5KW PAR S6 300w HFL	BOUNCE	R-20
82	GROUND ROW A-B-G-H	6"-9FT PAR 64 500w NFL	BOUNCE	R-32
83	GROUND ROW C-D-E-F	6"-9FT PAR 64 500w NFL	BOUNCE	R-32
84	3RD PIPE 1-3-7-10-14	8" 1000w F	SCRIM	N.C.
85	3RD PIPE 4-8-11-15	8" 1000w F	SCRIM	G-66
86	2ND PIPE -2-19	10" 2000w F	SKYLIGHT	117+
87	2ND PIPE 6-8-10	10" 2000w F	ROOF	117+
88	2ND PIPE 11-13-15	10" 2000w F	ROOF	117+
89	D.S. CATWALK 1	14" 5000w F	WASH	N.C.
90	D.S. CATWALK 12	14" 5000w F	WASH	G-60
91	4TH PIPE 11	14" 5000w F	BACK L	N.C.
92	LEFT PIPE UPPER	14" 5000w F	LEFT	R-35
93	LEFT PIPE LOWER	14" 5000w F	LEFT	N.C.
94	FLOOR L D.S	14" 5000w F	X IN 2	N.C.
95	1ST PIPE 7-8-9-10	10" 1000w F	KILLINGS ACT II	N.C.
96	RIGHT PIPE UPPER 4	14" 5000w F	RIGHT	R-35
97	FLOOR L U.S.	14" 5000w F	DOOR OPENING	N.C.
98	FLOOR R D.S	14" 5000w F	X IN 2	N.C.
99	RIGHT PIPE LOWER 4	14" 5000w F	DOOR	N.C.
100	2ND PIPE 4	20" 10,000w	ROOF FRESNEL	N.C.
101	4TH PIPE 1	20" 8,000w	ROOF	N.C.
102	FLY FLOOR L	20" 10,000w	ROOF	161
103	2ND PIPE 17	20" 10,000w	ROOF	N.C.
104	4TH PIPE 21	20" 10,000w	ROOF	N.C.
105	FLY FLOOR R	20" 10,000w	ROOF	161

Figure 5.41 *Sweeney Todd* switchboard hookup.

Figure 5.42 Production photo of *Sweeney Todd,* starring Angela
Lansbury and Len Cariou. (*Photo: © Martha Swope.*)

musical — nearly an opera in structure. Figure 5.42 is a production photo from *Sweeney Todd*. Color Fig. 32 is from the Broadway production of *Jesus Christ, Superstar*, with lighting design by Jules Fisher.[117]

Revues

The main differences between a revue and a musical are (1) a revue has no story line and instead deals with sketches and topical themes (a narrator or the equivalent may tie all the parts together) and (2) a revue is intended solely to entertain and amuse — through spectacle, music, dance, comedy, and, most of all, use of sex themes. The lighting design is not a great deal different from that used in other types of theatre. However, an examination of revues in Las Vegas or Atlantic City (currently the national capitols of revues) can be useful for understanding the genre. There were 10 casino theatres in Atlantic City in 1984, with more being built.[118] At present, Atlantic City attracts mostly patrons from a nearly 150-mile radius (*The New York Times*, June 9, 1985).[119]

In Las Vegas alone there are 27 large performance places (actually around 83, if you count all the smaller lounges, etc.), most of which have simplified lighting and staging. There are 25 more (5 of large proportions) in Reno, and 9 more in Tahoe, Lake Tahoe, Sparks, Carson City, Winnemucca, and Jackpot. These 117 places presenting theatre far surpass that which is available in New York City. "Show-biz" in Nevada is a large fertile field — but there are qualifications. The type of attractions is limited in Nevada; essentially there is no opera, no classical dance, and no drama in the usual sense. Instead one finds 5 places offering burlesque, at least 2 with ice shows, 1 with circus acts (the long-established Circus — Circus Clubs, in both Las Vegas and Reno), 1 or more with rock concerts, at least 3 with French revues (*Folies Bergères*, etc.), and many offering the standard format of over half of the performance places, i.e., an evening's entertainment with a band/orchestra onstage, a "big name" vocalist (or comedian), and a not as well known "second act" (juggler, pantomimist, etc.).

Something needs to be said about the performance places — the casino-hotels. In almost every case the audience's area consists of small tables and chairs rather than the more conventional rows of theatre seats. Dinner and/or drinks are served prior to or after the performance. A surprisingly large number of people can be crowded into a ballroom with a stage at one end if the tables are small and the customers are packed somewhat like sardines. (Since the majority of these performance places are located in large hotels — with adjacent gaming rooms — many *are* converted ballrooms.) The older places still have fairly low ceilings. Stage facilities were improved for presentation of live shows. Lighting equipment is likely to be mounted nearly anywhere, and backstage/offstage space is almost nonexistent.

The newer hotels and performance places are quite the opposite. The MGM Grand Hotel in Reno, for example, undoubtedly has some of the finest theatrical production facilities to be found in the United States. It was built in 1975 at a cost of $131 million in Reno, then a city of 150,000. George Howard was the theatrical consultant. The most up-to-date lighting equipment and memory control switchboards are to be found in this hotel.

None of this would exist were it not for the gambling casinos immediately outside the theatres. In every case it is necessary to pass through rooms filled with whirling slot machines to reach either the registration desk or the entrance to the theatre. The lavish, star-studded shows exist to draw customers to both Las Vegas and to each particular hotel, and also to provide either a break from the gaming tables or a place to go for accompanying husbands and wives who do not gamble. Yet the admission prices are comparable to those charged in New York City: tickets range from $15 to $40 dollars in most cases. An insight into the financial base: I learned that the Las Vegas Hilton and the newer Flamingo Hilton hotels in Las Vegas provide more than half of the profits of the entire worldwide Hilton hotel chain (see footnote 118, Lee Watson).

Not only do many of these hotels contain an important performance place, but many also have two or three other performance areas, e.g., nightclubs with live shows, corners of lobbies, etc. There is a lot of show business in Nevada, and much of it has designed lighting.

[117] *Jean Rosenthal*, The Magic of Light, *op. cit. (see footnote 110), Chap. Six: "Lighting the Musical," pp. 78–85, and "Hookup, Focus Chart and Light Plot for 'Hello, Dolly!'" pp. 178–201. The best material in print about designing lighting for musicals by a master of the art.*

Patricia MacKay, "Ain't Misbehavin'," Theatre Crafts, vol. 12, no. 6 (Oct. 1978), pp. 12–17, 66–69. Useful description of a Broadway musical with many helpful illustrations.

Richard Andrews, "Beatlemania," Cue, no. 3 (Jan./Feb. 1980), pp. 18–20. Illus., color. Robbie Monk's London lighting of the Jules Fisher musical.

"Oliver," TABS, vol. 18, no. 2 (Sept. 1960), pp. 6–18. While somewhat out-of-date, this article is useful because of its detail, length, and illustrations.

"A Ride on the Starlight Express," Lighting Dimensions, vol. 9, no. 2 (Mar./Apr. 1985), pp. 32–34, 37–40. Illus., color. Includes light plot. David Hersey's lighting of the London hit musical.

Patricia MacKay, "Evita," Theatre Crafts, vol. 13, no. 6 (Nov./Dec. 1979), pp. 14–19, 52–54, 59. Illus.

"The Dream Team on Collaboration," Theatre Crafts, vol. 16, no. 7 (Aug./Sept. 1982), pp. 12–15, 40, 42–43. An interview with Michael Bennett, Robin Wagner, Tharon Musser, Theoni V. Aldredge, and Bob Avian on their collaboration process. Useful insights into the process.

Susan Levi Wallach, "All Dolled Up," Theatre Crafts, vol. 16, no. 9 (Nov./Dec. 1982), pp. 22–23, 67–69, 71. Illus. See pp. 68–69, "Ken Billington on A Doll's Lights" for an interview in which Ken Billington explains his design approach to A Doll's House.

Ronn Smith, "Cats," Theatre Crafts, vol. 17, no. 1 (Jan. 1983), pp. 16–21, 36–39, 43–44. Illus.

Jules Fisher, "Dancin'," Lighting Design & Application, vol. 9, no. 6 (June 1979), p. 41. Illus., color. Lumen award writeup. Also in vol. 9, no. 9 (Oct. 1979), p. 23. Illus., color.

Wanda Jankowski, "Triumph Over Tradition — The Unconventional Lighting of 'Sweeney Todd'," Lighting Design & Application, vol. 9, no. 8 (Aug. 1979), pp. 26–30. Illus. Lengthy interview with Ken Billington. Includes light plot.

Richard Pilbrow, Stage Lighting. *London; Studio Vista; 1979 (revised ed. available from Drama Book Specialist, New York City). "Design Problems: Lighting the Musical" (pp. 104–134) contains production photos and a light plot for* Zorba, *a musical with sets by Boris Aronson and lighting by Pilbrow in New York City. Brief text.*

[118] *Lee Watson, "Nevada Showbiz!,"* Lighting Dimensions, *vol. 3, no. 3 (Mar. 1979), pp. 24–29, 32–35. An extensive report about revue lighting in the national capitol of revues, Nevada, including performance places, lighting equipment, and design comments. Illus., some color. Includes light plot and production photos for* Hello, Hollywood, Hello.

See also:

"Las Vegas Spectacular," Theatre Crafts, *vol. 10, no. 2 (Mar./Apr. 1976), pp. 6–9, 28, 30–31, 34. Illus. More about Las Vegas revue and theatre scene with additional details about* Hello, Hollywood, Hello, *lighted by Jules Fisher, and other shows.*

"Our French Connection," TABS, *vol. 34, no. 1 (Spring 1976), pp. 12–15. Several color photographs and text about the lighting and equipment used for French revue.*

Michael Knight, "Hallelujah Hollywood," TABS, *vol. 33, no. 2 (Summer 1975), pp. 11–15. Illus., color. Light plot in color. Excellent article about this Nevada spectacular revue with numerous color photos. Also, appended comments by Jules Fisher.*

Robert Macy, "Lighting up Las Vegas," Indianapolis Star, *Dec. 1, 1985, section G, pp. 1, 5. Illus., color.*

[119] *R. Bruce Dold (of* Chicago Tribune,) *"Casinos Thrive but Aren't Revitalizing Atlantic City,"* Indianapolis Star, *Sept. 5, 1983, p. 38.*

Jack Lloyd (Knight-Ridder Newspapers), "Casinos Turn Stalwarts into Has-Beens," Indianapolis Star, *Dec. 17, 1983, p. 37.*

"Atlantic City Report: The Stars Will Be Out in '84," New York Post, *Jan. 6, 1984, p. 33.*

[120] *Excerpted and abridged from this author's* Lighting Dimensions *column, "Nevada Show Biz!", op. cit. (see footnote 118).*

Having sketched the milieu, here is a description of one of the most lavish productions ever produced — Hello, Hollywood, Hello, which played for five years at the MGM Grand Hotel in Reno. Aside from the cost of the building, it is estimated that between 3 and 7 *million* dollars was spent on the production itself, for scenery, costumes, lighting design, and rehearsals. The show was in preparation for six months. As theatre goes, it is in a class by itself. Here is my description of the show, taken from my column "Nevada Show Biz!" in *Lighting Dimensions:*

> The opening is indeed spectacular. A full-sized DC-9 seems to fly in, land onstage, and disgorge showgirls from the 138-person cast. *That* is a boffo opening!
>
> In rapid succession, use was made of rear screen projections: front movie projection; a Steadylite (twinklelite) encrusted gauze drop. Costumes were most lavish. Side stages and ramps were much used by showgirls. Chaser-light circuits were built into much of the scenery.
>
> Next came fluorescent candelabra with flicker flame lights. This was followed by a spectacular, beautifully choreographed ballet sequence. Then, "Mr. Electric" appeared, a variety number with a wizard-performer making lighted bulbs appear everywhere in space.
>
> Good front projections of moving clouds with dancing beauties lighted behind it made a fine intro for "By The Light of the Silvery Moon." Dye-painted translucent scenery appeared for 'This Is Love.' The next number, "Barbarry Bums," featured multiple practical lamps, both on the set and battery operated. The Act I finale was a smasher! The San Francisco fire and earthquake, complete with sal ammoniac smoke, collapsing buildings, flames and fireworks, arc flashes and lightning, plus sound reinforcement.
>
> Act II also began with a bang. A starship number used "Peter Pan" flying rigs, a spaceship lowered in, extensive use was made of the side stages and lighting fluidity. China silk streamers were a centerpiece for a ballet which followed. Costumes were sprinkled with reflective mirrors combined with backlighting and creating "human mirror balls."
>
> The dragon's cave number combined dry ice fog, scenery sinking into the basement trap area under the stage, more fireworks (all stops pulled this time), several rainpipes going full blast, and the design-technical highlight of the whole evening. The entire stage was covered with a huge, multi-level flowing river and waterfall: *not* projections; *not* just a dribble, but water *several feet deep* cascading everywhere. Not only was it breathtaking, but ten seconds later (after a brief blackout), not a single drop of moisture was to be found anywhere as we moved into a juggling act!
>
> In the next act, a full-stage depth circus number, costumes were beyond belief. Performers working from the ceiling of the auditorium added more sensation and moved the show out of the confines of the proscenium. This was followed by "Great MGM Musicals on Parade." It consisted of short excerpts from all-time MGM movie greats (live, in costume) — with live horses! "Show Biz" featured a showboat with lighted practicals and many people wheeling around the stage. "Kiss Me Kate," "Ben Hur," "Louisa" were included, with "The Wizard of Oz" number with a full auditorium-width crossover bridge coming down on cables out of the ceiling over the heads of the audience for "Over the Rainbow," glistening with thousands of string beelights. Four circus girls using "teeth harnesses" next reeled into view on the ends of twirling cables over the heads of the audience. The grand finale, "The World of Entertainment — MGM," was capped by a *real* lion (presumably MGM's own) on a pedestal for perhaps the wildest curtain call ever devised.
>
> Nowhere else in the world of show business will you see anything like this spectacle. Not only is it lavish, but it is done with taste. Admittedly the book (if there is one) and structure are weak, but selectivity and imagination have been combined to make this one not to miss.[120]

Hello, Hollywood was the work of New York City lighting designer John McLain. The light plot is shown in Fig. 5.43. Color Fig. 33 is a production photo from this revue. Color Figs. 34, 35, and 36 are from *Grand Hotel,* the production preceding *Hello, Hollywood* at the MGM Grand Hotel in Reno (designed by New York City's Jules Fisher).

On a smaller scale, Figs. 5.44, 5.45, and 5.46 are from a *Folies Bergères* production by Nevada designer Robert Kiernan at the Tropicana Hotel in Las Vegas in 1976. It is a more typical Las Vegas revue.

Theatre people in Las Vegas or Atlantic City tend to be isolated from each other, and often do not even see the show playing next door. This is understandable; almost all casino-hotels offer two shows per night, seven days a week, leaving very little time for workers to "see what the others are doing." While casino-hotels spend money quite freely for splash and splendor — anything that the audience can see — they are too often reluctant to invest in necessary backstage facilities and equipment. Beautiful bodies, big stars, flashy costumes, nudity, elaborate scenery — and every lighting effect and trick in the book — is the order of the day. Nevada show business is a come-on and an adjunct for the gambling, but never the main attraction. This posi-

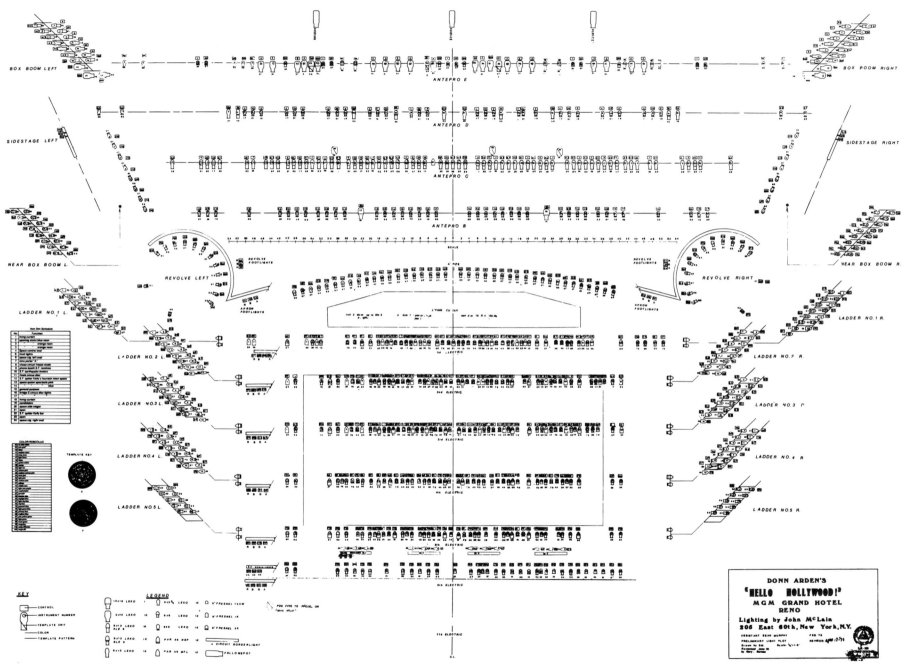

Figure 5.43 *Hello, Hollywood, Hello* at the MGM Grand Hotel in Reno, Nevada in 1978. Lighting designer: John McLain.

Figure 5.44 *Folies Bergères* at the Tropicana Hotel in Las Vegas, Nevada, in 1976. Producer: Alan Lee; director and choreography: Jerry Jackson; costumes: Nolan Miller; scenic design: William Morris; lighting design: Bob Kiernan.

Figure 5.45 (TOP RIGHT) *Folies Bergères.*

Figure 5.46 *Folies Bergères.*

tion in the hierarchy *does* make a difference. While big money *may* be spent, in the vast majority of the Nevada casino-hotels one will still find much that is lighted with rows of borderlights and footlights; garish use of color, rather than tasteful; and excessive emphasis on effects — basically, flashy illumination that is short on the true showmanship values implicit in tasteful lighting design. One can find the finest facilities and the best of revue lighting design next door to poor remanents of bygone vaudeville from another era.

Mention should also be made of the continued existence of the original grand home of the revue: New York City's Radio City Music Hall. Opened in 1932 as a "family entertainment" place to feature films and a live stage show, the Music Hall has fallen upon hard times. It is, however, still open and newly refurbished — and still offering the sedate version of revue.

Little more needs to be said about designing for revues. Revue lighting should be a combination of the best of lighting for musicals and dance, with a dash of effects and spectacle thrown in. Revues are meant to amuse and entertain and astound. And they do.

Operetta

Operetta is basically amusing, smaller opera. Usually comic in nature, it has a smaller orchestra than regular opera and deals in melody, music, and story line which are much less than grand tragedy. It is the farce/comedy section of the opera world. Not that it isn't popular. Every large city seems to have a Gilbert & Sullivan society producing at least one show a year. The St. Louis Municipal Opera (outdoors each summer) thrives on operetta. Many large grand opera companies throw one or two operettas into their season. Operettas mean packed houses, and they tend to reach a new, larger audience.

My lighting design for Johann Strauss Jr.'s *One Night In Venice* at the Pabst Theatre in Milwaukee is typical of lighting used for this genre. Figures 5.47 and 5.48 present the light plot and hookup. Color Figs. 37 through 46 offer full-stage views of the resultant lighting for selected key cues throughout the production. Portions of my text for "Gen-

esis of an Opera," from *Lighting Dimensions,* May 1981, will help make these views more useful for study:

One Night In Venice is the third most popular Johann Strauss, Jr. operetta in Europe, but is rarely produced in this country. It had been produced in New York as *A Wonderful Night* in 1929 and again in 1937, as *Venice At Night* in 1945, and as *A Night In Venice* by Todd at Jones Beach's Marine Theatre during the summer of 1952. However, this was to be a new translation by producer Colin Cabot of the Milwaukee Skylight Comic Opera, Ltd., with adaptation by director Roger Sullivan to be presented at Milwaukee's Pabst Theatre.

Scripts were forwarded to me February 16, along with all necessary technical and design information. We agreed to meet in Milwaukee a week later. With that information in hand, I was unable to resist doing a preliminary light plot and switchboard layout before going to Milwaukee. I already had plans for the opening scene (dry ice fog and a gaudy sunset fading rapidly into night) and the finale (a huge carnival fireworks display partly projected on a thick, moving fog curtain in front of the cyc). Actually, this preliminary study became the final plot although it was done prior to seeing either the theatre or a run-through.

I found Colin to be a charming, knowledgeable man of 30 with the appearance and enthusiasm of a teenager, not at all the elderly opera impresario I had expected. He is the glue that holds Skylight together. Harvard-trained, he is constructively busy 24 hours a day raising money, translating, selling tickets, loading trucks, overseeing every detail, and always available to answer any questions or make any needed decision. Beyond that, he makes a brief cameo appearance in each of his operas; he is the very tall Stilt-Walker in this production (see photographs).

A rapid tour of the Pabst Theatre followed. It is a charming, older unionized legit house, recently completely refurbished. Equipped with a new switchboard and adequate lighting equipment, it has a modest-sized orchestra pit and seats just under 1400 people. Front lights in more than sufficient numbers were located on a relatively high-angle balcony front position with good F-O-H side boom pipes at the end.

A complete cast run-through followed. I annotated my script with notes on all major light changes — actually the exact ones we ended up using. Details of available budget (color media, effects rental, etc.), design fee, housing, and transportation were agreed upon for submission as a letter of agreement to USA #350 (the local union).

I was upset that our budget allowed for only eight stagehands for two days of straight time set-up. This meant that in 16 working hours, eight stagehands from IATSE #18 were to fit up three complete sets of scenery, dress it, hang and focus nearly 140 pieces of lighting equipment, and write cue sheets. I was doubtful that this could be accomplished with the allotted crew size and set-up time.

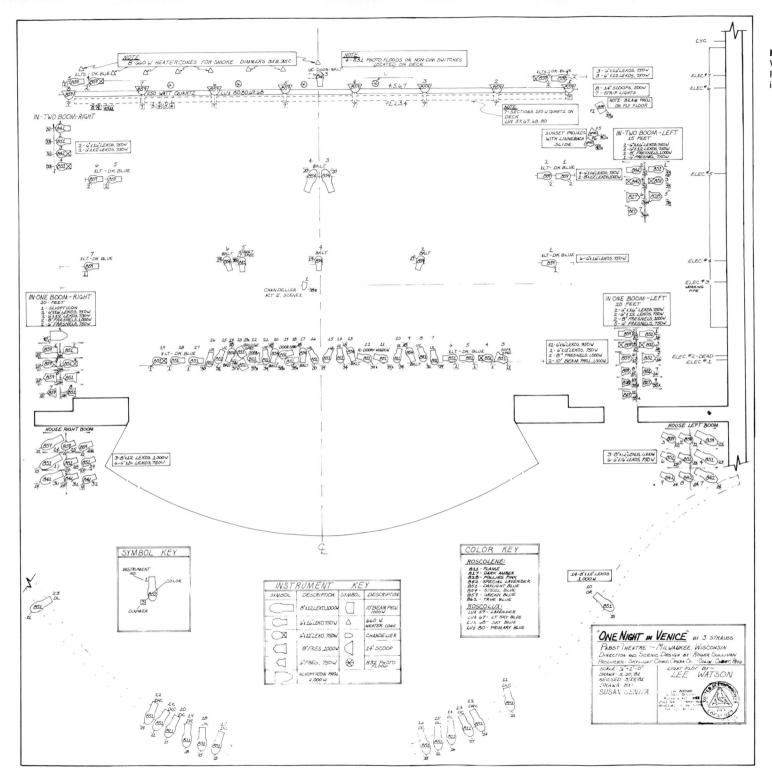

Figure 5.47 (RIGHT) Light plot by Lee Watson for *One Night in Venice* at the Pabst Theatre in Milwaukee, Wisconsin, in 1981.

Returning to Indiana, I began the search for the now approved "moving fireworks projection." Most firms had long ago discarded sciopticons in favor of the more efficient Great American Scene Machines. While these would undoubtedly be better than the older sciopticon effect head, the weekly rental price plus shipping would bring the total cost of a 2½-week rental for two units to over $1000, an amount in excess of our budget.

But as luck would have it, my old Yale classmate, Charles Levy of Strand Century, had carefully removed all of Century's 18-inch diameter sciopticon hand-painted effects discs and stored them in a locker before Strand Century junked the sciopticons themselves. Although he would not rent to me, he did loan two fireworks effects discs to me if I guaranteed their safe return. So problem number one was solved. Problem number two, where to obtain the sciopticons themselves, was resolved by renting from Kliegl. In my opinion, the older sciopticon would be bright enough to achieve the necessary effect. Our fireworks burst on the cyc (on both sides of the right column arch) is shown in illustration. The finale was smashing when bursts of intense colored light from R-32 Photoflood lamps were added to the multiple images on the disc-slide in rising motion and projected upon both the moving smoke curtain as well as on the cyc behind it.

On my return to Milwaukee on the first of March, the eight stagehands were busy finding out what needed to be done, breaking into small work teams (Milwaukee works "across department lines"). All of Monday went to hanging and cabling the lights and to assembling scenery prior to yielding the stage to the cast for an evening of "worklight" orchestra rehearsal.

The only shattering event of Monday was the discovery that the Kliegl rented sciopticon was missing the circular slide holder and motor drive. Frantic phone calls followed until we discovered that Midwest Scenic and Stage Equipment Co., Ltd., right there in Milwaukee, had a large stock of sciopticons and lamps. Shortly thereafter, John Dolphin, owner of Midwest, turned up at the theatre with a replacement lamp and effects disc.

On Tuesday morning, with an opening the next evening, in spite of really concentrated efforts by everyone involved, when it came time to go into the orchestra dress none of the four backstage booms had yet been focused. With the cast, sets, and costumes there, we did set all the light cues for Act I in final form and roughed out and recorded basic set-ups for Act II, with light levels for the booms to be added later. Keith Griswold, IATSE #18 electrician/stagehand, who is a top switchboard operator and a fine setup man, was of valuable assistance throughout, as was my assistant Susan Senita whose task Monday was to cut some 350 frames of color media.

On Tuesday, John Dolphin returned with some 30 sciopticon objective lenses from his stock. The projector had been relocated to the top of the #1 Stage right boom to get the best shot at the largest possible cyc area, yet avoiding the overhead teaser-

Figure 5.48 Switchboard hookup for *One Night in Venice*.

SWITCHBOARD LAYOUT: "One Night In Venice" by J. Strauss.   March 4, 1981.
For: Skylight Comic Opera Ltd., Milwaukee, Wisc.   PABST THEATRE.

Dimmer No.	Instrument Key Nos.	Units	Color	Focus
#1	2P4,5,6,27,28,29 4P1,7	#2 Elect: 6 --6x16" #4 Elect: 2--6x16"	859	Xlts., Entire--Dark Blue Pipe Ends, Dwnstg.
#2	5P1,2,5,6 7P1,2,4,5		859	Xlts., Entire--Dark Blue Pipe Ends, Upstg.
#3	6P4	#6 Elect: 7 sect. Xrays	Lux80	Cyc Top, Dark Blue
#4	6P5	#6 Elect: 7 sect. Xrays	Lux80	Cyc Top, Dark Blue
#5	6P6	#6 Elect: 7 sect. Xrays	Lux67	Cyc Top, Lt. Sky Blue
#6	6P7	#6 Elect: 7 sect. Xrays	Lux68	Cyc Top, Sky Blue
#7	6P1-3,8-12	#6 Elect: 8 Scoops, 500w.	859	Cyc Top, Moonlt, Blue-Green
#8	F1	Floor: 7 sects. Xrays	Lux80	Cyc Base, Dark Blue
#9	F2	Floor: 7 sects. Xrays	Lux57	Cyc Base, Lavendur
#10	F3	Floor: 7 sects. Xrays	Lux67	Cyc Base, Lt. Sky Blue
#11	F4	Floor: 7 sects. Xrays	Lux68	Cyc Base, Sky Blue
#12	R1-3,24-26	Booms,L&R: 2--8x12";4--6x16"	859	FRONT Xlts., Dark Blue
#13	R4-6,27-29	Booms,L&R: 2--8x12";4--6x16"	851	FRONT Xlts., Daylt. Blue
#14	R7-9,30-32	Booms,L&R: 2--8x12";4--6x16"	842	FRONTS Xlt., Spec. Lavendur
#15	LB2,4,6,8 RB1,3,5,7	Booms,#1 L&R: 2--6x16"; 2-- 6x12";2--6" Fres.;2--8" Fresnels	859	"In One" Booms, Moonlt. Blue Green
#16	LB1,3,5,7 RB2,4,6,8	Booms,#1 L&R: 2--6x16"; 2-- 6x12";2--6" Fres.; 2-- 8" Fresnels	851	"In One" Booms, Daylt. Blue
#17				Toning Strips, cut from show
#18	2P9,13,17,20,24	#2 Elect: 5--6x16"	854	Bklts.,Dwnstg.,Steel Blue
#19	4P2,4,6	#4 Elect: 3--6x16"	854	Bklts.,Midstg.,Steel Blue
#20	5P3,4	#5 Elect: 2--8x12"	854	Bklts.,Upstg., Steel Blue
#21	R15,23	Rail: 2--8x12"	851	DL FRONTS, Daylt. Blue
#22	R11,21	Rail: 2--8x12"	851	DLC FRONTS, Daylt. Blue
#23	R16,17	Rail: 2--8x12"	851	DC FRONTS, Daylt. Blue
#24	R12,22	Rail: 2--8x12"	851	DRC FRONTS, Daylt. Blue
#25	R10,18	Rail: 2--8x12"	851	DR FRONTS, Daylt. Blue
#26	R14	Rail: 1--8x12"	811	DL FRONTS, Flame
#27	R13,20	Rail: 2--8x12"	811	DC FRONTS, Flame
#28	R19	Rail: 1--8x12"	811	DR FRONTS, Flame
#29	2P7,15	#2 Elect: 2--6x16"	851	UL Area, Daylt. Blue
#30	2P16,26	#2 Elect: 2--6x16"	851	UR Area, Daylt. Blue
#31	2P8,25	#2 Elect: 2--6x16"	851	Ext. UC Area, Daylt. Blue
#32	#2 Boom,L: 2,4 #2 Boom,R: 1,3	#2 Booms,L&R: 2--6x16"; 2--6x12"	842	"In Two" Boom,Spec. Lav.
#33	#2 Boom,L: 1,3 #2 Boom,R: 2,4	#2 Booms,L&R: 2--6x16"; 2--6x12"	851	"In Two" Booms, Daylt. Blue
#34	2P10,14,21	#2 Elect: 3---6x12"	811	Upstg. Areas, Flame
#35A	#1 Boom,L: 9÷11	#1 Boom,L: 1--8" Fres.; 2--6" Fres.	817 828	Sunset, Pink & Amber (act I)
#36A	#2 Boom,L: 5-7	#2 Boom,L: 1--8" Fres.; 2--6" Fres.	817 828	Sunset, Pink & Amber (Act I)
#37A	2P23, 23A, F1	#2 Elect: 2--10" Beam Projs. Fly Floor: 1--10" BP	851 859	Bridge Specs., Daylt. Blue & Moonlt. Blue-Gn.(I)
#38A	2P18,19	#2 Elect: 2--6x16"	851	Bal. & Door Specs., L (I)
#39A	2P11,12	#2 Elect: 2--6x16"	851	Bal. & Door Specs., R (I)
#40A	F5,6 (on deck)	2--6" Fres. (remove lenses)	Slide	Sunset Linnebach, UL (I)
#35B	On deck	4--Heater cones, 660w. @		Smoke curtain, II-2
#36B	On deck	4--Heater cones, 660w. @		Smoke curtain, II-2
#37B	2P3,22	#2 Elect: 2--8" Fresnels	851	Sofa Spec., Act II-1
#38B	3P1	#3 Elect: Pract. Chandelier		Working Chand., II-1
#39B	7P3	#7 Elect: 1--6x16"	862	Ext.UC Door Bklt., Dark Blue
#38C	4P5	#4 Elect: 1--6x16"	811	Street Lamp Spec., II-2
#40C	#1 Boom, R	2000w. Sciopticon (Proj.)		Fireworks Disc, Effect II-2

On NON-DIMS: Proj. Fan Motor; Dry Ice Fog Machines (I); Fireworks Bursts (R-32s) (I)

121 *Excerpted and abridged from this author's "Genesis of an Opera,"* Lighting Dimensions, *vol. 5, no. 4 (May 1981), pp. 17–19, 21–23. Illus., color. Contains more complete text, light plot, switchboard layout, and three pages of color photographs, including several not included here.*

borders, side-masking legs, and set units. This required a new focal-length objective.

During Tuesday's dress rehearsal I had seen what I need to see—the effect of lights, color, and circuits on the costumed performers in front of the scenery. All basic cue levels had been recorded during dress.

On Wednesday, little time was left to finalize Act I cue sheets. Since director Sullivan had seen and approved of the general direction I was going in lighting design, it was agreed upon that I would be in the light booth with Keith Griswold during Wednesday evening's opening night performance to give final shape to the light cues for Act II during the performance. At the same time,

I could give the stage manager the exact location and time count for each cue, to be recorded in his script.

On opening night all ran smoothly and the audience could never have been aware that the lighting had not been recorded in stone for weeks.

While *One Night In Venice* is far from a major opera, it is fun with delightful music and lots of spectacle and humor. The opening sunset and the fireworks finale are challenging for any lighting designer. And while the Pabst Theatre is certainly not the Met Opera, it is a standard union house typical of the conditions lighting designers constantly encounter in their careers.[121]

PLATE 1 Projection for Act IV of *Carmen*, New Jersey State Opera. Projections, scenery, and lighting by Lee Watson. *(Photo: Steve Satterwhite)*

PLATE 2 Projection for Act II of *Carmen*. *(Photo: Steve Satterwhite)*

PLATE 3 Projection for Act I of *Carmen*. *(Photo: Steve Satterwhite)*

PLATE 4 Background projections. Original drawing used at Queen Elizabeth Theatre in Vancouver, Canada, for the North American premiere of Benjamin Britten's opera, *Midsummer Night's Dream,* August 1961. Scenery, costumes, and projections designed by Harry Horner; lighting design by Lee Watson.

PLATE 5 *Midsummer Night's Dream.*

PLATE 6 Projections replacing dye-painted scrim in *Tosca,* November 1975; New Jersey State Opera, Symphony Hall, Newark, New Jersey. Director: Jim Lucas; lighting design: Lee Watson; projections: Van Phillips.

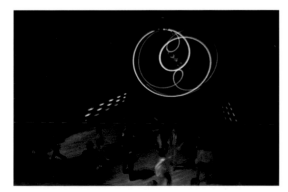

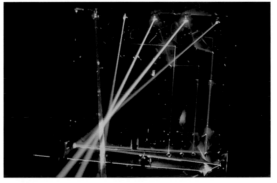

PLATE 7 Laser lighting by Science Faction Corporation, Inc. *(Photo: © Tetsu Okuhara)*

PLATE 8 Mixed-gas laser projection using an argon-krypton laser. Designed by Richard V. Werth and Steve Hectman of Spectrolaze, Los Angeles.

PLATE 9 An early use of fiber optics in the commercial theatre: Richard Pilbrow's fiber optics backdrop for the ill-fated musical, *Swing,* in Washington, D.C.

PLATE 10   *Electra* (1976), Purdue University Experimental Theatre. Lighting by Bridget Beier.

PLATE 13   *Tiny Alice* by Edward Albee (July 1968), University of Wisconsin at Madison. Sets and lighting designed by John Wright Stevens.

PLATE 11   *A Streetcar Named Desire* (1974), Picadilly Theatre, London. Director: Edwin Sherlin; scene designer: Patrick Robertson; costumes: Beatrice Dawson; lighting design: Richard Pilbrow; starring: Claire Bloom.

PLATE 14   *A Midsummer Night's Dream* (March 1976), Samford University, Birmingham, Alabama. Sets and lighting designed by Barbara and Eric Olson.

PLATE 16   *Romeo and Juliet* (November 1976), Rarig Center, Whitting Proscenium Theatre, University of Minnesota. Set design: Wendall Josal; lighting design: Jean A. Montgomery.

PLATE 12   *The Tempest* (Spring 1977), Loeb Playhouse, Purdue University. Director: Dale E. Miller; scene design: Van Phillips; costumes: Janice Stauffer; lighting design: Susan Dandridge.

PLATE 15   *Under Milk Wood* by Dylan Thomas, University of Michigan Theatre, Ann Arbor. Director: Caribel Baird; set designer: Alan Billings; costumes: Zelma Weisfeld; lighting design: R. Craig Wolf. *(Courtesy of Alan Billings.)*

PLATE 17   *Macbeth*, Miami University Theatre. Lighting by Geoffrey D. Fishburn.

PLATE 18   Metropolitan Opera production of *Tannhauser* by Wagner, December 1977. Director: Otto Schenk; scenic design: Gunter Schnieder-Sienssen; costumes: Patricia Zipprodt; lighting design: Gil Wechsler. *(Photo: James Hefferman)*

PLATE 19   *Salome* (1978), Santa Fe Opera. Director: Bliss Herbert; sets and costumes: A. Charles Klein; lighting design: Steven Ross.

PLATE 20   *L'Incorona Zione de Poppea* (November 1966), Dallas Civic Opera. Director: Peter Hall; scenic design: Attilio Colonnello; costumes: Luciana Novaro; lighting design: Nananne Porcher.

PLATE 21   *Prince Igor* (October 1962), Chicago Lyric Opera, Italian production. Director: Valadim Rosing; scenic design: Nichola Benois; lighting design: Nananne Porcher. Dancer Nureyev's North American premeire.

PLATE 22   *L'Incorona Zione de Poppea* (November 1966), Dallas Civic Opera. Director: Peter Hall; scenic design: Attilio Colonnelo; lighting design: Nananne Porcher.

PLATE 23   A 12-count build of lavender and pink crosslights, plus lavender front lights and light blue crosslights on the rear strings. The wing structure flies in. *(Photo: Robert Reid)*

PLATE 24   A 15-count build to full-up to pink and lavender crosslights for the *pas de deux*. Crosslighting on the strings is decreased. *(Photo: Robert Reid)*

PLATE 25   A 30-count build of blue crosslights to full with an increase of intensity on the cyc and pink crosslights on the strings added. *(Photo: Robert Reid)*

PLATE 26   A 30-count change to a red cyc with the closing and the wings moved to a new position. *(Photo: Robert Reid)*

PLATE 27 A 3-count bump-down to blue crosslight and full-up on an intense white (no color) pool of backlight on the strings. The wings moved to a high position. (*Photo: Robert Reid*)

PLATE 28 Cues 12 and 13: the final two cues, building in 28 counts to a bright pink full-up as the fans and wings move back to their original positions in sight. Cue 14 is a bump-off to black. (*Photo: Robert Reid*)

PLATE 29 *In Memory of Dear Companions* (September 1978), Schoenberg Hall, Momentum Dance Company at the Los Angeles Dance Festival, UCLA. Choreography: Carol Shiffman; lighting design: Fred Allen.

PLATE 30 *Quicksilver.*

PLATE 31 *Peter Pan* by John Munsell (November 1976), University of Wisconsin at Superior. Scenic design: Stewart Platner; lighting design: John J. Drott.

PLATE 32 *Jesus Christ Superstar.* New York City Broadway production. Lighting by Jules Fisher.

PLATE 33   *Hello, Hollywood, Hello;* MGM Grand Hotel, Reno. Production design: Brian Bartholomew and Ray Klausen; costumes: Bill Cambell and Pete Menefee; lighting design: John McLain.

PLATE 34   *Grand Hotel Revue;* MGM Grand Hotel, Reno. Lighting by Jules Fisher.

PLATE 35   *Grand Hotel Revue.*

PLATE 36   *Grand Hotel Revue.*

PLATE 37 *One Night in Venice.* Cue 1 with "follow" completed. Full-stage view showing dry-ice fog on the acting area and the Linnebach sunset projection behind the bridge. *(Photo: Mark Avery)*

PLATE 38 Cue 2: Full-up, sun already set, but late day in top moments of *One Night in Venice.* *(Photo: Mark Avery)*

PLATE 39 Cue 9: Light level for night, used throughout the remainder of Act I. *(Photo: Mark Avery)*

PLATE 40 Three views of the progressive one-minute light change as the set revolved between Scenes 1 and 2 of Act II in full view of the audience. *(Photos: Mark Avery)*

PLATE 41

PLATE 42

PLATE 43 Cue 21: Act II, Scene 1. Large group lighted upstage of the set of columns. This "ballroom" area was used often. *(Photo: Mark Avery)*

PLATE 44 Cue 44: Beginning of the darkening of the cyc. *(Photo: Mark Avery)*

PLATE 45 Cue 47: The fireworks finale. A projection of a fireworks burst is to be seen on both sides of the arch column upstage right (behind the street lamp). These projections were in continuous motion and appeared brighter to the audience than they do in this photograph. *(Photo: Mark Avery)*

PLATE 47 *Hill Cumorah Pageant (American Witness for Christ)*, "Destruction" scene, Palmyra, New York.

PLATE 46 Another view of cue 47: A burst of colored light from R-32 photoflood lamps on the cyc and sal ammoniac smoke curtain in front of the cyc for the final fireworks display. *(Photo: Mark Avery)*

PLATE 48a Italy's Arena di Verona during opera performance.

PLATE 48 Production of *La Gioconda* at the Arena di Verona, Verona, Italy.

PLATE 49 *Le Bourgeois Gentlemen* at American Conservatory Theatre (ACT), San Francisco, California, 1976. Director: William Ball; scenic design: Richard Seger; costumes: John Conklin; lighting design: Richard Devin.

PLATE 50 *Richard III.* Richard's nightmare scene, when all those he has murdered appear in his dream in silhouette. Lighting: Lee Watson. *(Photo: Mark von Wehrden)*

PLATE 51 *Richard III.* Scene from the numerous battle sequences. Smoke and rapid light cues presented a surrealistic scene during the battles. Richard lies dead center stage and victorious Richmond is on the "inner above". *(Photo: Mark von Wehrden)*

PLATE 52 *The Merry Wives of Windsor.* Final scene with Falstaff appearing through the magic door in the garden tree at midnight, disguised as Herne the Hunter. Lighting: Lee Watson. *(Photo: Mark von Wehrden)*

PLATE 53 *Merry Wives.* Same scene as in Plate 52, with the disguised fairies dancing about Falstaff tormenting him with their tapers; "inner above" also used. *(Photo: Mark von Wehrden)*

PLATE 54 *All's Well That Ends Well.* Exterior scene with sunlight leaf gobos. Lighting: Lee Watson. *(Photo: Mark von Wehrden)*

PLATE 55 *All's Well.* Scene using both forestage and full-stage depth. *(Photo: Mark von Wehrden)*

PLATE 56 *All's Well.* Full-stage scene set in Florence, Italy, with richly colored streamers unfurled in the background. *(Photo: Mark von Wehrden)*

PLATE 57 *All's Well.* Final curtain call, back in France with strings of garland lights on palace scene; principals in specials and portion of cast in silhouette. *(Photo: Mark von Wehrden)*

Chapter 6

Other Theatrical Forms

There are several specialized theatrical production forms and situations which do not readily fit into the category of nonmusical performance theatre, musical theatre, or any other production type presented in this *Handbook*. Among these forms are outdoor theatre (with its own special design problems), mime, miniature stages, children's theatre, repertory theatre production, and touring. An understanding of the special problems involved in each of these forms is an important part of a lighting designer's training, since these forms offer employment opportunities to the working lighting professional.

Outdoor Theatre

Mostly a summer activity in the United States, outdoor theatre came into prominence around 1900 when intense night illumination had become feasible. Since neither TV sets nor radios existed then, local entertainment consisted of (1) numerous local opera houses with theatres offering burlesque and vaudeville, and (2) socializing at the local tavern. (For the more serious-minded, there were religious revival meetings and Women's Christian Temperance Union meetings.) Citizens banded together to provide their own amusement. Stemming partly from a desire for festival or outing (as did the original Greek theatre) and partly from local pride (historical pageants, band concerts, choral groups — anyone who could "hold an audience"), community entertainment became popular. Many of today's well-known artists in theatre lighting started their careers with outdoor productions. Claude Bragdon designed "Song and Light" shows throughout the country for large choral groups. Ted Fuchs was active in outdoor historical pageants, as was Stanley R. McCandless.

Spectacle has usually been a major ingredient in any outdoor attraction for a large crowd. Even today, summer musical revivals at New York City's Jones Beach theatre end in fireworks displays.

Outdoor theatre has taken many forms from just plain pageantry through comedies, musicals, operettas, and operas. The St. Louis Municipal Opera is one. Jones Beach in New York City is another, and the Miller Outdoor Theatre in Houston yet another. The United States offers a multitude of historical dramas/pageants (*Lost Colony* in North Carolina is the ever-popular granddaddy). Dance and vaudeville are still to be found outdoors. There are numerous highly successful summer Shakespeare festivals. The Santa Fe Opera is world-famous. And the name Woodstock, New York, is enough to make almost anyone picture massive gatherings of young people at an outdoor summer concert.

Outdoor theatre during the winter months is in short supply in the United States. One would expect to find it prevalent in the sunny South or the far West, but such is not the case. Outdoor theatre is an important area of employment in its many different forms, but primarily during the summer months.

Design Considerations

Two basic elements affect outdoor productions: *size* and *weather*.

Outdoor theatre is large in scale. The average theatre is 1,500 to 3,000 seats; larger outdoor performance spaces accommodate 12,000 to 15,000 or more. The lighting required calls for units with more "punch" for longer throw distances. Broad design strokes rather than deft intimate touches are needed. Dramatic material must be bold, for it is difficult to convey subtleties. Outdoor drama usually consists of (1) historical or theme pageants, (2) musical comedy, (3) classics (Greek drama, Shakespeare), and (4) opera,[122] operetta, dance, and revues. Only infrequently do the works of Shaw, Schiller, Pinter, and Neil Simon or the standard Broadway comedies appear in outdoor production.

The alfresco nature of the performance site necessarily affects the lighting. The designer must focus lights after dark and plan accordingly. Many performances begin *before* dusk, and lighting levels can be affected well into Act I before darkness takes over. Performances can be rained out. I remember an evening performance at Long Island's Jones Beach Marine Stadium when ocean fog drifted in.[123] It was a magnificent sight for the 300 of us present in the 8,500-seat amphitheatre. Each shaft of colored light became crystal clear in space, creating a whole new wonderland for "lovers of light." In Bergenz, Austria, I saw *Flying Dutchman* in the rain. The stage was floating on Lake Constance, with the audience on the shore. The opera assumed an unequalled magical aura. A photograph of this production, not taken in the rain (Fig. 6.1), hardly captures the charm of that particular performance.

Communication Forms

Standard theatre light plots, switchboard hookup sheets, focus charts, and cue sheets are used for outdoor theatre. There are exceptions; for example, *Lost Colony* is focused from photographs taken the prior season. There are now few outdoor theatres at which the lighting is improvised or "worked out" without formalized plots and preplanning. Frequently the planning may only involve a basic season

repertory plot for all productions. Individual planning, per production, allocates specials. This is common in many outdoor theatres presenting a season of musical comedies. Season plots exist for such established places as the St. Louis Municipal Opera and many Starlight Theatres (Kansas City, Indianapolis) around the United States.

Techniques

Finding suitable places to mount lighting instruments is important and sometimes challenging. Since the usual theatre structure (proscenium, grid, auditorium ceiling) is not present, lights are mounted (1) in trees (low-budget) or on light towers around the audience seating area; (2) on light booths, bridges, or towers behind the audience; (3) in the usual footlight position; (4) on towers (stationary or on casters) on the sides of the stage opening and backstage within that structure; (5) around and on the scenery; and (6) on the ground or in a pit/trough upstage at the cyc/backdrop position. Backlighting is usually not possible. Lighting from a high, steep angle or from directly overhead is out of the question. Frontlighting tends to come from a flat, too-low angle and from too far away. Crosslighting therefore is very important. Accessibility for focus, adjustment, repair, and color is vital. All of these considerations clearly affect the lighting design.

The necessity for powerful luminaires for long throw distances changes instrumentation choice. Ordinarily the playing area (stage) is large-scale: 100 or more feet wide and quite deep. The vast audience assembly area usually places the nearest FOH (front-of-house) lights far from the stage. Powerful arc follow spotlights are needed. Front lights must be 3000- to 5000-watt elipsoidals rather than the 750-watt unit that is common indoors. Lenses are 10 to 12 inches in diameter, rather than the 6-inch size used indoors. Powerful 1000-watt PAR-64s in NSP (narrow spot) are vital, and older-style beam projectors also have a place. Backstage the 5-kilowatt and 10-kilowatt Fresnel is useful along with the more common 8-inch (2000-watt) Fresnel. The standard 6-inch Fresnel functions in outdoor theatre only as an "on set" special (replacing the 3-inch Fresnel used indoors). Footlights and cyc floodlights need to be of a heavier wattage than for indoors, and when it is necessary to

[122] *"Santa Fe Opera, Part II — Stephen Ross,"* Lighting Dimensions, *vol. 2, no. 1 (Jan. 1978), pp. 30–37.*

[123] *For photo and plan see Rubin and Watson, pp. 77–78, op. cit. (see footnote 3 or 125).*

Figure 6.1 Wagner's *Flying Dutchman* in 1975 on Lake Constance at Bregenz, Austria. (*Photo: © Foto-Hotter*)

Figure 6.2 Theatre Under the Stars (TUTS) *Gypsy.* Lighting design by Lee Watson. (*Courtesy of Frank Young/TUTS.*)

Figure 6.3 TUTS's *Boyfriend,* with Lee Watson's lighting. (*Courtesy of Frank Young/TUTS.*)

create comfortable, incisive visibility for an audience of 12,000, wattage increases. During my five years as lighting designer with the outdoor Miller Theatre in Hermann Park (Houston, Texas) we frequently checked visibility from the top of the hill, *behind* the seating area for 12,000 customers (or even, at times, from the overhanging balconies of the nearby hotel—a person couldn't *hear* from there, but we felt that someone that distance away ought to be able to *see*). Figures 6.2 and 6.3 are from those productions. Throw distances are long, and narrow beam spreads are important. The audience *must* be able to see clearly and easily, and this principle takes precedence over mood or effects.

The frequent absence of a "front curtain" necessitates other solutions. Two options are either a "light curtain" (striplights aimed *toward* the audience to momentarily blind the people while actors exit following the blackout at the end of a scene) or a "water curtain" (lights playing upon a controlled sheet of water at the curtain line—subject to the vagaries of wind and weather). Neither option is very satisfactory. Modern audiences adjust more readily to a simple blackout.

Equipment for outdoor theatre use is specialized in other respects. Weather and moisture are major considerations. Lighting units must frequently be cleaned. They must either be protected from rain, or else holes must be drilled in the instrument body to allow drainage. They must be painted often to minimize ever-present rusting. They tend to depreciate rapidly. Cables cannot have asbestos leads, since wet asbestos is a conductor, not an insulator. Cables must be rubber-covered and three-wire, grounded. Rain and moisture make this vital for *all* units used outdoors. This also means that all connectors need to be waterproof (usually three-prong, waterproof twist locks). Color media must be either glass (heat-resistant Pyrex) or one of the newer waterproof plastics, well-supported in color frames. With the high intensities used (PAR-64 lamps, for instance) which result in rapid fading, color media becomes a big expense item.

Outdoor theatres require larger switchboards with adequate load-carrying capacity and flexibility. Cost of control often leads to sacrifice of subtlety. Tiny "design touches" amount to very little for an audience of 15,000. Frequently a season plan of area control, crosslighting, cyc lighting, and specials is what is most needed. This is not meant to imply that striking, creative, imaginative lighting design is never to be found in outdoor theatres. The Hill Cumorah *America's Witness for Christ* pageant by the Church of Jesus Christ of the Latter Day Saints (Mormon) presented on four evenings each August in Palmyra, New York, is one of the most brilliant outdoor performances I have ever seen (see Figs. 6.4,

Figure 6.4 *Hill Cumorah Pageant (America's Witness for Christ)* at Palmyra, New York: "Christ's Arrest" scene. (*Photo:* © Rolf Photography, Inc.)

Figure 6.4a *Hill Cumorah Pageant.* (*Photo:* © Rolf Photography, Inc.)

6.4a, and Color Fig. 47). It is inspiring (and humbling) to remember that brilliant design work was being offered in outdoor pageants by Claude Bragdon and Theodore Fuchs as long ago as World War I (1916 to 1918), when lighting equipment and sources were primitive.

Procedures and Practices

Both visibility and spectacle play a large part in successful outdoor theatre lighting. Jones Beach each year packs an 8,500-seat theatre, the Marine Stadium, with the stage out on the water of Long Island Sound. Grandiose sets, lavish costumes, and a large cast combine with the use of the water between the stage and the audience. Underwater divers have been used; full stage sets sail — under their own power — into view for *Showboat.* The evening always ends with a fireworks display.

The skillful dramatic imagination of Theatre-Under-the-Stars (TUTS) producer Frank Young (Miller Theatre, Hermann Park, Houston) resulted in *South Pacific* being presented with half of the orchestra pit converted into a deep swimming pool — with a volcanic mountain and diving board erected on one of the side stages — and dozens of the most skillful and glamorous divers in Texas becoming part of the "Bali Hai" scene. For *Kismet,* Young began Act II with a processional of a cast of 50 (in fantastic Oriental costumes with sedan chairs, ostrich plumes, and a Mardi Gras look) coming slowly out of the nearby woods and moving onto the stage. Each member of the processional carried a lighted candle. It was an unexpected and breathtaking piece of spectacle. For *Gypsy,* Young topped them all. "Miss Electra's" burlesque costume in her big number contained miniature blinking lights (flashlight bulbs) concealed in all the usual places, but, as a climax, when "Miss Electra" did her final bump and grind, a concealed photoflash bulb fired — from the most strategic place possible! At each of the show's 12 nights, this effect brought never less than 10 full minutes of delighted applause. *That* is both spectacle and dramatic imagination.

In many ways, the Miller outdoor theatre in Houston, built and maintained by the city, is typical of most used for musical comedy. The partially covered main seating area holds around 2,000 seats. The sides and back are open so that another 10,000 people can arrange themselves informally on the hillside grass. Sound is amplified. The stagehouse, unlike many, has a proscenium and grid. It is even air-conditioned.

As an experiment, I designed several productions there with basic acting areas colored in the secondaries (cyan or blue-green, magenta, and yellow). The results looked much like the work of Nicholai Cernovitch in dance, and I was

Figure 6.5 *Lost Colony* historical pageant (1979) at Manteo, North Carolina. Lighting design: Nananne Porcher.

Figure 6.6 *Lost Colony;* Act I: "Plymouth Departure."

delighted and surprised by the range of usable saturated color readily available. One need not always light outdoor drama in pale pink, blue, or straw!

Color Fig. 48 shows the opera, *La Giaconda,* presented at the Arena di Verona in Verona, Italy. This huge ancient Roman amphitheatre is the second oldest in the world. Located in the center of the city, it is still in use each summer for really "grand" opera. Color Fig. 48a better shows the size of the amphitheatre. This is opera on huge scale. Few theatre experiences are as exciting as the intermission spectacle (at 2 a.m. under a night sky), when 23,000 people light extra-large wooden matches (distributed as souvenirs with the tickets) in unison. It is much like the intermission spectacle in which the entire audience lights matches at Soldier's Field in Chicago. Notice from the photographs that the lighting design is the equal of indoor production in mood, selective visibility, and dramatic use of light. Skillful use was made of fire and torches. Followspots and careful crosslighting kept the principals in focus.

A typically American outdoor theatre appears in Figs. 6.5 and 6.6, which show the annual *Lost Colony* historical pageant (the original and oldest) at Manteo, North Carolina. Nananne Porcher, lighting designer, provided these photographs. They show the 1979 version of lighting in a production form typical of over 100 annual summer historical dramas presented outdoors throughout the United States.

Outdoor theatre continues to thrive in the Sun Belt.[124]

Figures 6.7 and 6.8 are the light plot and hookup for *Salome* at the Santa Fe Opera done by lighting designer Stephen Ross. Figure 6.9 shows Ross's condensed hookup "cheat sheets." Figures 6.10 through 6.12 present production photos of the set and two scenes.

Not only are outdoor opera, operetta, and musical productions popular in the United States, but there are also numerous alfresco summer seasons of Shakespeare's plays. The Oregon Shakespeare Festival, the Utah Shakespeare Festival, the Shakespeare-in-the-Park by Joe Papp at Central Park in New York City are well-known examples. Summer is also a great time for outdoor theatre productions of both dance and Gilbert & Sullivan operettas. Some outdoor theatres provide many different types of productions on their stages in a single season. Wolf Trap, in Washington, D.C., provides a variety of production types, as does Saratoga Springs, in New York (which has presented ballet, musicals, and so forth, with Pepsico financing).[125]

Puppetry

Puppets (and puppetry) fall into four basic types: *marionettes* (string puppets), *rod puppets, hand puppets,* and *shadow puppets.* Puppets have been called an idealized

[124] *Consult the Institute of Outdoor Drama, University of North Carolina at Chapel Hill, 202 Graham Memorial 052A, Chapel Hill, NC 27514, for a complete listing. The listing is issued annually and gives complete details about many outdoor drama groups.*

[125] *Joel E. Rubin and Leland H. Watson,* Theatrical Lighting Practice. *N.Y.; Theatre Arts Books; 1954. "Open-Air Productions," pp. 67–76.*

Theodore Fuchs, Stage Lighting. *Boston; Little Brown & Co.; 1929. "Lighting Equipment for Outdoor Productions," pp. 203–205. "Outdoor Productions," pp. 452–58.*

Robert Ornbo, "Tattoos, Tournaments and Combined Operations," Cue, *no. 8, (Nov./Dec. 1980), pp. 9, 11. Illus. British designer Robert Ornbo's work on military tattoos.*

"Lighting (Outdoor Drama)," Theatre Crafts, *vol. 7, no. 2 (Mar./Apr. 1973), pp. 25–27.*

"Lighting—More Than a Paper Moon," Theatre Crafts, *vol. 9, no. 4 (Sept. 1975), pp. 26–28.*

"James Laws, Elretham Mysteries," Cue, *no. 2 (Nov./Dec. 1979), pp. 6–8. Illus., color.*

Alex de Jonge, "Swiss Spectacular," TABS, *vol. 36, no. 1 (Spring 1978), pp. 4–7.*

Ron Olson, "The Hill Cumorah Pageant," TABS, *vol. 34, no. 1 (Spring 1976), pp. 8–9.*

Jim Panos, "Germany: The Passion Play at Oberammergau," Travel & Leisure, *Nov. 1983, pp. 68–69. Illus. Produced since 1634, this is the oldest outdoor pageant.*

John Toogood, "Technical Review: Bartholomew Fair/A Midsummer Night's Dream," Sightline, *vol. 21, no. 2 (Autumn 1987), p. 38. Illus. A description of British designer Ian Callander's open air theatre lighting in Regent's Park, London.*

Kathy Matter, "Drama Forecast Improving," Lafayette Journal & Courier, *July 28, 1989. Critic Matter quotes Mark Sumner of the Institute of Outdoor Drama as saying: "So far attendance at outdoor dramas (1989) . . . is down from expectations. Some are as much as 30 percent below average for this time of the season."*

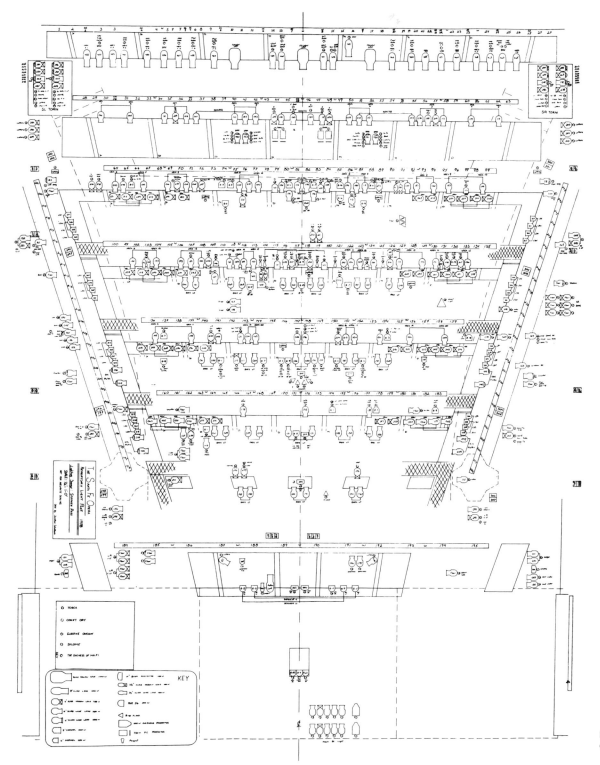

Figure 6.7 Light plot for *Salome* at the Santa Fe Opera. Lighting design by Stephan Ross.

Figure 6.8 *Salome* switchboard hookup.

Hook-Up REP

DIMMER	CIRCUIT	POSITION	TYPE	FOCUS		COLOR
1	31	2ᵈ COVE #046,005	2 - WIDES	A-1	(L)	NC
2	35	2ᵈ COVE #150,008	2 - WIDES	A-2	(L)	NC
3	43	2ᵈ COVE #143,073	2 - WIDES	A-3	(L)	NC
4	65	3ᵈ COVE #033,051	2 - WIDES	A-4	(L)	NC
5	70	3ᵈ COVE #016,012	2 - WIDES	A-5	(L)	NC
6	78	3ᵈ COVE #035,023	2 - WIDES	A-6	(L)	NC
7	102	4ᵗʰ COVE #122,153	2 - WIDES	A-7	(L)	NC
8	107	4ᵗʰ COVE #093,100	2 - WIDES	A-8	(L)	NC
9	114	4ᵗʰ COVE #109,107	2 - WIDES	A-9	(L)	NC
10	138	5ᵗʰ COVE #149,075	2 - WIDES	A-10		NC
11	141	5ᵗʰ COVE #049	1 - WIDE	A-11	(L)	NC
12	145	5ᵗʰ COVE #030,029	2 - WIDES	A-12	(L)	NC
13	47	2ᵈ COVE #028,110	2 - WIDES	A-1	(R)	NC
14	56	2ᵈ COVE #034,113	2 - WIDES	A-2	(R)	NC
15	60	2ᵈ COVE #134,115	2 - WIDES	A-3	(R)	NC
16	85	3ᵈ COVE #094,118	2 - WIDES	A-4	(R)	NC
17	94	3ᵈ COVE #151,052	2 - WIDES	A-5	(R)	NC
18	97	3ᵈ COVE #123,099	2 - WIDES	A-6	(R)	NC
19	121	4ᵗʰ COVE #106,055	2 - WIDES	A-7	(R)	NC
20	128	4ᵗʰ COVE #102,053	2 - WIDES	A-8	(R)	NC
21	132	4ᵗʰ COVE #061,086	2 - WIDES	A-9	(R)	NC
22	150	5ᵗʰ COVE #013,002	2 - WIDES	A-10	(R)	NC
23	153	5ᵗʰ COVE #001	1 - WIDE	A-11	(R)	NC
24	157	5ᵗʰ COVE #001,017	2 - WIDES	A-12	(R)	NC
25	67	3ᵈ COVE #217,213	2 - NAR	HSW-1	(L)	NC
	71	#283	1 - NAR	HSW-1	(L)	NC
26	103	4ᵗʰ COVE #218,220	2 - NAR	HSW-2	(L)	NC
	105	#233	1 - NAR	HSW-2	(L)	NC
27	137	5ᵗʰ COVE #297,286	2 - NAR	HSW-3		NC
	140	#222	1 - NAR	HSW-3	(L)	NC
28	161	6ᵗʰ COVE #85,042	2 - WD³	HSW-4	(L)	NC
	163	#271	1 - NAR	HSW-4	(L)	NC
29	96	3ᵈ COVE #274	2 - NAR	HSW-1	(R)	NC
	93	#263	1 - NAR	HSW-1	(R)	NC
30	134	4ᵗʰ COVE #251,261	2 - NAR	HSW-2	(R)	NC
	130	#225	1 - NAR	HSW-2	(R)	NC
31	158	5ᵗʰ COVE #215,253	2 - NAR	HSW-3	(R)	NC
	155	#216	1 - NAR	HSW-3	(R)	NC
32	181	6ᵗʰ COVE #119,003	2 - WD³	HSW-4	(R)	NC
	178	#211	1 - NAR	HSW-4	(R)	NC
33	66	3ᵈ COVE #231,257	2 - NAR	HSC-1	(L)	NC
	68	#299	1 - NAR	HSC-1	(L)	NC
34	100	4ᵗʰ COVE #258,226	2 - NAR	HSC-2	(L)	NC
	101	#295	1 - NAR	HSC-2	(L)	NC
35	136	5ᵗʰ COVE #249,268	2 - NAR	HSC-3	(L)	NC
	139	#276	1 - NAR	HSC-3	(L)	NC
36	160	6ᵗʰ COVE #163,209	2 - WIDES	HSC-4	(L)	NC
	162	#277	1 - NAR	HSC-4	(L)	NC
37	98	3ᵈ COVE #262,237	2 - NAR	HSC-1	(R)	NC
	95	#243	1 - NAR	HSC-1	(R)	NC
38	135	4ᵗʰ COVE #258,204	2 - NAR	HSC-2	(R)	NC
	131	#295	1 - NAR	HSC-2	(R)	NC
39	159	5ᵗʰ COVE #217,205	2 - NAR	HSC-3	(R)	NC
	156	#221	1 - NAR	HSC-3	(R)	NC
40	182	6ᵗʰ COVE #202,066	2 - WIDES	HSC-4	(R)	NC
	180	#202	1 - NAR	HSC-4	(R)	NC
41	254	TORM L #284,230	2 - NARS	TORM L. W.		NC
	248	#062	1 - WIDE	TORM L. W.		NC
	250					
42	262	TORM R #257,379	2 - NARS	TORM R. W.		NC
	263	#048	1 - WIDE	TORM R. W.		NC
	257					
43	255	TORM L #386,207	2 - NARS	TORM L. C.		NC
	249	#027	1 - WIDE	TORM L. C.		NC
	251					
44	260	TORM R #278,280	2 - NARS	TORM R. C.		NC
	261	#148	1 - WIDE	TORM R. C.		NC
	256					

DIMMER	CIRCUIT	POSITION	TYPE	FOCUS	COLOR
45	217	SL SIDE #320,309	2 - 6" FRES	LSW-1 (L)	NC
46	213	SL SIDE #334,374	2 - 6" FRES	LSW-2 (L)	NC
47	207	SL SIDE #342,323	2 - 6" FRES	LSW-3 (L)	NC
48	201	SL SIDE #332,318	2 - 6" FRES	LSW-4 (L)	NC
49	244	SR SIDE #311,315	2 - 6" FRES	LSW-1 (R)	NC
50	238	SR SIDE #306,301	2 - 6" FRES	LSW-2 (R)	NC
61	106	4ᵗʰ COVE #014,101	2 - WIDES	BL A-1	NC
	111	#067,102	2 - WIDES	BL A-1	NC
62	116	4ᵗʰ COVE #006,05	2 - WIDES	BL A-2	NC
	118	#145,037	2 - WIDES	BL A-2	NC
63	122	4ᵗʰ COVE #132,115	2 - WIDES	BL A-3	NC
	127	#138,070	2 - WIDES	BL A-3	NC
64	142	5ᵗʰ COVE #136,032	2 - WIDES	BL A-4	NC
	144	#111,064	2 - WIDES	BL A-4	NC
65	147	5ᵗʰ COVE #016,056	2 - WIDES	BL A-5	NC
66	151	5ᵗʰ COVE #160,108	2 - WIDES	BL A-6	NC
	154	#089,020	2 - WIDES	BL A-6	NC
67	166	6ᵗʰ COVE #021,029	2 - WIDES	BL A-7	NC
	168	#079,091	2 - WIDES	BL A-7	NC
68	172	6ᵗʰ COVE #121,139	2 - WIDES	BL A-8	NC
69	175	6ᵗʰ COVE #078,130	2 - WIDES	BL A-9	NC
	179	#097,080	2 - WIDES	BL A-9	NC
70	188	7ᵗʰ COVE #142,082	2 - WIDES	BL A-10	NC
81	8	1ˢᵗ COVE #461	1 - 8" Klieg	Fr Area 1	NC
	5	#450	1 - 8" Klieg	Fr Area 4	NC
	7	#467	1 - 8" Klieg	Fr Area 5	NC
	23	#455	1 - 8" Klieg	Fr Area 3	NC
	21	#462	1 - 8" Klieg	Fr Area 4	NC
	24	#468	1 - 8" Klieg	Fr Area 5	NC
82	6	1ˢᵗ COVE #458	1 - 8" Klieg	Fr Area 6	NC
	9	#464	1 - 8" Klieg	Fr Area 7	NC
	25	#469	1 - 8" Klieg	Fr Area 6	NC
	27	#465	1 - 8" Klieg	Fr Area 7	NC
83	253	TORM L #285	1 - NAR (I)	TORM SPEC LT	NC
84	252	TORM L #288	1 - NAR (I)	TORM SPEC LB	NC
85	259	TORM R #282	1 - NAR (I)	TORM SPEC RT	NC
86	258	TORM R #238	1 - NAR (I)	TORM SPEC RB	NC
87	40	2ᵈ COVE #750	1 - 6" 1000 w	6"Klieg Spec 1	NC
88	41	2ᵈ COVE #753	1 - 6" 1000 w	6"Klieg Spec 2	NC
89	49	2ᵈ COVE #751	1 - 6" 1000 w	6" Klieg Spec 3	NC
90	51	2ᵈ COVE #752	1 - 6" 1000 w	6"Klieg Spec 4	NC
91	187	8ᵗʰ COVE #84,34	2 - PAR 56	PAR BK LT	NC
92	193	8ᵗʰ COVE #84,61	2 PAR 56	PAR BK LT	NC
93	2	1ˢᵗ COVE #459	1 - 8" Klieg	8" Spec 1	NC
94	4	1ˢᵗ COVE #456	1 - 8" Klieg	8" Spec 2	NC
95	23	1ˢᵗ COVE #451	1 - 8" Klieg	8" Spec 3	NC
96	26	1ˢᵗ COVE #460	1 - 8" Klieg	8" Spec 4	NC

HOOK-UP SALOME

DIMMER	CIRCUIT	POSITION	TYPE	FOCUS	COLOR
1	31	2ᵈ COVE #046,005	2 - WIDES	A-1 {L}	62
2	35	2ᵈ COVE #150,008	2 WIDES	A-2 {L}	62
3	43	2ᵈ COVE #143,073	2 WIDES	A-3 {L}	03
4	65	3ᵈ COVE #033,051	2 WIDE	A-4 {L}	62
5	70	3ᵈ COVE #016,012	2 WIDE	A-5 {L}	62
6	78	3ᵈ COVE #035,023	2 WIDE	A-6 {L}	03
7	102	4ᵗʰ COVE #122,153	2 WIDE	A-7 {L}	62
9	114	4ᵗʰ COVE #109,107	2 WIDE	A-9 {L}	03
25	45	2ᵈ COVE #010,090	2 WIDES	R. PLATFORM	03
26	64	3ᵈ BAY-A #242	1 WIDE	DSL PLAT. Lower	62 Gobo
27	205	3ᵈ BAY	2 - 1000 w WIDES	DSL Finale	62 Gobo

DIMMER	CIRCUIT	POSITION	TYPE	FOCUS	COLOR
29	199	4ᵗʰ BAY	2 - 1000 w WIDES	USL Finale	62 Gobo
30	51	2ⁿᵈ #752	6" Klieg	THRONE FRONT {W}	03
	49	2 #751	6" Klieg		03
31	244	SR	4 6 Fres	LSW L 1R	017
	245				
32		#6 FRES		THRONE DN Lt.	03
36	238	LSR #306,301	2 - 6" FRES	LSW 2&3 {R}	017
	232	LSR #329,330	2 - 6" FRES		
37	131	4ᵗʰ H.S. #375	1 NARROW	L-WALL D.S.	62
41	239	LSR #302,326	2 - 6" FRES	LSC 2-3-{R}	017
	233	#333,324	2 - 6" FRES		
42	130	4ᵗʰ #205	1 - NW	COLUMN SPEC	62
	260	TORM R. #178	2 NARROWS	TORM R {C}	62
46	261	#269			
	256	#148	1 WIDE		
47	274	BACK DECK	2 WIDES	MOON LAV.	54
48	273	BACK DECK	2 NARROWS	MOON RED	27
50	271	BACK DECK	2 WIDES	MOON BLUE	62
51	275	BACK DECK	2 - WIDES	MOON ORANGE	23
52	272	BACK DECK	OVER HEAD	MOON O.H. PAT.	62
53	187	8ᵗʰ COVE	8" LeCo	FOLLOW SPOT	
56	113	4ᵗʰ BAY DECK	2 POINTS	HORSE EYES	03
57	73	3ᵈ BAY #250	1 NARROW	HERODUS NOTCH	03
59	74	3ᵈ BAY-A #240	1 NARROW	4' PLAT UPPER	62 Gobo
60	302	FLOOR #1000	1 WIDE	SHADOW	17
61	66	4ᵗʰ COVE #044,101	2 - WIDES	BL A-1	62
	111	#069,068	2 - WIDES	BL A-1	62 Gobo
64	142	5ᵗʰ COVE #136,032	2 - WIDES	BL A-4	62
	144	#111,064	2 - WIDES	BL A-4	62 Gobo
65	147	5ᵗʰ COVE #016,056	2 - WIDES	BL A-5	62 Gobo
66	151	5ᵗʰ COVE #160,108	2 - WIDES	BL A-6	03
	154	#089,020	2 - WIDES	BL A-6	03 Gobo
67	166	6ᵗʰ COVE #021,029	2 - WIDES	BL A-7	62
	168	#079,091	2 - WIDES	BL A-7	62 Gobo
69	175	6ᵗʰ COVE #078,130	2 - WIDES	BL A-9	03
	179	#097,080	2 - WIDES	BL A-9	03 Gobo
70	188	7ᵗʰ COVE #142,082	2 - WIDES	BL A-10	62 Gobo
71	170	7ᵗʰ COVE #081,141	2 WIDES	BL A-11	62 Gobo
74	212	4ᵗʰ COVE #404	8" Fres	CISTERN Top	62
75	212	TRAP ROOM #400	8" FRES	CISTERN Bottom	54
76	176	6ᵗʰ #B-1	1 - PAR 56	R. WALL	03
77	278	USR FLOOR STAND	1 - WIDE	GUEST SIDE	03
	198	4ᵗʰ #241	1 - WIDE		
	139	5ᵗʰ #296	1 - NW		
	162	6ᵗʰ #277	1 - NW		
	163	6ᵗʰ #271	1 - NW		
78	237	4ᵗʰ #266	1 - NW	R WALL (W)	03
	152	5ᵗʰ #B-3	1 - PAR 56		
79	109	4ᵗʰ 6 #232,237	1 - NW	L WALL (C)	62 Gobo
	165	5ᵗʰ 6 #230	1 - NW		
80	240	4ᵗʰ 6 #240	1 - NW	R WALL (C)	62
	183	5ᵗʰ #B-19	1 - PAR 56		
	174	6ᵗʰ #B-8	1 - PAR 56		
92	299	US LIFT	1 - WIDE	FLOOR US-X	62
93	222	8ᵗʰ #702	2" Klieg	SQUELCH BK LT	62
	286	700 3ᵈ DR.	1 - NW	SR DOOR	017
97	287	BOTH			
98	155	5ᵗʰ #216	1 - NW	HSW-3 {R}	62
	178	6ᵗʰ #211	1 - NW	HSW-4 {R}	62 Gobo
99	196		2 - WD³	Letters	27
		STAR COLUMN	2 NARROWS {L}	Letters	27
100	65		2 - NARROWS {R}		
	259				
	253	TORM SPEC R.	1 NARROW		
	252	TORM SPEC L.	1 NARROW		
	258				
	28				

NOTE: ALL MISSING NO'S. ON SALOME HOOKUP — SEE REP HOOKUP.

Cheat Sheet - Rep. Focus

#		#		#	
1.	Area 1 left	34.	High Side Cool - 2L	67.	BK. Area 7
2.	Area 2 left	35.	High Side Cool - 3L	68.	BK. Area 8
3.	Area 3 left	36.	High Side Cool - 4L	69.	BK. Area 9
4.	Area 4 left	37.	High Side Cool - 1R	70.	BK. Area 10
5.	Area 5 left	38.	High Side Cool - 2R	71.	BK. Area 11
6.	Area 6 left	39.	High Side Cool - 3R	72.	BK. Area 12
7.	Area 7 left	40.	High Side Cool - 4R	73.	
8.	Area 8 left	41.	Torm Left WARM	74.	USL Flutes
9.	Area 9 left	42.	Torm Right WARM	75.	DSL Flutes
10.	Area 10 left	43.	Torm Left Cool	76.	USR Flutes
11.	Area 11 left	44.	Torm Right Cool	77.	DSR Flutes
12.	Area 12 left	45.	Low Side WARM - 1L	78.	Kickers D.S.
13.	Area 1 right	46.	Low Side WARM - 2L	79.	Kickers U.S.
14.	Area 2 right	47.	Low Side WARM - 3L	80.	Front Area 1 L+R
15.	Area 3 right	48.	Low Side WARM - 4L	81.	Front Area 2 L+R
16.	Area 4 right	49.	Low Side WARM - 1R	82.	Front Area 3 L+R
17.	Area 5 right	50.	Low Side WARM - 2R	83.	Torm Spec. L.T.
18.	Area 6 right	51.	Low Side WARM - 3R	84.	Torm Spec. L.B.
19.	Area 7 right	52.	Low Side WARM - 4R	85.	Torm Spec. R.T.
20.	Area 8 right	53.	Low Side Cool - 1L	86.	Torm Spec. R.B.
21.	Area 9 right	54.	Low Side Cool - 2L	87.	6" Klieg Spec. #1
22.	Area 10 right	55.	Low Side Cool - 3L	88.	6" Klieg Spec. #2
23.	Area 11 right	56.	Low Side Cool - 4L	89.	6" Klieg Spec. #3
24.	Area 12 right	57.	Low Side Cool - 1R	90.	6" Klieg Spec. #4
25.	High Side WARM	58.	Low Side Cool - 2R	91.	Par BK. LT (cove 8)
26.	High Side WARM -	59.	Low Side Cool - 3R	92.	Par BK. LT (cove 8)
27.	High Side WARM - 3L	60.	Low Side Cool - 4R	93.	8" Spec. #1
28.	High Side WARM - 4L	61.	BK. Area 1	94.	8" Spec. #2
29.	High Side WARM - 1R	62.	BK. Area 2	95.	8" Spec. #3
30.	High Side WARM - 2R	63.	BK. Area 3	96.	8" Spec. #4
31.	High Side WARM - 3R	64.	BK. Area 4	97.	
32.	High Side WARM - 4R	65.	BK. Area 5	98.	
33.	High Side Cool - 1L	66.	BK. Area 6	99.	
				100.	

3KW (15), 5KW (49), 3KW (85), 12KW (98)

Figure 6.9 Simplified "cheat sheets" used by Stephan Ross at the Santa Fe Opera.

Cheat Sheet - Salome

#			#		
1.	Area 1 left	62	53.	Follow Spot #8	
2.	Area 2 left	62	54.		
3.	Area 3 left	03	55.		
4.	Area 4 left	62	56.	Horse eyes	03
5.	Area 5 left	62	57.	HERODIS notch	03
6.	Area 6 left	03	58.		
7.	Area 7 left	62	59.	Down stage left (upper)	03
8.			60.	Shadow	17 colour
9.	Area 9 left	03	61.	Back light area-1	62
10.-13	SEE REP.		62.		
14.	Area 2 right	62	63.		
15.	Area 3 right	03	64.	Back light area-4	62
16.-24.	SEE REP.		65.	Back light area-5	62
25.	Right Plat.	03	66.	Back light area-6	03
26.	Down Stage left Plat. (LOWER)	62	67.	Back light area-7	62
27.	Down Stage left Flutes	62	68.		
28.			69.	Back light area-9	03
29.	Up stage Flutes	62 gobo	70.	Back light area-10	62
30.	Throne front (warm)	03	71.	Back light area-11	62
31.	Throne Low Sides	017	72.		
32.	Throne down light	03	73.		
33.-35	SEE REP.		74.	Cistern (top)	62
36.	Low side (warm) bay 2 and 3-R	017	75.	Cistern (bottom)	54
37.	Left wall down stage	62	76.	Right wall up stage	03
38.-40.	SEE REP.		77.	Guest	03
41.	Low side (cool) bay 2 and 3-R	017	78.	Right wall	03
42.	Column special (gobo)	62	79.	Left wall	62
43.-45.	SEE REP.		80.	Right wall	62
46.	Torm right (cool)	62	81.-87.	SEE REP.	
47.	Moon (lav.)	54	88.	High side cool bay 1 and 2-R	62 (Gobo)
48.	Moon (red)	27	89.-91.	SEE REP.	
49.			92.	Up stage entrance cross	62
50.	Moon (blue)	517	93.	Soldier back	62
51.	Moon (orange)	23	94.-96.	SEE REP.	
52.	Moon over-head	62	97.	Stage right door	017
			98.	Left wall (cool)	62 (Gobo)
			99.	LETTERS US	027
			100.	Letters	27

gobo (67)

Figure 6.10 The 1978 Santa Fe Opera's production of *Salome*. Director: Bliss Herbert; scene and costume designer: A. Charles Klein; lighting design: Stephen Ross. (*Photo: © David Stein*)

Figure 6.12 Production photo of *Salome*.

Figure 6.11 Production photo of *Salome*.

imitation of life—nonrealistic creations with human attributes. Puppetry presents verisimilitude, but not reality.[126] Puppeteers of America, the national puppetry association, has around 2,000 members.[127] There are generally thought to be only 200 full-time professional puppeteers in the United States and Canada.

Design Considerations

Puppet Land is a fanciful, imaginative, and bold world—a world of colorful illusion, frequently not only for children but also for adults. Puppets appear everywhere: "live," on TV, in movies, in nightclubs, at amusement parks, at expositions, and in commercials. For the lighting designer, the ability to free design imagination and use smoke pots, projections, explosions—all the paraphernalia of spectacle—is refreshing.

As usual, budget must be considered. Only the largest established troupes can afford to carry on tour heavy, bulky, elaborate stages and catwalks, along with puppets, costumes, scenery, and effects. Most troupes are forced to travel much lighter, and lighting instruments and switchboards are usually the first items dispensed with. All equipment that tours with a troupe must be maximally portable.

Puppet professionals earn a large portion of their living by touring—going where the children are. Only a few, Bil Baird for example, have their own permanent theatres that attract recurrent audiences plus residual employment in TV and movies and commercials.[128]

The lighting designer designing for puppetry faces certain

[126] *David Currell*, The Complete Book of Puppetry. *London; Pitman; 1974. "Lighting and Sound," pp. 172–87. Best basic English text. Illus.*

"Special Issue: Puppetry for the Theatre," Theatre Crafts, *vol. 9, no. 2 (Mar./Apr. 1975), pp. 7–45. General background.*

William J. Plochy, "Who Moi? Miss Piggy and The Muppets Hit the Museum Circuit," Lighting Dimensions, *vol. 6, no. 1 (Jan./Feb. 1982), pp. 34–35, 37–39. Illus., color.*

Bil Baird, The Art of the Puppet by Bil Baird. *N.Y.; Macmillan Co.; 1965. Good basic volume. Little about lighting.*

Grenville Middleton, "Puppet Theatre Lighting," Cue, *no. 25 (Sept./Oct. 1983), pp. 9–10. Illus. How to light a puppet theatre on a riverboat.*

Mark Steinbrink, "Bil Baird and His Marionettes Are Busy With Stravinsky Now," The New York Times, *Sunday, June 26, 1983, section 2, pp. 19, 24. Illus.*

[127] *The address for the group is:*
IPPA (Institute of Professional Puppetry Arts)
O'Neill Theatre Center
305 Great Neck Road
Waterford, CT 06385
Also, the lighting specialist for the Puppeteers of America is:
Ken Moses (129)
Pickwick Puppet Theatre
1004 76th Street
North Bergen, NJ 07047

[128] *The Bil Baird Theatre [a Theatre Communications Group, Inc. (TCG) affiliate] operated with an annual budget of nearly $100,000. Such theatre names as Sheldon Harnick, Burt Shevelove, E. Y. Harburg, and Mary Rogers worked with the group. Peggy Clark frequently served as the group's lighting designer. The 194-seat theatre on Barrow Street in New York City's Greenwich Village served as a permanent performance place, a studio, and a warehouse. In addition to in-house performances, the group toured, performed on TV, etc. Bil Baird (the dean of American puppeteers—now deceased) and this author attended the State University of Iowa and I became acquainted with him at CBS-TV in the 1950s. Some of this information was obtained from* Theatre Profiles 3, *New York; Theatre Communications Group; 1977, vol. 3, pp. 40–41.*

[129] Ken Moses, "Lights," Theatre Crafts, vol. 9, no. 2 (Mar./Apr. 1975), pp. 13, 31–35. Most complete equipment and design information available.

basic problems. Puppeteers are forced to work with string puppets quite close to the scenic background or cyclorama (2 feet to 2 feet 6 inches away, maximum). This means that lighting should *not* come from low, flat-front sources. Crosslighting from the front removes the "marching shadows" on the background. When possible, backgrounds should be lighted separately with cyc striplights at the top of the drop and recessed in troughs at the base behind masking groundrows.

A second basic design consideration is the need for plasticity from heavy crosslighting. Ken Moses points out that puppet lighting is an offshoot of theatre and display lighting. He feels that it should be "much more related to dance lighting." [129] Puppets are fashioned from nonliving materials, just as is the scenic background surrounding them. Crosslighting helps model and mold the marionette figure and separate it from the nonmobile decor. Careful use of color and texture contrast by the puppet designer can aid in the process. Frequently the use of a black drape background does the utmost to make the puppets stand out. If a cyc or backdrop is used, restriction to darker colors helps increase separation. Unlike the human facial expression, the facial expression of a puppet does not change. Therefore, the usual theatre necessity for bright "face lighting" has less importance in puppetry than in human drama, and "side lighting" has more. Backlight is equally important but may accent unnecessarily the puppet control strings.

In puppetry, little use is made of standard theatre stage areas. The puppet playing space is too small for that kind of definition to matter. Concentration should be on overall illumination for clear visibility and sculpting. Puppet figures often require brighter visibility lighting than humans do, because puppets are much smaller in scale. Thus, dim scenes may be less dim than in a human show. Because puppets and costumes are painted or dyed to a desired color, intensity, and shade, beginning puppeteers should restrict their use of strongly saturated colors to "effects" in a limited number of scenes. The stage standard pastels usually suffice: steel blue, no-color pink, straw, lavender or violet, and bastard amber.

One final problem that concerns the designer is that lighting equipment mounting positions in puppetry are somewhat restricted. Front positions add little except shadow-producing flatness. For marionette stages, mounting positions are restricted to the ends of the stage, under the catwalks upon which human manipulators work, in standard footlight positions, and near the backdrop or background. Any other positions would result in operator's strings becoming tangled in the lights.

Shadow puppets are a different story. The puppets are often flat cutouts, and their shadows are projected from a rear light source upon a translucent screen. A single source (such as an overhead projector) is used.

Communications Forms

Since puppet troupes rehearse and prepare quite carefully, the often simple lighting requirements are usually worked out on the spot during rehearsal, without elaborate formal paperwork.

Techniques

Switchboards are often rather primitive. Frequently the lighting units themselves are miniature. The simplest puppetry lighting consists of a few floodlights and numerous R-20, R-30, and R-40 reflector lamps in swivel sockets with bullet housings, louvers, and color clips. Christmas tree lights, bee lights, and flashlight lamps find a ready use. On a more sophisticated level, extensive use is made of the smaller standard theatre units: the 3-inch Fresnel, the 3-inch Fresnel adapted into a "picture spot" with shutters, the 3½-inch quartz ellipsoidal reflector spotlights, low-voltage PARs, and standard ultraviolet (blacklight) fluorescent tubes and mercury-vapor lamps. Blacklight is often needed in puppetry. Projected backgrounds and gobo patterns in ellipsoidals also have their place.

Procedures and Practices

Puppetry finds wide application in television, movies, and commercials. Figure 6.13, showing the Rufus Rose Marionettes, illustrates studio photography of *Jerry Pulls the*

Figure 6.13 *Jerry Pulls the Strings.* The first full-length industrial film to use marionettes was this 1937 production by the Rufus Rose Marionettes. (*Courtesy of Margo Rose.*)

Figure 6.14 Pickwick Puppet Theatre production of *Sleeping Beauty* at the Avery Fisher Hall, Lincoln Center, New York City, in March 1976. Lighting design by Ken Moses. (*Courtesy of Ken Moses.*)

Strings with a typical stage in position. The larger lighting units in the photograph are those used by the movie camera operators for their filming. This was the first full-length film promoting a client's product to use marionettes (1937). Figure 6.14, presenting another variation of puppetry,

shows the Pickwick Puppet Theatre performing in conjunction with a symphony orchestra at Avery Fisher Hall, Lincoln Center, New York City, in March 1976. Ken Moses and Pickwick are well known for opera and classical music presentations. The lighting units, within the audience's sight, are owned and toured by Pickwick.

As far as I am aware, no one is engaged in full-time paid lighting design for the extensive world of puppetry, but working lighting designers may be called upon to assist the many puppet groups, whether it be for live presentation (at the home base or on tour) or for TV.[130]

Mime

Mime is almost the exact opposite of puppetry, in terms of lighting. With mime, clear, crisp visibility of the performer's face and body is all-important. Mime works with whatever the theatre and the lighting designer has available. Lighting for mime cannot really be considered a specialty. Standard (good) theatre lighting suffices for those troupes *not* performing impromptu on street corners (such as those performing at conventions and in university guest artists series or Marcel Marceau's professional troupe).

Miniature Stages

A brief look at miniature stages and their lighting is useful. I asked Professor Robert Segrin of San Francisco State University to supply illustrations and text for this *Handbook* concerning the model stage he uses both as a testing device for upcoming productions and as a highly valuable teaching instrument.[131] Professor Segrin's text follows:

One of the most frustrating aspects of teaching stage lighting is the lack of availability of the theatres during class time. The actual facilities are often in use by other classes. One solution is to bring the theatre (actually the stage) to the classroom where lighting is taught. This typical problem existed at San Francisco State University some years ago. The solution came when a graduate student, Raymon T. Stansbury, decided to design and construct a miniature lighting system and scale model of the stage in the Little Theatre. Since the lighting classroom is long and narrow, a

[130] See also:

Ray Da Silva, "Lighting Design for Puppet Theatre," TABS, vol. 32, no. 2 (Autumn 1974), pp. 3–4. Usable analysis of practical problems.

Joel E. Rubin and Leland H. Watson, Theatrical Lighting Practice. N.Y.; Theatre Arts Books; 1954. Chap. IV: "Puppetry," pp. 80–84. Basics.

[131] A detailed description of this miniature stage system appears in Robert L. Segrin, "Lighting in Miniature," Theatre Design Technology, no. 16 (Feb. 1969), pp. 12–14.

[132] *Mark M. Wohlwerth, "Museums—Stage Lighting in Miniature,"* Lighting Design + Application, *vol. 7, no. 4 (Apr. 1977), pp. 32–34. Lighting of miniature stage sets for a design exhibit at the Museum of the City of New York, by Mark Wohlwerth. Illus.*

Guy R. Williams, Making a Miniature Theatre. *Boston; Plays, Inc.; 1967. Illus.; 79 pages.*

Adolphe Winds, "Eine Versuchsliühne für Be-levchtungproben" ("A Trial Stage for Lighting Investigation"), Bühne und Welt, *Apr. 1910. Description of first model stage used by W. Bürgman in Leipzig, Germany.*

"Digital Palace," Electrosonic World, *#4 (1987), p. 4. Illus., color. The lighting of a miniature model of Britain's Buckingham Palace for a worldwide tour.*

[133] *"Special Issue: Theatre for Children,"* Theatre Crafts, *vol. 5, no. 2 (Mar./Apr. 1971), pp. 6–25. General background.*

scale of 1" = 1' was decided to be practical. Ideally, the miniature luminaries would have been designed in proportion to this scale, but practical considerations of available lamp/socket sizes and heat factors resulted in a larger scale (approximately twice as large as the 1" stage scale).

What are the parameters of an ideal miniature stage lighting system? In a word, accuracy. The small lighting units should be capable of creating the same characteristics of the full size equipment in terms of scaled-down intensity ratios, beam spread (and beam spread variability, where applicable), gobo potentials, soft edge (Fresnel), hard edge (ellipsoidal spotlight), linear (striplight), color filter holders, and, of course, subject to infinite dimming. By studying the important features of standard luminaires (models manufactured by Strand Century were chosen for the San Francisco State University project), a set of typical, albeit miniature, stage lighting luminaires were created: 6" Fresnels, 8" Fresnel, 6" × 9" ellipsoidal spotlights, 10" beam projectors and 14" "scoop" floodlights. Following the completion of the project, Linnebach projectors and 6' portable striplights were added to the set of miniature units.

The results of the miniature lighting equipment are amazing in terms of fidelity. When used in conjunction with carefully crafted model stage settings and properties (1" scale furniture has become exceptionally popular in recent years), a complete lighting design can be created with the miniature system before being implemented in the actual full-scale theatre. The benefits of such a system are worth the time and costs, especially in educational theatre. Lighting designs can be critiqued and alterations made before the technicians install and focus the actual lighting equipment in the theatre. Inexperienced lighting crew students can grasp a lighting concept when demonstrated on a model system prior to implementing to full-sized design. Lighting design light plot projects become infinitely more meaningful when the design is realized on an accurate model system (at San Francisco State, a 35-mm transparency is given to each student after the implementation of each lighting plot project, making a valuable contribution when added to the design portfolio in print form).

As an instructional device, the miniature system and model stage has proven to be a dynamic demonstration tool. Following typical discussions and chalkboard diagrams, the classroom lights are dimmed, the preset model lighting "scene" is brought up, and with the necessary "willing suspension of disbelief," a viable theatrical effect is demonstrated (if only those miniature scale figures could move and speak!)."

The accompanying photographs illustrate the model stage from various views. Figure 6.15 shows a full front view of

Figure 6.15 The model stage in use at the San Francisco State University. (*Photo: Robert Segrin*)

Figure 6.16 The model stage in use at the San Francisco State University. (*Photo: Robert Segrin*)

the model stage and FOH lights. Figure 6.16 illustrates the lighting and scenic setting used for a class demonstration.[132]

Children's Theatre

It is estimated that between 700 and 1,500 groups produce theatre for children on a regular basis each year. They play to an audience of over 10 million children.[133] (During the week of May 11, 1986, I found six companies performing in

Los Angeles.) About half of the groups are profit-making commercial ventures; the other half are nonprofit. Children's theatre exists in spite of the popularity and availability of its equivalent on TV. Why? Because theatre (1) educates children (and can be used as a teaching tool), (2) prepares children for "adult" theatre attendance (with a consequent higher level of sophistication and demands for "better theatre" as adults), and (3) provides children with live entertainment. As for adults, for children "live" theatre has an immediacy and impact not attainable in "canned" media.

Children's theatre deals with fairy tales, opera and music, dance, fantasy, classics of literature, and historical plays. It is an obvious place for spectacle in lighting design, given the child's unspoiled ability to suspend literality and enter the world of make-believe.

Children's theatre is an important part of the larger world of theatre but is rarely a source of employment for the lighting designer. All too many groups operate as "poor second cousins" on extremely limited budgets. The groups are forced to skimp and improvise, and often they are a "labor of love" of dedicated individuals rather than properly funded operations.[134]

There are exceptions. The Children's Theatre Company in Minneapolis, Minnesota, was founded in 1961. In 1977 its operating budget was over $1 million. It is heavily foundation funded and also operates an extensive accredited school. It has its own auditorium and tours widely its Moppet Players. It is involved in script writing for children's shows, direction, and all of the design/technical disciplines. Jon Baker and Karlis Ozols are the current lighting designers.[135] Other children's theatre companies that have permanent homes and adequate facilities are the Kay Rockefeller Traveling Playhouse and the First All Children's Theatre Co., New York City (a Theatre Communications Group member; lighting designers are Charles Willmott and Rick Belzer).[136] The Looking Glass Theatre in Providence, Rhode Island, is well known, and there are others. Most do not have a full-time lighting designer.

Trouping is the livelihood for many children's theatre companies. They usually travel light. Children's theatre lighting is a composite of those things dealt with elsewhere in this volume in discussions of adult theatre and of puppetry. The lighting designer must place added emphasis on crystal-clear vision of the performers' faces and catering to the free, open imagination of children.

Repertory Theatre

Repertory production (i.e., a single company producing a different play/opera/dance each performance, with two different ones on matinee days) has never been as extensive in the United States as in the rest of the theatrical world. No doubt this results from the much more limited and hesitant subsidization of the arts in the United States, largely traceable to the continued influence of our Puritan heritage and strong work ethic.[137]

Repertory ("rep") theatre does exist in the United States, however. It is to be found as the production pattern for the larger opera companies such as the Metropolitan Opera, for most dance companies, and for some well-established summer theatres (for example, the Missouri Repertory Theatre in Kansas City and the many summer Shakespeare festivals in Oregon, Virginia, Connecticut, and Utah). Rep has not yet established a firm foothold in the United States in serious professional nonmusical dramatic theatre. There have been many attempts but few successes.

Design Considerations

Because rep has been touched upon earlier in this volume (see discussions of opera lighting, dance and ballet lighting, and nonmusical theatre lighting), the treatment here will be brief. The five key design considerations are as follows:

1. Lighting equipment and layout must perform basic area/color/angle chores for many different productions. This means that the season's light plot must consist fundamentally of a *basic setup:* areas and color control. It must be flexible.

2. *Specials* are added to the basics. A few units, in readily accessible positions, must be available for changeover time.

3. Changeover time is extremely important. In rep it is not uncommon to put up one show in the morning and

[134] *"Lights On,"* Theatre Crafts, *vol. 5, no. 2 (Mar./Apr. 1971), pp. 26–27, 32–37. Very brief treatment of lighting for children's theatre.*

[135] *See* Theatre Profiles 3. *New York Theatre Communications Group, vol. 3, 1977.*

Ronn Smith, "Not for Children Only, The Children's Theatre of Minneapolis," Theatre Crafts, *vol. 17, no. 7 (Aug./Sept. 1983), pp. 31, 68, 70. Illus. Excellent short piece about one of the key professional children's theatre groups.*

[136] *John S. Wilson, "Stage: Children's Theatre in 'The Trip',"* The New York Times, *December 11, 1983, p. 48. Lighting for a First All Children's Theatre production by Stan Pressner and multimedia design by Joshua White.*

work on it, change over to a second show for a matinee performance, and change to yet a third show for the evening performance. Other groups beside the technical/design staff also need the stage. Exactitude—knowing how much *can* be changed in the allotted time and then not exceeding that time period—is the most vital element in lighting for repertory.

4. A fact of life in theatre is that there is never enough funding to match what the creative artist *could* do. In rep it's even worse. Repertory production is *the* most expensive way of doing theatre. The lighting designer must guard each penny spent and use stage crew, time, and materials economically.

5. *Preplanning.* Everything must be worked out carefully in advance on paper. Time on stage is vital. Those who are best at scheduling, anticipating disaster and coping with it and wringing the last bit of effort out of each moment are the only ones who will survive in repertory.

If all of this sounds rather grim—it is. Rep is the most challenging area of lighting design. The designer knows from the very beginning that compromise and simplification are necessary because there just isn't either the time or the money to achieve all that can be visualized. The designer also knows the great personal sense of achievement and pride that can result from "achieving the impossible" day after day, on schedule, within budget and with at least a modicum of creativeness.

Design Communication

A selection of repertory plots is included here. Figure 6.17 is the season light plot for the Mark Taper Forum in Los Angeles. Figure 6.18 is the season hookup. Figures 6.19 and 6.20 are the plot and hookup for *Black Angel,* designed by Tharon Musser within the season plot (which she prepares, being responsible for the entire season). Figure 6.21 is a production photo. The simplicity in equipment of the plot contrasts with the use of equipment in *Whose Life Is It Anyway?,* presented in Chap. 4 in the Broadway version (see Fig. 4.9). I saw *Black Angel.* It was among Musser's finest work, yet was done economically in terms of equipment used. That, not amount of design imagination, is a key to

rep. Figs. 4.19 to 4.21 in Chap. 4 present the plot, the hookup, and production photos for *Savages* at the Mark Taper Forum, designed by John Gleason using Tharon Musser's season light plot. Repertory does not mean that other lighting designers cannot work within a designer's season's framework. A study of this series of plots (season plot by Musser at Mark Taper; Musser's own *Black Angel* designed within that framework; John Gleason's *Savages* at Mark Taper) can provide any designer with some useful insights into repertory lighting.

An additional nonmusical repertory plot is included here: designer F. Mitchell Dana's season plot for the American Conservatory Theatre (A.C.T.) in San Francisco (Fig. 6.22). Figure 6.23 shows a section view. Figure 6.24 is the switchboard hookup for a specific play, *A Christmas Carol,* designed by Dana. Finally, Fig. 6.25 is a production photo. Two other production photos at the same theatre (the Geary in San Francisco) using a season repertory setup are Color Fig. 49, *Le Bourgeois Gentilhomme,* with lighting design at A.C.T. by Richard Devin, and Fig. 4.40, *Julius Caesar,* again by Devin. A.C.T. uses three separate lighting designers each season, all working within the confines of a single season plot.

Repertory is more common in opera. In Chap. 5, Figs. 5.1, 5.2, and 5.3 present the basic rep plot for the Metropolitan Opera, with Gil Wechsler as the designer. Figures 5.6 through 5.8 and Color Fig. 18 show Wechsler's use of this plot for a specific opera, *Tannhauser.* Stephen Ross's lighting design in outdoor repertory is also to be found in Chap. 5. Figures 6.7 through 6.12 and Color Fig. 19 are the plot, hookup, and "cheat sheets" for his lighting of *Salome* in Santa Fe. Other production photos from repertory theatres are found in Color Fig. 48a (the Arena di Verona in Italy), Color Fig. 21 (*Prince Igor* at the Chicago Lyric Opera), Color Fig. 48 (*La Giaconda* at the Arena di Verona), and Color Figs. 20 and 22 (*L'Incorona Zione de Poppea*) and Fig. 5.9 (*Aida*) (by Nananne Porcher). In Chap. 5, Fig. 5.4, showing *The Turn of the Screw* at the New York City Opera Co., is another good example.

Repertory is found most commonly in the world of dance. In Chap. 5, Figs. 5.15 through 5.18 are Thomas Skelton's plot, hookup, and production photos for the Ohio

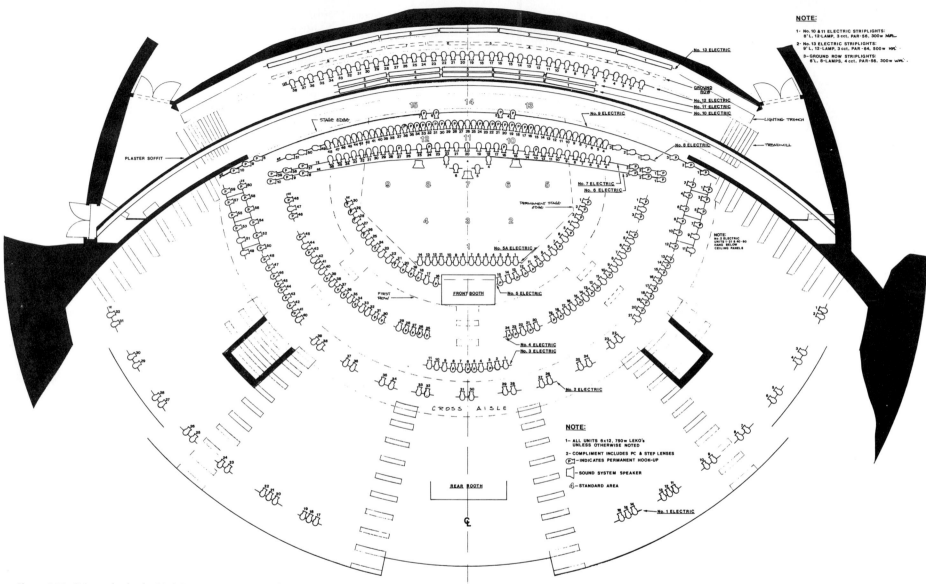

Figure 6.17 Season plot for the Mark Taper Forum, Los Angeles.
Lighting design: Tharon Musser.

SWITCHBOARD HOOK-UP SHEET — Mark Taper Forum

Revised August 1978

Gordon Davidson, Artistic Director
Center Theatre Group, Music Center

Dimmer Compliment: 1-60 = 7Kw, 4 way; 61-100 = 7Kw, 6 way; 101-120 = 12Kw, 12 way

SWITCH	POSITION – UNIT NUMBER	TYPE	FOCUS
1	3P – 6 4P – 12 – 37	3 6" Leko	Area 1 DDC
2	3P – 3 4P – 4 – 30 7P – 16	4 6" Leko	Area 2 DL
3	3P – 5 4P – 10 – 39	3 6" Leko	Area 3 DC
4	3P – 8 4P – 19 – 45 7P – 24	4 6" Leko	Area 4 DR
5	4P – 6 – 24 5P – 19 7P – 13	4 6" Leko	Area 5 SL
6	4P – 13 – 28 5P – 24	3 6" Leko	Area 6 L of C
7	4P – 18 – 31 5P – 2 – 29	4 6" Leko	Area 7 C
8	4P – 21 – 36 5P – 7	3 6" Leko	Area 8 R of C
9	4P – 25 – 43 5P – 12 7P – 27	4 6" Leko	Area 9 SR
10	4P – 3 – 23 5P – 18	3 6" Leko	Area 10 UL
11	4P – 15 – 34 5P – 5 – 26	4 6" Leko	Area 11 UC
12	4P – 26 – 46 5P – 13	3 6" Leko	Area 12 UR
13	4P – 1 5P – 15 – 21	3 6" Leko	Area 13 UUL
14	5P – 3 – 11 – 20 – 28	4 6" Leko	Area 14 UUC
15	4P – 48 5P – 10 – 16	3 6" Leko	Area 15 UUR
16-20 OPEN			
21	5P – 1 – 30	2 6" Leko	Area 1 DDC Back
22	8P – 17	1 6" Leko	Area 2 DL Back
23	8P – 21 – 23	2 6" Leko	Area 3 DC Back
24	8P – 35	1 6" Leko	Area 4 DR Back
25	8P – 19	1 6" Leko	Area 5 SL Back
26	8P – 22	1 6" Leko	Area 6 L of C Back
27	8P – 24 – 28	2 6" Leko	Area 7 C Back
28	8P – 30	1 6" Leko	Area 8 R of C Back
29	8P – 33	1 6" Leko	Area 9 SR Back
30	8P – 16 – 20	2 6" Leko	Area 10 UL Back
31	8P – 18 – 34	2 6" Leko	Area 11 UC Back
32	8P – 32 – 36	2 6" Leko	Area 12 UR Back
33	9P – 4	1 6" Leko	Area 13 UUL Back
34	9P – 5 – 6	2 6" Leko	Area 14 UUC Back
35	9P – 7	1 6" Leko	Area 15 UUR Back
36-39 OPEN			
40	6P – 1 – 2 – 3	3 6" Leko	US Ends SL
41	7P – 1 – 2 – 3	3 6" Leko	US Ends SL
42	9P – 1 – 2 – 3	3 6" Leko	US Ends SL
43	6P – 8 – 9 – 10	3 6" Leko	US Ends SR
44	7P – 37 – 38 – 39	3 6" Leko	US Ends SR
45	9P – 8 – 9 – 10	3 6" Leko	US Ends SR
46	2P – 1 – 4 – 5 – 8	4 6" Leko	US Sides SL
47	2P – 2 – 3 – 6 – 7	4 6" Leko	US Sides SL
48	2P – 13 – 15 – 17 – 19	4 6" Leko	Sides SL
49	2P – 14 – 16 – 18 – 20	4 6" Leko	Sides SL
50	2P – 54 – 55 – 58 – 59	4 6" Leko	US Sides SR
51	2P – 53 – 56 – 57 – 60	4 6" Leko	US Sides SR
52	2P – 41 – 43 – 45 – 47	4 6" Leko	Sides SR
53	2P – 42 – 44 – 46 – 48	4 6" Leko	Sides SR
54	2P – 10 – 12 – 50 – 52	4 6" Leko	Sides SL & SR
55-120 OPEN			
NON-DIM 1-10 OPEN			

Figure 6.18 Season switchboard hookup for the Mark Taper Forum.

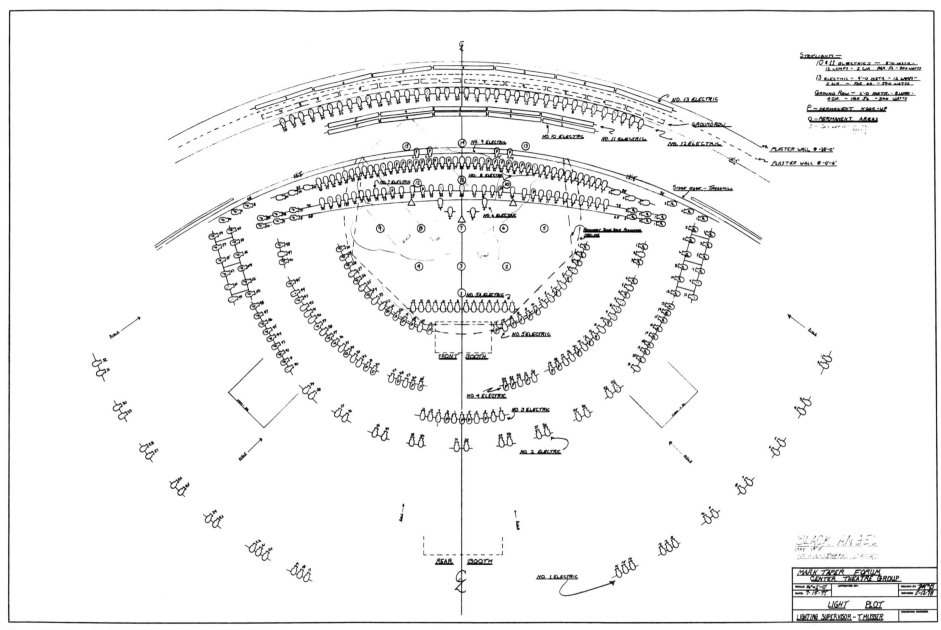

Figure 6.19 Light plot for *Black Angel* at the Mark Taper Forum in Los Angeles in May 1978. Lighting: Tharon Musser.

Figure 6.20 — Switchboard hookup for *Black Angel*.

MARK TAPER FORUM

PERMANENT HOOK-UP
"BLACK ANGEL"
Revised: July 1975

Switches 1 to 60 = 7000w / 4 way
Switches 61 to 100 = 7000w / 6 way
Switches 101 to 120 = 12000 w/12 way

Non Dims 1 to 10 = 4 way

SWITCH	POSITION	TYPE	FOCUS	COLOR
1	4 P - 12 - 37 / 3 P - 6	3/ 6" Leko	Area 1 DDC	4P-62R / 3P-06R
2	3 P - 3 / 4 P - 4 - 30 / 7 P - 16	4/ 6" Leko	Area 2 DL	4P-62R / 3P-06R / 7P-06R
3	3 P - 5 / 4 P - 10 - 39	3/ 6" Leko	Area 3 DC	4P-62R / 3P-06R
4	3 P - 8 / 4 P - 19 - 45 / 7 P - 24	4/ 6" Leko	Area 4 DR	4P-62R / 3P-06R / 7P-06R
5	4 P - 6 - 24 / 5 P - 19 / 7 P - 13	4/ 6" Leko	Area 5 L	4P-6 3P-19 }62R / 4P-24 7P-13 }-06R
6	4 P - 13 - 28 / 5 P - 24	3/ 6" Leko	Area 6 L O/C	4P-13 5P-24 }-62R / 4-28-06R
7	4 P - 18 - 31 / 5 P - 2 - 29	4/ 6" Leko	Area 7 C	4P-31 5P-2 }-62R / 4P-18 }-06R
8	4 P - 21 - 36 / 5 P - 7	3/ 6" Leko	Area 8 R O/C	4P-36 5P-7 }-62R / 4P-21-06R
9	5 P - 12 / 4 P - 25 - 43 / 7 P - 27	4/ 6" Leko	Area 9 R	4P-43 5P-12 }-62R / 4P-25 7P-27 }-06R
10	4 P - 3 - 23 / 5 P - 18	3/ 6" Leko	Area 10 UL	4P-3 5P-18 }-62R / 4P-23-06R
11	4 P - 15 - 34 / 5 P - 5 - 26	4/ 6" Leko	Area 11 UC	4P-34 5P-5 }-62R / 4P-15 5P-26 }-06R
12	4 P - 26 - 46 / 5 P - 13	3/ 6" Leko	Area 12 UR	4P-46 5P-13 }-62R / 4P-26-06R
13	4 P - 1 / 5 P - 15 - 21	3/ 6" Leko	Area 13 UUL	4P-1 5P-21 }-62R / 5P-15-06R
14	5 P - 3 - 11 - 20 - 28	4/ 6" Leko	Area 14 UUC	5P-3-20-62R / 5P-11-28-06R
15	4 P - 48 / 5 P - 10 - 16	3/ 6" Leko	Area 15 UUR	4P-48 5P-10 }-62R / 5P-16-06R
16	4 P - 9	1/ 6" Leko	ENGEL SAW HORSES	N.C.
17	4 P - 44	1/ 6" Leko	ENGEL PORCH	N.C.
20	8 P - 44	1/ 6" IRIS Leko	VERDICT UR	N.C.
21	5 P - 1 - 30	2/ 6" Leko	Area 1 DDC Back	60R
22	8 P - 17	1/ 6" Leko	Area 2 DL Back	60R

SWITCH	POSITION	TYPE	FOCUS	COLOR
23	8 P - 21 - 31	2/ 6" Leko	Area 3 DC Back	60R
24	8 P - 35	1/ 6" Leko	Area 4 DR Back	60R
25	8 P - 19	1/ 6" Leko	Area 5 L Back	60R
26	8 P - 22	1/ 6" Leko	Area 6 L O/C BK	60R
27	8 P - 24 - 28	2/ 6" Leko	Area 7 C Back	60R
28	8 P - 30	1/ 6" Leko	Area 8 R O/C BK	60R
29	8 P - 33	1/ 6" Leko	Area 9 R Back	60R
30	8 P - 16 - 20	2/ 6" Leko	Area 10 UL Back	60R
31	8 P - 18 - 34	2/ 6" Leko	Area 11 UC Back	60R
32	8 P - 32 - 36	2/ 6" Leko	Area 12 UR Back	60R
33	9 P - 4	1/ 6" Leko	Area 13 UUL Back	60R
34	9 P - 5 - 6	2/ 6" Leko	Area 14 UUC Back	60R
35	9 P - 7	1/ 6" Leko	Area 15 UUR Back	60R
36	2 P 49 - 51 - 40	3/ 6" Leko	HSE SL	60R
37	7 P 11-34 / 11 P 13-37	4/ 6" Leko	HOUSE COLOR II	52R
38	7 P - 10-33 / 11 P - 12-38	4/ 6" Leko	HOUSE COLOR II	03R
39	5 AP - 7	1/ 6" IRIS Leko	SIMONE END	62R
40	6 P - 1 - 2 - 3	3/ 6" Leko	US Ends L	60R
41	7 P - 1 - 2 - 3	3/ 6" Leko	US Ends L	06R
42	9 P - 1 - 2 - 3	3/ 6" Leko	US Ends L	60R
43	6 P - 8-9-10	3/ 6" Leko	US Ends R	N.C.
44	7 P - 37 - 38 - 39	3/ 6" Leko	US Ends R	62R

SWITCH	POSITION	TYPE	FOCUS	COLOR
45	9 P - 8 - 9 - 10	3/ 6" Leko	US Ends R	N.C.
46	2 P - 1 - 4 - 5 - 8	4/ 6" Leko	US Sides L	62R
47	2 P - 2 - 3 - 6 - 7	4/ 6" Leko	US Sides L	N.C.
48	2 P - 13 - 15 - 17 - 19	4/ 6" Leko	Sides L	62R
49	2 P - 14 - 16 - 18 - 20	4/ 6" Leko	Sides L	06R
50	2 P - 54 - 55 - 58 - 59	4/	US Sides R	60R
51	2 P - 53 - 56 - 57 - 60	4/ 6" Leko	US Sides R	06R
52	2 P - 41 - 43 - 45 - 47	4/ 6" Leko	Sides R	60R
53	2 P - 42 - 44 - 46 - 48	4/ 6" Leko	Sides R	N.C.
54	2 P - 10 - 12 - 50 - 52	4/ 6" Leko	Sides L & R	60R
55	TORM. L. 1-3-5	3/ 6" Leko	SIDE L	62R
56	TORM. L. 2-4-6	3/ 6" Leko	SIDE L	N.C.
57	TORM. R. 1-3-5	3/ 6" Leko	SIDE L	60R
58	TORM. R. 2-4-6	3/ 6" Leko	SIDE L	06R
59	LADDER L. 1-3-5	3/ 6" Leko	USL SIDE	62R
60	LADDER L. 2-4-6	3/ 6" Leko	USL SIDE	N.C.
61	LADDER R. 1-3-5	3/ Leko	USR SIDE	60R
62	LADDER R. 2-4-5	3/ Leko	USR SIDE	06R
63	4 P - 40 / 3 P 22-25	3/ Leko	SL ENDS	62R
64	4 P - 41 / 5 P - 23-27	3/ 6" Leko	SL ENDS	06R
65	4 P - 8 / 5 P - 4 - 8	3/ 6" Leko	SR ENDS	60R
66	4 P - 7 / 5 P - 6 - 9	3/ 6" Leko	SR ENDS	N.C.

SWITCH	POSITION	TYPE	FOCUS	COLOR
67	11 P - 3-4-5	3/ 6" Leko	USL ENDS	62R
68	11 P - 6-7-8	3/ 6" Leko	USL ENDS	06R
69	11 P - 34-35-36	3/ 6" Leko	USR ENDS	60R
70	11 P - 31-32-33	3/ 6" Leko	USR ENDS	N.C.
71	8 P - 23-25 / 11 P - 21-23	4/ 6" Leko	ROOF L	60R
72	8 P - 37-38 / 11 P - 29-30	4/ 6" Leko	ROOF R	62R
73	TORM L 7	1/ 6" Leko	3' OFF FLOOR	N.C.
74	TORM L 8	1/ 6" Leko	1'6" OFF FLOOR	62R
75	TORM R 7	1/ 6" Leko	1'6" OFF FLOOR	N.C.
76	8 P 11-15-41	3/ 6" Leko	3 TREES	60R
78	2 P 22-38 / 4 P 22	3/ 6" Leko	HSE MID	2P-62R / 4P-06R
79	3 P 9	1/ 6" IRIS Leko	SIMONE END	N.C.
80	7 P 5-6-7	3/ 6" Leko	SL TENT PUGET NT.	60R
81	7 P 20,21,22	3/ 6" Leko	SL TENT PUGET NT	62R
83	2 P 9-11	2/ 6" Leko	HSE SL	60R
101	12 P / GR ROW (4 micro sw)	4/ 1000W. Par	X HATCH BK WALL	
103	CYC 12P			N.C.
104	CYC 12P			60R
105	CYC 12P			62R
106	CYC GROUND ROW			N.C.
107	CYC " "			N.C.
108	CYC " "			72G
109 110 NO	CYC (NOT USED) - ND 1-10 (NOT USED)			62R OPEN

Figure 6.20 Switchboard hookup for *Black Angel*.

Figure 6.21 *Black Angel* production photo. Director: Gordon Davidson; scene and costume designer: Sally Jacobs; lighting design: Tharon Musser. (*Photo: Jay Tomson*)

Ballet. Figures 5.32 through 5.34 are Nananne Porcher's 1978 season road tour light plot, hookup, and focus charts for the American Ballet Theatre (ABT). Two other photos in Chap. 5 show repertory production lighting: Fig. 5.35 (Ronald Bates's lighting of *Serenade,* with the New York City Ballet) and Fig. 5.36 (Alwin Nikolais's *Crossfade*). Figures 5.23 through 5.31 and Color Figs. 23 through 28 are my own lighting of the ballet, *Poulenc Organ Concerto,* with the Cincinnati Ballet.

A reprint here of portions of my article, plot, hookup, and production photos from a 1982 season of repertory lighting for the Virginia Shakespeare Festival may help clarify repertory lighting by presenting an extended study of the sched-

ule and problems encountered in lighting a summer professional season of Shakespeare.

Repertory lighting is the ultimate challenge for the lighting designer. Using the number of lighting instruments and dimmers which a designer would consider adequate for one masterful production, he must produce sheer beauty for several shows, stay within budget and time limitations, and allow for simple but rapid changeovers from one production to the next. Repertory is not for beginners. But often it brings forth the finest artistry for the advanced designer. He must know lighting design, equipment, and how to deal with several different production teams in a minimum of time. The challenge forces the designer to make use of everything he knows — and then find additional resources to augment his talents.

In the summer of 1982, I had the opportunity to light the three-play Shakespeare repertory season for the Virginia Shakespeare Festival in Williamsburg, Virginia. The plays included *Merry Wives of Windsor, Richard III,* and *All's Well That Ends Well.* Fortunately, it was not my first season of repertory, since I have previously lighted many operas in rep in addition to spending some rep seasons with a major dance company and a summer many years earlier with the Missouri Repertory Theatre. There were many pluses at hand for this assignment. The Virginia Shakespeare Festival is a young, dedicated company performing in the well-equipped Phi Beta Kappa Theatre on the campus of William and Mary College. They employed an enthusiastic and creative staff for the summer — all underpaid, but dedicated to working together and to producing the best possible season. By stripping both campus theatres, 271 lighting units were made available. And by bringing the portable switchboard from the smaller theatre to a backstage position in the larger 763-seat Phi Beta Kappa Theatre, we had 48 dimmers (40 4-kW and 8 12-kW) possible in the back-of-house control booth and 32 (2.4-kW) more backstage. The only technical limitation was a shortage of places to plug in units in front of the proscenium — a circumstance readily overcome by making up additional portable cable and twofers. A single unit set, massively impressive in size, was used throughout the season.

Repertory designers who have a different set (or sets) for each show face additional challenges which I fortunately did not have to deal with. William and Mary staff designer J. H. Bledsoe designed the quite flexible basic set and with the assistance of graduate designer David Crank modified it with furniture, drapes, banners, steps, platforms, and an occasional piece which flew in. Costumes were by Rondi Hillstrom Davis and Lorraine Venberg. Each production had its own director: Jean Cutler for *Merry Wives,* John Cappelletti for *Richard III,* and Jack Clay for *All's Well.*

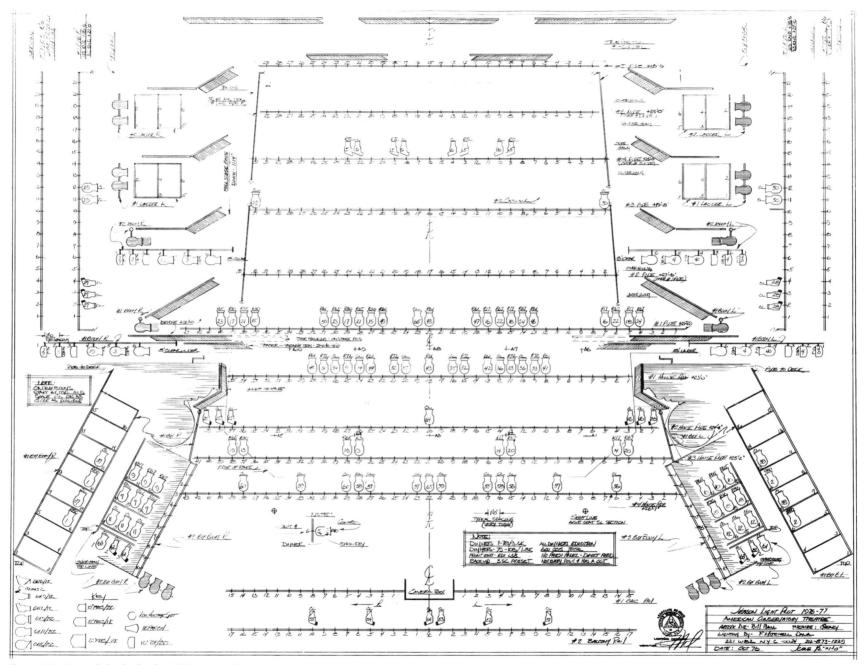

Figure 6.22 Season light plot for the ACT (American Conservatory Theatre) in San Francisco. Lighting: F. Mitchell Dana.

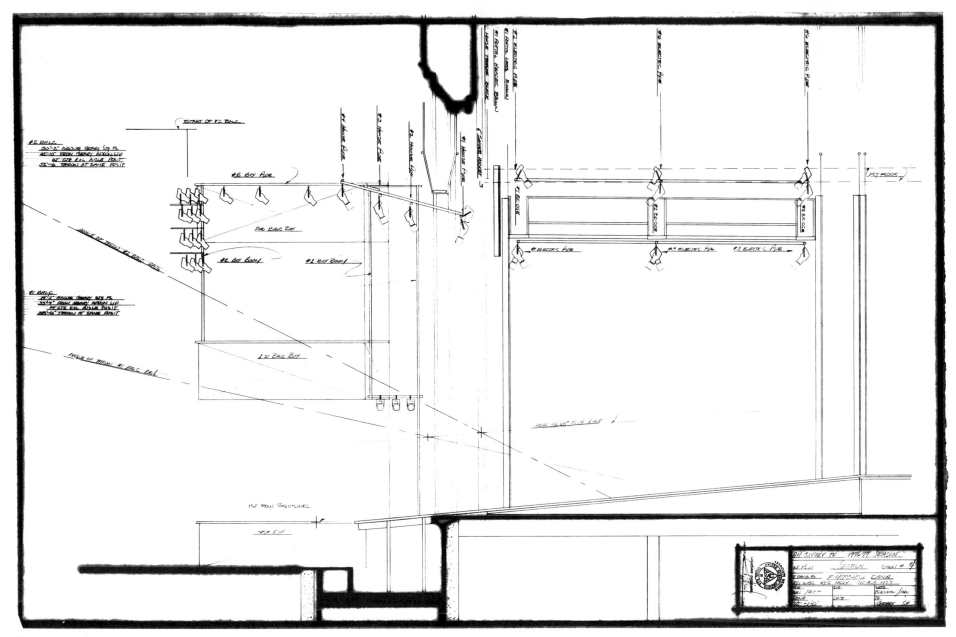

Figure 6.23 Lighting section for ACT.

Figure 6.24 Switchboard hookup for ACT season and A Christmas Carol. Lighting: F. Mitchell Dana.

SHOW: American Conservatory Th / Rep Plot   DATE: Oct 76
LIGHTING BY F. MITCHELL DANA, 221 WEST 82nd STREET, NEW YORK CITY (212) 873-1229

SW#	USE	TYPE	COLOR	POSITION	NOTES
1	LOW SIDE 1R BLUE	6X12/750	R80	1BBR 6·10	CUT AWAY TOP HATS
2	1L			1BBL 6·10	"
3	2R	6X12 10"BP		1BR5·2BR5 / 1BR2·2BR2	
4	2L	6X12 10"BP		1BL5·2BL5 / 1BL2·2BL5	
5	BLUE BK IN 2	6X12/1K	R72	4P 9·13·19·23	
6	CL BK IN L		CL	4P 10·14·18·22	
7	BOX WASH R WARM	6X12/750	R01	2BBR 7·8·9	TOP HATS
8	L WARM		R36	2BBL 7·8·9	
9	R COOL		R67	2BBR 10·11·12	
10	L COOL		R65	2BBL 10·11·12	
11	R CLEAR		CL	2BBR 4·5·6	
12	L CLEAR		CL	2BBL 4·5·6	
13	HIGH SIDE WARM 1R		R30	3H 27·37	CUT TH
14	1L		R17	3H 5·15	
15	HIGH SIDE WARM 2R	6X9/750	R30	1P 27·37	
16	2L		R17	1P 7·17	
17	3R		R30	1P 29·39	
18	3L		R17	1P 5·15	
19	HIGH SIDE COOL 1R	6X12/750	R65	3H 28·38	CUT TOP HATS
20	1L		R67	3H 4·14	"
21	2R	6X9/750	R65	1P 28·38	
22	2L		R67	1P 6·16	
23	3R		R65	1P 30·40	
24	3L		R67	1P 4·14	
25	CLEAR ENDS 1R	6X12/1KQTZ	CL	2H 37·38·39	CUT TOP HATS
26	1L			2H 1·2·3	"
27	2R	6X9/1KQTZ, 6X12		1PR2 / 1PR 3·4	
28	2L	6X9, 6X12		1PL2 / 1PL 3·4	
29	CL ENDS 3R	6X9/750, 6X12	CL	3P31 / 1PR 11·12	
30	3L	6X9, 6X12		3P1 / 1PL 11·12	
31	BACK BL 1R	6X9/750	R72	1H 25·27	CUT TOP HATS

LIGHTING BY F. MITCHELL DANA, 221 WEST 82nd STREET, NEW YORK CITY (212) 873-1229

SW#	USE	TYPE	COLOR	POSITION	NOTES
32	1C			1H 15·21	
33	1L			1H 9·11	
34	BACK CL 1R		CL	1H 24·26	
35	1C			1H 16·20	
36	1L			1H 10·12	
37	LOW SIDE CL 1R	6X12/	CL	1BBR 8·12	
38	1L			1BBL 8·12	
39	2R	6X12 10"BP		1BR4·2BR4 / 1BR1·2BR1	
40	2L	6X12 10"BP		1BL4·2BR4 / 1BL1·2BL1	
41	TOP A1/DL	6X12/750	R61	1H8	TOP HAT
42	A2/DC			1H 13	"
43	TOP A3/DC	6X12/750	R61	1H 18	TOP HAT
44	A4/DR			1H 23	"
45	A5/DR			1H 28	"
46	A6/L	6X9/750		1P 13	
47	A7/LC			1P 18	
48	A8/C			1P 22	
49	A9/RC			1P 26	
50	A10/R			1P 31	
51	FRONT A1/DL	6X12/750, 6X16/1KQTZ	CL	1H 27 / 2RAIL 10L	TOP HAT
52	A2/DC			2RAIL 51	
53	A3/DC			2RAIL 1L	
54	A4/DRC			2RAIL 5R	
55	A5/DR	6X12/750		2RAIL 10R / 4H 17	TOP HAT
56	A6/L	6X12/750		4H 6·15	
57	FRONT A7/LC	6X12/750	CL	4H 11·23	
58	A8/C			4H 16·28	
59	A9/RC			4H 21·33	
60	A10/R			4H 29·38	
61	IN 1 PUNCH L	6X12/750, 6X12/1KQTZ	CL	2BBL 1 / 2BBR 3	
62	C	6X12/1KQTZ		2BBR 2 / 2BBL 2	
63	R	6X12/1KQTZ, 6X12/750		2BBL 3 / 2BBR 1	

LIGHTING BY F. MITCHELL DANA, 221 WEST 82nd STREET, NEW YORK CITY (212) 873-1229

SW#	USE	TYPE	COLOR	POSITION	NOTES
64	DC SPEC	6X16/1KQTZ, 6X12/750		2RAIL CL / 2H 20	TOP HAT
65	CC SPEC	6X12/750		4H 22 / 1P 23	

CHRISTMAS CAROL
CHECK-OUT SHEETS   AS OF DEC. 2, 1976

DIMMER	DESCRIPTION	COLOR	TYPE	POSITION	CIRCUIT
074	CLOCK FACE	CLR	SPECIAL	1G10	1G10
075	LANTERNS	CLR	SPECIAL	1G9	1G9
076	CANDLES	CLR	SPECIAL	GRID	1G1
		CLR	SPECIAL	GRID	G3-8
077	BUSINESS MEN	R92	6 X 12	1BBR10	1BBR4
		R92	6 X 12	1BBL10	3BBL6
078	CAROLLER (6"FRES)	CLR	SPECIAL	3H29	3H32
079	DICKEN'S SPEC	CLR	PINSPOT	1BAL10	1BAL10
080	HANDCOCK SPEC	R72	6 X 12	4P15	4P10
		R65	6 X 12	2P22	2P18
081	GHOST SPEC	R65	6 X 9	1P20	1P13
082	BED	R65	6 X 12	2L5	2L3
		R65	6 X 12	2R5	2R1
083	SCROOGE DOWN	R71	10" B.F.	3H20	3H20
084	MINER	R17	10" B.F.	3H23	3H25
085	HOBBY HORSE	R18	6 X 12	1BBR14	3BBR1
086	GHOUL	R72	6 X 9	SHIN	SR3
087	HARPIES	R92	6 X 12	2R11	2R6
		R92	6 X 12	2L11	2L6
088	CANDLES -#2 UNIT	CLR	SPECIAL	GRID	1G2
089	CRATCHET FRONT L	R38	6 X 16	3BBL11	3BBL1
		R38	6 X 12	1BBL12	1BBL4
090	US CROSS LITES	CLR	10" B.F.	2R19	2R9
		CLR	10" B.F.	2L19	1L7
		R72	6 X 9	5P15	5P11
091	CC BACK (LEFT)	R18	6 X 9	1H1	1H3
		R18	6 X 9	1L5	1L4
092	CC WARM (LEFT)	R30	8" FRES.	2BL6	2BL3
		R30	8" FRES.	1BL6	1BL4
093	COOL BACK TNT	R72	6 X 12	8FB	6F5
		R72	6 X 12	6P22	6P5
		R72	6 X 12	6P12	6F11
		R72	6 X 12	6P18	6P11
094	WARM BACK IN3	CLR	6 X 12	6P13	6P12
		CLR	6 X 12	6P21	6P12
		CLR	6 X 12	6P9	6F17
		CLR	6 X 12	6F17	6P14
096	CC COOL (RIGHT)	R68	6 X 9	2R1	2P22
		R68	6 X 9	2R6	2R3
		R68	6 X 9	2R10	2R5
097	SKATING FRONT	R52	6 X 12	1BAL4	1BAL15
		R52	6 X 12	1BAL5	1BAL15
098	OFFICE BACK	CLR	6 X 9	1F21	1F14
		CLR	6 X 9	1P24	1P14
099	OFFICE FRONT	CLR	6 X 12	2H19	2H13
		CLR	6 X 12	4H25	4H29
100	ICE SKATING	R72	6 X 9	1L9	1L5
		R72	6 X 9	1L10	1L5
101	COOL SET	R81	6 X 12	1BAL7	1BAL 3
		R81	6 X 12	1BAL 8	1PAL 3
		R81	6 X 12	1BAL9	1BAL17
		R81	6 X 12	1BAL10	1BAL17
102	CC GOBOS DS	R71	6 X 12	3H6	3H6
		R71	6 X 9	3H10	3H9
		R71	6 X 12	3H29	3H30
		R71	6 X 12	3H35	3H14
103	CC GOBOS US	R71	6 X 9	1P8	1F6
		R71	6 X 9	1P12	1P5
		R71	6 X 9	1P32	1P24
		R71	6 X 9	1P36	1P25
104	CC GOBOS SET	R71	6 X 12	3P5	3P3
		R71	6 X 9	3P27	3P1B
		R71	6 X 12	2P26	2P21
		R71	6 X 12	2F8	2P7
105	CRATCHET FRONT R	R09	6 X 16	3BBR11	3BBR5
		R09	6 X 12	4H24	4H24
106	FRED'S HOUSE BACK	R30	6 X 9	1H29	1H20
107	FRED'S HOUSE FRNT	R11	6 X 12	3BBR10	3BBR4
		R09	6 X 12	3H9	3H8
108	FIREPLACE	915	6 X 12	3H22	3H22

Figure 6.25 Production photo of *A Christmas Carol* in December 1979 at the Geary Theatre, ACT, San Francisco. Director: Laird Williams; scene design: Robert Blackman; costumes: Robert Morgan; lighting: F. Mitchell Dana.

The lighting design problem was complicated by the fact that these three plays represent extremes of the many styles Shakespeare wrote in, with *Merry Wives* being basically a bawdy farce, *Richard III* a dark tragedy, and *All's Well* a light, fluffy "style" piece. No one color of light could conceivably be right for all three shows. The choice of these three shows immediately dictated certain "season" designer's choices: bastard amber and violet from the front overhead for the eight basic areas was the first choice. Bastard amber would work well for *Merry Wives* and much of *All's Well*. Violet could be the warm for *Richard III* and could also be a strong toning asset for both *Merry Wives* and *All's Well*. Crosslights (sidelighting from front-of-house and backstage booms) would work best in four colors — no color, light blue, moonlight blue-green, and strong pink. The raw white no color would be invaluable for *Merry Wives* and useful in parts of *All's Well*. The light blue could work in all three productions, as a toner in *Merry Wives* and *All's Well*, and as the basic warm in *Richard III*. The moonlight blue-green would be basic to the many heavy, dark scenes in *Richard III*, and the pink circuit would be of primary importance in *All's Well*.

Given those front and cross light choices, remaining available luminaires were sufficiently limited to dictate steel blue and dark blue as the two backlight circuit choices. Forty of the 271 lighting units were held back as specials. These included leaf gobo circuits used over the entire playing area in both night and day colors (useful for all exterior scenes), a "heater cone" smoke

circuit for the *Richard III* battle scenes, twinkling stars embedded in the huge back wall for some of the highly romantic scenes of *All's Well*, and an ample pool of narrow angle powerful ellipsoidals unassigned in all key positions. These unassigned specials were allocated show by show throughout the season as needed when located in inaccessible positions backstage or on the side walls front-of-house. A larger number of unassigned specials were placed in the three ceiling coves, readily reachable between performances on catwalks for color change and refocus. House border lights in primary color roundels of amber, red, green, and blue were used to provide a color wash on the massive back wall (dark blue for exterior night scenes) and to backlight scrim and gauze draperies flown in for *All's Well*. Four ancient and rusted 2000-watt beam projectors, inherited by William and Mary from the deceased outdoor pageant *Common Glory*, turned out to be a god-send. They were used to provide amber and blue diagonal slashes across the wood paneled back wall — a design/compositional tool used to enhance an otherwise dull scene.

We frequently replugged the circuits between shows, particularly on the readily accessible backstage switchboard. My experience with earlier repertory seasons had taught me the great value of keeping things simple — absolute minimum color and focus changes, replugging, etc. Except for a very minimum number of practical or decorative lights on the sets themselves, nothing changed the rest of the season once all shows had opened.

While all three directors were different in personality and approach, they were fully aware of the needs of the other shows and adjusted to those few artistic compromises which became necessary. All was made remarkably better by two team members — Chris Boll, the technical director and lighting educator at William and Mary, and Mary-Sue Gregson, the young stage manager who kept ironclad control over a large group of theatre people.

A frequent difficulty in working repertory is the scheduling. Since the same basic group of performers is simultaneously rehearsing and learning three different scripts, mastering fight sequences and choreography, having costumes fitted, and attending endless rehearsals, things tend toward madness. The technical crew comes in at dawn and puts one set and the lighting in place. Meanwhile the cast is rehearsing an entirely different show in the rehearsal hall. The show onstage is worked on during the late morning and early afternoon. Then it is struck and another set and lighting are put onstage for the evening's rehearsal or performance. And on a bad day, you can end up with all three productions (including sets, sound, lights, costumes, and performers) appearing on the same stage in one day. The possibilities for confusion abound.

[137] *"Lighting for Opera and Ballet in Repertory, An Interview with Hans Sondheimer at the New York State Theatre,"* Theatre Crafts, vol. 7, No. 1 (Jan./Feb. 1973), pp. 12–15, 34–38. *A chatty, well-written, rambling interview dealing with many of the basic considerations and problems of repertory production.*

Jim Tilton, *"Repertory Theatre: The Problems of a Complete Concept in Stage Design — Part I,"* Theatre Crafts, vol. 1, no. 1 (Mar./Apr. 1967), pp. 20–23. *Basic sketch for what repertory is, from the scenic designer's viewpoint. Illus.*

Gilbert V. Hemsley, Jr., *"Repertory Theatre: The Problem of a Complete Concept in Lighting and Sound — Part 2,"* Theatre Crafts, vol. 1, no. 2 (May/June 1967), pp. 15–21. *Very practical how-to tips on the realistic problems of rep. Well-written and well-illustrated.*

Helmut Grosser, *"The German Repertory Theatre,"* TABS, Part I: vol. 34, no. 1 (Spring 1976), pp. 5–7. Part II: vol. 34, no. 2 (Summer 1976), pp. 10–11. *Two brief articles by one of the world's leading experts on repertory. The German system is quite different from that used in the United States. Good background; informational reading.*

"The Seattle Repertory Theatre," Theatre Crafts, vol. 9, no. 6 (Nov./Dec. 1975), pp. 12–15, 29–32, 34–35. *Well-illustrated article which sketches the basics of repertory operation.*

Toni Goldin, *"Going the Limit: Realistic Repertory Lighting for Limited Facilities,"* Theatre Crafts, vol. 2, no. 6 (Oct. 1978), pp. 24–25, 58, 60–62, 64. *Handy how-to article about operating with limited facilities. Includes a light plot for rep.*

John Gleason, *"Lighting for Repertory at the Vivian Beaumont,"* Theatre Crafts, vol. 2, no. 6 (Nov. 1968).

"Speed, Simplicity Are Design Elements at NYC Opera," Rosconews, Spring 1986, pp. 2, 4. *A*

description by resident lighting designer Mark Stanley at the New York City Opera.

Susan Lieberman, "Northern Lights," Theatre Crafts, vol. 18, no. 7 (Aug./Sept. 1984), pp. 40–45, 95–98. Illus., color. Contains Duane Schuler's season repertory light plot for the Chicago Lyric Opera.

Bethany Haye, "Real Rep Comes to Broadway, Cyrano and Much Ado at the Gershwin," Theatre Crafts, vol. 19, no. 1 (Jan. 1985), pp. 38–41, 73–76. Illus., color. The rep work of British lighting designer Terry Hands and American Jeffrey Beecroft for the New York City run of the Royal Shakespeare Company's 1984 tour. Light plot included.

[138] *Lee Watson, "Light's Labours Not Lost," Lighting Dimensions, vol. 8, no. 2 (Mar./Apr. 1984), pp. 23–27. Illus., color. Light plot and hookup.*

It's difficult enough to please everyone involved in a production and still be happy with the quality of one's own work; take the whole set of problems, compromises, personalities, frustrations, all the pleasures and the pains, and everything else that goes into a show, multiply by three, and your work is cut out for you. As a test of a lighting designer's organizational skills, no experience is so valuable as the one offered by repertory theatre."[138]

Figures 6.26 and 6.27 give the light plot and switchboard hookup for Virginia Shakespeare Festival and Color Figs. 50 through 57 present selected production photos.

A careful study of this wealth of plots, hookups, and production photos should prepare any designer for the most difficult challenge — but often the most rewarding one — to be faced: repertory.

Touring

At best, touring is painful and it demands extensive technical know-how. From a design standpoint it is painful for the designer to face the necessity of simplifying beautiful designs. But it is inevitable! Managements cannot hope to endure on the road with today's high prices and frequently sparse audiences unless drastic economies are made. Lighting equipment must be consolidated (and eliminated) so as to fit available packing space — without sacrificing the design integrity of the show's "look." Personnel must be cut (weekly salaries for excessive electricians and followspot operators can lead to abrupt closings). While designers are aware of all of this, they often stand strongly opposed to any and all cuts. The producer and director may feel the same way, but reality wins in the end. The lighting designer must stay out of the middle of any conflict between the business staff and the artistic management. Furthermore, it should be kept in mind that if the show does tour successfully, the work of a master of lighting artistry will be seen many more places and by larger numbers of people than if the show did not tour.

The designer's point of departure is an extremely detailed analysis of the original lighting plan. Can anything be eliminated or simplified? Can one luminaire, at full intensity, replace two units at half intensity? Can color blends be done directly, with the color media producing the final color desired rather than having three colors carefully blended together? Only a detailed paperwork analysis of the designer's original plot, hookup, and cue sheets will yield the answers to these kinds of questions. It takes much time and care. At the request of the producer, I cut lighting equipment by nearly one-half and switchboards by one-third when we moved The Diary of Anne Frank from one Broadway theatre to another at the end of the first year. Careful redesign of the set by Boris Aronson was an important factor. Neither the cast nor that brilliant director, Garson Kanin, could detect any difference in the new simplified lighting. We had undertaken such a simplification for the second year of the New York City run to pretest the road tour version of the lighting. The simplification worked.

In addition to knowing how to approach design simplification, the lighting designer for a touring show needs to know a great deal technically about equipment. Luminaires or lamps must be found which are more powerful (in output), yet more compact than regular lamps. Setup time can be saved by using multiconductor cables. Nearly indestructable switchboards should be sought out. The designer should investigate ways of obtaining booms and sectional pipe-trusses which can carry luminaires in packing boxes, already locked in correct focus and carrying color and ready to be set up in a minimal amount of time. Electricians who tour regularly can guide a designer to shortcuts and offer advice about the latest time-savers — both equipment and practices. If a designer doesn't cut the lighting down to manageable proportions for the crew size and setup time available, much of the show will never be hung out of town, and damage to the designer's reputation may result.

Touring shows can put money in the designer's pocket. The designer is nearly always called upon to provide the tour light plot, because he or she is the one who best knows what cuts can be made. Union rules state that the minimum pay for preparing lighting for a touring show is an additional one-half of the original design fee. Designing for touring involves no more than (1) extensive knowledge of lighting equipment and road men and what both do; (2) detailed analysis of the original concept; and (3) lots of careful paperwork. Designers who do their tour preparation well

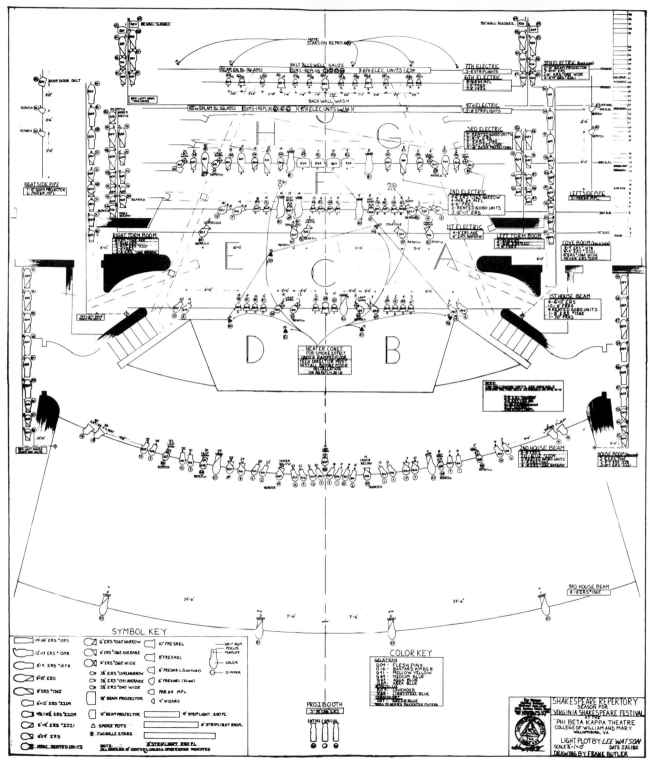

Figure 6.26 Season light plot for the Virginia Shakespeare Festival, by Lee Watson.

VIRGINIA SHAKESPEARE FESTIVAL Repertory HOOK-UP.   Phi Beta Kappa Theatre.   Williamsburg, Va.

DIMMER NUMBER	INSTRUMENT TYPE(s)	GANGED ON TWO-FER	INSTRUMENT LOCATION & KEY NUMBERS	COLOR	FOCUS
HOUSE SWITCHBOARD:	Dimmers #1-40 are 4 kw.; Dimmers #41-48 are 12 kw.				
#1	2--6x12" Cent.#2209 ERS	X	#2 Beam 6, 17	G 16	Area A Fronts, B. A.
#2	Ditto	X	#2 Beam 3, 15	G 16	Area B Fronts, B. A.
#3	Ditto	X	#2 Beam 12, 25	G 16	Area C Fronts, B. A.
#4	Ditto	X	#2 Beam 22, 34	G 16	Area D Fronts, B. A.
#5	Ditto	X	#2 Beam 20, 31	G 16	Area E Fronts, B. A.
#6	Ditto	X	#1 Beam 1, 19	G 16	Area F Fronts, B. A.
#7	2--6" Kl. #1365,Narrow ERS	X	#2 Beam 10; 2nd Elec.19	G 16	Area G Fronts, B. A.
#8	Ditto		#2 Beam 27; 2nd Elect.1	G 16	Area H Fronts, B. A.
#9	2--6x12" Cent.#2209 ERS	X	#2 Beam 7, 18	R 57	Area A Fronts, Violet
#10	Ditto	X	#2 Beam 4, 16	R 57	Area B Fronts, Violet
#11	Ditto	X	#2 Beam 13, 26	R 57	Area C Fronts, Violet
#12	Ditto	X	#2 Beam 23, 35	R 57	Area D Fronts, Violet
#13	Ditto	X	#2 Beam 21, 32	R 57	Area E Fronts, Violet
#14	Ditto	X	#1 Beam 2, 20	R 57	Area F Fronts, Violet
#15	2--6" Kl. #1365,Narrow ERS		#2 Beam 11;2nd Elect.20	R 57	Area G Fronts, Violet
#16	Ditto		#2 Beam 28;2nd Elect. 2	R 57	Area H Fronts, Violet
#17	2--8" Fres.,Cent. 3468	X	#2 Beam 1, 2	Various	ENTIRE, X-Lt. from Left
#18	Ditto	X	#1 Beam 36, 37	Various	ENTIRE, X-lt. from Right
#19					
#20	1--14x36" ERS, Kl. #1393		Proj. Booth 1, 2	Various	Fronts, Entire Wash
#21	1--14x36" ERS, Kl. #1393		Proj. Booth 3	Various	Fronts, Entire Wash
#22	1--8" ERS, Kl. #1365		#1 Beam 9		Spares
#23	2--8" ERS, Kl. #1365		#2 Beam 9, 29		Spares
#24	2--8" ERS, Kl. #1365		#3 Beam 1, 2		Spares
#25	2--8" ERS, Kl. #1365,Narrow ERS		#3 Beam 3, 4		Spares
#26	2--6" Kl. #1365,Narrow ERS		Rt. Portal Boom 12; #2 Beam 14,	G 16	"Rich III:"Inner Below, B. A.
#26B	3--Rental units, Template		#2 Beam 8, 30; #1 Beam 8	G 41 & Leaf Gobo	"Merry," "All's Well" Leaf Gobos on Stg. Floor & Rt. Wall, Yellow
#27	2--6" Kl. #1365,Narrow ERS		Rt. Portal Boom 11; #2 Beam 24	G 69	"Rich II:" Inner Below, Area Blue
#27B	3--Rental Units, Template	X	#2 Beam 13; 3rd Elect. 4, 19	G 41 & Leaf Gobo	"Merry," "All's Well" Leaf Gobos on Backwall & Left Wall, Yellow
#28	1--8x9" ERS, Cent. #1578 1--6x9" ERS,Cent.#2321 1--6" ERS, Kl. #1365,Narrow	X	House Boom Left 2,5,8	G 69	Box Boom L, Lt. Blue
#29	Ditto	X	House Boom Rt. 2, 5, 8	G 69	Box Boom R, Lt. Blue
#30	1--4x6" ERS, Cent. 2204 1--6" ERS, Kl. #1365, Wide 1--8x9" ERS,Cent.#1578	X	Cove L 2, 5, 8	G 69	Prosc.Boom L, Lt. Blue
#31	Ditto	X	Cove R 2, 5, 8	G 69	Prosc. Boom R, Lt. Blue
#32	1--8x10" ERS, Cent. 1--6x9" ERS, Cent. #2321 1--6" Fresnel	X	Torm Boom L 1, 5, 7	G 69	Portal Boom L, Lt. Blue
#33	Ditto	X	Torm Boom Rt. 1,5,7	G 69	Portal Boom Rt.,Lt. Blue
#34	Same as on Dimmer #28	X	House Boom L 1, 4, 7	D 57	Box Boom L,Mnlt.Bl.Gn.
#35	Same as on Dimmer #28	X	House Boom Rt. 1, 4, 7	D 57	Box Boom Rt.,Mnlt.Bl.Gn.
#36	Same as on Dimmer #30	X	Cove L 1, 4, 7	D 57	Prosc. Boom L,Mnlt.Bl.Gn.
#37	Same as on Dimmer #30	X	Cove Rt. 1, 4, 7	D 57	Prosc. Boom R,Mnlt.Bl.Gn.
#38	Same as on Dimmer #32	X	Torm Boom L 2, 4, 8	D 57	Portal Boom L,Mnlt.Bl.Gn.
#39	Same as on Dimmer #32	X	Torm Boom R 2, 5, 8	D 57	Portal Boom R,Mnlt.Bl.Gn.
#40					

VIRGINIA SHAKESPEARE FESTIVAL Repertory HOOK-UP. Phi Beta Kappa Theatre. Williamsburg, Va. Page 2

DIMMER NUMBER	INSTRUMENT TYPE(s)	GANGED ON TWO-FER	INSTRUMENT LOCATION & KEY NUMBERS	COLOR	FOCUS
#41	2--8x10" ERS, Cent.	X	3rd Elect. 3, 6	R 64	BKLT., Area A--Steel Bl.
	4--6" Fresnels	X	2nd Elect. 4,6; #1 Beam 3, 5	R 64	F'LT., Area B--Stl. Bl.
#42	2--Fresnel, Cent.		2nd Elect. 10, 12	R 64	BKLT., Area C--Stl. Bl.
	4--6" Fresnels	X	#1 Beam 10, 12		
	3--6" Fresnel	X	2nd Elect. 17; #1 Beam 15, 17	R 64	BKLT., Area D--Stl. Bl.
	2--8x10" ERS, Century		3rd Elect. 15, 17	R 64	BKLT., Area E--Stl. Bl.
	2--PAR 64, MFL, 500w.		6th Elect. 1,3,5,6	R 64	BKLT., Area E--Stl. Bl.
	2--18" BP, Altman		3rd Elect. 9, 11	R 64	BKLT., Area F--Stl. Bl.
	2--PAR 64, MFL, 500w.		6th Elect. 8,9,11,13	R 64	BKLT., Area H--Stl. Bl.
	1--8x10" Century		3rd Elect. 20	R 64	BKLT., Spare
#43					
#44	3--6x9" ERS, Century	X	3rd Elect. 2,5,7	G 64	BKLT., Area A--Dk. Bl.
	3--6" Fresnels	X	2nd Elect. 5; #1 Beam 4, 6	G 64	BKLT., Area B--Dk. Bl.
	1--6" PAR 64, MFL, 500w.		2nd Elect. 7		
	1--6" Fresnels		2nd Elect. 11	G 64	BKLT., Area C--Dk. Bl.
	1--6" PAR 64, MFL, 500w.		2nd Elect. 13		
	1--10" Fresnel, Cent.		#1 Beam 11		
	3--6" Fresnels	X	2nd Elect. 18; #1 Beam 16, 18	G 64	BKLT., Area D--Dk. Bl.
#45	2--8x9" ERS, Century	X	3rd Elect. 14,16,18,21	G 64	BKLT., Area E--Dk. Bl.
	2--18" BP, Altman		3rd Elect. 10, 12	G 64	BKLT., Area F--Dk. Bl.
	2--6" Fresnels	X	6th Elect. 2, 12	G 64	BKLT., Areas G-H, Dk. Bl.
	3--8" Fresnels, Cent.3468	X	6th Elect. 4, 7, 10	G 64	
#46					
#47	1--8x9" ERS, Cent. #1578	X	House Boom Left 3	G 04	X-LTS. from Left, Pink
	1--6x9" ERS, Cent.#2321	X	House Boom Left 6	G 04	
	1--8" ERS, Kliegl #1365, Narrow	X	House Boom Left 9	G 04	
	1--4x6" ERS, Cent. 2204	X	Cove Left 3	G 04	X-LTS. from Left,Pink
	1--6" ERS,Kl. #1365, Wide	X	Cove Left 6	G 04	
	1--8x9" ERS, Cent.#1578	X	Cove Left 9	G 04	
	1--8x10" ERS, Cent.	X	Torm Boom Left 3	G 04	X-LTS. from Left,Pink
	1--6x9" ERS, Cent. #2321	X	Torm Boom Left 6	G 04	
	1--6" Fresnel	X	Torm Boom Left 9	G 04	
#48	Same as Dimmer #47	X	House Boom Rt.3,6,9	G 04	X-LTS. from Rt., Pink
	Same as Dimmer #47	X	Cove Right 3, 6, 9	G 04	X-LTS. from Rt., Pink
	Same as Dimmer #47	X	Torm Boom Rt. 3, 6, 9	G 04	X-LTS. from Tr., Pink

BACKSTAGE SWITCHBOARD: 32 dimmers, 2.4 kw.

#50	Twinkle Stars		Mtd. on Backwall, F1		"Merry," "All's Well"
#50R	Heater Cones		Under Floor, F2		"Richard III" Smoke
#51	3--8' Xrays, 150w, R-40s		7th Elect. 1	Red	"All's Well" Scrim Bklts
#51R	Heater Cones		Under Floor, F3		"Richard III" Smoke
#52	3--8' Xrays, 150w, R-40s		7th Elect. 2	Amber	"All's Well" Scrim Bklts
#52R	2--6" ERS, Kl.#1365, Aver.	X	1st Elect. 4, 7	G 16	"Rich III" Inner Above
	1--6" ERS, Kl.#1365,Narrow		Portal Boom Rt. 1		
#53	3--8' Xrays, 150w, R-40s		7th Elect. 3	Green	"All's Well" Scrim Bklts
#54	3--8' Xrays, 150w, R-40s		7th Elect. 4	Blue	"All's Well" Scrim Bklts
#55	2--PAR 64, MFL, 500w.	X	Left Side Pipe 1,2	?	"All's" Window Bklts.,L
#55R	1--6" ERS, Kl.#1365,Narrow	X	1st Elect. 4	R 57	"Rich III" Stairs
	2--6" ERS,Kl.#1365,Average	X	1st Elect. 2, 5	R 57	

VIRGINIA SHAKESPEARE FESTIVAL Repertory HOOK-UP. Phi Beta Kappa Theatre, Williamsburg, Va. Page 3

DIMMER NUMBER	INSTRUMENT TYPE(s)	GANGED ON TWO-FER	INSTRUMENT LOCATION & KEY NUMBERS	COLOR	FOCUS
#56	2--PAR 64, MFL, 500w.	X	Right Side Pipe 3,4	?	"All's" Window Bklts.,R
#56R	1--6" ERS, Kl.#1365,Narrow		2nd Elect. 3	R 57	"Rich III" Ramp
#57	2--8x10" ERS, Cent.	X	5th Elect. Ladders, Left 5,7;Right 6,8		X-LTS., Area J, "In Four" Moonlt. Blue-Green
	2--6x9" ERS,Cent.#2321	X		D 57	
#58	2--8x10" ERS, Cent.	X	5th Elect. Ladders, Left 3,6;Right 4,5	R 16	X-LTS.,Area J,"In Four" Amber
	2--6" ERS,Kl.#1365,Wide				
#59	2--8x10" ERS, Century	X	5th Elect. Ladders, Left 4,8;Right 3,7	G 69	X-LTS., Area J, "In Four" Lt. Blue
#60	5--6" Xray,150w. R-40s		4th Elect. 1, 2	Red or Green	Backwall Wash
#61	5--6" Xray,150w. R-40		4th Elect. 3	Amber	Backwall Wash
#62	5--6" Xray,150w. R-40s		4th Elect. 4	Blue	Backwall Wash
#63					
#64					
#65					
#66	3--Template Lekos	X	1st Elect. 14; 3rd Elect. 1, 22	G 67-Gobo	NiteLeaf Gobos; 2 on back-wall, 1 on L , wall-NITE
#67	3--Template Lekos	X	#1 Beam 7; 2nd Elect. 8, 15	G 67-Gobo	Nite Leaf Gobos; 3 on up-stg. floor;1 on Rt. wall
#68	3--Template Lekos	X	#2 Beam 5,19,33	G 67-Gobo	Nite Leaf Gobos on stg.floor, Aqua Blue
#69	4--15" BP, 2000w.@		5th Elect. Ladders, Left 1,2;Right 1,2	G 64 R 57	Backwall Diag. Slashes; Replug as needed
#70	**				
#71	**				
#72	**				
#73	**				
#74	**				
#75	**				
#76	1--15" BP, Century,2000w.		Right Side Pipe 1	G 16	Rt. Door Bklt., Amber
#77					
#78					
#79					
#80	3--12x17" ERS,Cent.#1358		Fwd Elect. 9,14,18	?	Bkstg. Specials,as needed
#81	2--12x17" ERS,Cent.#1358		3rd Elect. 8, 13	?	Bkstg. Specials,as needed

** The following units should be kept on the deck to "float" as booms and specials,as needed:

6--6" Fresnels
2--6" ERS, Kl. #1365, Wide
3--6" ERS, Kl. #1365, Average
Miscellaneous Xrays

6--3½" ERS, Kl. #1340 with 2 Wide (46°), 2 Average (37°),
and 6 Narrow (32°) Lens barrels
4--9" Wizzards, 250w.

Figure 6.27 Season switchboard hookup for the Virginia Shakespeare Festival.

need not strip the "look" of the show or remove their names from the program.

Four types of attractions tour all the time, basically often having no real home base. These are concert shows (rock, jazz, etc.), industrial shows, ballet, and ice shows. A study of the plots, hookups, and production photos can give a designer a good background to the problems of touring. For comparison, Chap. 8 presents the touring version of John Denver's outdoor concert in Australia (Figure 8-5); the same concert at a proscenium theatre in Lake Tahoe, Nevada (Figures 8-6 and 8-7); in an arena version (Figure 8-8); and at New York City's Madison Square Garden (Figure 8-9)—all the work of designer Jim Moody and Sundance Corp. Chap. 8 shows the *Boston World Tour, 1979*, Color Figs. 72 and 72a, by designer Richard Ocean. Sometimes a touring concert attraction also becomes a television show. In Chap. 7 are various versions of the touring *Neil Diamond Show,* with lighting design by Imero Fiorentino (Figs. 7.6 through 7.9). Most industrial shows tour. In Chap. 10 is the plot, hookup, and photographs for the Pontiac '74 Show, Color Figs. 90, 91, 91a and 91b, which toured for several weeks (and for which I designed the lighting).

Ballet tours all the time. Chapter 5 presents examples, such as the Ohio Ballet by Thomas Skelton and the American Ballet Theatre by Nananne Porcher. Ice shows, too, are always "on the road." Chapter 9 focuses on ice shows and the *Ice Capades* tours.

These various light plots, production photos, and hookups provide a basic idea of how working designers cope with many of the problems enumerated above.[139]

[139] Tharon Musser, *"Cutting Lighting Without Losing Concept,"* Theatre Crafts, vol. 3, no. 6 (Nov./Dec. 1969), pp. 16–21, 38. The only material in print on this most practical subject. Musser not only analyzes the theory of simplification of lighting equipment, while retaining the original "look" or concept, for national tours (one-week-or-longer stands), but also deals with "bus-truck" touring (one-night stands). She deals with the how-to cutdown in practical terms and also outlines the practices and problems.

Susan Levi Wallach, *"They're Playing His Song—Tom Mallow Upgrades the Bus and Truck,"* Theatre Crafts, vol. 15, no. 5 (May 1981), pp. 16–17, 68–69. And *"Designs to Go, Reworking for the Road,"* pp. 18, 56, 58–59. Illus. This issue contains Tharon Musser's hookups (switchboard) for two touring shows. Pages 20–21 offer her light plots. Page 25 presents Dennis Parichy's touring light plot for the Acting Company's Midsummer Night's Dream.

Dan Butt, *"They Don't Pay To Watch a Set-Up, Do They?"* Lighting Dimensions, vol. 4, no. 7 (July 1980), pp. 16–17, 19–21. Illus. A description by the American Ballet Theatre's production manager, with photos of touring essentials.

Ross Cogswell, *"It Ain't 'Arf Hot Mum!,"* ADL # magazine, no. 7 (July 1988), pp. 15–18. Illus. A humorous description of British touring practices.

Alice M. Hale, *"Lights, Touring,"* Theatre Crafts, vol. 21, no. 7 (Aug./Sept. 1987), pp. 24–25, 72–75. Illus. Includes light plot. An interview with Marilyn Rennagel concerning the touring version of her Broadway show Social Security, with tour light plot. Useful information.

"American Productions in Europe," Theatre Crafts, vol. 23, no. 5 (May 1989), pp. 32–82. Illus., color. The entire issue is devoted to touring. Subjects include American Repertory Theatre in Europe by Susan Lieberman; Joffrey Ballet in Vienna by Beth Howard; Houston Grand Opera in Scotland and China by Michael S. Eddy; The Wagner Ring Cycle of the Deutsche Oper Berlin at the Kennedy Center in Washington, D.C., by Beth Howard; The Wooster Group in Germany by John Calhoun; worldwide touring by the Amnesty International's Human Rights Now concert group; *"Freightwork"* by Michael S. Eddy; *"Permission to Tour"* (government work permits) by John Calhoun; *"Insuring Touring"* by Michael Sommers; *"Customs"* by John Calhoun; *"Stage Labor Abroad,"* by Mark Loeffler. Several articles also include touring (or "house") light plots. An invaluable issue for those about to tour.

Chapter 7

Photographic Lighting Design

"Lighting, of course, does a great deal more than just energize a camera. The monitor/receiver screen being only two dimensional (height & width), illusions of depth and solidity are a function of lighting. The objectives of lighting include the separation of elements through varied intensities; textures and directional qualities of light; modeling for solidity with side angle sources; accenting for visual interest; providing adequate illumination for camera; and most important of all, directing and holding the eye to a predetermined center of interest. The eye is always attracted to the brightest area in the composition we are viewing.

"In television picture making, having the important area or subject just a touch brighter than its surrounds is a mighty important factor in communicating our visual message.

"You see, cameras and lighting hardware don't make pictures — you do!"

E. CARLTON WINCKLER[140]

[140] *E. Carlton Winckler, "On Television Lighting,"* Lowell Light News, *#3 (Fall 1983), pp. 1, 4. Excellent short summary of TV lighting basics by an expert who began in TV lighting in 1943.*

See also E. Carlton Winckler, "The Objectives of Lighting," SMPTE Journal, *vol. 94, no. 3 (Mar. 1985), pp. 305–308. Illus. A more recent basic summary by Winckler of TV lighting.*

Television

History

Over a relatively short span of years, television has become a primary international industry. CBS inaugurated its first regular schedule of television broadcasting on July 21, 1931. That program lasted exactly 15 minutes and featured New York City Mayor Walker, Kate Smith, the Boswell Sisters — and George Gershwin at the piano. During 1931 CBS TV was on the air 49 hours per week — 7 hours per day, 7 days per week. At that time there were only about 7,500 TV sets in New York City, and the TV picture was broadcast in 60 scan lines, rather than the 525 lines broadcast today. CBS TV (experimental W2XAB) suspended telecasting after 2,500 hours on the air on February 23, 1933, because of poor picture quality from the 60-line image. NBC's first scheduled telecast was on April 3, 1939 showing Franklin D. Roosevelt at the New York World's Fair. On October 10, 1939, CBS TV resumed transmitting — this time with 441 scan lines — from its new transmitter atop the Chrysler Tower (the studios were in New York City's Grand Central Terminal Building).

In 1941, broadcasting equipment was modified for 525 lines. The Federal Communications Commission (FCC) approved regularly scheduled commercial television on July

1, 1941. There were only two stations at the time. WCBS TV aired a 15-hour-per-week schedule. The programming was a mixture of news, documentaries, public service programs, and variety shows. During World War II, programming was cut back to 4 hours per week to conserve scarce tubes and manpower. Only film was aired. Live broadcasting was resumed on May 5, 1944.

By 1947 CBS was able to transmit TV programs from Washington to New York to Boston using combined coaxial cable and microwave facilities. Programs were also telecast to Baltimore and Philadelphia. Mass production of TV sets began. Live sports events were being telecast, as well as key special events (the opening session of Congress, United Nations opening ceremonies, and so on). The big year was 1948, when network programming began. From 28 affiliated stations, CBS expanded to 55 by 1949. TV was off and running![141]

As of 1988 there were 1,315 television stations in the United States. Cable TV in the United States reaches 42 million subscribers. In 1988, between 65 and 70 percent of all U.S. households owned video cassette recorders.[142]

The Camera versus the Eye

It is useful to keep in mind throughout this chapter the very real difference between *live* lighting and seeing versus *picture* lighting and seeing. The human eye is an amazingly flexible instrument—no camera can come close to equaling it. The human eye's ability to adjust to brightness and contrast differences far exceeds that of any camera. The eye also has built-in "zoom" focus which no manufactured lens assembly can equal. Thanks to the *fovea* area of the eye, the "human eye" can switch instantly from distant to closeup focus, while still retaining peripheral field of vision in a way that no camera can equal. Of course, the human brain (and its infinite card file of remembered past visual images) acts as a memory/identification interpretative screen in the seeing process.

These factors of human seeing and vision can in some ways be applied to the TV camera and the movie camera, both marvelous man-made *instruments* that can record light/shade/color radiant energy and pass it through a lens assembly onto either emulsified film or an electronic grid of hairlike wires (the energy thus becomes a transmittable electronic impulse). But these instruments are *not* the eye! Here are a few of the ways in which the differences between human seeing and camera "seeing" affect lighting design:

1. Because both film (a reconstituted light/shade/color image on a flat screen) and TV (same light patterns but on a flat tube surface) lack the *third dimension* (depth), lighting designers in photography must put extra effort into accentuating the clues to depth, space, and dimensionality, allowing each member of the human viewing audience to reconstitute these elements in his "remembered visual images clues" brain sector to interpret the seen picture. This necessity to eradicate "flatness" on the movie screen or TV tube accounts (in part) for the heavy use of backlighting in photographic lighting.

2. There are *time* differences in the three media (live, film, TV):

   a. Live is infinitely variable and not *exactly* reproducible. Anything may happen! Tonight's Hamlet may forget a page of lines. Last night the same Hamlet may have delivered his greatest, most definitive performance—but it is gone forever. The element of *chance* is always present (one of the strongest of *all* human drives). Limited dissemination and no repeatability are keys to live performance.

   b. TV is the middle route. Even if a broadcast is completely live (news, interviews, all early TV), it is still transmittable and reproducible (at first on kinescope recording, these days on videotape). While the true live performance mentioned above can be seen by only a maximum of perhaps 20,000 people at one time, the TV "light image" is an electronic signal which can be sent simultaneously all over the world, reaching millions of people at once. Widespread dissemination and possible repeatability are keys.

   c. Film lies at the other end of the road. An infinite number of "takes" allows the cinematographer to polish a production piece until the ultimate desired performance is "in the can." Even then what is on film can be modified in film developing and processing and then

[141] Hank Warner, "The First 21 Years of CBS-TV: From Henry Burbig to 'Lucy' ", Variety, Nov. 12, 1952, p. 36.

See also: Carl Gaiti, op. cit. (see footnote 144).

For a history of British TV from 1908 through 1939, see Bruce Norman, Here's Looking at You. This is a volume jointly published by the Royal Television Society and BBC, obtainable from Halligan Advertising Services, Ltd., 66 Addison Road, Bromley, Kent BR2 9TT, England. Covers the contributions of John Baird, Karl Braun, P. T. Farnsworth, C. F. Jenkins, and V. K. Zworykin. Excellent source material, well written and readable.

Hans Fantel, "Video: Television in the Beginning," The New York Times, May 7, 1989, p. 21.

David Cockayne, "Documenting Design, Some Thoughts On the Preservation of Theatre Design Records," Sightline, vol. 22, no. 2 (April 1988), pp. 27–31. Illus. A well-presented plea for better photographic documentation of theatrical presentations.

[142] Irwin W. Stelzer and Geraldine Alpert, "Let The New York Post Survive. . . . ", The New York Times, January 16, 1988, p. 15.

"VCRs Are in 65 Percent of Households," AP release in June 24, 1988, Lafayette Journal & Courier, p. A10.

[143] See Tony DiGirolamo in Wanda Jankowski interview, p. 33, op. cit. (see footnote 144).

James Ellis Studdiford, "Creative Television Lighting," thesis, University of North Carolina, 1959.

John Ransford, "Lighting Design for Television," Yale M.F.A., 1953.

[144] Walter Nurnberg, Lighting for Photography. N.Y.; Focal Press; 1968. Standard reference work. Excellent basic text, illustrated. Now in its eighteenth edition in five languages. 212 pages.

Ted Schwarz and Brian Stoppee, The Photographer's Guide to Using Light, N.Y.; Amphoto of Watson-Guptill Publishers, 1986. 144 pages, illus., color. Excellent beginners guide.

Gerald Millerson, TV Lighting Methods. N.Y.; Focal Press/Hastings House (Communications Arts Books); 1975. The basic how-to text; well-illustrated; text in simple language, understandable to the beginner. Covers all important areas. 150 pages.

Comprehensive Video Supply Corp., A Primer on Lighting for Video, Northvale, New Jersey; Comprehensive Video Supply Corp. (148 Veterans Drive, Northvale, NJ 07647; tel: (201) 767-7990); 1987. A 24-page, well-illustrated, quite readable beginner's guide to TV lighting. Available for $2.

Gerald Millerson, The Technique of Lighting for Television and Motion Pictures. N.Y.; Focal Press/Hastings House; 1972. Basic text. Excellent illustrations; highly readable. Deals more with fundamentals than Millerson's TV Lighting Methods (see above), but makes theory understandable to the layman. 336 pages.

James DuBois, Lighting for Television, Notes and Practical Applications on the Art of Television Lighting. San Juan Capistrano, Calif.; CDT Publications (P.O. Box 1677, S.J.C., CA 92693); 1985. 120 pp. Illus. Basic how-to book.

Tom LeTourneau, Lighting Techniques for Video Production, The Art of Casting Shadows. White Plains, N.Y. and London; Knowledge Industry Publishers, 1987. 172 pp., illus. Excellent basic text.

J. A. Carroll and Dr. R. E. Sherriffs, TV Lighting Handbook. Blue Ridge Summit, Penn.; TAB Books; 1977. 226 pp., illus., color. Contains glossary and multiplicity of illustrations.

Harry Mathias and Richard Patterson, Electronic Cinematography. Hollywood, CA; Tech Seminars, Inc. (1765 N. Highland Ave., #626, Hollywood, CA 90028); 1985; also available from Wadsworth, Inc. An excellent book about utilizing cinematography lighting in TV work.

Wanda Jankowski, "TTFL—Television Lighting Today—A Work of Art," Lighting Design & Application, vol. 9, no. 3 (Mar. 1979), pp. 32–38. A well-illustrated interview with three top practicing TV Lighting Directors from Fiorentino Associates: Tony DiGirolamo, Dave Clark, and Greg Bruton. Useful design ideas and attitudes.

Bill Lee, "Television Lighting in Britain," Lighting Dimensions, vol. 5, no. 6 (Sept./Oct. 1981), pp. 26–28, 30–33. Illus., color.

EITV (Educational and Industrial Television magazine), published by C. S. Tepfer Publishing Co., Inc., 51 Sugar Hollow Road, Danbury, CT 06810; telephone: (203) 743-2120.

Bob Anderson, "Colour Music!" Cue, #42 (July/Aug. 1986), p. 20. Illus., color. A description of Richard Dale's color spectacular and the TV recording of it.

"Personality Profile, The Lighter Side of Lighting," Lighting Design & Application, vol. 3, no. 7 (July 1973), pp. 39–41. A humorous interview with Imero Fiorentino about things that go wrong; includes photographs and cartoons.

Carl Gaiti, "T.V. Lighting Then and Now," Lighting Dimensions, vol. 1, no. 3 (Sept. 1977), pp. 17–18. Good, brief history by a pioneer.

Fred Humphrey, "Strand's Part in Breakfast TV," TABS, vol. 40, no. 1 (Aug. 1983), pp. 16–17. Illus., color. Excellent color photos and text on newest British TV studio.

Richard Glickman, "Automated Lighting Systems at Nippon Hoso Kyokai, Part I," Lighting Dimensions, vol. 3, no. 4 (Apr. 1979), pp. 26–29, 31; "Part II," vol. 3, no. 6 (June 1979), pp. 10–12, 14–17. Lavishly color-illustrated series about the equipment and operation of the

edited and spliced. The performance thus preserved can be repeated exactly for as long as the physical film maintains its integrity. In other words, limitless dissemination and infinite repeatability are the keys (and chance and immediacy are gone forever).

Each of the three media has advantages for the human viewer. Each has disadvantages. One media is not better than the other, nor worse; they're just all different—and so is the corresponding lighting design. For live performances, the person doing the lighting may spend days in preparation, but when performance time comes, he "takes what he can get." The production is, however, "live" and vibrant and variable. TV lies in the middle: there is some possibility of striving for perfection, but the end product is only a flat two-dimensional light-and-shade picture brought alive by the viewer's mind. Film offers the ultimate possibility for the maximum artistic polish and refinement, but all immediacy is gone, and the result is still a two-dimensional radiant energy picture reinterpreted by the viewer's mind.

These media differences are important, because much actual practice in each field is conditioned by the necessity for a thorough understanding of the particular receptor (eye or TV camera or motion picture camera) and for a lighting design which takes into account the limitations and advantages of that receptor.[143]

The Elements of TV Lighting Design

This discussion covers seven topics—lighting equipment, audio problems, video control problems, teamwork, camera mobility, special problems, and "keys to mastery"[144]—and then presents some specific examples and illustrations.

Lighting Equipment

Basic to TV is an understanding of what Millerson calls "hard" light as opposed to "soft" light.[145] In live theatre the equivalent of hard light is called specific illumination ("shadow-producing" light); the equivalent for soft light is called general illumination ("shadowless" light). Hard light is produced by spotlights with lenses, projectors, etc. Soft light comes from scoops, borderlights, fluorescent tubes,

ultramodern, highly automated and computerized TV lighting operation in Japan. See also Yukinobu Ujiie, "A New Television Studio," Journal of the SMPTE, vol. 8, (July 1972), pp. 522–28; and Hideo Moriyama and Yasuo Itow, "A New Multipurpose Hall: Theatre and Broadcasting Facilities," Journal of the SMPTE, vol. 83 (Mar. 1974), pp. 169–75.

E. Carlton Winckler, "TTFL—Television Lighting—You've Come a Long Way!" Lighting Design & Application, vol. 6, no. 7 (July 1976), pp. 44–47. "The story of the emerging skill in the use of light" in TV; illus.

William Klages, "Lighting for the Video Camera," American Cinematographer, Special Lighting Issue, vol. 64, no. 11 (Nov. 1982), pp. 1127, 1129, 1131. Invaluable comments from a top expert.

Bryan Wilkes, "Lighting the Royal Wedding," SMPTE Journal, vol. 91, no. 3 (Mar. 1982), pp. 253–259. Illus. Extensive photographs, lightplot, and text.

"Lighting the Royal Wedding," Lighting Journal 25, Summer 1982 (Published by Thorn EMI Lighting, Inc., Lawrence Road, London N15 4EG, England), pp. 2–7. Illus., color. Presentation of British TV lighting director Bryan Wilkes's lighting of the royal wedding. Extensive color graphics and text.

Steve Futers, "Recent Developments in Studio Lighting Suspension Systems," SMPTE Journal, vol. 91, no. 8 (Aug. 1982), pp. 730–32. Illus.

Ronn Smith, "Fifty Years of Live Television," Theatre Crafts, vol. 14, no. 5 (Nov./Dec. 1980), pp. 11, 74. Entire issue devoted to useful background summary of live TV by various authors. See also pp. 12–24. Illus. See particularly: "Gil Wechsler at the Met, Lighting Design for the Human and the Camera Eye," pp. 15, 86–87. Illus.

E. Carlton Winckler, "Television Lighting Tools, a Glossary of Basic Equipment," Theatre Crafts, vol. 15, no. 2 (Feb. 1980), pp. 26–27, 51–55. Illus. Excellent basic illustrated summary of TV luminaire and accessory terminology.

Mary Lucier, "Lighting Theatre for Television, Piaf Becomes a Videotape," Theatre Crafts, vol. 16, no. 4 (Apr. 1982), pp. 22–25, 30–32, 34. Illus. Includes Beverly Emmons's light plot for Piaf.

James Moody, "Close Ties—Adapting a Lighting Design for Video," Theatre Crafts, vol. 16, no. 8 (Oct. 1982), pp. 28–29, 55–57. Illus. Includes Moody's light plot.

C. Lee Jenner, "Dance in America, Choreography Moves from Stage to Television Studio," Theatre Crafts, vol. 13, no. 5 (Oct. 1979), pp. 22–23, 87–88, 90–92. Illus. Includes comments by lighting designer Ralph Holmes on his work for the PBS "Dance in America" lighting for TV.

Patricia MacKay, "Ralph Holmes," Theatre Crafts, vol. 13, no. 5 (Oct. 1979), pp. 25, 58–60, 62. Illus. Includes light plot.

Mark Levin, "How to Light a News Set," Lighting Dimensions, vol. 5, no. 7 (Nov./Dec. 1981), pp. 42–45. Illus., color.

"Sweeney Todd—Live on Tape," Lighting Dimensions, vol. 6, no. 1 (Jan./Feb. 1982), pp. 18–23. Illus., color. Includes William Klages's light plot.

E. Carlton Winckler, "Nobody Said Lighting Was Easy!" Lighting Dimensions, vol. 6, no. 6 (Sept./Oct. 1982), pp. 17, 42. Basics of TV lighting—well presented.

Richard Harris, "Setting a Television Lighting Trend," TABS, vol. 43, no. 1 (Feb. 1986), pp. 28–29. Illus., color. A presentation of the new BBC studios in Glasgow, Scotland.

"An Interview with Imero Fiorentino," Lighting Dimensions, vol. 6, no. 7 (Nov./Dec. 1982), pp. 26–27, 29–31, 41, 43. A wide-ranging interview with Fiorentino.

"Television Newsroom Lighting—Capital Broadcasting Co.," Lighting Design + Application, vol. 13, no. 1 (Jan. 1983), pp. 18–19. Illus., color.

William H. Seibel, "The Continuing Debate on the College TV Curriculum," Educational and Industrial Television, vol. 15, no. 5 (May 1983), pp. 110, 112. A summary of a symposium on training TV specialists.

Gary McClendon, "A 'Concert Look' for Willie Nelson's HBO Special," Lighting Dimensions, vol. 7, no. 2 (Apr./May 1983), pp. 50–55. Illus., color. Includes light plots. Useful comparison of lighting for live concert and for videotaping.

E. Carlton Winckler, "How to Improve Your News Image," Television/Broadcasting Communications, Nov. 1983, pp. 66, 68, 70.

"The Electronic Theatre," Theatre Crafts, vol. 17, no. 8 (Oct. 1983), pp. 16–38. Entire issue of magazine devoted primarily to TV/film. Illus.

"Faerie Tale Theatre," Lighting Dimensions, vol. 7, no. 6 (Nov./Dec. 1983), pp. 20–25. Illus., color. Description by Bill Klages, George Riesenberger, and Mark Levin of lighting for this videotaped "Showtime" TV series shot in single-camera, film technique.

"The Guiding Light of Solid Gold," Lighting Dimensions, vol. 9, no. 3 (May/June 1985), pp. 27–31, 33–34. Illus., color. Director of photography (of the Klages Group) combines concert and TV lighting techniques for the TV series "Solid Gold." Includes light plot.

"Breaking Into Music Video," Lighting Dimensions, vol. 9, no. 3 (May/June 1985), pp. 65, 67–70, 72. Illus., color. Lighting designer Pete Angelus and Richard Ocean on the subject of lighting for music videos.

Bentley Miller, "Lighting Design for Much Music," Broadcast Technology, vol. 11, no. 4 (Mar./Apr. 1986), pp. 62, 64, 66. A description of the newest Canadian pay TV studio facilities as a report of the Canadian Society of Television Lighting Directors. Continued in vol. 11, no. 5 (May/June 1986), pp. 56, 58–61 and titled "Day by Day" (written by TV lighting directors Miller and Sandy Carroll).

Verne and Sylvia Carlson, "A Lesson in Using the Fixture—The Fine Points of Achieving Lighting Effects for Film and Video," Lighting Dimensions, vol. 10, no. 1 (Jan./Feb. 1986), pp. 55–58, 60, 62, 64, 77–78, 80. Illus., color. Excellent basics of film/TV lighting by the authors of Professional Lighting Handbook.

"General Hospital: TV's Hottest Daytime Drama," Lighting Dimensions, vol. 7, no. 5 (Sept./Oct. 1983), pp. 36–39, 41–42. Illus., color. Grant Velie's lighting direction for this popular soap opera explained in detail. Extensive discussion of technical/lighting/camera techniques and scheduling, using input of three lighting directors.

Christopher Nash, "Scenes from Madison Square Garden," Lighting Dimensions, vol. 7, no. 5 (Sept./Oct. 1983), pp. 49–50, 52–55. Illus. A detailed description by Bill McManus of the permanent TV lighting setup in New York City's Garden.

Ross Lowell, "Video, Film and Still Lighting, Some Parallels and Divergencies," Lowell Light News, #3 (Fall 1983), pp. 1, 3. Good basic analysis.

"A Civil War Saga for Television—The Old South comes to life on ABC's adaptation of John Jake's North and South." Lighting Dimensions, vol. 9, no. 6 (Sept./Oct. 1985), pp. 18–25, 27. Illus., color.

"Industrial Television: A Primer." Lighting Dimensions, vol. 9, no. 6 (Sept./Oct. 1985) pp. 28–31, 32–36. Illus., color. One of the few pieces of merit on industrial/corporate TV.

"Germany's Studio of the Future," Lighting Dimensions, vol. 9, no. 6 (Sept./Oct. 1985), pp. 42–45. Illus., color. This material about the German ZDF broadcasting center is useful to the TV lighting designer.

Mike Williams, "Tales from the Oscars," Lighting Dimensions, vol. 10, no. 4 (July/Aug. 1986), p. 24–25, 45–48, 50. Illus., color. A well-illustrated, good text description of the lighting for the televised Oscar Award presentations.

Michael Cabana, "Illuminance Photometers, a Comparative Survey of the Marketplace," Lighting Dimensions, vol. 10, no. 6 (Nov. 1986), pp. 70, 72, 74–77. Buying guide chart showing comparative values of most illuminance photometers now on the market.

Eric Wallis, "Spotlight on Top of Pops," Society of Television Lighting Directors, #31 (Spring 1986), pp. 13–16. A description of the lighting of a leading British TV production.

Strand Lighting Corp., Lighting for Television. A 26-page booklet, available from any Strand outlet worldwide, presenting basics of television lighting.

Bentley Miller, "Light Sources: Softlights and Fluorescent Light," Society of Television Lighting Directors, vol. 13, no. 2 (Oct. 1987), pp. 48, 50–51. Another in Miller's series of basics published under the banner of the Canadian branch of the Society of Television Lighting Directors (STLD). Miller is a lighting director for City-TV/Much Music in Toronto.

Other applicable titles in Miller's series in the same journal include:

"'Tricks of the Trade'—Lighting Rock & Roll for Television," vol. 12, no. 5 (March 1987), pp. 44, 46–47.

"The Role of the Lighting Director in Television Production," vol. 12, no. 6 (April 1987), pp. 40–42.

"Of Lenses and Prisms: Optimizing Lens/Camera Performance," vol. 12, no. 7 (May 1987), pp. 44, 46–47.

"A Lens Primer for Lighting Directors," vol. 12, no. 8 (June 1987), pp. 42–44. Illus.

"Lighting Nomenclature/Jargon Explained," vol. 13, no. 1 (Sept. 1987), pp. 52–54, 56.

"Lighting Nomenclature: Controllers and Modifiers," vol. 13, no. 3 (Nov./Dec. 1987), pp. 58–60, 62.

"Nomenclature—Part III: Filters," vol. 13, no. 4 (Jan. 1988), pp. 57–59.

"More About Filters: Color Correction Media," vol. 13, no. 5 (Feb. 1988), pp. 45–47.

"Staging: Pitfalls Facing the Lighting Director," vol. 13, no. 7 (April 1988), pp. 50–53.

"Staging Is Critical to Lighting of Productions," vol. 13, no. 6 (March 1988), pp. 57–60.

"The Road Less Travelled. . . Some Thoughts on Creativity," vol. 13, no. 8 (May 1988), pp. 38–40.

"Hanover's Fully Automatic Studio Lighting System," Strandlight, no. 7 (Summer 1988), p. 1. Illus. A description of a high-technology TV studio equipped by Strand Lighting in Germany.

John Watt, "Denmark Goes Commercial," Society of Television Lighting Directors, no. 35 (Winter 1987–1988), pp. 5–12. Illus. Written by John Watt, head of lighting for BBC, about the new Denmark commercial TV station and a Denmark "Sound and Light" trade show, the article contains useful TV lighting basics presented by Watt.

Duncan Brown, "Allo Allo," Society of Television Lighting Directors, no. 37 (Autumn 1988), pp. 22–27. Illus., TV light plot. An article about the BBC TV series, Allo Allo, with useful information by BBC lighting director Duncan Brown.

Mat Irvine, "More Than Just Explosions," Society of Television Lighting Directors, no. 37 (Autumn 1988), pp. 31–33. Illus., color. Information by a leading BBC visual effects designer. Very useful.

Robert Battaile, "Neon and White Socks, DP Ron Garcia Helps Create the Retro Look of Crime Story," Lighting Dimensions, vol. 12, no. 3 (April 1988), pp. 41–45, 64–65. Illus., color. Details concerning a TV series.

Steve Weinstein, "Post Perfect: Potente/Koszalka Ltd. Lights a Video Post Production Workspace," Lighting Dimensions, vol. 12, no. 3 (April 1988), pp. 54–57. Illus., color. A well-illustrated description of the architectural lighting design for key editing studios, coping with the problem of work lights but minimum spill/glare on TV monitors.

Rod Litherland, "Automated Lighting," Society of Television Lighting Directors, no. 38 (Spring 1989), pp. 16–18. Illus. An extended presentation of automated lighting provided for TV studios in Germany and Britain by Strand Lighting, as narrated by Susan Dandridge and Michael Cawte.

Tony Escott, "Televisione Della Svizzera Italiana," Society of Television Lighting Directors, no. 38 (Spring 1989), pp. 20–21. Illus. Description of TV lighting in Italy.

Mark Loeffler, "Great Expectations—NBC Strives to Meet High Lighting Standards for Summer Olympics," Lighting Dimensions, vol. 12, no. 6 (September/October 1988), pp. 86–88. Illus. Describes the work of William McManus and Red McKinnon (Klages Group) for the Olympics in Seoul, South Korea.

"Robo Newsroom," Lighting Dimensions, vol. 12, no. 4 (May/June 1989), p. 15. Describes the automation of NBC's newsroom (home base for Tom Brokaw's Nightly News) by retired Robert Warren Davis with both preprogrammed camera movements and remotely controlled lighting.

Mark Loeffler, "Designer-Friendly, A Modular, Integrated System of Moving Lights Called Pan-Command," Lighting Dimensions, vol. 12, no. 4 (May/June 1988), pp. 44–47. Illus., color. William Klages' use of Morpheus Lights' Pan-Command remote-controlled units for the 1988 Grammy Awards Show.

Mike Williams, "Live at 5:00, John Gates Lights a TV Newsroom That Doubles as the Set for a Meandering Anchor," Lighting Dimensions, vol. 11, no. 7 (January/February 1988), pp. 82, 86–87, 89–90. Illus. Lighting for Boston's WNEV TV newsroom.

Martin Gardlin, "Late Night Light-Up, LDs Create an Image for Letterman and Carson Shows," Lighting Dimensions, vol. 11, no. 6 (Nov. 1987), pp. 58–60. Illus., color. Describes the lighting design for television of Cheryl Thacker and Robert Pohle.

Robert Battaile, "Dibie Deluxe: Master of Three-Camera Production," Lighting Dimensions, vol. 13, no. 3 (April 1989), pp. 76–79, 102, 104, 106. Illus., color.

Mike Williams, "Revealed: Chas. Norton's Secrets for Lighting Mystery! Introductions," Lighting Dimensions, vol. 13, no. 2 (March 1989), pp. 58, 83–85, 88. Illus., color.

Associated Press, "Music Videos' Usefulness Fades," Lafayette Journal & Courier, July 22, 1988, p. D6.

Bentley Miller, "'Tricks of the Trade,' Lighting Rock & Roll Television," Society of Television Lighting Directors, no. 34 (Summer 1987), pp. 14–16.

Mike Baker, "Commonwealth Fellowship Scheme to Cyprus," Society of Television Lighting Directors, no. 34 (Summer 1987), pp. 20–23. Illus. Humorous account of primitive TV lighting by BBC expert in Cyprus for six weeks.

"Videoconferencing," International Lighting Review, 38th year, 2nd quarter, 1987, pp. 44–49. Illus., color.

Lee Erskine, "Lighting the Olympic Ceremonies," Broadcast + Technology, vol. 13, no. 8 (May 1988), pp. 20–21. Illus., color. Lighting of the Calgary, Canada, Winter Olympics.

Scott Kenney, "Big Screen Video: A Picture Worth a Thousand Words," LS&V magazine, premier issue (November/December 1988), pp. 41, 48. Illus.

Bonnie S. Schwartz, "Actors First," Television Lighting, The Journal of the Society of Television Light Directors, no. 39 (Summer 1989), pp. 4–7. Also originally printed in Lighting Dimensions, under the title of "Actors First: Ryan's Hope LDs John Connolly and Candice Dunn Air for a Molded, Filmic Look," vol. 12, no. 2 (March 1988), pp. 72–75, 97, 99.

VIDEOTAPES

BBC, Society of Television Lighting Directors, An Introduction to Basic Television Lighting. Based on a lecture by former BBC senior lecturer Alan Bermingham, given at the Society's seminar held at BBC, Wood Norton, Evesham, England. Available from the Services Sound & Vision Corp., Chalfont Grove, Narcot Lane, Gerrards Cross, Bucks, SL9 8TN, England. Revised in 1988. Now titled: Basic Lighting for Film and Video. Telephone: 02407-4461. £22.95. Excellent. The best of the videotape training aids in lighting.

3M Company, Lighting for Video Tape Production, M-VC223, supplied by the Minnesota Mining & Manufacturing Co., St. Paul, MN 55101, 1977. Usable but not as good as the BBC tape.

Rosco Labs, Lighting In the Real World, A Program on Lighting Techniques for Better Video Images. 65 minutes. Dick Reizner, Emmy Award winning cameraman, narrates this tape from Rosco Labs, 36 Bush Avenue, Port Chester, NY 10573. Tel: (914) 937-1300. The tape is available in VHS for around $125. This is a very useful, well-written series, by an author active in television lighting direction.

Bentley Miller, "Lighting for Industrial Video Presentations," Broadcast Technology, vol. 11, no. 6 (July/Aug. 1986), pp. 30–32. Illus. The Canadian approach to lighting TV industrials.

Patricia Ackerman, "The Television Command Post, ABC-TV 3 News Studio Combines Architectural And Theatrical Lighting Techniques," Lighting Dimensions, vol. 11, no. 2 (Mar./April 1987), pp. 60–63, 86–89. Illus.

"The Creative Process From A to Z: A Television Pioneer and Friends Tell Us How It's Done," Lighting Design + Application, vol. 16, no. 12 (Dec. 1986), pp. 6, 42–45. Illus., color. A most useful question-and-answer interview with Imero Fiorentino, Alan Adelman, Randy Nordstrom, and Jim Tetlow — all practicing television lighting directors.

"A Television Son et Lumière as a Teaching Tool for Lighting Directors as David I. Taylor Reports on His Trip to Iraqi Television in Baghdad," ALD Newsletter, #4 (April 1987), pp. 9–12. Includes an Iraqi Son et Lumiere light plot.

"Spotlight on 'Top of the Pops,' Joanna Turner Talked with Robert Wright, Head of Television Lighting at the BBC, and Lighting Director Eric Wallis about the Background Work Involved in Setting Up Television's Major Light and Sound Show," Lighting + Sound International, vol. 1, no. 1 (Nov. 1985), pp. 27–30. Illus., color. Excellent insight into British television lighting practices and facilities.

[145] See Gerald Millerson, TV Lighting Methods, "Lighting for Clarity," pp. 76–77, op. cit. (see footnote 144).

[146] *See Gerald Millerson*, TV Lighting Methods, *"Measuring Light," pp. 128–29, op. cit. (see footnote 144).*

[147] *Another possibility has become a reality: remote control of focus. See Richard Glickman, op. cit. (see footnote 144).*

etc. Many hard lights can be softened by the addition of scrims, frost color media, and diffusers; however, soft light cannot easily be made to look like hard light.

In the realm of TV, the lighting artist is referred to as a "director," not as a "designer"—although he or she is both. The TV lighting director has available several controllable properties of light:

1. Direction. Where light comes from (in relation to the camera lens) is a key design tool. Flat front light (commonly called either "fill" or "base" light in TV), backlight, sidelight, and special effects (such as lighting from underneath the human face or flickering flames from a fire) all come into play. The general illumination which comes from the camera viewing angle is all-important to the camera. Unlike the human eye—which can see under an amazing range of intensity levels—the camera *must* have an overall threshold level of illumination to be able to "see" at all.[146] Lighting levels can range from that threshold point onward (brighter). The designer—within operable and acceptable levels for the camera—has a wide range of possibilities in *how* to employ light from differing directions.

2. Intensity. One of the designer's major means of controlling and determining lighting is an ability to select the wattage or power of illuminating units and then to modify that output at will with dimmers, filters, gobos, shields, and flippers. It is possible to paint any conceivable kind of picture, from brightest brights to darkest darks, as long as the designer stays within the allowable operational limits of the TV camera chain (system). Present TV cameras *can* operate with as little as 10 footcandles of light, but 75 to 100 footcandles is a better and more prevalent operational level.

3. Color. Since all camera/system adjustments (internationally) are based upon human skin *looking* (colorwise) like human skin, colored light is only rarely thrown upon an "on camera" performer, and then only for brief effects. The home viewer does (and is expected to) use "skin tone" as a criterion for set color and adjustment (as does the studio engineer). Any tampering with that will throw the whole system off. The designer may freely make use of colored light upon cycloramas, walls, or *any* surround area, as long

as color contrast and juxtapositioning laws of vision are kept in mind—that is, the appearance of skin tone may be affected by colored light projected nearby.

In addition to these three control variables, three other factors are important:

1. Mounting Positions. Unlike live theatre (where lights cannot readily be placed in the lap of the little old lady in the third row), TV has a wide range of equipment mounting positions (there *are* limitations, however). A few common approaches to mounting positions are discussed below:

- Lights can be mounted overhead. This point raises a classic argument in TV studio design: rigid mounting pipes overhead versus counterweighted pipe battens. A rigid grid of mounting pipes overhead with a catwalk has the advantages of ease of access—including during taping (for burnouts and emergency adjustments)—and stability of mounting position; it has the disadvantage of having a fixed mounting height. For theatre-type counterweighted pipe battens the advantage is that luminaires can be brought to the floor or deck with ease; the disadvantage is that these same luminaires are inaccessible (once the scenery is in place) except by ladder, use of which is impossible during taping. This debate will probably never be settled. "Extension pipes" and "lazy arms" extensions help make a rigid grid more flexible in mounting heights.[147] By far the largest proportion of lighting equipment in standard TV studios is mounted overhead, because it is necessary to keep the studio floor clear for camera movements, audio equipment (booms), performers, and scenery.

- A limited number of luminaires can be mounted either on the scenery itself or on castered movable floor stands (frequently requiring operators).

2. Communication Forms. Standard theatre-type light plots and switchboard hookup sheets are in common use in TV. Typical plots are presented later in this chapter accompanying the design work of Imero Fiorentino Associates, Ralph Holmes of CBS TV and PBS, and George Spiro Dibie of Hollywood.

3. Cues and Stage Crews. Another tool available to the designer is the setting up of "on camera" cues (lights turned on or off; lighting bursts; searchlights; etc.). In TV lighting the designer mustn't lose sight of the fact that union stage-hands who do the actual setup ("lash-up" in England) of lighting equipment and focus (under the lighting director's supervision) *are* exhaustible human beings. They are paid for their work. They do it—over and over—week in and week out. Unnecessary, unjustified, and excessive demands will readily "turn them off" and bring about maximum lack of cooperation—as is the case with any other highly skilled laborers in any industry.

Audio Problems

Audio designers and engineers are just as dedicated as lighting designers are. They want to send out the best possible sound to accompany pictures, free from "camera turret click," air-conditioning hum, and any other undesirable studio noise. The best quality (usually called "audio presence") would obviously result from the audio engineer's being permitted to drop a microphone down into the picture (in sight of the eventual viewer) as near as possible to a performer's mouth, thus allowing the engineer to turn the "gain" volume control way down to eliminate all extraneous sounds. Clearly this situation is not possible. While the audio engineer must have a portable microphone up "out of the picture," it should not be positioned any further away than is absolutely necessary, so a constant "war" results between the lighting director and the audio engineer over the available space. The audio engineer can get "sound" from a long distance away—but at the sacrifice of much quality. The smart and considerate lighting director takes the time and extra trouble to make sure that the audio engineer is aware from the very beginning that the designer understands the engineer's problems and desire for high standards. Then, if the designer discovers trouble with "boom shadows" on a specific shot, the engineer will most likely volunteer to sacrifice some audio quality to resolve the problem. It's a give-and-take world. In my 12 years as lighting director for network TV in New York City, I quickly found that consideration and friendly give-and-take with the audio man, the stagehands, and the video engineer could be a big asset in achieving quality lighting design.

Video Control Problems

Like the audio engineer, the video control engineer is a good person to have as a friend. Whatever the designer does with lighting that is good, the video control engineer can easily undo. Conversely, weakness and errors in lighting work can be made to look better by the video engineer. Fully half of lighting design in television is the work of the video engineer—and every good lighting designer knows it. Improperly set lens stops, mismatched cameras, poor control of "black clipper" (also called "minimum pedestal") or gain or blanking—any and all can ruin the best lighting work. Make a friend of the video control man.[148] In the last analysis, the two of you "paint a picture" together. As a team you can create sensational "high key" and "low key" scenes. *High key* involves fairly heavy use of flat front fill light or base level. Overall contrast is reduced. The end product is most suitable for daylight scenes, contest shows, sports events, etc. *Low key* maximizes stark, dramatic contrast and is used for night scenes, suspense, terror, and drama—or for its own visual compositional sake. E. Carlton Winckler has written:

> A composition in which all lighted areas are flatly lit and of equal intensity is dull and boring to look at. Providing intensity variation in areas, highlights, and "glints" adds visual interest. Some especially focused sources may be required to stress design features, a logo, a hanging plant, etc., but you may find that sources meeting other objectives provide these accents as well. The spill from a backlight may be plenty on the hanging plant, without adding an extra light for it.[149]

The lighting director not only has access to all the video control possibilities and control of direction, intensity, and color, but can also use gobos and patterns, rear-screen projections, and numerous special effects to enhance the picture. Also, the way a designer treats the scenic environs or background can become a design trademark. I am of the TV school of design which concentrates (in dramatic and musical shows) upon lighting the performers. There are other designers who like to light the performance place first: specials on wall scones and pictures; sunlight through the windows; slashes of light upon walls, furnishings, or architectural details. Either approach creates high-quality pictures, but the "look" achieved is different, depending upon

[148] *See Gerald Millerson*, TV Lighting Methods, *"Lighting and Picture Control," pp. 132–33, op. cit. (see footnote 144).*

[149] *E. Carlton Winckler, "How to Improve Your News Image," p. 68, op. cit. (see footnote 144).*

150 *Wanda Jankowski, p. 33, op. cit. (see footnote 144).*

where the individual designer placed the emphasis. A personal—and characteristic—touch in design style is possible in TV lighting.

Teamwork

More important in TV than lighting design ability or knowledge is the art of being a "team player," as has been alluded to in the previous discussions concerning the audio engineer and the video engineer. Often the lighting director is the lowest on the totempole in a large, complex team which must produce a production on schedule and within budget, and (hopefully) be ready to do this every day. Above the lighting director in authority are the technical director (the chief engineer to whom the video and audio contingent and the cameramen report); the director (who makes artistic decisions of mood and quality, rather than decisions about technical engineering standards); and, above the director, the producer, the advertising agency representatives (representing the client paying for the show), and, frequently, the client (advertiser) himself. The lighting director may also encounter stars with firm ideas of their own —plus all of their "hangers on." Stagehands are supposed to take orders from the lighting director, but they require respect and courtesy, too. David Clark said:

> I don't think that an award-worthy show can emerge from a production group that is not operating as a team. In a team atmosphere the normal friction between creative people results in a cohesive show look. The "things" work well together because the people did. Since the lighting design is only one part of a total production effort, and not an isolated process, developing a good rapport with the members of the production staff and the performers is vital.[150]

Camera Mobility

A basic difference between the live theatre production form (in which the audience remains seated in one place) and the forms of cinema (in which the camera is set up and the scene lighted for each shot) and TV is that the latter two use cameras, which allows for greater flexibility. TV cameras allow the most flexibility of all, for they are mounted on wheels or cranes or dollies. The director can electronically "cut" to any of several available camera shots, and the cameras can move nearly anywhere. The camera's mobility and its proximity to its subject produces quite a different effect for the viewer. The director can dissolve from one camera to another, put two or more cameras "on the line" simultaneously, fade/cut/dissolve to film or graphics, and go to remote camera pickups nearly anywhere in the world. While in some ways its possibilities are not quite as extensive as those open to film, the TV system just described allows an amazing range of possibilities for mobility and fluidity. All affect the TV lighting director. Often lighting directors may find that they are approaching situations similar to theatre arena lighting—but with camera eyes rather than audience everywhere. While this increases the exciting lighting possibilities of the medium far beyond those of live theatre, it may also create a corner from which the designers must gracefully extract themselves and their lighting. I remember lighting remotes from both the United Nations and Carnegie Hall with limited power available and no "free space" for mounting lighting equipment, and also several hours of TV shooting out on Broadway in a snowstorm for a Revlon commercial!

Special Problems

Different production situations present special lighting problems; for example, there is a separate art to lighting automobiles for TV commercials. Another special situation is the treatment of performers with script-derived or vanity-derived "problems" (too fat, too thin, too old, etc.). Also, the lighting for a news commentator at a desk is very different from that needed for a panel show, a national political speech, a sports event, a daily soap opera, musical and variety shows, and specials. And yet another artistry is called for to design TV lighting successfully for classical ballet, opera, or symphonic concerts. Some of these special cases are dealt with in Millerson (see footnote 144). Space does not permit extensive treatment of them here; however, a few pieces of advice from E. Carlton Winckler merit inclusion:

> There is a wonderful guideline used by thoroughly skilled designers that can avoid a mountain of 'lighting problems': "Materials used adjacent to faces, must be of a tonal value able to accept the same light striking the face, without becoming

brighter than, or as bright as, the face itself.' Use it, it always works!

Along the same line of preventing problems rather than trying to fix them is the guideline about keeping people at least six feet away from a background so you can light two elements with separate sources and control relative brightness." [151]

Backgrounds and surrounds for talent must always be of a reflectance value which is able to accept the same light that is falling upon the talent, without appearing brighter than the faces in the picture.

Remember, good lighting is simply well-defined and clean-cut." [152]

Keys to Mastery

The lighting designer should be sure to have a good understanding of the miscellaneous TV-related concepts and approaches listed below:

1. The only true test of picture quality is the master monitor in the control room. All other monitors may be of lesser quality, out of alignment, or else just basically hopeless. The lighting designer should never try to judge the picture quality of the lighting from the studio floor "by eyeball" (or even with a meter), because it just won't work! The eye is not your concern until it views the picture on a home television set. (And if you worry about what the home viewer may be doing with the set's contrast, brightness, or color controls, you will lose your sanity!) The master monitor — the only accurate place to judge the lighting work — must be the testing point.

2. Of vital importance are both *time* and *budget*. People in radio and TV learn to "live by the clock." Twenty seconds of dead space on a network show can literally seem like a whole lifetime — I know; I've been through it. "On Air" time does not move. The tradition of no dead air is as sacred as theatre's tradition that "the show must go on."

Budget is important, too. A TV show costs thousands of dollars to produce. Perhaps 50 to 150 people are simultaneously involved in making a show good within a designated hour of time. There is no room for delay, failures, and excuses. If a lighting director has a problem with this, there is always someone else who *can* deliver — and can take the incompetent lighting director's job.

3. Top lighting directors develop their own hallmarks. I have sometimes referred to these as the lighting director's own "bag of tricks," which is unfair in a way, since always the "tricks" are based upon skill, deep understanding, and long experience. For example, for two years I was on Arthur Murray's payroll, above and beyond my network salary. Kathryn Murray (his wife) was always picked up in all closeup shots on the #2 center camera only. It had a 5000-watt Dynabeam shooting straight in on her face beside the camera. In addition I had placed a small piece of a woman's silk stocking over the closeup lens (effectively softening and de-focusing the image). These two things added a dream-like "look of youth" to the close shots of the "star" of the show, who also was the producer's wife!

A few more examples of hallmarks are appropriate here. For years Paul Siatta lighted all of the Ted Mack Geritol commercials. The image of the Geritol product is youth. Siatta always used two carefully located TV scrimmed scoops on the floor below and in front of Mr. Mack. It did wonders to eradicate traces of age. Another well-known lighting director, Imero Fiorentino, long ago established a second hallmark to back up his very real talent and imagination: the Timex watch display. Fiorentino is one of the greatest in the business at skillfully and sincerely dealing with people and their private needs for reassurance. There are many, many other examples of the hallmarks of "good marketing," but those given should suffice.

4. TV is mostly a *business,* and only rarely an art. That statement doesn't mean that a lot of art doesn't go into good business. But TV is a commercial medium — shows are paid for by sponsors and watched (or not) as indicated by audience sampling. "Business first, art afterwards" must be a motto acceptable to any lighting designer who expects to be contented in TV.

5. *Quality* training and education are important in getting started in TV lighting. TV networks tend to hire graduates with broad-based degrees from prestigious schools and then train them "on the job" to do things the network's way. Specific training in either a university communications department or with one of the commercial "Radio-TV" trade schools usually helps little. In an article from *Lighting Design & Application,*[153] Greg Brunton was quoted as saying,

[151] E. Carlton Winckler, "On Television Lighting," (see footnote 140).

[152] E. Carlton Winckler, "How to Improve Your News Image," op. cit. (see footnote 144).

[153] See Wanda Jankowski, "TTFL," p. 38, op. cit. (see footnote 144).

"The more you know about everybody else's job, the better you'll be able to perform on your own." Dave [Clark], Tony [di Girolamo] and Greg agree that one of the best ways to learn a lot about everything is by working at a local television station in a small town. During the summers while he was in college, Greg gained two years experience working at a small station in Parkersburg, West Virginia. Dave wryly comments, "Start off at a local station in a small town, unless you know somebody and your uncle owns a network." "The best small station I can think of," says Dave, "is the flagship station of PBS in each state. For example, the University of Wisconsin, and the University of Nebraska. In those places the union situation is not as tight. Everybody gets to do everything and until you know a little bit about everything that's going on, you can't really get to know any one aspect of television production well. At these stations, you get to handle, build and fix your own equipment." Before joining Imero Fiorentino Associates, Tony had been in charge of all the lighting at the New Jersey Public Television studio.[153]

Specifics

Some illustrations can help clarify many of the topics discussed above. Figure 7.1 shows the set for the TV show *Fish in Hollywood*. This rare double-deck set offers a good interrelationship of typical light fixtures, cameras, audio boom, and studio setup. George Spiro Dibie (next to the woman operating the ABC camera) is the lighting director. Figure 7.2 is from the *Barney Miller* TV series from Hollywood, also by Dibie. Figure 7.3 is a self-explanatory (no hookup needed) light plot for Dibie's *Barney Miller*. Figures 7.4 and 7.5 present two photos from CBS's soap opera *Guiding Light,* by lighting director Lincoln John Stulik. The show originated in New York City and is produced by the Proctor and Gamble Company. One photograph illustrates scenery and hanging lighting equipment, while the other shows its use in the set.

Color Figs. 58, 59, and 60 show the *Neil Diamond* concert show televised from the Greek Theatre in Los Angeles. The lighting design made effective use of strong-colored backlight for maximum dramatic impact and also added a striking change of the scenic environment by varying the lighting of the city skyline. Figure 7.6 shows the light plot for the Greek Theatre television show. Unfortunately, the switchboard hookup sheets are not available. They are similar to the same show in world concert tour version presented in the light plot in Fig. 7.7 and the production photo Fig. 7.8.

The accompanying hookup sheets are in Fig. 7.9. These two plots present an interesting comparison. Each is exactly the same show in the same year. One version gives a clear indication of the units, wattages, and colors vital for telecasting in a large outdoor theatre. The other version (concert tour) is a modification to the units, wattages, colors, and mounting positions to perform the indoor (nontelecast) concert presentation in theatres, arenas, and auditoriums throughout the world. This set of plots and production photos and those by James Moody of Sundance for the John Denver concert tour (see Chap. 8) are excellent examples of a designer's adaptations of lighting equipment and design to different production media (TV, arena and proscenium presentation theatre, concert tours) in widely varying production places. They are well worth careful study and comparison. A comparison of plot and production photos for the same show in differing production types and various media has not appeared in any trade magazine or other lighting books.

Figure 7.10 is the light plot by CBS and PBS lighting director Ralph Holmes for the telecasting of Martha Graham's *Clytemnestra* (dance) taped at Opryland in Nashville, Tennessee, in 1979. Color Figs. 61 to 63 are production photos, as is Fig. 7.11. Holmes, in addition to his national reputation in TV lighting, has had extensive theatre training and experience.

The hit musical *Sweeney Todd, the Demon Barber of Fleet Street* offers yet another useful opportunity to compare lighting design for a live Broadway production with lighting for the show after it has been subjected to the necessary modifications for a TV taping. Figures 5.40 through 5.42 in Chap. 5 show the light plot, hookup, and a production photo of designer Ken Billington's brilliant original lighting of this musical on Broadway. Figure 7.12 offers Bill Klages's light plot (with no hookup needed, since it is self-explanatory) for the videotaping of *Sweeney Todd* during the road tour in California. Figures 7.13 to 7.15 show production shots during filming, with lights and cameras included. Because an interview granted by Klages explains so clearly — in relation to this specific production — the problems encountered by a lighting designer in redesigning lighting for the TV medium, I obtained permission to reprint here large portions of "Sweeney Todd — Live On Tape" from an arti-

Figure 7.1 *Fish.* Taped in Hollywood, with lighting by George Spiro Dibie.

Figure 7.2 *Barney Miller* television series taped in Hollywood. Lighting: George Spiro Dibie.

BARNEY MILLER

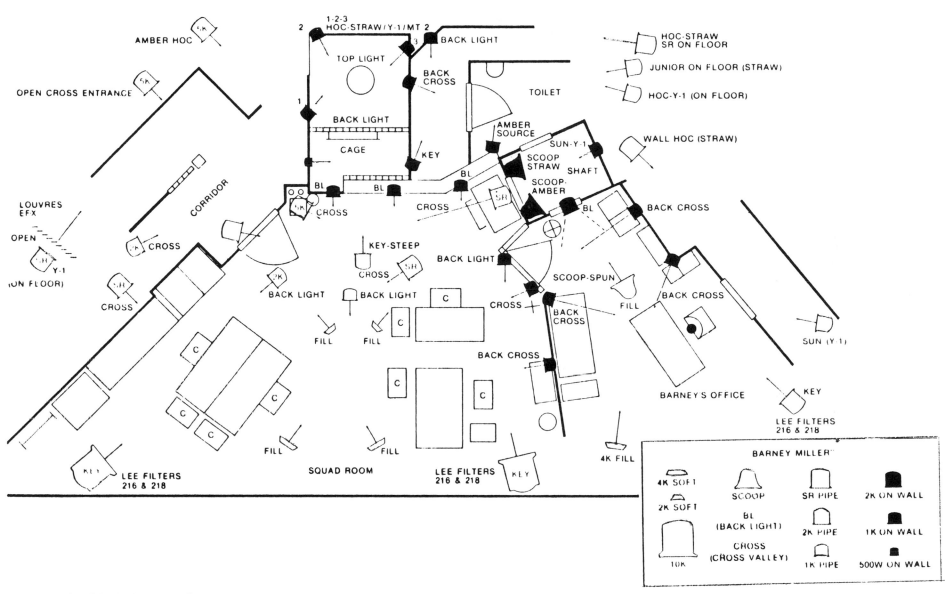

Figure 7.3 Dibie's light plot for *Barney Miller*.

Figure 7.4 CBS TV's soap opera *Guiding Light*. Lighting director: Lincoln J. Stulik; scene design: Harry Miller.

Figure 7.5 *Guiding Light*.

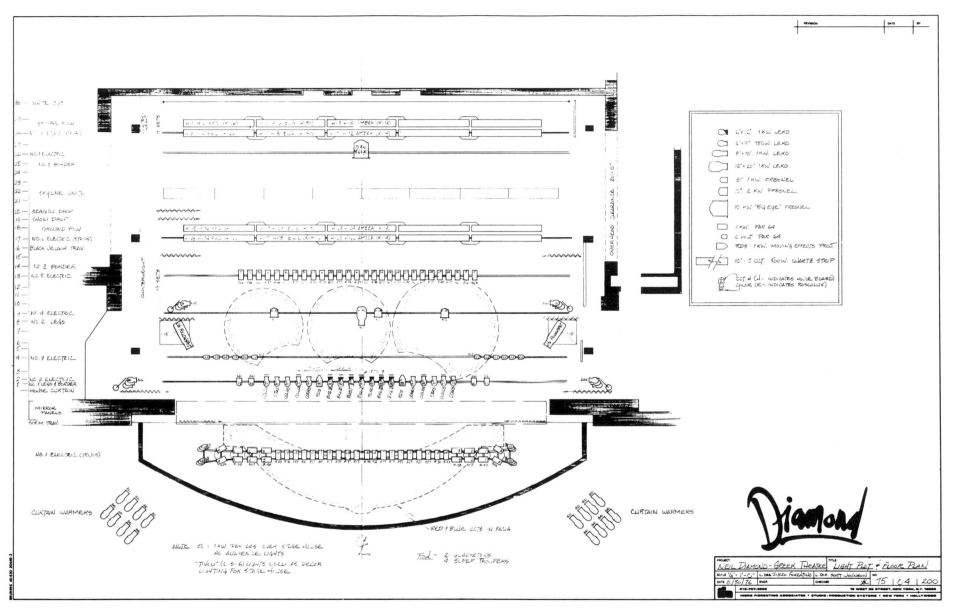

Figure 7.6 Light plot for the Neil Diamond TV special from the Greek Theatre, Los Angeles, 1976. Production director and stage design: George Honchar of Imero Fiorentino Associates; lighting design: Imero Fiorentino; lighting director: Scott Johnson.

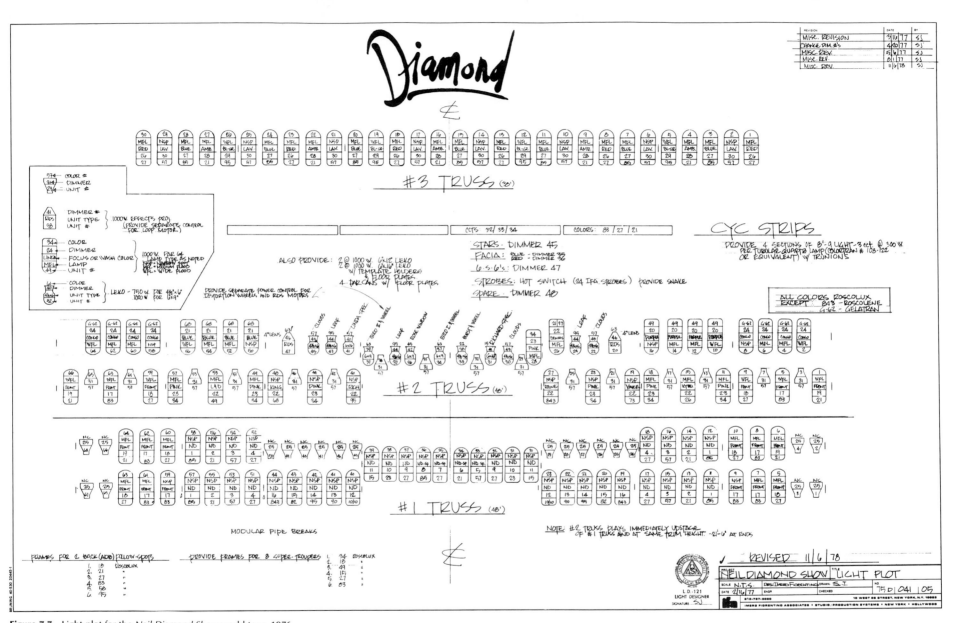

Figure 7.7 Light plot for the *Neil Diamond Show* world tour, 1976 to 1977.

Figure 7.8 The *Neil Diamond Show* in concert version for the 1976 to 1977 world tour. Notice the use of scenic panels behind Diamond to suggest that the performer is surrounded by audience, arena-style. Denver toured the United States, Australia, and New Zealand for seven months. This was a much simpler version of lighting than that used for the Aladdin Theatre for the Performing Arts appearance in Las Vegas or for the Los Angeles Greek Theatre TV Special at the culmination of the tour.

NEIL DIAMOND SHOW   **LIGHTING DESIGNER:** Imero Fiorentino

DIMMER SCHEDULE   **LIGHTING DIRECTOR:** Scott Johnson

REVISED 11-6-78

DIM #	POSITION & UNIT #	TYPE	FOCUS	COLOR	#	LOAD
1	1T 11,12,57,58	PAR 64 NSP	NEIL SIDES	85	4	4 KW
2	1T 13,14,55,56	NSP	" "	21	4	4 KW
3	1T 15,16,53,54	NSP	" "	57	4	4 KW
4	1T 17,18,51,52	NSP	" "	27	4	4 KW
5	1T 33	NSP	NEIL SP.	57	1	1 KW
6	1T 34	NSP	" "	21	1	1 KW
7	1T 35	NSP	" "	27	1	1 KW
8	1T 36	NSP	" "	85	1	1 KW
9	1T 32,37	NSP	NEIL PAIR	27	2	2 KW
10	1T 31,38	NSP	" "	23	2	2 KW
11	1T 30,39	NSP	" "	15	2	2 KW
12	1T 29,40	NSP	" "	12	2	2 KW
13	1T 22,41	NSP	" "	90	2	2 KW
14	1T 21,42	NSP	" "	95	2	2 KW
15	1T 20,43	NSP	" "	82	2	2 KW
16	1T 19,44	NSP	" "	843	2	2 KW
17	1T 7,8,9,59,61,62 2T 5,63	2WFL, 4MFL, 2NSP	BLUE FRONT	83	8	8 KW
18	1T 5,10,60,63 2T 9,59	4MFL, 2WFL	RED FRONT	27	6	6 KW
19	1T 6,64 2T 1,66	2MFL, 2WFL	AMBER FRONT	21	4	4 KW
20	2T 10,12,14,16	1NSP, 2MFL, 1WFL	PURPLE WASH	49	4	4 KW
21	2T 50,52,54,56	1NSP, 2MFL, 1WFL	BLUE WASH	68	4	4 KW
22	2T 15,19,26,27,40,48,53	3MFL, 4NSP	COLOR DOWN SPOTS	26,73,843 21,47,45,68,49	7	7 KW
23	2T 11,18,23,28,44,49,57	5MFL, 2NSP	PINK WASH	34	7	7 KW
24	2T 2,4,6,8,58,60,62,64	2NSP, 4MFL, 2WFL	CONGO WASH	G-62	8	8 KW
25	1T 1,2,3,4,24,25,26,27,28,29,45,46, 47,48,49,50,65,66,67,68	PAR 64 VNSP,6V,120W	BAND FACES	∅	20	~2.4 KW
26	3T 1,8,13,18,23,30	MFL	RED BACK	27	6	6 KW
27	3T 3,7,11,15,20,24,28	MFL	BLUE BACK	85	7	7 KW
28	3T 4,9,16,22,27	MFL	AMBER BACK	21	5	5 KW
29	3T 5,12,19,26	WFL	BL-GR. BACK	95	4	4 KW
30	3T 2,6,10,14,17,21,25,29	NSP	LAVENDER BACK	57	8	8 KW
31	2T 3,7,13,17,21,25,29,32,35 38,42,46,51,55,61,65	PAR 64 VSNP,6V,120W	HALO BACK	57	16	~1.6 KW
32	CYC STRIP BLUE	300W QUARTZ		83	16 LAMPS	4.8 KW
33	" " RED	" "		27	16 LAMPS	4.8 KW
34	" " AMBER	" "		21	16 LAMPS	4.8 KW
35	FACIA BLUE					
36	FACIA RED					
37	2T 34	6×9 AXIAL LEKO	BIRD I w/WHEEL	63	1	1 KW
38	2T 33	4½×6 " "	BURST w/WHEEL	22	1	1 KW
39	2T 39	6×9 " "	BIRD II w/WHEEL	63	1	1 KW
40	2T 40	6×16 " "	LINDA SPEC.	57	1	1 KW
41	2T 31	6×16 " "	RICH SPEC.	57	1	1 KW
42	2T 36	6×9 " "	ROSE WINDOW	45	1	1 KW
43	2T 22,30,45	4½×6 " "	CLOUDS	57	3	3 KW
44	2T 24,37,43	4½×6 " "	LEAVES	95	3	3 KW
45	STARS	IN CYC				
46	2T 20,47	RDS PROJ.-FILM LOOP 4" LENS	MOVING CLOUDS	63	2	2 KW
47	6·5·6 STRINGS		ON TRUSSES			

FLOOR STROBES (3 CCTS) AND CYC STROBES ON HOT SWITCHES

IMERO FIORENTINO ASSOCIATES, INC.
Consultants to the Performing Arts

Figure 7.9 Switchboard hookup for the *Neil Diamond* world tour.

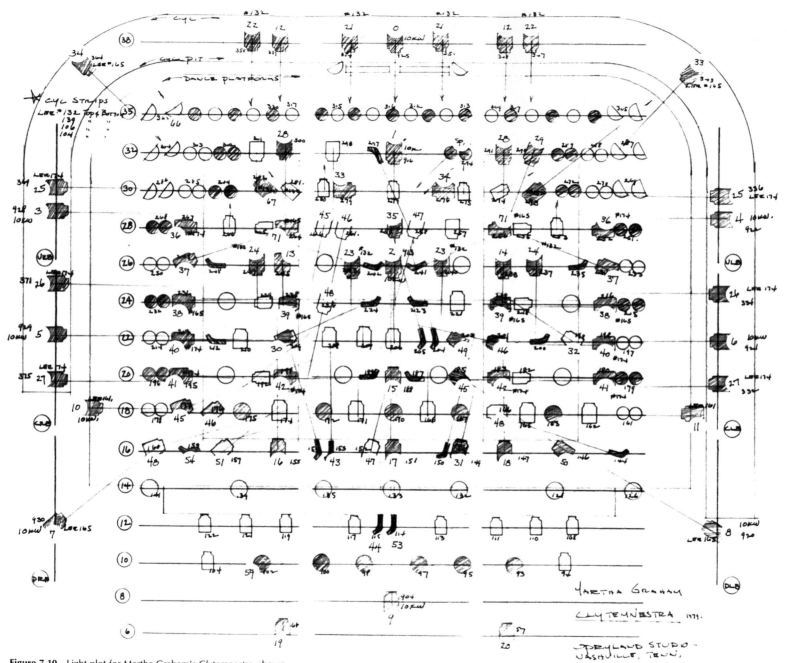

Figure 7.10 Light plot for Martha Graham's *Clytemnestra*, shown on Public Service Television's *Dance in America* series. Taped at Opryland, Nashville, Tennessee. Lighting director: Ralph Holmes. (*Courtesy of Ralph Holmes.*)

Figure 7.11   *Clytemnestra. (Courtesy of Ralph Holmes.)*

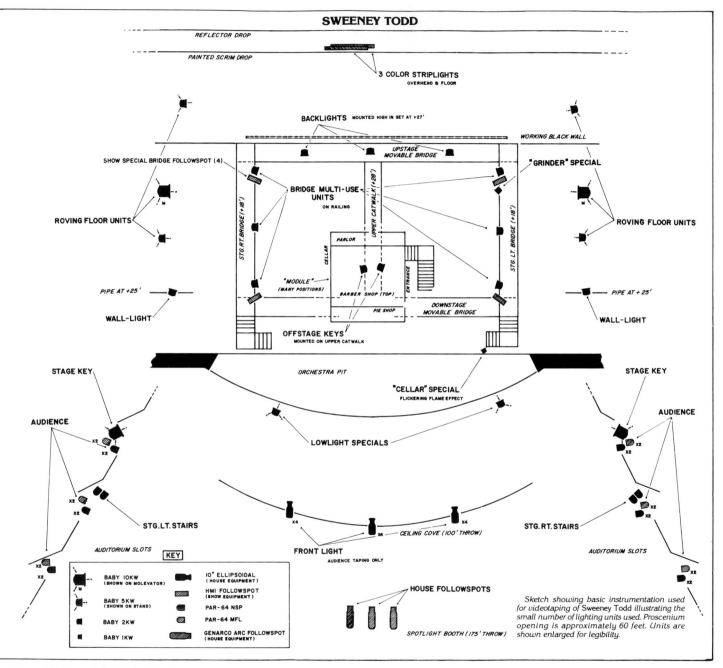

Figure 7.12 Bill Klages's light plot for the television videotaping of the musical *Sweeney Todd* at the Chandler Pavilion in Los Angeles in 1982. (*Courtesy of Bill Klages.*)

Figure 7.13 Videotaping of *Sweeney Todd*. Lighting director: William Klages. (*Photo: RKO/Nederlander*)

Figure 7.14 Videotaping of *Sweeney Todd* with Bill Klages's TV lighting. (*Photo: RKO/Nederlander*)

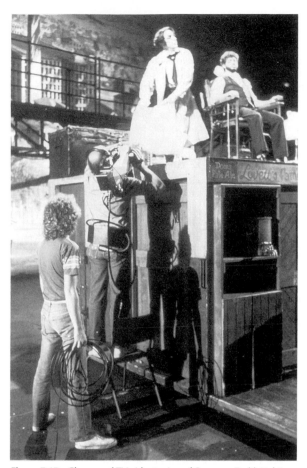

Figure 7.15 Closeup of TV videotaping of *Sweeney Todd*. Lighting director: Bill Klages. (*Photo: RKO/Nederlander*)

cle in the January/February 1982 issue of *Lighting Dimensions:*

Videotaping of *Sweeney Todd,* the macabre musical about the 19th century demon barber of Fleet Street and his accomplice who turned their victims into meat pies, has been completed. The show, produced by RKO-Nederlander, is the first major American musical to be taped while on tour. Angela Lansbury and George Hearn star in this show which was budgeted at well over half a million dollars.

There has been great interest in the last few years in finding more programming for television, due to the increased activity with cable companies. And one of the simplest solutions has been to think in terms of taking theatrical productions, such as Broadway shows, already in the making and taping them for rebroadcast on closed-circuit, as opposed to network programming. This is a desirable package because the show has already been developed and finished. And the show's success is also known as there has already been an audience reaction. Now, nearly all theatrical productions have some kind of agreement with cable production companies.

Sweeney Todd is interesting because it is not a typical Broadway musical. It is more operatic with rather extreme subject material. The music is very sophisticated, with one hearing really not sufficient to touch upon the surface of this complicated production. The show had moderate success and great critical acclaim when it first appeared on Broadway, and the show's success is still evident with the present stage company which includes a number of the original cast.

When the project was first conceived of, Bill Klages, Emmy-award-winning lighting designer with Fiorentino Associates, was asked to determine how easily the production, from a lighting standpoint, could be adapted to television. Klages says that the subject of how to approach the translation always comes up, with the producer's reply usually being, "Well, we can really augment the lighting of the theatrical production and in that way save a great deal of money; all we have to do is go in and tape the live performance."

But Klages believes, from his experience in this field, that there is no such thing as augmenting the light. "In every production I have done where we translated a theatrical event onto video tape, whether it be done in front of a live audience or done in the luxury of stop-and-go taping, I have completely relighted the show. And anybody who feels that they can get an adequate or presentable end result without doing this, I'm opposed to because I don't think it works.

"The most important thing to keep in mind is the lighting of the production for the eye. The eye has entirely different characteristics from the video camera. The eye has the ability to accept enormous ranges of brightness; so if we want something to re-main unseen in the theatre presentation, it must be painted a very dense black and receive absolutely no light whatsoever. This is very different from the television approach where the system has the capability of accepting a very narrow brightness range. There, we're not too overly concerned about unlighted areas, because they will not appear at all, whereas the eye would see into the depth of the shadows. So as a result, there is a certain light level that must be assumed if the camera is going to be exposed properly; and there is a wide variation in the acceptable qualities and quantity of light depending upon the camera used and the end result desired. Also, in taping from a live performance, the lighting intensity should be not only adequate for the camera, but also be quite well-balanced (particularly from scene to scene) because rapid adjustments of exposure changes put too much of a hindrance into the video operation."

Klages says that prior to taping the show, he saw the play seven or eight times. *Sweeney Todd's* very white stage makeup had to be altered slightly for the video production.

The elaborate staging of the play was done by Hal Prince. Set against a background of Hogarth's London with black boats frozen forever in the milk-white Thames was Mrs. Lovett's grungy pie shop with the butchering barber's chair upstairs center stage. For the original Broadway production, the set was huge, actually over-powering, for it had a working foundry interior built and used on stage. The set used by the road company was an adaptation of this and built as scenery. Represented again was the foundry interior, but on a much smaller scale.

Klages says that staging called for enormous amounts of movement and numbers of positions which make lighting and photography for television difficult. But in this case he says the set determined the ease of lighting for video. The set was basically a four-columned gantry enclosed with skylights above (generally out of view of the television camera). In addition, upstage and downstage were two movable bridges which were used as acting areas with different elevations; walls led from this main set off-stage to give a finished look. Upstage was a painted scrim with a Hogarth view of London. At times, a black wall closed off this scrim. The major playing element was a four-sided, two-story module. On one side of this module was Mrs. Lovett's small bake shop, another housed a parlor, with the third side the entrance to the barbershop upstairs, and the fourth side the cellar where the results of *Sweeney Todd's* work was disposed. The cellar comes to life (or death?) in the second act, probably the most interesting from a lighting standpoint. The intense feeling of gruesomeness and mysteriousness in the basement is achieved with a minimal number of set pieces.

A catwalk holding four follow spots went around the stage as part of the scenery. In addition to the four follow spots, Klages used 13 5ks [Fresnel spotlights] mounted in the set itself. These were refocused and readjusted for each sequence, so that basically the lighting was not unlike a film studio. There were also fixed units to light the scenery, four from the catwalk and two from off-stage areas. In addition there were three 5ks and a 10k on stands on each side which Klages placed as required. Three Genarco follow spots were part of the house complement. The corrected Genarcos were used for front light for the principals.

In translating Sweeney Todd to video, Klages felt that to do so in front of a live audience would require as much time to prepare a TV lighting performance as Billington had spent on his. But rehearsals for this could last up to a month, so with the limited time commitment available it was decided to do the show as a stop-and-go tape. The only way in which the audience would be shown was to alter the two opening and closing cues of the two acts in one evening's performance, light the audience prior to the house lights going down and balance the stage lighting to TV intensities. In addition, prerecorded tracks and audience reaction were recorded at that one performance.

Klages says his job was made easier in translating a play such as Sweeney Todd to video. Most of the work had already been done in Billington's interpretation of the lighting. For Klages, "My only job, then, was to make it look the same in front of the camera. Basically, the creative part of the show had been done and I was merely there as a translator. I was looking for the same emotional responses that the theatrical version provided."

Only four days were allotted for video-taping because of contractual agreements with all involved—the talent, musicians, stage crew, cameramen, etc. The show continued in performance each evening with videotaping taking place during the day. Working hours set-up and strike time were specified in order to prepare for the evening performance. With this very complicated schedule, there were four eight-hour taping days, plus one evening for taping of the live performance. The entire performance runs about two hours and 20 minutes in length.

For the time allotment and end result desired, the video lighting of Sweeney Todd was kept to a minimum. With stop-and-go taping, Director Terry Hughes could move the cameras much closer to the stage; an alley in the fifth and sixth rows accommodated a Nike crane and a crab dolly, as well as a pedestal camera. A hand-held camera was also used extensively. Four camera were used altogether and all were movable, with the ones left and right of the crane remaining relatively fixed. The crane did some movement and the hand-held provided numerous color shots.

The play has 37 scenes and in each of those scenes were a number of sub-scenes. An important thing in converting to video was to retain as much of these changes as possible. Klages says, "The transition between the individual scenes was a very important element in the stage production. This became more complicated for video because we didn't have the performance or the orchestra or the scenery to aid us. Many of the transitions had to

be eliminated because there was no way to achieve them. But by and large that feeling was retained. It is very important to make sure that the audience sees Sweeney Todd as a theatrical presentation rather than a movie of the week.

"Each day we would reset. We had to strike the cameras each night, as well as any of the lighting instruments which were bothersome as far as the view of the audience was concerned. The setup was usually done during the hour preceding camera time. Similarly each night we broke down all the cameras. Only about 10 instruments had to be struck each night, and we left the cabling in. So with the cooperation of the stage crew and the show's stage manager, in particular, we were spared having to strike too much."

The theatrical presentation of Sweeney Todd had close to 150 cues (dimmerboard only), not including the follow spot cues. So the show had a total of close to 300 cues altogether. For the video conversion those numerous cues were not necessary, because the camera becomes the cueing device; it takes your interest to what you are meant to see. Klages says, "Cues obviously occurred all during scene transitions. There were also balance adjustment cues, which you don't have at a theatrical performance, to balance the light intensities and make certain that all shots in a sequence are consistent with each other. As it was, within a sequence, very few adjustments were actually made."

The traveling show uses some 200 lighting instruments, but the television production used only one tenth of that. The lighting levels were all based upon what the Genarco follow spots were capable of giving in the filtered, corrected operation—about 50 footcandles. For each set-up only one reading was taken, then Klages would focus to make certain that everything was in range. The RCA TK 47 cameras that were operated normally at a sensitivity of 50 footcandles, well within their operating range. The four follow spots mounted in the gantry were used very sparingly, because for video purposes they were quite uneven and could have resulted in rather unpredictable results. They were used for effects instead, in many cases unfiltered so that the raw blue came through as startling. In one sequence, Sweeney Todd makes an unannounced appearance and scares the audience. When he pops up behind a piece of furniture, Klages hits him with one of the follow spots, uncorrected so as to be overexposed and blue, then fades it out to normal intensity and color balance.

A remarkable slide in a module of the set allows Sweeney to dispose of his victims in the barber's chair. The chair flattens out the body which slides into the trap door, the body reappearing in the basement. One sequence has one of the bodies suddenly appearing in the cellar, the actual execution not shown. To heighten the effect of the dead body suddenly appearing below, Klages again used an unfiltered follow spot for dramatic emphasis.

The talent was so professional that the change in lighting from stage to video didn't bother them. "They were most concerned, however," says Klages, "about seeing what it looked like on the monitor; they were quite pleased." Most of the actors had done a great deal of film and television work and were used to the differences. And their performances didn't change. However some of the actors' normal stage performances required alterations because of the magnification of the close-up camera.

The video crew would usually block a scene, then run it once or twice in sequence for rehearsal. Then they would make three or four recorded passes, a wide angle pass, a medium shot pass, a close-up pass, etc., each of those passes forming the basis of the final editorial. Many sequences were done with a live orchestra as well as the pre-recorded track.

Los Angeles' Dorothy Chandler Pavilion, where the play was videotaped, is a very unique theatre. Because of their tremendous array of productions, including the Oscar Awards, they have an enormous dimming system and a very sophisticated lighting control system. Sweeney Todd, however, troupes with an equally elaborate lighting control and dimming system of their own, because many of the theatres in which they play are not as well equipped as the Chandler. With all their equipment, it would take about 48 hours to load-in Sweeney Todd. The only instrumentation belonging to the show that Klages used were the strip lights used to light the reflector drop upstage of the painted scrim. Also used were some practical fixtures within the set that went through the traveling road company's dimmerboard. Head electrician James Eisner, who travels with the show, operated the show's board for the videotaping with Klages' additional equipment going into the house board operated by the master electrician for the Chandler, Peter Perricone.

Rather than use the television script, Klages worked from the script of the play. He says, "That worked out well because it gave me a way of learning the show and all its cues. Many of the light cues for the theatrical production were incorporated into the video production which was an added advantage. The memory boards were used to advantage because sometimes transitions were done on different days. This way, the transitions and scenes were memorized so that they could be reproduced accurately."

Klages emphasizes simplicity in his work. The success of this show, he feels (coupled with the ability to even do it), depended upon four 10ks, 24 5ks, and a few 2ks, a minimal amount of equipment. Klages, asked if he were to do the show over again would he make any changes, replied, "I would bring in my own striplight equipment of higher intensity for the scrim to get the blue to show." Klages had difficulty in getting the blue to read when lighting the upstage reflective white drop.

Special effects were used, in particular in the cellar. In the stage production, lights with a flame colored gelatin, supposedly emanating from the oven, were visible to the audience. Klages used this as a basis except he hid his lighting instruments. To heighten the dramatic effect Klages had a main light of low elevation—across the stage. As talent entered the cellar, they had a mysterious quality. As they got closer to the oven, Klages had a flame-colored Fresnel on the floor fed from a special effect module to give a random fire flicker effect. The only other element in that scene was a meat grinder lighted with a top light in steel blue. All in all, the scene was lighted with four units: the flickering oven light, the steel blue special on the grinder, the low light on the cellar entrance and a fill light from stage right. In order to get maximum dramatic quality, the instruments were placed and focused very carefully for each sequence, just as they would be for a theatrical production.

Tape was used rather than film to save on cost and time. It had to be shot multiple camera, and multiple camera on film is less controllable, especially in this circumstance according to Klages. He goes on to say that with the show's lighting intensities, video was easy; whereas 50 footcandles, although possible in film, is tricky to handle.

With video there can at last be a complete record of what could be the performance of a lifetime, a show rescued from the dimness of memory and faded reviews.[154]

[154] Lighting Dimensions, vol. 18, no. 1 (Jan./Feb. 1982), pp. 18–23. Illus., color.

The group of plots, hookups, and photographs in Figures 5.40 through 5.42 and 7.1 through 7.15 covers the many different variations and approaches to TV lighting design: network, local station, educational and public service networks, cable and movie channels. The group includes dramatic shows, dance and ballet, musical and cultural events, and soap opera. It also offers the basis for comparison of east coast and west coast lighting styles.

The established forms of TV continue: live, film, and videotape programming on network, local, and international facilities. Kinescope film recording has disappeared. Color has taken over. Pay TV, movie channels, and cable TV have established a firm foothold. Cable TV has become important in the telecasting of theatrical productions—classics, hits, and even new and untried scripts—largely as a result of TV's never-ending demand for new material. Important dance and opera company productions are now to be seen frequently, both on the commercial channels and on educational/public service channels. The production of commercials for TV continues to occupy much time and effort

[156] The "clearinghouse" for videodisc information is The Institute for Graphic Communication, Inc., 375 Commonwealth Avenue, Boston, MA 02115. This company also holds annual conferences.

C. Robert Paulson and Michael J. Doyle, "The Video Disc System," SMPTE Journal, vol. 91, no. 2 (Feb. 1982), pp. 180–85.

Philip Rice and Richard F. Dabbe, "Development of the First Optical Videodisc," SMPTE Journal, vol. 91, no. 3 (Mar. 1982), pp. 277–84. Illus. The most complete history of the evolution TV videodiscs.

"Special Report, Performing Arts and Video: The Cable Alliance," Theatre Crafts, vol. 15, no. 8 (Oct. 1981), pp. 17–32. Illus. See in particular Mary Lucier, "From the Proscenium to the Television Screen — Light Makes It Work," pp. 30, 61–63, and "Ralph Holmes: Illuminating Dance," pp. 30–31, 56–57. Illus.

[157] Ross Lowell, "Film, Video & Still Lighting . . . ", pp. 1, 3, op. cit. (see footnote 144).

by TV lighting directors. The 3½ million videotape cassettes in the United States (and the newer videodiscs) have become important in the marketplace.[156] Britain added Pay TV in 1984.

Whatever the reproduction or transmission facilities utilized, it still remains necessary to have TV lighting directors involved in the original recording and presentation. The newer marketing forms bear watching, since they are inevitably increasing the numbers involved in designing lighting for TV cameras.

Cinematography

TV lighting and cinematography lighting design are similar, yet in important ways different. Here are some of the similarities:

- Neither is live. Both can record a light-and-shade picture and reproduce it elsewhere at another time with no variations.
- Both have as basic good lighting design the specific necessity to know, understand, and utilize the potential of the intermediate "seeing" equipment (TV cameras or film cameras). The camera is the medium between the performance and its reproduction.
- Both utilize similar lighting instruments (luminaires), controls, and operational methods (similar, but not always identical).
- Both must depend upon light to create a sense of depth, space, and form (i.e., to suggest the third dimension).
- Both use light to help create and reinforce mood.
- Both normally use light to help create a sense of reality, i.e., to reinforce credibility by making the scene or shots seem to be lighted by natural sources present.

Here are some of the differences:

- The contrast ratios (the brightness contrast between the brightest element in the picture and the darkest element) differ vastly. Film can have a brightness ratio of 100 to 1, but control of "balance" is much more critical. TV normally will accept a contrast ratio of up to 30 to 1 (more like 8 to 1 for recorded color picture — the 30 to 1 applies to live and to black-and-white).

- There are variations in work methods. Lighting design in TV is indistinctly split between the engineers and the lighting director. In film work, the gaffer and crew will set up and "rough out" the lighting setup (usually after conference with higher-ups), but the director of photography, or the Cinematographer, or (sometimes) the first cameraman has the final design authority.

- The end product is quite different for the two media. TV is more mobile and frequently less polished. It is also more "instant." For TV, there are more limitations (decreasing each year) upon possible subsequent "lab modifications" (double exposures, cutting, editing, splicing, over and under printing synthesized images). Film tends to be more finished (polished) and to utilize more editing possibilities.

Ross Lowell writes:

> [Both] film and video are involved with the elements of time and motion. . . . Camera movement and editing are basic elements in the creative process in film and video. . . . The matching of light and mood is a major consideration for the cameraman or lighting director. . . . A lot can be done after shooting film and video to correct overall color imbalance, over and under exposure (film cameramen almost never "bracket" exposures the way still photographers often do) and, to some extent, overall contrast. . . . The size of the (film) screen also influences the way we light and compose.[157]

- TV features "instant" results, while film involves delayed editing. The lighting designer for TV can always instantly see the output. The film cameraman/lighting designer must await the following day's "rushes" to have even a rough idea of what the output looked like — and even that output is far from the final accepted film end product.

In spite of the differences between the two media, film and TV are each year trading more heavily upon their similarities. The two worlds continue to borrow the best from each other and adapt what they borrow as needed. As each year passes, TV has moved closer to using "film techniques." Tony Di Girolamo said in a *Lighting Design & Application* interview:

> When I say "film style" I mean the old method of shooting for the particular setup. Film style is the *old* method because this way of shooting for portraiture and lighting for each individual setup or scene was used in the motion picture industry long before television, the video medium was characterized by a multicamera method of shooting. That is, a scene had to be lighted "all around" and not only from one or two angles, so that several cameras could tape all the action of a scene from a variety of angles. The emphasis was on the general illumination of the scene with little attention paid to the particular details or movements.
>
> In contrast, "film style" shooting allows the lighting designer to produce dramatic and artistic results because he can concentrate on lighting for a particular moment in a scene. . . . The widespread use of "film style" shooting in the television industry in recent years has encouraged the development of the lighting designer's view of his profession as an art.[158]

Of the relationship between theatre lighting and film lighting, Gene Kelly, producer-director-choreographer, has said: "You can get away with more in theater than you can in motion pictures. . . . Dim a light in theatre and you get an effect. Do it in a movie, and someone will think there's something wrong with the projector. A movie is two-dimensional; the theatre is three-dimensional. One is like a painting. The other is like a sculpture." [159] In the "From the Editor" comments in the first Special Lighting Issue of *The American Cinematographer*, Richard Patterson wrote:

> The art of lighting is the cornerstone of all film and video production. Obviously without light there would be no recordable image, but even more importantly without the artistic use of light the images recorded either on film or videotape lose much of their impact and perhaps all of their meaning. The same people in the same environment can result in a totally different image depending on how the scene is lit. Lighting effects can not only turn an artificial setting into something believable; they can infuse everyday reality with an other-worldly or spiritual presence. A face can be made attractive or frightening through the use of light. Light can dazzle, mystify, clarify, glamorize, transform and dramatize.
>
> There is a tendency to assume that eventually high speed films or super-sensitive pick-up devices will eliminate the need for artificial lighting. . . . The mind's eye sees far more than is visible in the natural world, and the only way to create images seen by the mind's eye is through "artificial" means. Artificial does not mean just fake or phony; it means literally made by art. Artificial lighting is the means by which a cinematographer creates his images. At its best cinematography is still and will always be "painting with light."
>
> The video revolution (involves) the idea that the traditions of film lighting styles and techniques needed to be made more accessible to video production personnel. . . . Some of our readers apparently assume that Hollywood cameramen have secret lighting techniques which enable them to get the results we see on the screen. The truth of the matter is quite the opposite. There are no secrets. There is just the skill that comes from years of experience and in most cases of apprenticeship with other cameramen.[160]

Vilmos Zsigmond, cinematographer for *The Deer Hunter* and *Close Encounters of the Third Kind* said: "The most memorable moments of any film are created by light." The same can be said of both TV and film lighting.

The process also works the other way: film borrows from TV. One of the best examples of this is the increasing appearance of a TV Videcon camera fastened onto the film camera, allowing the cinematographer a "guesstimate" of focus on film and the director a chance to see the scene as the camera sees it. The lighting ratios are wrong on these TV monitors, so matching problems are still not solved with this method. Also, as mentioned above, while TV has moved closer to "single camera, single shot" shooting, several films have been made utilizing more than one film camera during shooting. The differences are disappearing, undoubtedly to the benefit of both industries.

Until recently there has been a minimal crossover between the film lighting group and the rest of the lighting design industry. Jules Fisher designed lighting for portions of the movies *Slow Dancing in the Big City* and *A Star Is Born* (see Color Figs. 64 and 65 and Figs. 7.16 and 7.17). These movies involved the use of a rock group whose lighting design was regularly the assignment of Fisher. Nananne Porcher was responsible for the lighting design for the movie *The Turning Point* (see Color Fig. 66) with cinematographer Robert Sertes. The movie consisted of lengthy ballet sequences, and Porcher was at that time the lighting designer for the American Ballet Theatre. In addition, the

[158] *Wanda Jankowski, op. cit. (see footnote 144).*

[159] *John Corry, "Gene Kelly Puts the Strut in 'Satchmo',"* The New York Times, *August 24, 1981, Chicago edition, p. 16.*

[160] *Richard Patterson, "From the Editor,"* American Cinematographer, *Special Lighting Issue, vol. 64, no. 11 (Nov. 1982), p. 1101.*

[161] *"The Crowd That Wasn't There and Other Secrets From . . . Rocky,"* Lighting Dimensions, *vol. 1, no. 1 (June 1977), pp. 12–15. Quote from page 14. A good, chatty interview with Ross Maehl about his lighting of the movie* Rocky. *Interview presents Maehl's design philosophy and many illustrations, both color and black and white.*

[162] *"Conrad Hall,"* Lighting Dimensions, *vol. 1, no. 2 (July/Aug. 1977), pp. 30–33, 36. Quote from page 31. A lengthy interview with one of the top cinematographers about his attitudes toward life and work, about lighting and his career and experiences. Very informative basic piece about the nature of the industry.*

[163] *Richard Eder, "To Bergman, Light, Too, Is a Character,"* The New York Times, *Wednesday, April 7, 1976. Interview and photography of Sven Nykvist, Bergman's cameraman.*

Figure 7.16 *A Star Is Born,* produced by Warner Bros. Lighting by Jules Fisher.

Figure 7.17 *A Star Is Born.*

filmed ballet sequences were shot on stage in New York City's Lincoln Center. James Tilton designed both scenery and lighting for the movie *Dear Dead Delilah* in Nashville, Tennessee, in 1970. Producer Jack Clemens was not an established film producer. He was familiar with Tilton and his work. All the filming was in Nashville. These are the only instances I am aware of involving a *theatre* lighting designer active in the world of cinematography. Many instances can be found of scenic designers (or scenographers) working in films as art directors, but the crossover has been rare in lighting design.

Design Considerations

Speaking of film lighting design, Academy Award–winner Ross Maehl says: "In (film) lighting, either you can see it or you can't. Soon your brain starts to look at the lighting as the film sees it, and that's a transition that must be made within yourself. You look at something, and you see how it will be on film." [161] Conrad Hall, whose work included *Butch Cassidy and the Sundance Kid,* says: "You don't ever learn much about light until you do it yourself, and I don't mean until you ask somebody else to do it for you, like a gaffer." [162] Ingmar Bergman's cameraman, Seven Nykvist, in an interview given to *The New York Times,* said:

[F]or example, there was the preparation of *Winter Light* (by Bergman and myself): A scene covering a period of three hours was to take place in a church. It was relatively early in the relationship, and Mr. Nykvist says he assumed that a single light setting would be enough for three hours. Every five minutes he had me take a photograph and when we finished I realized how all these tiny shifts of light worked out into what he was trying to do." [163]

The basic point is clear. Most (not all) movies require realistic, plausible, and believable lighting design. Theatre does not, nor does opera or dance. TV is somewhere in the middle. Cinematographers and directors of photography seek constantly to capture on film new, artistic ways of showing realism. A quick glance through a few volumes of *The American Cinematographer* provides plenty of evidence of this.

Secondly, the cinematographer's real "stock in trade" is a complete awareness of what the camera can record and how film can be processed and modified subsequently. Unlike the lighting director for TV, the cinematographer does not have the video engineer to lean upon but turns instead to the film processing lab. Light and photography are so closely intertwined that their practice is often one and the same. This is one reason why few lighting designers, trained in other areas, ever double over into the world of cinematography. The cinematographer must be a lighting designer and also a cameraman.

A brief glance at the *process* and *people* involved in lighting a film is appropriate at this point. Millerson writes:

> The lighting cameraman relates the film director's intended production treatment, and the story requirements, to the scenic design, and in evolving a lighting scheme giving life to his interpretations, considers the potential problems of the camerawork, time estimates and so on. For upon him rests the entire responsibility for production lighting, the visual image, and usually for selective camera set-ups and movements, as well as pictorial composition. . . . He is customarily . . . backed up by a team of electricians headed by the gaffer.

> Within the film studio, the chief electrician (gaffer) is responsible for lighting the setting to the lighting cameraman's requirements. Anticipating probable needs, he may rough-in the set lighting (i.e., rig suitable lamps for background lighting), ready for the lighting cameraman's final instructions. Rehearsal of the story-action (dialogue, moves, etc.) then takes place within the setting, and with this knowledge the lighting cameraman arranges for any background lighting modifications he deems necessary. Now the main portrait lighting is devised, lamps are positioned, set and balanced for the action the director has rehearsed perhaps with the help of stand-ins, who are lit in the principals' positions.[164]

It is clear from the above description that the cinematographer (who is the lighting designer in films) has much larger responsibilities than just lighting. When actual shooting begins, under the cinematographer and the director's supervision, the end product is a series of *shots,* each lasting from a few seconds to a few minutes. A full-length motion picture consists of from 600 to 1,500 *shots,* each lasting from 3 to 15 seconds with editing cuts every 3 to 10 seconds. A really top-notch film team can finish (at most) 120 shots per day (about 18 minutes running time); however, several days may be necessary to film an involved 30-second bit.

Some cinematographers plan their overall lighting treatment on paper in advance, modifying the plan as needed. Others evolve the lighting shot by shot. Each shot (action sequence) is "taken" several times until an optimum take —one which satisfies the performers, the director, and the cinematographer—is "in the can." The lighting is then modified and new camera positions/tracks are determined for the next shot. It is the cinematographer who has the ultimate responsibility for shots (sometimes taken months apart in time) "matching up" for the finished product (same time-of-day, etc.).

The cinematographer must also be very familiar with film processing. The "first prints" from the lab give the production group only a rough approximation of image quality, color values, lighting balance, content, and framing and composition. These first, uncorrected prints are called "rushes," or "dailies." The filming editor moves on to a "cutting copy" (rough cuts). From this evolves a "corrected print" (also called an "answer," "approval," or "grading" print). Sound tracks are added to complete the final "show" or "release" print. Many things can be done in the labs along the way to alter the final appearance of the lighting values of the film. The parallels in TV are the modifications possible by the video engineer—but modifications can be much more extensive in film.

Two other items should be kept in mind. Just as in theatre there are experienced and talented electricians who (in rather rare cases) end up as the production lighting designer (working under the guidance of either the director or the scenic designer), so also in film there are gaffers who determine the final lighting design by working closely with friendly and understanding cameramen and cinematographers. The final dividing line between the "cinematographer" or "director of photography" and the "gaffer" remains as indistinct as that between "electrician" and "lighting designer" in other parts of the business. Also the limitations of film response to light are very exact. The director of photography is as apt to be seen with a light meter in hand—checking brightness and distance prior to shooting—as is the operator of a color TV camera lining up in the morning on a test pattern.[165]

Techniques

Because scenery construction in film work is much more like enduring house construction than stage scenery, light mounting practices for film are somewhat different. Film studios are usually huge, barnlike structures. I designed

[164] *Gerald Millerson,* The Technique of Lighting for Television and Motion Pictures, *pp. 272–73, op. cit. (see footnote 144).*

[165] *Dennis Schaefer and Larry Salvate,* Masters of Light, Conversations With Contemporary Cinematographers. *Los Angeles; University of California Press; 1984. 355 pp.; no illustrations. Contains conversations with 15 leading contemporary cinematographers and a useful glossary of terms. Invaluable tool for those lighting feature films.*

Kris Malkiewicz, Film Lighting, Talks With Hollywood's Cinematographers and Gaffers. *N.Y.; Prentice Hall; 1986. 198 pp., illus. Interviews with over 20 industry leaders. Most useful.*

Nestor Almendros, A Man with a Camera, *N.Y.; Farrar, Straus Giroux; 1984. Illus., 306 pp. The best of the books about cinematography and light by a Spanish director of photography who has many award-winning feature films to his credit.*

Joseph Walker, ASC, and Juanita Walker, The Light On Her Face. *Hollywood, ASC Press; 1984. 290 pp., illus. Useful humorous stories and valuable information from a leading cinematographer.*

Verne and Sylvia Carlson, Professional Lighting Handbook. *Stoneham, MA; Focal Press (80 Montvale Ave. 02180); 1983. 224 pp., illus., color. A how-to approach to motion picture lighting on a professional level. Well-illustrated. Covers lighting equipment, lenses, controllers, and filters. Very useful.*

American Cinematographer, *Special Lighting Issue, vol. 64, no. 11 (Nov. 1982), 138 pages. Illus., color. Invaluable summary of current practices.*

Walter Kerr, "Films Are Made in the Cutting Room," The New York Times, *Sunday, March 17, 1985; p. 1 of Art & Leisure section. Kerr, a leading critic, stresses the vital contribution of editing for feature film.*

Jan Bone, Film Careers. *Lincolnwood, IL; National Textbook Co., VGM Career Horizons division; 1984. 147 pp., illus. A career guide handbook which sketches the development of the film industry; film business; training schools, seminars, workshops, and conventions; and film unions as a background to job hunting and opportunities abroad.*

Raymond Fielding, A Technological History of Motion Pictures and Television. *Berkeley, CA; University of California Press; 1967. Illus., 255 pp. An edited compilation of SMPTE articles. Well-documented and well-illustrated.*

Christopher Finch, Special Effects: Creating Movie Magic. *N.Y.; Abbeville Press; 1984. Illus., color, 252 pp. A lavishly illustrated (often in color) book on quality paper with a readable description of special effects in the art of film. Finch's text is very readable. Covers effects for many recent feature films.*

The Mystery of Filters II. *Published by Harrison & Harrison, 6363 Santa Monica Blvd., Hollywood, CA 90038. The standard reference manual on all photographic filters.*

David Samuelson, Motion Picture Camera & Lighting Equipment, Choice & Technique. *N.Y.; Focal Press/Hastings House; 1977. Readable; illustrated and detailed fundamentals plus necessary advanced technical information about cameras and lights. 220 pages.*

Alan J. Ritske, Lighting for Location Motion Pictures. *N.Y.; Van Nostrand Reinhold Co.; 1979. 224 pp., illus. Excellent study; good coverage of basics; choice illustrations; good text. The only American work in this area and very up-to-date.*

SMPTE, Elements of Color in Professional Motion Pictures. *N.Y.; SMPTE; 1957 (revised 1967). Contains 104 pp. of everything a lighting designer might need to know about color for motion pictures, compiled by a committee of the Society of Motion Picture and Television Engineers.*

Bernard Happe, Basic Motion Picture Technology (2d ed.). *N.Y.; Focal Press/Hastings House; 1975. Film technique in nontechnical language for both the artist and the technician.*

A. Arthur Englander and Paul Petzold, Filming for Television. *N.Y.; Focal Press/Hastings House; 1976. By two experienced experts.*

H. Mario Raimondo Souto, The Technique of the Motion Picture Camera (3d imprint). *N.Y.; Focal Press/Hastings House; 1976. Basic.*

John Alton, Painting with Light. *N.Y.; MacMillan Co.; 1949. While its technology is out of date, this full-length volume by a leading ASC member remains quite useful.*

Freddie Young and Paul Petzold, The Work of the Motion Picture Cameraman. *N.Y.; Focal Press/Hastings House; 1972. Technique.*

Sharon A. Russell, Semiotics and Lighting, A Study of Six Modern French Cameramen. *Ann Arbor, MI; UMI Press; 1981. 177 pp. For the advanced cinematographer only.*

Dennis R. Boknenkamp and Sam L. Grogg, Jr. (editors), American Film Institute Guide to College Courses in Film and Television. *Princeton, NJ; Petersen's Guides; 1978. 430 pages.*

Susan Todd, "The Jewel in the Crown," Theatre Crafts, *vol. 19, no. 1 (Jan. 1985), pp. 24–27, 98–99. Illus., color. Discusses the British (filmed) Granada TV 14-part dramatization and the work of lighting cameraman Ray Goode.*

Bethany Haye, "Structuring the Image, The Panoramas and Chiaroscuros of Billy Williams," Theatre Crafts, *vol. 20, no. 4 (Apr. 1986), pp. 77–80. Illus., color. Useful article about Williams's work.*

Bob Fisher, "Changing Concepts in Cinematography, Kodak Hosts 58 Cinematographers for a Technical Update on Film," On Location, *Feb. 1985, pp. 43, 45, 47, 158. Illus. Useful technical information.*

Barry Sonnenfeld, "A Cinematographer Talks Technical: Some How To's on Film Lighting," Lighting Design + Application, *vol. 16, no. 12 (Dec. 1986), pp. 21, 48. Brief, but useful.*

Laurance J. Roberts, "SMPTE Hollywood Section Presents a Tutorial Seminar on Production Lighting Techniques," SMPTE Journal, *vol. 92, no. 9 (Sept. 1983), pp. 954–960. Illus. Excellent description by Hungarian cinematographer, Vilamos Zsigmond (Close Encounters, The Deer Hunter) of lighting of a café interior for night and morning.*

"Zsigmond," SMPTE Journal, *vol. 91, no. 9 (Sept. 1982), pp. 850–51. Illus. Eastman Kodak advertisement featuring the cinematographer of The Deer Hunter, Close Encounters of the Third Kind, etc.*

"60th Anniversary Issue," SMPTE Journal, *vol. 85, no. 7 (July 1976). Entire issue still useful. See particularly: "Advancements in Motion-Picture and Television Set Lighting Equipment" by Daniel L. Aron, pp. 534ff.*

Rose Lowell, "Basic Lighting" Parts I–IV. Lowell Light News, Issues 3, 4, 5, and 6. Illus. *Lowell, owner of Lowell Light Manufacturing Co., Inc. (475 Tenth Ave., New York City 10018-1197) writes about the basics of film lighting from his many years of experience as owner of one of the largest film lighting equipment firms.*

"An Interview with David Holmes/Lee Filters," Lighting Dimensions, *vol. 7, no. 6 (Nov./Dec. 1983), pp. 12–14, 16. Illus. Noted British cinematographer discusses film lighting and filter use and discusses the differences between British and American techniques.*

Jerry McClain, "The Influence of Stage Lighting on Early Cinema," Lighting Dimensions, *vol. 9, no. 7 (Nov./Dec. 1985), pp. 36–38, 40–41, 43, 76. Illus. An excellently researched history with useful graphics.*

Follow Focus *magazine, published by the Professional Motion Picture Equipment Association, 6440 North Central Expressway, Suite 806, Dallas, TX 75206; telephone: (214) 696-1448.*

"Life on a Grand Scale — EXPO 86 Hosts the First 3-D IMAX Film," Lighting Dimensions, *vol. 10, no. 4 (July/Aug. 1986), pp. 18, 78. Illus.*

David Landau, "You're Giving Me Pretty Pictures: I Want Speed." Notes from a gaffer on a low budget. Lighting Dimensions, *vol. 5, no. 7 (Nov./Dec. 1981), pp. 14–17. Illus.*

"Jules Fisher," Lighting Dimensions, *vol. 2, no. 3 (Mar. 1978), pp. 22–27. An interview with Jules Fisher. Includes many color illustrations and a discussion with Fisher about lighting for the movie A Star is Born, from the viewpoint of a theatre/rock lighting designer working with film.*

Hal Trussell, "Lighting without Lights — The Lighting in the Film Blue Lagoon *Was Almost Totally Dependent on Natural Light. The Author Reveals Some of the Techniques,"* Lighting Dimensions, *vol. 5, no. 3 (Apr. 1981), pp. 29–31, 34–35. Illus., color.*

Hal Trussell, "Lighting the Day-for-Night Film Technique," Lighting Dimensions, *vol. 5, no. 7 (Nov./Dec. 1981), pp. 19, 21–22.*

"*John Alonso Sheds Light on* Runaway," Lighting Dimensions, *vol. 8, no. 7 (Nov./Dec. 1985), pp. 22–24, 26–30. Illus., color. Cinematography Alonso discuss his lighting philosophy.*

"*The Making of 2010,*" Lighting Dimensions, *vol. 8, no. 7 (Nov./Dec. 1985), pp. 34–41. Illus., color. Cinematographer-producer-director Peter Hyams discusses techniques used in the film 2010.*

"*Nestor Almendros—An Interview,*" Lighting Dimensions, *vol. 9, no. 7 (Nov./Dec. 1985), pp. 18–24, 27. Illus., color.*

"*The Filming of* Out of Africa," Lighting Dimensions, *vol. 9, no. 7 (Nov./Dec. 1985), pp. 28–29, 31–34. Illus., color. Cinematographer David Watkin explains his work.*

"*Backstage with* A Chorus Line," Lighting Dimensions, *vol. 9, no. 7 (Nov./Dec. 1985), pp. 44–46, 49–51. Illus., color. The filming of the Broadway musical.*

Mike Williams, "*A Trip to the Other Side: Cinematographer Andrew Laszlo on Poltergeist II,*" Lighting Dimensions, *vol. 10, no. 3 (May/June 1986), pp. 18, 52–57. Illus., color.*

Barbara J. Knox, "*Sid and Nancy: Cinematographer Roger Deakings Takes a Realistic Approach to This Story of Destructive Love,*" Lighting Dimensions, *vol. 10, no. 6 (Nov. 1986), pp. 46–49. Illus., color.*

Ric Gentry, "*The Eastwood Aesthetic: Cinematographer Jack Green Brings a Crisp Realism to the Latest Eastwood Adventure,* Heartbreak Ridge," Lighting Dimension, *vol. 11, no. 1 (Jan./Feb. 1987), pp. 20, 77–78, 80–82. Illus.*

Ric Gentry, "*Defining Shades of Gray: Robby Müller's Unique Use of Natural Light Makes For Effective Black and White Images in* Down By Law," Lighting Dimensions, *vol. 11, no. 2 (Mar./April 1987), pp. 44, 46–53. Illus.*

Tim Pulleine, "*Emotionally Correct Solutions: British Cinematographer Oliver Stapleton Explores the Subtleties of Light in* Prick Up Your Ears," Lighting Dimensions, *vol. 11, no. 3 (May/June 1987), pp. 116, 118, 120–123. Illus.*

Jill Kirschenbaum, "*News: Singing in the Purple Rain,*" Lighting Dimensions, *vol. 11, no. 4 (July/Aug. 1987), p. 16. Illus. Concerns Director of Photography Francis Kenny's use of color.*

Ric Gentry, "*Spaceballs: Cinematographer Nick Mclean Takes Stock of Special Effects,*" Lighting Dimensions, *vol. 11, no. 4 (July/Aug. 1987), pp. 44–47, 62–64. Illus., color.*

International Photographer, Film & Video Techniques. *Published monthly by Local #659, IATSE, in Hollywood, this quality journal with slick paper and color photos is devoted to cinematography and video techniques, "written by professionals for professionals." Volume 60 was published in 1988. Very useful journal.*

"*Dean Cundey, ASC, Making the Illusion Real,*" International Photographer, *vol. 60, no. 10 (Oct. 1988), pp. 14–15, 19–23. Illus., color. An excellent interview with a noted cinematographer.*

Michael S. Eddy, "*A Quality of Light,*" Cue International, *no. 59 (May/June 1989), pp. 21–25. Illus. An excellent presentation of the work of cinematographer Sven Nykist, active since 1963 for more than 60 films and cinematographer with Ingmar Bergman for 22 films during a 30-year period.*

Tim Pulleine, "*Nature's Call: Shooting Sun, Sand, and Sea in Castaway,*" Lighting Dimensions, *vol. 11, no. 5 (September/October 1987), pp. 55–57, 72–74. Illus., color.*

Ric Gentry, "*Mood Maker: Cinematographer Alex Thompson Creates the Otherworldly Look of High Spirits,*" Lighting Dimensions, *vol. 12, no. 7 (Nov. 1988), pp. 52–53, 68–71. Illus., color.*

Mike Williams, "*The Glass Menagerie: Michael Ballhaus Photographs Paul Newman's Film Version,*" Lighting Dimensions, *vol. 11, no. 6 (Nov. 1987), pp. 48–49, 68–71. Illus., color.*

Nicholas Pasquariello, "*Tucker: DP Vittorio Storaro Talks about His Latest Film with Francis Coppola,*" Lighting Dimensions, *vol. 12, no. 6 (September/October 1988), pp. 40, 42–45. Illus.*

Ric Gentry, "*DP Stephen Katz Lights Sister, Sister,*" Lighting Dimensions, *vol. 11, no. 7 (January/February 1988), p. 17. Illus.*

Tony Felton, "*Lenses and Lighting: The Clean, Crisp—and Often Wacky—Style of DP Barry*

Sonnenfeld," Lighting Dimensions, *vol. 12, no. 4 (May/June 1988), pp. 34–39, 59. Illus., color.*

Tony Felton, "*School Days to* School Daze, DP Ernest Dickerson Takes on Spike Lee's New Movie," Lighting Dimensions, *vol. 12, no. 2 (March 1988), pp. 44, 46, 48, 50. Illus.*

Michael S. Eddy, "*Lights, Camera, Action Films: Douglas Slocombe Shoots Last of* Indiana Jones Trilogy," Lighting Dimensions, *vol. 13, no. 4 (May/June 1989), pp. 54–55, 68, 70–71. Illus., color.*

Michael S. Eddy, "*Sven Nykvist: Cinematography Spanning Four Decades, from Ingmar Bergman to Woody Allen,*" Lighting Dimensions, *vol. 13, no. 1 (January/February 1989), pp. 42–45, 62, 64, 66. Illus., color.*

Adam Pirani, "*Holy Bat-Design!*" Cue International, *no. 60 (July/August 1989), pp. 16–19. Illus., color.*

Michael G. Uva, The Grip Book. *Published by Michael G. Uva, 1988. A semihumorous, semiliterate softcover 185-page booklet on "How To Become a Motion Picture Film Technician (i.e., Grip)," obtainable from: Independent Cinema Technology and Videos, 24307 Magic Mountain Parkway, Suite 40, Valencia, CA 91355. Tel: (805) 296-0276). Illus. throughout with black and white line drawings. Contains useful basic trade information from a working grip.*

Special Effects Business *magazine, a bimonthly magazine first published in August 1988. Contains useful information and trade news about film/TV special effects. Available on annual subscription from: 7943 Haskell, #11, Van Nuys, CA 91406. Tel: (818) 787-5939. Also available from P.O. Box 17180, Encino, CA 91416-7180.*

[166] "Streets *with Style,*" Lighting Dimension, *vol. 8, no. 3 (May/June 1984), pp. 27–34. Illus., color. Includes light plot. Quote from pp. 33–34. A lengthy interview with Cinematographer Andrew Laszlo and lighting designer Marc Brickman about the feature film* Streets of Fire. *Includes the first computer-generated light plot (see Chapter 3 of this Handbook, under "Computers").*

VIDEOTAPES

Vilmos Zsigmond, ASC, On Lighting. *A 50-minute videotape available from the SMPTE. It presents the 1983 Tutorial Seminar on Production Lighting Techniques in Hollywood, presented by a master cinematographer. Very useful.*

Richard Glouner, ASC, SMPTE Lighting Seminar. *Another SMPTE videotape, 25½-minutes in length. Very useful.*

Tiffen, Which Filter Should I Use? *A helpful videotape and booklet detailing uses of filters in photography. Available from: Tiffen Mfg. Corp., 90 Oser Ave., Hauppauge, NY 11788. Tel: (516) 273-2500. Tiffen is the manufacturer of Tiffen, Softnet, and Color-Grad photographic filters. Approximately $25.*

lighting for 26 half-hour recruiting films for the U.S. Army in the mid-1950s at the old movie studios in Long Island City (then the Army Pictorial Center). Throw distances were such that a 225-ampere arc spotlight (called a "Brute") was not an uncommon unit, even for the TV kinescopes we were producing. Thirty-foot-tall real trees were common for battlefield scenes. Luminaires were mounted on catwalks (readily accessible) in these huge studios or, even more commonly, on top of the set itself. Sturdy construction allows this. In addition, floor stand lights are used more freely than in TV because the camera track for a given shot is much more limited in space consumption and is known in advance.

Andrew Laszlo, cinematographer for 19 feature films in the past 20 years, wrote in *Lighting Dimensions* about his movie *Streets of Fire:*

There's nothing really new under the sun, but on a massive scale I think lighting has changed. The role of the cinematographer has become an artist, as opposed to someone who records an image, and I don't think I have to quote 10 pictures to illustrate this, because I'm sure you know of 20.

Lighting has traditionally fulfilled two major purposes, one of which is exposure, the other the artistry of the lighting. Today, the problem of exposure is slowly falling by the wayside as the new film emulsions, higher-speed lenses, and improved laboratory techniques enable us to have an exposure under just about any circumstances and conditions. I'm happy to say lighting now fulfills that larger portion I refer to as artistry, or the creation of the image with light, or the mood establishing the style of the film. When one examines lighting on a historical basis within the motion picture industry, we find there was a wave, a pendulum swinging back and forth on which exposure and artistry were constantly pushing one another. Many times, mainly by the dictates of the major studios, exposure would be more important, and the image would be sharp and crisp at the expense of what the mood of the lighting should have been.

Now the pendulum has swung the other way, so much so that our problem in many cases is not how to light up a set but how to light down a set. Light that a few years ago may have been considered minimal because of the emulsions, the lenses, and the laboratories is now too powerful for exposure. Consequently, instead of plopping that extra light in you have to devise ways to keep extra light off the subject matter, or to balance your light, for the sake of artistry, with the existing sources in the film. The existing sources may be neon (as it was in *Streets of Fires's*

street scenes), which you have very little control over. This is a big problem. In *Streets of Fire,* we had to resort to such means as using ordinary household bulbs in the lighting of major sets. We were using inkies to light three-story sets.

A few years ago, the tendency was to do everything in available light, or what we called the bounce light. We can't do that anymore.

Today, with 5293, we're not talking about shooting with 200 footcandles. We're talking about five footcandle; less than five in many cases.

There are radical changes going on in lighting, but the artistry has to be accommodated, because as film becomes more of an event . . . the audiences are more demanding. They want to see more films that are unusual and that stand out in their visual qualities.[166]

Communication Form

Almost no advance paperwork for lighting film exists or is standard practice. Lighting is generally just "worked out." Live locations are used quite regularly in film. Space to mount lights can be very limited. As film is also an outdoor medium, the sun, clouds, and general weather conditions are variables which consume time and money in the budget and can cause enormous matching problems with the lighting. Color Figs. 67 to 69 are from *The Deer Hunter,* by Academy Award–winning Director of Photography Vilmos Zsigmond, ASC (American Society of Cinematographers). Figures 7.18 to 7.20 present Nananne Porcher's light plot and switchboard hookup for the movie *The Turning Point* (see also Color Fig. 66). Figures 7.21 & 7.22 are of the movie *The Wiz* and are self-explanatory. Figure 7.23 is from the movie *Hurricane.*

Procedures and Practices

A brief letter I received in response to my Industry Survey, from Gerald R. McClain, is of considerable interest:

Everyone I know in the film business in Hollywood works part time no matter how successful they are. I know of no steady jobs in this business. That's a blessing or curse depending on your philosophy of life. I've been in it for fifteen years and I'd say it's a very hard business because of the great competition leading to the uncertainty of unemployment. Good financial years are followed immediately by disastrous ones. People are up for several

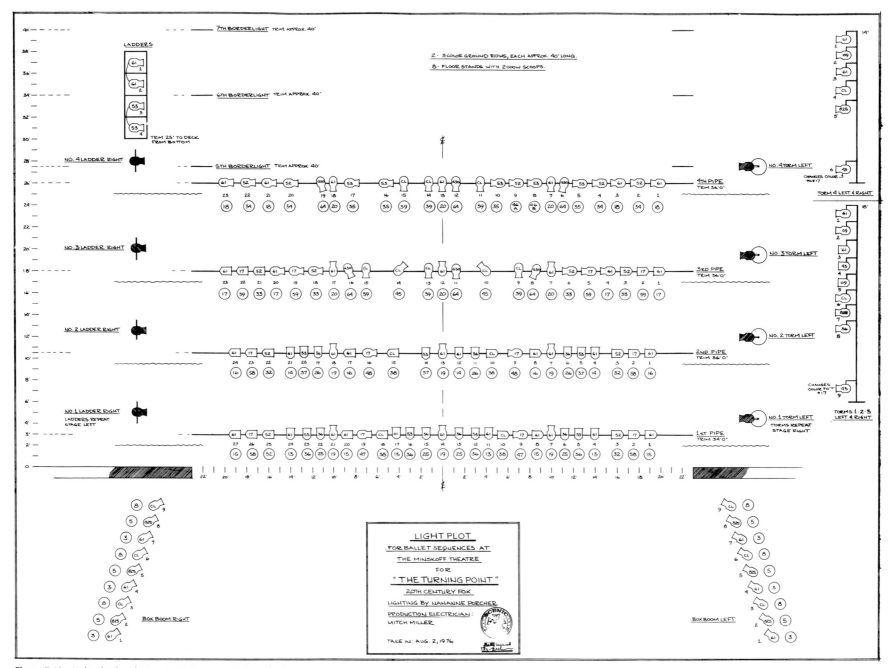

Figure 7.18 Light plot for *The Turning Point;* movie lighting by Nan Porcher.

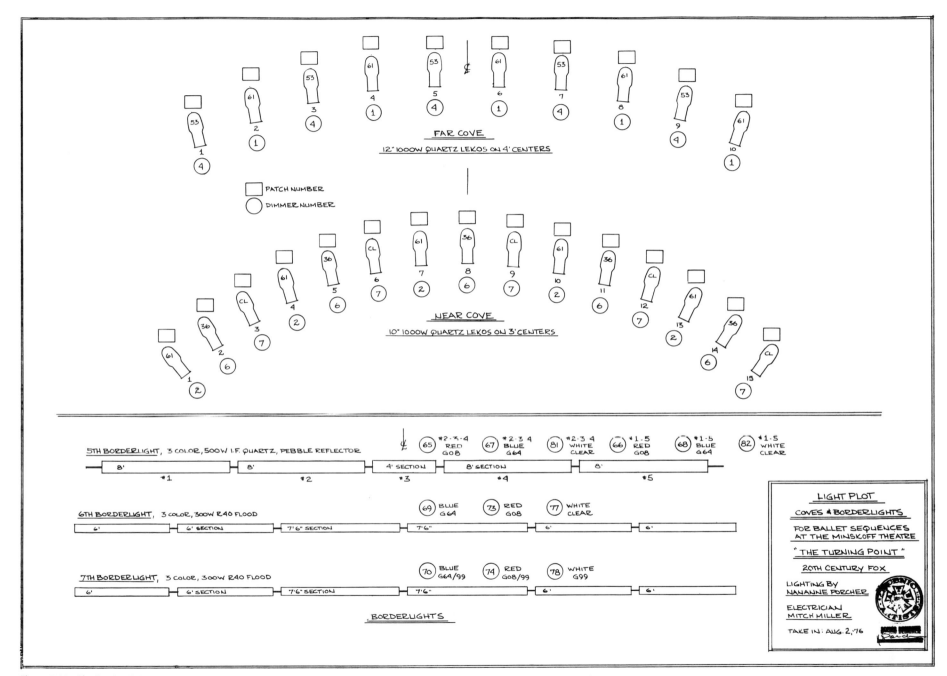

Figure 7.19 *The Turning Point.*

"THE TURNING POINT"   AUG. 2, 1976

HOOKUP   12 PLATE 5000W RESISTANCE

SWITCH	POSITION & UNIT NO.	TYPE	FOCUS NOTE	COLOR
1	FAR COVE 2·4·6·8·10	12" 1000W QUARTZ LEKO	FRONT BLUE WASH - DEEP	61
2	NEAR COVE 1·4·7·10·13	10" 1000W QUARTZ LEKO	FRONT BLUE WASH - D.S.	61
3	BOX BOOM LEFT 1·4·7 BOX BOOM RIGHT 1·4·7	6"X16" 750W LEKO	XLIGHT FRONT	61
4	FAR COVE 1·3·5·7·9	12" 1000W QUARTZ LEKO	FRONT WARM WASH - DEEP	53
5	BOX BOOM LEFT 2·5·8 BOX BOOM RIGHT 2·5·8	6"X16" 750W LEKO	XLIGHT FRONT	825
6	NEAR COVE 2·5·8·11·14	10" 1000W QUARTZ LEKO	FRONT LAV. WASH - D.S.	36
7	NEAR COVE 3·6·9·12·15	10" 1000W QUARTZ LEKO	FRONT CLEAR WASH - D.S.	CL
8	BOX BOOM LEFT 3·6·9 BOX BOOM RIGHT 3·6·9	6"X16" 750W LEKO	XLIGHT FRONT	CL
9	*1 LADDER LEFT 1·2 *1 LADDER RIGHT 1·2	6"X16" 1000W LEKO	HI DIAGONAL BACKLITE I	61
10	*2 LADDER LEFT 1·2 *2 LADDER RIGHT 1·2	6"X16" 1000W LEKO	HI DIAGONAL BACKLITE II	61
11	*3 LADDER LEFT 1·2 *3 LADDER RIGHT 1·2	6"X16" 1000W LEKO	HI DIAGONAL BACKLITE III	61
12	*4 LADDER LEFT 1·2 *4 LADDER RIGHT 1·2	6"X16" 1000W LEKO	HI DIAGONAL BACKLITE IV	61

HOOKUP 14 PLATE 6600W AUTOTRANSFORMER

SWITCH	POSITION & UNIT NO.	TYPE	FOCUS NOTE	COLOR
13	1ST PIPE 4·11·17·24	8" 1500W FRESNEL	COOL WASH MID STAGE	61
14	2ND PIPE 4·12·21	8" 1500W FRESNEL	COOL WASH UP STAGE	61
15	1ST PIPE 1·8·20·27	8" 1500W FRESNEL	XLIGHT D.S. IN I	61
16	2ND PIPE 1·8·17·24	8" 1500W FRESNEL	XLIGHT IN II	61
17	3RD PIPE 1·23 4·20	8" 1500W FRES. 6" 1000W LEKO	XLIGHT IN III	61
18 A	4TH PIPE 1·3·21·23	6"X12" 1000W LEKO	XLIGHT IN IV	61
19 A	1ST PIPE 7·14·21 2ND PIPE 7·13·18	6"X12" 1000W LEKO	DOWNLIGHTS D.S.	61
20 A	3RD PIPE 7·12·17 4TH PIPE 7·13·18	6"X12" 1000W LEKO	DOWNLIGHTS U.S.	61
21 A	*1·2·3 TORMS LEFT 1 *1·2·3 TORMS RIGHT 1	6"X12" 750W LEKO	LEFT & RIGHT BLUE ENTRANCE	61
22	*1·2·3 TORMS LEFT 3	8" 1500W FRESNEL	LEFT XLIGHT	61
23	*1·2·3 TORMS RIGHT 3	8" 1500W FRESNEL	RIGHT XLIGHT	61
24	*4 TORM LEFT 1·3 *4 TORM RIGHT 1·3	6"X12" 750W LEKO	L & R XLIGHT & ENTRANCES	61
25	1ST PIPE 6·13·15·22	8" 1500W FRESNEL	MID STAGE WASH	36
26	2ND PIPE 6·11·19	8" 1500W FRESNEL	UP STAGE WASH	36

HOOKUP 14 PLATE 6600W AUTOTRANSFORMER

SWITCH	POSITION & UNIT NO.	TYPE	FOCUS NOTE	COLOR
27	*1·2·3 TORMS L & R 9 *4 TORMS L & R 6	6"X12" 750W LEKO	SHINBUSTERS	43 OR 17
28	*1 LADDER LEFT 3·4 *1 LADDER RIGHT 3·4	6"X16" 1000W LEKO	L & R DIAGONAL BACKLITE IN I	53
29	*2 LADDER LEFT 3·4 *2 LADDER RIGHT 3·4	6"X16" 1000W LEKO	L & R DIAGONAL BACKLITE IN II	53
30	*3 LADDER LEFT 3·4 *3 LADDER RIGHT 3·4	6"X16" 1000W LEKO	L & R DIAGONAL BACKLITE IN III	53
31	*4 LADDER LEFT 3·4 *4 LADDER RIGHT 3·4	6"X16" 1000W LEKO	L & R DIAGONAL BACKLITE IN IV	53
32 A	1ST PIPE 3·25 2ND PIPE 3·22	8" 1500W FRESNELS	LEFT & RIGHT ENDS D.S.	52
33 A	3RD PIPE 3·21 6·18	8" 1500W FRES. 6"X12" 1000W LEKO	LEFT & RIGHT ENDS IN III	52
34 A	4TH PIPE 2·4·20·22	6"X12" 1000W LEKO	LEFT & RIGHT ENDS IN IV	52
35 A	4TH PIPE 5·10·16·17	6"X12" 1000W LEKO	SWAN LAKE ACT III U.S.	53
36	1ST PIPE 5·12·16·23	8" 1500W FRESNEL	MID STAGE WARM WASH	53
37	2ND PIPE 5·14·20	8" 1500W FRESNEL	UP STAGE WARM WASH	53
38	1ST PIPE 10·18 2ND PIPE 10·15	8" 1500W FRESNEL	D.S. CLEAR & XLIGHT	CL
39	3RD PIPE 9·13·15 4TH PIPE 11·14·15	6"X12" 1000W LEKO	CLEAR BACKLIGHT	CL
40	*1·2·3 TORMS L & R 6 *4 TORMS L & R 4	6"X12" 750W LEKO	CLEAR XLIGHT	CL

HOOKUP 14 PLATE 1500/3000W RESISTANCE

SWITCH	POSITION & UNIT NO.	TYPE	FOCUS NOTE	COLOR
41 A	*1·2·3 TORMS LEFT 7 *4 TORM LEFT 5	6"X12" 750W LEKO	XLIGHT	825
42 A	*1·2·3 TORMS RIGHT 7 *4 TORM RIGHT 5	6"X12" 750W LEKO	XLIGHT	825
43 A	*1·2·3 TORMS LEFT 8	6"X12" 750W LEKO	XLIGHT	36
44 A	*1·2·3 TORMS RIGHT 8	6"X12" 750W LEKO	XLIGHT	36
45 A	3RD PIPE 10·14	6"X12" 1000W LEKO	UP CENTER	CL
46 A	4TH PIPE 9	6"X12" 1000W LEKO	SLEEPING BEAUTY COLUMN ACCENT	52
46 B	4TH PIPE 8	6"X12" 1000W LEKO	SWAN ACT III COLUMN ACCENT	53
47	1ST PIPE 9·19	6"X12" 1000W LEKO	X & IN I	17
48	2ND PIPE 9·16	6"X12" 1000W LEKO	X & IN II	17
49	2 - FLOOR STAND SCOOPS	14" 1500W SCOOPS	U.S. DROP ACCENT	CL
50	2 - FLOOR STAND SCOOPS	16" 1500W SCOOPS	U.S. DROP ACCENT	G64
51	2 - FLOOR STAND SCOOPS	16" 1500W SCOOPS	U.S. DROP ACCENT	61
52	FOOTLIGHTS	HOUSE EQUIP.	MEDIUM BLUE	32
53	FOOTLIGHTS	HOUSE EQUIP.	LIGHT BLUE	61
54	FOOTLIGHTS	HOUSE EQUIP	PINK/AMBER	47

HOOKUP 14 PLATE 6600W AUTOTRANSFORMER

SWITCH	POSITION & UNIT NO.	TYPE	FOCUS NOTE	COLOR
55	*1·2·3·4 TORMS LEFT 2 *1·2·3·4 TORMS RIGHT 2	6"X12" 750W LEKO	LEFT & RIGHT ENTRANCES	09
56	*1·2·3 TORMS LEFT 5	8" 1500W FRESNEL	XLIGHT	09
57	*1·2·3 TORMS RIGHT 5	8" 1500W FRESNEL	XLIGHT	09
58	1ST PIPE 2·26 2ND PIPE 2·23	8" 1500W FRESNEL	COOL XLIGHT IN I & II	17
59	3RD PIPE 2·22 5·19	8" 1500W FRES. 6"X12" 1000W LEKO	COOL XLIGHT IN III & IV	17
60	*1·2·3 TORMS LEFT 4	8" 1500W FRESNEL	LEFT XLIGHT	43
61	*1·2·3 TORMS RIGHT 4	8" 1500W FRESNEL	RIGHT XLIGHT	43
62-63	OPEN DIMMERS			
64	3RD PIPE 8·11·16 4TH PIPE 6·12·19	6"X12" 1000W LEKOS	GOLD BACKLIGHT	G30
65	5TH BORDERLIGHT (3 SECTIONS LO/C, & R O/C)	500W I.F. QUARTZ	FACE OF DROP RED	G08
66	5TH BORDERLIGHT (2 SECTIONS · R END & L END)	500W I.F. QUARTZ	FACE OF DROP RED ENDS	G08
67	5TH BORDERLIGHT (3 SECTIONS · LO/C, & & R O/C)	500W I.F. QUARTZ	FACE OF DROP BLUE	G64
68	5TH BORDERLIGHT (2 SECTIONS · R END & L END)	500W I.F. QUARTZ	FACE OF DROP BLUE ENDS	G64

HOOKUP 14 PLATE 8000W AUTOTRANSFORMER

SWITCH	POSITION & UNIT NO.	TYPE	FOCUS NOTE	COLOR
69	6TH BORDERLIGHT (6 SECTIONS)	300W R40 FLOOD	FACE OF DROPS BLUE	G64
70	7TH BORDERLIGHT (6 SECTIONS)	300W R40 FLOOD	BACKLITE DROPS - BLUE	G64/99
71	GROUND ROW - D.S. STRIPS (6 SECTIONS)	300W R40 FLOOD	BACKLITE DROPS - BLUE	G64/99
72	GROUND ROW - U.S. STRIPS (6 SECTIONS)	300W R40 FLOOD	BACKLITE DROPS - BLUE	G64
73	6TH BORDERLIGHT (6 SECTIONS)	300W R40 FLOOD	FACE OF DROPS RED	G08
74	7TH BORDERLIGHT (6 SECTIONS)	300W R40 FLOOD	BACKLITE DROPS - RED	G08/99
75	GROUND ROW - D.S. STRIPS (6 SECTIONS)	300W R40 FLOOD	BACKLITE DROPS - RED	G08/99
76	GROUND ROW - U.S. STRIPS (6 SECTIONS)	300W R40 FLOOD	BACKLITE DROPS - RED	G08
77	6TH BORDERLIGHT (6 SECTIONS)	300W R40 FLOOD	FACE OF DROPS WHITE	CLEAR
78	7TH BORDERLIGHT (6 SECTIONS)	300W R40 FLOOD	BACKLITE DROPS - WHITE	G99
79	GROUND ROW - D.S. STRIPS (6 SECTIONS)	300W R40 FLOOD	BACKLITE DROPS - WHITE	G99
80	GROUND ROW - U.S. STRIPS (6 SECTIONS)	300W R40 FLOOD	BACKLITE DROPS - WHITE	CLEAR
81	5TH BORDERLIGHT (3 SECTIONS · L O/C, & & R O/C)	500W I.F. QUARTZ	FACE OF DROPS WHITE	CLEAR
82	5TH BORDERLIGHT (2 SECTIONS · R END & L END)	500W I.F. QUARTZ	FACE OF DROPS WHITE ENDS	CLEAR

Figure 7.20 Switchboard hookup for *The Turning Point*.

Figure 7.21 On-camera lighting for *The Wiz:* rubbish dump exterior set at Astoria Studios, New York City. (*From The American Cinematographer, November 1978.*)

Figure 7.23 Scene from *Hurricane,* using HMI bounce lights against large white reflectors for key light. (*From The American Cinematographer, March 1979.*)

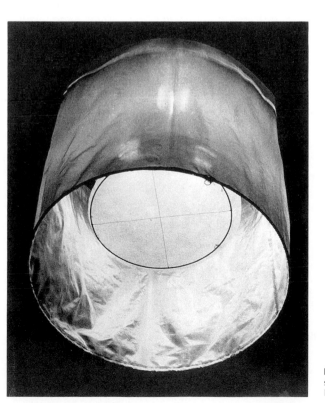

Figure 7.22 A silk-skirted light used in *The Wiz* to illuminate vast stage areas with shadowless light. Ossie Morris, ASC, Director of Photography. (*From The American Cinematographer, November 1978.*)

years and then hit a bad streak and drop to a survival level again. I assume the other areas of lighting work you mention are more stable. But film isn't and I doubt that it ever will be. TV's another matter. At least as far as tape shows go. They seem to have some measure of regularity. A lot of TV is on film and I've worked on a lot of it but the conditions seem to be very different from working on tape shows. At any rate, what I'm trying to say is, your book should delve deeper than job classifications and pay rates if it is to give some true insight into what makes the technical end of the film business work in Hollywood. The work is often good and a lot of money made; but . . . the other side should be mentioned.[167]

One final item deserves further mention here: the nature of and relative positions of The American Society of Cinematographers (ASC) and gaffer members of the American Society of Lighting Directors (ASLD), who frequently represent directors of photography. Both organizations deserve some clarification at this point.

The ASC was founded in 1919 for "social, fraternal, and educational" purposes. It is a club, not a union or a professional organization in the usual sense. Membership is around 200 including retired and inactive members. The ASC owns one of the few remaining historical mansions in Hollywood, which it uses as a clubhouse and as headquarters. Membership is extended—after careful selection pending attainment of stated qualifications—to the top cinematographers or directors of photography in the business. The club actively promotes dissemination of knowledge about cinematography through its monthly publication, *The American Cinematographer,* published continuously since November 1, 1920. The ASC is constantly active in elevating standards and in extending recognition to those who attain the highest level of work. A member may use the initials "ASC" after his name on a film. Five years of screen credits as "Director of Photography" is a minimum prerequisite to being considered for membership. Members in the "Associate" category are outstanding individuals in allied portions of the industry.

Many working directors of photography are not members of the ASC. Naturally an organization of this type with these stated aims guards its position in the industry very carefully. Unless gaffers go through the ranks to become cameramen, there is no way they will become members of the ASC.

Lighting director is a term used in the TV industry which is not applicable to cinematography. In England, a first cameraman or director of photography is called a "lighting cameraman." Gaffers who are using the title "lighting director" are men who are working with cinematographers who have abdicated their responsibilities.[168]

Show Photography

In the process of preparing this manuscript, Research Assistant William Roggenkamp and I handled well over 5,000 submitted photographs and graphics. Certain observations about photographs of lighting design (what is good, what gets instantly rejected) can be of potential value to designers who wish to obtain a photographic record of their own future work.[169]

1. If it is possible, *performers* should be evident in theatre/TV/movie photographs. A record of lighting on an empty setting is of little value. Shows are about people and are performed by people, and they should be present in photographs that represent a lighting designer's work. We rejected many, many submitted photographs because they did not include performers.

2. Shots should be *wide*. Close-ups (which is all one finds in the standard press department photography) are fine for selling a show but are of no use in showing the lighting. We rejected many shots because they could, for all intents and purposes, have been studio close-ups.

3. Show (or building or garden) photography should try to capture *contrast*. A brightly, evenly illuminated stage may contain pretty scenery and costumes and performers, but it shows nothing of value about the lighting. Show photographs should ideally display light and shadow contrast, color contrast, and "visual aliveness." Flatly illuminated performers make for dull visual presentation. Photographs with actors in follow spots should be avoided.

4. Show photographs should not include dark and underlighted faces of secondary performers onstage. While the human eye in the audience focuses these out, the camera does not. Such a photograph may be a very accurate record of the actual lighting, but there is little usable in a

[167] *Letter in my possession.*

[168] *"Six Decades of Loyalty, Progress, Artistry,"* American Cinematographer, *vol. 60, no. 6 (June 1979), pp. 576–77, and "The A.S.C. Clubhouse and Its Colorful History," pp. 580–81. A documented history of ASC on its sixtieth anniversary.*

R. G. Linderman, C. W. Handley, and A. Rogers, "Illumination in Motion Picture Production," Journal of the SMPTE, *vol. 42, no. 6 (June 1943), pp. 69–103. Early summary of film lighting.*

Charles G. Clarke, A.S.C., "History of the American Society of Cinematographers," Hollywood, CA: American Society of Cinematographers, Inc., *no date, 14 pages. Useful booklet outlining ASC's history.*

[169] *Paddy Cutts and Rosemary Curr,* Creative Techniques in Stage Theatrical Photography. *London; Batsford, Ltd.; 1983 (in USA: Drama Book Specialists, New York City). 168 pp., illus., color. The only book on show photography with a wealth of excellent photos and chapters such as "Gaining Access," "Equipment," "Films," "The Role of the Photographer," "Special Effects and Filters," "Filing," and "Storage." However, it is based upon British practice and equipment.*

See footnote 144, The Photographer's Guide To Using Light.

Linda Blase, "How to Photograph Your Own Show," Lighting Dimensions, *vol. 8, no. 2 (Mar./Apr. 1984), pp. 14–17, 19–21. Illus., color. Good brief article written and illustrated by a professional photographer/lighting designer. More detailed technically (concerning film, camera, filters, and lenses) than this* Handbook *can be.*

William Smith, "Photography for the Theatre, Some How-to's for the Photo Call," Theatre Crafts, *vol. 9, no. 6 (Nov./Dec. 1975), pp. 21–25. Good "dos and don'ts" with basic technical details. Deals more with closeup press photos than a lighting design record in a full stage photo. Illus.*

Tom Knowles and David Ulrich, "What's in a Picture," Light *magazine, vol. 30, no. 4 (1961), pp. 15–18. Illus.*

Jon Vickers, "Theatre Photography," TABS, vol. 18, no. 3 (Dec. 1960), pp. 23–28. Illus.

Robert S. Winkler, "What is the 'Right' Light?" Travel & Leisure, May 1984, pp. 18, 20–21. Illus., color.

David Derkacy, "Choosing the Right Lighting Technique," The New York Times, Jan. 22, 1984, section 2, p. 24. Illus.

Carl Purcell, "Some Filmy Advice," Signature, Nov. 1983, pp. 8, 150–151. Illus., color. On selecting film.

Jon R. Vernmilye, "Stage Photography," USITT Newsletter, vol. 34, no. 3 (Summer 1984), p. 10. Useful article by the technical coordinator at SUNY at Oswego, N.Y.

Stuart Nordheimer, Beginner's Photography, Simplified: A Modern Photo Guide. Garden City, N.Y.: Amphoto; rev. ed., Sept. 1978. Useful beginner's manual. Illus., 98 pages.

Leonard C. Watson, "Techniques of Set Photography," Theatre Design & Technology, no. 36 (Feb. 1974), pp. 27–29. Good basics. Illus.

Natalie Crohn Schmitt, "Recording the Theatre in Photographs," Educational Theatre Journal, vol. 28, no. 3 (Oct. 1976), pp. 376–88. Excellent source. Covers analysis of problem, history and objectives.

"The Image of Our Theatre," Theatre Crafts, vol. 4, no. 3 (May/June 1970), pp. 26–34, 41–42.

Terry R. Hayes, "Help for the Photo Call,: Theatre Crafts, vol. 19, no. 3 (Mar. 1985), p. 9. Useful technical notes concerning film to use for show call photography.

For a definitive article about photographing architectural lighting design, see "Ezra Stroller on Architectural Lighting," Light News, #4, Fall 1984, pp. 1, 3. Illus. Published by Lowell Light Manufacturing Co., Inc., 475 Tenth Ave., N.Y., N.Y. 10018-1197.

Michael Urbanek, "Lights, Camera Magic Make Architectural Photography," Architectural Lighting, vol. 1, no. 3 (Mar. 1987), pp. 30–36. Illus. color. Excellent graphics and text.

Ian Herbert, "Photographing Live Light," ALD # Magazine, no. 8 (Dec. 1988), pp. 16–17. Report of a British ALD meeting with theatre photographers Nobby Clark and Dave Atkinson. Useful.

Martin Gardlin, "Picture Looks, The Quest for Photographs That Reveal, Not Obscure, Lighting Design," Lighting Dimensions, vol. 12, no. 2 (March 1988), pp. 108, 110, 112. Illus., color. A most useful article about photography for architectural lighting.

Norman McGrath, Photographing Buildings Inside and Out. N.Y.; Whitney Library of Design; 1987. Approximately $32.50. The best source of information concerning photographing architectural lighting design.

Gerry Zekowski, "Good Photos Don't Fall From the Sky," Lighting Design + Application, vol. 18, no. 10 (Oct. 1988), pp. 8–10. Excellent article by an expert concerning architectural lighting design.

David Keene, "Nightclubs: Worth a Thousand Words: How to Photograph Your Club Lighting Design," Lighting Dimensions, vol. 13, no. 3 (April 1989), pp. 38, 40–42. Illus., color.

Margaret O. Kirk, "Folio: Picture This," US Air, vol. 11, no. 6 (June 1989), pp. 12–17. Illus., color. Well-written brief history of photography.

photograph showing two principals brilliantly lighted in a followspot surrounded by 50 other opera or musical chorus performers in half-light — unless that half-light is designed (sculpt, backlighted, or rim-lighted).

5. The lighting designer or a designated photographer should try for a sequence of shots throughout the show with the camera in a stationary position, covering full-stage width. One shot for each major light cue provides a viable record of the lighting design changes. Almost no one has done this. The examples in this *Handbook* of my own *Poulenc's Organ Concerto* for the Cincinnati Ballet (see Chap. 5) and the opera *One Night in Venice* (see Chap. 5) and the Virginia Shakespeare season (see Chap. 6) show what I mean. While this system of photographic recording is of little use to others connected with a production, it is the *only* type of photography which allows another designer or a student to "bring alive" a light plot and to understand how the designer used design tools. If more of these were available, teaching of lighting design would be easier. For this *Handbook*, we all too frequently found that only one close-up, sometimes of poor quality from a lighting design viewpoint, was all that was available to "bring alive" the light plots included in this text. The worst area for having any suitable graphics available continues to be the Broadway professional theatre.

Chapter 8

Nightclubs, Discos, and Concert Lighting

[169a] *Color-music has been a continuing attempt to combine human responses to color and to sound. Its genesis can be traced back to the work of Aristotle (384–323 B.C.), Leonardo da Vinci (1425–1519), Sir Isaac Newton (1642–1727), and Father Bertrand Castel (died 1763) in his book* Clavessin Oculaire. *Others in this field include Prof. A. Wallace Rimington (who published* Colour-Music, The Art of Mobile Colour *in 1912),* Adrian Bernard Klein *(who wrote* Colour-Music, The Art of Light *in 1926), and more recently the lifetime of work on color-music by Thomas Wilfred (1889–1968).*

[170] *"International Light Fairs: The Early Light Shows: Paris and London,"* International Lighting Review, *37th yr., 1st quarter 1986, pp. 30–33. Illus., color.*

For a fascinating account of a TV-music-light show, see "Global Village, a Multi-Media Rock Be-In," Houston Chronicle, *February 1, 1970, pp. 8–9 of Sunday Magazine section.*

See also "Bill McManus, Lighting Designer," Lighting Dimensions, *vol. 2, no. 1 (Jan. 1978), pp. 28–29.*

"Designers Forum," Disco Tech, *vol. 3, no. 3 (July 1987), pp. 6–7, 11. An important article covering a designer's roundtable discussion at the 1987 Night Club and Bar Exposition in Atlanta, Georgia. It deals extensively with design principles and theory.*

During the late 1970s, discos and concert lighting became the "biggest thing around," not only for lighting designers but also for equipment manufacturers, equipment salesmen, and development engineers. There is a continuous history of this type of lighting leading up to today from the early work in color music.[169a] In the mid-1980s nightclubs and cabarets began to come back into popularity, and although much less is heard about them, discos continue to be popular in cities and towns, large and small, throughout the United States. Concert lighting looms as large today as it did in the sixties and seventies, and concert groups are now recording performances on videocassettes and videodiscs. Thus, a combination of music and lighting (in some form) has been around for a long time, and it seems likely that that combination will continue to provide employment for lighting designers, equipment manufacturers, and salesmen for many years into the future.

Nightclubs

Early nightclub lighting was simple. It consisted of a stage/platform performance area and standard stage lighting units hung wherever possible, with the intention of colorfully illuminating the performers. The bar and the rooms were illuminated, and in most clubs the houselights could be dimmed during a performance. Nightclub acts were an "extra" — entertainment thrown in to attract more drinkers. Two things changed this: Las Vegas and psychedelic lighting.

Psychedelic lighting became popular around 1967.[170] Light shows and multimedia were also everywhere, outgrowths of the early color-music work combined with the rapid spread of the drug scene (lighting helped recreate the drug "trip"). Also, the sixties generation was "hooked on" music and had ready access to records, portable radios, and live performers. People of this generation had grown up exposed to massive doses of television, and they were thus prepared for multiple images, split concentration, and rapid shifts of locale or focus. These elements produced two things: (1) early rock concerts with lights and lighting effects added (leading up to Woodstock) and (2) light show performance places (which originated in Europe and California).[171] I am most familiar with Cliff Carlin, Jr.'s Love Street Light Circus club in downtown Houston, Texas.[172] The large room at the club had pillows and cushions everywhere. Beer and wine were served, and "pot" was freely smoked. A live orchestra played on a platform stage at one end of the room, with a constant pattern of ever-changing light playing upon the orchestra in tempo with the music. The light show was free-form and was different each time, depending upon the response of the control operator. Heavy use was made of overhead projectors with trays of mineral oil and dye at the slide position. Colored dyes were floated in the mineral oil and the resulting image projected on the band. Strobes were also used, as were flashing circuits of gaudy lights. Dense smoke in the air added to the "opium den with a beat" effect. All of this was an outgrowth of Thomas Wilfred's early work (see footnote 169a).

By the late 1960s changes were taking place. The one-night-stand rock concerts became more formalized and turned into organized national and international tours. (Current concert lighting is the subject of the last part of this section.) Light show ambience crept into nightclubs and prepared the ground for today's discos.

Least affected by the new lighting techniques were the traditional nightclubs. (They still exist in large numbers in Las Vegas and are discussed in Chap. 5, under "Revues.") During the late 1950s I designed lighting for one such night-club, with scenery by Peter Larkin, located in New York City's then-famous Latin Quarter. The differences between that nightclub-restaurant and today's Las Vegas clubs are minute.

Leading United States nightclubs have included Caroline's and Caroline's at the Seaport, Catch a Rising Star in Manhattan, Improvisation and the Comedy Store in Los Angeles, Second City and Zanies in Chicago, The Punch Line in Atlanta, and The Laff Stop in Houston.[173]

Discos

In 1987, Freddie Lloyd wrote in Lighting + Sound International: "The United States has been a slumbering giant for the past five years. Ever since that fateful day when 'Billboard' announced to the unsuspecting world that 'discotheque is dead,' the club industry has been in apparent recession, allowing the Europeans to leap far ahead in terms of technology and design."[174]

In 1977, the beginning of the disco "craze," Americans spent $5 billion building and attending discos. The International Discotheque Association estimated that there were then 10,000 discos nationwide. Disco Gossip magazine estimated that figure to be close to 20,000. The 1977 movie

Bonnie Schwartz, "Java Jive and Java Bay Nightclubs in Tokyo," Cue International, no. 58 (March/April 1989), pp. 28, 30. Illus. Details the nightclub design in Tokyo of lighting designers Ken Billington, John McKernon, and Jason Kantrowitz.

Barbara J. Knox, "Rainbow Room, $20-Million Facelift Restores Landmark's Glitter and Glamour," Lighting Dimensions, vol. 12, no. 4 (May/June 1988), pp. 48–49, 64, 67–68. Illus., color. Relighting of the Rainbow Room in Rockefeller Center, New York City, by Jules Fisher and Paul Marantz.

Michael Sommers, "Centerline: Ken Billington," Theatre Crafts, vol. 22, no. 8 (Oct. 1988), p. 22. Illus., color. More about Billington's Tokyo nightclub design.

Bonnie Schwartz, Mood Indigo: Understated Nightclub Lighting That Puts Patrons Center Stage," Lighting Dimensions, vol. 11, no. 5 (September/October 1987), pp. 24, 26, 28, 30. Illus., color. An excellent article for the lighting designer about newly restrained taste (as opposed to flash, glitz, and glitter) in nightclub design.

Bonnie S. Schwartz, "Dallas's Stark Club Lives On," Lighting Dimensions, vol. 12, no. 7 (Nov. 1988), p. 24. Illus., color. Another article about restraint in the designed use of light in new nightclubs.

Bonnie Schwartz, "A Place with a Smile: Java Jive and Java Bay Nightclubs Add Caribbean Whimsy to Tokyo Nightlife," Lighting Dimensions, vol. 12, no. 7 (November 1988), pp. 50–51, 66–67. Illus., color. More about Ken Billington's lighting of Tokyo nightclubs.

Robert Battaile, "The Stock Exchange: Historic Landmark Turns High Stakes Nightclub," Lighting Dimensions, vol. 11, no. 6 (Nov. 1988), pp. 50–53, 72. Illus., color. Conversion of the Los Angeles Pacific Stock Exchange to a nightclub, which opened in August 1987.

Adam Pirani, "Zig Zag: Aberdeen Nightclub Sets Theatrical Dance Floor Lighting Against Minimalist Decor," Lighting Dimensions, vol. 11, no. 7 (January/February 1988), pp. 58–60, 76, 78–79. Illus., color; includes light plot. A Scottish nightclub designed by Tony Gottelier with much use of neon is described.

Ann Daly, "Buffalo Nightclub," Lighting Dimensions, vol. 13, no. 3 (April 1989), p. 31. Illus., color. Lighting of The Late Show nightclub in Buffalo.

Bonnie Schwartz, "Back to the Future: Stage LD Malamud Takes on the Mars Club," Lighting Dimensions, vol. 13, no. 3 (April 1989), pp. 72–75, 99–100. Illus., color. Futuristic lighting of a contemporary Manhattan nightclub.

Mike Williams, "Love At First Light: Candace Brightman Brings the Grateful Dead Into the Nineties," Lighting Dimensions, vol. 13, no. 3 (April 1989), pp. 82–87. Illus., color.

Ann Daly, "The Annastasia Club," Lighting Dimensions, vol. 13, no. 1 (January/February 1989), p. 21. Illus. Turner Duncan of Dallas, Texas, designs for the Washington, D.C., Annastasia Club.

Bonnie Schwartz, "Nitelights Lights Up Nashville," Lighting Dimensions, vol. 13, no. 4 (May/June 1989), p. 20. Illus., color.

Bonnie Schwartz, "Primitive Customs: Boston's Hub Club Features Architect-Designed Fixtures," Lighting Dimensions, vol. 13, no. 4 (May/June 1989), pp. 60–61, 72–74, 77. Illus., color.

Mark Loeffler, "Under Control: New Console Technology Pushes Club Lighting to the Edge," Lighting Dimensions, vol. 13, no. 4 (March 1989), pp. 46, 48–49. Illus., color. A useful description of new controls centers (switchboards) available for nightclub lighting design installations.

Bonnie S. Schwartz, "Tremors: Detroit Area Club Features Both Flash and Familiarity," Lighting Dimensions, vol. 13, no. 4 (March 1989), pp. 66–67, 78. Illus., color. Another design by Dallas-based Turner Duncan.

[171] Bob Beck, Light Show Manual. Los Angeles; Pericles Press (1540 Cassil Place, L.A., CA 90028); 1966. This is an excellent basic study of the early days of light shows in California.

[172] John Gaines, "The Sight and Sound Clubs are in an Upswing," Houston Post, October 26, 1969, p. 4.

[173] *For the continuing classical music version, see Audrey Clinton, "A Bach Spectacular," New York Newsday, May 1, 1974, p. 2A. Described and illustrated is a combined Bach organ recital by organist Virgil Fox and a light show by David Snyder called "The Heavy Organ-Revelation Light Show" at the Callerone I theatre in Hempstead, Long Island (as part of a 50-concert tour that included Carnegie Hall).*

Sharon Jackman, "Watching and Listening: Lighting for Orchestras," Lighting Dimensions, vol. 10, no. 2 (Mar./Apr. 1986), pp. 72–73, 75, 77–78. Illus., color. The only printed piece I am aware of about designing lighting for symphony orchestras.

Michael Gross, "Night Life: The Latest Clubs," The New York Times, August 22, 1986, p. 24 (Chicago ed.). Illus.

Lawrence Sutin, "Just For Laughs," Sky (Delta Air Lines magazine), vol. 17, no. 6 (June 1988), pp. 20–22, 24, 26, 28. Illus., color. Sketches current comedy nightclubs throughout the United States.

J. Rutherford, "Installation Survey: Market Research, Data Processing and Other Information Collation," Pro Light & Sound, vol. 1, no. 2 (Spring 1987), pp. 21–24, 26–28, 31. Illus., color. In my opinion, the most complete collected information in existence concerning the size of the nightclub industry, its designers, and its equipment manufacturers. Twenty-five key installation and manufacturing firms were contacted for the survey.

Stephen Holden, "A New Golden Age for Cabaret," The New York Times, Chicago ed., pp. 15–16, March 1, 1985. Illus. Good summary of present status.

John S. Wilson, "A Comeback for the Old-Fashioned Nightclubs," The New York Times, January 27, 1984 (Chicago ed.), pp. 13, 16. Illus. A listing of nightclub activity in New York City with photos.

Fred Ferretti, "Where to Find the Funniest New Comics in Town," The New York Times, March 11, 1983 (Chicago ed.), pp. 15, 22. Illus. More of the same.

"Sensational Technology," Restaurant Design, vol. 4, no. 2 (Spring 1982), pp. 85–103. Illus., color.

Jon Pareles, "Dance and Music Clubs Thrive in Era of Change," The New York Times, November 12, 1982 (Chicago ed.), section C, pp. 1, 14.

James L. Moody, "Lee Ragonese on Saloon Lighting," Lighting Dimensions, vol. 3, no. 12 (Dec. 1979), pp. 26–28, 31–33. Illus., color.

Deborah Adams, "Lighting for 'Woman as Fantasy,'" Lighting Design & Application, vol. 10, no. 5 (May 1980), pp. 18–23. Illus., color. Lighting in the Latin Quarter nightclub in New York City.

Phillip Mazzurco, "The Palace—A Dazzling Nightclub," Lighting Dimensions, vol. 7, no. 3 (June 1983), pp. 26–27, 29–31. Illus., color. Spectacular relighting of Luchow's, a famous disco.

"Cabaret Spaces," a series of articles in Theatre Crafts, vol. 19, no. 2 (Feb. 1985), pp. 28–34, 40–44, 45–47, 50–54, 56–57 by various authors (Robert Long, Susan Lieberman, Steve Pollock, Pat Wadsley, and Craig Bromberg). Illus. Good basic overview of nightclub and cabaret productions.

Consult The New York Times, Sunday amusement section for advertisements of the key New York City nightclubs, including Cafe Versailles, the Blue Note, Caroline's, Fat Tuesday's, and the Village Gate.

Stephen Holden, "A Valentine Show with a Heart of Satire," The New York Times, February 6, 1987, p. 13. Illus. A description of a 65-minute show at New York City's Waldorf Astoria hotel Ballroom.

John Offord wrote a series of well illustrated articles about British clubs for Lighting + Sound International magazine. Offord is editor and publisher of the journal.

See:

"The Harlequin and Millionaire," vol. 2, no. 1 (Jan. 1987), pp. 12–14. Illus., color.

"Queues at the Quadrant," vol. 2, no. 1 (Jan. 1987), pp. 20, 23–24. Illus., color.

"Sweetings: The One-Man Mecca," vol. 1, no. 8 (July 1986), pp. 31–33. Illus., color.

Lighting + Sound International regularly runs listings and descriptions of principal supply sources in Europe for nightclub and disco lighting equipment.

Graham Walne, "Projecting the Right Image," Lighting + Sound International, vol. 1, no. 11 (Nov. 1986), pp. 11–12, 14, 16. Illus., color. In this article Walne writes about projected effects in nightclubs and discos and includes a most usable listing and description of sources of such equipment.

John Offord, "Design and Designers, The Atmosphere Creators," Lighting + Sound International, vol. 1, no. 11 (Nov. 1986), pp. 17–20. Illus., color. John Offord interviews Tony Kingsley, who is a designer with Europe's largest club lighting distribution company, Avitec. Excellent and numerous color illustrations.

"SIB Rimini 86—'Not to Be Missed',," Lighting and Sound International, vol. 1, no. 6 (Apr. 1986), pp. 51–52. Illus. Description of the fourth SIB International Exhibition of Equipment and Technology for discotheques and dance halls as a part of the Rimini (Italy) Trade Fair from May 6–9, 1986. Other trade shows for nightclubs and discos are listed on p. 53 of this article. PLASA is a large British trade organization that has an annual trade show. More about PLASA and its officers and structure appears in this article on pp. 53–54.

"Nightclub & Bar Expo: Show Exhibit Will Be Held in Las Vegas," Lighting Dimensions, vol. 11, no. 1 (Jan./Feb. 1987), p. 26. Lists exhibitors for the first U.S. nightclub and disco trade show and conference.

Mark Kruger, "Charting the 4th dimension, Kruger Associates Develops a High Energy Lighting Scheme for New York's Latest Nightclub," Lighting Dimensions, vol. 11, no. 1 (Jan./Feb. 1987), pp. 34–37, 49–52. Illus., color.

"Lighting No Ordinary Area," Lighting Dimensions, vol. 11, no. 2 (Mar./Apr. 1987), p. 16. Description of a new nightclub in New York City with phosphorescent paintings, stained glass collages, cement sculptures, neon wall figures, and waterfalls, with lasers by Dick Sandhaus.

Alice M. Hale, "Show Report: The Nightclub and Bar Expo—The First Annual Convention Had Close to 200 Exhibits and a Galaxy of Lighting Products," Lighting Dimensions, vol. 11, no. 2 (Mar./Apr. 1987), pp. 92, 94, 96. Illus. Report on the Las Vegas conference held January 5–7, 1987 and sponsored by Night Club and Bar magazine.

Nightclubs, Discos, and Concert Lighting / 239

Saturday Night Fever, starring John Travolta, both moved him into star status and gave disco a huge boost. An estimated 37 million people attended disco in 1977.[175] Why the disco "craze"? Because disco fulfills six basic needs:

1. *Relaxation.* Discos help release the day's tensions and provide escape from boredom. John Nadon calls discos a "hypo sensory encounter, designed to disorient a patron, releasing him or her from conventional restraints. . . . [Disco provides] a particular type of relaxation . . . rarely achieved in other recreation forms."[176]

2. *Socializing.* Discos allow patrons to meet new people in an informal atmosphere, and the atmosphere encourages personal interaction.

3. *Active Participation.* Disco allow people to take part in the action, rather than to observe passively. Disco dancing fits a generation with a high level of body-awareness and a physical fitness obsession that has led to a nation of joggers.

4. *Status Competition.* People's desire to be "chic," that is, to be with the "in" group at the "in" place, has been a major factor in the success of such discos as Studio 54 in New York City. To be where celebrities are and to mix freely with them becomes a social objective.

5. *Emotional Release/Fantasy Images/Sex.* Discos evoke a tremendously high level of emotional response, combining reactions to auditory stimuli, visual stimuli, and physical movement. Discos intentionally evoke a fantasy world of conditions, environment, and activities. George Bernard Shaw might well have been writing about discos when he wrote of: "[they are] vertical expression[s] of a horizontal desire." Discos have sometimes humorously been dubbed "meat markets."

6. *Entertainment.* Discos provide a "show" for which patrons are willing to pay a high admission price. The "performance" is created by the disc jockey, the light operator, and the customers themselves.

I wrote the following description of what occurs at a disco in *Lighting Dimensions,* as a part of my review of New York City's Studio 54: "contrived, forced action and simulated joy imposed by programmed sound and light used to stimulate and arouse."[177] The lighting designer needs to have this

---

Martin Gardlin, "A New Kind of Tunnel Vision: LD Robert Singer Turns an Old, Dark Railroad Station into a Tunnel of Light," Lighting Dimensions, *vol. 11, no. 3 (May/June 1987), pp. 18, 20, 22–23. Includes drawings of the relighting of New York City's Tunnel nightclub by designer Robert Singer.*

Mike Williams, "Filling the Space with Lasers, Laservision's Ron Alpert Transforms a Washington, DC, Nightclub with Custom Special Effects," Lighting Dimensions, *vol. 10, no. 5 (Sept./Oct. 1986), pp. 34–35, 58, 60–61. Illus., color.*

During its very brief publication history, Pro Light & Sound *magazine was a valuable resource concerning U.S. nightclub developments. Unfortunately, when it was sold soon after it began it changed its coverage and orientation.*

Glenn Pushelberg, "Stilife, Toronto, Ontario: From Warehouse to Night-Club," International Lighting Review, *39th year, 3rd quarter, 1988, pp. 109–111. Illus., color.*

Stephen Holden, "Who Says Cabaret is Passé?," The New York Times, *Living Arts Section, August 15, 1988, pp. 15, 20. Illus.*

L S & V Magazine *(Light, Sound & Video for the Nightclub & Entertainment Industries). Initial issue was the November/December 1988, vol. 1, no. 1. Subscription is obtainable from: 270 North Canyon Drive, Beverly Hills, CA 90210. Tel: (213) 278-7163. Published bimonthly. Illus., color. Best available source in this lighting design area for the United States.*

"Glamour Returns to the Rainbow Room," International Lighting Review, *39th year, 3rd quarter, 1988. pp. 109–111. Illus., color. IALD Award to Paul Marantz, Charles Stone, and E. Teal Brogden for relighting a famous nightclub.*

"Night Club & Bar Expo," Disco Tech, *vol. 4, no. 2 (August 1988), pp. 4–5. Illus., color. Color photographs and description of the annual trade show on nightclub lighting at Bally's Grand Hotel, Las Vegas, in 1988.*

Disco Tech, *a quarterly magazine published by Meteor Light and Sound, Inc., 8000 Madison Pike, Madison, Alabama 35758. Tel: (205) 722-9626. Distributed free to lighting, sound, and video stores, mobile operators, lighting designers, consultants, discotheques, lounge and resturant owners, roller rinks, and related*

entertainment facilities. Quality paper, color photos. Most useful for those working in these areas in the United States.

"Club Reviews, The Red Onion, The Wilsjire Club," Disco Tech, *vol. 4, no. 2 (August 1988), pp. 16–17. Illus., color. Description of a southwestern Mexican restaurant-bar-disco.*

"Design: Grazing on Sushi and Tapas," Disco Tech, *vol. 4, no. 1 (March 1988), pp. 10–11. Illus., color. Another California nightclub by designer Gilbert Konqui. Konqui has designed well over 200 nightclubs.*

"Sports Rock, Atlanta, Georgia," Disco Tech, *vol. 4, no. 1 (March 1988), pp. 12–13. Description of a bar-restaurant-nightclub-disco in Atlanta. Includes a light plot. Also: "Chameleon, Lynn, Massachusetts," pp. 14–15. Illus., color. A hotel nightclub. And: "Stripes, Edwards Air Force Base, California," p. 16. Illus., color.*

Night Club & Bar magazine, *305 West Jackson Avenue, Oxford, Mississippi 38655. Tel: (601) 236-5510. Another useful magazine about the United States nightclub and bar industry.*

"Élan, A Southern Success," Disco Tech, *vol. 3, no. 3 (July 1987), pp. 12–13. Illus., color. An award-winning Atlanta nightclub.*

[174] *February 1987 issue (vol. 2, no. 2), p. 39.*

[175] *Bruce Pollock, "Disco Sweeps the Nation,"* Family Weekly, *May 20, 1979, Lafayette Journal and Courier, pp. 4–5.*

Ron Butler, "America Puts on Its Dancing Shoes," TWA Ambassador *magazine, Aug. 1978, p. 16.*

[176] *John Nadon, "Designing the Discotheque,"* Lighting Design & Application, *vol. 9, no. 5 (May 1979), pp. 12–13, 63. Subtitle: "The peculiar requirements for the lighting design of a discotheque fall somewhere between the lighting demands of a bar/restaurant and a legitimate theatre house." This article offers a step-by-step approach to disco design.*

[177] *Lee Watson, "Six Discos Reviewed,"* Lighting Dimensions, *vol. 3, no. 4 (April 1979), pp. 17–19.*

[178] *John Nadon, p. 12, op. cit. (see footnote 176).*

[179] *Robert Lobi, "Disco, Orchestration of Light," Lighting Dimensions, vol. 2, no. 9 (Nov. 1978), pp. 51–53. Very useful information about disco controller design and its operation by a disco lighting designer. Also an interview with this author (Lee Watson).*

kind of analysis of and insight into the "whys" of discos before he begins to design for this specialized lighting area.

Design Considerations

John Nadon wrote: "More and more architects, interior decorators, and lighting designers are being drawn into the disco design field. The largest problem in planning a disco is just that — planning: the greatest error a designer can make . . . is to lack proper documentation . . . research and plan out a project — to know precisely what is trying to be done."[178] The designer needs to keep in mind that discos trade upon the elements of surprise or shock, constant change, and sparkle and rhythm (movement and variety stemming from the music). The lights and sound are not the show; the dancers are. Lighting is a part of the surrounding environment. The following design criteria can be set forth:

1. *Objective.* It is important to determine the objective of a particular disco, which involves a careful analysis by both the lighting designer and the client to define a disco's potential clientele. Different establishments draw widely different crowds. There are discos intended primarily for the teenage or collegiate set, while others intentionally have an "uptown" patronage in mind. Some cater to the over-30 set. Clientele greatly affects design, so the designer must get answers to some questions before beginning: (Who will the customers be? What style or class of dress? What age groups? What status or position in society? From a metropolitan area or a small town? "Rough" or "genteel"?)

2. *Budget.* How much does a particular client anticipate investing in a disco? If the figure is low, the designer is not only restricted in the number and types of units to be used but also may be limited to stock disco items readily available and low in price. Not surprisingly, most managements are interested in low initial cost, no upkeep or maintenance, and maximum sensational effects.

3. *Architect/interior designer's aims.* Obviously the disco lighting design must stem from the lighting designer's close cooperation with other involved designers, engineers, technicians, and contractors. Light must be used imaginatively in the available space. Design consideration

must be given to the customer flow through the entry space, the bar, the restaurant area, game rooms, lounge areas, and any observation areas, as well as through the space of the dance floor itself. Design style of the disco is another important factor. Is the disco to convey elegance? "Down to earth" relaxation? Fantasy and Never-Never Land? The lighting instruments must complement these determinable style decisions.

4. *Time available.* Disco investments are based upon an expected design-installation time with fixed opening dates in mind. This time factor may prohibit the designer from utilizing custom items or ordering from manufacturers and supply houses that cannot guarantee exact delivery dates.

Robert Lobi, president of Design Circuits, Inc., suggests only two design considerations: "orchestration of special effects and support lighting." Lobi, who has been designing discos since 1970, draws a clear distinction between those parts of the lighting instrument intended for spectacular, breathtaking effect and the surround devices intended to interpret and expand the music. This interpretation and expansion he calls "orchestration of light." Lobi says that to achieve this effect the designer should "create not a light show, but a lighting instrument. Follow rhythms — not volume."[179]

There are two basic schools of disco design: (1) use of large, lavish, complicated effects which combine to produce a satisfying spectacle (the same basic appeal is at the heart of ice shows, circuses, amusement parks, and expositions — i.e., a one-time thrill, not intended to be repeated often) and (2) design of the disco for night-in-night-out recurring appeal to a steady clientele. The latter school places a heavier emphasis upon lighting design accompanying and expanding the disc jockey's music rather than the light show "taking over." Clearly I have taken the liberty of reducing each theory to extreme examples for clarification. The ideal lighting for discos successfully combines both aims. The beginning disco designer needs to be aware of the possible differences in ultimate design objective and be certain that client–designer understanding is mutual on this point. Timothy Tunks expressed disco lighting objectives well: "The primary goals of the light show are to provide a visual interpretation of the recorded music and to excite the energies and imagination of the Disco customers."[180]

Communication Forms

The standard communications method is with drawings and specifications for the electrical contractor, as in architectural lighting design. Standard theatre light plots have no application here.

Techniques

Lighting design devices are rather standard. It is the individualistic uses and combinations of them which produce artistry. The devices can be grouped as follows:

Units:
Lasers
Mirror balls
Strobes[181]
Ultraviolet (blacklight) lights
Dry-ice fog
Flasher lights (police or ambulance "whirlers")
Standard stage Fresnels and ellipsoidals

Projections:
Carousel slide projectors
Multiple gobos (steady and changing in ellipsoidals)

Movement- and Control-Activated Devices:
Flashing lights (colored and clear)
Chaser circuits
Revolving PAR heads ("whirlers")
Lighting unit beams redirected from rotating mirrors
Rotating color wheels
Color change from separate circuits
Follow spotlights

Architectural Features:
Extensive use of mirrors, mylar, and plexiglass
Flown (counterweighted) drops, objects
Multilevel dance floors that are expandable/contractable
Lights *within* dance floor area (bee lights, neon, fluorescent, panels)
Highly confined dance floor area *(essential)*
Elaborate treatment of chandeliers and structural columns (neon encircles, for example)
Intricate treatment of bar illumination (stained glass panels, downlights, etc).

Light Sources:
Neon tubing
Bee lights ("grain of wheat" lights — flashing, twinkling, chasing)
Xenon or HMI (light "bursts")
LED (light-emitting diode) lights

Effects:
Waterfalls and fountains in entrance lobby
Voice-activated color synthesizers
Color music display panels

For more complete and technical descriptions of how these elements are combined, see the many available specialized publications listed in the footnotes.[182]

The most important device is the controller (switchboard) activated by the light operator. Its counterpart in music is the organ keyboard. These are the heart of both the system and its effective use. Controllers have become increasingly complex and are constantly being improved, but they are somewhat removed from the subject of this volume, lighting *design*[183].

Procedures and Practices

Light operators have no easy task. They must be capable of infinitely flexible use of the controller. They must be able to respond both to the music and to the mood of the patrons. Usually they work four to six hours per night, five to six nights per week, under pressure and in a confined space. These specialists are being paid $200 to $300 per night in the larger metropolitan areas.[184] Their job is not an easy one.

The design of lighting discos has reached out to a wide group of lighting designers. There are many established industry specialists: Robert Lobi, of Design Circuits, Inc., has been designing discos since 1970 (see Fig. 8.1); Brian Edwards of Wavelength, Inc., has been designing discos since 1972 (his first was in Oxnard, California); Graham Smith, of Graham Smith Associates, Ltd., New York City, is another early pioneer (see Figs. 8.2 and 8.3). Well-known "name" designers in the theatre world have also designed discos: Jules Fisher, Paul Marantz, Imero Fiorentino (see Color Fig. 70), and Abe Feder, to name but four. A panel of six disco designers at Lighting World IV in Los Angeles in May 1986 listed as outstanding discos the following: the Astral in Dallas, Texas; the Palladium in New York City; and the Ocean Club in Houston, Texas.

In the short space of ten or so years discos have become an important industry. Lighting designers involved with discos continuously ask themselves and each other how long the disco fad will last and what will replace it. Large conventions sponsored by "Billboard" (International Disco Forums) seek answers, gathering together 2,000 to 3,000

[180] "A New Disco Light Controller," Lighting Dimensions, *vol. 2, no. 7 (Sept. 1978), pp. 55, 57, 59–60. Usable analysis of controller design for discos by Wavelengths system designer Timothy Tunks and electronics designer William Ward.*

[181] *Frank Dawe, "Stroboscopes for Illusion Lighting," TABS, vol. 33, no. 1 (Spring 1975), pp. 20–21. Illus. Excellent basics of strobe equipment and use.*

[182] *Brian Edwards, "Dillion's Making the Disco Beat Better," Lighting Dimensions, vol. 3, no. 2 (Feb. 1979), pp. 28–30. Usable history of Edwards's career in disco design from 1972 on. Edwards is president of Wavelength, Inc.*

John Nadon, "Disco Lighting Design: More is More, A Guide to Instruments for the Industry," Theatre Crafts, vol. 14, no. 1 (Jan./Feb. 1980), pp. 31–33, 74–77. Includes a list of sources. Illus.

John Nadon, "Designing the Discotheque," Lighting Design & Application, vol. 9, no. 5 (May 1979), pp. 12–13, 63. Nadon lays out, step-by-step, the disco design process.

"Dixie Disco," Lighting Design & Application, vol. 9, no. 11 (Nov. 1979), pp. 13–15. Illus., color. Robert Lobi design.

Ed Constanty, "A Pleasure Dome for Dance," Lighting Dimensions, vol. 8, no. 4 (July/Aug. 1984), pp. 37–42. Illus., color. A description of one of New York City's largest and newest discos, The Saint, which has a planetarium dome.

"The Look of Limelight," Lighting Dimensions, vol. 9, no. 4 (July/Aug. 1985), pp. 48–54. Illus., color. A detailed and well-illustrated presentation of one of New York City's newest discos.

Craig Bromberg, "An Evening in Four Acts: The Palladium Lights Up the Night," Theatre Crafts, vol. 19, no. 8 (Oct. 1985), pp. 29, 54–57. Illus., color. Description of one of New York City's newer and larger discos.

Paul Goldberger, "The Palladium: An Architecturally Dramatic New Manhattan Discotheque," The New York Times, Chicago ed., p. 12, May 12, 1985.

The Design Trust catalog (750 ½ Pier Ave.,
Santa Monica, CA 90405. Telephone: (213)
396-1400). Color brochure of the disco designs
of Timothy Tunks and Kelley W. Forde, with an
article by David N. Flaten: "The Design Trust."

"The Power of the Palladium," Lighting
Dimensions, vol. 9, no. 7 (Nov./Dec. 1985), pp.
62–65, 67–72, 74. Illus., color. Includes light
plot.

Jill Marks, "Boise's Gastation, Houston's Ritz:
Two Designs by Graham Smith," Lighting
Dimensions, vol. 3, no. 7 (July 1979), pp. 26–
29. Illus., color. Includes light plot.

Robert Lobi, "Emerald City," Lighting Dimensions, vol. 3, no. 7 (July 1979), pp. 30–31.
Illus., color.

John Nadon, "Special Effects in Disco,"
Lighting Dimensions, vol. 3, no. 7 (July 1979),
pp. 32–33, 35–37. Illus., color.

Mark Kruger, "Heaven . . . A Rather Unique
Space," Lighting Dimensions, vol. 4, no. 7
(July 1980), pp. 26–28, 41. Illus., color.
Discusses and illustrates the disco design process.

Mike Callahan, "The Savoy: Aging Legit Finds
New Life as Unique Club," Lighting Dimen-
sions, vol. 6, no. 3 (April 1983), pp. 26–28.
Illus., color.

"Auto Headlights Give Disco Go," Lighting
Design + Application, vol. 16, no. 10 (Oct.
1986), pp. 28–29. Illus., color. Describes the
disco in the Fiesta Americana Hotel in
Tijuana, Baja California, which won a 1986
Edwin M. Guth Memorial Award of Excellence
from the IES.

Lisa W. Foderaro, "Glitz, Funk and Victoriana
Enliven New York's Discos," The New York
Times, Weekend, March 27, 1987, pp. 15, 20.
Illus.

Figure 8.1 *Emerald City* in Philadelphia, Pennsylvania, by designer Robert Lobi. (*Courtesy of George Hayward.*)

Figure 8.2 The "Gastation" in Boise, Idaho, by designer Graham Smith. (*Photo: Gloria Swanson Gruesen*)

Figure 8.3 The Ritz in Houston, Texas, by Graham Smith. (*Photo: Gloria Swanson Gruesen*)

specialists and well over 200 exhibitors each year. The best discos are now appearing in city suburbs. Video cameras and monitors have become important to disco, and there is a discernible trend toward *interactive* discos which allow the patrons to trigger or control the effects in the environment.

Concert Lighting

Concert lighting is basically the "road show" touring version of the best of light shows, vaudeville/burlesque shows, night-club/Las Vegas and Broadway revues, utilizing all the disco equipment they can transport. Design elements of all of these types of production may be present in concert lighting.

Normally there are over 800 musical artists/bands on the road. Perhaps 90 to 140 of these bands toured with lights and sound; 150 to 200 carried a lighting designer/supervisor/electrician and either rented lights or used those available where they were playing; and another 30 to 40 played well-equipped Atlantic City–type clubs.[185] Concerts frequently gross over $1 million for a single evening with over 80,000 cash customers present. Cecil Richmond paints a picture of hundreds of concerts shows each week playing in theatres, college gyms, outdoor festivals, racetracks, con-

cert halls, and arenas, with a basic pool of 400 to 500 touring groups, large and small.[186] The concert industry is a billion-dollar business. According to James L. Moody of Sundance Lighting Corporation:

> The rock concert is coming of age . . . as a permanent theatrical medium. It [has] begun to set entertainment standards and proven that it has lasting entertainment as well as cultural ability . . . whatever the state of the economy, the production values, budget, and complexity of design continue to expand in

"The 1986 IALD and IESNA Awards," International Lighting Review, 1987/1 (first quarter 1987), p. 31. Illus., color. The Heart Throb Cafe in Philadelphia won a 1986 International Association of Lighting Designers (IALD) Honorable Mention award.

Michele Lo Scotto, "Show Preview: Magis/SIB, the Two International Trade Shows Will be Held May 4–8 in Rimini, Italy," Lighting Dimensions, vol. 11, no. 2 (Mar./Apr. 1987), pp. 98, 100–101. Illus. Details concerning the fifth annual SIB International Discotheque and Dance-Hall Equipment and Technology Exhibition and the Magis Exhibition of Theatre and Cinema Equipment and Technology in Italy.

Lighting + Sound International magazine, published in England, is an excellent source of information about British and European disco designers, equipment, and manufacturers. Specific articles which merit special attention are:

"All The World's A Stage: Tony Gotellier Asks Why No One Has So Far Designed and Implemented a Truly Flexible Discotheque Environment Based on Theatrical Principles of Stage Sets to Create New Scenes or Productions," vol. 1, no. 1 (Nov. 1985), pp. 35–36. Illus.

"A Night Out at the Dome—John Offord Visits First Leisure's 'Most Spectacular Discotheque in the World,'" vol. 1, no. 1 (Nov. 1985), pp. 37, 39, 40, 42–45. Illus., color. Includes light plot.

"Discom 85—Paris, La Certitude—The Certitude?" vol. 1, no. 1 (Nov. 1985), p. 49. Illus. Discusses Parisian disco.

"Hippodrome on the Road," vol. 1, no. 1 (Nov. 1985), p. 48. Illus. About a British touring disco light and sound show.

"Show Page with PLASA News," vol. 1, no. 1 (Nov. 1985), pp. 58–61. Illus., color. PLASA (Professional Lighting and Sound Association) in England publishes Lighting + Sound International, the monthly magazine for the disco-club area. Contact John Offord Publications, Ltd., 12 The Avenue, Eastbourne, East Sussex, BN21 3YA, England. Telephone: (0-323) 645871. PLASA can be reached through Roger Saunders, 1 West Ruislip Station, Ruislip, Middlesex, WA4 7DW, England. Telephone: (08956) 34515.

"Upstairs to Paradise—John Offord Visits First Leisure's 'Most Beautiful Discotheque in the World,'" vol. 1, no. 2 (Dec. 1985), pp. 21–23. Illus., color. A continuation of the article cited above in vol. 1, no. 1.

"The Point Lights Up—UK's First Multiplex Opens at Milton Keynes," vol. 1, no. 2 (Dec. 1985), pp. 24–26. Illus., color. A British disco combined with 10 movie theatres, a restaurant, a bar, and a social club. Technical details and drawings included.

"Creating the People Magnets," vol. 1, no. 3 (Jan. 1986), pp. 18–23. Illus., color. A more definitive investigation of the disco design process, with excellent accompanying color photos.

"From Porno to Paparazzi—John Offord Goes to Glasgow with Tony Gottelier," vol. 1, no. 4 (Feb. 1986), pp. 22–25. Illus., color. Discusses discos in Scotland.

"Terry's Wheel," vol. 1, no. 4 (Feb. 1986), pp. 26–28. Illus., color. Discusses a gyroscopic lighted wheel installed in Cinder's nightspot at Willenhall in the West Midlands.

Roger St. Pierre, "Stringfellow in New York," vol. 1, no. 5 (March 1986), pp. 25–33. Designer Stringfellow offers his opinion of New York City discos, the Hippodrome in London, and discos in Croydon. Illus., color.

"Getlit Down Under—The Aussie's Hottest Disco Show?" vol. 1, no. 5 (March 1986), pp. 34–35. Illus. Gives details about Australian discos.

"Limelight in London—John Offord Looks at Peter Gatlen's New London Venue," vol. 1, no. 9 (Aug. 1986), pp. 13–16. Illus.

Andrew Brooker, "From Pictures to Palaces—Cinemas Provide a Major Source for New Discotheque and Club Venues," vol. 1, no. 9 (Aug. 1986), pp. 24–25. Illus.

Francis Reid, "A Theatre Man at PLASA," vol. 1, no. 10 (Sept./Oct. 1986), pp. 35–36. Illus. British Reid relates the theatre lighting designer to the disco world with his usual wit and wisdom.

Roger St. Pierre, "Dick Carrier—Colour and Chrome," vol. 1, no. 11 (Nov. 1986), pp. 21–25. Illus., color. The story of Light and Sound Distribution and their designs by Dick Carrier. Lavishly illustrated in color.

"The Escape—Amsterdam's Latest Discotheque," vol. 1, no. 12 (Dec. 1986), pp. 8–11. Illus., color. Includes light plot.

"Pattemore's Palace—John Offord looks at Blackpool's Latest Lights," vol. 1, no. 12 (Dec. 1986), pp. 32–34, 37. Illus., color.

Graham Fathers, "Lights on the Ocean Wave," vol. 2, no. 2 (Feb. 1987), pp. 30–32. Illus., color. Describes a disco on shipboard on a cruise ship.

"Home Grown in Derby: Roger St. Pierre Talks to Club Manager Anthony Walker at the Pink Coconut in Derby," vol. 2, no. 3 (March 1987), pp. 16–27. Illus., color.

"A Great Day Out Indoors: John Offord Visits the New Leisure World Complex at Bridlington, Where the Local Authority Has Installed a Major Discotheque Operation," vol. 2, no. 4 (April 1987), pp. 13, 17. Illus., color.

"The Frontier Club: Batley's New Style in Variety," vol. 2, no. 4 (April 1987), pp. 19, 20. Illus., color.

William George Wilson, "The Red Parrot, Where All The World's a Stage," Lighting Dimensions, vol. 6, no. 4 (May/June 1982), pp. 18–19, 22–23. Illus., color. Excellent example of where disco design is going.

"Club Splash: Tijuana's Newest Tourist Attraction," L S & V magazine, vol. 1, no. 1 (November/December 1988), p. 27. Illus., color.

Doug Shannon, "The Definitive History of Disco," Part I, L S & V magazine, vol. 1, no. 1 (November/December 1988), pp. 39, 49. Shannon traces early disco from the Nazi banning of jazz, to secret caves in France where jazz recordings were played, through dancing to recorded music in the United States in the 1950s. Part II appears in vol. 1, no. 2 (January/February 1989), pp. 23, 57–58. Part III is printed in vol. 1, no. 3 (March/April 1989), pp. 46–47.

Mike J. Love, "How To Start a Mobile DJ Company," L S & V Magazine, vol. 1, no. 2 (January/February 1989), Part I: pp. 22, 59. Part II: vol. 1, no. 3 (March/April 1989), pp. 17, 56, 59. Also in vol. 1, no. 3: "Blackjack, Rock of the Ozarks," pp. 21, 58. These two "how to" articles are about mobile travelling disco companies and their lighting.

"Light Concert Spectacular Comes To Clubs," L S & V magazine, vol. 1, no. 1 (November/December 1988), pp. 31, 51. Illus., color. A description of San Francisco's Parhelion, which combines fireworks, lasers, and music. A citywide light spectacular is described in detail.

Norman Kelley, "The Twilight Club," L S & V magazine, vol. 1, no. 3 (March/April 1989), p. 25. Illus., color. Also: "Skate Reflections," pp. 26–27. Illus., color. About a disco in a roller rink.

"Projected Effects," L S & V magazine, vol. 1, no. 3 (March/April 1989), pp. 29–31, 57. Illus., color. A most useful article with good illustrations concerning suitable projectors for disco use.

"Club Marilyn," L S & V Magazine, vol. 1, no. 3 (March/April 1986), pp. 36–37. Illus., color. About a disco in Milwaukee, Wisconsin. Also in the same issue: "Cocoacabana Lounge — New Concept Captivates Cocoa Beach," p. 38. Illus., color. A Florida Disco. And: "The Ultimate Private Club," pp. 40–51. Illus., color. A private disco in the home of a wealthy Orange County, California, retail-clothing-chain mogul with a 36,000 square-foot dance floor, disco, fountain lighting, etc.

"Hawkins," Disco Tech, vol. 3, no. 1 (Jan. 1987), pp. 7–10. Illus. A reprint from Disco & Club International, February 1986, about the Birmingham (Britain) Hawkins Cafe Bar (disco), "Britain's Best Known Cafe Bar."

"Teen Discotheques," Disco Tech, vol. 3, no. 1 (Jan. 1987), pp. 12–13, 16, 18. Illus., color. Not only deals with lighting for a successful teen disco, but details basic business practices for a successful club. Also in the same issue: "Trussing," p. 17. Illus., color. About Meteor trusses. And: "—And More Major Effects," pp. 20–26. Illus. Presents details useful for the designer about the newest in disco controllers and effects units.

"Spectrum, Toronto — Bingo Is Dead! Long Live Disco!," Pro Light + Sound magazine, vol. 2, no. 6 (April/May 1988), p. 30. Illus., color. This magazine, published briefly from 5302 Vineland Avenue, North Hollywood, CA 91601, as a bimonthly publication by Mountain Lion Publications, no longer exists.

"Installation, USA vs. UK," Disco Tech, vol. 3, no. 3 (July 1987), pp. 4–5, 29. Illus. An interview of Keith Hardy (United Kingdom) and David Milly (United States), conducted by Colin Hammond, about differences in discotheque equipment installation. Continued in: vol. 4, no. 1 (March 1988), pp. 6–7, 29–30. Illus.

"Proof Disco Lives!" Disco Tech, vol. 4, no. 1 (March 1988), pp. 18–19. Information on the ADIA (American Discotheque Industry Association) and the continued popularity of discos in the United States.

"Alcohol Sales vs. Cover Charges: Are Discotheques Heading Down the Wrong Road?" Disco Tech, vol. 4, no. 2 (August 1988), pp. 10–11. Illus., color. Basic information on disco objectives and management, which any disco lighting designer should be familiar with before designing.

"Club Reviews: Circus Disco, Hollywood, California," Disco Tech, vol. 4, no. 2 (August 1988), pp. 18–19. Illus., color. Also: "Carnivale, Glendale, California," pp. 20–21. Illus., color. Descriptions of two unique theme discos in California.

Michele Lo Scotto, "Transatlantic Trade: Italian Disco Manufacturers Testing U.S. Waters," Lighting Dimensions, vol. 11, no. 6 (Nov. 1987), pp. 84, 86, Illus. Useful information for the disco or nightclub lighting designer concerning technologies and films (Clay-Paky, for example) supplying units for this market.

Michele Lo Scotto, "Disco Italian Style: Fiber Optics, Intimate Venues, and Other Trends in Italian Nightclubs," Cue International, no. 58 (March/April 1989), pp. 23–26, Illus. More about Italian sources for nightclub/disco luminaires.

Mark Loeffler, "Disco Renewal: Michael A. Fink Renovates Lighting at Studio 54 and Merlin," Lighting Dimensions, vol. 12, no. 6 (September/October 1988), pp. 58–59, 78–79. Illus., color. A description of the third lighting design for New York City's Studio 54 by Fink.

183 John Gaudio, "Designing a Disco Control System," Lighting Dimensions, vol. 3, no. 7 (July 1979), pp. 39, 41–42. Illus.

"Controlling the Palace," Lighting Dimensions, vol. 3, no. 7 (July 1979), pp. 44–45, 47, 49, 51. Illus.

184 Author's interview with Robert Lobi.

185 James J. Moody, "Rock and Roll Tour Lighting: What You Need to Know Before You Begin to Design," Theatre Crafts, vol. 12, no. 3 (Mar./Apr. 1978), p. 80.

186 Cecil Richmond, "Rock Concerts Keep Rolling In Big Bucks," Indianapolis Star, August 4, 1978, p. 36.

the concert field. And with this expansion will come the education and growth of the concert technician.[187]

Design Considerations

The essentials of concert lighting can be reduced to five factors:

1. *Mobility and Time.* Concert lighting differs from theatre lighting in a major way: mobility. A concert schedule may demand 30 complex performances in 30 cities over 30 days. Portability and rapid setup and loadout are key to the concert business. Theatre shows rehearse longer, involve more setup time, and stay longer in one place. Concert technicians and designers have no such luxury, yet they must produce equally demanding artistic results.

2. *Enhancement of Music and Performers/Artists.* Concert lighting is not for the designer who doesn't *love* contemporary music—whatever trend is predominant in the ever-changing styles. Like theatre lighting, which *should* assist the playwright and production rather than be a show in itself, concert lighting must reinforce, expand, and extend the work of the musical artists—not take over. The end product may well be spectacle, but the design objective is not to create spectacle at the expense of the performers.

3. *Variety of Performance Places.* Theatre usually performs in physical plants which have proper power supplies, counterweighted grids, and all the other expected appurtenances for production. Concerts can and do take place anywhere a sufficient number of cash customers can be assembled. Since the audiences are huge and since the people come expecting to *see* as well as to hear, *clear visibility* is a prime design consideration.

4. *"Theatrical" Production Values.* Concerts are "shows"—they are *not* just performers in T-shirts and blue jeans under work lights. For the designer this leads to highly complex cues (both on control boards and followspots—frequently every 10 to 15 seconds) and heavy technical emphasis. The world of concert lighting is a maze of technical complexity: trusses, controllers, luminaires, and scheduling.

5. *Cost.* Some major attractions and some concert designers make "the sky the limit," as far as lighting costs go. In any case, it still is necessary to keep the show mobile enough for short, multiple playing dates—unlimited money does *not* solve that problem. (Of course, most concert attractions *do* work within cost limitations).

James L. Moody lists the key design considerations somewhat differently.[188] I have slightly modified and expanded his list, as follows:

1. Where will the concert play?
2. What is the budget or cost?
3. What are the needs of the artist? (How can artist/designer rapport be achieved?)
4. What are the staging limitations (as set by the artist)?
5. What crewing is available, in terms of number and time allowed? (Usually two to four crew people are allowed in electrics on tour traveling with the show, plus locals.)
6. What is the opening act, and how can it be fitted into the planned lighting design?
7. What is the prep time available (pretour and on the road) for designing?
8. How much rehearsal time, as opposed to prep time, is available (prior to the tour with lights)?
9. What are the contract rider provisions (i.e., the business necessities of compensation and organization)?

The concert lighting designer, once a design objectives and production parameters are in hand, turns to the standard theatre issues and choices: color concepts and media selection; mounting positions and lighting angles; cues and their fluidity and complexity (frequently different for each performance and mood as the musical selections change); the selected controller (switchboard) and its flexibility response; the overall structure, flow, and climax of the totally designed show (the artist's "concept"); plus necessary adaptation to potential performance places and the designer's relations with both the artists and their music.

The Concert Lighting Director

The position of a concert lighting director *does* differ from that of a theatrical lighting designer. The main difference

[187] *James L. Moody, "Rock Tour Lighting: General Road Problems and Scheduling," Theatre Crafts, vol. 12, no. 5 (Sept. 1978), p. 87.*

[188] *Moody, p. 78, op. cit. (see footnote 185).*

[189] *At the author's (Lee Watson's) request, this quote was sent by James L. Moody for inclusion in the* Handbook *in a letter dated June 27, 1979. Text in author's possession.*

[190] *James L. Moody,* Concert Lighting, Techniques, Art and Business. *Boston and London; Focal Press; 1989. 191 pages, illustrated, color. The definitive source by a master of concert lighting who writes well. Invaluable.*

Karen Hunter, "Solid Gold Brilliance," Video Systems, *vol. 8, no. 5 (June 1982), pp. 28–34. Illus., color. Presents light plots and photographs of a weekly TV concert lighting series, lighted by Bob Dickinson.*

David Kerr, "Lighting in the Rock 'n Roll Business," Cue, *no. 1 (Sept./Oct. 1979), pp. 14–15. Illus., color. British practice. Good technical/business information.*

Brian Croft, "Rock 'n' Roll is Here to Stay," Cue, *no. 16 (Mar./Apr. 1982), pp. 4–6. Illus., color. More on British practice.*

Patricia MacKay, "Bill McManus, On the Concert Circuit," Theatre Crafts, *vol. 15, no. 5 (May 1981), pp. 26, 59–62, 64–66. Illus. Also see in the same issue William McManus, "Concert Tour Management," pp. 27, 66 (illus.) and "Packaging a Show to Troupe: Into the Truck and on the Road," by Michael Esmonde, pp. 28–29, 46–48, 50 (illus.).*

Ronn Smith, "The Rolling Stones on Tour," Theatre Crafts, *vol. 16, no. 3 (Mar. 1982), pp. 25, 34–35, 39. Illus.*

"'The Who'—Lighting for Rock's Outer Limit," Lighting Dimensions, *vol. 5, no. 1 (Jan./Feb. 1981), pp. 46–49. Illus., color. Includes light plot.*

Mike Williams, "Rock Touring with England's Yes," Lighting Dimensions, *vol. 5, no. 3 (Apr. 1981), pp. 25–27. Illus. color.*

"The Rolling Stones—Electronic Extravaganza," Lighting Dimensions, *vol. 6, no. 3 (Apr. 1982), pp. 18–25. Illus., color. Includes Allen Branton's light plot.*

Mike Williams, "Styx: Paradise Theatre Revived and Alive on the Road," Lighting Dimensions, *vol. 6, no. 3 (Apr. 1983), pp. 30–33, 41–42, 46. Illus., color. Includes Jeff Ravitz' light plot.*

Bob Peterson, "Bob Seeger and The Silver Bullet Band 'Against the Wind,'" Lighting Dimensions, *vol. 6, no. 3 (Apr. 1983), pp. 34–39. Illus., color. Includes light plot.*

"Vegas Scrapbook," Lighting Design & Application, *vol. 10, no. 8 (Aug. 1980), pp. 14–18. Illus., color. Interview with designer Stig Edgren.*

"Van Halen: Hard Rocks and Stylish Raunch," Lighting Dimensions, *vol. 7, no. 2 (Apr./May 1983), pp. 18–24. Illus., color. Light plot by Pete Angelus and equipment list for the elaborate Van Halen tours.*

Michael Callahan, "Bright New World?," Lighting Dimensions, *vol. 7, no. 1 (Mar. 1983), pp. 62–64, 66, 72–73, illus.; vol. 7, no. 2 (Apr./May 1983), pp. 27–32, 35, 38–39, illus.; vol. 7, no. 3 (June 1983), pp. 35–42, illus. Brilliant analysis of the potentialities and limitations of improved control of intensity, color, form, and movement in light sources as seen through the eyes of a concert lighting designer/engineer. Also a sketchy history of the evolution of concert lighting (vol. 7, no. 1).*

Sherri English, "Oh, No! It's Devo," Lighting Dimensions, *vol. 7, no. 2 (Apr./May 1983), pp. 42–43, 45–49. Illus., color. Includes light plot. Description of a group which combines video, film, and live techniques.*

Patricia MacKay, "Serious and Stunning—Moonlight: Allen Brant on Lights (for) David Bowie's Concert Tour," Theatre Crafts, *vol. 18, no. 1 (Jan. 1984), pp. 17, 19, 66, 68–71. Illus., color. Includes light plot and switchboard layout. Excellent photographs and text.*

"Lighting the Audience at The Who's Final Concert," Lighting Dimensions, *vol. 8, no. 1 (Jan./Feb. 1984), pp. 46–52. Illus., color.*

centers around responsibilities; the concert lighting designer is often the only design artist associated with the show (although larger concerts can afford to have a separate scenic artist), so the lighting designer may be looked to for all visual concepts. The second big difference is that for concerts there is rarely a very extended rehearsal period, certainly nothing equal to theatrical rehearsal schedules. Often one day is all the rehearsal the concert lighting designer will see, and sometimes that rehearsal is carried out without the lighting to be used on the road.

The concert lighting designer must be very involved in music. A native aptitude for musical interpretation is generally found at the core of the better lighting designers. Most of them go on the road with the shows they design. A few do use a lighting console operator, but most of them run their own shows completely and do not use a stage manager to call cues during the run of the production.

Concert lighting is an immediacy art! The lighting designer can't put a color on the canvas or chip a piece of stone away from a block and stand back to think about it for an hour, a day, or a week. Instantaneous reaction is called for. Often there is not even time to write down what was done for a particular number or show. Frequently the lighting is executed intuitively, never to be exactly reproduced again. Preparation is the key. The fact is that every day brings new buildings and hence new problems for the designer to work out. Adaptability in the designer is a *must.* The most important lesson is that "there is no such thing as a wrong decision; the only wrong decision is to hesitate." [189] If the designer is prepared for all conceivable disasters, then he or she can deal logically and calmly with ordinary problems.

While creative artists in any field come and go in a constantly changing flow, certain names from the first few years of concert lighting deserve mention. These designers formed the specialty, and in the future they will continue as important factors in the industry. They are (in no particular order) Bill McManus (who formed the first concert lighting firm in 1964), Lee Bonomy, James L. Moody, Chip Largman, Jules Fisher, Tony Mazzucchi, Chip Monck (who was the first to light any concert touring group, The Rolling Stones, in 1972), and Imero Fiorentino. [190]

Includes light plot. This concert spectacular was also televised with Alan Adelman of Fiorentino Associates as lighting designer.

"Bette Midler — The Divine Miss M and De Tour '83," Lighting Dimensions, vol. 7, no. 5 (Sept./Oct. 1983), pp. 28–30, 33–34. Illus., color. Includes light plot. Lengthy description of Chip Largman's lighting with plot and numerous color photographs. Extensive use of gobos and remote color changers explained, along with Largman's design philosophy.

Mike Williams, "The Styx — World Tour 1983," Lighting Dimensions, vol. 7, no. 6 (Nov./Dec. 1983), pp. 37–43, 51. Describes Jeff Ravitz' sets and lighting for the tour, including use of a film sequence.

Ronn Smith, "Concert Lighting: Singing in the Rain," Theatre Crafts, vol. 17, no. 9 (Nov./Dec. 1983), p. 10. Illus. An amusing account of the rained-out Diana Ross concert in New York City's Central Park and its effect upon lights.

Bob Anderson, "Colour Music!" Cue, #42 (July/Aug. 1986), pp. 20. Illus., color. Thorough coverage of a spectacular British concert with Richard Dale's elaborate color lighting.

Steve Pollock, "Programming Madonna," Theatre Crafts, vol. 19, no. 9 (Nov. 1985), pp. 38–39, 41, 44. Illus., color.

"From Genesis — A Revolution," Lighting Dimensions, vol. 8, no. 3 (May/June 1984), pp. 18–24. Illus., color, light plot. Detailed interview with Alan Owens, lighting designer for the rock group Genesis since 1973. Lavish color illustrations and light plot.

"Getting David Bowie on the Road," Lighting Dimensions, vol. 8, no. 3 (May/June 1984), pp. 36–39, 41–45. Illus., color. Includes light plot. Useful description, color photographs, and light plot of designer Allen Branton's work with this concert group.

Mike Williams, "On the Road with Live Video: Kieran Healy Lights the Annual Marlboro Country Music Tour," Lighting Dimensions, vol. 10, no. 5 (Sept./Oct. 1986), pp. 80, 82–83. Illus., color.

Craig Bromberg, "RUSH on Tour: Rocking with the Rapid Deployment Lighting Module," Theatre Crafts, vol. 18, no. 9 (Nov./Dec. 1984), pp. 36–37, 92–94. Illus., color. Detailed description of new touring lighting truss.

"Lighting Critical in Rock Concert Design," Rosconews, Spring 1985, p. 2. Descriptions by

Marc Brickman (film lighting for Bruce Springsteen) and Jeff Ravitz (Styx) of their use of color.

"The Thrill of Victory," Lighting Dimensions, vol. 9, no. 1 (Jan./Feb. 1985), pp. 24–26, 28–34, 36–37. Illus., color. Includes light plot. A description of the 1984 Michael Jackson concert tour of the United States.

"Panorama: A Window on the World of Arts," Kansas City Star, February 22, 1987. A short piece on classical singer Luciano Pavarotti's plans, as presented by his manager Herbert H. Breslin, to tour with Handel's Messiah and Wagner's Ring Cycle, accompanied by lasers, light poles, etc., in arenas.

Keith Dale, "On Tour," Lighting + Sound International, vol. 1, no. 1 (Nov. 1985), pp. 46–47. Illus., color. Gives brief details of British concert (rock) groups on tour.

Mike Williams, "Japan's Follow Spot Spectacular," Lighting Dimensions, vol. 10, no. 4 (July/Aug. 1986), pp. 26–29, 52, 54. Contains scale drawing of Kazuo Inoue's stunning rock lighting with good text and vivid graphics.

Mike Williams, "Rock 'n' Roll History: Genesis Takes to the Road and Leaves the PAR 64s at Home," Lighting Dimensions, vol. 10, no. 6 (Nov. 1986), pp. 50–52. Illus., color. Details designer Alen Owen's work for the 1986–1987 Genesis world tour.

Mike Williams, "A Meeting of the Minds: LD Jonathan Smeeton and Peter Gabriel Collaborate Quickly for a Unique Tour," Lighting Dimensions, vol. 11, no. 2 (Mar./Apr. 1987), pp. 64–66, 82, 84–86. Illus., color. An analysis and description of designer/musician collaboration in lighting design. Good analysis.

"Light Fantastique!" Lighting Dimensions, vol. 9, no. 3 (May/June 1985), pp. 18–23, 25. Illus., color, light plot. French designer Jacques Rouverollis used both British and American technology for a light show for the Johnny Hallyday tour.

"Springsteen Keeps It Simple," Lighting Dimensions, vol. 9, no. 3 (May/June 1985), pp. 37–39, 41, 43–44, 48. Illus., color. Includes light plot. Jeff Ravitz' design for the 1984–1985 Springsteen tour.

"Lighting Prince's Purple Reign," Lighting Dimensions, vol. 9, no. 3 (May/June 1985), pp.

50–51, 53, 55–56, 58, 60. Illus., color. Includes light plot. Roy Bennett's lighting for the Prince film, Purple Rain.

Mark Loeffler, "'Bad' Lighting," Lighting Dimensions, vol. 12, no. 6 (September/October 1988), p. 22. Illus., color. A description of Allen Branton's lighting for the Michael Jackson Bad tour.

Mike Williams, "The Bigger, the Better? For David Lee Roth's Tour, Phil Ealy Aims For a Larger Look On Less Equipment," Lighting Dimensions, vol. 12, no. 6 (September/October 1988), pp. 64–65, 83–84. Illus., color.

"Short Circuits," Lighting Dimension, vol. 11, no. 7 (January/February 1988), p. 21. A description of recent work by concert lighting designer Richard Ocean of Ocean, Rose and Associates.

Mike Williams, "Floyd Droids: LD Marc Brickman and Set Designer Paul Staples Drench Pink Floyd in Technological Wonder, Lighting Dimensions, vol. 11, no. 7 (January/February pp. 66–68, 70–71. Illus., color. Marc Brickman's lighting for the Pink Floyd tour.

Ric Gentry, "Jeff Ravitz: An LD Comes Full Circle from the Theatre to Preprogrammed Rock Shows," Lighting Dimensions, vol. 12, no. 7 (November 1988), pp. 56–60, 62. Illus., color. A definitive article about the lighting design work (both theatre and concert) of a leading designer since 1976.

Allen Branton, "In Search of . . . . . Coherency: What the Arena Rock Concert Needs Is Creative Direction," Lighting Dimensions, vol. 12, no. 7 (November 1988), pp. 98, 105. An important "think piece" by a major concert lighting designer, now in his 16th year; designer for Michael Jackson. His thoughts about where concert tour lighting is going are of value.

Mike Williams, "Double Duty: Allen Branton Designs Two Presentations for Whitney Houston Tour," Lighting Dimensions, vol. 11, no. 5 (September/October 1987), pp. 60–63, 77–78. Illus., color. More about Branton's work.

Mike Williams, "Stephen Bickford: Portrait of the Artist as a Rock and Roll LD," Lighting Dimensions, vol. 12, no. 3 (April 1988), pp. 58–63. Illus., color. Excellent, well-illustrated article about a lighting designer who has worked in concert lighting, film, video, and industrial shows.

Beth Howard, "Lighting For One: Solo Singers Require the Designer's Subtle Touch," Lighting Dimensions, vol. 12, no. 2 (March 1988), pp. 68–71, 94, 97. Illus., color, includes light plot. A definitive article about lighting the one-performer show.

Mike Williams, "Low-Tech Lighting: Ken Mednick Gives Robert Plant Tour a Psychedelic Look." Lighting Dimensions, vol. 13, no. 1 (January/February 1989). pp. 58–59, 61–62. Illus., color.

[191] "Bill McManus, Lighting Designer," Lighting Dimensions, vol. 2, no. 1 (Jan. 1978), pp. 28–29, 52, 54–55, 57. Useful information about the early history of concert lighting by the founder of the first principal concert lighting firm. Extensive discussion of luminaires used for the Boz Scaggs group and for touring.

"TTFL, Lighting Rock and Pop: 'Anyone Who Designs for a One-Night Touring Rock Group Should Be Required to Go on the Road for at Least a Year with Three Different Acts and Work a Show That He Didn't Design . . . ,'" Lighting Design + Application, vol. 8, no. 1 (Jan. 1978), pp. 14–19. Valuable illustrations, discussion of TV lighting for concert groups, and useful information for beginners or Broadway lighting designers.

"TTFL, Profile of a Master Communicator: Bill McManus Revisited," Lighting Design & Application, vol. 3, no. 3 (Mar. 1979), pp. 12–16. Discusses the problem of lighting concert attractions for both live audiences and the TV camera.

Zoe Paine, "Kiss," Lighting Dimensions, vol. 3, no. 1 (Jan. 1979), pp. 24–26. Detailed description of equipment, personnel, and schedule for one of the larger, more elaborate concert tour groups.

Rosemary Kalikow, "Fiorentino Adds New Light to a Sparkling Diamond," Lighting Dimensions, vol. 1, no. 1 (June 1977), pp. 20–22, 32. Useful description of the development of performer/designer rapport, plus a detailed, careful analysis of adaptation of design to widely varying performance places. Good analysis of the development of the design process.

"Eagles, Parts 1, 2, 3," Lighting Dimensions, vol. 1, no. 5 (Nov. 1977), pp. 22–30. Part 1 deals with Jim Johnson (the lighting director) and his philosophy of design; also gives an account of equipment and touring. Part 2 by John C. Gates is about the lighting control system used. Part 3 by Michael Callahan and Fred Jason Hancock concerns the luminaires (lighting units) used and tour problems.

Mary Wilson, How To Make It In the Rock Business. London; Columbus; 1987. Approximately $5 in paperback. Covers the basics for those in concert lighting: gigs, records, managers, pluggers, charts, videos, accountants, contracts, royalties, etc., which anyone designing lighting in this area needs to be familiar with.

Patricia MacKay, "Beatlemania: Reconstructing the Sixties in Projections, Lighting, and Song," Theatre Crafts, vol. 12, no. 1 (Jan./Feb. 1978), pp. 16–19. Photographs of and Jules Fisher's light plot for the Broadway production of Beatlemania; Fisher applied concert lighting techniques for this show.

Communication Form

In its basics, concert lighting is so similar to theatre lighting that the standard light plot and hookup are used. However, concert lighting is much freer and is more flexible and more fluid in both setup and performance. The light plot frequently is the same type of "intentions guide" that the theatre plot is when a standard theatre show is "on the road."

Techniques

The technical specifics are so subject to constant modification and improvement that I refer the reader to James L. Moody's book cited in footnote 190. Moody deals with crew requirements, International Association of Theatre and Stage Employees (IATSE) "yellow cards," and "pink contracts"; setup time; preplanning for emergencies and "getting the show on"; power service problems; followspots and operators; stage size and structure; special effects; lifestyle (drugs and alcohol); transportation; and trusses and lifts. These are all things the designer *must* be in complete command of; however, they do not properly belong in a basic book dealing with lighting *design* (rather than technology). Designers can expand their knowledge of concert lighting technology and design by becoming familiar with the work and writings of today's top concert lighting artists.[191]

Procedures and Practices

Figures 8.4 to 8.9 present James L. Moody's light plot, hookup, and production photos for the John Denver tour under three separate sets of conditions: (1) for the Australian tour (Figs. 8.4 and 8.5), (2) at Lake Tahoe, Nevada, as a nightclub show in a well-equipped theatre (Figs. 8.6 and 8.7), and (3) as presented "in the round," arena-style (Figs. 8.8 and 8.9). This series provides a good opportunity to study the modifications of a given concert attraction performing in three different "specialty" areas. Illustrations in Chap. 7 present a similar sequence for Imero Fiorentino's lighting for Neil Diamond's show, shown in light plot and photographs as a TV show and at the outdoor Greek Theatre in Berkeley, California. A careful study of the modi-

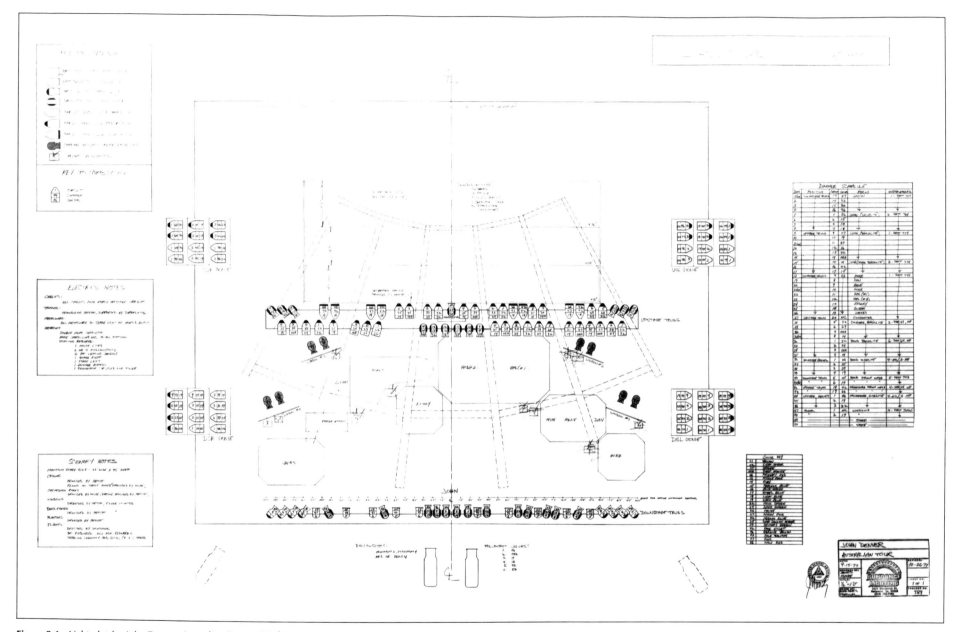

Figure 8.4 Light plot for *John Denver,* Australian Tour, 1977, by
James L. Moody.

Figure 8.5 *John Denver* during rehearsal at an outdoor cricket field in Australia, 1977. Lighting director: James L. Moody. (*Courtesy of Sundance Lighting Corp.*)

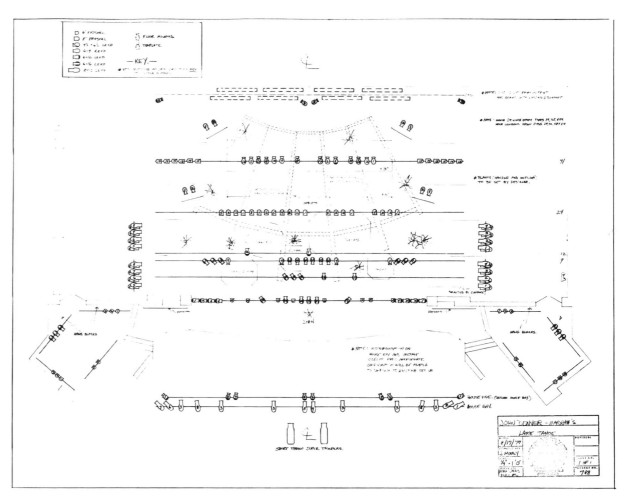

Figure 8.6 Light plot for *John Denver* at Harrah's, Lake Tahoe, Nevada, 1977, by James L. Moody.

Figure 8.7 *John Denver* at Harrah's, Lake Tahoe, Nevada, with lighting by James L. Moody. (*Courtesy of Sundance Lighting Corp.*)

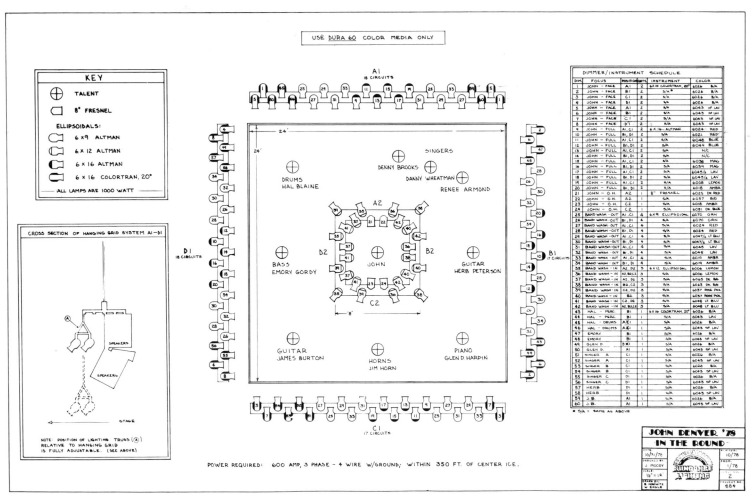

Figure 8.8 Light plot for *John Denver,* In-the-Round, 1978, by James L. Moody.

[192] *Netta Gelfman, "Music-Light-Space: A Production without Actors," Cue, no. 25 (Sept./Oct. 1983), pp. 19–21. Illus., color. Includes light plot. A description of a contemporary light show in England with technical details elaborated.*

"Thunder and Lightning," ABTT News, Mar. 1984, p. 23. Professors Cundall (Salford University) and Nicholas Phillips (Loughborough University) presented a demonstration of explosives and "incredible lighting and laser effects" (their words) on June 19, 1984, at the Theatre Royal, during the York Festival.

fications for each performance place can be most useful. Moody's design for The Eagles in "Hello Sailor" is shown in Color Fig. 71. Color Fig. 72 is the work of brilliant young West Coast designer, Richard Ocean. Figure 8.10 is Bill McManus's design for the 1978 Barry Manilow concert.

Aspiring lighting designers need not fear specialization in concert lighting. In spite of occasional written doubts by some established concert lighting experts, there has been a sufficiently large number of young designers moving freely from concert lighting to theatre, or from theatre to concert, to remove any doubts about specialization limiting the designer. Both Marilyn Rennagel and Martin Tudor worked with Sundance Lighting Corp. before coming to Broadway, and Imero Fiorentino and Jules Fisher went from theatre to concert. Such examples abound.

With the wealth of discos and concert groups in action and the beginnings of a revival of the traditional nightclub, light shows are not—at this time—in vogue. However, they are in the process of revival. Present-day versions are dealt with in the next chapter.[192]

Figure 8.9 *John Denver* show In-the-Round, 1978, at Madison Square Garden, New York City.

Figure 8.10 Bill McManus's lighting for a Barry Manilow concert, 1978.

Chapter 9

Spectacle

The Place of Spectacle in Design

What *is* spectacle? *Spectacle* is that which is shocking, unexpected, delightful, lavish, and/or astounding — usually on a large scale. In short, any use of light which greatly surprises or pleases can be called spectacle. Examples of spectacle are fireworks (see Color Fig. 72A), a stage filled with cascading water, and the blissful luxury of any Never-Never Land of Disney. Spectacle is as diverse as human beings are, but people usually know it when they see it or create it.

Clearly the production types discussed in Chaps. 4 through 8 lean heavily upon spectacle as a design element. Those production types have a serious side and yet employ spectacle, and it should not be forgotten that each production type discussed in *this* chapter also can have a serious secondary purpose — for example, expositions and amusement parks in many cases inform and summarize, rock or country western concerts are tied to their music, and ice show performances exhibit great trained daring and skill, just as circus acts do.

The beginning designer must be careful when using spectacle, because it can be overdone, which just makes the designer look like a show-off. Any attempt to make a whole evening that consists of one smashing effect topped by another is destined to fail, in terms of good design. Just as Shakespeare wrote plays with careful structure — in one place adding a touch of humor and relief, in another inserting a quiet scene to contrast with and build to the next big moment — so must the lighting designer husband available resources. The motto for use of spectacle is "Don't overdo."

Spectacle is usually quite attractive to the untried, insecure lighting design novitiate because the designer's efforts and effects are noticed and admired and praised by the cash customers, the critics, and the management. The designer can "show what can be done" with spectacle. However, the appropriate and judicious use of spectacle requires restraint. In comparison, artistry achieved in the theatre or dance or opera more often goes unnoticed.

Spectacle has its place in almost every kind of show business, although some production types call for greater reliance upon razzle-dazzle, and creative imagination than others do. Spectacle *can* be a trap, however; overdone, it can be a bore.

Light Shows

During the last few years light shows have reappeared in an entirely new form, as citywide (or nationwide) celebrations of anniversaries and other special events. Now they may involve nationwide telecasting, film, laser displays, fireworks on a spectacular scale, and often leading internationally known performers and celebrities participating in a staged "show." Examples which readily come to mind are the Los Angeles Olympics, the Houston Festival for the

150th anniversary of Texas, and the 4th of July nationwide celebration of the refurbishing of the Statue of Liberty in the New York City harbor.[193] At the statue of Liberty event the passing by of the tall mast ships in the harbor took place in daylight, but the numerous evening festivities, such as laser displays and fireworks, required intricate lighting and involved many lighting designers. The gala event was attended by the presidents of the United States and France, plus numerous other celebrities and officials. This is today's version of the once-popular light show, which has a lengthy, ongoing history.

Among light shows, the California-based IBM tour of the "Exploratorium" should be mentioned.[194]

Theme (Amusement) Parks

Considering the popularity of theme/amusement parks in the United States and worldwide, and the increasing number of multimillion dollar parks, one would expect this to be a primary design area for lighting, but it has only recently become so.[195]

Disneyland was the first giant-scale amusement park. There are now a string of amusement emporiums throughout the country, including the $1 billion, 260-acre Epcot Center created by Disney in Florida. Such parks are largely located in the more favorable climates of the South and West. A number of lighting designers have been involved in planning the initial design of such parks, both interior and exterior, but only two designers currently are employed year-round. They are Dahl C. Brown, whose duties consist primarily of design of lighting for theatre-type shows on the amusement ground, and John R. Haupt at Disney's Epcot Center in Florida. Other designers have designed for the opening of theme parks, including Imero Fiorentino Associates (King's Island) and John Watson (Six Flags over Texas, Six Flags over Georgia, Six Flags over Mid-America at St. Louis, and Great Adventure in New Jersey). Watson's work has only been on exterior areas. Randall Duell & Associates, which plans most of the big parks, does not have a full-time lighting design specialist on its staff. Opryland, in Nashville, Tennessee, is an example of this group's work (see Color Fig. 73).

Tivoli Gardens in Copenhagen, Denmark, is a masterpiece of older night lighting design, indoors and outside (see Color Fig. 74). In Europe the lesser mobility of people (because of innumerable borders to cross, passports to be examined, and changing regulations) has been a factor in the night lighting of amusement parks and the popularity of the parks. Tent carnivals and circuses still travel *to* the people, moving from town to town. With the huge geographical space and great individual mobility in the United States, the customer more frequently goes *to* the attraction (Disneyland, Opryland, Disney World, Epcot, Astroworld, Animal Kingdom, Six Flags, etc.).

A big reason why lighting designers have not been more involved in amusement parks is that amusement parks sprang out of the carnival and circus tradition, which does not rely very heavily on lighting *design*. Illumination takes precedence over artistry. A comparison of touring ice shows (which carry extensive lighting and rely on lighting designers) with circuses suffices to make this difference clear. Consequently, the huge new amusement parks have usually assigned responsibility for exterior illumination (streets, walks, buildings) to electrical contractors and illumination engineers. When indoor theatrical attractions are used (music concerts, haunted houses, ice shows, country and western music performances, etc.), only reluctantly do managements call in lighting design specialists. Also, many amusement parks are either not open during the dark night hours or else consider this to be a period of lesser economic importance, with general street lighting sufficing. (Old Country in Williamsburg, Virginia, is an example of this approach.) Amusement parks consist of highly controlled, preprogrammed visits to the Never-Never Land of dreams. They represent a large capital investment. Disney has invested over $1 billion in Epcot Center at Lake Buena Vista, Florida. Epcot is similar to a permanent world's fair. Normally redesigning takes place only between seasons. The attraction is "prepackaged" and standardized. Disneyworld and Magic Kingdom gross over $500 million each year and alone attracted 13 million visitors in 1981. Lighting for amusement parks *should* be a larger area of employment for lighting designers than it is. Even in times of economic hardship, business continues to be rather "bullish" at

[193] See "A City in Concert: Designer Jacques Rouverollis Brings Houston to Life," Lighting Dimensions, vol. 10, no. 4 (July/Aug. 1986), pp. 12, 60, 62. Illus., color.

[194] Michael Cabana, "New York's Own Exploratorium," Lighting Dimensions, vol. 10, no. 3 (May/June 1986), pp. 66, 68. Illus. The exhibit, called "Seeing the Light," from San Francisco's Exploratorium and exhibited in New York City's IBM gallery of Science and Art, contains much on the threshold of light as art and is priceless in exhibiting fundamentals of optics and vision.

"The Night the Light Died—NYC's Urban Light Festival," Lighting Dimensions, vol. 10, no. 1 (Jan./Feb. 1986), pp. 67, 69, 71, 73–74. Illus., color.

"The Liberty Weekend Fête—How the Production Crews Pulled It Off," Lighting Dimensions, vol. 10, no. 5 (Sept./Oct. 1986), pp. 72, 74. Illus.

"A New York Sound and Light Show," The New York Times, May 13, 1988, p. C24. Illus. A description of the New York City–wide light show held during the convention there of the AIA (American Institute of Architects). Organized by architect Richard Hayden and lighting designer Howard Brandston, it involved lighted buildings (40), lasers, and a "solo performance" by the Empire State Building.

Walter Gundy, "Producing the World's Largest Laser Show: A Gold Medal Performance at Seoul 1988," L S & V magazine, vol. 1, no. 2 (January/February 1989), pp. 45, 54, 60. Good description of today's version of a light show.

Glen Goodwin, "A Countdown to Remember," Focal Point, (a publication by Vincent Lighting Systems), p. 4. A description of the various light shows in celebration of Cincinnati's Bicentennial. May be ordered from Vincent Lighting Systems, 20810 Miles Parkway, Cleveland, Ohio 44128. Tel: (216) 475-7600.

Peter McLean, "The Australian Bicentennial," International Lighting Review, 40th year, 1st quarter of 1989, pp. 6–7. Illus., color. Excellent color photos of the light show which celebrated "A Legacy to the Future," Australia's bicentennial.

"Theatre at Sea," Theatre Crafts, vol. 23, no. 3 (March 1989), pp. 40–45, 59–65. Illus. Excellent series of articles concerning presentation shows on cruise liners with both design and tech information about shipboard lighting to be found nowhere else.

The most elaborate nightly light show in the United States at this time (1989) is the IllumiNations presentation in Orlando, Florida —a joint effort of Disney's Epcot Center and General Electric. The 20 minute presentation of lasers, fireworks (more than most July 4th exhibits elsewhere), water fountain illuminations (all presented in the International Pavilion lagoon), wide-angle scenic projections, and illuminations of the twelve International buildings (Germany, France, United States, China) which light up with thousands of tiny lights outlining each building's structure (and flashing, chasing and blinking), cost an initial $10 million and has an operating cost of $7,000 per night (over $2 million per year). It is truly dazzling.

"Short Circuits," Lighting Dimensions, vol. 12, no. 6 (September/October 1988), p. 34. Description of the Somerville, Massachusetts, laser company which provided a laser show for a Boston American–Soviet symphonic premiere.

"Olympian Light Celebration," Lighting Dimensions, vol. 12, no. 3 (April 1988), p. 10. Illus., color. Description of Dick Sandhaus's laser show contribution to the Calgary, Canada, Winter Olympics. Useful description of the entire light show.

Mary Burke, "Psychedelic Light Show Returns," Lighting Dimensions, vol. 11, no. 6 (Nov. 1987), p. 18. Description of the revival of a San Francisco filmaker's 15-year-old light show.

"Lasers over the Grand Coulee," Lighting Dimensions, vol. 13, no. 3 (April 1989), p. 36. A permanent laser light show has been added nightly at Grand Coulee Dam in Washington state.

[195] There are around 50 major amusement parks grossing nearly $1 billion per year and attended by nearly 75 million cash customers. See:

Gary Kyriazi, The Great American Amusement Parks. Secaucus, N.J. Citadel Press; 1976.

Theme Parks, Theatre Crafts, vol. 11, no. 4 (Sept. 1977), pp. 26. Ten major articles; excellent basic information.

"Opryland," Lighting Dimensions, vol. 1, no. 4 (Oct. 1977), pp. 28–35. Opryland is not strictly an amusement park; a theme park, its facilities for TV and live stage shows really place it in another category.

J. Robert Wills, "Mass Audience Entertainment Events," Theatre Design & Technology, vol. 13, no. 1 (Spring 1977), pp. 9–13. Illus.

Robb Resler, "Epcot Center," Theatre Crafts, vol. 16, no. 9 (Nov./Dec. 1982), pp. 12–21. Illus. Special issue. See particularly Tom Craven, "Carnaval de Lumiére," p. 15; John Haupt, "Parade Route Lighting," p. 16; "Customizing a Lighting Console," p. 17; and H. Lee Pharr, "Sound and Lighting Enclosures for the American Adverture," p. 20.

"Baltimore's Amazement Park," Lighting Dimensions, vol. 10, no. 1 (Jan./Feb. 1986), pp. 42–51, 74–78, 80. Illus., color. Designer Dan Flannery's work for an unusual theme park at Baltimore's Pier 4.

Peter Bleasby, "Spaceship Earth," Lighting Design + Application, vol. 13, no. 1 (Jan. 1983), pp. 10–12. Illus., color. Disney's Epcot Center in Florida.

Susan Lieberman, "Focus: Theme Parks," Theatre Crafts, vol. 17, no. 9 (Nov./Dec. 1983), p. 12. Illus. Discusses holiday decoration of Cincinnati's King's Island.

Maggie Riechers, "If a Theme Park's Your Thing, United States Has 10 Top Draws," Gannett News Service in the Lafayette Journal & Courier, April 29, 1984, p. D2. General information.

"The Adventures of Conan—A Sword and Sorcery Spectacular," Lighting Dimensions, vol. 8, no. 1 (Jan./Feb. 1984), pp. 36–42, 44, 52–54. Illus., color, light plot. Describes in detail this centerpiece show at Universal Studios Theme Park in Hollywood, designed by Daniel Flannery and opened in the summer of 1983.

"Epcot Center Pavilions," Lighting Design + Application, vol. 13, no. 10 (Oct. 1983), pp. 21–24. Illus., color. Fiorentino landscape lighting of the Epcot "World Showcase" area in Orlando, Florida, described in text and color photographs, including design approach. Award-winning design.

"Spaceship Earth—Lighting the Geodesic Sphere," Lighting Design + Application, vol. 13, no. 10 (Oct. 1983), pp. 19–20. Illus., color. Description of the outdoor lighting of the central symbol of Epcot by WED (Disney) in Orlando, Florida. Award-winning design.

John Roderick, "Tokyo Disneyland," Associated Press release in Lafayette Journal & Courier, March 11, 1984, p. D8. Illus. General information on the new Disney Theme Park in Japan.

David Hanly, "Tivoli!" Travel & Leisure, July 1981, pp. 62–63, 65, 67, 69–70. Illus., color. Excellent color photographs of Copenhagen (Denmark) "Danish Pastry," the original theme or amusement park, which is still in operation.

"Fabulous Fantasies," Travel & Leisure, Feb. 1982, pp. 44–55. Illus., color. Excellent roundup of background information with extensive photographs (including night fireworks) of key United States theme parks.

Mark Schacter, "London Landmark to Become Theme Park," United Press International release in Indianapolis Star, July 6, 1984, p. 19. The 50-year-old Battersea power station on the bank of the Thames River in London is being converted into a $50 million theme park.

Francis Reid, "Experimental Prototype Community of Tomorrow," Cue, May/June 1984, pp. 6–8. Illus., color. Excellent article with color graphics about the Disney's Epcot Center in Florida.

Alice M. Hale, "Naturally Effective," Theatre Crafts, vol. 20, no. 5 (May 1986), pp. 10. Illus., color. A description of the theme park volcano at the New Mexico Museum of Natural History, which uses fog, lasers, fiber optics, and holograms. It was created by former Disney employees.

Clyde Haberman, "In Japan, Mickey-San Is Right at Home: New Subjects for the Magic Kingdom," The New York Times, September 25, 1986. Amusement section, p. 37, Illus. A feature piece on Disney's new theme park in Tokyo, in the eastern suburb of Urayasu.

Bob Deitel, "Christian Theme Park Puts on the Ritz," Lafayette Journal & Courier, October 26,

amusement parks, having only dropped 7 to 14 percent during the early 1980s recession.

American firms have been expanding their amusement theme parks worldwide, to Japan (Disney and Landmark Entertainment Group) and to Australia (Kings Entertainment Co.). Others are now planned for Europe.

Included in the category of theme parks should also be such fringe operations as Knott's Berry Farm, Marineland, the Queen Mary, the Spruce Goose, and Universal Studio's Tours, all of which are in Los Angeles. Others are Sea World in Florida; new parks in California, Ohio, and Texas; plus Boardwalk, and Baseball in Florida.

In his article "Mass Audience Entertainment Events," J. Robert Wills points to another factor which may be responsible for the virtual absence of theatre-trained lighting specialists in the amusement or theme park area. He writes:

> Each also depends for total success on an audience of groups rather than individuals: they are not the kind of entertainments you do by yourself. They offer shared, spontaneous *fun*, devoid of pre-planned rigor. Just being there is enough; and once present, the event happens to you. It's what Sanford and Law in their book, *Synthetic Fun*, call "pre-canned, precubed, pre-heated, pre-gutted, pre-hygienized, emasculated, dialed-for instant experience, that state in which the real world can be forgotten, replaced by a dream world, synthetic euphoria."
> Within the confines of Disneyland (or while seated watching *Hello Hollywood*) there is no reality other than the present moment. Fantasy reigns. Escape occurs, not by transforming the real world, but by ignoring it, pretending wholeheartedly that it doesn't exist, while simultaneously striving to create an alternative reality of here and now.[196]

Wills stresses that mass audience events utilize huge amounts of available capital and have at their disposal the most advanced technology. He also says that theatre technology and personnel are utilized (for painting, building, and creating special effects); however, "[these employees] are not working in theatre. They are not dealing with artistic concerns." One would expect that the creation and operation of the "ideal world of complete fantasy" would be an important attraction to lighting design artists from other areas, but such is not the case. Amusement or theme parks remain almost exclusively in the hands of businessmen and master manipulators of popular culture, even more than in the allied world of circus and world's fair expositions.

Considering the increasing popularity of amusement parks and the huge capital investment, it is my opinion that a great potential for both gainful lighting employment and artistic creativity awaits anyone who can "open the door wider" and that amusement parks are "missing a good bet" by largely ignoring the world of lighting design.

Expositions and World's Fairs

Lighting designers do not have unlimited opportunities to design for world's fairs and expositions. When such assignments do come along, they are huge in size and demanding of artistic creativity. I was lucky to be involved in such an endeavor. I was engaged by RCA in 1962 as part of the design team working on *Century 21*, the theme centerpiece of the Seattle World's Fair, so I will use *Century 21* to illustrate this category of design. The scope and techniques involved in this undertaking in 1962 have not changed markedly over time.

The Washington State Coliseum building which housed *Century 21* is shown in the lower right foreground of Fig. 9.1. It was 11 stories high and a block square.[197] Seattle in 1962 was a small city of 600,000 and was relatively unknown in a worldwide sense. The planners of the fair decided to create a permanent usable civic center addition to Seattle as well as to "put the city on the map." Thus, the four-acre fairgrounds overlooking Puget Sound incorporated a modernistic monorail to downtown Seattle (still in use), a symbolic Space Needle restaurant, the Playhouse theatre, the Seattle Opera House, an art gallery, a plaza with a magnificent water fountain (with 100-foot high water jets), food pavilions, and a sports stadium. The fair was science-oriented, giving a look at the possible wonders of "The World of Tomorrow—Century 21." This fair ranks as one of the very few World's Fairs which turned a profit.

Figure 9.2 shows a view of the interior of the Washington State Coliseum building. Inside stood a huge, free-form structure composed of 3,700 aluminum cubes, each 4-foot square, bolted together and standing midair on slender

1986, p. B-6. *Illus. A description of the Heritage USA theme park in Fort Mill, South Carolina.*

"IllumiNations Puts World Showcase in Brand New Light!" The New York Times, March 6, 1988. Advertisement on p. 2 of Amusement section. Photographs of and text describing "IllumiNations" at Epcot Center in Florida: "presented by GE . . . it happens every evening . . . [and involves] a visual treat [with] 25 computer systems, synchronized special effects projectors, lasers, searchlights, fountains, fireworks, strobelights and over 50,000 lightbulbs."

Kings Productions advertisement in Theatre Crafts, *vol. 20, no. 8 (Oct. 1986), pp. 63. Kings Productions during 1987 produced 50 shows with a budget over $8 million for industrial clients (AT&T, Procter & Gamble, IBM, etc.), as well as productions at their six theme parks: Kings Island in Cincinnati, Kings Dominion in Richmond, Carowinds in Charlotte, Great America near San Francisco, Canada's Wonderland in Toronto, and Australia's Wonderland in Sydney.*

Imero Fiorentino, "The Spruce Goose, Long Beach," International Lighting Review, *37th year (4th quarter 1986), pp. 128–131. Illus., color.*

[196] *J. Robert Wills, "Mass Audience Entertainment Events,"* Theatre Design & Technology, *vol. 13, no. 1 (Spring 1977), pp. 9–13.*

[197] *See:*

"Space-Age Wonders in Seattle," Life, *vol. 52, no. 6 (Feb. 9, 1962), pp. 74–75.*

"Fabulous Fair in Seattle," Life, *vol. 52, no. 18 (May 4, 1962), pp. 30–39.*

Frank J. Taylor, "The Show of Tomorrow," Saturday Evening Post, *vol. 234, no. 47 (November 25, 1961), pp. 36, 38, 42, 45.*

Carolyn Bennett Patterson, "Seattle Fair Looks to the 21st Century," National Geographic, *vol. 122, no. 3 (Sept. 1962), pp. 402–427.*

Figure 9.1   Aerial view of Seattle World's Fair grounds, now a part of the Seattle Center.

Figure 9.2   Interior cube structure of *Century 21.*

steel support columns. There were reflective water pools underneath, which were illuminated with over 100 R-40 Spots with revolving color wheels concealed in the open underside of selected cubes. The reflective pools constantly, subtly changed color.

At the audience assembly point stood a waiting "Bubbleator," shown in Fig. 9.3. (As the picture shows, the holes in some cubes' housings concealed lights and projectors.) The Bubbleator was a plexiglass ball operating on a vertical drive shaft (plunger) as an elevator to raise 100 people at a time up inside the cube structure. As the passengers ascended, the narrator's voice (on tape) intoned: "Utopia Century 21 . . . First Floor, threats and thresholds, frustrations and fulfillments, challenges and opportunities. . . ." [198] Using concealed overhead 5-Kilowatt Fresnels, the interior of the plastic Bubbleator changed from pearly light to pink as control panel lights twinkled. It changed again to amber as the audience exited. The entire inside of the cube structure consisted of a series of winding pathways threading through futuristic glimpses of Seattle in 2001: a twenty-first-century home, and the work, education, transportation, and leisure of the future. Taped narration with music was the background, but the actual physical movement of each group of 100 people through the length of the structure (seven groups were inside at seven different points at any one time) was controlled *solely* by the device of areas illuminating just ahead of the group and dying out behind them. In

Figure 9.3   "Bubbleator" rising into maze of cubes. (*Photo:* © *National Geographic Society*)

Figure 9.4 Cubes with rear projections. (*Photo: © National Geographic Society*)

early design conferences we decided that the compulsive human tendency to move toward lights and away from darkness would be sufficient for crowd control —and it worked! As the groups progressed through the structure, the narration was reinforced by 4-foot cube sections concealing interior color transparencies lighting up and by massive "time-of-day and weather" changes projected by light (clouds, snowfall, sunset, sunrise, night, dawn) taking place and constantly changing in a given area (see Fig. 9.4). The second area, for example, contained a recessed 60-foot diameter miniature model of Seattle as it might look in 2001 A.D. Constructed over many months at a cost of $250,000, this lifelike model had moving autos and buildings which lighted up at night in a complete sequence from night through day into sunset and back to night. The theme script tied together links with the past (seen in lighted cube transparencies) and glimpses into the future. Twinkling stars (thousands of them), huge bursts of flowers, lightning and warfare and shellbursts, a mirror chamber, sunlight through the trees, actual model airplanes flying on tracker wires over

audience's heads, Christmas trees (inside cubes)—these and many other effects known to theatrical lighting designers and graphics, model, and special-effects experts were combined. The total budget in 1962 (for lighting equipment only) was $300,000. Over 200 electricians worked on the installation and focus. The RCA-built sequential time controller (which was quite unlike today's more sophisticated memory switchboards) took two weeks to program for 226 cues with overlapping, differing time-sequence changes programmed throughout the structure. Color Fig. 75, a sketch by artist Stanley Neltzoff, depicts the "feel" of the exhibit. In Fig. 9.4 it can be seen that some transparencies extend throughout the surface of several adjacent cubes.

Figure 9.5 shows a portion of the instrument schedule. It would be impossible to reproduce the "light plot" since it consisted of several hundred scaled drawings of the cube arrangements (to scale) in both vertical and horizontal views with lighting equipment indicated inside each cube. There were also many pages of cue sheet guides and programmer time-sequence duration charts. Three draftsman worked all night (with daytime jobs at Century Lighting, Inc.) for two months preparing finished plates from my "roughs."

Designers encounter unique problems on a job of this scale. In one afternoon I received two rush phone calls from engineers requesting me to supply the following data: (1) How many BTUs (British Thermal Units) of heat would the total mass of over 1,500 lights create during the span each was lighted? and (2) What was to be the total weight of *all* lighting equipment within the cube structure (instruments, cable runs, switchboard-controller, accessories)? By phoning Century and having them run heat tests on some typical lighting units, I was able to supply a workable answer. Since the air conditioning proved to be adequate, the estimates must have been accurate. (I have since learned from Frank A. Florentine of the Smithsonian Institute, National Air and Space Museum in Washington, D.C., that each watt of electrical energy in light generates 3.1415 BTUs). Century engineers also provided weights of typical units, cable runs of selected lengths, etc. The resulting slender steel columns specified by the structural engineers did support the struc-

Key No.	Unit Type	Accessories	Wattage	Color	Location	Function	Cue No.	Weight	Control CCT. No.	Lamp Life	Cost Unit	Dim.
1	12" Lekolite Century #1540	Funnel - Color Frame 8" Long - 12" Lens	5000 W	517 & 536	Cube 1/7-24 These cubes open top - bottom	Pearly light on Bubblelator	1	200 lbs.		75 Hrs.	$800	1
2	12" Lekolite Century #1540	Funnel - Color Frame 8" Long - 12" Lens	5000 W	517 & 536	Cube 1/7-22 This cube open top - bottom	Pearly light on Bubblelator	1	200 lbs		75 Hrs.	$800	2
3	Twinkle lites Oscilloscope Flashers (Xmas tree types)	Control Panel in Bubblelator	Approx 500W Total	Various	Control panel in Bubblelator	Control panel effect	Initiated by operator push button	Negligable	Operated by actor	Various		No dim
4	12" Lekolite Century #1540	Funnel - Color Frame 8" Long for 12" Lens	5000 W	507	Cube 1/8-22 Cube open top - bottom	Bubblelator rises 10'-0" Changes color to pink	4	200 lbs.		75 Hrs	$800	3
5	12" Lekolite Century #1540	Funnel - Color Frame 8" Long for 12" Lens	5000 W	507	Cube 1/8-24 Cube open top - bottom	Bubblelator rises 10'-0" Changes interior color to pink	4	200 lbs.		75 Hrs	$800	4
						Bubblelator door closed begins rise, controlled by operator	2-3		Actor			
6	14" Featherlite Century #554	Concentric spill rings - color frame	5000W	533	Cube 1/8-25 Cube open top - bottom	Bubblelator rises 20'-0" changes interior color to amber.	5	21 lbs.		500 Hrs	$230	5
7-47	40-20 Lamp Starburst twinkle lamp strings	From Noel Mfg. Co. #UL3610-20. Transformer comes with each string	5W per string 800W Total	No color	Cubes 1/1-3, 1/2-9, 11, 12, 1/3-12, 14, 18, 1/4-14, 16, 17, 19	Star Burst	5			Long	Approx $6 per string Total $240	6
					1/5-14, 16, 19, 20, 22, 1/6-15, 17, 19, 20, 23, 25, 1/7-15, 18, 21, 25, 29	Twinkle light	5 Low Reading	Negligable		"		
					1/8-16, 19, 20, 23, 30 1/9-17, 20, 22, 23, 24	Circuit for 1st Half	"			"		
					1/10-17 & 18 1/9 & 20, 23, 25 & 26 1/11-17 & 18 & 19 & 20 & 21 24 & 25	Of chamber appears	"			"		
					1/12-14 & 15 & 16 & 17, & 20 & 21 NOTE: All these cubes can be covered on three sides (leave top open for ventilation and access) with standard perforated grill facing.	In 60 cubes in varying densities - total of 800 individually blinking stars.	"			"		
48	Special effect Moving star proj.			None	Cubes 1/10-22 & fake below 22	Moving stars effect	5 Low Reading					7
49-67	19-6 Fresnels Century #520 or 500	Barn doors - 4 way color frames	500 W	533 (frost) (529)	Cubes 1/2-10 (open on bottom) Cubes 1/3-11, 19 (open on interior side) Cubes 1/5-15, 25 (open on interior side) Cubes 1/7-17, 27 (open on interior side) Cubes 1/9-16, 27 (open on interior side) Cubes 1/11-18, 26 (open on interior side) Cubes 1/13-13, 21 (open on interior side) Cube 1/8-16 (open on bottom) On top of cube 1/7-3 (under ramp) On top of cube 1/9-5 (under ramp) On top of cube 1/11-4 (under ramp) On top of cube 1/13-5 (under ramp) On top of cube 1/13-28 (under ramp)	Interior of cube structure lights up in amber.	5	12 lbs.		500 Hrs.	$34 each Total $646	8-9
68	1-8' Featherlite Century #546	Barn doors - 4 way	2000 W		On top of cube 1/11-42 (under ramp)	Interior of cube structure lights up in amber.	5	12 lbs each		800 Hrs.	$130	10
69-87	19-6' Fresnel Century #520 or 500	Barn doors - 4 way color frames	500 W	505A & Frost (529)	Cubes 1/2-10, 1/3-11, 19 1/5-15, 25, 1/7-11, 27 open on interior sides 1/9-16, 27, 1/11-18, 26 1/13-13, 21 On top of cubes 1/7-3, 1/9-5 1/11-4, 1/13-4, 1/13-28 under ramp Cube 1/8-16 open at bottom	Interior changes to deeper orange	6 Med. reading	12 lbs each		500 Hrs.	$34 each Total $646	11-12
88	1-8' Featherlite Century #546	Barn doors - 4 way color frames	2000W	505A & Frost (529)	On top of cube 1/11-42 under ramp	Interior of cube structure changes to deeper orange	6 Med. reading	12 lbs.		800 Hrs.	$130	13
89	Motor driven sequentially lighted slimline tubes in floor	Tubes light up progressively under translucent false floor.		None	Under false flooring - translucent	As Bubblelator doors open - leads audience into chamber	7		Sequential motor drive impulse actuated	Lengthy		No dim actuation
						Orange circuit up full (Key No. 89-108) maybe Amber circuit out (Key No. 69-88) Bubblelator descends. Return to pearly light for loading (Key Nos. 1-2)	8					11, 12, 13 ↑ 7, 8, 9 ↓ 1, 2, ↑
90-108	19-6' Fresnels Century 500 or 520	Barn doors - 4 way color frames	750 W	520 & Frost (529)	Cubes 1/2-10, 1/3-11, 19 1/5-15, 25, 1/7-17, 27 open on interior sides 1/9-16, 27, 1/11-18, 26 1/13-13, 21 Cubes (on top of) 1/7-3, 1/9-5 1/11-4, 1/13-4, 1/13-28 under ramp Cube 1/3-16 (open at bottom)	Amber & orange circuits out, (dims 7-13) stars up higher (dims 6-7) interior of cube structure becomes deep blue	9	12 lbs. each		500 Hrs	$34 each Total $346	14, 15, 16
109	1-8' Featherlite Century #546	Barn doors - 4 way color frames	2000W	520 & Frost (529)	On top of cube 1/11-42 (under ramp)	Interior of cube structure becomes deep blue	9	12 lbs		800 Hrs.	$130	17
110	Quartz line lamps in cross in lucite	Special effect	2000W Approx	None	Below cube 1/7-17B	Single bright star comes on.	9			2000 Hrs.		18

Figure 9.5 Century 21, "World of Tomorrow" cue schedule.

ture adequately, so the weight estimate must have been correct. I have always suspected that the engineers to whom I gave the information added a healthy extra "safety factor," just as I did prior to supplying the estimates. These actual cases illustrate the offbeat type of information which has little or nothing to do with lighting design but which may be within the scope of a designer working on a design assignment of this size.

Obviously this is the type of lighting design assignment a designer dreams of. Unfortunately there are few such opportunities in a lifetime. Fellow designers could recount similar design challenges with the New York World's Fair of 1964; the San Antonio Hemisfair or the 1979 Canadian National Exposition; the 1982 Knoxville, Tennessee, Fair; and the 1984 New Orleans Fair. One of the most recent projects of this magnitude is the permanent Great Savannah Exposition in Savannah, Georgia.[199]

Son et Lumiére

The first sound and light — son et lumiére — show was produced in France. French architect Paul-Robert Houdin, in residence at the Chateau de Chambord in the Valley of the Loire, created the first such show in 1952. Son et lumiéres gradually spread throughout Europe — some good, some poor imitations of the original. None seemed to endure for any long period of time.[200] Light and sound shows have not been of much importance in the United States so far. The best-known ones in this country were Jean Rosenthal's work at Boscobel, New York, and the reconstruction and addition of a son et lumiére show at the same time in the Ford Theatre in Washington, D.C., by David Mintz and Charles Levy.[201] Both are no longer in operation. This is a form of spectacle (combined with great visual artistic imagination) whose time has not come yet in the United States.

According to Rosenthal, son et lumiére "is used to people the darkness through the imagination, not to create effects for their own sake." [202] TABS magazine said that "the aim of the lighting designer in Son et Lumiére is to capture the attention of the audience and to direct their attention in such a way as to complement the spoken words and to show the structure in a new and revealing fashion." [203] Robin Close, writing about British sound and light produc-

[199] "Exhibitions: Expo '86: Images of an Exhibition," International Lighting Review, 37th year (4th quarter 1986). pp. 122–125. Illus., color.

"Exhibitions: B.C. Pavilion, Vancouver," International Lighting Review, 37th year (4th quarter 1986), pp. 125–127.

C. M. Cutler, "Why a Fair," Light magazine, vol. 33, no. 2 (1964), pp. 11–24. Whole issue devoted to the New York World's Fair. Excellent text and illustrations, many in color.

"Expo '67," Light magazine, vol. 36, no. 2 (1967), entire issue. Twenty pages with color photos. Good summary treatment of one major expo.

James R. Benya, "Ghosts of the Globe at the Canadian National Exhibition — Lightning bolts, trap doors into the depths of hell, bursts of flame and smoke, "animation" by light and color — all are a part of this 2200-cue, 32-minute production," Lighting Design & Application, vol. 9, no. 1 (Jan. 1979), pp. 12–15. Color photographs and text narrate the design of Michael Hooker & Associates, Oak Park, Illinois.

Caskie Stinnett, "Water, Whimsy and All That Jazz," Signature, May 1984, pp. 75, 77–79, 107 ff. Illus., color. General discussion of the 1984 New Orleans World's Fair.

William E. Schmidt, "The Desolate Legacy of Knoxville's World's Fair," The New York Times, May 18, 1984, p. 8. Illus. Summary review of the financial disaster of the Knoxville Fair.

Douglas Welch, "Inside and Out Expo 86: Three Challenges in Vancouver," Lighting Design + Application, vol. 17, no. 1 (Jan. 1987), pp. 24–25, 50–51. Illus., color.

"Ice Palace Grows With Momentary Magic," Lighting Design + Application, vol. 16, no. 10 (Oct. 1986), pp. 30–31. Illus., color. An IES Edwin M. Guth Memorial Award of Excellence winner in the lighting of the 1986 St. Paul (Minnesota) Winter Carnival Ice Palace by designers Patricia Hunt and Charles Hopwood.

"Lighting an Olympiad of Art," Lighting Dimensions, vol. 8, no. 6 (Sept./Oct. 1985), pp. 36–46. Illus., color. Includes light plot. Elaborate lighting of the 1984 Los Angeles Olympics, much by designer John De Santis.

"The Sign is a Star," Lighting Dimensions, vol. 8, no. 6 (Sept./Oct. 1985), pp. 53–55, 57. Illus., color. More about the Hollywood Olympics.

Richard Harris, "EXPO 86, Vancouver Makes an Exhibition of Itself," Cue, no. 42 (July/Aug. 1986), pp. 14–15. Illus.

Chris Heath, "Southern Exposure: A World's Fair Below the Mason-Dixon Line Opens in — Of All Places — Knoxville, Tennessee," Signature, May 1982, pp. 39–44. Illus., color. Not only summarizes the Knoxville Fair but has brief treatment, with photographs, of the Chicago 1933 Century of Progress, the 1958 Brussels World's Fair, 1962's Century 21 in Seattle, the 1964 New York World's Fair, Expo '67 in Montreal, and Expo '70 in Osaka, Japan — all in color.

Kathy Matter, "Kings Island Doesn't Go into Hibernation in Winter," Lafayette Journal & Courier, November 25, 1988. Illus.

Michael Sommers, "Centerline: John Haupt," Theatre Crafts, vol. 23, no. 3 (March 1989), p. 14. Information about John Haupt, Disney's chief lighting design/show production head in Florida, with photograph.

Mark Loeffler, "Disney Deslights," Lighting Dimensions, vol. 12, no. 3 (April 1988), p. 17. Illus. Further information about the Disney–General Electric IllumiNations light show in the Epcot Center lagoon in Florida.

"Coasting and Sliding at 12 of America's Amusement Parks," The New York Times, Travel section, August 13, 1989. pp. 14–16, 18–19. Illus. Covers: New Jersey's "Great Adventure;" Pennsylvania's "Dorney Park" in Allentown; "Water Country U.S.A." in Williamsburg, Virginia; "Adventure Island" in Tampa, Florida; "Six Flags Over Glorgia" in Atlanta; "Astroworld" in Houston, Texas; "Worlds of Fun" and "Oceans of Fun" in Kansas City, Missouri; "Cedar Point" in Sandusky, Ohio; "Kings Island" in Kings Island, Ohio' "Knott's Berry Farm" in Buena Park, California; "Great America" in Santa Clara, California; "Enchanted Parks" and "Wild Waves" in Seattle, Washington.

Fred Loessel, "Theme Parks," Lighting Dimensions, vol. 13, no. 1 (January/February 1989), p. 14. A report on the Lighting Dimensions International '88 conference session containing a panel discussion by William Barbour (Landmark Entertainment Group), John Haupt (Disney), Don McCrary (Battaglia Associates). McCrary discussed a 19-acre facility completely enclosed by a skylight, being built by Battaglia in South Korea.

Peter McLean, "World Expo '88, Brisbane," International Lighting Review, *40th year, 1st quarter 1989, pp. 21–25. Illus., color. Description of a winter exposition in Australia which leaned heavily upon lighting design.*

[200] *I have located records of the following: "The Creation of Ancient Athens" at the Acropolis in Athens, Greece; Greenwich Observatory, London, England; "The Story of Istanbul," Istanbul, Turkey; "Shade of Glory" at Invalides, France; Belvedere Palace in Vienna, Austria; Merimere Castle in Trieste, Italy; Gruuthuse Museum in Bridges, Belgium; "Saga of the Sword and Cross" at Middlebury Abby, Province of Zeeland, Holland; Palace of the Grand Master, Rhodes, Greece; Strasbourg Cathedral, Biarretz, France; Luxembourg; The Hague, Holland and Neckar-Steinch, Germany. In the United States: "The Thomas Wolfe Home, Ashville, North Carolina; Boscobel, New York; "Lincoln" in Springfield, Illinois (the only one active at this writing); Ford's Theatre in Washington, D.C.; "The Father of Liberty" at Independence Hall, Philadelphia, Pennsylvania (1976); George Washington Home in Mt. Vernon, Virginia. There was a brief sound and light show (with fireworks) which ran from May 24 through October 10 of 1985 in New York City to celebrate the anniversary of the Brooklyn Bridge, called "The Eighth Wonder." The sound and light spectacle called "Jerash" opened in the Jordanian desert in 1983. John Jacobson, Yale graduate of 1969, and president of White Oak Design, a firm specializing in sound and light shows, designed "Timespell" for the Watkins Glen State Park in New York in 1979 and "The World of Shakespeare," a pageant at Stratford-Upon-Avon, England (from Yale Drama Alumni Newsletter, Fall 1973). See also Harry Ryan, "Watkins Glen Adds Light Show," Indianapolis Star, September 4, 1983, p. 10E, illus. A more recent sound and light show opened during August 1984 at Hampton Court Palace outside London (see Keith H. Hammonds, "Sound and Light on Henry VIII and Company," The New York Times, August 12, 1984, p. 3 in Leisure section; illus.). Also there was a Son et Lumiére at Wake Forest University in North Carolina in 1985 and one at Stone Mountain in Georgia.*

Sarah Stoddart, "Son et Lumiére," Travel and Leisure, June 1980, pp. 58–59. Illus. Lists attractions internationally. Performance details available are given.

"Europe's Sound and Light Pageantry," The New York Post, *June 3, 1975, p. 36.*

J. H. Jensen, "Celebrating . . . 50 Years of Nela Park," Light *magazine, vol. 32, no. 3 (1963), pp. 14–21. Lavish color illustrated and text of General Electric's Son et Lumiére.*

Jean Rosenthal and Lael Wertenbaker, The Magic of Light. *Boston; Little, Brown and Co.; 1972. Chapter 8: Lighting the House. Light Plot and text for Jean Rosenthal's Son et Lumiére design for a Hudson River house in Boscobel, New York. (lighting done in 1963). Describes her work and Clyde Nordheimer's. A thorough analysis of sound and light production values and of evolution of the script. Boscobel's sound and light show no longer exists.*

"Stone Mountain Comes Alive," Lighting Dimensions, *vol. 9, no. 1 (Jan./Feb. 1985), pp. 42–43, 45, 47, 49. Illus., color. Includes light plot. Details of a recent sound and light show at Stone Mountain, Georgia.*

Steve Pollock, "Son et Lumiére at Wake Forest University," Theatre Crafts, *vol. 19, no. 3 (Mar. 1985), pp. 10, 66–67. Illus. Details about the Wake Forest University sesquicentennial sound and light show at Winston-Salem, North Carolina, by designer Howell Binkley.*

Sarah Shankman, "Egyptian Temples of Philae Celebrated in Son et Lumiére, Third Century BC temples reclaimed from Nile (Egypt)," Lighting Design + Application, *vol. 16, no. 4 (April 1986), pp. 13–15. Illus., color.*

David I. Taylor, "A Television Son et Lumiére As a Teaching Tool for Lighting Directors: David I. Taylor Reports on His Trip to Iraqi Television in Baghdad," ALD Newsletter, *no. 4 (April 1987), pp. 9–12. Illus. Light plot in Iraqi.*

"Son et Lumiére in Geneva," Electrosonic World, *no. 4, p. 6. Illus. A Son et Lumiére production done in Geneva, Switzerland, in 1986 to celebrate the 450th Anniversary of the Reformation in Geneva.*

See also "A City in Concert," *footnote 193.*

"A Futuristic History Lesson: The history of Quebec was written on the walls of Parliment last summer in an award-winning presentation of sound, light, and lasers," Lighting Dimensions, *vol. 9, no. 4 (July/Aug. 1985), pp. 32–34, 36. Illus., color.*

Simon Corder, "Hot Nights Out East, Staging Fragile Forest in Singapore Zoo," Sightline, *vol. 23, no. 1 (January 1989). pp. 22–25. Illus. A son et lumiere in Singapore.*

A show of the 20-year history of Lincoln Center in New York City opened May 21, 1979. Designed by Robert Rubinawitz and Bob Gill (film), Christ Langhart (sound), John Chester, and Jim Hamilton. George Tresohler, Associate Producer. It ran 35 minutes each weekend. (Information from Bob Gill in phone conversation on July 9, 1979.)

[201] David A. Mintz and Charles Levy, "Ford's Theatre Sound and Light Presentation," *Lighting Design & Application, vol. 1, no. 2 (Aug. 1971), pp. 27–30. Complete technical description of equipment used for one of the few Son et Lumiéres in the United States in 1970.*

"Automated Theatre, the Sound and Light Show at Ford's Theatre," Theatre Crafts, *vol. 5, no. 2 (Mar./Apr. 1971), pp. 28–31. Designed by David Mintz, Charles Levy, and Roger Morgan.*

[202] Rosenthal, p. 110, *op. cit. (see footnote 200).*

[203] "The Church Visible," TABS, *vol. 34, no. 2 (Summer 1976), pp. 14–16. Illus., color. Includes light plot. Guy Hawkins's Son et Lumiére at St. Nicholas Church in Sturry, England, performed with rented lighting equipment.*

tions, stated: "It is a static medium, more suited to the painter and radio producer than the many who undertake it. . . . nothing 'happens' except in the audience's imagination. . . . Lamps are tools used to create atmosphere, effect, to heighten the meaning of the words — all by painting pictures that constantly change."[204]

I saw the production of *son et lumiére* at the Royal Greenwich Observatory on the outskirts of London in the fall of 1973. This one-hour presentation with 12 historical scenes and an epilogue hardly stands in my memory as satisfying, but perhaps the fact that it was raining with a bitter cold wind influenced my reaction.

Communication Forms

Since *son et lumiére* design assignments are few and far between, each designer does best just to utilize a workable combination of standard theatre light plot and architectural plot practice. Controllers (switchboards) are different from one show to another, and even cue sheets are not standard.

Design Considerations

Robin Close suggests two vital rules:

1. Always remember *Son et Lumiére* is an abstract medium; a medium of illusion. It is not a play with the actors missing but an 'art' in its own right;

2. Never forget that boredom does not have to be worked for; but an audience's interest does.

Son et Lumiére can only succeed if it is treated as an entertainment.[205]

For the designer three items are paramount: (1) cost, (2) script, and (3) cues. Sound and light shows are very expensive to produce. A creative imagination, given a noble historic monument, can come up with unlimited ideas; however, the budget is not unlimited. Just as important as budget is close rapport between the script writer, the lighting designer, and the sound designer. Without real ability and teamwork on the part of all three, the project is destined for costly failure. Since there are no actors and the auditory portion is on tape, fluidity of light cues is essential

— not just for their own sake but to keep the story moving and to hold the audience's attention. *Son et Lumiére* is not for everyone; a negative view of it is presented by Fred Bentham in *The Art of Stage Lighting*.[206]

Techniques

Important is the availability on the site of sufficient power supply. Speaker locations and central control location must be decided early on. Lighting mounting positions *not visible to the audience* must be selected. Visible luminaires break the illusion. The audience should see without knowing *how*. The designer must make provision for adequate setup and installation time, sufficient time for focus and programming, and plenty of final rehearsal time. Multiple, simultaneous cues of sound, lights, and mechanized effects are not easily made "performance-smooth" on even the most versatile programmer. The audience area must not be lighted, and the audience should not be asked to either turn around or look high in the air for any length of time. Most sound and light shows happen within or near priceless historic buildings and monuments, and great care must be taken to avoid altering or damaging these heritages of the past when planning and mounting equipment.

Procedures and Practices

Robin Close's article "An Audience Will Accept Almost Anything Except Boredom," cited earlier, provides many practical tips (see footnote 204). Also available is a good article in *TABS* on *temporary* sound and light shows in British churches and cathedrals.[207] *Theatre Crafts* dealt at some length with *The Spokane Story,* a hybrid creation which combines elements of an industrial exhibition, a sound and light show, and a minor amusement park.[208] It remains to be seen if any artists — playwrights or environmental designers or lighting designers — will find a workable formula in the United States to popularize the sound and light form of artistry/spectacle.

At this writing there are two *son et lumiéres* in operation in the United States: (1) the story of the battleship *North Carolina* in Charlotte, North Carolina, and (2) the *Story of*

[204] Robin Close, "An Audience Will Accept Almost Anything Except Boredom," TABS, vol. 35, no. 1 (Spring 1977), p. 9.

[205] Ibid., p. 10.

[206] Frederick Bentham, The Art of Stage Lighting. N.Y.; Taplinger Publisher; 1969, 1st ed. Chap. 13 discusses colour music and Son et Lumiére (pp. 361–62). Brief comments.

[207] "The Church Visible," op. cit. (see footnote 203). See also "The Power of the Glory," Lighting Dimensions, vol. 8, no. 2 (Mar./Apr. 1984), pp. 42–47, 49. Illus., color. Includes light plot. A useful description of Ken Billington's lighting of an annual Easter religious pageant in the Crystal Cathedral at Garden Grove, California. Sets by Charles Lisanby. Opened April 1, 1984, it includes 14 tableaux in a one-and-a-half-hour presentation. This is a true spectacle using lights, lasers, and strobes in a huge space.

[208] F. A. Rothschild, "The Spokane Story, A New Approach to Computerized Exhibitry and Multi-media Control," Theatre Crafts, vol. 13, no. 2 (Mar./Apr. 1979), pp. 32–33, 90–94. The story of Riverfront Park's renovation for Spokane's 100th anniversary on Hovermale Island. While this was also a part of Expo '74, it is a series of 13 exhibits through which the audience moves in a one-hour show. This $6 ½ million exhibit opened 10 hours per day in 1979 with 1,200 cues. Technical details explained at length.

[210] *William Keller generously supplied the following information:*

In a small room 25 feet under the stone walk at Old Capitol's south gate, a sophisticated electronic control unit activates Sound and Light at the Old State Capitol. A one-inch, 8-track tape unwinds at 15 inches per second playing a control track and six separate audio tracks. Voices, sound effects, and music are played so that the sound actually moves from one place to another. The unit's computer console "reads" the control track of the 3400-foot-long tape for cues to activate thousands of sound and light effects through the eleven speakers and the more than 160 exterior and interior lighting fixtures.

The Old State Capitol was the principal forum of Abraham Lincoln's public life for the twenty years that ended in 1861 with his departure for Washington and the Presidency. . . . Sound and Light was produced by Guggenheim Productions, Inc., of Washington, D.C. The story is narrated by the late Lee J. Cobb — it was his last professional performance.

[211] *"Sound and Light Spectacle 'Jerash,' Special Effects Bring the Ancient World to Life in the Jordanian Desert,"* Lighting Design + Application, *vol. 13, no. 9 (Sept. 1983), pp. 12–16. Illus., color. Well-illustrated article about the newest* Son et Lumiére *spectacle in Jordan.*

Peter Applebome, "Sound-and-Light Show on a Scale Fit for Houston," The New York Times, *April 7, 1986, Chicago ed. p. 8. Illus.*

New York City's *"Urban Light Show" was sponsored by the Illuminating Engineering Society's New York Section and the International Association of Lighting Designers. See "Urban Lights,"* IALD Newsletter, *Oct. 1985, p. 1.*

[212] *A listing of indoor arenas in the United States can be found in the annual* Audareana Stadium, International Guide & Directory, *published annually by the Amusement Business*

Lincoln at the Old State Capitol Plaza in Springfield, Illinois.[210] The latter was designed by Hugh Lester, formerly of Washington, D.C. (see Fig. 9.6). It is open six nights per week in the summer and is free to the public. It was conceived by the Illinois State Historical Library and is operated by them. The newest show abroad is *The Henry VIII Son et Lumiére* at Hampton Court Palace in London. What is becoming popular in the United States are one-night *son et lumiéres* celebrating a special event with lasers, fireworks, and sound. Such was the *Urban Light* show celebrating New York City's Bicentennial, November 6–9, 1985.[211]

Ice Shows

Few other entertainment forms depend upon spectacle more extensively than do ice shows. Large skating areas are common (40 feet by 150 feet is not unusual).[212] Some smaller ice shows perform on restricted rinks in Las Vegas or Atlantic City and as nightclub acts, but large arenas (seating 15 to 30 thousand) or large legitimate theatres are more common as performance places. Ice performance has a long history of extensive use of top-quality lighting design.

Design Considerations

Lighting for ice shows must consider the massive audiences and the necessity for clear, crisp visibility of the graceful and skillful performances of the skaters, particularly for solos and duets. The rapid mass movement involved in skating adds another challenge for the lighting designer. *Selective visibility* (focus of the audience's attention on where the action is in the skating space) is important, and color, splash, pomp, and pageantry also come into play. Little attention is directed toward detailed visibility of the performer's face. This broadening of scale causes the designer to concentrate upon mass effect. Strong use of both color and intensity contrasts between solo performers and the mass of skaters around the solo artists (or a darkened rink) is important. An overall pattern of color and intensity variations is needed to structure the show (usually the show format alternates between intimate acts, such as a comedy act or a specialty

Figure 9.6 *Son et Lumiére* production at the Old State Capital Plaza in Springfield, Illinois. (*Photo: © William Keller, Illinois State Historical Library*)

duo, and full-rink production numbers. Lighting design practices for ice shows most closely resemble practices used in theatrical arena production; areas, specials, color washes, and effects predominate. In addition to being concerned about lighting design, the designer is inevitably concerned for the safety of the performers, who are moving at high speeds in a restricted area and must not be blinded by bright lights at low angles. Also, the skaters must know at all times the location of the edges of the skating rink.

Communication Forms

The standard light plot and hookup are used. Cue sheets are very important. Not only are there numerous light changes on exact cues, but also up to 20 powerful followspots are often used. Since the design pattern involves frequent color changes plus rapid switches from following a soloist to widening to cover a mass of skaters, design imagination and calling followspot cues is at the heart of most good ice show lighting.

Figure 9.7 shows the 1979 season's light plot for all companies of *Ice Capades* (several identical companies are out on the road throughout the year). Dick Troxler (staff designer/electrician) plans and assembles all *Ice Capades* road

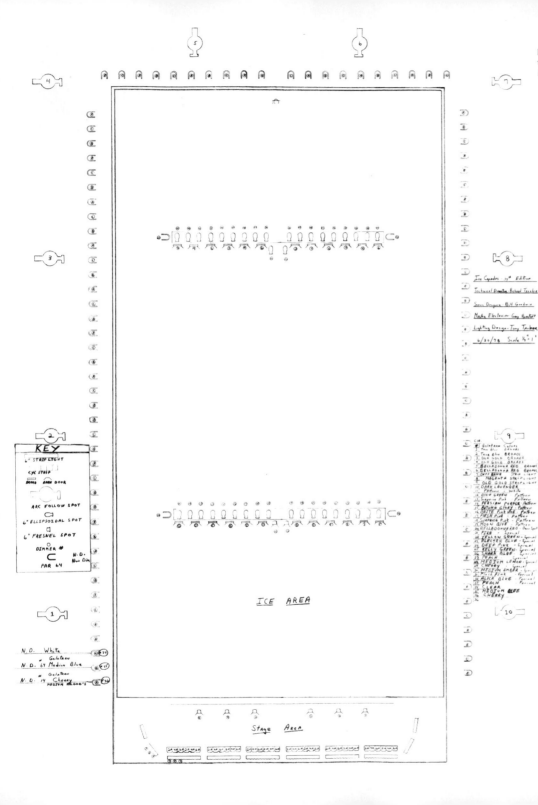

KEY

6" STRIP LIGHT

CYC STRIP

BARNS BARN DOOR

ARC FOLLOW SPOT

6" ELLIPSOIDAL SPOT

6" FRESNEL SPOT

DIMMER #   N.D.
                  Non Dim
PAR 64

ICE AREA

Stage Area

N.D. White
    " Gelatran
N.D. 64 Medium Blue
    " Gelatran
N.O. 14 Cherry
    MEDIUM FLOOD'S

Figure 9.7 Light plot for *Ice Capades,* 1979. Lighting: Tony Tauber; technical director: Dick Troxler. This was the 39th edition of the East Company show.

Figure 9.8 Metromedia production of Robert Turk's *Ice Capades,* 1979. Scene design: Bill Goodwin; lighting: Tony Tauber; costumes: David Doucette; technical director: Dick Troxler. The 39th edition of the East Company show. (*Photo: Larry Secrist, Grafcom & Associates*)

Division of Billboard Publications, Inc., 1515 Broadway, New York, NY 10036.

See also:

Anita Finkel, "Choreography on Ice Comes to the Metropolitan," The New York Times, Leisure section, p. 7. Illus. About John Curry's work.

"Edinburgh International Festival," TABS, vol. 33, no. 1 (Spring 1975), p. 13. Illus., color. British ice rink lighting.

[213] *This history is excerpted and revised from "Lighting the Ice Capades," Lighting Dimensions, vol. 8, no. 1 (Jan./Feb. 1984), pp. 18–25. Illus., color. Includes light plot. Three pages of color photos of Ice Capades productions and technology and an interview and light plot by current lighting designers Marilyn Lowey and Aubrey Wilson.*

[214] *"New Black Magic," Collier's, vol. 134, no. 5 (September 3, 1954), pp. 56–57.*

[215] *Radiant Rink," Life, vol. 34, no. 2 (January 12, 1953), p. 38.*

"A Movie Plus . . ." New York Sunday News, March 1, 1953, pp. 16–17 (Rotogravure section).

companies at their California home base each year. Figure 9.8 is a production photo.

Ice Capades has been around for 44 years. The first professional ice revue was produced by Frank Bearing in 1914 at Chicago's Sherman Hotel. In 1915 Broadway impresario Charles Dillingham froze the 45- by 90-foot stage of the New York Hippodrome to present the original skating musical, *Flirting at San Moritz,* starring Charlotte Oelschlagel. Oelschlagel later appeared in the first skating film, a six-part serial called *The Frozen Warning.*

Sonja Henie, from Oslo, Norway, revived ice shows as a popular attraction when she first appeared in the United States in 1936. Holder of 10 world, 10 European, and 3 Olympic championships, she began a film career with *One in a Million.* Many more skating films starring Henie followed. America's first *touring* skating show, which was opened in 1936 by Oscar Johnson and Eddie and Roy Shipstad, was called *Ice Follies.* Shortly thereafter Sonja Henie appeared in a rival touring show, *Hollywood Ice Revue,* produced by Chicago sportsman Arthur M. Wirtz. This production also appeared annually at New York's Center Theatre from 1940 to 1950.

On Valentine's Day, 1940, several arena owners, including John H. Harris, met in Hershey, Pennsylvania and formed the original *Ice Capades,* which is still running today. In 1964, Metromedia, a broadcasting and entertainment company, bought *Ice Capades.*[213]

Techniques

The catalog of rather common special effects used in ice shows is extensive: (1) black light (ultraviolet) production numbers,[214] (2) use of both motion picture projection (most frequently combined with the "living screen" technique popularized by Ralph Alswang, in which the screen is made up of vertical strips through which a skater can pass) and gobo patterns, (3) costumes or accessories in a production number festooned with miniature light bulbs and battery packs concealed within the skater's costume — all to suddenly light up on cue as the other illumination is doused or dimmed, and (4) the standard mirror ball, flash pots, and explosions (popular in both fairy-tale witches' scenes and science-fiction numbers). Fog and smoke are rarely used, since they tend to disorient the skaters. Fire and lightning seem to have no proper place.

Base lighting, sometimes controllable by areas, frequently comes from either the older beam projector – type units or the newer PAR lamps. Often these are the in-place house units at each arena played. Sometimes an ice show supplements house equipment with additional units of its own. All too frequently the base lights are mounted directly over the skating area and become "downlights," rather than the more desirable 45° angle lights used in theatre. Almost always they are colored in very bland, standard pastels: blue, pink, straw or amber, and clear. Stronger color comes only from the followspots. A few companies may carry a limited number or more specialized ellipsoidals or Fresnels, to be used either as specials or to further boost the intensity of the center area. If the designer has 20 followspots available, there is much that can be done. Ice shows are noted for brilliant and imaginative use of strong color contrast (spots on different parts of the perimeter of the arena covering the same target, in contrasting colors). This use of strong color, combined with extreme precision and frequent color changes, is the major element enhancing spectacle.

One other special effect deserves mention. Various ice shows have frozen either neon tubes or fluorescent tubes in several different colors *within* the ice itself (neon is more common).[215] This must be done prior to freezing the rink. It allows the designer to play a wide range of spectacular design tricks: flashing colors, chasing color sequences, or simply providing a soft rosy glow (or icy blue, or cool green) from underneath the skaters which emanates from the ice itself. This device is time-consuming, takes lots of preplanning, and adds to the cost — but it gets the applause every time.

The designer must also be certain that the entire rink is surrounded by lights that look like footlights, but aren't. These lights are boxes with frosted glass coverings which contain circuits of colored lamps (many different types are used). Figure 9.9, depicting *Holiday on Ice,* shows these circuits. One of these circuits must remain on at all times, because the skaters "fix" or "guide" upon these footlights

Figure 9.9 *Holiday on Ice,* International, 24th edition. Lighting design: D. Scott Linder.

during high-speed spins, and the lights also help the skater know the safe usable dimensions of the rink. These lights do not ordinarily serve any important purpose in lighting either the skaters or the performance area.

Ice shows often consist of multiple touring companies. They are planned each year at a home location, and several identically planned shows then go "on the road" for the balance of the season. The companies carry scenery, costumes, props, and some lighting equipment and switchboards. Normally one to two days of setup time take place in each new city, followed by a week-long run (or longer in large metropolitan areas). The Disney organization often has an ice show on tour.

A second type of ice show is also common: the ice show presented in a standard proscenium theatre. Figures 9.10, 9.11, and 9.12 are Marilyn Rennagel's light plot and hookup for *Ice Dancing* at the Minskoff Theatre (New York City) in December 1978. Here the design approach is a hybrid one. Elements of the arena approach are combined with standard theatre lighting. The availability of legitimate theatre house mounting positions and the fact that the audience does not surround the rink allows more design freedom.

Ice show "bits" are inserted as part of some Las Vegas and Atlantic City revues, sometimes making up the major portion of the show. Such bits are not uncommon in night-club presentations. The lighting for these smaller rinks, which have a limited number of skaters, is often simply an adaptation of available lighting. Ice shows are also frequently televised.[216]

Circuses and Carnivals

If any entertainment form thrives on spectacle, it is circus. The history of circus lighting is both long and colorful.[217] Up until the 1840s adequate illumination and performer safety were the main lighting objectives. Torches and candles were used. Then gas lighting took over, with some use of the limelight. Electricity arrived when circuses were still playing under canvas, and many absorbing tales exist of portable generators and rapidly improvised, unsafe wiring.

E. Carlton Winckler cites John Murray Anderson's production of the Billy Rose musical *Jumbo,* at New York City's Hippodrome Theatre, as the real beginning of lighting design in the circus. The musical had a full complement of circus performers. Winckler was technical director. Norman Bel Geddes was also involved in early circus lighting.

When the big circuses (such as Ringling Bros. and Barnum & Bailey) moved indoors into the large arenas, circus lighting began to be similar to both ice show and arena lighting. General illumination from banks of floodlights (more recently PAR-64s) and Fresnels illuminated the three major rings and surrounding parade areas. In well-equipped arenas, these were pink, blue, and white. Amber was added for the center ring only. Less well equipped arenas tried to use mercury vapor lamps (which cannot be rapidly reignited once extinguished) and complete elimination of any color in floodlights. Merely sufficient visibility was often all that was possible. The ever-present arc follow-spots (a minimum of six, but preferably ten to twelve or more) became the standby for introducing richer color as well as directing focus to star and solo acts as needed.

Because *safety* for the performer tops all else in importance, such acts as teeterboard, trapeze, high-wire, and animal shows demand flat, bright illumination which does not hamper the performer's orientation. This has always meant lighting from very high angles. The literature is re-

[216] *For TV lighting of ice shows, see "Bill Klages" and "Pete Edwards,"* Lighting Dimensions, *vol. 1, no. 6. (Dec. 1977), pp. 25–36, 42.*

[217] *"The Grand, the Wonderful, the Amazing, and Ever Glorious Electric Circus Light,"* Theatre Crafts, *vol. 6, no. 4 (Sept. 1972), pp. 23–26, 40–42. This entire issue is devoted to the circus.*

"Circus," Lighting Dimensions, *vol. 1, no. 3 (Sept. 1977), pp. 20–36, 50. Extensive treatment of circus lighting for TV; history of circus lighting; an interview with Erich Powers, Lighting Director with Ringling Bros. and Barnum & Bailey Circus.*

Steve Brown, "Stand By . . . and Hit It," Lighting Dimensions, *vol. 1, no. 5 (Nov. 1977), pp. 54, 48.*

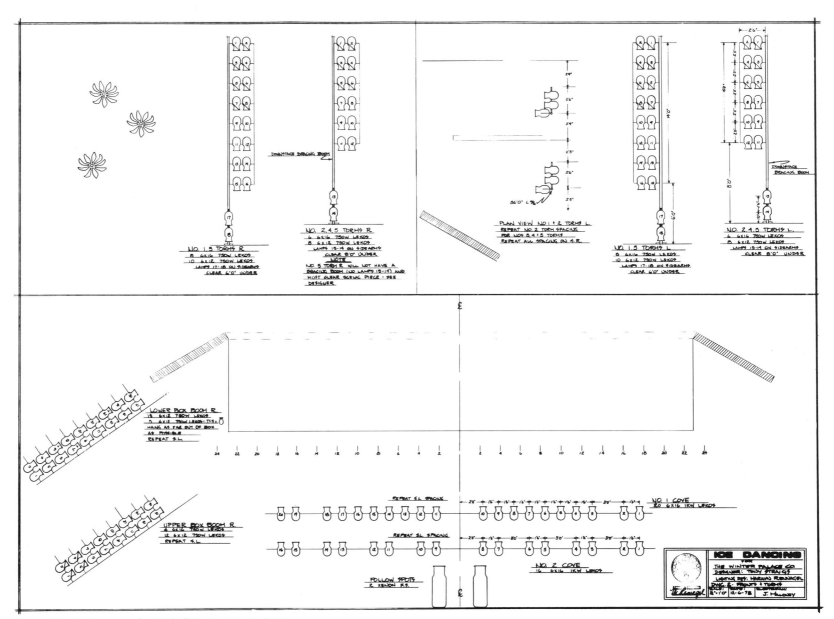

Figure 9.10 *Ice Dancing* at the Minskoff Theatre, New York City, December 1978. Scene design: Tony Straiges; lighting design: Marilyn Rennagel. Drawing of front-of-house and torm hanging positions.

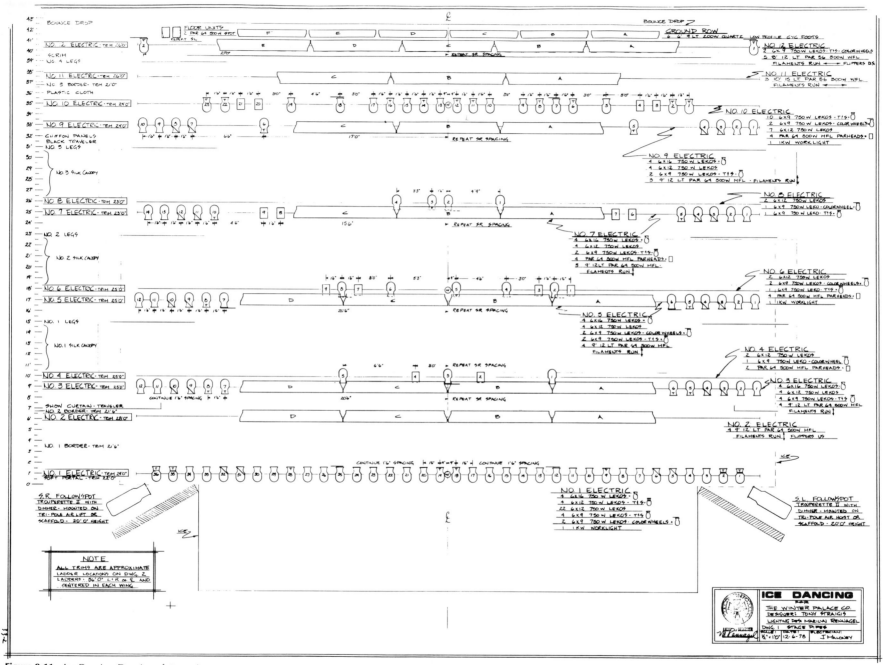

Figure 9.11 *Ice Dancing.* Drawing of stage pipes.

Figure 9.12 *Ice Dancing.* Switchboard hookup by Marilyn Rennagel.

"Ice Dancing" BDNY — REVISED 12-15-78 / 12-20-78 — 1 OF 4

HOOK-UP LIGHT PALETTE - 87 CONTROL CHANNELS

Left table:

CIRC	POSITION & UNIT NO.	TYPE	FOCUS	COL
31	No.1 Torm R 2-3-10-11	6x16/6x12 750WL	X	R17
32	No.1 Torm R 6-8-14-16	6x16/6x12 750WL	X	852
33*	No.2 Torm R 1-4-7-10 / No.3 Torm R 1-4-9-12	6x16/6x12 750WL	X	R58
34*	No.2 Torm R 2-3-8-9 / No.3 Torm R 2-3-10-11	6x16/6x12 750WL	X	R17
35	No.2 Torm R 5-6-11-12 / No.3 Torm R 6-8-14-16	6x16/6x12 750WL	X	852
36*	No.4 Torm R 1-4-7-10 / No.5 Torm R 1-4-7-10	6x16 750WL	X	R58
37*	No.4 Torm R 2-3-8-9 / No.5 Torm R 2-3-8-9	750WL	X	R17
38*	No.4 Torm R 5-6-11-12 / No.5 Torm R 5-6-11-12	6x16 750WL	X	852
39	No.1 Torm R 5-7-13-15	750WL	DIAG	R64
40	No.3 Torm R 5-7-13-15	6x16/6x12 750WL	DIAG	R64
41	No.1 Elec. 3-4-5-6	6x12 750WL	ENDS L	R03
42*	No.3 Elec. 1-2-3-4 / No.5 Elec. 1-2-3-4	6x12 750WL	ENDS L	R03
43*	No.7 Elec. 1-2-3-4 / No.9 Elec. 1-2-3-4	6x12 750WL	ENDS L	R03
44	No.1 Elec. 31-32-33-34	6x12 750WL	ENDS R	R80
45*	No.3 Elec. 9-10-11-12 / No.5 Elec. 9-10-11-12	6x12 750WL	ENDS R	R80
46*	No.7 Elec. 11-12-13-14 / No.9 Elec. 7-8-9-10	6x12 750WL	ENDS R	R80
47	No.2 Elec. A-D	8'12 LT PAR 56 300W Q HFL	BK-SIDES	126
48	No.2 Elec. B-C	"	BK-HID	126
49*	No.3 Elec. A-D / No.5 Elec. A-C	10'16 LT PAR 56 300W HFL	BK-SIDES	126
50*	No.3 Elec. B-C / No.5 Elec. B	"	BK-HID	126
51*	No.7 Elec. A-C / No.9 Elec. A-C	10'15 LT PAR 56 300W HFL	BK-SIDES	126
52	No.7 Elec. B / No.9 Elec. B	"	BK-HID	126
53	No.2 Elec. A-D	8'12 LT PAR 56 300W Q HFL	BK-SIDES	R79
54	No.2 Elec. B-C	"	BK-HID	R79
55*	No.3 Elec. A-D / No.5 Elec. A-C	8'12 LT PAR 56 300W HFL	BK-SIDES	R79
56*	No.3 Elec. B-C / No.5 Elec. B	"	BK-HID	R79
57*	No.7 Elec. A-C / No.9 Elec. A-C	10'16 LT PAR 56 300W HFL	BK-SIDES	R79
58	No.7 Elec. B / No.9 Elec. B	"	BK-HID	R79
59	No.2 Elec. A-D	8'12 LT PAR 56 300WQ HFL	BK-SIDES	NC
60	No.2 Elec. B-C	"	BK-HID	NC
61*	No.3 Elec. A-D / No.5 Elec. A-C	8'12 LT PAR 56 300W HFL	BK-SIDES	NC

Middle table:

CIRC	POSITION & UNIT NO.	TYPE	FOCUS	COLOR
62*	No.3 Elec. B-C / No.5 Elec. B	•	BK-HID	NC
63*	No.7 Elec. A-C / No.9 Elec. A-C	10'16 LT PAR 56 300W HFL	BK-SIDES	NC
64	No.7 Elec. B / No.9 Elec. B	•	BK-HID	NC
65A	#2 Torm L 17 / #3 Torm L 17 / #4 Torm L 15	6x12 750WL	LO SIDE L	R62
B	#2 Torm L 14 / #3 Torm L 18 / #4 Torm L 14	6x12 750WL	LO SIDE L	827
66A	#1 Torm R 17 / #2 Torm R 13 / #3 Torm R 17 / #4 Torm R 13	6x12 750WL	LO SIDE R	R82
B	#1 Torm R 18 / #2 Torm R 14 / #3 Torm R 18 / #4 Torm R 14	6x12 750WL	LO SIDE R	817
67A	Lower Bx Bm L 14 / Lower Bx Bm L 13	6x12 750WL	DS ROSES	13+14: R44 / 18: R36
B	Lower Bx Bm L 7 / Lower Bx Bm R 6	6x12 750WL	DS LEAVES	L7: R32 / R6: R84
68A	No.3 E. 5-8/No.6E.5	6x9 750WL	MID ROSES	
B	No.1 Elec. 9-19-28 / No.3 Elec. 6-7	6x9 750WL	MID LEAVES	
69A	No.7 Elec. 5-10 / No.10 Elec. 12	6x9 750WL	US ROSES	
B	No.5 E. 5-8/No8E.3 / No.10 Elec. 2-14	6x9 750WL	US LEAVES	
70	No.10 Elec. 16-22 / No.10 Elec. 6-8-11	6x9 750WL T&S	CYC LEAVES	
71*	No.1E.12-25/No.5E.67 / No.10 Elec. 7-18	LEKO COLORWHEEL	RING CW	SEE P7
72A	No.1E.3/No.6E 2-8 / No.8 Elec. 2	6x9 750 LEKO COLORWHEEL	CW	SEE P7
B	S.L. Floor Units 1-2 / S.R. Floor Units 1-2	PAR 64 120W SP PARHEAD	CYC SLASH	1: R23 / 2: 164
73A	No.9 Elec. 5-6 No.10 Elec. 1-23	GRD 750WL T&S	"ICE MOVES" DNS	R64
B	No.10 Elec. 10-13-15	6x12 750WL		10: R31 R6: R36
74A	No.12 Elec. 1-2	6x9 750WL T&S	"FEUX FOLLETS" CYC TEMPS	½ FR R23 ½ FR R44
B	Moon Box	24 100W FROST HOUSEHOLDS		GST
73AA	No.8 Elec. 1-4	6x12 750W.L	UC "PALAIS" PRINCE	N/C
75	No.4 E.2/No.6E 1-8 / No.7E 6-7/No.10 E 3-4	PAR 64 800W HFL PARHEAD	BK DIAG L	R23
76	No.4E. 4/No.6E 7-9 / No.7E. 8-9/No.10E 20-21	PAR 64 800W HFL PARHEAD	BK DIAG R	164
77	No.1 Elec. 1-2-35-36	6x12 750WL LEKO T&S	CURTAIN	R80
78	Lower Bx Bm L 15 / Lower Bx Bm R 14 / No.1 Cove 8-13	6x12 750WL LEKOS / 6x16 1KW LEKOS	"MOON"	R62 / R64
79	No.11 Elec. A-B-C	10'16 LT PAR 56 300W WFL	SCRIM TOP	119
80*	No.11 Elec. A-B-C	"	SCRIM TOP	R81
81*	No.11 Elec. A-B-C	"	SCRIM TOP	G63
82	No.12 Elec A-B-C-D-E	8'12 LT PAR 56 300W WFL	BOUNCE TOP	R80
83*	No.12 Elec A-B-C-D-E	"	BOUNCE TOP	R85
84*	No.12 Elec A-B-C-D-E	"	BOUNCE TOP	843

Right table:

CIRC	POSITION & UNIT NO.	TYPE	FOCUS	COL
1*	No.2 Cove 1-3-5-7-9-11-13-15	6x16 1KW LEKO	DS FRONTS	R52
2*	No.2 Cove 2-4-6-8-10-12-14-16	6x16 1KW LEKO	DS FRONTS	R64
3*	No.1 Cove 1-3-6-9-11-14-17-19	6x16 1KW LEKO	FRONTS	R52
4*	No.1 Cove 2-4-7-10-12-15-18-20	6x16 1KW LEKO	FRONTS	R64
5	Upper Bx Bm L 1-4-5-8	6x16/6x12 750WL	DIAG	R52
6	Upper Bx Bm L 2-3-6-7	750WL	WASH	R03
7	Upper Bx Bm L 9-10-11-12	6x12 750W LEKO	WASH	NC
8	Upper Bx Bm R 1-4-5-8	6x16/6x12 750WL	DIAG	R64
9	Upper Bx Bm R 2-3-6-7	6x12 750WL	WASH	R80
10	Upper Bx Bm R 9-10-11-12	6x12 750W LEKO	WASH	NC
11	Lower Bx Bm L 1-4-9-12	6x12 750W LEKO	X	R36
12	Lower Bx Bm L 2-3-10-11	6x12 750W LEKO	X	142
13	Lower Bx Bm L 5-8-13-16	6x12 750W LEKO	X	G64
14	Lower Bx Bm R 1-4-9-12	6x12 750W LEKO	X	R58
15	Lower Bx Bm R 2-3-10-11	6x12 750W LEKO	X	R17
16	Lower Bx Bm R 5-8-15-16	6x12 750W LEKO	X	852
17*	No.1 Elec. 7-10-13-16-20-23-26-29	6x12 750W LEKO	US FRONTS	R52
18*	No.1 Elec. 8-11-14-17-21-24-27-30	6x12 750W LEKO	US FRONTS	R64
19	No.1 Torm L 1-4-9-12	750WL	X	R36
20	No.1 Torm L 2-3-10-11	6x16/6x12 750WL	X	142
21	No.1 Torm L 6-8-14-16	6x16/6x12 750WL	X	G64
22*	No.2 Torm L 1-4-7-10 / No.3 Torm L 1-4-9-12	750WL	X	R36
23*	No.2 Torm L 2-3-8-9 / No.3 Torm L 2-3-10-11	6x12 750WL	X	142
24*	No.2 Torm L 5-6-11-12 / No.3 Torm L 6-8-14-16	6x16/6x12 750WL	X	G64
25*	No.4 Torm L 1-4-7-10 / No.5 Torm L 1-4-7-10	6x16 750WL	X	R36
26*	No.4 Torm L 2-3-8-9 / No.5 Torm L 2-3-8-9	750WL	X	142
27*	No.4 Torm L 5-6-11-12 / No.5 Torm L 5-6-11-12	750WL	X	G64
28	No.1 Torm L 5-7-13-15	6x16/6x12 750WL	DIAG	R52
29	No.3 Torm L 5-7-13-15	750WL	DIAG	R52
30	No.1 Torm R 1-4-9-12	6x16/6x12 750WL	DIAG	R58

plete with vivid narrations of near death and disaster when all lights went out at crucial moments. The consideration of safety overrides all others in circus lighting.

Added to safety concerns are the problems of limited budgets and tight time schedules for touring setups. The circus is constantly on the move. It does not carry a large amount of lighting equipment nor any great number of lights. Local men, unfamiliar with the circus routine, must set up and operate a hugely complicated spectacle in a minimum amount of time. Each arena played requires adjustments: different arc mounting positions, different lighting equipment for floodlights, and different control networks.

The April 1979 stand of the Ringling Bros. and Barnum & Bailey at Madison Square Gardens is a good example of circus lighting. It involved 48 beam projectors in red-green-blue in an overhead inner ring position; 350 beam projectors as downlights and around the rings in lavender-green-straw-and-clear; 100 or more ceiling slot ellipsoidal reflector spotlights; and an additional 56 beam projectors for the ring ends. The Garden's followspots are HMI (hydrargyrum-medium iodides; see Chap. 3). Red and blue footlights sections (of low intensity) were used around the ring (for performers to guide on, just as in ice shows).

All of these concerns together — design, safety, budget, and time — make it clear that the highly skilled lighting director for a circus show must

- Have an exact knowledge of the show and be able to sense and deal with crisis, change, or even disaster
- Have a sense of color and of showmanship (since the lighting person directs all followspots on a closed-circuit headset)
- Be quick in setup, flexible in adjusting to each new arena, and able to deal effectively with constantly changing setup and operations men in each new city
- Above all, keep performer safety foremost in mind and act upon it as needed.

Steve Brown, in Lighting Dimensions,[218] said that the circus lighting director was similar to an air traffic controller. Precision of timing and fluidity of response are the key to good lighting design for the circus. While there are (and probably always will be) very exact limitations upon the artistic possibilities, it is an exciting world in which to work for those with the necessary temperament and training.

Figure 9.13 is a production photo of The Flying Segreras, in Ringling Bros. and Barnum & Bailey Combined Shows.

Light As an Art Form

In Light in Architecture and Decoration, published in 1930 by the IES (Illuminating Engineering Society), Professor Albert Charles Schweizer wrote:

> The time is approaching for lighting to take another important step, that from the status of a decorative medium to the new place of the art. The word, art, is not used here in any loose or petty sense but in the specific sense of a medium of artistic creation. Lighting should take its place as an important "fine art" alongside painting, ceramics, sculpture and other recognized arts. It will be an abstract art, governed by the same principles as govern the other abstract arts and should produce equally vital aesthetic and dramatic works.
>
> Great ages have produced great specialized aspects of art. Thus the glory of the Byzantine style was in its brilliant mosaics and that of the Romanesque and Gothic styles in the marvelous stained glass windows of the cathedrals. In both these instances, light played an important role in bringing forth the full effectiveness of the technique. Light, through its perfected control, could play a still greater part in the distinctly modern art which, by use of the imagination, one can picture as rivalling these earlier media. Art in illumination developed on a foundation of scientific achievement would be a fitting artistic expression of the twentieth century, the great age of Science and Industry.[219]

Just over 100 years age, Thomas Alva Edison and Sir Joseph Swan each developed (independently) a workable electric light. This breakthrough led to ever more powerful sources of artificial illumination and the increasingly complex technology which followed. Inevitably, electric light influenced the fine artist (painter, sculptor, etc.).

The earliest history of "light art," or "luminism," goes back to work in color music (see Chapter 8). The earliest work in color music was done by Father Louis Bertrand Caster in Paris, in 1734, with his clevessin oculaire. Edward Gordon Craig wrote in 1908: "The only true material for the art of the theatre is light, and by means of light, move-

[218] Steve Brown, op. cit. (see footnote 217).

[219] "Reflections from the Past," Lighting Design + Application, vol. 13, no. 8 (Aug. 1983), p. 9. Professor Schweizer was a professor of architecture at New York University and a member of the Winold Reiss Studios.

[220] John F. Maguire, "Light in Art," Lighting Design & Application, vol. 1, no. 1 (July 1971), pp. 24–32. The first basic article on fine art use of light as design media. Illus., some color. Excellent survey and bibliography. Quote from p. 25.

[221] Rudi Stern, Let There Be Neon. N.Y.; Harry N. Abrams, Inc.; 1979. Illus., color; 160 pages. Lavishly illustrated volume on the history and uses of neon as a decorative use of light, in sculpture, in signs, in architecture, and as a technical craft. Includes glossary and bibliography.

Michael Webb, The Magic of Neon. Salt Lake City, Utah; Gibbs M. Smith, Inc. and Peregrine Smith Books (P.O. Box 667, Layton, Utah 84041); 1984. 87 pp., illus., color. Includes history, technique, design and use, bibliography, and listing of sources for neon.

Michael Webb, "The Magic and Art of Neon," Lighting Dimensions, vol. 8, no. 1 (Jan./Feb. 1984) pp. 28–29, 31–35. Illus., color. Excerpted from his book, The Magic of Neon.

The University of California, Los Angeles (UCLA) offered beginning and advanced courses in "Drawing With Lights: Neon Design and Fabrication" by neon artist Richard John Jenkins in September of 1983. Student creations were exhibited at the Museum of Neon Art in Los Angeles. (From IALD Newsletter, Nov. 1983, p. 3.)

The American School of Neon, 212 Third Ave. North, Minneapolis, MN 55401 [Telephone: (612) 338-5045] offers extensive instruction in this specialty.

"Neon—A Revival," International Lighting Review, 38th year (1st quarter of 1987), pp. 2–5. Illus., color. Also in this issue see A. L. C. Vreven and G. A. C. Trommar, "The Craft of Neon," pp. 5–7; "Neon—Raffles City, Singapore," by K. Seshadri and Peter Wang, pp. 7–9; "Neon—MONO, Museum of Neon Art, Los Angeles" pp. 10–11; and "Neon—Light, Colour and Movement, Edison Brothers Headquarters, St. Louis, USA," pp. 12–17. All illustrated, in color. Excellent summary of neon usage worldwide, both as an art form and commercially.

Patricia Pinckney, "Light as Art—Stephen Antonakos Explores the Many Facets of Neon in His Colorful, Geometric Sculptures," Lighting Dimensions, vol. 11, no. 1 (Jan./Feb. 1987), pp.

ment."[220] Shortly thereafter came the work of Thomas Wilfred with his Claviux, performing "Lumia" concerts (which began in 1905 and were highly refined by 1919).

The English chemist, Sir William Ramsey, discovered neon gas in 1898, and the rise of neon in art paralleled that of electricity. Frenchman George Claude patented neon lights prior to World War I. In 1921 the first neon sign (from France) appeared outside a Packard dealer's showroom in Los Angeles, and by 1929 neon signs were common in the United States. From that grew a whole different branch of light art: neon art.[221] Through the thirties, forties, fifties, and into the sixties—and even up to today—several prominent artists have used neon as their media; Cryssa, Paul Mohr, Joseph Kosuth, Bob Watts, Maurice Grosman, Stephen Antonakos (he began using neon sculpture in the 1950s, and since 1962 he has worked only with neon), and Bruce Nauman are the most prominent. Others producing neon artwork include Rudi Stern, Michael Webb, Annika Bernhard, John Harris, Joe Leitze, and Roger Mazzuchelli (there were and will continue to be many others). John F. Maguire has labeled the use of neon as "environmental light art" (Maguire cites fireworks as the oldest form of environmental light art). Neon signs are kinetic, that is, they incorporate motion. To this is added design and color, making neon sculpture a highly potent luminous media for the fine artist.

With electric artificial illumination (and the accompanying technology) evolving and becoming important in peoples' lives, it was inevitable that what Maguire calls "self-contained light art" would evolve in the forties and fifties. Light sculptures which plug in, light up, and introduce kinetic motion and color and design make up this art form. Willard Huntingdon Wright wrote in 1923 that the emphasis in painting would change from color to "real light."[222] This prediction was no doubt influenced by Laszle Moholy-Nagy's kinetic light sculpture (the first we have records of), "Lichtrequist," displayed from 1922 to 1930. A replica of this motor-driven sculpture with hundreds of colored light bulbs is on display in the Howard Wise Gallery in New York City.

Poet-engineers of art and light and energy followed in rapid profusion. Ann Holmes, critic at the Houston Chroni-

Figure 9.13 The Flying Segreras of Ringling Bros. and Barnum & Bailey Circus. (Photo: Ringling Bros. and Barnum & Bailey Circus)

Figure 9.14 A Found Evening, March 1974. A classroom project at Courtyard Theatre, SUNY at Buffalo, New York; neon by Paul Brown.

cle, wrote in 1970 that these light sculptures "light up your imagination." [223] Making use of all types of light sources (incandescent, neon, fluorescent), of coated glass and mirror reflective surfaces (creating an illusion of the vastness of space and infinity by reflection and refraction repeated endlessly), and of motion and movement (flashers, motors, timed and controlled movement), the beginnings of a new art were created. Prominent were the works of Dan Flavin, Charles Ross (who used light through prisms in the 1960s), Stanley Landsman, Julie Le Parc, John Maguire, Gunther Uecker, Nicholas Schoffer, Frank Malina, James Turrell, Forrest Myers, Les Levine, and Marvin Torffield. Flavin, who began making light sculptures in 1961, made the light source itself (often fluorescent tubes), designed and arranged in space as a "found object," the center of his designs. Flavin had created 84 fluorescent tube sculptures by 1963. [224]

Robert Whitman was perhaps the first "fine artist" to create his light art designs around today's increasingly popular laser. Sites for the exhibition of Charles Ross's work include the U.S. Customs House in New York City (1973); a display in Jerusalem, Israel (1973); the Nebraska Federal Building (1976); the Spectrum Building in Denver; and "Star Axis" on a mesa in New Mexico. [225] The laser art trend is only now in its early stages (see Chap. 3).

In 1982 a production, *Red and Blue*, appeared at Papp's Public Theatre's Other Stage featuring only a red light bulb, a blue light bulb, and a voice. [226]

John Maguire writes:

> That all visual art is dependent on light is immediately evident, but working directly in light rather than creating objects visible in light provides new opportunities as well as some unique limitations. [227]
>
> The richness of light art as a medium extends even further than light itself. Time is an important factor as well. Interval control, time extension, rhythm are often involved. The extension to actual sound has been for some a logical step. [228]

If all of this sounds quite close to the modern world of disco design, it is. The multiple strands of color music, developed by (mostly) theatre-trained designers; of disco; and of light art in galleries, museums, homes, and offices are all closely related. Figure 9.14 shows a contemporary example

44–47. Illus., color. Includes a listing of Antonakos's work in various museums.

Jeffery Black, "NEON, NEON, Sign Shop and Gallery Showcase Light and Art," Lighting Design + Application, vol. 17, no. 6 (June 1987), pp. 4–5. Illus., color.

"Light & Designs: Energetic Art: A recent exhibit of neon art at the Owens-Illinois Arts Center in Toledo, Ohio, reveals the medium's versatility," Interior Design, vol. 55, no. 11 (Nov. 1984), pp. 26–61. Illus., color.

Vilma Barr and Barbara Welanetz, "Lighting the Marketplace—II, Neon Sculptures Lend Instant Identity to Boston's Quincy Market," Lighting Design & Application, vol. 8, no. 11 (Nov. 1978), pp. 16–18. Illus.; one in color.

Malcom Preston, "Gallery Turn-on: Neon, Old and New," Newsday, N.Y., June 26, 1973, p. 13A. Illus.

Amei Wallach, "Working with Neon, the Light Fantastic," Newsday, N.Y., July 8, 1973, Part II, p. 15. Illus.

April 21 through May 9, 1986 eleven artists displayed their neon work at New York City's Fashion Institute of Technology; the display was called "Luminous Visions."

Baltimore's Brightstar Gallery makes custom-designed neon art forms from $160 and up.

"Art & Science: Neon Lights Up Greenwich," IALD Newsletter, March 1987, p. 3. News of the Bruce Museum in Greenwich, Connecticut, hosting the "Neon: New Artistic Expressions" show with twenty neon sculptures by Stephen Antonakos and Cork Marcheschi.

[222] John F. Maguire, p. 26, op. cit. (see footnote 220).

[223] Ann Homes, "Lights in Boxes and No Limit on Imagination," Houston Chronicle, February 15, 1970, p. 20 in Sunday Magazine. Illustrated article about Stanley Landsman's "light boxes" at the Houston Contemporary Arts Museum exhibit.

[224] "Dan Flavin," Lighting Design & Application, vol. 3, no. 1 (Jan. 1973), p. 57. Photograph of Flavin's "Light Painting" in Houston, Texas.

"E. F. Hauserman Showroom," Lighting Design + Application, vol. 13, no. 10 (Oct. 1983), pp. 12–15. Illus., color. Designer Flavin's award-winning showroom design, which makes lavish use of abstract colored light, is presented in detail. It is an outstanding design, based upon light use. Flavin received the 1983 IES (Illuminating Engineering Society) Lumen Award as "Lighting Installation Artist" for the Hauserman Showroom, a Vignelli Associates design by Lella and Massimo Vignelli.

Further color illustrations of Flavin's work while employed by Sunar, Ltd. (an Ontario-based office furnishings maker) in the late 1970s can be found in William Wilson, "Office Politics," Ambassador, vol. 16, no. 6 (June 1983), pp. 57–66. See particularly p. 65.

See also Lighting Dimensions, vol. 8, no. 1 (Jan./Feb. 1984), pp. 53–54. This outlines Daniel Flannery's part in The Adventures of Conan, a 20-minute film/live spectacular at Universal Studios Theme Park in Los Angeles produced in the summer of 1983. In 1977 Flannery established Daniel Flannery, Inc., in Los Angeles, as a producing and design service. Earlier Flannery had been a student at the Lester Polakov Studio and Forum of Stage Design in New York City. He later attended Columbia University, where he studied film-making. He has participated in lighting design and effects for over 70 theatrical productions for Broadway, Off-Broadway, and opera, as well as having many TV credits on ABC, NBC, specials, sitcoms, soap operas, and news shows. He was involved in the E. T. at the Hollywood Bowl show, and he created concepts, staging, direction, and design for the The Great Symphonic Visual Fantasy at the Blossom Music Center (Cleveland). In 1978 he directed the Mardi Gras in the New Orleans Superdome, a concert show which turned the Superdome into the world's largest disco. He was project lighting design consultant to W.E.D. Enterprises (Disney) for Epcot Center in Orlando, Florida, including the American Adventure Pavilion and two others. In 1984 he was deeply involved in the Victorian Arts Centre in Melbourne, Australia, as lighting design consultant for one of the world's largest multi-theatre complexes.

John Russell, "Art: In the Hamptons, Dan Flavin's Works," The New York Times, August 2, 1985, p. 14 (Chicago ed.). A lengthy piece on Flavin's latest efforts: the Flavin Institute in Bridgehampton, a large permanent exhibition of Flavin's light sculptures. Lengthy description of the museum's contents.

Patricia Pinckney, "Light As Art: Dan Flavin Creates 'Icons' of Light with Fluorescents," Lighting Dimensions, *vol. 11, no. 2 (Mar./Apr. 1987), pp. 76-78. Illus., color. Pinckney taught "Light as an Art Form" at the Parsons School of Design in New York City. This article includes a listing of Dan Flavin's exhibitions.*

[225] *"News,"* Lighting Dimensions, *vol. 11, no. 1 (Jan./Feb. 1987), pp. 14-15. Includes "Heaslip Lights George Benson's Tour," "Laser Companies form ILDA" (International Laser Display Association), and "Neon Art Exhibit Scheduled at Bruce Museum," (in Greenwich, Connecticut).*

"News," Lighting Dimensions, *vol. 11, no. 1 (Jan./Feb. 1987), pp. 16-17. Includes "Setting a Bird on Fire," which describes the lighted sculpture for the Orange County Performing Arts Center; the sculpture is by Richard Lippold (60 feet high, 120 feet wide, and 100 feet long), and the lighting is by Paul Marantz and Tom Ruzika. Illus.*

"Lightmobile," International Lighting Review, *38th year (1st quarter of 1987), pp. 34-35. Color illustration of Eric Staller's 1967 VW Beetle decorated with 1,659 lights. It won a 1986 IES award.*

Andrew Hayden, "Colour Music—Back to the Future?" ALD Newsletter, *#4 (Apr. 1987), pp. 5-6. A good analytical piece about color music as a light art form.*

"Statement: Commercial—Lighted Art Glass Prevents Hallway Boredom," Architectural Lighting, *vol. 1, no. 5 (May 1987), pp. 18. Illus., color.*

"Statement: Institutional—Illuminated Sculpture a Standout on Charles River Skyline," Architectural Lighting, *vol. 1, no. 0 (Nov. 1986), p. 22. Illus., color. The artistic illumination of "Lupus," a 40-foot steel sculpture by John Raimondi at the Lotus Development Corp. headquarters in Cambridge, Massachusetts. Lighting by Karen Langendorff of Horton-Lees Lighting Design, Inc.*

Information about Daniel Engelke's light sculpture in Lake Michigan (Professor Engelke is a member of Purdue University's Creative Arts Department) can be found in:

Norm Bess, "Unusual Art Destined for Lake Shore: Sound of Waves to Trigger Show of Lights on Water," Indianapolis News, *April 9, 1987, p. 28 Illus.*

Kathy Matter, "Sculpture Lights Up Lake: Floating Art Is Professor's Labor of Love," Lafayette Journal & Courier, *September 29, 1987, Life & Times section, B1 and B3. Illus.*

Kathy Matter, "Light Sculpture Returning to Sparkle Once More," Lafayette Journal & Courier, *February 9, 1988, Life & Times section, C1 and C4. Illus.*

James Gleick, "Vision of Times Square Calls for Dancing Lasers," The New York Times, *April 12, 1987, p. 14 (Chicago ed.). Illus. David Katzive, formerly of the Museum of Holography and now teaching at Cooper Union School of Art, offers plans to use light as the design media to enhance Times Square. Interesting sketches present use of light as an art media.*

Alan Lapidus, "Let There Be Light in Times Square," The New York Times, *February 21, 1987, p. 15. Illus.*

"Electronic Creation," Lafayette Journal & Courier, *November 17, 1986, page E-1. Illus. Bill Parker's electronic sculpture (a "plasma generator" electronic sphere) is illustrated while on exhibit at the Philadelphia Civic Center.*

Phillip Evans-Clark, "Messages Sent in the Medium of Light," The New York Times, *August 17, 1986. Art & Leisure section, p. 29. Illus. Information about the Paul Hunter "Lights: Perception   Projection" exhibit in Montreal, presented by the International Center of Contemporary Art.*

"Future Memories" was an Immedia exhibition of Carlos Rodriguez's light paintings held in New York City in 1988 from February 17 through March 5, at the Immedia Galleries, 578 Broadway, 5th Floor. First of a series of artists' "Light As Art" showings.

Bruce Weber, "Works in Progress: Spreading Sunshine," The New York Times Sunday Magazine, *May 1, 1988, Section 6, p. 118. Color illustrations of designs created by light and colored glass at the Oregon Institute of Technology in Klamath Falls by designer Michael R. McCulloch. This was a skylight project, part of 22 exhibits headlined as "Architectural Art."*

"American Falls' Illumination May Light Up Tourists," Lafayette Journal & Courier, *April 5, 1988, p. A5. Lighting of the upper Niagara River rapids at Niagara Reservation park by William Marshall, of Imero Fiorentino Associates.*

Barbara J. Knox, "Designer Fixtures: Adam Tihany Introduces His Off The Wall Ideas," Lighting Dimensions, *vol. 10, no. 3 (May/June 1986), pp. 14, 16-17. Illus., color. Vibrant colored lamps (luminaires),*

Susan Nielsen, "News: It's a Buoy, It's a Plane, It's a Bubbleboat!" Lighting Dimensions, *vol. 10, no. 6 (Nov. 1986), p. 12. Illus. Eric Staller (creator of the Volkswagen with lights—see "Lightmobile" earlier in this footnote) creates a water vehicle sculpture that can carry five passengers and is covered with hundreds of lights and control circuits. It is intended as a light art piece.*

"Annual Christmas Tree and Crèche at Met," Lighting Dimensions, *vol. 10, no. 6 (Nov. 1986), p. 14. Illus. Metropolitan Museum of Art lighting designer William Riegel turns the museum's Christmas tree into a light art work.*

"News: New Light Exhibition at Alternative Museum," Lighting Dimensions, *vol. 10 no. 6 (Nov. 1986), p. 20. "Luminosity" was the exhibit at New York City's Alternative Museum featuring the work of the following seven light artists: Caterina Bertolotto (projected dots and mirrors), Cork Marcheschi (programmed neon), Leni Schwendinger (light and sand sculpture), Paul Seide (neon), Eric Staller (miniature light sculpture suspended from the ceiling), Ted Victoria (camera obscura), and Ingrid Wagner (suspended lighted crystals refracting light).*

Susan Nielsen, "News: Lighting No Ordinary Area," Lighting Dimensions, *vol. 11, no. 2 (Mar./Apr. 1987), p. 16. Illus. A redesign of a nightclub by designer Rhett Butler involving phosphorescent paintings, stained glass collages, neon wall figures, and lasers (by Dick Sandhaus).*

Patricia Pinckney, "The Art of Light: Two Recent Museum Exhibitions Explore Contemporary Works by Artists Who Work with Light." Lighting Dimensions, *vol. 11, no. 2 (Mar./Apr. 1987), pp. 38, 40, 42. Illus.*

"Dates: Exhibitions," Lighting Dimensions, *vol. 11, no. 1 (May/June 1987), p. 10. Lighting Dimensions began listing "Light As Art" exhibitions in museums around the New York City area with this issue.*

John Davis Moody, a light sculptor artist from Minneapolis, demonstrated his "light as art" work at the IES (Illuminating Engineering Society of North America) annual conference in Minneapolis in August of 1988.

Thomas B. Hess and John Ashbery, editors, Light in Art. N.Y.; Collier Books—Art News Series, Collier-MacMillan, Ltd.; 1969. A collection of essays, the most useful of which is "Dan Flavin: Fiat Lux" by William S. Wilson, pp. 137–49. Illus.

"New King of Painting Uses Light as Medium," The New York Times, December 8, 1931.

Wanda Jankowski, "Art: Seeing Space in a New Light," Lighting Design & Application, vol. 9, no. 11 (Nov. 1979), pp. 8–12. Light used as an art in the University Art Museum, Berkeley, California.

"Art: Lighting a 'Stairway to the Stars'," Lighting Design & Application, vol. 11, no. 12 (Dec. 1981), pp. 16–19. Illus., color. By Chicago artist John David Mooney.

Eleanor Freed, "Dimensions in Light: Stanley Landsman's Light Sculpture Repeats Patterns Endlessly, Mesmerizing the Spectator, Dissolving Before His Eyes," Houston Post, February 15, 1970, p. 6 in Spotlight section. Illus.

"Light, Architecture and Aesthetics: Architecture and Lighting: That the Two Should Meet," Lighting Design & Application, vol. 8, no. 11 (Nov. 1978), pp. 12–15. Illus., color. Article on the use of light sculptures as part of a modern architectural office design by designer Paul Rudolph.

"Festival of Lights," Lafayette Journal & Courier, December 5, 1983, page B4. An Associated Press Laserphoto of sculptor Larry Goodridge's light sculpture at the entrance to the Cincinnati Zoo, a part of its International Festival of Lights.

"Whitney Museum Sued over 1980 'Light Show'," IALD Newsletter, June 1982, pp. 1–2. Lawsuits over a light show by artist James Turrell called "James Turrell: Light and Space" in December 1980.

Ronald Pellegreno, The Electronic Arts of Sound and Light. N.Y.; Van Nostrand Reinhold; 1984. 256 pp., illus. A study combining computers, lasers, videographics, film, and oscillographics into today's version of color music. Detailed, encyclopedic work of great value in this field.

Burt Supree, "Light on the Subject," Village Voice, June 5, 1984, p. 88. A review of the Mel

Wong Dance Co. at the Whitney Museum of American Art reviewing a multimedia work by Wong and sculptor Cathey Billian.

Traci Sampson, "Bill Parker, Light Sculptor," Lighting Dimensions, vol. 9, no. 1 (Jan./Feb. 1985), pp. 50–51. Illus., color. A discussion by artist Bill Parker of his unique light sculptures, with color photographs. Parker's work in this specialty merits serious consideration.

Steven Winn, "SEE HERE NOW, George Coates' Rare Performance Work," Theatre Crafts, vol. 20, no. 4 (April 1986), pp. 37–38, 40–43. Illus. A well-illustrated description of George Coates's multimedia experimental art with lighting by Larry Neff and Jeff Hunt.

Michael Cahana, "Brilliant Bubble," IALD Newsletter, Sept. 1986, pp. 2–3. Illus. The work of artist Eric Staller, creator of both the "Lightmobile" (a 1967 Volkswagen covered with 1,659 chasing white lights) and the "Bubbleboat" (a lighted unidentified floating object).

"Brooklyn Bridge Fireworks," Lighting Design + Application, vol. 15, no. 9 (Sept. 1985), pp. 22–23. Illus., color. Photographs and text about the fireworks display May 24, 1983, at the Brooklyn Bridge (New York City).

Paul Hosefros, "New Wave of Holgraphers Work to Expand the Art, IALD Newsletter, Sept. 1984, p. 3. Reprint from The New York Times on holograms as an art form. Excellent source.

"Holographers Explore Process as an Art Form," The New York Times, July 22, 1984, Art & Leisure, p. 27. Illus. Two artists, Sam Moree and Dan Schweitzer, are using holograms as their art form of expression in conjunction with the New York Holographic Laboratories.

Tracy Reese, "Project Makes Temporary Water Sculpture Permanent Art," Purdue Exponent (campus daily newspaper of Purdue University in West Lafayette, Indiana), July 14, 1989, p. 3. Describes elaborate night lighting of Daniel Engleke's "Lightpath," now permanently recorded on videotape by Marvin Diskin (26-minutes).

"LIGHTPATH, A Sculptural Installation for Lake Michigan," A pamphlet by Purdue University sculptor Dan Inglekey. Color, illus.

Johan Jansen and Otto Lührs, Art in Light, Lighting Effects In Painting and Sculpture, Art

and Technology. Deventer, Netherlands; Kulwer Technical Books; 1985, 125 pp. Illus., color, glossy paper. Excellent study, written in English, with fine illustrations of the interrelationship of light and art.

"Light Flashes." International Lighting Review, 39th, 1st quarter, 1988, pp. 3–4. Illus., color. See "Modal Space of Consciousness" photos and text.

Thomas B. Hess and John Ashbery, editors, Light In Art. N.Y.; Collier Books—Art News Series, Collier Macmillan, Ltd.; 1969.

Ronald Pellegreno, The Electronic Arts of Sound and Light. N.Y.; Van Nostrand Reinhold; 1984.

"Kelly Grant Winners," Lighting Dimensions, vol. 12, no. 3 (April 1988), p. 12. Illus., color. Information about the Richard Kelly annual award grants, one of which was given to New York City sculptor Chris Freeman for his neon sculpture.

Myriam Weisang, "Noctures, Keiichi Tahara Turns Searchlights on Nature to Capture Nighttime Photos," Lighting Dimensions, vol. 11, no. 7 (January/February 1988), pp. 45–47, 72. Illus., color. Tahara's photos are almost entirely light compositions.

"Interactive Art," Lighting Dimensions, vol. 12, no. 6 (September/October 1988), p. 26. Description of a light show at the Aldrich Museum of Contemporary Art in Ridgefield, Connecticut. Exhibiting were Clyde Lynds, Art Spellings, Jon Kessler, Milton Komisar, Alejandro Sīna (neon), and Wen Ying Tsai.

Mark Loeffler, "Light Art Gallery Opens," Lighting Dimensions vol. 12, no. 4 (May/June 1988), p. 17. Description of Carlos Rodriguez's light paintings at the Dome Gallery, 578 Broadway, New York City. Illus., color.

"Halogen Surf'n'Turf," Lighting Dimensions, vol. 11, no. p. 18. Illus., color. A combination restaurant and aquarium with light art added.

Patricia Pinckney, "Light As Art: Using Natural Light and Prisms, Charles Ross Sculpts "Living" Spectrums," Lighting Dimensions, vol. 11, no. 6 (November 1987), pp. 54–55, 73. Charles Ross's light sculpture, well described and illustrated.

"Light Flashes," International Lighting Review, 2nd quarter, 40th year (1989), pp. 44–45. Illus., color.

Judith Gor and Erik Hehenkamp, "Designing With Sunrise and Sunset: In Search of an Ambience on the Banks of the IR in Amsterdam," International Lighting Review, 2nd quarter, 40th year (1989), pp. 74–79. Illus., color. Very interesting use of artificial light and daylight in architectural artistic design.

Bonnie Schwartz, "Illuminating Designs," Lighting Dimensions, vol. 13, no. 3 April 1989), p. 22. Use of glass, acrylic, brass, wood, and synthetic materials with fluorescent and quartz-halogen sources for innovative lighting fixtures in architectural lighting.

Fred Loessel, "The Art of Light: Sculptor Christopher Freeman Redefines Neon," Lighting Dimensions, vol. 13, no. 3 (April 1989), pp. 80–81, 106. Illus., color. Very inventive use of neon as an art form by 27-year old Christopher Freeman.

Michael S. Eddy, "Light over the Holland Tunnel," Lighting Dimensions, vol. 13, no. 4 (May/June 1989), p. 18. Imaginative work in New York City by light artist/designer Leni Schwendinger.

Barbara J. Knox, "Akari: Isamu Noguchi's Light Sculptures Make a Comeback," Lighting Dimensions, vol. 13, no. 2 (March 1989), pp. 92–97. Illus.

[226] Frank Rich, "Stage: 'Red and Blue,' 2 Light Bulbs," review in The New York Times, May 12, 1982.

[227] John Maguire, p. 31, op. cit. (see footnote 220).

[228] Ibid., p. 32.

[229] Martin Garon, "Light Sculpture," International Lighting Review, vol. 22, no. 2, Amsterdam, The Netherlands. Brief article with color photographs of the light sculpture for the Lopez Administration Building at Rizal, Philippines (Manila Electric Co. headquarters).

[230] For a complete illustrated description, see Rollo Gillespie Williams, Lighting for Color and Form. N.Y.; Pitman; 1954. 340 pp., illus., color (see color frontispiece and "The Lobby Lighting at 383-5 Madison Avenue, N.Y., N.Y.," pp. 259–264).

of this interrelatedness in theatre. Called *A Found Evening*, it is an onstage arrangement of objects, light sources, and neon created under the direction of Paul Brown at the State University of New York (Buffalo) in 1974 by his lighting design students.

Some recent artists who are using light as a design medium include Annalee Koehn, Divilo Passariello-Caceres, David Winfield Wilson, Leni Schwendinger, Cork Marches-Chi, Eric Staller, Milton Komisar, Caterina Bertolotto, Joe Augusta, Cathy Billian, Chris Freeman, Beth Galston, and Ron Rocco.

Light art has had a marked effect on one other area of lighting design: architectural lighting. Figure 9.15 is a photograph of the light sculpture in the lobby of the Lopez Administration Building at Rizal, Philippines, the corporate headquarters building of the Manila Electric Co.[229] It is the work of Martin Garon, a former president of Wheel-Garon, Inc., New York City. The entire exterior facade of this building was treated as a huge illuminated light sculpture. Another example, which can be seen daily in New York City, is Gyorgy Kepes's light mural in the KLM (Netherlands) Airlines New York office at the corner of Fifth Avenue and Forty-ninth Street, installed in 1959. In the early 1950s, while he was an employee of Century Lighting, Rollo Gillespie Williams designed a computer-controlled bank of thousands of colored lights (each in individual open-ended conelike containers) to provide an ever-changing luminous ceiling pattern for an office building on Madison Avenue.[230] It is no longer in use.

Mention should be made of the "pop art" variation of light art, in the form of the Living Pictures annual presentation at Laguna Beach, California.[231] Begun in 1933 and presented for seven weeks in July and August each summer, Living Pictures recreates art masterpieces using live bodies. Laguna Beach locals, adorned with body paint and makeup and costumes, vie to pose in the full-sized masterpiece reproductions. The Living Picture Pageant sells out each year — and usually most of the tickets are reserved a year ahead by residents and tourists. Masterpieces such as Da Vinci's "Last Supper" are reproduced down to the last detail — which necessitates very elaborate lighting. The annual presentation, sponsored by the Laguna Beach Art Festival,

Figure 9.15 Environmental light sculpture at Corporate Headquarters and Theatre of Manila Electric Co., Lopez Administration Building; design by Wheel-Gersztoff, Inc.

raises approximately $200,000 yearly for scholarships and grants to local artists and performers. Since 1949 the presentation has raised over $4 million for the Ballet Pacifica, the Laguna Museum of Art, and scholarships. Much of the audience fascination stems from watching the performers hold absolutely "frozen" poses — in spite of all adversity. Linda Deutsch in an Associated Press release wrote: "Once . . . a pigeon landed on the painted breast of a woman frozen in the pose of a statue. The pigeon slid down the greasy body makeup, across the woman's leg and onto the stage. The performer, a real trouper, never flinched and received a standing ovation.[232]

Living Pictures was originated by John Hinchman, a local artist. The lighting and technical direction is currently in the hands of Carl Callaway, operations manager. For color photographs and additional details, the reader should refer to the extensive articles cited in footnote 231.

Other examples of light art abound — in museums, discos, lighted signs, and architectural work — but this new art form is only at its beginnings. Progress in such an art form frequently depends upon a close collaboration between the designing artist, who usually is limited in knowledge of and utilization of current technology, and engineering experts.

[231] *"Living Pictures,"* Lighting Dimensions, *vol. 4, no. 9 (Sept./Oct. 1980), pp. 16–20 and cover. Color illus.*

Linda Deutsch, "People Flock to See 'Frozen' Summer Theatre," Associated Press release, August 23, 1981, Indianapolis Star, *p. 8, Section 8.*

[232] *Deutsch, op. cit. (see footnote 231).*

Chapter 10

Architectural/Commercial/ Industrial Lighting

[233] *Gerry Zekowski, "The Undeification of the Calculation,"* Lighting Design + Application, *vol. 14, no. 2 (Feb. 1984), pp. 27–33.*

[234] *William Dombroski, "Lighting Education: An Overview,"* Lighting Design + Application, *vol. 15, no. 3 (Feb. 1985), p. 32. Professor Dombroski is from the Ohio University Interior Design Department.*

[235] *Leslie Larson writes of the IES Code of Recommended Minimum Levels of Illumination: "Codes should be viewed with proper respect bordering on suspicion. While they have often been formed to protect the public from inferior work or products, they have usually ended up by straitjacketing the imagination." Leslie Larson,* Lighting and Its Design. *N.Y.; Whitney Library of Design; 1964. 288 pp. Fine illustrations of light as a design element and good text. Important study. Quote from pp. ix–x.*

[236] *William M. C. Lam,* Perception and Lighting as Formgivers for Architecture. *N.Y.; McGraw-Hill; 1977. The basic book. Should be in every lighting designer's library, whether he is designing for theatre, TV, discos, or films. Keystone of current theories of architectural lighting. 310 pp.; lavishly illustrated.*

Fran Kellogg Smith and Fred J. Bertolone, Bringing Interiors to Light, The Principles and Practices of Lighting Design. *N.Y.; Watson-Guptill Publications, Whitney Library of Design;*

> "The lighting profession . . . has been overly preoccupied by footcandle prediction and has used the computer as a modern day divining rod. *Illumination engineering* is only a small part of *lighting design!* . . . Lighting and the environment are an interactive human perceptual phenomenon that cannot be evaluated by simple pass/fail scores."
> GERRY ZEKOWSKI[233]

> "Because lighting controls so many aspects of a space, you cannot design that space properly without designing the lighting for it, too."
> WILLIAM DOMBROSKI[234]

Architectural, commercial, and industrial lighting make up the largest and most diverse lighting design field. This chapter considers design for architectural and interior design lighting; landscape architectural lighting; lighting for sales merchandising; lighting for industrial shows, trades shows, and conventions; employment in lighting equipment manufacturing/sales/distribution; the work of lighting consultants to architects for theatre buildings, studios, and places of entertainment; and energy conservation.

Half of the designers in architectural lighting have either a theatre background or training in theatre lighting. Yet there are big differences—that greatly affect the lighting designer—between the architectural/commercial/industrial lighting field and the lighting fields that concern the entertainment industry.

Architectural lighting designers must have a comprehensive knowledge of light sources, available luminaires, and illumination calculations. Familiarity with calculations is a part of designing.[235] Since, however, this volume deals with design, rather than technology, the reader is referred to any of the eight basic volumes listed in the footnotes which can provide the needed technical information.[236] Space does not permit the treatment of technology here other than to list the common architectural lighting design constraints enumerated by Stefan Graf at the 1989 Lighting World International conference in New York City. The constraints are: (1) the project schedule, (2) the project budget, (3) integration of architectural and system requirements with lighting, (4) interior design considerations, (5) system flexibility, (6) Underwrighter's Code requirements, (7) energy

1986. 224 pp., illus., color. The most recent and probably the most usable, both on a theoretical and a practical level, of the texts about architectural lighting. Readable and well-illustrated. Most useful for the nonengineer.

Lightolier, Lessons in Lighting, A Basic Course by Lightolier, Incorporated. Jersey City, N.J.; Lightolier, Inc.; 1982. 110 pp., illus. A looseleaf workbook with student problems (and supplied answers) covering all of the basics of architectural lighting. A handy quick reference summary of the essentials of this specialized area of lighting design.

M. David Egan, Concepts in Architectural Lighting. N.Y.; McGraw-Hill; 1983. 270 pp., illus. Very readable and clearly illustrated basic text by an illumination engineer. Covers vision and perception, light sources, measurement, light and form; lighting systems; daylight and design; and models. Contains glossary and bibliography. Somewhat technical for the nonengineer but more understandable for the designer than most basic illuminating engineering texts.

James L. Nuckolls, Interior Lighting for Environmental Designers, 2d ed. N.Y.; John Wiley & Sons; 1983. Dated basic text. Good balance between necessary illumination knowledge and the lighting design consultant's approach. Useful reference source for the beginner. More practical than theoretical. 407 pp., illus.

Ronald N. Helms, Illumination Engineering for Energy Efficient Luminous Environments. Englewood Cliffs, N.J.; Prentice-Hall; 1980. 322 pp., illus. Requires considerable engineering skills to understand. Chap. 8, "Lighting and Energy Conservation," pp. 201–209, is most useful.

Edward Effron, Planning & Designing Lighting. Boston; Brown and Co.; 1986. 144 pp., illus., color. With a heavy emphasis on fixtures (luminaires), this excellently presented volume (both text and graphics) deals primarily with residential (home) lighting.

John E. Kaufman (editor), IES Lighting Handbook, 1981. Vol. I: Reference (1981). Vol. II: Application (1984). Published by the Illuminating Engineering Society, New York City. Vol. I contains lighting terminology, physics, vision, measurement, color, control and luminaire design, daylighting, light sources, and calculations. Vol. II covers lighting

design, systems design, economics, energy management, office lighting, educational facilities lighting, institution and public building lighting (banks, churches, health care facilities, hotels, libraries, museums), merchandise areas, industrial lighting, residential lighting, outdoor lighting, sports and recreational areas, roadways, aviation, transportation, advertising, underwater, nonvisual effects of radiant energy, and searchlights. Both volumes are illustrated and are the committee work of experts from all segments of the industry. These two volumes are invaluable basic reference works.

Joseph B. Murdoch, Illumination Engineering: From Edison's Lamp to the Laser. N.Y. and London; Macmillan; 1985. 541 pp., illus. Intended for the engineer (either illumination or electrical) with an engineer's command of math. Of much less use for the lighting designer. Covers sight and seeing, lighting calculations and measurements, light as radiant energy, vision and color, lamps, interior design by IES formulas, daylighting, optics and light control, exterior lighting; also offers student problems (and provides answers).

Other basic informational sources, beyond these eight texts, include:

Barbara J. Knox, "An Interior Designer Looks at Light—Susan Forbes Knows the Value of a Lighting Consultant," Lighting Dimensions, vol. 10, no. 4 (July/Aug. 1986), pp. 30–33, 54–56. Illus., color. A sketch of Forbes's career by a very active interior designer who also is widely acquainted with and respected in the lighting design field. Many of Forbes's design projects involve Wheel-Gersztoff Associates as lighting designers.

"Architects on Lighting: It's Time to Let the Architects Speak for Themselves," Lighting Dimensions, vol. 11, no. 3 (May/June 1987), p. 31ff.

Barbara J. Knox, "Architectural Lighting: The Dramatic Influence," Lighting Dimensions, vol. 10, no. 3 (May/June 1986), p. 23 ff.

Nora Richter Greer, "Light as a Tool of Design," Architecture, Oct. 1984, pp. 54–67. Illus., color. Six case studies are included in an excellent overview of the 1984 contribution of light design to contemporary architecture in this special issue (devoted to lighting) of the American Institute of Architects magazine. Case studies include museums, restaurants, re-

search laboratories, and an office building. Good history and summary of architectural lighting's development and purpose. Covers daylight integration with artificial sources.

"Interview: Motoke Ishii," International Lighting Review, 1985/1, pp. 16–21. Illus., color. A lavishly illustrated interview with the Japanese woman who has won worldwide awards for her lighting designs. Ishii fields key questions concerning architectural lighting design. Numerous color illustrations of the artist's work.

J. B. Harris, "Professionalism in Lighting," International Lighting Review, 1985/1, pp. 28–33. Illus., color. A highly useful summary of what professionalism means in architectural lighting design with 17 strikingly reproduced color photos of outstanding design in many areas.

John Marsteller, "Lighting Design: An American's View from Abroad," Lighting Design + Application, vol. 15, no. 5 (May 1985), pp. 19–22. Illus., color. A most cogent overview concerning the existence and practices of architectural lighting designers in Europe and Asia.

Raymond Grenald, "Perception—The Name of the Game, Architecture Lives in the Seeing," Lighting Design + Application, vol. 16, no. 7 (July 1986), pp. 21–24. Illus., color. An architect/engineer, specializing in lighting, writes about basics of architectural lighting.

"Interview with Raymond Grenald: Lighting Design as a Discipline," Lighting, vol. 2, no. 3 (June 1988), pp. 32, 34–35, 37. Subtitled: "Raymond Grenald is an outspoken proponent of lighting design professionalism. In an interview, he gives his views on problems and issues facing lightning designers across North America, and how the future my impact particularly on the Canadian scene."

Forrest Wilson interview with Ron Keenberg, "Architecture, Light, Color, Form and Function—Generating Attitude and Comprehension," Lighting Design + Application, vol. 16, no. 7 (July 1986), pp. 30–33. Illus., color. A prominent Canadian architect and educator, Ron Keenberg, offers extensively illustrated comments about lighting design basics and lighting.

Barbara J. Knox, "Giving the Customers What They Want: At Harry Gitlin, Inc., Custom Furniture Design Has Been a Way of Life Since WWII," Lighting Dimensions, vol. 10, no. 5 (Sept./Oct. 1986), pp. 36–37. Illus., color.

Johan van Kemenade, "New Concepts: A Visual Beam Definition," International Lighting Review, 2d quarter 1986, pp. 53–56. Illus., color. A valuable study for accent lighting design.

"Edwin F. Guth Memorial Award of Merit Projects, 1984," Lighting Design + Application, vol. 14, no. 11 (Nov. 1984), pp. 14–35. Illus. Describes and often illustrates regional award-winning lighting designs for offices/ banks, public places, interiors, restaurants, residences, landscapes, roadways, churches, hospitals, recreational areas, libraries, and industrial buildings.

Paul Goldberger, "The Relationship of Light to Architecture," Lighting Design + Application, vol. 15, no. 9 (Sept. 1985), pp. 14–25. Illus., color. A very important series of articles concerning the basics of architectural lighting.

Louis Erhardt, "Views on the Visual Environment," Lighting Design + Application, "Illuminance" in vol. 14, no. 11 (Nov. 1984), p. 50. A brilliant debunking of many previous studies that attempt to prove that increased work efficiency corresponds with higher light levels. Erhardt, a leading theoretician, defends the lighting designer and questions the basis of lighting engineering claims. This is a continuing series. See also Erhardt's "Views" in all following issues of this magazine. In the Dec. 1984 issue he points out the dubious value of luminance measurements, etc.

Barbara J. Knox, "Architectural Lighting: The Dramatic Influence," Lighting Dimensions, vol. 10, no. 3 (May/June 1986), pp. 23–43, 45–46. Illus., color. A series of eight useful articles, lavishly color illustrated, about the architectural lighting design of Abe Feder, Paul Marantz, Leslie Wheel, Donald Gersztoff, David Mintz, and James Nuckolls.

K. Seshadri, Peter Wang, et al., "About Singapore," International Lighting Review, 38th year, 3rd quarter, 1987, pp. 80–103. Illus., color. Most of issue devoted to architectural lighting in Singapore, including roadways (streets), corporate headquarters buildings, sports areas, office buildings, exterior building illuminations, shopping centers, and residences. Lavishly illustrated in color on glossy paper; good text.

IES, IES Lighting Ready Reference. N.Y.; IES; 1985. Edited by John E. Kaufman and Jack F. Christensen. Available from the Illuminating Engineering Society of North America, 345 East 47th Street, New York, NY 10017. A paperback short version of IES information in the Reference and Application volumes, intended for students. Quite useful, much less expensive and easier to carry.

Videotape:

Lighting Fundamentals, I, II, III, IV. Two videotapes (I, II, and III run 60 minutes; IV runs 20 minutes) covering basic illumination fundamentals. Well done, understandable (with concentration) by nonengineers. Most useful in architectural lighting work.

Susan S. Szenasy, Light, The Complete Handbook of Lighting Design. London; Columbus Books: 1986. 141 pp.; illus. in color throughout. Covers seeing light, using light, diffusing light, concentrating light, and the enduring lamp. Readable, well presented, most useful.

Motoko Ishii, My World of Lights. Tokyo; Libro Port Co., Ltd. 1985. 124 pp., glossy paper, color throughout. Printed in both Japanese and English. Presents the architectural design lighting of Japan's (and the Orient's) leading practitioner today. Available through Motoko Ishii International, 9171 Wilshire Blvd., Suite 606, Beverly Hills, CA 90210. Tel: (213) 275-7710.

John E. Flynn, Arthur W. Segil, and Gary Steffy, Architectural Interior Systems. New York; Van Nostrand Reinhold: 2nd edition, 1988. 326 pp., illus. The definitive volume on the integration of lighting, acoustics, and air conditioning in architectural lighting.

Mark D. Kruger, "Theatrical Techniques in Architectural Lighting." A 7-page handout by Mark Kruger, 9 Murray Street, 9N-E, New York, NY 10007. Tel: (212) 571-0617. Covers his presentation at Lighting World International in New York City in 1989.

"A Tour of Manhattan Light Spots," Lightview International, vol. 2, no. 1 (Spring 1989). pp. 1–3. Illus., color. Good summary of outstanding

consumption and conservation requirements, (8) maintenance and unkeep schedules, and (9) emergency lighting systems.

Anyone engaged in architectural lighting design practice should also be familiar with the judging criteria used by IALD (International Association of Lighting Designers, the professional organization of architectural lighting specialists) in selecting those to be honored at their annual awards presentation. These include:[236a]

- Does this project reinforce the architectural concept?
- Does the design reinforce the natural mood of the activity or situation to create a sense of well-being?
- Is the lighting solution appropriate for the activities of the space?
- Are the lighting elements (i.e., fixtures, coves, etc.) integrated well into the architectural framework?
- Has the appropriateness or inappropriateness of the design as it relates to the culture or geographic location been considered?
- Does this project exemplify technical expertise?
- Is there a satisfactory level of illumination for the specific tasks performed in the space?
- In addition to providing the correct quantity of light, have the more subtle aspects of viewing comfort been addressed, such as glare and contrast ratios?
- If energy conservation was an issue, was it handled appropriately?
- If the budget restrictions were an issue, was the solution successfully executed within the limitations?
- If color or unusual effects with the lighting were considered, were they executed successfully?
- Does this project exemplify high aesthetic achievement?

There is a further objective to this chapter. While the material is not intended for the practicing professional in architectural lighting, other than to supplement available design knowledge, it is intended for those designers trained in nonarchitectural lighting areas, to familiarize them with design criteria and the extent of the architectural field. Most designers in lighting fields other than architectural lighting are untrained in engineering and in the scientific manner of

[236a] Taken from: Lightview International, vol. 1, no. 4 (Winter 1989), p. 2.

thinking. Since basic illumination engineering texts presume a familiarity with the formula approach to a design problem, this chapter is intended to serve as a *transition* for the nonengineer into the practices, objectives, and literature of architectural lighting. Designers *can,* and do, master illumination calculations. This chapter will help make the concepts required for transition more comprehensible.

Who Does Architectural Lighting?

Client/Contractor/Vendor. The client/contractor/vendor makes up the largest group. James Jewell said at a 1978 Illuminating Engineering Society (IES) convention: "Only a negligible portion of the lighting design is actually done by the lighting designers. The majority of design is done by architects, electrical engineers and contractors, and sales representatives."[237] Because local electrical contractors are still the day-to-day authorities on cost of installation, materials, and upkeep (all places where the buck is spent), they act as advisory designers. They are in direct contact with the client on smaller jobs. They know what pleased and what displeased past customers. And they care. They are in a highly competitive position. They need to be certain that the client gets what the client can afford and is comfortable with. However, electrical contractors are not apt to have an in-depth design knowledge. Often a contractor may work in conjunction with an interior designer/decorator, who can contribute developed taste, based on a knowledge of what the client wants, and add creative inventiveness. All too often it is the local electrical contractor, with the assistance of an interior designer and the added help of a vendor (be it the manufacturer of lighting equipment or the local outlet), who "gets the job" if it is small in size (such small jobs can include gardens, residences, stores, offices, and factories). A firm which manufactures and sells lighting equipment may already know the customer, and the firm is most happy to have its staff specify equipment (part of designing), as long as what is specified is a product which the firm produces or markets. If an assignment involves either a large expenditure of money or a firm's prestige image, the lighting design duties may go to a specialized lighting design consultant firm.

Illumination/Architectural/Electrical Engineers. Illumination/architectural/electrical engineers make up another group that does architectural lighting. *Illuminating* (rather than designing the lighting for) a building exterior, a factory, a library, a parking lot, a shopping mall, a sports arena, or a roadway was by past tradition the province of the engineer —not the designer. When light is used to bring pleasure, productivity, or beauty, the illuminator (engineer), who is expected to provide only even visibility, is increasingly yielding to the designer. Nonetheless, illuminating engineers are the backbone of this industry as they research vision (with physicists and vision specialists), develop new instrumentation and technology, and continue to provide the basic knowledge from which the designer works. The contribution of the illumination engineer is extensive and critical. The illumination engineer is concerned with

- Lighting as it affects heat ventilation and flexibility of building use
- Technical knowledge about power factors, distribution and control of current, lighting fixtures, and fittings
- Visual task requirements (enough light being delivered where needed to enable the user to see and to accomplish necessary tasks)
- Cost — of initial installation, operational requirements during a building's life cycle, maintenance and upkeep, and energy consumption

The engineer is uniquely qualified to research and make judgments about these concerns. Day in and day out the engineer deals with obtaining and installing lighting equipment. These lighting scientists/engineers came into prominence with the successful development of the incandescent lamp. Early use of electricity required someone trained in science—not an artist. Engineers rapidly branched out and began intensive, useful studies of *amounts* of radiant energy needed for optimum visual performance. They postulated stated minimum levels of illumination for a wide variety of tasks. Engineers were, and continue to be, at the forefront in developing increasingly better light sources and luminaires (fixtures). R. G. Hopkinson, an engineer who has a broader artistic perspective than many of his fellow engineers, wrote in 1970:

architectural lighting design highlights in Manhattan, with excellent color photos.

"The Profession of Lighting Design: A Roundtable Discussion," Lightview International, *vol. 2, no. 1 (Spring 1989), pp. 4–6. Illus. Subtitle is: "What is a lighting designer, exactly? Why should I include a lighting designer on my project team? And if I decide to use one, how do I find the right lighting designer for my particular project?" The panel consisted of: Peter Barna (Light & Space Assoc., Ltd.), Garen Goldstick (Gary Gordon Architectural Lighting Design), Jules Horton (Horton-Lees Lighting Design, Inc.), John Lijewski (ISD, Inc.), Hayden McKay (Hayden McKay Lighting Design), Anthony Romeo (Wm. Nicholas Bodouva & Assoc.), Sara Schrager (Sara Schrager Lighting Consultants), and D. W. Schweppe, Jr. (Schweppe Lighting Design, Inc.). The moderator was Barbara Ciance (Horton-Lees Lighting Design Inc.). The comments of these six architectural lighting designers, an architect, and an interior designer are probably the best statement in print of what the architectural lighting designer does and why.*

"Focus on Australia," International Lighting Review, *40th year (1989), 1st quarter, entire issue. Illus., color. This summary of architectural lighting in Australia covers bridges, atriums, libraries, a bicentennial celebration, landscape lighting, building exterior illumination, sports facilities, restaurants, and a world exposition. Excellent text and color photos.*

"Lumen Awards," Lighting Dimensions, *vol. 12, no. 4 (May/June 1989), pp. 42–43. Illus., color. Lumen Awards to Howard Branston (relighting of Statue of Liberty), Francesca Bettridge, and Stephen Bernstrin's office tower in Minneapolis, Jerry Kugler's Herman Miller Showroom, and Babu Shankar's Willard Hotel in Washington, D. C.*

[237] *"Light, Architecture, and Aesthetics,"* Lighting Design & Application, *vol. 8, no. 11 (Nov. 1978), p. 21.*

[238] *R. G. Hopkinson and J. B. Collins,* The Ergonomics of Lighting. *London; McDonald Technical and Scientific; 1970. Excellent text on fundamentals of vision and illumination engineering. Scholarly and well-illustrated. Not for the nonengineer or anyone weak in math. Covers seeing, light production and measurement, fixtures (luminaires), and applications. Professor Hopkinson is one of the world's leading researchers in the fields of optics, vision, and illumination. Quote from p. 17.*

[239] *Dr. Walther Köhler and Wassili Luckhardt,* Lighting in Architecture. *N.Y.; Reinhold; 1959. Progresses from theory to practice. Lavishly illustrated. Invaluable study by an illuminating engineer. Quote from p. 116.*

[240] *Leslie Larson, p. 1, op. cit. (see footnote 235).*

[241] *Ibid., p. 2.*

[242] *"Lighting Design,"* Progressive Architecture, *Sept. 1973. Entire issue devoted to lighting, pp. 73–121. Quote by Brandston from pp. 76 and 86–89.*

The science and art of lighting depends upon the adaptability of the eye to function with reasonable efficiency in a wide range of conditions. The eye is able to make use of very high and of very low levels of light, but there are certain optimum conditions in which it works best, and the aim of the lighting research is to find out exactly what are these optimum conditions. The aim of good lighting is to provide them.[238]

Lighting Designers/Consultants. Lighting designers/consultants are practitioners of architectural lighting whose training and experience are concentrated in *uses of light* and *responses to light.* The lighting designer is likely to be well-versed in uses of light for theatricalism and merchandising. While technical background may be strong, a key asset is artistry. Early training was most likely either in theatre or in illuminating engineering. There are engineers who are artists who practice lighting *design.* There are designers whose only strength is mastery of technology. The gifted lighting designer combines concern with artistry, a solid grounding in technology, an ability to utilize IES illumination calculations, and, above all, the skills to deal equally well with an architect, an electrical contractor, and a client. The lighting designer keeps in mind those things which will have maximum usable impact upon the customer. Köhler and Luckhardt summed up the issue of lighting designer traits as follows: "We strive for a collaboration between the artist creative in engineering and the artistically creative engineer."[239]

The lighting designer is a relatively new breed—not a contractor, yet one who specifies equipment (but does not install it). The designer is not an engineer but should be thoroughly familiar with the engineer's accumulated knowledge and research. The lighting designer deals with "spatial design." According to Leslie Larson, "The power of visualization distinguishes the designer from the engineer,"[240] and "lighting must be designed before it is engineered."[241] Howard Brandston writes:

In the hands of a skilled designer, lighting creates a planned sequence of visual revelations, clearly expressing the architect's aesthetic intent, and provides visual understanding of the functional elements of the architect's space. Lighting can, if its inherent dramatic and psychological qualities are exploited with sensitivity and imagination, add fresh visual and emotional dimensions to an architectural solution. This is not to say that the medium is the message—only that the medium can significantly reinforce the message.

What is a lighting designer? He is not a mechanical, electrical or illuminating engineer—though he is thoroughly conversant with all of these specialties. He is not a footcandle calculator—though illumination adequate for specific functions is certainly one of his concerns. He is not a fixture broker—though selection or design of fixtures appropriate to a given space is one of the services he provides. A lighting designer is what the term says he is—a *designer* whose field of specialization is light, an independent professional who earns his living solely by providing a design consultation service. The good lighting designer does not think in terms of equipment, wattage or illumination level. He thinks in terms of space.

The lighting practitioner has not always been a lighting *designer.* As a separate and distinct professional service, lighting design has evolved over the past four decades from a minor specialty most commonly offered by sales representatives (but not infrequently practiced by unqualified "consultants") to its present status as an independent discipline similar to landscape architecture, acoustical engineering, graphic design and other professional services.[242]

Jules G. Horton, president of Jules G. Horton Lighting Design, Inc., and himself an engineer, wrote these incisive thoughts and (which are an applicable summary of this discussion) in the May 1974 *Lighting Design & Application:*

Can we all agree on a definition of a lighting designer? . . . [A] lighting designer is a person (not a group or corporation) who designs lighting systems (not just components of a system) and does not manufacture, distribute, or sell any product—tangible (lamps, fixtures, components) or intangible (electric power).

Some of my respected and/or successful fellow practitioners come from the fields of architecture, interior design, theatre, electrical engineering, and fixture design. Each professional gives the convert some very valuable knowledge and experience that others have to acquire the hard way. . . . that brings me to the list of requirements that, in my opinion, have to be fulfilled if one is to qualify as a lighting designer:

■ Interest in human psychology; ability to analyze and predict human behavior in a varying visual environment.

■ Interest in art and architecture; knowledge of their history and variables of style.

■ Interest in varying human tasks (this includes leisure activities) and conditions: ability to analyze and predict the effect of visual environment upon the performance of tasks and response to conditions.

- Ability to see and interpret the effect of visual environment upon the appearance of people and spaces.
- Ability to communicate with the architect, interior designer, and landscape architect, on their terms, and to translate their design successfully into mental images in which light becomes the key variable.
- Ability to communicate to these professionals, again on their terms, concepts of lighting design that he, the lighting designer, considers best suited to the requirements.
- Ability to relate his design concepts to the economic technical and maintenance aspects of the project.
- Knowledge of building materials and methods affecting his trade.
- Up-to-date knowledge of lighting hardware (lamps, fixtures, components, finishes).
- Knowledge of manufacturing processes and problems affecting lighting specifications.
- Ability to analyze local conditions and to correctly interpret their possible effects on design and specifying decisions.
- Ability to apply correctly all relevant tools and methods of illuminating engineering to the process of design.
- Ability to produce optimal design within the given parameters of first and operating costs as well as the criteria of energy conservation.
- Ability to produce a set of contract documents that give the owner what he paid for the project and protect him from unwarranted extras. At the same time, these documents should help the contractor to plan his work without undue surprises or need for endless clarifications.
- Ability to produce a concise and clear set of information for the operating personnel after the completion of the project.[243]

Design Objectives

The largest number of lighting designers are employed in the architectural lighting industry. Lighting design theories and practices of the more esoteric portions of our industry influence, modify, and enhance architectural lighting practices, but the base objective remains *lighting spaces at night.*

Picasso said that light is "a measuring instrument in the world of shapes." Derek Phillips wrote in 1964: "Natural lighting [daylight] is becoming a luxury."[244] The American Associates of the Blind estimates that seven-eighths of *all* our perceptions are through sight. Sight is design! "Obviously, there is no sight without light," wrote James Nuckolls.[245] Abe H. Feder notes that in too many cases lighting design tends to forget people. He believes that lighting de-

sign should create "a world designed for people. We create places for living where we work. The central cause is people, *not* walls and ceilings."[246] Frank Lloyd Wright could have been speaking of lighting design when he wrote: "A doctor can bury his mistakes, but an architect can only advise his client to plant ivy." William M. C. Lam writes:

> We are comfortable when we are free to focus our attention on what we want or need to see, when the information we seek is clearly visible and confirms our desires and our expectations, and when the background does not compete for our attention in a distracting way.
>
> A good luminous environment helps us to do what we want to do and makes us feel good while we do it. . . . [It] provides a comfortable, pleasant, reassuring, interesting and functional space for the people who inhabit it.[247]

Willard Thompson wrote in the 1930s: "I wish that architects and lighting designers had a better understanding of each other's objectives and problems. Lighting is so much a part of a building that close liaison between them is necessary if the building is to function and aesthetically serve its purpose."[248] *Progressive Architecture* devoted its September 1973 issue to lighting design. In that issue the editors wrote:

> But what is "good" lighting? The criteria vary from place to place, from situation to situation. It cannot be measured by its effectiveness, appropriateness and allowances for adjustment by the individual user, who is apt to have needs or preferences different from the average. The research must go on, the body of knowledge must grow. Facts must be separated from opinion, scientific criteria from subjectivity. Probably the most important input will come from the lighting designers—those who earn their livings by mixing scientific principles, technical know-how and educated tastes into what becomes a technical art form, applying it to real, not theoretical, situations.[249]

Designers are aware that light can be used to modify spaces. Light can unify space, reveal or conceal and control surfaces, and heighten or diminish spaces. Light can add the following features to an architectural space:

- *Variety.* Variations of intensity (bright places and dark shadow areas) and variations of color and direction (or distribution) are important. They are vital to the architect in revealing, organizing, and emphasizing the space he has

[243] *Julius G. Horton, "Views and Opinions: What Is a Lighting Designer?" Lighting Design & Application, vol. 9, no. 5 (May 1974), p. 14.*

[244] *Derek Phillips, Lighting in Architectural Design. N.Y.; McGraw-Hill; 1964. Excellent study with emphasis on designing, theory, and current practice, by England's leading designer. Lavishly illustrated. Solid, useful. 310 pp. Quote from p. 13.*

[245] *James Nuckolls, p. vii, op. cit. (see footnote 236.).*

[246] *Abe H. Feder, "Lighting, Awareness and Discipline," Lighting Dimensions, vol. 2, no. 4 (Apr. 1978), pp. 38–39, 43, 48–49. Good discussion of the place of the theatre-trained lighting designer in architectural lighting consultation by a noted practitioner. Quote from pp. 38, 48–49.*

[247] *William M. C. Lam, p. 14, op. cit. (see footnote 236.).*

[248] *"A Salute to Willard Thompson," Light magazine, vol. 26, no. 3 (May/June 1957), p. 4.*

[249] *"Lighting Design," p. 73, op. cit. (see footnote 242).*

250 *R. G. Hopkinson and J. D. Kay*, The Lighting of Buildings. *London; Farber & Farber; 1969. Best of the older British texts. Includes schools, hospitals, offices and laboratories, factories, residential buildings, and — buildings in the tropics. 318 pp. Quote from p. 21.*

251 *Excerpted from the introduction to the Wheel-Garon, Inc., Lighting Consultants brochure.*

252 *William M. C. Lam, p. 2, op. cit. (see footnote 236.).*

253 *William M.C. Lam, pp. 5–6, op. cit. (see footnote 236.).*

created. Variations are of great importance to the person who eventually works in a building, for they add rest, relief, focus, and comfort — and sometimes charm and beauty.

• *Visibility.* The architectural place, the objects therein, and the detailing thereof are shaped by, and the appearance of things revealed, clarified, and modeled by, *organized visibility* (not just flat, even footcandles of illumination). The needs of the user of the building are of more importance than those of the architect, the constructor, or the client.

• *Color.* Hopkinson and Kay state that a "rich colour can be a bass note to counterpoint an otherwise high color scheme."[250] Often both emotional response and mood are a result of light and color. A lively or restful place, a neutral or intimate environ, a high-key or low-key atmosphere, an overall look of excitement or repose or sparkle — all are the province of the lighting designer, who can articulate a building's space, uses, and meaning.

• *Efficiency, Comfort, and Safety.* These are as much design factors as they are illumination objectives. The consultant must always be concerned with the needs of heating and ventilation, air conditioning, acoustical control, electrical distribution, fire control, and variable partitioning of interior spaces. These are as much the concern of the lighting designer as they are those of the illuminating engineer.

A Wheel-Garon brochure expresses the lighting designer's objectives:

> The luminous environment should evolve out of the essential character of the structure, the functions it performs, and the people for whom it is created. Experienced through light and shadow, it becomes an intangible bridge between the forms created by the designer, and the sensory perception of the individual. Light is experienced not only through vision but also through the emotions. This planned experience in light should be as varied and dynamic as the architecture itself.[251]

William M. C. Lam writes forcefully on the side of design (versus illumination). Speaking of his own development as a designer, Lam writes:

> I became increasingly aware that the difference between sparkle and glare, like the difference between music and noise, did not lie in measured intensity ratios or absolute intensity levels,

the conventional criteria for the luminous environment. More light was, indeed, often less pleasant, less comfortable, and even less safe. Yet lighting handbooks, codes, and the spokesmen of the power and lighting industries all seemed to be saying that more light was a good thing under all circumstances — something to strive for in design of the luminous environment.[252]

[A]s human beings we evaluate an environment according to how well that environment is structured, organized, and illuminated to satisfy all of our needs for visual information. These needs derive from both the activities in which we choose to engage and the biological information needs related to the very essentials of human nature which are present regardless of the specific activity which holds our attention at one time. . . . In the relevant, appropriate luminous environment, those things which we want or need to see are clearly visible and emphasized, while those things which are distracting or unpleasant are de-emphasized or hidden from sight. The relevant environment is comfortable and reassuring — it makes us feel at ease, while helping us to do the things we do.

Until those who own, design, finance, build, regulate, and maintain our physical environment base their work on a deeper understanding of the principles of perception and of the true, total nature of human perceptual needs, they will continue to grind out bad luminous environments.[253] (Italics are this author's.)

There is no *real* differentiation between lighting designers and architects specializing in lighting other than attitudes and approaches stemming from different initial training. Both have the same objectives, and each has made noteworthy contributions to the architectural lighting industry. That master architect, Le Corbusier, said in 1927: "Architecture is the masterly, correct and magnificent play of masses brought together in *light*." Wanda Jankowski, editor of *Lighting Design + Application* said in an editorial in the April 1983 issue: "The age of specifying standard lighting solutions to a broad range of problems is virtually gone. Clients will demand personalization, and increased 'humanness' in their environments. The 'design' part of lighting is not going to go away."[254]

Landscape Architecture

Landscape illumination stands out as one of the foremost challenges facing the lighting professional today. Whether it be gardens, patios, or extensive residential or corporate grounds, the questions and limitations are complex. But the payoffs in terms of design statement and satisfaction are grand.[254A]

A relative newcomer to the field of lighting design, the landscape architecture lighting designer was in many cases trained as a landscape architect. If specializing in lighting, landscape architects are concerned with

- Walks, paths, and steps
- Driveways and parking areas (but not streets)
- Gardens: trees, shrubs, flowers, fences, and walls
- Water: pools, fountains, and waterfalls
- Porches, terraces, and patios; places for outdoor work and domestic sports areas
- Parks and outdoor professional sports areas
- Building exteriors; bridges, tunnels, airports, and transit systems; shopping malls; signs

The earliest garden lighting was created with Japanese lanterns and floodlights tacked onto buildings. The first extensive outdoor artificial illumination was for the Chicago Columbian Exposition in 1893. By 1916 the elaborate night lighting of the James L. Breese estate in Southampton, Long Island, New York, existed as an early example of domestic landscape lighting in the United States. In 1928 Clarence Mackay brought Rudolph Wendel to the United States from Europe. Wendel was a lighting artist who perceived his mission in life to be the artistic illumination design of gardens, painting, sculpture, tapestries, and other works of art. The foundations of both garden lighting and museum lighting trace back to his work. When John Watson, today's major artist in this field, began his work, he found it necessary to describe his occupation as "landscape architecture lighting design." Until that time Wendel had called it "garden lighting." In a letter from Wendel to John Watson for inclusion in Watson's thesis (finished in 1947), Wendel wrote:

In regard to outdoor lighting, our aim . . . has been to create moonlight. The light sources are concealed even in daylight itself.[255] The leading idea of garden lighting is to give not only distinctive separate light effects but to achieve a unified, artistic composition. The landscape architect attains the impression of an artistic but not artificial illumination. He is able to create the fascination and mystery of a garden bathed in moonlight. The lighting harmonizes with the style and flora of each garden.[256]

Wendel summarized many of today's garden lighting design objectives when he wrote the following in the June 1936 *House and Garden*:

As the plan of a garden is the expression of a landscape artist which an individual has chosen because it expresses a portion of his personality, so the lighting of a garden can be equally an achievement of art, which by its form, natural or even unreal can be for that individual a continuous source of inspiration.

Garden lighting attempted without a thorough study of its reason and without the vision of its final effect may end in a complete failure. . . . The use of different reflectors and their placement can determine the appearance of a statue, either as a natural decoration or a ghost visiting over regions, or as a gem clearly outlined against the night sky.[257]

Why light outdoors at night? Six basic reasons can be set forth:

1. *Visibility.* To help people see where they are going outdoors at night and to direct attention (to a garage, pool, statuary, etc.).

[254] *Prafulla C. Sorcar*, Rapid Lighting Design and Cost Estimating. *N.Y.; McGraw-Hill; 1979. Absolutely invaluable to the student in lighting who is not an engineer. Provides readable tables of all standard luminaire distribution and cost factors. Handy reference and application volume. Illus.*

"Engineers vs. Designers—A Lighthearted Debate with a Message," Lighting Design & Application, *vol. 12, no. 8 (Aug. 1982). pp. 21–19. Illus. A worthwhile look at the question, Who is the right person for a client to hire to do the lighting for a project—a designer or an engineer? See also* "Letters," *vol. 12, no. 11 (Nov. 1982), p. 2.*

Wanda Jankowski, *"The Importance of Considering Psychology in Design,"* Lighting Design & Application, *vol. 12, no. 9 (Sept. 1982), pp. 10–19. Illus., color. Important design concepts.*

V. C. Gulati and S. P. Tambe, *"Tourist Attractions: Marble Rocks Valley, India,"* International Lighting Review, *4th quarter 1986, pp. 144–147. Illus., color. Lighting an Indian natural environment.*

Louis Erhardt, *"Views on the Visual Environment—Design Process Part I—Project Analysis,"* Lighting Design & Application, *vol. 13, no. 10 (Oct. 1983), pp. 8–9. Absolute* must *reading for any architectural lighting designer. Erhardt presents a list of essential questions to ask prior to proposing any design solution. He expands upon basics of William M. C. Lam. See also* "Design Process Part 2," Lighting Design & Application, *vol. 13, no. 11 (Nov. 1983), p. 6; and* "Design Process Part 3," Lighting Design & Application, *vol. 13, no. 12 (Dec. 1983). Erhardt concludes the series with* "20 Questions of Design," Lighting Design & Application, *vol. 14, no. 1 (Jan. 1984), p. 8, a very useful checklist of fundamentals of architectural lighting design.*

John E. Flynn, AIA/IES, *"Reflections from the Present on the Past: Concepts Beyond the IES Framework,"* Lighting Design + Application, *vol. 13, no. 6 (June 1983), pp. 34–40. Illus. A reprinting of Professor Flynn's January 1973 statement which, when he became president of IES, changed the institute's direction. Followed by (same pages) Ronald Goodrich,* "Concepts Reconsidered: An Environmental Psychologist Comments on the Applicability of Flynn's Ideas and Approach in 1983."

Jane Rottenbach, "They Say the Neon Lights Are Bright on Broadway—Advertising, Art and Magic," Lighting Design + Application, *vol. 17, no. 4 (Apr. 1987), pp. 33–35. Illus. A rare article about lighted signs.*

Michel Quointeau, "Presentation Techniques: Artists' Impressions in Lighting," International Lighting Review, *1984/4, pp. 116–121. Illus., color. The best article in print of designer's use of light/shade/color sketches for client presentation of a design concept. Accompanied by nine beautifully reproduced artist's sketches and readable text.*

Randy Burkett, "Presentation Techniques: Presentation of Lighting Designs with Back-lighted Transparencies," International Lighting Review, *1984/4, pp. 127–129. Illus., color. Another useful technique, well presented, for the architectural lighting designer's use in client presentation.*

2. *Safety and Protection.* To discourage prowlers and provide additional night security.

3. *Fun, Work, Play, and Entertainment Outdoors.* To make the outdoors usable after dark, whether for a picnic, swimming, reading, or sports — in all, for "outdoor living" at night.

4. *Visual Beauty.* To create an artistic ambience or to illuminate a strikingly beautiful garden, flowers, statuary, etc.

5. *Prestige.* To solicit attention or admiration in order to enhance the property owner's prestige, or increase property value, by the addition of something "extra" representing taste and lavishness.

6. *Control Insects.* To decrease annoying insect presence by use of "insect lights."

There is a difference between landscape *illumination* (the type of floodlighting that can be done by the electrical contractor or the talented homeowner) and landscape *design.*

Design Considerations

The eleven basic design considerations are touched upon below:

1. The designer must consider the *personality* of the individual for whom the garden is to be illuminated. What colors affect the owner? What is the owner's taste level? Is the client quiet, studious, sincere, and meek or aggressive, bold, and blunt? What are the client's likes and dislikes? Does the client prefer formalism or abandon?

2. What are the *intentions* of the owner for the finished garden? (What is the garden to be used for? Sports? Entertaining? Meditation?)

3. Garden lighting should *harmonize* with the style and period of decoration of the owner's building and with suitable decor for the time designed (fashion). A modern penthouse garden *could* justify the use of neon tubing; an old Tudor garden never.

4. *Activity areas* — terraces and dining patios or areas for reading or card playing — should be bright. Eye strain must be avoided.

5. Consider the *observer's viewpoint.* Is the garden to be seen from a picture window (fixed viewpoint) or while moving within the garden (mobile viewpoint)?

6. The spectator must be unaware of the light sources, so *indirect* light should be used. At least 90 percent of all sources should be hidden from view.

7. The designer needs to have adequate *technical knowledge.*

8. The designer must study and understand the layout of the garden, both by day and by night, before beginning to design. The designer should seek a *focus,* and it is the designer's task to control and plan emphasis and accentuation. Watson says: "Spatial expression of the relationships of lines, tones, colors and textures [are the key to garden lighting]. When the lighting I have designed simply illuminates something, I've made a mistake, and change it so that the illumination interprets part of a scene. I make it do something more than light up a subject. I bring it out."[258]

9. Lighting units must be selected which are *sturdy* in construction, *weatherproof* and *watertight, safe* in operation (electrically), and *tamperproof* (when used in exposed or public places).

10. The designer should use many *small light sources* rather than high-powered floodlights (design versus illumination). Watson quotes from an earlier General Electric pamphlet: "Sustained brightness destroys aerial perspective. Decreasing brightness increases the apparent depth." Do not be afraid of using shadow and areas of darkness.

11. The designer must consider *cost* and *energy consumption.* Factors involved, besides initial cost of units and installation, are long lamp life and low energy consumption.

Communication Forms

As might be expected, theatre light plots are not used here. Architectural site studies are; so, too, are electrical contractor wiring and unit drawings. John Watson, for example, executes his designs by having the electrical installation performed by contractors but doing the final focus and adjustment himself (or having a trained staff member do it). Usually the client is presented with a written, illustrated "prospectus" (discussed later in this chapter).

Techniques

Some specific additional notes may be useful. Water and pools should be illuminated from within the water for maximum effectiveness, because illumination of the bottom makes the water appear luminous (lighting from outside opaques the surface). In fountain lighting, illumination of each water jet or spray from within, with the water jet *surrounding* a directional light source, works best. In determining relative wattage (or intensity) color balance for fountains to overcome color output of standard light sources, Watson suggests the following relative (proportional) amounts: amber, 1.5; red, 2; green, 3; and blue, 5. In other words, 500 watts of blue light should be used for every 150 watts of amber light (due to low output in most light sources and low transmission of filters).[259] In addition to using intricately designed pumps and controllers for the fountain water jets themselves, designers of water displays also employ mobile and changing light patterns, which can be controlled by flashers, dimmers, rotary controllers, or (the ultimate) electronic memory programmers. For waterfalls and cascades, it is best to illuminate from immediately under the crest of the waterfall. See Color Fig. 74 in Chap. 9 of the Tivoli Garden fountains in Copenhagen, Denmark. Figure 10.1 and Color Figs. 76 and 77 are the 1979 relighting of Niagara Falls. This lighting is a continuing project by Jean Rosenthal Associates designers Nananne Porcher and engineer Clyde Nordheimer.

Some specifics concerning night lighting levels might be useful in some cases. Moonlight is usually around 1 footcandle. To "pull out" an outdoor object in moonlight levels of light, 4 footcandles is a minimum level, 5 to 8 footcandles represents medium brightness, and 8 to 30 footcandles is generally considered to be quite bright. A small sculpture can be adequately illuminated using 15 footcandles. These basic landscape lighting levels were suggested by designer Tim Coppola at the Lighting World International conference in New York City on May 13, 1987.

When lighting around trees, shrubs, and flowers it is wise to keep in mind the varying reflectivity of plants. For example, the top surface of a rhododendron leaf (in midsummer) reflects 9.7 percent of incident *daylight,* while the undersurface of each leaf reflects 34.5 percent. Bright flowers will reflect from 50 to 75 percent of incident daylight. Green grass reflects 10 percent. These levels all change throughout the season as the various plants grow and fade.

John Watson and I vary slightly in the colors we suggest for night garden illumination. John Watson leans toward the pale blues and greens and unaltered white. My choices stem from my Landscape Architecture Lighting Design class at Purdue University, in which classroom experiments indicated a heavy student preference for pale lavender (violet) and pale blue on plants, flowers, and greenery. John Watson and I are in accord on some fundamentals: tints should be used; only *rarely* are strong, saturated colors appropriate. The designer should *not* try to reproduce daylight — it just isn't possible or desirable.

The landscape architectural lighting designer should give positive consideration to *mobility* and change of light and light patterns. Static, inflexible lighting lacks a vital element. Perhaps this description of the lighting of the first large lighted garden (on the Breese estate, 1916) best illustrates the point:

> The garden is left in darkness until the family and guests are gathered on the terrace back of the house. Then, nearly a half a mile away, a great marble vase, filled with gay-colored flowers, begins to glow in an intense blue light which grows brighter and paler until pure white is reached, and then a tremulous variation between pale blue and old ivory, as the blue and amber lights rise and fall. The vase is flanked by two tall Hermae, which, from a distance give the whole groups the aspect of some fairy shrine. Hardly is this impression fixed, when the path from the group to the house becomes slowly illuminated, followed by the peculiar gray-blue of the pergolas and the evenly diffused general illumination of the foliage in the inner garden. The water fountain is still out of range of any of the lights, the most brilliant spot being the group at the far end of the long path; but now a soft rose color melts into the white of the marble, changing almost instantly to pale orange, and a fleeting touch of green, but so imperceptibly that one cannot tell when the variations take place. The fountain dominates the picture, and the illumination is complete.[260]

One final note: At various times successful use has been made of ultraviolet light (black light) in garden designing.

Procedures and Practices

The work of John Watson[261] is shown in Figs. 10.2 through 10.5 and Color Figs. 78 to 81. These photographs represent a wide range of work. Figure 10.6 shows a quality restaurant, the Rainbow Lodge, in a lovely sylvan setting in Hous-

J. F. Caminada, "Architectural: About Architectural Lighting," International Lighting Review, 1984/4, pp. 132–135. Illus., color. One of the most important articles of recent vintage about design principles in architectural lighting, with color sketches and photos illustrating all key design basics.

Sara Schrager and Ann Lurie Berlin, "Troubleshooting Lighting Design," Lighting Design + Application, vol. 16, no. 6 (June 1986), pp. 52–58. Illus. A prominent Canadian architectural lighting designer writes about unusual design assignments. Useful for those already in practice.

"Getting Ready for Outdoors: A Preview of Outdoor Lighting for 1987," Home Lighting & Accessories, vol. 70, no. 3 (Mar. 1987), pp. 52–75. Illus. Very useful text along with "new products" presentation.paper; good text.

[254a] From the Designer's Lighting Forum of New York and the New York IES poster for the March 15, 1989, Landscape Lighting Product Revue.

[255] John R. Watson, Garden Illumination for the Landscape Architect. M.S. thesis, Agricultural and Mechanical College of Texas, June 1947. 184 pp., illus. Definitive earliest work by Watson. First study on subject. Quote from p. 73.

[256] Ibid., pp. 73–74.

[257] Ibid., pp. 75–77.

[258] Frenchy Falik, "Landscape Illumination: A Light Touch for Beauty and Security," Houston Home/Garden magazine, March 1979, pp. 83–88.

[259] John Watson, p. 26, op. cit. (see footnote 255.). See also "Fountains of Light," Lighting Dimensions, vol. 8, no. 4 (July/Aug. 1984), pp. 20–24, 26, 42. Illus., color. A description of Pierre du Pont's Longwood Gardens in Kennett Square, Pennsylvania. This is the only lengthy piece on fountain lighting readily available.

[260] "The Garden At Night," Country Life in America, vol. 31, no. 3 (Jan. 1917), pp. 26–27.

Figure 10.1 Niagara Falls Illumination Building with modified Xenon spots installed inside old arc housings from original 1950s units. Lighting by Clyde Nordheimer and Nananne Porcher.

Figure 10.3 Town North Townhomes in Dallas, Texas (1974). Lighting by John Watson.

Figure 10.5 The LBJ Ranch in Johnson City, Texas (1972). Lighting by John Watson.

Figure 10.2 The George Brown Residence in Forth Worth, Texas, 1975. Lighting by John Watson.

Figure 10.4 The Registry Office Complex in Dallas, Texas, 1972. Lighting by John Watson.

Figure 10.6 Exterior lighting by the restaurant owners of the picturesque grounds surrounding the Rainbow Lodge, Birdsall Drive, Houston, Texas. (*Courtesy of Dr. Sandra Montgomery.*)

261 *To give the reader some concept of the range of work handled by John Watson, here is a selected pre-1980 summary of his designs:*

26 Clubs, including the Aspen Club (Colo.), Big Canoe Country Club (Atlanta, Ga.), Birnham Wood Golf Club (Santa Barbara, Ca.), 19 others in Texas (Dallas, San Antonio, Fort Worth, Houston, Austin, etc.).

14 National headquarters buildings, including Atlantic-Richfield Plaza (Los Angeles, Ca.); Gulf States Paper Co (Tuscaloosa, Ala.); and Pepsico, Inc. (Purchase, N.Y.).

7 Universities, including Auburn University (Auburn, Ala.), Cornell (Ithaca, N.Y.), Hendricks (Conway, Ariz.), Texas A&M (College Station, Tex.), Texas Christian University (Fort Worth, Tex.), Trinity University (San Antonio, Tex.), and University of Texas (Austin).

31 Community Developments (major housing complexes) in Texas, Florida, and Georgia.

8 Hospitals in Texas and Louisiana.

9 Religions Centers in Texas and Massachusetts (Christian Science Mother Church).

14 Parks in Texas, Georgia, and Missouri, including Queen Victoria and Regina (Saskatchewan), Canada. These include Six Flags Over Georgia, Mid-America (St. Louis), and Texas, plus Great Adventure *in Jackson, N.J.*

13 Restaurants in Texas and Louisiana.

Plus assorted camps, hotels, office buildings, banks, and museums.

Headquartered in Dallas, Texas, John Watson has offices in 19 cities, (1989), including Houston, Austin, and San Antonio, Texas; Atlanta, Georgia; New Orleans, Louisiana; Honolulu, Hawaii; Connecticut; and Mexico City. His firm handles approximately 500 design assignments each year.

See also Wanda Jankowski, Inside Lighting *(obtainable from: Wanda Jankowski, P.O. Box 1823, Murray Hill Station, N.Y., NY 10156), preview issue, p. 7 (May 1986), for an illustration of Watson's lighting of CenTrust Tower in Miami, Florida.*

262 *Basic reference works:*

Bernard Gladstone, The Complete Book of Garden and Outdoor Lighting. *N.Y.; Hearthside Press; 1956. 120 pp. Illus. Good volume for the "do it yourself" outdoor amateur; discusses planning; wiring; fixtures and equipment; gardens, patios, terraces, pools, walks, and entrances; "build your own" lighting equipment; Christmas lighting; insect repellant lights; and safety and maintenance. Good illustrations. Out of print.*

Stanley Schuler, Outdoor Lighting for Your Home. *N.Y.; D. Van Nostrand; 1962. 192 pp.,* *illus. Another "do it yourself" guidebook. Covers same subjects as Gladstone (above). Excellent illustrations from the work of John Watson. Also numerous illustrations of the design work of others. Out of print.*

"Japanese Garden Light," Lighting Design + Application, *vol. 15, no. 10 (Oct. 1985), pp. 18–19. Illus., color. An Edwin F. Guth Memorial Award of Excellence by the IES for garden lighting.*

"Mr. Moonlight," Houston Chronicle, *Texas Magazine, Sunday, September 1, 1968, pp. 8–11. Excellent color photographs and text about John Watson's work.*

F. B. Nightingale, Lighting As an Art. *Skyforest, Calif.; Knight Publishing Co.; 1962. 320 pp. Also see* Garden Lighting *by Nightingale, no date. Privately printed curiosity by an early garden lighting authority. A well-illustrated, disorganized memorabilia. Out of print.*

Contemporary Lighting: Selected Projects from the Second Philips International Lighting Contest, *Eindhoven, Netherlands; Centrex Publishing Co.; 1961. 190 pp. "Outdoor Lighting," pp. 88–181. Photos and descriptions of outstanding foreign lighting of streets, tunnels, service stations, railroad yards, docks, festivals, stadiums and sports arenas, fountains, and buildings. Excellent summary of lighting design artistry abroad.*

Harry B. Zackrison, Jr., "Outside Lighting Systems Design," Lighting Design & Application, *vol. 10, no. 5 (June 1980), pp. 29–38. Illus. Fine basic article.*

Derek Phillips, Floodlighting Buildings. *Published by the Royal Institute of British Architects, 66 Portland Place, London, W1N4AD, England; 1983. 33 pp. Illus., color. Presents page after page of text, color photographs, and lighting descriptions of the key night-lighted buildings exteriors in England. Valuable addition to the sparse literature in this field.*

"Fury of the Nile," Lighting Design + Application, *vol. 15, no. 10 (Oct. 1985), p. 46. Illus. A Guth Award of Merit by IES for exterior lighting.*

Elaine C. Cherry, Fluorescent Light Gardening. *N.Y.; D. Van Nostrand; 1965. 256 pp. Useful volume for those interested in "grow light" gardening.*

"The Great Illuminator," Lighting Dimensions, *vol. 9, no. 4 (July/Aug. 1985), pp. 44–47. Illus., color. An interview with Douglas Leigh,* *foremost building illuminator in the United States, with photographs of his work.*

"Chrysler Building Night Lighting," Lighting Design + Application, *vol. 12, no. 8 (Aug. 1982), pp. 11–12. Illus., color.*

"The Light at the End of Park Avenue," Lighting Design + Application, *vol. 9, no. 6 (June 1979). Douglas Leigh's lighting of the Hemsley Building, in New York City—a Lumen Award winner.*

Wout van Bommel and Joop van Dijk, "Security Lighting for Domestic Exteriors," Lighting Design + Application, *vol. 15, no. 5 (May 1985), pp. 39–44. Illus. Two Netherlands experts give in-depth treatment of home security lighting.*

Wanda Jankowski, "Exterior Lighting: Two Approaches," Inside Lighting *(obtainable from Wanda Jankowski, P.O. Box 1823, Murray Hill Station, N.Y., NY 10156), preview issue, p. 6. Illus.*

John Marsteller, "Documenting the Lighted Landscape," Lighting Design + Application, *vol. 16, no. 4 (April 1986) pp. 16–21. Illus., color. A leading international lighting designer suggests and illustrates in sketches and color photos how to organize design ideas.*

D. W. Atwater and Alfred Paulus, "Artificial Light as an Aid to the Landscape Architect," Transactions of the Illuminating Engineering Society, *March 1983, pp. 223–38. Early basic treatment. Well-illustrated. Much stress on early available luminaires. Good historical survey. Outdated technical information.*

C. M. Cutler, "Why a Fair," Light *magazine, vol. 33, no. 3 (1964), pp. 11–26. Numerous illustrations, many in color, of lighted fountains and reflecting pools at world's fairs.*

P. Gergely, "Outdoor: Lighting Gems Along the Danube," Lighting Design + Application, *vol. 9, no. 12 (Dec. 1979), pp. 6–10, 12. Illus., color.*

"Outdoor," Lighting Design + Application, *vol. 11, no. 6 (June 1981), pp. 6–7. Illus., color.*

"Outdoor—Cleveland's Terminal Tower," Lighting Design + Application, *vol. 13, no. 3 (Mar. 1983), pp. 20–23. Illus., color. See also pp. 40–43 for "Optimization Techniques for Outdoor Lighting Design."*

J. M. Casal, "Spain: Floodlighting Design and Influence," Lighting Design + Application, *July*

1972 (pp. 4–19) and reprinted in vol. 13, no. 5 (May 1983), pp. 27–28, 30, 32–36. Illus. The best design statement in print about lighting design for ancient edifices, national monuments, and spiritual shrines, written by a leading Spanish designer.

A. T. Baker, "Architecture: Shaping Water into Art: A Fantasia of Fountains Adorns Downtown, U.S.A.," Time, vol. 11 (September 12, 1977), pp. 32–33. Illus.

"New Lighting Fixture Design for NY's Central Park," IALD Newsletter, Oct. 1983, p. 1. Reprinted from the The New York Times, August 2, 1983, "How Design Was Decided for Central Park's Lamps," by Joseph Giovanni.

"Guth Memorial Awards," Lighting Design + Application, vol. 13, no. 10 (Oct. 1983), p. 46. Illus. Outdoor lighting for the Cuyahoga Falls, Ohio, riverfront.

"Lumen Awards," Lighting Design + Application, vol. 9, no. 6 (June 1979), p. 34. A Niagara Falls "Winter Garden." Illus., color.

"A Festival of Lights — Niagara Falls, N.Y.," Lighting Design + Application, vol. 13, no. 12 (Dec. 1983), pp. 10, 12. Illus., color. A description of the lavish Christmas lighting of a whole city.

Christos C. Mpelkas, "Indoor Landscaping for Healthy, Beautiful Workplaces," Architectural Lighting, vol. 1, no. 2 (Feb. 1987), pp. 42–44. Illus., color. Indoor plant lights discussed with charts. Very useful for the designer.

Tom O'Mahony, "Rockefeller Center: Midtown Glows," Lighting Design + Application, vol. 15, no. 4 (Apr. 1985), pp. 20–24. Illus., color. An article on the lighting of Rockefeller Center by Abe Feder, with extensive photographs and description.

A. E. Tanner, "Light Trespass? What the Heck Is That? Astronomers and Light Sleepers Can Give Ready Definitions," Lighting Design + Application, vol. 16, no. 4 (Apr. 1986), pp. 22–23. Illus., color. An electrical engineer writes about unwanted light "spill."

William J. Locklin, "Outdoor Lighting: One Man's View of an Honest Art," Lighting Design + Application, vol. 17, no. 2 (Feb. 1987), p. 22. Illus. Brief but useful article by an IES member who is a licensed electrical contractor and registered electrical engineer practicing in California.

Gary Gordon, "The Design Department," Architectural Lighting, vol. 1, no. 0 (Nov. 1986), pp. 64–66. Regular columnist turns his attention to suitable lamp criteria (in chart form) for lighting evergreens and deciduous plants. Very useful. See also vol. 1, no. 2 (Feb. 1987), pp. 45–46, for further basics of architectural lighting design.

"Letters to the Editor," Architectural Lighting, vol. 1, no. 5 (May 1987), p. 12. Explanation of a legal change in the law banning lighting fixtures installed on trees.

"Detroit Lights Up: The Most Comprehensive City Plan in the US," Lighting Design + Application, vol. 17, no. 5 (May 1987), pp. 17–19, 53. Illus., color. A master project by Howard Brandston Lighting Design, Inc., for the relighting of all of Detroit.

William J. Locklin, "The Honest Art of Good Outdoor Lighting — The Client is the Expert," Lighting Design + Application, vol. 17, no. 5 (May 1987), pp. 20–21, 54. Illus., color.

"Desert Hotel Achieves Oasis Look — Meets Tough Codes with Low-wattage Outdoor Lighting," Lighting Design + Application, vol. 17, no. 5 (May 1987), p. 45. Illus.

Chip Israel, "To Find Landscape Solutions, Define the Problem," Architectural Lighting, vol. 1, no. 3 (March 1987), pp. 40–42. Illus., color. Israel is an associate of Grenald Associates, Inc., an architectural lighting firm in Los Angeles, Philadelphia, and New York City.

Kay Keating, "Let There Be Light Outside Your House," from the Gannett News Service in the Lafayette Journal and Courier, April 12, 1987, p. C10 of Life & Times section. Illus.

Aldo Paoletti, "Public Lighting: Lights in Venice," International Lighting Review, 2d quarter 1986, pp. 40–44. Illus., color. A lavishly illustrated article sketching the history of outdoor lighting in Venice up to present times.

Gilbert Quéré, "Grand Palais, Paris: Blue light — White light — the Irreversible Rhythm of Time," International Lighting Review, 39th year, 1st quarter, 1988, pp. 8–11. Illus. color. Exterior illumination of a glass museum.

"Towers: Sparkling Spires, Melbourne and Sao Paulo," International Lighting Review, 39th year, 1st quarter, 1988, pp. 12–15. Illus., color. Lighting of the Victorian Arts Centre spire in

ton. The owners provided their own night illumination with reflector lamps fastened to trees and building structures. This picture serves as a good example of two things: (1) even amateur night lighting is better than no lighting at all, and (2) glare and unevenness and obvious lack of trained design is readily apparent in amateur lighting.

The 1977 project for the relighting of the Krannert Courtyard of the Purdue University campus in West Lafayette, Indiana, is shown in Figs. 10.7, 10.8, and 10.9. This outdoor area had existing (vandalized) fixtures in a planned garden-courtyard between the Krannert Industrial Management Building and the adjoining Graduate House dormitory. The area, which is at a main intersection of the campus, sees heavy use at night. It was an ideal area for redesign. The project is the work of Professor Phillip E. (Gene) DeTurk, formerly head of the Division of Landscape Architecture at Purdue, and former theatre graduate student Kirk Bookman. Accompanying the project were a number of other drawings plus a 22-page bound "prospectus." The prospectus, a standard form submitted to clients, usually includes a presentation of project objectives, the design narrative (concept), fixture-color schedule of selected instruments and materials, a cost estimate, maintenance data, and proposed fees.[262]

Figure 10.10 presents John Watson's illumination of an underground cavern. The design is unusual.

Building Exteriors

The origins of building lighting were the festooning of strings or rows of low-power lamps upon the exterior of a building. Denmark's Tivoli Gardens employs this approach effectively today (see Color Fig. 74 in Chap. 9). Soon more powerful floodlights on adjacent buildings or atop poles became the vogue. Eventually these gave way to powerful units containing carefully designed reflectors with incandescent and high-intensity discharge lamps (mercury, etc.) and the ever-widening range of PAR and R reflector lamps. Abe Feder calls night lighting "pushing back the darkness," but there are many additional reasons for using night lighting on building exteriors:

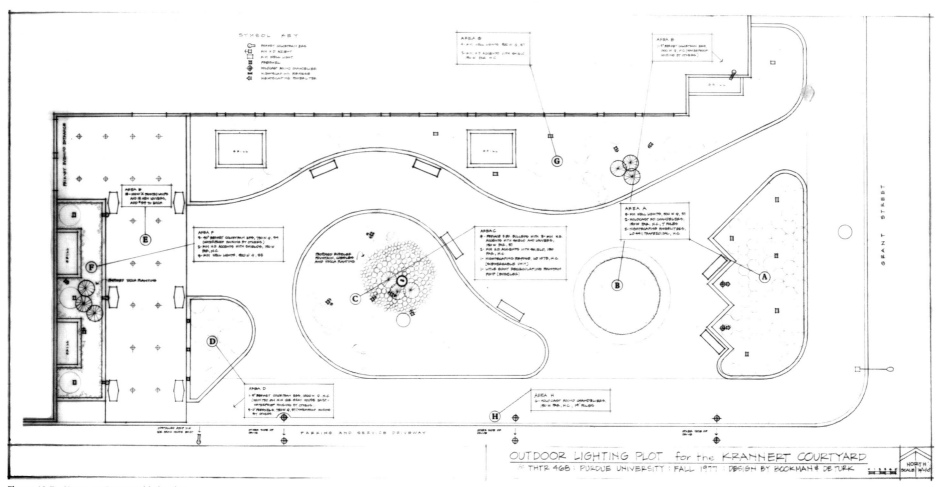

Figure 10.7 Krannert Courtyard light plot.

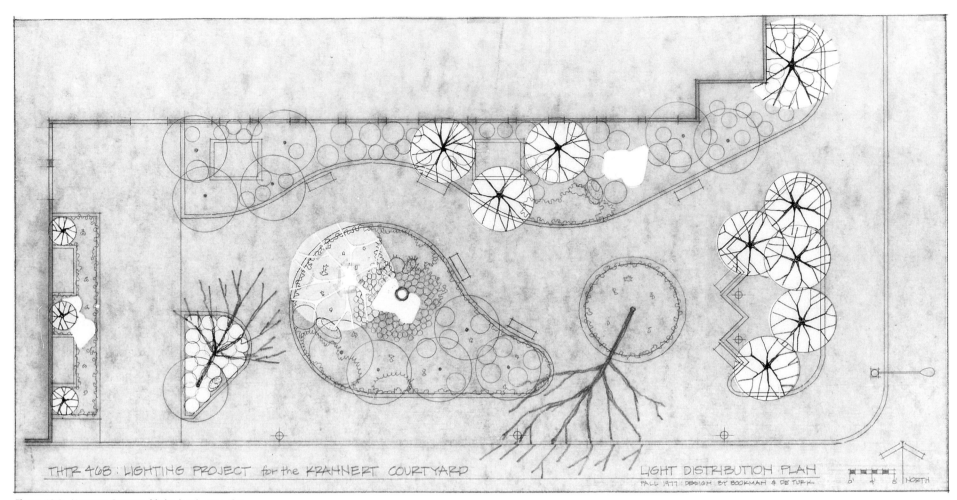

THTR 468: LIGHTING PROJECT for the KRANNERT COURTYARD   LIGHT DISTRIBUTION PLAN
FALL 1977 DESIGN BY BOOKMAN & DE TURK

NORTH

Figure 10.8 Krannert Courtyard light distribution plan.

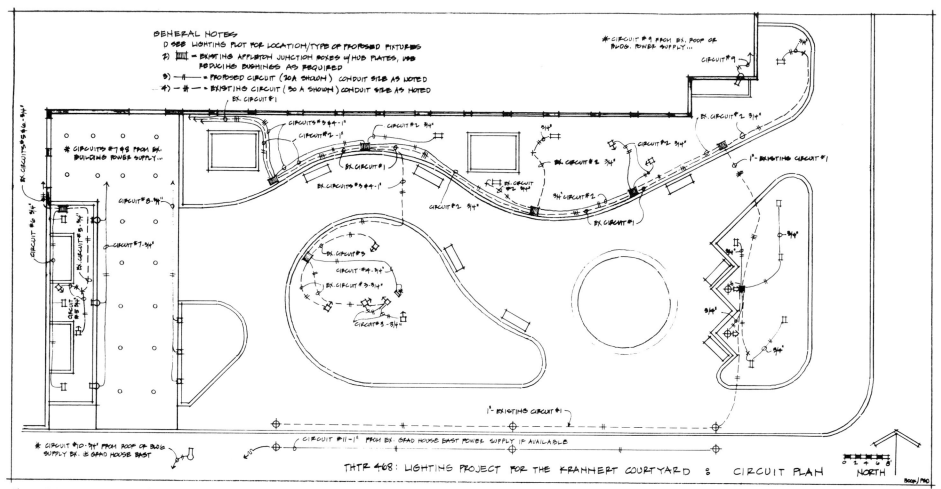

Figure 10.9 Krannert Courtyard circuit plan.

Melbourne, Australia, and the Globo TV tower in Sao Paulo, Brazil.

"Towers: Tower of Wind, Yokohama, Japan," International Lighting Review, 39th year, 1st quarter, 1988, pp. 16–18. Illus., color. A Japanese ventilation tower has been enhanced by night lighting.

"MBB Building, Kuala Lumpur, Malaysia," International Lighting Review, 39th year, 3rd quarter, 1988, pp. 94–97. Illus., color. Stunning night lighting of a building in Malaysia, a bank headquarters, and the tallest building in the country.

Kirsten Stevenson, "Landscape: The Effect, Not the Source, Is the Key," Lighting, vol. 1, no. 3 (Nov. 1987), pp. 20–21, 33. Illus., Basic article on landscape lighting by the principal of Nightdecor Landscape Lighting. Useful for the designer.

Dana Dubbs, "Starry night: Jan Moyer Sculpts San Francisco Bay Estate with Light," Lighting Dimensions, vol. 12, no. 7 (November 1988), pp. 54–55, 72–73. Illus., color. Good example of recent landscape lighting.

"Minneapolis Sculpture Garden," Lighting Dimensions, vol. 12, no. 6, (September/October 1988), p. 30. Illus. An excellent landscaped garden lighting design by Howard Brandston's firm.

Kari-Johan Grönholm, "Dynamic River-bank Lighting in Tampere, Finland," International Lighting Review, 2nd quarter, 40th year (1989), pp. 80–81, Illus., color. Really outstanding exterior city lighting. Also: Jean Muller and Volmer Rose, "Dam at Esch-sur-Sûre, Luxembourg," pp. 82–83. Illus., color. Security-conscious, yet artistic, lighting of a hydroelectric station and dam in Luxembourg.

Figure 10.10 Inner Space Caverns in Georgetown, Texas (1966). Lighting design by John Watson.

■ *Attention*. Night lighting is used to attract passersby to stores, shops, or factories, either for immediate point-of-contact sales or for image identification (usually for factories and industry headquarters complexes). Nighttime focus on the building and its individuality are involved.

■ *Attractiveness*. Industry headquarters complexes, shopping malls, historical buildings and monuments, churches, and outstanding architectural edifices are expensive to erect. They are lasting. They involve pride and beauty. Obviously the design tool of light can add much. Use of designed light portrays pride of ownership and strong corporate image. It also gives pure visual pleasure to the nighttime viewer.

■ *Unification*. Such utilitarian edifices as parking lots, industry complexes, university campuses, and large hospitals can and do benefit from the lighting designer's ability to focus and direct attention and movement. Selective visibility comes into play here. Just as the play director expects help from the lighting designer for control of focus of attention, the client and the architect have a right to expect assistance from lighting in unifying an architectural edifice.

■ *Security and Safety*. Security has to do with the prevention of robbery, rape, and riot. Safety (a much tamer objective) has to do with preventing broken hips, legs, arms, etc. from occurring because of unseen obstacles (or open manholes) lurking in the dimness. Safety and security are both important design considerations.

Given these objectives, an electrical contractor can (and frequently does) supply *workable* answers. An illuminating engineer can supply *inventive* technological solutions, imaginative to the degree that the engineer creates beyond the limits delineated by charts and tables and client's instructions. The architectural lighting designer is much at home in this area. When a client particularly desires creative theatrical imagination for a project, he or she may turn to Douglas Leigh (the foremost building illuminator today) or any of many other architectural lighting specialists.

Building lighting from three categories is illustrated here. Figure 10.11 shows the General Electric (GE) Building in New York City. Figure 10.12 is Abe Feder's design for Rich's department store in Knoxville, Tennessee. Notice how imaginatively he has painted with light and the variegated play of light and shade. Figure 10.13 is Feder's work for New York City's Pan Am Building. Color Fig. 82 shows the use of changeable color as a design element used on New York City's Empire State Building (lighting by designer Douglas Leigh). The dividing line between landscape architecture lighting and architectural lighting nearly disappears for some of the more lavish private residences and some motel/community development housing. Figures 10.3 and 10.4 show John Watson's work for an apartment and an office building. Figure 10.14 presents Abe Feder's striking design for the John F. Kennedy Center for the Performing Arts in Washington, D.C. The 50-foot-high overhung portico surrounds all four sides of this 300-foot-by-700-foot building. Monumentality is greatly enhanced by the lighting design. Figure 10.5 exhibits an entirely different kind of monumentality: John Watson's lighting of the LBJ Ranch in Texas. Here softness and subtlety dominate in presenting a national shrine in proper context. Yet Watson is equally capable of "hard sell" commercialism in his lighting design, when it is called for. Color Fig. 78, which pictures a restau-

Figure 10.12 Rich's department store, now Miller's, in Knoxville, Tennessee. Lighting by Abe Feder.

Figure 10.14 John F. Kennedy Center for the Performing Arts, Washington, D.C. View of the entrance plaza showing Abe Feder's imaginative lighting.

Figure 10.11 Night lighting of the GE Building in New York City.

Figure 10.13 Pan Am Bulding in NYC. Lighting by Abe Feder.

[263] *See the most recent printing of* GE Building Floodlighting, *Bulletin TP-115.*

[264] *"Floodlighting of Historic Buildings in Istanbul,"* Lighting Design + Application, *vol. 12, no. 5 (May 1982), pp. 12–17. Illus., color. Outstanding.*

"Light for Freedom," Light *magazine, vol. 23, no. 5 (Sept./Oct. 1954), pp. 5–15. Diamond Jubilee issue with a panorama of outdoor building lighting illustrated. Monuments, government and historical buildings, commercial buildings, and assorted others are shown.*

Abe Feder, "Lighting the Nation's Capitol . . . in the 70's," I.E.S. Capitol Section Newsletter, *June 6, 1971.*

"In Focus," Lighting Design + Application, *vol. 13, no. 11 (Nov. 1983), p. 12. Illus. Night lighting of the California State Capitol Building and the Philadelphia Independence Mall with technical and energy conservation details.*

See also: "Focus On Australia," Footnote 236.

"As the Sun Goes Down, Citicorp Center Lights Up," IALD Newsletter, *Sept. 1982, p. 1. About Douglas Leigh's building illumination.*

Paul Goldberger, "New York, the New City of Lights," The New York Times, *March 4, 1983, pp. 15, 20. Illus. Eight photographs and a map of New York City night building illumination with accompanying text.*

Pierre Bideau, "Monuments, the Eiffel Tower," International Lighting Review, *37th year, 1st quarter, 1986, pp. 16–20. Illus., color. Relighting Paris's Eiffel Tower.*

W. T. Scheinman, "Renovations—Queen's Quay Terminal, Toronto," International

rant in Texas, provides a striking example of his design work for a commercial operation.

Color Fig. 83 shows the stunning night illumination of beautiful Salzburg, Austria. Nestled in the mountains, the entire city looks like a *real* Walt Disney world at night, with churches and ancient buildings lighted throughout the city, "string of pearls" bridges soaring across the midcity river, and the castle on the mountaintop dominating all.

Design Considerations

Buildings themselves should attract attention—not garlands of lights or festooned flashing neon. The designer must carefully study and react to a building's reflectivity (Is it brick, glass, chrome, marble, or composite? Is it smooth or rough, rustic or sophisticated?). Careful consideration must be given to ambient light (streetlights and the general illumination of the neighborhood). Much lower levels of overall illumination are needed for a building in the woods (for example, the LBJ Ranch) as opposed to one surrounded by gaudy signs (as in Times Square in New York City, for example).

Some specifics about luminaire selection follow:

1. Luminaires must be weatherproof, durable, tamperproof, and accessible.

2. Luminaires should be selected which will throw all their lumen output on the target building (not off in wasted space). Catalogs and IES tables are most helpful when the designer is considering this point. Misdirected light is irretrievable.

3. The designer should be able to calculate reflected brightness and anticipate the end-product design. Standard formulas exist to help the designer obtain accurate information.

4. All lighting units should be concealed from normal viewing angles. Floods can be mounted on the ground (and concealed in shrubbery), in trees, on top of marquees or building ledge recesses and cornices, and on adjacent buildings (if legal rights are cleared). In no case should the luminous flux from a luminaire splash heavily over into adjacent property. Blinding passing motorists is as bad as floodlighting the bedroom of a nearby residence.

5. *Design* is always called for, not just illumination. In the lighting of a large building, variations of light level (bright at the bottom and dimmer above to accent a building's height for example) are useful. Columns can be silhouetted to increase their apparent slenderness or frontlighted to emphasize their strength and solidity. Niches and offsets can be used inventively. The designer should not be afraid of variations of intensity—bright areas and reposeful shadow areas. Color can often be used as a design element. All design must stem from a careful study of the building's structure, form, pattern, and texture.

6. Preplanning is unbeatable, when it is available. It is much less expensive for mounting positions, wireways, and luminaires to be provided when a building is being constructed (or rebuilt) than it is for this equipment to be added later. Also, the end product is much more attractive when lighting units are not ill-concealed or look to be added on as an afterthought. Unit placement *is* design.

7. The designer needs to be familiar with all standard luminaires. Consideration must be given to a fixture's beauty, suitability, cost, durability, and maintenance and lamp-life factors.

8. The designer should consider the different uses of floodlighting: "flat-on illumination" versus "grazing" light, and single-source illumination versus multiple sources versus lineal line sources. These approaches and their artful combination are important design factors.[263] The deliberate and controlled use of shadows (on bricks, masonry, etc.) and surface highlights separates the designer from the illuminator.[264]

Parking Lots, Street Lighting, Underground Transit Systems, and Tunnels

Parking lot illumination presents the designer with these objectives: (1) to provide overall uniform illumination with reduced shadows (for advanced design ideas see the work of Feder, discussed in the next section, "Shopping Malls"), (2) to minimize distraction for the driver from adjacent signs and store windows, (3) to select attractive and appropriate fixtures for the luminaires (there are hundreds of styles and

Lighting Review, *36th year, 3d quarter, 1985, pp. 84–88. Illus., color.*

"Monterrey's Rivers of Light," Lighting Dimensions, *vol. 10, no. 1 (Jan./Feb. 1986), pp. 22–25, 27. Illus., color. Exterior lighting of the Monterrey, Mexico, Lighthouse of Commerce, including laser use.*

Jerry Cooper, *"The Light of Liberty: Howard Brandston Brings the Lady Up to Date,"* Lighting Dimensions, *vol. 10, no. 4 (July/Aug. 1986), pp. 20–23, 40–44. Illus., color. Includes light plot.*

"Howard Brandston Talks to LD + A About Lighting THE LADY," Lighting Design + Application, *vol. 16, no. 7 (July 1986), cover and pp. 14–18, 42. Illus., color.*

"Interview: Howard Brandston," International Lighting Review, *3d Fall quarter of 1986, pp. 89–93. Illus., color. Text and many color photographs. Concerns the lighting of the Statue of Liberty.*

Sue Berg, *"Gil Reiling, '53, and GE team, Statue of Liberty's Renewed Splendor,"* Alumni Review, *University of North Dakota, Sept. 1986, p. 6. GE engineer developed special lamp to light Statue of Liberty.*

Larry Swasey, *"Relighting the Lady,"* Lighting Design + Application, *vol. 15, no. 12 (Dec. 1985), pp. 11–13. Illus., color. Use of computers and computer graphics in planning relighting of Statue of Liberty. Also reprinted in* IALD Newsletter, *July 1986, pp. 2–3.*

"Flattering Light for Liberty," Lafayette Journal & Courier, *September 25, 1985, p. C-1. Illus. About GE lamps used to light the Statue of Liberty.*

"Central Trust Tower Stands Out In Cincinnati's Night-Time Sky," Lighting Design + Application, *vol. 16, no. 2 (Feb. 1986), pp. 29–31. Illus.*

Aldo Paoletti, *"Public Lighting: Lights in Venice"; see footnote 262 for this entry and for several others concerned with lighting building exteriors.*

Ekrem Akkus and Haldun Demirdes, *"Monuments: Floodlighting in Turkey,"* International Lighting Review, *2d quarter of 1986, pp. 45–49. Illus., color. Excellent graphics, text.*

Oddvar Johansen, *"Monuments: Frederiksten Fortress, Halden, Norway,"* International Lighting Review, *2d quarter of 1986, pp. 50–52. Illus., color. Excellent graphics.*

Vincent J. Faiella, *"Columbus City Hall Washed with Gold and White: Architectural Detailing Comes to Life,"* Lighting Design + Application, *vol. 17, no. 1 (Jan. 1987), pp. 18, 46. Illus., color. The relighting of the exterior of the city hall in Columbus, Ohio.*

"Building Pride Through Lighting," Lighting Spectrum, *vol. 2, no. 2 (Mar./Apr. 1987), pp. 65–72. Illus., color. High-quality color photographs of numerous exterior lighted buildings in the United States, plus technical details supplied by GE.*

"Living Above the Store Dallas-Style, an Edwin F. Guth Memorial Award of Excellence (by the IES) to Designer Craig A. Roeder, Dallas," Lighting Design + Application, *vol. 16, no. 10 (Oct. 1986), pp. 8–10. Illus., color. Imaginative lighting of an art gallery exterior with the owners living above.*

"Skylines Shine As Lights Glow Across the Midwest," The New York Times, *Chicago ed., p. 9, February 3, 1986. Illus.*

E. J. Kahn, Jr., *"Profiles: Lights, Lights, Lights,"* The New Yorker, *June 7, 1941, pp. 23–20. A lengthy profile of Douglas Leigh, responsible in just New York City alone for the night lighting of the Empire State Building, the Hemsley Building (230 Park Ave.), Con Edison Towers (Irving Place and 14th St.), the St. Moritz Hotel Tower, the Crown Bldg. (57th St. and Fifth Ave.), Citicorp Center (Lexington Ave. and 53rd St.), the Madison Square Garden Tower and sidewalk lighting and motor entrance, the Waldorf-Astoria Hotel (Park Ave. and 50th St.), the Greenwich Savings Bank (36th St. and Broadway), Grand Central Terminal, and many others. See also a special issue of* Playbill *(Dec. 9, 1982) for the presentation of the Golden Scroll Award by the Broadway Association to Douglas Leigh.*

Caskie Stinnett, *"A Feast of Diversities,"* Signature, *March 1982. Illus., color. Color photographs of the night lighting of Notre Dame Cathedral in Paris, pp. 65–68.*

Carl Purcell, *"On Camera: Architectural Exposures,"* Signature, *July 1982, p. 26. A color photograph of the night lighting of Trafalger Square fountain and the National Gallery in London.*

Peter Ross Range, *"The Caress of Constance,"* Signature, *March 1984, pp. 88. Color photograph of night city lighting of Constance (Lake Constance on the border of Germany, Austria, and Switzerland).*

Catherine M. Hamm, *"City Lights: Kansas City,"* Signature, *Dec. 1983, pp. 81–82. Color photo of the extensive Christmas night lighting in Kansas City.*

Jim Davidson, *"Dallas After Dark: From Argon to Strobes, The Nighttime Skyline Shimmers,"* Lighting Dimensions, *vol. 12, no. 7 (November 1988), pp. 76–77, 84–85. Illus., color. Useful, well-written, well-illustrated article on nighttime lighting of a major city.*

"Sun (Bank) Shine," Lighting Dimensions, *vol. 12, no. 6 (September/October 1988), p. 26. Illus. Nighttime lighting of the SunBank Center in Orlando, Florida, by Bruce Yarbell.*

Jim Davidson, *"Las Vegas: Forty-Two Miles of Neon and Two Million Light Bulbs,"* Lighting Dimensions, *vol. 12, no. 3 (April 1988), pp. 50–53, 70–71. Illus., color.*

"Night Moves," Lighting Dimensions, *vol. 12, no. 6 (September/October 1988), p. 30. Illus., color. Award-winning night lighting of Miami's Brickell Building by John McGuire Associates.*

Arthur Erickson, *"Enlightenment: The Art of Lighting Design as a Means of Revealing the Truth of a Space,"* Lighting Dimensions, *vol. 12, no. 6 (September/October 1988), pp. 46, 88–93. Illus., color. Very perceptive article concerning the design portion of lighting by a leading architect.*

"Las Vegas," International Lighting Review, *39th year, 4th quarter, 1988, p. 136. Illus., color. Includes signs as well as building exteriors.*

"Light Flashes," International Lighting Review, *40th year, 2nd quarter (1989), pp. 46–47. Illus., color. Outstanding exterior lighting examples.*

PLATE 58 *The Neil Diamond Concert,* televised from the Greek Theatre, Los Angeles, California. Production director and stage designer: George Honchar, Imero Fiorentino Associates; lighting designer: Imero Fiorentino; lighting director: Scott Johnson.

PLATE 59 *The Neil Diamond Concert.*

PLATE 60 *The Neil Diamond Concert.*

PLATE 61 Martha Graham's *Clytemnestra,* shown on Public Service Television's *Dance in America* series; taped at Opryland, Nashville, Tennessee. Lighting director: Ralph Holmes. *(Courtesy of Ralph Holmes.)*

PLATE 62 *Clytemnestra.*

PLATE 63 *Clytemnestra.*

PLATE 64 *A Star Is Born,* produced by Warner Bros.. Lighting by Jules Fisher. *(Photo: © Warner Bros., Inc.)*

PLATE 65 *A Star Is Born.* *(Photo: © Warner Bros., Inc.)*

PLATE 66 *The Turning Point,* produced by 20th Century Fox. Lighting by Nananne Porcher. *(Photo: © 20th Century Fox)*

PLATE 67 Street scene near steel mill from *Deer Hunter* with supplemented lighting.

PLATE 68 Wedding reception sequence in St. Theodosis' Cathedral, Cleveland, from filming of *Deer Hunter.* Lighting units concealed behind hanging banners in low-ceilinged room.

PLATE 69 Night lighting of city block for the movie *Deer Hunter.* Used masterlights and HMT.

PLATE 70 Electric Circus, New York City. Lighting designer: Imero Fiorentino. *(Courtesy of Imero Fiorentino Associates.)*

PLATE 71 *Hello Sailor* (punk rock) concert, 1979. Lighting designer: James L. Moody. *(Courtesy of Sundance Lighting Corp.)*

PLATE 72 *Boston World Tour '79.* Lighting by Richard Ocean. *(Photo: © Ron Pownall)*

PLATE 72a Spectacle in concert. Pyrotechnics in action. *Boston World Tour '79* with lighting by Richard Ocean. *(Photo: C. Ron Pownall)*

PLATE 73 Night lighting of Tivoli Gardens fountain, Copenhagen, Denmark.

PLATE 74 *Opryland* at night, Nashville, Tennessee.
Lighting by R. Duell and Associates.

PLATE 75 Artist Stanley Neltzoff's impression of *Century 21*, centerpiece of the 1962 Seattle World's Fair.

PLATE 76 Niagara Falls (American side) at night.
Relighting by Clyde Nordheimer and Nananne Porcher,
1979. *(Photo: Stuart Nordheimer)*

PLATE 77 The backlighted "plume" at
Niagara Falls. *(Photo: Nananne Porcher)*
Lighting by Nananne Porcher and
Clyde Nordheimer, 1979.

PLATE 78 The Casa Rio Mexican Restaurant
in San Antonio, Texas (1971). Lighting
by John Watson.

PLATE 80   The John Watson residence in Dallas (1975). Lighting by John Watson.

PLATE 81   The Elton Hyder residence in Fort Worth, Texas (1972). Lighting by John Watson.

PLATE 82   Empire State Building lighted for the Fourth of July. Lighting by designer Douglas Leigh.

PLATE 79   The Mary Crowley residential entrance in Dallas, Texas (1975). Lighting by John Watson.

PLATE 83a   St. Thomas Aquinas Church, Indianapolis; Wollen Associates, architect. Lighting by Wm. M. C. Lam Associates, Inc.

PLATE 83   Night lighting of Salzburg, Austria.

PLATE 84 Interior of California First Bank, San Francisco. Lighting by Jules G. Horton Lighting Design, Inc. (1977). *(Photo: Jaime Ardiles Arce)*

PLATE 85 An office in complex "G" of the Cite' Parlementaire, Quebec, Canada; Fiset and Deschamps-Cathier, Guite and Jean-Marie Roy, architects. Lighting by Wm. M. C. Lam Associates, Inc.

PLATE 86 Charlotte Hungerford Hospital Addition in Torrington, Connecticut (1973). Architects: Isadore & Zachary Rosenfield. Lighting by Wm. M. C. Lam Associates, Inc.

PLATE 86a The lobby of the Omni Hotel in Miami, Florida. Lighting by James L. Nuckolls.

PLATE 87 Interior of Touche Ross office complex, New York City. Lighting by Wheel-Garon, Inc.; interiors by the Space Design Group. *(Photo: Bernard Liebman)*

PLATE 88 The Upjohn Executive Office Building, Kalamazoo, Michigan; Skidmore, Owings and Merrill, architects. Lighting by Edison Price, Inc.

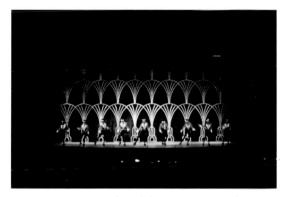

PLATE 90 *Pontiac '74* industrial show, Masonic Temple, Detroit, Michigan. Scene design: David Ballou; lighting design: Lee Watson.

PLATE 89 Burdine's, Tampa, Florida. Lighting by David A. Mintz, Inc.; interior design by the Walker Group/CNI. *(Photo: Harry Hartman)*

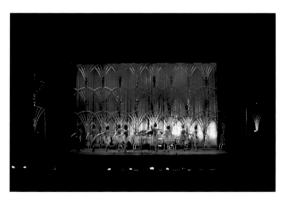

PLATE 91 *Pontiac '74.*

PLATE 91a *Pontiac '74.*

PLATE 91b *Pontiac '74.*

PLATE 92 *Milliken Fabrics* industrial show, grand ballroom of the Waldorf-Astoria Hotel, New York City. Lighting by Imero Fiorentino.

PLATE 92a *Anheuser-Busch Command Performance* industrial show, San Francisco; designed and produced by George Honchar of Imero Fiorentino Associates. Lighting consultant: Imero Fiorentino; lighting director: Marilyn Lowey.

PLATE 92b *Miss U.S.A. Beauty Pageant,* Biloxi, Mississippi. Lighting director: Carl Vitelli of Imero Fiorentino Associates.

[265] *W. M. J. van Bommel and J. B. deBoer,* Road Lighting. *London; MacMillan Press, Ltd.; 1980 (or Scholium International, Inc., 265 Great Neck Road, Great Neck, NY 11021). 328 pp., illus., color. Basic reference on road lighting.*

"Recommended Practice for Roadway Sign Lighting,"Journal of the IES, vol. 12, no. 3 (Apr. 1983), pp. 141–145. Same issue: "Proposed American National Standard Practice for Roadway Lighting," pp. 146–196. The latest IES-approved standards; includes charts, tables, glossary, and bibliography.

Normal Nadel, "Street Lights: More Than Glass on Pole," Fort Worth Press, December 20, 1971. Jules Horton's work.

S. Howard Young, "Lighting of a Special Purpose Urban Freeway," Lighting Design + Application, vol. 11, no. 6 (June 1981), pp. 18–21. Illus.

"Oerkvitz on Roadway Lighting: Chairman of the IES Roadway Lighting Committee Discusses State-of-the-Art of Street and Roadway Lighting." Lighting Design + Application, vol. 9, no. 7 (July 1979), pp. 16–17. Other articles on pp. 18–41. Illus. Includes information on "high-mast" lighting.

Theo Megens, "Area Lighting: New ECT Container Terminal, Rotterdam," International Lighting Review, 1984/4, pp. 136–139. Illus., color. Illustrations, plans, and sketches of the lighting of the Rotterdam ECT/Delta Airlines outdoor airport freight terminal with accompanying technical information.

G. De Cleroq, "Public Lighting: Fifteen Years of Road Lighting in Belgium," International Lighting Review, 1984/4, pp. 2–7. Illus., color. Useful roadway article, very well illustrated.

Jean Gue, "Public Lighting: A New Solution for Two Streets in Bordeaux," International Lighting Review, 1984/4, pp. 8–9. Mixing light source types in an ancient street in France.

Anne Laidebeur, "Public Lighting" Lighting, Pedestrians and the City, International Lighting Review, 38th year, 2nd quarter, (1987), pp. 50–53. Illus., color. An excellent study on the psychological interrelationship of lighting, streets and public squares, and human response.

"Outdoor: Roadway Lighting: History Comes Alive," Lighting, vol. 2, no. 6 (December 1988), pp. 14–15. Useful information concerning research in replacement of older streetlighting poles and lamps.

Michael S. Janoff and Norman L. Zlotnick, "Reduced Freeway Lighting: Costs, Benefits, and Legal Implications," Lighting Design + Application, vol. 15, no. 8 (Aug. 1985), pp. 35–42.

Charles A. Oerkvitz, "Relighting the 30th St. Station Underpass, Philadelphia", Lighting Design + Application, pp. 32–35. Illus., color.

"British Columbia Place Site Lighting," Lighting Design + Application, vol. 15, no. 10 (Oct 1985), p. 44. Illus.

[266] *"Mass Transit—Lighting Design—the Key to MARTA's New Mass Transit System," Lighting Design + Application, vol. 10, no. 8 (Aug. 1980), pp. 36–40. Illus.*

G. Giesbers, "Tunnel Lighting—Ten Years On: A Look at How International Lighting Recommendations Have Influenced Tunnel Lighting Design," International Lighting Review, 39th year, 1st quarter (1988), pp. 18–24. Illus., color. The definitive, well-illustrated, up-to-date text on this subject.

W. K. Adrian, "A Note on the Suggested IES Recommendations for Tunnel Lighting in North America," Journal of the I.E.S., vol. 17, no. 1 (Winter 1988), pp. 62–66. Highly technical article for the engineer on current tunnel lighting requirements.

"Light Flashes," International Lighting Review, 2nd quarter, 40th year (1989). p. 47. Illus., color. Outstanding street (roadway) lighting.

Anne Laidebeur, "Public Lighting: Lighting Pedestrians and the City," International Lighting Review, 38th year, 2nd quarter, (1987).

Harry B. Zackrison, Jr., "Revisions and Technological Updating of the Washington, D.C. Metro System Lighting," Lighting Design + Application, vol. 12, no. 3 (Mar. 1983), pp. 17–24. Illus. The technical implementation of William M. C. Lam's Washington Metro design to improve performance and lower life-cycle costs. Detailed presentation.

"Metrorail," Lighting Design + Application, vol. 15, no. 10 (Oct. 1985), p. 46. Illus. A Florida underground transit design.

"Public Transport: The Lille Metro," International Lighting Review, 3d quarter of 1986, pp. 99–107. Illus., color. Also see "Public Transport: Marseilles Metro: Second Line," pp. 107–108. Illus., color; and "Public Transport: Underground Railway in Calcutta," p. 109. Illus., color. Three well-illustrated articles in a roundup of contemporary public transit lighting design worldwide.

types), (4) to produce a clean, uncluttered look (a minimum number of light poles), and (5) to create the atmosphere of a pleasant place (the color output of the luminaires may be a key factor).

Street lighting is similar to parking lot lighting but largely remains a specialized field for the illuminating engineer. Both Abe Feder (designer for shopping malls and the Kennedy International Airport) and Jules Horton (designer for several New York City bridges, the Cincinnati Airport, and the Dallas–Fort Worth Airport and access highway) have had an important design influence in this area.

Forty percent of a person's life is spent in periods of darkness. The extreme mobility in the United States puts people out on the roads a sizable portion of these hours. On a yearly average there are 4,100 hours of darkness. The basic lighting consideration for streets is *safety* for the driver and the pedestrian. The IES has continually conducted studies in this area. Because it is an important market, the larger manufacturers are constantly developing improved luminaires. In 1955 GE first introduced fluorescent street lighting. That same year, interchangeable reflectors for standard fixtures were developed for mercury luminaires to alter beam spread for different roadway widths. Today there may be within a few short blocks street lighting from filament sources, from high-intensity discharge mercury and sodium lamps, and from constantly improved fluorescents.[265]

From time to time an architectural lighting designer encounters a quite unusual design assignment. For example, William Lam Associates has been involved for the past 12 years in the lighting of the Washington, D.C. Metropolitan Area Transit System (see Figs. 10.15 and 10.16).[266]

Shopping Malls

Shopping malls are numerous throughout the United States. These bustling places of activity, now to be found worldwide, involve the best lighting practice for streets, parking lots, stores, and buildings, along with requirements specific to the shopping mall. While sometimes the province of the electrical contractor or the illuminating engineer, some of the most progressive advances in mall lighting have come from the vision of Abe Feder and Tom

Figure 10.15 Washington Metropolitan Area Transit. Lighting by Wm. M. C. Lam Associates, Inc. (*Photo: Paul Myatt*)

Figure 10.17 Lincoln Road City Mall renovation project in Miami Beach, Florida, 1961. Lighting by Abe Feder.

Figure 10.19 Center fountain and mall between extensive parking lots at the Kennedy International Airport, New York City (1978). Lighting design by Abe Feder.

Figure 10.18 Columbia, South Carolina, Main Street Mall with 150-feet high-mast street lighting designed by Abe Feder.

Figure 10.16 Washington Metropolitan Area Transit. (*Photo: Paul Myatt*)

267 "City Mall—Key to Downtown Miami Beach Revival?" Illuminating Engineering, vol. 56, no. 6 (June 1961), pp. 370–72.

268 "High-Mast: Theatrical Lighting Drama Comes to Main Street, Columbia, South Carolina," Lighting Design + Application, vol. 8, no. 4 (Apr. 1978), pp. 20–24. Complete technical/design details and illustrations.

269 "City Mall—Key to Downtown Miami Beach Revival?" pp. 371–72, op. cit. (see footnote 267).

270 Abe Feder, "Outdoor Lighting: Creative Lighting of Miami Beach Mall," American City, Mar. 1961, pp. 135–36.
"Clearly Attractive," Interiors, Vol. CXLI, no. 7 (Feb. 1982), pp. 74–75. Illus., color.
Sylvan R. Shemitz, "The Mixing Game—Daylight and Lighting Techniques in Shopping Malls," Interiors, Vol. CXLI, no. 7 (Feb. 1982), pp. 94, 100. Illus.
"Flatz Ohizumi," Lighting Design + Application, vol. 14, no. 10 (Oct. 1984), pp. 21–23. Illus., color. Latest in shopping mall lighting in Tokyo. IES Award of Excellence, 1984.
Jill Herzfeld, "South Coast Plaza Crystal Court," Lighting Dimensions, vol. 11, no. 1 (Jan./Feb. 1987), pp. 62, 64, 66–67. Illus., including architectural light plot by Tom Ruzika. Also in Strand, vol. 2, no. 1 (Spring 1987), p. 6. Illus.
"Light Flashes: Crystal Court Mall, Costa Mesa," International Lighting Review, 39th year, 1st quarter (1988), p. 3. Illus., color. Steve Weinstein, "Poughkeepsie Galleria: Dramatic Mall Attracts Affluent Shoppers," Lighting Dimensions, vol. 12, no. 2 (March 1988), pp. 66–67, 101–102. Illus., color. Derek Phillips, "Shopping Centres, London," International Lighting Review, 2nd quarter, 40th year (1989), pp. 57–61. Illus., color. Two European award-winning shopping centers.
"Omaha's Central Park Mall: Light for Fun and Games, Safety and Growth," Architectural Lighting, vol. 1, no. 5 (May 1987). p. 22. Illus., color.
"High-Mast Lighting," Lighting Design + Application, vol. 6, no. 12 (Dec. 1976), pp. 5–11. Two articles, "Do's and Don'ts of

Ruzika. Feder was an advocate of "high-mast" lighting years ahead of most others. High-mast lighting involves unusually tall light poles for outdoor street and parking lot lighting—it gets the luminaires high in the air, allowing for both even illumination and minimum glare or direct light into the eye. Feder's work for the eight-block-long Lincoln Road City Mall in Miami Beach, Florida, is outstanding[267] (see Fig. 10.17). This mall includes lavish tropical foliage, 10 pools, fountains, waterfalls, and exhibit areas. The most outstanding feature is the even, overall illumination which issues from luminaires mounted atop eleven 60-foot poles. This design approach has been called "nighttime unification of areas through the use of light."[268] *Illuminating Engineering* wrote:

> One interesting economic sidelight of this high-level general illumination system is that it requires considerably less power than the lower-level lower-mounted standard street lighting system which it replaced.
> The visual effect of the illumination design—cascading colored waters, high-mounted lighting playing on the tree tops and flower beds, the blend of interior and exterior lighting which turns the shelters into dark silhouettes—is a dramatic addition to the nighttime appearance of the mall.[269]

Figure 10.18 pictures another mall by Feder in Columbia, South Carolina.

The following are required for mall lighting: easy, safe parking lot lighting for good traffic-flow patterns; clear directional signs for exit/entrance/parking; a unifying *theme* and mall identification sign or logo; use of light for customer mobility from parking to mall; and safety and convenience for customer ease with clear visibility in all weather. Storefronts can theme-unify the entire mall through lighting design.

Garden lighting may come into use in malls, with indoor and outdoor planting areas utilizing the wide range of fixtures available. Sculptures, fountains, pools, and waterfalls may be included in areas of relaxation and comfort provided by the management. Trees, shrubs, flowers, murals, and—in some cases—small, portable stages may be called for. These auxiliary areas demand artistic and creative treatment. The client usually has a specific intention for each auxiliary area, whether it is to incite gaiety, or repose, or excitement. The areas and their lighting must be tasteful, attractive, and distinctive. Lighting can also be an important design element in guiding customer flow patterns throughout and in design unity. Summarized, lighting design has the following objectives: *selling, attention-getting, identification, comfort, mobility, attractiveness, safety,* and *convenience.*[270] That's a big order! Cutler and Dorsey write:

> Good lighting design helps to identify the center at close range and from a distance. It simplifies parking and provides safe circulation for pedestrians in the parking area. It serves to direct traffic flow and guide customers to specific areas. It beautifies walkways and malls, landscaping, and recreational areas, attracting crowds and lending distinction to the entire center. Floodlighting buildings contributes to over-all attractiveness, in addition to identification and advertising features.[271]

Airport and Nautical Lighting

In the past this design area was frequently left to the illumination engineer, but the design work of Abe Feder in 1957 for New York International Airport (now Kennedy International Airport) changed all that. Kennedy consists of 655 acres with 10 large passenger terminal buildings, a 160-acre plaza with parking areas, a reflection pool, and a botanical garden. Numerous other designers were approached prior to Feder's receiving the final design assignment. Unity, beauty, and brightness were desired. For the project, Feder and GE designed a new mercury lamp. Forty-three stunningly attractive 75-foot-tall pylons topped by a total of 338 newly designed floodlights were designed and erected. These were Feder's first venture into "high-mast" lighting and were used as the design theme for the airport. They provided an *even* 1.5 to 5 footcandles of illumination over all utilized areas. Figure 10.19 illustrates this airport, now familiar to millions. While the execution leaned heavily upon the cooperation of top illumination engineers, the breadth of concept came from Feder, a theatre-trained lighting designer.[272] Jules Horton has since designed the lighting for both the Cincinnati and the Dallas–Fort Worth airports. The very specialized requirements of nautical lighting are referred to at length in footnote 273.

High-Mast Lighting" by Jules Horton and "State of the Art of High-Mast Lighting" by Daryl Sullivan. Illus.

"Guth Memorial Award," Lighting Design + Application, vol. 13, no. 10 (Oct. 1983), p. 32. Illus. An outstanding shopping mall lighting design in Upper Arlington, Ohio.

"Photobiology: Christian Mall—Lush and Lovely," Lighting Design + Application, vol. 10, no. 6 (June 1980), pp. 12–15. Use of metal halide lamps to promote plant growth in a shopping mall.

"Stanford Town Center," Lighting Design + Application, vol. 14, no. 10 (Oct. 1984), pp. 39–41. Illus., color. An IES "Special Citation" mall design in Stanford, Connecticut.

271 C. M. Cutler and R. T. Dorsey, "How We Design Lighting for Today's Modern Shopping Centers," GE Review, vol. 59, no. 3–4 (May/July 1956), pp. 11–13. Quote from p. 13.

272 Abe Feder, "Outdoor Lighting Design for New York International Airport," Illuminating Engineering, vol. 53, no. 3 (Mar. 1958), pp. 142–51. Detailed, illustrated. Complete technical details and narration of design process.

"Guth Memorial Awards," Lighting Design + Application, vol. 13, no. 10 (Oct. 1983), p. 38. Illus. Contemporary airport lighting in Davenport, Iowa, and Winston-Salem, North Carolina.

"1983 Gold Medalist Charles A. Douglas," Lighting Design + Application, vol. 13, no. 9 (Sept. 1983), p. 32. Douglas was the pioneer in developing aviation lighting.

"John W. Simeroth, IES Fellow," Lighting Design + Application, vol. 13, no. 9 (Sept. 1983), p. 38. Simeroth made an important contribution to aviation lighting.

Norman D. Witteveen, "US Airport Runway and Taxiway Lighting Systems—An Engineer's Overview of Their History, Development, and Design Considerations," Lighting Design + Application, vol. 15, no. 5 (May 1985), pp. 36–38. Illus.

"Flying into Flint, Where Lighting Makes a Good Impression," Architectural Lighting, vol. 1, no. 5 (May 1987), p. 16. Illus., color. Lighting designer Dean Welch's work for airport in Flint, Michigan.

"Innovations in Lighting Distinguish San Antonio International Airport," Lighting Design + Application, vol. 16, no. 8 (Aug. 1986), pp. 34–37. See also vol. 15, no. 10 (Oct. 1985), p. 44. Illus.

Frank Schink, "Airport Taxiway Lighting System Improved," CEE, vol. 40, no. 4 (April 1988), pp. 16–17. Illus., color.

"McCarran International Airport Award of Excellence," Lightview, vol. 1, no. 1 (Spring 1988), p. 4. Illus., color. Description of Stephen W. Lees' IALD Award-winning airport design for Las Vegas, Nevada.

"Exterior Airport Lighting," Lighting, vol. 1 no. 3 (November 1987), color cover and pp. 12, 17. Illus. Useful technical information about airport-lighting safety and durability controls.

Bruno Salvi, "Airports: Leonardo da Vinci Airport, Rome," International Lighting Review, 39th year, 4th quarter, 1988, pp. 130–132.

"Esplanade of McCarran International Airport," Lighting Dimensions, vol. 11, no. 7 (January/February 1988), p. 50. Illus. A design by the Horton-Lees firm in New York City.

273 Karl-Johan Grönbolm, "Ships: Cruise Liner M/S Birka Princess," International Lighting Review, 3d quarter of 1986, pp. 78–88. Illus., color. Extensively illustrated in color with good text, this is the definitive article currently in print regarding large ship lighting design.

Laurence Swasey, "Ocean Depth Mysteries Unlocked by Research Ship—The JOIDES Resolution Provides Creature Comforts As Well As Answers to Scientific Questions," Lighting Design + Application, vol. 16, no. 8 (Aug. 1986), pp. 28–31. Illus., color.

Robert A. Lewis, "Ships: See and Be Seen—Relighting U.S. Aircraft Carriers," International Lighting Review, 36th year, 4th quarter, 1985, pp. 139–143. Illus., color.

"Sea Currents," Theater Crafts, vol. 23, no. 7, (August/September 1989), pp. 6–7. A technically useful "Letter to the Editor" from Steven R. Terry, vice president of Production Arts Lighting, Inc., concerning shipboard power supply.

274 "Lighting for Soldier Field Stadium (Chicago)" and "B.C. Place Stadium," Lighting Design + Application, vol. 15, no. 10 (Oct. 1985), p. 43. Illus.

Laurence Swasey, "Superbowl Halftime Show Shines" and "Superbowl XX," Lighting Design + Application, vol. 16, no. 4 (Apr. 1986), pp. 28–31. Illus., color.

Laurence J. Maloney, "Sports Lighting, Some New Ideas on Quantity and Quality," Lighting Design + Application, vol. 16, no. 4 (Apr. 1986), pp. 37–41. Illus.

Charles Linn, "Light Leads the Way for Horse Racing's New Image," Architectural Lighting, vol. 1, no. 2 (Feb. 1987), pp. 14–21. Illus., color. New Jersey's Garden State Park.

See also: "Focus On Australia," Footnote 236.

"Exhibitions—The Gym Lesson," International Lighting Review, 36th year, 3d quarter, pp. 107–109. Illus., color. Lighted gym exhibition in Vienna.

"Sports: Tanah Merah Century Club, Singapore," International Lighting Review, 1984/4, pp. 145–47. Illus., color. A recent design including lighting of a golf course, swimming pool, and tennis courts—all outdoors in Singapore. Lavishly illustrated.

"Sports: The Paris-Bercy Sports Palace," International Lighting Review, 1985/1, pp. 22–27. Illus., color. Lavishly illustrated presentation of the Palais Omnisports, opened in December 1983 in France.

"A Show for All the World," Lighting Dimensions, vol. 8, no. 6 (Sept./Oct. 1984), pp. 20–27, 29–31, 33, 35. Illus., color. A lengthy description of the elaborate lighting of the 1984 closing ceremonies of the Los Angeles Olympics by designer Bill Klages.

"The Yacht Regina," Lighting Design + Application, vol. 14, no. 10 (Oct. 1984), pp. 36–38. Illus., color. An IES Award of Excellence yacht design using mostly neon.

"Relighting Pompano Harness Track," Lighting Design + Application, vol. 14, no. 7 (July 1984), pp. 13–14. Illus., color. Winner of the 1983 IES Section Award and an Edwin F. Guth Memorial Award of Merit.

"Community Recreation Sites in Plymouth, MN, Economize with HSP Lighting," Lighting

Design + Application, *vol. 14, no. 7 (July 1984), pp. 35–39. Illus. Lighting sports fields.*

M. F. Oldham, "Sports: Floodlighting the Melbourne Cricket Ground," International Lighting Review, *36th year, 3d quarter, pp. 78–83. Illus., color. In Australia.*

"Guth Memorial Awards," Lighting Design & Application, *vol. 13, no. 10 (Oct. 1983), pp. 39–40. Recent sports lighting of a race track, sports arenas, and stadiums.*

"Night Skiing, the Hows and Whys of Lighting Ski Mountains," Lighting Dimensions, *vol. 5, no. 2 (Mar. 1981), pp. 32–34. Illus., color.*

"Sports Lighting: Silent Stars at Madison Square Garden," Lighting Design + Application, *vol. 10, no. 2 (Feb. 1980), pp. 8–10, 12–13. Illus., color.*

"Sports Lighting: Relighting Seattle's Kingdome," Lighting Design + Application, *vol. 12, no. 2 (Feb. 1982), pp. 26–30. Illus., color.*

Jennifer M. Lowell and Laurence J. Maloney, *"Illuminance Selection Procedure for Sports Lighting,"* Lighting Design + Application, *vol. 13, no. 5 (May 1983), pp. 38, 40, 42–43.*

Michael De Mello, *"Holiday Spa Health Club, Riverside, California,"* International Lighting Review, *38th year, 4th quarter, (1987), pp. 140–145. Illus., color. Excellent graphics, useful text.*

Paul Enthrop and George Szeker, *"XV Winter Olympics, Calgary, Canada,"* International Lighting Review, *39th year, 2nd quarter (1988), pp. 46–57. Illus., color. Also in the same issue: A Th Snoek, "Sports City Complex, Latakia, Syria," pp. 58–65. Illus., color. And: Max Oldham, "The WACA Cricket Ground, Perth, Australia," pp. 66–69. Illus., color. And: Max Oldham, "National Tennis Centre, Melbourne," pp. 70–73. Illus., color. This series of beautifully illustrated articles is accompanied by readable, useful text for a good composite background concerning the lighting of sports structures.*

"Light Flashes: Lighting the Arena," International Lighting Review, *39th year, 3rd quarter (1988), p. 87. Illus., color. Lighting of a Netherlands soccer club (outdoors) in Eindhoven with a new type metal halide PAR lamp.*

"Sports: Thialf Ice Stadium, Heerenveen, The Netherlands," International Lighting Review, *38th year, 2nd quarter (1987). pp. 70–75. Illus., color. Lighting of an indoor ice stadium.*

Monica Buchholz, "Understanding Today's Sports Lighting," CEE, *vol. 40, no. 4 (April 1988), pp. 14–15. Illus., color. Most useful technical/artistic summary of sports lighting.*

Paul Entrop, *"Philips Stadium, Eindhoven: The Stadium Is a Theatre,"* International Lighting Review, *39th year, 4th quarter (1988), pp. 152–159. Illus., color. Well-illustrated article about both the design and technology of stadium lighting, interior and exterior.*

Sports Lighting: The Year of the Olympics: Challenges Posed by Olympic Design and Engineering Tasks for Outdoor Lighting Were Considerable, *Lighting, vol. 2, no. 6 (December 1988), pp. 10–12. Illus. Details about the lighting of the Calgary, Canada, Olympics.*

"The Dome: Sport Facility Gets Latest in Lighting Design," *Lighting, vol. 1, no. 1 (June 1987), pp. 34–35. Illus. Information about Toronto, Canada's, new domed stadium lighting.*

[275] "Necklaces of Light," Lighting Design + Application, *vol. 9, no. 6 (June 1979), p. 46. Lumen Award bridge lighting in New York City.*

"Lighting Eads Bridge," Lighting Design + Application, *vol. 14, no. 8 (Aug. 1984), pp. 17–19. A newly lighted bridge in St. Louis, winner of IES and Guth Memorial Awards of Merit.*

"The Lighting of the John A. Roebling Suspension Bridge (Cincinnati)," Lighting Design + Application, *vol. 15, no. 11 (Nov. 1985), pp. 10–12. Illus., color. See also vol. 15, no. 10 (Oct. 1985), p. 45. Illus.*

"Ben Franklin Struck by Lighting," Lighting Dimensions, *vol. 11, no. 2 (March/April 1987), p. 12. Illus. Lighting of the Benjamin Franklin Bridge across the Delaware River between Philadelphia and Camden, New Jersey, by Steven Izenour and Miles Ritter.*

"Bridge Lighting Concealed by Day, Controlled from River by Night," Architectural Lighting, *vol. 1, no. 0 (Nov. 1986), p. 24. Illus., color. The lighting of the Eads Bridge across the Mississippi.*

Stan Ward, *"Vancouver's Lions Gate Bridge: Solving Problems 400 ft Up,"* Lighting Design + Application, *vol. 17, no. 2 (Feb. 1987), pp. 17–18. Illus., color.*

Michael S. Janoff, *"Bridge Lighting: Low-Mounted Lineal vs. Overhead,"* Lighting Design + Application, *vol. 16, no. 11 (Nov. 1986), pp.*

Sports Lighting

Sports lighting is another area which formerly belonged almost exclusively to the illumination engineer. The objective here is bright, even illumination of huge stadia, tennis courts, and all types of playing areas by floodlighting from multiple pole locations at very high mounting positions. The key considerations are lamp selection, desired illumination levels, pole spacing/height/location, luminaire focus, cost (initial and operating), and maintenance. Figure 10.20 shows Wm. McManus Enterprises' lighting design for a Texas swim meet.[274]

Bridges

New York City lighting consultant Jules Horton was the designer of the Triborough Bridge, the Bronx-Whitestone Bridge, and the Throgs Neck Bridge in New York City (see Figs. 10.21 and 10.22). While one might expect that illuminating engineers would always be sufficient for this task, bridge lighting design *can* call for design imagination. Anyone who has been in New York City and is familiar with the end product of lighting design on bridges can testify to the resultant nighttime beauty.[275]

Technical Data

A quick summary of types of floodlight lamps and luminaires is appropriate at this point. The three types of luminaires are floodlights (there are many types and beam spreads), spotlights, and decorative fixtures.

The types of light sources are *incandescent* (including quartz), *fluorescent,* and *high-intensity discharge* (mercury, sodium, metallogen). Incandescent is best for accurate color reproduction but has limited operational time. Its advantages are low initial cost and good optical control (PAR and R lamps, for example). Disadvantages are short life expectancy (500 to 4,000 hours) and low efficiency (15 to 25 lumens per watt). Fluorescent is in the midrange of life expectancy and efficiency. Its advantages are reasonably good color rendition, higher efficiency (70 to 75 lumens per watt), and long life (900 to 17,000 hours). Its disadvantages are long optical length (and less control), initial expense (ballasts, starters), and severe affectation by temperature

Figure 10.20 Special lighting for a Texas swim meet by Bill McManus. (*Photo: Bob Lenkowski*)

Figure 10.21 Triborough Bridge, New York City. Lighting by Jules G. Horton Lighting Design, Inc. (*Courtesy of Triborough Bridge & Tunnel Authority.*)

Figure 10.22 Throgs Neck Bridge, New York City. Lighting by Jules G. Horton. (*Courtesy of Infranorof North American, Inc.*)

variations. Also, fluorescent fixtures are usually not interchangeable and are inflexible (ballasts, etc.). High-intensity discharge (HID) lamps have the advantages of long life expectancy (24,000 hours) and high luminous efficiency (75 to 125 lumens per watt). The disadvantages of many HID lamps are poor color rendition, a slow warmup cycle with time delay in coming to full intensity, added cost of auxiliary equipment such as ballasts, and poor optical control. A more lengthy discussion of these important factors can be found in GE Bulletin TPC-34, "Lamps for Outdoor Lighting."[276]

These are basic design considerations involved in lamp and luminaire selection:

- Purpose (desired lighting level)
- Design criteria (desired evenness of field — illumination versus design)
- Color rendition
- Optical and energy efficiency (and hours in use)
- Maintenance and lamp life
- Cost (funds available)

Safety and security in outdoor night lighting are touched upon in a specific way under other topics in this chapter, but a few general words may be useful. Security has to do with protection from illegal activities. Intruders rarely attempt to outwit lighting security systems. Bright night light around a factory or home can serve as a crime deterrent. Lighting can either come from inside or outside the building. For example, the approach grounds can be floodlighted from the roof of the building with light directed *away from* the building when there are night guards inside. Lighting directed *toward* a building is often used for a private residence or factory which does *not* have guards on duty. Stray light must be kept within a building's property line — in no instance should light be allowed to "spill" over and blind neighbors or passing traffic. Any good engineer or contractor can direct the designer to properly shielded luminaires that can eliminate this concern.[277]

Interior Lighting Design

Lighting for spectacle, for TV and movies, for the theatre, and for outdoors is but the tip of the lighting iceberg. The

46–49. *Contains charts. Most useful article for bridge lighting design.*

"The New Bridge on Brush Creek," Lighting Design & Application, *vol. 14, no. 2 (Feb. 1984), pp. 18–20. Illus., color. A contemporary bridge lighting design in Kansas City, Missouri.*

"Guth Memorial Awards," Lighting Design + Application, *vol. 13, no. 10 (Oct. 1983), p. 39. Illus. Lighting of the Eads Bridge in St. Louis in 1983.*

Bram Koebrugge, "Tower Bridge, London," International Lighting Review, *39th year, 3rd quarter (1988), pp. 88–93. Illus., color. See also, p. 45 for color illus. and brief text on this same bridge-lighting design in* International Lighting Review, *39th year, 2nd quarter (1988). Illus., color.*

George A. Bury, "Controls Animate Lighting for Ben Franklin Bridge, Complex Lighting Project Completed in Time for Philadelphia's Bicentennial Celebration," CEE, *vol. 40, no. 4 (April 1988), pp. 20, 33. Illus., color. Major recent bridge lighting by Steven Izenour, son of George Izenour. Detailed text, good graphics.*

"Animation Energizes Bridge Lighting Scheme," Lightview International, *vol. 1, no. 4 (Winter 1989), pp. 4–5. Illus., color. Designer George C. Izenour and son Steven Izenour's work, receiving an IALD Award of Excellence in 1989. Good text and color photos.*

See also: "Focus on Australia," Footnote 236.

Steve Pollock, "Suspended Animation," Lighting Dimensions, *vol. 11, no. 7 (January/February 1988), p. 14. Color illustration and some details about the relighting of the Ben Franklin Bridge in Philadelphia by George Izenour and son Steven Izenour, Jim Reed, and Duane Wilson.*

"Glasgow Lights Up," Lighting Dimensions, *vol. 12, no. 3 (April 1988), p. 10. Illus., color. Bridge over the River Clyde in Glasgow, Scotland.*

"More Moonlight over Austin," Lighting Dimensions, *vol. 13, no. 3 (April 1989), p. 28. Illus. Celebrating the 150th anniversary of Austin as the Texas state capital, this lighting of the tall towers on the Congress Avenue Bridge over Town Lake won a design competition.*

"Light Flashes," International Lighting Review, *2nd quarter, 40th year (1989), p. 46. When two bridges meet — and pass — in Rotterdam. Illus.*

[276] *See also:*

Tom Lemons, "Update on Fluorescents," Interiors, *vol. CXLIV, No. 9 (Apr. 1985), pp. 134–135. Illus., color. Useful update on 20 different fluorescent lamps.*

David Winfield Willson, "The Control of Light," Interior Design, *a three-part article in vol. 55, no. 11 (Nov. 1984), pp. 248–253, and vol. 56, no. 1A (Jan. 1985), pp. 292–297 and vol. 57, no. 4 (April 1987), pp. 190–191. Illus., color. Useful "observations, evaluations and applications" of lighting control, including low-voltage lamps, in architectural lighting.*

Harry B. Zackrison, "Trends in the Lighting Industry: A Look at Available Lamps and Their Development," Lighting Design + Application, *vol. 14, no. 11 (Nov. 1984), pp. 42–47. Illus. A readable summary of new lamps and their relationship to energy-efficient cost savings.*

Harry Zackrison, "Today's Current Lighting Technology," Lighting Design + Application, *vol. 15, no. 7 (July 1985), pp. 25–36. An update to article listed above; much more detailed.*

Sidney M. Pankin, "The Parts Department," Architectural Lighting, *vol. 1, no. 2 (Feb. 1987), pp. 50–51. Latest advances in fluorescents, ballasts, and rapid-start lamps. See also vol. 1, no. 6 (June 1987), pp. 44–45, illus.; and vol. 1, no. 4 (April 1987), pp. 40–41, illus.*

Randal E. Swiech, "Lighting Control Technology Grows in Importance," Architectural Lighting, *vol. 1, no. 0 (Nov. 1986), pp. 49–50. Illus.*

Sidney M. Pankin, "The Parts Department," Architectural Lighting, *vol. 1, no. 1 (Jan. 1987), pp. 58, 60. More about improvements in fluorescents and the history of this light source.*

"1985 Progress Report," Lighting Design + Application, *vol. 15, no. 11 (Nov. 1985), pp. 24–39. Illus. This IES annual report on new equipment appears in* Lighting Design + Application *each November. It is updated by a large IES committee.*

R. R. Verderber, "Review of Lighting Control Equipment and Applications," Lighting Design + Application, *vol. 16, no. 2 (Feb. 1986), pp. 45–49. Charts. Excellent summary of basics in architectural lighting control units.*

H. A. Lee, "The 'New' Low Voltage, a Short History of Current Use," Lighting Design + Application, *vol. 15, no. 9 (Sept. 1985), pp.*

28–29. Illus. Useful brief summary of low-voltage lighting.

Tod Swormstedt, "A Case for Cold Cathode," Visual Merchandising & Store Design, *vol. 117, no. 5 (May 1986), pp. 82–85. Illus., color.*

"New Lamps For Old?" ABTT News, *June 1985, p. 14. About gold-finished MR16 low voltage and PAR 36 lamps available in Europe.*

[277] *Richard J. Healy,* Design for Security. *N.Y.; Wiley & Sons; 1983. 280 pp., illus. Complete volume by an authority on security lighting (see "Security Lighting," Chap. 6).*

"New Lighting Reduces Accidents, Vandalism, and Burglaries," Lighting Design + Application, *vol. 15, no. 7 (July 1985), pp. 50–52. Useful factual information concerning crime and accident reduction by security lighting.*

Gordon D. Rowe, "A Crime Time Show," Light *magazine, vol. 38, no. 3 (1969), pp. 19–23. Very important article on light levels needed in a parking lot for video surveillance systems along with a cost comparison for incandescent versus multivapor versus lucalox light sources.*

"Vandalproof Lighting," Lighting Design & Application, *vol. 9, no. 6 (June 1979), pp. 48, 50. Illus., color.*

James M. Tien, "Street Lighting: Lighting's Impact on Crime," Lighting Design + Application, *vol. 9, no. 12 (Dec. 1979), pp. 20–30. Illus. Excellent informative study.*

W. van Bommel and J. van Dijk, "Security Lighting: Security Lighting for Domestic Exteriors," International Lighting Review, *1985/1, pp. 10–15. Illus., color. The most extensive, up-to-date coverage of security lighting with excellent color illustrations and technical details.*

George J. English and Robert E. Levin, "Infrared Floodlighting—Significant Application for Security Lighting," Lighting Design + Application, *vol. 15, no. 12 (Dec. 1985), pp. 48–51. Illus.*

M. F. Oldham, "Security Lighting: Housing Estates, Melbourne," International Lighting Review, *38th year, 2nd quarter (1987), pp. 54–57. Illus., color. Well-illustrated and -written article about security lighting in Australia.*

Owen B. Stevens, "First Lines of Defense, Lighting Design is a Primary Consideration in Crime Prevention and Detection," Lighting, *vol. 3, no. 3 (June 1989), pp. 12, 14–16. Tables. Useful.*

body of that iceberg is the illumination and design of interiors during both daytime and nighttime hours.

There are in existence several books which deal with interior lighting *design* (as well as technology), a situation not often the case in the other lighting design specialties covered in this volume. In view of that fact, I refer the reader back to footnote 236. The first books listed there cover interior architectural lighting design in excellent fashion. I will, therefore, somewhat restrict coverage of this area in this study to outstanding graphic examples of lighting design in the many interior architectural specialties (banks, museums, hospitals, places of worship, etc.); an enumeration of these specialty areas (both for the newcomer to interior architectural lighting and the present practitioner); and, finally, extensive annotated footnotes listing other existing sources of information about design in each specialty.[278]

Communication Forms

Unlike the theatre practitioner, the designer of architectural lighting does not communicate through a light plot. I referred earlier in this chapter to necessary elements in a client/architect prospectus (see "Procedures and Practices" under "Landscape Architecture"). In addition to a prospectus, frequently newly designed fixture drawings are needed. The examples of a prospectus sketch and detailed drawings of fixtures shown in Figs. 10.23, 10.24, and 10.25 are from the work of Howard Brandston Lighting Design, Inc. James Nuckolls devoted 12 helpful pages in his book *Interior Lighting for Environmental Designers* to a detailed discussion, with examples, of drawings, prospectus, reports, and layouts needed from the architectural lighting designer.[279] That information is not repeated here, but the reader is referred to Nuckolls's book. A beginning designer may wish to solicit sample client presentations from some of the larger firms as a way of becoming familiar with the accepted forms. Most firms spend much time in preparation of these presentations. They have top graphics specialists on their staffs and are justly proud of both their sales presentations and the resultant communication forms necessary to yield proper actualization of a finished project.

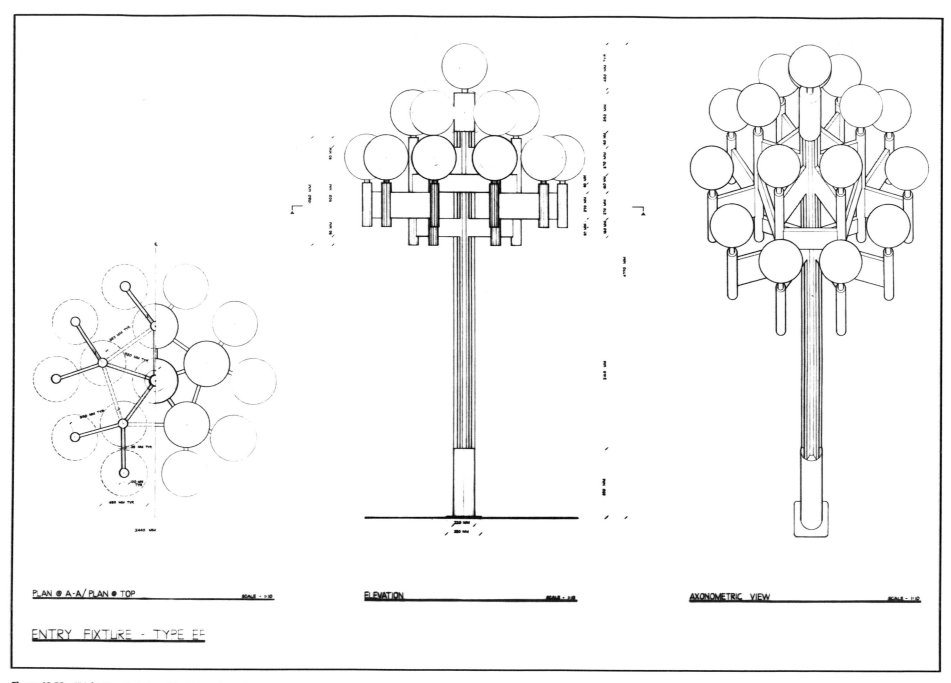

PLAN @ A-A/ PLAN @ TOP   SCALE - 1:10

ELEVATION   SCALE - 1:10

AXONOMETRIC VIEW   SCALE - 1:10

ENTRY FIXTURE - TYPE EF

Figure 10.23 "Light Trees" designed by Howard Brandston.

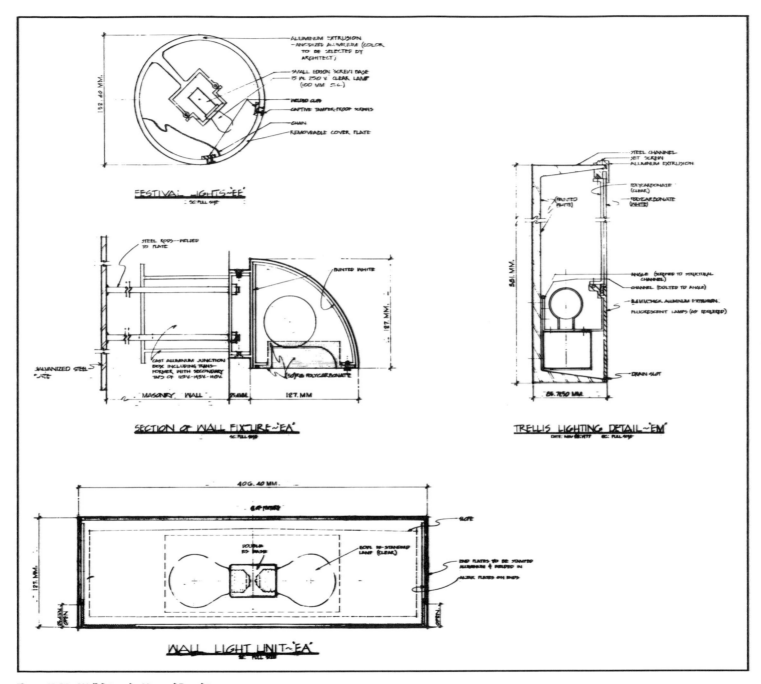

Figure 10.24 Wall fixture by Howard Brandston.

Figure 10.25 Prospectus for Transitway Mall, Denver, Colorado, by Howard Brandston Lighting Design, Inc.

[278] Barbara J. Knox, "An Interior Designer Looks at Light — Susan Forbes Knows the Value of a Lighting Consultant," Lighting Dimensions, vol. 10, no. 4 (July/Aug. 1986), pp. 30–33, 54–56.

"Let There Be Light," Interiors, Vol. CXLII, no. 9 (Apr. 1983), pp. 85–107. Illus., color. A summary of the present status of architectural lighting design in hotels, restaurants, showrooms, banks, a greenhouse, a shopping center and a unique use of color. Outstanding color photographs and design suggestions.

"1986 Lumen Awards Program," Visual Merchandising and Store Design, vol. 117, no. 5 (May 1986), pp. 62–69. Illus., color. Well-reproduced color photographs and credits for the 1986 (19th annual) IES Lumen Award winners.

John E. Traister, Practical Lighting Applications for Building Construction. New York; Van Nostrand Reinhold; 1982. 215 pages, illus. A valuable tool for the architectural lighting specialist.

"Interview: On Common Sense Designing," Lighting Design & Application, vol. 9, no. 11 (Nov. 1979), pp. 18–21. Illus. Interview with Jules Horton on architectural lighting design.

Susanne Selsin, "The Lighting Designer: Bright New Star," The New York Times, November 8, 1979, Home section, pp. C1, C8. Excellent illustrated article about the importance and work of today's interior lighting designers and IALD.

Ernest Wotton and Dr. Ben Barkow, "The Cheerfulometer, or The Psychology of Lighting," IALD Newsletter, Dec. 1980, pp. 1, 2. Should be read by all interior lighting designers. Concerns nonmeasurable human responses to lighting.

"IES 1984 Progress Committee Report," Lighting Design + Application, vol. 14, no. 12 (Dec. 1984), pp. 18–28. Illus., color. An IES committee summary of new lamps, control units, and applications changes for the year.

Harry Zackrison, Jr., "Today's Lighting Control Techniques Will Light Our Tomorrows: Recent Technological Advances Offer a Wide Choice of Energy-saving Techniques in Lighting," Lighting Design & Application, vol. 15, no. 3 (March 1985), pp. 29–36. Illus. Extended report on newer control devices.

M. A. Cayless and A. M. Marsden (editors), Lamps and Lighting. Baltimore; Edward Arnold (300 N. Charles St., Baltimore, MD 21201); 1983. 521 pp., illus. A full-length reference work about lamps, frequently revised. Basic reference tool.

D. L. DiLaura, D. P. Igoe, P. G. Samaras, and A. M. Smith, "Verifying the Applicability of Computer Generated Pictures to Lighting Design," Journal of the I.E.S., vol. 17, no. 1 (Winter 1988), pp. 36–61. Highly technical analysis of computer verification. Illus.

Louis A. Carriere and Mark S. Rea, "Economics of Switching Fluorescent Lamps," IEEE Transactions on Industry Applications, vol. 24, no. 3 (May/June 1988), pp. 370–379. A careful, lengthy study which basically establishes that frequent "on/off" of fluorescents does not materially shorten lamp life. This is a key point in energy conservation planning.

Steve Pollock, "The Age of Refinement: Manufacturers' Innovations Drive the Future of Architectural Lighting," Lighting Dimensions, vol. 11, no. 7, (January/February 1988), pp. 96–105. Excellent article about the interrelationship between architectural lighting design and technical innovation.

Mark Loeffler, "Full Circle: Stage Manufacturers Rediscover the Architectural Market," Lighting Dimensions, vol. 11, no. 6 (November 1987), pp. 30, 32–34, 36. Illus., color. An analysis of the history and firms involved in manufacturing architectural lighting dimmers and control. Useful.

Bryan S. Rogers, "Programmable Lighting Controls," Lighting, vol. 1, no. 1 (June 1987), pp. 12–16, 18, 32. Illus.

"Light Pipe: Bringing the Sun Indoors," Lighting, vol. 1, no. 1 (June 1987), pp. 28, 30. Illus.

Steve Pollock, "Architectural Lighting Control," Theater Crafts, vol. 21, no. 8 (October 1987), pp. 43, 76, 78–83.

"Hazardous Lighting: Some of the Products Available in the Canadian Marketplace," Lighting, vol. 3, no. 2 (April 1989), pp. 26, 28. Illus.

W. Glen Geiger, Jr., "When is a Tree Not a Tree!" Lighting Dimensions, vol. 13, no. 3 (April 1989), p. 15. Geiger, President of Geiger Engineering, Inc., in Charleston, South Carolina, and Jan Moyer explain the quite complicated ruling under the National Electrical Code (NFPA 70-87, Article 225-26), regarding mounting lights on live vegetation (trees, for example). This is an extremely important "Letters" correspondence on a subject which every landscape lighting designer should be familiar with!

Edward Effron, "Smaller Is Better: Compact Fluorescents Quickly Gaining Visibility," Lighting Dimensions, vol. 13, no. 3 (April 1989), pp. 110–111, 113–114. A comparison chart of compact lamps by watts in fluorescents from various manufacturers. Useful information for the lighting designer.

Barry H. Slinker, "Art and Commerce: Robert Sonneman on the Business of Modern Fixture Design," Lighting Dimensions, vol. 13, no. 3 (April 1989), pp. 116, 118. Explains somewhat the business of fixture (luminaire) manufacture and sales and design.

See also: "Focus On Australia," Footnote 236.

"DLF Annual Workshop 1985," a 58-page spiral-bound presentation to students involving lighting design for the executive offices and showroom of a manufacturer/importer of glassware. Includes suggested design solutions by three prominent New York City professional designers. Available from the Designer's Lighting Forum, New York City. Excellent student project. Quality graphics.

Parry Moon and Domina Eberle Spencer, Lighting Design. Cambridge, Massachusetts; Addison-Wesley Press; 1948. The older basic American illumination engineering text. Somewhat out of date.

J. B. deBoer and Dr. D. Fisher, Interior Lighting. London; Macmillan (Philip Technical Library); 1978. (Available in the United States from Scholium International, Inc., 130-30 31st Avenue, Flushing, New York). Good basic book on illuminating engineering by two prominent Dutch experts. Valuable for detailed discussion of IES standards variations throughout the world. Not for the nonengineer, or anyone weak in math. Excellent illus. Of use to established consultants. 336 pages.

E. M. Feher, "Light-Space-Architecture," TABS, vol. 33, no. 2 (Spring 1977), pp. 7–9. The best *philosophical/historical analysis yet written about architectural lighting.*

Prafulla C. Sorcar, Architectural Lighting for Commercial Interiors. *N.Y.; John Wiley & Sons, Interscience; 1987. 249 pp. Illus. Basic text covering light and vision, seeing color, light sources and accessories, photometrics and measuring light, lighting calculations, lighting layouts, electrical circuiting, lighting control, incandescent/luminaires and fluorescent and high-intensity discharge lighting patterns and forms, human reaction to light, and applications (task lighting, office environment, ambient light, perimeter lighting) for offices and for merchandising. Excellent basic volume. Well written and illustrated. Belongs in every architectural lighting library.*

"Lighting: By Design or by Default?" Workshop booklet used at Lighting World International, Javits Convention Center, New York City, May 12, 1987. Published by New York Designers Lighting Forum. Contains the expressed comments of Connie Jensen (Lighting Professionals, Inc.), Lesley Wheel (Wheel Gertsztoff Friedman Associates, Inc.), and Gerry Zekowski (Lighting by Design, Inc.). While only 18 pages long and folder-bound, it contains a very good basic summary of light sources, color temperature, developing a design, things to avoid, task lighting, avoiding glare, wall lighting, mirrors, and a checklist for good lighting.

"Show Preview: Nineteen Years of Neocon, the Annual Contract Furnishings Show in Chicago's Merchandise Mart is June 9–12," Lighting Dimensions, *vol. 11, no. 1 (May/June 1987), p. 16. Illus. A trade show of great value to architectural lighting specialists. Also covers (in an advertisement) the Internation Lighting Fair at the Dallas Convention Center, July 11–14, 1987 (of much less importance than Lighting World International annual conference/trade show sponsored by IES and IALD).*

James Nuckolls, "Feedback: IES Papers Report—James Nuckolls Reports on the Significant Aesthetic Points of the Papers Presented at the 1986 IES Conference," *Lighting Dimensions, vol. 11, no. 1 (Jan./Feb. 1987), pp. 25, 82–83. A useful report by Nuckolls about papers entitled "Wall Lighting Placement: Effect on Behavior in the Work Environment," "Preferred Luminances in Offices," and "The Effects of Light on Decision Making."*

Jules Horton, "The Lighting Consultant, Welcome to the Team," *The Designer magazine, vol. 12, no. 145 (Dec. 1969).*

"Young Designers, '79," Lighting Design & Application, *vol. 9, no. 5 (May 1979), pp. 20–24. An interview with nine young architectural lighting designers. Questions and answers. Excellent overview for a beginner.*

"Light, Architecture, and Aesthetics," Lighting Design + Application, *vol. 8, no. 11 (Nov. 1978), pp. 7–23. Central theme of this issue. Still useful information in spite of the 1978 date.*

"Lighting 1979," Designers West *magazine, vol. 26, no. 12 (Oct. 1979), entire issue. Contains 190 pages of quality photographs and articles about interior lighting design in the 17 western states. Excellent.*

Interiors *magazine, vol. CXLI, no. 7 (Feb. 1982). Illus., color. Entire issue devoted to commercial lighting. Very useful.*

Alec Feder, "Breaking out of 'The Bottle Era'," *and* "Dialogues with Light," *Lighting Design & Application, vol. 12, no. 8 (Aug. 1982), pp. 15–20. Illus., color. Vivid demostration and photographs of designing with light.*

R. T. Dorsey, "Design Approach—The New Thrust in Lighting Practice," *Lighting Design & Application, vol. 1, no. 1 (July 1971), pp. 9–13. An early article encouraging engineers to understand the lighting design approach (rather than just the engineering approach).*

Arnold Nicholson, "Mr. Kelly's Magic Lights," *The Saturday Evening Post, vol. 231, no. 1 (July 5, 1958), pp. 28–29, 61, 64–65. Illus. Interview with Richard Kelly about his work and philosophy.*

Robert T. Dorsey and H. Richard Blackwell, "Visual Performance: A Performance-oriented Approach to Lighting Specifications," *Lighting Design + Application, vol. 5, no. 2 (Feb. 1975), pp. 13–27. An important article. A plea to tailor lighting to task requirements, not formulas; heavily illustrated.*

"Philosophies of Architectural Lighting, Parts 1, 2, and 3" Lighting Design + Application, *vol. 6, no. 5 (May 1976), pp. 12–27. Important basic discussion articles by Der Scutt, Viggo Bech, and James L. Nuckolls about differing approaches to architectural lighting design.*

J. F. Caminada, "Architectural Lighting," *Lighting Design + Application, vol. 13, no. 8 (Aug. 1983), pp. 16–21. Illus., color. Caminada, editor of International Lighting Review and architect/lighting designer with Philips, Holland, analyzes architectural lighting objectives. Many simplified sketches and useful text. Should be read by all architects and lighting designers in this area.*

Interior Design *magazine. Excellent source of the latest interior design trends and lavishly illustrated color photos on quality paper. Devotes great attention to lighting design and designers. 12 issues per year. P.O. Box 1970, Marion, OH 43305. Telephone: (800) 624-9200. The December "Buyers Guide" issue is a comprehensive listing of manufacturers nationwide.*

"Winning Ways," Lighting Dimensions, *vol. 11, no. 7 (January/February 1988), pp. 48–51. Illus. IALD Award-winning interior designs for 1988, including hotels, atriums, showrooms, New York City's Carnegie Hall, and a restaurant.*

Bonnie S. Schwartz, "Washington's Union Station Reopens," *Lighting Dimensions, vol. 12, no. 6 (September/October 1988), p. 20. Lighting design by Robert Friedman (of Wheel Gersztoff Friedman) and by Wm. M. C. Lam.*

Edward Effron, Planning and Designing Lighting. *Boston, New York, Toronto; Little, Brown and Co.; (1988). A "Demystification" of lighting as an interior design element for the novice. Around $23.*

And the Winner Is . . . New York's Lumen Awards Are Announced," Lighting Dimensions, *vol. 13, no. 4 (May/June 1989), pp. 66–67. Illus. Offices, an office building, a restaurant, and the Club Zanzibar in Newark, New Jersey, won awards with "crackle" neon, glass beads, prisms, dichroic mirrors, UV, etc.*

[279] James L. Nuckolls, Chap. 22, *"Lighting Layouts and Design Reports," pp. 286–98, op. cit. (see footnote 236).*

[280] Progressive Architecture, *pp. 76, 78, op. cit.* *(see footnote 242).*

[281] *William M. C. Lam, p. 83, op. cit. (see footnote 236).*

Procedures and Practices

Howard Brandston provided the following pertinent material concerning specific architectural lighting design practices in *Progressive Architecture:*

> If the experience of my own firm is typical, the lighting designer receives half of his commissions from the owner and half from the architect. The ideal arrangement is selection by the architect (who will feel more secure with a lighting designer of his own choice) and payment by the owner, with whom the lighting designer negotiates his own contract.
>
> Fee arrangements vary, the most common being (again using experience of my own office): (1) upset fee and hourly rate, (2) flat fee with schedule of payments contingent on job progress, (3) flat fee with monthly payments. Each contract is based on a proposal specifying all services.
>
> The lighting designer should be equipped to create a lighting system for all areas outlined in the contracted scope of work, following consultation with the architect, landscape architect, interior designer and graphic designer. He will also consult with the electrical, structural and mechanical engineers on all phases of electrical design affecting the lighting plan. He should perform the following services:
>
> 1. Provide complete lighting plans for all spaces outlined in the scope of the work, showing location and type of all fixtures necessary to complete the lighting system.
> 2. Prepare a dimmer or control diagram as required by the lighting design.
> 3. Prepare a lamp schedule using currently available lamps.
> 4. Prepare scale drawings or specifications suitable for competitive bidding of all fixtures shown on the lighting plan.
> 5. Prepare dimmer specifications suitable for competitive bidding on all dimmers shown on the lighting plan.
> 6. Prepare a budget estimate on specified fixtures and dimmers.
> 7. Check shop drawings of specified fixtures and dimmers.
> 8. Supervise and inspect all work as requested (supervision by the lighting designer should be distinguished from the continuous personal superintendence by the contractor).
> 9. Furnish all information available about the lighting system, including calculations, mock-ups, renderings, etc.
>
> Because lighting is so important to the architectural solution, the lighting designer should be a full working member of the design team from the outset of a commission. To limit his range of solutions through controls set by feasibility or preliminary design studies in which he has not participated is to risk incorporating dubious expediencies or courting expensive changes to achieve the optimum solution.

> In practical terms, lighting affects heating and air conditioning requirements and, in certain situations, structural requirements. Light sources and air conditioning ducts frequently vie for the same space. Failure to establish at the outset various lighting system criteria—watts per square foot, ceiling heights, restrictions on crossovers, requirements for mechanical and electrical closets, etc.—invites problems later on. Where the architect, lighting designers, structural engineer and mechanical-electrical engineer are working together throughout, and where the role and responsibilities of the lighting designers are clearly understood by all members on the team, there are fewer conflicts and cross-purposes; design-engineering decisions may be coordinated at every stage to generate a smooth-flowing operation, a logical progression of drawings and, ultimately, a successfully and economically executed project.
>
> Worthy of special mention is the lighting designer's role vis-a-vis the general contractor and the electrical subcontractor, who sometimes look upon lighting specifications as the key to sound family financial planning. Lighting fixtures are particularly vulnerable to price-shaving and to the substitution of equivalents which are not precisely equivalent. The reason for this stems from the nature of the lighting industry itself. It is replete with small operators competing fiercely for contracts. This affords advantages, of course, but it can also lead to abuses. To assure that the integrity of the design will not be compromised, the lighting designer must approve all shop drawings and samples submitted pertaining to the system, and it must be clearly understood that he has the right of refusal.[280]

The standard proposal (contract) of Jules G. Horton Lighting Design, Inc., is reproduced in edited form as a guide in Fig. 10.26. William M. C. Lam provides a somewhat more condensed checklist. He suggests to the designer the following six steps:

1. Introduce lighting design as a design factor at the beginning. Opening communication is *vital.*
2. Use architect/client education as a tool. Take clients on tours. Give brief illustrated lectures about light and its design.
3. Use diagrams, models, and test mock-ups for testing, lectures, field trips, demonstrations, and instruction.
4. Plan and program space needs and design objectives clearly rather than just providing equipment lists and illumination levels.
5. Use renderings, fixtures, and job-site mock-ups.
6. Do cost-benefit studies and energy-conservation studies.[281]

JULES G. HORTON LIGHTING DESIGN, INC.

450 PARK AVENUE SOUTH   NEW YORK, NEW YORK 10016

STANDARD FORM OF THE PROPOSAL

We are pleased to submit the Proposal for Professional Services as lighting consultants and designers for the above project.

1. The Proposal is based on:

2. The Proposal is limited to the following areas:

3. The Proposal is based on the scope of services as described below and is divided into Phases I, II, III and IV.

4. PHASE I (Schematic Design) will consist of the following:

    (a) Conceptual design conferences with the Architect, his Consultants and the Owner (time for all necessary trips is included in the fee).

    (b) Conceptual studies.

    (c) Written report outlining the recommended program for lighting design.

    (d) Special renderings and other visual presentation elements, if required and as authorized by the Architect.

5. PHASE II (Design Development) will consist of the following:

    (a) Design conferences with the Architect, his Consultants and the Owner.

    (b) Lighting Section of Power Budget as required by governing authority.

    (c) Layouts of typical areas.

    (d) Daylight and artificial light calculations.

    (e) Preliminary layouts of proposed lighting on transparencies provided by the Architect (including emergency lighting concept).

    (f) Fixture Schedule with preliminary fixture cuts and sketches.

    ⌈(g) Providing Owner's Contractor with information required to prepare a guaranteed maximum cost.

    or

    ⌊(g) Preliminary cost estimate.

    (h) Intent diagrams for circuiting and control.

    (i) Design, observation of construction, testing and evaluation of mockups, if required, and as authorized in writing by the Architect.

6. PHASE III (Contract Documents) will consist of the following:

    (a) Coordinating lighting design with architectural, structural and mechanical design.

    (b) Final layouts of proposed lighting on working drawing transparencies provided by the Architect.

    (c) Final cuts and sketches of proposed lighting fixtures.

    (d) Summary of illumination levels.

    (e) Final specifications for the lighting fixtures.

    (f) Review of final Contract Documents as prepared by the Architect and his Consultants, and related to the lighting system.

    (g) Assistance in evaluating proposals by the Bidders.

7. PHASE IV (Construction) will consist of the following:

    (a) Conferences with the Architect, the Owner and the Contractor, as required.

    (b) Checking of shop drawings of lighting fixtures, control equipment and associated architectural elements.

    (c) Review and testing of fixture samples.

    (d) Shop and field inspections, if required and as authorized in writing by the Architect.

    (e) Final review of lighting installation and supervision of fixture targeting (including time for necessary trips to the project site).

    (f) Final lamp schedule for the Building Maintenance Crew.

8. Our fee will be based on the following hourly rates:

    | Principals: | Jules G. Horton | @ | $50.00 per hour. |
    | | Stephen W. Lees | @ | $40.00 per hour. |
    | | Joseph A. DiBernardo | @ | $40.00 per hour. |

    Associates/Designers/Draftsmen: $15.00 to $30.00 per hour, subject to salary increases during the life of the project.

    All bills will be submitted monthly and will be payable within thirty (30) days.

9. The estimated maximum fee will be _____.

    The fee will cover the following items:

    (1) Items (a) through (c) of Phase I.   (3) All items of Phase III.

    (2) Items (a) through (h) of Phase II.   (4) Items (b), (c), (e) and (f) of Phase IV.

    Before exceeding the above fee due to changes, revisions or an increase in the scope of the project, we will notify the Architect in writing in order to secure his written approval.

10. Time required for Item (d) of Phase I, Item (i) of Phase II and Items (a) and (d) of Phase IV is not included in the fee and will be billed according to actual time spent and based on a prior written authorization by the Architect.

11. Additional time spent in out-of-town travel in connection with the project after Phase I other than listed above is not included in the fee and will be billed at the rate of $500.00 per day for the Principals and $300.00 per day for technical personnel.

12. All incidental expenses such as travel, lodging and meals, toll telephone calls, blueprints, computer charges, messengers, express mail, Xerox copies, mockups and tests are not included in the fee and will be billed at cost.

13. At the time of signing the Proposal we will be paid a retainer fee of _____.

14. It is understood that all publicity about the project where credits are given shall include the name of Jules G. Horton Lighting Design, Inc., as Lighting Consultants.

15. Attached Riders 1 and 2 form an integral part of this Proposal.

Figure 10.26 Standard contract form developed by Jules G. Horton Lighting Design, Inc.

[282] "Stadia," Lighting Design + Application, vol. 3, no. 2 (Feb. 1973), pp. 6–38. Major feature of this issue. Several articles; well illustrated.

"Stage—Abe Feder, Part I," Lighting Design + Application, vol. 5, no. 12 (Dec. 1975), pp. 24–28. Abe Feder's thoughts on lighting arenas and auditoriums plus a detailed, informative, illustrated interview with Feder about his career and work.

J. B. deBoer and D. Fisher, "Sports Buildings," pp. 299–309, op. cit. (see footnote 278). Basic illuminating engineering. Excellent illustrations, some color.

Jane Ganter, "Unexpected Bonus with Instant Restrike Metal Halide Lighting," Architectural Lighting, vol. 1, no. 4 (April 1987), pp. 34–37. Illus., color. New installation in the Philadelphia Spectrum Arena.

Barbara J. Knox, "The Javits Convention Center: Paul Marantz Lights New York's Latest 'Big Deal' ", Lighting Dimensions, vol. 10, no. 4 (July/Aug. 1986), pp. 34–35, 50. Illus.

[283] "Tube-Mounted Metal Halides Set Devotional Mood in Synagogue," Architectural Lighting, vol. 1, no. 2 (Feb. 1987), p. 10. Illus., color.

Stephen P. Schuber, "Let There Be Light: A Design for Meditation," Architectural Lighting, vol. 1, no. 2 (Feb. 1987), pp. 24–26. Illus., color. Lighting of Our Lady of Grace Church in Edina, Minnesota. Excellent color photographs and text.

"A Dim Religious Light: Three Environ Church Projects," Strand Light, vol. 2, issue 1 (Spring 1987), pp. 2–3. Illus. Lighting of the Manchester Cathedral, First Assembly of God in Phoenix, and Old South Church in Boston.

"Lighting and Liturgy, Three Views: Clergymen, Architect and Lighting Designer," Light magazine, vol. 41, no. 1 (1972), pp. 3–9. Useful basic text. Fine illustrations, many in color. Includes light plot.

Robert E. Fischer, "The Crystal Cathedral: Embodiment of Light and Nature," Architectural Record, Nov. 1980, pp. 77–85. Illus., color. Lengthy, well-illustrated exposition of an ultramodern "drive-in" California church used for TV.

Specific Techniques

While the overall philosophy and practices of interior architectural lighting have been defined above, there are specific practices which apply to particular areas. The requirements for hospital lighting, for example, are far different from those for a sports arena. Therefore, several specialized areas — and the specifics thereof — are presented in most of the balance of this chapter.

Arenas, Amphitheaters, and Sports Complexes

These structures are sometimes the province of the illuminating engineer. In other cases a unified uniqueness of style has been desired which only the lighting designer can provide. Howard Brandston designed the entire New Jersey Sports Complex near Hackensack, New Jersey, including the first racetrack. Abe Feder was the designer for the New York Coliseum, a huge exhibit and trade show building. David Mintz designed the Athletic Building for SUNY (State University of New York) at Potsdam.[282]

Places of Worship

For the lighting of places of worship people frequently turn to lighting designers. A place of worship should involve taste, focus, monumentality, and flexibility. Most churches are multipurpose gathering places. The formalized services benefit from mobile, changeable lighting. The lighting objectives are

1. To create an atmosphere that is conducive to worship.
2. To allow for variations in levels of lighting for different uses and different portions of the worship service.
3. To provide the ability to shift focus as desired (to the alter, the choir, etc.). Control panels and dimmers can be used.
4. To limit required maintenance — frequently fixtures in churches are not readily accessible due to room height.
5. To place architectural emphasis on building form, texture, etc.

6. To emphasize decorative elements, such as a dramatic cross, stained glass windows, arches, and transepts.

Places of worship usually have both adequate funding and high standards. The people involved are concerned with that which is durable and in good taste for many years into the future. See Color Fig. 83a, a church lighted by Wm. Lam Associates, Inc.[283]

Banks and Government and Public Buildings

Banks often have large profits. They are frequent contributors to charity and worthy community causes, and they do not hesitate to spend money for their business buildings. Banks have these lighting requirements:

- Attract customers by presenting a warm, inviting appearance
- Present a prestige image of dignity, solidarity, and style
- Provide efficiency (high light levels) in work/customer areas.

Figure 10.27 is Wheel-Garon, Inc.'s work for the Philadelphia National Bank. Color Fig. 84 is the California First Bank in San Francisco lighted by Jules G. Horton Lighting Design, Inc. Color Fig. 85 is the Cite Parlementaire by Wm. M. C. Lam Associates, Inc. Government and public buildings also aim for monumentality and have some of the same lighting concerns that banks do. "Build the best," seems to be the motto, "for the customer is the unidentifiable taxpayer."[284]

Factories and Industrial Buildings

Justice Louis Brandeis said in 1910, "The greatest source of waste in the industrial world is unused, underdeveloped, or misdirected human effort. . . . [I]f you waste human effort, you make the product cost more." Köhler and Luckhardt wrote:

The lighting of factories cannot readily be understood and evaluated, let alone satisfactorily solved, unless the illuminating engineer has gained a clear mental picture of the plant as a living organism. He must understand the nature of the work and work-

Figure 10.27 Philadelphia National Bank renovation. Lighting by Wheel-Garon, Inc.; interiors designed by the Space Design Group. (*Photo: Bernard Liebman*)

ing conditions, the cycle of operations, and the peculiarities of the industry. This he can do only through conversations and consultations with management, foreman, and working men and women, and above all by spending time on the job at various job stations.[285]

These are but a few of the reasons cost-conscious managements often turn to the designer rather than the engineer. Such managements have the philosophy that a lighting system is a production tool, and this approach usually motivates the selection of the best lighting the budget can handle. The lighting of two types of areas must be considered: (1) the overall building lighting, including corridors and storage facilities, and (2) work lighting for specific production tasks. There are three good reasons behind well-de-

signed factory lighting:

1. *Increased production.* Good lighting helps eliminate fatigue, lowers product rejection rates, and may reduce absenteeism and accident rates. An increase in lighting level to 200 footcandles has been established to increase productivity up to 10 percent.

2. *Prestige.* Employee morale and production is important, but public image is also of concern. For example, General Motors built literally the best that money could buy in Detroit, employing top lighting designers to ensure the best lighting possible.

3. *Economics.* There are provable economic advantages to spending money on lighting. Group relamping (rather than sporadic relamping) reduces overall lamps costs by 10 percent. Proper maintenance—cleaning, repairs, and upkeep—of lighting fixtures can more than pay for its cost. Lighting planned properly can reduce costs for heat, air conditioning, and humidification/dehumidification. Planned wall, floor, and ceiling reflectivity, plus that of machinery and furnishings, can be employed as a design (and economic) tool to reduce lighting requirements.

The IES states that good factory lighting enhances safety, facilitates seeing, and influences emotional response.[286] Figures 10.28 and 10.29 show an RCA factory before and after relighting.[287]

Hospitals

A hospital has been called "a city in itself." Four objectives apply to hospital lighting: (1) to meet physical needs (clear visibility), (2) to meet psychological needs (atmosphere), (3) to meet budget needs (most hospitals lose money), and (4) to meet service needs (in kitchens, offices, labs, operating rooms, and patient areas). The two basic areas to deal with are patient/visitor areas, which include parking lots, waiting areas and corridors, gift/coffee shops and restaurants, chapels, patients' rooms, and medical service areas, which include libraries, laundry rooms, kitchens, operating rooms, examination areas, and staff and office quarters. In addition to having lighting design knowledge about a wide range of use areas, the designer must know the technical require-

Derek Phillips, "Lighting for Churches," IALD Newsletter, *Sept. 1982, pp. 2–3. Very useful basic outline of church lighting by this leading British architect and lighting designer.*

"The Crystal Cathedral," Lighting Dimensions, *vol. 5, no. 1 (Jan./Feb. 1981), pp. 32–34, cover. Illus., color.*

"Let There Be Light . . . at Rosary Cathedral," Lighting Design + Application, *vol. 12, no. 3 (March 1982), pp. 14–16. Illus., color.*

John Adams and John Flynn, "Light and Form, Their Relation to Modern Church Design," Light *magazine, vol. 27, no. 1 (Jan./Mar. 1958), pp. 3–9. Excellent.*

Richard C. Peters and Sarah Shankman, "Innovative Planning Meets Tradition in St. Matthews Design (Pacific Palisades, CA)," Lighting Design + Application, *vol. 16, no. 7 (July 1986), pp. 10–12. Illus., color.*

"Churches," Lighting Design + Application, *vol. 15, no. 10 (Oct. 1985), p. 34. Three IES Guth Awards of Merit designs.*

"The Luthern Brotherhood Building," Lighting Design + Application, *vol. 14, no. 10 (Oct. 1984), pp. 34–35. Illus., color. Church headquarters building in Minneapolis—an IES Award of Excellence winner.*

"St. Anselm's Church," Lighting Design + Application, *vol. 14, no. 10 (Oct. 1984), pp. 28–29. Illus., color. An IES Award of Excellence winner in Tokyo.*

"First Presbyterian Church Sanctuary," Lighting Design + Application, *vol. 14, no. 1 (Jan 1984), pp. 22–23. Illus., color. Award-winning church lighting design in London, Ohio.*

"Guth Memorial Awards," Lighting Design + Application, *vol. 13, no. 10 (Oct. 1983), pp. 42. Illus. Presentation of the outstanding 1983 church lighting.*

"Public Places—Santa Clara Mission: Theatrical Lighting in a Religious Setting," Lighting Design + Application, *vol. 13, no. 7 (July 1983), pp. 26–28. Illus., color.*

"Bagai House of Worship, New Delhi, India," International Lighting Review, *38th year, 4th quarter (1987), pp. 157–159. Illus., color. Description of the lighting of a uniquely contemporary place of wosrhip in the capital of India.*

Sarah Platero, "Aula Magna, Bologna, Italy: Church Interior Scene of University Celebra-

tions," International Lighting Review, *2nd quarter, 40th year (1989), pp. 62–64. Illus., color. Relighting of a cathedral in Bologna, Italy. Well presented.*

[284] D. Walter Köhler and Wassili Luckhardt, "Administration and Banking Rooms," *pp. 179–92, op. cit. (see footnote 239). Good illustrations and analysis.*

"Guth Memorial Award," Lighting Design + Application, *vol. 13, no. 10 (Oct. 1983), p. 32. Illus. Outstanding lighting of Centerre Plaza Bank in St. Louis, Missouri. Also see p. 33 for two savings and loan interiors.*

"New York Stock Exchange Main Trading Floor," Lighting Design + Application, *vol. 14, no. 2 (Feb. 1984), pp. 21–22.*

"Home Federal Savings & Loan," Lighting Design + Application, *vol. 15, no. 5 (May 1985), pp. 27–28. Illus., color. A California institution.*

"Calcasieu Aglow," Lighting Design + Application, *vol. 15, no. 10 (Oct. 1985), pp. 24–26. Illus., color. Guth Award of Excellence by IES for the Lake Charles, Louisiana, Calcasieu Marine National Bank.*

"Allied Bank of Texas," "Amerifirst Federal-Oakland Park," "Farm Credit Banks of Wichita," Lighting Design + Application, *vol. 15, no. 10 (Oct. 1985), p. 31. Illus. All IES Guth Award of Merit designs.*

"Meeting Rooms: Banque Paribas, Paris," International Lighting Review, *2d quarter 1986, pp. 63–66. Illus., color. Excellent graphics and text concerning the lighting of numerous banks worldwide.*

Jeffrey I. L. Miller, "The Glow of a Neon 'Sky' Lights a Seattle Banking Hall," Architectural Lighting, *vol. 1, no. 0 (Nov. 1986), pp. 42–45. Illus., color. Lighting of the Washington Federal Savings and Loan in Seattle.*

"Lighted Breastplate Symbol of Bank's Tradition, Stability," Architectural Lighting, *vol. 1, no. 5 (May 1987), p. 14. Illus., color.*

"Fidelity Faithful to Good Design," Lighting Design + Application, *vol. 16, no. 10 (Oct. 1986), pp. 24–25. Illus., color. Philadelphia's Fidelity Bank, an Edwin M. Guth Memorial Award of Excellence (IES).*

Xiao Huigan and Sun Yannian, "A Few Problems on the Lighting of Large Public Build-

ings," Lighting Design + Application, *vol. 16, no. 2 (Feb. 1986), pp. 20–26. Illus.*

"Powerful Simplicity," Lighting Design + Application, *vol. 14, no. 10 (Oct. 1984), pp. 30–31. Illus., color. Lighting of the Memorial Center for Holocaust Studies in Dallas. An example of light as a major design element in a public memorial. A 1984 IES Award of Excellence winner.*

"Ridgeway Center Atrium Adorns St. Louis Botanical Gardens," Lighting Design + Application, *vol. 14, no. 9 (Sept. 1984), pp. 22–25. Illus., color.*

"Court Curves-The Jefferson County Courthouse in Beaumont, Texas," Interiors, *vol. CXLI, no. 7 (Feb. 1982), p. 72. Illus., color. The work of Wheel-Gersztoff Associates.*

"The Station Lights Up — Philadelphia's 30th Street Station," Interiors, *vol. CXLI, no. 7 (Feb. 1982), p. 71. Illus. Design work of David A. Mintz.*

"Kips Bay Boy's Club Showhouse," Lighting Design + Application, *vol. 15, no. 9 (Sept. 1985), p. 24. Illus., color.*

Hans T. Von Malotki, "Public Buildings — Karlsruhe Civic Hall," International Lighting Review, *37th year, 1st quarter, pp. 2–9. Illus., color.*

"The Council House," Lighting Design + Application, *vol. 12, no. 9 (Sept. 1982), pp. 23–27. Illus., color.*

"Public Places: Lighting Design for Public Spaces in Asian Countries," Lighting Design + Application, *vol. 10, no. 4 (April 1981), pp. 21–26. Illus., color.*

"Public Places: Something Bright and Beautiful — Industry Exhibit Conference Center," Lighting Design + Application, *vol. 11, no. 9 (Sept. 1981), pp. 14–19. Illus., color.*

"Green Bay Correctional Institution: High-Mast HPS Luminaires Increase Efficiency and Provide Flexibility and Better Control," Lighting Design + Application, *vol. 13, no. 8 (Aug. 1983), pp. 28–29. Illus., color.*

"Guth Memorial Awards," Lighting Design + Application, *vol. 13, no. 10 (Oct. 1983), pp. 43–44. Illus. Outstanding lighting for a botanical garden in St. Louis' Sunsphere at Knoxville, Tennessee; an Algerian monument in Montreal, Canada; a 32-acre outdoor sculpture in Dallas, Texas; a public hall in*

Milwaukee; *and a horticultural building in Canada.*

"New Roles for Old Halls: St. Louis Station and Palladium," Lighting Design + Application, *vol. 16, no. 10 (Oct. 1986), pp. 16–19, 56. Illus., color. Conversion of existing lighting design to a disco and a refurbished Grand Hall by designers Paul Marantz and Steve Hefferan, winning an IES Guth Award of Excellence and a Special Citation.*

Charles Linn, "The Best of Both Worlds: Historic Luminaires and Modern Illumination," Architectural Lighting, *vol. 1, no. 3 (March 1987), pp. 20–25. Illus., color. Relighting of the Colorado State Office Building.*

"Public Buildings: Graf-Zeppelin-Haus, Friedrichshafen," International Lighting Review, *2d quarter 1986, pp. 58–62. Illus., color. Lighting of the Graf-Zeppelin Cultural Centre in Friedrichshafen on Lake Constance.*

"Public Places — Horticultural Building at the Canadian National Exhibition," Lighting Design + Application, *vol. 13, no. 11 (Nov. 1983), pp. 16–19. Illus., color. An award-winning specialized design — interior and exterior — in Toronto.*

"MBB Building, Kuala Lampur, Malaysia," *see footnote 262. A bank corporate headquarters in Malaysia.*

Bram Koebrugge, "TOWERS, Hofuf Water Tower, Saudi Arabia; An Oasis of Colour; A Gigantic Sculpture," International Lighting Review, *39th year, 1st quarter (1988), pp. 5–7. Illus., color.*

[285] Köhler and Luckhardt, *p. 158, op. cit. (see footnote 284).*

[286] "IES Transaction — Proposed American National Standard Practice for Industrial Lighting," Lighting Design + Application, *vol. 9, no. 5 (May 1979), pp. 24–58. Essential reading.*

[287] Stanley L. Lyons, Handbook of Industrial Lighting. *London; Butterworths; 1981. Illus., 213 pp. Technical; intended for the lighting engineer. Comprehensive; basic to extensive practice in this area.*

Figure 10.28 RCA factory before relighting.

Figure 10.29 RCA factory after relighting.

ments for specific medical facilities. Individualized lighting arrangements must be planned for rooms occupied by two or more patients. Color Fig. 86 shows the Charlotte Hungerford Hospital Addition in Torrington, Connecticut, 1973, with lighting design by Wm. M. C. Lam Associates, Inc.[288]

Hotels and Motels

A hotel or motel can also be considered a city in itself. It is both a temporary home and a public institution. Designers must be concerned with (1) the approach, grounds, entrance, and "street image"; (2) the foyer area and lobby, reception desk, and public lounges; (3) in-house restaurants, bars, and discos; (4) corridors, stairs, elevators, and escalators; (5) the treatment of the various guest rooms; and (6) ballrooms, ice rinks, theatres, gaming rooms (Las Vegas and Atlantic City), or other places of entertainment. Most architectural lighting specialists have designed for a hotel or motel. Basically such design utilizes the approaches outlined throughout this chapter, with particularly careful attention to the specific aims and needs of the individual client. Color Fig. 86a is James L. Nuckolls's design for the lobby of the Omni Hotel in Miami, Florida.[289]

Museums and Art Galleries

Many architectural lighting specialists have designed one or more museums. Funds are usually available for both an enduring structure and one with a designed viewpoint. The late Richard Kelly held an international reputation as the foremost lighting designer of museums. He frequently worked with Edison Price as his master technician. Today LeMar Terry at the New York City Metropolitan Museum is considered a leading museum practitioner. Frank A. Florentine, lighting designer for the National Air and Space Museum at the Smithsonian Institution in Washington, D.C., presented very useful information at the 1987 Lighting World International conference in California. His "Recommended Maximum Exposure Levels" for museums include:

Material	Exposure footcandles
Silk, paper, lace, water color paintings, and fugitive dyes or adhesives	15
Cotton, wool, wood, stable dyes, and leather	20
Treated wood, rubber, oil paintings, and treated fabrics	30
Painted wood, painted fabric, and nonfugitive dyes	40
Glass, metal, rock, bronze, and stable material	50

Stanley L. Lyons, Management Guide to Modern Industrial Lighting, *2d edition. London; Butterworths; 1983. Illus., 140 pp. Intended for the nontechnical nonengineer. Comprehensive and well written.*

National Lighting Bureau, Industrial Lighting Handbook. *Washington D.C.; National Lighting Bureau, 2101 L St., N.W., Suite 300; 1983. Illus., 40 pp. Good beginners handbook. Strong on energy saving.*

"Proposed American National Standard Practice for Industrial Lighting," Lighting Design + Application, *vol. 13, no. 7 (July 1983), pp. 29–68. Illus.*

"W. W. Grainger Warehouse—More Than Just Good Lighting," Lighting Design + Application, *vol. 15, no. 8 (Aug. 1985), pp. 18–19. Illus., color.*

"Sloss Furnace: Lighting an Industrial Museum," Lighting Design + Application, *vol. 15, no. 7 (July 1985), pp. 10–12. Illus., color. In Birmingham, Alabama.*

H. E. Th. Bakker, "Renovations: CERN, Geneva," International Lighting Review, *36th year, 4th quarter, 1985, pp. 135–138. Illus., color. Lighting of CERN laboratories in Geneva, Switzerland.*

Patricia E. Goodwin and Herbert A. Fouke, "Industrial Lighting: Superior Environment from Luminaires Producing Uplight—New Design Emits More of the Total Lamp Lumens," Lighting Design + Application, *vol. 15, no. 7 (July 1985), pp. 17–24. Illus.*

Patricia E. Goodwin, "Warehouse Aisle Lighting: Significant Variables and Actual versus Predicted Measurements—The Unique Factors of Warehouse Lighting Create Intriguing Problems," Lighting Design + Application, *vol. 15, no. 6 (June 1985), pp. 30–42. Illus., color.*

"Relighting the Corhart Refractories Plant—Boosting Lighting Levels from Below Industry Standards with Metal Halide Lamps Increases Workers' Safety, Productivity and Morale While Cutting Energy Costs," Lighting Design + Application, *vol. 15, no. 5 (May 1985), pp. 45–46, 48–49. Illus.*

Köhler and Luckhardt, "Rooms for Working," pp. 158–68, op. cit. (see footnote 284).

"Industrial," Lighting Design + Application, *vol. 9, no. 11 (Nov. 1979), pp. 22–29. Illus. Useful basics.*

deBoer and Fisher, "Industrial Lighting," pp. 251–60, op. cit. (see footnote 282). Excellent illustrations, some in color. Good text.

"Industrial," Lighting Design + Application, vol. 9, no. 8 (Aug. 1979), pp. 53–54. Illus.

"Guth Memorial Awards," Lighting Design + Application, vol. 13, no. 10 (Oct. 1983), pp. 40–41. Illus. Lighting for warehouses, shipyards, a steam plant, and a factory.

"Industrial" Lighting Design + Application, vol. 15, no. 10 (Oct. 1985), pp. 38–39. Illus. Six IES Guth Award of Merit designs.

Robert Zeller, "Selecting Luminaires for Hazardous Locations," Architectural Lighting, vol. 1, no. 6 (June 1987), pp. 28–31. Illus.

Martyn K. Timmings, "Industrial Lighting Needs More Than Cost Analysis: How To Evaluate Industrial Lighting Systems With an Eye to Improving Productivity While Reducing Lighting Costs," Lighting, vol. 2, no. 3 (June 1988), pp. 22, 24, 26–28, 30–31. Illus.

Carl Rath, "Accuracy of Lighting Design in the Industrial Workplace," Lighting, vol. 2, no. 5 (Oct. 1988), pp. 26, 28, 30, 32. Illus.

[288] R. G. Hopkinson, Hospital Lighting. London; Heinemann; 1964. Complete volume on this subject by a leading British illumination engineer.

IES, Lighting for Health Care Facilities. N.Y.; IES; 1985. Publication IES CP-29-1985; ISBN 0-87995-023-4. 81 pp. Illus. Prepared by the IES Health Care Facilities Committee and also to be found in the IES reference manuals.

"Prescription Lighting Helps Reduce Hospital Stress at St. Michael's," Architectural Lighting, vol. 1, no. 1 (Jan. 1987), p. 20. Illus., color. St. Michael's is in Stevens Point, Wisconsin.

deBoer and Fisher, "Hospitals," pp. 291–298, op. cit. (see footnote 282). Excellent text and illustrations.

"Nurses, Doctors Help Plan Surgery Unit Lighting," Architectural Lighting, vol. 1, no. 6 (June 1987), p. 14. Illus., color. The Condell Memorial Hospital in Libertyville, Illinois.

"Hospital," Lighting Design + Application, vol. 10, no. 1 (Jan. 1980), pp. 14–18. Illus., color.

William C. Beck, Joy Schreckendgust, and John Geffert, "The Color of the Surgeon's Task Light," Lighting Design + Application, vol. 9, no. 7 (July 1979), pp. 54–57. Illus.

"Lumens Awards' 80: Coronary Care Unit, Lenox Hill Hospital," Lighting Design + Application, vol. 10, no. 6 (June 1980), pp. 21–23. Illus.

"San Antonio Community Hospital," Lighting Design + Application, vol. 14, no. 1 (Jan. 1984), pp. 20–21. Illus., color. Award-winning Texas hospital design.

"Guth Memorial Award of Merit Projects — Hospitals," Lighting Design + Application, vol. 13, no. 10 (Oct. 1983), p. 31. Outstanding 1983 hospital lighting presented in text and illustrations.

"Kaiser-Permanente Medical Care Program — Mililani Clinic: Combining Comfort and Function," Lighting Design + Application, vol. 15, no. 6 (June 1985), pp. 20–27. Illus., color.

Brian Clarkson, "Hospitals — Basement Hospital Suite, Belleville (Ontario, Canada)," International Lighting Review, 36th year, 4th quarter, 1985, pp. 132–134. Illus., color.

"Institutional," Lighting Design + Application, vol. 15, no. 10 (Oct. 1985), pp. 40–41. Three IES Guth Awards of Merit designs.

Dorothy Kamm, "Changing Hospital Environments — Revolutionary Uses of Color and Light," Lighting Design + Application, vol. 15, no. 11 (Nov. 1985), pp. 15–18. Illus., color.

William C. Beck, MD, FACS, FIES, "The Lighting of the Birthing Room," Lighting Design + Application, vol. 14, no. 7 (July 1984), pp. 40–41. Illus.

"Audio/Visual Bombardment Room — School for Exceptional Children," Lighting Design + Application, vol. 13, no. 10 (Oct. 1983), pp. 25–27. Illus., color. This facility in Orlando, Florida, is designed for visual stimulation instruction training. It is the most extensive facility of its kind. Described and illustrated in detail, this facility is of great interest to lighting designers concerned with the vision process. An award-winning design.

Fred Loessel, "No Place Like Home," Lighting Dimensions, vol. 12, no. 7 (Nov. 1988), p. 16. Lighting of the New York City Foundling Hospital in 1988. Contains useful design tips.

"A Different Colour For Each Floor: Bronovo Hospital, The Hague," International Lighting Review, 2nd quarter, 40th year (1989), pp. 68–69. Illus., color. Excellent new design direction is presented for a Netherlands hospital.

[289] deBoer and Fisher, "Hotels," pp. 284–90, op. cit. (see footnote 282). Excellent text. Illus., in color.

Howard Brandston, " . . . Lighting the Public Rooms of the Helmsley Palace Hotel," Lighting Design + Application, vol. 11, no. 12 (Dec. 1981), pp. 20–26. Illus., color.

"The Sheraton Park Hotel, Washington, D.C.," Lighting Design + Application, vol. 12, no. 3 (Mar. 1982), pp. 8–13. Illus.

"The Lounge of Aurora," Lighting Design + Application, vol. 12, no. 5 (May 1982), pp. 18–19. Illus., color. Hotel lobby in Tokyo.

Der Scutt, "Grand Hyatt: New York Hotel Design Pomp and Circumstance," Lighting Design + Application, vol. 10, no. 4 (Apr. 1981), pp. 14–20. Illus., color.

"South Bay Club Condo: Lighting under Deadline," Lighting Design + Application, vol. 13, no. 5 (May 1983), pp. 25–26. Illus., color. A lobby relighted.

"New Illuminations — San Francisco's Sir Francis Drake Hotel," Interiors, vol. CXLI, no. 7 (Feb. 1982), p. 65. Illus., color.

"Guth Memorial Awards," Lighting Design + Application, vol. 13, no. 10 (Oct. 1983), p. 33. Illus. Description of two outstanding hotels' interior lighting.

"On Target — The Lighting Design for Arrowhead Hilton Lodge," Lighting Design + Application, vol. 14, no. 2 (Feb. 1984), pp. 13–15. Illus., color. An award-winning lighting design.

"Tripping the Light Fantastic — At the Wyndham Hotel," Lighting Design + Application, vol. 14, no. 1 (Jan. 1984), pp. 12–13. Illus., color. A prize-winning hotel lobby and restaurant lighting design in Dallas, Texas.

John Marsteller, "Three New Hotels for Hong Kong," Lighting Design + Application, vol. 13, no. 8 (Aug. 1983), pp. 22–25. Illus., color. Marsteller, president of Spatial Light Environments, Ltd., in Munich and Hong Kong (he is a United States citizen) has lighted three Hong Kong hotels on different price/ambience levels: classic, de luxe, and regular. The well-illustrated text of this article offers much useful guidance on contemporary hotel lighting design.

Since it is UV (ultraviolet or black light) which is most damaging to artwork, he also offered the following "Percentage of UV to Visible Light" figures:

Type of light	Ratio of UV to visible light, %
North-sky daylight and mercury vapor, (clear)	20
Sunlight and total daylight	10
Mercury vapor, (coated) and metal halide (all types)	10–20
Fluorescent (deluxe and natural)	12
Fluorescent (cool white)	8
Fluorescent (warm white)	4
Tungsten halogen incandescent	8
Low-voltage incandescent	4–8
Standard incandescent	4
Sodium vapor	½
Fluorescent (rare earth and Triphosphors)	½

Florentine attributes these statistics to Edwin K. Robinson, Lighting Engineer at the National Museum of American History, Smithsonian Museum.

Special problems must be addressed by the designer. Paintings on exhibit must be glare-free. They are subject to potential permanent damage by prolonged exposure to either daylight or improper artificial illumination. The surroundings of a gallery or museum should be conducive to comfort and relaxation and should suggest prestige. The lighting artist needs to consider the original viewing conditions prevalent at the time each particular artist painted. Each generation of artists has worked in ever-changing kinds of illumination over the years. In fairness to the creator, present-day lighting must take contemporary lighting into consideration. The lighting of sculpture and statuary is still another special case. Frequently theatrical and/or display design techniques come into play. I remember well sculptress Louise Nevelson's praise to me (as did the press reviews) concerning the quality of my own design work when lighting a major exhibition of Nevelson's life's work for the Houston Museum in October 1969. The form, texture, and mass intended by the sculpture can be brought forth and reinforced by lighting.

The lighting designer for museums must carefully consider human eye adaptation times as a design factor. Eyes must be allowed to adjust when people come indoors from a brightly illuminated outdoors to the level of light most frequently found desirable for proper display and prevention of light damage to priceless masterpieces.

Among the museums for which lighting was designed by Richard Kelly were the Yale Center of British Art and British Studies and The Yale Mellon Museum; the Kimball Museum in Fort Worth, Texas; the Norton Simon Museum in Pasadena, California; and the Munson Williams Proctor Institute in Utica, New York, designed in 1960 with Edison Price (see Figs. 10.30 and 10.31). Kelly's combined love of fine art and his obsession with power and pleasure of light made him a master of design in this specialty.[290]

Office Buildings

Offices and office buildings provide another highly important area for architectural lighting designers. Office buildings must both be attractive and highly utilitarian to attract renters. They represent a large capital investment. For headquarters buildings for major corporations a prestige image factor is important. All of the usual criteria apply: comfort, attractiveness, and cost plus work efficiency. Specific factors to be considered are energy consumption, first cost versus life-cycle cost, relative sophistication of the owners and/or tenants; the need for flexibility (open-plan versus office "compartments"), the demand for quality, and "fast-track construction" (quick delivery of standardized parts). Obviously the lighting designer can modify the apparent size (height, width, length) of an office, working in conjunction with the other designers (architect, interior, etc.). Concealed ceiling lighting (with many different systems, light sources, and potential products available) is important here. There has been an increasing trend toward localized inconspicuous light sources rather than flat IES-recommended "football-field" illumination. The newest trend in this direction (task/ambient lighting) has led to the arrival on the market of furniture that claims to have all necessary lighting sources built into the furniture (wall partitions, desks, filing cabinets, etc.). The claimed advantages are (1) elimination of the necessity for overall ceiling illumination of a space; (2) the ability to adapt the space to each new client's needs (or to change the space for an existing client) without the expensive modification of the electrical/

Figure 10.30 Gallery of the Munson Williams Proctor Institute Museum in Utica, N.Y. (1960). Lighting design by Richard Kelly and Edison Price. (*Courtesy of Edison Price*)

Figure 10.31 Another view of the Munson Williams Proctor Institute Museum. (*Courtesy of Edison Price.*)

Lesley Wheel and John Aspromonte, "Lighting an Art Deco Masterpiece," Lighting Design + Application, vol. 14, no. 9 (Sept. 1984), pp. 16–19. Illus., color. The Omni-Netherlands Hotel in Cincinnati.

Alan Gilbert, "The Xiyuan Hotel, China: Lighting Design for Industrially Developing Countries." Lighting Design + Application, vol. 15, no. 5 (May 1985), pp. 14–18. Illus., color.

Candace Kling, "Before the Ball Begins— Lighting for Ballrooms and Meeting Rooms," Lighting Design + Application, vol. 16, no. 5 (May 1986), pp. 27–30. Illus., color.

John Marsteller, "Candlelight and Tropical Breezes Are Not Enough: Modern Technology Combines with Native Motifs in Far Eastern Hotel Design," Lighting Design + Application, vol. 16, no. 9 (Sept. 1986), pp. 16–21. Illus., color. Excellent text and graphics on this subject by Marsteller.

"Setting the Scene in Hotels," Electrosonic World, #4 (1987), p. 4. Illus.

"The Drama Lives On in Grand Hotels," Lighting Design + Application, vol. 16, no. 10 (Oct. 1986), pp. 32–34. Illus., color. Text and graphics of IES Guth Memorial Award of Excellence hotel designs by Lesley Wheel and John Aspromonte.

Peter Crossley, "Regent Melbourne Hotel Grand Ballroom," TABS, vol. 40, no. 1 (Aug. 1983), pp. 34–35. Illus., color.

"Recreating the Past—'A Labor of Love.' Willard Intercontinental Hotel—Citation," Lightview, vol. 1, no. 1 (Spring 1988), p. 7. Illus., color. Babu Shankar's lighting design for the modernization of the Willard Hotel in Washington, D.C., which received an IALD Citation Award.

"Lighting Control System Brightens Hotel: Programmable Unit Allows Quick Changing of Illumination Levels," CEE, vol. 40, no. 4 (April 1988), pp. 32, 34. Illus. An energy-saving lighting system for the Beverly Hills Hotel ballroom in Hollywood, California.

See also; footnote 275.

"Lumen Awards," Lighting Dimensions, vol. 12, no. 4 (May/June 1988), pp. 42–43. Illus., color. Willard Intercontinental Hotel in Washington, D.C., wins a Lumen Award for designer Babu Shankar.

William Weathersby, Jr., "Shadow and Light: Chicago's Hotel Nikko Uses Theatrical Techniques for Dramatic, Japanese-Flavored Setting, Lighting Dimensions, vol. 12, no. 4 (May/June 1988), pp. 50–51, 68–69. Illus., color. A prize winning design by Imero Fiorentino Associates' designer Maggie Giusto.

William Weathersby, Jr., "Hyatt on Collins: Design of Melbourne Hotel Starts with Australia's Clear, White Light," Lighting Dimensions, vol. 13, no. 2 (March 1989), pp. 60–61, 80. Illus., color.

290 Maureen O'Malley, "Report on LeMar Terry Tour," IALD Newsletter, Sept. 1982, p. 1. From page 2:

Three different light sources were used [in the Met's Astor Court]. . . . Fluorescent, mercury vapor, and quartz [were] used together and singularly to create the realistic effects of daylight, dusk, and moonlight which work compatibly with the skylight above. The light control system is a photocell computerized control which turns the light(s) on or off according to the amount of light given from outside. . . . Lemar spoke of problems (dealing) with the conservation of artifacts made of natural materials. Filters are essential to shield the ultraviolet rays from damaging pieces. Organic artifacts also dictate a use of 5 foot-candles and sometimes less. LeMar also has to deal with the Museum's budget restrictions.

deBoer and Fisher, "Museums and Art Galleries," pp. 278–83, op. cit. (see footnote 282). Good text from illumination engineering viewpoint; excellent illustrations, many in color.

"Museums," Lighting Design + Application, vol. 3, no. 8 (Aug. 1973), pp. 18–32. Major feature of issue is museum lighting; several illustrated articles.

Isaac Goodbar, "Museums: Possible Reduction of the Fading of Art Objects by Elimination of the North Skylight," Lighting Design + Application, vol. 6, no. 6 (June 1976), pp. 30–33. Useful study.

"Lumen Awards," Lighting Design + Application, vol. 9, no. 6 (June 1979), pp. 30–33, 35–36. Illus., color. Two articles on museum lighting, one the work of the Metropolitan's LeMar Terry.

"The Clockwork Universe," Lighting Design + Application, vol. 12, no. 2 (Feb. 1982), pp. 12–15. Very effective lighting of a museum of timepieces. Illus., color.

"Lighting the Spruce Goose," Lighting Dimensions, Vol. 7, no. 3 (June 1983), pp. 18–19, 21–23, 32. Illus., color. A graphic word presentation of a unique museum-type lighting assignment for Imero Fiorentino.

"Shade and Shadow—West Wing of Boston Museum of Fine Arts," Interiors, Vol. CXLI, no. 7 (Feb. 1982), pp. 66–67. Illus., color. The museum design work of Paul Marantz and Jules Fisher.

"Guth Memorial Awards," Lighting Design + Application, vol. 13, no. 10 (Oct. 1983), p. 44. Illus. Outdoor lighting of a huge Charles Perry sculpture on a 32-acre site in Dallas, Texas. See also vol. 13, no. 11 (Nov. 1983), pp. 20–22. Illus., color.

At a Nov. 14, 1983 meeting of the Indiana section of IES, guest speaker and expert Martin J. Radecki, Chief Conservator of the Indianapolis Museum of Art, stressed that ultraviolet light energy is the element which does the most damage to paintings.

Allen Freedman and Keyes Condon Florence, "The National West: Gleaming New Galleries"; Andrea Oppenheimer Dean, "The National East: An Evaluation"; Robert Campbell, "A Special Kind of Classicism, GBQC's Museum Addition, Louisville, Ky.," Architecture, Oct. 1984, pp. 68–73; 74–79; 80–86. Illus., color. Excellent graphics and text.

Mark M. Wohlwerth, "Lighting the 'First Ladies'—A Lighting Challenge: Making the Intricate Details of Ballgowns Visible, While Preserving the Delicate Fabric," Lighting Design + Application, vol. 14, no. 12 (Dec. 1984), pp. 8, 10–12. Illus., color. Lighting an exhibit in the Smithsonian's National Museum of American History in Washington, D.C.

"The Invisible Visual Art: The Best Display Lighting Can Often Be Found in an Art Museum. In This Report, We Look at Two of the World's Finest, MoMA and The Metropolitan," Lighting Dimensions, vol. 9, no. 4 (July/Aug. 1985), pp. 20–28, 31. Illus., color. Treats New York City's Museum of Modern Art and the Metropolitan Museum.

Geraldine Kiefer, "Focus on Light: New Addition to the Cleveland Museum of Art— Meeting the Challenge of Lighting an Entire New Wing," Lighting Design + Application, vol. 15, no. 5 (May 1985), pp. 23–26. Illus., color.

"Fishing for Answers—Lighting the New York Aquarium," Lighting Design + Application, vol. 15, no. 11 (Nov. 1985), pp. 13–14. Illus., color.

Figure 10.32 Task/ambient lighting with the Westinghouse ASD open office system.

Figure 10.33 The Upjohn Executive Office Building in Kalamazoo, Michigan; Skidmore, Owings and Merrill, Architects. Lighting design: Edison Price, Inc.

lighting system; and (3) provision of illumination where needed (on work spaces), rather than everywhere. All that is necessary is sufficient wall electrical outlets of adequate capacity. In some senses this is an adaptation to the office of Abe Feder's lighting solution for the New York Coliseum: providing mobility in lighting for a constantly changing series of exhibitors. Whether this trend will assume increasing importance in office lighting remains to be seen. Figure 10.32 shows the Westinghouse task ambient system. Color Fig. 87 shows Wheel-Garon's design for Touche Ross. Color Fig. 88 shows Edison Price's illumination of the Upjohn Executive Office Building in Kalamazoo, Michigan, as does Fig. 10.33. Notice the deeply recessed ceiling bays and the one fixture visible in the upper left corner— concealed fixtures, yet ones that provide high-ambience, even illumination of the work area.[291]

Private Residences

Every architectural lighting designer seems to have designed at least one private residence, usually at the beginning of his or her career. Richard Kelly did the New York City Rockerfeller apartment, for example. Even I (whose field this definitely is not) designed the lighting for the elaborate living room of Mr. and Mrs. L. George in Houston. Generally only the smaller firms or interior designers/electrical contractors work in this area, because only the wealthy can afford the lighting specialist's services and also because homes are private places that are highly subject to the tastes and preferences of the individual homeowner. Residences frequently have better task lighting (versus overall illumination) than do many commercial buildings. Why? Because the individual owner puts lamps and light sources exactly where they are wanted and where they will meet specific lighting needs. The resident, particularly if a renter, has very little control over indirect (structural) sources (such as ceiling lights; cove/valance illumination; and fixtures built into sinks, stoves, and baths), but does have complete control of direct (portable) lamps and ornamental sources. The trained lighting designer can add a wide variety of structural sources: wall-washers on fireplace walls, cove/valance/cornice lighting as needed (or de-

Stephen M. Goldberg, "Light and Architecture Enhance Communication with Art—Alaskan Light and Darkness Pose Special Questions for Gallery Designer," Lighting Design + Application, vol. 16, no. 7 (July 1986), pp. 7–9. Illus., color.

"Portland Museum of Art, Charles Shipman Payson Building," Lighting Design + Application, vol. 16, no. 7 (July 1986), p. 15. Illus., color.

Edwin K. Robinson, "Spotlight on after the Revolution—Trend-Setting Museum Design Moves Both Viewer and Story Along," Lighting Design + Application, vol. 16, no. 5 (May 1986), pp. 23–25. Illus., color.

Tom O'Mahony and Sarah Shankma, "Holocaust Memorial Center—Lighting Helps Create Legacy of Personal Freedom," Lighting Design + Application, vol. 16, no. 1 (Jan. 1986), pp. 13–15. Illus., color. Memorial in West Bloomfield, Michigan.

Michael Webb, "Museum of Contemporary Art: Paul Marantz and Charles Stone Illuminate Isozaki's New L.A. Museum," Lighting Dimensions, vol. 11, no. 2 (March/April 1987), pp. 55–59, 80, 82. Illus., color. Excellent text and graphics.

Steven Weintraub, Robin Zieb, and Mary Ballard (editors), "Museum Lighting and Deterioration," Art and Archaeology Technical Abstracts: Supplement, vol. 15, no. 1 (Summer 1978).

"Museums: The City of Science and Industry, Paris/La Villete," International Lighting Review, 4th quarter 1986, pp. 116–121. Illus., color. See also "The Spruce Goose, Long Beach," pp. 128–131, illus., color; and "Cologne's New Cultural Centre: Wallraf-Richartz-Museum with Museum Ludwig and Philharmonic Hall," pp. 132–143, illus., color. Excellent text and graphics.

Steve Pollock, "An Underwater Challenge: Don Maxcy Explores the Art of Aquatic Lighting at the Monterey Aquarium," Lighting Dimensions, vol. 10, no. 5 (Sept./Oct. 1986), pp. 48–50, 52–54.

"Hollywood on the Road: Richard Nelson Lights the Smithsonian's Traveling History of Film," Lighting Dimensions, vol. 10, no. 4 (July/Aug. 1986), pp. 36–40. Illus.

"The Tent of Meeting—Lighting for a Traveling Art Show," Architectural Lighting, vol. 1, no. 5 (May 1987), p. 20. Illus., color.

Charles Linn, "Loyd-Paxton Galleries: Optimum Lighting for Peerless Antiques," Architectural Lighting, vol. 1, no. 0 (Nov. 1986), pp. 30–38. Illus., color.

"New Light Sources at the London Planetarium," p. 6, and "Daley Superstar" p. 9., Electrosonic World, #4 (1987). "Superstar" is about Mme. Tussaud's Waxworks. Illus., color.

"From Warehouse to Art Gallery," Lightview International, vol. 1, no. 4 (Winter 1989), p. 7. Illus., color. Description of designer Richard Gluckman's conversion of a warehouse space to the Dia Art Foundation in New York City. It won an IALD Citation Award.

"Showpiece Lighting Meets All Criteria," Lighting, vol. 1, no. 3 (Nov. 1987), pp. 25–26. Illus. Description of the lighting for the $37 million Museum of Civilization in Quebec City, Canada.

Michael S. Eddy, "Worklight: Art & Technology," Theatre Crafts, vol. 23, no. 3 (March 1989), pp. 16–17. Illus., color. Lighting of the New Mexico Museum of Natural History in Albuquerque, New Mexico.

Barry H. Slinker, "Museum Daylighting Aided by New Technology, Museums Return to Natural Lighting, Lighting Dimensions, vol. 13, no. 1 (January/February 1989), pp. 54–57, 71. Illus., color.

291 Gary Gillette, "Evaluating Office Lighting Environments," Lighting Design + Application, vol. 17, no. 5 (May 1987), pp. 4–6, 46–47. Illus., color. Gillette, a research associate at the National Bureau of Standards, has written the best basic article on office lighting design. Invaluable and essential for all working in this specialty.

Douglas Davis and Maggie Malone, "Offices of the Future," Newsweek, May 14, 1984. Reprint. In color.

"Task/Ambient Lighting—The Issue Persists," Lighting Design + Application, vol. 9, no. 1 (Jan. 1979), pp. 18–40. Entire issue devoted to this trend.

Harry B. Zackrison, Jr., PE, "Furniture-Mounted Task/Indirect Ambient Lighting—Has Its Time Expired? Application and Prior Analysis of Each System Can Best Assure Peak Efficiency and Quality," Lighting Design + Application, vol. 13, no. 8 (Aug. 1983), pp. 30–

37. Illus. Useful reading for all architectural lighting designers. Zackrison discusses at length both the advantages and disadvantages of the "fad" of task/ambient lighting and suggests a midpoint "wedding" for low-energy expenditure. Well-illustrated; good text.

Gary R. Steffy, "Lighting the High-Tech Office," Building Operating Management, June 1984. 5 pp. reprint. Illus., color. Excellent presentation by an expert specialist who communicates well.

"What's Beyond Task/Ambient Lighting?" Lighting Design + Application, vol. 11, no. 11 (Nov. 1981), pp. 14–19. Illus., color. Other articles on office lighting on pp. 20–38. Illus., color.

Gary R. Steffy, "Office renovation in the Information Age: Lighting for Electronic Tasks," Lighting Design + Application, vol. 15, no. 8 (Aug. 1985), pp. 20–23. Illus., color. A very important article. Steffy is a leading architectural lighting designer for offices and the computer situation and writes well.

Stephen P. Schuber, "Down the Tubes: Solar Light Goes Indoors," Architectural Lighting, vol. 1, no. 2 (Feb. 1987), pp. 32–35. Illus., color. Useful article about the use of solar tubes (the latest variation of fiber optics) to light the office complex at Victoria Park Place in Toronto.

National Lighting Bureau, Lighting Energy Management for Offices and Office Buildings. Washington, D.C.; National Lighting Bureau (Suite 300, 2101 L St. N.W., 20037). 40 pp. Illus. The National Lighting Bureau issues useful pamphlets as well as useful news releases in the area of energy conservation and lighting.

H. J. Hentschel, E. Klein, J. Leibig, and K.-F. Roll, "Energy Effective Direct/Indirect Office and VDU-Lighting Systems: Test and Application," Journal of the IES, vol. 16, no. 2 (Summer 1987), pp. 89–105. Illus. A rather technical but important report delivered at an annual IES conference by a group of Siemens engineers from the Federal Republic of Germany (West Germany).

Corwin A. Bennett, "Lighting, Comfort, and Performance in the Workplace: Human-VDT interaction Requires Special Considerations," Lighting Design + Application, vol. 16, no. 8 (Aug. 1986), pp. 40–44. Charts.

P. E. Goodwin, "Evaluation of Methodology for Evaluating Lighting for Offices with VDTs," Journal of the IES, vol. 16, no. 1 (Winter 1987), pp. 39–51. Illus. Includes comments from Gary Steffy following this IES annual conference paper presentation.

Douglas Bulleit and Kenneth Fairbanks, "Offices: An Ambient/Task High-intensity Source Office Lighting System," Lighting Design + Application, vol. 10, no. 6 (June 1980), pp. 41–49. Illus.

G. K. Brabson, "An Evaluation of Lighting Systems for the Electronic Office," Journal of the IES, vol. 13, no. 1 (Oct. 1983), pp. 220–229. Illus. A scholarly paper presented at the 1983 IES annual conference.

"Architectural Character Builder—Wall Lighting," Light magazine, vol. 29, no. 3 (July/Sept. 1960), p. 21. About the work of Edison Price and a bank by Richard Kelly.

Sylvan R. Shemitz and Gladys Walker, "Lighting the 'Communicators': The Special Problems of Elevator Lobbies, Reception Areas and Passageways," Interior Design, vol. 55, no. 3 (Mar. 1984), pp. 72, 74, 76. Brief, useful summary of lighting design for areas which make an initial impression on clients.

Sonny Sonnenfeld, Sal Bonsignore, George T. Howard, Robert J Nissen, and Charles Clark, "Lighting for Teleconference Rooms: An Introduction to the Lighting of an Exciting, New Kind of Communications Facility," Lighting Design + Application, vol. 15, no. 5 (May 1985), pp. 31–35. Illus. Also in IALD Newsletter, March 1984, pp. 1–3.

deBoer and Fisher, "Offices," pp. 261–268, op. cit. (see footnote 282). Excellent text and illustrations.

"Offices," Lighting Design + Application, vol. 12, no. 4 (Apr. 1982), pp. 12–25. Three articles on contemporary office design problems. Illus., color. Pages 27–60 present the proposed IES standards for office lighting.

"Offices," Lighting Design + Application, vol. 13, no. 3 (Mar. 1983), pp. 10–19, 24–36. Illus., color. Four articles.

Thomas M. Lemons and Anne V. Robinson, "Offices: Exploring Indirect Lighting," Lighting Design + Application, vol. 9, no. 12 (Dec. 1979), pp. 37–43. Illus.

"Guth Memorial Award of Merit projects — CRT Applications and Offices," Lighting Design + Application, vol. 13, no. 10 (Oct. 1983), pp. 29, 34–38. Illus. Details and illustrates outstanding lighting design for both general office situations and those involving the specialized problem of office computer illumination.

"Lighting up the CRT Screen — Problems and Solutions, Three Lighting Design Systems Offer Award-Winning Alternatives to the Challenge of New Electronic Offices," Lighting Design + Application, vol. 14, no. 1 (Jan. 1984), pp. 14–17. Illus., color.

Mark S. Rea, "Behavioral Responses to a Flexible Desk Luminaire," Journal of the IES, vol. 13, no. 1 (Oct. 1983), pp. 174–190. Illus. Another useful scholarly study.

"Merrill Lynch: Educating the Client for a Successful Solution," Lighting Design + Application, vol. 15, no. 7 (July 1985), pp. 15–16. Illus., color.

"Legal Lighting for Law Firm: Meeting Strict Guidelines Set by a Lease Agreement," Lighting Design + Application, vol. 15, no. 5 (May 1985), pp. 29–30. Illus., color.

"Offices," Lighting Design + Application, vol. 15, no. 10 (Oct. 1985), pp. 27–30. Illus. Eleven IES Guth Awards of Merit Designs.

Sarah Shankman, "California's Sunshine Daylights Office Tower;" Thomas O'Mahony and Laurence Swasey, "Ergonomics Sheds New Light on Office Productivity — Lighting Engineering for Humans in Work Places" Lighting Design + Application, vol. 16, no. 2 (Feb. 1986), pp. 10–12, 14–19. Illus., color.

"King Broadcasting — Communicating through Light," Lighting Design + Application, vol. 13, no. 7 (July 1983), pp. 22, 24–25. Illus., color.

"With An Eye to the Future, General Motors Lights Its New Technical Center," Light magazine, vol. 25, no. 5 (Sept./Oct. 1956), pp. 4–11. A 25-building complex occupying 330 acres, strikingly designed by architect Eero Saarinen with lighting by Richard Kelly. Good text and illustrations.

"Georgia-Pacific's New Headquarters," Lighting Design + Application, vol. 14, no. 9 (Sept. 1984), pp. 26–28. Illus., color.

"Royal Insurance Takes High-Pressure Sodium Inside," Lighting Design + Application, vol. 11, no. 6 (June 1981), pp. 22–24. Illus.

Der Scutt, "Public Places: Trump Tower's Simple Lighting," Lighting Design + Application, vol. 14, no. 7 (July 1984), pp. 8–12. Illus., color. Atrium lighting by an architect/lighting designer.

Christian Friedrich Appenheiner and Wolfgang Sypplie, "Control Rooms: Lighting Architecture in Modern Control Rooms," International Lighting Review, 1st quarter 1987, pp. 22–24. Illus., color. See also "Control Rooms: Borssele and Leiden, The Netherlands," by H. de Ranitz and A. van Gils, pp. 24–28, illus., color; and "Control Rooms: Regional Dispatching, Nancy, France," by Daniel Dieudonne, pp. 29–30, illus., color. Useful articles with fine text and graphics on a rarely covered design area.

"Integrating Lighting and Architecture for a Dramatic Flourish," Architectural Lighting, vol. 1, no. 1 (Jan. 1987), p. 14. Illus., color. About the Procter & Gamble General Offices Complex in Cincinnati with emphasis on the lobby and conference auditorium.

"More Light at Less Cost for Airport Postal Facility," Architectural Lighting, vol. 1, no. 1 (Jan. 1987), p. 22. Illus., color. Airport postal facility in San Francisco.

"Innovative Sconce Provides Customized Lobby Lighting," Architectural Lighting, vol. 1, no. 1 (Jan. 1987), p. 24. Illus., color. The lobby at 400 Montgomery St. in San Francisco with design by Horton-Lees.

Bruce Yarnell, "Uplighting Gives Arches Even Wash Lighting," Architectural Lighting, vol. 1, no. 1 (Jan. 1987), pp. 35–37. Illus., color. Dominion Plaza in Dallas.

"Lighting Reveals Tones of Cool Bronze, Warm Copper," Architectural Lighting, vol. 1, no. 6 (June 1987), p. 18. Illus., color. Lighting of the Atlas sculpture in the International Building lobby of Rockefeller Center in New York City by designer Abe Feder.

"Bringing the Outside into a Windowless Space," Architectural Lighting, vol. 1, no. 5 (May 1987), p. 28. Illus., color. Remodeling of Wisconsin Bell Telephone in Milwaukee with the architect creating an illusion of window lighting.

Barbara J. Knox, "A Delicate Balance: Diane Berrian Viola's Lighting Plan Brings Out the Architectural Complexities of the Site Offices," Lighting Dimensions, vol. 11, no. 1 (Jan./Feb. 1987), pp. 42–43, 54–55. Illus., color. Includes architect's plan/light plot for the site offices in New York City.

George Stahl, "Four Light Levels Illuminate Corporate Boardroom," Architectural Lighting, vol. 1, no. 2 (Feb. 1987), pp. 28–31. Illus., color. Useful article about the Ameritech corporate headquarters boardroom in Chicago.

"Shepley, Bulfinch, Richardson & Abbott," Lighting Design + Application, vol. 14, no. 5 (May 1984), pp. 24–25. Illus., color. An energy-saving relocation of an architectural firm's offices in Boston.

"Reflecting Bright Ideas at Weslayan Towers," Lighting Design + Application, vol. 14, no. 1 (Jan. 1984), pp. 18–19. Illus., color. Award-winning office building lobby in Houston, Texas.

W. S. Fisher, "New Concepts for Town and Country: An Analysis of the Lighting Design for Two Famous Office Buildings," Light magazine, vol. 27, no. 4 (Oct./Dec. 1958), pp. 3–7. The early work of Richard Kelly and Willard Thompson. Both of historical interest and still useful.

Rudolph Stenner, "Offices — The New VEW Building, Münster (Germany)," International Lighting Review, 1st quarter 1986, pp. 25–29. Illus., color.

W. T. Scheinman, "Renovations — Queen's Quay Terminal, Toronto," International Lighting Review, 1st quarter 1986, pp. 84–88. Illus., color.

Larry Swasey, "Technological Center Showcases Plastic Products — Design and Materials Do General Electric Proud," Lighting Design + Application, vol. 16, no. 7 (July 1986), pp. 26–29. Illus., color.

Gary Steffy, "Lighting for Architecture and People: A Case Study — Steelcare Headquarters Addresses Lighting Issues Early for Cohesive Solution," Lighting Design + Application, vol. 16, no. 7 (July 1986), pp. 38–40. Illus., color. Very useful "application" article.

"Light & Design: Eye Opener, Color, Light, and Symbolism Are Set in Play by Louis Nelson for the Sunglass Division of Corning," Interior Design, vol. 55, no. 11 (Nov. 1984), pp. 256–57. Illus., color.

"Light & Design: Brilliant Future: An M.I.T. Exhibition Design by Ted Williams & Associates," Interior Design, vol. 55, no. 11 (Nov. 1984), pp. 262–63. Illus., color.

"Light & Design: High Charge, An Artful Blend of Light and Form Animates the Offices of Kleinberg Electric by Seth Robins," Interior Design, vol. 55, no. 11 (Nov. 1984), pp. 266–67. Illus., color.

"Offices: PCGD Office, Leeuwarden, The Netherlands," International Lighting Review, 1984/4, pp. 140–144. Illus., color. An outstanding design in the Netherlands.

"Offices: Kwasha Lipton, Stepped Design Theme Becomes Basis for Interior and Lighting Design, and Architecture," Lighting Design + Application, vol. 14, no. 12 (Dec. 1984), pp. 13–15. A design by Paul Marantz/Jules Fisher. Illus., color.

"Teamspace Design — Pacific Telephone and Telegraph," Interiors, vol. CXLI, no. 7 (Feb. 1982), p. 70. Illus. The design work of John Brass of Lighting Research and Development, Inc., in California.

Editors of PCB International, Lighting The Workplace, New York; PBC International and Rizzoli International Publishers in New York City or Letraset USA in Paramus, New Jersey, or Letraset Canada, Ltd., in Markham, Ontario, or Hearst Books International in New York City; 1988. 255 pages; oversized volume on glossy paper; lavishly illustrated in color throughout. Covers corporate headquarters, small private offices, daylighting, reception areas, meeting rooms, executive suites, public areas, and future trends. Most useful and comprehensive.

Prafulla C. Sorcar, Architectural Lighting for Commercial Interiors. New York; John Wiley & Sons, Inc; 1987. 249 pages, illustrated with black and white drawings. Covers same ground as some prior Sorcar volumes: foundations (vision, color), engineering tools (light sources and accessories; calculations; drafting and circuiting and control), architectural tools (luminaires — incandescent, fluorescent, HID, patterns, human reaction to light and color), applications (task lighting in offices, ambient lighting, perimeter lighting), and merchandising environments. However,

the accent in this volume is centered on the lighting of commercial spaces. Because Sorcar writes well and with a simplicity which is of value to the nonengineer, this volume is very useful even if it falls somewhat below his other works, which are well-illustrated in color.

Manfred Geisler-Hansson, "Wilhelf-Lehmbruck Museum, Duisburg," International Lighting Review, 39th year, 3rd quarter (1988), pp. 112–115. Illus., color.

John Russell, "The Frick's West Gallery is Given a New Old Look," The New York Times, May 12 (1989), p. C24. Illus. A useful description of how assistant electrician Bryan Knowles modernized the lighting in the Frick Museum's West Gallery in New York City.

Dale K. Tiller, "Toward Better Office Design Standards," Lighting, vol. 3, no. 3 (June 1989), pp. 23–24, 62. Subtitle is: "The National Research Council (Canada) Is Conducting Experiments in a New Subjective Reactions Laboratory Facility Aimed at a Deeper Understanding of the Psychological Aspects of Lighting in the Office Environment."

"Classical Modernism Highlights Bow Valley: Office Tower Renovations in Calgary Allowed the Interior Designer to Use Quality Materials and Special Lighting Effects for Simplicity and Purity," Lighting, vol. 3, no. 1 (February 1989), pp. 11–12. Illus., color. Also: Ernest Wooton, "Lighting for Interior Spaces: Office Lighting and Store Lighting Are Two Areas Where Eye Comfort, Lamp Efficiency and Proper Colour Rendering Are Critical," pp. 14, 17, 20. Illus., color.

Ernest Wotton, "Lighting the Electronic Office: Traditional Lighting Systems Are in Many Cases Unsuitable for Today's Electronic Office. Here Are Some Recommendations For Proper Lighting Techniques," Lighting, vol. 2, no. 1 (February 1988), pp. 10–11, 28. Illus.

Jim Dixon, "Visual Environments and the Office," Lighting, vol. 2, no. 2 (April 1988), p. 26. Brief but useful article by the Projects Manager, Occupational Health & Safety, Canadian Standards Association, Toronto.

Mark Loeffler, "An Uneasy Partnership: Researchers, Designers, and Manufacturers Work Toward Optimal Office Lighting," Lighting Dimensions, vol. 11, no. 5 (September/October 1987), pp. 64–68, 70. Illus., color. A useful article (with excellent color

illustrations) about Peter Barna's Lumen Award winner (1987) for the Tensil Lighting Environment in Cleveland, Ohio.

"Survey: Workers' Control Over Personal Lighting Aids Productivity," Lighting, vol. 2, no. 6 (December 1988), p. 30. Illus. Report on a government survey (Canada) about workers' desire for control of their office lighting. "Adjustable Lighting" is available for 33% of the office workers in North America. 71% believe that it "helps get more done." Useful study.

Dana Dubbs, "A Balancing Act: Bringing the Outdoors Into a San Francisco Residence," Lighting Dimensions, vol. 13, no. 2 (March 1989), pp. 68–69, 75. Outstanding residential lighting design by Randall Whitehead of Light Source in San Francisco.

Bonnie S. Schwartz, "Jerrystyle: Lighting Is Not the Icing — It's the Cake," Lighting Dimensions, vol. 13, no. 1 (January/February 1989), pp. 18–19. Illus., color. Interesting unique luminaires (fixtures, lamps) by two New York City designers, Jerry Van Deelen and Jeff Brown.

Bonnie S. Schwartz, "Urban Village: Film Production Study Challenges Lighting Designer to Give Form to Interior Cityscape," Lighting Dimensions, vol. 13, no. 3 (April 1989), pp. 88–89, 109. Illus., color. Describes the lighting of Propaganda Films' new production studio in Hollywood.

George Berne, "Interior Landscape, Nanterre, France," International Lighting Review, 38th year, 4th quarter (1987), pp. 148–149. Illus., color. An interior garden in a corporate office building in France. Rick Tzui Hin-Fai, "Shun Tak Centre and Macau Ferry Terminal, Hong Kong," in the same issue, pp. 151–156. Illus., color.

"Singapore: NOL Building," International Lighting Review, 38th year, 3rd quarter (1987), pp. 86–91. Illus., color. Several buildings. And in the same issue: "Tung Centre," pp. 92–95. Illus., color. Also: "MAS Building," pp. 96–103. Illus., color.

H. H. Angus, "Lighting in the Contemporary Workplace." A useful mimeographed 7-page study produced by H. H. Angus & Associates, Limited, Consulting Engineers, 1127 Leslie Street, Don Mills, Ontario, M3C 2J6, Canada. Tel.: (416) 443-8200.

sired), brackets, luminous panels, and ceiling-recessed downlights. The designer should have ready access to Wendelighting's *System Photographique,* an ingenious method of designing luminaires to highlight paintings, statuary, etc. Wendelighting, a firm that has been following the path of founder Wendell for over 40 years (Wendell was a leading early designer; see discussion of landscape architecture lighting earlier in this chapter), has its counterpart in stage "photospots" and small optical ellipsoidal reflector units. Residential lighting can add style, change mood, modify the appearance of a room, and focus attention in any home, as well as providing task illumination.

Köhler and Luckhardt said of residential lighting, "Correct lighting is an art." They list five objectives for residential lighting. It must

1. Provide vision
2. Meet hygienic requirements (provide adequate illumination to achieve proper sanitation)
3. Meet esthetic standards
4. Provide good spatial impression
5. Meet its objectives economically

In 1977 Joan Kron of *The New York Times* interviewed Tharon Musser, a well-known Broadway lighting design artist, about home lighting. Musser's views provide an amusing look at home lighting:

"There is no place you can read a magazine in this house," said Tharon Musser, "except at the drawing board."

Miss Musser . . . likes bright light in the kitchen and in her workroom, but in the rest of her Early American-furnished house in the Village "I like it dim. A home is still a place to relax. I like dark corners.

"Most modern light sources are hideous. I won't eat in a restaurant that has fluorescent light. What's more, actors can't make up in fluorescent light."

So what does she use for light? . . . Her collection includes Venetian street lights, an old railroad lantern, an antique bicycle lamp, hanging oil lamps (she electrifies them herself), sandwich glass globes, teardrop globes, old crystal shades—and to reflect light in her Connecticut pool room, there is a mirrored ball on order.

In the city, over the drafting table there are two Luxe architect's lamps, but her staple is a "lot of candles."

"Light," said Miss Musser, "is the atmosphere we live in. I'm such a fanatic, I don't wear sunglasses ever because I want to see and remember things the way they are. I never carry a camera either," she confided. "It's a crutch. Lighting design is learning how to see. I learn to hear the lights in music in my mind."[292]

Restaurants

Another popular area for lighting designers, restaurants must be special, portraying images of class, festivity, or relaxation. Commercial success can depend as much upon a restaurant's decor as on its service and food. If all three aspects are excellent, business is assured. If any one is weak, customers may go elsewhere. Some of the finest restaurant designs have been lighted by Richard Kelly. Figures 10.34 and 10.35 are his work. (See also Color Fig. 78 earlier in this chapter, which is John Watson's design for a Mexican restaurant in Texas.)

Critic Thomas Goldthwaite, writing about Morristown, Indiana's Kopper Kettle Restaurant (which is 125 years old), brings up an interesting point. He writes:

[The Kopper Kettle] is a scheme of improvised lighting fixtures that resemble an Eastern European auction salon. . . . I counted 10 different kinds of lighting within view of the restaurant's three major dining rooms. . . . Candles, leaded-glass shades, twinkle bulbs, chandeliers, milkglass and flickering sconces generate a special aura. . . . Everyone looks incredibly rosy and polished. . . . How often do you see that in your local bistro where the lighting is apt to be so dim from recessed spots and stark windowless walls that the customers blend into the grey houseplants?[293]

Schools and Libraries

Like a hospital, a university (and some high schools) is like a city within itself. Much that has been said earlier about other lighting areas applies to school lighting as well. Particular emphasis has been placed upon task visibility — having enough light of the correct kind to enable people to see to read, type, or work in a laboratory. Visual comfort goes hand in hand with task visibility. Economy is a factor, as in most lighting areas. It is interesting that A. Sorsby in England conclusively established through documented studies at the Royal College of Surgeons that "vision problems can not, in any major degree, be attributed to lighting condi-

Figure 10.34 The Four Seasons Restaurant, New York City. Lighting by Richard Kelly.

Figure 10.35 The Four Seasons Restaurant.

[292] Joan Kron, "A Lighting Touch," The New York Times, vol. 126, no. 43,580, May 19, 1977, page 26.

See also:

William F. Rooney, Practical Guide to Home Lighting. N.Y.; Van Nostrand Reinbold; 1980. 142 pages, illus., color. Useful; well-written and well-illustrated.

Derek Phillips, Planning Your Lighting. London; Design Center (28 Haymarket); 1976. 71 pp. Illus., color. Basic book for the layman on architectural, residential interior lighting by England's leading designer.

Mary Gilliatt and Douglas Baker, Lighting Your Home: A Practical Guide. New York; Random House; 1979. 175 pp., illus., color. Excellent text and illustrations.

American Home Lighting Institute, Guidelines to Good Lighting. AHLI, 435 N. Michigan Ave., Chicago, IL 60611; 1983. 20 pp. Illus., color.

IES, Design Criteria for Lighting Interior Living Spaces, RP-11. N.Y.; IES; 1980. 50 pp., illus. Useful summary of IES recommendations.

Home Lighting & Accessories magazine is published monthly by Ebel-Doctorow Publishers, Inc., P.O. Box 2147, 1115 Clifton Ave., Clifton, NJ 07015. It is most useful in this area.

"Residences — Lighting for Living," International Lighting Review, 36th year, 3d quarter 1985, pp. 89–100. Illus., color. A most useful summary of residential lighting design philosophy and problems; well-illustrated.

Barbara J. Knox, "Designer Fixtures, Adam Tibany Introduces His Off the Wall Ideas," Lighting Dimensions, vol. 10, no. 3 (May/June 1986), pp. 14, 16–17. Illus., color. Useful noveaux household fixtures.

Walter Köhler and Wassill Luckhardt, "Rooms for Living," pp. 192–95, op. cit. (see footnote 239).

"Bulbs That Can Provide Lighting Without Glare," The New York Times, Chicago ed., p. 21, April 10, 1986. Several professional New York City architectural lighting designers comment on available light sources including neodymium bulbs from Finland and halogen sources as well as new fluorescents.

"Light & Design: San Francisco Update: Alan Lucas Gives New Finishes and Furnishings to a Penthouse Overlooking Nob Hill," Interior Design, vol. 55, no. 11 (Nov. 1984), pp. 254–255. Illus., color.

"A Dream House in Dallas," Lighting Dimensions, vol. 8, no. 4 (July/Aug. 1984), pp. 12–13, 15–18. Illus., color. Designer Tully Weiss lighted a Texan's home with lasers and "fantasy lights." Includes light plot.

"Ski Residence: Simple, Unobtrusive Lighting for a Second Home," Lighting Design + Application, vol. 15, no. 6 (June 1985), pp. 17–19. Illus., color.

"Lower Level of Lake Residence: Incorporating Negative Structural Elements and Energy Efficiency," Lighting Design + Application, vol. 15, no. 6 (June 1985), pp. 26–27. Illus., color. IES Award–winner in New York.

"'Toad Hall' The de Menil Residence," Lighting Design + Application, vol. 14, no. 10 (Oct. 1984), pp. 26–27. Illus., color. IES Award–winner in New York.

"Edwin F. Guth Memorial Award of Merit Projects," Lighting Design + Application, vol. 13, no. 10 (Oct. 1983), p. 28. Illus. Outstanding residential lighting including one by Carroll B. Cline.

"The Laboratory," Lighting Design + Application, vol. 14, no. 10 (Oct. 1984), pp. 24–25. Illus., color. An experimental residential lighting installation involving 300 lighting instruments, 75,000 watts, and a cost of $300,000, including a laser. 1984 IES Award–winner in Dallas.

Tony M. Napoli, "New Jersey Residence and Poolhouse," Lighting Design + Application, vol. 13, no. 6 (June 1983), pp. 14–17. Illus., color. Modernistic residential lighting described in detail with nine color photos.

"Residential: Long Island Residence," Lighting Design + Application, vol. 6, no. 10 (Oct. 1976), pp. 4–9. Lighting design of an elaborate Long Island home by designer Jim Nuckolls involving lighting of major works of art, indoors and outdoors.

Carol Levine, "Fresh Ideas about Lighting For the Home," The New York Times, October 7, 1982. Home section, pp. 21–22. Illus.

"Design Criteria for Lighting Interior Living Spaces, Part I," Lighting Design + Application, vol. 10, no. 2 (Feb. 1980), pp. 31–49, 50, 52, 54, 56, 58, 60–61. Illus.

Nancy Christensen, "Homelighting, Focus on Aesthetics, Energy and Quality — Flexibility, Safety, and Security are Also Paramount," Lighting Design + Application, vol. 16, no. 5 (May 1986), pp. 33, 35, 37, 39. Illus., color. Well-presented basics.

Joseph Giovannini, "For Theatre Set Designers, All the Home's a Stage," The New York Times, February 24, 1983, pp. 15, 17.

Paulette R. Hebert, "A Southern Accent By Design: Residential Lighting by and for Southern Design Professionals," Lighting Design + Application, vol. 17, no. 1 (Jan. 1987), pp. 6–9, 45–46. Illus., color.

Tom Miears, "Dining Room Serves Up More Than Meals: Functions-Based Approach to Planning," Lighting Design + Application, vol. 17, no. 1 (Jan. 1987), pp. 12–13, 47. Illus., color.

Deyan Sudjic, The Lighting Book, A Complete Guide to Lighting Your Home. London; Mitchell Beazley Int'l.; 1985. 192 pp., illus., color. Covers lighting basics, sources, hardware, and designing. Sudjic is architectural correspondent for the (London) Sunday Times and editor of the British design magazine Blueprint. He writes well; the volume is excellently illustrated; quite a valuable source in this area of lighting design.

Barty Phillips, Christopher Wray's Guide to Decorative Lighting. London; Michael Joseph Ltd., or Webb & Bower; 1987. 144 pp., illus., color throughout. Covers mostly lamps, fixtures, and luminaires. Excellent study for research or reference in lightshades, period designs, etc. Useful.

Ronn Smith, "Timeless elegance," Lighting Dimensions, vol. 12, no. 2 (March 1988), pp. 76–81, 102–107. Illus., color, includes light plot. Lighting of an elegant East Side residence in New York City by V LeMar Terry, Jr., and Neil Chassman. For many years Terry was lighting designer for the New York City Metropolitan Museum. The residence lighting earned the first annual House & Garden Award for them and French designer Patrick Naggar.

tions [but] better lighting unquestionably led to better visual performance and particularly to more accurate and easier reading. . . . [B]etter lighting led to a feeling of freshness and buoyancy . . . and better learning."[294] A rather startling new study by Rita Dunn and Jeffrey Krimsky, entitled "Schools Light Up Their Lives—And Sometimes Dim Their Chances for Success,"[295] offers extensive scholarly documentation for the thesis that children's vision varies as much as their fingerprints. "Many students report that they can concentrate only in bright light; low light makes them lethargic. Others find that the reverse is true; low light calms them and permits them to learn easily, whereas bright light makes them 'nervous and fidgety'." At the end of the study, Dunn and Krimsky state: "Certainly light is an element of learning style. It is likely that we have not yet begun to recognize its full potency." Should this study prove to have merit and become more widely disseminated, it could have a destructive effect upon the entire IES set of standards. It is a whole new ballgame for the lighting designer if further studies verify that individual responses to overall light levels vary from person to person, with half of our population—whether in the office or classroom or factory—responding better to lower levels of light and half responding better to higher levels of light.

Perhaps we have overdone (both in initial cost and in recurrent energy consumption) the illumination of classrooms by following the recommended minimums of the IES. Better campus lighting has been designed—without the factory-like approach—by several lighting designers who paid maximum attention to lighting various areas for specific needs and functions. It is possible to avoid massive "even" illumination and turn out a visually better environment.[296]

For more specifics on library lighting, see footnote 296.

Stores, Merchandising, and Display Windows

There are a variety of lighting areas in which lighting's main function is to *sell*. These specialized areas include stores and merchandising, industrial shows, trade shows, and conventions. TV and film commercials also use lighting to promote sales, but these areas were covered earlier, in Chap. 7.

Barbara J. Knox, *"The Home as Art Gallery: Randall Whitehead Lights People First, Architecture Second, and Paintings Last,"* Lighting Dimensions, *vol. 11, no. 6 (November 1987), pp. 56–57, 76. Illus., color. Lighting of the Wright residence in San Francisco, containing important art works.*

[293] Thomas Goldthwaite, *"Gastronomy, Goodness Amid Glitter,"* Indianapolis Star magazine, *October 21, 1984, p. 13.*

"LIGHT Pictorial," Light magazine, vol. 29, no. 2 (Apr./June 1960), pp. 12–13 and color cover photo. Richard Kelly's work.*

"Decorating with Lighted Plants!" Light magazine, vol. 24, no. 1 (Jan./Feb. 1955), pp. 10–13. Richard Kelly's designs.*

"Sun Sensations at La Fonda Del Sol," Light magazine, vol. 31, no. 1 (1962), pp. 3–4. Richard Kelly.*

"Drama at the Dynasty—Lighting Plays Starring Role at Restaurant," Lighting Design + Application, vol. 15, no. 12 (Dec. 1985), pp. 8–9. Illus., color. A restaurant in Milwaukee.*

"The 1986 IALD and IESNA Awards," International Lighting Review, 1st quarter 1987, pp. 31, 33. Illus., color. An award-winning restaurant and a bar.*

Barbara Hillier, *"Programmed Lighting Important Ingredient in Restaurant,"* Architectural Lighting, vol. 1, no. 6 (June 1987), pp. 32–35. Illus., color. Restaurants in Jenkintown, Pennsylvania. Excellent color graphics.*

"Your Outside Is In: They're Eating Up the Pizza Sign in San Francisco," Architectural Lighting, vol. 1, no. 1 (Jan. 1987), p. 18. Illus., color. Lighting of the Escape from New York Pizza Restaurant in San Francisco.*

"Setting the Stage for Sushi-Zen," Lighting Design + Application, vol. 16, no. 10 (Oct. 1986), pp. 5–7. Illus., color. A strikingly lighted sushi restaurant in New York City.*

Craig A. Roeder, *"Light Cuisine: From Fast-Food to Fine Dining, What You See Is What You Eat,"* Lighting Design + Application, vol. 16, no. 9 (Sept. 1986), pp. 4–6, 42–43. Illus., color. Several restaurants.*

Jane Rottenbach, *"Fitting Form and Function: Lighthouse Restaurants Are a Beacon of Good Taste,"* Lighting Design + Application, vol. 16, no. 9 (Sept. 1986), pp. 8–11, 48. Parker's Lighthouse Restaurant in Palm Beach Gardens, Florida. Contains ground plan/light plot.*

Sarah Shankman, *"Aurora: The Payoff of Love's Labor—Masters of Cuisine, Design, and Light Create a Work of Art,"* Lighting Design + Application, vol. 16, no. 9 (Sept. 1986), pp. 12–15. Illus., color. New York City's Aurora Restaurant.*

"Light & Design: Corporate Consolidation: Worrell Associates Combines Conoco's Separate Food Service Areas into a Single Facility on One Floor," Interior Design, vol. 55, no. 11 (Nov. 1984), pp. 258–59. Illus., color.*

"Light & Design: American Cafe, Chevy Chase," Interior Design, vol. 55, no. 11 (Nov. 1984), pp. 268–69. Illus., color.*

"Light & Design: Swan Dive, Theatrical Lighting Is the Key Element in This Portland, Maine, Restaurant by Dana Johnson of Lightworks," Interior Design, vol. 55, no. 11 (Nov. 1984). Illus., color.*

"Light & Design: Stage-Set Sushi, American Architect David Rockwell Designs a Japanese Restaurant in New York," Interior Design, vol. 55, no. 11 (Nov. 1984), pp. 272–73. Illus., color.*

"Light & Design: The Commons at Copley Place, A Cafeteria-and-a-bar in a Make-believe Park Setting Designed by Graham/Meus, Inc.," Interior Design, vol. 55, no. 11 (Nov. 1984), pp. 274–277. Illus., color.*

Aileen Robbins, *"Restaurants as Theatre,"* Theatre Crafts, vol. 19, no. 1 (Jan. 1985), pp. 28–29, 62–67. Illus., color.*

Steve Pollock, *"Ken Billington on Restaurant Lighting Design,"* Theatre Crafts, vol. 19, no. 1 (Jan. 1985), pp. 30–31, 67–86. Illus., color. Broadway designer's architectural work in restaurant lighting.*

"Sushi-Zen Restaurant," Lighting Design + Application, vol. 15, no. 9 (Sept. 1985), p. 17. Illus., color.*

"Sleek Deco Electricity," Lighting Design + Application, vol. 12, no. 9 (Sept. 1982), pp. 20–22. Illus., color.*

"Le Cygne Restaurant," Lighting Design + Application, vol. 13, no. 10 (Oct. 1983), pp. 16–18. Illus., color. This award-winning lighting design by Jules Fisher and Paul Marantz, Inc.,*

of New York City is detailed in text and offers excellent color photographs. Also see p. 48 in the same issue for five more restaurants and bars.

"White Castle: Restaurant: A Wider View on Fast Food Lighting," Lighting Design + Application, vol. 13, no. 8 (Aug. 1983), pp. 26–27. Illus., color. Winner of a 1982 Section Lighting Design Award and an Edwin F. Guth Memorial Award of Merit, this design solves many of the more common lighting problems of a less-than-glamorous space.

"'Shogun' Revisited: Discovering Japan in Northbrook, IL," Lighting Design + Application, vol. 13, no. 5 (May 1983), pp. 22–24. Illus., color. Award-winning restaurant.

"Art deco at Metropol Reflects Lighting Ingenuity," Lighting Design + Application, vol. 14, no. 9 (Sept. 1984), pp. 20–21. Illus., color. The Metropol Restaurant in Houston.

Harrods Dress Circle Restaurant: Fresh and Elegant—Citation," Lightview, vol. 1, no. 1 (Spring 1988), p. 5. Illus., color. IALD Citation Award to Johnathan Spiers for the lighting of this British restaurant.

Cliff Isbii, "Bubles Balboa Club, Newport Beach, California," International Lighting Review, 38th year, 4th quarter (1987), pp. 137–139. Illus., color.

Ann Daly, "Casual Quilted Giraffe," Lighting Dimensions, vol. 11, no. 5 (September/October 1987), pp. 52–53, 70–72. Illus., color. Lighting of New Yorks City's Casual Quilted Giraffe restaurant in the AT&T Building by Jerry Kugler Associates.

Barry H. Slinker, "China Grill: A Ceiling of Floating Fixtures Unites a Fragmented Restaurant Space," Lighting Dimensions, vol. 12, no. 4 (May/June 1988), pp. 30, 32. Illus., color. Another Kugler project in New York City.

"Glamour Returns to the Rainbow Room," Lightview International, vol. 1, no. 4 (Winter 1989), pp. 6, 8. Illus., color. Relighting of New York City's famous Rainbow Room by Paul Marantz (of Jules Fisher-Marantz), Charles Stone, and E. Teal Brogden.

"Two-time Winner," Lighting Dimensions, vol. 12, no. 6 (September/October 1988), p. 34. Illus. Michael K. Souter's award-winning design for the Ho-Chow Restaurant in Fremont, California. It won the 1987 Edison Award and the 1988 Halo/Metalux National Lighting Competition. Souter is with Luminae of San Francisco.

Mark Loeffler, "Aureole, Restaurant Design Features Concealed Linear Lighting Wall Grazing Systems," Lighting Dimensions, vol. 13, no. 3 (April 1989), pp. 94–95. Fashionable restaurant in New York City lighted by Mark Kruger Associates, Inc., Illus., color.

Alice M. Hale, "A Safe, Warm Place: Pat Kuleto Designs Restaurants That Are Both Beautiful and Successful," Lighting Dimensions, vol. 13, no. 2 (March 1989), pp. 54–57, 88, 90. Illus., color. Very useful presentation of restaurant lighting design.

[294] Hopkinson and Kay, Lighting of Buildings, pp. 169–70, op. cit. (see footnote 250).

[295] Rita Dunn and Jeffrey Krimsky, with A. Raymond Barretto, Mary Ellen Freeley, Louis Primavera, and Richard Sinatra, "Schools Light Up Their Lives—And Sometimes Dim Their Chances for Success." Available to me in a 14-page mimeographed report sent to me by Dr. Joel E. Rubin, Kliegl Bros. Original source unknown.

[296] "The Classroom—From A-lamps to HID," Lighting Design + Application, vol. 9, no. 8 (Aug. 1979), pp. 36–42. Illus. Excellent history of classroom lighting.

"Lumen Awards '80: New York University, School of Continuing Education," Lighting Design + Application, vol. 10, no. 6 (June 1980), pp. 15–16. Illus.

"Lighting Design for Brookhaven College," Lighting Design + Application, vol. 11, no. 6 (June 1981), pp. 15–17. Illus., color.

Vilma Barr, "Lighting the Kennedy Years," Lighting Design + Application, vol. 10, no. 1 (Jan. 1980), pp. 2–6, 8, 10–13. Illus., color. Museum-library lighting.

deBoer and Fisher, "Schools," pp. 268–271, op. cit. (see footnote 282). Brief; Illus.

"Classrooms," Lighting Design + Application, vol. 6, no. 3 (Mar. 1976), pp. 9–24. Several articles on the same theme.

"A Case for Rarities," Light magazine, vol. 33, no. 1 (1964), pp. 19–21. Lighting design for the Yale library, one of Richard Kelly's last assignments (done in conjunction with Stanley R. McCandless). Illus.

"Markham Village Green Community Library," Lighting Design + Application, vol. 12, no. 11 (Nov. 1982), pp. 12–16. Illus., color.

"Edwin F. Guth Memorial Award of Merit Projects" schools (pp. 29–31), libraries (pp. 44, 46), Lighting Design + Application, vol. 13, no. 10 (Oct. 1983). Illus. Details and illustrates outstanding lighting design in 1983 in these specialized areas. Also see p. 32 for a display area and training room in Alabama.

"Projects in Progress," Lighting Design + Application, vol. 13, no. 11 (Nov. 1983), pp. 14–15. Illus., color. New Lawrence Institute of Technology building in Southfield, Michigan.

"Relighting for the Future: Erie Community College," Lighting Design + Application, vol. 13, no. 6 (June 1983), pp. 18–21. Illus., color, drawings.

"Stanford Main Library—Efficient and Uncompromising Lighting," Lighting Design + Application, vol. 13, no. 5 (May 1983), pp. 18–21. Illus., color.

"Westside High School: Remodeling the Corridor and Cafeteria," Lighting Design + Application, vol. 15, no. 8 (Aug. 1985), p. 17. Illus., color.

"Public Buildings—San Juan Capistrano Library, California," International Lighting Review, 1st quarter 1986, pp. 10–15. Illus., color.

"John Fiske Elementary School (library)," "Florida Jr. Univ. Auditorium," Lighting Design + Application, vol. 15, no. 10 (Oct. 1985), pp. 40–41. Illus. Also "Main Reading Room of Cedar Rapids Public Library," p. 44. Illus.

Ken Loach, "Good Lighting Design Speaks Volumes: Speciality Lighting Design for a Library Had to Take into Account General Area Lighting As Well As Vertical Illuminance for the Bookshelves," Lighting, vol. 3, no. 2 (April 1989), pp. 12, 14. Illus., color.

How does *sales* lighting differ from other lighting? Köhler and Luckhardt list two lighting objectives:

1. To sell, feature, glamorize, and emphasize the product, and always put the product in a favorable light

Figure 10.36 Burdine's Department Store, Clearwater, Florida. Lighting by David A. Mintz, Inc.; interior design by the Walker Group/CNI. (*Photo: Alexandre Georges*)

Figure 10.37 Burdine's Department Store, Clearwater, Florida.

2. To create a favorable psychic climate that encourages purchases (puts the customer in the mood to buy)[297]

GE describes the objectives somewhat differently, calling them the "Three A's":

1. *Attraction* lighting (getting the customers' attention using contrast, color, animation, etc.)
2. *Atmosphere* lighting (using patterns, mirrors, chandeliers, architectural lines, etc.)
3. *Appraisal* lighting (to allow for careful inspection of the merchandise)

Involved in appraisal lighting are easy visibility of the product and labels, the texture of the merchandise, and the accurate colors of the items offered for sale. Allowing for proper merchandise evaluation by the customer can reduce returns.

In addition to these "selling" objectives, lighting is used to assist in the control of movement and traffic flow throughout the selling place. Light should also be used to enhance decor and architecture—to give the store "personality" (this can be highly individual: bright and lively for children's toys, somber for a funeral home, staid or friendly for a bank, conducive to studiousness for a bookstore, etc.). Store areas to be dealt with include circulation areas (aisles), merchandising areas, case and counter displays, and featured item displays throughout the store.

One of the aspects of store design that deserves careful consideration is ceiling treatment. A huge, bright ceiling draws attention away from merchandise. Adequate illumination is solved by using concealed sources (egg-crate louvers, cornice and cove lighting) plus accent spotlights. The basic lighting considerations set forth earlier in this chapter also apply: cost, energy consumption, taste, and design. Added is the element of sales imagination. Frequently theatre-trained lighting designers are at their very best in sales lighting because their specialty has been a study of the use of light to evoke responses from audiences. An added strength is such a designer's sense of theatricalism and drama.[297A]

Color Fig. 89 presents David Mintz's lighting design for Burdines department store in Tampa, Florida (the domestics department). Figures 10.36 and 10.37 are Mintz's work

[297] *Köhler and Luckhardt, p. 168, op. cit. (see footnote 284).*

See also: Wm. Weathersby, "Aged Futurism: Alena Appia Lights the Landscape of Archilla Men's Store," Lighting Dimensions, vol. 12, no. 4 (May/June 1988), pp. 40–41, 61, 63. Illus., color. Santa Monica, California, Men's Store lighted by Alena Appia.

Jill Dolan, "Craig Roberts: Discreet Lighting for Elegant Environments," Lighting Dimensions, vol. 12, no. 4 (May/June 1988), pp. 52–54, 57, 59. Illus., color. Polo, Ralph Lauren's New York City store, lighted by Los Angeles–Dallas based Craig Roberts.

Joseph R. Zaharewicz, "Place Ville Marie Gets Facelift: Corridor Lighting Utilizing Ceiling Vault Surfaces for Reflection Create a Sense of Height and Spaciousness," Lighting, vol. 2, no. 6 (December 1988), pp. 18, 20. Illus.

Mark Loeffler, "The Randolph Duke Boutique: Ya Ya Ho Light Trapeze Adds Whimsy to Formal Design," Lighting Dimensions, vol. 11, no. 5 (September/October 1987), pp. 58–59. Illus., color.

Design for a Manhattan clothier's shop, lighting consultant Corinne Strumpf made use of a whimsical Ingo Maurer's Ya Ya Ho light trapeze.

A. F. M. Gils, "The Four-Corner Philosophy: A Matrix for Shop Lighting," International Lighting Review, 2nd quarter, 40th year (1989), pp. 48–56. Illus., color. A most important presentation of design philosophy for store lighting.

"News," Lighting Dimensions, vol. 13, no. 4 (May/June 1989), p. 26. Illus. Gregory Ballweg's visual merchandising lighting in a company showroom in Manhattan.

"Lighting Filene's," Lighting Dimensions, vol. 13, no. 2 (March 1989), p. 16. Illus. Gilbert Whalen's lighting of Filene's flagship retail store in Chestnut Hill, Massachusetts. Also: Michael Cahana, "MR-16's: Revolutionary Tiny White Light Source Sparks Civil War," pp. 50, 52–53. Illus., color. And: Bonnie S. Schwartz, "Star Quality: In the World of High Design: Johnson Schwinghammer," pp. 62–65, 82–83. Illus., color. And: William Weathersby, Jr., "New and Improved: Lighting Proves Key to Supermarkets' Good Looks," pp. 70–72, 74. The best magazine article available concerning the lighting of supermarkets.

[298] Alfred Makulee, "The Shop Window . . . Looking Glass or . . . Look-in Glass," Part 1, Light magazine, vol. 28, no. 4 (Oct./Dec. 1959), pp. 11–14; Part 2 in vol. 29, no. 1 (Jan./Mar. 1960), pp. 17–20. Illus. Excellent series also covering automobile showrooms, luminous backgrounds and display decor, and ventilation and fading. Part I, p. 11.

[299] Enid Nemy, "Windows That Light Up the Holidays," The New York Times, Chicago edition, pp. C1, C10, Friday, December 7, 1984. Illus. Excellent article about New York City's outstanding store window illumination.

"Merchandise Lighting," Lighting Design + Application, vol. 10, no. 9 (Sept. 1980). Contains: "(David) Mintz on Merchandising— An Energy Update," pp. 8–11, illus., color; "Window Wizard," pp. 12–15, 18–19, illus., color (store window work of designer Adam Hayes); "The Brickyard Mall," pp. 20–22, illus.; "J. C. Penney's 'Energy Management Process','" pp. 23–24, illus.; "The Indiana Mall," pp. 26–27, illus.

IES, Recommended Practice for Lighting Merchandising Areas, RP-2. N.Y.; IES; 1976. Illus., 35 pp. Useful summary of store lighting.

Köhler and Luckhardt, "Sales Rooms," pp. 168–179, op. cit. (see footnote 284).

deBoer and Fisher, "Shops and Stores," pp. 272–77, op. cit. (see footnote 282). Excellent text. Many illustrations, in color. Covers store windows.

"Lighting for Merchandising," International Lighting Review, 2d quarter 1985. Illus., color. Entire issue, pp. 39–69, contains articles on lighting for shops, mannequins, foodstuffs, etc. by various authors. Lavishly illustrated; good text. Invaluable reference source.

"Guth Memorial Award," Lighting Design + Application, vol. 13, no. 10 (Oct. 1983), p. 32. Illus. An award-winning supermarket interior's lighting design discussed and illustrated for Foodarama. See also "Lighting up the aisles at Foodarama," Lighting Design & Application, vol. 14, no. 2 (Feb. 1984), pp. 16–17. Illus., color.

"Eat at Dino's!" Lighting Dimensions, vol. 8, no. 2 (Mar./Apr. 1984), pp. 30–31, 33, 37–39.

Illus., color. Film producer Dino De Laurentis has created three "DDL Foodshows" (two in New York City and one in Beverly Hills, California) which are combination deli-display "galleries" lighted entirely with stage lights. Color illustrations and extensive text.

"Corning Glass Showroom," Lighting Design + Application, vol. 14, no. 5 (May 1984), pp. 28–33. Illus., color, drawings. The Corning Glass Corp.'s New York City showroom was turned into a unique showcase/display area with constantly changing projections, light, and color. A most innovative and workable solution.

"E. F. Hauserman Showroom," Lighting Design + Application, vol. 13, no. 10 (Oct. 1983), pp. 12–15. Illus., color. An outstanding award-winning lighting design by Dan Flavin presented in colorful detail. The design is based almost entirely on color and light.

"Merchandising: Arizona State University Bookstore," Lighting Design + Application, vol. 14, no. 11 (Nov. 1984), pp. 11–13. Illus., color.

Lighting Manual for Department & Specialty Stores: A Guide to Better Lighting & Energy Savings. Indianapolis; Indy Lighting, Inc., 8431 Castlewood Drive, Indianapolis, IN 46250. At a price of $95 per copy, this remains a useful source in this specialty.

A. van Gils, "A House Style Through Lighting, Profoot Chain, The Netherlands," International Lighting Review, 38th year, 4th quarter (1987), pp. 132–133. Illus., color. Lighting design for a shoestore chain in Holland. Also in the same issue: A. van Gils, "Fashions in a New Light, Jos Hoes, Veldhoven, the Netherlands," pp. 134–136. Illus., color. Store window lighting.

"Showing a Room to Advantage—Award of Excellence," Lightview, vol. 1, no. 1 (Spring 1988), p. 3. Illus., color. Chris Ripman's Advantage Showroom in Waltham, Massachusetts, won an IALD 1988 Award of Excellence. See Also: Chris Ripman, "Advantage Showroom, Waltham, USA," International Lighting Review, 39th year, 3rd quarter (1988), p. 104–106. Illus., color. Subtitled: "Imaginative Lighting Enhances Sales Area." Designer Ripman also makes good use of neon. Also: "Light Flashes,"

for the Burdines in Clearwater, Florida (the men's clothing and women's accessories departments). State by state, maximum allowable energy consumption levels are becoming law. The current California legal energy code for retail lighting allows an average 3.1 watts per square foot for major store areas and 4.1 watts per square foot for minor display areas.

All that applies to lighting for stores and merchandising applies to display windows, but there are a few added factors. It is not uncommon for a well-located department store to spend $20,000 (or more) for one window display. Alfred Makulec offers the designer these objectives for lighting window displays:

- Make the display maximally visible and attention-attracting, day or night.
- Add dramatic effects: color contrasts, movement, texture emphasis.
- Emphasize details.
- Consider window ventilation and merchandise fading, because technically, high light levels are needed.[298]

Store window lighting design is almost always the province of the design and display staff of the store. It is, however, up to the building designer to provide these staffs with decent lighting tools and the necessary electrical power for creative design.

Sales/merchandising/display lighting design requires a rare combination of talents: extensive lighting design knowledge, technical know-how, originality and inventiveness, dramatic imagination, and, most of all, the true salesman's innate sense of "selling." Those lighting designers who have these qualities will always find employment awaiting them.[299]

Industrials, Trade Shows, and Conventions

Industrials

Industrial shows are a funny breed. They could have been included in Chap. 8, "Spectacle," or in Chap. 4, under "Musicals" or "Revues," but instead they are treated here, because they have one objective: *sales*. While they are often in many ways identical to a Broadway musical, the "star" of the industrial production is always "the product." Industrials are often performed in theatres or in ballrooms or similar spaces not primarily intended for theatrical production. They make use of Broadway costume designers and construction houses; professional scenic designers, shops, and painters; union lighting designers; and stars, dancers, singers, choreographers, directors, and authors from the traditional world of legitimate show business. There are only four elements which set industrials apart from Broadway shows:

1. Spectacle. Since the product is the "star," maximum spectacle is needed from the designer for the all-important "reveals." This means maximum splash and splendor — not schmaltz or glitz. Having the skill and experience to make the leading lady look great onstage is not the same as having the taste, inventiveness, and originality to assist the client/producer in an effective and appropriate "reveal" of, say, a new-model automobile. The client has several years of expensive research and design invested in the product, and assembled is the group that is expected to market the end product of millions of dollars of investment. Effective lighting is vital.

2. Money. Funding is not nearly as tight for industrials as it is for Broadway shows. That doesn't mean that there is no set budget or that cash is thrown around freely, but it *does* mean that "selling" the product is all-important. The available resources of General Motors or Milliken far exceed those of *any* Broadway production group. The lighting designer thus faces an unusual situation. He or she is *not* designing light for Shakespeare's *Romeo and Juliet,* and most likely the "book" is weak and trite. The star is not Barbara Streisand (but still is a talented working professional). On the other hand, for once in a lifetime the designer *can* have what is needed to work with. Is an extra switchboard needed? Get it. Need another pipe of lights? Rent them. If new custom-built specials fabricated in the shop are needed, order them. *The only real limitation is the designer's own imagination.* It is not often that lighting artists (or any artists) find themselves in *that* situation. In addition, the original designer's fee is high (frequently double the fee for the same amount of work on Broadway). There is not a long

International Lighting Review, *39th year, 1st quarter (1988), p. 2, for another color photo. Also: "Light Flashes," same issue, p. 4, illus., color. Lighting of a fashion show in Milan, Italy.* A. F. M. van Gils, *"Shops: De Bijenkorf, Utrecht, The Netherlands,"* International Lighting Review, *39th year, 1st quarter (1988), pp. 32–36. Illus., color. Subtitled: "A Leisure Shop with an Aura of Exclusiveness."*

"Fairs: EuroShop 87, Dusseldorf," International Lighting Review, *38th year, 2nd quarter (1987), pp. 58–69. Illus., color. Excellent layout covering display lighting for several firms in numerous cities.*

Ronn Smith, *"Larger Than Life: Steven Hefferan Does Windows — for Barneys and Bergdorf Goodman,"* Lighting Dimensions, *vol. 12, no. 6 (September/October 1988), pp. 52–57, 77–78. Illus., color. Undoubtedly the best magazine article in print about store window lighting design.*

"Winning Ways: IALD Awards," Lighting Dimensions, *vol. 11, no. 7 (January/February 1988), p. 48. Illus. An award-winning showroom in Waltham, Massachusetts, by Chris Ripman and Nancy Polcari in Belmont, Massachusetts. While they are not show windows, showrooms utilize the same design principles.*

M. Toho, E. Shiobama, H. Imamura, S. Wada, K. Nakai, and Y. Namikoshi, *"High Brightness, Color Variable Lighting Element for Large Outdoor Displays,"* Journal of the I.E.S., *vol. 18, no. 2 (Summer 1989), pp. 23–31. Illus. Good study of outdoor signs.*

"Commercial Display Lighting and Shop Lighting," International Lighting Review, *1985, #2, pp. 38–69. Illus., color. Includes "Globe-Shopping," by J. F. Caminada; "Lighting for Merchandising," by Alex Bonvini; "The Grafton Centre, Cambridge, England," by Derek Phillips; "Fresh Lighting for Foodstuffs," by Heinz Jochens (Germany); and "Shop Lighting," "Display Mannequins," and "The Shop," by Peter von der Horst (Netherlands). Excellent text and a profusion of quality color graphics on glossy paper presenting the best in merchandise sales lighting in the 1980s worldwide.*

See also Visual Merchandising & Store Design *magazine, published monthly by Signs of the Times Publishing Co., 407 Gilbert Ave., Cincinnati, OH 45202. Vol. 117, no. 5 (May

1986) contains a complete issue devoted to lighting designs including "Designing For Designers" by David Mintz, pp. 86–87. Excellent color graphics of the most advanced contemporary design.*

"Times Square to Stay Bright," IALD Newsletter, *Sept. 1986, p. 2. New law in New York City will require moving lighted signs of large dimension to keep Times Square festooned colorfully.*

"A Store Lighting Guide: Recommended Practice for Lighting Merchandising Areas," Lighting Design + Application, *vol. 16, no. 5 (May 1986), pp. 18–21. Illus., color.*

"Low Voltage Delivers High Impact," Lighting Design + Application, *vol. 16, no. 1 (Jan. 1986), pp. 10–11. Illus., color. A Honolulu, Hawaii, specialty shop.*

"Sontini e Dominici," Lighting Design + Application, *vol. 15, no. 10 (Oct. 1985), pp. 20–21. Illus., color. A Florida shoe store. Also "Merchandise," pp. 35–38. Illus. Fine IES Guth Awards of Merit for 35 designs.*

Dorothy Kamm, *"Colored Renditions — Light as Decoration,"* Lighting Design + Application, *vol. 15, no. 12 (Dec. 1985), pp. 15–19. Illus., color. An excellent article on store lighting reprinted from* Visual Merchandising & Store Design *magazine.*

Frank Lagiusa, *"Holiday Lighting Creates the Sparkle: A Step-by-Step Procedure for Planning a Holiday Lighting Display,"* Lighting Design + Application, *vol. 16, no. 4 (April 1986), pp. 25–27. Illus., color. Christmas lighting in merchandising.*

Charles Linn, *"Calculating Daylight for Successful Retail Design,"* Architectural Lighting, *vol. 1, no. 1 (Jan. 1987), pp. 28–34. Illus., color.*

Sarah Shankman, *" 'Goodnight, Mrs. Calabash, Wherever You Are' — Theo Kondos Lights the Shopping Center As Theatre,"* Lighting Design + Application, *vol. 16, no. 9 (Sept. 1986), pp. 26–29. Illus., color. A useful article on the "sales glamorization" of shopping centers.*

Bernard V. Bauer, *" 'Murphy's Law' Sabotages Merchandise Lighting Plans: Bullock's Teaches Maintenance and Operation,"* Lighting Design + Application, *vol. 16, no. 8 (Aug. 1986), pp. 6–8, 58, 59. Illus., color. Includes the "Ten Commandments of Merchandising." Also* includes the following: Edmund Feldman, "Sizing Things Up, Down, and Elsewhere," pp. 10–13, illus., color; Dick Holm, "A Window Into Herman Miller—Using Light to the Advantage of Clients and Employees," pp. 14–18, 60, illus., color; David Mintz, "Lighting What's For Sale: In Retail and Architecture the 'Big Laws' of Lighting Remain Constant," pp. 19–21, illus., color; Robert O'Brien, "Lazarus Update With Relighting: Ambient, Perimeter and Accent Layers Bring New Look to Life," pp. 22–23, illus., color; Jules Horton with Sarah Shankman, "Lighting Helps Create New Image For Fanny Farmer: Chocolate Must Be Handled with a Special Touch," pp. 26–27, illus., color; "Dominick's Sella in a True Light—Tracks with Low Voltage Make Produce Shine," pp. 38–39, illus.

Charles Linn, "A Flexible Lighting System for a Dynamic Display Environment," Architectural Lighting, vol. 1, no. 4 (April 1987), pp. 18–25. Illus., color. An excellent article on the lighting design for the Herman Miller Pavilion (furniture) in Grand Rapids, Michigan.

"Champagne Taste Shows in Upscale Men's Clothing Store," Architectural Lighting, vol. 1, no. 2 (Feb. 1987), p. 12. Illus., color. The C. T. Man store in Sonoma, California.

"Retail Lighting: Some Rules of Thumb for Lighting Merchandise and Interior Architecture in Retail Environments," Lighting Dimensions, vol. 10, no. 6 (Nov. 1986), pp. 37–41. Illus., color. The Saks department store in Palm Springs, California.

"Presentation & Lighting Major Markets," Electrosonic World, #4 (1987), p. 1. Illus., color. Also "Lighting Control in Retail Takes Off," p. 4. Illus. A London china and glass shop.

National Lighting Bureau, Lighting Energy Management in Retailing. Washington D.C.; National Lighting Bureau, Suite 300, 2101 L St., N.W.; 1981. 24 pp., illus. Good beginner's manual with stress on energy economics.

"Renovations—Sleep Country—Low Voltage Lighting Receives High Marks," Lighting Design + Application, vol. 13, no. 6 (June 1983), pp. 22–24. Illus., color. Detailed presentation of energy-saving low-voltage lamps used in store modernization.

"Pillow Talk—A Showroom," Interiors, vol. CXLI, no. 7 (Feb. 1982), pp. 68–69. Illus., color.

run, so the designer does not receive royalties; however, designers can come close to being paid an original fee as large as they may have always felt they deserved (but never got)—and that "ain't gonna happen" in many other circumstances.

3. The Performance Run. Industrials do not open, garner smash hit notices, and run for four years. In fact, no one even charges admission for the performances—the audience is all invited to attend free of charge. So, the designer need not worry about "the national company," four "road" companies, etc. The industrial show is a two- to two-and-a-half-hour commercial on a stage in theatrical form. It may only perform once (and most likely in the worst possible performance place: see Fiorentino's article concerning the Milliken show in the Waldorf-Astoria Hotel's ballroom, or the account of James Moody's Amway Corp. show on the road and in the Los Angeles Sports Arena, both cited in footnote 300). Or the industrial may go forth into the countryside in as many as five duplicate companies for an extensive road tour. The Chevrolet shows I designed sent two large companies out each season (to the big cities on both the East Coast and the West Coast) plus three slightly smaller "cut down" companies to play the smaller cities. All five had to be lighted and rehearsed in two adjacent theatres each August at the Masonic Temple in Detroit. While the scheduling was carefully planned, nonetheless I did find myself lighting five complete shows on two stages in one week in a single city.

The designer must also give careful design consideration to the fact that the industrials tour. He must know where (city and theatre) the industrials are to perform and must be aware of any specific theatre limitations. For the show to be magnificent in Detroit for the "big corporate brass" is not enough. It may be playing 11 other stands for which the designer will not be present. Should word drift back that it "looked pretty tacky" in Des Moines, Iowa, and Tampa, Florida, the designer can be very certain that another lighting designer will be hired the next season!

4. Heavy Technical Emphasis. An industrial is intended to entertain and arouse, so eye-catching technical effects are important. Corporations have discovered that the manner in which they present their newest product to "the troops" must result in the same type of emotional arousal associated with the winning of football games, pep rallies, Fourth of July celebrations, etc. An example of a basic corporate goal for an industrial is to "send the troops forth excited about the new 'Spitfire 99,' anxious and eager to get the product in their showrooms and to sell." That is why all those dancers and singers and comedians and costumes and scenery and lights were hired! Critical acclaim and taste (while still important) are not at the top of the priority list. Attention-getting newness is. Consequently, all design and technical elements of the show strive for the unique, the unusual, and the unexpected—and always for maximum effect. The industrial is no place for formula lighting, tried and true. It is a place for the lighting designer with new ideas—if the ideas are practical and feasible. It's a hard, cold world of cash, and the impractical dreamer just doesn't last long.

Each of these four elements affects the lighting designer and the design.

For the purpose of clarity I have defined industrials as those musical/revues presented in traditional theatres (or equivalent performance spaces) with a production style similar to the Broadway musical. Several examples of treatments of industrials are shown in the figures. Figure 10.38 is the light plot (Detroit only) for the Pontiac '74 Presentation Show, with scenic design by David ("Tex") R. Ballou and lighting design by the author. Figure 10.39 is the switchboard hookup. Notice the heavy use of PAR striplights and x-rays. They are quick to hang and easy to troupe and focus. Tex Ballou had intentionally designed the production relying heavily upon light to tone, color, and modify a limited number of "flown" scenic elements. Color Figs. 90, 91, and 91a show two views of the same production number with the background changed by lighting: alternately either the (1) the backdrop or (2) the "built, three-dimensional" filigree curtain a few feet in front of it. This kind of highly effective spectacle and mobility of light and color is common in industrials.

Color Fig. 91a also presents one production number in which 10 stunning female dancers worked with reflective mylar mirror panels on casters—the movement of the mir-

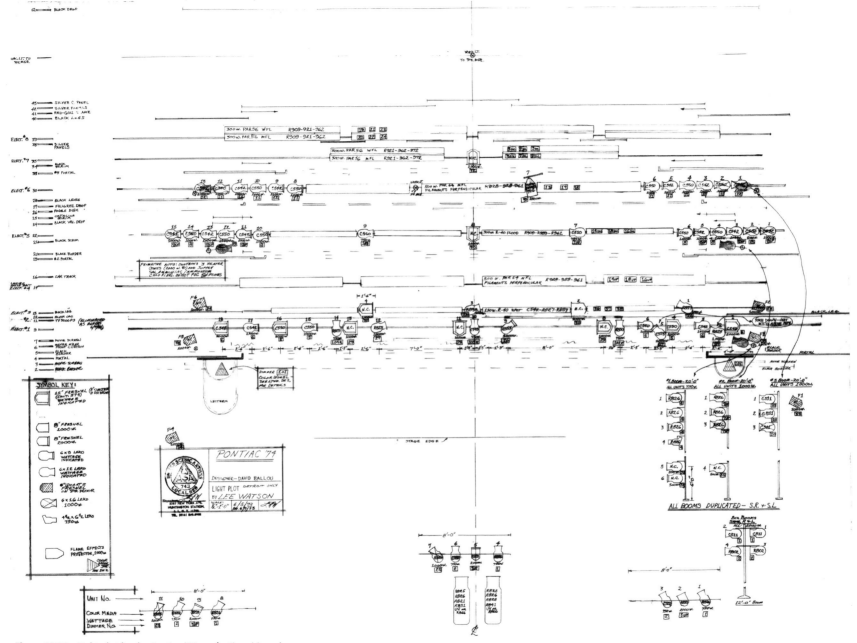

Figure 10.38 Light plot for the *Pontiac '74* production, Masonic Temple, Detroit, Michigan. Lighting design: Lee Watson; scene design: David Ballou.

"PONTIAC '74"

DIMMER NO.	UNIT NOs.	USE	COLOR	INSTRUMENTS & notes
#1	R1,4,8;BL&R1,2	PINK FRONTS	Bal.R826 Box C511	3--8x10, 750w. 4--6x12, 1000w.
#2	R3,6,10;BL&R3,4	BA FRONTS	Bal.C552 Box R802	3--8x10, 750w. 4--6x12, 1000w.
#3 UP	R2,5,9	MYLAR CURTAIN WASH	R859	3--8" Fres.,2000w.B/D
#3 DN	7th El. Xrays	SILVER PANELS, Red	R921	2--10' 300w.PAR56WFL 2--10' 300w.PAR56MFL
#4	1stL&RB1,2,3,4	"IN ONE" BOOMS, Pink	R826	2--4½x6½--2--6x9 4--6x12 All 750w.
#5	1P4,6,15,16	"IN ONE" Pipe Ends Xlts., Yellow	C550	2--8" Fres.,2000w.B/D 2--6x9, 1000w.
#6	1P1,3,17,18	"IN ONE" Pipe Ends,Xlts., Lav.	C542	2--8"Fres.,2000w. B/D 2--6x9, 1000w.
#7 UP	2ndL&RB1,2,3	"IN TWO" BOOMS, Pink	R826	2--6x9---2--6x12 2--6x16 All 1000w.
#7 DN	6th Elect. Xrays	SILVER PANELS, Blue	R962	2--10' 300w.PAR56WFL 2--10' 300w.PAR56MFL
#8	4P2,4,6,10,12,14	"IN TWO" PIPE Ends,Xlts., Yellow	C550	2--6x9---2--6x12 2--6x16 All 1000w.
#9 UP	4P1,3,5,11,13,15	"IN TWO" PIPE ENDS, Xlts., Lav.	C542	2--6x9---2--6x12 2--6x16 All 1000w.
#9 DN	6th Elect. Xrays	SILVER PANELS, Green	R972	2--10' 300w.PAR56WFL 2--10' 300w.PAR56MFL
#10	3rdL&RB1,2,3	"IN THREE" BOOMS, Pink	C511	2--6x9---2--6x12 2--6x16 All 1000w.
#11	5P2,4,6,1,10,12	"IN THREE" PIPE ENDS,Xlts., Yellow	C550	2--6x9---2--6x12 2--6x16 All 1000w.
#12	5P1,3,5,9,11,13	"IN THREE" PIPE ENDS, Xlts., Lav.	C542	2--6x9---2--6x12 2--6x16 All 1000w.
#13	5th Elect. Xrays	BKLTS.,Upstg.,Pink	R928	3--9' 500w.PAR64MFL
#14 UP	3rd Elect. Xrays	BKLTS.,Dwnstg.,Pink	R928	4--9' 500w.PAR64MFL
#14 DN	4th Elect. Xrays	FILIGREE CURTAIN, Amber	R909	4--7'6" 300w.R-40FL
#15	5th Elect. Xrays	BKLTS., Upstg.,Blue Green	R961	3--9' 500w.PAR64MFL
#16 UP	3rd Elect.,Xrays	BKLTS.,Dwnstg.,Blue Green	R961	4--9' 500w.PAR64MFL
#16 DN	4th Elect. Xrays	FILIGREE CURTAIN, Blue	R962	4--7'6" 300w.R-40FL
#17	5th Elect. Xrays	BKLTS.,Upstg.,Blue	R958	3--9' 500w.PAR64MFL
#18 UP	3rd Elect. Xrays	BKLTS.,Dwnstg.,Blue	R958	4--9' 500w.PAR64MFL
#18 DN	4th Elect. Xrays	FILIGREE CURTAIN,Blue Gn.	R959	4--7'6" 300w.R-40FL
#19	7th Elect. Xrays	BKDRP.& GLAME, Amber	R909	4--10' 300w.PAR56WFL
#20	7th Elect. Xrays	BKDRP.& GLAME, Amber	R909	4--10' 300w.PAR56MFL
#21	7th Elect. Xrays	BKDRP.& GLAME, Red	R921	4--10' 300w.PAR56WFL
#22	7th Elect. Xrays	BKDRP.& GLAME, Red	R921	4--10' 300w.PAR56MFL
#23	7th Elect. Xrays	BKDRP.& GLAME, Blue	R962	4--10' 300w.PAR56WFL
#24	7th Elect. Xrays	BKDRP.& GLAME, Blue	R962	4--10' 300w.PAR56MFL
#25	R7,11	LECTERN FRONTS	R825	2--6x16, 1000w.
#26	1P9, 2P1, 3	TV SET	C553 R077 R832	1--6x9, 1000w. 1--6x12, 1000w. 1--6x12, 1000w.
#27	1P2,5,12	TV SET	R825 C553 R825	1--6x12,1000w. 1--6x9 , 1000w. 1--6x12, 1000w.
#28	MASTER: Aux. 101-104			
#29	1P8,11,13	CAR REVEAL	NC	3--8" Fres.,1000w.B/D
#30	2P2,4; 5P13	CAR REVEAL	NC	3--8" Fres.,1000w.B/D
#31	2ndL&RB4 1stL&RB5,6	CAR SHIN BOOMS	NC	4--6x12, 500w. 2--6x9, 500w.
#32	6th Elect. C	"CATALINA" REVEAL,Dwnlt.	NC	1--8" Fres.,2000w.B/D
#33	F1,2,3	CAR SHIN BOOMS, L	NC	3--8" Fres.,1000w.B/D
#34	F4,5,6	CAR SHIN BOOMS, R	NC	3--8" Fres.,1000w.B/D
#35	5P7	MOVING FLAME EFF.PROJ.	Disc	1--1500w.Proj.,Motor
#36	2nd Elect. Xrays	BORDERLTS., Lav.	C542	4--7'6" 150w.R-40SP
#37	2nd Elect. Xrays	BORDERLTS., Pink	R827	4--7'6" 150w.R-40SP
#38	2nd Elect. Xrays	BORDERLTS., Blue	R857	4--7'6" 150w.R-40SP
AUX. #101-104: Mastered by Dimmer #28:				
#101	L&R Lecterns	COLOR WHEELS		See Designer
#102	1P7	MIRROR BALL Lt.	C510	1--6x12, 750w.
#103	1P10	POOL SPEC., C	C549	1--6x12, 750w.
#104	Mirror Ball Motor			
#104R	1P14	POOL SPEC., R	R829	1--6x12, 750w.
#105	4P7	MIRROR BALL Lt.	C510	1--6x12, 750w.
#106	4P9	MIRROR BALL Lt.	C510	1--6x12, 750w.

ON HOT SWITCHES: CO_2 TRIGGER; MIRROR BALL MOTOR

Figure 10.39 Pontiac '74 switchboard hookup.

rors was carefully choreographed, as was the movement of the dancers. The costumes were semitransparent and quite revealing. The costumes were pink, and I used only heavy pink backlight and pink crosslight, with nothing from the front. Consequently, the audience saw mostly idealized faceless female figures. The double presence of bosoms and posteriors — seen from the front and reflected in the mirrors — was considered quite effective by the producers. When the dancers formed a final silhouetted lineup at the curtain line, *everything* was visible except faces. Color Fig. 91*b* also shows the all-important "reveal" (one of several in the production) of that year's new cars. A designer who can't handle car illumination (which involves avoiding unwanted reflections and adding crystal-clear crisp beauty) shouldn't do auto industrials!

Color Fig. 92 shows Imero Fiorentino's lighting design for the *Milliken Fabrics Industrial Show,* presented annually the first two weeks of June to 30,000 top retail executives in the garment business in the Grand Ballroom of the Waldorf-Astoria Hotel in New York City. Color Fig. 92*a* is from the *Anheuser-Busch Command Performance* show in San Francisco. Designed and produced by George Honchar of Imero Fiorentino Associates with Imero Fiorentino as lighting consultant and Marilyn Lowey as lighting director, many of the elements pointed out in illustrations of other industrials are evident: the use of light for spectacle, change, and mobility, as well as focus. Color Fig. 92*b* and Fig. 10.40 show the *Miss U.S.A. Beauty Pageant* (which is also televised) in Biloxi, Mississippi, with Carl Vitelli of the Fiorentino Associates staff as the lighting director.

For the designer who does not demand pure "art" in his lighting design efforts but does want to be involved in theatre, industrials are indeed a lucrative and challenging opportunity.[300]

Trade Shows

Trade shows are similar to industrials, but they are not normally presented in theatres and theatre-like places. Trade shows take place at regional or national sales meetings, usually in ballrooms, at some 28,000 meeting per year. In the United States alone approximately 26 million people

Figure 10.40 *Miss U.S.A. Beauty Pageant,* Biloxi, Mississippi. Lighting director: Carl Vitelli of Imero Fiorentino Associates.

attended 250,000 different gatherings, accounting for $15 billion spent in 1978. Hotel and convention facility ballrooms (or any other large room) do *not* normally have either high ceilings or stages (as such). The lighting designer has two additional challenges. First, he or she must be technically gifted and imaginative to cope adequately with the lack of height for mounting lights and the absence of all of the accessories of a stage (proscenium, fly space, adequate power, etc.); second, frequently the room is booked either immediately before or after a trade show performance, which calls for all of the mobility and efficiency of setup which is required for concert lighting. Trade shows do not often have elaborate scenery. Members of a trade show cast, rather than being working professionals, are sales executives and engineers from the product's higher echelon. There may be no costumes, no choreography, and/or no book. There is always, however, a script and a product, and frequently there is a film or other graphics/charts/demonstration material and special lighting. The "reveal" may or may not be presented in the traditional form. These "shows" are halfway between a sales convention and theatre. Business has long since learned that a little "flash" from the world of show business keeps everyone awake and presents the sales message to those assembled with maximum effectiveness.

Conventions

Almost all industries have an annual gathering. During 1983, 53 million delegates attended a total of 100,000 meetings in 170 cities in the United States and spent over $20 billion.[301] In the world of show business, the "big" conventions are the national meetings of the United States Institute for Theatre Technology (USITT), the National Association of Broadcasters, the Society of Motion Picture and Television Engineers (SMPTE) Exposition, the IES conference, and IES's Theatre, Television and Film Lighting (TTFL) and Lightfair (International Association of Lighting Designers [IALD]) conferences. Several of these organizations also have regional meetings.

Manufacturers flock to trade shows and spend a good deal of money to rent exhibit space. Franc Dutton's article (cited in footnote 300) explains the great sales effectiveness of these trade shows and their importance to the manufacturer/producer/distributor. At the show, the products of all large competing firms are available in the same exhibit space. Each firm exhibits its new products and tries to attract customers. This is the place for a company to "put its best foot forward." Enter the lighting designer. All of the things mentioned about sales lighting previously apply here. The trade show may only run three to five days, but it is a critical time, and effective display/sales/lighting is important.

Trade shows are a big factor not only in our industry but in *all* industries. Name for me an established professional who has not designed lighting (and frequently obtained and put the equipment up himself) for trade shows in the textile, furniture, floral—you name it—business and I will be certain that the designer is either shy, independently wealthy, unimaginative, or lazy. Lighting designers' theatrical ability to attract crowds and move merchandise through use of light has provided many practitioners with unexpected additional cash that enabled them to design that low-paying but artistically rewarding Off-Off-Off-Broadway show friends had been insisting they do.[302]

300 "The Milliken Industrial Show," Lighting Design + Application, vol. 5, no. 7 (July 1975), pp. 28–31. Illustrated discussion of Fiorentino's lighting which won him the IES Award of Excellence.

Gail Hardman, "Triumph Acclaim—A Theatrical Triumph!", TABS, vol. 39, no. 1 (May 1982), pp. 26–27. Illus., color. A graphic narration with color photographs of a British industrial show with elaborate lighting design for the 1982 Triumph Acclaim Auto.

Richard Andrews, "Trade Off," Cue, no. 7 (Sept./Oct. 1980), pp. 4, 6–7. Illus., color. Light plot, text, and photographs for British touring industrial shows.

Richard Pilbrow, "The Smile on the Face of the Tiger," Cue, no. 11 (May/June 1981), pp. 27–28. Illus., color. Theatre Projects design of the Leyland bus show.

"Fiorentino's Lighting for Industrial Shows: Details on the 1972 Buick Show," Theatre Crafts, (Oct. 1973), pp. 11–14, 34–37. Well-illustrated, detailed discussion of Fiorentino's work.

James L. Moody, "Corporate Theatre," Lighting Dimensions, vol. 2, no. 9 (Nov. 1978), pp. 31–39. Well-illustrated (including color illustrations and a light plot) with good text by Moody about a Sundance Lighting industrial.

Franc Dutton, "Trade Shows: Money Well Spent?" Lighting Dimensions, vol. 3, no. 3 (Mar. 1979), pp. 18–20. An excellent analysis of the fiscal effect of trade shows upon the manufacturer; includes charts and facts.

Gene E. Diskey and Mary B. Moore, "Trade Show Techniques—Lighting for Video Magnification," Lighting Design + Application, vol. 9, no. 3 (Mar. 1979), pp. 39–42. A trade show in the Dallas Convention Center for Mary Kay Cosmetics using extensive video magnification. Detailed text; numerous color illustrations.

Mary Lucier, "Industrials, The Theatre of Persuasion," Theatre Crafts, vol. 15, no. 1 (Jan. 1981), pp. 12–29. Illus. Special report. See particularly "Lighting—Seeing the Product," pp. 26, 74–76, illus., and Ronn Smith, "Myron Sanft: A Historical Perspective," p. 79 (gives a detailed history of industrial shows).

"A Conversation with Cassandra Henning and Coca-Cola USA," Lighting Dimensions, vol. 4, no. 6 (June 1980), pp. 16–17.

Cassandra Henning, "Developing an Indoor Spectacular for Coca-Cola," Lighting Dimensions, vol. 4, no. 6 (June 1980), pp. 18–22, 49. Illus., color.

John Hagan, "Lighting the Industrial Show," Lighting Dimensions, vol. 4, no. 6 (June 1980), pp. 25, 28–33. Illus.

Robert L. Barber, "Industrial Theatre," Lighting Dimensions, vol. 4, no. 6 (June 1980), pp. 34–35, 37, 41. Illus.

Mike Williams, "The Boston Flower Show," Lighting Dimensions, vol. 6, no. 1 (Jan./Feb. 1982), pp. 26–28. Illus., color. Includes light plot.

"Hard Graft Gets Acclaim," ABTT News, July 1984, p. 16. Account of the British Austin Rover Industrial show, reprinted from Audio Visual monthly.

"Industrial Theatre," ABTT News, July 1984, p. 17. More about the Austin Rover show.

"See What You Can Hear: In This Exhibit Describing Communication at the Olympics, Light was the Medium of the Message," Lighting Dimensions, vol. 8, no. 6 (Sept./Oct. 1984), pp. 47–51. Illus., color. Detailed description of the AT&T exhibit at the 1984 California Olympics.

Stephen Chambers, "Foot Notes," Cue, Jan./Feb. 1986 (#39), pp. 9–10. A very amusing description of convention shows by a British stage manager.

Barbara J. Knox, "The Javits Convention Center, Paul Marantz Lights New York's Latest 'Big Deal,'" Lighting Dimensions, vol. 10, no. 4 (July/Aug. 1968), pp. 32–33, 50. Illus.

J. A. Chrysler, "Meeting Places—Metro Toronto Convention Centre," International Lighting Review, 4th quarter, 1985, pp. 144–147. Illus., color.

"Hands Across the Water," Lighting Dimensions, vol. 10, no. 1 (Jan./Feb. 1986), pp. 28–34, 36–38, 40. Illus., color. All about designer Stephen Bickford's lighting of the Toyota automobile show for Japan.

"Theatrical," Lighting Design + Application, vol. 15, no. 10 (Oct. 1985), p. 47. Illus. Three IES Guth Awards of Merit designs.

Mike Williams, "Birthday Bash for an American Classic: John Ingram Lights Up the Coca-Cola Centennial in Atlanta," Lighting Dimensions, vol. 10, no. 5 (Sept./Oct. 1986), pp. 42–47, 60–61. Illus., color. Includes light plot.

"New Rover Walks on Water," Light + Sound International, vol. 1, no. 8 (July 1986), pp. 28–30. Illus., color. The British industrial show featuring the 1986 Rover automobile.

"Michael Faraday's One-Man Show: Alan Russell Explains the Background to the 1986/87 Faraday Lecture, Currently Touring the UK," Light + Sound International, vol. 2, no. 4 (April 1987), pp. 36–37. Illus., color. See also "Peter Clarke," pp. 41–42, for an interview with a prominent British fashion show lighting designer.

"The Toyota Dealers' Presentation: Made from the Right Stuff," Lighting Dimensions, vol. 6, no. 4 (May/June 1981), pp. 33–36. Illus., color. Includes light plot.

"The Phoenix International Premier," Lighting Design + Application, vol. 12, no. 6 (June 1982), pp. 16–21. Illus., color. Computer design–oriented industrial show.

Michael Sommers, "C. Henning Studios," Theater Crafts, vol. 22, no. 3 (March 1988), pp. 57, 74–75. Illus., color. More about Cassandra Henning's shop in Atlanta, one of the largest in the country producing industrial shows primarily.

[301] Walter Roessing, "America's Amazing (New) Convention Centers," Delta Air's Sky magazine, vol. 13, no. 8 (Aug. 1984), pp. 80–82. Illus., color. A survey of the convention field.

[302] "America Gets Together, A Special Section on Meetings and Conventions," TWA Ambassador, vol. 12, no. 8 (Aug. 1979), pp. 51–54, 56, 71–72. Factual information about the size and nature of the convention business.

Richard Thompson, Ted Jones, Joseph Tawil, and James Davis, "Supply, Demand, and the Performing Arts: A Critical Look at the Business of Supplying Show Business," Theatre Design + Technology, no. 43, (Winter 1975), p. 27.

The more important trade shows of interest to lighting designers include:

Show Tech by the International Trade Fair and Congress for Entertainment Technology, Equipment, and Management. Usually held in May. In Berlin in 1988. See: Lighting Dimensions, vol. 12, no. 2 (March 1988), p. 14.

Discotec, usually held in November. In Düsseldorf, West Germany in 1988.

Theatrical Dealers Association, held in Anaheim, California, in 1988 in conjunction with USITT. World Light Show, a portion of the Hanover (West Germany) Fair Industry, held April 20–27 in 1989, with over 300 exhibitors. See: Lighting Dimensions, vol. 12, no. 2 (March 1988), p. 22.

Lighting World International, held in April variously in New York City, Los Angeles, and Chicago. Now in a state of flux since both the IES and IALD pulled out (1989), leaving only National Expositions (New York City) to "run the show." Remains to be seen whether this large and (until now) successful architectural lighting trade show and conference will survive.

Lightfair, now sponsored by IES and IALD in New York City. It replaces Lighting World International (1989) and promises to draw away most architectural lighting exhibitors and panelists.

SEIL, the 7th international trade show of equipment and technology for the entertainment industry and leisure places is held in Paris, France, usually in April. In 1989 it was combined with the 4th Theatrical Services Exhibition in Paris, April 9–12, with 300 exhibitors and 20,000 visitors expected. See: "Readying for Paris. SEIL, April 9–12, 1989," CUE International, no. 58 (March/April 1989), p. 40–41.

ABTT, the trade show and conference of the Association of British Theatre Technicians, has been growing each year. It is held in or near London in April or May. See: "The ABTT Trade Show 89, May 18–20," in CUE International, no. 59 (May/June 1989), p. 34.

International Laser Display Association, held in Stone Mountain, Georgia in November in 1988.

International Hotel/Motel and Restaurant Show, held in New York City in November in 1988.

Nightclub & Bar Expo, sponsored by Night Club & Bar magazine, held in Oxford, Mississippi, in 1989.

Visual Merchandising, Store Planning and Design Market, held their 93rd Conference in New York City in December, 1989.

International Lighting Exposition, held in May in 1988 in Toronto. The first of the big Canadian shows and quite successful.

Electric 88, held by the International Electrical Exposition and Congress in New York City in June in 1988.

Other Careers in Lighting (Besides Design)

Manufacturing, Sales, and Engineering

Approximately one-third of those who study lighting design in school end up as employees of the multitude of firms which design, build, manufacture, and sell lighting equipment — be it for TV, film, theatre, or discos. They may be employed by one of the big manufacturers, or they may be part of the even larger group of regional distributors and sales/service firms. The hours are predictable (if sometimes lengthy, as in all aspects of show business); the income steady; and having such a job is certainly superior to going hungry because of unemployment. The United States is filled with first-quality lighting-related firms that employ people who enjoy their occupations and perform their jobs exceedingly well. Many, many of these faithful and devoted people have incomes and lifestyles that far surpass those of any but the top few established designers. Designing will always be the tip of the iceberg in the lighting business. The remainder that is "underwater" is what keeps everything afloat!

One way people trained in lighting design get into non-design aspects of lighting is by developing a product — for example, a fine new lighting unit or switchboard — and going into business producing and selling that product. This approach can succeed, but it is important to know that an idea alone is not enough. Three of the most imaginative and inventive engineers in the United States are Ariel Davis, Edison Price, and Steve Skirpan, and most people involved in lighting envy both their broadness of vision and their ability to turn ideas into the "hard machinery" designers need. Yet Ariel Davis has never exhibited outstanding strength as either a businessman nor as a hard-headed administrator. Hard-headed business types have taken over firms he has created, along with his innovations.

Many smaller sales/service/distribution firms survive down through the years because they have learned the secret of cordial, efficient *service*. Somehow they get the customer what is needed when it is needed. And the same customers come back year after year. A person trained in lighting who can provide such service and enjoys the work may find it more satisfying and more profitable to use light-ing knowledge in this area rather than in a hopeless pursuit of "designing." Such people are needed.

When one enters the world of the key manufacturing firms (Kliegl, Colortran, Strand, etc.), there are available many really good positions for administrators/executives, salesmen, and engineers. Since I became involved in Purdue University's MFA program in "Theatre Engineering" originated by Professor I. Van Phillips, we have noted a constant stream of inquiries to both of us from these firms for "an engineer who knows something about theatre." Such engineers are in very short supply. The manufacturing firms are constantly designing, developing, and improving highly sophisticated electronic equipment. Not only that, but they must provide drawings and specifications for clients on numerous new jobs, and they run their own servicing and repair operations. Certified engineers who can cope with, appreciate, and understand "show folks" and their needs are not being produced in any adequate quantity by M.I.T., Stanford, Rice, Purdue, or other schools of engineering. Furthermore, pay scales are such that graduating engineers are lured to other parts of industry at rates the theatre firms cannot hope to match. The entertainment firm's only salvation frequently lies in locating a qualified engineer who has been "bitten by the theatre bug" (or disco "bug," etc.) and will thus be available at a price the firm can afford.

Several prominent theatre names *are* engineers. Tom Lemons graduated from Purdue University in Electrical Engineering. He went on to be the co-developer of the tungsten halogen ("quartz") lamp while employed at Sylvania. Now Tom Lemons Associates in Salem, Massachusetts, is a group of busy and prominent theatre engineering consultants. Lemons has been the leading proponent of HMI (metallogen) lamp usage in this country. George T. Howard of Howard Associates in Los Angeles is also an engineer, as are Lenny Auerbach, Theodore (Ted) Fuchs, and Richard Thompson. There are many others.

A letter from Fred M. Wolff, who is retired from his position of many years as production manager with Century Lighting (during the Edward Kook days), gives his perspective:

> I am a mongrel. I have a BS in electrical engineering, an MFA in theatre production, and a year of architecture in between. This

Light + Sound Show, sponsored by PLASA (Professional Light and Sound Assn.) held in London in 1989. This is the largest British trade show for nightclub, disco, and concert lighting experts. Held in September. The 1989 version was their 12th year.

AIA, the annual gathering of the American Institute of Architects. Held in New York City in May in 1988.

Euroluce, held annually in Milan, Italy, in conjunction with the Milan furniture fair in September. In 1988, held September 12th.

Pan Pacific Lighting Exposition, held in San Francisco in September 1988.

Lighting Dimensions International, held in November in Dallas in 1988 and in Nashville in 1989, is perhaps the newest but one of the most successful trade show/conferences. See: "LDI89 Set For November 17–19 in Nashville," CUE International, no. 58 (March/April 1989), p. 46.

USITT, the annual trade show and conference of the U.S. Institute for Theater Technology, is held in April (sometimes May) and moves to various cities in the U.S. and Canada. This trade show for theater people is one of the larger ones. Held in Milwaukee in 1990.

NAB, the trade show of the National Association of Broadcasters, has been known to draw between 40,000 and 50,000 attendees. Usually meets in Las Vegas, Nevada, in April/May and is the largest trade show in the U.S. in the entertainment field. See: "Broadcast Views, NAB Meets April 9–12 in Las Vegas," Lighting Dimensions, vol. 12, no. 3 (April 1988), pp. 22, 24.

Photokina, or the World's Fair of Imaging Systems, was held in Cologne, West Germany, in October in 1988. It is the largest of the European trade shows dealing with film and television.

SMPTE, the annual trade show of the Society of Motion Picture and Television Engineers, was held in New York City in 1988 in October. Concerned with television and motion picture work, it moves to different cities.

International Lighting Exposition is the Canadian trade show. Sponsored by IES (Toronto Section) and Kerrwil Publications (publishers of Lighting magazine), it was first held May 25–27, 1988, at the Toronto Convention Centre. See: "Canada's First:

Internaional Lighting Show Set for Toronto in 1988," Lighting, *vol. 1, no. 1 (June 1987), p. 26.*

SIB/MAGIS. *Held in Italy, the SIB International Exhibition of Equipment and Technology for Discotheques and Danceballs has been combined with the MAGIS Exhibition of Equipment and Technology for Theatres, Cinemas, and Show Business. The 1989 edition opened April 10th. The exhibition is now in its 7th year (1989) and in 1988 attracted over 400 exhibitors and 13,000 visitors from 40 countries. See: "SIB/MAGIS Preview,"* CUE International, *no. 57 (January/February 1989), p. 9. See also: Andrew Shearer, "SIB/MAGIS and SIEL Ready for 89,"* CUE International, *no. 58 (March/April 1989), pp. 36–39.*

Showlight, *last held in Amsterdam in May 1989, is an international television, theatre and film lighting colloquium for professional lighting designers. The accompanying trade show by manufacturers tends to be on the small side. See: "Showlight 89 in Amsterdam,"* CUE International, *no. 59 (May/June 1989), pp. 32–33. See also: "Showlight 89 in Amsterdam,"* CUE International, *no. 58 (March/April 1989), p. 44.*

International Auditorium and Arena Managers' Annual Conference and Trade Show, *held in July/Aug. in Las Vegas, Nevada.*

International Hotel/Motel and Restaurant Show *(the 73rd in 1989), held in November, in New York City in 1989.*

Restaurant Hotel International Exposition, *formerly in Chicago, is now moved to Los Angeles.*

Showbiz Expo, *held in Hollywood in April, deals largely with the film industry.*

Further information concerning the annual dates and locations of these and other trade shows of interest to lighting designers can regularly be found in such magazines as Lighting Dimensions, *with particulars on whom to contact for further information.*

[303] *Letter to the author dated June 21, 1979.*

[304] *"U.S. Lighting Device Shipments to Total $29 Billion by 1995,"* Lighting Design + Application, *vol. 13, no. 4 (April 1983), pp. 4–5. Predicasts, Inc., is located at 11001 Cedar Ave., Cleveland, OH 44106. Their annual reports are available for $900, and an international version can be obtained from England.*

took place at a time when such cross breeding was automatically suspect. And yet, it all ties in with the field of lighting. I helped write the last edition of "Artificial Light and Its Application" for the Westinghouse Lamp Division. I have also written articles on "The Illumination of Jewelry and Tableware," "Methods of Controlling the Intensity of Incandescent Lamps," and "Simplified Solid State Dimmers." My major work has been in the design and production of lighting and lighting control equipment. Isn't it better if the person who is responsible for the equipment knows what the person who will use it wants to achieve? I think so.[303]

Nothing more need be said here about the personality qualities which move employable individuals into administration or sales or engineering. You either "have it" or you don't. Those who do, and find contentment therein, will find their theatre training backgrounds invaluable. The *really* talented who can "deliver" are employable anywhere. Lighting training only adds to their marketability. Predicasts, Inc., a Cleveland-based business information and market research firm, reported that the 1980 manufacturers' shipments of lighting devices amounted to $9 billion and predicts a $29 billion market by 1995. There's a huge market and a lot of jobs out there for those trained in lighting design who choose to move into the supply side of the industry![304]

Theatre Building Consulting

Consulting has already been discussed twice in this chapter, but there is still another group of highly specialized consultants: those whose consultation services involve the renovation or construction of new theatre buildings/public performance places or television studios. What do theatre consultants do? USITT, in an official policy statement in 1971, said:

> Moreover, a theatre is often a public trust, financed through contributions and designed to serve and enrich its home community or the educational institution to which it is attached. It therefore demands the same, if not greater degree of specialized knowledge than do facilities in other fields, especially in view of the rapid development of technology and practice in recent years. The consultant, in close liaison with the architect, owner, and where possible, the user, can provide supplementary information and guidance even when all parties concerned have a high degree of expertise in the field. The consultant brings to the project a valuable objectivity which can do much to assist in

creating a truly effective theatre and a viable program within the structure.

A theatre consultant is a person or firm offering consultation services for a fee in one or more fields related to any facet of the theatre and the performance arts. It is the function of the consultant to provide the owner and the architect knowledge and judgement in matters of use, equipment, and operational techniques in order to arrive at the most satisfactory solution possible in the planning and equipment of a theatre building and in scheduling operations appropriate to the theatre program. His ability to do this stems from his experience with the working theatre and an active interest in the problems of theatre operation, programming, architecture, and technology.[305]

Webster's Dictionary defines a *consultant* as an "advisor." Consultants *may* be but usually are not licensed architects or engineers. Licensing for consultants does not yet exist.[306] The consultant is acknowledged to be an expert about theatres. If a consultant is not an architect or an engineer, his or her training was generally within the art form of performance/theatre, although it may not have been strongly concentrated in the areas of lighting and lighting design. The consultant should be receptive to untried solutions and familiar with new approaches, yet have a comprehensive knowledge of existing materials and their availability and adaptability. Above all the consultant should have an established track record for dependability, service, and "teamplay" with architects, owners, contractors, and other consultant specialists (acousticians, for example).

USITT adds:

> [T]he consultant may assist with the design of the new facilities or the improvement of existing structures. . . . The consultant must have experience with practical theatre and ample knowledge of theatre architecture, administration, education and technology. . . . In the process of advising the client, the consultant is obliged to explain the advantages and disadvantages inherent in various forms current in the theatre, including differences in cost of construction of one form as opposed to another, and the degree to which each is supportive of varying program modes and objectives. He has a similar obligation in his recommendations of specialized equipment. It is one of his basic responsibilities to keep abreast of current developments in order to fulfill this obligation.[307]

It should be kept firmly in mind that rarely is there a "lighting consultant" *only* on a new or a rebuilt theatre building. There have been such cases, but generally the client also hires a "theatre consultant" who is thoroughly qualified to handle many areas of consultation: overall building design and use advice, sightlines, materials, the entire range of specialized theatre equipment (not just lighting and switchboards but also shops/construction/machinery, etc.). The fact that many theatre individuals with an established reputation in lighting have served as consultants does *not* imply that each was not equally well versed in other areas of theatre technology. Van Phillips writes:

Many young people make this mistake of assuming that having simple experience and an idea of what *they* would desire in a building makes them a consultant. In consulting, the owner/user's needs (generally referred to as the "program") establish the base, much as a script relates to a play. To ignore these needs, no matter how brilliantly to fulfill personal goals, will ultimately court failure.

There are many approaches to establishing one's self as a consultant: (1) by working for an established consultant then slowly forming your own business: (2) by holding another job (generally in production) and slowly taking on some consulting work, ever increasing in scope and frequency until it can represent a full-time income: (3) by reaching the top of a production field so that you can use your reputation to add a consulting line (e.g., the way Jean Rosenthal did). Each of these routes, however, takes time, and most established consultants have 10 to 20 years of experience before they become self-sustaining financially. The consultant generally starts with small projects such as community or high school theatres and by building a track record graduates to bigger projects.[308]

There are many types of lighting consultants. The subject was first covered in this volume under "Landscape Architecture." All that was presented previously concerning architectural lighting consultants and designers (including many provisions of the sample contract from Horton Associates) also applies here.

USITT stated:

Depending upon specific qualifications, consultants can be divided into two broad categories:

(a) General or coordinating consultant: one who works on the overall plan and concept of a theatre, assisting with the arrangement of spaces, guiding in the selection of lighting, rigging, and other specialized equipment and other operational needs. He or the client may call upon additional specialists in specific areas according to the needs of the project.

(b) Specialist consultant: one who has undertaken particular study and experience in a single aspect of theatre architecture or technology, education or administration. Specialists are available in such diverse fields as acoustics, lighting, seating, rigging, administration, community relations, fund-raising, and audience development.[305]

The process of consultation has been divided into five distinct phases by the firm Jones and Phillips. These, and the approximate portion of total time consumed, are:

Phase 1: Design and concept (20 percent)

Phase 2: Specification and bid preparation (50 percent)

Phase 3: Bid review/bid letting (10 percent)

Phase 4: Construction/installation (15 percent)

Phase 5: First major program and review phase (5 percent)

Firms other than Jones and Phillips might separate the tasks differently or evaluate the time consumed on each phase differently. For a good consultant, consulting is highly profitable. Consulting is an important aspect of the lighting design business for those few individuals qualified to participate in helping to create better performance places for the future of our industry. Van Phillips states an added value when he writes:

A building, unlike a production, usually has a life spanning years — even decades. Mistakes and poor judgement therefore may come back to haunt the consultant long after a poor production has been struck and forgotten. Even wise choices that have not allowed for future growth may appear at some point to be a fault, yet the consultant's name is on the building plans for better or worse. No consultant can put a disclaimer on a building's face, and even though you might like to put up a sign saying "Did you know the lighting budget was cut by $100,000.00 to put in marble bathroom fixtures!" it cannot be done. Being forced to say "it looked like a good idea at the time" will not get many new clients.[308]

Communication Forms, Techniques, Procedures, and Practices. A typical consulting presentation is shown here. These drawings are only selected examples of the much larger mass of bids, drawings, and consultations (with constant careful attention to detail) necessary in the overall job.

[305] "The Role and Function of a Theatre Consultant," Theatre Design + Technology, no. 27 (Dec. 1971), pp. 11–12. An official USITT policy statement by the Institute's Executive Council, the result of a series of committees chaired by Richard Thompson, David Weiss, David Thayer, and Joel Rubin.

[306] About licensing, USITT writes:

Licensing . . . is generally not required unless specific engineering or architectural work is done by the consultant. . . . At this time, the legal responsibility for professional services does not reside in an unlicensed consultant but with the architect or engineer who must be licensed and practice under law. This should be understood by both those who seek to engage consultants and those who provide such services (see footnote 305).

Van Phillips writes: "You have a legal liability for counsel given, services in the contract, expectations created and appraisals made." All drawing and papers processed by Jones and Phillips (as with most firms) carry the printed disclaimer: "Contract conditions place the responsibility for dimensions, coordination, and compliance with contract documents on the contractor." Their standard contract reads as follows:

It is understood that Jones & Phillips Associates, like most Theatre Consultants, are NOT licensed Architects or Engineers. Because of this, our services are advisory only, and specific reference to type, size, distribution of structural, mechanical, and electrical components will be left to qualified Architects and Engineers as hired by the owner or his representatives. . . . We will provide advice pertaining to expectations for performance, suggesting probable demands, logistic concerns, and relationships so that Architects & Engineers may develop their specifications. In some cases we will suggest solutions or equipment types to be considered for inclusion because of proven use elsewhere. In such cases the Architect and Engineers must review these items for appropriateness to the situation for safe operation. (From pages 2–3 of the Jones & Phillips contract, supplied by the firm and in my possession.)

Such contractual disclaimers arise because many noted theatre consultants are neither licensed architects nor engineers. An additional problem for them becomes the obtaining of adequate risk liability insurance.

[307] "The Role and Function of a Theatre Consultant," p. 11, op. cit. (see footnote 305).

[308] Letter from Professor Van Phillips to this author.

[309] See "Roger L. Stevens Center for the Performing Arts," Theatre Crafts, vol. 13, no. 4 (Sept. 1979), pp. 73, 120, 122.

[310] Harold C. Schonberg, "Have Cultural Centers Benefitted the Arts?" The New York Times, Sunday, July 10, 1983, Arts and Leisure section, pp. 1, 26.

[311] Michael A. Neighbors, How to Become a Successful Consultant in Lighting Engineering. Published by Association of Technology, Rt. 2, Box 448, East Springs, TN 37330. A spiral-bound, mimeographed work, approximately 200 pages in length. This is not a guide to the technology of consulting. It does cover business basics, selling, contracts, interviews, legal matters, and a wealth of readily readable tips concerning the business of consulting. Since it is the only work available about consulting, it is a starting point. It is well written and contains much pertinent information.

H. de Ranitz and A. F. M. Gils, "Theatres: Music Theatre, Dance Theatre — The Haque," International Lighting Review, 39th year, 1st quarter (1988), pp. 25–31. Illus., color.

"IALD Citation Award: The Chicago Theater: A Return to Glory," Lightview International, vol. 1, no. 4 (Winter 1989), p. 3. Illus., color. Details of the restoration of the Chicago Theater, an IALD Award Winner in 1988.

Ian Mackintosh, "How the Committees and Consultants Hijacked Theater Architecture in the '60s Plus a Rescue Plan for the Late '90s," CUE, no. 50 (November/December 1987), pp. 7–10. An important article, excerpted from the December Theatre Crafts by one of England's leading theatre architectural consultants.

Bob Anderson, "Theatre Design Consultants," CUE, no. 52 (March/April 1988), pp. 6–9. Illus. Another important article about British practices, John Wyckham, and the Society of Theatre Consultants. A useful description of the evolution of JWA (John Wyckham Associates).

"Renovations/85," Theatre Crafts, vol. 19, no. 10 (Dec. 1985), pp. 20–60, 62–75. Illus. Lengthy articles by nine expert consultants with examples of renovations. A wealth of usable information.

Robert T. Loewy, "Renovations — The Fabulous Fox," International Lighting Review, 4th quarter, 1985, pp. 116–122. Illus., color. Reno-vation of the Fox (movie) Theatre in Atlanta, Georgia.

Patricia MacKay, "Who's Who in Theatre Consulting," Theatre Crafts, vol. 17, no. 5 (May 1983). Illus. Theme of entire issue. Includes articles by Susan Levi Wallach. Describes many consultants, with illustrations of their work (but misses some key ones). Articles on insurance law. For 21 firms lists date of founding, fee structure, and major jobs in the last few years, as well as architects and engineers. Extensive illustrations and plans. Included are Jules Fisher, Nananne Porcher, Roger Morgan, George Howard, and Richard Pilbrow. Useful basic reference tool for consultants.

Revised list of consultants who are members of the American Society of Theatre Consultants, in Theatre Crafts, vol. 17, no. 7 (Aug./Sept. 1983), p. 14. Lists addresses and telephone numbers.

Theatre Consultants, First Edition, 1973. N.Y.; U.S. Institute for Theatre Technology Publ.; 1973. 60 pp. Listed firms and individuals experienced in the problems of theatre operation, programming, architecture, and technology. Now somewhat out of date and out of print.

Bob Anderson, "Theatre Consultants," Cue, #45 (Jan./Feb. 1987), pp. 7–9. Illus. The most definitive British article about England's numerous theatrical consultants.

S. Leonard Auerbach, "Architecture 86: In Search of Excellence," Theatre Crafts, vol. 20, no. 10 (Dec. 1986), pp. 17 ff. Main theme of entire issue. Illus., color. Includes "Orange County Performing Arts Center," by Douglass F. Sisk; "Where the Money Comes From" and "Working With the General Contractor," by Michael Sommers; "Marquis Theatre: Broadway's Newest Baby"; "Horton Plaza Lyceum Theatre: Only in Southern California," by Alice M. Hale: "F. J. Harquail Theatre: The Caymans Pearl In a Shell," by Michèle La Rue; "Bidding the Building," by Hisan X. Pert; "Alabama Shakespeare Festival: Montgomery's Estate of the Art"; "Fire Safety Systems"; "Selecting the Seats"; and "The World Theater Rejuvenation in St. Paul." Issue loaded with good text and graphics, most useful for any consultant.

ABTT, Theatres: Planning Guide for Design and Adaptation. London; ABTT (Association of British Theatre Technicians, 4 Great Pulteney

Figures 10.41 and 10.42 are the work of Jean Rosenthal Associates (Clyde Nordheimer, Nananne Porcher, and others) for the rebuilt Roger L. Stevens Center for the Performing Arts in Winston-Salem, North Carolina.[309] Formerly the Old Carolina Theatre (see Fig. 10.43), built in 1929 for vaudeville and film, the theatre is now the property of the North Carolina School for the Arts. The former 2,500-seat proscenium theatre was modernized by architects Newman, Calloway, Johnson, Van Ettan, Winfree Associates to house 1,500 seats at a cost of $6 million. Piedmont Publishing Co. gave the old theatre and hotel to the school. The stage house was enlarged, front light positions added, a new proscenium added, one balcony eliminated, sight lines improved for the remaining balcony, and a sound and light control booth added, along with dressing rooms and storage and wardrobe space. The proscenium was enlarged and an orchestra pit lift added. A portable acoustical shell for musical performances was added. The architects redesigned the exterior and added a lobby restaurant. Former hotel space became lecture halls, studios, and offices. Nananne Porcher of Jean Rosenthal Associates was the primary consultant. Figure 10.44 shows the projected exterior of the building. This type of consulting project is as common a consulting commission as is a project for an all-new theatre building complex.

Theatre consulting has become one of the most profitable areas for many trained in lighting design. Prior to the creation of the Lincoln Center in New York City in 1962 there were few national community cultural centers. Today there are some 2,000 arts/cultural centers in the United States. They often combine one or more theatres (or performance spaces) with libraries, museums, and art galleries in a revitalized city center.[310] And more are being built every year. Because most architectural firms (with a few firms as exceptions) can expect to design only one or two theatres over a great many years, it has become necessary for them to turn to the specialized knowledge and advice of theatre consultants (just as they turn to specialists when they get the very rare assignment of designing a hospital). Consulting provides many employment opportunities for those trained in lighting design who choose to and are qualified to move into this specialized area.[311]

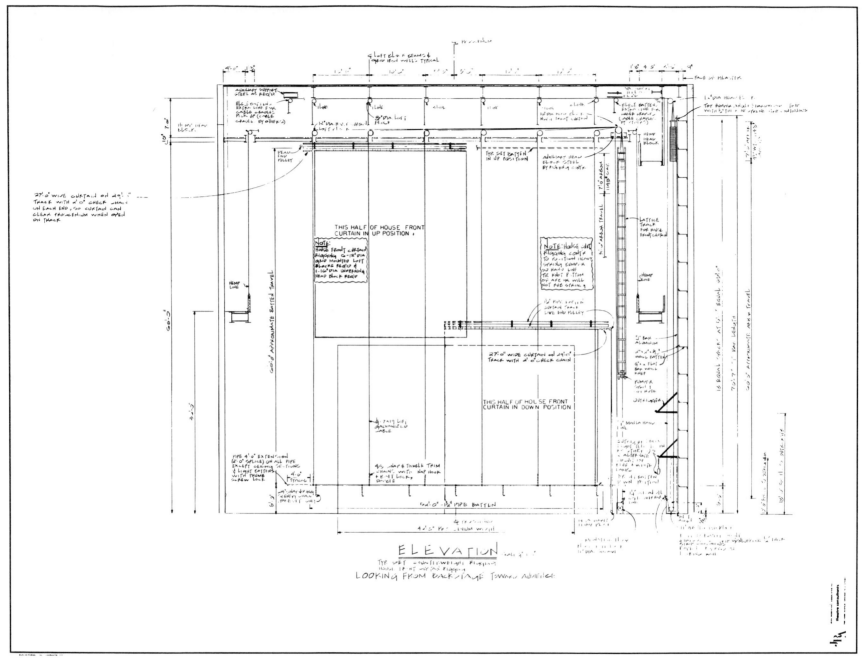

Figure 10.41 Roger L. Stevens Center, Winston-Salem, North Carolina. Consultants: Jean Rosenthal Associates.

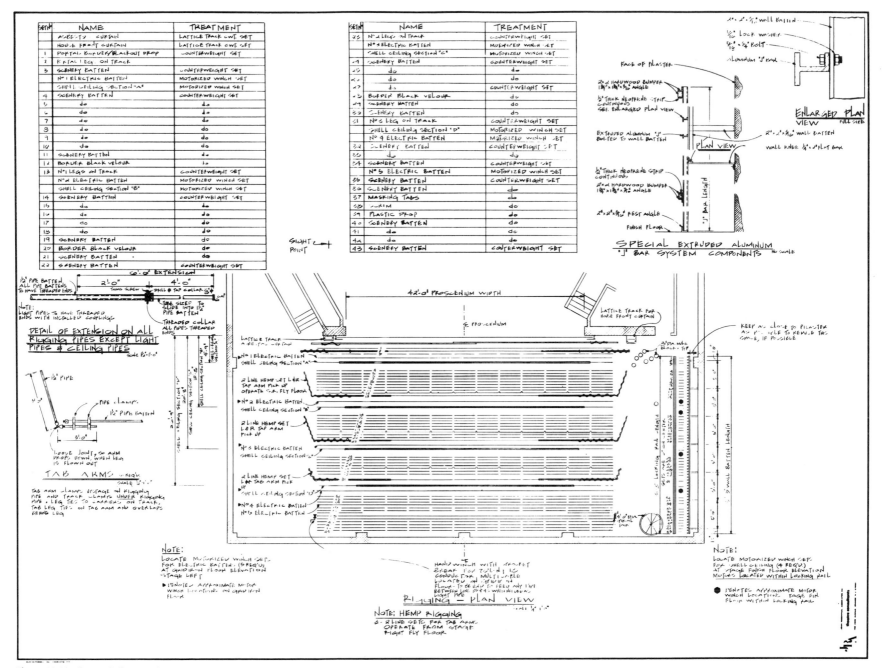

Figure 10.42 Rogers L. Stevens Center.

Figure 10.43 Interior of the Old Carolina Theatre before renovation. (*Courtesy of North Carolina School of the Arts.*)

Figure 10.44 Exterior of Roger L. Stevens Center, Winston-Salem, North Carolina. (*Courtesy of Charlie Buchanan.*)

Energy Conservation

It might seem that only the illuminating engineer needs to be concerned with the ever-increasing need to reduce energy consumption, but such is not the case. Working lighting designers can and do play as vital a role in energy conservation as the engineer does.

The 1973 oil import shortage with its resultant gasoline lines brought to public attention a fact which forward-looking experts had known for years: the supply of fossil fuels (coal, oil, and gas) is finite and exhaustible. In the United States, 85 percent of the energy utilized is generated from resources that are not replaceable — 45 percent from coal, 20 percent from natural gas, and 20 percent from petroleum. An additional 5 percent is produced hydroelectrically, and 13 percent is produced from geothermal (hot water and air) and nuclear sources. Only a tiny percentage is currently produced by solar energy sources.

Of the total energy consumed, about 25 percent is used to generate electricity. Even here there are important energy losses, since electricity generation is only about 34 percent efficient (the amount of energy consumed in the process of generating electricity versus the amount of electrical energy produced). Only 20 percent of the 25 percent of total energy that is used to produce electricity ends up as lighting. Automobile energy consumption, for example, represents use of 25 percent of all energy used. Translated, this means that only 5 percent (20 percent of 25 percent) of all energy consumed in this country each year is used for electrical lighting. Of that, only 9 percent is generated from gas and oil energy sources. Only 3 percent involves critical fuels. Thus energy used for lighting is not a very big factor in the total energy picture.

When one considers the statistics given above and the fact that electrical energy used for heating and air conditioning of buildings (environmental control) is approximately *double* that used for lighting, it becomes clear that lighting consumes a *relatively* small amount of energy.[312]

However, the energy consumption of electric light is much more apparent to the general public than are other uses of energy, so lighting is a big target for energy conservationists. Masses of electric signs in big cities, powerful

St., London W1R 3Df, England); 1988. A revised and updated edition of Theatre Planning, edited by Roderick Ham. Costs £40 to £50, plus postage and packing.

David W. Weiss, "Consulting in the Theatre," Theatre Design & Technology, no. 6 (Oct. 1966), pp. 38–43. A USITT convention panel report. Comments by Jean Rosenthal, David Peacock, Gary W. Gaiser, and Don Swinney.

"Lighting the Darkened Palaces," Time, May 5, 1980, pp. 82–83. Illus., color. An excellent short, lavishly illustrated article concerning restoration of old "movie palaces" throughout the United States.

John Wyckham, "Ten Days to Tales," TABS, vol. 33, no. 1 (Spring 1975), pp. 14–17. A highly amusing day-to-day account of a theatrical consultant's life. Should be read by all prospective consultants!

C. Jay Burton, "Recycling: Found Spaces to Theatre Spaces," Theatre Crafts, vol. 13, no. 4 (Sept. 1979), pp. 39–90. Illus. Issue devoted to theatre construction. Very useful article from the consumer's viewpoint.

Robert Benson, "Buying Consulting Services," Theatre Crafts, vol. 13, no. 6 (Nov./Dec. 1979), pp. 86–88.

"Cleveland Arts Center Lives Again," Lighting Dimensions, vol. 8, no. 4 (July/Aug. 1984), pp. 28–33, 35. Illus., color. Roger Morgan's rebuilding of three older commercial theatres in Cleveland.

"Kansas City Music Hall," Lighting Design + Application, vol. 15, no. 1 (Jan. 1985), pp. 12, 14, 16. Illus., color. Refurbishing of a 1936 building in Kansas City.

"Consultants Update," Theatre Crafts, vol. 19, no. 2 (Feb. 1985), p. 8. Makes mention of the Theatre Projects Consultants' (London, Richard Pilbrow) renovation of the Paramount Theatre in Portland, Oregon.

Jane Bauschard, "Van Dijk Paints a Fair Face for Cleveland; The Playhouse Square Redevelopment and TRW Guest House Restoration," Lighting Design + Application, vol. 17, no. 1 (Jan. 1987), pp. 14–16, 48–49. Illus., color.

Jane Rottenbach, "'Curtain Up, Light the Lights . . .' Roger Morgan Talks about Designing Theatres and Theatrical Lighting Design," Lighting Design + Application, vol. 16, no. 12 (Dec. 1986), pp. 10–11, 46–47. Illus., color.

Ron Jerit, "Catfish and Lighting System Design," Lighting Dimensions, vol. 3, no. 8 (Aug. 1979), pp. 20–21, 32. About consulting.

H. T. von Malotki, "Lucens—Lux Ludens for the Frankfurt Opera," Lighting Design + Application, vol. 12, no. 6 (June 1982), pp. 6–14. Illus., color.

Iain Mackintosh, "Putting the Clock Back," Cue, May/June 1983, pp. 20–22. Illus., color. A description of the redesign of the St. Lawrence Theatre in Toronto, Canada, by Theatre Projects Consultants.

"IES Transaction, Stage Lighting—A Guide to the Planning of Theatres and Public Building Auditoriums," Lighting Design + Application, vol. 13, no. 9 (Sept. 1983), pp. 17–27. IES committee report on recommended standards. Basic but useful.

Theatre Projects Bulletin is published quarterly by Theatre Projects, Ltd., and distributed through its London office (14 Langley St., London WC2H 9JG, United Kingdom), its New York City office (27 W. 67th St., N.Y., NY 10023), its Los Angeles office (6758 Eddinghill Drive, Rancho Palos Verdes, CA 90274), and its Toronto office (Toronto Dominion Centre, Suite 4650, P. O. Box 77, Toronto, Ontario M5K 1E7).

The American Society of Theatre Consultants was formed in New York City on Jan. 14, 1983. For further information contact Mr. Ned Lustig, Secretary, at Ned Lustig & Associates, 1226 Mentz Hill Road, St. Louis, MO 63128.

For a listing of British theatre consultants, see "Society of Theatre Consultants," pp. 457, in John Offord's British Theatre Directory, 1983. Eastbourne, England; John Offord Publisher, Ltd.; 1983.

[312] Information drawn from Helms pp. 201–202, op. cit. (see footnote 236); Nuckolls, pp. 333–345, op. cit. (see footnote 236); and other sources.

[313] Helms, p. 202, op. cit. (see footnote 236).

[314] "Progress' 78," Lighting Design + Application, vol. 8, no. 12 (Dec. 1978), pp. 18–23. Sum-

illumination in TV and movie studios and theatres, blinding lighting at roadside service stations, and lights at night athletic games are all such a visible use of energy, while the energy waste from faulty heating and cooling systems or poorly maintained automobiles and badly planned buildings is much less apparent. Buildings which do not make wise use of insulation and sunlight are harder to spot and bother the conservation-minded observer less than do buildings which use many lights. The world of illumination, which is of vital concern to the lighting designer, is thus highly vulnerable to the energy conservationist's cry of "Turn off the lights!"

Operating costs are another factor which needs to be mentioned. In the words of Ronald N. Helms:

> In terms of the end user, lighting represents 30–50 percent of the operating cost of a building. Lighting energy conservation is important in terms of the total resource reserves and in terms of operating costs for the building owner. As utility rates continue to increase, the impact of lighting on operating costs will become painfully apparent. Make no mistake, much lighting is wasteful.[313]

The "Lawrence Berkeley Update," published by the IES from research done at the University of California in Berkeley, adds:

> The lighting of buildings in the residential, commercial, industrial and public sectors accounts for roughly 440 billion Kw of energy consumption annually, or about 25% of the electricity sold in the United States each year. . . . It is estimated that 40% . . . could be saved by a concerted conservation effort.[314]

A specific example:

> Macy's (in NYC) converted sources resulting in an equal amount of light using ½ the lamp wattage and reductions in air conditioning costs (by modernizing lighting fixtures). Macy's will be saving over one-quarter of a million dollars in operating costs the first year (1978).[315]

The National Lighting Bureau cites an almost endless group of cases in which knowledgeable lighting designers have markedly influenced energy consumption. For example, Central Michigan University saved $12,000 per year through lighting modifications; a $51,000 modification of

an indoor Pennsylvania shopping mall repaid the investment in six days; the Pillowtex Corporation's showroom in the Dallas World Trade Center paid for itself in just 19 hours of use; Merrimack College physical education center in North Andover, Massachusetts, reduced its lighting costs by 70 percent and saved $20,000 per year; the relighting of two Washington State ski areas (at a cost of $115,000) increased revenues by $150,000 per year and reduced lighting operating and maintenance costs by 71 percent; lighting costs in a Wisconsin elementary school were reduced 80 percent (while student performance and safety improved). These are but a few selected case studies which vividly demonstrate the value of involving a knowledgeable, energy-consumption–conscious lighting designer in a project.

There are at least three approaches available in any attempt to conserve energy: (1) development of new and more energy-efficient sources, power generation, and distribution (mostly the work of illuminating engineers and manufacturers); (2) better energy management and utilization for more useful consumption (largely the province of the lighting designer); and (3) development of non–fossil fuel alternate energy sources, such as solar, thermal, hydroelectric, and nuclear (mostly the task of the government and power generation companies). All three approaches are important — no one solution provides an adequate answer.

William M. C. Lam has some comments about the function of lighting designers in promoting wise use of energy:

> As lighting levels across the country have been reduced in response to the energy crises, there has been substantial evidence of increase in comfort and productivity as a result of the decrease in light levels. People are finding out for themselves that if they turn off their lights (at least, some of their lights) they can see just as well — if not better — and more comfortably.[316]

In 1972 the first of what was to become a long series of conservation efforts by both the IES and the U.S. government began. Various "Energy Conservation Guidelines" were drawn up, discussed, and modified. A number of these proposals have been adopted as law by certain states. In other states they serve as a federal guideline or are in the process of becoming law. I have condensed the 12 IES recommendations of 1972 into the following list applicable today:

1. Design lighting for the expected activity. Use less light on surround, nonworking areas (corridors, storage, circulation). Employ task-ambient lighting with resulting nonuniform light patterns.
2. Provide for relocation of luminaires as needed.
3. Use more efficient luminaires.
4. Use more efficient light sources.[317] There is a need for "cooler" sources with less heat exhaustion problems, plus better utilization of energy in light production (see Fig. 10.45).
5. Use more reflective ceilings, walls, floors, and furnishings (with a lighter finish).
6. Provide for flexible control. Make better use of switching and dimming networks with such devices as photoelectric control and other means of extinguishing unneeded light sources when alternate adequate lighting is present (e.g., daylight).
7. Make better and increased use of daylight.
8. Ensure better maintenance of luminaires and sources for higher continued efficiency (this can improve output by as much as 20 percent).

These are factors the lighting designer should be aware of. These parameters do *not* apply to just architectural and landscape lighting. They are equally important for those designing in theatre, film, and TV. Using energy only where it is needed, where it makes a necessary contribution, is as much a job for these designers as it is for the engineer. For example, should energy shortages so dictate, it is possible to reduce greatly the lighting power used for marquees, signs, lobbies, and circulation areas without endangering safety. Any reductions should be approached with great caution, however, when they affect the appearance of what is on stage, on TV camera or on film. This example emphasizes the basic approach: Utilize energy where it matters, and eliminate energy consumption that is nonessential.

Jim Nuckolls offers his own list of criteria for the evaluation of economical light output: (1) effectiveness, (2) energy use, (3) initial cost (including interest, taxes, and insurance), (4) installation labor and materials costs, (5) lamp replacement costs, (6) maintenance and repair cost (labor and materials), (7) depreciation, and (8) impact on the environment.[318] Reducing energy consumption is no simple matter. It involves factual knowledge plus careful consideration of each of these eight factors. Lighting designers should be aware that their role in conservation is an increasingly important one and prepare accordingly.[319]

Among the energy-conservation technologies available to the practicing lighting designer/consultant are: (1) personnel presence sensors that switch lights on and off, (2) infrared sensors which respond to the presence of body heat, (3) ultrasonic sensors which respond to the presence of sound, and (4) other acoustic sensor devices. A typical installation of infrared sensors, for example, can result in a 63% energy saving. Outdoor microwave sensors can set off safety and security lighting around a critical exterior area when an intruder enters the area. National security installations are particularly interested in this control device.

New Technical Solutions

The stream of new technological developments by scientists and manufacturers, plus improved design possibilities, is nearly endless. While this volume cannot hope to cover them all — that is a task for technical texts and current journals — presentation of a few will give the lighting designer a better idea of what to keep an eye on:

Task-Ambient Lighting. As mentioned previously, many firms are marketing modular office furniture which contains lighting fixtures. By using properly located lamps and fluorescents, energy reductions are achieved because (1) the needed amount of illumination for task achievement and visual comfort is available at the point where the task is accomplished (with much lower wattage consumption), (2) eliminated is the necessity of providing an expensive high overall "room lighting level" (only a lower overall intensity is needed to supplement the individual work areas), and (3) considerable flexibility is at hand for office or work area reassignment and rearrangement as needs change, without expensive redesign and rewiring. If sufficient wall outlets are available in structural columns and an adequate overall lower lighting level is present, redesigning the use of space

mary of technological energy-saving developments. Quote from p. 39.

[315] *Ibid., quote from p. 21.*

[316] *William M. C. Lam, Perception and Lighting As Formgivers in Architecture, pp. 78–79, op. cit. (see footnote 236).*

[317] *Jack Brett, Raymond P. Fontana, Peter J. Walsh, Steven A. Spura, L. J. Parascandola, Wolfgang E. Thouret, and Luke Thorington, "Radiation — Conserving Incandescent Lamps," Journal of the IES, vol. 9, no. 4 (July 1980), pp. 197–204, illus.; also by the same authors, "Development of High Energy — Conserving Incandescent Lamps," Journal of the IES, vol. 10, no. 4 (July 1981), pp. 214–218. Illus.*

[318] *Nuckolls, p. 335, op. cit. (see footnote 236).*

[319] *Prafulla C. Sorcar, Energy Saving Lighting Systems. N.Y.; Van Nostrand Reinhold; 1982. 346 p., illus. Very useful complete text.*

National Lighting Bureau, Getting the Most from Your Lighting Dollar. Washington, D.C.; NLB (2101 L St., N.W., Suite 300, Washington, D.C. 20037); 1982. 24-page illustrated booklet. NLB also provides useful News releases on current energy-saving installations and publishes Lighting Energy Management in Retailing (24 pages), and The Energy-Saver's Guide to Good Outdoor Lighting (24 pages), illus., color).

"Energy Utilization," Lighting Design + Application, vol. 13, no. 2 (Feb. 1983), pp. 7–37. Illus., color. Nine articles on energy conservation and recent design projects reports.

M. S. Rea, "Switch the Lights Off!" Lighting Design + Application, vol. 16, no. 12 (Dec. 1986), pp. 36–37. Charts. Well-written article on energy conservation by the head of the lighting program for the National Research Council of Canada.

R. Arnold Tucker, "The Parts Department," Architectural Lighting, *vol. 1, no. 3 (Mar. 1987), pp. 51–53. Charts. Proper maintenance is a key factor in energy conservation.*

Michael J. Leite, "California Leads the Nation with Efficient Lighting Programs — Energy Talks at Pan Pacific Lighting Exposition," Lighting Design + Application, *vol. 16, no. 9 (Sept. 1986), pp. 38–39. Illus.*

Charles Linn, "Calculating Daylight for Successful Retail Design," Architectural Lighting, *vol. 1, no. 1 (Jan. 1987), pp. 28–34. Illus., color.*

Vito Racanelli, "ASHRAE To Round Up Protocol Pioneers," Energy User News Magazine, *vol. 12, no. 13 (March 1987), p. 8. A report on the Standards Committee of the American Society of Heating, Refrigerating and Air-Conditioning Engineers (ASHRAE).*

Richard Mullin, "Old News, 'New' News, and a New Tool for Users," Energy User News Magazine, *vol. 1, no. 1 (Nov. 1986). Entire issue is devoted to articles on lighting energy conservation. This issue also celebrates the tenth anniversary of the Association of Energy Engineers establishment. Deals with ballasts, switching and dimming, fixtures, halides, and an overview of lighting energy consumption and conservation.*

James L. Nuckolls, Interior Lighting for Environmental Designers, *op. cit. (see footnote 236). See Chap. 26, "Architectural Lighting and Associated Phenomena," which contains a section on "Conservation of Lighting Energy,"*

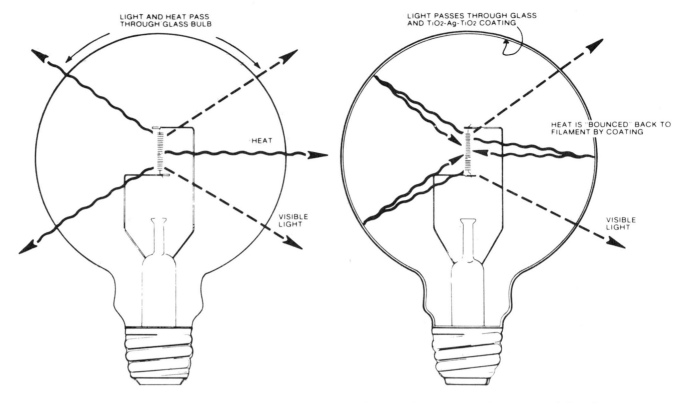

IN CONVENTIONAL BULB, Incandescent filament emits 90% heat and 10% light. Heat and light pass through bulb wall. For more light, filament must be heated more, requiring higher wattage consumption.

IN LOW-ENERGY BULB, invisible coating on bulb wall will allow light to pass through, while reflecting heat back to the filament. The filament then will give the same light with 60% less wattage.

Figure 10.45 Low-energy lamp.

becomes possible at much lower energy consumption costs. While putting light where the work is rather than just all over is not a workable answer in *all* cases, it represents the kind of design thinking that illuminating engineers and working lighting designers have been bringing to bear on the twin problems of better vision (not just less light) combined with lower energy needs. Only the trained lighting designer is in a position to have and use this knowledge.

Technical Improvements in Fluorescent Luminaires. Solid-state high-intensity discharge (HID) ballasts have been developed. High-frequency electronic ballasts which consume less energy and operate at a cooler temperature (reducing heat control energy expenditure) have been fabricated. Electrodeless fluorescent light bulbs (the Litek lamp from Lighting Technology Corp., for example) with transistorization are available. The introduction into fluorescent tubes of krypton gas and new phosphors offers an 11 to 15 percent improved efficiency. Johnson Industries of Los Angeles produces a "Killer Watt" adapter for circleline tube fluorescents which reportedly saves 50 percent in energy consumption with no loss of intensity, burns cooler, and increases lamp life.

New Light Sources. New light sources developed recently promise large energy savings. The amazing light output of the new short-arc lamps (see lengthy discussion of HMI metallogen lamps in Chap. 3, under "Projections") is an example. In 1978 GE brought out a new elliptical reflector lamp and new PAR lamps which save a claimed 20 to 66 percent in power costs compared to previous models yet produce an identical amount of light output in specific situations. A new 1000-watt mercury lamp claims a possible 12 percent reduction in electric energy consumption with 62 percent more lumen output. Low-voltage lamps offer big potential savings.

Technological Breakthroughs. In November 1978 GE announced results of test operations of an electrical generator tested at an operating temperature of −452°F. With special metals in the generator, operation at this sub-zero temperature reduces the inherent resistance of metals to the free flow of electricity. This discovery promises to increase

pp. 333–45. A basic, earlier work in this area. Good analysis and specific solutions.

Scott Churchill, "Symposium Report on Energy Efficient Sources," IALD Newsletter, Dec. 1982, p. 3. An Oct. 1982 meeting on "Energy Efficient Sources for the Illumination of Interior Spaces" in New York City with reports by Dr. Ron Helms, Dr. Gerald Howett (National Bureau of Standards), Dr. Morris Waxler (Biological Effects Bureau of Radiological Health of the Federal Drug Administration), John J. Neidhart, and Tom Lemons.

Robert W. Sant, Dennis W. Bakke, and Roger F. Naill, Creating Abundance: America's Least-Cost Energy Strategy. N.Y.; McGraw-Hill; 1984. 176 pp., illus. Basic survey book.

William Pierpoint, "Energy Conservation from Lighting Maintenance," Journal of the IES, vol. 8, no. 4 (July 1979), pp. 195–201. Illus.; graphs. Highly technical study of increased light output by proper maintenance.

Howard Brandston, "What Environmental Price Do We Pay to Conserve Energy?" Lighting Design + Application, vol. 11, no. 8 (Aug. 1981), pp. 35–38. Good design versus energy conservation discussed.

"A State-by-State Listing of Energy Offices," Lighting Design + Application, vol. 14, no. 2 (Feb. 1984), pp. 48–51. Useful reference.

F. Rubinstein, M. Karayel, and R. Verdeber, "Field Study on (Office) Occupancy Scheduling As a Lighting Management Strategy," Lighting Design + Application, vol. 14, no. 5 (May 1984), pp. 34–38, 40–45. Illus. An in-depth study of hours of use and quantity of illumination needed for a major office space. This research was underwritten by the U.S. Dept. of Energy and is of value to all architectural lighting designers.

"Light Switching for Energy Conservation in an Office Environment," Lighting Design + Application, vol. 14, no. 2 (Feb. 1984), pp. 35–40. Illus. An actual Dec. 1979 case study in Ottawa, Canada, demonstrating a 40 percent energy consumption saving created solely by introducing controlled decentralized switching.

Thomas L. Williams, "A Quality Education," Lighting Design + Application, vol. 14, no. 1 (Jan. 1984), pp. 24–26. In a reprinted address to the 1983 IES Annual Conference in Los Angeles, Williams (vice president of GE) lays

out both the history of government-imposed lighting energy standards (including ASHRAE) and the lighting industry's objections to imposed standards which stress quantity *and* degrade quality *of architectural lighting. He stresses the difference between* efficient *and* effective *use of light.*

Robert A. Meyers (ed.), Handbook of Energy Technology and Economics. N.Y.; Wiley; 1984. Illus., 1089 pp. Basic volume in this field. Contains little of direct, immediate application to lighting design but offers useful basic information.

Howard Brandston, "Open Letter to the Membership of ASHRAE," Lighting Design + Application, vol. 13, no. 12 (Dec. 1983), pp. 6, 8. Outlines IES's objections to ASHRAE (American Society of Heating, Refrigeration and Air-Conditioning Engineers) and SP41 lighting energy standards being considered by the U.S. Dept. of Energy as maximums *allowable for new buildings. Of importance to all concerned with proposed government standards.*

Harry Zackrison, Jr., "Today's Lighting Control Techniques Will Light Our Tomorrows—Recent Technological Advances Offer a Wide Choice of Energy-Saving Techniques in Lighting," Lighting Design + Application, vol. 15, no. 3 (Mar. 1985), pp. 29–36. Illus. Excerpts from Zackrison's book, Energy Conservation Techniques for Engineers, *published by Van Nostrand Reinhold.*

"Energy—A State-by-State Listing of Energy Offices," Lighting Design + Application, vol. 15, no. 3 (Mar. 1985), pp. 38–40. An invaluable listing of addresses for those working in this area of lighting design.

Harry B. Zackrison, Jr., Energy Conservation Techniques for Engineers. N.Y.; Van Nostrand Reinhold; 1984. 332 pp., illus. See above.

Tom O'Mahony, "Energy Optimization—Education and Collaboration," Lighting Design + Application, vol. 15, no. 8 (Aug. 1985), pp. 28–29. An excellent summary of the history of energy conservation in lighting.

"Group Maintenance Saves Big Bucks—Design and Contracting Lower Costs for R. J. Reynolds Tobacco Company," Lighting Design + Application, vol. 16, no. 6 (June 1986), pp. 49–51. Illus.

IALD Argues Controversial Energy Mandate, Standard 90.1P Under Review," Lightview, vol. 1, no. 3 (Fall 1968), pp. 1–5. Illus., color.

IALD's objection to Standard 90.1P: "Energy Efficient Design of New Buildings Except Low-Rise Residential Buildings" presented in detail. These government standards and codes with minimum energy demands and minimum design flexibility greatly affect the work of practicing lighting designers in the architectural field.

Dana Dubbs, *"Energy: Watts the Matter— California Energy Commission Institutes Display Lighting Restrictions,* Lighting Dimensions, vol. 12, no. 4 (May/June 1988), pp. 24, 26, 28. Illus., color. *A useful report about the California Energy Commission's restrictions on energy usage for display lighting under the California State Building Code (Title 24).*

"Retrofit: Emphasis on Energy Efficiency: One Contractor's Experience in Relamping at Toronto's Pearson International Airport," Lighting, vol. 3, no. 2 (April 1989), pp. 36–37.

Albert Thumann, Lighting Efficiency Applications. *Lilburn, Georgia; AEE Energy Books; 1988. Book published by the Association of Energy Engineers, 4025 Pleasantdale Road, Suite 420, Atlanta, GA 30340. Basic work in this area.*

Jules Horton, "A Statement on Energy Conservation," *available in mimeographed form from Horton-Lees Lighting Design, Inc., 200 Park Avenue South, Suite 1401, New York, NY 10003. Useful statement by one of the first architectural lighting designers in the United States who became concerned about energy conservation as a design element.*

Albert Thumann, Lighting Efficiency Applications, *Lilburn, Georgia; Fairmont Press, Inc. (700 Indian Trail, Lilburn, GA 30247); 1989. 330 pages, illus. A rather technical, somewhat engineer-oriented definitive manual covering ways to maximize energy conservation yet provide adequate lighting design. Well-written and most useful for the architectural lighting consultant.*

[320] *"GE Testing Generator to Operate at − 452° F.,"* Indianapolis Star, November 8, 1979.

[321] Polarized Corp. of America, 8921 Quartz Avenue, Northridge, CA 91324. Telephone: (213) 341-0300. See the company's bulletins: "Energy Savings, Recommended Levels of Illumination"; Myron Kahn's "Questions and Answers, Polarized Lighting Concept," (reprinted from the Sept. 1978 Building Operating Management magazine); and "Polarized Lighting."

[322] *"Demand-Controlled Lighting,"* Lighting Dimensions, vol. 1, no. 4 (Oct. 1977), p. 10. An energy-saving method of switching indoor lighting off and on as needed to supplement sunlight.

"New Energy Saving Light Bulb," Lighting Dimensions, vol. 1, no. 4 (Oct. 1977), p. 44. Description and drawings of a bulb developed by Duro-Test Corp. which has inside the glass bulb a chemical coating which redirects infrared, potentially reducing electrical energy consumption by 60 percent without any loss of light output. Developed by MIT and Corning Glass (see Fig. 10.45). See also "New Super-Efficient Light Bulb Makes Cents," Lafayette Journal and Courier, April 27, 1980, p. D-8.

"The Infrared-Reflecting Incandescent—An Update," Lighting Design + Application, vol. 9, no. 1 (Jan. 1979), p. 44. More details about the Duro-Test–MIT lamp.

[323] Abe II. Feder, p. 49, op. cit. (see footnote 246).

greatly generator output and to reduce the energy needed to run a generator.[320]

Polarized Panels. The Polarized Corp. of America in Northridge, California, claims a maximum 50 percent reduction in lighting operating costs while simultaneously *improving* visual quality through the use of their polarized panels. These panels reduce direct and reflective glare and improve color rendition, increasing visual effectiveness and eye comfort. This is yet another approach to the overall problem.[321]

It is impossible for a book of this type to cover the constant technological improvements that are made every day. Those presented above are indicative of the type of constant change taking place. The combined efforts of inventors, engineers, and manufacturers increasingly offer ways for the informed lighting designer to reduce energy consumption. Added to new lighting breakthroughs are developments with new energy sources, such as nuclear and solar power generation. It is a combination of these innovations which will best deal with the energy problem, rather than dependence on any one.[322]

Summary

Those readers interested only in film, TV, and stage lighting design—who are still wondering why they have encountered Chap. 10—should rest assured that almost *all* professional lighting designers do *some* work in the areas covered in this chapter during their careers. More than half of the best known "names" in architectural lighting *started out* in the theatre, discovering along the way that they liked being employed and that architectural lighting has its own challenges and rewards. In the words of Abe Feder, one of the first generation of lighting designers in the United States and a practitioner today in theatre/TV/disco/architectural lighting and illumination engineering wrote: "The stage Lighting Designer offers the architectural design world a good many things, particularly his belief in a world designed for people. In that respect, the stage is a great teacher."[323] Tony Corbett, Managing Director of Light Ltd. (a part of Theatre Projects Group in London, England), specializes in architectural lighting design. Writing in *TABS* on the virtues of a stage lighting training, Corbett says:

> Adaptability is an important part of the lighting designer's make-up, [with the designer] able to work together and interpret other people's thoughts and ideas. [The designer is] ready and prepared, all the time, for any changes that may occur, [this adaptability] produces an alert yet fluid mind, which through its apparent calmness and self-assurance (an absolute necessity) is able to produce the most visually exciting and imaginative end result under sometimes extreme pressures. This discipline and versatility, combined with him always wanting to go one better, always wanting more and better equipment, never prepared to sit around and accept what is given to him, pushing and demanding all the time, is what is too often lacking in architectural lighting and is where the stage lighting designer can make a very important contribution.[324]

[324] Tony Corbett, ''From the Green to Site,'' TABS, vol. 33, no. 2 (Summer 1975), p. 3.

See also Ken Billington, ''Theatrical vs. Architectural Lighting—Bridging the Gap,'' Lighting Design + Application, vol. 13, no. 1 (Jan. 1983), pp. 13–17. Illus., color.

Part 3

The Business
of Lighting Design

It is nearly impossible to estimate the size of the lighting industry. An acceptable rough figure would be 50,000 individuals. Of this number, probably 3,000 can be considered part-time or full-time *designers* of light. The USA (United Scenic Artists) union (based in New York, Chicago, Los Angeles, and Florida) has approximately 260 members who hold "Lighting Designer" cards. The IALD (International Association of Lighting Designers), made up of full-time specialists in architectural lighting design, has nearly 400 members. The Hollywood ASC (American Society of Cinematographers) has a membership of nearly 200. The British ALD (Association of Lighting Designers) has a membership of 110. The Canadian STLD (Society of Television Lighting Directors) has 120 members; the Australian branch has another 120, and the British membership is around 400. The ASLD (Association of Lighting Designers, formerly Association of Lighting Directors), which is composed mostly of West Coast film and television lighting specialists, has nearly 500 members. The ADC (Associated Designers of Canada), which includes all professional designers, has roughly 100 members who specialize in lighting. It is impossible to estimate the number of designers in other parts of Europe, Asia,

and South America, but the figures above plus some estimates give a rough total of 3,000 people concerned almost exclusively with lighting *design*.

The waters become more murky when an attempt is made to estimate the number of individuals engaged in manufacturing and installing lighting equipment and the number of purveyors (salesmen of lighting equipment worldwide), engineers, and scientists. The IESNA (Illuminating Engineering Society of North America) alone has 9,000 to 10,000 members. Another 8,000 are active members of SMPTE (the Society of Motion Picture and Television Engineers). A former Purdue University graduate student of mine, Glen Goodman, recently completed an extensive investigation and listing of nearly 500 lighting educators worldwide. There are another 400 members of the British Society of Theatrical Lighting Designers and an unknown number of individuals worldwide serving as stagehands, operators of power distribution firms, and employees of such companies as General Electric, Osram, Philips, Westinghouse, Sylvania, etc.

If one adds the known thousands of stagehands in IATSE (International Association of Theatre and Stage Employees) and

NABET [National Association of Broadcast Engineers and Technicians (television)], plus local television station personnel who also are involved part-time in lighting, a conservative estimate of the number of people worldwide with an extensive interest in lighting design and technology gets up into the range of 50,000 people.

Lighting Spectrum magazine, during its all-too-brief existence, presented an article by Robert Preston in the Summer 1986 issue about the nine largest lighting conglomerates (manufacturers) in the United States, which control 50 percent of the $4 billion lighting market. In the Fall 1986 issue, *Lighting Spectrum* reported an annual 8.3 percent growth in the lighting industry, with a $7 billion lighting market in 1986 and a projected $14.4 billion market by 1995.

Whichever of these figures one chooses to "go with," little doubt remains that the lighting industry is huge, that the position of the lighting designer (be it as engineer or artist of light) increases each and every year, and that in slightly over 100 years since the discovery of a practical incandescent electric light (1879) a large and diverse industry has arisen. Nonetheless, almost no instruction anywhere in the worldwide educational system deals with the practical *business* information associated with this area of employment, and even very few professional practitioners of the art/craft are informed on the subject beyond occasional exposure to a very limited number of magazine articles in widely scattered sources.[325]

Realizing this lack of business information, I have organized Part 3 of this volume to present the results of an Industry Survey I conducted (as a means of learning more about both the extent and the nature of the lighting design business) and to cover such practical business matters as taxes, agents, professional organizations, unions, lighting training and education. The last chapter in Part 3 (and in the book) takes a speculative look at the lighting world of tomorrow.

Chapter 11

Employment and Career Prospects

[325] *The following books and articles are useful additional references to accompany this volume:*

Michael A. Neighbors, How to Become a Successful Consultant in Lighting Engineering. *Published by the Association Technology, Rt. 2, Box 448, East Springs, TN 37330. A spiral-bound, mimeographed work, approximately 200 pages in length. This work is not a guide to the technology of consulting. It covers business basics, selling, contracts, interviews, legal matters, and a wealth of readily readable tips concerning the business of consulting. As the only work available about lighting consulting, it is a good starting point. Besides, it is well written and contains a wealth of pertinent information.*

James L. Moody, "The Business of Lighting Design," Lighting Dimensions, *vol. 9, no. 7 (Nov./Dec. 1985), pp. 56, 58, 60. A quick overview of résumés, portfolios, clients, interviews, and job connections.*

James L. Moody, "Money, Money, Money," Lighting Dimensions, *vol. 10, no. 1 (Jan./Feb. 1986), pp. 17–20. More by Moody in a six-part series on lighting design business.*

James L. Moody, "Setting Up Your Business," Part III, Lighting Dimensions, *vol. 10, no. 2 (Mar./Apr. 1986), pp. 21–24, 26–27. Continu-*

The first business of a lighting designer is to find a job. The second is steadily to build a career. If you are a recent graduate (or a newcomer to the field), you must first make a basic decision: Are you, at the moment, looking for steady employment and a regular paycheck? Do you wish to free-lance in lighting design, and do part-time work (presumably of a temporary nature) on the side to pay the bills? Or will you try for both (which is much more difficult)? Your answer to these questions depends upon (1) your immediate financial situation, (2) your long-range goals and objectives (both dreams and reality), (3) your established inventiveness in surviving hardship, and (4) your relative adventurousness (comfort with gambling or chance-taking). Only you can analyze what you want — and only you can answer the tough questions.

Steady Employment

These days, most graduates are in debt when they leave school. There are others who may not be in debt but are just not comfortable living with constant financial insecurity. For these people a regular income is the answer. If you are a person who requires a regular income, you can still continue to learn and grow, to design (in your spare time), and to make valuable contacts for the future. If you are seeking employment with a regular income, here are some strategies:

1. Check the lighting equipment manufacturers: Kliegl, Strand, Colortran, Altman — any firm, in or out of New York City. These firms have both constant turnover and constant expansion. Don't rule out the smaller firms or the firms that aren't in New York City. For example, consider Grand Stage Lighting in Chicago, and Little Stage Lighting in Dallas, Texas. Disco firms and rental-supply houses are everywhere, and they *need* employees who know an ellipsoidal from a Fresnel. It isn't designing — but you can pay the bills and the loans.

2. Look at the charts presented later in this chapter. If you look at "Relative Employment in Major Areas of Lighting Design," in Fig. 11.12 (it is the final part of the Industry Survey), you can see that lighting design isn't just in theatre. Make "house calls" on firms involved in your areas of interest or areas in which you feel you are competent to make a contribution. The Industry Survey is based upon statistically accurate information concerning the relative strength of employment in the many lighting design specialities. The chart was prepared in 1980. However, trends change, and no one really knows exactly how many people are employed in each specialty.

3. Take a steady job anywhere, in any field. The classic "side" jobs in New York City are selling toys at Macy's during Christmas or waiting tables in a restaurant. In your off-duty hours, whether you are in New York or elsewhere, continue studying. Light anything — for free if need be.

Light anything anyone will let you do: dinner theatres, store windows, community theatre, museum exhibits, local opera groups, local dance companies, *anything*. Watch for an opening. Make friends in all areas of show business and lighting design. Attend conventions when you can. Go to meetings. (Get the picture?) If you are in New York City, take classes at New York University or Pace University. Outside New York there are similar opportunities in *any* metropolitan area. Just look for them. Ask around. My students at Purdue have designed lighting for operas in Richmond, Indiana; in Indianapolis; in Chicago; with the Lafayette Civic Theatre; for parties and banquets; etc. The same kinds of experiences were almost certainly shared by Gil Hemsley's students at the University of Wisconsin–Madison, by John Gleason's students at New York University, and by Randy Earle's students at San Jose State University in California. Just ask. Most theatre groups are always both broke and shorthanded. They welcome talented "freebies." And you will be able to learn and to widen your circle of friends and admirers — while holding a steady job. So you don't get any sleep. Next year, maybe.

Free-Lancing

Should you decide to take the big chance and free-lance (in which case you are either rich, think yourself to be quite gifted, or just have a lot of "guts"), you must tackle one of the biggest questions of all: Should you try New York City or go elsewhere? Hint: *Try to begin outside of New York City.* Stay where you are known, where you grew up or were educated, because you are potentially more readily employable there. Competition in New York is keen. Making contacts in the unfriendly metropolis usually takes a long time. The people in New York don't need you. They already have 14 million bodies — probably half of them would-be thespians!

If you *must* begin in New York City, here are some places to check:

Opportunity Resources for the Performing Arts
1501 Broadway, New York, NY 10019
Telephone: (212) 575-1688

This nonprofit corporation was founded in 1971 and is as-
sisted by grants from the National Endowment for the Arts, Washington, D.C.; the N.Y. State Council on the Arts; the Rockefeller Brothers Fund; and the Edward John Noble Foundation. Its function is to help people associated with the performing arts find work. There is a registration fee.

USITT (United States Institute for Theatre Technology)
10 West 19th St., Suite 5A
New York, NY 10011
Telephone: (212) 924-9088.

USITT publishes the constantly updated "Theatre Design Internship Clearinghouse."

National Arts Jobbank
207 Shelby St., Suite 200
Santa Fe, NM 87501

The National Arts Jobbank publishes Jobbank, *a monthly placement bulletin (available for around $30 per year) of The Western States Art Foundation, 141 East Palace Avenue, Santa Fe, NM 87501. Telephone: (505) 988-1166.*

USA #829 (United Scenic Artists, Local Union #829)
575 Eighth Avenue
New York, NY 10018
Telephone: (212) 736-4498.

The office bulletin board often has listings of job openings, posted for members, *as does the monthly* Newsletter.

TCG (Theatre Communications Group, Inc.)
355 Lexington Avenue
New York, NY 10017
Telephone: (212) 697-5230.

Designers can make an appointment with TCG to show their portfolios in order to gain access to the top regional theatre jobs in the country. A subscription to TCG's Art Search, *a placement bulletin from its National Employment Service, costs around $25 per year.*

TAP (Technical Assistance Project)
570 Seventh Avenue
New York, NY 10018
Telephone: (212) 586-1925.

Broadway lighting designer Beverly Emmons and her associates have become a quasi-official clearinghouse for potential beginning employment, particularly in dance lighting, as

ation of Moody's well-written, useful series of articles.

James L. Moody, *"Contracts and Letters of Agreement,"* Part IV, Lighting Dimensions, vol. 10, no. 6 (Nov. 1986), pp. 60, 62, 64–69. *Includes a sample contract.*

James L. Moody, *"Expanding the Operation . . . Business Advice for the Growing Firm,"* Part V, Lighting Dimensions, vol. 11, no. 1 (Jan./Feb. 1987), pp. 68, 70–76. *Includes an income statement.*

James L. Moody, *"Effective Communication Skills,"* Part VI, Lighting Dimensions, vol. 11, no. 2 (Mar./Apr. 1987), pp. 120, 122, 124–126. *Moody discusses how good interpersonal relations can help designers get jobs.*

David Hale Hand, *"The Joys of Export Contracting — One Engineer's View of Business in the Far East,"* Lighting Design + Application, vol. 17, no. 6 (June 1987), pp. 6–7, 56. *Illus., color. An amusing and informative article concerning doing lighting business in the Orient.*

Robert Preston, *"The Lighting Giants Are Here,"* Lighting Spectrum, vol. 1, no. 1 (Summer 1986), pp. 12–15, 56–62. *Illus., color. A look at the nine largest conglomerates (Lithonia, Cooper Industries Group, Genlyte Group, U.S. Industries, Kidde, Thomas Industries, Emerson Electric, Hubbell, and Jac Jacobsen) in a special report. These conglomerates control many subsidiary firms whose names are familiar, such as Crouse-Hinds, McGraw, Halo, SPI, Lightolier, Keene, Stonco, Prescolite, Moldcast, Kim, etc. Useful basic information about the extent of the industry.*

"What a Business," Lighting Spectrum, vol. 1, no. 2 (Fall 1986), pp. 17–20. *Illus. Another definitive article about the extent of lighting sales and annual growth of key firms. Includes numerous useful charts.*

Mary F. Lovett and James M. Stone, *"Seminar on Freelancing: Protecting Your Legal and Business Interests,"* a mimeographed 7-page summary of a presentation at the Ohio USITT Spring Conference, April 12, 1986. *These two attorneys touch all bases in a most useful study.*

"The Lighting Biz; Bigger and Smaller," IALD Newsletter, July 1985, pp. 2–3. *An overview of*

the $43-billion-a-year architectural business involving some 400 fabricator manufacturing companies.

Wanda Jankowski, "How's Business?" Inside Lighting, May 1986, preview issue, pp. 4–5. Illus. Comments by Gary Steffy, Jeff Milham, James Benya, and Jane Moyer about starting and expanding architectural lighting firms. Useful.

[326] Jean Dalrymple, Careers and Opportunities in the Theatre. N.Y.; Dutton & Company; 1969.

"Special Report: The Business of Working," Theatre Crafts, vol. 17, no. 3 (Mar. 1983), pp. 15–25. Special issue on the business of theatre. See particularly Susan Levi Wallach, "Clearing Houses for Art Jobs," p. 16; "Agents and Agencies," p. 17; Hope Hanafin, "Glorified Go-Fer Being an Assistant," p. 17; "Contracts," p. 18; Joseph Melillo, "Exempt or Non-Exempt," p. 22; Garritt D. Lydecker, "Finding a Job," p. 22. Illus.

Ann Folke and Richard Harden, Opportunities in Theatrical Design and Production. Lincolnwoods, Illinois; VGM Career Horizons (a division of National Textbook Co.); 1985. Illus., 148 pp. Deals with the structure of theatre organization and production, unions, education possibilities, and job seeking. Contains a useful listing of theme parks in the appendix.

Steve Pollock, "Living and Working in Los Angeles," Theatre Crafts, vol. 19, no. 1 (Jan. 1985), pp. 34–37, 70–73, 90–97. Useful information about unions and job opportunities in Los Angeles.

Robert Long, "Working: How to Find a Job in Resident Theatres," Theatre Crafts, vol. 20, no. 4 (Apr. 1986), pp. 18, 96, 98, 100–105. Includes useful information and addresses of key regional theatres.

Career Handbook for Those Beginning Careers in the Performing Arts. Compiled under the auspices of the Executive Committee of the Yale Drama Alumni Association, Spring 1977; pp. 26–49, "Design." Available from 90/A Yale Station, New Haven, CT 06520. 98 pp. Portions excerpted in

well as in theatre and opera. TAP is foundation-supported. TAP publishes a useful newsletter and is part of The American Dance Festival organization.

Theatre joblist, The National Employment Service Billboard for Theatre Arts published monthly by ATHE, includes administrative/management positions, assistanceships and internships, and listings under "Design/Technology" each of which is of interest to lighting designers. Contact: Theatre Service, P.O. Box 15282, Evansville, IN 47716 [Telephone: (812) 474-0549] or 1451 Audubon Drive, Evansville, IN 47715.

For an electronic bulletin board as well as assistance in resume writing, contact: ARTS Employment Referral Service, P.O. Box 12484, Atlanta, GA 30355-2484. Telephone: (404) 876-1823.

In Britain, contact: Framework, 340 Old Street, London EC1V 9DF. Telephone: 01-739-4384. They operate a temporary placement agency which services lighting designers, among others. ABTT (Association of British Theatre Technicians) also publishes each month a listing of those seeking tech/design employment, their age, years of experience, and area of employment interest. See Chapter 13 for ABTT's address.

"Showcasing" and making contacts — in New York City or elsewhere — is vital. Find some group which will let you "show your stuff." Here's an example. A friend of mine dropped by the Cubiculo Theatre in New York City on West Fifty-first Street. He did not ask for a job, and he did not leave a résumé. He did not even indicate that he was interested in lighting design. Instead he met the management. He indicated that he was aware of the group's work and admired it, and he offered to help. He was put to work unloading trucks, hanging lights, putting up scenery, and distributing posters, as well as taking tickets. He kept coming back when he was requested to. Within a very short time, the management — finding him trained, willing, and dependable — offered him pay (a low hourly compensation). Shortly thereafter, when he had become an underpaid "regular," he was asked "what he really wanted to do." Soon he was given sporadic opportunities to design, and eventually he became part of the paid staff. Get the

idea? Most theatre groups are over budget. The tasks a group needs to have done when you first appear may be sweeping the floor or taking tickets or distributing posters. But if you can be counted upon, your efforts and dependability will soon lead you where you want to go. And you will make valuable contacts this way.

Another hint: You are being watched everywhere, by everyone. Those who work with you form opinions of you and of your work. Here is an example of how this can be advantageous. I was hired to design the lighting (under a union contract) for the Broadway-bound play Harbor Lights. I was hired before either the director or the scenic designer! Why? Ten years earlier, while working in summer stock at the Pocono Playhouse, I had regularly stopped by the soft drink and candy stand in front of the theatre, spending two to three minutes saying "hello" to the fat, pimply 16-year-old attendant. We'd talk about the weather or the mass of cars in the parking lot. Idle chitchat. Nearly everyone else ignored him. Ten years later he was production assistant to Broadway Producer Anthony Parella. It was Parella who produced Harbor Lights (with Robert Alda and the late Linda Darnell as stars), and his production assistant remembered me. I was hired — at a price above union minimums. These kinds of connections are the reason it is important to try (none of us succeeds as much as we would like) to leave good impressions with everyone you work with in the theatre, not just the boss.[326]

Getting Paid

While it might seem gratuitous to add comments about collecting all payments due, it certainly is part of the business of lighting design. Producers and clients have long been notorious for not paying the monies owed to the designer. For example, lighting designer Robert Brand remembers well the day in Boston when it was necessary for him to remove the large switchboard main fuses and take them to his hotel room to assure that the artistic director of a prominent New England opera company would come through with the designer's fee in cash on opening day. She did, but Bob did not work there again.

I was staff lighting designer at the Queens Playhouse, Flushing Meadows, New York City, in the summer of 1974, for a "star" season with big names. The season ended over $250,000 in debt. *I* managed to collect all that was owed to me through the union bond. Four Star Stage Lighting (renters of the season's lighting equipment) did not.

In 1959 David R. ("Tex") Ballou (scenic designer) and I were in Europe with Harold Arlen's musical, *Free and Easy*. The producers were Robert Breen (of *Porgy and Bess* fame) and Stanley Chase (the original *Three Penny Opera* revival Off-Broadway). With us were 15 tons of American switchboards and lighting equipment from Century Lighting (Ed Kook). The entire show was moved from Belgium to The Netherlands *on the producer's Diners Club credit card in rented cars!* Yet I collected all the show owed me. Why? I had a return-trip air ticket in hand at my insistence (and United Scenic Artists') *before* I left New York. At any time, if the management did not pay, I could leave for the United States. What, then, would they do for a lighting designer who was knowledgeable about American lights?

In 1966 I designed and supervised the installation of elaborate interior lighting for the living room of Mrs. Johnny George (Houston producer who began with Margo Jones and Nina Vance). Her husband, Larraine George, was an important construction contractor, worth $5 to 6 million. It took one-and-a-half years of monthly "collection calls" on Mr. George, but I finally was paid in full. His money was tied up in construction equipment and jobs. His cash flow problem once resulted in a bounced check to me, yet Mr. George was Chairman of the Galveston (Texas) National Bank!

Only once, in nearly 40 years of lighting, have I failed to be paid. In 1979 Producer Jerry Brandt had a $2 million musical called *Got Tu Go Disco* one week away from a postponed official opening at the Minskoff Theatre in New York City.[327] He phoned me and offered transportation and expenses if I would come to New York City from Indiana and discuss the lighting. I arrived for the first preview night. At curtain time the agreed-upon $300 expense money was not with the pair of tickets. I tore up the tickets and left for Indiana. While I lost $300, I *did* have the satisfaction of hearing from the associate producer: "You'll see. We'll get the money to you in the morning. We'll prove that we can play with the grown-ups!" But they did not pay my ex-

penses. Quite an expensive compliment — but worth it. In short, the world of lighting is fraught with perils. Learn to protect yourself. Chapter 12 explains (among other things) that protection for monies due is one of the main reasons for the existence of theatre unions.

Duration of Career

Contrary to popular belief, in most cases the career of a theatre lighting designer on Broadway does *not* necessarily soar to better shows and higher pay as the designer becomes a "name" in the business. Often the opposite applies. As designers become successful, they may find fewer and fewer challenges coming their way as their careers lengthen. True, they *know* more. But, on the other hand, producing managements are eager to utilize newcomers who will work at union minimum rates. Often Broadway is used to establish a designer's artistic merit and credentials, and then the mature, middle-aged designer moves on to teaching, regional theatre, or an established staff position with one of the larger dance or opera or repertory companies. These positions offer both a steady income and often a greater opportunity to work over a period of time with a production group the designer enjoys creating for. It also begins to remove the designer from the (sometimes) deadly cutthroat competition for the few new shows available on Broadway, "The Main Stem."

Examples abound. While they still design lighting professionally, the following well-known designers have also created careers as educators: John Gleason, William Mintzer, Lee Watson, Peggy Clark, Hugh Lester, Richard Devin, Neil Peter Jampolis, Pat Simmons, Jim Nuckolls, Lloyd Burlingame, Louise Guthman, Klaus Holm, William Allison, Charles Elson, Howard Bay, and many others. Jennifer Tipton, Jules Fisher, and Tom Skelton have all taught at times in their careers. Other great designers have become corporate heads of lighting design empires, for example, Richard Pilbrow in England (founder and former chief executive officer of Theatre Projects, Ltd.) and Jules Fisher who both produces and is a partner in an architectural lighting firm. Imero Fiorentino, Jim Moody, (with Sundance Lighting, Inc., in California and much concert lighting) and Bill

"Joining the Union: United Scenic Artists Local 829," Theatre Crafts, *vol. 12, no. 4 (May/June 2978), pp. 70–72.*

"Careers: Getting a Design Job in New York," Theatre Crafts, *Part I, vol. 13, no. 1 (Jan./Feb. 1979), p. 8.*

"Careers: Getting a Job in New York: Part II," Theatre Crafts, *vol. 13, no. 3 (May/June 1979), p. 91.*

Lee Watson, "Retrospect, I," Lighting Dimensions, vol. 2, no. 2 (Feb. 1978), pp. 16–17.

Lee Watson, "Retrospect, II," Lighting Dimensions, vol. 2, no. 3 (Mar. 1978), p. 14.

Marguerite Feitlowitz, "Working: Summer Madness, Getting a Job in the Theme Park," Theatre Crafts, vol. 18, no. 4 (Apr. 1984), pp. 18, 60, 62–65. Useful guidance.

Jan W. Greenberg, Theatre Crafts, A Comprehensive Guide to Non-Acting Careers in the Theatre. N.Y.; Holt, Rinehart & Winston; 1983. 206 pp. Contains a useful interview with Ken Billington.

Theatre Crafts *(editors), Summer Theatre Jobs. N.Y.; Drama Book Specialists; published annually. Complete summer theatre employment information. Revised annually.*

ABTT (Association of British Theatre Technicians, London), So You Want to Work in Theatre. Useful 14-page booklet (1983), free to members. Published by ABTT, 4–7 Greater Pulteney St., London W1R 3DF, England. Clarifies British unions, practices, and training facilities.

Marjorie Bradley Kellogg, "Opinion: Designing Money," USITT Sightlines, vol. 29, no. 7/8 (July/August 1989), pp. 6–7. A carefully presented analysis of the underpayment of scenic designers by a working freelance professional. Reprinted from the June 1989 issue of American Theatre *magazine.*

[327] *See Steven Gaines, "Go Tu Go Hustle: Presenting the Grand Man,"* New York, *vol. 12, no. 26 (June 25, 1979), pp. 54–58. Reviews of* Got Tu Go Disco *appear in* The New York Times *(Richard Eder),* New York Post *(Clive Barnes), and the* Daily News *(Patricia O'Haire) for Tuesday, June 26, 1979.*

328 *See Lee Simonson, Part of a Lifetime. N.Y.; Duell, Sloan and Pearce; 1943. p. 67.*

Lee Watson, "Contrasts," Lighting Dimensions, vol. 5, no. 7 (Nov./Dec. 1981), pp. 58–59.

McManus (with a major firm in the concert/rock field) are other examples of designers who have businesses. Some designers have moved into architectural theatrical consulting: Jules Fisher and Nananne Porcher, for example. A few have taken permanent staff positions; Gil Wechsler with the Metropolitan Opera and the late Ron Bates with the New York City Ballet are examples. Even Tharon Musser—Broadway's leading lighting designer—also lights the season (or assigns the task to others under her overall supervision) for the Mark Taper Forum in Los Angeles, the Miami Opera, and the Dallas Opera. She also spent several seasons with the Stratford (Connecticut) Shakespeare Festival. Yet she is one of the very few who can be said to derive her primary income from Broadway lighting, year after year.

The career pattern is somewhat different in the other lighting design fields. Those in TV lighting tend to stay there, with little mobility. Those in architectural lighting usually start their own consulting firms and stay in that area. Work for leading cinematographers is so sporadic that it is difficult to generalize. Many cinematographers, however, work in other (lesser) capacities between their employment on feature films.

So, the beginner is warned not to make a lifetime career designing lighting on Broadway as a career objective. I wrote in the 1981 November–December issue of *Lighting Dimensions:*

> Jo Mielziner was nearly unemployable toward the end of his career. The last show which he saw executed was *Marathon 33* at Purdue University. True, he was working on the Broadway musical, *The Baker's Wife,* which was far from a success. Not exactly an auspicious climax for the longest, most successful (in his earlier years) scenic design career on Broadway. Norman Bel Geddes found that he had to leave designing scenery and lighting in the theatre, establishing a new career as the first industrial designer of products. Yet his theatre contributions (*The Divine Comedy* designs, for example) were more than monumental. Leo Kerz, after many years as a prominent Broadway and Washington Area and TV scenic designer, became USA #829's Assistant Business Agent during his final years because he was no longer in demand as a designer. Howard Bay, another noted Broadway figure, also taught at Brandeis University—having publicly expressed his bitterness at the few professional design opportunities which came his way late in his career. Remember Sam Leve? Does Oliver Smith, *the* most contributory designer of American musical comedies, get engaged for more than one or two Broad-

way productions per season these days? Fortunately he has had a lengthy career as co-producer of the American Ballet Theatre and designed several movies. *Pacific Overture,* certainly not a hit, was the last production designed by Boris Aronson—rarely called upon by Broadway after *Applause, Company, Fiddler,* etc. Robert Edmond Jones found very few calls for his services during his prime of maturity. Donald Oenslager was restricted largely to high fashion Broadway drawing room sets during his late years—yet had a remarkable record of brilliant design for classics and serious drama at Yale. Klaus Holm now teaches in Pennsylvania—yet had several years in professionalism. Why is this the case?

. . . The answer is twofold and simple: (1) the theatre-going public constantly expects and demands newcomers: new ideas, new approaches, constant change in our rapidly jaded entertainment industry (ask yourself how long the disco fad has lasted; or look at what is happening to concert productions); (2) new designers, while less certain and lacking a fund of experience, work at (or near) minimums—better-established designers do not. You think that is not a factor? You are wrong. Producers have long known that sets and costumes and sound and lighting do not a hit make—yet they cost a lot of money. Words by the playwright, acting by the cast and direction by the stars of directing make a hit. So why commit large sums of money on expensive designers with an untried product? Ask Peter Larkin or Rouben Ter Arutunian or even David "Tex" Ballou what happens when you come close to "heavy design" [high fees and elaborate, expensive scenery] in the early, most successful days of your evolving career. Each of these fine designers has come back closer to the prices and output of "newcomers," and thus continued or revived fading creative careers. How often have you seen Jules Fisher's name as a Broadway lighting designer lately? Yet he has three Tonys.

Lee Simonson, another of America's four major designers, expressed it better than I can. His early career was phenomenal with the Theatre Guild and the Met Opera. I knew him well (he lived in the next block in New York City and we worked together at USA #829) during his latter years. In *PART OF A LIFETIME* (page 67), he wrote:

> The careers of scenic designers in the New York theatre reflect its box office rhythms. A few are "hits" and settle down to a run. The rest, often equally talented, appear sporadically for "limited engagements" and are rarely given enough consecutive opportunity to mature as artists. Their debuts have been uniformly brilliant. By the time they near 50 and might be doing their best work if in any other field of design, they are likely to find themselves unable to practice their profession unless they happen to have, in the meanwhile, become directors or managers and employ themselves. Otherwise the overwhelming odds are that they will find their careers as abruptly terminated as though they were sent to the storehouse with one of their stage-settings. Scott Fitzgerald remarked, "There are no second acts in American lives." There are rarely any third acts in the careers of American designers for the theatre.[328]

Apprenticeships

Certain unions have apprenticeships. Designers who have passed the entrance exams of United Scenic Artists #829 are on their way. They will be regularly employed as assistant lighting designers by harassed, overcommitted union designers at $350 to $770 per week under union contract. Many designers are reluctant to stop working as assistants and begin designing shows on their own because they become so accustomed to a steady paycheck. What do assistants do? Anything the employer wants them to do — from drafting to "gofer" to you name it (within reason, of course) — cheerfully and helpfully. Assistants gain two invaluable things from an apprenticeship: (1) priceless on-the-job training while learning from an established master and (2) excellent contacts in the world of professional theatre. (Not to mention a paycheck!) Assistants are almost always the ones that an established designer passes jobs along to, either when the designer thinks the new show being offered is a potential turkey, or when he or she is already too busy to undertake additional design assignments. Who cares if it *is* a turkey? Not the new designer, if it's a first Broadway credit. The number of established designers who started as assistants to either Jean Rosenthal or Nananne Porcher or Tharon Musser or Ken Billington or Marilyn Rennagel is legion. Serving as an assistant is the greatest "training ground" around. The assistant's primary duty is to keep an absolutely infallible and accurate record on paper of everything the designer does. It will be needed, not only while the production is being designed, but also for subsequent road companies, etc. Remember that a designer must be a union member to become an assistant. Background training, prior to passing the USA Entrance Examination and serving as an assistant, usually includes attendance at a good school plus lots of practical experience (in nonunion situations: Off-Broadway, Off-Off-Broadway, regional theatre, opera and dance, concert lighting, etc.). One member of a panel of union assistant designers at the American Theatre Association convention in New York City at the Statler-Hilton Hotel in August 1979 put it in a nutshell: "As an assistant, you gain the experience without assuming the [design] responsibility." [329]

Internships

An internship differs from an apprenticeship in two ways: (1) it may pay more, and (2) it is often intended as a "tryout" and training period for a new member of a firm with the intention, should the beginner be a tolerable employee with satisfactory work, that the intern will join the employing firm and remain on its staff at a regular salary. Internships are always for a prespecified time period, while apprenticeships may be open-ended. Many universities now require an internship period as a portion of the work toward an advanced academic degree. They frequently help students locate a suitable place of employment for the internship. The New York City Opera Company offers a competitive (paid) internship each year in memory of lighting designer Gilbert Hemsley, Jr.[330] The IALD has for several years placed up to 20 outstanding prospective architectural lighting designers with member firms. This program has been highly successful. In 1986, for example, the IALD intern program received 86 submitted portfolios. Of the portfolios, 26 were from seniors in colleges and universities, 53 from juniors, and 7 from nonstudents. Thirteen internship applicants (nine seniors, four juniors) were placed with firms owned and/or operated by IALD members. The thirteen applicants were engaged by nine firms — three in San Francisco and ten in New York City.[331] In 1988 IALD placed 15 interns on both coasts: 11 in New York City, 2 on the West Coast, and 2 in Washington, D.C. Many interns have remained with the firm that first employed them, and some have later gone on to establish their own design firms.

The British handle internships much better than they are handled in the United States. ABTT (Association of British Theatre Technicians) runs a government-subsidized training program, helping to place beginners in proper places for training and then following through by using its newsletter as a constant update for those seeking employment (older and established members as well as interns). The design industry in the United States would do well to emulate the British system. In Canada, ADC has begun placing intern/apprentices. The British ALD (Association of Lighting Designers, London) has begun a program of "Lighting Design Assistants." [331a]

[329] Theodore G. Ohl, "The Santa Fe Opera's Apprentice Technical Program," Lighting Dimensions, vol. 2, no. 6 (July/Aug. 1978), p. 33.

Among the groups which annually hold auditions for apprenticeships are the following:

The Children's Theatre Co. and School, Minneapolis, Minnesota

The League of Outdoor Drama (for dozens of summer outdoor pageants nationwide)

Asolo State Theatre, Sarasota, Florida

Almost all summer theatres

Almost all theme parks

The USITT now sells a constantly updated internship listing with detailed, specific information about each internship (its TDTICH Internship list). This listing is constantly updated on a computer at Florida State University, Tallahassee, Florida. Listings for "Lighting Design" and "Lighting Technology" internships can be obtained through USITT's national office, 10 West 19th Street, Suite 5A, New York, NY 10011. Tel.: (212) 924-9088.

Loren Ginsberg with Alice Hale, "Resources: Getting the Experience: A Guide to Internship Programs," Theatre Crafts, vol. 20, no. 1 (Jan. 1986), pp. 18, 62, 64–73. Most usable list of organizations and addresses with further information about internships.

Craig Miller, "A Guide For Assistant Lighting Designers: Some Modestly Proffered Notes," Theatre Crafts, vol. 23, no. 1 (Jan. 1989), pp. 10, 22–27. Very useful tips for apprentice (assistant) lighting designers from a working professional.

Paul L. Butler, "Letters: More Advice For ALDs," Theatre Crafts, vol. 23, no. 3 (March 1989), p. 7. Additional comments and suggestions about Craig Miller's article (see listing above).

[330] See "New York City Opera Accepting Internships Applications," Lighting Dimensions, vol. 11, no. 2 (March/April 1987), p. 20.

[331] Heidi Galassini, "Intern — In Turn a Career," IALD Newsletter, Oct. 1984, pp. 2–3. An intern describes her internship.

"Education: IALD Intern Program Educates Prospective Lighting Designers 'in the Field'," Lighting Design + Application, vol. 11, no. 2 (Feb. 1981), pp. 25–27. Illus., color. Program in operation for training architectural lighting designers.

News release from IALD in 1988 by chairperson Brad Chilcote.

"IALD Intern Program Survey Results," IALD Newsletter, July/August 1987, p. 1. The Intern Committee's survey disclosed that lighting firms preferred senior students over juniors; selected interns in the following order (from areas of collegiate training): architecture, interior design, architectural engineering, architectural lighting, and theatre. Employers were only slightly interested in part-time interns during the school year; firms provided stipends in line with industry levels; firms wanted IALD to continue their Interm Program.

Internship information, both for New York and for San Francisco, is available from IALD in 6-page mimeographed form.

331a Warren Christensen, ed. National Directory of Arts Internships, 3rd edition, National Network for Artistic Placement, 1988. 300 pp. Lists over 850 producing groups offering over 2000 internships, plus information on how to design internships and prepare resumes, portfolios, letters of recommendation, etc., for theatre, management, dance, film, video, music, design, and technology.

See also:

"Lighting Design Assistants," ALD #Magazine, No. 8 (1988), p. 7.

332 Taken from the USA #829 "Lighting Design Internship Program" bulletin.

333 Burdette E. Bostwick, Resume Writing: A Comprehensive How-To-Do-It Guide, 3d edition. Somerset, NJ; John Wiley & Sons; 1985. Illus., 352 pp.

Robert G. Nesbit, "Strategies: Rate Your Resume," USAir, vol. 11, no. 3 (March 1989), pp. 88, 90–91.

The United Scenic Artists, Local Union #829, initiated its internship program in lighting design in 1986. The program was authorized by the union's membership in October 1985. Two interns were selected in 1986 to begin the program. As of March 1988, both were full Lighting Design members. Applications for admission are now accepted twice yearly, addressed to the Lighting Design Internship Committee, USA #829, 575 Eighth Avenue, 3d Floor, N.Y., NY 10018. Interviews are in April and October. Those selected begin work in June or September and in January. Interns are assigned to working union designers who have chosen to participate in the program. Normally 40 weeks of work as assistants to professional designers over a period not to exceed two years is required. Initial screening looks at the applicant's educational and professional background, confidential letters of recommendation, and a portfolio. An interview follows for those determined to be eligible.

During 1988 there were three interns in the program. The initial two selected earlier had already achieved membership in the union. The Internship Committee stresses that "the Program is not a training program for designers, but is geared towards those who have already completed their training in a university or nonunion professional situation and are ready to move into the Union's area of jurisdiction." [332] Each intern is required to work with a minimum of four designers during the internship period.

Résumés

The form of a résumé is a matter of almost simplistic logic. The prospective employer first wants to know an applicant's name, address, and telephone number. Next the potential employer wants a brief personal sketch to get an idea of the person represented. The sketch should include age; education; any pertinent facts like marital status, children (if any), armed forces and disability record (laws, you know), and possibly religion; and probably information regarding any permanent physical disability. After that the employer wants an employment record (which sometimes is short or nonexistent for graduating students): where the applicant last worked and for how long, plus each job preceding the most recent (getting more generalized as the farther back in time it goes). Following that the employer needs to know (in reverse chronological order) other (nonpaid) activities bearing upon the application for employment (for example, shows and responsibilities with collegiate productions, or computer training and skills). Lastly the employer wants to see the miscellaneous goodies: awards, citations, publications, lectures, special skills or training, and organizations (unions and professional or even social) to which the applicant belongs (all presented in reverse order, that is, starting with most recent). If the employer is interested and wishes to know more than those things listed above, it is likely that the applicant will be asked in for an interview. [333]

Portfolios

The approach for portfolios is not quite so simple. You need two different portfolios: one for the interview committees of USA, class instruction, etc. and another for potential employers.

Portfolio for the Union. It is important to know which USA group you wish to approach before you assemble your portfolio. USA in New York City wants no drawings of less than half-inch scale, while USA in Chicago likes them in quarter-inch scale. The New York City group doesn't really like photographs, slides, and transparencies, because it is convinced that photographs of a show never (or almost never) look anything like the original artistry; however, the Chicago group likes photographs and transparencies. USA in New York City hates to see theatre programs in a portfolio. They are rather mistrustful of press reviews (but may glance at them) since to them "no critic knows very much about good lighting design anyhow." Both unions want to see your light plots, section drawings, switchboard hookup sheets, etc. Both have on their interview committees people as qualified as any to be found anywhere in the art of interpreting your mysterious scribblings and visualizing what your lighting was like. Both want a range of work. Provide at least one of as many of the following as you can carry:

- Plots, etc., from shows actually produced and designed by you

- A plot from an arena production, and also from a thrust stage production if you have done one
- A plot showing your dance work or your opera work
- A really finished (large-scale) plot showing what you can do with few limitations of budget, theatre size, etc. (this *can* be your big final project from your last class in lighting)
- Anything else in any area which will show you in your best light.

Read Warfel's *Handbook of Stage Lighting Graphics,* the bible of light plot terminology and presentation.[334] Include *both* a Broadway-type plot and a classroom-type plot.[335]

Portfolio for the Employer. Most employers are not trained experts at reading lighting drawings. On the other hand, they have jobs to offer and money to pay. Show them photographs, reviews, letters of admiration from your following—and a snazzy sampling of your mastery of the mysterious art of plotting lighting. Show them anything which will make them view you as their new, inexpensive (of course), and shatteringly talented "artist of light."

Besides following the tips provided above, you should take a careful look at Yale's *Careers Handbook,* in which there is much that is of great value. Good luck and—"get a job."[336]

An Industry Survey

No one really knows how many individuals are in the field of lighting. We in the business are beginning to discover that it is a lot more than we thought. Like Topsy, the industry has grown in many different directions, specialists in any one area all too often being only somewhat aware of who and what are involved in other specialties.

Added together, those who design, manufacture, and market light sources and luminaires (fixtures); those involved in power production design, distribution, and sales (from power companies down to local electricians); and those involved in research and in the development and utilization of lighting equipment (lighting designers) make up a big industry.

While I estimate the total size of the larger lighting industry to be well above 50,000 individuals, I have made an attempt to discover and define that smaller group: the light-

ing designers. These are the individuals whose specialty is the utilization of power and luminaires to achieve specific desired human benefits. Until now there has been available precious little information concerning this group. A more accurate picture would benefit: (1) manufacturers and power producers/distributors, by identifying potential customers; (2) manufacturers and designers of fixtures, fittings, accessories, and luminaires (for the same reason); and (3) students giving serious thought to a lifetime career in this area (whose parents all too often ask, Why do you want to study that?).

To try to define this group of designers, I prepared an Industry Survey. A copy is reproduced as Fig. 11.1. While only eight basic questions were asked by the survey, the replies provided more solid, statistically verifiable information than has been available up to this time.

A total of 2003 surveys were sent to the following people: 105 active lighting design members of United Scenic Artists, Local Union #829, New York City; 150 members of United Scenic Artists #350, Chicago; 150 members of the International Association of Lighting Designers (architectural lighting), New York City; 280 individuals listed in the May 1979 "Who's Who In Lighting" directory published by *Lighting Dimensions* magazine; 51 network television lighting directors from CBS, NBC, and ABC in New York City (local station TV Lighting Directors replied, contacted through other sources); 52 names from the *Dance Annual '79;* 300 selected lighting equipment manufacturers (selected from my files and the *Theatre Crafts* listing in *Theatre Crafts Directory, 1979–80);* 500 educators (selected from American Theater Association's *Directory of American College Theatre, 1976* and Robert L. Smith's *USITT's Directory of Graduate Programs in Theatre Design and Technology, 1978);* 150 nonprofit professional theatre companies who are members of TCG (Theatre Communications Group, Inc.) taken from *Theatre Profiles/3, 1977;* and 235 members of ASLD (American Society of Lighting Directors), Los Angeles. *Lighting Dimensions* ran a courtesy advertisement soliciting names and addresses from those who might have been overlooked. While this survey is now almost 10 years old, the data derived is still valid today.

The survey was directed toward *lighting designers.* No attempt was made to reach workers (manufacturing em-

[334] *William B. Warfel,* Handbook of Stage Lighting Graphics, *op. cit. (see footnote 16).*

[335] *A Broadway-style plot shows only units (luminaires) on mounting pipes with a key identification number. A classroom-type plot also gives focus, color, dimmer number, etc. You need to be able to do both. Samples of each should be included in your portfolio.*

[336] *Alice Hale, "Portfolio Pitfalls: Do's and Don't for Preparing Your Portfolio,"* Theatre Crafts, *vol. 19, no. 8 (Oct. 1985), pp. 28, 51–54. Sketchy. Illus.*

"What Should Your Portfolio Communicate," a portion of the information sheets supplied to internship applicants available from IALD. Contains a good analysis of the requirements for a portfolio in architectural lighting design.

Note: If you received more than one copy of this Survey,
EACH member of your firm/organization should fill out a separate form
ALL REPLIES WILL REMAIN CONFIDENTIAL!

Personal Data:

Age: _____

Sex: ☐ F ☐ M

Education: ☐ BA or ☐ BFA; ☐ MA or ☐ MFA; ☐ Ph.D.

Occupational Description:

Percent of paid time devoted to lighting: _____ %
(for part-time and educators)

Percent of paid time devoted to (indicate %):

_____% Educator   _____% Mfg. Lighting Equipment
_____% Student   _____% Sales/Promo of Lighting Equip.
_____% Author,   (Marketing/Distribution)
Lecturer,   _____% Designer/Engineer of Lighting
Critic,   Equipment & Systems
Publisher   _____% Laser/Holography Specialist
_____% Consultant, Specify type: _____

LIGHTING DESIGNER for:

_____% Discos _____% Rock Concerts _____% Film
_____% TV   _____% Ice Shows   _____% Other
_____% Interiors (homes, offices, factories, stores)
          Specify specialties: _____
_____% Exteriors (buildings, gardens, monuments)
          Specify specialties: _____

THEATRE:

_____% B'way or Professional (unionized)
_____% Regional Theatre
_____% Community Theatre
_____% Outdoor Theatre & Pageants
_____% Amusement Parks, Circus, etc.
_____% Dinner Theatre
_____% Other. Please Specify: _____

Number of years employed in Lighting: _____ (yrs.)

Are you a union member ☐ Yes ☐ No. What unions?

Please list unions: _____

Industry Incomes:

Please state your current annual income from Lighting:

☐ $10,000 or under   ☐ $30-40,000
☐ $10-15,000   ☐ $40-50,000
☐ $15,-20,000   ☐ $50-60,000
☐ $20-25,000   ☐ $60-70,000
☐ $25-30,000   ☐ Over $70,000

Figure 11.1 Lighting industry survey.

ployees "on the production line"), power companies and/or distributors, or the large mass of lighting-related manufacturers. The memberships of certain established groups were not contacted — not IES (Illuminating Engineering Society of North America), ASC, or SMPTE, nor the large membership of IATSE — partly because mailing lists were not available. Also, contact with these groups would bring responses from relatively few lighting *designers*. Those who were actively designing were reached through the channels used. Careful attention was devoted to avoiding multiple mailings to single individuals who belonged to several of the organizations contacted. The mailing was restricted to 2,000 individuals (contacting a larger group was beyond the means available). A small sampling of students was included. The 2,000 individuals who were selected serve as a valid cross section of those involved primarily in lighting design.

A total of 603 individuals responded (a 30.1 percent reply rate). From a statistical accuracy standpoint, this is a sufficient number to validify the factual matter based on the survey. Surprisingly, 94 percent of those responding answered the quite personal "Industry Incomes" question.

Results of the Industry Survey

Age. See Fig. 11.2. Age did not seem to be an important factor among the various specialty areas of the industry.

Sex. See Fig. 11.3. Sex distributions provided interesting information in relation to the various employment specialties. See Fig. 11.4. While there are individual exceptions, the overall pattern is one of a higher percentage of women employed in lighting design and quite a limited number employed in education, television, and manufacturing (with the exception of sales).

Sex/Income. The average income reported for all men and women is shown in Fig. 11.5. *Remember that these are 1978 incomes* (there is roughly a $2,000-per-year difference between 1978 incomes and current incomes). There were only two women in the "over $70,000" bracket (one each in manufacturing and professional theatre). In several areas almost all women were in the "under $20,000" income range: dance, disco, education, manufacturing, outdoor theatre, opera, regional theatre, and television.

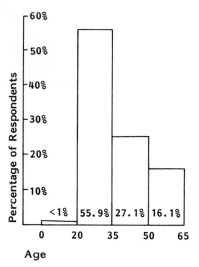

Figure 11.2 Lighting industry survey results: breakdown according to age.

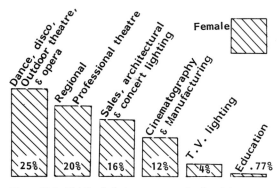

Figure 11.4 Lighting industry survey results: breakdown according to sex and area.

[337] *Marjorie Bradley Kellogg, prominent Broadway scenic designer, conducted a 1983 survey of female scenic designers which concentrated on the question of whether or not women felt that they were discriminated against in training and in hiring. The results were published in Marjorie Bradley Kellogg, "Opinion: Betting on a Dark Horse — 'Are There Old-Boy Networks from Which You Feel Excluded?' 'Yes,' said 93 percent,'"* American Theatre, *May 1984, pp. 28–29. Illus.*

Figure 11.3 Lighting industry survey results: breakdown according to sex.

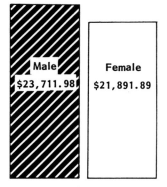

Figure 11.5 Lighting industry survey results: average income breakdown by sex.

Women were to be found in the "over $20,000" income range only in architectural lighting, sales, and professional theatre areas. In professional theatre a much better distribution of incomes in the higher brackets was to be found for women than for the men. Only two women were found to be working extensively in television, and those two had widely separated income levels.[337]

Among the men certain trends were discernible. Incomes tended to be preponderantly in the lower ranges in dance, disco (unless the designer was the owner of a large firm), education, outdoor theatre, opera, and regional theatre. There was a much heavier concentration of incomes over $20,000 in architectural lighting, consultation, manufacturing, cinematography, and (particularly) television. Professional theatre is fairly even throughout the income ranges. The "over $70,000" incomes for men are found most often in television, manufacturing, cinematography, architectural lighting, consulting, and sales. The ranks of the very well paid thin in dance, disco, outdoor theatre, and opera, and none at the "over $70,000" level was found in regional theatre or professional theatre. *Note:* These figures were compiled by "tabulating" the *multiple* sources of income from most lighting designers. Very few designers work in only one specialty.

Education. See Fig. 11.6. I expected that further training and advanced degrees would produce higher average incomes, but such is not the case. No correlation between education and income could be established statistically. When earned degrees were checked against the 23 specialty areas, no pattern was apparent, with one exception: there was a marked preponderance of M.A., M.F.A., M.S., and Ph.D. degrees among educators.

Part-Time versus Full-Time Employment in Lighting. See Fig. 11.7. The purpose of this question was to separate those who spend all of their gainfully employed time in lighting/lighting design from those whose activity in this area makes up only a portion of their total employment. Educators are an example. Much lighting design is taught by educators who also teach scenic design, costume design, technical theatre, etc. Only a fraction of their total teaching time is involved in lighting classes and the lighting of productions. The same can be said of other specialties: for example, some TV lighting directors double as engineers (audio men, camera or boom operators, etc.).

When the total number of individuals in each specialty was checked to determine areas of predominant full-time employment, this was the result: 75 percent of those in television were full-time; 67 percent of those in sales; 50 percent of those in professional theatre, manufacturing and cinematography; 20 percent of those in architectural lighting and consulting. It drops to 6 percent full-timers in regional theatre, and the lowest of all is in education, in which only 4 percent of those responding replied that they worked full-time in lighting. The areas of dance and disco were about evenly divided between part-time and full-time

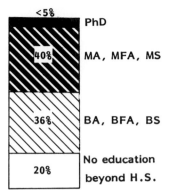

Figure 11.6 Lighting industry survey results: educational breakdown.

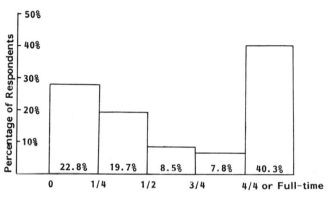

Amount of employed time spent in lighting or lighting design

Figure 11.7 Lighting industry survey results: full-time versus part-time employment.

workers. Outdoor theatre and opera reported very few part-timers.

Number of Years in the Lighting Industry. Is the lighting industry, a rather new industry with a relatively short history, an industry of youngsters who move in their mature years to other fields? See Fig. 11.8. A number of survey respondents did not answer the question about years in the lighting industry (46 out of 603). Worthy of note is the fact that nearly 80 percent of those who answered the question have been in the lighting design industry for only 20 years or less.

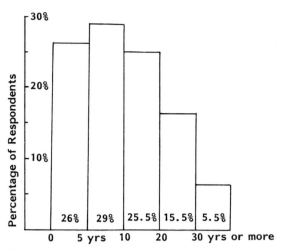

Figure 11.8 Lighting industry survey results: number of years in the lighting industry.

There were two specialty areas in which replies tipped heavily toward prolonged periods of employment: television and education. There were three specialty areas where most respondents had been active 20 years or less: dance, disco, and regional theatre. All other areas showed a reasonable spread of all "length of service" categories.

Union versus Nonunion. See Fig. 11.9. Of those responding, 34.5 percent were members of at least one of the theatrical unions, and 8.2 percent belonged to two or more

unions. This gives a total of 42.7 percent unionization. The unions listed were USA, IATSE, NABET, IBEW (International Brotherhood of Electrical Workers), AEA (Actors Equity Association), AGMA (American Guild of Musical Artists), SSDC (Society of Stage Directors and Choreographers), AFTRA (American Federation of Television and Radio Artists), Scenic and Title Artists, and Director's Guild of America. Unfortunately, although we were only seeking union membership, several professional organizations were also listed: IES, IALD, International Photographers, and Radio-TV-Recording Employees Association. However, these professional organizations were too small in number to affect the total statistical picture.

A marked difference was apparent between the average income of union versus nonunion responders. Those who were union members received an average annual wage of $29,000 in 1978 figures. Those who were nonunion received $21,000. Obviously union membership is important. This is statistically verifiable and is an important factor in the industry.

Two specialty areas were *heavily* unionized: television and professional theatre (see Fig. 11.10). Others were only lightly represented by union membership: dance, disco, education, manufacturing, cinematography, and sales. Viewed in terms of specialty areas, TV had the highest number of union members and the highest average salaries. Three areas show income ranges across all reported catego-

Figure 11.9 Lighting industry survey results: percentage of unionization.

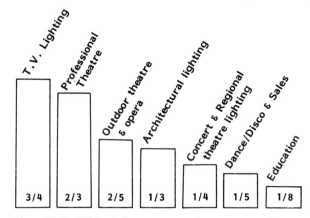

Figure 11.10 Lighting industry survey results: percentage of unionization by areas of specialization.

ries from union members: manufacturing, cinematography, and sales. Those who belong to unions in architectural lighting are to be found up to the $30,000 to $40,000 income range, with only one above that. In six specialty areas the income range of those belonging to a union is largely in the lower brackets ($30,000 and under): dance, disco, education, outdoor theatre, opera, and regional theatre. Professional theatre has a preponderance of "$20,000 or under" salaries among union members, but this is balanced by an even scattering of salary ranges right up to the top category ("over $70,000") among union members.

Looking only at the salary ranges of those who do not belong to any union, again the preponderance of salaries is in the lower ranges for dance, disco, educators, outdoor theatre, opera, regional theatre, and professional theatre (nonunion). There is a much sharper tilt toward higher income ranges for nonunion members in architectural lighting, consulting, manufacturing, cinematography, and TV.

Areas that might be expected to be nonunionized (education, manufacturing, sales, and consulting) are, for the most part, just that. Other specialties are highly unionized (TV, professional theatre). In some areas of lighting design, union membership is obviously a prerequisite to reaching higher income levels. Unionization versus nonunionization is roughly 40 percent versus 60 percent. *On the average, union members earn $8,000 more per year than nonunion members do.*

Concluding Remarks on the Industry Survey

I have broken down the Industry Survey for clarification (see Fig. 11.11). Remember that the survey was intentionally sent to those who derive at least some of their income from lighting design.

A basic objective of the survey was to determine *how many* individuals were involved in lighting design and in what specialties. The percentages in Fig. 11.12 are statistically accurate as to relative *sources of income* for all who answered the survey.

Professional theatre *may* have been influenced by designers wishing to think of themselves as employed in this area when they could, more aptly, have checked regional

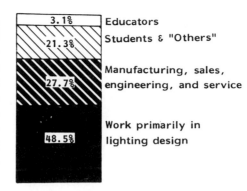

Figure 11.11 Lighting industry survey results: areas of activity.

theatre. The number responding to the survey was so small in the area of author, publisher, and lecturer that figures related to this area are questionable. The figures of relative areas of employment are quite accurate and can serve as a guide to students in their training and to professionals seeking opportunities to design.

The employment opportunities in the architectural lighting design area were touched upon by a survey IALD conducted. In the March/April 1989 issue of *IALD NEWS,* "The Business of Lighting Design" article indicated that 86 percent of the IALD members were principals of lighting design firms (rather than working for engineering, architectural, or interior design firms as lighting specialist employees). Most indicated that business volume improved each year. Among them, 30 percent were members of one-person firms; 27 percent were with firms of two to five employees; 20.5 percent with six to ten employees; 20.5 percent with eleven to twenty employees; and 2 percent with architectural lighting firms with more than twenty employees. Of the firms, 2 percent had been in business for one to two years; 31 percent for three to five years; 24 percent for six to ten years; and 43 percent were members of firms in business for more than ten years — indicating that architectural lighting firms are not as much newcomers to the design field as one might think. Almost all firms worked on either a fixed-fee or hourly basis for billing, rather than a percentage of construction costs. Hourly rates ranged from $100 per hour for principals; $50 to $74 for senior designers; and $25

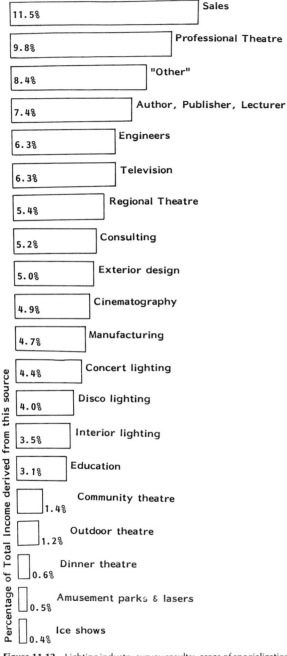

Percentage of Total Income derived from this source

11.5%	Sales
9.8%	Professional Theatre
8.4%	"Other"
7.4%	Author, Publisher, Lecturer
6.3%	Engineers
6.3%	Television
5.4%	Regional Theatre
5.2%	Consulting
5.0%	Exterior design
4.9%	Cinematography
4.7%	Manufacturing
4.4%	Concert lighting
4.0%	Disco lighting
3.5%	Interior lighting
3.1%	Education
1.4%	Community theatre
1.2%	Outdoor theatre
0.6%	Dinner theatre
0.5%	Amusement parks & lasers
0.4%	Ice shows

Figure 11.12   Lighting industry survey results: areas of specialization.

to $49 for staff and drafters. Average project fees in 1988 were $24,925, with median fees of $17,500. In terms of computer graphics, 86 percent used Computer Illumination Calculations; 43 percent used CADD; 43 percent used Computer Graphics; 36 percent used Database Specification Programs; and 25 percent used Daylighting Analysis Equipment.

It should be further added that no attempt was made through the survey to quantify the total number of individuals working in each of the lighting specialty areas. What was demonstrated reiterates one of the basic themes of this volume: *POTENTIAL lighting designers should not aim to work just in theatre, or just in film, or just in TV, or just in architectural lighting;* lighting design income is most often derived from design work in many of these areas *for each designer.* American education makes a tragic error in the instruction and preparation of future professionals in the lighting design industry if each student or trainee is not adequately prepared to practice lighting design in *all* of the specialty areas.

Chapter 12

Unions

[338] *Michael H. Moskow*, Labor Relations in the Performing Arts, An Introductory Survey. *N.Y.; The Associated Council of the Arts; 1969. p. 34. The Council of the Arts may be contacted at 1564 Broadway, N.Y., N.Y. Labor Relations provides useful background information.*

[339] *Howard Carson, "How Relevant Are the Unions? Do They Hurt More Than Help?"* Theatre Crafts, *vol. 12, no. 7 (Nov./Dec. 1978), p. 82. An antiunion viewpoint, well presented.*

Beeb Salzer, "Contrast," Lighting Dimensions, *vol. 2, no. 2 (Feb. 1978), pp. 70, 64–66 Pros and cons of union exams.*

Since we are in a period of relative antiunionism and a decline in union power, see also:

Henry Weinstein, "Organized Labor Taking a Beating but Says It Isn't Down for the Count," from the Los Angeles Times, *reprinted in the* Indianapolis Star. *National union membership has dropped from 35 percent of the working populace in 1954 to 23 percent in 1980 and 18.8 percent in 1985.*

William Serrin, "The Union Movement Looks in the Mirror," The New York Times, *Feb. 24, 1985, p. E5. Illus.*

Most *theatrical* lighting designers encounter unions and decide to become members. A few lighting areas that do not have much to do with unions are the fields of architectural lighting, display, disco design, and sales and engineering in a lighting equipment manufacturing firm. It is possible to earn a living as a theatrical lighting designer without ever joining any unions; however, those who follow the nonunion route find themselves unable to work in several of the professional areas which offer big money, reputation, and more interesting and challenging design assignments.

What Do Unions Do?

The performing arts (live) are strongly unionized.[338] Lighting designers, being part technicians and part creative-artist designers, frequently have mixed emotions about unions.[339]

Theatre unions became strong in the early 1900s. They gained their present power as a result of two factors: (1) frequent blatant exploitation of theatre workers by both producers and theatre owners, including nonpayment for work performed; and (2) the casual nature of show business, involving short-term jobs for constantly changing employers in widely separated geographical locations. Unionization became the employees' means of obtaining adequate compensation, job security, fringe benefits, and decent working conditions. Employers found unionization acceptable because the unions could offer ready access to the pool of top available skilled and talented labor.[340]

Unions only negotiate and enforce *minimum* standards and employment rates, which primarily protect beginners. They are guaranteed an acceptable "living wage" commensurate with their skills and the knowledge accumulated from lengthy study plus practical experience. Unions act to prevent design jobs from falling into the hands of transient, untrained nonmembers. For example, a huge number of people in allied fields would leap at the opportunity to design lighting for a Broadway show. Some would even pay the management for this privilege because of the glamour and credit involved. And most would immediately afterward return to their usual field of employment. This would be unfair to the dedicated lighting designer who has suffered through university training and additional years working with assorted theatre groups while polishing and acquiring skills — the individual who has selected lighting design as a life career.

Unions are less concerned with members who have established international reputations and are in constant demand. These artists work above minimum scale, and they can command additional conditions and privileges: royalties, "house seats" held for them to assign for their hit show, prominent program and advertising billing, etc.

Theatre unions frequently expend as much effort, time, and money policing their own members as they do negotiating better contracts with employers for their members.

There is a human temptation for newcomers or for designers in the midst of an "at liberty" stretch to want to find ways to get around their own union's posted minimums.

Unions are organized democratically. In the last analysis the union's officers must always bow to the demands of the membership in general meeting. Even if union officers feel the demands are unjustified or destructive to the industry they must go along or be voted out of office.

In summary, unions negotiate and protect minimums for fair employment. Through signed contracts with employers a union organizes and extends its jurisdiction for exclusive employment of its members where the union can effectively exercise control. Some designers join unions willingly. Others reluctantly belong because membership is the only way to get choice jobs. Unions are composed of humans. The faults, flaws, and abuses which humans are capable of can occasionally lead to bad or unfair decisions in any union. Such individual cases have helped to produce the existing antiunionism on the part of employers and nonmembers and are often at the root of charges of union "featherbedding," "favoritism," "laziness," and "exorbitant salaries."

From the employer's standpoint, ideally all lighting designers would work for nothing because they love theatre. Designers don't, but unions simplify things by supplying employers with access to the top creative people, at rates and terms of employment that are a known absolute for purposes of budgeting and planning a production. I have often sat on the union side of the table during negotiations with the TV networks, the League of New York Theatres, and the New York City Opera. Except in those rare cases where important new negotiation directions are being pursued and negotiations may lead to bitterness at the table and a labor strike, the meetings are very businesslike. There is normally an unexpressed underlying appreciation on the part of both parties of their need for each other and of the necessity of arriving at a compromise acceptable to both.

The next few sections cover some specific unions, answering the questions, What are these unions? How do they operate? and How does one gain membership?

IATSE

Jurisdiction

The International Alliance of Theatrical Stage Employees (IATSE) is an older union representing around 75,000 stagehands and all motion picture projectionists. It has approximately 830 locals nationally.[341] As of August 1988, up to 60 percent of all IATSE members were unemployed. One-third of all members were based in Los Angeles. In recent years IATSE has expanded in metropolitan areas to embrace craftsmen in a wide range of film and television positions. For example, in New York City IATSE represents both lighting directors and special effects employees at CBS and elsewhere (members of IATSE Theatrical Protective Unions #1).[342] A potential basic conflict has always existed between IATSE and USA (United Scenic Artists) concerning jurisdiction over lighting designers. The conflict has been carefully downplayed by both sides. Prior to World War I, shows were lighted by the electrician with input from the director, scenic designer, and producer. When the United Scenic Artists, which was a guild from 1896 on, became a union in 1918, a conflict of jurisdiction regarding lighting design was inevitable. IATSE has local unions throughout the country. Some are "mixed locals" representing both stagehands and projectionists. In metropolitan areas two separate locals exist. In most instances working lighting designers encounter IATSE members almost exclusively as talented, dedicated, imaginative electricians and stagehands who perform the arduous task of assembling and operating the designer's "lighting machine."

Membership

Provisions for membership vary somewhat in detail from local to local throughout the country. Membership traditionally involved the applicant placing his/her name on a waiting list. When the name came up for consideration, the applicant was either voted in or blackballed (i.e., rejected). Ultimately legal charges of both favoritism and discrimination arose under newer labor laws, and IATSE has contin-

James J. Kilpatrick, "Hard Times For Organized Labor," Indianapolis Star, May 18, 1985, p. 8.

William Serrin, "New Federal Statistics Show Union Membership Has Continued to Decline," The New York Times, Friday, Feb. 8, 1985, p. 11. Illus.

340 James L. Nuckolls, "Theatre Unions," Theatre Design & Technology, no. 5 (1966), pp. 3–11. Good basics; bibliography.

James L. Nuckolls, "Theatre Employment Contracts," Theatre Design & Technology, no. 2 (Dec. 1965), pp. 16–23. Good article, detailed; bibliography.

Klaus Holm, "Lighting—The Broadway Practice," Theatre Design & Technology, no. 11 (Dec. 1967), pp. 21–23. Good background material; worth consulting.

James Maronek, "The Ins and Outs of a Labor Union, USA Local 350, Chicago," Theatre Crafts, vol. 13, no. 5 (Oct. 1979), pp. 6, 94, 96.

341 1501 Broadway, N.Y., NY 10036. Telephone: (212) 730-1770 (international office).

342 1775 Broadway, N.Y., NY 10036. Telephone: (212) 489-7710 (Theatrical Protective Union #1 office).

[343] *111 West 50th Street, N.Y., NY 10020. Telephone: (212) 265-3500 (L.U. #15, New York City).*

[344] *575 Eighth Ave., 3rd Floor, N.Y., NY 10018. Telephone: (212) 736-4498 (L.U. #829, New York City).*

[345] *343 So. Dearborn St., Chicago, IL 60604. Telephone: (312) 431-0790.*

[346] *L.U. #829 in Los Angeles: 5410 Wilshire Blvd., Suite 407, Los Angeles, CA 90036, Telephone: (305) 444-5170.*

[347] *Holiday Inn, Golden Glades, 148 NW 167th St., North Miami Beach, Fla. Telephone: (305) 232-6801.*

[348] *The Eastern Region includes Ala., Conn., Del., Fla., Ga., Maine, Md., N.H., N.J., N.Y., N.C., Pa., R.I., S.C., Vt., Va., and W.Va., with offices in New York City. The Midwest Region, with offices in Chicago, embraces Ark., Colo., Ill., Ind., Iowa, Kan., Ky., La., Mich., Mo., Minn., Neb., N.Dak., Ohio, Okla., S.Dak., Tenn., Tex., and Wis. The West Coast Region, with offices in Los Angeles, covers Alaska, Ariz., Calif., Hawaii, Idaho, Mont., Nev., N.Mex., Oreg., Utah, Wash., and Wyo.*

Claudia Eller, "At Long Last Merger," Theatre Crafts, vol. 20, no. 7 (Aug./Sept. 1986), p. 10.

Claudia Eller, "USA All the Way," Theatre Crafts, vol. 21, no. 3 (March 1987), pp. 14–15, 74–77.

ued to adapt to reality by modifying admission procedures. An apprenticeship system has now been widely adopted. Apprentice tests are used, followed by a three-year period of apprenticeship, work training, and experience. This leads to an admissions list from which new full members are drawn as the need arises. With a long waiting list of qualified applicants, it is possible to work five or more years prior to receiving a card and full membership.

Within the geographical area represented by an IATSE local, the first choice of jobs goes to full members of that local. When all are employed, the local next turns to available card-carrying members from other IATSE locals. When demand is heavy the local's business agent calls upon members of other (allied or friendly) unions and, finally, calls upon non-card-carrying friends, relatives of members, and anyone who can handle the job. First choice of the prime jobs *always* remains with the card-carrying members of the local in whose jurisdiction the work is performed.

There is one exception to this process. Any member of any local (throughout the country) may file an IATSE contract with the New York City international office covering a key position (electrician, soundman, followspot operator) for a road (touring) production. This member is paid and employed by the management of the attraction. Terms of employment are different. A much higher pay rate is involved for a production contract with the international office. It allows "unlimited hours" plus specific provisions for travel and expenses. These are the "plum jobs." Production men are the cream of the industry: ambitious, experienced, dedicated. They have "saved the skin" of many a beginning lighting designer. Membership in *any* IATSE local is advantageous to a working lighting designer.

NABET

The National Association of Broadcast Employees and Technicians (NABET) represents a wide range of engineers, directors of photography, cameramen, electricians, etc., both for film and TV.[343] NABET Local Union #15 represents lighting directors at ABC, NBC, and some other locations in videotape and film in New York City. Since the basic union (L.U. #11) includes cameramen and video engineers, locals are to be found throughout the country. Traditionally, lighting directors at ABC and NBC begin as cable men, camera men, boom pushers, etc. They must hold a NABET card before specializing in lighting. Those among the engineers with either an obvious aptitude or a strong interest in lighting direction are allowed or encouraged to specialize in lighting. Both unions (IATSE and NABET) negotiate good salaries and prime working conditions for their lighting directors. Membership in NABET is conditional only upon "having a job." An apprentice exam is available for properly trained engineers.

USA

The United Scenic Artists (USA) union, the key union involving lighting designers, had a total membership of 2,129 in 1989. A merger agreement is underway which divides the union into four regions: the Eastern Region (headquartered in New York City with Local #829),[344] the Midwest Region (headquartered in Chicago with Local #350),[345] a West Coast Region (Los Angeles),[346] and a Southern (Florida) section.[347] The proposed merger structure, making USA function as a national union, is quite complex. The merger, however, is not yet (1989) in full effect. Local #829 was founded June 24, 1918, and #350 on January 19, 1927. Both are members of the International Brotherhood of Painters and Allied Trades.[348] Local Union #350 has approximately 360 members.

Jurisdiction

USA represents scenic designers, scenic artists (painters), costume designers, lighting designers, and people in allied crafts (including projection designers, storyboard artists, mural and diorama workers, etc.). In the television field the union represents designers and painters but not lighting directors. In feature film the union's jurisdiction includes art directors (scenery) and costume designers and scenic artists nationwide, but not lighting designers (called "directors of photography" or "cinematographers"). Since the merged union will be a member of the International Brotherhood of Painters and Allied Trades, in a strike situation its traditional allies are other painters, construction unions, and (frequently) teamsters. USA has frequently received less positive support from other theatre unions, such as Equity, musicians, IATSE stagehands, etc.

USA #829 has a lot to look after with jurisdiction in five different design/craft specialties and involvement in theatre, film, TV, cable, commercials, etc. It also has some Canadian members. Operating with one business agent (elected), two to three assistant business agents, and an office staff of 8 to 12 (handling records, dues, contracts, and general office work), plus retained attorneys and accountants, #829's real strength rests in the fact that the top employable artists/craftsmen in the business are members. All unions *claim* broad jurisdiction control, but *actual* control is often limited to those places of employment where the union's membership is willing to act in unison to enforce conditions (or the management presumes that they will). Local #829 created a separate category of membership for lighting designers in 1963.[349]

Local #350 in Chicago, representing the Midwest (in TV and legitimate theater, but not in feature film), has an even larger geographical area. It operates with one business agent and part-time office help. Nonetheless, #350 remains an effective force.

USA #829 normally has signed employment-jurisdictional contracts with key feature film producers; the TV networks; free-lance and cable TV; the lesser independent and commercial producers; the New York City scenery suppliers (the shops that build and paint theatre scenery); the Metropolitan Opera; Radio City Music Hall; the New York City Opera and several regional opera companies; the major ballet companies (American Ballet Theatre, New York City Ballet, Joffrey Ballet, Alvin Ailey Dance Co., etc.); the League of New York Theatres (Broadway producers and theatre owners); the Children's Television Workshop; Channel 13; and miscellaneous Off-Broadway, regional and dinner theatres. Less secure is their jurisdictional control for industrial shows, trade shows, and expositions. Contracts have in the past existed with the Ringling Bros.

Circus in Florida. USA #829 exercises quite effective control in the larger East Coast metropolitan centers: New York City, Washington (D.C.), Philadelphia, and Boston. As is the case with all unions dealing with a large geographical area, the further away a situation is from New York (or Chicago or Los Angeles), the weaker the union's control over it is.

Financing

USA #829 and USA #350 are supported by (1) initiation fees, (2) monthly dues and assessments, and (3) a percentage (usually 2 percent) of each member's weekly earnings. USA #829 members and their employers contribute to a separately administered Pension and Welfare Fund, which provides group health insurance, major medical coverage, GHI dental care, Blue Cross-Blue Shield, and life insurance for those members whose regular employment (a low yearly minimum) qualifies them to participate. Also there is an emergency Sick and Benefit Fund.

Conditions

Both USA #829 and USA #350 enforce proper program, poster, and advertisement credit for lighting designers. Each has "Working Rules" which protect members from improper working conditions or employer abuse. Both require the filing of three *separate* contracts for each show: one for scenic design, one for costume design, and one for lighting design (although all three contracts may involve a single designer if the designer is certified to work in several areas). Since all three positions must be filled by union members and all three contracts must be approved by the union's business agent before work can proceed on a show, this effectively prevents nonunion members from working on unionized productions. The penalty for violation is formal "charges" against that member by the union's elected business agent with the executive board sitting as a "trial jury" to determine guilt and to assess penalty fines or other strictures. Such fines must be paid by any member found guilty prior to any further acceptance of regular dues by the union. Failure to pay can result in loss of union membership and loss of all accumulated benefits and pension rights with the local and the international union.

[349] *Letter to me from Secretary Elmon Webb, dated June 18, 1979: "With the I.A. (International Association of Theatrical and Stage Employees) threat growing, a committee was appointed on January 9, 1962, to explore the problems of lighting design in the theatre and report back. Appointed: Musser, Rosenthal, Feder, Oenslager, Mielziner, Polakov and Gurlitz." I also served on that committee along with Peggy Clark and Charles Elson. "Later proposals were made to formulate a lighting exam, and November 16, 1962, was the initial deadline for applications–of which there were 64. The Exam was in January 1963, and reported (to the floor) on March 5. Passing: Hemsley, Benson, March, Collins, Hunt, Dunham, Ronstadt, Steele, Gallenstein, and Batchelder. They were obligated in May 1963."*

Members in good standing of #350 for one year's time are allowed to accept employment within #829's jurisdiction with #829's approval. A member of #350 may not, however, transfer membership from Local Union #350 into #829 (that is, receive a "clearance card" for transfer of membership from the jurisdiction of one local union within the international into another local) before having been a member of #350 (in good standing) for three years.

Dues

Monthly dues for #829 members are around $15 per month or $180 per year (1989). Inflation or other factors resulting in action by the voting membership can change this at any time through prescribed constitution procedures. Initiation fees are $1,000 for lighting designers who have passed the annual entrance exam; these fees are $2,500 for those who enter the union "organizationally," as a working professional (this is called a "professional" membership and is described in detail later in this chapter). Members also pay 2 percent of all *gross* earnings received for a union job (including royalty payments). Life membership is available for members in good standing for 25 years and upon application at the age of 60. In 1989 there were 120 Life Members. Life members, however, may not continue to work actively under the union's jurisdiction without paying dues.

Admission to Membership

Prior to July 2, 1972, the only *approved* method of joining USA #829 was by passing the annual USA #829 Entrance Examination. Only during one year in the long distant past did the general membership vote to bypass offering the exam because there was a surplus of unemployed members. This has not happened recently and does not seem likely to reoccur. There is now another legal way to join the union. In 1972, then-president Jim Ryan and I coauthored a change in admission policy which was sent to the members in a mail referendum, passed, and became a part of the present union constitution. The change came about as a result of the Taft-Hartley "Right to Work" laws. If a producer wishes to hire a nonunion designer and cannot be dissuaded, by law the union can choose to (1) allow the nonunion designer to work but dissuade *all* other members

of USA #829 (scenic artists, for example) from working on that production (meanwhile informing the nonunion designer that USA #829 does not wish him or her as a member), or (2) allow the nonunion designer to join the union (the business agent proposes the potential designer for membership at a monthly union meeting, recommending the designer for acceptance "for organizational purposes as a professional," i.e., to expand control of places of employment). Here are the pertinent portions of the July 1972 admissions policy:

It is the intention of this Union to include within its membership all professionals working in areas where we have collective bargaining agreements, and that therefore, when it shall come to the attention of our Business Agents that an individual is found to be so working, said individual shall be proposed to the floor for membership.

That the initiation fees of this local shall be: **LIGHTING DESIGNER $2,500.00**

That an examination shall be offered annually. That this examination shall be geared toward Designers and Artists, as a method of determining their professional qualifications.

That in consideration of the money and time that is normally required for an applicant to successfully complete the examination, then those new members who are admitted upon the recommendation of the examination committee as having passed the examination shall receive a credit of $1,500.00 on the above listed initiation fees, and the total initiation fee for such new members shall not exceed $1,000.00.[350]

Obviously producers do not wish to be subjected to the first alternative listed previously (the entire production done with nonunion designers and scenic artists), and the union does not wish to be representing a working nonmember. So the second alternative ("professional" membership) is now widely used. By 1980 more than 50 percent of the new members were admitted "professionally." This "professional" route presents no problem when the designer applying already has an international reputation (Salvadore Dali, Marc Chagall, Oliver Messel, or Richard Pilbrow, for example). It presents few problems when the applicant has established a successful track record of some duration in this country (several years of noteworthy work with a key regional or educational theatre, for example). Thus the "professional" route is invoked when (1) a noted foreign designer works in this country, or (2) a successful "hit" production is moved from a regional theatre, university theatre, or Off-Broadway to a Broadway theatre and the producer insists upon using the original designer. This route is *not* intended to provide membership in the union to the untried recent university graduate nor the "bush league" designer with a long string of mediocre work. (See Fig. 12.1 for earlier membership trends.)

The Union Entrance Exams

The USA #829 Entrance Exam

Application. While there has been some discussion concerning the eventual elimination of the Lighting Design Entrance Examination, the exam in some form will undoubtedly be with us for several more years. Democratic unions move very slowly in modifying tradition. The separate category of union membership, "Lighting Designer," was created in 1963, thanks (in large part) to persistent efforts by those "All-Category" members specializing in lighting design, particularly Tharon Musser and Jean Rosenthal (see footnote 349). The exam itself has been modified each year by a committee of working designers appointed by the #829 president. Applicants wishing to take the exam should apply in writing to The Examination Committee, United Scenic Artists, 575 Eighth Ave., N.Y., NY 10018, and request an application form and the available information booklet. Each year's exam committee establishes its own applications cutoff date.

The exam committee is appointed by the president of #829. Members are paid only a token amount for serving; working on the exam committee is a "labor of love." The president each year selects a few willing "old-timers" (with prior experience and an established standing in the industry) and a few new members. Since the committee serves only during a portion of the year and operates mostly with volunteers, an applicant shouldn't expect a prompt reply.

The Interview. If an applicant is selected for interview, he or she needs to supply by the time of the interview (1) three letters of recommendation from the references listed on the application, (2) an up-to-date professional résumé, (3) a portfolio of past work, and (4) a completed interview project (if one was assigned). The applicant then receives a

RECENT ADMISSIONS TO MEMBERSHIP,
UNITED SCENIC ARTISTS, LIGHTING

L.U. #829

Year	Number of applicants taking exam	Number admitted to membership through exam	Number in lighting admitted to membership professionally-organizationally
1970	21	3	
1971		(4)	
1972	22	4	
1973	23	3	1
1974	18	1	1
1975	26	2	1
1976	33	3	1
1977	31	6	2
1978	38	8	4
1979	53	12	2

SUMMARY:

Average no. taking Lighting Exam each year (10 yr. period): approx. 30

Average no. passing Lighting Exam each year and admitted to membership: 4.6

Entered by exam: 77%

Total no. admitted to memvership in lighting organizationally/
Professionally in 7 year period: 12

Entered Prof./Org.: 22%

Source: Elmon Webb, Secretary. from minutes for U.S.A.A. #829

L.U. #350

Year	Number of applicants taking exam	Number admitted to membership through exam	Number in lighting admitted to membership professionally-organizationally
Fall 1974	4	3	
Spring 1975	6	1	
Fall 1975	3	2	
Spring 1976	7	2	
Fall 1976	4	2	
Spring 1977	11	6	
Fall 1977	4	1	
Spring 1978	4	0	
Spring 1979	6	0	

SUMMARY:

Average no. taking Lighting Exam each year (6 year period): approx. 8

Average no. passing Lighting Exam each year and admitted to membership: 2.8

Entered by exam: 85%

Total no. admitted to membership in lighting organizationally/
professionally in 6 year period: 3

Entered by Prof./Org.: 15%

Source: Caryl Esteves, Office Manager, U.S.A.A. #350.

NOTE: Professional/organizational entrance to union not available by year.

Figure 12.1 Admissions to the United Scenic Artists in Lighting.

letter from the exam committee chairman with information about of the date, time, and place of the scheduled interview. The letter will also list what the applicant should bring to the interview. Photographs of lighting, programs, and press notices are frowned upon. If the applicant chooses to bring slides, they should be accompanied by a viewer. All drawings should be half-inch scale (one-half inch equals one foot) or larger. If an applicant cannot be present for the scheduled interview, for valid reasons (such as a job or the prohibitive expense of making two trips from California or Florida, etc.), the exam committee must be notified immediately. In such a case, the committee often will reschedule the interview for the date immediately prior to the exam and will send the individual all the necessary information. Applicants who have not heard from the union as deadlines near should contact the exam committee by telephone, because sometimes letters get lost. The committee schedules exams for a huge group of applicants. Eighty people applied for the 1982 New York City interview, and 69 were actually interviewed. Sixty-two were interviewed in 1985.

Interview Day. Each applicant is seen for 15 minutes by at least three professional working lighting designers. They look at the applicant's résumé, read letters of recommendation, ask about background and training, and perhaps ask questions about design concepts and views of theatre lighting. They usually ask about the applicant's reasons for wishing to join the union. They will examine, in careful detail, any required scaled drawing light plot the applicant brings showing instruments selected, color, wattage, mounting positions, and intensities. Also, the interviewers will allow some time for the applicant to ask questions. At the end of the interview it is *possible* for the interviewers to rule that an applicant is not ready to take the exam, perhaps because they believe that the applicant falls far short of minimum qualifications for admission. In such a case the interviewers may suggest either (1) further study (they may suggest places to study) or (2) acquisition of further nonunion work and experience. At the other extreme, the interviewers sometimes suggest that an applicant's presentation indicates immediate readiness for union membership with no need to take the exam! (A total of 15 applicants were so admitted in 1985.)

Those of us who have served for many years on the annual exam committee despair of the large number of applicants who wish to take the exam who obviously are not yet ready. One has only to sit through four solid 12-hour days of judging practicals (described later in this chapter) to understand the annoyance of poorly paid volunteers watching the work of masses of unqualified applicants.

Following the interview the applicant may be informed about the exam fee being charged (around $150 – $200, but subject to change). This fee is nonrefundable. It is a minimum charge which barely covers the cost to the union of space to give the exam, as well as all that is involved in the practical: a theatre, rented lighting equipment, color media, actors and actresses, stagehands, costumes and scenery, etc. The applicant is told what play or opera or production has been selected for the practical portion of the exam.

I have included later in this chapter (Fig. 12.5) portions of the 1976 and 1977 USA #829 Lighting Exam — not because they are in any important way similar to the exams now in use, but as an example of the level of presentation, knowledge, and design imagination the union expects of those who wish to become new members. In 1976, for the now-discontinued "home project," applicants were supplied with information about theatre and scenery for a production of *The Member of the Wedding* at the Zellerbach Theatre in Philadelphia. Applicants were given both a ground plan and section drawing of the Zellerbach, an instruction sheet, and a section and a line drawing for the scenery (these are shown later in the chapter, in Fig. 12.5). What used to be the home project has now become a part of the interview, but the examples of the old home project given in Fig. 12.5 are a good indication of the competence expected from those whom the committee recommends for USA #829 membership (the examples offered are the work of three designers who are now established successful professionals).

The interview has assumed more importance in recent years. Since 1980 it has been possible for a limited number of interview applicants to be excused from taking the full examination if, in the opinion of two teams of three interviewers (who are working professional lighting design members of the union), the applicant's work and résumé and conduct during the interview process indicate that the applicant is already fully qualified for membership in the union (see footnote 351 under "professional membership"). These applicants, from 4 to 15 in number yearly since this policy was adopted, are then recommended for full membership in the union without going through the rest of the exam process. This modification has greatly increased the importance of the interview, and has allowed the union to reduce the number of applicants taking each year's full exam. The full exam is an expensive and time-consuming process for the union, particularly in view of the growing number of new applicants each year due to the extensive instruction in lighting design now available throughout the educational system. Further, a cautious legal check established that the procedures used by the union do, indeed, allow the union to certify—during the interview process—that an applicant is not yet qualified to undertake the full exam.

In the past, the numbers of applicants grew continuously from year to year due to three factors: (1) educators and members of other avocational designer groups who had no real intention of practicing the art/craft full-time were taking the exam because they desired the "certification" which a USA #829 card conveys; (2) applicants, most just out of school, who knew that they would not pass the exam the first time, were taking it because they wished to familiarize themselves with its process and contents so as to be better prepared for "the next time"; and (3) a small group of applicants were taking the exam each year who were not then qualified for either the exam or union membership and who showed little promise of ever attaining that status. The union's careful reaction to these growing numbers, through the efforts of those long-connected with the annual exam (myself included), was to do two things: (1) strengthen the interview process as indicated above and (2) simplify the extent of the exam during the two-day exam period to speed up the lengthy grading process. The first obvious move was to eliminate the "Dance Problem." Other changes have been made by each year's exam committee. By 1984 the actual exam had been reduced to only the practical exam and an examination of the home project submitted at interview time by the applicant to selected judges. Further modifications followed. The exam is modi-fied each year; the text which follows indicates several modifications which have taken place up to the 1986 entrance exam.

The Exam Days. See footnote 351 for recent dates on which the interviews and practical exam were offered. The exam is now given, not only in New York City and Chicago, but also on the West Coast, although the Chicago local is the only union that continues to require the exam as of this writing. Figures 12.2, 12.3, and 12.4 are action photographs of the 1982 Chicago (#350) Lighting Exam. Sufficient time is allowed the applicant so that the home project, when used, represents the designer's best work. The purpose of the home project is to determine what the applicant can do when not under intense pressure. Looked for is a careful and detailing reading and analysis of the script; an ideal light plot, section, and hookup; a shop order; quality drafting and presentation; and mastery of technical/design details. It is always presumed that the applicant does all of the work submitted, with no help from friends or advisors. None of this work is signed. The applicant is assigned a code number. The union intends to ensure that the applicant's work is judged without any influence from a union judging member's personal acquaintanceship with an applicant or knowledge of an applicant's previous design work. Later the applicant is given an alphabetical letter designation for the practical problem. The judges should not however know the applicant's written work code number or code letter. It is common practice for any judges present at the practical who have had an applicant as a student or are well-acquainted with an applicant's work to disqualify themselves from scoring that applicant's practical. The exam is intended to judge the applicants' work—not their personality. Judges are not allowed to mix with, closely observe, or engage in prolonged conversation with applicants until all parts of the exam have been completed. In recent years the exam has been held at Pace College's Schimmel Center Theatre in New York City.

Example: The 1976 USA #829 Entrance Exam. Caution: The 1976 exams presented in Fig. 12.5 should be used *only* as an indication of the level of ability and preparedness necessary to undertake the exam. Each year the play and

[351] *At this time, the entrance exam has been divided into three groups:*

Track A Exam: Professional qualifications determined by an Interview and analysis of the applicant's Resume (for Experience) and Portfolio. Held in March/April of 1989.

Track B Exam: The traditional "Exam" wherein applicants do some sort of practical project (generally a home project and/or an on the spot practical exam) determined yearly by the Exam Committee. This is the exam generally chosen by recent graduates and those without a professional "track record" (i.e., fewer battle scars).

Professional: Application to the Union is made by any designer, scenic artist, stylist, craftsperson on the basis of a bona fide Union Contract. That is, anyone found working under one of our Collective Bargaining Agreements is required to make application to the Union and is then submitted by the Business Representative to the membership for approval."

The quote above is from the July 1988 membership Newsletter. During 1987 the "Track A" Lighting Design Exam was offered January 24 and September 19. The "Track B" Exam Interview was on April 25 to 26 and the Design Practical on May 16 to 17. The dates for the lighting entrance exam vary somewhat from year to year.

Figure 12.2 Judges at their table at Northwestern University for the 1982 Chicago (USA #350) Lighting Entrance Examination. (*Courtesy of Van Phillips.*)

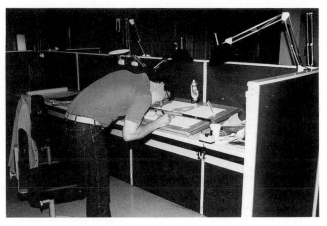

Figure 12.3 An applicant working on a light plot during the 1982 Chicago (USA #350) Lighting Entrance Examination at Northwestern University. (*Courtesy of Van Phillips.*)

theatre conditions are decided upon by that year's exam committee, and each year the exam-day problems are modified.

Those applicants who have only worked in one (or a few) university theatres during their training period often find the interview and exam to be a real challenge. Notice on the accompanying instruction sheets from the 1976 exam that a new, brief concept was called for. The new theatre was the Royale. The applicant was asked to modify with colored pencils a *print* (not the original drawing) of the Home Project light plot. A new hookup was called for (on rented switchboards — the Zellerbach has electronic memory switchboards permanently installed). A shop order was called for. Sketches and diagrams were required in response to specific questions which show (visually) the lighting design intention for particular scenes, and the applicant was also required to supply and explain further details (specified) concerning equipment placement and selection, control, and color to solve the problem posed in specific cues within the terms of his or her own concept of the play. Examples of the exam-day *Member of the Wedding* light plot, section, hookup, answers to questions, shop order, and sketches appear in Fig. 12.5.

(Text continues on p. 389)

Figure 12.4 Applicant lighting the practical portion of the Chicago (USA #350) Lighting Entrance examination in Northwestern University's "Black Box" Theatre in 1982. (*Courtesy of Van Phillips.*)

UNITED SCENIC ARTISTS LOCAL 829

LIGHTING DESIGNER'S ENTRANCE EXAMINATION - HOME PROJECT - 1976

The formal examination will take place on two days of the Memorial Day weekend starting Saturday, May 29th through Monday, May 31st at Schimmel Center Theater, Pace College, Spruce Street between Park Row and Williams Street (near the Brooklyn Bridge) in Manhattan. The examination will begin at 9:00 A.M. each day. Due to the large number of applicants, some may be called to take the "Practical" on Friday, May 28th. We advise you to hold the entire four-day span open.

Your Home Project must be completed and brought with you to the examination.

The 1976 examination will be based on Shakespeare's KING LEAR and Carson McCullers' THE MEMBER OF THE WEDDING.

(1) Concept:
Prepare a written dissertation on the lighting concept you would employ in designing the lighting for KING LEAR. This concept is part of your examination and will be used in grading your work. It should be a written expression of the artistic contribution to the production which will be made by the Lighting Designer and a statement of the visual communication of the playwright's ideas as interpreted by the Lighting Designer. The essay should be 250 words or less, typed and double spaced. It is understood that the judges are familiar with the plot and that they do not expect a "book report" or an equipment list.

(2) Lighting Design:
Using the Ground Plans and Sections provided and the equipment available from a standard Broadway rental house, design the lighting for the play THE MEMBER OF THE WEDDING for the Zellerbach Theatre, Philadelphia, to include:
1. Light Plot. All drafting to be in the scale of $\frac{1}{2}$" = 1'-0", using the standard lighting templates.
2. Complete Lighting Designer's Section.
3. Board Hook-up

Bring two (2) clear prints (blue line or black line) of your designs of the above to the examination.

Please limit your color on all parts of this examination to Cinemoid, Roscogel or Roscolene.

GENERAL INSTRUCTIONS FOR THE HOME PROJECT:

DO NOT SIGN ANY OF THE PROJECT PAPERS -- THIS WILL DISQUALIFY YOU!

Your Home Projects must be brought with you to the exam on the first day. The United Scenic Artists reserves the right to retain any and all materials submitted.

That you will not solve any of the problems of the production with any other person(s) is understood to be a tacit and honorable agreement between the applicant and the United Scenic Artists Local Union 829. ANY VIOLATION of this understanding will immediately disqualify you for membership.

GENERAL INSTRUCTIONS FOR THE FORMAL EXAMINATION:

Bring to the examination the following: Drawing Board large enough to work on a Broadway production, drawing pencils, color pencils, pencil sharpener, erasers, T-square, triangles, paper, scale rule, standard $\frac{1}{2}$" lighting template, color books (for Cinemoid, Roscogel or Roscolene) and any other drafting material you normally use. Bring Drafting Table Light and extension.

Bring your scripts of KING LEAR and THE MEMBER OF THE WEDDING.

It is advisable for you to bring lunch.

Do not forget that payment is required by May 10, 1976. Please check the accompanying sheet for the appropriate fee.

Scripts for KING LEAR for $1.25 and for THE MEMBER OF THE WEDDING for $1.50 are available at the Drama Book Shop, 150 West 52nd Street, New York City, or may be purchased for the same price at the time of your Interview, from the Union.

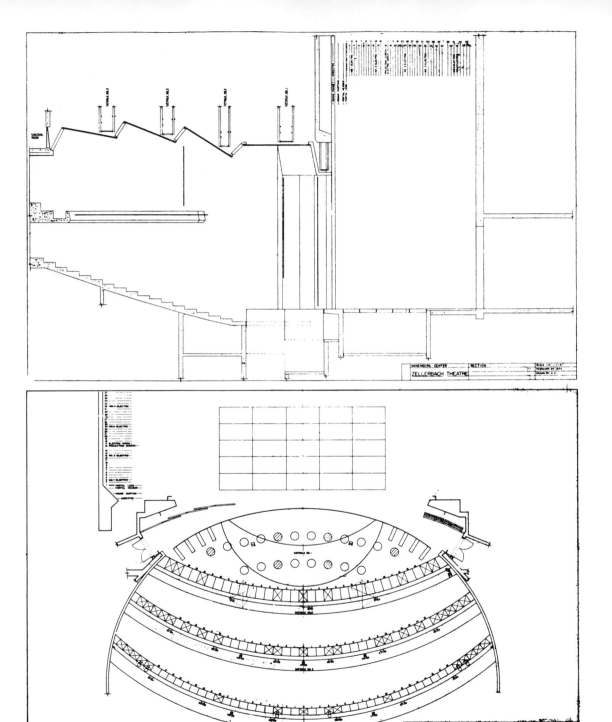

Figure 12.5 A sample of the United Scenic Artists Lighting Design Entrance Examination.

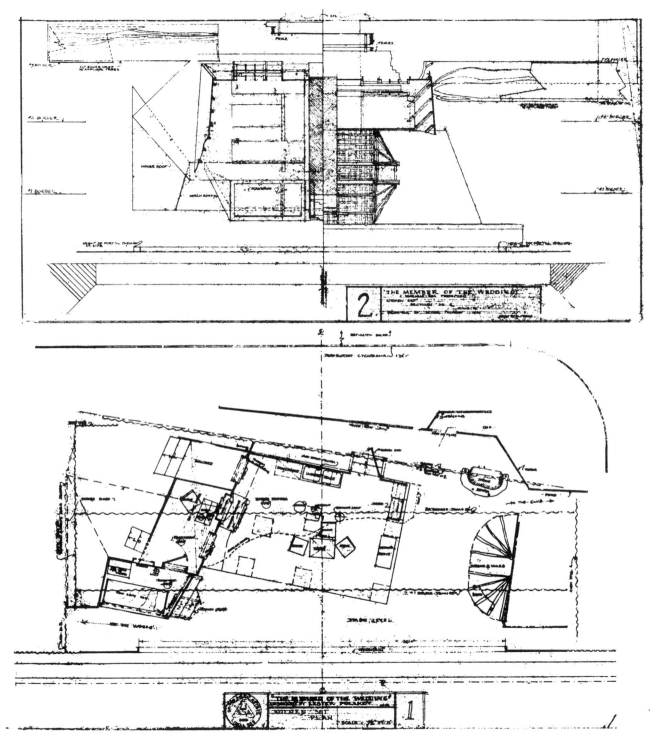

THE MEMBER OF THE WEDDING — LIGHTING CONCEPT

The Member of the Wedding is a lyric drama portraying the growth of an adolescent girl from extreme loneliness to a mature self-reliance. Because of Berenice's unselfish understanding and own sense of belonging, Frankie breaks through a wall of isolation and goes outward with a new feeling of belonging and human companionship.

Frankie is like the light of a single flickering candle. Her mind and spirit leap: they stretch, dance, dart and fly. She is all at once bright, gay, pretty and sad (to borrow from Harold Clurman). Like the candle flame, she is extremely sensitive to the atmosphere and events around her; her moods are easily intensified or smothered.

The lighting of the play can exhibit similar qualities. Just like a flickering candle flame, the light in the back yard (and hence the house) is ephemeral and fleeting, always changing in angle, color, and intensity depending on time of day, weather, and season. Every visual moment should be significant of Frankie's inner state; consequently, the production style is not altogether realistic. Just as a candle flame is heightened at times, specials can be employed to heighten certain visual moments. The color palette is generally warm (with warm blues and warm greens), pale, and soft, echoing the candle flame. Just like the flame of a candle, Frankie is affected by the atmosphere around her. The balmy Southern atmosphere continually changes, exploding in a thunder storm as Frankie is deserted by the wedding party and runs away. As the storm clears, the season changes. The candle stops flickering and glows with a new strength and sureness. In the final scene, the warm, steady glow of the kitchen light sustains itself and endures against the bleak November evening. As the season changes, we detect a change within Frankie herself, achieving freedom from loneliness in an adult reliance upon herself.

ABOVE: Applicant's written concept submitted with home project.
BELOW: Sketch of original set given to applicant.

THE MEMBER OF THE WEDDING   DESIGNED by LESTER POLAKOV

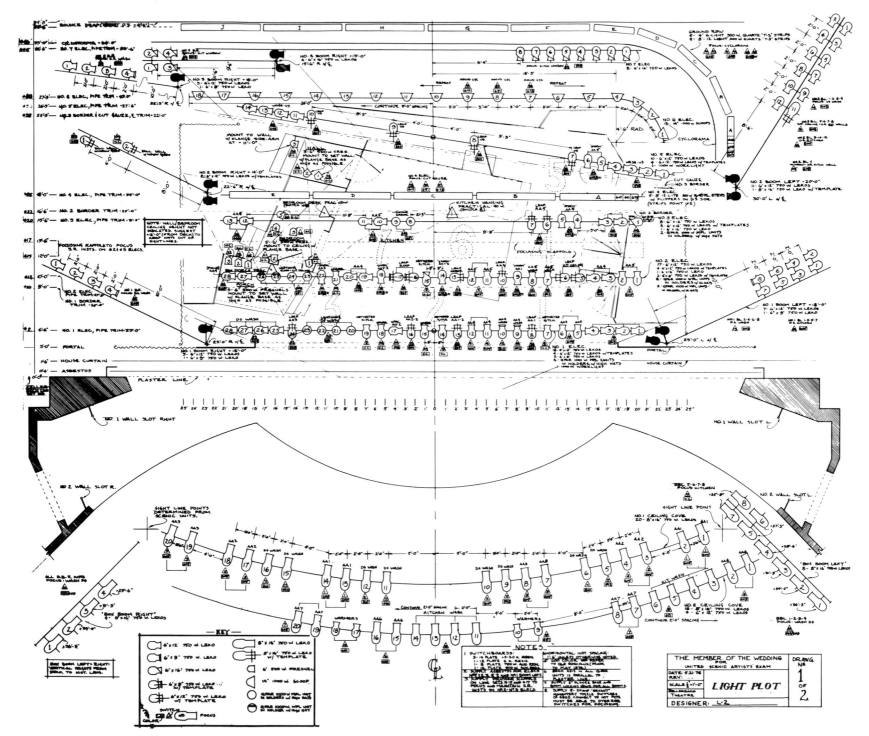

Figure 12.5 A sample of the United Scenic Artists Lighting Design Entrance Examination. *(Continued)*

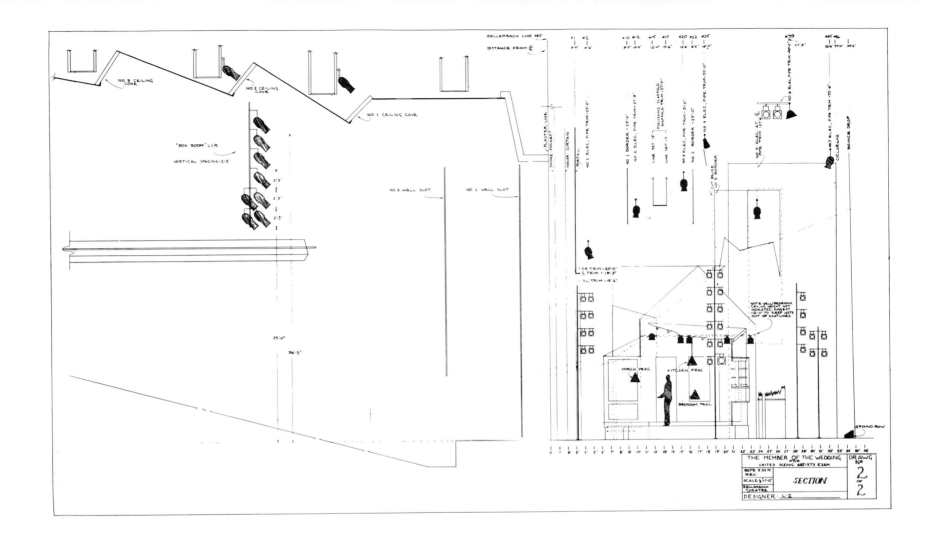

THE MEMBER OF THE WEDDING
UNITED SCENIC ARTISTS EXAM

SECTION

DRAWG N°
2 OF 2

Handwritten Hook-Up Sheet

ZELLERBACH   DESIGNER: L-2
MEMBER OF THE WEDDING HOOK-UP
PRODUCTION: USA. EXAM '76   BOARD #1   TYPE: RESISTANCE   14-PLATE 1500–3000 W.

SWITCH	LOCATION-#	TYPE-WATT	COLOR	FOCUS	NOTES
1	#1 COVE 1-2-13-14	4-8×16 750W LEKOS	605	A.A.1	
2	#1 COVE 3-4-17-18	4-8×16 750W LEKOS	605	A.A.2	
3	#1 COVE 7-8-19-20	4-8×16 750W LEKOS	605	A.A.3	
4	#1 ELEC 11-12	4-6×12 750W	605	A.A.4	

Member of the Wedding - HOOK-UP
Production: U.S.A. Exam '76
Board #1: 14-Plate 1500-3000W. Type: Resistance

Switch	Location-#	Type-Watt	Color	Focus
1	#1 Cove/1-2-13-14	4-8×16 750 W Lekos	605	A.A. 1
2	#1 Cove 3-4-17-18	4-8×16 750W Lekos	605	A.A. 2
3	#1 Cove 7-8-19-20	4-8×16 750W Lekos	605	A.A. 3
4	#1 Elec 5-6-11-12	4-6×12 750W Lekos	605	A.A. 4
5	#2 Elec 1-2-11-12	4-6×12 750W Lekos	605	A.A. 5
6	#2 Cove 1-2-15-16	4-8×16 750W Lekos	649	(Kitchen) A.A. 6
7	#2 Cove 7-8-19-20	4-8×16 750W Lekos	649	(Kitchen) A.A.7
8	#1 Elec 7-14-19	40W Prac.	N.C.	Motivated Kitchen + Prac
		3-6×12 750 W Leko		
	#2 Elec 15	1-6×16 750 W Leko		
9	#2 Cove 3-4-5-6	4-8×16 750W Lekos	651	Kitchen Wash (Afternoon)
10	BBL 5-6-7-8	4-8×16 750W Lekos	N.C.	Kitchen (BBL)
11	#1 Cove 6-10-12-16	4-8×16 750W Lekos	810	DS Wash (Afternoon)
12	#1E10/#2E8	2-6×9 750W Lekos	810	AA 4-5 Wash (Afternoon) *
13	#1 BL 2-4-6	3-6×12 750W Lekos	603	DS Wash (Late Aft Key)
	#1BL 8	1-6×9 750W Leko	603	
14	#2B L 1-2-3-4	4-6×12 750W Lekos	603	U S Wash (Late Aft Key)

Board #2: 14-Plate 1500-3000W Type: Resistance

Switch	Location-#	Type-Watt	Color	Focus
15	#2 Cove 9-10-17-18	4-6×12 750W Lekos	651	Curtain warmers
16	#2 Cove 11-12-13-14	4-8×16 750W Lekos	503	Kitchen Wash (Evening)
17	#1 Cove 5-9-11-15	4-8×16 750W Lekos	542	D S Wash (Evening)
18	1E9/2E7	2-6×9 750W Lekos	542	AA4-5 Wash (Evening) *
19	#1 Elec 1-2-3-4	4-6×12 750W Lekos	503	DS Wash "Ends" (Early Aft Key)
20	2E 3-4/3E 2-3	4-6×12 750 W Lekos	503	AA 4-5 "Ends" (Early Aft Key)
21	#5 Elec 1-2-3-.4	4-6×12 750 W Lekos	503	US Wash "Ends" (Early Aft Key)
22	#1 Elec 25-26-27-28	4-6×12 750W Lekos	648	DS Wash "Ends" (Aft Fill)
23	2E 19-20/3E 10-11	4-6×12 750W Lekos	648	AA 4-5 "Ends" (Aft Fill)
24	#5 Elec 11-12-13-14	4-6×12 750W Lekos	648	US Wash "Ends" (Aft Fill)
25	Aux 101-104 26 Aux 105-108 27 Aux 109-114 28 Aux 115-120			

Board #3: 14-Plate 1500-3000W Type: Resistance

Switch	Location-#	Type-Watt	Color	Focus
29	BBL 1-2-3-4	4-8×16 750 W Lekos	542/649	Wash (BBL-Evening)
30	BBR 1-2-3-4	4-8×16 750W Lekos	542/649	Wash (BBR Evening)
31	#2 B L 5-6-7-8	4-6×12 750W Lekos	603	Wash: Ext Walls, Roof, Kitch. Ceiling.
32	#2 Elec 9-14-18-22	4-6×12 750W Lekos	642/671	AA 1-2-3 DN Light (Storm)
33	3E 4-5/5E 5-6	4-6×12 750W Lekos	642/671	7AA 4-5 DN Light Storm
34	4B R 1-2-3-4	4-6×16 750 W Leko	669	U.S. Window -Kitchen- (Dawn)
35	1 BR 1-2-3	3-6×12 750 W Leko	669	D.S. Wash. (Dawn)
	1 BR 4	1-6×9 750 W Leko	669	
36	2E 27-28/3E 12-13	4-6×12 750W Lekos	669	AA 4+5 (Dawn)

Switch	Location-#	Type-Watt	Color	Focus
37	3 BR 1-2-3	3-6×12 750W Lekos	669	US Wash (Dawn)
	3 BR 4	1-6×9 750W Leko	669	
38	#5 Elec 7-8-9-10	4-6×12 750W Lekos/ w/Templates	869	US-Leaf Template
39	2E 5-6	2-6×12 750W Template Lekos	869	Ext Walls, Roof, Kitch. Ceiling - Leaf Template
	2E 16-17	2-6×9 750W Template Lekos		
40	Ground Row A-B-C-D-E	5-4' 6-Lt/300W Q-T3 Strips	603	Cyclorama (Curved Area)
41	Ground Row A-B-C-D-E	5-4' 6-Lt. 300W Q-T3 Strips	649	Cyclorama (Curved Area)
42	Ground Row	5-4' 6-Lt 300W Q-T3 Strips	607/607	Cyclorama (Curved Area)

Board #4: 12-Plate 6000W Type: Resistance

Switch	Location-#	Type-Watt	Color	Focus
43	Ground Row F-G-H-I-J	5-8' 12-Lt 300W Q-T3603 Strips		CYC (Flat Area)
44	Ground Row F-G-H-I-J	5-8' 12-Lt 300W Q-T3649 Strips		CYC (Flat Area)
45	Ground Row F-G-H-I-J	5-8' 12-Lt 300W Q-T3607/607 Strips		CYC (Flat Area)
46	#6 Elec 3-6-9-12-15-18	6-14" 1000W Scoops	610	CYC Wash
47	#6 Elec 2-5-8-11-14-17	6-14" 1000 W Scoops	651	CYC Wash
48	#6 Elec 1-4-7-10-13-16	6-14" 1000 W Scoops	673	CYC Wash
49	#4 Elec A-B-C-D-E	5-8' 12 Lt 300 W R-40FL Strips w/ Flippers	610	Cut Gauze Wash
50	#4 Elec A-B-C-D-E	5-8' 12-Lt. 300W R-40 FL Strips w/ Flippers	651	Cut Gauze Wash
51	#4 Elec A-B-C-D-E	5-8' 12-Lt. 300W R-40 FL. Strips w/ Flippers	673	Cut Gauze Wash
52	#7 Elec 1-2-3-4 5-6-7-8	8-6×16 750W Lekos	503	Kitch. Windows
53	1E 8-13-16-24 2E 10-13 3E 6-7	8-6×12 750W Lekos w/ Templates	869	-Leaf- AA 1-2-3 AA 4+Arbor AA 5+Tree
54	1 BL 1-3-5-7 2 BL 9-10-12	7-6×12 750W Lekos	605	Kitchen AA 6-7 *

Board #5: 8-Plate 750W Aux Type: Resistance

	Switch	Location	Type-Watt	Color	Focus
MASTER 25	101	1E17	1-6×12 750W Leko	542	Yard-Act I - Spec (Curtain Lines)
	102	3E1	1-6×16 750W Leko	503	Kitchen - Act II + III Spec (Curtain Lines)
	103	#2 BR 1	1-6×12 750W Template Leko	649	Hall Wall Window Template (Early Aft)
	104	#2 BR 2	1-6×12 750W Template Leko	N/C	Hall Wall Window Template (Late Aft)
MASTER 26	105	#2 BL 11	1-8×16 750W Template Leko	603	Kitchen Floor + Sr Wall Window Template
	106	1 E 18	1-6×12 750W Leko	N.C.	Spare
	107	1 E 15	1-6×12 750W Leko	N.C.	Spare
	108	2 E 21	1-6×12 750W Leko	N.C.	Spare

Supply: 5-20A "Bryant" Momentary Toggle Switches (#4921) Connect to 2-6K Hot Pockets for Lightning Effects

	Switch	Location	Type-Watt	Color	Focus
H.P. 1	A	2E 23-24	2-QPAR 1000W MFL Holder w/Hi.Hat	651	Kitch. Ceiling (Lightning)
	B	2E 25-26	2-QPAR 1000W WFL unit in Holder w/ High Hats	651	House Roof (Lightning)
H.P. 2	C	1E 20-21	2-QPAR 1000W MFL unit in Holder w/ High Hat	651	AA 1-2 (Lightning)
	D	1E 22-23	2-QPAR 1000W MFL unit in Holder with High Hat	651	AA 2-3 (Lightning)
	E	3E 8-9	2-QPAR 1000W MFL unit in	651	AA 4-5-Arbor (Lightning)

Board #6: Aux. Type: 12-Plate 500W Resistance

	Switch	Location	Type-Watt	Color	Focus
Master 27	109	Bedroom Desk Prac. Practical	100W Bedroom Desk	N.C.*	
	110	Bedroom #1	1-6" 500W Fres	N.C.	Bdroom Wash
	111	Bedroom #2	1-6" 500W Fres	N.C.	Bdroom Wash
	112	Bedroom #3	1-6" 500W Fres.	N.C.	Porch Door
	113	Bedroom #4	1-6" 500W Fres.	N.C.	Porch Window
	114	Bedroom #5	1-6" 500W Fres.	N.C.	Kitch. Door
	115	Porch Prac. and Porch #1	40 W Prac + 1-6" 500 W Fres	N.C.	Porch Wash
Master 28	116	Porch #2	1-6" 500W Fresnel	N.C.	Porch Wash
	117	Porch #3	1-6" 500W Fresnel	N.C.	Porch Wash
	118	Hall #1	1-6" 500W Fresnel	N.C.	Hall Wash
	119	Hall #2	1-6" 500W Fresnel	N.C.	Hall Wash
	120	Hall #3	1-6" 500W Fresnel	N.C.	Kitch Door

*Load as Needed

Figure 12.5 A sample of the United Scenic Artists Lighting Design Entrance Examination. (*Continued*)

DIRECTIONS:

Read the entire examination THOROUGHLY to make certain you understand everything. Your time should be budgeted so as to complete
each part of the exam; never leave any section blank as this will
affect your final grade. There are two days to complete this examination. Saturday until 6:00 P.M. and Sunday until 6:00 P.M.
Because of the great number of applicants, it will be necessary for
some to return Monday for your "Practicals". On Saturday you may
leave everything at your table since you are not permitted to take
any portion of your project home. All work on MEMBER OF THE WEDDING
will be collected Sunday night. All work on KING LEAR will be collected
as soon as you complete your "Practical". Take a lunch break when
you wish.

DO NOT SIGN YOUR NAME TO ANY PART OF THIS TEST!

Put your examination NUMBER on all paper work except the Concept
for KING LEAR and the "Practical" for which you will be assigned
a practical LETTER. Be certain to put your number on all paper
work so there will be no question as to whom it belongs.

ANSWER ALL QUESTIONS, INCLUDING THE PRACTICAL, ACCORDING TO YOUR
WRITTEN CONCEPTS. IN THE EVENT YOUR CONCEPT WILL NOT WORK WITH THE
SETTING PROVIDED, INDICATE HOW YOU WOULD CHANGE YOUR CONCEPT TO
SUIT THIS SITUATION. YOUR CONCEPT FOR KING LEAR WILL BE COLLECTED
AT THE TIME OF YOUR PRACTICAL EXAMINATION. REMEMBER TO PUT YOUR
PRACTICAL LETTER ON YOUR CONCEPT FOR KING LEAR. IT IS PART OF THE
EXAMINATION AND WILL BE USED BY THE JUDGES IN EVALUATING YOUR WORK
AND HOW YOU TRANSLATE IT INTO CREATIVE DESIGN.

1. PRACTICAL: KING LEAR

Approximately one hour prior to your scheduled time, you will
be given your "Practical" problems and light plot. After 45 minutes
the proctor will pick up your color list   and concept for
KING LEAR and at your scheduled time you will be conducted into the
theatre.You will have a total of 40 minutes to focus and set cues
for the problem you have chosen. Be sure to put your practical
letter on all papers concerning this part of the test as all work
in this area will be collected.

CHOOSE ONLY ONE OF THE PROBLEMS GIVEN.

For those taking the PRACTICAL on Monday; your examinations will
be collected and you will be excused at 4:20 P.M., Sunday.

2. THE MEMBER OF THE WEDDING

(A) In 200 words or less, write (legibly or print) your concept
for your lighting design for THE MEMBER OF THE WEDDING. Use the
guidelines for this dissertation as explained in your Home Project.

(B) Your production of THE MEMBER OF THE WEDDING in the Zellerbach Theatre in Philadelphia is a hit! A new Producer has bought the
production and is bringing it to New York into the Royale Theatre.
With color pencils of your choice adapt your light plot and section
for this new theatre on one set of your prints from your home project.
Specifications for the Royale Theatre:

Balcony Rail: 40' from plaster line, 10' above stage level
                 24 circuits, @ 20 Amps each

No. 1 Box Booms: 10' from plaster line, 6' above stage level (21')
                 28' left and right of center
                 4 circuits aside

No. 2 Box Booms: 20' from plaster line, 8' above stage level (21')
                 30' left and right of center
                 8 circuits aside

Service: Ample DC Current, 100 Amps of AC.

(C) Do a new Hookup for the Royale Theatre.

(D) Make a Shop Order for all equipment necessary for the
New York Production (Cable lengths not necessary.)

(E) QUESTIONS:
    (1) Through the use of simple line drawings, sketches or
        diagrams show how you intend to light the following scenes:

    (a) Act I, start of the show, from the first revealing of
        the set (Berenice in the kitchen, the family in the
        yard) for the Wedding Announcement till the family
        exit and John Henry enters the kitchen.

    (b) Act III Scene 1, end of scene, from Berenice and
        John Henry alone in the kitchen to (Cue) lights go
        out (gloom) and (Cue) Berenice lights candle. Meanwhile
        outside; storm, lightning flashes and thunder.

Also indicate approximate intensities of each circuit in
relation to the composition of each scene. Other verbal
descriptions will not be accepted.

    (2) Describe, in terms of your Hook-up, the circuits used in
        each of the above scenes in Question (1) in terms of:
        (a) Type of equipment used
        (b) Focus of equipment
        (c) Color choice
        (d) How each circuit implements your concept.

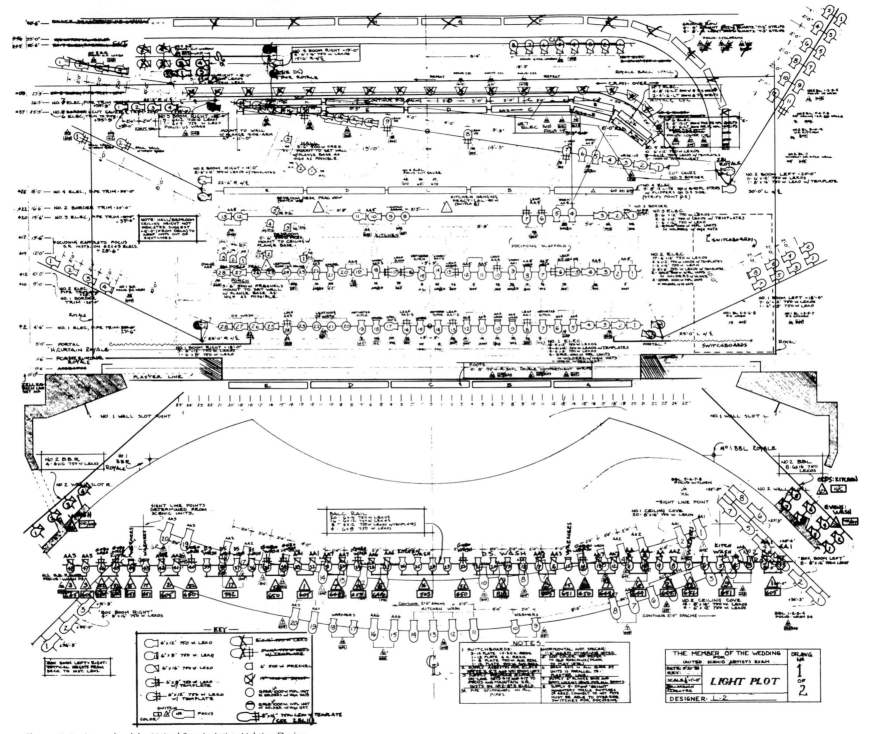

Figure 12.5 A sample of the United Scenic Artists Lighting Design Entrance Examination. *(Continued)*

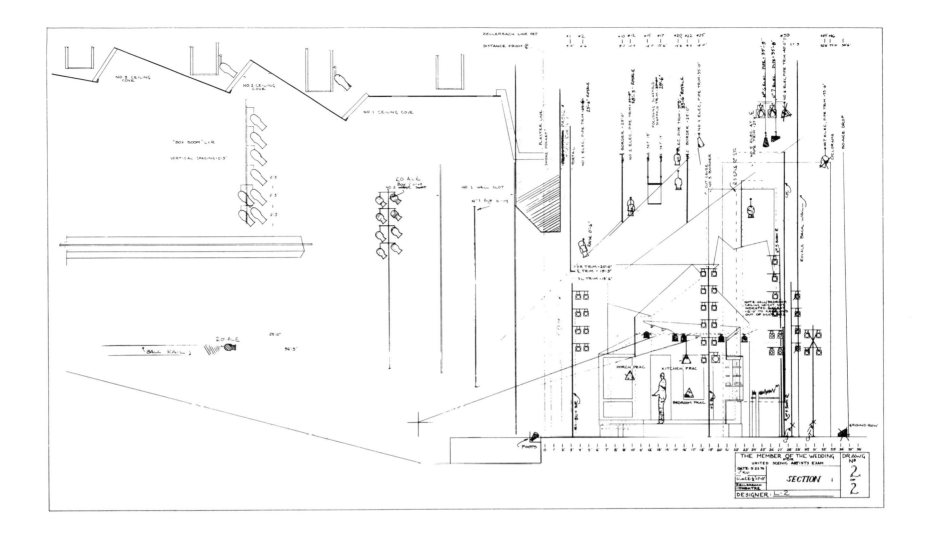

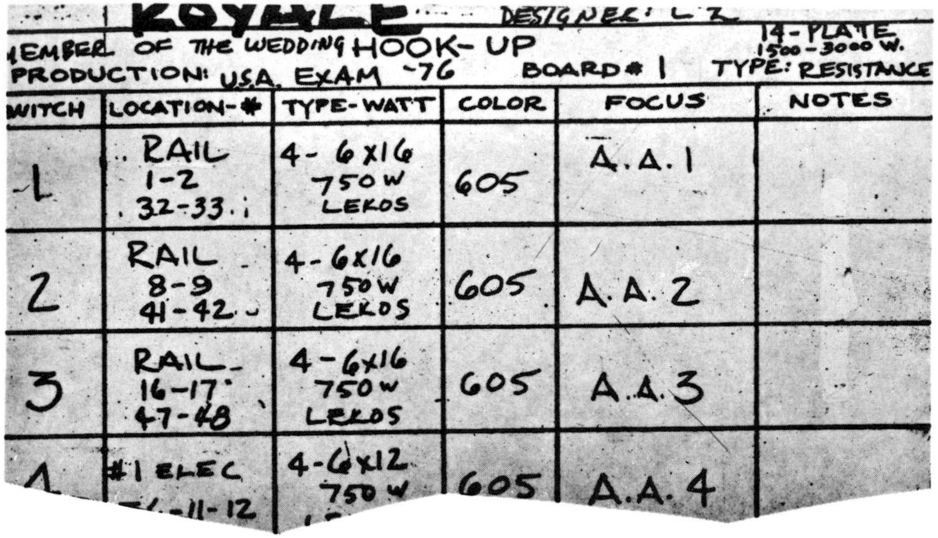

SWITCH	LOCATION-#	TYPE-WATT	COLOR	FOCUS	NOTES
1	RAIL 1-2 32-33	4-6x16 750W LEKOS	605	A.A. 1	
2	RAIL 8-9 41-42	4-6x16 750W LEKOS	605	A.A. 2	
3	RAIL 16-17 47-48	4-6x16 750W LEKOS	605	A.A. 3	
4	#1 ELEC -11-12	4-6x12 750 W	605	A.A. 4	

DESIGNER: L Z
MEMBER OF THE WEDDING HOOK-UP
14-PLATE 1500-3000 W.
PRODUCTION: USA EXAM -76
BOARD # 1
TYPE: RESISTANCE

Board #1: 14-Plate 1500-3000W. Type: Resistance

1	Rail 1-2,-32-33	4-6×16 750W Lekos	605	A.A. 1
2	Rail 8-9,-41-42	4-6×16 750W Lekos	605	A.A. 2
3	Rail 16-17,-47-48	4-6×16 750W Lekos	605	A.A. 3
4	#1 Elec 5-6-11-12	4-6×12 750W Lekos	605	A.A. 4
5	#2 Elec 1-2-11-12	4-6×12 750W Lekos	605	A.A. 5
6	Rail 10-11,-27-28	4-6×16 750W Lekos	649	(Kitchen) A.A. 6
7	Rail 12-13,-30-31	4-6×16 750W Lekos	649	(Kitchen) A.A. 7
8	#1 Elec 7-14-19 #2 Elec 15	40 W Prac. 3-6×12 750 W Leko 1-6×16 750W Leko	N.C.	Motivated Kitchen + Prac
9	Rail 3-4-5-6	4-6×12 750W Lekos	651	Kitchen Wash (Afternoon)
10	BBL 1-3-5-7	4-6×16 750W Lekos	N.C.	Kitchen (BBL)
11	Rail 18-19-20-21	4-6×12 750 W Lekos	810	DS Wash (Afternoon)
12	#1 E 10 #2 E 8	2-6×9 750W Lekos	810	AA 4-5 Wash (Afternoon) *
13	#1 BL 2-4-6 #1 BL 8	3-6×12 750W Lekos 1-6×9 750W Leko	603	DS Wash (Late Aft. Key)
14	#2 B.L. 1-2-3-4	4-6×12 750W Lekos	603	U.S. Wash (Late Aft Key)

Board #2: 14-Plate 1500-3000W Type: Resistance

15	Rail 7-15-43-44	4-6×9 750W Lekos	651	Curtain Warmers
16	Rail 23-24-25-26	4-6×12 750W Lekos	503	Kitchen Wash (Evening)
17	Rail 36-37-38-39	4-6×12 750W Lekos	542	D.S. Wash (Evening)
18	1 E 9/2 E 7	2-6×9 750W Lekos	542	AA 4-5 Wash (Evening)*
19	#1 Elec 1-2-3-4	4-6×12 750W Lekos	503	DS Wash "Ends" (Early Aft Key)
20	2E 3-4/3E 2-3	4-6×12 750W Lekos	503	AA 4-5 "Ends" (Early Aft Key)
21	#5 Elec 1-2-3-4	4-6×12 750W Lekos	503	US Wash "Ends" (Early Aft Key)
22	#1 Elec 25-26-27-28	4-6×12 750W Lekos	648	DS Wash "Ends" (Aft Fill)
23	2E 19-20/3E 10-11	4-6×12 750W Lekos	648	AA 4-5 "Ends" (Aft Fill)
24	#5 Elec 10-11-12-13	4-6×12 750W Lekos	648	US Wash "Ends" (Aft Fill)

25 Aux 101-104   26 Aux 105-108   27 Aux 109-114   28 Aux 115-120

Board #3: 14-Plate 1500-3000W Type: Resistance

29	BBL 2-4-6-8	4-6×16 750W Lekos	542/ 649	Wash (BBL-Evening)
30	BBR 1-2-3-4	4-6×16 750W Lekos	542/ 649	Wash (BBR Evening)
31	#2 B.L. 5-6-7-8	4-6×12 750W Lekos	603	Wash: Ext Walls, Roof, Kitch. Ceiling.
32	#2 Elec 9-14-18-22	4-6×12 750W Lekos	642/ 671	AA 1-2-3 Dn Light (Storm)
33	3E 4-5/5E 5-6	4-6×12 750W Lekos	642/ 671	AA 4-5 Dn Light Storm
34	4 B.R. 1-2-3-4	4-6×16 750W Lekos	669	U.S. Window -Kitchen- (Dawn)
35	1 BR 1-2-3 1 BR 4	3-6×12 750W Lekos 1-6×9 750W Leko	669	D.S. Wash (Dawn)
36	2E 27-28/3E 12-13	4-6×12 750W Lekos	669	AA 4+5 (Dawn)
37	3 BR 1-2-3 3 BR 4	3-6×12 750W Lekos 1-6×9 750W Leko	669	US Wash (Dawn)
38	#5 Elec 7-8-9	3-6×12 750W Lekos W/Templates	869	US - Leaf Template*
39	2E 5-6 2E 16-17	2-6×12 750W Template Lekos 2-6×9 750W Template Lekos	869	Ext Walls, Roof, Kitch. Ceiling - Leaf Template
40	Apron-Foots A-B-C-D-E	5-8' Strips 75W R-30 FL Dbl. Com.	643/ 648	Wash
41	Apron - Foots A-B-C-D-E	"	649/ 649	"
42	Apron Foots A-B-C-D-E	"	605	"

Figure 12.5 A sample of the United Scenic Artists Lighting Design Entrance Examination. *(Continued)*

Board #4: 12-Plate 6000W Type: Resistance

43	No 7 Elec A B C D E F	4-8' 12-Lt and 2-4' 6-Lt 300W Q-T3 Strips	610	CYC Wash
44	"	"	651	CYC Wash
45	"	"	673	CYC Wash
46	No 6 Elec ABCDEF	4-8' 12-Lt and 2-4' 6-Lt 300W Par-56 MFL Strips	603	Lower CYC Wash
47	"	"	605	Lower CYC Wash
48	"	"	649	Lower CYC Wash
49	#4 Elec A-B-C-D-E	5-8' 12 Lt 300W R-40FL Strips W/ Flippers	610	Cut Gauze Wash
50	#4 Elec A-B-C-D-E	5-8' 12-Lt. 300 W R-40 FL Strips W/ Flippers	651	Cut Gauze Wash
51	#4 Elec A-B-C-D-E	5-8' 12-Lt. 300 W. R-40 FL Strips W/ Flippers	673	Cut Gauze Wash
52	Rail 14-22-29-34 35-40-45-46	8-6×12 750 W Lekos W/Templates	650	Template Wash
53	1E 8-13-16-24 2E 10-13 3E 6-7	8-6×12 750W Lekos W/Templates	869	-Leaf- AA 1-2-3 AA 4 + Arbor AA 5 + Tree
54	1 BL 1-3-5-7 2 BL 9-10-12	7-6×12 750W Lekos	605	Kitchen/AA 6-7*

Board #5: Aux 8-Plate 750W Type: Resistance

Master 25	101	1E 17	1-6×12 750W Leko	542	Yard-Act I - Spec (Curtain Lines)
	102	3 E 1	1-6×16 750W Leko	503	Kitchen - Act II + III Spec (Curtain Lines)
	103	#2 BR 1	1-6×12 750W Template Leko	649	Hall Wall Window Template (Early Aft)
	104	#2 BR 2	1-6×12 750W Template Leko	N/C	Hall Wall Window Template (Late Aft)
Master 26	105	#2 BL 11	1-8×16 750W Template Leko	603	Kitchen Floor + Sr Wall Window Template
	106	1 E 18	1-6×12 750W Leko	N.C.	Spare
	107	1 E 15	1-6×12 750W Leko	N.C.	Spare
	108	2 E 21	1-6×12 750 W Leko	N.C.	Spare

Supply: 5-204 "Bryant" Momentary toggle switches (#4921) Connect to 2-6K Hot Pockets for lightning effects

H.P. 1	A	2E 23-24	2-QPAR 1000 W MFL Holder W/Hi. Hat	651	Kitch. Ceiling (Lightning)
	B	2E 25-26	2-QPAR 1000W WFL unit in holder W/high Hats	651	House Roof (Lightning)
H.P. 2	C	1E 20-21	2-QPAR 1000W MFL unit in holder W/High Hat	651	AA 1-2 (Lightning)
	D	1E 22-23	2-QPAR 1000W MFL unit in holder with High Hat	651	AA 2-3 (Lightning)
	E	3E 8-9	2-QPAR 1000W MFL unit in holder W/Hi. Hat	651	AA 4-5-Arbor (Lightning)

Board #6: Aux 12-Plate 500W Type: Resistance

Master 27	109	Bedroom Desk Prac.	100 W Bedroom Desk Practical	N.C.*	
	110	Bedroom #1	1-6" 500W Fres	N.C.	Bdroom Wash
	111	Bedroom #2	1-6" 500W Fres	N.C.	Bdroom Wash
	112	Bedroom #3	1-6" 500W Fres.	N.C.	Porch Door
	113	Bedroom #4	1-6" 500W Fres.	N.C.	Porch Window
	114	Bedroom #5	1-6" 500W Fres.	N.C.	Kitch. Door
Master 28	115	Porch Prac. and Porch #1	40 W Prac + 1-6" 500W Fres	N.C.	Porch Wash
	116	Porch #2	1-6" 500W Fresnel	N.C.	Porch Wash
	117	Porch #3	1-6" 500W Fresnel	N.C.	Porch Wash
	118	Hall #1	1-6" 500W Fresnel	N.C.	Hall Wash
	119	Hall #2	1-6" 500W Fresnel	N.C.	Hall Wash
	120	Hall #3	1-6" 500W Fresnel	N.C.	Kitch Door

*Load as Needed

MEMBER OF THE WEDDING — APPROX. INTENSITIES OF
TOP OF SHOW — CIRCUITS USED IN SKETCHES

Switch	Intensity	Equip. Color	Focus	Concept
19-20-21	F	12-6×12 750W — 503	ENDS "WASH"	SOFT/PALE/WARM COLOR LIKE THAT OF A CANDLE
38-39-53	F	13-6×12 750W Template / 2-6×9 750W Lekos — 869	WASH	BROKEN LIGHT LIKE FLICKERING CANDLE. WILL FADE OUT AS SUN SETS - DIFF ATMOSPHERE.
1-2-3-4-5	5	12 6×16 750W / 8 6×12 750W — 605	AA EXTERIOR	CANDLELIGHT COLOR PALE/SOFT/WARM

Switch	Inten.	Equip.	Color	Focus	Concept
19-20-21	F	12-6×12 750W	503	"Ends" Wash	Soft/pale/warm color like that of a candle
38-39-53	F	13-6×12 750W 2-6×9 750W Template Lekos	869	Wash	Broken light like flickering candle. Will fade out as sun sets - diff atmosphere.
1-2-3-4-5	5	12 6×16 750W 8 6×12 750W	605	AA Exterior	Candlelight color pale/soft/warm
22-23-24	7	12-6×12 750W	648	Ends wash fill →	Cool tone cleans comp. and emphasizes warms. Diff color and diff angle emphasizes ephemeral quality of flickering candle.
31	F	4-6×12 750W	603	Ext. walls + roof	Pale/soft/warm like candlelight.
118-119-120	F	3-6" 500W Fres.	N/C	Hall Bking	Room lighted from Sr. in next Q, dominant light is from S.L. change in angle and color like flickering candle.
43-49	5	300W Qt3 Strips	610	CYC. and Cut Gauze	CYC changes color as time of day + weather changes - ephemeral quality of candle
44-50	F	and 300W R-40FL	651		
46	F	300 W PAR -56 MFL Strips	603	Lower CYC	Horizon paler and brighter - changing atmosphere affects Frankie like it does a candle.
47	F	"	605		
19-20-21	F	12-6×12 750W	503	Wash ←	Soft/pale/warm color like that of a candle.
38-39-53	F	13-6×12 750W Templates 2-6×9 "	869 / 869	Wash / "	Broken light like flickering candle. Will fade out as sun sets - diff atmosphere.
1-2-3-4-5	Out	12-6×16 750W 8-6×12 750W	605 / 605	AA Ext.	Candlelight color pale/soft/warm
22-23-24	7	12 6×12 750W	648	Fill Wash	Cool tone cleans comp. and emphasizes warms. Diff color and diff angle emphasizes ephemeral quality of flickering candle.
31	F	4-6×12 750W	603	Roof/Walls	Pale/soft/warm like candlelight.
6-7	5	8-6×16 750W	649	AA-Kitchen	Warm blue like the blue at base of candle flame.
54	F	7-6×12 750W	605	"	
118-119-120	F	3-6" 500W Fres	N/C	Hall/Bking	Candle flame palette slight accent from Sr - contrasting angle to dominant lighting (5L) — contrast in color also — like a flickering candle.
43-49	5	300W QT3 strips	610	CYC and Cut Gauze	CYC changes color as time of day + weather changes - ephemeral quality of candle
44-50	F	and 300W R-40FL	651		
46	F	300 W PAR -56 MFL Strips	603	Lower CYC	Horizon paler and brighter - changing atmosphere affects Frankie like it does a candle.
47	F	"	605		

Switch	Inten.	Equip.	Color	Focus	Concept
105	F	1-8×16 window 750W Template	603	kitch wall	Color of candle this fades out as sun sets - changing atmosphere
118-119-120 115-116-117	F F	3-6" 500W Fres " and Prac	N/C	Hall Backing Porch Bking	W/Dark exterior, these shafts of light symbolize Frankies walls of isolation - she has to break thru them to survive.
8	F	1 6×16 750W 3 6×12 750W Prac	N/C	Kitchen motivated	Just as a candle flame is heightened, so too are the table + chairs in the kitchen
16	F	4-6×12 750W	503	Kit. Wash	Color of candle - makes SW 8 above less harsh.
32-33	7	8-6×12 750W	642/671	Ext Wash "Storm green"	Warm blue 642/green 671/warm Warm palette of candle.
35-36-37	5	10-6×12 750W 2-6×9 750W	669	"	At reading of 5, color nears "yellow" - candle flame.
45-51	F	300W QT3 Strips + 300W R-40 FL "	673		CYC changes as weather changes (candle affected by atmos. conditions)
44-50	4	"	651		CYC changes as weather changes (candle affected by atmos. conditions)
48	F	300W PAR-56 MFL	649		
8	out	1 6×16 750W 3 6×12 750W Prac	N/C	Kitchen motivated	Just as a candle flame is heightened, so too are the table + chairs in the kitchen
118-119-120 115-116-117	Out Out	3-6" 500W Fres " and Prac	N/C	Hall Backing Porch Bking	W/Dark exterior, these shafts of light symbolize Frankies walls of isolation - she has to break thru them to survive.
16	Out	4-6×12 750W	503	Kit. Wash	Color of candle - makes SW 8 above less harsh.
32-33	5	8-6×12 750W	642/671	Ext Wash "Storm green"	Warm blue 642 green 671 warm Warm palette of candle.
35-36-37	Out	10-6×12 750W 2-6×9 750W	669	"	At reading of 5, color nears "yellow" - candle flame.
45-51	6	300W QT3 Strips + 300W R-40 FL "	673		CYC changes as weather changes (candle affected by atmos. conditions)
44-50	4	300W QT 3 Strips + 300W R-40 FL "	673		CYC changes as weather changes (candle affected by atmos. conditions)
48	3	300W QT 3 Strips + 300W R-40 FL "	673		CYC changes as weather changes (candle affected by atmos. conditions)
9	4	4-6×12 750W	651	Kitch wash	At reading of 4-651 which is a warm blue becomes yellower - the colors found in flame of candle. Also 651 at 4 pts will look muddy or gloomy -
9 A-B-C-D-E Flash	Out (Full) Non-Dim	" Q PAR 64 1000W MFL units	651	Wash	Lightning flashes just like when candle is almost extinguished - every once in a while there is a new burst of energy as flame gets more oxygen (candle affected by atmosphere just like Frankie)
16	4	4-6×12 750W	503	Kitch. Wash.	At reading of 4, very warm amber - like flame of candle.
32-33	5	8-6×12 750W	642/671	Ext Wash "Storm green"	Warm blue 642 green 671 warm Warm palette of candle.
45-51	O	300W QT3 Strips + 300W R-40 FL "	673		CYC changes as weather changes (candle affected by atmos. conditions)
44-50	6	300W QT 3 Strips + 300W R-40 FL "	673		CYC changes as weather changes (candle affected by atmos. conditions)
48	O	300W QT 3 Strips + 300W R-40 FL "	673		CYC changes as weather changes (candle affected by atmos. conditions)
10	5	4-6×16 750W	N/C	Kitchen	N/C at reading of 5 is soft candle lite color

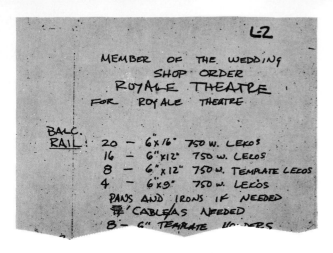

MEMBER OF THE WEDDING
SHOP ORDER
ROYALE THEATRE
FOR ROYALE THEATRE

BALC.
RAIL: 20 — 6"x16" 750 W. LEKOS
16 — 6"x12" 750 W. LEKOS
8 — 6"x12" 750 W. TEMPLATE LEKOS
4 — 6"x9" 750 W. LEKOS
PANS AND IRONS IF NEEDED
#'CABLE AS NEEDED
8 — 6" TEMPLATE HOLDERS

MEMBER OF THE WEDDING
SHOP ORDER
FOR ROYALE THEATRE

Balc. Rail:	20—6"×16" 750 W. Lekos 16—6"×12" 750 W. Lekos 8—6"×12" 750 W. Template Lekos 4—6"×9" 750 W. Lekos Pans and irons if needed Cable as needed 8—6" Template holders
No. 2 Box Boom Left:	21'-0" Boom 8—6"×16" 750 W. Lekos Boom Locking Hdwe 4—Double side arms Pans if needed Cable as needed
No. 2 Box Boom Right:	21'-0" Boom 4—6"×16" 750 W. Lekos Boom locking hdwe 4-side arms Pans if needed Cable as needed
Apron:	5—8' 75W. R-30 FL; Double compartment strips Hanging irons and masking cable as needed
No. 1 Electric	18—6"×12" 750 W. Lekos 4—6"×12" 750 W. Template Lekos 2—6"×9" 750 W. Lekos 4—Q-Par 64 1000 W MFL units in holders by high hats 1—1000W Worklight Pipe stiffeners Asbestos 42'-0" Pipe 4—6" Template holders Cable as needed

No. 2 Electric	17—6"×12" 750 W. Lekos 4—6"×12" 750 W. Template Lekos 1—6"×16" 750 W. Leko 2—6"×9" 750 W. Template Lekos 4—6" Template holders Cable as needed 42'-0" Pipe 2—Q-Par 64 1000W. WFL units in holders by high hats 2—Q-Par 64 1000W. MFL units in holders by high hats Pipe stiffeners Asbestos
No. 3 Electric	8—6"×12" 750 W. Lekos 2—6"×12" 750 W. Template Lekos 1—6"×16" 750 W. Leko 2—Q-Par 64 1000W MFL units in holders by high hats 42'-0" Pipe & Pipe stiffeners Asbestos 2—6" Template holders Cable as needed
No. 4 Electric:	5—8' 12-Lt. 300W R40 FL strips by flippers on D.S. side (strips point U.S.) Pipe stiffeners 42'-0" Pipe Cable as needed
No. 5 Electric:	10—6"×12" 750 W. Lekos 3—6"×12" 750 W. Template Lekos 1—1000W. Worklight Pipe stiffeners Asbestos 35'-0" Pipe 3-6" Template holders Cable as needed
No. 6 Electric:	4—8' 12-Lt 300W Par 56 MFL strips 2—4' 6-Lt 300W Par 56 MFL strips Pipe stiffeners Curved pipe (radius & dimensions on plot) Cable as needed
No. 7 Electric:	4—8' 12-Lt. 300W QT-3 strips 2—4' 6-Lt 300W QT-3 strips Pipe stiffeners Asbestos Curved pipe (radius & dimensions on plot) Cable as needed
No. 1 Boom Left:	7—6"×12" 750 W. Lekos 1—6"×9" 750 W. Leko 18'-0" Boom by 6" flange base Boom locking hdwe 4—Double side arms Asbestos Cable as needed
No. 2 Boom Left:	11—6"×12" 750 W. Lekos 1—8"×16" 750 W. Template Lekos 12—side arms 20'-0" Boom by 6" flange base Boom locking hdwe Cable as needed 1—8" Template holder

No. 1 Boom Right:	3—6"×12" 750 W Lekos 1—6"×9" 750 W. Leko 18'-0" Boom by 6" flange base 4—side arms Boom locking hdwe Cable as needed
No. 2 Boom Right:	2—6"×12" 750 W. Template Lekos 14'-0" Boom by 6" flange base Boom locking hdwe 2—side arms 2—6" Template holders Cable as needed
No. 3 Boom Right:	3—6"×12" 750 W. Lekos 1—6"×9" 750 W. Leko 22'-0" Boom by 6" flange base Boom locking hdwe 4—side arms Cable as needed
No. 4 Boom Right:	4—6"×16" 750W Lekos 13'-0" Boom by 18" flange base Boom locking hdwe 2—Double side arms Cable as needed
Kitchen:	1—40W Practical
Hall:	3—6" 500W Fresnels 2 Wall-mounting plates 1—Wall mounting side arm
Bedroom:	5—6" 500W Fresnels 1—100W Practical 5—Wall mounting plates
Porch:	3—6" 500W Fresnels 1—40W Practical 3—Wall mounting plates
Switch-boards: (Aux)	3—14-Plate 1500-3000W Resis. 1—12-Plate 6000W Resis. 1—8-Plate 750W Resis. 1—12-Plate 500W Resis. Main boards w/clearing bars

Switchboard position: DSL

Supply focussing scaffold on line sets #15 and #17 (see plot w/Zellerbach line set #'s).

Supply extra sheets #600 Roscolux for Fresnels

Supply 5-20 amp double-throw "Bryant" momentary toggle switches #4921. Connect 2 (A+B) to 6K hot pkt #1. Connect 3 (C,D+E) to 6K hot pkt #2. Must be able to over-ride switches for focussing.

Supply double set of color

Supply cable for all practicals

Figure 12.5 A sample of the United Scenic Artists Lighting Design Entrance Examination. (Continued)

STORY BOARD
FOE
"MEMBER"...
II A + B
III A - B - C

TOP OF SHOW I A

TOP OF III A

II B

III B

II B   X-FADE TO INTERIOR
J. HENRY ENTERS

—LIGHT GOES OUT—

"MEMBER OF THE WEDDING - TEMPLATE DESIGNS
U.S.A. EXAM 1976   DESIGNER No. L-2
CUT OUT WHITE AREAS

MAKE 1
(SWITCH #103)

MAKE 1
(SWITCH #104)
SCALE 1"=1"

MAKE 1
(SWITCH #105)

BERENICE LIGHTS A CANDLE

III
C

L-2

3. BALLET

A small, talented Ballet Company, enchanted with your lighting for THE MEMBER OF THE WEDDING has created a new twenty minute ballet, based on your concept, which they plan to tour in a bus and small truck. It is "FRANKIE'S DREAM BALLET", expressing her feelings about her brother's wedding and honeymoon. The music is by an American Composer in romantic style.

For the simple setting you have available for use, if desired, black legs and borders, a backdrop and a scrim of your specifications, a table, two chairs, a hanging kitchen light (which may fly out, if you desire) and a grape arbor with bench and trellis.

It will play houses with 40' × 18' proscenium stage opening and 30' depth.

They have hired you to design the lighting which must be limited to not more than 64 focusing units, three 6-pack, 3600 watt dimmers to be worked by one electrician. Set-up time; four hours.

(A) Draft a complete plan and section at ½" - 1'-0" scale, including masking, drops, scenery and props; showing instrumentation, placement, color and hookup for your lighting for this ballet.

(B) On a yellow pad indicate cues and rough time indications for this ballet as you imagine them and how this evolves from your concept.

PUT YOUR EXAMINATION **NUMBER** ON ALL YOUR WORK RELATING TO **THE MEMBER OF THE WEDDING** INCLUDING BOTH SETS OF PROJECT PRINTS.

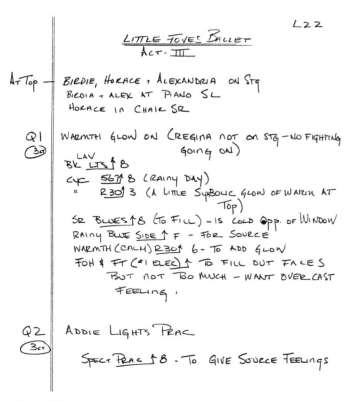

L22

LITTLE FOXES BALLET
ACT - III

At Top — BIRDIE, HORACE + ALEXANDRIA ON STG
BIRDIA + ALEX AT PIANO SL
HORACE IN CHAIR SR

Q1 (30") — WARMTH GLOW ON (REGINA NOT ON STG — NO FIGHTING GOING ON)

BK LAV LTS ↑ 8
CYC 567 ↑ 8 (RAINY DAY)
" R30 ↑ 3 (A LITTLE SYMBOLIC GLOW OF WARM AT TOP)
SR BLUES ↑ 8 (TO FILL) - IS COLD OPP. OF WINDOW
RAINY BLUE SIDE ↑ F - FOR SOURCE
WARMTH (CALM) R30 ↑ 6 - TO ADD GLOW
FOH & FT (#1 ELEC) ↑ TO FILL OUT FACES
BUT NOT TOO MUCH - WANT OVERCAST FEELING.

Q2 (3") — ADDIE LIGHTS PRAC

SPECT PRAC ↑ 8 - TO GIVE SOURCE FEELINGS

Q3 (10") — REGINA ENTERS

X-FADE GLOW WARMTH ON CYC + SIDE W/ GREEN CYC + SIDE — SUBTLE CHANGE

NOTE: THE WARMTH (HARMONY) + GREEN (DISCORD) PLAY LOW TO BE FELT & NOT NEC. "SEEN" - ESP. ON CYC

OTHER DIMMERS ADJUST FOR PROPER BLEND KEEPING 567 SIDE + PRAC HOTTEST FOR SOURCES

Q4 (20") FOLLOW → (50") — HORACE + REGINA'S FIGHT

BUILD GREEN TO HIGHEST LEVEL ON HORACE'S COLLAPSE (BENCH)
ADJUST OTHER DIMMERS — GREEN BUILD ONLY ON SIDES — NOT CYC

IN FOLLOW BRING 567 ↑ & ADD SR BLUE FOR EVENING
CYC GOES BLK EXCEPT FOR HINT OF EMOTIONAL COLORS

Q5 (10") — WHEN REGINA FEELS SHE HAS GOTTEN WHAT SHE WANTS AFTER FIGHT + DURING MEETING W/ BEN ETC,

X-FADE GREENS OUT & WARMTH UP
NIGHT BLUE SR UP + 567 COMPLETELY OUT

Q6 (5") — AS REGINA TRIES TO GET BACK DAUGHTER'S AFFECTION + ALEX SAYS/DANCES "ARE YOU AFRAID MAMA?"

GREEN CYC + SIDES ↑ X-ING WITH WARMTH OUT

DURING THIS Q START FADING EVERYTHING OUT IN A (5) SO GREEN SEEMS TO LAG IN (2)
LAG SIDE GREEN (DIS) ONLY

NOTE: EMOTIONAL COLORS ON CYC TO ADD FLAVOR (IT'S DANCE AFTER ALL) BUT SOURCE COLORS MUST PREVAIL TO STAY TRUE TO CONCEPT

Figure 12.5 A sample of the United Scenic Artists Lighting Design Entrance Examination. (Continued)

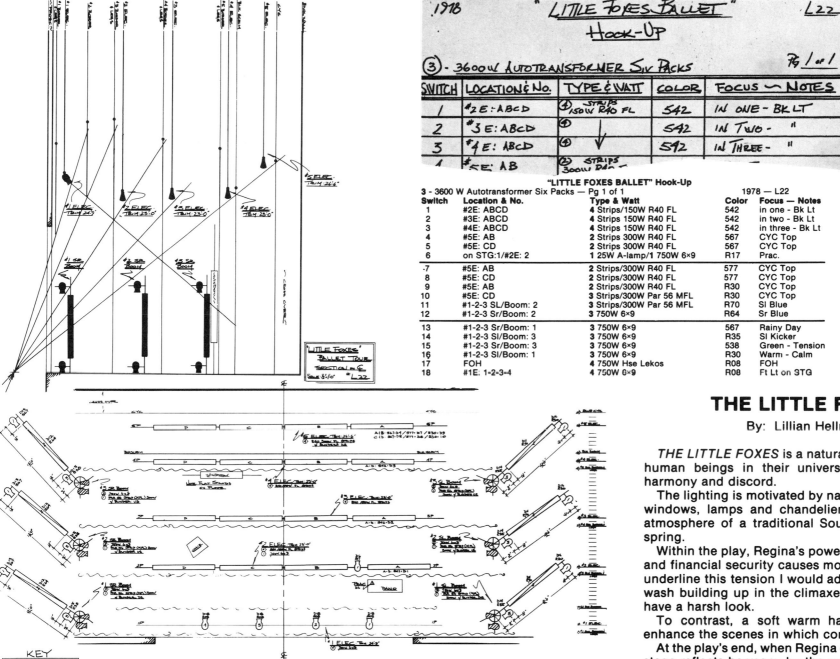

1978 "LITTLE FOXES BALLET" Hook-Up   *L22*

③ - 3600 W AUTOTRANSFORMER SIX PACKS   Pg 1 of 1

SWITCH	LOCATION & No.	TYPE & WATT	COLOR	FOCUS — NOTES
1	#2 E: ABCD	④ STRIPS 150W R40 FL	542	IN ONE - BK LT
2	#3 E: ABCD	④	542	IN TWO - "
3	#4 E: ABCD	④	542	IN THREE - "
4	#5E: AB	② STRIPS 300W R40 —		

"LITTLE FOXES BALLET" Hook-Up

3 - 3600 W Autotransformer Six Packs — Pg 1 of 1   1978 — L22

Switch	Location & No.	Type & Watt	Color	Focus — Notes
1	#2E: ABCD	4 Strips/150W R40 FL	542	in one - Bk Lt
2	#3E: ABCD	4 Strips 150W R40 FL	542	in two - Bk Lt
3	#4E: ABCD	4 Strips 150W R40 FL	542	in three - Bk Lt
4	#5E: AB	2 Strips 300W R40 FL	567	CYC Top
5	#5E: CD	2 Strips 300W R40 FL	567	CYC Top
6	on STG:1/#2E: 2	1 25W A-lamp/1 750W 6×9	R17	Prac.
·7	#5E: AB	2 Strips/300W R40 FL	577	CYC Top
8	#5E: CD	2 Strips/300W R40 FL	577	CYC Top
9	#5E: AB	2 Strips/300W R40 FL	R30	CYC Top
10	#5E: CD	3 Strips/300W Par 56 MFL	R30	CYC Top
11	#1-2-3 SL/Boom: 2	3 Strips/300W Par 56 MFL	R70	Sl Blue
12	#1-2-3 Sr/Boom: 2	3 750W 6×9	R64	Sr Blue
13	#1-2-3 Sr/Boom: 1	3 750W 6×9	567	Rainy Day
14	#1-2-3 Sl/Boom: 3	3 750W 6×9	R35	Sl Kicker
15	#1-2-3 Sr/Boom: 3	3 750W 6×9	538	Green - Tension
16	#1-2-3 Sl/Boom: 1	3 750W 6×9	R30	Warm - Calm
17	FOH	4 750W Hse Lekos	R08	FOH
18	#1E: 1-2-3-4	4 750W 6×9	R08	Ft Lt on STG

THE LITTLE FOXES

By: Lillian Hellman

THE LITTLE FOXES is a naturalistic play; it is about human beings in their universal struggle between harmony and discord.

The lighting is motivated by natural sources such as windows, lamps and chandeliers, thus creating the atmosphere of a traditional Southern home in early spring.

Within the play, Regina's powerful drive for freedom and financial security causes most of the discord. To underline this tension I would add a contrasting color wash building up in the climaxes so that they would have a harsh look.

To contrast, a soft warm harmonic glow would enhance the scenes in which conflict is not present.

At the play's end, when Regina obtains her goals, the stage reflects harmony by the warm glow. But in the final moment, when she tries to regain her daughter's affection, the discord color returns to leave a lingering doubt.

1. PRACTICAL, KING LEAR:

Put your EXAMINATION LETTER on your concept for KING LEAR and on all the paperwork you do for your PRACTICAL.

Your Concept for KING LEAR will be collected at the time of your Practical Examination. It is part of the Examination and will be used by the Judges in evaluating your work and how you translate it into creative lighting design.

(A) Approximately one hour prior to your scheduled time, you will be given your practical problems and light plot. After 45 minutes the proctor will pick up your color list and concept for KING LEAR and at your scheduled time you will be conducted into the theatre. You will have a total of 40 minutes to focus and set cues for the problem you have chosen. Be sure to put your Practical Letter on all papers concerning this part of the test as all work in this area will be collected.

(B) CHOOSE ONE of the following PROBLEMS for your Practical. Write the number of the Problem you have chosen on your Concept for KING LEAR. You are expected to utilize the Light Plot which is given you and to follow all instructions. You should allot yourself sufficient time during the Practical to create the cues implicit in the Problem chosen.

PROBLEMS:

I. Act I Scene 1 Throne Room, general torch lighted chamber, Lear in throne chair. Scene begins with Lear's: "To thee and thine hereditary ever remain this ample third of our fair kingdom..." through "...be as well neighbored, pitied and relieved, as thou my sometime daughter."
   Problem: Set up a fully lighted chamber with torches.
   Cue: Isolate throne area for Cordelia, Lear scene.

II. Act II Scene 4 Courtyard, dawn, Kent being set free from the stocks. Scene begins with Regan's: "I am glad to see your highness." through Lear's: "...Strike her young bones, you taking airs, with lameness."
   Problem: Scene starts just as sun is rising.
   Cue: Morning sun rises.

III. Act III Scene 2 The Heath, famous storm scene. Scene starts with Lear's: "Blow, winds, and crack your cheeks..." through Fool's: "For there was never yet fair woman but she made mouths in a glass."
   Problem: Scene starts in violent storm.
   Cue: Acting light comes in and storm diminishes to play scene.

Figure 12.5 A sample of the United Scenic Artists Lighting Design Entrance Examination. *(Continued)*

UNITED STATES ARTISTS' LIGHTING DESIGN EXAMINATION GRADING SHEET

APPLICANT LETTER_____

JUDGE_____ PROBLEM NUMBER_____

==

GRADING INFORMATION: Please circle a numerical score for each section. Do not circle between numbers. The grade of 6 is a borderline pass. Please write in as many comments as you can, since it helps us at the review.

1. ESSAY   COMMENTS:

   Validity of point of   1 2 3 4 5
   view, visual image,   6 7 8 9 10
   technical approach.
----
2. INSTRUMENTATION/UNIT PLACEMENT

   Correct choice of units   1 2 3 4 5
   and position for the job?   6 7 8 9 10
----
3. ABILITY TO HANDLE CREW

   Professional communica-   1 2 3 4 5
   tion and productive use   6 7 8 9 10
   of crew.
----
4. ORGANIZATION/PREPARATION

   Well thought out approach   1 2 3 4 5
   of scene. Prepared to   6 7 8 9 10
   work efficiently.
----
5. PROFESSIONAL ATTITUDE

   Need we say more?   1 2 3 4 5
                                 6 7 8 9 10
----
6. ACCURACY OF FOCUS

   Hot spots cover action.   1 2 3 4 5
   Obvious shutter cuts   6 7 8 9 10
   executed.
----
7. COMPOSITION   COMMENTS:

   Ability to create a stage   1 2 3 4 5
   picture using angle,   6 7 8 9 10
   color, and intensity.
----
8. SENSE OF CUEING

   Are the cues logical,   1 2 3 4 5
   in the right place,   6 7 8 9 10
   in reasonable counts?
----
9. OVERALL LOOK

   Do all the elements of   1 2 3 4 5
   the entire scene work   6 7 8 9 10
   together?
----
10. FAITHFULNESS TO ESSAY

   Did the applicant achieve   1 2 3 4 5
   his stated intentions?   6 7 8 9 10
   If not, was there a valid
   reason?
==

ADDITIONAL COMMENTS:

Example: The 1984 USA #829 Entrance Exam. In 1984, the home project selected was Hugh Leonard's play, *Da* (in 1985 it was Jo Mielziner's *Cat On a Hot Tin Roof*). Applicants mailed the home project to the union office prior to the interview and it was graded by the exam committee members in advance of the interview. The exam fee was $150, nonrefundable. Only blueprints (not originals) of the home project were acceptable — and folded, not rolled. The union supplied each applicant with complete details about the theatre to be used for *Da* (light mounting positions, power, line sets, etc.). A written "Director's Approach" was included. So were ground plans and set sketches. An essay (a modification of the older "concept") was required "outlining [the applicant's] intellectual and artistic approach to this production" as it would be explained to the director. No house curtain was to be used. Notes were included about the set texture and materials. Called for was a *light plot* (half-inch scale) with details given by the union about symbols to be used and style of presentation (similar to the 1976 example in Fig. 12.5). Only Roscolene, Roscolux, Lee Filters, and Geltran could be used. Also required were the following: a *section;* a *board hookup* (using any equipment currently available for rental in New York City and allowing soft patch but no repatches or replugs); a *cue synopsis* (a list of all cues the applicant planned to use in *Da,* including cue number, time duration or count in seconds, and a brief description of what the cue does); *magic sheet* (a graphic magic sheet that would be used to cue the show); a *shop order* (minus cable lengths, but including pipe); *value study/diagrams* for union-specified selected "moments" in the script (value study sketches showing use of light, tied in with the submitted plot, hookup, etc.), using three or six moments offered.

The Practical. At the beginning of the exam days, all applicants are assembled in the theatre that is to be used for the practical exam. The applicants have familiarized themselves with a selected play or opera (in 1976 the selected work was *King Lear;* in 1982, *The Fantastics;* in 1984, the opera *The Medium;* in 1985, *Pelleas and Melisande*). They have prepared an essay (concept). Each applicant is assigned a practical alphabetical letter, to be used in identifying all work on the practical. Three selected scenes, approximately three to five minutes long, are performed by professional actors and actresses in costume on stage with a simple set under work lights. The committee always selects scenes that are challenging for a lighting designer. One hour prior to the practical the applicant is brought into the theatre lobby and handed the following items: (1) a list of color media available — frame sizes, quantity, and selected colors; (2) a light plot of the theatre showing all lighting units available, with information on each light's wattage, ganging, type, mounting position (i.e., balcony front, ceiling cove, backstage pipes, cyc area, rovers, etc.), as well as the dimmer to which each has been assigned. The applicant has elected to design lighting for one of the three scenes previously performed. The applicant has the remaining time to plot (in any manner chosen) the lighting he or she wishes to use for the selected scene. The applicant hands in a list of colors to be used at a designated time. When the hour is up, monitors usher the applicant into the theatre. The judges (eight to twelve well-known working lighting designers) are introduced. The crew (partly IATSE stagehands) is introduced. Crew members are in position to operate the switchboard, focus backstage on a roving ladder, and focus front-of-house (FOH) lights. The necessary colors have already been pulled. The applicant has exactly 40 minutes to (1) direct the focus of all units to be used and color them; (2) step out into the house and, from a lighted control board with talk-back, give the switchboard operator the levels and timing desired for each cue (performers are available in costume to stand in or "walk" any scene at the applicant's request); and (3) play the scene back for the judges with full lighting and with the actors performing the selected scene. The applicant can at any time ask how much time remains. The applicant is warned when there are 15 minutes left, and an alarm rings when only 5 minutes are left. The applicant's work is carefully observed by the judges, who note such things as the clarity, civility, and speed of focus directions; overall utilization of time; preplanning; and knowledge of equipment and procedure. At the end of the 40 minutes the judges ask the applicant what he would have done differently if there had been available a wider range of color, a different selection of equipment or mounting positions, etc. This brief question period frequently serves to indicate to the judges how clearly applicants understand where they have fallen short of the "ultimate" and whether or not they know how to correct any obvious flaws induced by time and pressure. More than any other element of the Lighting Design Entrance Exam, the practical separates the qualified from the not-yet-ready. It is an expensive but realistic test of an applicant's ability to design under the actual pressure of typical professional conditions.

The revised 1984 judges scoring sheets used by USA #829 for *The Medium* scored applicants (from 1 to 10) on essay; instrumentation (did the applicant pick the right unit for the job?) and unit placement; ability to handle crew; organization, preparation, and attitude; accuracy of focus; validity of composition; validity of cueing; overall look; and faithfulness of result to the essay.

Exam Judging and Critique. Following the exam in New York City teams of judges assemble (as individual schedules permit) at the union office and score the paperwork or tally up scores. The grading sheets allow space for comments by the judges. Such comments may be helpful to the applicant in understanding where mistakes were made and why points were lost. This scoring process takes several days. Each applicant's paperwork takes approximately an hour and 15 minutes for each team to score. Frequently judges pencil comments concerning errors on the drawings and paperwork to help the applicant on the next attempt to pass the exam (these have been deleted from all examples presented). Scores of the separate teams are averaged. Finally, the exam committee presents to the regular monthly union meeting its recommendations for those applicants who, in the committee's best collective judgement, are qualified for membership. Members present vote to accept (or reject) the exam committee's recommendations. Those who pass are so informed. They receive a bill for the initiation fee and are invited to a regular meeting for formal obligation as new members of the union and for an indoctrination and orientation session about union practices.

Those who did not qualify are also informed. They may, if they wish, meet briefly with a small group of judges at specific dates for a constructive critique of their exam and final score.

Some Comments about the #829 Exam. Peggy Clark and John Gleason, writing in *Theatre Crafts*, summarized the Lighting Design Entrance Exam very aptly: "We attempt to set up an examination that comes as close as possible to simulating the various elements of a lighting designer's craft that are necessary to create the design and to deliver credible, workable, viable lighting for first-class productions." [352] The exam has been widely misunderstood. It is neither an attempt by the union to set itself up as an absolute and final judge of artistic ability and creative inventiveness nor part of a plan to keep the union small by excluding newcomers. Quite the opposite, the exam measures professional competence, knowledge, and workability in the "real world" industry, prepared and judged by those who know its reality best, and also the New York City exam is based heavily upon New York practices and techniques, because that is where the union headquarters is located, where the union has jurisdiction, and where most jobs originate. In simplest terms, the exam is, in a sense, the equivalent of the lawyer's bar exam or the medical qualifying exams for a physician. An "M.D." after a person's name does not mean that he is a great doctor. It *does* attest to the fact that he has mastered certain basics and is competent to step into an operating room in an emergency to remove an ailing appendix. The union has no interest in severely restricting membership. If it did, in the long run it would lose control of the craft. Christopher A. Thomas, technical director and designer for the Schimmel Center for the Arts, Pace University, New York City, wrote in *Lighting Dimensions:*

The entrance examination tests for three very specific facets of being able to work within [the union's] jurisdiction. Passing this examination proves only that, in understanding light as a designer, the individual can work within the Broadway format as a professional and can communicate *as* an artist and *to* the technician.

The Broadway designer is an interpretative artist in collaboration with other artists — his function must not be that of a technician. And he must be professional. This means he must be fully prepared: to know what each light will do before he reaches the theatre, and if necessary, to focus the entire show without a set, to give the stage manager all the cues and counts before the

[352] *Peggy Clark and John Gleason, "Training the Lighting Designer,"* Theatre Crafts, *vol. 10, no. 6 (Nov./Dec. 1976), p. 28.*

Figure 12.6 USA Local #829 union stamp.

[353] Christopher A. Thomas, "Contrast," Lighting Dimensions, vol. 2, no. 10 (Dec. 1978), p. 44.

[354] See also Elmon Webb's, "Joining United Scenic Artists Local 829: Follow Up," Theatre Crafts, vol. 12, no. 5 (Sept. 1978), pp. 9–12.

Elmon Webb, "Unions, Questions and Answers," Theatre Crafts, vol. 12, no. 7 (Nov./Dec. 1978), p. 16.

Elmon Webb, "Unions, Questions and Answers," Theatre Crafts, vol. 13, no. 3 (May/June 1979), pp. 91–94.

[355] Information presented concerning USA #350 (Chicago) Lighting Design Entrance Examination was obtained during my attendance at the May 19–20, 1979, exam at Northwestern University's Evanston (Illinois) campus and from exam documents released by USA #350's executive board and in my possession.

Lee Watson, "Chicago USA Lighting Exam," Lighting Dimensions, vol. 3, no. 7 (July 1979), pp. 19, 21–22, 24.

technical rehearsal, to cue the entire show in one dress rehearsal without stopping the actors, to change theatres![353]

It is these aspects of the art and craft which are tested by USA #829.[354] In 1982 eighty people applied to take the exam. Of those, 69 were interviewed, 36 took the practical, and 12 were admitted. The exam fee was $200.

The USA #350 (Chicago) Lighting Design Exam

USA #350 has somewhat modified its exam practices to bring them into closer conformity with #829's, yet still retain an individuality which suits the differing employment practices and needs of #350's area. The Chicago group currently offers its exam only once a year (late in May), and only in Chicago (actually on Northwestern University's campus in nearby Evanston, Illinois). USA #350 does not use an interview. Instead, applicants are asked to submit three color photographs or slides of productions they have done. Applicants deposit with the union half of the initiation fee of $250 and a nonrefundable exam fee of $75. The initiation fee is refunded if the applicant does not pass. Applicants are sent a code identification number for all of their submitted work. Applicants are told of the year's selected production for the exam (a play or opera, changing each year). In 1979 Puccini's La Bohème was selected, and Chekhov's The Seagull was used for the practical.

The Home Project. USA #350 sends the applicant the drawings (plan and section) for a "project theatre." (In 1979, for example applicants were asked to assume that The Seagull was a road show with rented lighting equipment.) Applicants are asked to provide a ground plan for the project theatre, a light plot, a section lighting drawing, an instrument schedule and/or hookup sheets, and bid specifications (shop order) — all in quarter-inch scale. Thumbnail sketches are required showing major lighting compositions and their progression and orchestration. Also a prose cue synopsis (indicating light changes and progression of areas, washes, and specials, with cue sheets included if the applicant wishes) is required. (An acceptable alternative for this portion of the home project has been submission of five- by seven-inch color photographs or 35-mm slides of a scale model showing lighting and a typewritten concept description.) Also required is a set of color schemes for scenery and costumes for the total production (on 15- by 20-inch board) indicating relative amounts of color. Electrical service for the project theatre is specified; color media is limited to Roscogel, Roscolene, and Cinemoid. A lighting symbol key is requested from a standard lighting template on the light plot. The home project is graded by three judges (scoring separately) on the basis of artistic values (originality, competence, and appropriateness), technical values (practicality, usability for the director and actor, and quality of graphics — drafting and painting), completeness of work, and portfolio.

The Exam Day. Seven and one-half hours are allowed for the single exam day. Each section of the exam is allowed a varying number of score points by the judges, and additional points are given for competence of presentation (graphics, completeness), originality, and technical practicality.

The Practical. Given the day following the exam, USA #350's practical is similar to #829's, yet much more condensed. Applicants were given 20 minutes, prior to their practical, for planning and organization. The actual theatre practical consumed approximately 25 minutes. Three judges filled out rating sheets on the basis of hookup (control board use, instrument selection, and color choice), focus (attitude, logical process of execution, speed of execution, precision and clarity of requests, and knowledge of mechanics), cueing (time spent on setting cues, logic of cue placement, and timing or count of cue), and overall effect (dramatic appropriateness and dramatic originality).[355]

Some Comments about the #350 Exam. In my opinion, Chicago's Lighting Design Entrance Examination, adapted to the specific employment needs and practices of their Midwest area, is comprehensive and is approached with great integrity and seriousness of purpose. The Chicago group deals with arena lighting and also asks for considerable ability to sketch and more mastery of the fundamentals of scenic design than does the New York City group. USA #850 also places added emphasis on equipment specifications as a consultant and upon budgeting. Less emphasis is placed on adaptation of a light plot to differing performance places. This shift in emphasis involves only details — both groups test equally for design competence, knowledge, and imagination.

Contracts and Wage Scales

Minimum union rates for lighting design are just that: *minimums*. As with any union, USA minimums are based upon long-term awareness of the hours and effort needed to do a particular job. No member of a union can work for less than the minimum rate unless (1) the design job is in a design area in which the union does not *claim* (or is unwilling to *exercise*) jurisdiction (for example, teaching, lecturing, and sometimes industrial shows and trade conventions), or (2) the union member has permission from the union's business agent to accept a lower fee — for example, the Syracuse Stage is a LORT (League of Regional Theatres) theatre with Actor's Equity performers; its seating capacity is only 202 seats, and union members, each in an individual case, have been allowed to design there on a "letter of agreement" for less than standard minimums). *In all cases, union members must contact the union's business agent if they have doubts about the minimum rates they may accept.* Most well-established union lighting designers normally work at rates *above* the minimum.

Contract Provisions

Rates. What are the minimum rates? There are many. They differ for the various contracts (Broadway, Off-Broadway, Metropolitan Opera, opera, ballet, etc.). Most are based upon the "Standard Lighting Design Contract," drawn from the signed agreement between the union and the League of Broadway Theatres (producers and owners of theatres in New York City) and traditionally the union's highest "first class" rates. The present contract in force provides the following:[356]

Lighting design assignment	Compensation, $
Dramatic single set	$2,880
Dramatic multiset	$4,230
Dramatic unit set with phases	$5,420
Musical single set	$3,390
Musical multiset	$7,610
Musical unit set with phases	$5,080

As this was written the Union was in the process of negotiating a new first class rate and work conditions with the League of Professional Theatres. In addition, there are AWC (Additional Weekly Compensation) provisions which apply the first week after the investors have recouped their investment, but no later than the 11th week following the official New York City opening or the 21st week following the first paid public performance (whichever occurs first). These continue for the run of the production, subsequent productions, or a touring production, with specific modifications. AWC is *not* paid in any week a production is losing money. For a lighting designer's *first* Broadway production he or she receives AWC of $50 per week for weeks 1 through 5, $60 per week for weeks 6 through 15, and $70 per week for weeks 16 through 26. For the designer's *second* Broadway production he or she receives AWC of $75 per week, and for the third or all subsequent Broadway productions, AWC begins at $100 per week. All payments now involve standard weekly withholding: federal income tax, state tax, sometimes city tax, social security, workman's compensation, etc. Designers are valid labor union members, not independent contractors.

Other Contract Provisions. Many other provisions of the contract and agreement are worth outlining here. For example, the producer must contribute to the United Scenic Artists Pension and Welfare Fund 11 or 12 percent of the contract fee and all weekly compensation (from the producer's funds, not from the designer's fee). However, there is a contribution ceiling of $1,440 for each designer. This is exclusive of Pension and Welfare Fund contributions, for which the 11 or 12 percent is deducted from the total weekly payment by the producer. The designer receives the balance. These Pension and Welfare Fund contributions increase throughout the life of the contract under a complex series of agreements that will not be elaborated upon here.

The agreement spells out the services (and documents) the lighting designer is expected to provide. For example,

[356] *Information presented concerning the League Contract I have excerpted (and edited and condensed) from "Agreement Between the League of New York Theatres & Producers, Inc., and United Scenic Artists, Local 829 — Effective Mar. 20, 1978 until Dec. 31, 1989." Copy in my possession. Rates are as of 1988.*

Figure 12.7 USA Local #350 union stamp.

the designer is expected to (1) provide a light plot and equipment list in scale drawing; (2) provide a color plot and additional necessary information as needed by the electrician; (3) provide a control plot; (4) supervise and plot special effects; (5) supply specifications and obtain estimates from contractors to a maximum of three, with additional details enumerated; (6) supervise hanging and focus, plus set cues; (7) be present at pre-Broadway and Broadway setups, technical and dress rehearsals, and the first public performance and opening — both out of town and in New York City — and conduct a reasonable number of lighting rehearsals, if requested (additional specifics are enumerated); and (8) attend public performances from time to time to conduct a "normal check" of the lighting (within reason). Any additional work by the designer is paid for at $217 per day. All transportation costs plus $125 per day for expenses are paid by the producer.

Assistants are engaged by the producer, not the lighting designer. The designer requests an assistant from the producer. The producer "shall not unreasonably withhold" such approval. A separate contract is filed for assistants. Minimum for assistants (lighting) is $600 per week, plus detailed provisions for compensation for expenses "on the road" for Broadway and $85 *per diem* plus transportation. For a key ballet (such as the American Ballet Theatre, the New York City Ballet, and the Joffrey Ballet) rates are $490; for the Metropolitan Opera rates are $883.47 for staff and $789.29 for free-lance; for regional opera rates are $475; for standard ballet, Off-Broadway, and regional/dinner theatre rates are $485 to $490; for free-lance and Cable TV rates are $935 per week or $243 for seven hours.

The contract enumerates specific conditions concerning subsequent use of a design. These involve the following: moving a production to a different theatre in New York City, formation of additional "duplicate" (road) companies, reuse of the original lighting (involving additional work by the designer), and sale or lease or license of rights to the original production. These provisions are complex. Several pages of the contract are required to enumerate the specifics which apply for concert presentations (for example, Hal Holbrook in *Mark Twain,* one-performer attractions such as Frank Sinatra or Diana Ross, etc.). Provisions are

included for cost-of-living adjustments and for reopening (modifying) provisions of the contract at specific times.

The contract is quite specific: Individual agreements must be signed for scenic design, costume design, lighting design, and assistant designers. They must be filed with the union's business agent and approved by the union. Designers are specifically forbidden from "commencing any work whatsoever, until said agreement has been approved in writing by the Union." This provision exists because of the danger of a less-than-reputable producer suggesting to a gullible designer that he or she will be employed and then soliciting drawings, sketches, and plots from that designer *and* a number of other designers. The unscrupulous producer then turns all the drawings over to a newcomer in the union (who will work at minimum rates) and says, "Take the best ideas from each of these, and you will do the show." Meanwhile, several top designers' ideas have been stolen and misused without compensation. This scenario may seem to be purely hypothetical, but it is not. A few years ago a prominent Broadway producer (who will remain unnamed) handed *seven complete sets* of sketches and even shop drawings for his upcoming musical to a fellow union scenic designer and me when he retained us to design his show. They were *all* the work of well-established designers. Young designers should remember that the union exists to prevent this kind of misuse and piracy of ideas.

The contract also spells out method of payment. Bonds are posted with the union by the producer to protect and assure payment. The design fee is paid to the designer by the union (from a separate "Stock Bonding Funds" account used by the union to guarantee absolute honesty while the union has in its possession funds collected for the designer). The system of payment is elaborate and is not detailed here. An important point, however, is that designers are *weekly employees* of the producer and *not* independent contractors. Major points of law (involving the Taft-Hartley Law, basic labor law, and many thousands of dollars of legal time) are involved. The details of all this law are neither necessary to the designer nor readily understandable to the laymen or someone who is not schooled in legal matters.

Several pages in the contract are given over to spelling out "other Use of Designs." This section defines rights for reuse of a design in motion pictures, TV cassettes, television, live broadcasts, closed-circuit and subscription TV, simulcast, tapes, film, film cassettes, etc. Designers in many cases are entitled to additional payments for reuse of their designs. The union maintains that the designer *leases* the right to use design ideas to the producer. Actual *ownership* of that design remains the exclusive property of the designer. This subject is dealt with in detail.

The producer "shall not alter nor permit anyone to alter or make substitutions . . . for the light plot, or lighting cues after the official New York opening without the Designer's consent." Broadway practice has always been based upon this premise. The director should have decided what he desires by the time of the official opening. If the director wishes to continue experimenting past that date, the producer must pay an additional design fee at *per diem* rates. The lighting designer, whose name is on the show, has a right (and a legal contract to back him up) to be sure that *anyone* who sees that production at a later date will see *his exact lighting* — not his design modified ("played with") by well-intentioned directors, stage managers, and electricians. (Because the educational theatre situation is quite different, a university production is frequently modified throughout its run in the interests of learning, experimenting, and improving — professional theatre is a completely different ball game!)

There are contract provisions that spell out terms for the importation of a production, including lighting and lighting designs (these are too complex to warrant enumeration here). Billing is dealt with in great detail. Included are discussions of theatre house boards, programs, and New York City display and newspaper advertisements. The union has long fought for (and usually obtained) proper recognition for the work of its creative artists. The specifics are complex.

The contract sets forth methods of adjusting disputes (usually arbitration through the American Arbitration Association). Producer rights to discharge a union member are enumerated.

An important provision is the following: "The Designer and Producer may negotiate for any additional provision or payments of monies providing that such provisions shall in no way lessen, abrogate or contradict any of the terms (within the Agreement). Such provisions shall be placed on a Rider to this Agreement and shall be deemed a part hereof."

The usual "acts of God" clauses are provided (strikes, accidents, fire, and other unavoidable delays). The designer agrees not to accept kickbacks from suppliers, upon penalty of discharge. Strikes and lockouts are forbidden during the period when the agreement is in force. No discrimination (for race, age, sex, creed, color, national origin, or *union activities*) is permitted.

Signed by Irving W. Cheskin (executive director of the League of Broadway Theatres) and Domingo Rodriguez (business representative of the union in 1978) on behalf of the members of the two groups, the current agreement was 24 printed pages long and was in effect from March 20, 1978, until December 31, 1989, with modification in payment rates during the contract's lifetime. The contract was modified January 1, 1987 (the modified rates have been presented here).

Only the highlights of the contract have been set forth, and any inaccuracy or error in summarization is (of course) my fault. Specifics beyond this general outline reside with the union; however, both access to the agreement and guidance in its interpretation and application are available to #829 members only. It is my belief that, since the terms of this agreement are not secret, both students and those earning a living as lighting designers can benefit from a better understanding of the generalities of this agreement and of how the union acts on behalf of its members in determining and enforcing workable minimums.

Other Contracts

Most other union contracts are based upon the League Agreement. The union has many contracts, and the specific provisions differ in details from contract to contract. The duration of each contract varies. Contracts are constantly being renegotiated. To obtain specific details a designer must be a member of the union and must consult the union's business agent for current provisions in effect. *As a guide only,* presented below are some selected design rates (in effect in 1989 unless otherwise indicated). For comparison, at the top of the pay scale are staff lighting designers at

357 *Specific rate structures presented in table form are excerpted from current contracts in my possession.*

the Metropolitan Opera, who earn $1,983.77 per week with holidays and vacation pay and regular workday hours specified in the contract.

Off-Broadway Rates for Lighting Design

Theatres with 199 or fewer seats
  Single set: $1,000
  More than one set: $1,200

Theatres with 200 to 299 seats
  Single set: $1,585
  Multiple set: $1,850

Theatres with 300 to 349 seats
  Single set: $1,600 (dramatic); $1,900 (musical)
  Multiset: $2,350 (dramatic); $4,260 (musical)
  Unit set with phases: $3,000 (dramatic); $2,800 (musical)

Theatres with 350 to 399 seats
  Single set: $1,850 (dramatic); $2,175 (musical)
  Multiset: $2,730 (dramatic); $4,900 (musical)
  Unit set with phases: $3,500 (dramatic); $3,275 (musical)

Theatres with 400 or more seats
  Single set: $2,100 (dramatic); $2,500 (musical)
  Multiset: $3,100 (dramatic); $5,565 (musical)
  Unit set with phases: $4,000 (dramatic); $3,700 (musical)
  AWC (Additional Weekly Compensation, i.e., Royalties)
0 to 199 seats or less

In the Broadway area: first five weeks, $45; 6th to 16th week, $55; 16th week on, $65

200 to 299 seats

In the Broadway area: $55, $65, $75

300 or more seats

In the Broadway area: $65, $75, $85
Design Assistants: $510 weekly.

Regional/Residential and Educational Theatre Rates and Dinner Theatre Rates

For a single set with 199 or fewer seats: $1,200; 200 to 299 seats: $1,458; 300 to 499 seats: $1,960; 500 to 999 seats: $2,375; over 1000 seats: $2,970.

For a multiple set or unit set with phases in a house with 199 seats or less: $1,300; 200 to 299 seats: $1,670; 300 to 499 seats: $2,210; 500 to 999 seats: $2,745; over 1000 seats: $3,505.

Regional opera lighting designer rates are a flat $2,883.20 plus 12 percent Pension and Welfare, transportation, and out-of-pocket expenses (in *all* contracts mentioned herein), hotel accommodations, and a daily allowance of $50 for food. There are other complicated provisions governing reuse, and also lease or sale of an opera light plot to another opera company ("shared" productions). Covered are the Baltimore Opera, Los Angeles Music Center, Greater Miami Opera, and the Opera Company of Philadelphia. Other regional operas tend to use the same contract.

Lighting Design Rates for the American Ballet Theatre, New York City Ballet, Joffrey Ballet, and Other Major Ballet Companies

  Full-length ballet: $3,765
  More than one-third of the evening: $2,510
  One-third of an evening: $1,255
  Pas de Deux/Trois: $855

Unit set, full-length: above fee or one-half of scenic design fee. The Major Ballet Contract also calls for a minimum rate of $225 per day for a prearranged number of days for any additional work, 12 percent Pension and Welfare to a maximum of $1,500 per contract, royalties at 8 percent of the original fee to be paid for five years only up to a maximum of $750, and a provision of considerable complexity governing subsequent use of lighting designs.

The Standard Ballet Company Lighting Design Rates

  Full-length ballet: $2,570
  More than one-third of the evening: $1,755
  One-third of the evening: $850
  Less than one-third of the evening: $645

This contract includes 12 percent Pension and Welfare, transportation at the prevailing government rate, $35 *per diem* (or some other reasonable amount) for each night spent out of town by the lighting designer or any assistants, and "subsequent" reuse rights provisions.357

LORT Rates. Finally USA was able to complete an agreement with LORT covering the numerous regional theatres throughout the United States. The contract was signed on September 1, 1987, and it runs for five years. Each of the many LORT theatres was designated as falling into category A, B, B+, C-1, or C-2 in a listing available to members and in the hands of the business agents. Some of the regional theatres which have more than one stage fall into two or more categories. Some 70 theatres are involved. Lighting design fees are for 1988:

    A theatres: $2,545
    B+ theatres: $2,225
    B theatres: $1,830
    C-1 theatres: $1,390
    C-2 theatres: rates not applicable until 9/1/91

There are other provisions covering excluded productions, staff designers, revivals, transfers to other theatres, etc.

At various times the union has also had (or has now) contracts with The Acting Company, Brooklyn Academy of Music, the American Shakespeare Company, Channel 13, the Pittsburgh Civic Light Opera, Wolftrap Light Opera Season, PAF (Performing Arts Foundation in Long Island), Burt Reynolds Dinner Theatre, Harlequin Dinner Theatre, Buffalo Studio Arena, Washington (D.C.) Arena Stage, New York City Opera, etc.

Contracts, in Summary

In all cases, contracts constantly change and are constantly being renegotiated. Details vary. Only *guidelines* derived from information readily available have been sketched here. *Complete, accurate information can only be obtained by union members consulting with the business agent.* The condensed summaries offered here are only guidelines presented so that the reader may better grasp union structure and more fully understand the huge task faced daily by the business agent of the union, assistants, and by union-selected contract-negotiating committees (made up of knowledgeable, concerned individuals working primarily in the area or place under negotiation). Ultimately *all* contracts must be negotiated and then presented to the general membership for approval or rejection before they are in force. The complex task of then *interpreting* the contents is a primary duty of the business agent assisted by the union attorneys and the executive board, when needed. (The examples provided have been taken from USA #829, but sim-ilar information about the operation, contracts, and procedures of USA #350 is not necessary here, as it varies only in specifics.)

USA Wrap-up

In the March 1980 *Newsletter,* Recording Secretary Elmon Webb presented an outline of the total number of USA #829 members working regularly in the various areas during all of 1978. Here are his figures:

    Theatre lighting: 42 members
    Total Working Members: 553
        Scenic design: 157
        Scenic artists (painters): 184
        Costumes: 111
        Design/artists: 18
        Diorama and display: 6
        Lighting: 42
        Industrial members: 25
        Mixed design: 10
        Mural artist: 0

It must be kept in mind that there are *many* paid-up card-carrying members of USA #829 who are educators or are working primarily in other (nonunion design or painting) areas of the industry.

In 1986 USA #829 sent a questionnaire from an "Oversight Committee on Admission Policies" to union members. The replies of those responding (approximately 700 in number) are of interest: 60 percent had been in the Union more than five years, with 92 percent considering lighting their lifetime career area. While 81 percent considered work under USA #829's jurisdiction as their major source of income, 58 percent had some income from other sources. Of the 700 responding lighting designers, 88 percent considered an apprentice program a good idea; 70 percent felt that the entrance exam they took was a valid test of their abilities and #829 standards; 80 percent felt that some applicants should be admitted to the union on the basis of past professional experience; 67 percent felt that the present exams do not assure the employer of hiring a skilled artist or designer; and 69 percent felt that an increase in union membership would not make it any more difficult for them

358 *11–13 Neal's Yard, London, England WC 2H 9DP.*

359 *I am a full, dues-paying member of The Society of British Theatre Designers and the Association of Lighting Designers. Information presented herein is excerpted from documents in my possession.*

Barbara Tumarkin Dunham, "Unionizing British Designers," Theatre Crafts, vol. 18, no. 9 (Nov./Dec. 1984), pp. 22, 104–107. A detailed explanation of the unionization of British costume, scenic and lighting designers through SBTD and British Actors Equity Association. Gives latest design fees.

For information about international architectural lighting design, see "International: Views on Lighting from Around the World," Lighting Design & Application, vol. 12, no. 5 (May 1982), pp. 27–42. Reports from 17 countries. Illus.

359a *Taken from ALD magazine, no. 8, December 1988, p. 8.*

360 *"Organizations, NATTKE," reprinted in the ABTT News, Feb. 1985, p. 15. Contains a detailed history of NATTKE. (National Association of Theatrical, Television, and Kine Employees).*

Figure 12.8 Seal of the Society of British Theatre Designers.

to obtain work. Only 33 percent felt that admissions to membership in the union should be restricted in times of sustained lack of work. The committee handling the survey was headed by Virginia Dancy Webb, and the results of the survey (here only excerpted and summarized) were published in USA #829's February 1986 *Newsletter*.

I outline details of union matters in this volume not to disclose union secrets or issues, but rather to make the reader aware of the fact that unions — just like theatre itself — are composed of humans and are in a constant state of flux. The information presented in this chapter provides both additional knowledge and a deeper understanding of the nature and functions of theatre unions. (Of course, the information contained herein can only reflect what is fact as this text goes to print.)

Foreign Unions

Finally brief mention should be made of the Society of British Theatre Designers (SBTD).[358] An outgrowth of the earlier Society of British Theatre Lighting Designers, founded in 1961, it was organized by Joe Davis, Richard Pilbrow, and (later) John Bury. It expanded from a professional organization of lighting designers to include all theatre designers (scenery, costume, and lighting) in 1976. I met with the union's executive board in London in 1973 and 1975 as a quasi-official representative of United Scenic Artists #829.[359] USA #829's position was to encourage the British union to move toward becoming a trade union — a move which it was considering and would have pursued in any case. Eventually the union became a branch of British Equity, and it has, at this writing, formulated union contracts and procedures. The 1988 lighting design rates in an ALD, British Actor's, Equity, TMA, SWET (Society of West End Theatres), and BETA agreement are:[359a]

 Royal Shakespearean Theatre and National Theatre:
  (full) £682.56, (small) £341.28
 Commercal theatre (West End): £512.47 to £284.95
 Subsidized theatre: £125.68 to £398.70
 Opera and ballet:
 Royal Opera House and English National Opera:
  £398.70 to £796.32

 Opera North/Glyndebourne/Welsh National
  Opera/Southern Opera: £227.52 to £455.04
 Smaller opera companies: £136.51 to £227.52
 Royal Ballet/London Festival Ballet/Saddler Wells
  Royal Ballet: £227.52 to £455.04
 Smaller Ballet (Rambert/London Contemporary
  Dance Theatre/Northern/Scottish): £171.18 to
  £398.70
 Smallest Ballet and Dance Companies: £136.51 to
  £199.35.

At the present time, if any member of a British theatre group is a member of Equity, an Equity lighting design contract must be filed. Lighting design fees are normally only 25 percent of those for the production's scenic designer. However, any reuse of a lighting design is not allowed without the original lighting designer's consent and additional payment. Also, no changes in the lighting are permitted following opening night in the West End without further designer compensation. Three working professional lighting designers now serve on the Equity Designer's Committee.

SBTD is an active organization embracing the top British designers. Several Americans are full members (Jules Fisher, Tharon Musser, Neil Peter Jampolis, myself, etc.). SBTD has extended maximum gracious assistance to American designers working in England. Particularly of concern to both groups is the necessity for any American designer working in England to obtain a work permit from the Ministry of Labor. The SBTD is not yet in a position to guarantee granting of such permission but has been most helpful in all ways possible.

During 1983 a suborganization of SBTD was formed by those members involved in lighting: The Association of Lighting Designers (ALD), headed by Richard Pilbrow. This group does not intend to become a union — instead it serves as a social group within SBTD. Its members have common experience and interests to further the lighting design industry in England. The group has a dues structure which makes dues higher for those in England (near London) who can attend meetings regularly and lower for those in touch by mail and outside of England. (Professional organizations are discussed in the next chapter.)

The British stagehands union (equivalent of IATSE in the United States) is NATTKE, (National Association of Theatrical, Television and Kine Employees), an "open union" with ready admission requirements. It was formed in 1890.[360]

ADC

The Associated Designers of Canada (ADC) adopted a new constitution in June 1983, widening its activities. In existence since around 1965, ADC now has a membership of 125 professional designers of sets, costumes, and lighting. ADC is rapidly becoming the union of designers in Canada. Its constitution provides for several regional councils (British Columbia, Alberta, Saskatchewan, Manitoba, Atlantic, and Toronto), and it has signed contracts with the Professional Association of Canadian Theatres specifying working conditions, royalties and fees, reuse rights, etc. ADC publishes a quarterly newsletter and has set up a structure quite similar to USA #829 in the United States. They have a producer-paid (disability) accident insurance program. ADC does not, at this time, have an entrance examination. Membership is obtained upon recommendation of three present members of ADC and approval by the membership committee and the board. They publish an annual Membership Directory and information bulletins. Annual dues are about $230 plus a percentage of all earned design fees. ADC has also been active in organizing exhibitions (and sales) of members' designs and is the focal point for Canadian exhibition in the Prague Quadriennale. The address of the ADC is 651 Queen St., East, Toronto, Ontario M4M 1G4, Canada; (416) 469-3544 is the telephone number. Recently ADC began placing apprentice/intern trainees in Canadian jobs with leading designers as their assistants. As of 1988, ADC had on file the names of 40 potential assistants, mostly from the Toronto area. Ron Francis was appointed as full-time executive director of ADC in October 1988. As of 1989, ADC was evolving an improved designer's fee structure.

Chapter 13

Professional Organizations

361 *Lee Watson, "Alphabet Soup" Lighting Dimensions, vol. 1, no. 5 (Nov. 1977), p. 15.*

"Groups Are Sources of Lighting Information," Architectural Lighting, *vol. 1, no. 5 (May 1987), pp. 38, 40, 42, 44, 46–47.*

362 *USITT, 10 West 19th Street, Suite 5A, New York, NY 10011. Telephone: (212) 924-9088.*

For an extended history of USITT, see Donald H. Swinney, "USITT at 25," Theatre Design & Technology, *vol. 21, no. 1 (Spring 1985), pp. 6– 10. Illus. A discursive article about the aims and evolution of USITT. Good documentation— more extensive than that recorded in this Handbook.*

Immediately after a new industry springs into being (light-ing design, for instance), trade guilds and professional organizations blossom (unions come later). There are many such societies in lighting. This chapter takes a brief look at why professional organizations exist and what they do, and then presents descriptions of many specific professional organizations related to the lighting design field.

Humans are social beings — particularly those in the per-forming arts. They gather to become acquainted; exchange trade information; gossip; recognize outstanding achieve-ments of fellow practitioners; and enhance, strengthen, and publicize the accomplishments of their field.

All professional organizations form committees, under-take studies to expand available knowledge, write constitu-tions and bylaws, collect dues, and elect officers. National or international bodies are a composite of regional and local branches/chapters/affiliates. The local's problems are dealt with by the parent group. All professional organiza-tions have meetings and national conventions which fre-quently feature speakers of international repute. Many publish trade journals, scholarly reports, books, brochures, and pamphlets of primary interest to the specialist. Some become involved in the training of newcomers or in estab-lishing standards and systems. Frequently a professional group becomes involved with being a liaison between its members and the government, businesses, foundations, and other professional groups in affiliated areas. Often pro-fessional organizations are concerned with the basic stan-dards and/or criteria of the industry, as well as with its

vocabulary and means of common communication. Those are a lot of objectives. Like most things human, professional organizations often fall short of their goals. And most have members who pay dues but contribute little except attend-ance at the annual convention. Yet professional organiza-tions are the backbone of the lighting craft, and their contri-butions to lighting design's progress and public acceptance are far out of proportion to the limited number of their members who are willing to be elected to office, serve on committees, undertake research, write reports, and add im-provements for their total membership. Professional orga-nizations (like humans) are born, flourish, and finally may wither and die. The available pool of organizations is an ever-changing "alphabet soup." [361]

USITT

The United States Institute for Theatre Technology (The American Association of Design and Production Profes-sionals in the Performing Arts) was born on the campus of Columbia University in the midst of a blizzard in New York City in 1961.[362] It sprang from an expressed desire of several American designer-technicians (while attending a meeting in Germany) to band together, and prior to the organiza-tional meeting at Columbia University most of the members of the founding group had met informally in the living room of the late Hans Sondheimer (technical director/stage man-ager/lighting designer for the New York City Opera).

Membership is now 3,200 (1989) members, nationally

and internationally. There are 20 regional sections including Canada, plus several student chapters. Dues are approximately $60 per year for an individual member (plus local dues, if any) and are lower for students. The annual national meeting is held each spring with the geographical location moving around the country on a pattern which complements that year's meeting places for SMPTE (Society of Motion Picture and Television Engineers — see below) and NAB (National Association of Broadcasters).

USITT is composed of several basic groups: manufacturers and distributors of theatre equipment, working professional designers and technicians, educators, theatre architects and consultants, a small group concerned with theatre business and arts administration, and a scattering of others (performers, directors, and playwrights, for example) who are "just interested." Agreements exist with other professional organizations.

USITT publishes two journals. The *USITT Newsletter* is published 10 times yearly. This is a "house letter" containing news and notes primarily of interest to USITT's members. USITT's scholarly journal is the quarterly *Theatre Design & Technology*. USITT maintains an extensive network (both regional and national) of work/study commissions in a wide range of specialties (theatre health and safety, architecture, costume design and technology, scenic design, theatre and production, management, education, engineering, technical production, sound design and lighting design, national liaison, and international liaison) plus subgroups (such as scenography exhibits and publications) as needed.

Lighting and lighting design is only a portion of USITT's area of interest; however, most lighting equipment manufacturers recognize that USITT embraces key people in the performance part of the theatre and entertainment industry and thus utilize USITT's annual spring convention as an important arena for displaying their complete line of wares. Lighting designers in all areas can gain much from membership in USITT.

IOSTT

USITT is a member of IOSTT, the International Organization of Scenographers and Theatre Technicians, which is based in Prague, Czechoslovakia, and founded in 1970.[363] It is composed of member national groups from approximately 25 countries. National groups embrace theatre architects and consultants, designers, audiovisual specialists, engineers and acousticians, scene painters, model makers, carpenters, machinists, costumers, lighting and scenic technicians, stage managers, technical directors, chief electricians and directors, and those with an interest in history and theory of design and technology, training and safety. The organization has inherent difficulties since it embraces both communist and noncommunist parent governments and Arab and Jewish governments. That this organization has continued to exist, to grow, to meet, and to work may be one of the finest testimonials to the value of today's world of artists and technicians. IOSTT was organized in Prague, and both Josef Svoboda (Czechoslovakia) and Dr. Joel E. Rubin (United States) have been important factors in the organization's history. Its continued existence has constituted an invaluable bridge between artists and technicians with common interests but different philosophical and political bases.

IOSST has numerous congresses and colloquies each year. Its work commissions coordinate a wide variety of activities. Its objective is improvement of theatre on an international level. Annual meetings are held. Every two years IOSTT meets in congress. Every second congress takes place in Prague and is concurrent with the international Quadrienalle of Scenography, an international exhibit and trade show that is attended by 20 or more nations, including USITT representatives. USITT has regularly underwritten part of the expenses for 5 to 12 U.S. student members to attend the Quadrienalle, primarily as a result of efforts by a past-president of IOSTT, Dr. Joel E. Rubin. IOSTT does not have individual memberships. As national sections evolve, they apply to IOSTT for membership.

ILDA

The International Laser Display Association was formed by 34 laser entertainment firms and laser professionals at Lake Tahoe, California. They had met earlier (August 1986) and incorporated in May 1987. Ron Goldstein of Laser Media became president. The laser industry is a $50 billion a year

[363] *Secretary General, IOSTT, 110 01 Prague 1, Celetna ul. 17, Czechoslovakia.*

IOSTT member groups are located in Austria, Belgium, Bulgaria, Canada, China, Czechoslovakia, Finland, France, German Democratic Republic, German Federal Republic, Great Britain, Holland, Hungary, Israel, Japan, Mexico, Norway, Poland, Romania, Sweden, United Arab Republic, and the United States.

[363a] "ILDA Formed by 34 Laser Pros," Pro Light & Sound, no. 3 (Summer 1987), p. 44.

"Laser Group Meets," Lighting Dimensions, vol. 11, no. 6 (November 1987), p. 17. ILDA met November 13–14, 1987 and had 50 members at that time.

"ILDA Meeting," Lighting Dimensions, vol. 12, no. 6 (September/October 1988), p. 24.

[363b] "Theatrical Dealers Association Formed," Theatre Crafts, vol. 22, no. 3 (March 1988), p. 20. Also: Lighting Dimensions, vol. 12, no. 2 (March 1988), p. 22.

[364] American Society of Lighting Designers, 4947 Hollywood Blvd., Hollywood, CA 90027. Telephone: (818) 783-3530.

[365] Excerpted from ASLD's "Application for Membership."

[366] International Association of Lighting Designers, 18 E. 16th St., N.Y., NY 10003. Telephone: (212) 206-1281.

See the IALD Newsletter, Nov. 1986, for an eight-page summary of IALD activities ("What's Going On . . . ").

[366a] Taken from the IALD Constitution and By-Laws.

market. Advancement of laser safety regulations and public awareness of the ever-increasing laser media are objectives of the organization. Membership is in five categories: corporate, affiliate, associate, individual, and subscriber. The Association can be reached through: Barbara Inatsugu, ILDA, 1126 Ashland Avenue, Santa Monica, California 90405. Telephone: (213) 826-3838. As of 1989, the organization had 41 members.[363a]

TDA

The initial meeting of the Theatrical Dealers Association was held November 1987 in Las Vegas with 25 members. It met again on March 23, 1988, in Anaheim, California. The organization, which now has 130 individual members from 50 theatrical dealers and 12 manufacturers, publishes a quarterly newsletter. The Association can be reached through: Steve Butler, Membership Chairperson, 406 East 18th Street, Kansas City, Missouri 64108. Telephone: (816) 474-1751.[363b]

ASLD

ASLD was the American Society of Lighting Directors Inc., but now is the American Society of Lighting Designers.[364] Consisting of approximately 450 film and TV gaffers and miscellaneous lighting designers, this West Coast group is quite active. Formed to "facilitate the interchange of information," it has as its "sole aim to foster the advancement of the art and science of lighting by encouraging technical development and honoring aesthetic achievement in this field."[365] Annual dues are approximately $35. Although basically representing the film and TV industry, this group crosses into the interest areas of many other professional organizations. Its strengths are the compactness of its geographical area and its active group of members.

IALD

IALD is the International Association of Lighting Designers.[366] Formed January 1969 by a group of 14 architectural lighting design practitioners as a result of a telephone conversation between David A. Mintz and Marton Garon, it now has a membership of approximately 390 (from 33 states and 5 foreign countries). Concerned with the aesthetics of lighting, behavioral psychology, human physics, and the physiology of light perception and seeing, IALD members are employed by architects, interior designers, and other environmentalists. IALD does not allow manufacturers or suppliers to join — only designers. This membership criterion distinctly separates it from the IES (Illuminating Engineering Society — discussed below). "Corporate" members are working professionals with a proven record of successful design of lighting. Each must have established a minimum of four years as chief designer. "Senior associate" members must have had a minimum of two years at the level of job captain. Only these two membership categories carry voting privileges. "Associate" members are employees of architectural lighting design firms. "Affiliate" members are employed lighting consultants, who must move into another category within three years. "Student" members are usually still in school. Lastly, "collaborating professionals" are those who do not meet the criteria for voting, but "whom IALD deems have contributed to the profession." A Western committee was formed on May 18, 1989, and a European committee earlier. The annual dues and the initiation structure vary with each membership category. "Corporate" members pay dues of $100 per annum. IALD defines its goals as being to

Advance understanding of the role of light as a design material and of the impact of lighting on architectural design and the quality of the environment; promote . . . the importance of the function of lighting designers; further the acceptance of lighting designers by architects and owners as a valid and necessary discipline on every project so as to ensure high professional standards of lighting design; develop a code of professional conduct; further the growth of the ranks of the profession and work to improve the training available to those entering the profession; work towards development of educational programs offering a degree in lighting design; develop guidelines for agreement between lighting designers and their clients and define the areas of responsibility; promote equipment installation standards for the industry; promote licensing and professional certification of lighting designers.[366a]

Quite an undertaking. The IALD's goals are not just platitudes, however, for the IALD has an active and widely publicized internship system, established in 1977. This system provides job training in architectural lighting design with member firms. IALD also sponsors an annual Award of Excellence program for outstanding lighting design, which was begun in 1983 and is separate from the IES Lumen Awards. IALD continues to come to grips with the very specialized needs of newcomers in this field who have both strong architectural training (drafting ability, for example) and strong visual design skills (frequently individuals who are theatre-trained or trained in interior design or illuminating engineering).

IALD, in conjunction with IES, held the first architectural lighting trade show, called *Lighting World International*,[367] in New York City in December 1981; the second was held in April 1983; the third, in New York City in 1985; *Lighting World IV* was held in Los Angeles, California in 1986. Over 12,000 attended to view the 400 company exhibits and attend 14 seminars. These trade shows have been quite successful. The fifth show, held at Jacob K. Javits Convention Center in New York City in May 1987, was attended by over 14,000 people; it had 450 exhibitors, 17 seminars, and 3 workshops. In 1989 both the IES and IALD separated from Lightworld and offered Light Fair, a trade show and conference, in April 1990 at the New York City Hilton Hotel. Lightworld continues under the sponsorship of National Expositions.

A sizable percentage of IALD's members were theatre-trained prior to moving into architectural lighting design: Abe Feder, the late James Nuckolls, Donald Gersztoff, Howard Brandston, Jules Fisher, Tom Lemons, Paul Marantz, David A. Mintz, William Nelson, Edison Price, and William Warfel, to name but a few. In May of 1984 IALD began forming a regional committee (outside New York City). Present active committees concern such things as the IALD Awards Program, Lighting World International, energy, education, membership, the intern program, the newsletter, and long-range goals. For a short period of time IALD published *Lightview*, a quarterly journal initiated in the spring of 1988 and discontinued in 1989.

CIE

CIE stands for *Commission Internationale de L'Éclairage* (International Commission on Illumination). Founded in 1913,

it is composed of member committees from 42 countries. Its functions are the setting of international technical standards in photometry, colorimetry, spectral distribution, and other data areas concerning the measurement of light and color. Its second function is the free exchange of information between scientists in this area from the member countries. It works through 23 technical committees covering such subjects as ultraviolet radiation, discomfort, glare, daylight, and sports lighting. The CIE established a Stage and Studio Lighting Committee in Scheveningen, Holland, in 1939.

Individuals cannot belong to CIE unless they are official representatives of member countries' national illumination organizations. International conferences are held every four years, and individual study committees meet more often. The CIE has attracted the services of leading figures concerned with illumination through the years. It is a most useful scientific research and dissemination center for those in the fields of architectural lighting, TV and film lighting, and theatrical lighting equipment design and production.

CIE began publishing the *CIE Journal* in three languages in 1983.[368] *Euroluce,* the largest international display of lighting products, is held each September in Milan, Italy, at the city's fairgrounds, in conjunction with the Salone Del Mobile (residential furniture and accessories show). The first *Euroluce* was held in 1976. Around 350 exhibitors from Italy and other countries display their products. Roughly 140,000 visitors — 40,000 from foreign countries — attend this annual combined lighting/furniture show.[369]

TCG

Theatre Communications Group (TCG) is not really a professional organization.[370] It is a foundation-supported national service organization, founded in 1961, which services most of the United States' nonprofit professional theatres. TCG runs its own interview/placement service, but for employer theatres, not for the job applicants. The service exists to assist member producing groups in locating directors, scripts, performers, designers, and technicians. TCG publishes books and newsletters and magazines. In most ways it performs many of the functions of a profes-

[367] *"Industry Event—Lighting World 2"* Interiors, Vol. CXLII, no. 9 (April 1983), pp. 43–45, 46, 48, 50, 54.

"The First Great Show," Interiors, Vol. CXLI, no. 7 (Feb. 1982), pp. 40, 42, 50, 52. Illus. Photographs of IES (NY)-IALD's first "Lighting World International" trade show.

"Leading Lights—IALD," Interiors, Vol. CXLI, no. 7 (Feb. 1982), p. 73. Illus. Outlines IALD's aims and personnel.

[368] Charles L. Amick, *"The CIE in the USA,"* Lighting Design + Application, vol. 15, no. 7 (July 1985), pp. 43–44. Illus.

K. R. Ackerman, *"C.I.E. — 1975,"* TABS, vol. 33, no. 2 (Summer 1975), pp. 21–22. Very concise, helpful exploration of the CIE.

Fred W. Billmeyer, Jr., *"The CIE — Where It's At and Where It's Going,"* Lighting Design & Application, vol. 12, no. 5 (May 1982), pp. 24–26.

"CIE," SMPTE Journal, Vol. 92, no. 4 (April 1983), p. 360. Details of SMPTE and CIE coordination.

"Anniversary: International Lighting Body Celebrates 75 Years," Lighting, vol. 2, no. 5 (October 1988), pp. 25, 37. "Gas lighting engineers and scientists founded the Commission Internationale de Photometrie (CIP) on September 3, 1900, in Paris. . . . [the actual] CIE was formalized at the 4th meeting of the CIP on August 27–30, 1913, in Berlin . . . with statutes and rules of operation." As of 1989, 38 countries belonged to the CIE, with over 100 technical committees in seven divisions.

Sylvester K. Guth, *"The Commission Internationale de l'Éclairage: A Short History,"* CIE Journal, vol. 2, no. 1 (July 1983), pp. 2–4. An extensive and detailed history of the CIE, its objectives, and its activities by a past president.

"Interview: Mike Marsden," International Lighting Review, 1st quarter of 38th year (1987), pp. 18–21. Illus., color. A well-written and well-illustrated interview with the president of CIE (Marsden) with much more detail concerning the organization than is offered in this Handbook.

[369] Edie Cohen, *"Euroluce in Milan,"* Lighting Dimensions, vol. 10, no. 6 (Nov. 1986), pp. 82–85. Illus.

370 *355 Lexington Avenue, N.Y., NY 10017. Telephone: (212) 697-5230.*

371 *Michele Larue, "Theatre Educators Meet in Chicago,"* Theatre Crafts, *vol. 21, no. 9 (November 1987), p. 22. ATHE, formed April 1985 with 1200 members, can be contacted through Vincent Angotti, Administrator, Theatre Service, P.O. Box 15282, Evansville, IN 47716. It publishes a* Newsletter, *is involved in a* THEatre JOBLIST *(a placement service listing published nineteen times yearly since January 1987), and has annual dues of $50 for individuals and $75 for organizations.*

372 *"ADIA Update,"* Disco-Tech, *vol. 4, no. 2 (August 1988), p. 8.*

"Proof Disco Lives!" Disco-Tech, *vol. 4, no. 1 (March 1988), pp. 18–19. This article also outlines the purposes of ADIA. For more information contact: Patricia O'Connor, Membership Coordinator, American Discotheque Industry Association, Inc., P.O. Box 7063, Huntsville, AL 35807.*

373 *345 E. 47th St., N.Y., NY 10036. Telephone: (212) 644-7926.*

374 *"Howard Brandston Elected IES President,"* Lighting Design + Application, *vol. 13, no. 8 (Aug. 1983), pp. 38–41. Illus. An excellent short history of IES and architectural lighting design/engineering with a forthright statement of IES objectives in this energy-conscious era by a former IES president. This is intended as a guide to present practices for architects and engineers.*

Mike Williams, "IES Celebrates 80 Light Years — Boston Played Host to the 1986 Illuminating Engineering Society's Annual Conference," Lighting Dimensions, *vol. 10, no. 6 (Nov. 1986), pp. 78–80. Illus.*

Mark Loeffler, "Show Report: Spotlight 1987, Symposium and Exposition Draw Theatre and Television Lighting Professionals to Montreal," Lighting Dimensions, *vol. 11, no. 7 (January/February 1988), pp. 92–93.*

sional society, except that it exists to service the needs of the employer, not the individual. Its list of member theatres is extensive. TCG is the clearinghouse for many of the most important nonprofit theatres in the United States. There is no way an individual can become a member — only producing groups belong. However, awareness of TCG — its scope and activities — is important for a lighting designer.

ATHE, AATSE, AATY and AATE

When the long-enduring American Theatre Association (ATA) disbanded in April of 1986, it was replaced by ATHE (Association for Theatre in Higher Education), AATSE (American Association for Theatre in Secondary Education), AATY (American Association of Theatre for Youth) and AATE (American Alliance for Theatre and Education). These new organizations, mostly founded in 1988 and with roughly 800 members each, are still evolving as a rallying place for the educators in theatre who were for many years members of ATA.[371]

ADIA

The American Discotheque Industry Association, Inc., is tied in with *Nightclub & Bar* magazine. In 1988 the organization and the magazine exhibited in a trade show together in Las Vegas. The organization's first annual meeting was held in May 1989 with the Sound and Video Contractors Association convention in Nashville, Tennessee.[372]

SRES

The Specular Reflector Engineering Society deals with testing and verfication of luminaire reflectors. Membership categories include: sustaining, professional, industry, associate, student, and retired. SRES is contactable through: P.O. Box 23130, 3223 Greyling Drive, San Diego, CA 92123.

IES

IES (also IESNA) is the Illuminating Engineering Society of North America.[373] It is the oldest of the professional societies, and lighting designers are a very small part of its total membership. Founded in 1906, IES embraces educators, manufacturers, electrical contractors, engineers, scientists, utility personnel, suppliers — workers in all those disciplines concerned with the technology of illuminating engineering. Current membership is between 9,000 and 10,000. Since the artist who uses light needs to master the technology of the craft, membership and knowledge of IES is important. IES publishes *The Journal of the IES* and the more popularized *Lighting Design + Application* magazine. *Lighting Design + Application* is an invaluable publication for *any* lighting designer, and it is absolutely essential for those in either architectural or landscape lighting. Additionally, IES publishes the *Lighting Handbooks,* both *Reference* and *Application* volumes, and numerous shorter works.

IES has an extensive network of commissions and 12 regional groups throughout the country which meet regularly and investigate, evaluate, and report on industry standards, criteria, and new developments. There are over 100 local sections in Canada, Mexico, and the United States. IES's basic annual dues are $100 for full members, $35 for retired members, and $30 for students. Membership categories include Fellow, Member, Associate Member, Honorary Member, Member Emeritus, and Student. A membership application requires sponsorship by three present IES members. The IES has more than 70 technical, research, and design committees and subcommittees. One of the commissions of IES is the Theatre, Television and Film Lighting (TTFL) Committee of IES. Annual meetings of this group (separate from the IES conference) resemble a "family reunion" of the lighting engineers of show business and manufacturing. TTFL also brings together television workers, architectural engineers, and some film specialists. It also crosses over into the lighting designer groups and is in general an amalgamation.[374]

Lighting Research and Education Institutes

Under the presidency of Howard Brandston (architectural lighting designer and former student of mine) during 1983, IES began raising several million dollars to support its newly created Lighting Research Institute and Education Fund.

These two separate corporations represent a forward thrust by IES to improve the lighting industry. The Lighting Research Institute is a nonprofit organization created in 1982 (with Dr. Maxine Savitz as president) to promote and sponsor basic and applied research and development in lighting and vision in the areas of photobiology, systemic effects of light, physical/chemical hazards of light, vision, systems applications, and the psychology of human responses to light through scientific investigation.[375] In 1984 a similar Canadian Lighting Research Institute was founded by IES. Both the American and Canadian Lighting Education Foundations are of even more recent creation. They are intended to subsidize advanced educational instruction in illumination engineering and interior lighting design. They have begun their work both by contributing funds to strengthen outstanding existing programs of instruction (upgrade faculty and libraries, fund scholarships and grants) and by holding brief summer workshops for both instructors and students of architectural and interior design lighting to improve the level of instruction in these fields. Several national panel sessions of lighting experts were underwritten by the IES and the U.S. National Bureau of Standards to formulate the structure, objectives, and methods to be utilized by both the Research and Education Foundations.

SMPTE

The SMPTE (Society of Motion Picture and Television Engineers)[376] was founded in the summer of 1916 by C. Francis Jenkins and 25 associates at the Hotel Astor in New York City. Present membership is around 9,000. SMPTE is, in some ways, the counterpart of IES in the motion picture and TV fields, but basically it is more restricted to engineers. SMPTE expanded to include television engineers in January, 1950.[377]

SMPTE's publication is the scholarly SMPTE Journal. SMPTE has 20 regional branches, and base membership costs around $50 per year. Its annual conference is in October.

During its existence, SMPTE has remained committed to five basic objectives: (1) to advance the theory and practice of engineering in motion pictures, television, and allied arts and sciences; (2) to establish standards and practices in the industry; (3) to maintain and enhance high professional standards; (4) to guide students and improve standards of education; and (5) to disseminate scientific knowledge through publication.[378] The SMPTE has been quite successfully making progress toward each of these objectives.

The SMPTE's counterpart in England is BKSTS — the British Kinematography, Sound, and Television Society, founded in 1931. BKSTS, which grew out of the former London Branch of SMPTE, publishes the BKSTS Journal.[379] The Canadian branch of SMPTE was founded in 1916.[380]

ASC

The American Society of Cinematographers (ASC) was founded in 1919.[381] Its membership stays around 180. Membership is by invitation only. Members carry the letters "ASC" after their names on screen credits. Active members are those invited who have had five years or more with screen credit as either "Cinematographer" or "Director of Photography." Associate members (again by invitation) are other members in the industry. Dues are $15 per quarter. There is no regional structure nor strong affiliation with other organizations. ASC defines its purposes as "social, fraternal and educational." ASC's publication is The American Cinematographer, published monthly since 1919 for $9 per year.[382]

PMPEA

Those who work in film/TV lighting design need to know of the Professional Motion Picture Equipment Association (PMPEA).[383] This organization publishes Follow Focus magazine each March and September. PMPEA was formed in 1973 by Mrs. Lee Duncan, then president of Victor Duncan, Inc. She became PMPEA's secretary/treasurer but retired on November 10, 1982.

The membership of PMPEA consists of importers, distributors, and manufacturers of motion picture products. Active members pay $250 per year dues; associate (individual) members pay $50. PMPEA's primary purpose is "to promote film and the film industry." Not only does the organization publish a journal, but it also has a speakers bureau,

[375] "Research Agenda," Lighting Design + Application, vol. 14, no. 7 (July 1984), pp. 23–26. IES objectives for the new Lighting Research Institute.

Maxine Savitz, "LRI—After Two Years, Here's Where We Are," Lighting Design + Application, vol. 15, no. 7 (July 1985), pp. 39–42. Illus. The first president of LRI reports on projects, research, and progress.

"LRI Research Agenda," Lighting Design & Technology, vol. 14, no. 7 (July 1984). A reprint available from the Lighting Research Institute concerning its structure.

"L.R.I. Project Summaries," an 11-page mimeographed report about specific LRI projects funded for 1984 and 1985. Available from LRI.

"LRI Annual Report, 1984," a four-page booklet available from LRI.

[376] 862 Scarsdale Ave., Scarsdale, NY 10583. Telephone: (914) 472-6606.

[377] General Electric Review, vol. 59, no. 3-4 (May/June 1956), p. 45. SMPTE history.

[378] Freely adapted from SMPTE Journal, "1916–1981," vol. 90, no. 12 (Dec. 1981), p. 1191. See also:

Herbert E. Farmer, "Education and the SMPTE," SMPTE Journal, vol. 91, no. 2 (Feb. 1982), pp. 139–40.

"Education and Training," SMPTE Journal, Part I, vol. 91, no. 5 (May 1982), p. 464. Progress report on SMPTE scholarships.

Frederick M. Remley, "Education," SMPTE Journal, vol. 92, no. 4 (April 1983), p. 411. A detailed report by SMPTE on training film and TV engineers, proposing SMPTE internship-apprenticeships.

Mary Eginton, "What is SMPTE? The Society of Motion Picture and Television Engineers Gathers for its 70th Annual Conference," Lighting Dimensions, vol. 10, no. 6 (Nov. 1986), p. 30.

Janet Staiger, "Historical Note: Standardization and Independence: The Founding Objectives of the SMPTE," SMPTE Journal, vol. 96, no. 6 (June 1987), pp. 532–537. An authentic, extensive history of SMPTE; article also discusses the SMPTE's objectives and presents a progress report.

SMPTE began a day-long "Production Lighting Techniques" Tutorial Seminar sponsored by the Hollywood Section of SMPTE. In May 1983 this was held at the Universal Studios with noted ASC directors of photography and cinematographers as leaders. For further information (or participation) contact Jack Spring, Eastman Kodak Co., 6706 Santa Monica Blvd., Hollywood, CA 90038, telephone: (213) 464-6131; or Howard La Zare, Consolidated Film Industries, 959 No. Seward St., Hollywood, CA 90038, telephone: (213) 462-3161.

Alex E. Alden, "Our Society — Its Beginning, Its Growth," SMPTE Journal, vol. 96, no. 7 (July 1987), pp. 687–691. More detailed history of SMPTE from the pen of their former Manager of Engineering. Well-presented, useful history.

[379] John B. Aldred, "The Role of the BKSTS," SMPTE Journal, vol. 91, no. 1 (Jan. 1982), p. 59.

[380] Gerald Graham, "A Retrospective Look at Canadian Participation in the SMPTE," SMPTE Journal, vol. 91, no. 4 (April 1982), pp. 332–37. An extended history of the Canadian SMPTE.

[381] 1784 North Orange Drive, Hollywood, CA 90023. Telephone: (213) 876-5080.

[382] Information about ASC verified in a telephone conversation with Ms. Three Tyler on June 13, 1979, and in a subsequent West Coast meeting.

[383] Ten Thousand Riverside Drive, Suite 17, Toluca Lake, CA 91602. Telephone: (213) 761-6690.

[384] The Designers Lighting Forum in New York City can be contacted through IALD or at the address given below. DLF addresses and membership rates include:

BOSTON: Paul Chabot, P.O. Box 6406, Boston, MA 02102. Telephone: (617) 367-0910. Dues: $35 (students $10).

DETROIT: Joan Bradley, Detroit Edison, 2000 Second Ave., Detroit, MI 48226. Telephone: (313) 237-7136. Dues: $35.

LOS ANGELES: Susie Caron, P.O. Box 6175, Malibu, CA 90265. Telephone: (213) 837-4149. Dues: $40.

NEW YORK CITY: Ruth Drachler, Louis Baldinger & Sons, Inc., 19-02 Steinway Street, Astoria, NY 11105. Telephone: (718) 204-5700 or (212) 678-0414. Dues: $40 (students $25).

ORANGE COUNTY: Committee of IES Orange Section, Sheldon Liss, Liss Engineering, 2862A Walnut Ave., Tustin, CA 92680. Telephone: (714) 730-0222. Dues: $95.

conducts seminars and workshops, conducts research, and promotes the film industry. In 1984 there were 98 active member firms worldwide and 20 associate members. PMPEA has been constructively active in the film industry.

DLF

DLF is the Designers Lighting Forum, in New York City and other cities, which is affiliated with IALD. DLF meets regularly and offers quality programs for its architectural lighting design members, as well as annual awards for outstanding design.[384] There are chapters of DLF in New York, Boston, Detroit, Los Angeles, San Diego, San Francisco, and Orange County, California. In the past there were DLF chapters in Atlanta, Cleveland, Nashville, and Toledo. DLF grew out of IES Residential Lighting Forums of the 1930s and 1940s. DLF's membership includes interior designers, architects, engineers, lighting designers, consultants, manufacturers, contractors, distributors, utility personnel, and students. DLF of New York, Inc., can be reached through Janis Axnes, Treasurer, 58 Stratford Avenue, Greenlawn, NY 11740. Telephone: (516) 368-5470.

ASTC

The American Society of Theatre Consultants (ASTC) was formed in 1983 with consultant S. Leonard Auerbach as president, Vincent Piacentini as vice president, Edgar L. Lustig as secretary/treasurer, and Robert Davis and Ron Jerit as directors-at-large.[385] The organization's address is ASTC, 12226 Mentz Hill Road, St. Louis, Missouri 63128.

The National Archives of Theatre Lighting

The National Archives of Theatre Lighting is not a professional organization,[386] but it properly deserves attention in this chapter. William Allison established the Archives at Penn State in 1975 as a museum and research base. The Archives contain lighting units (luminaires) and accessories, files and records (much from Strand Century), and data, all of which is catalogued, stored, and made available for research. Kliegl Lighting & Engineering, Carnegie-Mellon University, George Izenour Associates, and others also contributed. Documents include original engineering drawings, transparencies, and data sheets. Some of this information is filed in the Rare Book Room of Pattee Library. A catalog is available. There is no charge for use to students of theatre research. Other lighting research collections can be found at the University of Texas, the University of Missouri — Kansas City (USITT's archives), and Brigham Young University in Provo, Utah.

AMI

AMI, the Association for Multi-Image, International, Inc., holds an annual conference. Contact Marilyn Kulp, (813) 932-1692.

NAB

The National Association of Broadcasters (NAB) holds the largest trade show in the United States (including lighting equipment) held each year and is an organization of interest to those in TV lighting. Lighting is only a small part of this large professional organization. NAB's annual convention and exposition is held in April of each year.

TLA

Educators will be interested in another organization which has been active for many years: the Theatre Library Association (TLA). TLA publishes Broadside quarterly. The group is composed mostly of librarians. Annual dues are $20. TLA can be contacted at 111 Amsterdam Ave., New York, New York 10023.

ALA

Formerly the American Home Lighting Institute (AHLI), this organization is now the American Lighting Association. As the AHLI, it was founded in 1945. The organization unites manufacturers, retail showrooms, and manufacturers' representatives with the aims of developing a larger demand for lighting products, providing educational programs, and increasing the consumer's awareness of lighting.

As of 1985 it had a membership of more than 500 and was "a major educational force in the industry, offering a variety of seminars on the technical, functional, and aesthetic aspects of lighting."[387] The 1989 convention was held in Washington, D.C., in September. Contact: Helen L. Closs, ALA, 435 North Michigan Avenue, Chicago, IL 60611. Telephone: (312) 644-0828.

FOREIGN ORGANIZATIONS

MALE

The Mexican Association of Lighting Engineers (MALE) was formed in Monterrey, N.L., Mexico, in November 1986. It can be contacted through Juan De La Barrera NTE, 1008, Colonia Modelo CP, or P.O. Box 6842, Laredo, Texas 78042.

BSTLD

The British Society of Television Lighting Directors came into existence on October 30, 1974.[378] Organized to provide a forum for exchange of ideas, to encourage discussion of TV lighting techniques and equipment, to provide social gatherings, and to publish a journal. It now has over 500 members. The membership meets regularly and publishes a journal. BSTLD members are active in international meetings. They have no union or political affiliations. In 1989 BSTLD began giving an annual award for outstanding TV lighting. An affiliated organization is the Canadian Society of Television Lighting Directors, formed in 1978.[388] It had in 1982 around 120 members. Annual dues are $25. The Australian Society of Television Lighting Directors, which is also affiliated with BSTLD, was formed in Victoria in July of 1980. It has a current membership numbering approximately 120. All three also have had ties with the British Society of Cinematographers since 1981. There are also affiliated branches in Denmark, France, Italy, Israel, New Zealand, Norway, South Africa, Sweden, and the United States. The BSTLD can be contacted through Eric Wallis, The Cot, Ditton Road, Langley, Berks SL3 8PR, England.

ABTT

The Association of British Theatre Technicians (ABTT) was founded in 1961 and incorporated in 1975.[389] In 1989 it had around 1,300 members. Annual dues are £35 (approximately $60) per year. Membership categories include Fellows, Members, Associate Members, (£35 dues); Organizational Members, (£85 dues); Honorary Life Members, and students (£17.50 dues). ABTT publishes both *Sightlines* (a quarterly journal) and *ABTT News* (a monthly newsletter). The organization has four regional divisions: North, Scotland, Midlands, and Wales. It is registered as a nonprofit charity and is partly subsidized by the British Arts Council. ABTT gives annual awards for outstanding work, has research and study commissions, operates an extensive (and most effective) intern trainees program in conjunction with the British Arts Council, serves as a job placement agency for members, organizes both lectures of general interest and regular meetings, and disseminates much useful technical/design information through its two publications. Since 1978 it has also offered an October national trade show, attended by over 1,800 people and 50 exhibitors in 1982. In 1986 ABTT added a second annual trade show in Belfast, Ireland. ABTT is the British member of OISTT and is quite active internationally. It not only sends a British scenographer exhibit abroad but also arranges trips for interested members to places such as India, Japan, and Australia. ABTT is the British equivalent of USITT, but it has a far wider focus.[390] The organization has many active committees, concerning such areas as finance, awards, publications, training, sound, safety, theatre planning, archeology, and regional groups.

BSTD

The British Society of Theatre Lighting Designers (BSTLD), organized by Joe Davis and Richard Pilbrow in 1961, evolved into the British Society of Theatre Designers (BSTD) in 1976 when the scenic and costume designers wished to join the long active lighting designers group. BSTD now has 100 members (1985). British designer John Bury assumed leadership for a social/informational gather-

SAN DIEGO: Committee of San Diego IES, Pat Silver, 5720 Mott Street, San Diego, CA 92122. Telephone: (619) 453-3905. Dues: $5.

NORTHERN CALIFORNIA: Paula Goodell, P.O. Box 1429, San Francisco, CA 94101-1429. Telephone: (415) 550-0333. Dues: individual $30, firm $50.

See "Groups Are Sources of Lighting Information," op. cit. (see footnote 36) for more information.

Barbara J. Knox, "Designers Lighting Forum: Chapters Across the Nation Welcome All Interested in Lighting Design," Lighting Dimensions, vol. 11, no. 6 (November 1987), pp. 90, 93–94.

[385] ASTC, 12226 Mentz Hill Road, St. Louis, MO 63128. Telephone: (314) 843-9218.

[386] Pennsylvania State University, Ihlseng Cottage, University Park, PA 16802. See also:

"National Lighting Archives Established," Theatre Crafts, vol. 9, no. 5 (Oct. 1975), p. 2.

"For the Love of Light," Lighting Dimensions, vol. 10, no. 2 (Mar./Apr. 1986), pp. 95–96, 98–99. Illus. A report about Connie and Margarita Stevens, Los Angeles Stage Lighting, who have a treasure trove of antique equipment.

The British equivalent of the archives in Penn State is the firm Ancient Lights in Atteborough, Norfolk County. See TABS, vol. 43, no. 1 (Feb. 1986), pp. 24–25. Illus.

[387] See Lighting Design + Application, vol. 15, no. 4 (Apr. 1985), p. 2.

[388] See:

Bill Lee, "The Long Slow Fade," Society of Television Lighting Directors, Winter 1984, pp. 6–8.

Alan Homes, "Society of Television Lighting Directors," TABS, vol. 38, no. 1 (June 1981), p. 24. More detailed information than that presented here.

"Society of Television Lighting Directors — The History," mimeographed. Available from STLD.

"Aims of the Society," Society of Television Lighting Directors, no. 38 (Spring 1989), p. 50. Outlines the aims, structure, and affiliates of SMPTE and the countries it represents within its membership (Australia, Brazil, Canada, Cyprus, Denmark, France, India, Israel, Italy, Malaysia, New Zealand, Netherlands, Norway, South Africa, Spain, Sweden, and the United States).

Bill Lee, "From Dreams Such Stuff Is Made," Society of Television Lighting Directors, *no. 36 (Summer 1988), pp. 7–9. Illus. A more personal history of STLD by a former editor.*

[389] *The Canadian Society of Television Lighting Directors holds an annual spring trade show. Contact Tom Nutt, Canadian Broadcasting Corporation, 7925 Cote St., Luc Road, Montreal, Quebec H4W 1R5, for further information.*

[390] *4 Great Pulteney St., London W1R 3DF, England. Telephone: 01-434-3901. For a complete listing of British professional societies and organizations, see pp. 437–451 in John Offord's and The British Theatre Institute's* British Theatre Directory, *London; John Offord Publs., Ltd; 1983.*

[391] *Information taken primarily from ABTT's annual reports.*

For a history of ABTT (and early USITT), see ABTT News, *July 1982, by Richard Pilbrow.*

Richard Pilbrow, "The Way We Were", Sightline, *vol. 20, no. 1 (Summer 1986), pp. 19, 21–25. Illus. Pilbrow reviews ABTT's history on its Silver Anniversary.*

Ethel Langstreth, "Nostalgia", ABTT News., *April 1982.*

[392] *% Theatre Projects, Ltd., 10 Longacre St., London WC2 EqLN, England. Telephone: (01-240-5411).*

[393] *ALD address is: 3 Apollo Studios, Charlton Kings Road, London NW5 25W, England. Telephone: 01-482-4224.*

"Association of Lighting Designers," Cue, *no. 16 (Mar./Apr. 1982), p. 10.*

See ALD Newsletter, *#4 (April 1987), p. 3, for details concerning ALD's connections with British Actors Equity. Concerns contracts and designers' rights.*

[394] *See "PLASA Presents . . . London's Light + Sound Show,"* Lighting + Sound International, *vol. 1, no. 10 (September/October 1986), pp. 21–33. Illus., color. Little text, mostly photographs.*

Adam Pirani, "Light and Sound Show '87: British Club Manufacturers Court American Buyers," Lighting Dimensions, *vol. II, no. 6 (November 1987), pp. 96, 98, 100–102. Illus. Description of a PLASA show in London in 1987.*

ing organization of those interested in lighting design. BSTD remained the same with the addition of the other designer disciplines in 1976. In addition to Joe Davis and Richard Pilbrow, other founders of the original BSTLD were John Wychham, Charles Bristow, William Bundy, Michael Northern, and 24 other members, including Jo Mielziner and Jean Rosenthal (United States). BSTD has evolved to semi-union status (and is discussed briefly in Chap. 12) and has become a part of British Equity. In conjunction with Equity, BSTD establishes contracts and terms of employment in many areas. BSTD is also quite active with IOSTT and in membership meetings.[391]

ALD

The British lighting designers in 1984 formed a new association—separate from the British Society of Theatre Designers—called the Association of Lighting Designers (ALD). It was organized with the late Joe Davis as president and Richard Pilbrow as chairman. In addition to Full Members, ALD also has Associate Members (those interested in lighting but not professionally employed), Affiliated Members (companies concerned with promoting the interests of stage lighting), Fellows, and Honorary Members. Annual dues are approximately $40 (£15 for Full Members, £12.50 for Country Members; £5 for Associate Members, and £100 for Affiliated Members). ALD does not intend to become a union and so does not deal with wages and working conditions. "The Association's purpose is to further the art of lighting design for the theatre, live entertainment, and associated industries. To represent the art and to promote a professional code and terms of contract." ALD is a group of lighting designers who meet for "discussion, debates, exchange of ideas and experiences, all in a very informal atmosphere." It had nearly 250 members as of 1988, including most full-time professional lighting designers in the United Kingdom plus enthusiastic semiprofessional amateurs, students, and people involved in manufacturing and sales of lighting equipment. Entrance fees in 1984 were £10 (approximately $14) plus annual dues of approximately $20. For those of us not in London, ALD has a "Country" membership.[392] ALD also publishes a journal.

APIAD

The Italian Associazione Produttori Italiani Attrezzature per Discotheque e Teatri (Italian Association of Discotheque and Theatre Equipment Manufacturers) holds an annual trade show. See *CUE International,* no. 58 (March/April 1989), p. 26. See Also "Spotlight on APIAD," *LS&V* Magazine, vol. 1, no. 2 (January/February 1989), pp. 14, 58.

PLASA

The British Professional Lighting and Sound Association (PLASA) publishes *Lighting & Sound International* magazine (P.O. Box 628, Eastbourne, East Sussex BN21 2PZ, England). PLASA has an annual trade show, held in August/September, which was attended by over 4,000 people in 1986 (with 90 exhibitors participating).[394] PLASA is an association of manufacturing and rental companies in the world of live pop music, roadshows, and discos.

Chapter 14

Lighting Design Training and Education: Textbooks and Teachers

While this volume was in preparation, a prominent editor from a leading publishing firm said to me, "You must remove that chapter on education. Teachers won't buy a book which tells their students how training could be better. The students are already enrolled in a school, and educators do not want *their* teaching and *their* school contrasted with others." My 50 years in professional theatre, in television, and as an author/educator tells me she was wrong, for the following reasons:

- The lighting design educators I know (myself included) are constantly looking for new and better ways to teach. We will "steal" from anyone who has a better way or idea!
- Students, unless human nature changes, will always look for ways to improve their department and to get more from the time and money they spend on training — yet they are quite reasonable when a "no" is explained to them about proposed changes.
- A volume of this type is intended for undergraduates, graduates, *and* working professionals. Undergraduates can make use of this chapter in selecting a graduate school. Professionals can be guided toward sources of *further* training (seminars, workshops, lectures, etc.). Those of us who are professionals never cease growing and learning. We attend conferences and conventions and workshops to learn *more*. We want to know what is going on elsewhere in lighting education. We all hope to continue learning until our final days.

Clearly, I strongly disagree with that editor's advice, and so this chapter remains in the text. It should be used wisely. It is a *guide* to growth — not a list of places to study.

Once someone has decided that he or she wants to be a lighting designer, how should one go about it? On-the-job training and lots of practical experience with good people as mentors? That's where most people start: working in the theatre backstage or in TV/film studios and kindling the twin fires of interest and ambition. Next comes the desire to obtain more solid training from acknowledged masters (to learn what they already know so as to build on it and be even better). The would-be designer must then decide what school to go to, and for how many years.

For the lighting student, four to seven or more years in a college or university involves considerable expense and the possibility of not being accepted by the place of his choice; yet these college years are the most valuable career preparation period of his life. They provide the designer with a last opportunity to make mistakes and profit from them, without extreme repercussions (employers do not look kindly upon "growth" mistakes). College is probably the last time when a student may be financially subsidized by parents or loans to take the time to learn and experiment and shape personal objectives — and to prepare for the selected potential career. All this is obvious — but what is the best approach?

The *first step* is a questioning of what to study and how to develop personal creative abilities. The next few paragraphs are devoted to an analysis of such things. It is hoped that the student will use what follows as a checklist to determine the suitability of the schools he or she is considering. Can the schools supply the needed training? The *second step* is consideration of those training places which have a track record of fine instruction. Each student should assemble some personalized criteria concerning their suitability. The *third step* is to take a look at the available textbooks in the lighting design field.

Step One: What the Student Needs to Know

Knowledge which lighting designers need to have at their command falls basically into three areas: (1) technical/theoretical facts, (2) artistic/design concept development, and (3) systems for working within a teamwork structure (specific established procedures).[394]

Technical/Theoretical Facts

The lighting designer in training needs to understand and have enough knowledge to use each of the following:

1. What *light* is and how it behaves.
2. How light is *produced* and *controlled* (fluorescence versus incandescence versus neon, for example; lenses and reflectors; electricity and its production, distribution, and use).
3. How humans *see* (vision), both directly and through the intervening media of TV cameras and film cameras.
4. How humans *respond* to what they see (the human eye is *not* a mechanical "seeing machine" — it is governed by a conditioned, trained human mind which interprets).

5. *Color* production, color use, color theories, color perception, and response by the viewer.
6. The specific lighting *luminaires* or equipment in common use in the various fields (spotlights, floodlights, and borderlights in theatre; standard fixtures in architectural lighting; effects units in disco and concert lighting; etc.).
7. *Control devices* (switchboards, louvers, barn doors, kukoloris, gobos, irises, etc.).
8. The basic *history* of lighting design.
9. The traditional established *systems* used to achieve a lighting design assignment on schedule, within budget, and in an orderly — yet creative — fashion (i.e., light plots, switchboard layouts, architect's drawings, etc.).
10. Mechanical *drafting skills* and/or computer fluency (i.e., control of the established symbols and communications methods in presentation).
11. *Rendering* skills. Since lighting is a visual medium (rather than a word and symbol medium), increasingly lighting designers need to be able to "chalk talk" their ideas visually and present simple light/shade/color sketches.
12. Existing highly *specialized technical media*: lasers, holograms, scenic projection, strobe units, pyrotechnic effects, etc.
13. Established procedures and practices in the various *specialties*, e.g., theatre, television, film, disco, etc. It is essential for the designer to have a basic knowledge of practices, procedures, unions, problem solving, etc., in the "world past the classroom."

That is quite a variety of knowledge — but it *is* all teachable. Most of this information is to be found in the half-dozen basic textbooks of lighting design. This information is all available in print, which may explain why there are a few lighting designers in the highest income brackets who have only a high school education.

Odd as it may seem, a student who attains all of the knowledge and skills outlined above — who can successfully "illuminate" a stage or a building or a film — is *not* yet a lighting designer. That person is a highly trained and skilled *technician,* but not an artist of light. However, before considering the artistic/designer concept development training needed, a student should use the knowledge listed above to evaluate the schools under consideration. Does

[394] *Susan Lieberman, "A Roof without a House: Assessing Current Graduate Training,"* Theatre Crafts, *vol. 19, no. 3 (March 1985), pp. 26–29, 51–52, 54. Illus. A very perceptive and important article concerning the need for a broad academic base for all designers.* Lieberman writes:

MFA students . . . suffer from familiar problems: poor communication skills, inadequate attention to dramatic texts, weak foundation in general liberal arts subjects, inability to synthesize information or to integrate production elements, limited understanding or interest in related arts or world events, and an overall lack of passion and drive in executing an idea. . . . Artistic quality cannot be manufactured; it can only be nurtured and preserved.

Tom O'Mahony, "Education: University of Kansas and Parsons School of Design — Two Approaches to the Lighting Education," Lighting Design + Application, *vol. 15, no. 2 (February 1985), pp. 24–26. O'Mahony outlines and contrasts two outstanding educational programs for training architectural lighting specialists: an illuminating engineering program (Kansas) and a lighting design program (Parsons).*

Alice M. Hale, "Special Report: What's In It for You? Three Years without Sleep," Theatre Crafts, *vol. 19, no. 9 (November 1985), pp. 26–35, 48–58, 60–79. Illus. Useful information and evaluation of the theatre training programs at Boston University, Brandeis, California Institute of the Arts, Carnegie Mellon, Florida State, Indiana University, North Carolina School of the Arts, New York University, Rutgers University, Southern Methodist, Temple, University of California at San Diego, University of Southern California, University of Texas at Austin, University of Washington (Seattle), University of Wisconsin at Madison, and Yale University. While this series overlooks several outstanding training programs and is at times almost a promotional piece for the schools presented, it does contain useful basic information.*

Michael White, "Merging Two Disciplines — Architects Can Learn Much from the Accumulated Experiences of Lighting Designers Versed in the Theatre," Lighting Dimensions, *vol. 11, no. 1 (January/February 1987), pp. 56, 60–61.*

Paulette R. Hebert and Andrea Daugherty, "Studying Light and Color, System Variables

Are Interdependent—Color Projects for Interior Design Students, Daugherty and Hebert Write about Teaching at LSU," Lighting Design + Application, vol. 17, no. 4 (April 1987), pp. 12–13. Illus., color. Vital article for all who plan to work in architectural lighting.

Peter Ruffett, *"Lighting Education: An Overview—Nine Educators Speak Out on the Current State of Education in Lighting,"* Lighting Design + Application, vol. 15, no. 2 (February 1985), pp. 31–43. An in-depth question-and-answer analysis of lighting education by five lighting design educators, three engineering lighting educators, and two architectural lighting educators. The educators discuss both strengths and weaknesses of present programs. A vital discussion for students wishing to select between lighting engineering and lighting design programs and educators in both disciplines. The nine educators involved are James Benya (California University, architecture), David Butler (University of Florida, interior design), David DiLaura (University of Colorado, Architectural Engineering), William Dombroski (Ohio University, interior design), Dee Ginthner (University of Minnesota, interior design), James Long (Virginia Commonwealth University, interior design), Robert Meden (Ball State University, architecture), Joseph Murdoch (University of New Hampshire, electrical engineering) and Robert Smith (University of Illinois, architecture). Benya says:

I know there are some academic people out there who are doing a fine job. . . . I don't want to take anything away from the programs they've attempted to put together. The problem is that none of them is generating credible lighting design professionals. When they walk out the door, I can't take them and put them to work. I've got to train them in areas in which their particular programs are lacking, because that program is not a program in lighting design, it's a program in architectural engineering with an emphasis on lighting design, or a program in architecture with a specialty in lighting, etc. As a result, the student usually misses some aspect that is necessary to make a successful, working lighting designer. . . . Lighting design is a profession, not a part of anything else. Designing is something that

you can't just pick up a book and study like ABCs or mathematics. . . . DiLaura said: "Education, once you get beyond the high school level, must be handled by individuals who not only know something about lighting, but who are trained educators. The notion that one need only be knowledgeable about the field to transmit information is seriously misguided. It continues to be an unfortunate aspect of most western higher education."

"Illumination Roundtable III, 'Lighting Research and Education for the Eighties,'" Lighting Design + Application, vol. 14, no. 7 (July 1984), pp. 27–34. Illus. A summary of an IES national conference about the training of lighting (illumination) engineers and interior designers; also includes research.

Peggy Clark and John Gleason, *"Training the Lighting Designer,"* Theatre Crafts, vol. 10, no. 6 (November/December 1976), pp. 28, 30–34. Excellent analysis of the problems of training lighting designers and objectives by two leading working professionals who teach. Partly about preparation for the annual United Scenic Artists #829 Lighting Entrance Examination.

John Gleason, *"The Training of Lighting Designers, Part II,"* Theatre Crafts, vol. 11, no. 5 (October 1977), pp. 71–76. A continuation of the earlier article with emphasis upon the nature and contents of training. Excellent.

"Letters: Training the Lighting Designer," Theatre Crafts, vol. 11, no. 1 (January/February 1977), pp. 2–3.

Stephen M. Goldman, *"CONTRAST: How We're Failing the Students,"* Lighting Dimensions, vol. 1, no. 1 (June 1977), pp. 46, 38. A plea for memory switchboards in training students to free their design imagination.

Rich Sassone, *"Needed: A New Approach to Teaching Lighting,"* Lighting Dimensions, vol. 2, no. 9 (November 1978), pp. 44–49. A highly logical, well-presented argument by an expert about training in film and TV. Illus.

Dorian Kelly, *"A Time to Consolidate,"* Cue, no. 15 (January/February 1982), pp. 14–15. A British viewpoint.

"OISTT Reports on Theatre Training: German Democratic Republic; Great Britain; Japan; Czechoslovakia; Hungary," Theatre Design & Technology, vol. 12, no. 3 (Fall 1976), pp. 13–25. An international report about training abroad.

Francis Reid, *"Light Training,"* TABS, vol. 33, no. 2 (Summer 1975), p. 2. British thoughts on training lighting designers.

Patricia MacKay, *"Approaching Performing Arts Training: A Focused Training Program at North Carolina School of the Arts,"* Theatre Crafts, vol. 12, no. 6 (October 1978), pp. 36–39, 70–72, 74. Illustrated description of one school's approach to training.

"Tech Training at Carnegie-Mellon University," Theatre Crafts, (October 1973), vol. 7, no. 5, pp. 23–30. Good description of a training program in a plant with limited facilities.

Peggy Clark, *"For Our Students: A Memory Board is a Panacea, But Not the Answer,"* Lighting Dimensions, vol. 1, no. 3 (September 1977), p. 54. Clark replies to Stephen M. Goldman (see above).

Howard Bay, Stage Design. N.Y.; Drama Book Specialists; 1974. See Chap. V, *"Lighting Design,"* pp. 132–147. Chatty but excellent. Basics presented clearly.

Lee Watson, *"Teaching Techniques for Tomorrow's Lighting Designers,"* Lighting Dimensions, vol. 4, no. 10 (November/December 1980), pp. 15–16.

Howard Brandston, *"Some Thoughts on Lighting Design,"* Lighting Dimensions, vol. 5, no. 1 (January/February 1981), pp. 43, 45, 54.

the training facility have the physical plant and the trained, qualified faculty to provide instruction in these fundamental areas? If not, that facility should be rejected as a place to study, because its graduates will not be able to compete for design jobs successfully with others who are better trained. The student should not be "led astray" by places which offer magnificent physical plants with memory switchboards, revolving stages, multiple theatres, and monumental facilities, yet have an inadequately trained faculty. The student should also be wary of heavy production schedules and a "friendly and fun" group — it is difficult to learn to be an employable lighting designer through lots of "learning by doing." Unless a student is carefully instructed, that student will simply keep repeating the same mistakes and will lack a solid theory base with which to compete with those who are better trained. There are 2,822 accredited higher education institutions in the United States — choosing the right one may not be easy.

Artistic/Design Concept Development

It is vital for a chosen training place to have experienced instructors who can help the student to grow in the following three areas:

1. Learning how to see. Observation powers must be developed and sharpened. For example, each year at Purdue University I take a class of landscape architect students on a bus tour of Lafayette (population of 100,000), and they are amazed at the vast amount of night lighting which they really had not "seen" before: lighted smokestacks, fountains, a funeral home, parks, playing fields, gas stations, parking lots, private residence walkways and driveways, the county courthouse, streets, signs, and on and on. Another example: For several years I was a lighting director at CBS TV in New York City. I soon learned how to watch 8 to 10 TV monitors simultaneously, detecting vital details involving lighting in each. The student who wants to grow as a lighting design artist must develop this trained skill, whether the aim is theatre, architectural lighting, film, or TV.

2. Production Analysis. This topic should be considered broadly. For someone preparing to design lighting for an architectural edifice, the same factors apply as in theatre. A student who has not learned to do "homework" is not prepared to design lighting. No designer is prepared to meet with the producer, the director, the scenic designer, the prop person, the costume designer, the client/architect or contractor, or even the business manager before having developed the ability to read, research, analyze, and understand the project at hand. Only then can designers meet with fellow artists and contribute their specialty: a knowledge of how light and shade and color use can contribute to the total effectiveness. Not only do they need as deep and broad an understanding of the project at hand as their collaborating fellow artists have, but they also should have developed a broad understanding concerning how humans (audiences or building users) *respond* to light. This aspect of lighting enters the area of psychological behavior responses, an area about which too little is known. At the present time this vital element of lighting design knowledge is acquired the slow and painful way: through a lifetime of study and observation. The student should select a training facility which can be a guide in developing patterns of expanding and deepening both of these vital skills: production analysis and human response to light.[395]

3. Broadening of the Artist. This aspect of design is the most difficult thing to teach. It is also often the most difficult objective to get the student to understand. In essence, a top lighting designer (whether in garden lighting or disco lighting) needs a perspective that is much broader than simply a command of a lighting specialty in order to have anything worthwhile to contribute. As a lighting artist, the designer needs to "flesh out" a basic knowledge of theatre history, dramatic history, dramatic literature, architecture, music, art, dance, philosophy, religion, economics, psychology, history, etc. Without a broad range of interests and an even broader range of knowledge, the designer has only an infinite amount of knowledge about a very little thing: lighting.

Of paramount importance is seeking out and finding a *particular* educator of lighting design from whom one can learn. This is a highly personal matter. Different educators use differing methods of instruction. The trainee needs to find the one the trainee trusts, respects, and can communi-

Designer Brandston discusses the place of the designer and of the engineer in lighting.

Lee Watson, "Through the Looking Glass," Lighting Dimensions, vol. 15, no. 2 (March 1981), pp. 13–14. Watson discusses lighting engineers versus design artists.

Robert L. Smith, "Education: Learning the Art and Science of Illumination: An Associate Professor of Architecture Discusses the University of Illinois' Approach to Introducing Students to Lighting Design," Lighting Design + Application, vol. 9, no. 8 (August 1979), pp. 12, 14. Illus., color. An illuminating engineer's approach presented.

Robert L. Smith, "Education: Lighting Education and Professional Development — a Survey of Illumination Courses Indicates a Need for Broader Scope, Improved Educational Materials, More Testing Equipment, and Advanced Training," Lighting Design + Application, vol. 9, no. 8 (August 1979), pp. 60–61. A thoughtful proposal for revitalizing illuminating engineering instruction.

Gerry Zekowski, "The Art of Lighting Is a Science/The Science of Lighting Is an Art — Part I," Lighting Design + Application, vol. 11, no. 1 (January 1981), pp. 10–15. Illus. Zekowski maintains that lighting is both an art and a science. "Part II" appears in vol. 11, no. 3 (March 1981), pp. 39–45. Illus.

Stephen S. Squillace, "The Time Is NOW!", Lighting Design + Application, vol. 11, no. 8 (August 1981), pp. 40–42. Key article by a former president of IES analyzing the need and method to improve lighting research and education.

Ken Billington, "Theatrical vs. Architectural Lighting — Bridging the Gap," Lighting Design + Application, vol. 13, no. 1 (January 1983), pp. 13–18. Illus., color. Work of a designer who bridges two fields.

Andrea Daugherty, "A 'Learning-by-Doing' Aid to Teach Lighting Design," Lighting Design + Application, vol. 12, no. 2 (February 1982), pp. 20–25. Illus., color. Invaluable for any teacher of interior lighting design.

Craig A. Bernecker, "Instructional Objectives for Lighting Education within an Architectural Engineering Curriculum," Lighting Design +

Application, *vol. 13, no. 11 (November 1983), pp. 23–31. By applying the best principles from the field of education, Professor Bernecker presents a structure for both formulating and evaluating lighting design instruction.*

"Brandston Speaks on Lighting Education," Lightview, *vol. 1, no. 1 (Spring 1988), p. 6. Mr. Brandston, both as a former student of this author and a frequent critic of today's lighting education, offers comments concerning discipline, dedication, experience, simplicity, the lighting design processes, tools and technology, and mock-ups and simulations. Brandston stresses the designer's intuition as of paramount concern among the other observations he offers.*

Jill Charles, *Directory of Theatre Training Profiles, of College and Conservatory Programs throughout the United States. Dorset, Vermont; Dorset Theatre Festival & Colony House, Inc.; 1987. 107 pp. A most useful guide to theatre training programs.*

John Ezell and Felicia Londré, "Training: What Went Wrong in Stage Design Training and 11 Ideas for How to Fix It," Theatre Crafts, *vol. 22, no. 8 (October 1988), pp. 42–46. A well-formulated attack on the concentration upon teaching contemporary drama while largely ignoring the classics. Eleven rabble-rousing but highly constructive suggested changes in design instruction.*

John Gleason, "Another Voice," Theatre Crafts, *vol. 22, no. 8 (October 1988), pp. 42, 46–47. Constructive comments by Prof. Gleason about the article listed above by Ezell and Londré. Gleason believes that much of the present generation's deficiency in knowledge of dramatic literature must be dealt with in high school and undergraduate education.*

Nick MacLiammoir, "Bristol Meeting: Training the Lighting Designers," ALD # Magazine, *no. 9 (May 1989), pp. 3–10. Illus. The author is lighting designer at the Albany Empire Theatre, Deptford. Other panelists included Dee Kyne (freelance lighting designer), David Taylor (American-trained British lighting designer), Nigel Morgan (Central School of Speech and Drama), Wyn Jones (director of Southern Lights Theatre Co.), and Rick Fisher (consultant on lighting training for the Central School of Art and Design). The article ends with a one-page "Statement on Lighting Design Education in Britain," adopted by the ALD at the Bristol meeting.*

"Lighting Education at the Bartlett," Strand-light, *No. 8 (Spring 1989), p. 4. Illus. A lengthy description of Professor David Loe's program in architectural lighting at the Bartlett School of Architecture and Planning at University College, London, by Strand representative David Brooks. Loe heads the program (one of England's best) at the International Philips Centre for Lighting Education and Research, Bartlett School of Architecture and Planning, University College, London, 22 Gordon Street, WC1H 0QB England. In the same issue, page 6, see "Jonathan Miller to Launch Lighting Symposium." The one-day symposium, with Jonathan Miller, Frances Reid, Bob Anderson, David Taylor, and John B. Read, is sponsored by Bartlett.*

Bonnie S. Schwartz, "Parsons MFA Lighting Design Program Schedules Weekday Classes," *Lighting Dimensions, vol. 12, no. 2 (March 1988), p. 18.*

"Technical Training and Standards Move to Centre Stage," Cue, *no. 55 (September/October 1988), p. 10. About AETTI (Arts and Entertainment Technical Training Initiative). AETTI consists of union, employers, industry organizations (much like ABTT), institutes, and trade associations, pressuring in England for better training of lighting designers in all areas. In October 1988, they began soliciting information about extant training places and programs by questionnaire.*

Lucy Terry Nowell, Frank Silberstein, John Carr, Gary Gaiser, Leon Brauner, and Adel Migid, "Promotion and Tenure Evaluation of the Theatrical Design and Technology Faculty: Issues and Recommended Guidelines," *Theatre Design & Technology Supplement, vol. 23, no. 3 (Fall 1987), pp. 33–1 to 33–15. See section on Lighting Designers, pp. 9–10. The first attempt at setting up an evaluation process concerning promotion and tenure for teachers of lighting design. A most important study.*

Ernest Wotton, "Meeting the Demand for Lighting Specialists: A British Response," *Lighting, vol. 2, no. 6 (December 1988), p. 36. More about the British Bartlett program under the direction of Professor David Loe, by a prominent Canadian designer/consultant.*

"Letters: Good LD Programs Needed in All Design Schools," *Lighting Dimensions, vol. 12, no. 6 (September/October 1988), pp. 6–8. A response by Professor Robert L. Smith (Univer-*

cate with. Teaching is communication. There is no *one* successful way of teaching. Many approaches work. The trainee must find a person whose work and methods he or she admires and then meet with that person to find out if the give-and-take process of learning can work between instructor and student. This is *the most vital factor* in selecting a place to study—not physical plant, or number of theatres, or amount of productions, or size of faculty, or extent of the library facilities. Trainees who can find, within the range of choices open to them, one good educator, are well on the way toward utilizing wisely one of the few big choice areas they have in life, their education.

Systems

The third area of information the trainee must master is teamwork systems and procedures. Step by step, how *does* a show (or building) get designed and lighted? There are established methods of working and communicating that have evolved out of a prolonged period of trial and error. Most are teachable, although some are not. A student can be taught about light plots, drawings, and diagrams and also about preplanning and organization and anticipation of disaster. The trainee must seek qualified and experienced personnel for guidance in these systems and procedures.

All lighting design involves *teamwork*. Strong, creative, opinionated people pool their knowledge and ideas to create a production (or TV show or disco or building). There are sometimes clashes and even intense arguments—not personally motivated—about possible alternative solutions. Two opposites must always be at work in the design process: team play and cooperation toward a common objective *and* freewheeling creative individuality. The ways of treading these treacherous waters are not readily teachable, but a good educator can help guide a student in being comfortable with and making maximum effective use of that student's own "ways of working." Most tasks involving a lighting designer are highly structured and organized—much like tasks performed in the army. Someone *must* be the boss, accept the ultimate responsibility, and make the final decisions. The designer must be willing to be a team player within that structure; however, that does *not* mean that individual creativeness is eliminated. Good ideas must be properly marketed! No facet of lighting design has any need of *prima donnas,* who must be the center of attention and have everything their way. For people who have that kind of temperament, there are important places in the creative world — they can write a novel, paint a picture, or compose music — but they should *stay out of* theatre, architectural lighting, television, films, etc. A good educator can *help* students deal with this necessary balance between opposites and guide them toward having both employability and striking creativity in the lighting design industry.

Step Two: Training Places

Good training places are hard to find. For example, in "Needed: A New Approach to Teaching Lighting," by Rich Sassone (see footnote 394), Sassone points out that television is a *$10 billion industry;* yet, according to a 1977 American Institute survey, 1,075 colleges and universities teach 4,218 film and TV courses with 2,622 instructors and *fewer than a dozen* offer any full course in lighting design! No course is offered that deals with lighting design training for the student who wishes to work in both film and television. Some "short courses" are available, but that is all. And no place offers even the beginnings of instruction in lighting design for discos, concert lighting, or ice shows.

Here are a few of the training place specifics a student should look for:

- The better educators not only encourage their students to design lighting away from the classroom and campus, but they also help students find such opportunities. For example, the late Gil Hemsley, while at the University of Wisconsin, took his students all over the country with him on professional shows; John Gleason at New York University critiques Off- and Off-Off-Broadway lighting design work of his students in New York City; and I take my students to Richmond, Indiana, to design lighting for the Whitewater Opera and other groups throughout the midwest. Randy Earle, at San Jose State (California), has the same approach as does Tom Ruzika at the University of California – Irvine.

Trainees should encounter a wide range of design jobs and training conditions.

- Top-notch educators bring in prominent guest lecturers and designers when available. I know that my way of designing lighting is not the *only* way and that others will benefit from exposure to a wide range of design viewpoints and practices.
- Training courses should make use of field trips (to lighting firms, TV studios, etc.) and instructors should insist that students see and critique available "road" attractions, TV specials (for example, the *Dance in America* series and other PBS attractions), and outstanding films with exceptional lighting. If possible, instructors should also arrange trips to New York City or Chicago or Los Angeles to see professional productions.[396]
- Someone who takes the time and has the interest to critique a student's lighting design work makes the very best instructor. Without such educated critique, the student will not grow. Professionals do this for each other.
- A good place to study will have a proven track record in the placement area. Do educators use their contacts to help students find summer employment? Do they help open the doors to find graduates their first job?
- What is the track record of others the place has trained in lighting design? Does the employment record of past students bode well for the training offered?
- A training place should have either a light lab or a miniature stage. A place to experiment with colors and various luminaires and some switchboard control is vital. Lighting design is a visual art. Education that is restricted to textbooks and lectures is not enough. Hands-on training is vital. Even a large number of projects or productions by trainee designers is hardly sufficient. Increasingly good instruction in lighting design must include an equipped space to test and experiment with the real thing: lights, colors, and control.

Fortunately for the industry, if the student has received good training in the fundamentals of lighting design — as outlined in this chapter thus far — much of that training can be readily adapted to the various lighting specialties. An understanding of the uses and methods of lighting is basic, whether that understanding is applied to buildings or ballet.

sity of Illinois) to Gad Giladi's article surveying Schools of Architecture offering lighting design training (listed next).

Gad Giladi, "Architecture Schools: Survey Finds Few Programs Include Required Lighting Course," Lighting Dimensions, *vol. 12, no. 4 (May/June 1988), pp. 72, 75–79, 81. Giladi surveyed architecture schools worldwide, finding one school in the United States and six in England and Australia requiring architecture students to take a full course dedicated solely to lighting. He lists elective courses available in ten worldwide universitites (five in the United States). He also suggests eleven topics which should be included in the instruction. A most useful study.*

Jill Dolan, "The Recruitment Trail: My MFA Design Program's Better Than Yours," Theatre Crafts, *vol. 23, no. 7 (August/September 1989), pp. 22, 24–28, 30. An analysis which maintains that there are too many MFA programs in design and that it is now a buyer's market for the students rather than a seller's market for the universities. This is an excellent 1990s analysis of MFA recruiting by various schools (Yale, Carnegie Mellon, New York University, University of Wisconsin at Madison, University of Michigan at Ann Arbor, DePaul University in Chicago, University of Texas in Austin, University of Missouri in Kansas City, University of Delaware, Boston University, Ithaca College in New York, USITT and U/RTA). Also discusses why students select certain schools and what various universities offer as their instructional strengths when recruiting prospects.*

David Loe, "On the Subject of Lighting," Lighting Dimensions, *vol. 13, no. 2 (March 1989), p. 10. Professor David Loe, Director of the International Philips Centre for Lighting Education and Research in London, writes of his outstanding training course at the Bartlett School of Architecture and Planning, University College, London.*

[395] *Robert L. Benedetti, "The Designer–Director Relationship: Form and Process,"* Theatre Crafts, *vol. 13, no. 1 (January/February 1979), pp. 36, 58–65. Overly discursive, but useful.*

Robert L. Beneditti, "The Designer–Director Relationship: The Integration of Action and Environment," Theatre Crafts, *vol. 13, no. 5 (October 1979), pp. 30–33, 42–44, 46, 51.*

Jean Rosenthal and Lael Wertenbaker, The Magic of Light. *Boston; Little, Brown and Co.; 1972. Chap. 5, pp. 59–72. Excellent analysis; very readable.*

J. Michael Gillette, Designing with Light. *Palo Alto, Calif.; Mayfield Publishing Co.; 1978. See Chap. 9, "Analyzing the Script," pp. 107–113. Good basics.*

Willard F. Bellman, Lighting the Stage, Art and Practice, *2d edition. N.Y.; Chandler Publishing Co.; 1974. See Chap. 18, "Design Procedures," pp. 371–375. Very basic; sketchy. See also "Return to the Script," p. 416.*

Jo Mielziner, Designing for the Theatre, *N.Y.; Bramhall House; 1965. See pp. 7–9 for an excellent presentation of the ramifications and importance of script analysis.*

See also the ABTT mimeographed report by Pamela Howard on the OISTT Commission meeting, March 7, 1983, at London's Central School of Art and Design, Theatre Dept., for a summary of educational training in Czechoslovakia, Egypt, Japan, Finland, USSR, Hungary, and Poland.

Bently Miller, "Training TV Lighting Designers, Evesham Shows the Way," TABS, vol. 40, no. 1 (August 1983), pp. 32. Illus. A reprint from the Canadian Society of Lighting Directors newsletter about Canadian TV lighting training.

John Offord (editor), British Theatre Directory, 1983, *op. cit. (see footnote 389). See pp. 413–426 for a complete listing of British sources of training.*

"UNH Lighting Research and Development Center," a pamphlet published by the University of New Hampshire at Durham explaining the school's training program, faculty, and facilities.

"NYU Designer Gleason Sees New 'Visual Language' A Factor In Theatre," Rosconews, Spring 1987, p. 2. Illus. More about the New York University training program.

Bonnie S. Schwartz, "Lighting Education: The Struggle for Identity at Parsons," Lighting Dimensions, *vol. 11, no. 3 (May/June 1987), pp. 103–107. An extensive presentation of the Parsons School of Design (New School for Social Research) two-year M.F.A. lighting program in New York City.*

Gareth Fenley, "Neon: A Hands-on Craft with Its Own Vocabulary," Architectural Lighting, *vol. 1, no. 2 (February 1987). Page 40 contains*

LIGHTING DESIGN EDUCATION: A TIME FOR CHANGE

"It is necessary to improve educational programs for lighting design. Design complexities and energy constraints require special instruction with a broader foundation than present curricula provide. Lighting design education should cross departmental lines.

Lighting design encompasses esthetics, perception, illuminating engineering and specific technical expertise. These are used to reinforce project goals. Improvement in lighting design education must fulfill the needs of the designer and those served.

Design for the arts, architecture, industry and other applications requires a thorough understanding of the psychological, psycho-physical and physical aspects of lighting. The characteristics of human, photographic, and photo-electric receptors must be addressed.

Properly trained people are readily employable but job entry requirements are significantly more stringent than in the past. Educators must respond.

Lighting design is the process of creatively using the qualities and functions of lighting to affect people, objects and space. The qualities of lighting are intensity, form, color and movement. The functions of lighting are visibility, mood/atmosphere, composition and motivation. Study should include at least a fundamental understanding of the following:

Design Technique and Application:
color, light sources; photometrics; brightness relationships. Introduction to, and evaluation of, typical lighting applications. Drafting and visualization.

Human Responses to Light:
sight; esthetics; behavior; photobiology.

Electrical Control and Distribution

Optical Control and Distribution

Lighting Equipment Types and Application

Specialized Topics:
Conservation of energy and materials; safety codes and regulations; history; photographic and photo-electric reproduction technology.

Today's instruction in specialized areas —theatre, communications (TV & film), interior design, architectural and engineering departments — is no longer sufficiently broadly inclusive for the actual needs of the industry nor for the needs of graduates seeking employment."

This statement was formulated at the T.O.L.D. (Training of Lighting Designers) Conference on January 11, 1981, at Purdue University. Sponsored by U.S.I.T.T. The following lighting industry leaders attended. Each helped form this statement and support it:

Prof. Robt. Allen, Dept. of Arch., Wash. State Univ., Pullman

Prof. James J. Andrews, Univ. of Calgary, Canada, representing USITT-Canada

Prof. John Bracewell, Theatre Arts Dept., Ithaca College, Ithaca, NY, and USITT National Liaison

Howard Brandston, IES (Illuminating Engineering Society of No. Amer.) Vice-Pres. and Howard Brandston Lighting, NYC

Prof. Andrea Daugherty, Interior Lighting, Louisiana State Univ., Baton Rouge, LA

Lou Erhardt, engineer-author, Camarillo, CA

Prof. Charles Firmin, Dept. of Theatre and Film, Penn State Univ., State College, PA

Prof. J. Michael Gillette, Theatre Dept., Univ. of Ariz., Tucson, and USITT Education Commission

Prof. Ron Helms, Arch. Engineering, Univ. of Colorado, Boulder

James H. Jensen, GE Lighting Institute, Cleveland, OH

Thomas Lemons, TLA Consultants, Salem, Mass. IES-TTFL (Theatre, Television and Film Lighting) Commission Chairperson

Charles Levy, Strand Century Lighting, Inc., Elmwood Park, N.J.

James Moody, Sundance Lighting, Chatsworth, Calif. and President of P.E.P.S. (Professional Entertainment Production Society) and representing ASLD (Amer. Soc. of Lighting Directors), Los Angeles

James Nuckolls, Inc. Consultants, Ltd., NYC, Parsons School of Design, NYC spokesman for the IALD (International Association of Lighting Designers, NYC)

Dr. Joel E. Rubin, Kliegl Bros. Lighting, NYC

Prof. Robt. Smith (represented by Randy Swanson), Arch. Engineering, Univ. of Ill., Urbana

Wm. Tracy, ABC-TV, NYC

Prof. Lee Watson, Pres. of USITT, and Theatre Dept., Purdue Univ., West Lafayette, Ind.

Fred Weller, owner and publisher of LIGHTING DIMENSIONS magazine, South Laguna, CA

Leslie Wheel, Wheel-Gertzoff Lighting, NYC, and IALD Intern Committee

E. Carlton Winckler, Imero Fiorentino Associates, NYC

Roland Zavada, Eastman Kodak, Rochester, NY and Vice Pres. of S.M.P.T.E. (Society of Motion Picture and Television Engineers)

In addition, this statement has since received the official support or endorsement of the following lighting industry organizations:

American Society of Lighting Directors, North Hollywood
American Theatre Association, Washington, D.C.
International Association of Lighting Designers, NYC
Illuminating Engineering Society of North America, NYC
Professional Entertainment Production Society, Los Angeles

Society of Motion Picture and Television Engineers, NYC
U.S. Institute for Theatre Technology, NYC
United Scenic Artists, L. U. #350, Chicago
University/Resident Theatre Association, Washington, D.C.
General Electric Lighting Institute, Cleveland, Ohio

This request, formulated by 22 lighting representatives, now bears the official support of professional organizations representing over 50,000 members of the industry. We ask American educators to put it into action at the earliest possible date.

Send inquiries concerning T.O.L.D. to: USITT, 330 W. 42nd St., NYC 10036.

Figure 14.1 TOLD Conference Report.

Any student who has doubts concerning what the fundamentals of lighting design *are* should study carefully the TOLD ("Training of Lighting Designers") Conference report, appended here as Fig. 14.1.

The boxed areas of study constitute a checklist which should be used in training selection. I am reluctant to name specific schools or educators, because programs and instructors change with each passing year. Some schools have great teachers and artists who are nearly impossible to get along with. Other schools employ teachers who are just marvelous people, but have little ability to teach. It is hoped that this analysis has helped the student understand the all-important point: *an individual must find the right teacher.* This volume gives some good criteria for training selection. A list of present-day major training programs is available from USITT (see Chap. 13 for the address).

Step Three: Textbooks

The vast majority of texts are improved rewrites of theories and practices admirably laid out by Stanley R. McCandless and Theodore Fuchs (which were fine for another day and age, but now do not represent the accepted practice). Over time theory changes very little, but practice and equipment can change quite a bit. Such authors as Willard Bellman, Oren Parker, Harvey Smith, Craig Wolf, and Hunton D. Sellman have kept the equipment facts up-to-the-minute, although since none of these authors is a practicing professional in lighting design, there are weaknesses in the area of practice. Nonetheless, these texts are an invaluable starting point for familiarization with existing theory and equipment.

Except for my earlier text with Dr. Joel Rubin, *Theatrical Lighting Practice,* Jean Rosenthal's *The Magic of Light,* Jim Moody's *Concert Lighting,* and Richard Pilbrow's *Stage Lighting,* only scattered magazine and journal articles have made any serious attempt to supply the needs of the lighting design student who has moved *beyond* the first course. Exceptions can sometimes be found in a given specialized area (film or TV, for example), but such offerings deal only with a particular specialty.

As the reference footnotes listed in this volume attest,

existing useful knowledge about lighting design is now so extensive that *no one text is the answer.*

Training for the Specialties

Most of the information supplied in this chapter so far applies to those intending to pursue careers in theatre, industrial shows, or disco. A few words of advice are needed for those intending careers in architectural lighting design, landscape architectural lighting design, film, television, or illuminating engineering. Basics are basics. Any lighting designer will profit from instruction in the basic areas of light and design, whether it be in a theatre/drama department, an engineering/physics instruction program, a communications/film/TV school, an architectural/landscape architectural program of instruction, or any similar program. The rest of this chapter offers a few further notes to guide those pursuing careers in any of the lighting specialties.

Illumination Engineering/Architectural Engineering/Interior Design

The key architectural/illuminating engineering programs can be found at the following schools: Rensselaer Polytechnic Institute (Dr. Mark S. Rea, Lighting Research Center, Troy, New York); University of Kansas (Lawrence; Dr. Ronald Helms, Architectural Engineering Program); Penn State University (State College, Pennsylvania; Craig Bernecker); University of New Hampshire (Durham, New Hampshire; Electrical Engineering Department; Joseph B. Murdock); University of Illinois (Urbana, Illinois; School of Architecture; Robert Smith); University of Colorado; University of Wisconsin — Madison (Department of Engineering and Applied Science); University of Virginia (Charlottesville; Randy Davis); Georgia Institute of Technology – Atlanta (Alexander F. Styne); and Clemson University (Clemson, South Carolina; M. David Egan). Some of these schools offer "short course" workshops in illumination engineering aspects from time to time, including the University of Kansas and the University of Wisconsin — Madison, Extension Division. Schools, faculty, and programs change constantly; therefore, the preceding is *not* a list of recommen-

a listing of the schools and programs in neon education in California, Kansas, Minnesota, Missouri, New Jersey, New York, North Carolina, Oregon, Rhode Island, Texas, Washington, and Wisconsin with addresses, telephone numbers, and brief information about each program.

Martin Carr, "Theatre Technology in the Hong Kong Academy for Performing Arts," Lighting + Sound International, vol. 1, no. 7 (May/June 1986), pp. 26–27, 29. Illus., color. Excellent description of training now available in Hong Kong.

Donald Walker, "'Give Me Some Light'—The Essential Training," Lighting + Sound International, vol. 1, no. 6 (April 1986), pp. 45–46. Illus. An excellent article about the British ABTT training program by an English educational expert.

Michael Neighbors, How to Become a Successful Consultant in Lighting Engineering. Estill Springs, TN; Associated Technology (Rt. 2 Box 448, Estill Springs, TN 37330); 1984. Presents basic business details: fees, ethics, finding clients, advertising, contracts, etc.

[396] *A lighting instructor should be willing to take students to any of several excellent lighting lab/display facilities in the United States, such as:*

GE's Lighting Institute in Nela Park, Cleveland, Ohio. All year long this program offers excellent instructional seminars to both students and professionals in excellent facilities with a top staff.

Philips Lighting Center, Somerset, New Jersey. A unique new showroom and training center which costs over $750,000 per year to operate and represents an initial investment of $4 million.

Halo/ELA Tech Center, 6 West 20th Street, New York, NY 10011. Telephone: (212) 645-4580.

Luminatae, Inc., 8515 Keystone Crossing Avenue, Indianapolis, Indiana 46204. Telephone: (317) 251-1100. Contact: Barbara Baebler.

Moto-Light, 3119A South Scenic, Springfield, Missouri. Telephone: (417) 883-4549.

York Lighting Corporation, St. Laurent (Montreal), Quebec, has opened a large showroom at their head office.

University of Kansas, Lawrence, Kansas.

Capri Lighting of Los Angeles. At 6430 East Slauson Avenue, Los Angeles, CA 90040. Telephone: (213) 726-1800). This firm specializing in low-voltage lighting installations has excellent facilities.

Stan Scherr, Plunket & Lynch, 15 West 26th Street, New York City. Telephone: (212) 684-3240.

Lightolier, Inc., S. L. Bollinger, 1071 Ave. of the Americas (6th Ave. at 41st St.), N.Y., NY 10018. Telephone: (212) 719-1616. Lightolier has excellent showrooms in Kentucky, Illinois (Chicago), and on the West Coast. Look up your nearest Lightolier distributor.

The Fashion Institute, 227 West 27th Street, N.Y., NY 10001. Telephone: (212) 760-7800. New York State has provided its Interior Design Department with one of the best-equipped labs in the United States.

See: "Showrooms," Interior Design, April 1987. Illus., color.

Also, a visit to the Exploratorium in San Francisco or the Museum of Holography in both New York City and Chicago (see Chapter 3) is valuable training.

See: "Seeing the Light," Lighting Design + Application, vol. 16, no. 7 (July 1986), pp. 36–37. There are many other light labs and showrooms, with new ones being added weekly around the country. This list serves only as a beginning point for the many others not listed here.

"Four Young Lighting Designers Speak Out: What Did You Learn in School? What Do You Wish You Had Learned?" Lighting Design + Application, vol. 16, no. 3 (March 1986), pp. 10–12. Illus. The four young designers are: Robert Prouse (formerly a student at the University of Colorado, now with Fisher & Marantz in New York City); Thomas Thompson (now with Howard Brandston Lighting Design, Inc., in New York City; formerly a student at Penn State); Mark L. Roush (formerly a student at the University of Illinois; now with Holophane); and Helen K. Diemer (formerly a student at Penn State; now head of the lighting department with Flack & Kurta in New York City). This is a very useful article for practicing lighting educators.

See also "Letters", Lighting Design + Application, vol. 16, no. 5 (May 1986), p. 2. An astute commentary by a veteran lighting designer on the above article listing methods and materials architectural lighting design students need to know.

Instructors should also take or send students to as many of the annual trade shows as possible:

Lighting World International. Sponsored annually by IALD and IES, either in New York City or on the West Coast, this was the key trade show for those in architectural lighting. Then IES and IALD withdrew from Lighting World International (now owned by National Expositions in New York City) and began their own trade show, Lightfair.

dations. There are other good training places not listed. The list does, however, guide the student toward those *present* programs which are generally acknowledged to be outstanding in this lighting area. For those already practicing architectural lighting design, some tips toward further growth are to be found in footnote 396. Former student views concerning the adequacy of their training should be studied.[397] Consideration should be given to developing rendering skills.[398]

The interior designer/architectural lighting designer should give serious consideration to Parson's School of Design (the New School for Social Research in New York City at 66 Fifth Ave.) and its three-year M.F.A. program in lighting design, instructed by a faculty of leading practitioners from New York City. Professor Andrea Daugherty at the University of Louisiana in Baton Rouge is rapidly building a nationally recognized program of instruction in interior design lighting. California State Polytechnic in Pomona offered a four-year lighting program in the spring of 1985. I offer such a program at Purdue University, in West Lafayette, Indiana, leading to a three-year M.F.A. degree. Further, the Yamagiwa Art Foundation in Tokyo has held 10 International Lighting Design Competitions, awarding prizes and scholarships for outstanding work, as well as an excellent curriculum. These are exhibited throughout Japan. Those who wish to enter should contact the Yamagiwa Art Foundation, 3-12-4, Sotokanda, Chiyoda-ku, Tokyo 101, Japan.

The IES now annually offers a $1,500 prize (the Howard Brandston Award) to the best student architectural design. This award was won in its second year by two former students of mine, Glen Goodwin and Kim Nibeck. Also, regional sections of the IES frequently have annual student architectural lighting design competitions with prizes. My own Purdue University students annually compete at the Indiana IES chapter in Indianapolis with students from the University of Illinois, Butler University, Ball State University, and the Purdue undergraduate program in the Interior Design Department. Thus far we have once won the Grand Prize (Goodwin and Nibeck) of IES membership and the IES *Reference* and *Applications* handbooks, plus assorted lesser prizes for first and second place winners.[399]

Other Specialties

Obviously, those who wish to work in film should first study with any top photography program. Students should check to see if the program offers *any* instruction in the use of light and fill in the void (if one exists) by taking such instruction in other departments. Training for work in the TV field involves mostly specific instruction in the media. Lighting design–specialized training *per se* is almost nonexistent. The interested student should arrange to get as many of the basics as is possible. TV networks — and even local stations — often have no set pattern for hiring and prefer to train those whom they have selected for lighting direction in their own evolved methods. If a student's intention is lighting outdoors, both training in illumination engineering and at a top landscape architecture school is valuable. There are two training routes for designing lighting indoors (depending upon the scope of the student's intended career): study in a good school of architecture (hoping that it also offers instruction in the designed use of light) or study in a department of interior design (again, filling in lighting training elsewhere, if necessary). The second choice will more severely limit the future range of employment. Lastly, a student who is interested in the film world should find a good department of cinematography/film such as the one at UCLA in Los Angeles or the one at NYU in New York City. Imero Fiorentino Associates (New York City) offers useful training films and workshops in TV lighting. Harry Mathias, cinematographer of Victor Duncan, Inc. (2659 Fondren, Dallas, Texas 75206), has offered a series of workshops around the country in "Cinematic Approach to the Use of Video Cameras." Victor Duncan, Inc. also offers film seminars in "Lighting As a Language."

Recently the West Coast SMPTE (Society of Motion Picture and Television Engineers) combined with the PMPEA (Professional Motion Picture Equipment Association) to offer an extensive tutorial seminar at Universal Studio's stages 31, 42, and 43 on production lighting techniques for film and TV with top cinematographers/directors of photography as the speakers. It was a hands-on program and is likely to be repeated each year. It is available on videotape.

Two excellent videotapes on lighting for TV are available:

"An Introduction to Basic Television Lighting," produced by the British Society of Television Lighting Directors and based upon lectures by BBC Senior Lecturer, Alan Bermingham, from the Society's Seminar at BBC's Wood Norton, Evesham, England; and "Lighting for Video Tape Production," an instructional tape prepared by and available from 3M Co. (Minnesota Mining and Manufacturing Co., 1977). I use both with my classes, making it possible to bring the subject of TV lighting alive and make it visual even when adequate TV studio facilities are not at hand.

An increasing number of educational institutions offer two-year "certificate" programs for trained stagehands in lighting—among them are Indiana University (Bloomington, Indiana), the Conservatory of Theatre Arts at Webster College (St. Louis, Missouri), American University (Washington, D.C.), and Bergen Community College (Paramus, New Jersey). These programs are not of great concern to lighting designers, however.

Those in architectural lighting should be aware of the many seminars nationwide offered by the Designers Lighting Forum (DLF—see Chap. 13). SMPTE offers several grants and scholarships for the training of film and TV engineers (but not designers). ABTT (Association of British Theatre Technicians) in England conducts an extensive training program, for both beginners and pros.[400]

Summary

As this chapter makes clear, preparation for a career in lighting design is not yet a unified course of study anywhere. Light as a design element is itself a newcomer to the arts. Architects complain about those they hire for lighting design, saying hirelings have too little background in architecture, architectural drafting, illumination engineering, etc., and often too much training in theatre. The other specialties have similar complaints. Trainees can be most certain of employment (and perhaps even of job satisfaction) if (1) they are aware of the conflict and difference between training in *engineering* and training in *design* (and make whatever choices their own abilities dictate or master both), and (2) they soundly ground themselves in the basics of light and vision. Many individuals successfully cross today's arbitrary walls dividing the specialties, and it is hoped that their number will keep increasing.

USITT's annual conference. Usually held in April or May in different cities (sometimes countries) each year, this is the big trade show for those in theatrical lighting.

Lighting Dimensions International in Dallas, Texas, in 1988 and in Nashville, Tennessee, in November 1989. Trade show sponsored by *Lighting Dimensions* magazine..

Pan Pacific Lighting Exposition in San Francisco. (See *International Lighting Review*, 4th quarter of 1986, p. 148.) Contact Pan Pacific Lighting Exposition Producers, 2 Henry Adams St., San Francisco, CA 94103. Telephone: (415) 621-4761.

Workspace 87. A 1987 tradeshow about office environment lighting. See *Lighting Dimensions*, vol. 11, no. 4 (July/August 1987), p. 20.

International Lighting Fair in Dallas, Texas. See *Lighting Dimensions*, vol. 11, no. 4 (July/August 1987), pp. 30, 32–35. Contact PSA Show Management, PO Box 214, Sea Girt, NJ 08750. Telephone: (201) 974-1900.

Francis Reid, ". . . and at Photokina," *Light + Sound International*, vol. 1, no. 10 (September/October 1986), pp. 38, 41. Illus. Details about the annual Photokina trade show, the largest in Europe dealing with film and video.

In 1988 Scott Wightman was named manager of GE's Lighting Institute at Nela Park, Cleveland.

GTE (General Telephone & Electronics—Sylvania lamps) in 1988 opened a 23,000-square-foot exhibit and meeting facility in Dallas, Texas.

John Offord "SIB Rimini—'The Best Show,'" *Lighting + Sound International*, vol. 1, no. 7 (May/June 1986), pp. 20–21, 23, 25. Illus., color. A review of the annual trade show at Rimini, off Italy's Adriatic coast, attended in 1986 by over 12,000 people. Covers theatre, film, and television lighting worldwide, with a total of over 350 exhibitors in 1986.

PLASA, the British Annual trade show of the Professional Lighting + Sound Association. See *Lighting + Sound International*, vol. 1, no. 10 (September/October 1986), pp. 21–33. Contact P.O. Box 628, Eastbourne, East Sussex BN21 2PZ, England. PLASA is an association of manufacturing and rental companies for live pop music, roadshows, and discos.

[397] *See Lee Watson, "Lighting Design Educators,"* Lighting Design + Application, *vol. 14, no. 7 (July 1984), pp. 27–40.*

[398] *William Rupp, "Toward the Rendering of Lighting Design,"* Lighting Design + Application, *vol. 13, no. 11 (November 1983), pp. 33–35. Illus. Professor Rupp (University of Massachusetts, Department of Art/Design, Amherst) provides useful beginning suggestions about how architectural lighting designers can communicate light and shade design intentions.*

[399] *"Jeannine M. Fisher Wins 1986 Student Competition,"* Lighting Design + Application, *vol. 16, no. 10 (October 1986), pp. 38–39. Illus.*

[400] *British designers should see:*

Ruth Tenne, "A Study of Technicians in the British Theatre," Reprinted in ABTT News, *January 1985, pp. 4–9. Originally printed in the January 1985 Employment Gazette, the official monthly journal of the Department of Employment. An excellent, detailed study of British employment conditions.*

Datec Directory of Drama Courses in Higher Education, *1984 edition. Published by and obtainable from Publications Secretary, British Theatre Institute, 61 Surbiton Court, St. Andrews Square, Surbiton, Surrey KT6 3ED, England.*

Chapter 15

Agents and Taxes

[401] *Lee Watson, "Agents for Lighting Designers,"* Lighting Dimensions, *vol. 2, no. 9 (November 1978), pp. 16–17.*

Agents

Until recently, no one paid much attention to agents for lighting designers. In 1978 my curiosity about agent use was aroused when I needed a representative in New York City.[401] Accordingly, I mailed 75 questionnaires to working members of United Scenic Artists #829 known to concentrate in lighting design. Fifty replied (a 66 ⅔ percent response rate).

To the first question — "Do you now, or have you ever, retained an agent?" — 33 percent replied yes. At the time of the survey, 17.6 percent of the respondents had an agent.

The next question dealt with an agent's expected duties, which generally are (1) to find jobs, (2) to negotiate contracts and payment, and (3) to guide career growth. Almost all survey respondents replied that, while they had hoped an agent would be instrumental in increasing design assignments, in fact agents were *not*. Many designers responded that agents (or attorneys) were most useful in negotiating contracts and securing full payment. Bob Davis said, "An agent could do the ugly negotiating so I would not have the risk of damaging the good relationship I must retain with the manager, director, and producer." Bill Mintzer wrote: "Keeps me separated from money discussions, etc., with producers." F. Mitchell Dana replied, "I do use a lawyer who negotiates for me for a set fee. I use a lawyer because I find it easier to let him handle selling me. Also my relationship with management is based around the show, not a difficult and potentially damaging confrontation about me." Roger Morgan said, "I use an attorney. . . . I know several other designers who also do this. He also gives me

financial advice and recently he handled all of my taxes and prepared the annual tax forms." Others who suggested using an attorney rather than an agent included Martin Tudor, Barry Arnold, Patrika Brown, and Jules Fisher.

Among those respondents who had used or were using an agent, most indicated disappointment in the area of securing employment. Some designers were bitter, and several had changed agents. One wrote: "1st agent never found work and almost lost a major star contract at the time; 2nd only obtained me one job." John Gleason said tersely, "You don't get B'way jobs via agents." Tharon Musser wrote, "Remember that seldom is it possible for an agent to obtain a job for a designer, since someone on the production usually knows who they want, i.e., the director, designer, producer. . . . There are exceptions, naturally, such as some industrials." Another designer wrote: "I got some job applications from dancers she [my agent] handled . . . possible jobs which would not be heard of otherwise." It can be concluded that at this moment agents are not of much value in expanding employment for the lighting designers they represent. Many agents recognize this reality and are quite hesitant to represent lighting designers. There are cases that are exceptions, usually involving an agent who represents a "stable," i.e., a group of stars, directors, authors, scenic designers, and costume designers (usually only one artist from each of the design areas). The producer hires all of the agent's suggested clients for a given production. Few in number, these agents do find some work for the lighting designers they represent.

In light of the numerous negative views on the value of personal experience with agents, I used the survey question "In your opinion, is an agent necessary (or helpful or unnecessary) for a lighting designer, and do you believe that *other* lighting designers would profit from having an agent?". The tabulated results were surprising. A total of 6 percent of respondents felt that an agent was "necessary," while 44 percent replied "helpful" and only 38 percent responded "unnecessary" (an additional 12 percent didn't have an opinion). As to the question of whether an agent would be of value to other lighting designers, 44 percent answered yes, 40 percent answered no, and the rest added (gratuitously), "It depends." Lighting designers seemed to be split fifty-fifty on the desirability of an agent for any purpose.

Helpful or not, what do agents exact for their services? Almost all responses indicated that agents received a 10 percent standard service charge. Details did vary, however. Most agents receive 10 percent of *everything* earned by any client on the agent's roster, including work not generated by that agent. Others ask only 10 percent of all royalties and monies over minimum union scale (these agents negotiate their client's contracts). One designer reported giving his agent only 7 percent of funds received, but his agent was used only to negotiate contracts. Tharon Musser stated her view well: "If one feels they cannot negotiate a contract, just remember that they will pay 10 percent on *all* income from a production for its lifetime. This seems a lot to pay someone for a few phone calls and perhaps two or three hours of work." Robbie Monk wrote: "It depends on who you deal with and your ability to talk and handle money. If you deal with big time producers, it can be helpful and prestigious. If you deal with regional theatre companies, an agent can get in the way."

Agents seem to be of most value to a number of constantly working designers who prefer to have an agent to handle the "business matters." Yet it is the unknown designer who most needs an agent's services and frequently can't obtain them. Tony Quintavalla's opinion makes a useful summary here: "Right now, the only use for an agent is negotiating contracts and that only in levels of business high enough to warrant hiring someone to handle contracts. If many designers begin using agents, then agents may become more useful or even necessary as they have in other fields."

Taxes

Lighting designers should discover early in their careers the advantages inherent in the present income tax structure. It is imperative to keep accurate records to make use of the potential deductions. This subject has been well covered by R. Brendan Hanlon in the Drama Book Specialists volume *A Guide to Taxes and Record Keeping for Performers, Designers, Directors*.[402] Hanlon writes with relaxed humor but great caution. Tax laws change each year, so his more recent comments are listed in footnote 402.

Lighting designers need to be concerned about tax laws as soon as they begin to design. Lighting designers are from that half-world between the employed laborer and the independent contractor. Unlike most laboring people, lighting designers do not have employer-provided office space or work space (other than the theatre during production), tools or supplies of their trade, or research facilities — nor do they even have regular daily hours of labor. Yet by current legal (and tax) practice, the designer is an employee. The standard deductions (income taxes, social security, etc.) are regularly withheld from their wages. However, as the tax laws are now written, the designer is legally entitled to deductions commonly available only to the self-employed. Transportation and living expenses directly related to the job (unless they were reimbursed by the employer), craft tools (professional organization dues, trade journals, work supplies), some office overhead (under stringent restrictions), telephone costs, plus other expenses too numerous to list are deductible. Hanlon's main point is well taken: the designer should keep detailed records of everything and use the services of a knowledgeable tax consultant. Those artists fortunate enough to have income from writing and publication (as I do) fall under amazingly liberal deduction clauses that are a valid part of the tax laws.

The IRS keeps a wary eye on employees of show business. Since designers fall in a category between the regularly employed and the self-employed, they are especially liable to audit and tax "interpretation" of the rules.

In summary, the designer who wants to get a handle on taxes should read Hanlon, keep accurate and extensive records, find a good tax authority, and understand that this is a career area that is vulnerable to tax investigation.

[402] *Marjorie O'Neill Butler, Ingrid Sonnichsen, and Gary Marc*, The Tax Guide for Performers, *Boston, MA. Telephone: (617) 482-1280. Approximately $8.*

R. Brendan Hanlon, The New Tax Guide for Performing Artists, Designers, Directors and Other Show Biz Folk, *Wolfeboro, NH; Proscenium Publishers/Limelight Editions; 1988. Approximately $8.*

Brendan Hanlon, "Taxes — The Code is Dead! Long Live the Code," Theatre Crafts, *vol. 21, no. 3 (March 1987), pp. 12, 73 – 74.*

Brendan Hanlon, "After Tax Reform, What?" Theatre Crafts, *vol. 21, no. 1 (January 1987), p. 12.*

"Finances: The Designer As Taxpayer," Theatre Crafts, *vol. 12, no. 1 (January/Febuary 1978), pp. 69 – 72.*

"Finances: Getting Audited! Show and Tell with IRS," Theatre Crafts, *vol. 12, no. 6 (October 1978), pp. 90 – 92.*

"Finances: Keep the Receipts! Record Keeping for the Performing Arts Taxpayer," Theatre Crafts, *vol. 12, no. 7 (November/December 1978), pp. 80 – 81.*

"Finances: Transportation and Travel Expenses," Theatre Crafts, *vol. 13, no. 1 (January/February 1979), pp. 75, 78.*

Irving L. Blackman, "The Great Tax Bite," Lighting Dimensions, *vol. 5, no. 2 (March 1981), pp. 49, 51 – 53.*

Chapter 16

The World of Tomorrow

[403] Lee Watson, "The World of Tomorrow —A Vision," Lighting Dimensions, vol. 3, no. 12 (Dec. 1979), pp. 24–25.

Joel E. Rubin, "Stage Lighting and the State of the Art in Twenty Years," Theatre Design & Technology, vol. 18, no. 3 (Fall 1982), pp. 5–10. Excellent overview. See also Lighting Dimensions, vol. 7, no. 1 (March 1983), pp. 52–53, 55, 57–58, 60. Illus. A perceptive insight from the manufacturers' point of view by an industry leader.

"Overseas: OISTAT Amsterdam," ABTT News, November/December 1987, pp. 5–8. Report of a seminar from the Congress for Stage Technology by the Netherlands Centre of OISTAT on "The Future of Lighting Techniques." Participants were Richard Pilbrow, chairperson, Bob Davis (New York City consultant), Andy Meldrum (United Kingdom), Steve Kemp (lighting designer from Holland), and Henk van der Geest (also Holland). The remainder of the report is in ABTT News, January 1988, pp. 3–6.

Cameron Harvey, "Glimpsing the Future: Symposium Discusses Prospects for Automated Lighting on the Legitimate Stage," Lighting Dimensions, vol. 12, no. 2 (March 1988), pp. 30, 32, 34–43. Also contains: Richard Pilbrow, "A Designer's Viewpoint"; Steve Terry, "A Technical Commentary." A series of introspective and evaluative articles about the first use of moving Vari*Lites for productions by the Los Angeles Music Center in the Dorothy Chandler Pavilion in 1988. Useful insights.

Any study of history has only one purpose: to summarize and interpret what has thus far been done, learned, and mastered, as a guide to doing things better (more creatively) tomorrow. Further, a study of history points toward those things which a particular group has not yet achieved to its ultimate satisfaction, thus giving its members guides for further growth and improvement. Thus it is fitting that this business volume should close with a speculative look at the potential world of tomorrow.[403]

What does lighting design consist of *today*? A trained specialist receives basic information as follows: place of performance or design; scenic environment or building; limits on time, money, personnel, and equipment available; and a script/plans. This information is studied, and the conferences are held with other artists: the architect/director/producer, other designers (costume, scenic, etc.), interior decorator/designers, business managers, camera or film directors, etc. From this gathered information, plus his own informed personal experience, a lighting designer derives a light plot (or drawings) which is basically a work order for the creation of a "lighting machine." Then the agony begins!

Every lighting designer wishes to begin a designing job immediately, using light to evoke the response desired from an attendant audience (or users, if it is an architectural job). First, however, the "lighting machine" must be created, which always seems to involve endless hours of noncreative drudgery. There is very little that is fascinating or productive about the process of mounting tin cans with magnifying glasses at one end (spotlights or luminaires) on pipes (or in the ceiling) from rickety ladders or shaky lifts. From each of these lights wires must be strung and plugged into the proper place. Then comes the process of inserting little bits of colored media, pointing the can in the right place (focus), and attending to any necessary final adjustments.

The next-to-last step is that highly mysterious period when the lighting designer sits for endless hours at a talk-back directing the construction of an elaborate network of levels and cues (programming), properly recorded or memorized, rehearsed, checked out, and executed.

Nine-tenths of the designer's time is spent working with very primitive and inadequate technology. Maybe, if the designer is very lucky, one-tenth of the time is devoted to creative designing and utilization of accumulated knowledge and experience. This chapter looks at some of these primitive technology tools and reveals what more is possible in the predictable future.

Light Sources

The present tungsten sources are only 10 to 12 percent efficient. In other words, only about 10 percent of the electrical energy input becomes usable visible radiation. Tungsten sources are often bulky, and they generate tremendous quantities of unneeded heat. The color curve output is deplorable and is subject to modification with dimming. The light source (filament) is far from the "point" source in dimension needed for optimum utilization of the laws of optics.

Another light source, the fluorescent tube (a basic in architectural lighting), is much cooler in operation and much more efficient in visible light output versus energy consumption, as compared to tungsten sources. However, it is a *line* source, not a point source. Also, the color output is not a satisfactory continuous spectrum, and the fluorescent light cannot be readily dimmed (economically).

The lighting industry's greatest need is for a highly compact, highly efficient energy source, with close to a "point" source, operating with minimum heat generation at a reasonable initial cost and with long life (burning time). Recent discoveries are moving technology closer to those goals. The newest line of short-arc lamps, such as HMI (hydrargyrum-medium iodides) metallogen, HID (high-intensity discharge), etc., offer great promise and are increasingly being used in followspots, wide-angle scenic projectors, and location shooting for films and TV. Currently quite expensive with rather short lamp life, these short-arc lamps produce a highly concentrated (close to a "point") light source that is much more energy efficient than tungsten, reasonably cool in operation, compact in size, and with an ideal color curve output. They cannot, however, be electrically dimmed — only mechanical dimmers can be used. Both cost and dimming problems offer promise of acceptable solutions in the relatively near future. The use of short-arc lamps could change the whole nature of luminaires in the lighting industry.

Increasing attention is being given to low-voltage quartz sources. There are numerous advantages to 12- and 14-volt tungsten quartz light sources, long known to Europeans but underutilized in the United States. The filament can be much more compact than regular tungsten sources (and thus nearer the ideal "point"). Color temperature is better, with more output in the blue end of the spectrum (usually 3200° to 3250° Kelvin). Low-voltage quartz sources are also 15 percent more efficient in terms of usable visible light output versus current consumption than regular tungsten. Because the low-voltage filament is usually smaller and thicker, the resultant lamps both have more durability (longer life) and less tungsten evaporation (resulting in an

overall lower cost factor), and the filament exhibits greater resistance to physical damage. These sources produce less heat for an identical amount of visible radiant energy (as compared to regular tungsten sources), a very important factor. The smaller size of both the filament and the overall lamp makes the low-voltage quartz source better suited to luminaire design utilizing reflectors and lenses. The new MR-16 low-voltage lamps have appeared in a variety of wattages and beam spreads and are being increasingly introduced into architectural lighting. The 36-watt PAR36Q tungsten halogen is now available in narrow and wide flood configurations. Further, as John Foley of Phoebus Manufacturing Co. wrote in *Theatre Crafts*:

> New developments in low voltage/high intensity lamps will enable dimmers to become a part of each lighting instrument without being damaged by ambient heat. This will eliminate the backstage dimmer pack and enable the instruments to be connected directly to the controller with low voltage cables, resulting in less weight, expense, and energy consumption.[404]

Such a direction for improvement of light sources was clearly outlined by Erwin Feher in his "Advances in Stage Lighting" paper in the early sixties (see footnote 403). The lighting industry in the United States is just now catching up with his conclusions and widely used European practices.

Attention must be paid to the proliferation of PAR reflector lamps. Richard Pilbrow in his chapter on "Tomorrow" in *Stage Lighting* writes: "PAR lamp[s] . . . are revolutionizing display and architectural lighting, and becoming highly useful in the theatre. . . . [T]he variety and sophistication of the sealed beam lamp perhaps indicates that future stage lighting units might increasingly rely, for their performance, upon the lamp they contain."[405]

Improved light sources also include lasers and fiber optics, which have many *potential* — but few realized — applications in lighting design. Both technologies are discussed briefly later in this chapter.

Color

Present color practices could not be more primitive. After the color wheel and additive color mixing from a multiplic-

"Interview: Whither the Canadian Lighting Industry?" Lighting, vol. 1, no. 1 (June 1987), pp. 20, 22. Illus. An interview with Ernest Wotton, leading Canadian designer, consultant, psychologist, engineer, researcher, and educator about his views of the future of lighting design in Canada.

Robert Long, "Amsterdam OISTAT Conference," Theatre Crafts, vol. 21, no. 9 (November 1987), p. 24. A report about a panel session chaired by Richard Pilbrow on "The Future of Lighting" at the 1987 conference of the International Organization of Scenographers, Theatre Architects and Technicians (OISTT) in Amsterdam during August 1987.

Robert Long, "Amsterdam OISTAT Conference," Theatre Crafts, vol. 21, no. 9 (November 1987), p. 24. A panel discussion about "The Future of Lighting" chaired by Richard Pilbrow. See "Overseas" in ABTT/News entry above in this footnote for names of panelists.

Robert Wills, "The Turn of the Decade," Theatre Crafts, vol. 14, no. 1 (January/February 1980), pp. 19, 61–63. Illus.

R. T. Dorsey, "The New World of Light," Light magazine, vol. 42, no. 2 (1973), pp. 3–8. Illus. Concerns mostly architectural lighting.

Beeb Salzer, "In 25 Years," Lighting Dimensions, vol. 3, no. 12 (December 1979), pp. 49, 51. Beeb peers into the future.

Donald Oenslager, "Let There Be Light," reprint from the September 1947 Theatre Arts. Available from USITT. One of the most poetic, inspirational statements ever made about the power and influence of light in all aspects of our lives.

Richard B. Glickman, "The Future of Entertainment Lighting," Lighting Dimensions, vol. 5, no. 6 (September/October 1981), pp. 47–49. Glickman predicts technological advances in the lighting specialties.

Erwin Feber, *"Advances in Stage Lighting."* An undated (around 1961–63), mimeographed study prepared for AETA (Stage Design and Technical Developments Project) and USITT. Never published. AETA (American Educational Theatre Association) is the predecessor of ATA (American Theatre Association).

Richard Pilbrow, Stage Lighting. *London; Studio Vista; revised edition, 1979. See Part I, Chap. 10, "Tomorrow," pp. 139–144. Excellent analysis and predictions.*

Richard Pilbrow, *"Lighting in '81,"* TABS, *vol. 38, no. 2 (October 1981), pp. 16–17. Illus., color. Devotes more attention to film and TV.*

"Richard Pilbrow: A View of Lighting from Across the Water," Lighting Dimensions, *vol. 6, no. 2 (March 1982), pp. 16–17, 45, 52–54.*

Francis Reid, *"Saying Sooth,"* TABS, *vol. 33, no. 1 (Spring 1975), p. 2.*

"What Will the Future Bring?" Lighting Design + Application, *vol. 11, no. 1 (January 1981), pp. 34–44. The opinions of 32 leaders in architectural lighting, lighting research, and education.*

Michael Callahan, *"Bright New World?"* Lighting Dimensions, *vol. 7, no. 1 (March 1983), pp. 62–64, 66, 72–73; no. 2 (April/May 1983), pp. 27, 32, 35, 38–39; no. 3 (June 1983), pp. 35–42. Illus. An astute analysis of the pragmatic realities affecting advances in luminaires and control.*

John Brass, *"Forecast for Lighting 1993,"* Interiors, *vol. CXLII, no. 9 (April 1983), pp. 108–109. Designer Brass postulates the position and facilities of architectural lighting design's future.*

Graham Walne, *"Light Years Away,"* Sightlines, *vol. 18, no. 1 (January 1984), pp. 6–7. A brief, well-stated plea for cooler light sources.*

[404] *The complete records on this quote are not available at this time. The author has been unable to locate John Foley.*

[405] *Richard Pilbrow, p. 140, op. cit. (see footnote 403).*

[406] *Michael Wolfe and John Schwiller, "Instant Colour," TABS, vol. 35, no. 2 (Summer 1977), pp. 18–19. Illus., color. Key research for tomorrow.*

[407] *Francis Reid, p. 3, op. cit. (see footnote 403).*

ity of sources were invented, color innovation just came to a halt. Even Vari-Lite only begins to come to grips with modernization, using dichroic color filters. On the bright side, Michael Wolfe and John Schwiller (of the Thorn Theatre Lighting Division and Thorndike Theatre in Leatherhead, both in England) presented the results of some early investigations in an article in *TABS* in 1977 called "Instant Colour."[406] Their system, called MIC (modulation-induced color), is still far from being commercially acceptable, but it does offer a hope for the future. By electrochemical processes (electronic control of liquid crystal dyed molecules), the MIC system can produce any color of light from a single instrument by remote control—including blackout. In the future, such an approach could completely revolutionize lighting design when combined with the new short-arc light sources. The dimmer, as such, would disappear. At the designer's fingertips at a control console would be both an infinite range of color modification and intensity control—all combined with memory recording. Delaying further progress along these research lines are initial high research costs, the potential high costs of each electrochemical color modification unit, and present high light-loss levels of output in the system. MIC's time *will* come, however—expanding beyond belief the color modification potentials for the artist-designer and markedly modifying present switchboard, control, and available color. What an improvement for the designer to be able to obtain *all* colors, as desired, from any single luminaire; to modify color from a luminaire at will; and to reproduce any desired color upon command! In 1975, Francis Reid wrote: "Why use a colour filter? Can we not break up the spectrum electronically?"[407]

A separate but important aspect of color in lighting in the future is the need for much more extensive solid data from the behaviorists (psychologists) concerning human responses (emotional and intellectual) to colored light. This research exists only in the most primitive state. Current practice is for designers to hope that, by experience and intuition, they can predict audience response to color usage. When the science of human behavioral investigation becomes more exact, designers will be guided in color use by solid information rather than only the present "educated guesses" based upon past experience.

Distribution

If current control of color can be called primitive, the current ability to control distribution (focus spread and movement) is *pre*-primitive. At the lighting designer's disposal is the follow spotlight (movement), the Vari-Lite and its relatives, a very limited selection of newer luminaires with multiple lens trains allowing variations in beam spread, and the mounting of additional expensive and time-consuming luminaires when we want a different focus or coverage. However, since the early 1970s both ADB (Adrian de Backer in Belgium) and Ludwig Pani in Vienna have been mass-producing and successfully marketing remote control of beam sharpness, spread, and focus effected by highly sophisticated motor and gear drives (servomechanics)—all accurately reproducible, with memory control included. These units, of the highest quality, control horizontal and vertical tilt (direction), enable spot/flood or barrel focus, and provide a five-color selection changer. While the units are expensive, they have found a ready market in European television studios, film locations, and several larger theatres (the Bolshoi Theatre in Moscow has them; so does the National Theatre in London). In the mid-seventies, ABD quoted to me a price per unit of $5,000 per luminaire for ellipsoidal spotlights with memory remote control of insertion *and* tilt of all four shutters, plus horizontal and vertical direction of the instrument. Today that price would be $10,000 to $12,000 per unit. Of course the price is high. But in a television studio, film studio, or busy opera house, such technology soon repays its cost many times over in increased efficiency and reduced labor charges. The manufacturers in the United States can, and will, provide such mechanization "when a client is ready to pay for it." The sooner that day comes the better, for the sake of improved lighting design. Tentative beginnings belatedly are to be seen in the U.S.-produced Vari-Lite and its imitators.

The ability to refocus lighting units *between* cues, rather than hanging additional units, would simplify the designer's life and free his or her design imagination to grapple with bigger and better ideas. Memory-motorize these functions and the lighting designer can step into the theatre and begin designing with complete remote memory control of the three controllable properties of light: intensity, color, and distribution. Today we frequently can control only intensity variations to any desirable degree.

In 1975 Francis Reid wrote: "Lighting is still held in chains by the theatre industry's historical dependence on abundant cheap labour rather than capital investment: lighting equipment is primitive because it has been traditionally cheap. The days of a labour intensive theatre are over and in terms of efficient working on a repertoire stage, we believe that a focusing improvement of, say, 5 seconds per lantern can justify considerable capital outlay."[408] Richard Pilbrow wrote in 1979:

> Many major theatres in Germany and Eastern Europe employ a limited number of remote pan, tilt and focus lanterns. . . . Japan possesses several theatres heavily equipped with remote control lanterns. . . . Time must produce a breakthrough in this sphere. Present control systems employ considerable sophistication to record and repeat the intensity of stage lighting instruments. Surely in the near future systems will become available, at reasonable cost, that will control not only intensity but also the position, direction, shape and colour of every unit."[409]

Any nation which has mastered the technology for remote "robot" control of nuclear fission materials could do the same for remote control of luminaires, but such advances are hindered by the relative lack of "necessity" for improved lighting design technology.

Intensity

The developments of the last 10 years in the addition of memory control and computer technology, leading to ever more complex control networks, have already been discussed. These trends will continue, and the evolving lighting designer will have to be respectful of tools which, misused, will overwhelm any theatrical production or architectural edifice until the end result is simply a razzle-dazzle mélange of excessive light cues, effects, and tricks — obliterating all meaningfulness as the "show-off" in lighting takes over.

Special Effects

Several specialized lighting areas could make great use of lighting-related improvements in some of the tools and technologies already at hand, such as holograms, lasers, projection, multimedia, and fiber optics. Product developers are far from reaching any practical application of evolving hologram technology for the lighting craft; however, that day will come. While much has been developed in the area of controlled projections (better wide-angle scenic projectors, gobos, polarized motion in patterns, etc.), there is still far to go in more extensive application of film projections with continuous motion (either reproduced from film or from video images evolving through TV). That day will come, too. Laser technology is evolving at such a rapid rate that it boggles the mind to consider all of the possibilities which may soon be available in sources, luminaires, and control/power devices once lasers cease to be primarily an "effect" and become a part of our everyday expanding working technology. The fiber-optics industry had grown to a $1.2 billion industry by 1989. We are not too far away from the day when a bundle of fiber-optic cables can snake around the stage set, in sight, and deliver a bundle of radiant energy on the face of a performer (or wherever desired). How long have designers *wanted* to be able to get light to go around corners? Such a feat may soon be possible. Current uses of fiber optics have been mostly decorative, for effect, but that will change soon, too. The evolving multimedia field offers many challenges in new techniques and equipment not yet fully utilized in the theatre. Pilbrow wrote: "Multi-screen set-ups with three projectors to each screen; complex interweaving timing; automatic homing; facilities for adding, skipping and reversing cues — all these are readily available."[410]

Nontechnical Areas

Pilbrow also said, "Lighting equipment, be it computer or spotlight, is just a tool; and no tool ever produced a masterpiece. Just as the quality of the brush probably added little to Rembrandt's paintings, so lighting equipment cannot produce fine lighting. All is in the designer's imagination and talent."[411] Other areas which offer possibilities for change include education (lighting design training), professional organizational structures (the business of lighting design), expansion of areas of employment, and the nature of design itself.

[408] *Ibid., p. 2.*

[409] *Richard Pilbrow,* Stage Lighting, *p. 140, op. cit. (see footnote 403).*

[410] *Ibid., pp. 142–43.*

[411] *Ibid., p. 143.*

[412] *Ibid.*

[413] *Ibid., p. 144.*

[414] *Francis Reid, p. 2, op. cit. (see footnote 403).*

[415] *There has been a continuing slump in Broadway theatre in recent years; Britain's West End is also in the doldrums as a result of cuts in British subsidies to the arts. Regional theatre, both in the United States and England, has also been affected, but to a lesser degree. Amusement parks continue to update their facilities and offer continuing employment, as do world's fairs and exhibitions. During 1985 it was apparent that the commercial television networks were beginning to face increasing competition from home video systems. Cable TV, which now reaches half of the homes in the United States, has been in a slump, frequently offering little that is new in specialized programming and few new employment opportunities. Music video was the "rage" of the 1980s. Discos continue to be built, ever larger and more complex. The worlds of opera and dance seem to have reached a plateau in attracting new audiences. Yet the latest Louis Harris poll shows more Americans attending live performances (in one form or another) than ever before. For current trends, which will of course affect future employment possibilities, see:*

Samuel G. Freedman, "Broadway Economic Season Is Called Worst in a Decade," The New York Times, Chicago ed. pp. 1, 14, May 20, 1985.

Anna Kisselgoff, "Has the Dance Boom Run Its Course" The New York Times, Art & Leisure section, March 3, 1985, pp. 1, 32.

John J. O'Connor, "Where's That Promised New World of Cable?" The New York Times, Art & Leisure section, November 25, 1984, pp. 1, 22.

Douglas C. McGill, "More Americans Attend Performances of Arts," The New York Times, Chicago edition, December 4, 1984, p. 26.

Benedict Nightingale, "British Theatre Faces a Lean Future," The New York Times, Art & Leisure section, C1, C22, April 22, 1985.

Samuel G. Freedman, "Losses Double in a Year at Regional Theaters," The New York Times, Art & Leisure section, p. C-17, March 13, 1985.

Samuel G. Freedman, "Is Broadway in Trouble or in Clover?" The New York Times, Art & Leisure section, pp. C1, C8, Sunday, December 9, 1984.

Education. Commenting on education, Pilbrow writes:

In both Britain and the States, dissatisfaction has been expressed about the formal training available. All too often this training is concerned with technology, equipment and techniques. Indeed, all too often where enthusiasts of lighting find themselves together, the conversation turns in the same direction. But these things are peripheral to lighting design. The designer has a creative role to play in interpreting the drama, dance or opera and aiding the director in his interpretation. The designer's preoccupation must be with *seeing* every facet of light, and with listening to, reading, and understanding the material upon which he is working, and grasping the purpose behind his unique art."[412]

The technician has a vital role to play, his job is indispensable. But lighting design is a fundamentally different process, requiring intuition, sympathy, talent and, above technological knowledge, the ability to hear and to see."[413]

American educators have called for a shift in emphasis away from indoctrination in technology and toward development of artistic/design ability in the stage-lighting education process. Professor John Gleason has predicted that "more universities will pick up the banner in training lighting designers and not tech-jocks." Professor Charles E. Williams, past president of USITT (United States Institute for Theatre Technology), said, "We are producing technicians, not artists." The TOLD (Training of Lighting Designers) Conference encouraged the training movement to broaden educational instruction in lighting design to include the needs of all the many specialties (TV, film, theatre, interiors, architectural, disco, amusement parks, etc.). Increasingly, those concerned with light use and design in the many different fields will be in touch with each other, and educators will respond by placing design training first and technology second, and by broadening their instruction to include all the areas of practice. This is, however, a slow process. Francis Reid wrote in 1975: "Learning to light is becoming too big a subject to be left to trial and error experiments on live actors and audiences: we predict the growth of proper sophisticated training facilities."[414]

Professional Organizations. In the United States the power of labor unions is decreasing, as has been the case in England in the face of a worldwide recessive economy. USA #829 will ultimately become the center of a more effective nationwide union network centered in a single local in New York City. USA #829 affects mostly newcomers to the industry (ensuring them minimum standards). The newer British Society of Theatre Designers (BSTD) has moved rapidly toward full union status and effectiveness. Since British lighting designers have traditionally been vastly underpaid for their efforts and abilities, British Society of Theatre Designers and the companion British Society of Television Lighting Directors are likely to become effective instruments for improvement in working conditions and industry stature. The multitude of professional societies are increasingly finding ways to cooperate for mutual effectiveness and gain. This cooperation is likely to increase.

Areas of Employment. The largest potential area of expanding employment for lighting designers continues to be in architectural lighting. The increased emphasis upon lighting for safety from crime and injury and the likely continued stress on economical energy consumption are two factors which justify predictions for growth. In addition, architectural lighting is the largest market around and is a comparative newcomer to the lighting design scene, so it is safe to predict that the lighting field will be a large growth area in the years to come. There will *always* be an excess of potential lighting designers (some skilled, some creative, others just technologically competent) in all facets of lighting in the world of entertainment (theatre, IV, film, and spectacle). The "glamour" of "show-biz" seems likely to continue to attract more applicants than needed.[415]

Of architectural lighting, in his article "The New World of Light" R. T. Dorsey wrote in 1973:

Better lighting creates a more agreeable working environment —generates pride in the workplace and a will to better housekeeping—generally tending both to motivate and to facilitate productivity. Facts support that point; facts emerging from literally hundreds of examples of improved productivity. Ample documentation from all over the country cites increases ranging between 5% and 20%, providing overwhelming conviction that better lighting increases productivity [and] better lighting improves the quality of life . . . from our homes to the whole city. . . . The lighting industry is faced with a heroic task: providing lighting . . . through lighting designs that use energy with increasingly better efficiency . . . there remains the need to make the best use possible of energy."[416]

Design. The late Professor Donald Oenslager provides a suitable note upon which to close, penned in 1947:

"The role we assign to light in the theatre today may be curtailed by technical deficiencies, but in the theatre of tomorrow it will shine as a new force as surely as did that first dawn. It will come sweeping in on our own winged trial-and-error insistence on new forms of expression. In the meantime Jake is still up there on the ladder and Joe is on the dimmers. Give them a hand. Let there be light—not tomorrow but today."[417]

[416] *R. T. Dorsey, pp. 3–4, op. cit. (see footnote 403).*

[417] *Oenslager, final paragraph, op. cit. (see footnote 403).*

[418] *From* Lighting Dimensions. *Reprinted by permission of Beeb Salzer and* Lighting Dimensions *magazine.* ©

Some Humor in the Industry

Those who have patiently struggled thus far through this *Handbook*—particularly students—are entitled to a final moment of trivial relaxation. Our lighting industry is much like all others: we have our relaxed moments of humor—if for no other reason than to retain tiny bits of sanity in a business noted for hysteria, tension, pressure and (frequently) the irrationality of *all* artists.

Accordingly, I have here appended a brief epilogue. It is an assemblage of a few cartoons and one literary piece by Beeb Salzer which greatly amused me. Let us hope that it has the same effect upon you, the patient reader.

2 VIEWS OF THE SAME SUBJECT

BASED UPON A SKETCH BY LEE PILCHER,

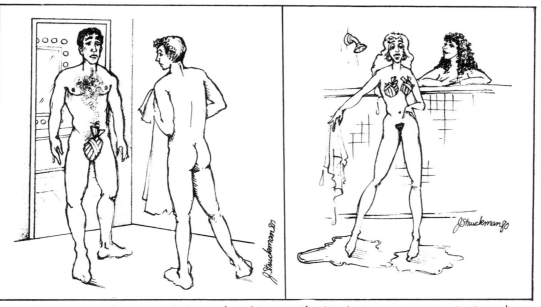

"THE LIGHTING DESIGNER OF 'OH CALCUTTA' FOCUSED EVERYTHING THERE!"

LIGHTING DESIGNER

I.R.S.

"I DON'T CARE HOW VITAL SHE IS TO YOUR CREATIVE ABILITY — A MISTRESS IS NOT A DEDUCTIBLE ITEM!"

BASED UPON A SKETCH BY LEE PILCHER, U.S.A. F-829

SIGH!

"YOU MEAN I DIDN'T HAVE TO BUILD A MODEL FOR THE LIGHTING EXAM!?!"

CITIZEN SMITH By Dave Gerard

1-21

"The beauty of this design is when your nuclear power is cut off, your oil reserves give out and coal becomes too expensive — this bank of windmills takes over!"

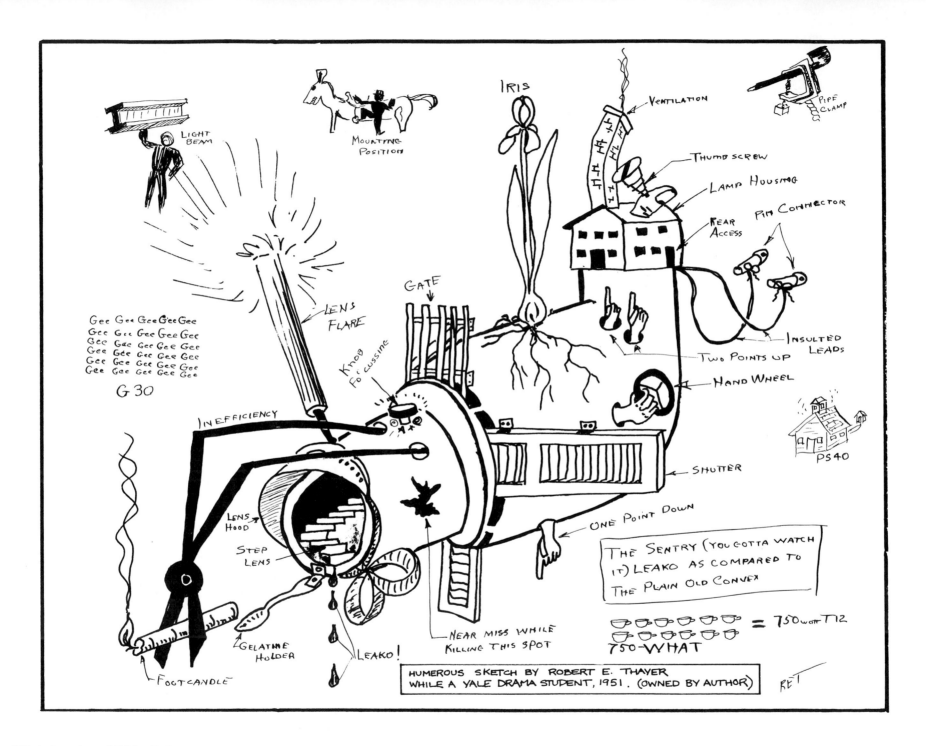

HUMEROUS SKETCH BY ROBERT E. THAYER
WHILE A YALE DRAMA STUDENT, 1951. (OWNED BY AUTHOR)

Education At Last

By Beeb Salzer

The following was received by mail and is reprinted here in its entirety.

POST GRADUATE EDUCATION IN THEATRE TECHNOLOGY THE UNIVERSITY OF SOUTHERN FORTY-SECOND STREET

A proliferation of theatre schools and drama departments since the Second World War has dumped into the market place masses of graduates trained in all areas of theatre technology. None of these graduates, however, has received formal training in those subjects which truly prepare them to function in the professional world. The University of Southern Forty-Second Street is now offering post graduate courses designed to supplement a diet of theatre courses deficient in practical vitamins and minerals.

Coping 104
5 hours 3 credits

The basic course is designed to help the student get his own way in dealing with colleagues. Starting with positive techniques such as flattery (sometimes known as ass kissing), it moves into giving and getting sexual favors, voice training for screaming, when and how to cry, and finally to negative techniques of law suits, both real and threatened.

Guest lectures are given by Supreme Court justices, several residents of Forty-Second Street area, and a four-year-old tantrum expert.

Coping 206
3 hours 3 credits

This course, titled "Looking Good," covers the important area of outward appearances. The student is encouraged to design a persona for himself, taking various forms of either "sloppy-genuine" or "elegant-a-la-mode". Some time is spent discussing the proper instruments to carry to look professional and efficient. Training is given in the ostentatious use of light meters, slide rules, calculators, scale rules, and view lenses.

Coping 207
3 hours 3 credits

The second term of "Looking Good" is devoted solely to the use of an entourage. Concrete examples are presented by various experts and their assistants (often known as foot pads). This course will prepare the student to recognize when to appear himself, when to send an assistant, or when to appear with assistants and how many.

Coping 307
3 hours 3 credits

The advanced course in this series deals with the extra-physical process of "Looking Good". Starting with techniques of getting publicity without advertising, it leads the student to discover ways of starting rumors which aid his career. The course ends with subtle ways of bad-mouthing the competition. As was widely said, "It is not enough to succeed yourself; your best friend must fail."

Coping 308
2 hours 2 credits

The most advanced course in Coping involves techniques of getting others to do your work. The expert in this area will know ways of taking credit for the work and ideas of others.

Early Years 116
6 hours 3 credits

For the student just starting his career, practical techniques of solving real problems are explored. Going further that just an attractive resume and portfolio, this course aids the young professional in beefing up his resume with non-checkable items and shows how to write letters of recommendation from deceased celebrities.

Early Years 117
2 hours 1 credit

After the portfolios and resumes are ready, weekly field trips give the student experience in how to carry a portfolio in a high wind, how to get on and off a crowded bus or subway with a portfolio. Advanced work at the end of the semester covers transporting models in taxis and through rain storms.

Support Systems
6 hours 6 credits

The basic course in support systems is a key to a successful career. It explores ways of providing income while looking for work. (If a student is fortunate enough to have wealthy parents and has convinced them to be generous, this requirement can be waived on presentation of an up to date bank book.) The major emphasis of the term is on finding a rich mate. The procedures learning include: frequenting the watering holes of the rich; how to tell a wealthy man/woman from a door to door salesman/airline stewardess; checking Dun and Bradstreet; overcoming the fortune hunter image; wooing the rich; and marriage contracts.

Support System 232
3 hours 3 credits

The value of a suitable environment which reflects the taste and position of the student is discussed. Class tours of private homes, lofts, and Bloomingdale's rooms are required along with a subscription to *Architectural Digest*. Prerequisite: "Looking Good" Series.

Support System 302
3 hours 3 credits

A natural progression through #223, #224, #232, culminates in this class devoted to entertaining producers and network officials. Frequently termed the "Who You Know" course, ways are explored to entice useful people to your home, obligate them, impress them, and follow up the contracts. Also covered are suitable presents, called bribes.

Support Systems 303
3 hours 3 credits

As an extension of #302, the student is taught the importance of the barter of favor system of operation. Those in a position to employ others are often won over by personal favors. Covered are: designing lighting for a party, a bar mitzvah, a wedding, a funeral.

Ivied Walls 125
3 hours 3 credits

The basic course for those seeking academic careers should be taken in the same term as #116. This class takes the place of Coping 206 and stresses the first impression made by an academic job applicant. Attention is paid to tweed jackets, length of hair, beard maintenance, and pipe smoking for non-smokers.

Ivied Walls 230
4 hours 6 credits

"Stepping Over the Bodies" is the popular name for this course, which offers information about promotion and tenure procedures. The uses of publication are stressed. Methods are explored by which the student can write articles which sound impressive without saying anything. It is shown why articles in *The Drama Review* are most likely to win promotions while articles in *Lighting Dimensions* lead to demotion.

Ivied Walls 231
3 hours 3 credits

Professional work while teaching is discussed in this important class. While some faculties deplore any activity that makes money, others are very impressed by the glamour of professional experience. The student is taught to arrange his teaching schedule so that he can travel around the country on professional jobs and hardly ever meet a class. The advanced work in this course explores ways to use students as unpaid assistants.

Ivied Walls 340
2 hours 3 credits

To complete the academic series, this course proposes ways to recruit students. Areas covered are: jokes and witty anecdotes for the classroom, giving higher grades than other professors, X-rated films for classroom use.

Advanced Technical Problems 425
12 hours 12 credits

Affectionately known as "Making Mountains out of Molehills", this course covers those difficult lighting tasks which are not dealt with in most lighting courses. Ways are examined to best light aging stars, dogs, and sea lions. Special attention is paid to Restoration cleavages. Because new styles of theatre have made new demands, lighting techniques are proposed for increasing the size, three dimensionally, and importance of pudenda.

Application forms and further information are available from the University of Southern Forty-Second Street, Box 0, Times Square Station, New York, Iowa 470978652.

"Education At Last"!!

Appendix A

Shop Orders

Basics. The most important thing to remember about a shop order is that it is a legally binding rental order. Any reputable electrical equipment rental shop will bid on and then deliver *only* the things the shop order specifies. If the designer does not list C-clamps or sidearms, all units will arrive with only the yoke — and no way of mounting the units. If the designer does not call for a work light, or switchboard feeder cables, or worklights for the switchboard, he simply won't get them, which can be very awkward if he happens to be opening in Ashtabula, Ohio, or Keokuk, Iowa! Pages 433 to 435 present an actual shop order (from the *Pontiac '74* auto show) which will be used as an example in the discussions that follow.

The Title Page. The first page of a shop order needs to contain the following information:

1. show title
2. producers or producing firm (who will sign the checks for payment)
3. load-in date and place (the rental firm figures out how to pack and deliver the rented items to the designated theatre in time for load-in
4. load-out date and place (final performance and place, so the rental firm can calculate the return of equipment to their place of business)
5. the lighting designer's address and telephone number (in case the rental firm has questions)
6. a shorthand summary of major rental items (switchboards and luminaires — not accessories, etc.) used for quick calculations of the rental bid price.

Equipment Breakdown. A brief introductory note is useful before the actual equipment breakdown is listed. For example, if all luminaires in the order are to be 750 watt, the shop order should say so in the introductory note to avoid repetition in the equipment list. If the designer wishes to have a double set of color frames (for a color change on the road), this should be mentioned in the introductory note. As a last example, if a designer wishes all units to have quartz lamps rather than incandescent, the introductory note should make it clear up front.

Next the shop order should list *all* units (luminaires) and *all* accessories by mounting position. The designer wants the rental firm to pack everything in properly labeled boxes so that they will be sent to the right part of the theatre while the show is being hung. The "balcony rail" portion of the sample shop order at the end of Appendix A calls for an additional five 8-foot pipe lengths and ten extension stands 6 feet tall (not used in theatres where balcony front spotlights are placed in existent "pans"). With an automobile industrial show, some of the theatres may not have a proper balcony front mounting position, or a production may be playing to a small, select audience that is not using the balcony for seating. It is much quicker (saving expensive stagehands' time) to hang fixtures in a balcony this way, rather than attempting to fit spotlights into the theatre's existent "pans" or "cones."

There is a difference between cables and jumpers. A *cable* has a female pin connector (or twistlock) on one end and a stage plug (also called "pocket-plug" because it fits the old standard floor pockets) on the other. A *jumper* has a pin connector or twistlock on *both* ends.

On the equipment list, cable lengths and bundles are specified. These are easy to calculate by using the ground plan of the theatre and light plot and measuring the distance to the switchboard location. Vertical runs (the drop down to the stage floor from an electrical pipe, for example) must be added. For safety, and to cover the fact that a given cable may plug into the most distant part of the switchboard, 20 feet of extra cable should be specified. Nothing is more frustrating (nor better proof to the electrician of a designer's amateur status) than feeder cables from lighting luminaires which are two to three feet too short to plug into the switchboard.

As for bundling: Good rental firms will bundle cables into groups of four to eight cables with friction tape ties every two to three feet, and then coil and tie the resulting cable bundle (and label it). More than eight to ten cables per bundle tend to make the bundle awkward to handle and unmanageable. One bundle will be the "short run" to the luminaires on an overhead electrical pipe which are nearest to the switchboard. One bundle is apt to be the "middle run" for the luminaires in the middle of the pipe. And the "long run" supplies power to those most distant from the switchboard on a given pipe. Specifications for the FIRST ELECTRIC PIPE call for 18 cables in bundles of 6, 100 feet to 125 feet long. The rental shop can (and will) work out the rest. Multiconductor cables are now available from the better rental houses.

"Pipe stiffeners" are also called for under FIRST ELECTRIC PIPE. A pipe stiffener is basically a sidearm without the T fitting. It is clamped to the electric pipe and then tied to the steel cable or hemp supporting the pipe. It prevents the electrical pipe from turning or revolving when luminaires are clamped to it and "winged out."

"Pipe bumpers"—C-clamps that each have a circular pipe (or band of steel) circle—clamp to the electric pipe and deflect flying scenery or drops past the luminaires when there is a working (moving) pipe of scenery near the lights. Without pipe bumpers scenery would inevitably either knock out the color frames, refocus the luminaires, or hang up on shutter knobs.

The work light (a standard 1000-watt PS lamp in a metal cage guard with a C-clamp for attachment to the electric pipe) terminates at the stage manager's desk. The rental house knows to supply this with a household toggle switch and a standard household (rather than stage) male plug that *does not* go through the show switchboard.

When x-rays or striplights are called for, the designer should *be specific* (see specs for SEVENTH ELECTRIC PIPE.) The designer should indicate the lengths wanted, the exact lamp type, the number of color circuits, and (if it is not obvious) how the units are to be hung (hanger irons with C-clamps or chain hangers?). If PAR reflector lamps are involved, indicate which way the filament length is to be turned. (Those who are somewhat confused by these details should obtain a standard rental firm catalog from Four Star Stage Lighting, 585 Gerard Avenue, Bronx, New York 10451 *or* 3935 North Mission Road, Los Angeles, California 90031.)

The SEVENTH ELECTRIC PIPE also calls for a 30-foot *asbestos cloth* with ties. The rental firm will (reluctantly) supply asbestos, but only when the designer specifies it. Asbestos or other fire retardant cloth should be called for whenever an electric pipe is near working scenery or flammable drapes.

The presention of the bid specs should move logically from front-of-house (FOH) through to the final overhead pipe; then give specs for all vertically mounted boom (tree or tower) units, from FOH to upstage; and then give specs for units on the stage floor or those attached to the scenery.

On the booms each sidearm and its size is specified. In addition, extra C-clamps are called for since the show might well play in houses on the tour that do not have side box mounting positions. In that case, the electrician uses C-clamps instead of sidearms and mounts these luminaires on the extreme ends of the balcony front.

The lighting designer *must be prepared for any eventuality,* should specify the height and required pipe lengths and pipe threading for each boom, as well as the type of boom base (flange or 50-pound bell base). "Tie-off rings" should be specified for the top of the booms. The show carpenter will "spot" boom "safety" tie-off lines to each boom backstage from the grid. If the rental firm does not have tie-off rings (and frequently they do not), the specifications at least make it aware that the designer wants *something* to tie off the boom support rope, and accordingly the firm will provide extra C-clamps to use to prevent the rope tie from sliding off the end of the boom pipe.

Often there is a need for "ganging" two or more luminaires in a given mounting position to go to the switchboard on a single cable. In this case the designer must specify a "twofer" (also called a "martingale" and a "spider" in some places). The shop order may call for three-way females; however, most rental firms stock very few of these.

Details on floor- and set-mounted specials must be quite specific. If the design calls for striplights on the stage floor, the designer must remember to call for trunnions (legs), or none will arrive. If the strips are to set and strike, call for castered trunnions; if castered floor stands or units with an iris are needed, call for them, too. The same goes for barn doors (two-door or four-door?) and funnels (hi-hats). The shop order should be specific concerning followspots: the type, spare lamps or carbons, and cables to connect them to power sources. If gobos are in the plan, "pattern slots" should be called for each luminaire which will receive a gobo. Anything that the designer leaves out (because it was in his mind and not on paper), the rental firm will leave out, and that can get to be most awkward.

Switchboards. The designer must also be specific about switchboards. Include the anticipated feeder cable run to the theatre's source of power, and also specify work lights (commonly "backing" or "entrance" striplights — those small 2-4-6-8 lamp portable striplight units with hooks on one end).

Most rental firms stock switchboards in standard sizes. Since the advent of memory switchboards and SCR (silicon controlled rectifiers) electronic dimmers in compact packages, switchboard use is in a state of flux. The designer should find out what the rental firms to be used or from whom bids are being solicited have available. The designer can call for wooden "cable racks" to surround the board, which will help everyone to cope with the large mass of "spaghetti" which centers there.

Spare equipment is vital and should be specified. A few extra luminaires, some spare cables, some extra jumpers —

these items are most handy to have along! The director may come up with a "life-and-death" need for "just one more special," or some of the rented equipment may be defective. There should be spares along for *any* emergency.

Perishables. Supplies which must be purchased (rather than rented) are listed at the end of the shop order. These include all color media, spare lamps, spare fuses, tie-line, friction and electrical tape, masking tape (to label the switchboard), gaffer's tape (to tape down cables on the floor), shipping or label tags (to tie on cables if "replugs" are involved), etc. Anything the designer does not order will not show up in the neatly labeled wooden shipping crates that come from the rental firm.

The following is an actual shop order from the *Pontiac '74* auto show.

Shop Order

EQUIPMENT LIST
PONTIAC '74
2 companies

PRODUCED BY: Communico, Inc., 1315 North Hwy. Drive, Fenton, MO 63026

PRODUCERS: Ed Powell & Larry La Rue
(314) 938-5450

LIGHTING DESIGNER: Lee Watson, 2387 N.Y. Ave., Huntington Station, NY 11746
(516) 549-8925

FOR LOAD-IN: Co. #1 — Mon., July 16th at Ford Auditorium, Detroit, Mich.
Co. #2 — Load-out Fri., July 27th to Boston

FINAL PERFORMANCE: Co. #1 — Lake Tahoe, Nev., Aug. 15th
Co. #2 — Atlanta, Ga., Aug. 13th

TOTAL UNITS SUMMARY:

To assist in bids only — checklist for exact numbers and wattages:

4½" × 6½"	2
6" × 9"	22
6" × 12"	44
6" × 16"	14
8" Fresnels	16
10" or 12" Fresnels	4
Effects projector	1
7' 6" R-40 x-rays	8
10' PAR 56 x-rays	12

9' PAR 64 x-rays 7
Switchboards

Note: All units with lamp, clamp or sidearm, and color frame. Bundle all cables.
* *Must* be quartz lamp units
** *Should* be quartz lamp units
† *Must* be 10–12" Fresnels, only

BALCONY RAIL:

6 . . . . . . 6" × 12" ERS, 750-watt
2 . . . . . . 6" × 16" ERS, 1000-watt
3 . . . . . . 8" Fresnels, 2000-watt quartz
5 . . . . . . 8' pipes
10 . . . . . . 6' extension stands with C-clamps
1 . . . . . . bundle of 7 cables, 250' long (asbestos-wrapped, if available)
1 . . . . . . bundle of 4 cables, 230' long (asbestos-wrapped, if available)
3 . . . . . . 4-way barn doors, 8" Fresnels

FIRST ELECTRIC PIPE:

6 . . . . . . 6" × 9" ERS, 1000-watt
3 . . . . . . 6" × 12" ERS, 750-watt
2 . . . . . . 6" × 12" ERS, 1000-watt
3 . . . . . . 8" Fresnels, 1000-watt quartz
4 . . . . . . 10" Fresnels, 2000-watt quartz
50' . . . . . . asbestos
18 . . . . . . bundles of cables, 100–125' long
4 . . . . . . pipe stiffeners
4 . . . . . . pipe bumpers
3 . . . . . . 4-way barn doors, 8" Fresnels
4 . . . . . . 4-way barn doors, 10–12" Fresnels

Note: Other pipes deleted in this presentation.

SEVENTH ELECTRIC PIPE:

2 . . . . . . 10' sections PAR 56 WFL, 300-watt striplights, 3 color circuits
2 . . . . . . 10' sections PAR 56 MFL, 300-watt striplights, 3 color circuits
4 . . . . . . short pipe hangers for striplights (strips hang 2 above, 2 below, on same pipe)
4 . . . . . . long pipe hangers for striplights (see above)
3 . . . . . . pipe stiffeners
3 . . . . . . pipe bumpers
25' . . . . . . asbestos
*1 . . . . . . 10" Fresnel, 2000-watt quartz
1 . . . . . . 4-way barn door, 8" Fresnel
13 . . . . . . bundle of cables, 150–120' long

BOX BOOMS (FRONT-OF-HOUSE), L & R:

8 . . . . . . 6" × 12" ERS, 1000-watt
8 . . . . . . 18" sidearms

8 . . . . . . C-clamps (carried as extra for use when boxes not used)
2 . . . . . . 12' boom pipes (threaded both ends) with 50 lb. Bell bases
2 . . . . . . threaded couplings and 8' additional lengths of pipe (threaded at both ends) to extend booms to 20' when needed
2 . . . . . . boom tie-off rings (threaded)
2 . . . . . . boom asbestos, 5' each
1 . . . . . . bundle of 4 cables, 150' (asbestos wrapped, if possible)
1 . . . . . . bundle of 4 cables, 75' long (asbestos wrapped, if possible)

FIRST BOOMS SL & SR:

2 . . . . . . 4½" × 6½" ERS, 750-watt
2 . . . . . . 6" × 9" ERS, 750-watt
2 . . . . . . 6" × 9" ERS, 500-watt
4 . . . . . . 6" × 12" ERS, 750-watt
2 . . . . . . 6" × 12" ERS, 500-watt
12 . . . . . . 18" sidearms
2 . . . . . . 20' booms with 6" flange base
6 . . . . . . twofers
1 . . . . . . bundle of 3 cables, 150' long
1 . . . . . . bundle of 3 cables, 75' long

FLOOR EQUIPMENT:

1 . . . . . . cable, 75' long for color wheel, Lectern R (scene shop provides unit)
1 . . . . . . cable, 125' long for color wheel, Lectern L (scene shop provides unit)
1 . . . . . . cable, 200' long (*must be* 3-wire throughout) for control circuits in Primitive Car (flys out; travels in traveller track)
2 . . . . . . 5-lb. jars of ammonium chloride (sal ammoniac) for 2 heater cones
*6 . . . . . . 8" Fresnels, 1000-watt quartz
6 . . . . . . 8" Fresnel floor bases
6 . . . . . . 4-way barn doors for 8" Fresnels
6 . . . . . . squares of asbestos to cover Fresnels
3 . . . . . . 150' long cables
3 . . . . . . 75' long cables

FOLLOWSPOTS:

2 . . . . . . Strong Trouper Arc Follow Spots with color booms, etc.
2 . . . . . . 100' cables, hub to hub with adapters for male Edison two-prong and three-prong twistlock
2 . . . . . . glass UV (blacklight) filters

SWITCHBOARDS: (All boards to have feeder cables that make up to 100' feeders. See designer.)

1 . . . . . . cable rack for boards
2 . . . . . . backing strips for worklights

SPARE EQUIPMENT:

2 . . . . . . 100' cables   12 . . . . . . 6–15' jumpers

```
2 . . . . . . 25' cables        6 . . . . . . twofers
10 . . . . . . 25' jumpers      3 . . . . . . pipe bumpers
```

PERISHABLES:

10% spare lamps
spare boxes of switchboard fuses
tieline
friction tape
masking tape
2 cases spare carbons for Strong Troupers (4 performances & rehearsal time for each company)

COLOR:

```
48 . . . . . .sheets Roscolene
83 . . . . . .sheets Roscolar
12 . . . . . .sheets Cinemoid
```

PERISHABLES BREAKDOWN:

COLOR MEDIA: See attached COLOR LIST for sheets needed.

FUSES: 3 boxes, 15-amp buss fuses
       2 boxes, 20-amp plug fuses

4 200-amp buss fuses
4 400-amp buss fuses
2 600-amp buss fuses

TIELINE: 3 balls tie-on twine

TAPE: 24 rolls friction tape
      6 rolls electrical tape

MASKING TAPE: 4 rolls 2" masking tape
              2 rolls 1¼" masking tape

CARBONS: 2 cases, 250 per case, L0700 carbons

LAMPS:

```
3 . . . . . . R-40 Spot, 150-watt
3 . . . . . . PAR 64 MFL, 500-watt
3 . . . . . . R-40 Flood, 300-watt
6 . . . . . . PAR 56 WFL, 300-watt
6 . . . . . . PAR 56 MFL, 300-watt
```
Spare lamps for focusable units (ERS and Fresnels) cannot be exactly
specified until 10% of quartz supplied and number of 10–12" Fresnels
is determined. *Estimate 10% spare lamps* for these units.

Appendix B

Buying Guides

By Robert Benson

THEATRE LIGHTING INSTRUMENTS[419]

Determining Your Needs and Evaluating Units

As a general statement, you get what you pay for when buying lighting instruments, as you do when buying most products. How the value is received for the money spent can vary from one manufacturer to the other. One may give you superior optical (light output) performance, and another excellent mechanical construction. Should you get both, and an attractive price as well, the manufacturer may well have reached the "Acme of Perfection" that one famous New York company claimed in a 1905 advertisement.

The long term cost of equipment is an equation that balances the first cost, the durability of the equipment versus its intended use; the cost per hour of lamp operation, and the projected replacement cost of such items as lenses, shutter blades, reflectors, wiring, etc.

On occasion, the expensive product may be the one that requires the least long-term maintenance, and uses the best range of lamps for the most economical operation. If you are purchasing what could be considered disposable equipment, for short-term use and disposition, the least expensive units might be the likely choice, given adequate light output.

In analyzing a piece of lighting apparatus for potential purchase, several factors may be considered for any type of unit being selected:

1. The specific purpose to which the equipment will be put.
2. Overall light output, field quality and light distribution, and general operating efficiency.
3. The mechanical construction, including size, weight, and durability.
4. The energy consumption vs. output of light.
5. Lamp availability. Range of wattages, lamp lives, Kelvin temperatures. Local purchasing availability.
6. Adherence to local codes, and/or Underwriters' Laboratories, Inc. listings.
7. First cost.
8. Long-range cost.

Use of Equipment

All equipment should be selected for purchase with specific uses in mind. In the beginning, a theatre may be sup-

[419] Robert Benson, "Theatre Lighting Instruments: Determining Your Needs and Evaluating Units," Theatre Crafts, vol. 12, no. 3 (March/April 1978), pp. 13, 72.

plied with a large number of basic units. These can consist of 6″ or 8″ ellipsoidal reflector spotlights, and 6″ or 8″ fresnel lens spotlights. Obviously the size and type of theatre will govern the precise choice. Striplights of one or more wattages and reflector types may be needed for general washes and drop lighting, and in some theatres, a permanent cyclorama lighting rig may be required.

There will likely be a need for using striplights on the floor as ground row lighting, and for lighting translucencies, rear projection screens, the bottom of the cyclorama, backings, etc. General purpose scoops or floodlights are often purchased in this basic list, as well as more specialized units like beam projectors and high wattage PAR-lamp holders.

How Much Light?

Evaluate the lighting job to be done from each lighting position, then determine the type of instrument you wish at that location. A rule of thumb used by many designers requires each spotlight, at each location, to deliver 50 footcandles in white light to its designated acting/playing area. If this is achieved from all locations (or nearly so), you will have an evenly blended basic lighting scheme over the entire area from all directions and sources.

This is not the way to light a show, but having this even field of light forms a solid foundation for an overall lighting plan. This formula is advanced for the purpose of equipment selection only. Clearly, the moment we use any color, the relationships all change.

Be realistic about the mounting location, the throw distance, and the wattage selected. It is foolish to put a 2000w fresnel spotlight on a pipe with a 15′ throw unless you are specifically looking for an intense blaze of light. It would be terrible as an acting area light at that distance. Conversely, using a 750w fresnel to achieve that blaze of light is bound to be a big disappointment.

There are units that can span these needs where some compromise seems necessary. One series of fresnels can accommodate a 500/750/1000w lamp series. Another, the 1000/1500/2000w lamp types. Keep in mind that dimming a lamp that is too bright shifts the color (in some cases quite a lot). If you are trying to achieve sparkling clarity of color, your lamps will have to run at or near full brightness (i.e., very white light) to make this work. This is another reason to carefully select the proper wattage in the beginning.

There will be a time when you need framing units for quite long throws. It is impractical to buy a wide angle unit, and shutter down to the field you need. The light output will be pretty tepid. There are some new units on the market that offer variable lens positions, or zoom optics for variable field diameters. These might be a better choice if you feel you must have a multi-purpose unit. Otherwise, buy the single purpose, narrow angle units for that long throw, and the wide angle units for the short throws. The size of the acting area field will vary with each designer and each show and theatre. A lighting area from 10′ to 15′ in diameter is typical, with plenty of overlapping of adjacent areas.

There are large differences in the light output, range of field angles, flatness of field, ability to shutter cleanly, presence or lack of chromatic aberration, extraneous halos, or lighting patterns and the like, among the various manufacturers' products. Not all items of any one manufacturer will be bad or good. Most can provide you with data taken, either by an independent testing laboratory, or in conformance with those practices. On a large job, you can request that this be verified with a sample unit, to be held against the completion of the order.

Mechanical Considerations

The approach to mechanical assembly varies with the equipment designers. Some rivet everything together, presuming it will never have or need any service. Others see it differently and bolt or screw the assemblies together.

Some obvious things to look for could begin with the gauge of the metal used. Is it sturdy enough for your purposes? If it is a sheet metal housing, will small dents affect the optical performance? Will the unit retain end-to-end optical alignment after rough handling?

Does the hardware look durable? Is the attachment secure, and the underlying metal adequate to hold it? Is the finish durable? Is the wiring sound and well restrained as it enters the housing? Is it protected from excessive heat? Is relamping easy?

As the equipment is built, is it maintainable? With ease, or with difficulty? What kind of tools would be required? Can you accommodate the size and weight of the unit in the locations you plan for it? Where do replacement parts come from?

Performance/Energy Consumption

The optical design area is where some of the manufacturers go into rhapsodies of one-upping in their advertising efforts. Some with justification, but others may only be doing semantic tarantellas. However, for you, as the potential victim/buyer (and you can determine which you are), this is the most fertile area to explore when evaluating equipment.

Some of the newer ellipsoidal spotlights are considerably more efficient in terms of light output than those of only a few years ago. Careful selection in this area can mean a difference of about 50% in your light bill and your lamp costs. In new installations lower initial wiring costs, lower air conditioning requirements, and a lower initial demand factor from the utility company will be the rewards for careful buying.

For theatrical purposes, long life lamps are generally more desirable than those with shorter lives and high Kelvin temperatures. If you are doing television broadcasts, and using the equipment un-gelled, lamping with 3200° Kelvin lamps is practical. It is essential that the color temperatures be consistent on the performer's faces.

If no television taping or broadcasting is being done in the facility, the 2000-hour 3000° Kelvin lamps are a greater value. Some equipment is designed to take lamp ranges that offer all these combinations, some do not. Assess your real needs, and compare them to the available equipment. It goes without saying that equipment requiring special or exotic lamps may have down time if the lamp supply is remote or undependable.

Codes and Safety

No manufacturer is knowingly going to build equipment that is hazardous to use. However, competitive pressures cause some to cut corners pretty sharply. This will continue to happen as long as the dominant pressure in the market place is "cost first."

One assurance (at least of electrical safety in construction) is the listing of the unit by the Underwriters' Laboratories, Inc. or the Canadian Standards Association. U/L is a private, profit making firm operated by several fire insurance companies. Its function is to inspect products and set standards for electrical safety (in this case). If the product meets the criteria, they "list" it in their guides. Technically, they do not "approve" any product. Manufacturers whose products are listed can give you evidence of that fact with a listing number, or a guide card number. On direct inquiry U/L will advise if a specific catalogue numbered item is listed. It is interesting to note that the given manufacturer pays for the cost of the inspection and a fee to maintain the listing annually.

First and Last Cost

Generally speaking, the lighting equipment we use in our theatres today is less well made than the equipment our fathers used fifty years ago. Those were the days of heavy durable castings. Russian iron housings, manganese bronze fittings, and beautifully machined brass spindles and operating parts. But with all that durability, came weight and cost.

Today we don't want that weight, and we can't afford the cost of that beautiful machine work. After World War II, the reopened market for lighting equipment was characterized by a highly competitive race to recapture the customer. Inevitably the goal was to make something cheaper than the other guy in order to build up sales volume, not to make something better. This pressure was generated by the purchasers as well, and like many other industries and crafts, the quality began to disappear because few would pay for it. Many buyers gave lip service to high quality, but not many opened their wallets while speaking.

It is remarkable that in spite of these pressures some very innovative designs and manufacturing processes did evolve. Significant gains were made in the area of performance.

Bidding/Substitutions

Most public institutions require that equipment be purchased through open bidding processes. This does not preclude your writing clearly defined performances and mechanical specifications.

Once your real needs have been determined, assemble a realistic specification that is clear, to the point, and one that you know one or more manufacturers can supply as you wish. Don't make a fruit salad of it so no one can legitimately bid honestly. Do not pick one feature from each of 10 units and expect anyone to build it.

If you are purchasing a large complement of equipment, and you feel that the integrity of the specifications and the bid may be jeopardized by bidders who have no real intention of meeting your requirements, it is common to require that any successful bidder post a performance bond, guaranteeing his obligation to meet your performance specifications.

PURCHASING GUIDE FOR ELLIPSOIDAL REFLECTOR SPOTLIGHTS[420]

[420] Robert Benson, "Purchasing Guide For Ellipsoidal Reflector Spotlights," Theatre Crafts, vol. 12, no. 5 (September 1978), pp. 13–14, 16.

This spotlight unit, so named because it uses the efficient ellipsoidal reflector, is more frequently known in the trade as a Leko, a Klieglight, or by one of the other manufacturer's trade names.

It characteristically is a unit with framing shutters, a fixed field angle, and is often equipped with an iris and/or a pattern slot for the projection of gobos. In North American lighting practice, it is the workhorse unit for most theatrical applications. Field angles available vary from 50 degrees down to 5 degrees in width.

In this article I will not discuss why you would choose one field range or another, that being a design decision which can initiate this purchasing and comparison study. Once the decision is made to purchase units of a particular type, the following material should be helpful to you in comparison shopping.

As a lighting designer you are most concerned about light: light output, quality of light, flatness of field, ability to adjust this field, sharpness or softness of shutter lines, and chromatic aberration at the edge of the field or on shutter lines. These are the things you see as the designer, and the audience sees as representative of your intent. Behind that, however, is a lot of metal, glass, and wiring to make it happen.

These ellipsoidal reflector spotlights (the manufacturers call them fixtures) are commonly made as die-cast aluminum housing or with spun aluminum and steel housing. The die-cast units tend to be more rugged, but heavier.

The choice of lenses supplied falls into two general categories: plano-convex, or stepped. The first tends to give sharp shutter lines (cuts) and the latter a softer line. A good unit with P.C. lenses can be adjusted from sharp to soft edges. A Step lens unit goes from soft to softer.

Stepped lenses are usually molded with a low expansion borosilicate glass; Pyrex* is a similar formulation. Plano-convex lenses are available to the manufacturer in several grades; those with no treatment for heat stress; tempered glass, or heat-resistant material, again of the low expansion borosilicate type. The latter is by far the best and the most costly. The gain is freedom from frequent cracking of lenses and their subsequent regular replacement.

Some care is required to select lenses that do not have internal coloration (usually yellow or green). The spotlight manufacturer should do this grading, but the buyer should be aware that this is an inherent problem with heat-resisting lenses, and certain glass types. You do not have to accept off-color lenses. Currently the best quality lenses come from France and Japan.

Step lenses have vertical risers molded into the lens construction. To minimize surface brightness on the lens, these risers are often painted dark gray or black, with a baked-on finish. These painted risers also reduce flare from the shutter blade images and in general, bring more control to the beam, but may (in some units) produce soft rings of light in the field. In any event, the painting does reduce the light transmission by about 10%. Be aware that certain lenses are almost useless as spotlight lenses unless they are supplied with the risers painted. Without this treatment, most shuttering control is lost.

The mechanical assembly will vary from one manufacturer to another, and the ease of disassembly for maintenance or repair should be considered. Some make it easy to remove a reflector, others, almost impossible. Some take great care in protecting the wiring from excessive heat, and others take little care at all. Some manufacturers use the Alzak† plating process for reflector surfacing, others use equally efficient electro-brightening processes, and others much less expensive (and probably less durable) finishes. Most reflectors look good when new. Heat is the ultimate destroyer of the surface.

Traditionally shutter blades have been made of nichrome steel or stainless steel alloys. Generally the life and durability of the blade has been a function of the thickness of the material. One manufacturer is currently offering aluminum shutterblades; however, as yet there is little field experience to establish the reliability of this material.

Several companies have placed zoom-optic spotlights on the market in the last few years. The units offer variable field angle adjustments by either moving lenses manually in a lens tube, or by operating rack and pinion gears, or slide adjustments to change the relationship of two internal lenses to each other and to the gate. These provide varying field diameters, and can provide the operating function of two or more fixed field units. The units tend to be rather larger than the conventional spot, and more expensive. However, for certain installations, they are very satisfactory. In most cases the light output is quite high.

If the equipment being purchased is to be used out of doors, especially without rain protection, consideration should be given to those units that are made predominately of aluminum. Steel can be primed with zinc chromate before the normal finish is applied, but unless good maintenance is provided, they will deteriorate more rapidly than the aluminum units.

One application for the ellipsoidal reflector spotlight that has assumed somewhat larger importance in the last few years is that of a pattern projector. With the increased availability of good stock patterns, and the more widespread knowledge of the use and preparation of patterns, designers are making more and more use of light and shade in basic lighting concepts. The typical plano-convex lens units will project considerable detail in these patterns. The step lens units will handle adequately large scaled or bolder patterns.

When making comparison between units that you may buy, be realistic. If your primary consideration is buying light, i.e., a field angle and a light level, you may find that one manufacturer can give you this with a 3½" lens unit, while another may require a larger 6" unit to produce the same results. One may be able to produce the same light level with a 6" unit that another manufacturer can only provide in a more expensive 8" unit. Begin with the lighting performance for comparison, then work back toward the hardware.

You generally get what you pay for in equipment. Don't expect the finest hardware and construction detailing to be compatible with the lowest price. Don't expect the highest light output or the best overall performance to be the cheapest. But it is possible to select those features and performance characteristics you need from many of the units on the market.

The Checklist

1. What lamp type/socket series is used in the unit? Are long-life lamps, as well as shorter life (higher Kelvin temperature) lamps available? Do these lamps interchange with any other units in your inventory?

2. How well is the lamp housing ventilated?

[421] *Robert Benson, "Selecting a Lighting Control System,"* Theatre Crafts, *vol. 11, no. 6 (November/December 1977), pp. 84, 86–88, 90, 92.*

3. How is the housing built? Die-cast, sheet metal, etc?

4. What metal(s) are used in the construction?

5. Is the assembly put together with rivets, screws, bolts? How does this affect reasonable maintenance requirements?

6. What brightening or plating process is used for the reflector? (Presumably, they will all be aluminum.)

7. Is the reflector faceted? Flatted or double-flatted? (This kind of surface treatment usually produces a smoother field of light.)

8. What material is used for the shutter blades? How thick is it?

9. Do the blades operate in two or four planes? (Is there any opposite shutter interference in actual operation?)

10. Is the shutter area provided with good ventilation?

11. Is there a pattern slot? Standard/optional?

12. Can an iris be installed if required? If so, do you lose either the shutters or the pattern slot in doing so?

13. Is the inside of the lens tube painted or treated in such a way as to minimize internal light reflections?

14. Is the unit well-balanced and/or provided with secure locking hardware?

15. Is the yoke rigid? Will the unit turn 360° under the C-clamp? Will it pass through the yoke rotating vertically?

16. How are the lenses mounted? Are they easy to replace? Is expansion room provided for the lens to expand and contract during heating and cooling?

17. Does the unit make any mechanical noises during this heating and cooling process?

18. What type of lenses are provided? Step? Plano-convex?

19. What type of glass is used in the lenses? Heat-resisting? Tempered? No treatment? Are the lenses clear of color or imperfections? (Molding swirls in step lenses will produce aberrations in the field, as well as poorly defined shutter lines.)

20. Is the hardware (nuts and bolts) to U.S. thread standards or metric?

21. Is the wiring protected internally from heat? Protected as it leaves the housing? Good strain relief?

22. What are the leads made of? (Type of wire and insulation)

23. Are the leads protected with sleeving from damage?

24. Is the unit grounded? (3-wire)

25. How convenient is the re-lamping system? Does it require tools? Can it be done from the rear; the front; from above or below, or from a ladder?)

26. Is the lamp adjustable in the reflector? How? Are tools required?

27. Are there operating handles on the unit? Are they insulated? Do they appear rugged enough for the service you intend?

28. How much light leaks out of the unit in operation?

29. What comes with the unit as standard equipment in the normal price quoted? Clamp? Connector, installed? Color frame? Lamp?

30. Is the unit UL listed? If so, to what maximum wattage lamp?

31. What warranty does the manufacturer offer on the unit?

---

* Pyrex is a registered trademark of Corning Glass Works.
† Alzak is a registered trademark of the Aluminum Co. of America.

SELECTING A LIGHTING CONTROL SYSTEM[421]

For many theatre directors and technical personnel, the day the board of directors or the financial office says that you can buy that new lighting control system is one mixed with joy, relief, and no little apprehension.

Fifteen years ago, there were six companies in the U.S. that were considered the major suppliers of lighting control systems. There were also a number of smaller, regional firms who did occasional stage lighting control installations. Today there are at least 50 companies supplying stage lighting equipment. The original six are still around, dividing the total business into ever-decreasing shares with all the new companies. The dilemma faced by the buyer today is no different than it ever was, but his choice of equipment is dazzling.

In the educational theatre, being "part of the learning process" is the norm. You, however, shouldn't expect to be part of the manufacturers' learning process, at your expense. We are a society trained to anticipate and welcome new things quickly, including complex technological developments. The fact is that all these developments require some proving time, in the lab, and in the field. If you choose to be part of this proving process, do it with your eyes open.

We are in an era of rapidly advancing technology, and it seems that each month brings some new and exciting device, circuit, gadget, or supplier, that has a moment of glory. Ultimately, of course, the decision must be made, equipment and companies evaluated, and an order placed. Today the combined joy and curse is that there may be something better available two years hence, but if you need a system today — you need it today.

So with a plethora of goodies, how do you make a selection? As a buyer of technical products you can establish some guidelines that can justify your final decision. Those that would satisfy a prudent comptroller, or yourself, if you are spending your own hard-to-come-by cash.

Evaluating Needs

First, you do have to evaluate realistically your own needs. This means taking a hard look at the size of your facility, its operating schedule, its operating staff, the complexity of the productions, the scale of their mounting (scenery, costumes, and lighting), and your overall operating budget.

Then, draw up the outline requirements as to numbers of dimmers, capacity of each, feeder capacity and arrangement (if special), size of patch panel including size and number of branch circuitry and finally, but most importantly, the kind of control unit you want to operate these dimmers.

Ideally, at this point, one should hire a competent theatre consultant to work with you on all of these needs. For the purpose of this discussion however, let us presume that you must handle this yourself.

In some cases the technical sales staff of the larger manufacturers can assist you with outlining these basic require-

ments and if you wish, they will prepare detailed specifications for bidding purposes, when that is required. You should realize the manufacturer's specifications will, of course, reflect their particular equipment designs and features, to the exclusion (generally) of most other suppliers. If this is understood and acceptable to you, then proceed.

If you find yourself in the position of having to prepare so-called "open" specifications, you will have to sanitize all the special features and gimmicks the manufacturer put in, and leave just the basic system requirements standing before the job is to be bid. This is not to say that you should remove all operating or electrical standards.

Choosing a Company

How do you choose the specific company to buy from or with which to work? This is the toughest part, but there are some rational ways to proceed. How you answer these questions will tend to guide you to the appropriate suppliers:

1. Is the equipment to be portable or fixed?
2. Is it to be purchased for short-term special purpose use, or for a permanent installation with a long life projected? (20 years is certainly reasonable).
3. What is the technical competence of the operating staff?
4. How much money do you have to spend?
5. Does the manufacturer, supplier selling the equipment actually manufacture the items? If not, where are they made? Where is the source of parts and service? Who will support the warranty?

As you will soon discover, some manufacturers will make only portable equipment, some only fixed systems, and several make both types. Some companies are new, some are old, some large, some very small.

Portable Systems

The question about short-term long-term use may determine how much you initially spend for a portable system. If you are producing a one-shot rock concert tour, and need the equipment to just last the tour, knowing it will be written off at the end, you may not wish to purchase high-priced equipment. You may be satisfied with selling it for whatever value remains at the end of the tour. If however — due to the nature of the tour, the reputation of performer or the size of the rooms being played — you cannot hazard potential system failures, you should buy the best you can get.

A rental house making the same judgments would likely buy the most rugged equipment (mechanically and electrically), and the easiest to service. Availability of parts might be more important in their consideration than the initial cost.

Once you have identified two or three manufacturers that make portable equipment to your liking, ask these questions:

1. Where can service be obtained on the equipment (under the manufacturer)? Are maintenance manuals available?

2. How easy is the equipment to service for the buyer/user?

3. Is it well built for the use intended? Check the knobs, connectors, lifting handles, enclosure.

4. Does it perform to your satisfaction, electrically? Dimmer response, curve, noise filtering, operating voltage, etc.?

5. Does the equipment work well as a system? Are the cable interconnections simple and reasonable? Do the parts work well together? Do they stack, or physically attach to each other? Is it compact? How much does it weigh? How long would it take to set it up?

6. What is the manufacturer's system experience with the model you are interested in? How long has it been in service? How many units are in the field? Who is using them?

7. How do the users of the equipment rate it?

8. Is the equipment U/L Listed?

9. What is the cost relative to similar systems offering similar construction and operating features? You will never get precise comparisons. Do the most thorough evaluation you can.

Fixed Systems

Many of the questions above are also applicable to the consideration of a manufacturer of a large fixed system. Those concerning service, experience, system reliability, U/L Listing, and maintenance manuals among them. Others that are useful could be:

1. Are the dimmers plug-in modules, partially plug-in, or totally wired in place?

2. What is the size of the rack required for the system you need? What is the height (check door clearances, stair wells, and overall access to the dimmer room), the width and depth.

3. Can the bank be placed against a wall? Is rear access required? Desirable?

4. Can the dimmer modules be completely withdrawn from the rack where you plan to place the system?

5. Is the system convection cooled or forced-air cooled? What is the actual heat load generated by the dimmer rack? Should the room be air conditioned in your climate?

6. Is the dimmer module constructed for easy maintenance?

7. How do the operating characteristics of the dimmers compare with others being considered? Dimmer response time, curve, rise time (filtering), rating of rectifiers?

8. Is the equipment completely pre-wired when it arrives, or does it require assembly or wiring on the job site?

9. What kind of warranty is offered with the system?

10. Is the system U/L Listed? Are the dimmer modules U/L Listed as components?

11. How long has this particular dimmer module or system type been in service? Where? How many systems? Ask for names and users for reference.

12. What is the cost feature comparison with other systems being considered?

13. What is the service record of the company after the installation is complete? Get this from present users.

14. Does the company have the financial and engineering resources to supply installation assistance information? A thorough check-out at system turn-on time and good follow-up after that time? Check with other users on follow-up experience.

From this list you can see that a comparative analysis chart listing features may be the simplest approach to making this presentation of data for your own review.

A User Report

When asking opinions of users about their equipment you have to determine the basic technical competence (or interest) of the opinion-giver. You may also want to ascertain (clairvoyance would help) if they tend to function analytically or by-the-seat-of-their-pants. It is probably a good idea to find out if they actually bought or recommended the purchase of the equipment being discussed. Beware of both lavish praise of equipment, and glib showbiz put-downs. Try to ascertain from a user:

1. Did the equipment come in for the estimated, quoted, or projected cost?

2. Did it arrive when promised?

3. Were there any initial operational problems of a serious nature? Solid state equipment often has small scale start-up, or early life component failures. The operative word here is *serious*.

4. If there were, were they resolved promptly by the manufacturer/supplier?

5. Does the equipment perform up to the specifications promised?

6. Were there any unauthorized substitutions or changes in the equipment?

7. Is it holding up well mechanically and electrically?

8. Is it operationally stable?

9. Did adequate maintenance/service/operating manuals come with the equipment?

10. Would you buy another system of this type from the same manufacturer/supplier? This last question is the expression of the buyer's evaluation of the company that supplied him the equipment.

The practice of all aspects of the theatre-craft is one requiring discrimination in the selection of colors, scale, placement, and texture of everything that is placed on the stage. Stage lighting is the visual glue that binds all the other visual elements together, and its control and selection of control equipment should be subject to the same degree of discrimination, which can also be defined, as the exercise of good judgment.

The evaluation of the company you plan to buy from is probably more important than the specifics of the equipment itself. A number of firms have come and gone in the stage lighting industry. It seems to the industry leaders, who have millions invested in physical plant, engineering departments, research and development efforts and sales assistance programs, that anyone with a hot soldering iron and the G.E. circuit handbook thinks he is in the dimming system business. I might add that the same feeling is also true concerning the mini/micro-processing systems being offered. Here the stakes, and hazards, are even greater for the buyer.

The bottom line of this discussion is a charge to be realistic in your approach to these purchases. Having worked in the theatre most of my life, I know we often demand reliability from the lighting equipment we buy in excess of what we ask (or expect) from our cars. Yet, I regularly see derelict systems in the field, and agonizingly unhappy users. Most of this can be avoided, with thought and prudence.

THE LIGHTING CONTROL SYSTEM WARRANTY[422]

You've bought it, and now it doesn't work. It is usually a system that cost a lot of money — and one that you need in operation today. Most things bought for the theatre (except the obvious consumable items) do have some kind of warranty coverage. All lighting systems are covered in some manner. The manner of coverage varies with the manufacturer and the type of system. A statement about warranty is

[422] Robert Benson, "The Lighting Control System Warranty," Theatre Crafts, vol. 11, no. 5 (October 1977), pp. 8–10.

frequently printed in company literature but will be supplied on request from each manufacturer.

Starting Date

The date the warranty takes effect will vary with the type of equipment bought, the supplier's standard terms of sale, the terms of the construction specifications, or the client/user's terms set when the equipment was purchased.

Portable lighting control systems are usually under factory warranty for one year from date of shipment. For permanently installed control systems, that starting date can be the day the system was shipped or the first turn-on (preferred by the manufacturer), or the date the entire installation is complete and officially accepted by the architect/owner/user. The latter is usually preferred by the client group. In any case, one clearly identifiable date can and should be established that starts your own warranty clock ticking.

Shipping and Damage

In the case of equipment being installed permanently in a building, the electrical contractor usually receives and handles this apparatus, and will report any apparent or concealed shipping damage to the carrier, and file the necessary claim. If you are receiving portable dimming equipment yourself, check the shipping cartons or crates for any obvious damage, and uncrate it promptly to inspect for possible concealed damage.

Most equipment is shipped f.o.b. the factory. This means that the responsibility for the safe transport and arrival is in the hands of the carrier, and the shipper has no legal responsibility for its safety. If there is damage, the receiver (you) must file a claim with the carrier for compensation. This could mean replacement or repair. The manufacturer's invoice is usually required to support these claims. Very expensive equipment should be insured by the receiver/purchaser. The normal liability of common carriers rarely covers a major loss.

Troubleshooting Checklist

Assume the equipment arrived safely and was installed correctly. It has been working for a period of time before trouble arises and still is definitely covered by the warranty. What to do?

1. Check the operating instructions. Make absolutely certain that the problem is with the equipment and not with the operator. Operator error, however well-meaning, has sold a lot of airline tickets to field engineers.
2. Check the maintenance information supplied by the manufacturer. Determine if there are test procedures or troubleshooting guidelines to follow. Frequently the problem is an obvious one. You may not be able to solve it, but identifying the problem can save a lot of time.
3. Call your supplier, if this is not the original manufacturer. Ask for their suggestions.
4. Determine if there is a local or regional repair facility for this manufacturer's equipment. Call them and discuss the problem. This must be a factory-authorized repair facility to do in-warranty (i.e., no charge to you) repairs.
5. Failing all the above, call the factory.

Tell the factory operator you have a field maintenance problem and you want to talk to a technician or engineer. Give the technician or engineer as much of this data as you can:

1. The type, model, and serial number of the defective or malfunctioning item.
2. When it was bought and from whom.
3. The purchase order numbers, or the factory's shop order, work order, or invoice numbers. This will speed up the access to the files, and, hopefully, the solution to your problem.
4. Tell the technician/engineer as carefully, accurately, and precisely as possible, what is happening, or not happening with the equipment. Hysterics will probably make you feel better, but have them before you call the technician.
5. Tell the technician/engineer if you have a specific date by which the equipment must be operational. Be very

honest and realistic. Many manufacturers will fly a field service engineer to your theatre at their expense if they believe you are really in trouble. If they find you aren't, you may be billed for the trip. Certainly, if another problem occurs, don't be surprised if they are not super-responsive.

6. If the technician/engineer asks you to perform certain tests, checks, or procedures, or to investigate some part of the equipment, please do it. It may be that you have overlooked something fairly obvious (like a blown fuse), and can resume operation without his personal presence.

7. Give him your complete name, address, and telephone number, and an alternate person to speak to if you are not available. Likewise, get the technician/engineer's complete name, position, and telephone number.

8. Ask for a specific recommendation or plan of action as a result of your conversation.

Word of caution: Do not exceed your technical ability while testing, or attempting to check out the equipment. If you don't feel comfortable taking the covers off the units, and probing about, don't do it! Under no circumstances should you work alone. Coincidentally, if you do anything without supervision or instruction of the manufacturer, you will probably void the warranty.

Now What?

Now that you have called the heavies for assistance, what should they do for you? The manufacturer is concerned with two things when considering in-warranty repair work. Is the equipment still within its guarantee period? And, is this a legitimate claim? By legitimate, he will want to know if the failure seems to be from "natural" causes, i.e., from normal use, as opposed to abuse or damage to the equip-

ment. Damage can be caused in shipment, in original connection, or in operation by a careless electrician. This is a real concern, and one that usually can be resolved on inspection of the equipment.

It is incumbent on the manufacturer to use his best efforts to produce a prompt solution to your problem. It may be that you can handle it or it may have to be done by his staff. If it is an item that should be repaired at the factory, he may ask you to return it. The client usually pays the shipping charges both ways. If you must have a replacement part at once, the manufacturer may bill you for it; and then cancel the billing on the return of the defective item.

If you have an operational deadline and must have this equipment running, the manufacturer should do his best to bring this about. If this must be done on a weekend, or outside of "normal" working hours for non-theatre civilians, you may be asked to share in the cost of the manufacturer's overtime.

Fortunately, much of today's equipment is made with plug-in components and easily interchangeable parts. A lot of this maintenance can be telephone-diagnosed and performed by the user. If your problem is more serious, ask for on-site assistance from the manufacturer at his expense.

No reputable manufacturer is short-sighted enough to want to deliberately abuse the customer or ignore real needs. The industry is too small and the buying public too closely knit.

Some factories are quicker to respond than others. Some have better internal systems to handle this kind of service. They all must authenticate the in-warranty claim before processing, and you play a large part in how quickly this is done. What is being decided is not whether repairs will be done, but whether they should be done at no cost under your warranty.

Sources of Information

Both lighting design students and active practitioners need to be familiar with basic sources of information. These divide into four groups: (1) craft journals and periodicals, (2) standard basic reference works, (3) manufacturers and purveyors of equipment, and (4) reference material (for theatre, TV, film) concerning period lighting fixtures. While addresses (and subscription/purchase prices) change from time to time, a list of basic sources in each of these four categories is a helpful starting point.

Journals and Periodicals

Six are basic:

Theatre Crafts. Published nine times yearly (single copies $2.50) by Theatre Crafts, 135 Fifth Ave., N.Y., N.Y. Subscriptions: P.O. Box 630, Holmes, PA 19043–0630. Annual subscription rate: around $24. Telephone: (212) 677-5997. A quality publication; well edited, good paper, quality text and illustrations. It covers *all* theatre crafts: scenery, props, administration, sound, costumes, etc. An adequate amount of space is given over to articles involving lighting. Lighting coverage is wide-ranging in scope, frequently definitive, and sometimes most useful on the how-to level. Good regular departments covering new products, book reviews, and production reviews.

Lighting Dimensions. Published nine times yearly (single copies $3, $20 per year) by Lighting Dimensions, Inc. Same address as *Theatre Crafts.* Subscriptions: P.O. Box 425, Mount Morris, IL 61054–0425. A relatively new publication (1977) devoted exclusively to lighting. Quality paper; quality illustrations. Covers all fields of lighting, not just theatre. Has heavy emphasis on architectural lighting now. Formerly had heavy emphasis on lasers, holograms, television, concert lighting, disco lighting. Good regular departments covering industry activities, book reviews, and new products.

Theatre Design & Technology. Published quarterly (free to United States Institute for Theatre Technology members; available to libraries for $28 per year) by the USITT, 10 West 19th Street, Suite 5A, New York, NY 10011. Telephone: (212) 924-9088. Established scholarly journal covering all technical/design arts and crafts. Fair coverage of lighting, but major emphasis is on other tech/design areas.

Lighting Design + Application. Published monthly ($30 per year for members of IES; $35 per year for nonmembers) by the Illuminating Engineering Society of North America, 345 East 47th Street, New York, NY 10017. Telephone: (212) 705-7926. Intended for engineers and designers in architectural and display lighting in all areas of the lighting industry. It is also the house organ of the IES. Good illustrations; articles vary from a "Popular Mechanics" how-to level to a level that is quite scholarly and technical. This is the popular journal in this field. Information about regional IES activities, new products, upcoming conferences and events, obituaries, etc. Founded in July 1971.

Cue, Technical Theatre Review. Published six times yearly by Twynam Publishers, Ltd., Kitemore, Faringdon, Oxfordshire SN7 8HR, England. Telephone: 0367.21141. Subscription: $10.50 per year. Good paper and illustrations, some color. In-depth articles and news from British viewpoint. Book reviews, new products. Useful new publication.

TABS. House publication of Rank Strand Electric, Ltd., in London, P. O. Box 51, Great West Road, Brentford, Middlesex TW8 9HR, England. Good illustrations; quality paper; definitive writing with an emphasis upon new equipment, installations, and practices involving Rank Strand products (but worldwide in scope and coverage). Useful reference tool. Founded in 1937. Quarterly. Approximately 13,000 copies are distributed free each quarter by Rank Strand. Now replaced by *Strandlight,* a trade journal for Rank-Strand, Ltd.

Architectural Lighting. Published by Gralla Publications, 1515 Broadway, New York, NY 10036. Telephone: (212) 869-1300. Subscriptions: Around $50 per year for 12 issues. This is an invaluable new magazine (first published in January 1987) for all those in architectural lighting. *Lighting* magazine. A monthly Canadian magazine published by Kerrwil Publications, Ltd., 501 Oakdale Road, Downsview, Ontario, M3N 1W7 Canada. Telephone: (416) 764-1421. Subscription rate in 1989 was $24 (Canadian) per year in Canada, $48 outside. This publication, tied in with the IES (Toronto section), has slick paper, good graphics, and color photographs. It covers *all* aspects of lighting design and lighting designers in Canada. Most useful publication.

Three others, now discontinued, are of value for reference and can be found in libraries. They are as follows:

Light. The Magazine of Light. Published as a house organ for many years by the Lamp Department of the General Electric Co. Quality publication with good illustrations and definitive articles by GE engineers, designers, and sales personnel. Good research tool. Discontinued in 1977. Largely superseded by *Lighting Design + Application* magazine.

G.E. Review. Published for many years by General Electric six times each year. Another quality house organ and valuable reference tool. Even more slanted toward GE's output than either *TABS* or *LIGHT.*

Light Spectrum. 15 Park Circle, Centerport, NY 11721. A journal for lighting manufacturers. The Summer 1986 issue contains a "Lighting Buyers Guide" pp. BG1–BG32.

There are several quality magazines in selected specialty areas which from time to time contain some coverage of lighting. Check with libraries or magazine subscription dealers for the publication addresses and rates of the following:

SMPTE Journal. House publication of the Society of Motion Picture and Television Engineers. Highly technical, scientific house organ.

Opera News. Vital publication for keeping abreast of opera productions and reviews worldwide. A Metropolitan Opera Guild publication.

Dance magazine. Broad coverage of the world of dance by an established publication. The *Dance Annual* issue is an invaluable reference tool.

The American Cinematographer. Long-time, top publication by the American Society of Cinematographers. Well-illustrated; quality paper and writing. Covers the field of contemporary feature motion pictures in exemplary manner.

CIE Journal. Published by the Commission Internationale de L'Éclairage, Bureau Central, 52 Boulevard Malesherbes, 75008 Paris, France. Published twice yearly. Highly technical research articles on light and vision.

International Lighting Review. Published quarterly since 1949 by the Stichting (Foundation) Prometheus, Amsterdam, The Netherlands. P.O. Box 721, 5600 AS, Eindhoven, The Netherlands.

E-ITV (Educational and Industrial Television, The Techniques Magazine for Professional Video), P.O. Box 427, Dalton, MA 01227-9990.

LS&V magazine (Light, Sound & Video for the Nightclub & Entertainment Industries), 270 North Canon Drive, Beverly Hills, CA 90210. Telephone: (213) 278-7163. Published bimonthly since November/ December 1988.

These are several key magazines of quality in the fields of interest to the lighting designer. The architectural lighting specialist will find occasional lighting-related articles in: *Architectural Record, Interiors, Interior Design, Contract, Electrical Systems Design, Designers West, Restaurant and Hotel Design, Visual Merchandising and Store Design, Interior Design* (England), *Electrical Construction and Maintenance,* and *New York Construction News.* Other trade magazines (in the areas of disco, film, etc.) tend to deal less consistently with lighting design and to be more concerned with either the industry business news (arenas, industrial shows, conventions, etc.) or to be presented on a "newsstand" level. A few others exist for highly specialized areas, such as lasers and holograms.

Reference Books

There are many reference books available in specific areas of the industry. They are cited in footnotes throughout this handbook. The handbook itself is intended to serve partially as a basic reference source. Of particular note among reference books is *Lighting Issues in the 1980's,* National Bureau of Standards (NBS) publication #587. Edited by Arthur I. Rubin, it presents the results of the "Lighting Round-table" conference held by NBS and IES at the Shoreton Center, in New York City, June 14–15, 1979. Issued July 1980, the publication is available from the U.S. Department of Commerce.

See also: Christopher Edwards (editor), *The World Guide to Performing Arts Periodicals.* London; British Centre of the International Theatre Institute; 1982. A useful research tool listing in detail 636 periodicals. Already somewhat inaccurate and out of date, since information changes rapidly. No other such source exists, however.

Theatre Words, An International Vocabulary in Nine Languages. Published by IOSTT, compiled and edited for the Nordic Theatre Union, and formerly available in the United States from USITT (New York City) for around $15. It is now out of print. This handy 156-page booklet contains common theatre terminology in English, French, Spanish, Italian, German, Swedish, Hungarian, Czech, and Russian. It is also illustrated with line drawings. A separate supplement in Japanese is available. See also Verne Carlson, *Professional Cameraman's Handbook,* (Los Angeles; Birns & Sawyer, Inc.; 1984), which offers 2,500 film and TV terms in French, German, Italian, Spanish, Japanese, and English.

There are numerous volumes which cite and often describe the main theatre reference collections of designs in key (and sometimes obscure) public libraries. Theodore Fuchs's papers are at Brigham Young University in Provo,

Utah; Norman Bel Geddes's papers are at the University of Texas—Austin; both the Abe Feder and Jean Rosenthal collected papers are still available. Particularly of note are the theatre collections of the New York Public Library (Lincoln Center); Yale University Drama Library; the University of Wisconsin Center for Theatre Research at Madison; and the Library of Congress in Washington, D.C. Consult any good library reference center for more specific information needed by the advanced researcher.

Arriving here too late for inclusion in the main text of this *Handbook* (footnote #3, for example), is a fine basic text that deserves mention.

Ian McGrath, *A Process for Lighting the Stage*. Boston, London, Sydney, Toronto; Allyn and Bacon; 1990. 331 pages, illustrated, color.

Purveyors and Sources

Sources, prices, and sales literature should be obtained from two groups of suppliers: (1) those who assemble, manufacture, or fabricate lighting equipment and (2) local dealers and suppliers who serve as a marketing network (sometimes (1) and (2) are the same firm). Since addresses, phone numbers, and firms are ever-changing, consult any of the basic texts listed throughout this handbook (they almost always contain "Directories of Manufacturers"), or consult the following:

Theatre Crafts Directory. An annual, separate publication with nearly everything a designer might need to know. Invaluable.

Lighting Dimensions Manufacturers' and Buyers' Guide. Summer issue of the magazine. Newer and not as compactly organized as the *Theatre Crafts* directory but of value because of *Lighting Dimensions'* wider range of lighting interests: disco, film, TV, lasers, holograms, etc.

Simon's Directory of Theatrical Materials, Services, Information. Published by Package Publicity Service, Inc., 1564 Broadway, New York, NY 10036. Revised from time to time since initial publication in 1956, this is the "bible" of complete source information. Currently nearly 400 pages with 22,000 entries, it is invaluable.

Motion Picture, TV and Theatre Directory. Published by Motion Picture Enterprises Publications, Inc., Tarrytown, NY, 10591. Published frequently in the handbook form, this is a valuable source supplement.

Festivals in Great Britain. London; John Offord Publishers; 1985.

John Offord (editor), *British Theatre Directory, 1983*. Eastbourne, England; John Offord Publishers, Ltd.; 1983. 575 pp. A complete reference manual of British theatre organizations, manufacturers, dealers, etc.

"Interiors Lighting Equipment Directory," *Interiors*, vol. CXLI, no. 7 (Feb. 1982), pp. 29–39. Compiled by Professor James Nuckolls, this is a master list (kept updated on a computer) of interior architectural lighting equipment in 90 categories, listing 289 manufacturers in 29 states. It is updated annually in *Interiors*. Invaluable to the architectural lighting specialist.

Interior Design Buyers Guide. Published by *Interior Design* magazine, 275 Washington St., Newton, MA 02158 or P.O. Box 1970, Marion, OH 43305.

New York Feature Film & Video Guide. Published by Olga Barrekette, 90 Riverside Drive, N.Y., NY 10024. Telephone: (212) 362-7773. Contains addresses and telephone numbers of New York City film unions and production firms.

Lighting Design + Application. The annual January issue contains a directory listing of sources of lighting equipment and accessories with manufacturers' addresses, divided into light sources, luminaires, and accessories (listed both alphabetically and geographically).

"1989 Directory of Suppliers," *Lighting*, vol. 3, no. 3 (June 1989), pp. 27–31, 38–42, 44–48, 50–52, 54, 56, 58–59. This is an excellent Canadian directory of manufacturers and suppliers, printed as a portion of *Lighting* magazine.

Jill Charles (editor), *Summer Theatre Directory 1985: A National Guide to Summer Employment for Professionals and Students*. North Adams, Mass.; Lamb Printing; 1985. 204 pp. Issued annually.

Lisa S. Hulse (editor), *1985 Internships*. Cincinnati, Ohio; Writer's Digest Books; 1984. 384 pp. Includes a 36-page section of theatre internships in the United States.

Josie Caruse and Karen McDuffee (editors), *The New York Theatrical Sourcebook: 1985 Edition*. N.Y.; Broadway Press; 1985. 562 pp. Compiled by the Association of Theatrical Artists and Craftspeople, the *Sourcebook* lists nearly every imaginable theatrical supply source in the greater New York City area.

Richard Harlin and Anne Folke Wells, *Opportunities in Theatrical Design & Production*. Chicago; National Textbook Co.; 1985. Part of the Career Horizons series.

A Glossary of Commonly Used Terms in Theatre, Television and Film Lighting. IES publication CP-44 (1984, 7pp). A good, useful glossary.

Period Lighting Fixture Research

When dealing with scenic naturalism or realism in the theatre or film or TV, lighting designers often need access to the very limited source material describing period lighting fixtures. Such information is not easy to locate. Lighting texts have overlooked this research need. Here is a list of good sources:

Leroy Thwing, *Flickering Flames, A History of Domestic Lighting through the Ages*. Rutland, Vermont; Charles E. Tuttle Co. (published for Rushlight Club); 1958. Printed in Japan. Also available from 15 Edogawa-cho, Bunkyo-ku, Tokyo. Includes 97 plates, 8 figures, and 42 sketches. Excellent, illustrated narration of domestic lighting. 138 pp.

Viggo Bech Rambusch, "The History of the Electric Light Fixture," *Lighting Design + Application*, vol. 14, no. 8 (Aug. 1984), pp. 20–26. Illus., color.

Arthur H. Hayward, *Colonial Lighting*. Boston; B. J. Brimmer Co.; 1923.

Contains 81 full-page half-tone plates; 8 drawings by the author. Excellent source material and good text concerning light fixtures of the Colonial period. 160 pp.

F. W. Robins, *The Story of the Lamp (and the Candle)*. N.Y.; Oxford University Press; 1939. Contains 28 full-page half-tone plates. Excellent narrative text. 156 pp.

Mr. and Mrs. G. Glen Gould, *Period Lighting Fixtures*. N.Y.; Dodd, Mead & Co.; 1928. Good narrative history; all countries. Well-illustrated. 174 pp.

Matthew Luckiesh, *Lighting Fixtures and Lighting Effects*. N.Y.; McGraw-Hill Book Co., Inc.; 1925. A complete outline of light sources and light fixtures in various periods and places. Illustrated with line drawings. 330 pp.

Alastair Duncan, *Art Nouveau and Art Deco Lighting*. N.Y.; Simon and Schuster; 1978. An art book, lavishly illustrated in color. Covers this period definitively. 208 pp.

Gabriel Henriot, *Encyclopedia du Luminaire, Formes & Decors Apparentes Depuis L'Antiquite Jusqu'a 1870*. Paris; "Les Editions Guerinet"; 1934. 2 vols. Folio-bound large engraved plates (12" × 16") of lighting fixtures on quality paper. This set is in the rare book class but where available is a classic reference source.

Warren E. Cox, *Lighting and Lamp Design*. N.Y.; Crown Publishers; 1952. Basically dealing with other subjects, this volume contains a section of approximately 50 pages of quality half-tone illustrations of lighting fixtures.

Stanley Wells, *Period Lighting*. London; Pelham Books; 1975. 166 pp. Good coverage of subject; useful text and illustrations.

Alastair Laing, *Victoria and Albert Museum: Lighting, the Arts and Living*. London; Her Majesty's Stationery Office; 1982. Illus., color. 72 pp. Good source material on period lighting fixtures in the Museum's collection.

Lawrence S. Cook, *Lighting in America*. Pittstown, N.J.; Main St. Press (Wm. Case House, Pittstown, NJ; 08867); 1984. 176 pp., illus. Colonial and Victorian lighting techniques are covered.

Index